Proceedings of the 9th International World Wide Web Conference

Conference Proceedings

9th International World Wide Web Conference

THE WEB: THE NEXT GENERATION

Amsterdam, The Netherlands

May 15-19 2000

http://www9.org.

Conference Organization:

FORETEC SEMINARS
Suite 100, 1895 Preston White Drive
Reston, VA 20191-5434
USA

2000
ELSEVIER
Amsterdam - Lausanne - New York - Oxford - Shannon - Singapore - Tokyo

ELSEVIER SCIENCE B.V.
Sara Burgerhartstraat 25
P.O. Box 211, 1000 AE Amsterdam, The Netherlands

ISBN: 0-444-50515-6

Transferred to digital printing 2006
Printed and bound by Antony Rowe Ltd, Eastbourne

Welcome to WWW9!

After several years, the World Wide Web conference comes back to Europe, this time to the beautiful city of Amsterdam. Since the last time the conference was in Europe, the Web has changed significantly, both technologically and in its applications. It has become part of everyday life, influencing society, business, politics, national and international law, art, and scientific development. And the development goes on: we can safely predict that the Web will remain an exciting world far into the future.

The integration of Web technologies into other areas of our daily life has just begun. For instance, the synergy between the Web and the traditional entertainment industries such as television, movies, radio, and printed media will revolutionize the way we perceive and personalize content. The appearance of Web services on our mobile phones and PDAs, in our cars, boats and other vehicles and, in the future, on wearable computers and various electronic appliances is another example of where the integration will certainly open up new perspectives.

The programme of the 9th International World Wide Web conference truly reflects some of these exciting developments. We have five keynote speakers, representing not only the Web industry, but also the telecommunication world, palm computing, and society. We offer a very rich Web & Industry track addressing E-commerce, the mobile Web, publishing, and Web & TV. Representatives of various industrial segments of our society will share with us their vision of the future and point to the challenges that must be addressed by our community to turn these visions into reality. We have also organized five panels on various topics, addressing issues like accessibility, multilingualism, and mobile applications. A separate track looks at the relationship of the Web and culture in general, inviting representatives of musea and art galleries to tell us about their experiences.

Of course, the backbone of the conference is the technical programme. We have 57 high quality technical papers selected, by an International Programme Committee, from a pool of 280 submissions. A strenuous task, which was superbly accomplished by the Chair and the Vice-chairs of the Programme Committee, with the help of a large number of technical reviewers. We hope you will enjoy listening to the paper presentations and read the papers. We also have a rich poster programme, including 65 posters and demonstrations. As in previous years, a separate poster proceedings is also available. These poster papers may be short, but they contain exciting ideas — do not forget to read them!

The W3C track has become a traditional part of these conferences. This track provides a unique opportunity to get first-hand information on the excellent work done by the World Wide Web Consortium in developing new specifications and guidelines to move the Web towards its full potential. We can safely say that this track will again be one of the highlights of this conference.

WWW9 follows the same pattern as earlier conferences; a rich tutorial programme, as well as a series of workshops where researchers can exchange their ideas and their latest results, precedes the core conference. The conference is followed by a Developers' Day, allowing developers to show and discuss their latest ideas and tools, and give further impetus to all developers around the world. The topics chosen for all these events duly represent the variety of technologies and applications that proliferate around the Web.

Organizing such a conference is a huge team effort. The credit goes to all the track chairs, vice-chairs, reviewers, and all those who have taken part in this endeavour. We can only thank them for their cooperation and dedication. Please take a moment and scan through the list of organizers just to appreciate the international character and variety of people who were involved! We owe thanks to our Meeting Planner, Web Developer, Conference Registrar, and Sponsor and Exhibition Coordinator who were instrumental in ensuring a smooth operating conference. Our very special thanks goes to the Conference Coordinator, who kept the whole organizing team together, and reminded us of our shortcomings, errors, and missing deadlines; she played a central role in the success of this conference.

We, the Conference Co-chairs, wish to express our gratitude to the conference sponsors and exhibitors without whom we would not have been able to bring such a successful conference to fruition.

Amsterdam truly represents the new European economy hosting the European headquarters of numerous Asian and North American companies, as well as a major hub on the European part of the Internet, and is home to a large number of exciting new Web related ventures. It is also a beautiful city, rich with historical buildings and neighbourhoods, with a special and appealing atmosphere. We hope all of you will find the time to walk around the canals, visit Amsterdam's Musea, and enjoy your evenings in one of the numerous restaurants or pubs. Welcome to Amsterdam, and enjoy the conference!

IVAN HERMAN (CWI)
ALBERT VEZZA (CNRI)

WWW9 Conference Co-chairs

Message from the Program Committee Chair

On behalf of the entire program committee, I am happy to welcome you to WWW-9 in Amsterdam.

This year's program continues in the trend started a year ago in Toronto toward greater quality and higher selectivity in the set of technical papers at the conference. Thanks to the dedicated efforts of the entire committee, we were able to put together a balanced program containing papers across a broad spectrum of professional interests.

This being the 9th conference in this series, it is natural to wonder if the relative maturity of the Web has led to the stagnation that one sometimes finds in other 'hot' areas as they begin to cool down. Luckily, the Web remains a very diverse place and the range of papers we received has allowed us to put together a program that reflects this diversity. We have been able to do this while maintaining sufficient depth to be of interest to both authors and participants.

Approximately 300 papers were submitted for consideration in the technical program. Of these, only 19% were selected for presentation at the conference. This reflects the goal of the WWW-X conference series to remain a highly selective – and probably the most selective – forum for researchers and practitioners. Each of the authors can be justifiably proud that their work has been selected.

The program committee for WWW-9 consisted of one program Chair and seven Vice-Chairs, each of which was responsible for a general area of Web technology, and a world-wide set of reviewers. The Vice-Chairs and their areas of responsibility were:

Ann Bassetti, Boeing Commercial Airplane Company (Practice and Experience)
Stephan Fischer, Darmstadt University of Technology (Content and Coding)
Lynda Hardman, CWI/Amsterdam (Hypermedia)
Hannes Marais, Alta Vista (Browsers and Tools)
Arun Iyengar, IBM Research (Performance)
Max Mühlhäuser, Darmstadt University of Technology (Applications and UI)
Ethan Munson, University of Wisconsin/Milwakee (Languages and Standards)
Mary Ellen Zurko, Iris (E-Commerce and Security)

Each of these members were responsible for the initial review and ranking of papers within their areas. The final program was selected at a meeting in Amsterdam in mid-January, based on the reviews of the entire program committee. At this meeting, the desire to reflect a balance in the presentations across all of the topic areas meant that a number of high-quality papers needed to be cut from the program. While this is always a problem at popular conferences, the limited space given to papers in each subject area meant that only between three and six submissions could be accepted per topic. I am grateful to the entire group of Vice-Chairs for their constructive work in helping to define the final selection.

Many of the authors who could not present in the main technical program were invited to present posters at the conference. Frans Heeman of Elsevier Science B.V. served as Poster Chair, and was able to put together an interesting collection of work-in-progress posters that are worth your attention during the conference.

In addition to the members of the program committee, several other persons played constructive roles in putting together this year's technical program. First, I would like to thank Ivan Herman of CWI/Amsterdam and Al Vezza of CNRI (the conference general chairs), who provided a range of incentives to make sure that all of the pieces of the program puzzle fell into place on time. Their patience and (relative) sense of humor is appreciated. Also greatly appreciated were the efforts of Eric Tang of Foretec, who handled the vast administrative details associated with the collection, distribution, coordination, notification, and proding of papers and authors for the conference. Jan Kastelein of Elsevier Science B.V. was responsible for putting together the publication you are holding in your hands from the soft-copy provided by authors. Even in this era of style sheets, putting together a polished printed proceedings is no small task.

At this point in a Program Chair's message, one is left wondering: whom did I forget? There are probably many people, and if you feel that you are one of them – thanks!

All that is left for me to do is to remind you that the much of the responsibility for making WWW-9 a success now resides in your minds and mouths: I encourage you to sample many presentations, look at many posters, ask many questions and to enjoy both your visit to the conference and your stay in Amsterdam!

DICK C.A. BULTERMAN
Program Committee Chairman
WWW-9 / Amsterdam

Credits

Conference Co-Chairs

Ivan Herman, CWI
Albert Vezza, CNRI

Program Committee Chair

Dick Bulterman, Oratrix

Program Committee Vice Chairs

Practice and Experience
Ann Bassetti, Boeing

Content and Coding
Stephan Fischer, Technical University, Darmstadt

Hypermedia
Lynda Hardman, CWI

Performance
Arun Iyengar, IBM Research

Browsers and Tools
Hannes Marais, AltaVista Company

Applications and UI
Max Mühlhäuser, Technical University, Darmstadt

Languages and Standards
Ethan Munson, University of Wisconsin–Milwaukee

Electronic Commerce and Security
Mary Ellen Zurko, Iris Associates

Posters Chair

Frans Heeman, Elsevier Science

Tutorials Co-Chairs

Richard Binder, Foretec Seminars
Dieter Fellner, Technical University Braunschweig

Workshops Co-Chairs

David Duce, Oxford Brookes University
Richard Binder, Foretec Seminars

Developers' Day Co-Chairs

Murray Maloney, Muzmo Communication
Sean McGrath, Digitome

Panels Chair

Håkon Lie, Opera Software

Keynote Speakers Chair

Robert Cailliau, CERN

Awards Chair

Simon Phipps, IBM UK Laboratories

The Web/Internet and Society Co-Chairs

Jaap Bloem, ISOC.NL
Daniel Weitzner, W3C at MIT LCS

The Web and Industry Chair

Michael Dreisch, UPC

W3C Chair

Janet Daly, W3C at MIT LCS

Culture Track Co-Chairs

Alfredo Ronchi, EC MEDICI Framework Secretariat
Judith Gradwhol, Smithsonian Institution

Program Committee Members

Ken Anderson, University of Colorado at Boulder
Helen Ashman, University of Nottingham
Rob Barrett, IBM – Almaden Research Center
Nina Bhatti, Hewlett-Packard Labs
Bert Bos, W3C at INRIA
Niels Olof Bouvin, University of Aarhus
Anne Brüggemann-Klein, Technische Universität München
Pei Cao, University of Wisconsin

Mark Wood, Eastman Kodak Company
Uffe Kock Wiil, Aalborg University Esbjerg
Martina Zitterbart, University of Braunschweig

Additional Reviewers

Martin Arlitt, HP Labs
Gerhard Austaller, University of Linz
Jan Borchers, University of Linz
George Candea, IBM
Catherine Chronaki, ICS-FORTH
Brian Dennis, Northwestern University
Michail Flouris, ICS-FORTH and University of Crete
Ralf Hauber, University of Linz
Andrew Huang, IBM
Shyam Kapur, AltaVista Research
Emre Kiciman, IBM
Theo Kopetzky, University of Linz
Håkon Lie, Opera Software
Manolis Marazakis, ICS-FORTH and University of Crete
Philip Marden, University of Wisconsin-Milwaukee
Mikhail Mikhailov, WPI
Tien Nhut Nguyen, University of Wisconsin-Milwaukee
Dionisios Pnevmatikatos, ICS-FORTH and University of Crete
Sigi Reich, University of Linz
Rimbert Rudisch, University of Linz
Sandeep Sibal, AT&T Labs
Christoph Trompler, University of Linz
Greg Vernon, Boeing Commercial Airplane Company
Simon Vogl, University of Linz
Michael Welzl, University of Linz

Volunteers Co-Chairs

John Miller, Southern Cross University
Mark Nguyen, Foretec Seminars
Gioacchino La Vecchia, Link s.r.l.

International WWW Conference Committee

Jean-Francois Abramatic, Chairman of W3C, INRIA
Tim Berners-Lee, Director of W3C, MIT/LCS
Jon Bosak, SunSoft
Dick Bulterman, Oratix
Robert Cailliau, Treasurer of IW3C2, CERN
Allan Ellis, President and Chair of IW3C2, Southern Cross University (SCU)
Wendy Hall, Vice President of IW3C2, University of Southampton
Joseph Hardin, University of Michigan
Ivan Herman, CWI
Robert Hopgood, W3C at INRIA
Murray Maloney, Muzmo Communication
Peter Plamondon, Microsoft Corporation
Albert Vezza, CNRI
Bebo White, Stanford Linear Accelerator Centre (SLAC)
Mary Ellen Zurko, Iris Associates

Graphic Design

Marcia Ciro, Paper Trace Studios

Conference Management by Foretec Seminars

Registration: Julie Kirchhoff
Planning: Marcia Beaulieu
Coordination: Barbara Fuller
Exhibitor/Sponsor Liaison: Amy Katherine Vezza
Web Developer: Eric Tang
Network Design: Mark Nguyen

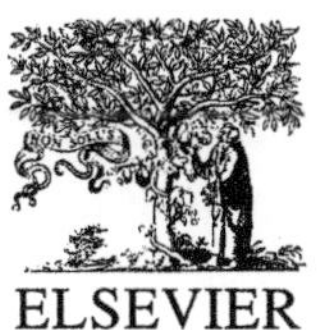
ELSEVIER

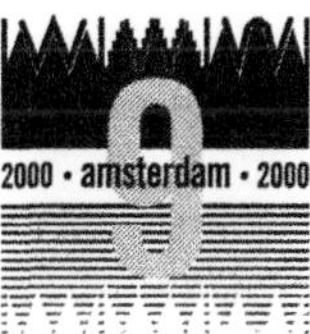
2000 · amsterdam · 2000

Contents

Content and control

ELSEVIER

Integrating user-perceived quality into Web server design

Nina Bhatti *, Anna Bouch [1], Allan Kuchinsky [2]

Hewlett-Packard Laboratories, 1501 Page Mill Road, Palo Alto, CA 94304, USA

Abstract

As the number of Web users and the diversity of Web applications continues to explode, Web Quality of Service (QoS) is an increasingly critical issue in the domain of e-commerce. This paper presents experiments designed to estimate users' tolerance of QoS in the context of e-commerce. In addition to objective measures, we discuss contextual factors that influence these thresholds and show how users' conceptual models of Web tasks affect their expectations. We then show how user thresholds of tolerance can be taken into account when designing Web servers. This integration of user requirements for QoS into systems design is ultimately of benefit to all stakeholders in the design of Internet services.

Keywords: Quality of service; User perception; E-commerce; Server design

1. Introduction

The success of any scheme that attempts to deliver desirable levels of Quality of Server (QoS) for the future Internet must be based, not only on technology improvements, but on users' requirements [16,21]. To date, the majority of research on QoS is systems oriented, focusing on the scheduling and routing of network traffic. Although it is often recognized that a measurement of user satisfaction must be included in assessing network efficiency [22], relatively minor attention has been paid to user-level QoS issues. The number of Electronic Commerce (e-commerce) users is rising. As the e-commerce industry grows the topic of providing adequate QoS for the Internet becomes increasingly critical to businesses. To provide the flexibility needed to respond to customer requests, Web pages that support e-commerce applications typically are dynamically computed. This means that the delays witnessed by users are directly affected by server performance, and not simply due to download times. Inevitably, more requests are made of servers than they can immediately handle; the magnitude of user demand outstrips server capacity. The outcome of this situation is that often some users are denied access to the server, or the accessed service is unacceptably slow.

As the World Wide Web is rapidly increasing with numbers of users expected to reach 320 million by 2002 [34], the increase in network usage is paralleled by a growing diversity in the range of supportable applications. Because of its accessibility, the future Internet offers the potential to break traditional barriers in communications and commerce. However, the

* Corresponding author. E-mail: nina_bhatti@yahoo.com

[1] Current address: Department of Computer Science, University College London, Gower Street, London, WC1 E6BT, UK. E-mail: a.bouch@cs.ucl.ac.uk

[2] E-mail: kuchinsk@hpl.hp.com

current service to users is often unacceptable [12,27] and is likely to remain so in at least the near future [5].

The components of QoS systems are extremely difficult to integrate. For example, server utilization cannot be divorced from the requests made to that server from applications, or from network conditions. For example, providing another 5% worth of server utilization may require a considerable amount of computational effort, but have minimal incremental benefit to users. A difficult but central question for server designers in the future is to what degree user perception of improved quality of service can be translated into metrics that can be used to inform service providers in designing resource allocation strategies. The real challenge for future network designers, therefore, may not solely lie in maximizing utilization of servers, but in ensuring that the service provided is both efficient and subjectively valuable to users [7].

This paper reports results from a set of studies into how users define and perceive Internet QoS. We describe empirical work that shows that a mapping can be developed between objective and subjective expressions of latency. Latency is defined as the delay between a request for a Web page and receiving that page in its entirety. We chose to study latency, not simply because it is associated with the most common cause of poor QoS, but because it represents a problem that is likely to escalate as Internet usage inevitably grows [24]. We use qualitative data to elucidate the motivations behind behavior observed in empirical work. We then show how these results can be included in server design to improve realized QoS. Our server designs use prioritization schemes that attempt to meet the increasing demand for access to network bandwidth and server resources according to the QoS needs of applications [4,15,17,35]. Priority scheduling schemes can be implemented in the server using mechanisms that queue and service traffic from particular applications in a specific order. Schemes such as differentiated services exploit this ability by classifying packets of information in certain service profiles [4]. It should not be assumed that the requirements of applications regarding QoS can be divorced from the requirements of those who ultimately use those applications [35]. However, it was not known to what extent objective QoS metrics relate to user perceptions of quality and impact the behavior of users. Only by understanding this relationship can we define the potential trade-off between the cost of resource allocation for the service provider, and the benefits in increased business gained by providing a level of QoS perceived as valuable by users.

The rest of this paper is organized as follows. Section 2 describes the objectives and design of experiments to assess user's tolerance for delay in an e-commerce setting. Section 3 describes the results of these studies. Section 4 shows how these results can be incorporated into server designs to achieve improved perceived QoS for users. Finally, Section 5 wraps up with some remarks about future work and our conclusions.

2. Experimental assessment of users' tolerance for delay

2.1. *Objectives*

Measured thresholds for QoS are increasingly important to system designers [19]. Establishing a mapping between objective and subjective QoS is perhaps the most direct way research can enable servers to be designed to provide maximum utility. A common finding from previous research is that QoS delivered by servers must accord with users' expectations in order to be perceived as acceptable [7,8,18]. Objective measurements, such as response time and delay cannot, however, fully characterize the factors that drive these expectations. A consistent finding is that QoS received by users should concur with their expectations but that these expectations change according to the pattern of quality received [8,10]. The characterization of factors that impact users' expectations is complicated by the fact that many such factors are interrelated. For example, Web pages that are retrieved faster are judged to be significantly more interesting than their slower counterparts [32], and users may judge a relatively fast service to be unacceptable unless it is also predictable, visually appealing and reliable [8]. Indeed, the weight of evidence from prior research suggests that there is no direct correlation between objective levels of quality received by users and their perceptions of that quality. To predict users' tolerance for QoS it is therefore necessary to understand what motivates users' judgements of QoS. We selected study participants that met the profile for e-commerce users that were moderately experienced Internet users. The measures of QoS were established during a representative set of e-commerce tasks. We set out to define the minimum latency users would tolerate before they find that level of QoS unacceptable and potentially take their business to a competitor.

Our study enabled us to address the following questions.

- Are there objective measures for user's tolerance of delay?
- Is this tolerance affected by the task?
- Is this tolerance affected by the duration of interaction with the site?
- What is the perception of businesses that have poor QoS?
- Does Web site design influence user's tolerances?

2.2. *Experimental design*

We set out to design experiments that would allow us to assess whether we can measure a user's tolerance for delay and what affects this tolerance. To gather this information we created a Web site with delay and bandwidth programmability. This provided a self-contained and consistent Web shopping experience.

Because we focused our interest on Web QoS for e-commerce, we selected participants that would match a profile of Internet shoppers. There were 30 male participants, between the ages of 18 and 68 [10], in the study. It was essential that a homogeneous group of users was selected, because users with different amounts of knowledge and experience of Web QoS have different expectations of QoS [8]. We restricted our sample to participants who:

- use the Internet for at least two hours per week;
- have made at least two purchases on the Internet in the last year;
- have at least an intermediate level of self-assessed skill with using computers.

Male participants were selected for the study to eliminate any confounding effects due to gender differences in visual perception and learning [25]. Males were identified as the most frequent users of Internet services [31].

The participants were given the same task series so that their path through the site would be consistent. The task involved configuring and purchasing a home computer system. We wanted the task to be as ecologically valid as possible. We therefore chose an e-commerce site currently in operation, the HP Shopping Village [20]. This busy site is ranked first for retail revenue generated by e-commerce [19]. This situated the task strongly in a real-world context. During the task participants were asked to purchase each component of the computer separately. To answer the research questions, it was necessary that the chosen task meet certain criteria. To study whether users' requirements for QoS were similar for similar subtasks, a set pattern of actions was repeated through the task. For each component purchased, participants were required to:

(1) view a class of similar products;
(2) select a specific product from a class of products;
(3) add the chosen product to their shopping cart;
(4) view the contents of their shopping cart.

We needed a consistent set of tasks to determine if users' tolerance changes over time. If the tasks had been widely variable, then any change in tolerance could be ascribed to the variation in what participants were asked to do, and not to a genuine accumulation of frustration. The task was designed so that all participants followed the same path through the Web site.

Participants gave feedback on Web performance satisfaction through:

- interaction with a quality rating browser extension;
- verbal protocols — participants talked aloud while performing the experimental tasks;
- participation in focus group discussions.

We correlated user feedback with actual known delay measurements and built a model of users' tolerance. The capture of QoS acceptability information, in our study, was driven by the correlation of user interface button clicks for rating of QoS, and verbal protocols. The inclusion of verbal protocols enabled us to gather feedback from users during interaction with the Web site. Focus group studies enabled us to explore in a wider context the issues raised during the protocols.

2.3. *Experimental conditions*

The first condition in the study investigated how the latency between requesting a page and receiving it is perceived by users. Varying the latency in this condition has the effect that the page where the link has been clicked remains displayed in the browser until the next page has been loaded. This next page is then brought up in its entirety. Predetermined delays ranging from 2 to 73 seconds were injected into the loading process. The choice of this range of speeds was guided by speeds that users had perceived to be qualitatively different in previous research [13, 32]. There were two sequences of delay for latency. Pattern 1 mimicked a random pattern of delay. In pattern 2, the delay generated on the Web pages was relatively smooth.

Experiment 1: Classification of latency. Participants were asked to perform the shopping task and rate the latency received for each Web page access. An interface was developed to register ratings. The interface contained gray buttons labeled 'high', 'medium', 'low', as well as a black button, marked with an 'X'. Participants were directed to click one of the buttons in this interface for each Web page accessed. Participants were told that the black button, marked with an 'X', should be used to indicate that the quality was totally unacceptable.

Experiment 2: Control of latency. In this condition, users were told that if they found the delay of the Web page unacceptable they could click a button labeled 'Increase Quality'. The effect of this button was to immediately bring up the requested page. Previous research suggested that this would be a valid measure of users' requirements for speed [6]. This experimental set-up contrasts users' opinions about tolerance of QoS, captured in classification conditions, with what can be implied about users' tolerance from their behavior when they controlled the quality.

Experiment 3: Incremental loading. This part of the study investigated whether users would be more tolerant of delay when Web pages were loaded incrementally instead of all at once. Previous research suggests that providing continuous feedback reassures users that the system is working and gives them something to look at while waiting [26]. However, [30] points out that standard browser feedback, provided in the form of progress bars, fails to communicate the amount of the page that has been completed. Loading Web pages incrementally can address this shortcoming, while providing users with visually interesting feedback. The flow of information between Web server and client was manipulated to cause the Web pages to load in parts. In our task, participants would receive the banner of the next page as soon as they clicked a link. This was followed by text, and later, graphics. Participants were asked to evaluate the time it took for the whole Web page to complete using the same GUI as in Experiment 1. The time taken for specific pages to complete was random. Fig. 1 shows the mean delay taken by each Web page to complete in condition 3. These measurements were taken using client-based software that captures latency received by users with 100% accuracy [14].

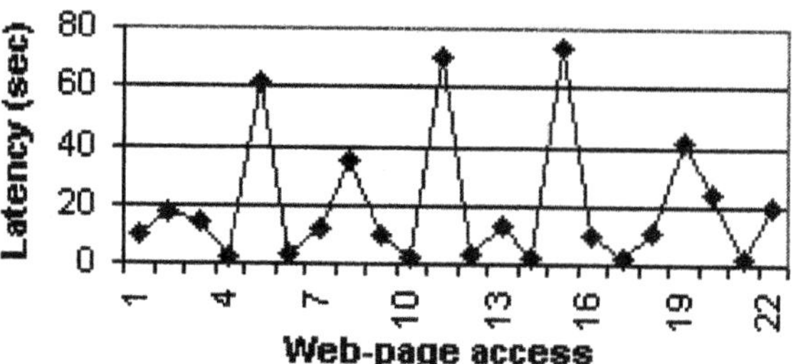

Fig. 1. Incremental loading latency.

Participants were split into two groups for the investigation of latency in Experiments 1 and 2. 15 participants received pattern 1 for both the classification and control of latency, while the remaining 15 participants received pattern 2 for both the classifications and control of latency. Table 1 summarizes the experimental conditions applied.

Table 1
Experimental conditions

Experiment	Pattern	Participants
1 (classify)	Random	15 (Group 1)
2 (control)	Random	15 (Group 1)
1 (classify)	Regular	15 (Group 2)
2 (control)	Regular	15 (Group 2)
3 (classify)	Random and Regular	30

3. Results

The key finding of the research was a mapping between objective QoS and users' subjective perceptions of QoS. The data we gained from verbal protocols and focus groups indicates that participants were strongly influenced by their expectations of the delay when responding to the QoS they received in the experiment. Additional discussion of experimental design and results can be found in [9].

Focus group data indicated that tolerance of delay was decreased when there was a conflict between the level of quality expected and that received. We found that there was almost unanimous agreement among participants concerning the factors that help form these expectations. These expectations are influenced by contextual factors including the type of task, the method of page loading, and cumulative time of interaction. We also found that there are very real business consequences of slow server response times. Users believe that if performance is poor, the security of the site may be compromised. Poor performance also leads to loss of customers.

3.1. Measures of users' tolerance for delay

Verbal protocols indicated that participants used the 'Low' button when they found that the QoS was unacceptable; very few participants used the black button labeled 'X'. We took this into account by aggregating the 'Low' button and 'X' button responses when conducting a set of Chi-squared tests for statistical significance. Table 2 lists the ratings of specific delays and shows that the threshold where QoS is judged as 'Low' is around 11 seconds. This finding is consistent with previous work that established this threshold for holding users' attention to the task [11].

Table 2
Rating of latency

Rating	Range of latency (in s), Experiments 1 and 2 (non-incremental loading)	Range of latency (in s), Experiment 3 (incremental loading)
High	0–5	0–39
Average	>5	>39
Low	>11	>56

The range of latency assigned by participants to each classification in condition 3 (incremental loading) is almost 6 times higher in each case compared to the classifications made in condition 1 (see Table 2). This indicates that users are more tolerant of latency when Web pages load incrementally than when there is a delay followed by the display of the page in its entirety. These results indicate that incremental loading may help to maintain users' attention to the task at hand, rather than to the QoS they receive. Furthermore, Table 2 shows us that, relative to the selection of 'Low' or 'Average', quality of service is more likely to be classified as 'High' in condition 3 (incremental loading); this category is proportionately much larger in Experiment 3 compared to Experiment 1 (classification of latency).

We observed, in Experiment 2 (control of latency) that there was a large standard deviation among participants in terms of their tolerance of latency. Although the average tolerance was 8.57 seconds in this experiment, the standard deviation was 5.85 seconds. It is not possible for us to conclude from Experiment 2 that users will tolerate a specific amount of latency before finding that QoS unacceptable. Multiple regression analysis revealed that the number of hours participants used the Web significantly influenced their tolerance for latency. Higher levels of Web usage were associated with less tolerance for delay during interaction ($p < 0.01$). The large standard deviation observed when participants were asked to control latency may have been due to the differences among participants in terms of their risk-taking behavior. Participants differed in terms of whether they took advantage of the fact that there was no penalty for pushing the button to increase quality. This difference is also suggested by the fact that there was no correlation between participants' tolerance when classifying latency and their tolerance when controlling latency. To gain useful insights from this condition, we therefore investigated the levels of tolerance demonstrated by each individual participant.

Previous research has established three thresholds relating to users' tolerance for delay [30]. For delays of 0.1 seconds or less, users perceive the response as immediate. A delay of 1 second corresponds to the pace of an interactive dialog. A threshold of 10 seconds was identified as the point at which a significant number of users perceive the delay to be unacceptable. According to this research, a 10 second delay corresponds to thresholds where users lose their attention to the task at hand. These findings fit with the literature on cognition [11]. Two stimuli within 0.1 second of each other fuse into a single precept, e.g. two pictures seen within 0.1 second fuse into a perception of motion; animation breaks down if longer than 0.1 second per frame. The coarsest level of interaction is the 'unit task', the pace of routine cognitive skill, e.g. 10 seconds is about the time needed to select text on a screen and modify it. Thus, a delay of over 10 seconds constitutes a disruption in the 'unit task' and may cause disorientation and reduced performance. Other research has described thresholds that are perceived as qualitatively different over a wider range of latency [32].

3.2. The duration of time users interact with the site

Investigating whether tolerance for delay is influenced by the length of a session is especially pertinent in the area of e-commerce. On the one hand, users' frustration at delays incurred may accumulate. This would mean that they would tolerate less delay as the session time increases. This is a likely scenario because it has been shown that users conceptualize the quality of their interaction according to their ability to reach the top-level goal. In the case of e-commerce this goal often is to make a purchase. Furthermore, in e-commerce, subtasks are by nature structured so that the act of purchasing is normally the last in a chain of related operations. If users' tolerance for delay decreases over time, then this has a clear impact on loss of business on the site. On the other hand, as the length of the session increases, users have invested more time towards reaching their goal of purchasing a product and thus have an incentive to continue. It may be that, as the time remaining to complete their task decreases, users' tolerance for delay goes up.

The first condition in the study investigated how the latency between requesting a page and receiving it is perceived. In all conditions we found that users' tolerance for delay decreased as the length of time they spent interacting with the site increased. In all cases this finding is statistically significant ($p < 0.01$). The effect is more powerfully significant for condition 3 ($p < 0.001$). Fig. 2 is an example

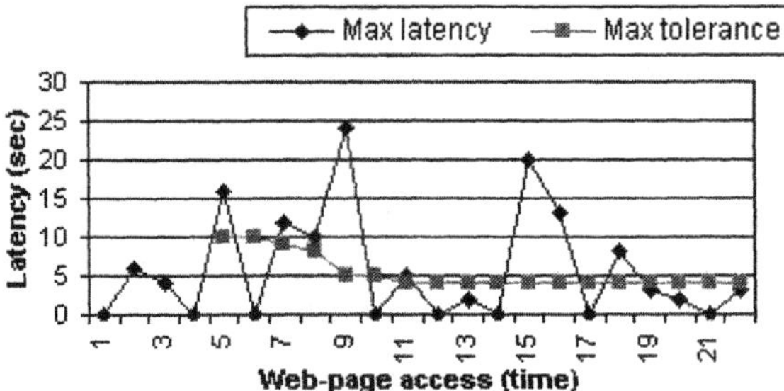

Fig. 2. Tolerance of latency over a session.

of the maximum delay tolerated by a participant in condition 2. Maximum tolerance for delay is represented by the point at which the participant clicked the 'Increase Quality' button.

Our results suggest that users become increasingly frustrated with delays incurred during interaction. Qualitative data shows that although users are less likely to leave an on-line shopping site once they have placed objects in their shopping cart, they are no more tolerant of delay. In fact, users are more likely to become annoyed in this situation as they feel they have less control over interaction and have been manipulated into being forced to endure poor QoS:

"I'm already half way through what I wanted to do, now I'm caught because I can't leave, but I won't come back." [3]

3.3. Expectations based on task

The user's goal, when interacting with any network application, has been shown to affect not only the level of QoS that the user will tolerate but the very definition of quality [35]. For example, requirements for high video performance are more prominent in interactive tele-teaching tasks than in listening to lectures [23]. Furthermore, it has been established that large quality variations should be avoided for audio transmission [36]. We set out to investigate the influence of users' tasks on their tolerance of delay in the e-commerce environment. Our findings suggest that there is a distinction to be made between a situation where a user interacts with a Web site for information-gathering purposes and where a

[3] To illustrate key points, we have included quotes taken from the verbal protocols and focus groups.

user interacts to undertake a specific action (in our context, to buy an item):

"... it depends on the intent. If I'm browsing for something then the (quality) I get isn't so important as if I've got a definite mission in mind."

The type of real-world task in which they are engaged is likely to be involved in forming expectations of QoS and therefore have an influence on the amount of delay tolerated:

"When I've added stuff to the list ... I would expect it to take a little longer than when it's got preset pages."

"Like when you're comparing I expect that to take a little longer because it's going to have to go out and get information."

Qualitative data suggests that participants expect different tasks to take longer than others. From this information we were able to classify tasks according to participant's expectations of the latency each task should incur. High-tolerance tasks were:

- comparing several items;
- viewing the shopping cart.

By comparison, low-tolerance tasks were:

- returning to a previously accessed page;
- viewing a class of products;
- adding to the shopping cart.

During the experiments we found that users tolerated different levels of latency depending on what they were doing. As can be seen from Fig. 3, participants classified response with an 8 second delay (corresponding to comparing different printers) as of higher quality than that with a 6 second delay (corresponding to viewing a class of monitors). Statistical tests show that users will accept more delay when

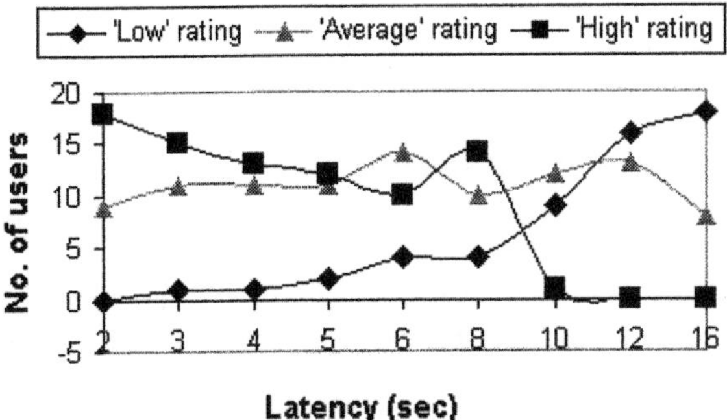

Fig. 3. Rating of latency by users.

they are comparing products or viewing the contents of their shopping cart than when they are viewing a class of products or adding to the shopping cart ($p < 0.01$).

Qualitative data showed that participants had a conceptual model of the way that networks store and access information. This conception influenced users' tolerance for delay. For example, our data indicated that tolerance for delay associated with specific tasks was dependent on (a) if the user believed that the task required accessing a database, e.g. from which to compare products, (b) if the task involved a calculation to be made, e.g. in calculating the total spent from the items placed in the shopping cart.

"when I brought up my shopping cart I figured it would have to compile a bit longer so I was more willing to wait a little bit for it to come up."

In an e-commerce environment different tasks imply different levels of economic incentive on the part of the company whose products are sold. For example, participants expected tasks like adding to the shopping cart to be relatively fast because of the company's motivation to encourage user's to make a purchase. Although no pages were cached in the experiment, participants awareness of this technology made them relatively intolerant of delay when re-visiting previously accessed pages.

Our findings suggest that users anticipate the amount of time it will take them to perform particular on-line tasks. This anticipation helps form their expectations of the time it should take them to complete a whole task. Our results suggest that when the process of completing a task is disrupted by unanticipated delays, a conflict arises between users' expectations and the QoS they received. This conflict results in a rating of poor QoS:

"So I'll be sitting there for half an hour so I'm set for that ... so a lot of it depends on the time I anticipated I had when I set out."

"If I'm going to buy something that I need to do research on, mentally I'll allocate more time."

3.4. Feedback

If delivered quality is to concur with users' expectations, that service must be predictable [28]. Previous research has established thresholds by which

Web page response times can be classified, and related these thresholds to the need for browser feedback to enable users to predict response times [22]. If the delay from request to the display of a Web page in the browser is one second or less, then there is no interruption of the users' flow of thought. Users perceive this response to be immediate and therefore do not require feedback in the browser. However, in the frequently occurring situation where servers cannot provide an immediate response, continuous feedback must be provided. Feedback is especially important if the delays incurred are likely to vary, as in [6]. Feedback enables users to predict the amount of time they will have to wait. We investigated the interaction between providing feedback to the browser and overall judgements of QoS by comparing users' tolerance for delay under two conditions.

(1) *Page loads incrementally.* The Web page would be brought up in parts. In our study this meant that users would receive the banner heading the site first, followed by graphics and, later, textual information.
(2) *All information displayed together.* The Web page from which users clicked the link would remain displayed in the browser until the entire next page could be downloaded.

Consistent with previous research [30], we found that, in circumstances where feedback is provided (Experiment 3) tolerance of delay is significantly higher.

Qualitative data suggests that the value of feedback is that it:

- promotes confidence that users' requests are being processed: *"As long as you see things coming up it's not nearly as bad as just sitting there waiting and again you don't know whether you're stuck."*
- enables users to estimate how long they will have to wait until they can interact with the site: *"Well I know if it's saying 33% or whatever then I'll have to wait a couple of seconds."*
- focuses their attention by giving them something to look at while waiting: *"at least you're not sitting there with nothing to look at, while I'm waiting for it to come up, I can be reading."*.

Some participants in our study used the standard browser feedback, i.e. messages of percent download completed within a small status bar to assess activity in the network. Typically, these participants did not prefer incremental loading. This finding confirms the strength of incremental loading as being indicative of the processing of a request. Either browser feedback or incremental loading can provide this feedback.

3.5. Business implications of poor QoS

Recent assessments of Web usability indicate that the same QoS dimensions are responsible for the greatest number of degradations in users' perceptions of overall QoS for over three years [29]. Several prominent Internet sites such as www.ebay.com, www.schab.com and www.brittanica.com have all experienced publicly embarrassing unavailability and poor performance. In a review of twenty prominent sites it was found that what is called the greatest 'design mistake', slow download times, was committed by an average of 84% of Web sites. This figure is likely to be even greater for the aggregate of Web sites, since smaller companies often provide lower levels of QoS than prominent companies. A recent study of nearly 3000 on-line shoppers found that people use e-commerce sites because they are convenient. If systems designers cannot understand the limits of users' tolerance for slow download times they risk not only promoting users' frustration but also an eventual and significant loss of business.

We found that users' perceptions of the QoS they receive affects not only the likelihood of going to a competitor's Web site but also their opinion of the company's products and of the company itself. A failure to understand users' on-line QoS requirements, therefore, may affect users' conception of a company's stature and commercial viability. As more and more people use the Internet for commerce, service providers must integrate users' QoS requirements into their server design in order to meet the needs of *their* customers, the retailers whose products are sold on-line.

Data from users suggest that blame for poor QoS is placed on the server, even though the users in our study possessed a conception of the manner in which data was routed on the network. Indeed, although participants said that they could reason that poor QoS could be due to the amount of traffic on the network, they nevertheless did not intuitively associate this situation as the cause of delay. When participants were questioned about the causes of delay they did not blame network traffic demands, networking infrastructure, ISPs or even their own modem connections; instead they placed the blame on the individual businesses represented by the sites.

3.5.1. User's expectations of corporate Web sites

Inevitably, if poor — or unpredictable — QoS is habitually experienced at the site of a particular company, the products of that company are likely to be viewed as inferior. Participants in our study believed that companies that are more commercially successful should possess the financial means to supply at least adequate levels of QoS 100% of the time. This expectation means that users are less likely to accept delays, or refused admissions, to a site that promotes the products of high-status companies:

"Because the companies are so huge they should pour money into their web-sites, they should have fast sites. If I try to get on those sites and they're slow then I'm not as patient."

"This is the way the consumer sees the company ... it should look good, it should be fast."

Qualitative data also shows that users who frequently purchase products from particular Web sites habituate to the typical levels of quality they receive from those sites. Conceptually, this leads to a sense of betrayal if the QoS delivered is not according to what is expected. Users describe this situation as compromising their conception of the customer loyalty shown to them by the company from whom they are buying:

"If I've been going to you for a long time and you suddenly can't perform ... well then you've sort of betrayed me and I won't be going back."

Unpredictable service therefore compromises users' trust in the company. Failure to provide a consistent level of QoS that is needed to maintain users' sense of customer loyalty means that users will not return to that site. Maintaining acceptable levels of QoS is not just the problem of the service provider. The companies whose products are sold on-line, and the advertisers who are their sponsors, are also affected by the ability of Web servers to provide acceptable QoS to users. Our data show that the ultimate consequence of falling short of this goal is loss of customers.

Users have too many Web sites that they can use as alternatives if they are either refused entry to one site or are given particularly slow service. There are almost no barriers to switching to another site if performance is unacceptable. This makes performance critical to attracting and keeping customers:

"There's just too many alternatives, I can't think of anything that I can't just go and get somewhere else."

3.5.2. Compromised security

Another finding in our focus groups was that users made a connection between poor performance and compromised security. Participants in this study felt that cumulative slowness on Web pages suggested not only that the products being sold were of inferior quality, but that the security of their purchase was compromised:

"If it's slow I won't give my credit card number."

"I'd say, you haven't got your resources figured out, you're a poorly managed outfit, I don't trust you any longer."

Once users perceive that security has been compromised, no purchase will be made and the main purpose of any commercial Web site becomes critically compromised. It is therefore crucial for systems designers to understand the effect of cumulative frustration, especially as it is typically in the later stages of interaction that users are likely to commit to a purchase.

3.5.3. Deferring users

There are inevitable spikes of traffic that can overwhelm a server and therefore admission control may be used occasionally. We asked participants about their opinions regarding being denied access to a site. Opinions were very negative:

"Could you imagine going to store and someone saying, 'oh, too many people waiting in line, come back in an hour'. "

"You're going to go to the next store."

Users' conception of the Internet is that it provides service on demand. Indeed, the success of the Internet is in part due to its convenience. Our evidence shows that users define *convenience* as 'accessibility' and 'ease of use'. In the same way there is a conception that companies want to encourage visitation to their site. This is especially the case in the realm of Internet commerce. Asking users to defer their requests is therefore in direct opposition to users' concept of service on demand. We found that if sites must defer customers then some sort of incentive should be offered to return to the site.

Participants suggested that they would be more willing to defer their request if a discount or 'coupon' was offered as an incentive to go back to the site:

"We'll give you 5% off if you come back, well, that would be a different story."

3.6. The effects of Web site design

Data from the verbal protocols suggest that the actual design of a Web site can have a profound effect upon the perceived Quality of Service in several areas as outlined in the subsections below.

3.6.1. Page structure

Previous work has shown that users judge the speed of the service they receive according to their ability to accomplish the overall goal of their task [28]. Verbal protocols taken while participants performed the task indicates that the time taken to scroll down a specific page to locate a link detracts from users' perceptions of page latency. For example, participants reported annoyance with situations that required them to scroll a page to reach the desired information. They were particularly disconcerted in cases where they had to scroll in order to locate the selection to make for adding an item to the shopping cart. This is an example of an interaction effect between page structure and overall perceptions of QoS:

"The speed wasn't bad except (when getting) the paper ... plus the fact that you have to scroll down to view your basket."

3.6.2. Iconic representation

The use of icons in interactive applications has the benefit that they are more easily associated with real-world metaphors than text-based information [33]. The functionality of a real-world metaphor can be encapsulated in a simple pictorial representation. The use of icons is, therefore, especially relevant when the intention is to associate the functions of a real-world metaphor with a well-known image. A prime candidate in our study would be the use of a shopping cart. Indeed, many participants suggested that this would have been an intuitive use of graphics, enabling them to clearly see the functionality of the site.

In our task users wanted an 'Add to Shopping Cart' button be placed prominently on all pages of the Web site and be easily accessible throughout all phases of the shopping experience. This would certainly be in the interests of the proprietors of an Internet commerce sites, who wish users to add items to their shopping carts. The fact that this was not the case in our study often led users to associate the site with an overall lower standard of service.

3.6.3. Number of links

Another issue for Web site design, which affects perceived quality of service, is the number of link traversals necessary for a user to reach information of interest [29]. It should be noted that improvements to server and/or network performance can only improve the delivery of each individual Web page. If there is an excessive number of Web pages that have to be visited before the item of interest can be retrieved, then the benefits of server and/or network performance improvements will go unnoticed. This implies that the proprietors of electronic commerce sites should apply sound principles of information structuring; e.g. link trees should be wide, rather than deep and that such information-structuring decisions are as crucial as server performance is to the perception of quality of service.

The point to stress is that the quality of the Web site design is inextricably bound with the perception of quality of service and that any attempts to improve quality of service should include site design as one of the parameters to be considered. Inevitably, providing users with optimum levels of QoS involves sometimes subtle trade-offs between maximizing the ease of use of a site and the speed at which it can be delivered. An obvious example of this is providing iconic as opposed to text-based information. What our results show is that users' overall perceptions of the performance of a site is affected, not just by the objective latency of each page, but by the delay incurred during their interaction with that page. This latter delay can be due to poor Web site design.

4. Implications for server design

The perspective of this work is not only to understand user behavior relating to QoS, but to interpret those findings into solutions for real-world problems. Our findings have implications for the way that servers dynamically control the processing and delivery of information in response to users' requests. For example, Web servers can be altered to modify the scheduling of requests so requests are served more selectively than with the traditional FIFO mechanism. [1,2,6] give architectures for modification of Web servers to allow control of scheduling of requests and resources given to these requests. There are also several operating systems efforts underway to account for and control system resources given to each class of Web request [2,3]. While we have the technology to better control the level of service each Web request receives, little work has been done to define and implement policies based on user perceptions of quality of service. In this section, we provide some insights into appropriate policies for Web server QoS controls that can adjust the server response time to more closely match the expectations of users, therefore maximizing the utility of the sever.

4.1. Meeting latency requirements

To facilitate user satisfaction all requests should be processed within the latency requirements for high QoS rating given in Table 2. We propose to modify the scheduling algorithms of Web servers to ensure that tasks complete within their deadlines. This can be accomplished, for example, by Earliest Deadline First scheduling. Each request that enters the Web server has an associated deadline for completion. The association of deadlines with requests can be fairly fine-grained; the deadline associated with the request can be based on the task. From the results of our study it was clear that users have different models in their mind about which tasks 'should' take a while and which tasks 'should' be fairly quick. These different deadlines can be assigned by parsing the URL for the request, where the URL has been encoded to indicate task urgency (see Section 4.3), and then associating the correct deadline. The server is given fine-grained information about which tasks are expected to finish quickly.

Current Web servers such as Apache are a collection of processes and execution threads that all implement a fairly simple model: wait for a new request, accept the request, process the request, send the results to the client. There is no control over which request completes first. Requests are simply executed as soon as a server process/thread is available and can accept the connection. This means that a potentially important request with very low latency requirements can be waiting in the queue with no process assigned to service it. By the time a process accepts the request and determines its scheduling precedence, the deadline may have passed. This is an especially critical problem when servers are busy and therefore the delay increases before a process is available to handle the request. Web servers can be modified to accept all connections quickly for classification, then, after consulting QoS policies, calculate deadlines for each request. The server processes then can select the next *most urgent* request to complete.

One of the most efficient ways to improve server resources is to complete work that has higher value. We can use our findings of objective thresholds to enable servers to process requests while they still have utility to users. It does not benefit users if server resources are wasted on requests that have been waiting so long that it is likely that the user has long since moved on to other Web pages. The ability to associate timeliness data with each request allows the server to be more selective in its scheduling.

In addition to providing better service to all users, our objective measures can associate target performance for different classes of service. Current proposals for differentiated QoS [2,6] are driven by relative measures of performance, e.g. in best-effort vs. premium service. They are not based upon absolute measures of performance. We can only assure that a premium client was receiving better service than a best-effort class of service client. When a premium client receives slow responses it is not reassuring to tell the client that there are users who have lower priority. Using our data for high, average, and low response time ratings we can associate specific deadlines with different classes of service. Each request can be marked with not only the priority of the request but also with a specific deadline that satisfies the specific class of service. This allows the server to offer differentiated services, based not on relative priority scheduling, but upon actual performance within defined objective measures.

In the case of differentiated services where a server provides OS-level support for allocation of resources based on class of service, the performance of each class can be compared to what the targets are for the class. If the target performance is not attained, then the server will have to allocate more resources to the premium class. This is an important auditing and control mechanism. Otherwise we know only that a class of service has been given a certain share of say CPU resources; it may still be failing to achieve the performance goals.

4.2. Duration and latency requirements

A central finding in our study is that users' tolerance for latency decreases over the duration of interaction with a site. Fig. 4 shows that this effect is apparent for both relatively low and relatively high levels of delay. A 16 second latency is acceptable to 60% of the participants during the first 4 Web page accesses, but not acceptable to anyone for accesses over the 13th page. This is extremely significant, as e-commerce sites often have a fairly complex organization where a transaction is composed of many Web page accesses. A 6 second latency was rated as acceptable for all participants until the 3rd page access and then the number of users that rated it as acceptable declines steadily to 80% for 20 or more accesses.

If an e-commerce site wishes its customers to rate their shopping experience as acceptable, then the site must assure that the performance does not degrade. This can actually mean that the latency must improve

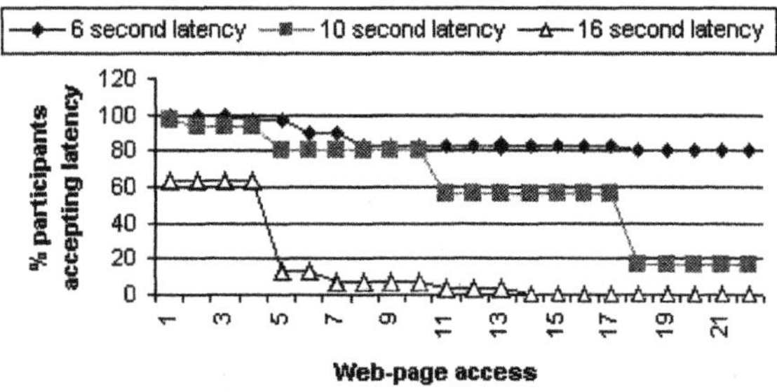

Fig. 4. Tolerance for latency over time.

over the duration of a session. This has a particularly profound effect upon the maintaining of ongoing customer relationships, i.e. ensuring repeat business. Our focus groups found that users will complete a shopping transaction even while the site has poor performance, if only because they have loaded up their shopping cart and therefore have a significant investment of time and energy at the site. However, if performance is perceived as not acceptable, the customer will remember that shopping experience and actively avoid the specific site again. This results in perhaps one completed sale but, more importantly, one customer who will not come back to the site. This information about a repulsed customer is not contained in any log; only a successful transaction is recorded, providing misleading information to the e-commerce site operator. To ensure repeat business, the transaction must complete with acceptable performance for each page access. The phenomenon of duration causing users to be more critical of performance can be expressed as a function that takes into account the duration of the session. Here we express the 'utility' of a session of requests as a number between 1 and -1, where utility > 0 indicates that acceptable performance thresholds have been exceeded, utility $= 0$ indicates that the service is exactly acceptable, utility < 0 is unacceptable performance. Total utility of a session of length N can be expressed as:

$$\text{Utility} = \frac{\displaystyle\sum_{i-1}^{N} \frac{\text{threshold}(i) - \text{latency}(i)}{\text{threshold}(i)}}{N}$$

where threshold(i) = threshold of acceptability of access i; latency(i) = delay in completion of page i; N = length of session.

Based on our data, threshold(i) decreases as i increases which implies that latency(i) must improve as i increases, just to maintain the same utility over a session. This relationship is illustrated in Table 3.

An e-commerce site generally has a notion of a session which is typically implemented using cookies. A cookie is used to associate a user with a shopping cart and profile. The cookie can directly encode a session duration field and be used to index into a table of session duration. With this information the server can schedule response times to maximize

Table 3
Utility values for different latencies over time

Page number	Threshold(i) (s)	Utility at latency of		
		6 s	10 s	16 s
1	16	0.63	0.38	0
2	16	0.63	0.38	0
3	16	0.63	0.38	0
4	16	0.63	0.38	0
5	10	0.58	0.30	−0.12
6	10	0.55	0.25	−0.20
7	10	0.53	0.21	−0.26
8	10	0.51	0.19	−0.30
9	10	0.50	0.17	−0.33
10	10	0.49	0.15	−0.36
11	10	0.48	0.14	−0.38
12	10	0.48	0.12	−0.40
13	10	0.47	0.12	−0.42
14	10	0.47	0.11	−0.43
15	10	0.46	0.10	−0.44
16	10	0.46	0.09	−0.45
17	10	0.45	0.09	−0.46
18	6	0.43	0.05	−0.53
19	6	0.41	0.01	−0.59
20	6	0.39	−0.03	−0.64
21	6	0.37	−0.06	−0.69
22	6	0.35	−0.08	−0.73

the utility for each user, for the average of all users, or for a premium class of users. The server can use the session length as an indication of the tolerance of the user to delay. At a minimum, this calculation of utility can be used to more exactly assess the performance of the site by taking into account the session duration. An alternative to this cookie method is the use of URL parameters that encode the length of the session. This is described below in Section 4.3.

4.3. Task expectations and latency requirements

Although we did not specifically set out to measure the difference in latency based upon task differences, we nevertheless found significant differences in tolerance and this was confirmed during focus group discussions. The importance of the finding is that users' expectations are different, based on their beliefs about the complexity of the task, the slowness of access of remote information, or the effects of caching. We can apply this to Web site performance by classifying requests by the kind of access type and then apply appropriate deadlines to the task. To establish the expectations of users, the task sets for each site can be profiled through user testing. A table can be established that maps quality ratings to the latencies of specific tasks. This information can be used in conjunction with duration information as well.

The association of tasks to deadlines can be encoded in the URL. There are several ways that this can be done. The simplest is to embed this information in parameters for the URL so that servers can classify requests with minimum performance penalty. For example http://www.shopping.hp.com/cgi-bin/shopping/scripts/general/shopping_basket.jsp is an URL that our participants believed could take some time to process because it retrieves a shopping basket. On the other hand, the main home page http://www.shopping.village.hp.com was one they felt should load up immediately. We can associate a deadline with the URL by passing this information as a parameter that can be quickly parsed and does not require consulting a table of URLs for the appropriate deadline. For deadlines that can be calculated once such as task-based deadlines the URLs can be included in the parameter, for example:

```
http://www.e-shopping.com/
  lots_of_goodies?task_deadline=3
```

The parameter could also specify a *task-type* flag that can be interpreted by the servers, for example:

```
http://www.e-shopping.com/
  lots_of_goodies?task_type=fast
http:/www.e-shopping.com/
  calc_cart_costs?task_type=calc
```

This *task-type* flag technique allows the deadline to be calculated by the task using other information, such as client class of service or duration of the session for this client. For sites that do not maintain client-based session information, the URLs can be dynamically generated to include session duration as well as task deadline parameters, for example by incrementing counters embedded in the URLs. Many e-commerce sites dynamically generate all URLs in each page and include client-specific parameters, so there may already exist a framework under which these parameters can be conveniently added.

4.4. *When to send feedback?*

Using our measures of the latency users will tolerate, we can modify servers to provide feedback to users. Our results have shown that providing information concerning the processing of a request can significantly increase users' tolerance of poor QoS. The experiments in incremental loading show that people are willing to classify the service as high for up to 39 seconds instead of 5 if they have some notion that progress is being made. If the request has not completed within 5–10 seconds the user should be sent some indication that the request is still being processed. At this threshold the user is unsure whether the request has not been received correctly, if the site is down, or if the transaction has failed. The feedback to the user can be delivered as a multi-part HTML reply and can keep the client informed of the progress. It can even include boiler plate information that will be included in the final complete response. Without knowledge about when feedback is or is not to be expected, many users abandon long-running requests. Informing the user if their request will be delayed above the established threshold for tolerance implicates that the QoS of the task as a whole is seen as better:

"I think it's great ... saying we are unusually busy, there may be some delays, you might want to visit later. You've told me now. If I decide to go ahead, that's my choice".

4.5. *QoS auditing*

While a site may make every effort to provide high quality of service, the measurement and interpretation of actual performance is essential. Using the thresholds of acceptability of response time, the objective performance to Web server monitoring data such as log files can be interpreted. For example, if the response times are less than 5 seconds 95% of the time and we know from our study that this constitutes high performance, then we can conclude that users experience high QoS 95% of the time at that site. Web servers can categorize and report very specifically for how many users it delivered high, medium, and low qualities of service, over time based on transaction volume. Servers can even identify specific pages for which service has deteriorated. For example, if the QoS was high during all the page viewings up to checkout, but checkout drops to medium or low, this change in performance can be noted. This can point out aspects of Web server and application servers that may need additional capacity to boost performance. The session QoS can also be reported and correlated to specific tasks that experience poor performance at the site. The QoS auditing information could also be used to give feedback to the users. For example, if the server maintains historical data about site access patterns, then when it sees itself under a heavy load it can compare that load to typical load measures for the particular time of day/week/month. It can then provide feedback to the user about what level of service they can expect to get. The server might even be able to suggest a time when the server is less likely to be so heavily loaded, or predict what the response time will be. This interpretation of log and real-time monitoring data is critically important as it provides a user's perspective of performance. The interpretation of objective thresholds of performance can also be used to decide when a site should be upgraded if the goal of the enterprise is to assure high QoS. Without these objective measures, the enterprise is only presented with absolute server response numbers, with no way to associate this data with user perceptions of QoS.

5. Conclusions and future work

This study was designed to investigate users' requirements for Internet QoS. We have shown that:

- the task in which users are engaged, the length of time they have been interacting with a site, and the method of page loading affect the acceptability of QoS;
- tolerance of delay is influenced by the conceptual model users have of how the system works;
- poor Web site performance leads to poor corporate image and often compromises users' conceptions of the security of the site;
- the findings of users' perception can be integrated into server design and therefore result in QoS controls that reflect users' perception of quality.

We have shown that users' behavior in reaction to the level of QoS can be objectively quantified. Our findings have outlined a set of objective thresholds that reflect users' subjective assessments of quality. We were also able to identify salient parameters to a utility function. This function can be used to predict users' dynamic reactions to the QoS they receive. Predicting such reactions is a crucial step in accommodating user demand.

Our study focused on a Web-shopping task and the implications for server performance. We now have data to modify the server to give performance based on the absolute measures of latency for high, average, and low quality of service. To further validate these results, empirical work is needed to test these technical assumptions; for example, observing user interaction with a modified server, to determine if a server that consistently meets the objective thresholds for high QoS is in fact perceived by users as providing a high QoS experience.

Our experience with duration of Web site interaction indicates that thresholds of acceptability change over time. A more precise mapping of these changes is needed. Again, it would be interesting to modify a server to improve the completion times of pages as the session time increases. Ideally, we would then be able to analyze the logs of the site and note that there was an increase in completed sessions and therefore successful buying operations.

There are a number of areas in which the study could be made more comprehensive. An obvious improvement would be a larger study that includes female subjects. Female e-commerce shopping is growing rapidly and they may have different user perceptions which should be measured and incorporated into the findings. Our study covered one specific e-commerce site, but certainly the experiment needs to be repeated with a variety of sites to be confident of the generality of the results. This study was also specific to a Web shopping task. Further study of users' perceptions of QoS should investigate the validity of our findings in different genres of Web usage, such as entertainment. The combination of results from different genres would make it possible to create more comprehensive conceptual models to predict how tolerance changes over the length of a session. Our research represents an important first step in identifying that such a relationship exists, and therefore indicating the need for technology to meet this requirement.

Acknowledgements

We thank Ilja Bedner for invaluable assistance with system configuration, Sharad Singhal, Ed Perry and Ilja Bedner for their help with experimental design, and members of HP Labs for participating in pilot studies. We also thank the WWW9 reviewers for their helpful comments.

References

[1] T. Abdelzaher and N. Bhatti, Adaptive content delivery for Web server QoS, in: Proc. of IWQoS'99, London, May 1999.

[2] J. Alameida et al., Providing different levels of service in Web hosting, in: Proc. of the Internet Server Performance Workshop, March 1998.

[3] G. Banga and P. Druschel, Resource containers: a new facility for web content hosting, in: Proc. of the Internet Server Performance Workshop, March 1998.

[4] Y. Bernet, A framework for end-to-end QoS combining RSVP/Intserv and differentiated services, IETF, March 1998.

[5] J. Berst, Bandwidth progress report, Available at http://www.zdnet.com/anchordesk/story/story_1384.html.

[6] N. Bhatti and R. Friedrich, Web server support for tiered services, IEEE Network (September/October 1999).

[7] A. Bouch and M.A. Sasse, Network QoS: what do users need, in: IDC'99, Madrid, September 1999.

[8] A. Bouch and M.A. Sasse, It ain't what you charge it's the way that you do it: a user perspective of network QoS and pricing, in: Proc. of IM'99, Boston MA, May 1999.

[9] A. Bouch et al., Quality is in the eye of the beholder: meeting users's requirements for Internet quality of service, in: Proc. of ACM Conference on Human Factors in Computing Systems (CHI 2000), to appear April 2000, The Hague.

[10] D.L. Boyer, J.G. Pollack and T.F. Eggemeier, Effects of aging on subjective workload and performance: determinants of age differences in cognitive performance, in: Proc. of Human Factors Society 36th Annual Meeting 1 (1992).

[11] S.K. Card, T.P. Moran and A. Newell, The Psychology of Human-Computer Interaction, Lawrence Erlbaum Associates, Hillsdale, NJ, 1983

[12] P. Cullinane, Ready, set, crash, Telephony (November 1998).

[13] M.D. Dunlop and C. Johnson, Subjectivity and notions of time and value in interactive information retrieval, Interacting with Computers 10 (1) (1998).

[14] ETE Watch for Web Browsers, http:/www.candle.com/ete watch.

[15] P.C. Fishburn and O.M. Odlyzko, Dynamic behavior of differential pricing and Quality of Service options for the Internet, Proc. of ICE-98, ACM Press.

[16] R. Fox, News track, Communications of the ACM (May 1999) 9–10.

[17] D.O.A. Stahl and A.B. Whinston, Pricing of services on the Internet, http://cism.bus.utexas.edu/alok/pricing.html.

[18] Graphic, visualization, and usability center's WWW user surveys, http://www.cc.gatech.edu/gvu/user_surveys.

[19] M. Hogan, The first ever report on the top 100 e-commerce businesses and the secrets of their success, PC Computing Magazine (June 8, 1999).

[20] HP Shopping Village, http://www.shopping.hp.com.

[21] J. Kawalek, A user perspective for QoS management, in: Proc. QoS Workshop, 16 September, 1995, Crete.

[22] J.J. Keller, Ex-MFs managers plan to build global network based on Internet, Wall Street Journal (January 20, 1998).

[23] A. Kokotopoulos, Subjective assessment of multimedia systems for distance learning, in: Proc. of the European Conference on Multimedia Applications, Services and Techniques, Milan, May 1997.

[24] J.K. Mackie-Mason and H. Varian, Economic FAQs about the Internet, in: L.W. McKnight and J.P. Bailey (Eds.), Internet Economics, MIT Press, Cambridge, MA, 1997.

[25] K. Morgan, R.L. Morris, H. Macleod and S. Gibbs, Gender differences and cognitive style, human–computer interaction, in: Proc. of EWHCI'92, 1992.

[26] B.A. Myers, The importance of percent-done progress indicators for computer–human interfaces, in: Proc. of CHI'85, San Francisco, CA, April 1985.

[27] Network reliability steering committee annual report 1998, http://www.nric.org.

[28] W. Newman and H. Lamming, Interactive Systems Design, Prentice-Hall, Englewood Cliffs, NJ, 1995.

[29] J. Nielsen, Top ten mistakes of Web design, http:/www.usei t.com/alertbox/9605.html.

[30] J. Nielson, Usability Engineering, AP Professional Press, Boston, MA, 1994.

[31] C. Perry, Travelers on the Internet, A survey of Internet users, Online 19 (2) (1995).

[32] J. Ramsay, A. Barbesi and J. Preece, Psychological investigation of long retrieval times on the World Wide Web, Interacting with Computers 10 (1) (1998).

[33] Y. Rogers, Evaluating the meaningfulness of icon sets to represent command operations, display based systems, in: Proc. HCI'86 Conference on People and Computers II, 1986, pp. 586–603.

[34] The Internet, Technology 1999, Analysis and Forecast, IEEE Spectrum, January 1999.

[35] Z. Wang, USD: Scalable bandwidth for differentiated services, http://www.ietf.org/drafts-wang-00.txt.

[36] A. Watson and M.A. Sasse, Multimedia conferencing via multicast: determining the quality of service required by the end-user, in: Proc. International Workshop on Audio–Visual Services over Packet Networks (AVSPN) 15–16 September, 1997, Aberdeen.

Analyzing factors that influence end-to-end Web performance

Balachander Krishnamurthy [a,1], Craig E. Wills [b,*]

[a] *AT&T Laboratories – Research, 180 Park Avenue, Florham Park, NJ 07932, USA*
[b] *Computer Science Department, Worcester Polytechnic Institute, Worcester, MA 01609, USA*

Abstract

Web performance impacts the popularity of a particular Web site or service as well as the load on the network, but there have been no publicly available *end-to-end* measurements that have focused on a large number of popular Web servers examining the components of delay or the effectiveness of the recent changes to the HTTP protocol. In this paper we report on an extensive study carried out from many client sites geographically distributed around the world to a collection of over 700 servers to which a majority of Web traffic is directed. Our results show that the HTTP/1.1 protocol, particularly with pipelining, is indeed an improvement over existing practice, but that servers serving a small number of objects or closing a persistent connection without explicit notification can reduce or eliminate any performance improvement. Similarly, use of caching and multi-server content distribution can also improve performance if done effectively.

Keywords: Web performance; Web protocols; End-to-end performance; Active measurement

1. Introduction

Several projects have studied factors that influence the performance of the Web using Web server logs, proxy logs and client traces. Significant effort has gone into improving the protocol on which the Web is based and the new version of HTTP, namely HTTP/1.1 has been recently upgraded to a draft standard by IETF [4]. However, to the best of our knowledge, no one has performed an end-to-end test of the Web in terms of the factors that influence performance as perceived by users when they visit various Web sites.

This work grows out of independent work by the authors for testing different aspects of Web performance. It is a natural follow-up PROCOW study [9], an original large-scale study examining if the Web servers running at popular Web sites around the world claiming to run HTTP/1.1 were indeed compliant with the HTTP/1.1 protocol specification. The PROCOW study examined the compliancy of the servers by sending valid HTTP/1.1 client requests from several places in the world. The major conclusion of the PROCOW study was that many sites were not fully compliant with the HTTP/1.1 protocol and some sites were turning off the new features in HTTP/1.1. The work described in this paper also follows up on the methodology of the work examining content reuse and server responses relevant for Web caching [19].

In this work we build on the PROCOW infrastructure and use nine client sites around the world to test how various factors affect the *performance*

* Corresponding author. E-mail: cew@cs.wpi.edu
[1] E-mail: bala@research.att.com

of the Web. Our study is based on the key set of changes between HTTP/1.0 and HTTP/1.1 [10] to test their impact on performance. We also examine their impact on performance in conjunction with other factors such as caching and distributed Web content.

Our study is significant in that it examines the performance of various protocol options by measuring end-to-end response for actual Web servers from a variety of client sites. This is a significantly broader study compared to that of Nielsen et al. [17], which measured the performance of HTTP/1.0 and HTTP/1.1 in a controlled setting for a single synthesized Web page. We gathered a set of active measurements by sending requests from various client sites around the world to over 700 popular sites to help quantify the benefits of HTTP/1.1 features in conjunction with other factors. These include persistent connections, persistent connections with pipelining, range requests, caching and responses from multiple servers for a single Web page.

The collection of Web servers tested are representative of the *interesting* set of Web servers since we attempted to include servers to which a significant portion of the request traffic is addressed. We do not claim that our client sites are representative of all users, but they do include a variety of sites. We ensured that there is some degree of control in our experiment but given that the Web experience changes fairly often, our study mimics real life. In analyzing the results, we look for trends rather than absolute numbers. The fact that the results are relatively consistent over multiple clients and that we make some measurements from the same client/server pair over multiple days at the same time gives us some degree of belief in the repeatability of our experiments.

In the remainder of this paper we describe the factors studied in our work, followed by a discussion of the methodology we used in performing the study. The middle portion of the paper presents the results from our study on the test sets we use followed by a discussion on possible implications of these results for Web servers, caches and the HTTP protocol. The paper concludes with a description of related work followed by a summary and our own directions for future work.

2. Study

There are numerous factors involved in the end-to-end performance of retrieving a Web page over the Internet. In the following we describe the specific factors we study (and those we do not) in this work and our reasons for doing so. In addition, there are many factors that we do not explicitly study, but consider in the testing and analysis of the various factors.

2.1. Factors studied

The factors we explicitly study are the following.

- *Protocol options.* What is the effect of different HTTP options on performance? HTTP/1.0 has been used by clients and servers for a long time, but clients and servers have been moving to HTTP/1.1. The de facto standard use of HTTP/1.0 has been for clients to open multiple parallel connections to the same server in order to improve performance over serialized connections. In HTTP/1.1 persistent connections are supported, which can either be used for serialized request/response pairs or for pipelining multiple requests and then receiving multiple responses. The relative performance of these protocol options was studied by Nielsen et al. [17] but it was done on a limited basis with a single artificially created page with 40 embedded objects. The experiment was useful to isolate specific low-level issues on the impact of TCP on HTTP/1.1 and demonstrated the usefulness of pipelining/persistent connections under the test conditions. A primary goal of our work is to study these protocol options using real-life servers.
- *Caching.* We do not study expected cache hit rates nor particular policies for cache replacement and coherency. These issues have been studied in numerous pieces of previous work such as [3,11]. Rather we focus on studying the relative performance gains for different levels of caching effectiveness. These relative gains may vary according to the protocol option being used, the cache hit rate and whether validation of cached content is required.
- *Multi-server content.* Rather than serve the base page and all embedded images from the same

base server, Web sites are serving some or all of the embedded objects from different servers — both servers located at the same site and on servers located at different sites. This approach reduces the load on the base server, but does it improve the response time for the end user?

- *Byte range requests*. This feature of HTTP/1.1 allows a client to request only parts of an object rather than the entire object. Obviously, there is a clear gain in bandwidth usage since fewer bytes are shipped. But does this translate into significant savings in user-perceived latency? For example, would a proxy cache be better off retrieving the entire object in response to a client request for a specific byte range request? If the time to respond to a byte range request is not significantly less than the time to respond to a full content request then the proxy could retrieve the entire contents for possible later use.

2.2. Factors considered

In studying these factors there are numerous other factors that must be accounted for in our testing and analysis. These factors are as follows.

- *Network delay*. The magnitude and variance of network delay between a client and server can have a major influence on the total response time for serving a set of Web objects from the server to the client. In an ideal study we would be able to control this variable as we conduct various tests, but to do so requires an artificial testbed, which would raise questions about the applicability of any results to actual networks. Rather, our approach is to test with real networks and account for effects of variable network delays in our analysis. Tests of the different protocol options to the same server are tested consecutively so they are done under similar network conditions. We also tested client/server pairs at different times of day to vary the network conditions under which measurements were taken.
- *Server load*. The server load can have a major influence on the time to service a request. As is the case for network delay, we do not control, or even know, the load of a server under test, but we always test different protocol options between a client and a server at approximately the same time and we do vary the time of day in which testing is done.
- *Number of objects and total bytes*. The time to retrieve a Web page is dependent on the number and size of objects it contains. In our study we do not specifically control this variable, but rather we select a test set of Web pages and then account for the number and size of objects in our analysis.

2.3. Factors not examined

There are many other factors influencing the end-to-end performance in retrieving a Web page. The following are some that we considered for our current study, but did not include.

- *DNS lookup time*. Once a server to IP address mapping has been obtained and is cached, the DNS lookup time is a trivial contribution to the overall performance. If the mapping is not cached then this contributes some time to overall performance. Because we expect most mappings to be cached in our study we did not explicitly study the lookup time.
- *Redirection*. Some Web sites use HTTP redirection to direct user requests to another URL. We did not consider the cost of this redirection, but rather dropped such sites from our study.
- *Dynamic content*. The amount of time for a server to serve an object stored as a static file should be less than the time to serve an object of the same size that must be dynamically generated. We plan to study this issue in the future.
- *Packet level performance*. Examining packet level performance through tools such as *tcpdump* would be useful in understanding reasons for observed delays and variance in network performance. However, to keep a simpler test set up for distribution to a number of client sites around the world we chose not to include packet level performance issues at this time.

3. Methodology

Our basic methodology is to make active measurements on the effect of different protocol options for a large number of client/server pairs at different times. The previous study on HTTP/1.1 performance improvements used an artificial environment for testing [17]. Other Web performance studies have used logs and packet traces to obtain timing information, but this approach does not allow a controlled set of requests to be issued. Our approach was to identify a set of client and server sites for our tests.

We came to an early conclusion that it would be difficult to have a set of representative client sites since information about the distribution of clients and their network connections is both hard to obtain and verify. Additionally, to obtain a fair sampling of clients around the world would involve significant effort. We chose to sample from a set of client sites where we had professional connections. The client sites used in our study along with their location and network setup are given below.

(1) AT&T Research Labs, NJ USA, with multiple T-1 connections to the Internet.
(2) A commercial site in Santiago, Chile (10 Mbps via fiber to Telefonica Net which has a slower link to the Internet and links to Cable and Wireless and Alternet via two hops of 45 Mbps ATM link).
(3) Hewlett-Packard Labs, Palo Alto, CA, USA, connects to the public Internet via one of four major ISPs depending upon the traffic's destination, each ISP being connected with one or more T-3 circuits.
(4) ACIRI: AT&T Center for Internet Research at ICSI, Berkeley, CA, USA (10 Mbps link from ACIRI to UCB, then UCB to Internet over Calren).
(5) University of Kentucky, Lexington, Kentucky, USA, connected via UUNET over a DS3 (45 Mbps link).
(6) A site belonging to an academic network UNINETT AS, in Trondheim, Norway (10 Mbps link to UNINETT-GW and increasing speed links to the Internet via NORDUnet).
(7) University of Western Australia, Nedlands, Western Australia.
(8) A private site in Cape Town, South Africa with a 64K Digital connection, similar to a US-standard 56K connection, to the Internet.
(9) Worcester Polytechnic Institute, Worcester, MA, USA, with multiple T-1 links to the Internet.

The choice of servers is a bit easier since there is a necessary concurrence in the notion of 'popular' sites. Advertisers depend on this information and sites would attempt to demonstrate that studies significantly lowering their standing in any ranking are incorrect. Accordingly, we went with a subset of the collection done for the PROCOW study [9], which used a combination of collection techniques. Briefly, it merged a combination of recognized rating sites (MediaMetrix [13], Netcraft [16], Hot100 [18]) and a set of sites that are likely to be popular given their business prominence (Fortune 500 [5] and Global 500 [7]). The end result was a list of 711 popular server sites for which we retrieved the home page and all embedded objects. In creating the list, we did not try to distinguish whether a server site was supporting HTTP/1.0 or HTTP/1.1.

The basic engine for making all retrievals in our study is httperf [15]. We obtained a publicly available copy of the software and modified it slightly to print out additional information needed for our study. The httperf software is attractive because it allows a set of objects to be retrieved from a server using the variety of 1.0 and 1.1 protocol options of interest to our study. The native software collects and prints out a number of statistics about the status and performance of retrieving the set of objects. Of particular interest to our study is that it records the number of server connections made and for each retrieved object, the time the request was sent, the time receipt of the response began and the time the complete response was received. For small objects the last two times may be the same.

The algorithm in Fig. 1 describes the method used for a single test between a client and a server. It exploits features of httperf and overcomes certain limitations of httperf for the purposes of our study. The two primary limitations that we had to overcome was that httperf does not parse HTML code to retrieve embedded images and a single run of httperf could communicate with only one server. However, we exploited httperf's feature of retrieving a fixed set of URLs from a server using serial requests over separate connections, parallel requests over separate connections, serial requests over a persistent connection and pipelined requests over a persistent connection. The resulting algorithm starting with a base URL for a given server is shown in Fig. 1.

There are a number of points to note about the algorithm. The initial retrieval in Step 1 is used to

```
1. Use httperf to retrieve the base URL from the server and store the results.
2. Parse the base URL code to determine all unique embedded objects.
3. Separate the base and embedded objects according to their server.
4. For each server containing needed objects {
    5. (serial-1.0) Use httperf to retrieve all objects using
       serialized HTTP/1.0 requests.
    6. (burst-1.0) Use httperf to retrieve all objects using
       up to four parallel HTTP/1.0 requests.
    7. (serial-1.1) Use httperf to retrieve all objects using
       serialized requests over an HTTP/1.1 persistent connection.
    8. (burst-1.1) Use httperf to retrieve all objects using
       pipelined requests over an HTTP/1.1 persistent connection.
}
```

Fig. 1. Basic algorithm to test a server from a client.

determine the set of objects to fetch. If all embedded objects are from the same server as the base URL then there will be only one server list in Step 3. The server list for the base server includes the base object. The burstiness of parallel connections in Step 6 and pipelined connections in Step 8 does not begin until the first object in the list is retrieved. Step 1 retrieves and stores the object contents. Steps 5–8 retrieve, but do not store object contents. Steps 5–8 are used for all performance measurements.

We used four parallel connections in the burst-1.0 method since that appears to be the default in the popular browsers (Netscape and Internet Explorer). With each additional parallel connection, there is a necessary load on the client and the server (more on the server since it has to have free TCP slots to handle several client connections in parallel).

This basic test is used to compare performance of each protocol option for a specific client and server. While the comparison of response times for an individual test may not be meaningful due to variation in network and server load, we use these individual tests as building blocks for measuring the relative performance of the protocol options over a large number of tests.

We used this basic test over two sets of test data. All tests were made in November, 1999. The first set of test data consists of the 711 previously identified servers. Tests of each of these servers were run once from each of the client sites. The tests last several hours so each client/server test may be run under different network conditions, but the four protocol options of each test are run under approximately the same conditions.

In addition, we ran the test in a more controlled setting from the AT&T, Chile and WPI client sites. For these tests we selected 72 server sites from a list of 200 sites identified on the current MediaMetrix, Netcraft and Hot100 sites. The selected sites were chosen because they supported pipelining and persistent connections in a test run on these sites. The controlled tests were run on the same fixed 6 h intervals from each site for a week. This controlled test was designed to study caching and time of day factors.

4. Results

This section provides results to address the factors for study that were identified in Section 2.

4.1. Test sets

The initial part of our results is analyzing the base set of statistics for our client/server test sets, and is shown in Table 1 for client/server pairs. The clients are our test sites, the servers are either PROCOW indicating that we tested the 711 servers from the earlier PROCOW study or 'select' indicating that we tested with 72 servers repeated every 6 h.

Focusing on the PROCOW test set, the second column indicates the number of servers out of the 711 that returned an HTTP 200 response code (success) when the base URL was retrieved. Those not returning this value either returned 302 (redirection), 404 (not found), or the client timed out. Once the base URL is retrieved, all objects contained on this

Table 1
Test sets

Client/server set	Successful retrieval of base URL	Servers with successful object retrieval	Multiple object servers	Perfect connection persistent servers	Imperfect connection persistent servers
att/procow	670	855	674	167 (25%)	121 (18%)
aciri/procow	673	858	667	223 (33%)	73 (11%)
aust/procow	667	854	664	201 (30%)	56 (8%)
chile/procow	674	862	671	200 (30%)	74 (11%)
hp/procow	665	854	662	201 (30%)	73 (11%)
uky/procow	645	824	635	196 (31%)	84 (13%)
norway/procow	668	856	662	128 (19%)	38 (6%)
safrica/procow	663	848	654	194 (30%)	92 (14%)
wpi/procow	657	834	662	192 (29%)	66 (10%)
att/select	1515	2588	1975	858 (43%)	206 (10%)
chile/select	1873	3161	2423	910 (38%)	288 (12%)
wpi/select	1897	3223	2456	1049 (43%)	274 (11%)

page were retrieved. As shown in Fig. 1 multiple servers may be accessed to retrieve all objects. The third column of Table 1 shows a count of these servers that successfully returned all objects. The fourth column shows the number of these servers that return more than one object. We focus on these servers because persistent connections will not have an effect on client access time if only one object is retrieved. The last two columns in Table 1 show the number and percentage of multiple object servers exhibiting persistent connections.

The last two columns need further explanation: one focus of our study is to compare the performance of the four protocol options. Thus for a client/server test, we only want to consider cases where all objects needed from that server are successfully retrieved for all protocol options. If one or more of the four protocol option tests retrieves fewer than all objects then we discount that test (all four protocol options) for further study. In addition to the number of objects retrieved we also examine the number of TCP connections that are used. If an HTTP/1.1 test used as many TCP connections as objects then all objects have been retrieved, but not with any persistent connections. These test cases are also eliminated from further study. The remaining tests are classified as showing some connection persistence. These tests retrieve all objects for all protocol options and use fewer TCP connections than objects needed for both 1.1 options. Of this category, we classify tests using only one TCP connection for both HTTP/1.1 tests as 'perfect' indicating all objects are retrieved in a single persistent connection. We characterize tests exhibiting some connection persistence, but not perfect connection persistence, as 'imperfect' meaning that one or both of the 1.1 options used more than one TCP connection.

The last three rows of Table 1 show the same statistics for the selected set of servers tested periodically from three client sites. The last two columns indicate that these tests are a bit better in exhibiting a higher percentage of persistence, but the percentages are not as high as we would expect from a 'select' group. These reduced numbers come from the inclusion of servers not exhibiting persistence in our initial tests due to an early error (subsequently fixed) in one of our analysis scripts. In addition, just because the base server supports persistence, it is possible that other servers providing its embedded objects may not. Again only tests exhibiting persistence are considered for further analysis.

As a final point on summarizing the test sets we note that the Nielsen et al. paper on HTTP/1.1 also described two other performance improvements — cascading style sheets (CSS) and portable network graphics (PNG). As an interesting sidelight to our study we examined penetration of these improvements to the set of PROCOW servers. Examination of the AT&T results (typical for other results) showed 82 (12%) of the 670 base URLs using style sheets. A similar examination for PNG images found zero usage.

4.2. Protocol options

In examining the various issues influencing end-to-end Web performance we first examined the impact of the four protocol options described in Fig. 1. For this analysis we only consider the client/server tests exhibiting persistence. Results for the four protocol options from three of the client sites using the PROCOW test set are shown in Table 2 for servers that exhibit perfect connection persistence in the retrieval of objects. Results from the remaining client sites are shown in Table 8 at the end of the paper.

Table 2 shows four lines of results for each client site. For each client, the first three lines are classifications based on the number of objects to be retrieved while the fourth line is a summary for all multi-object server tests exhibiting perfect connection persistence. The categorization is introduced to examine variations that occur due to the number of objects retrieved. The ranges of 2–5, 6–15 and 16+ are intended to reflect a small, medium and large number of objects for retrieval. The second column in the table reflects the relative percentage of servers with the given number of objects relative to the total count of servers (column 3 in Table 1). The fourth column in the table indicates the percentage of servers exhibiting perfect connection persistence among all servers with the given range of objects. For example, 49% of servers with 2–5 objects showed perfect connection persistence when tested from the AT&T client. The fact that only 3% of the servers with 16+ objects exhibited perfect connection persistence from the AT&T client is out of line with the performance of all other client sites in Tables 2 and 8. We do not have a clear explanation for this behavior, but do note that the percentage of the servers with 16+ objects exhibiting imperfect connection persistence from the AT&T client in Table 4 is actually higher than for other client sites.

The last four columns show the average retrieval time for each of the four protocol options in seconds. The number in parentheses is the ratio of the given time to the time for the burst-1.0 option. The ratio is intended to show the relative performance of each option relative to common HTTP/1.0 usage. Again illustrating with an example, the burst-1.1 option (pipelining with persistence) for 6–15 objects from the AT&T client took on average 1.40 s to retrieve. This time is approximately 60% (0.6) of the time taken to retrieve the same objects using burst-1.0.

Table 3 shows an alternate approach for presenting the relative performance of the four protocol options for perfect connection persistence servers. The table shows the relative variation in the results shown in Table 2. The retrieval times for each protocol option from a client site are compared against the time for the burst-1.0 option. If the absolute value of the difference is less than 1 s then the relative performance of these two options is considered the 'same'. If the protocol option exhibits better than 1 s performance improvement then this option is

Table 2
Servers exhibiting perfect connection persistence from three client sites

Client site	Object count range	Range percentage for range (%)	Percentage persistent (%)	Average retrieval time (s) (ratio with burst-1.0)			
				serial-1.0	burst-1.0	serial-1.1	burst-1.1
att	2–5	26	49	1.83 (1.1)	1.65 (1.0)	1.68 (1.0)	1.73 (1.0)
att	6–15	22	26	2.96 (1.3)	2.28 (1.0)	1.74 (0.8)	1.40 (0.6)
att	16+	28	3	3.71 (1.4)	2.70 (1.0)	1.72 (0.6)	1.21 (0.4)
att	Multi	76	25	2.25 (1.2)	1.88 (1.0)	1.70 (0.9)	1.61 (0.9)
chile	2–5	26	48	9.23 (1.5)	6.27 (1.0)	6.45 (1.0)	6.24 (1.0)
chile	6–15	22	25	23.45 (2.0)	11.73 (1.0)	12.08 (1.0)	9.13 (0.8)
chile	16+	28	18	45.11 (2.9)	15.52 (1.0)	23.51 (1.5)	13.06 (0.8)
chile	Multi	76	30	20.47 (2.1)	9.59 (1.0)	11.53 (1.2)	8.42 (0.9)
wpi	2–5	26	46	5.24 (1.1)	4.90 (1.0)	3.69 (0.8)	3.60 (0.7)
wpi	6–15	21	25	14.23 (1.7)	8.15 (1.0)	7.49 (0.9)	5.87 (0.7)
wpi	16+	28	18	26.87 (2.1)	12.87 (1.0)	14.28 (1.1)	8.20 (0.6)
wpi	Multi	75	30	12.24 (1.6)	7.46 (1.0)	6.97 (0.9)	5.18 (0.7)

Table 3
Variation in performance for servers exhibiting perfect connection persistence from three client sites

Client site	Object count range	Better/same/worse% performance relative to burst-1.0			
		serial-1.0	burst-1.0	serial-1.1	burst-1.1
att	2–5	15/75/9%	0/100/0%	15/76/8%	15/74/11%
att	6–15	10/42/48%	0/100/0%	16/84/0%	22/70/8%
att	16+	29/29/43%	0/100/0%	43/29/29%	57/43/0%
att	Multi	14/63/22%	0/100/0%	17/77/7%	19/71/10%
chile	2–5	12/18/70%	0/100/0%	15/58/28%	23/59/18%
chile	6–15	06/00/94%	0/100/0%	32/21/47%	62/21/17%
chile	16+	00/00/100%	0/100/0%	07/00/93%	73/02/25%
chile	Multi	08/10/82%	0/100/0%	17/37/47%	43/38/20%
wpi	2–5	23/46/31%	0/100/0%	31/50/19%	33/54/13%
wpi	6–15	15/07/78%	0/100/0%	28/41/30%	41/48/11%
wpi	16+	12/02/86%	0/100/0%	30/21/49%	53/23/23%
wpi	Multi	19/27/55%	0/100/0%	30/41/29%	40/46/15%

classified as ‘better’ than burst-1.0 and if its performance is more than 1 s worse then it is classified as ‘worse’. Table 3 shows the percentages of servers that are classified as better, the same and worse for each protocol option from the three client sites in Table 2. The results are consistent with the ratios given in Table 2, except they reduce the significance of differences for relatively well-connected clients such as AT&T where the retrieval times for all protocol options are relatively small.

Overall, the burst-1.1 option generally exhibits the best performance with the burst-1.0 and serial-1.1 options in the middle and the serial-1.0 option exhibiting the worst performance. These results are as expected and consistent with those presented in [17]. However, a number of other results come out of examination of the results in Tables 2, 3 and 8.

(1) The percentage of servers that exhibit perfect connection persistence goes down as the number of objects retrieved increases.
(2) The relative performance of burst-1.1 (compared to burst-1.0) improves as the number of objects increases. Thus pipelining and persistence improves relative performance with more objects, but also causes more problems in correctly obtaining all objects with a single connection.
(3) The percentage of servers that support perfect connection persistence is relatively low. Looking at the ‘Multi’ row for each client site (or the fifth column in Table 1), we see the range to be 25–31% of servers. Variations occur because tests were run at different times from different clients under different network and server conditions.
   - To better understand this result we retested and analyzed results from the WPI client with the PROCOW test set. We found that all objects were successfully retrieved from multiple object servers in 99% and 98% of the cases for the serial-1.0 and burst-1.0 options. However, only in 29% of the cases did we find that objects were successfully retrieved from these servers with only one TCP connection using the burst-1.1 option. We found that objects were successfully retrieved for 40% of the cases for the serial-1.1 option. These results confirm that the failure of the burst-1.1 option to use only one connection is largely responsible for the small percentage of servers classified as perfect connection persistence servers.
   - In looking for reasons that persistence was not present, we found that in 36% of the cases for the burst-1.1 option, the server either reported it was using HTTP/1.0 or explicitly included `Connection: close` in one of its response headers. In 23% of cases for this option, the server did not exhibit any persistence nor was there any reason given based on the server response. These cases indicate that the TCP connection was closed or reset without explicit warning. The two figures were 24% and 11% for the serial-1.1 option.

Table 4
Servers exhibiting imperfect connection persistence from three client sites

Client site	Object count range	Range percentage (%)	Percentage persistent for range (%)	Average retrieval time (s) (ratio with burst-1.0)			
				serial-1.0	burst-1.0	serial-1.1	burst-1.1
att	2–5	26	5	7.57 (3.7)	2.05 (1.0)	2.75 (1.3)	4.89 (2.4)
att	6–15	22	15	4.78 (1.5)	3.15 (1.0)	3.03 (1.0)	2.61 (0.8)
att	16+	28	33	8.87 (2.0)	4.51 (1.0)	4.36 (1.0)	2.48 (0.6)
att	Multi	76	18	7.73 (2.0)	3.93 (1.0)	3.87 (1.0)	2.75 (0.7)
chile	2–5	26	8	17.82 (2.1)	8.69 (1.0)	10.92 (1.3)	12.25 (1.4)
chile	6–15	22	15	32.14 (2.0)	16.36 (1.0)	20.27 (1.2)	21.86 (1.3)
chile	16+	28	12	60.51 (2.6)	23.57 (1.0)	33.33 (1.4)	34.02 (1.4)
chile	Multi	76	11	39.39 (2.3)	17.22 (1.0)	22.94 (1.3)	24.13 (1.4)
wpi	2–5	26	7	5.77 (1.3)	4.28 (1.0)	7.32 (1.7)	6.44 (1.5)
wpi	6–15	21	14	19.14 (2.1)	9.04 (1.0)	11.69 (1.3)	12.64 (1.4)
wpi	16+	28	11	33.11 (2.6)	12.63 (1.0)	18.01 (1.4)	18.98 (1.5)
wpi	Multi	75	10	21.60 (2.3)	9.37 (1.0)	13.19 (1.4)	13.73 (1.5)

Table 4 shows results from three client sites for servers that exhibit imperfect connection persistence. Results for the additional client sites are shown in Table 9 at the end of the paper. Servers are classified as imperfect from a client site when the number of needed TCP connections is more than one, but fewer than the number of retrieved objects, for at least one of the 1.1 options. The results show that the relative performance of the serial-1.1 and burst-1.1 options is worse than the perfect connection persistent sites. These results indicate that the reconnection costs for dropped or lost connections impact the overall performance to the point that imperfect persistence servers generally exhibit worse performance with the 1.1 options than with the burst-1.0 option.

4.3. Time of day analysis

The previous analysis used results from retrievals by a client to a large number of servers. The various protocol options were tested at approximately the same time for each client/server pair, but there was no control when these tests were run. To have more control on when tests were run we created the smaller, select set of servers and created a script to test each server at precise six-hour intervals for one week. This script was run from the AT&T, Chile and WPI client sites. A test for the first server in the list was started at 0:02, 6:02, 12:02 and 18:02 GMT each day. Tests for subsequent servers in the list were started at three-minute intervals for an approximate testing period of three and one-half hours for a single round of testing. Results for each round from each of the three client sites are shown in Table 5, which is of similar format to Tables 2 and 4, but includes average object and byte count. Note that the results shown are only for servers exhibiting perfect connection persistence during at least one of the seven days in each time period.

The results show that average performance is generally best for the 6:00–9:30 GMT time period (1:00–4:30 on the east coast of the U.S.). WPI results show that the 12:00–15:30 time period is best. Performance is generally the worst for the 18:00–21:30 time period (13:00–16:30 EST). These variations are expected with an approximate ratio of two between the worst and best time periods for a protocol option. Of more interest to our study are the variations in relative performance of the four protocol options. The results show little variation in the relative performance of the options as network/server activity varies other than results from the AT&T client, which shows relatively fast access so small variations have a larger effect on the ratio.

4.4. Caching

We again used the select set of servers to analyze the end-to-end performance effects of caching and restricted our analysis to those server tests exhibiting perfect connection persistence. The performance of each of the protocol options is shown in the first row

Table 5
Servers exhibiting perfect connection persistence tested at different times of day

Client site	Time range (GMT)	Percentage persistent (%)	Average object count	Average object bytes	Average retrieval time (s) (ratio with burst-1.0)			
					serial-1.0	burst-1.0	serial-1.1	burst-1.1
att	00:00–03:30	42	7.4	32,248	1.85 (1.4)	1.30 (1.0)	2.06 (1.6)	1.74 (1.3)
att	06:00–09:30	42	7.7	33,093	1.60 (1.4)	1.18 (1.0)	2.22 (1.9)	1.68 (1.4)
att	12:00–15:30	43	7.5	32,886	3.47 (1.6)	2.22 (1.0)	2.51 (1.1)	2.14 (1.0)
att	18:00–21:30	42	7.3	31,754	3.81 (1.6)	2.31 (1.0)	2.64 (1.1)	2.32 (1.0)
chile	00:00–03:30	32	9.0	33,004	30.80 (1.9)	16.59 (1.0)	17.13 (1.0)	12.98 (0.8)
chile	06:00–09:30	40	9.1	35,322	19.60 (2.0)	9.67 (1.0)	10.80 (1.1)	7.00 (0.7)
chile	12:00–15:30	38	9.3	35,225	25.17 (1.9)	13.11 (1.0)	14.09 (1.1)	9.46 (0.7)
chile	18:00–21:30	35	9.1	34,658	30.09 (1.9)	16.25 (1.0)	17.69 (1.1)	12.86 (0.8)
wpi	00:00–03:30	41	8.7	33,963	16.11 (1.8)	8.76 (1.0)	8.71 (1.0)	6.25 (0.7)
wpi	06:00–09:30	42	9.0	34,889	12.70 (1.9)	6.54 (1.0)	7.09 (1.1)	5.05 (0.8)
wpi	12:00–15:30	43	9.4	36,526	9.28 (1.8)	5.20 (1.0)	5.73 (1.1)	4.04 (0.8)
wpi	18:00–21:30	40	9.6	37,143	22.04 (1.9)	11.56 (1.0)	11.04 (1.0)	8.33 (0.7)

Table 6
Caching impact for servers exhibiting perfect connection persistence

Client site	Cache use	Average retrieval time (s) (ratio with burst-1.0)				Retrieved objects	Retrieved bytes
		serial-1.0	burst-1.0	serial-1.1	burst-1.1		
att	no cache	3.05 (1.7)	1.83 (1.0)	2.39 (1.3)	1.91 (1.0)	7.6	32,405
att	with cache	0.51 (1.9)	0.27 (1.0)	0.27 (1.0)	0.28 (1.0)	0.5	6,550
att	validate cache	2.44 (1.8)	1.37 (1.0)	1.23 (0.9)	0.74 (0.5)		
chile	no cache	25.88 (1.9)	13.58 (1.0)	14.51 (1.1)	10.32 (0.8)	8.9	33,810
chile	with cache	2.91 (1.3)	2.24 (1.0)	2.11 (0.9)	1.63 (0.7)	0.5	6,210
chile	validate cache	19.14 (2.0)	9.41 (1.0)	9.92 (1.1)	5.13 (0.5)		
wpi	no cache	13.95 (1.8)	7.54 (1.0)	7.55 (1.0)	5.45 (0.7)	8.9	34,873
wpi	with cache	1.35 (1.1)	1.24 (1.0)	1.00 (0.8)	0.80 (0.6)	0.5	6,704
wpi	validate cache	10.57 (1.9)	5.65 (1.0)	4.97 (0.9)	2.57 (0.5)		

for each client in Table 6. The relative performance of the four protocol options are relatively the same as found in the PROCOW test set for the given number of objects.

Of interest is the second row in the table for each client. This row predicts the performance results if a client cache was used. Because the select data set has a number of tests between the same client and server we can determine when an object from that server has been previously retrieved. For this study, we assume that the cached contents can be reused if the size of the object has not changed. While this assumption is not always valid it is sufficient for the scope of this analysis. The number of objects and bytes retrieved in the presence of a cache is significantly reduced from the results in our test. The results include all of the initial cache misses. These results indicate that the set of Web pages in the select set were relatively static over the week of our study. The performance for each of the protocol options were not measured directly, but derived from the test data with an assumption of zero time for a cache hit. The results show that such a high cache reuse percentage leads to much better performance for all protocol options. As expected, caching has the most relative impact for the slowest serial-1.0 option.

The last row for each client in Table 6 again shows derived costs if each cache hit also incurred a validation cost where the client must send a GET If-Modified-Since or a GET If-None-Match request to the server and receive a 304 response before reusing the cache content. While this assumption is unrealistic, it examines the impact of validation requests on end-to-end performance. Our measured results for an object retrieval differentiate between when the first byte of response is received and when all bytes are received. For our derivation we used the time when the first byte is received as an approximation to the time for a header-only 304 response. The results show that the derived validation costs significantly increase the overall time, particularly for the serial-1.0 option. However, the relative performance of serial-1.1 improves relative to the other options.

In summary, the impact of caching is to reduce the number of objects retrieved. We can use the results in Tables 2–4, 8 and 9 to see that as the number of objects is reduced there is less relative difference between the protocol options. As the tables show, this reduction is not uniform so caching will yield the most cost reduction for serial-1.0 and the least for burst-1.1. The results also show that validation costs can be significant, particularly when connection and request times are in the critical path. As one measure of the validity of our assumption for deriving validation costs, we also issued a 'GET If-None-Match: *' request to servers from the AT&T client. The ratio between average If-None-Match and full retrieval times for an object was 0.6. Hence the derived costs for validation shown in Table 6 do not appear unreasonable, but further testing is warranted.

4.5. Multi-server content

In analyzing the end-to-end performance impact of embedded objects served by servers other than the base server we use the PROCOW set of servers. The first part of our analysis is to determine the extent to which content is being served from multiple servers. These results are shown in Table 7 where the second column shows the number of cases where the base object includes embedded objects by servers other than the base server. These numbers are relative to the count of base servers in column 2 of Table 1. For example, the HP site shows that 99 out of 665 (15%) base URLs use more than one server to serve content.

We label content servers separate from the base servers as *auxiliary*. To further explore these results, we classified each of the auxiliary servers used. We did this classification through a combination of looking at the auxiliary server's name and IP address (results from the AT&T client are not shown because of problems due to masking when the IP address is printed). If the network portion of auxiliary server IP address matched the network portion of the base server's address it was classified as a *local* server (i.e., local to the *base* server, not the client). We realize that such a classification may not always be correct but we were able to verify by hand most of the sample. Non-local servers containing the string 'ad' in the server name (such as 'adforce') were classified as ad servers. Non-local servers containing the string 'akamai' were another category. Akamai [1] is a commercial company, which serves content for contracted sites. All other non-local servers were grouped in the final category as *Other*. The purpose of these other sites is unknown — some may also serve ads or contracted content.

Results in Table 7 show the count of non-local servers in each category as well as the percentage of

Table 7
Use of multi-server content

Client site	Multi-server count	Local servers			Ad servers			Akamai servers			Other servers		
		count	object percentage (%)	byte percentage (%)	count	object percentage (%)	byte percentage (%)	count	object percentage (%)	byte percentage (%)	count	object percentage (%)	byte percentage (%)
aciri	97	31	42	25	34	11	3	10	55	33	42	14	9
aust	95	32	49	29	34	12	5	7	54	40	38	12	8
chile	103	33	39	20	34	11	4	7	63	40	45	13	7
hp	99	31	45	24	38	11	4	11	59	33	40	12	7
uky	90	27	39	19	36	9	4	8	69	43	39	14	10
norway	96	30	44	27	36	11	4	11	60	37	37	16	9
safrica	92	28	55	31	37	11	3	9	53	38	39	13	8
wpi	92	28	42	23	33	12	7	8	63	44	37	21	12

Table 8
Servers exhibiting perfect connection persistence from additional client sites

Client site	Object count range	Range percentage (%)	Percentage persistent for range (%)	Average retrieval time (s) (ratio with burst-1.0)			
				serial-1.0	burst-1.0	serial-1.1	burst-1.1
aciri	2–5	27	52	2.18 (1.0)	2.17 (1.0)	1.79 (0.8)	1.90 (0.9)
aciri	6–15	21	29	5.40 (2.7)	2.00 (1.0)	2.15 (1.1)	1.26 (0.6)
aciri	16+	28	20	9.64 (2.7)	3.59 (1.0)	5.21 (1.5)	3.05 (0.9)
aciri	Multi	76	34	4.62 (1.9)	2.45 (1.0)	2.64 (1.1)	2.01 (0.8)
aust	2–5	26	48	10.61 (1.4)	7.42 (1.0)	7.10 (1.0)	6.16 (0.8)
aust	6–15	21	27	27.28 (2.4)	11.40 (1.0)	13.24 (1.2)	10.93 (1.0)
aust	16+	28	18	59.80 (2.8)	21.06 (1.0)	28.11 (1.3)	19.20 (0.9)
aust	Multi	75	31	25.11 (2.2)	11.29 (1.0)	13.06 (1.2)	10.09 (0.9)
hp	2–5	26	50	1.61 (1.3)	1.20 (1.0)	1.69 (1.4)	1.37 (1.1)
hp	6–15	21	27	5.18 (2.2)	2.32 (1.0)	2.55 (1.1)	1.52 (0.7)
hp	16+	28	17	10.22 (2.5)	4.07 (1.0)	3.80 (0.9)	2.45 (0.6)
hp	Multi	75	31	4.24 (2.1)	2.06 (1.0)	2.33 (1.1)	1.63 (0.8)
uky	2–5	25	49	6.64 (1.3)	5.07 (1.0)	4.27 (0.8)	3.59 (0.7)
uky	6–15	20	28	14.00 (2.4)	5.80 (1.0)	5.62 (1.0)	3.88 (0.7)
ky	16+	27	18	38.76 (2.8)	13.69 (1.0)	15.69 (1.1)	7.01 (0.5)
uky	Multi	72	32	15.53 (2.2)	7.15 (1.0)	7.11 (1.0)	4.41 (0.6)
norway	2–5	26	48	3.50 (1.6)	2.19 (1.0)	2.65 (1.2)	2.23 (1.0)
norway	6–15	22	9	8.00 (2.1)	3.79 (1.0)	3.97 (1.0)	2.63 (0.7)
norway	16+	27	2	19.18 (2.9)	6.57 (1.0)	11.24 (1.7)	8.09 (1.2)
norway	Multi	75	20	4.55 (1.8)	2.53 (1.0)	3.09 (1.2)	2.46 (1.0)
safrica	2–5	26	49	14.22 (1.4)	10.45 (1.0)	10.35 (1.0)	10.71 (1.0)
safrica	6–15	21	26	35.43 (2.1)	16.95 (1.0)	22.36 (1.3)	17.20 (1.0)
safrica	16+	27	16	83.90 (2.8)	29.79 (1.0)	47.13 (1.6)	30.28 (1.0)
safrica	Multi	73	31	32.90 (2.1)	15.78 (1.0)	20.40 (1.3)	16.08 (1.0)

objects and bytes served by this category relative to the total number of objects and bytes for the base Web page. The percentages only include Web pages where the given category of servers are present. All cases show that auxiliary servers serve relatively more objects than bytes.

We also examined the impact of these categories on end-to-end performance. Because the base server and its auxiliary servers serve different numbers of objects and bytes it is not possible to compare the response times directly. Rather we determined the rate at which objects and bytes are served from each category of server using the best case time of the supported protocol options for each server. We found that local servers in the same network as the base servers have a higher object rate but a lower byte rate. Ad servers are mixed on object rate and lower on byte rate. Some of the servers that we categorized as *other* could be ad servers as well. Their byte rate is often less than the base servers.

The results also show that content distribution servers (which happen to be only Akamai servers in our test set) almost always show improved data rates relative to the base server. The relative object rate for the Akamai servers ranged from 2.0 for the Chile client to 20.0 for the HP client. The relative byte rate for the Akamai servers ranged from 0.7 for the Chile client to 7.5 for the Australia client. To further investigate these results we exploited the mechanism used to name Akamai-served objects where the object name includes the base server URL for these objects. This naming scheme allowed us to design a test where we retrieved from each client site the *same* set of objects from an Akamai server and their original base server. In this test the Akamai servers always yielded relatively better data rates. The relative object rate ranged from 1.9 for Chile to 15.2 for AT&T. The relative byte rate ranged from 2.1 for South Africa to 15.6 for AT&T.

Translating the impact of these improved data rates to end-to-end response time is more difficult and dependent on the strategy used by a server in

Table 9
Servers exhibiting imperfect connection persistence from additional client sites

Client site	Object count range	Range percentage (%)	Percentage persistent for range (%)	Average retrieval time (s) (ratio with burst-1.0)			
				serial-1.0	burst-1.0	serial-1.1	burst-1.1
aciri	2–5	27	5	2.77 (0.9)	3.05 (1.0)	3.80 (1.2)	3.98 (1.3)
aciri	6–15	21	16	6.48 (2.0)	3.32 (1.0)	3.58 (1.1)	4.59 (1.4)
aciri	16+	28	13	7.16 (2.7)	2.69 (1.0)	3.83 (1.4)	3.46 (1.3)
aciri	Multi	76	11	6.16 (2.0)	3.01 (1.0)	3.72 (1.2)	4.01 (1.3)
aust	2–5	26	8	11.10 (1.5)	7.58 (1.0)	8.55 (1.1)	10.00 (1.3)
aust	6–15	21	10	40.56 (2.7)	15.00 (1.0)	23.51 (1.6)	20.52 (1.4)
aust	16+	28	8	61.44 (3.1)	20.03 (1.0)	33.77 (1.7)	21.66 (1.1)
aust	Multi	75	9	37.27 (2.6)	14.10 (1.0)	21.73 (1.5)	17.32 (1.2)
hp	2–5	26	6	1.75 (0.9)	2.05 (1.0)	3.29 (1.6)	3.19 (1.6)
hp	6–15	21	13	7.31 (2.1)	3.55 (1.0)	3.79 (1.1)	4.81 (1.4)
hp	16+	28	15	9.94 (2.4)	4.16 (1.0)	4.32 (1.0)	5.32 (1.3)
hp	Multi	75	11	7.62 (2.1)	3.58 (1.0)	3.96 (1.1)	4.77 (1.3)
uky	2–5	25	7	5.80 (1.9)	3.12 (1.0)	3.21 (1.0)	7.09 (2.3)
uky	6–15	20	17	19.65 (1.7)	11.86 (1.0)	12.63 (1.1)	10.68 (0.9)
uky	16+	27	17	38.74 (2.5)	15.65 (1.0)	15.04 (1.0)	12.69 (0.8)
uky	Multi	72	14	26.27 (2.2)	12.10 (1.0)	12.10 (1.0)	11.00 (0.9)
norway	2–5	26	5	4.87 (2.3)	2.10 (1.0)	4.54 (2.2)	11.06 (5.3)
norway	6–15	22	9	13.86 (2.2)	6.39 (1.0)	6.89 (1.1)	18.21 (2.8)
norway	16+	27	4	14.89 (2.1)	7.26 (1.0)	9.09 (1.3)	16.80 (2.3)
norway	Multi	75	6	11.53 (2.1)	5.38 (1.0)	6.79 (1.3)	15.77 (2.9)
safrica	2–5	26	6	29.21 (1.4)	20.57 (1.0)	28.13 (1.4)	25.19 (1.2)
safrica	6–15	21	17	50.55 (1.9)	26.31 (1.0)	38.97 (1.5)	29.21 (1.1)
safrica	16+	27	21	84.44 (2.4)	34.57 (1.0)	58.05 (1.7)	46.57 (1.3)
safrica	Multi	73	14	65.22 (2.2)	29.81 (1.0)	47.39 (1.6)	37.70 (1.3)

distributing objects and a client in retrieving these objects from multiple servers. If a client retrieves objects from one server at a time then improvements in data rates for the remote content servers might be mitigated by increased costs to establish new connections with these servers, particularly if the client already has a pipelined, persistent connection with the base server. If on the other hand, the client retrieves objects in parallel from all servers then total response time will be controlled by the server spending the most time serving content. Results in Table 7 show that the base server is still serving most of the bytes, if not the objects, when multiple servers are used. In the case of most of the content coming from the base server then offloaded content does reduce response time, but then the importance between distributing content to a *faster* server versus simply a *different* server is less clear.

In summary, the performance impact of multi-server content is dependent on how multiple servers are used (for example performance is not a key consideration for ad servers) and how multi-server content is retrieved by clients. More study is needed on this issue, but it is important to consider that the use of multi-server content is still relatively small at the time of this study with it being used by 15% of base URLs, including less than 1.5% using it for remote content distribution.

4.6. Range requests

We examine a subset of requests sent to HTTP/1.1 servers that were able to handle `Range` requests to see if there was appreciable reduction in latency in getting just the first hundred bytes and the first thousand bytes of an object as compared to a full retrieval. For the first hundred bytes test, among the servers that responded correctly with the 206 Partial Content response, the average latency for a `Range` response was 60% that of a full response for the AT&T Labs data, though the average full response time was only half a second. The numbers for South Africa are 53% with an average full response time of 3.84 seconds, and for Norway 65% with an average response time of 0.72 seconds. For the thousand bytes range test the numbers are similar (AT&T 59% with the average full response time of 0.71 seconds, South Africa 57% with 3.84 seconds average, Norway 59% with 1 second average). So it is clear that there is improvement in user-perceived latency but the appreciable nature of improvement depends on the speed of the link from a client site and its location in the Internet relative to server sites.

5. Discussion

The results from this study lead to a number of interesting observations about the factors that influence end-to-end Web performance. Focusing on the protocol option used, the results show that the best end-to-end performance is obtained when servers support persistent connections with pipelining (burst-1.1 option) and the connection persists over the lifetime of object retrieval from the server. The improved performance for this protocol option grows relative to other protocol options as more objects need to be retrieved from a server. The amount of this improvement is relatively constant over different times-of-day with different network and server conditions.

However, there are issues with this expected result that dampen its effect. First, the likelihood that a server is able to support pipelining over a single persistent connection for the lifetime of object retrieval decreases as the number of objects increases. Second, the performance benefit of persistent connections is generally lost relative to the parallel HTTP/1.0 (burst-1.0) option if the connection is reset by the server and a new one (or ones) must be reestablished by the client. These results are highlighted by differences between perfect connection persistence results in Tables 2, 3 and 8 and imperfect connection persistence results in Tables 4 and 9. Finally, the potential performance benefits of the burst-1.1 policy are only available for about 50% of the servers we tested, as approximately 25% of servers served only one object and another 25% served a small number of objects. End-to-end performance for these servers will differ little based on what protocol option is used.

Our results also show that the interactions between various factors are important in end-to-end performance. The relative impact of caching for a client will vary according to the protocol option being employed by the client. Caching without the need for validation of the contents with the server can significantly improve all options, particularly the serial-1.0 option. However, if validation is needed then the cost of each TCP connection is significant and the burst-1.1 option performs even better than the other options.

Interactions are also important in measuring the impact of multi-server content on end-to-end performance. If a client already has a persistent, pipelined connection with a base server, then retrieving a small amount of content from a different server, even if access to that server is faster than the base, may actually increase the total response time to retrieve all objects. However, if a significant amount of content does not need to be retrieved from the base server, but can be retrieved from a server closer to the client then the client should gain in performance if comparable protocol options are available from the servers.

In summary the study raises a number of issues for further investigation, but the results do point at some recommendations that we can make for clients and servers to improve end-to-end performance based upon the factors we studied.

- Servers should continue to move towards support for HTTP/1.1 and its new performance features such as byte ranges, persistent connections and particularly pipelining. When these features are available and when they work correctly then clients see real performance improvements.
- Clients and servers need to make the management of TCP connections more deterministic so that a connection is at least not reset during the lifetime of retrieving all objects for the given page from the server. The absence of a policy on when to close persistent connections in the HTTP/1.1 protocol standard is understandable; however, this close and the subsequent client recovery can eliminate any performance benefits of pipelining. If the server cannot support the connection over this lifetime then overall performance could be improved if an explicit `Connection: close` header was sent by the server on retrieval of the first object so that the client could pursue an

alternate strategy, such as parallel retrievals, for subsequent objects.

- The cost of validating cached objects is significant, particularly if pipelining over a persistent connection is not available. Servers and caches need improvements so that unnecessary invalidations of cached objects are reduced [11,20].
- Base servers can distribute content to auxiliary servers and improve end-to-end performance for a client if the amount of content is significant, and the auxiliary servers are faster, closer to the client or support improved protocol options compared to the base server. Unless the base server is at full capacity then distributing content without these conditions will not improve and may reduce client performance.

6. Related work

There have been many studies to examine Web performance from various perspectives. Nielsen et al. published the first work on measured performance of the HTTP/1.1 protocol. A related piece of work studied the performance interactions of persistent HTTP with TCP. Both of these studies found significant interaction problems that needed correction before persistent HTTP performed as expected. These works build on prior work to examine the impact of persistent connection HTTP [14].

More recent work has examined how bottlenecks in the network, CPU and the disk system affect the relative performance of HTTP/1.0 and HTTP/1.1 [2]. This work describes a controlled experiment to understand the relative impact of these subsystems on the protocol versions. One of the results of this work is a recommendation that HTTP/1.1 clients implement an 'early close' policy where the client closes a connection after retrieving all objects associated with a Web page.

A number of other studies and tools directly examine the user-perceived performance of the Web. Keynote makes available a tool to visualize the performance of a Web retrieval [8]. Kruse et al. examine the impact of interleaving requests on user-perceived performance [12]. Gilbert and Brodersen demonstrate the benefits of progressive delivery of Web images in Web page rendering [6].

7. Summary and future work

In this work, we have examined factors contributing to end-to-end delay for a client's Web experience by performing a large-scale study of popular Web sites. We have built on the PROCOW infrastructure by adding additional clients to the collection of client sites around the world. We have presented results on performance improvements due to the changes in the HTTP/1.1 protocol and for the impact of caching and multi-server content distribution in conjunction with different protocol options.

Our results show that the HTTP/1.1 protocol, particularly with pipelining, is indeed an improvement over existing practice, but that servers serving a small number of objects or closing a persistent connection without explicit notification can reduce or eliminate any performance improvement. Similarly, use of caching and multi-server content distribution can also improve performance if done effectively.

We believe that our work is a step in the right direction of measuring end-to-end performance. Our global testing infrastructure is solidifying and our process is largely automated. Clearly, further work is warranted. We expect more content diversification on the Web and the dependence on DNS for such methods needs to be examined more closely. We need to investigate the contribution of network aspects of the latency and see how they interact with the HTTP layer. This includes passive measurements to examine the variance against the observed measurements at the application layer. We also plan to test other types of target servers such as those responsible for server objects requiring a larger portion of the bandwidth usage and those serving dynamically generated objects.

Acknowledgements

The authors would like to thank several people who were helpful in getting us access to machines in many parts of the world — the study would not be possible without their help. They include Martin Arlitt, Alan Barrett, Steven Bellovin, Randy Bush, Jim Griffioen, Eduardo Krell, Anders Lund, Mark Murray, Scott Shenker, Graeme Yates. We thank Mikhail Mikhailov for assistance in setting up the testing framework and David Finkel for consultation on the analysis. We thank Bruce Maggs for answering questions related to Akamai.

References

[1] Akamai, http://www.akamai.com.

[2] P. Barford and M. Crovella, A performance evaluation of hyper text transfer protocols, in: Proc. of the ACM SIGMETRICS '99 Conference, Atlanta, GA, May 1999.

[3] P. Cao and S. Irani, Cost-aware WWW proxy caching algorithms, in: Symposium on Internet Technology and Systems, USENIX Association, December 1997, http://www.usenix.org/publications/library/proceedings/usits97/cao.html.

[4] R. Fielding, J. Gettys, J.C. Mogul, H. Frystyk, L. Masinter, P. Leach and T. Berners-Lee, Hypertext Transfer Protocol — HTTP/1.1, RFC 2616, HTTP Working Group, June 1999, ftp://ftp.ietf.org/rfc2616.txt.

[5] 1999 Fortune 500 companies, Fortune 139 (8) (1999), April 26.

[6] J. Gilbert and R. Brodersen, Globally progressive interactive web delivery, in: Proc. of the IEEE Infocom '99 Conference, New York, March 1999.

[7] 1998 Global 500 companies, Fortune Magazine 1998.

[8] Keynote lifeline, http://lifeline.keynote.com/Lifeline/buyitonline/snapshot.asp.

[9] B. Krishnamurthy and M. Arlitt, PRO-COW: protocol compliance on the web, Technical Report 990803-05-TM, AT&T Labs, August 1999, http://www.research.att.com/~bala/papers/procow-1.ps.gz.

[10] B. Krishnamurthy, J.C. Mogul and D.M. Kristol, Key differences between HTTP/1.0 and HTTP/1.1, in: Eighth International World Wide Web Conference, Toronto, May 1999, http://www.research.att.com/~bala/papers/h0vh1.ps.gz.

[11] B. Krishnamurthy and C.E. Wills, Piggyback server invalidation for proxy cache coherency, in: Seventh International World Wide Web Conference, Brisbane, April 1998, pp. 185–193; published in Computer Networks and ISDN Systems 30 (1–7) (1998) 185–193, http://www.cs.wpi.edu/~cew/papers/www7/www7.html.

[12] H. Kruse, M. Allman and P. Mallasch, Network and user-perceived performance of web page retrievals, in: Proc. of the First International Conference on Telecommunications and Electronic Commerce, Nashville, TN, November 1998, http://roland.lerc.nasa.gov/~mallman/papers/ecom98.ps.

[13] Media metrix, http://www.mediametrix.com.

[14] J.C. Mogul, The case for persistent-connection HTTP, in: Proc. of the ACM SIGCOMM '95 Conference, August 1995, http://www.acm.org/sigcomm/sigcomm95/papers/mogul.html.

[15] D. Mosberger and T. Jin, httperf — a tool for measuring web server performance, in: Workshop on Internet Server Performance, Madison, WI, June 1998, http://www.cs.wisc.edu/~cao/WISP98/final-versions/davidm.ps.

[16] The netcraft web server survey, http://netcraft.co.uk/survey/.

[17] H. Frystyk Nielsen, J. Gettys, A. Baird-Smith, E. Prud'hommeaux, H. Lie and C. Lilley, Network performance effects of HTTP/1.1, CSS1, and PNG, in: Proc. of the ACM SIGCOMM '97 Conference, September 1997, http://www.acm.org/sigcomm/sigcomm97/papers/p102.html.

[18] 100hot.com, http://www.100hot.com.

[19] C.E. Wills and M. Mikhailov, Towards a better understanding of web resources and server responses for improved caching, in: Eighth International World Wide Web Conference, Toronto, May 1999, http://www.cs.wpi.edu/~cew/papers/www8.ps.gz.

[20] C.E. Wills and M. Mikhailov, Studying the impact of more complete server information on web caching, Technical Report WPI-CS-TR-99-36, Computer Science Department, Worcester Polytechnic Institute, November 1999, http://www.cs.wpi.edu/~cew/papers/tr99-36.ps.gz.

Balachander Krishnamurthy is a member of technical staff at AT&T Labs — Research in Florham Park, New Jersey, USA.

Craig E. Wills is an associate professor in the Computer Science Department at Worcester Polytechnic Institute. His research interests include distributed computing, operating systems, networking and user interfaces.

SPREAD: scalable platform for reliable and efficient automated distribution

Pablo Rodriguez [*,a,1], Sandeep Sibal [b,2]

[a] *Institut EURECOM, 2229 Route des Cretes, 06904 Sophia Antipolis Cedex, France*
[b] *AT&T Labs Research, B-129, 180 Park Avenue, Florham Park, NJ 07932, USA*

Abstract

We introduce SPREAD — a new architecture for distributing and maintaining up-to-date Web content that simultaneously employs three different mechanisms: client validation, server invalidation, and replication. Proxies within SPREAD self-configure themselves to form scalable distribution hierarchies that connect the origin servers of content providers to clients. Each proxy autonomously decides on the best mechanism based on the object's popularity and modification rates. Requests and subscriptions propagate from edge proxies to the origin server through a chain of intermediate proxies. Invalidations and replications travel in the opposite direction. SPREAD's network of proxies automatically reconfigures when proxies go down or come up, or when new ones are added. The ability to spontaneously form hierarchies is based on a modified transparent proxying mechanism, called *translucent* proxying, that sanitizes transparent proxying. It allows proxies to be placed in an ad-hoc fashion anywhere in the network — not just at focal points within the network that are guaranteed to see all the packets of a TCP connection. In this paper we (1) describe the architecture of SPREAD, (2) discuss how proxies determine which mechanism to use based on local observations, and (3) use a trace-driven simulation to test SPREAD's behavior in a realistic setting.

Keywords: Content distribution; Consistency; Automated; Hierarchy; Caching; Replication

1. Introduction

Due to the explosive growth of the World Wide Web, internet service providers (ISPs) throughout the world are installing proxy caches to reduce user perceived latency as well as bandwidth consumption. Such proxy caches are under the control of the ISP, and usually cache content for its client community, irrespective of the origin server. These proxy caches are often called *forward proxy* caches to distinguish them from *reverse proxy* caches, which we discuss next.

More recently, several vendors, such as Akamai [1] and Sandpiper [17] have begun offering proxy-based solutions to content providers, as opposed to ISPs. The business model here is that improving a user's browsing experience, is not only in the ISP's interest, but in the content provider's interest as well. This is becoming increasingly important as the number of content providers multiply and compete for the attention of end users. Proxy caches used in such a scenario are often called *reverse* proxy caches, to underline the fact that they are controlled by and

* Corresponding author. E-mail: rodrigue@eurecom.fr
[1] During the period of this work, he was at AT&T research labs as an intern.
[2] E-mail: sibal@research.att.com

represent the interests of the content provider (or its agent). Reverse proxy caches serve content on behalf of the content provider, usually to any arbitrary client on the Internet.

In the rest of the paper we use the term proxy, cache, and proxy cache interchangeably, since the proxying and caching functions are co-located in a single entity.

SPREAD can be realized in both the forward proxying and reverse proxying contexts. In this paper we consider the forward proxying context. Applying SPREAD in a reverse proxying context would need minor alterations, which we point out at various points in the paper.

1.1. Object consistency

One of the tenets of SPREAD is that the system provides *strong* object consistency. This means that content served is always fresh. Technically it is impossible to guarantee *absolute* freshness, since there is a non-zero delay between the time a proxy cache receives an object from an origin server, and the instant it serves it to a client. The term *strong* is used to distinguish it from *weak* schemes, which improve consistency but do not provide guarantees. We believe strong consistency is imperative, especially now that people have begun to rely on the Web in timely information for conducting business, and because an increasing number of sites have begun to offer time-sensitive information.

Forward proxies have been known to be notoriously sloppy in this area. While mechanisms exist within the HTTP protocol for maintaining cache consistency, in practice, forward proxy caches administered by ISPs, use their own time-to-live (TTL) heuristics [8,22] that are engineered in a rather arbitrary fashion. Historically, part of the effect (or some say the cause) has been that content providers often misuse or abuse features of the HTTP protocol, using techniques such as *cache-busting*. Regardless of how one sees this tension between ISPs and content providers, we believe that adhering to strong consistency mechanisms in accordance with the HTTP guidelines is important. This is a fundamental design guideline in SPREAD.

SPREAD uses three primary mechanisms to achieve strong consistency:

- *Client validation (V):* In this mechanism, for every client request that a proxy receives the proxy always checks back with the origin server to see if the object copy is fresh. This is typically accomplished by an *If-Modified-Since (IMS)* HTTP Request. If the origin server finds the object in the proxy fresh, the proxy cache will respond to the client with its cached copy. If the object has expired, the client will receive the master object from the origin server and the cache will keep an object copy. The only exception to this rule is if the object has been explicitly marked as cacheable, and a Max-age, Expires, or an equivalent piece of metadata has been set to a value by the origin server that indicates a non-zero time-to-live (TTL). In such a situation the proxy will not need check back with the server to validate the cached copy of the object for the stipulated TTL.
- *Server invalidation (I):* With invalidation, a proxy cache first subscribes to an invalidation service for that object (or range of objects) with the origin server, or an agent for the origin server that is responsible for signaling the expire of the object. In this case, the proxy cache assumes that the object is fresh unless an invalidation message from the origin server is received by the proxy to explicitly expire the object. Using invalidation, the first client request after the object is invalidated experiences high latency since the object needs to be retrieved from the origin server.
- *Replication (R):* With replication, updated versions of the object are explicitly pre-loaded in the proxy cache by using *push*, or equivalently a *pseudo-push* that can be implemented with a periodic-pull. As with invalidation, a proxy cache must express interest in the object (or a range of objects) a-priori, by subscribing to the replication service. Using replication, clients always experience very small latencies, however, the bandwidth consumed can be wasteful in cases where there are more updates than requests.

To save on bandwidth, instead of sending the entire object, one may send just the *diff*, or some encoded form of the *change* between the old and new versions. This may be applied to all of the above mechanisms. The results of this paper remain valid under such a scenario as well.

1.2. Our approach

A novel feature of SPREAD is that its proxies *dynamically* choose between client invalidation, server invalidation, and replication, on a per-object basis. This is discussed in detail in Section 3. Earlier studies [23,9] have analyzed the benefits of server invalidation versus client validation, but their comparisons were in a context where strong cache consistency was not imperative. More importantly, their evaluation had been focused on assessing stale hit-rate using trace-driven simulations at a *macroscopic* level. In our work, we evaluate the competing mechanisms to keep strong consistency from a more fundamental perspective, analyzing the problem at the level of individual reads and writes of each object, which we believe yields substantial insight. The authors of [13] propose unicast invalidations instead of adaptive time-to-live mechanisms to keep strong consistency, however, using unicast communication from the server to the clients makes their approach non-scalable. The authors of [24] study the efficacy of server invalidations using a scalable distribution infrastructure, and provide several insights into the general problem of cache consistency. Our work advances the state-of-the-art beyond [24] in three major respects. First, proxies in our system *dynamically* choose the consistency mechanism based on their own observation of the request rates and update rates of objects. Prior knowledge of these statistics is not assumed. Second, our analytic results, help us define the thresholds of the optimal control policy at which proxy caches switch from one mechanism to another, which in turn helps us in building a smarter overall system. A third novel feature of SPREAD is its ability to spontaneously build content distribution hierarchies, without prior knowledge of the existence of other proxies. If a proxy lies along the natural path from an edge proxy to the origin server, it intercepts communication between them. Communication includes Web requests, as well as subscriptions for invalidation and replication. Such incremental actions by intermediate proxies builds sophisticated multi-level hierarchies rooted at origin servers. The interception is at the TCP layer. While the possibility of using Layer-4 transparent proxying for building hierarchies has been considered in [12], the scope of such an architecture is limited because of the problem that all packets of a TCP connection may not always follow the same path. If a transparent proxy intercepting a connection is unable to see all the packets of the connection, it cannot sanely proxy the TCP connection, which is a well known limitation [5]. A partial solution is to deploy transparent proxies at *focal points* within the network, which are guaranteed to see all packets of a connection. This makes the ad-hoc placement of proxies infeasible. SPREAD solves this problem by using what we call *translucent* proxying, which guarantees that a proxy that sees the SYN of a TCP connection, will see all subsequent packets as well. This is accomplished by a novel use of IP tunneling and TCP-OPTIONS which we will discuss later.

2. SPREAD architecture

The SPREAD architecture is based on a scalable content distribution network that spontaneously builds proxy caching hierarchies. In SPREAD, edge proxies connect to servers using a chain of proxies which are on the natural path from the edge proxy to the origin server (see Fig. 1). Any given edge proxy may be a part of multiple proxy caching hierarchies rooted at different origin servers. In this section we discuss the basic principles that enable this. Unless otherwise mentioned, we assume a forward proxying scenario.

It is important to note that SPREAD is not concerned with how clients reach edge proxies. This is considered orthogonal to SPREAD. While this is indeed a non-issue in the case of forward proxies (which typically have a fixed or long-term mapping of clients to edge proxies), the reverse proxy scenario is trickier. With the advent of dynamic DNS tricks, the mapping of clients to edge proxies can be more fluid.

2.1. Spontaneous hierarchies

A proxy caching hierarchy acts as an *application-level multicast* distribution tree [20], reducing the bandwidth usage in the network, the load at origin servers, and also reducing client latency. In the absence of a proxy caching hierarchy, origin servers need to directly communicate with all edge proxies,

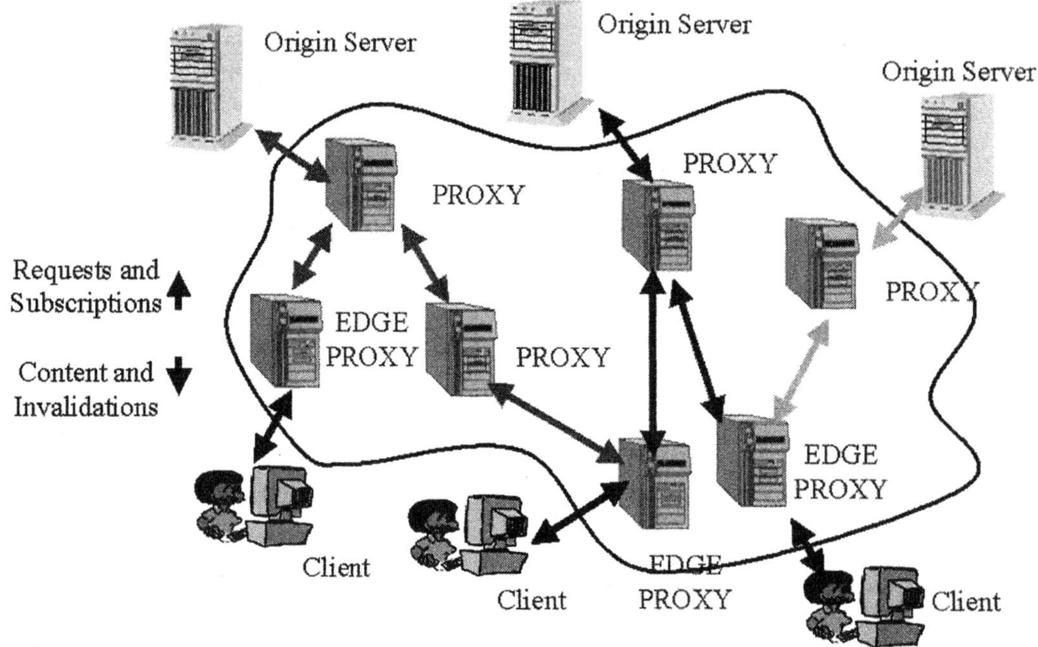

Fig. 1. SPREAD architecture.

creating a huge burden on the origin server and the network. Using reliable multicast between the origin server and edge proxies would require an infeasible large number of multicast groups, and in addition reliable multicast is not yet available everywhere and has unresolved congestion control problems.

Proxy caching hierarchies already exist in the current Internet [2]. However, current hierarchies are static and require substantial manual configuration and maintenance. To generate caching hierarchies that automatically configure themselves and forward packets to the origin servers through the shortest path routes, a routing architecture at the application level can also be implemented. Caches would then exchange application-level costs and calculate the best path to every origin server [15]. However, building an application level routing infrastructure is non-trivial, since route changes in the underlying network layer, will impact application-level routing. In contrast, SPREAD uses network layer routing and transparent proxies to build its proxy caching hierarchies. Requests travel from the clients to the origin servers following the shortest network path, and intermediate transparent proxies automatically pick up the connections for Web traffic (port 80). A transparent proxy that picks up a connection directly satisfies the document request if the document is stored in its cache, or lets the request travel towards the origin server if the document is not stored in its cache. As the request travels towards the origin server, the document request may be intercepted again by other transparent proxies, automatically forming a caching hierarchy. Changes in routes will create new hierarchies spontaneously, which will obey network level routing. No extra signaling is required to maintain the hierarchy.

Naively building a hierarchy using transparent proxies is elegant, but has a serious problem. Since routing in an IP network can lead to situations where multiple paths from client to server may have the lowest cost, it can happen that packets of a connection follow multiple paths. In such a situation, a transparent proxy may see only a fraction of packets of the connection. Occasionally it is also possible that routes change mid-way through a TCP connection, due to routing updates in the underlying IP network. This problem limits the scope, requiring transparent proxies to be deployed exclusively at the edges or *focal* points within the network where they are guaranteed to see all the packets of the con-

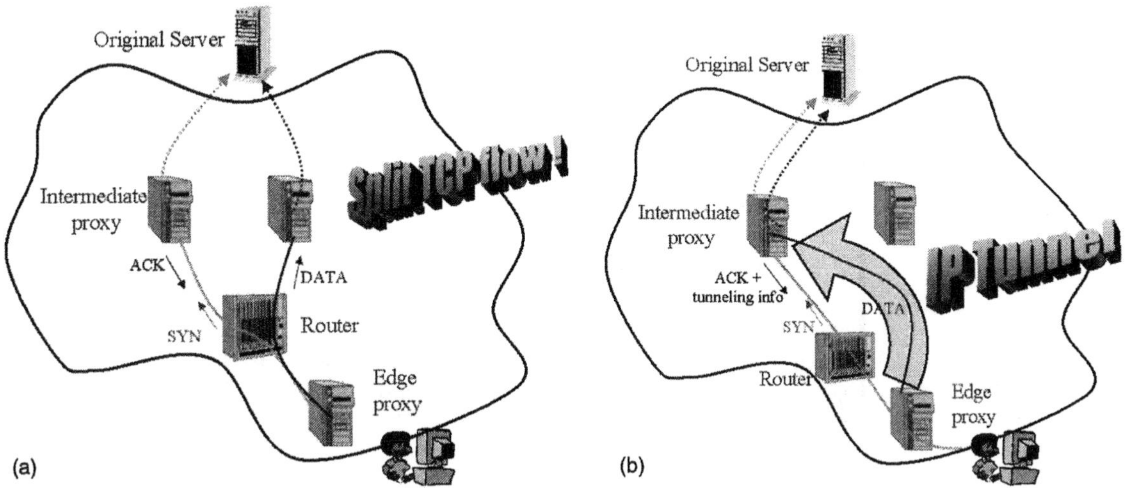

Fig. 2. Translucent proxying solves the split flow problem using IP tunneling.

nection. SPREAD addresses this limitation by using translucent proxying, which allows the placement of proxies *anywhere* in the network.

2.1.1. Translucent proxying

Translucent proxying of TCP (TPOT) is a more sophisticated transparent proxying mechanism that allows proxies to be cascaded and networked together transparently, eliminating split TCP flows. Fig. 2a provides a high level overview of the problem of split TCP flows and how translucent proxying solves the problem. When an edge proxy intends to connect with an origin server as shown in Fig. 2b, it issues a SYN packet, which reaches the intermediate proxy on the left. If the next packet of the TCP connection should be routed towards the proxy on the right, we have a situation where the proxy on the left cannot properly proxy the TCP connection. In translucent proxying, the proxy on the left sends back in the ACK, a signal to the edge proxy providing its IP address. The edge proxy will then use the IP address, to *tunnel* all remaining packets via the proxy on the left.

Before describing the TPOT protocol, we provide a brief background of TCP/IP, which will help in better understanding TPOT.

Each IP packet typically contains an IP header, and a TCP segment. The IP header contains the packet's source and destination IP address. The TCP segment itself contains a TCP header. The TCP header contains the source port and the destination port that the packet is intended for. This 4-tuple of the IP addresses and port numbers of the source and destination uniquely identify the TCP connection that the packet belongs to. In addition, the TCP header contains a flag that indicates whether it is a SYN packet, and also an ACK flag and sequence number that acknowledges the receipt of data from its peer. Finally, a TCP header might also contain TCP-OPTIONs that can be used for custom signaling.

In addition to the above basic format of an IP packet, an IP packet can also be encapsulated in another IP packet. At the source, this involves prefixing an IP header with the IP address of an intermediate tunnel point on an IP packet. On reaching the intermediate tunnel point, the IP header of the intermediary is stripped off. The (remaining) IP packet is then processed as usual.

We now describe the TPOT protocol. Consider a source S that intends to connect with destination D via TCP, as shown in Fig. 3. Assume that the first (SYN) packet sent out by S to D reaches the intermediary TPOT proxy P. (S, S_p, D, D_p) is the notation that we use to describe a packet that is headed from S to D, and has S_p and D_p as the source and *destination* ports respectively.

To co-exist peacefully with other end-points that do not wish to talk TPOT, we use a special TCP-OPTION 'TPOT,' that a source uses to explicitly

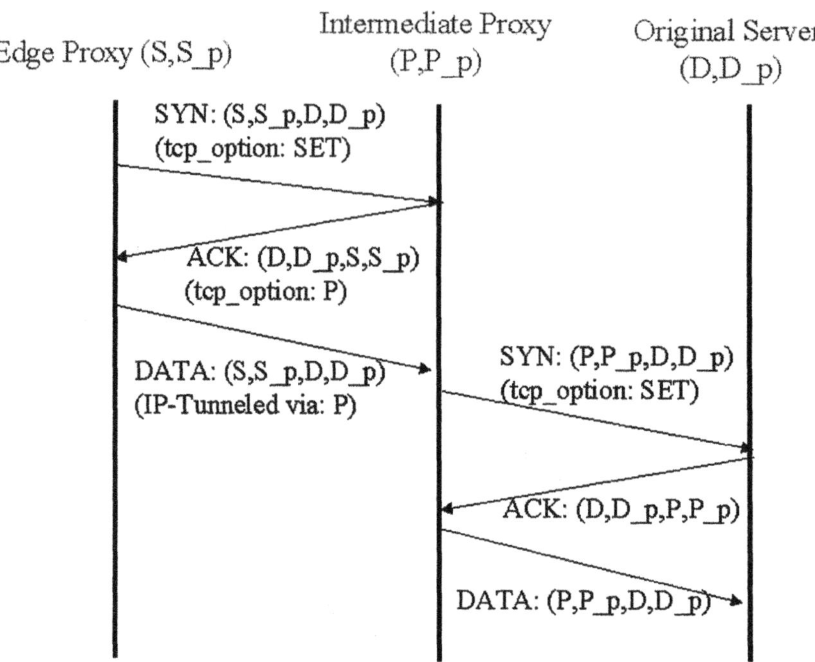

Fig. 3. The translucent proxying protocol.

indicate to TPOT proxies within the network, such as P, that they are interested in using the TPOT mechanism. If P does not see this option, it will take no action, and simply forwards the packet on to D on its fast-path. If P sees a SYN packet that has the TCP-OPTION 'TPOT' set, it responds to S with a SYN-ACK that encodes its own IP address P in the TCP-OPTION field. On receiving this packet, S must then send the remaining packets of that TCP connection, IP tunnelled to P. From an implementation standpoint this would imply adding another 20 byte IP header with P's IP address as destination address to all packets that S sends out for that TCP connection. Since this additional header is removed on the next TPOT proxy, the total overhead is limited to 20 bytes regardless of the number of TPOT proxies intercepting the connection from the source to the final destination. This overhead can be further reduced by IP header compression [14,10].

In SPREAD we use TPOT both for regular HTTP Requests as well as for subscriptions and unsubscriptions. Consider the case of a regular HTTP Request. For a cache hit, P is able to satisfy a request from S, and the response is simply served from one or more caches attached to P. In the case of a cache miss, P communicates with the destination D as shown in Fig. 3. Note that the proxy P sets the TCP-OPTION 'TPOT' in its SYN to D to allow possibly another TPOT proxy along the way to again proxy the connection. In Fig. 3 we do not show such a scenario.

A more comprehensive description of the TPOT protocol, its variants, scalability and performance issues, as well as a prototype implementation may be found in [21].

2.2. *Automated content distribution*

In this section we describe the basic content distribution in SPREAD. Edge proxies request objects from origin servers and requests are transparently intercepted by intermediate translucent proxy caches en-route to the origin server.

Proxies periodically calculate the expected number of requests per update period for every object, or for a volume (set of objects). Depending on the number of requests per update period, proxies may subscribe to invalidation or replication (see Section 3).

As the subscription travels to the origin server, an intermediate translucent proxy en-route intercepts the subscription (unless the intermediate proxy is overloaded — in which case it lets the subscription pass through). On intercepting a subscription for invalidation, the intermediate proxy will subscribe itself to such a service, which in turn may be re-proxied by yet another proxy. Note that it is possible to limit this recursion by adding a hop-count field to the subscription, which gets decrement at each proxy. Once the counter hits zero, no other proxy will intercept it.

In the case where an invalidation (I) subscription arrives at a proxy, the proxy is forced to subscribe itself, unless of course it is already subscribed to I, or to Replication (R) — since R *implies* I. In the case where an R arrives at a proxy, it must subscribe to R, if it is not already subscribed to R. As we will see later, one may order mechanisms, in the increasing order V, I, R. If a child proxy finds a certain mechanism optimal, then a parent must, *at least*, use that mechanism. This assumes that children proxies are self-regulating as per SPREAD's optimal control policy. This will be discussed in a later section. Thus when a child proxy subscribes to I or R, all proxies on the path to the origin server are also automatically subscribed to *at least* that mechanism. Invalidations and replications themselves travel in the opposite direction. When an object is updated at the origin server, the server sends invalidations and/or replicas to proxy caches that are subscribed to I or R. Proxy caches that receive invalidations or replicas will themselves propagate the invalidations or replicas to children subscribed to I or R at the next tier. The process is repeated until the invalidation or document replica arrives at the edge proxy. Thus strong consistency is maintained.

2.2.1. Leases

Subscriptions have leases associated with them. On expire, a subscription must be renewed. These leases are set large enough so that repeated subscriptions do not overburden the network. At the same time, they are not so large that proxies commit themselves so far into the future when the changing statistics of the request and update rates suggest another mechanism. This is an implementation issue, that we do not discuss further.

2.2.2. State information

Parent proxies need to keep state information about the children proxies that are subscribed to invalidation or replication. However, the amount of state information required to keep track of subscribed children proxies is negligible compared to the disk capacity needed to store objects. Objects are usually subscribed and unsubscribed infrequently, and therefore, the amount of processing required is very small [24]. In addition, if multicasting is used, the load and state information at parent proxy caches is very small since only one object copy needs to be distributed to a set of children proxies. To further reduce the load and the state information, objects can be grouped into volumes at the cost of a coarser granularity for optimization and control. Here, a whole volume is invalidated or replicated instead of an individual object.

2.3. Reliability and load balancing

To ensure strong consistency even in the case of proxy cache failure, parent proxies periodically send *heart beats* to their children proxies. When a parent proxy dies, children proxies set the corresponding objects that the parent was responsible for as stale and re-send subscriptions towards to the origin server. The next (alive) proxies in the path to the origin servers then pick up the new subscriptions and become the new parents. This mechanism makes SPREAD reliable against even under catastrophic outages. A failed proxy or link, gracefully degrades the performance of SPREAD, without corrupting its correctness and guarantee of strong consistency.

Alternately, when a new proxy surfaces, it joins SPREAD incrementally. While existing subscriptions are not disturbed (since they are tunnelled using TPOT to the existing parent), new subscriptions and Web requests that it sees can be proxied. Existing subscriptions also ultimately get re-proxied once their lease expires.

SPREAD automatically redistributes the load among its proxy caches, since every proxy cache is only responsible for those objects for which it sees requests, and then again only to its children. A last resort for an overloaded proxy server, is simply to stop intercepting any new Web requests and subscriptions, effectively going into *invisible* mode for all future services.

3. Optimizing SPREAD

To develop an appreciation for why and how SPREAD may optimize its performance, consider the scenario shown in Fig. 4. An object is considered hotter than another if it is requested (read) more times than its is updated or modified (written).

Imagine that we want to minimize bandwidth consumption. For objects that are so cold, that every request appears after one or more writes/updates of the object, invalidations are useless, since every new object request sees a new object update. Replication, on the other hand, wastes even more bandwidth since objects are replicated on every write though they are rarely requested. In such a situation, it appears that client validation is probably the best policy. Note that what is important is the relative frequency of reads to writes. Objects that are hot, are objects for which there are one or more reads per write. In such a situation, replication is always preferred to client validation. Validation suffers from the problem that the second and future reads in an update/write interval will each require an *If-Modified-Since* poll, even if the object has not changed. The poll consumes bandwidth and causes additional delays. While invalidation performs better than validation, invalidation also wastes some bandwidth due to invalidation messages that perform no constructive function when compared to replication. Indeed, as we will see more rigorously later, invalidation is optimal for warm objects whose frequency of reads/requests is on the same order as the number of writes/updates. Note that in situations where not all three mechanisms are supported by the origin server, SPREAD will simply choose the best from what is available.

3.1. Analytic model

We now build a mathematical framework to investigate how one might formulate the problem of deciding which mechanism to use for a given object. Since these choices will be made at each proxy, the issue of how a proxy estimates the various parameters relating to an object is an important one. These estimation issues will be dealt with in later sections.

We start with the case of an edge proxy that sees requests for some arbitrary object. We will extend our analysis to the case of an Intermediate proxy (not just an edge proxy) in later sections. We argue that requests for the object from all the clients connected to an edge proxy cache are Poisson distributed with average request rate λ. The assumption of Poisson arrivals is a reasonable one [7,3]. We also assume that objects are updated either periodically in a deterministic fashion, or randomly in an exponential distribution. This assumption will be discussed in a later section (Section 3.2). The average update period is denoted Δ.

We denote N to be the number of requests for the object per update period from all clients connected to the edge proxy. In the case when the object is updated exponentially, the probability that there is at least one object request per update period from an edge proxy is then given by:

$$\Pr\{N > 0\} = 1 - e^{-\lambda\Delta}$$

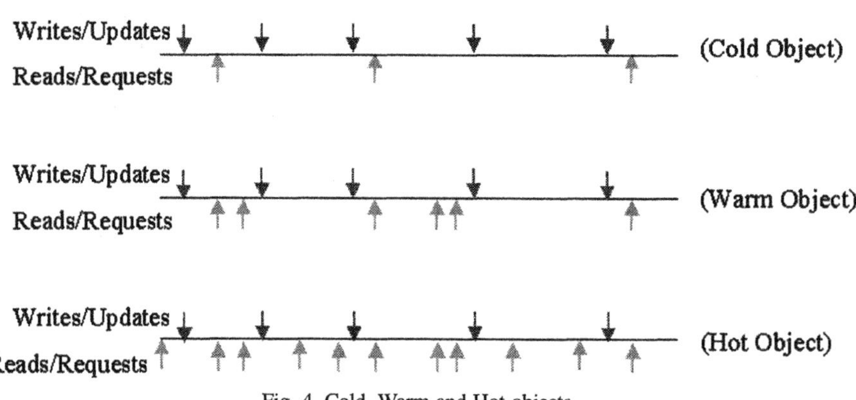

Fig. 4. Cold, Warm and Hot objects.

Note that $\lambda\Delta$ is the average number of requests per update period Δ.

When the object is updated periodically, the probability that there is at least one object request per update period from an edge proxy is given by:

$$\Pr\{N > 0\} = \frac{\lambda\Delta}{\lambda\Delta + 1}.$$

To determine whether to use validation, invalidation, or replication, caches need to estimate the average number of requests per update period on a per-object basis. To calculate the average number of requests per update period, caches need to estimate the average request rate of an object and the average update period of an object.

To estimate the request rate of an object, edge proxies can use the access logs from client access. The problem of estimating the request rate for an intermediate proxy is more involved (since it may not see direct hits from clients), and is discussed in a later section. It is of course possible for edge proxies to inform intermediate proxies about their request rates (and in fact this was our initial design), but as we shall see later, one can do without such communication.

3.2. *Estimating update rate*

Proxy caches that are subscribed to invalidation (I) or replication (R) for an object, see all updates, and can therefore estimate the update rate in a straight-forward fashion. However estimating the update period of an object that uses validation (V) is more complex. Since the proxy can only inspect the *Last-Modified* time of an object when it is requested, information on updates that are never requested are lost. However, proxies can use the difference between the time of a request (or Date field) and the Last-Modified time, to infer the average update period of an object if they know the probability distribution of object updates.

We should point out that headers such as the 'Expires' header which explicitly provide consistency information, cannot be used here for two reasons. First, our own study of the Web and those of others have shown that most cacheable documents have their Expires headers at a value that effectively makes the TTL zero anyway. Further, such protocol headers (even when non-zero) do not provide realistic values for update rates, since, these headers only need to provide a lower bound. In other words, a document whose TTL is set to 10 seconds (via an Expires header or some other metadata) may update itself after 10 days, and yet be perfectly in line with the HTTP protocol.

Previous work on the distribution of object updates suggested that objects are approximately updated randomly following an exponential distribution or periodically [6]. However, these results were performed with client traces that did not see all server updates. To better study the distribution of object updates we polled different sites once every minute for a period of 10 days, recording the last-modified-time stamp of the object on every poll. Then we calculated the update period of an object as the time difference between two different last-modified-time stamps. This experiment gave us the real update pattern of an object within a resolution of one minute. Our results confirm the ones presented in [6]. We found that there are a large number of Web sites that update their information periodically, e.g. every 15 or 30 minutes. However, we also found a large number of Web sites that update their Web sites randomly following an exponential distribution. In Fig. 5 we present the distribution of object updates for two different news sites. We clearly see that the distribution of object updates in both sites approximates an exponential distribution.

Note that proxy caches can easily determine if an object is updated periodically or is exponentially distributed by studying the variance of object updates. Once they have determined if the object is updated periodically or exponentially, they can use the time difference between object requests and the last-modified-time stamps to estimate the average update period [11].

Fig. 6 shows how rapidly the estimate of the average update period converges with the number of samples. Each sample measures the time difference between every request and the last-modified-time, and computes a simple average. We observe that after 200 samples, the estimate of the average update period converges to 600 seconds in Fig. 6a, and 1500 seconds in Fig. 6b. This warm-up time is small enough to make such estimators viable.

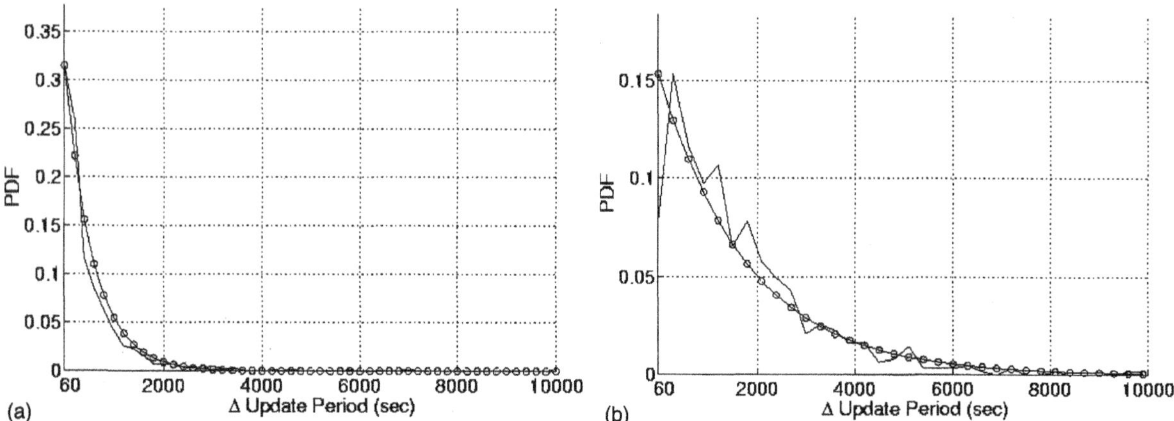

Fig. 5. Distribution of object update intervals. 10 day logs. Servers are polled every minute. (a) Spanish newspaper Web site. (b) BBC News Web site.

3.3. Optimizing bandwidth

Next, we compute the bandwidth usage by each mechanism. We define the bandwidth usage B as the average number of bytes consumed per update period Δ in a proxy's link.

Let S_o be the actual size of a Web object. Let S_h be the size of an HTTP header, which is considered to be the same as the size of an IMS request. Let S_i the size of an invalidation message.

The bandwidth usage for validation B_V, invalidation B_I, and replication B_R can be easily shown to be:

$$B_V = \Pr\{N > 0\}S_o + E[N]S_h,$$

$$B_I = \Pr\{N > 0\}(S_o + S_h) + S_i,$$

$$B_R = S_o.$$

Note that in our analysis we have assumed that the object has a TTL of zero. In a situation where this is non-zero, the analysis would need to be modified accordingly, though the qualitative results of our paper would still hold.

Fig. 7 shows the bandwidth usage of validation, invalidation, and replication depending on the average number of requests per update period $\lambda\Delta$. The values for S_i, S_h and S_o are representative of what is typical for the Web today. For objects with few

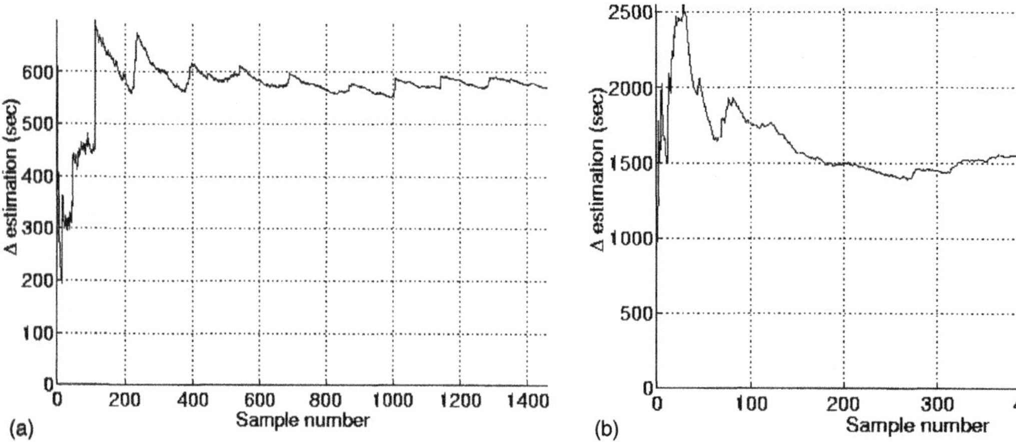

Fig. 6. Estimation of the average update interval as a function of the number of samples. (a) Spanish newspaper Web site. (b) BBC News Web site.

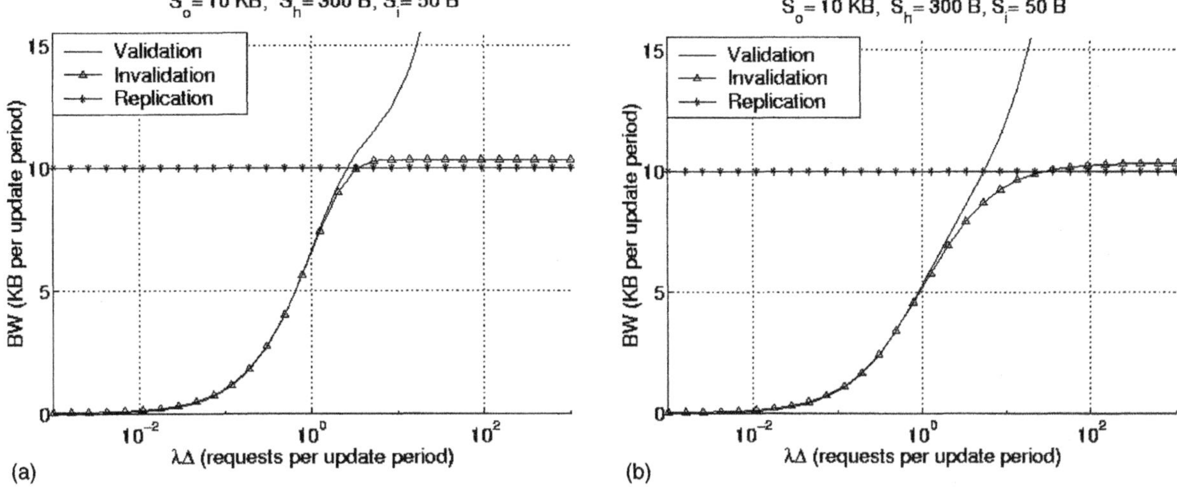

Fig. 7. Bandwidth usage. (a) Periodic updates. (b) Exponentially distributed updates.

requests per update period, replication wastes a lot of bandwidth compared to validation or invalidation, since the object is preloaded into the caches even when it is not requested by the clients. On the other hand, validation and invalidation have a low bandwidth usage since the object is only fetched into the caches when it is requested by a client. For a large range of values for $\lambda\Delta$ from about 0 to 1 request per update period, validation uses slightly less bandwidth than invalidation since every request finds a new object update and therefore the overhead of IMS requests to the origin server is almost zero. For values above about 1 request per update period, replication does well, trailed by invalidation, which suffers because of the extra invalidations that are sent out. Validation works poorly, due to the fact that every request generates an IMS request which is typically much heavier than an invalidation. Fig. 7 shows us that the mechanism that consumes the least bandwidth is different in different regimes of $\lambda\Delta$. It appears that the order in which they are optimal is V, I, and R as $\lambda\Delta$ increased.

3.4. Switching thresholds

Let the switching thresholds between V and I, and I and R, be denoted by Th_{VI} and Th_{IR} respectively. Table 1 shows the thresholds to switch among the different policies at an edge proxy.

From Table 1 it is easy to prove that for all reasonable values of S_{i}, S_{h} and S_{o}, we have the property that: $Th_{\mathrm{VI}} < Th_{\mathrm{IR}}$. Further, since λ increases as one moves closer to the origin server, we have the property that at any level of the hierarchy if a given mechanism is optimal for a proxy, it must be *at least* good for the parents above. That is:

- if a proxy finds V optimal, then its parent may find V, I, or R optimal;
- if a proxy finds I optimal, then its parent may find I, or R optimal;

Table 1
Thresholds to switch between validation and invalidation Th_{VI}, and between invalidation and replication Th_{IR}

Perspective	Th_{VI} (req. per update period)	Th_{IR} (req. per update period)
Edge proxy (deterministic update period)	$\sqrt{\frac{2S_{\mathrm{i}}}{S_{\mathrm{h}}}}$	$\ln\left(\frac{S_{\mathrm{o}}+S_{\mathrm{h}}}{S_{\mathrm{h}}}\right)$
Edge proxy (exponential update period)	$\frac{S_{\mathrm{i}}+\sqrt{S_{\mathrm{i}}^2+4S_{\mathrm{h}}S_{\mathrm{i}}}}{2\cdot S_{\mathrm{h}}}$	$\frac{S_{\mathrm{o}}-S_{\mathrm{i}}}{S_{\mathrm{h}}+S_{\mathrm{i}}}$

- if a proxy finds R optimal, then its parent will find only R optimal.

By the above result, if a proxy subscribes to a certain policy, it must also be in its parent's best interest to at least have that policy in place. Therefore it always makes sense to proxy subscriptions on behalf of a child proxy. This clearly validates SPREAD's design model, even if by serendipity.

3.5. Estimating request rate at an intermediate proxy

As we discussed earlier, estimating the request rate of an object at an Intermediate proxy may be complicated because it does not see direct hits from clients. However, we argue here that given the observations of the previous section, this can be substantially simplified by breaking down the possibilities into two cases.

- *Case 1:* If *any* of the children are in the R state, then, the parent proxy is also in the R state and cannot go to I until all of its children unsubscribe from R. No decision need be made by the proxy, and therefore estimating request rate is not essential. (Note that when the last child proxy unsubscribes from R, we can seed the estimator with the estimated request rate from that child to be Th_{IR}/Δ.)
- *Case 2:* In this case, children proxies are in the I or V state. For those in the V state the estimation of the request rate is straightforward, since the proxy sees all the requests (HTTP GETs or IMS requests). For proxies in the I state, the request rate may be computed in a more sophisticated fashion. Here, the proxy estimates the time interval between an invalidation and the immediate following request. For both exponentially distributed and periodic (deterministic) update periods, we may compute an estimate for the request rate from that child proxy using standards results for residual life from the area of Renewal Theory [4]. For reasons of space we omit a lengthier discussion.

3.6. Latency

In this section we investigate the latency experienced by the clients when validation, invalidation, or replication are used. Let t_{os} be the transmission time of an object when it is retrieved from the origin server. Let t_{pc} and t_{cc} be the transmission time of an object when it is transmitted from the parent proxy and from the children proxies respectively. Let RTT_{os} be the round-trip-time between the origin server and any proxy cache. The expected latency experienced by a client depends on the tree level where the object is hit. Let L be the number of links traversed to find a object. In this section, we consider a simple two-tier caching hierarchy, however, the analysis can be easily extended for a different number of cache tiers. The exact calculation of the probability distribution function of L can be found in [20] and has been omitted due to space limitations. Given the distribution of L we can calculate the expected latency experienced by a client for validation T_{V}, invalidation T_{I}, and replication T_{R} as:

$$
\begin{aligned}
T_{\mathrm{V}} &= \Pr\{l = \mathrm{cc}\}\,(t_{\mathrm{cc}} + RTT_{\mathrm{os}}) \\
&\quad + \Pr\{l = \mathrm{pc}\}\,\left(t_{\mathrm{pc}} + RTT_{\mathrm{os}}\right) + \Pr\{l = \mathrm{os}\}t_{\mathrm{os}}, \\
T_{\mathrm{I}} &= \Pr\{l = \mathrm{cc}\}t_{\mathrm{cc}} + \Pr\{l = \mathrm{pc}\}t_{\mathrm{pc}} + \Pr\{l = \mathrm{os}\}t_{\mathrm{os}}, \\
T_{\mathrm{R}} &= t_{\mathrm{cp}}.
\end{aligned}
$$

To consider real values for the latency, we analyzed 10 days of logs on the local proxy at Eurecom, which is connected to a caching hierarchy through a parent proxy. We averaged the latencies during the 10 days of the trace to obtain the following values:

- Transmission time from the local proxy: $T_{\mathrm{cc}} = 117$ ms,
- Transmission time from a parent proxy: $T_{\mathrm{pc}} = 585$ ms,
- Transmission time from the origin server: $T_{\mathrm{os}} = 1183$ ms,
- Round-Trip-Time to the origin server: $RTT_{\mathrm{os}} = 300$ ms.

We considered the case of a caching hierarchy with 64 children caches and a single parent cache. Based on these values, Fig. 8 shows the latency experienced by a client for validation, invalidation, and replication. Using replication, clients always experience small latencies since the edge proxy always has the object replicated to it. This, as we have seen earlier, may be extremely wasteful of bandwidth. As the number of requests per update period increases, the probability of finding an object at proxies closer to the client increases, thus, reducing the latency experienced. Invalidation offers better latencies than

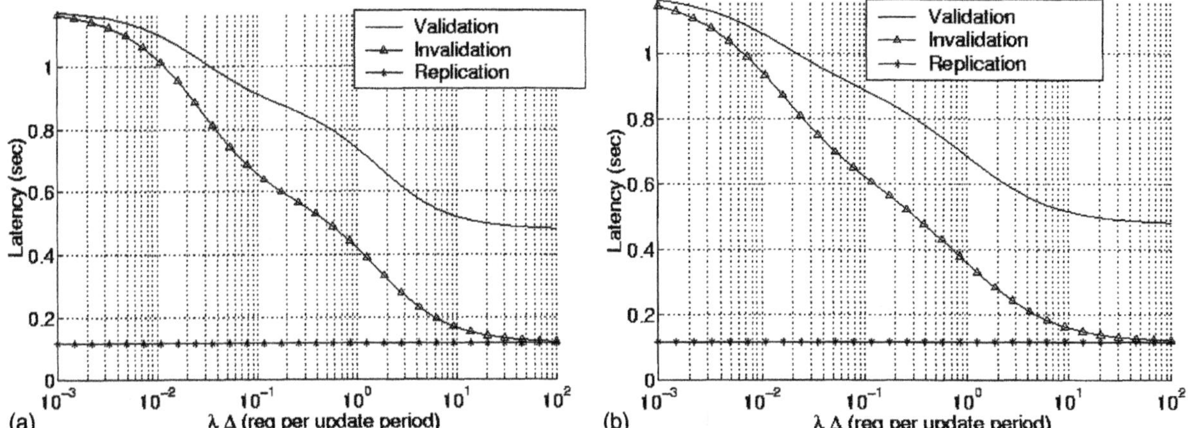

Fig. 8. Expected latency. (a) Periodic updates. (b) Exponentially distributed updates.

validation since client requests do not need to contact the origin server every time. However, for invalidation to provide similar latencies as replication, the number of requests per update period needs to be very high (i.e. approx. 100 requests/update period). For such popular objects, using invalidation to reduce client's latency is not the best option since replication generates slightly less traffic in the network (see Fig. 7), providing very small latencies for *all* receivers.

3.7. Multicast extensions

In this section we consider the case when the network supports multicasting. If multicasting is available, parent proxies may decide to multicast invalidations and replicas to their children proxies instead of sending them via unicast. For validation, objects and IMS messages are distributed via unicast. For invalidation, the actual object is fetched via unicast by the children proxies, however, invalidation messages are multicast to all proxy caches. For replication, object updates are pushed via multicast from the parent proxy cache to all children proxies.

The decision to use multicast or unicast depends on the multicast gain $G = C_{\mathrm{mc}}/C_{\mathrm{uc}}$, that is the multicast cost C_{mc} divided by the unicast cost C_{uc}, which is a function of the network topology, the number of children proxies and their location. Several studies have shown that the multicast gain in a wide range of network topologies can be approximated by $G = M^{-0.2}$, where M is the number of receiving proxies [18]. Therefore, it is enough for a parent proxy to know the number of subscribed children proxies to estimate the multicast gain and therefore decide whether to turn on multicast or not.

The bandwidth usage in the network of validation B_{V}, invalidation B_{I}, and replication B_{R} to deliver one byte from a parent proxy to the children proxies with multicast is:

$$B_{\mathrm{V}} = \Pr\{N > 0\} S_{\mathrm{o}} C_{\mathrm{uc}} + E[N] S_{\mathrm{h}} C_{\mathrm{uc}},$$
$$B_{\mathrm{I}} = \Pr\{N > 0\} (S_{\mathrm{o}} + S_{\mathrm{h}}) C_{\mathrm{uc}} + S_{\mathrm{i}} C_{\mathrm{mc}},$$
$$B_{\mathrm{R}} = S_{\mathrm{o}} C_{\mathrm{mc}}.$$

To study the effect of a multicast distribution we analyze the case where the network connecting the parent proxy with its M children proxy caches is a full O-ary tree with height H [19] (a full O-ary tree has proved to be a good model for network topologies, providing very realistic results [16]). In Fig. 9 we present the bandwidth usage inside the network for validation, invalidation, and replication when multicast is enabled.

Comparing Figs. 7 and 9 we observe that the relative performance of validation is not modified since validation does not benefit from the fact that multicast is enabled. We also observe that the relative performance of invalidation is slightly smaller since invalidation messages are now multicasted. For replication, the bandwidth savings are very high, since the cost of replication is small. Of course, the multicast gain depends on the network topology and

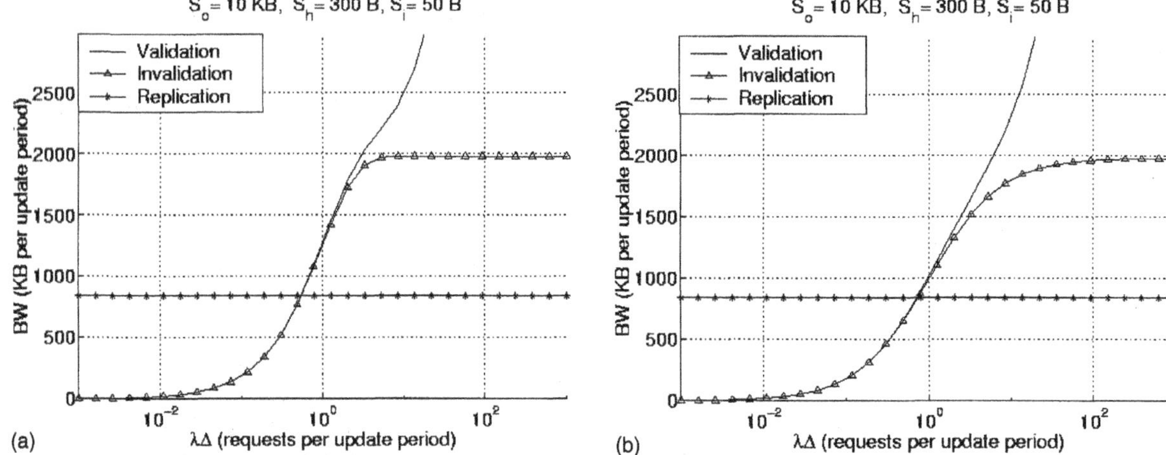

Fig. 9. Bandwidth usage with multicast enabled. (a) Periodic updates. (b) Exponentially distributed updates.

the number of receivers; however, even in the worst case a multicast distribution performs no worse than unicast, and the relative performance of validation, invalidation, and replication would then be the same as the one in Fig. 7.

4. Trace-driven simulation

Based on the switching thresholds calculated in Section 3.4, we now perform a trace driven simulation to get a feel for how SPREAD will behave in a real-life setting. To that end, we analyze log traces from one access node (POP) at AT&T Worldnet (Bridgeton) over a period of 10 days, collected in May 1999. The total number of requests in the trace is roughly 10 million. From the logs we extract all the cacheable requests that contain last-modified information. We then extract objects of type text/html and image/gif to study how the control algorithm we use in SPREAD will perform. These two object types constitute an overwhelming majority (over 90%) of the accesses. For every single object in the log-file we estimate the average request rate and the average update period. To calculate the average update period we use the average time difference between every request for the same object and the last-modified-time, which is the average update period in the case of exponentially distributed update periods, and is equal to the half of the average update period for periodic updates. In reality, a SPREAD proxy would continuously monitor the request and update rates; however, using the average update period during the trace was a suitable approximation for the purpose of our simulation study.

In Fig. 10a we show the distribution of objects of type text/html that have a certain number of requests per update period. We see that most objects have a value which is concentrated between 10^{-4} requests per update period and 10^{4} requests per update period.

Combining the results presented in Fig. 10a and Table 1, we can calculate the percentage of objects that would use validation, invalidation, or replication to minimize the bandwidth usage.

Table 2 shows the percentage of objects requiring every scheme in the case of periodic updates, and the

Table 2
Percentage of objects that require validation (V), invalidation (I), and replication (R). Periodic and exponentially distributed updates

Perspective	Threshold (req. per update period)	V (%)	I (%)	R (%)
Bandwidth (Periodic)	$Th_{VI} = 0.7$, $Th_{IR} = 3.6$	18.4	19	62.2
Bandwidth (Exponential distribution)	$Th_{VI} = 0.55$, $Th_{IR} = 29$	16	52	32

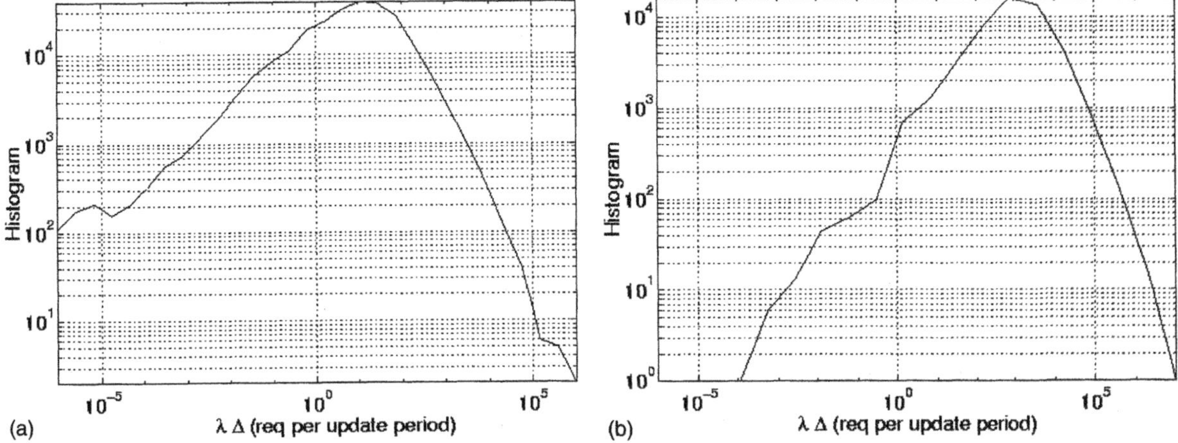

Fig. 10. Distribution of requests per update period $\lambda\Delta$. (a) HTML. (b) GIF.

value of the switching points in terms of requests per update period (Th_{VI} and Th_{IR}) for a sample HTML document of size 10 KB.

From Table 2, we see that in the case of periodic updates, 19% of the objects would require invalidation to minimize bandwidth usage, and 63% would require replication. In the case of exponentially distributed update periods we also calculated the percentage of objects that would require each scheme, and see that the percentage of objects that would require invalidation increases to 86%.

In the Optimization section, we calculated the bandwidth usage in a proxy's link for a single document with varying requests per update period $\lambda\Delta$, and the average client's latency for a simple two-tier cache hierarchy. Next, we calculate the total average bandwidth usage and the expected latency for validation, invalidation, replication, and SPREAD. We sum up the bandwidth used by *all* objects, and scale the bandwidth we obtain per update period — to per second — by dividing the result by the object's update period Δ.

Table 3 summarizes the results for bandwidth usage, and the corresponding client latency. From Table 3 we see that the bandwidth needed to deliver all documents with validation is quite small since most of the documents in the trace have few requests per update period. Invalidation, on the other hand, has a higher bandwidth usage than validation, since invalidation messages are sent for documents that are never requested. Replication has the highest

Table 3
Bandwidth consumption and resulting latency for validation (V), invalidation (I), replication (R), and SPREAD for HTML documents. Periodic updates

Perspective	V	I	R	SPREAD
Bandwidth (KB/s)	1.6	5.3	803	1.4
Client latency (s)	0.58	0.28	0.11	0.26

bandwidth usage since all documents are being replicated, and many are not requested. SPREAD, has the minimum bandwidth usage since proxies automatically select validation, invalidation, or replication to optimize bandwidth. The benefits in terms of bandwidth of SPREAD compared to validation are not very high since there are not many hot documents in the trace that produce a large number of IMS requests (the bandwidth usage of validation would be much higher in the case of more popular documents). However, the latency experienced by the clients with SPREAD is about half the latency experienced with validation. Even though SPREAD is not optimized to minimize latency we see that the latency offered by SPREAD is smaller than for validation or invalidation. As SPREAD proxies subscribe to invalidation or replication to minimize bandwidth usage, the latency reduces, since the origin server is not contacted so often. Of course, replication has the lowest latency at the cost of high bandwidth usage. We have also calculated the same parameters than in Table 3 for the case of exponentially update periods, and the

Table 4
Bandwidth consumption and resulting latency for validation (V), invalidation (I), replication (R), and SPREAD for GIF images. Periodic updates

Perspective	V	I	R	SPREAD
Bandwidth (KB/s)	7.6	2.4	72	1.6
Client latency (s)	0.45	0.14	0.11	0.12

results for exponentially update periods do not differ much from those for periodic updates.

Next, we also study the case for objects of type image/gif (see Fig. 10b). GIF objects tend to change less frequently, and therefore the number of requests that a GIF object receives before it is updated is much higher than for HTML objects (Fig. 10a). Table 4 shows the total bandwidth usage by GIF objects using validation, invalidation, replication, and SPREAD. From Table 4 we see that validation performs worse than it does for HTML documents, since validation results in a higher number of IMS queries to the origin server (since GIFs see more requests per update). Replication performs better than it does for HTML documents for the same reason. This also causes SPREAD to improve on validation much more than it did with HTML. As before, we see that though SPREAD is tuned to optimize bandwidth, it has an average latency which is very close to that achieved with replication.

Finally, in Table 5 we add the total bandwidth usage and calculate the average latency for text/html and image/gif objects to see how the various schemes perform. We see that the bandwidth savings and the reduction in latency for SPREAD compared to validation, invalidation, and replication are much more relevant than for either text/html or for image/gif objects alone. That is, while one of the mechanisms may be suited for one type of object, e.g. validation to reduce bandwidth usage for text/html or invalidation for image/gif, SPREAD does well overall, distancing itself from the other mechanisms when a mix of objects are considered.

Table 5
Bandwidth consumption and resulting latency for validation for validation (V), invalidation (I), replication (R), and SPREAD for HTML documents and GIF images. Periodic updates

Perspective	V	I	R	SPREAD
Bandwidth (KB/s)	9.2	7.7	875	3
Client latency (s)	0.49	0.18	0.11	0.16

5. Conclusions and future work

In this paper we introduced SPREAD, a new architecture for content distribution. SPREAD uses a network of proxies that automatically configure themselves and make autonomous decisions on how to maintain cache consistency. They dynamically choose between client validation, server invalidation and replication to optimize bandwidth usage. One key component of SPREAD is that it uses a new class of transparent proxies called translucent proxies. Translucent proxies can be cascaded and networked together transparently, without requiring them to be placed at focal points in the network.

SPREAD is also showing promise as a base platform for a large set of other wide-area applications for which self-organization, scalability and robustness are important. To explore this further, we are currently pursuing the use of SPREAD for streaming media. In the future we hope to also use it as a dissemination mechanism for global event notification systems.

Acknowledgements

We thank Anja Feldmann for collecting and providing traces from AT&T Worldnet.

References

[1] FreeFlow: How it Works, Akamai, Cambridge, MA, USA, November 1999.
[2] National Lab of Applied Network Research (NLANR), http://ircache.nlanrnet/.
[3] M.F. Arlitt and C.L. Williamson, Web server workload characterization: the search for invariants, in: Proc. of the ACM SIGMETRICS, New York, May 23–26, 1996.
[4] D.R. Cox, Renewal Theory, 1962.
[5] P. Danzig and K.L. Swartz, Transparent, scaleable, fail-safe Web caching, Technichal report, Network Appliance, Santa Clara, CA, USA, 1999.
[6] F. Douglis, A. Feldmann, B. Krishnamurthy and J. Mogul,

Rate of change and other metrics: A live study of the World Wide Web, in: Proc. of the USENIX Symposium on Internet Technologies and Systems, December 1997.
[7] S. Gribble and E. Brewer, System design issues for Internet middleware services: deductions from a large client trace, in: Proc. of the USENIX Symposium on Internet Technologies and Systems, December 1997.
[8] J. Gwertzman, Autonomous replication in wide-area internetworks, M.S. Thesis, Harvard, Cambridge, MA, April 1995.
[9] J. Gwertzman and M. Seltzer, World-Wide Web cache consistency, in: Proc. of the 1996 USENIX Technical Conference, San Diego, CA, January 1996.
[10] V. Jacobson, Compressing TCP/IP headers for low-speed serial links, RFC 1144, 1990.
[11] L. Kleinrock, Queuing Systems, Volume I: Theory, Wiley, New York, 1975.
[12] P. Krisnan, D. Raz and Y. Shavitt, Transparent en-route caching in WANs, in: Work-in-progress in the 4th International Caching Workshop, San Diego, March 1999.
[13] C. Liu and P. Cao, Maintaining strong cache consistency in the World-Wide Web, in: Proc. of ICDCS, May 1997.
[14] B.N.M. Degermark and S. Pink, RFC 2507: IP header compression, February 1999.
[15] S. Michel, K. Nguyen, A. Rosenstein, L. Zhang, S. Floyd and V. Jacobson, Adaptive Web caching: towards a new global caching architecture, in: 3rd International WWW Caching Workshop, June 1998.
[16] J. Nonnenmacher and E.W. Biersack, Performance modelling of reliable multicast transmission, in: Proc. of the IEEE INFOCOM'97, Kobe, Japan, April 1997.
[17] F. Overview, Sandpiper, Thousand Oaks, CA, USA, October 1999.
[18] G. Phillips, S. Shenker and H. Tangmunarunkit, Scaling of multicast trees: comments on the Chuang-Sirbu Scaling Law, in: ACM SIGCOMM'99, Vol. 29, Harvard University, MA, USA, September 1999.
[19] P. Rodriguez, E.W. Biersack and K.W. Ross, Automated delivery of Web documents through a caching infrastructure, Technical Report, EURECOM, June 1999.
[20] P. Rodriguez, K.W. Ross and E.W. Biersack, Distributing frequently-changing documents in the Web: multicasting or hierarchical caching, in: Selected Papers of the 3rd International Caching Workshop, Comput. Networks ISDN Syst. 30 (1998) 2223–2245.
[21] P. Rodriguez, S. Sibal and O. Spatscheck, TPOT: Translucent Proxying of TCP, Technical report TR 00.4.1, AT&T Research Labs, 2000.
[22] D. Wessels, Squid Internet Object Cache: http://www.nlanr.net/Squid/, 1996.
[23] K. Worrel, Invalidation in large scale network object caches, Master's Thesis, University of Colorado, Boulder, 1994.
[24] H. Yu, L. Breslau and S. Shenker, A scalable Web cache consistency architecture, in: Proc. of ACM SIGCOMM'99, Cambridge, September 1999.

Pablo Rodriguez is a senior graduate student at the Institut EURECOM, finishing up his thesis on scalable content distribution in the Internet. He has been active in the areas of Web caching and replication, satellite dissemination of Web documents, caching infrastructures for delivering up-to-date content, and scalable broadcasting solutions.

Sandeep Sibal is a senior technical staff member in the Internet and Networking Systems Center at AT&T Labs — Research. His general interests are Internet technologies and services, and he is currently working on topics in content distribution and Layer-4 proxies.

Risks of the Passport single signon protocol

David P. Kormann [1], Aviel D. Rubin [1]

AT&T Labs, Research, 180 Park Avenue, Florham Park, NJ 07932, USA

Abstract

Passport is a protocol that enables users to sign onto many different merchants' Web pages by authenticating themselves only once to a common server. This is important because users tend to pick poor (guessable) user names and passwords and to repeat them at different sites. Passport is notable as it is being very widely deployed by Microsoft. At the time of this writing, Passport boasts 40 million consumers and more than 400 authentications per second on average. We examine the Passport single signon protocol, and identify several risks and attacks. We discuss a flaw that we discovered in the interaction of Passport and Netscape browsers that leaves a user logged in while informing him that he has successfully logged out. Finally, we suggest several areas of improvement.

Keywords: Web security; Single signon; Authentication; E-commerce

1. Introduction

It has become common practice for retailers, banks, service providers, and just about everyone else to provide customers with a way of shopping on the Web. To ensure the security of these customers' financial data, the online vendors often require a username and a password to access an account. Users are faced with a dilemma when creating multiple accounts. Do they use the same name and password for all the accounts? If so, that means that, for example, their online grocery store will have access to their stock trading account. The alternative is to maintain a list of usernames and passwords. This list must be written down, as so many names and passwords are cumbersome to remember. As such, compromise of this list constitutes potential for a serious loss.

Single signon is the term used to represent a system whereby users need only remember one username and password, and authenticated it can be provided for multiple services. Kerberos [3] is an example of a system where users provide a password and receive a ticket in exchange. The ticket can be used to authenticate users to different network services. Kerberos single signon is possible because all of the services are under the same administrative control. There is a centralized database containing keys that are shared with each service, and tickets can be issued, encrypted under the keys of the target services.

Single signon on the Web is much more difficult. Different Web sites are under completely different administrative control. Thus, it is not natural to imagine signing in once, and gaining authenticated access to multiple, independent Web services. Passport is Microsoft's ambitious attempt to provide this service. While the overall architecture makes sense given the constraints of the protocol (namely, to use

[1] E-mail: {davek,rubin}@research.att.com

only existing Web technologies that are present in most browsers and servers), there are some risks associated with using this protocol that are not pointed out in the paper. We refer to the online description of **Passport**[2]. The draft we refer to is the one at the time of this writing. We were unable to locate a paper copy to reference.

As just mentioned, one of the constraints of Passport is that it was designed to use existing Web technologies, so that clients and servers need not be modified. The protocol leverages HTTP redirects, Javascript, cookies, and SSL. While Javascript is not absolutely required, it is highly recommended. Some of the attacks described below result from some fundamental problems with security on the Web, and in particular, the public key infrastructure that is built into browsers. As such, they are not specific to Passport, but nonetheless represent risks of using that system (and any system subject to these constraints).

2. The problem with SSL

SSL is a wonderful protocol. It is well designed, has withstood much analysis and scrutiny [4], and its deployment is probably the single most positive step towards anything resembling security on the Web. While we find no fault in the SSL protocol or its implementations in browsers and servers, we believe that the certification model and user interface can lead to problems.

Browsers come with many default 'root' public keys. For example, Netscape Navigator 4.5 comes with 58 root public keys. Anyone who controls the corresponding private keys can issue certificates that are automatically trusted by all major browsers. All it takes is for one of the certifying authorities with a weak policy, security breach, or intentional compromise (e.g. bribe) for the certification process to be meaningless. If an entity can obtain a certificate from a trusted authority, then the only recourse of the user when presented with a 'secure' Web site is to check the security information and determine that the root CA that signed the certificate is one it trusts, and that the name in the certificate corresponds to the actual entity with which it wants to have a secure session. Most users are not qualified to determine either of these things, and are probably not even aware of SSL or certificates anyhow.

As it stands, the SSL model does not lend itself naturally to the problem of delegation. This is exactly the feature that Passport requires. So, Passport uses the existing Web technologies to the best of its abilities. Unfortunately, the resulting protocol poses several risks to the user, and these are the focus of this paper.

3. How Passport works

In this section, we describe the Passport single signon and wallet protocols. In the Passport model, there are three entities: the client at a Web browser (usually a consumer who has previously registered with the Passport service), the merchant (a store or collection of stores wishing to market to the consumer), and the Passport login server. The login server maintains authentication and customer profile information for the client and gives the merchant access to this information when permitted by the customer. Passport divides client data into profile information (such as addresses, shoe size, and so on) and the *wallet*, which contains credit card information. Passport's protocols are designed to enable the secure transfer of this profile and wallet information between the Passport server and the merchants.

3.1. Single signon protocol

Passport's interaction with a user begins when a client, visiting a merchant site, needs to authenticate (to provide some personal information or make a purchase). The merchant Web server redirects the customer's browser to a well-known Passport server. The Passport server presents the user with a login page over an SSL connection. The user logs into the Passport server and the Passport server redirects the user back to the end server. Authentication information is included in the redirect message in the query string. This information is encrypted using triple DES with a key previously established between Passport and the merchant server. The end server then sets an encrypted cookie in the client's browser. This is illustrated in Fig. 1.

[2] http://www.passport.com/business/content_whitepaper2.html

The idea is that when a user returns to the IBM site, for example, the encrypted cookie is returned as well. The site can decrypt the cookie and verify the user is already authenticated. The Passport server also sets a cookie. Thus, if a user visits another site, say dell.com, when the browser is redirected to the Passport server, the user is no longer presented with a login screen because the previous Passport cookie is used. If this cookie contains valid credentials, the client is redirected back to the merchant server without user intervention.

3.2. Wallet protocol

The wallet protocol is very similar in nature to the single signon protocol. Instead of just authenticating, however, the user can insert all sorts of personal and credit card information. Then, when the user is shopping on an end server site, the user can select which information to include for that merchant. The user never needs to enter the information again for participating end servers.

4. Risks of Passport

In Sections 4.1 and 4.2 we look at some practical risks of the Passport protocol and some specific attacks.

4.1. Practical matters

In this section, we look at some security issues related to the chosen architecture and protocols. These are meant to highlight some of the risks of using Passport, without discussing specific attacks. Those are covered in Section 4.2.

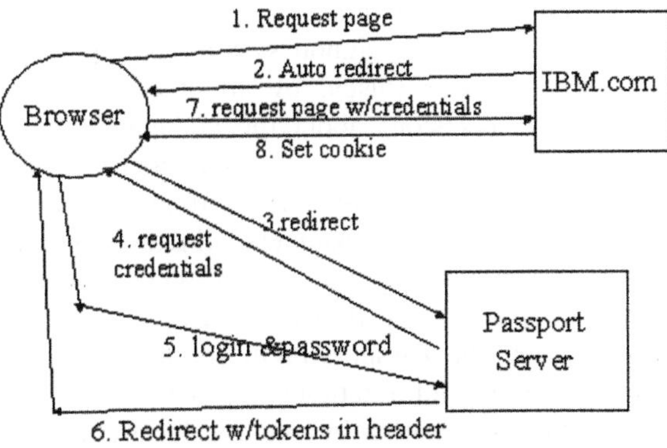

Fig. 1. The Passport architecture.

4.1.1. User interface

In security systems, the user interface is one of the most crucial and frequently inadequate parts. For example, any merchant site that uses Passport displays a Passport signout icon which is supposed to remove Passport cookies. One of the most popular Passport services currently deployed is the Hotmail e-mail service from Microsoft. We set up some Hotmail accounts and did some experimentation. One thing we discovered is that in addition to the Passport signout icon, there is also a Hotmail logout option on the page. So, what does this mean to a user? Presumably, the Hotmail logout button is used to remove the Hotmail credentials, while the Passport signout button is used to remove the Passport credentials to all services. While this may be clear to computer security experts, it is unlikely that the average non-expert computer user will understand the distinction. A user making the mistaken, but reasonable, presumption that the Hotmail Logout button will remove Passport credentials could easily walk away from a browser still able to authenticate on behalf of the user.

A curious interaction between Netscape's browsers and the Passport signout process demonstrates how difficult it is to design a user interface that makes sense and works correctly. After signing in to Hotmail with our Passport credentials, we clicked on the Passport signout icon. The redirect occurred, and our screen said that the Hotmail credentials were being removed. The point was made with a page that said Passport credentials were being removed and which displayed a check mark next to the Hotmail service. We were then redirected to a generic page with links, news stories and shopping opportunities. One of the links on that page was to Hotmail. When we clicked on that link, we found ourselves back in our Hotmail account, without reauthenticating. We tried this on several different machines. It turns out that regardless of whether we clicked on the Passport signout button or the Hotmail logout button, the message that we were logged out appeared, but in reality, we were not logged out. We tried this in Internet Explorer, and the logout was successful. There is something about the interaction of Passport and Netscape that invalidates the Passport logout procedure (at the time of this writing).

The risk of this flaw in Passport on the Netscape platform is clear. Imagine a user reading Hotmail e-mail from a public browser. When finished, the user clicks the signout button and is told that the credentials have been removed and that he is signed out from the account. The user confidently walks away from the machine. Then, when another user steps up to that machine and goes to Hotmail, he is automatically logged into that account.

It turns out that the flaw that we discovered was a problem with the Microsoft Passport server when running Netscape with the option to only return cookies to the server from which they came. We pointed out this flaw to Microsoft. Microsoft indicated they were already aware of the flaw, and that it was fixed that same day. Nonetheless, the problem makes an important point: the Passport user interface indicated that the signout process had succeeded without ensuring that it had. The value of the data maintained by Passport (its users' identities) turns this otherwise relatively minor and obscure user interface gaffe into a potentially dangerous flaw.

4.1.2. Key management

In this section, we identify areas of potential concern with regard to the usage of keys in Passport. The Passport protocol requires that the Passport server shares triple DES keys with each merchant. The keys are used to encrypt information transferred from Passport to the merchants in redirect messages. These keys must be generated securely, i.e. randomly, and assigned out of band. Many systems have been broken because poor randomness was used to generate keys (e.g., [2]). It is a difficult problem that requires careful attention.

Assigning the secret keys out of band is a nontrivial task. The mechanism for transferring keys is not stated in the current version of the specification. Ideally, these keys are transferred by physical mail or over the phone. The intuitive solution, to transfer the keys over an SSL connection, requires authentication of the merchant in some way, and is likely to lead to potential breaches.

Passport encrypts information for itself and stores the information in Passport cookies on client machines. A single key is used to encrypt all of the cookies. This represents an unnecessary risk of exposure of that key. A better solution is to use a master key to generate a unique key per client. This is accomplished as follows: using the master key that is currently used to encrypt cookies, generate a unique key per client by encrypting the client address with the master key, and using the resulting ciphertext as the encryption key for that client. Thus, the master key is used only as a key encryption key. If an individual key is compromised, Passport cookies on other clients are not directly vulnerable.

To illustrate, take three clients, CLIENT_1, CLIENT_2, and CLIENT_3, and say that the passport master key for storing keys in the browsers is MK. Assume that CLIENT_n represents the IP address of client n. To store a cookie on client CLIENT_1, Passport computes K_1 = 3DES(MK, CLIENT_1) and uses K_1 to encrypt the cookie that is stored on CLIENT_1. Likewise, Passport computes K_2 = 3DES(MK, CLIENT_2) and K_3 = 3DES(MK, CLIENT_3). Now, if Passport later receives a cookie from CLIENT_n, it first uses MK to compute the key for that host and then decrypts the cookie. Of course, this solution would not work for clients whose IP addresses change frequently, so perhaps using the domain name is a better idea. The main point is that a compromise of one of the keys does not compromise cookies stored on other hosts.

Since triple DES is used, the three keys needed can be obtained by encrypting the client address with each of the three keys in the master key in turn and using the resulting three ciphertexts as the triple DES keys.

4.1.3. Central point of attack

As with all single signon systems, Passport establishes a service trusted by all others to make authoritative decisions about the authenticity of a user. Whereas in traditional Web authentication each merchant is responsible for safeguarding the authentication information of customers, all data is centralized in Passport. Compromise of this central service would be particularly disastrous. Besides authentication data, the Passport login service maintains consumer profile information on all registered users. Storing this information in a central location, while convenient, makes the server an extremely attractive target for attack, both for denial of service and unauthorized access. The centralized service model is antithetical to the distributed nature of the Internet that has made it so robust and so popular.

The effects of a denial of service attack on the login server are particularly acute. Obviously, the usefulness of a system like Passport increases in direct proportion to the number of merchants who subscribe. But as the number of merchants supporting the service grows, the effects of an outage (deliberate or accidental) increase. An operator of a large online shopping site not affiliated with Passport might see a significant increase in traffic (and hence income) by making it impossible (or even difficult) for Passport users to access their wallet and Passport. The unscrupulous competitor might accomplish this by simply flooding the Passport site with bogus profile registrations or logins.

The usual response to such problems of service availability is to replicate the service sufficiently to make catastrophic failure unlikely. No information is provided on how the system could handle the fundamental problems of key distribution and database replication in scale. Furthermore, replicating the service would require multiple copies of the secret keys shared with the merchant and the master secret key of Passport, thus increasing the exposure of those keys to risks of compromise.

One specific denial of service attack that exists is due to the fact that single signon tokens are stored as cookies in the browsers. An active attacker can impersonate the Passport server and delete cookies at will on the clients. Furthermore, attacks such as the **Cookie Monster bug**[3] for domain names outside of .com, .org, .gov, .edu, .net and .mil could easily overwrite merchant cookies on any client.

4.1.4. Cookies and Javascript

The Passport white paper describes two Web technologies used in support of Passport. Cookies are used to store encrypted credential information in the browsers, and Javascript is used to "make certain transactions more efficient (fewer redirects) and also to enable co-branding for participants on most centralized Web pages". According to the white paper, Javascript may be disabled without significantly impairing the function of Passport (the system is said to 'gracefully degrade'), but the system will not function without cookies.

Usually, the danger with cookies is limited to the exposure of sensitive cookie payloads to unintended recipients. Because the Passport cookie contains sensitive data, the system encrypts these cookies using triple DES (as described above). Passport cookies, though, are also proofs of authentication whose lifetimes are determined only by the lifetime of the Web browser and the (encrypted) time window in the cookie. On a public machine, a user who forgets to log out of a Passport account could leave valid authentication tokens behind on the machine for any user to recover.

The most important problems, however, with cookies and Javascript are more social than technological. Regardless of their actual value or security, these technologies have been shown to compromise user privacy. Dictating (or even strongly recommending) the use of technologies which are not felt to be trustworthy in a system whose purpose is to establish trust can undermine significantly the perceived value of that system.

4.1.5. Persistent cookies

Passport leaves authenticators, in the form of browser cookies on the client machine. As the white paper states: "This option keeps a consumer signed in to Passport at all times on that computer even if the consumer disconnects from the Internet, closes the browser, or turns off the computer." The idea is to have a persistent authenticator so that users are not required to retype in their passwords. The Passport server does not have to reissue credentials if the cookie has not expired yet. As mentioned in the introduction, this is reminiscent of single signon in Kerberos.

Kerberos uses tickets, which are encrypted credentials, to establish continuous authentication within a specified amount of time, without requiring a return trip to the authentication server. However, Passport is lacking one of the fundamental properties of single signon with tickets. Namely, there is no concept of an *authenticator*. In Kerberos, the client must send an authenticator that proves knowledge of the key inside the ticket. To accomplish this, the

[3] http://help.netscape.com/kb/consumer/981231-1.html and http://homepages.paradise.net.nz/~glineham/cookiemonster.html

client simply encrypts a timestamp. If the timestamp can be decrypted, the client must have used the correct key. This prevents theft and misuse of a ticket found lying on a machine. In Passport, where cookies stand in for tickets, possession of the cookie is all that is necessary to impersonate the valid user of that cookie. No further proof is required. Furthermore, the breach is undetected, and the attacker gets unlimited use of the victim's authentication information and wallet. This is especially dangerous if a user uses Passport on a public machine, or if the user's machine is broken into. Given the recent surge in e-mail viruses that compromise integrity and privacy, it is not unreasonable to assume that attackers may get access to a user's cookie file.

4.1.6. Automatic credential assignment

To demonstrate the ability of Passport to scale, all of Microsoft's Hotmail accounts were automatically moved on top of Passport. In a sense, every Hotmail user id and password became Passport credentials, and when users log into Hotmail, they actually run the Passport protocol, with the Hotmail server acting as the merchant. Unfortunately, Hotmail has been fraught with security problems. One compromise allowed an attacker to log into any Hotmail account without knowing the password[4]. This presents a problem if users use their Hotmail credentials, which are already automatically usable as Passport credentials, to shop online with other merchants. Any compromised account, and for that matter any future compromise of Hotmail, could result in abuse of their account at these other merchants.

4.2. Attacks

In this section, we look at some specific attacks on the Passport protocol that can result in compromise of user credentials and wallet information.

4.2.1. Bogus merchant

The bogus merchant threat is probably the weakest aspect of Passport. Imagine that users get accustomed to using Passport. They enjoy the convenience of single signon and wallet services, while trusting that the service is secure. Perhaps the first time that they use the service and authenticate to the Passport server they actually bother to check the certificate in the SSL connection. It is unlikely that they will do this. It is even more unlikely that they will continue to check this certificate every time they return.

Now, to attack the system, a merchant sets up a phony Web store, selling something attractive. In addition, the attacker obtains a certificate for a domain he has set up, called pasport.com. Notice that pasport.com is an incorrect spelling of passport.com. The attacker must convince some legitimate certificate authority to certify his use of the domain name. Given the aforementioned quantity of root certification authorities, the existence of one vulnerable to deception seems likely. The attacker sets up his Web site with all of the Passport images that would appear on a legitimate Passport customer site. When the user visits the phony Web site, the server simulates a redirect to pasport.com, and the user is prompted for his credentials on a page that looks exactly like the legitimate Passport server. The user is in the habit of filling this out every once in a while, so he does not notice the misspelled URL, or check the certificate. Even if he did check the certificate, he might not notice the misspelling. In practice, any URL, even one that does not resemble the word 'passport' would probably work as well.

After the user fills in all of his information and submits it, the bogus Web site can proceed to process the request any way the attacker wants. The important thing to note is that the attacker has obtained the user's valid authentication information, and he can now authenticate to Passport on behalf of the user, use wallet services, sell the credentials, or exploit them any way he pleases.

The fundamental problem is that users tend to inherently trust the Web, and services such as Passport serve to increase that confidence. However, by simply simulating a valid merchant, an attacker can abuse this confidence to bypass the entire system.

4.2.2. Active attack

An attacker with access to the network between the client's Web browser and the merchant server (and able, therefore, to rewrite packets passing between the two hosts) can take advantage of this access to achieve the same result described above while permitting the client to interact normally with

[4] http://www.zdnet.com/zdnn/stories/news/0,4586,2323960,00.html

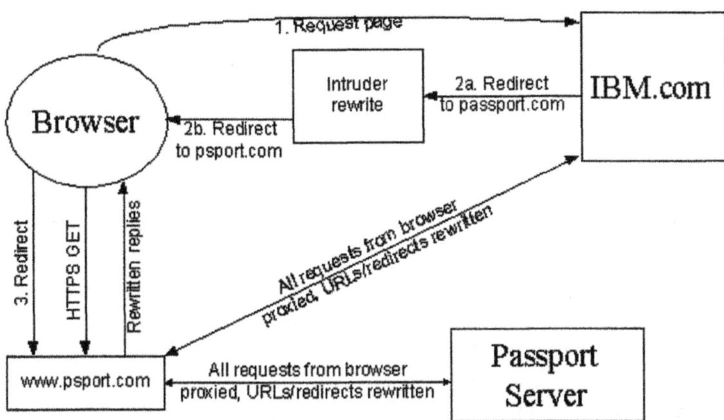

Fig. 2. Rewriting and proxying requests.

the merchant site. Such access is not prohibitively difficult to obtain. Large ISPs concentrate the traffic of thousands of users through a fairly small set of routers and servers. Obtaining unauthorized access to one of these hosts interposes the attacker between these users and all services they wish to access. Any traffic passing through such a compromised host could potentially then be read and rewritten.

As before, this attack makes use of the fact that users are unlikely to check the contents of URLs or certificates except under extraordinary circumstances (such as when the Web browser complains of a mismatch between the certificate and server URL). The attack also relies on the attacker's ability to identify when the Passport authentication process begins. This is fairly simple. Imagine a client communicating with a merchant server, using a login service at `www.passport.com`. The attacker, waiting between the client and merchant site, watches for an HTTP redirect to `www.passport.com`. The merchant site is required to perform this redirection at the beginning of a Passport session, and the redirection is not protected by SSL. Seeing this redirection, the attacker intercepts the packet and rewrites the URL in the redirection to a previously established bogus Passport server, perhaps again making use of creative domain names and legitimate certificates to make the service appear genuine. This server then acts as a proxy between the client and `www.passport.com`, and between the client and merchant site, impersonating the Passport service to the client and vice versa while rewriting all URLs and HTTP redirects to force traffic through the proxy. Passport's use of SSL cannot at this point prevent the proxy from reading and possibly rewriting each packet, as all SSL connections are terminated on the proxy, and the user is unlikely to notice the proxy acting on her behalf.

While an intruder who accomplishes this attack cannot read the contents of the encrypted cookies (and so cannot directly extract credit card or personal information), it would be quite simple to store the user's password and use it to retrieve the information from the stored customer profile.

Fig. 2 shows the intruder's rewriting process and proxy service as a component of the Passport architecture shown in Fig. 1. The attacker has established a bogus authentication service at `www.psport.com`, and has compromised a host in the path between the client browser and the merchant site, at `www.ibm.com`.

A common (if weak) protection against this sort of attack, which involves having the server receiving the redirection inspect the HTTP `Referer:` header to ensure the referral comes from a legitimate site, will not help here, as this can be rewritten as well.

4.2.3. DNS attacks

Passport's security model depends heavily on the Domain Name System. In addition to the well-known problem of SSL's dependence on the DNS, HTTP redirects generally specify a host to receive the redirection in the form of a DNS name. An intruder who controls a client's DNS service could transparently perform the rewriting process described in the previous section by simply aliasing www.passport.com to the IP address of a server controlled by the intruder. Specifically:

- The attacker inserts the bogus record in the local DNS server
- A client is redirected by the merchant service to www.passport.com
- Resolving this hostname, the client receives and connects to the IP address of the attacker's fake Passport service
- The attacker's Passport service proceeds as described above, acting as a proxy between the client and the Passport and merchant services.

Another form of attacking the DNS is to append bogus DNS information to valid DNS replies from the legitimate DNS server. This attack was identified in [1]. Until there is widespread adoption of DNSSEC, which provides digitally signed DNS information, such attacks will be possible.

5. Conclusions

As e-commerce proliferates, the need for a tool to help users manage authentication and personal information across a variety of sites becomes increasingly critical. Passport is an ambitious attempt to meet this need while requiring no changes to existing browsers and servers. However, the system carries significant risks to users that are not made adequately clear in the technical documentation available.

The bulk of Passport's flaws arises directly from its reliance on systems that are either not trustworthy (such as HTTP referrals and the DNS) or assume too much about user awareness (such as SSL). Another flaw arises out of interactions with a particular browser (Netscape). Passport's attempt to retrofit the complex process of single signon to fit the limitations of existing browser technology leads to compromises that create real risks.

Some improvement is possible in Passport without violating the system's goals of supporting unmodified browsers. Rotating the keys used to encrypt cookies would significantly increase the difficulty of retrieving cookie contents, as would using the master key to generate encryption keys instead of encrypting all cookies with the same key. Requiring SSL for all transactions would eliminate the possibility of forged redirects (at the cost of significantly increased load on merchant servers). Replacing password-based authentication with a challenge–response scheme (such as HTTP digest authentication) would make it impossible for an attacker to reuse passwords to impersonate a user.

In the end, Passport's risks may be inevitable for a system with its requirements. We believe that until fundamental changes are made to underlying protocols (through standards such as DNSSEC and IPSec), efforts such as Passport must be viewed with suspicion.

References

[1] D. Dean, E.W. Felten and D.S. Wallach, Java security: from HotJava to Netscape and beyond, 1996 IEEE Symp. on Security and Privacy, 1996, pp. 190–200.

[2] I. Goldberg and E. Wagner, Randomness and the Netscape browser, Dr. Dobb's J., 1996, pp. 66–70.

[3] J.G. Steiner, B.C. Neuman and J.I. Schiller, Kerberos: an authentication service for open network systems, Usenix Conf. Proc., 1988, pp. 191–202.

[4] D. Wagner and B. Schneier, Analysis of the SSL 3.0 Protocol, 2nd USENIX Workshop on Electronic Commerce Proc., 1996, pp. 29–40.

Dave Kormann is a senior technical staff member at AT & T Labs, Research in the Online Platforms Research department, where his work includes systems administration and Internet services development. He received the M.S. in Computer Science from Northeastern University in 1996.

Aviel D. Rubin is a principal technical staff member at AT & T Labs, Research in the Secure Systems Research Department, and an adjunct professor of computer science at New York University, where he teaches cryptography and computer security. He is the co-author of the Web Security Sourcebook. Rubin holds a B.S., M.S.E., and Ph.D. from the University of Michigan in Ann Arbor (1989, 1991, 1994) in computer science and engineering. He has served on several program committees for major security conferences and as the program chair USENIX Security '98, USENIX Technical '99, and ISOC NDSS 2000. Rubin is a frequent invited speaker at computer security conferences, industry groups, and on Wall Street.

Design and implementation of an access control processor for XML documents

Ernesto Damiani [a,1], Sabrina De Capitani di Vimercati [b,*,2], Stefano Paraboschi [c,3], Pierangela Samarati [a,2]

[a] *Università di Milano, Polo Didattico di Crema, Via Bramante 65, Crema (CR), Italy*
[b] *Università di Brescia, Dip. Elettronica per l'Automazione, Via Branze 38, 25123 Brescia, Italy*
[c] *Politecnico di Milano, Dip. Elettronica e Informazione, Piazza L. da Vinci 32, 20133 Milano, Italy*

Abstract

More and more information is distributed in XML format, both on corporate Intranets and on the global Net. In this paper an *Access Control System* for XML is described allowing for definition and enforcement of access restrictions directly on the structure and content of XML documents, thus providing a simple and effective way for users to protect information at the same granularity level provided by the language itself.

Keywords: Security; Access control model; XML

1. Introduction

As more and more information is made available in *eXtensible Markup Language* (XML) format, both on corporate Intranets and on the global Net, concerns are being raised by developers and end-users about XML security problems. Early research work about XML was not directly related to access control and security, because XML was initially introduced as a data format for documents; therefore, many researchers assumed well-known techniques for securing documents to be straightforwardly applicable to XML data. But the way XML is being positioned has caused some to question if additional measures will be necessary.

For example, in the scenario of the oncoming FASTER (*Flexible Access to Statistics, Tables, and Electronic Resources*) project, end-users will be able to control their interaction with Web sites by pulling the information they are interested in out of dynamically generated XML documents. However, different users may well have different interests or access authorizations, and XML enabled servers will need to know which data each user should get, at a finer level of granularity than whole documents. In other words, some FASTER applications will need to block or allow access to entire XML instances, while others will control access at the tag level. The control residing at the tag level is particularly important in the view of wider use of the *XLink* and *XPointer* standards, which enable applications to re-

* Corresponding author.
[1] E-mail: edamiani@crema.unimi.it
[2] E-mail: {decapita,samarati}@dsi.unimi.it
[3] E-mail: parabosc@elet.polimi.it

trieve portions of documents. Indeed, a clean model for dynamic access control with granularity control is needed to allow XML documents to link against arbitrary XML chunks. It is interesting to remark that the same observation applies to authentication and encryption-based techniques, that naturally complement access control in our usage scenario. With authentication, the server will know what information can be sent to the user based on that user's identity or certified property (e.g., group membership), whereas encryption will only let users with adequate decryption keys see the message. Therefore, XML security should support the entire range of coarse- to fine-grain granularity. In the remainder of this section, we propose five basic requirements for standardizing XML access control at the tag level. Our requirements take into account the experience of other FASTER consortium partners, and are directed at large-scale knowledge management within organizations using XML, as well as at XML-based Internet applications.

(1) *Support of authorizations at different organizational levels.* Organizations may need to enforce security policies on huge document-bases, often dynamically created from heterogeneous datasources; on the other hand, site administrators require full control on authorization specifications on single documents.
(2) *Extension to existing Web server technology.* XML documents are usually made available by means of Web sites, using a variety of HTTP-based protocols. XML access control must exploit current solutions in much the same way as cryptography-based services, without interfering with existing APIs and development tools.
(3) *Fine-grained access control.* Access control policies should be supported at all levels of granularity, including documents and individual XML elements.
(4) *Transparency.* The access control system operation should be as transparent as possible to the requesters. The requester should not be aware of the information within a document which is being hidden to them by the access control system. The transparency of the access control must be preserved by the presentation and rendering phases and may therefore impose constraints on the behavior of technologies such as CSS and XSL [18]. In particular, access control should preserve the *validity* of the documents with respect to their DTDs.
(5) *Smoothless integration* with existing technologies for user authentication (e.g. digital signatures). Access control should complement tag-level authentication based on digital signatures.

Fig. 1 depicts the conceptual architecture of our approach. A *central authority* uses a pool of XML DTDs to specify the format of information to be exchanged within the organization. XML documents instances of such DTDs are defined and maintained at each site, describing the site-specific information. The *schema–instance relationship* between XML documents and DTDs naturally supports the distinction between two levels of authorizations, both of them allowing for fine-grained specifications. Namely, we distinguish: (1) low-level authorizations, associated to XML documents, providing full control on authorizations on a document-by-document basis; (2) high-level authorizations, associated to XML DTDs, providing organization-wide and department-wide declarations of access permissions. Centrally specified DTD-level authorizations can be mandatory, stating *impositions* of the central authority to lower organizational levels where XML documents are created and managed, usually by means of a network of federated Web sites. This technique allows for easy, centralized modification of access permissions on large document sets, and provides a general, abstract way of specifying access authorizations. In other words, specifying authorizations at the DTD level cleanly separates access control specified via XML markup from access control policies defined for the individual datasources (e.g., relational databases vs. file systems) which are different from one another both in granularity and abstraction level. Each departmental authority managing a Web site retains the right to define its own authorizations (again, at the granularity of XML tags) on individual documents, or to document sets by means of wild cards. In our model local authorities can also define authorizations at the DTD level; however, such authorizations only apply to the documents of the local domain.

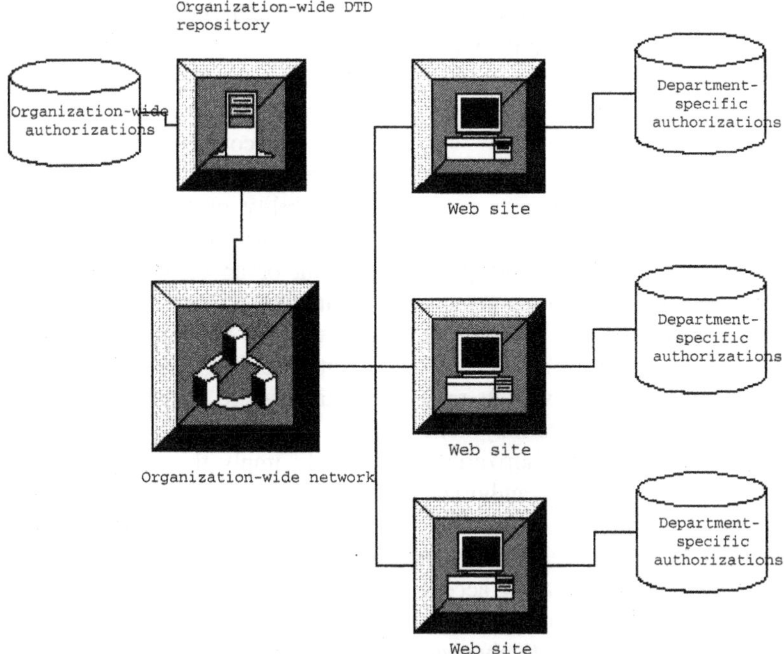

Fig. 1. Conceptual architecture.

2. Authorization specification

The architectural framework depicted in Fig. 1 describes the basic components taking part in the specification of access and protection requirements. We now discuss their specification. Before introducing the form and semantics of the authorizations supported by our model, we describe the basic features that they need to provide to satisfy requirements 1 and 3 discussed in the introduction.

2.1. Collection based vs instance based authorizations

The different protection requirements that different documents may have call for the support of access restrictions at the level of each specific document. On the other hand, requiring the specification of authorizations for each single document would make the authorization specification task much too heavy. The system should support, beside authorizations on single documents, authorizations on collections of documents. The concept of DTD can be naturally exploited to this end, by allowing protection requirements to refer to DTD or XML documents, where requirements specified at the level of DTD apply to all those documents instance of the DTDs. The use of DTDs as a primary way to refer to sets of documents as opposed to the use of file system structures (directory) used in previous approaches, is consistent with the fact that our approach takes advantage of the data semantics, departing from the limitations of storage-based structures. The fact that instances of DTDs share a common (semi)structure, allows the association with DTD-level authorizations of conditions that limit the documents/elements to which the authorization applies. This way authorizations can be specified which apply only to certain instances of a DTD. While using DTDs as a primary way to reference classes of documents, we do not discard other methods. In particular, our model also supports the use of wild cards in the specification of document URIs and the possibility of referencing and evaluating meta-properties, such as RDF markup [19]. The use of wild cards allows the specification of authorizations that apply to all documents matching a given path expression, depending on the file system organization. The reference to meta-properties allows the specification of authorizations that apply to all documents satisfying specific properties, expressed by means of meta-information associated with the documents (e.g., creator, creation date, and so on). Meta-properties can also be used to provide organization of documents in domains [13].

2.2. *Organization's wide vs. site-specific authorizations*

Access and protection requirements can be specified both at the level of the enterprise, stating general regulations that should hold, and at the level of specific domains (part of the enterprise) where, according to a local policy, additional constraints may need to be specified or some constraints may need to be relaxed. Organizations specify authorizations with respect to DTDs; sites can specify authorizations with respect to specific documents as well as to DTDs. The two types of DTD-level authorizations have complementary roles in increasing access control flexibility. *Global* DTD-level authorizations stated by a central authority can be effectively used to implement corporate-wide access control policies on document classes. *Local* DTD-level authorizations specified by departmental authorities allow for department-wide access control policies complementing the corporate ones. Moreover they alleviate administration chores by allowing concise specification of site-wide authorizations.

2.3. *Document vs. element/attribute authorizations*

The identification of elements and attributes within a document provided by XML tags can be exploited to specify authorizations at a fine-grained level. Authorizations specified for an element are intended to be applicable to all its attributes. Again, to avoid the need of specifying authorizations for each single element in a document, the document structure can be exploited by supporting a recursive interpretation of authorizations by which an authorization specified on an element applies to its whole content (attributes and subelements). Our model allows to specify whether an authorization specified for an element is local to its own data (PC data and attributes) or applies recursively to all its subelements. The authorization on a document in its entirety is specified as a recursive authorization on its root.

2.4. *Exception support (permissions and denials)*

The support of authorizations at different granularity levels allows for easy expressiveness of both fine- and coarse-grained authorizations. Such an advantage would however remain very limited without the ability of the authorization model to support exceptions, since the presence of a granule (document or an element/attribute) with protection requirements different from those of its siblings would require the explicit specification of authorizations at that specific granularity level. For instance, the situation where a user should be granted access to all the documents of a DTD but one specific instance, would imply the need of stating the authorizations explicitly for all the other documents as well, thereby ruling out the advantage of supporting authorizations at the DTD level. A simple way to support exceptions is by using both positive (permissions) and negative (denials) authorizations, where permissions and denials can override each other. According to intuition, overriding typically occurs when going to a finer granularity level, according to the 'most specific takes precedence' principle [11,8]. Finer-grained authorizations override coarser ones, each document being at a finer grain than its DTD and each element/attribute being at a finer grain than the elements in which it is contained.

2.5. *Hard and soft statements (ruling out exceptions and filling the blanks)*

The support of exceptions while clearly adding to the expressiveness of the model, allows stated protection requirements to be possibly overridden. When authorization specification spans different administrative competencies and authorities, as it is the case of organization-wide authorizations vs. site-specific authorizations, there might be cases where such a capability needs to be restricted. The 'most specific takes precedence' principle dictates that authorizations specified on a document override (where conflicting) authorizations specified on its DTD. In organizational terms, the authorization specified at a site would always override the authorizations specified at the organization level. We can imagine two scenarios where such a behavior is not wanted. First, at the organization level certain specifications may need to be declared as mandatory, meaning they should be obeyed at all the sites, no site discretionary statement being allowed. Second, at the site level, certain specifications may need to be declared as *soft*, meaning they should be applied only if nothing has been stated at the organization level. In both scenarios the need is to subvert the 'most specific takes precedence' principle. The fact that the need may come either from the organization or from the site, requiring the ability to support its expression in association with the both DTD and document authorizations. In particular, the enterprise can specify DTD authorizations as hard, sites can specify document authorizations as soft. (For the sake of simplicity of the model, we do not allow sites to specify hard DTD authorizations as it would introduce complications while not adding in expressiveness.)

3. Authorizations

The list of features illustrated in the previous section outlines the form and semantics of the authorizations supported by our model. We can then summarize the discussion above and introduce our authorizations as follows:

- Authorizations can be specified at the level of a DTD (schema) or specific documents (instance). DTD authorizations can be specified either at the global organization level or at the local site. Document authorizations can be specified at the local site.
- Both DTD and XML authorizations can be specified with reference to each single element/attribute in a document. Authorizations on an element can be declared as *recursive* (apply to its subelements) or *local* (apply only to its direct attributes and PC data).
- DTD-level authorizations specified at the global level can be declared as *hard*.
- Document-level authorizations can be declared as *soft*.

Authorizations specified for each XML document /DTD (elements within) are stored in an XAS (*XML Access Sheet*) associated with the document/DTD, bringing to the organization illustrated in Fig. 2. The representation and storage of authorizations in a component XAS separate from the document they protect follows the well-known design principle requiring clean separation between data model and access control model [4]. Also, it has the great advantage of allowing the specification of authorizations on dynamically generated XML documents. Besides, enclosing authorizations in the documents themselves would compromise readability of both the documents and its access restrictions.

We anticipate that, in the access control processing, DTD-level authorizations specified at the global level and those specified at the local level are, with respect to each DTD, merged by performing a *flat union*. In other words, organization-wide and site-specific authorizations are treated in the same way (although, remember that organization-wide authorizations apply to all the documents in the network while site-specific authorizations apply only to documents stored at the site). Given this, in the future we will simply refer to DTD authorizations without making any distinction of where they have been specified. The reason for merging the two sets of authorizations with a simple flat union is simplicity. We do observe that, in principle, even at this level some notion of 'specificity' could be applied. This reasoning could also be possibly extended by considering any number of intermediate organizational levels which could be reflected in priorities associated with the authorizations. We note, however, that the most specific principle of DTD vs XML, together with the possibility of specifying hard and soft options subverting it, does already provide, on the two organizational levels considered which were of interest in our project, such expressiveness. As it may be clear from the previous discussion, we allow the specification of hard authorizations only at the global level. In this way no unresolvable conflict can arise. This does not limit expressiveness: site administrators that want their authorizations to override global authorizations can simply do so by going to the instance level (wild-card characters and meta-properties allow doing so without the need of specifying an authorization for each instance).

The XAS associated with a document/DTD contains the set of authorizations specified for the document/DTD or elements within. The authorizations are expressed in XML and comply to the DTD illustrated in Fig. 3. Each authorization states the permission or denial (depending on the value of

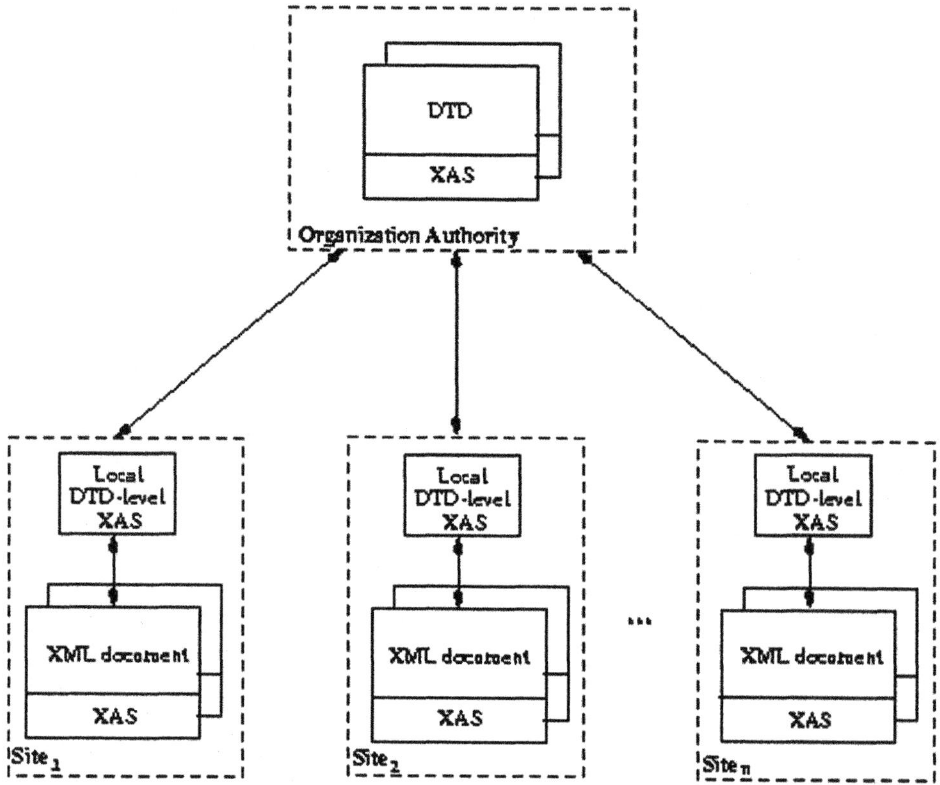

Fig. 2. Authorization information stored at the different levels.

```
<!ELEMENT set_of_authorizations (authorization)+>
<!ELEMENT authorization (subject,object,action,sign,type,priority)>
<!ELEMENT subject (#PCDATA)>
<!ELEMENT object (#PCDATA)>
<!ELEMENT action empty>
<!ELEMENT sign empty>
<!ELEMENT type empty>
<!ELEMENT priority empty>
<!ATTLIST set_of_authorizations about CDATA #REQUIRED >
<!ATTLIST action    value (read)             #REQUIRED>
<!ATTLIST sign      value (+|-)              #REQUIRED>
<!ATTLIST type      value (local|recursive)  #REQUIRED>
<!ATTLIST priority  value (hard|soft)        #IMPLIED>
```

Fig. 3. XAS syntax.

`sign`) for a `subject` to execute a certain `action` on an `object`, together with the priority (`soft` vs `hard`) and type (`recursive` vs `local`) of such a statement. Here `object` identifies an element or set of elements in a document or set of documents.

We now describe in more details how documents and elements/attributes within them are references to the purpose of specifying authorizations. We then discuss authorization subjects.

3.1. Identifying authorization objects via path expressions

In the traditional Web security setting, Uniform Resource Identifiers (URI) [2] are used to denote the resources to be protected. Each document and DTD is characterized by a single URI. As we go to a finer level of granularity we need to reference specific elements and attributes in documents. Elements/attributes in a document can be referenced by means of *path expressions*. A straightforward way of writing path expressions is by using the XPath language [20]. The reason for this choice is that several tools are currently available which can be easily reused to produce a functioning system. XPath expressions make reference to the tree organization of documents/DTDs which is obtained in a simple way by interpreting elements and attributes as children of the element in which they are directly contained. Each element and attribute can be then referenced by means of the tree path that must be followed to reach it. An XPath on an XML document tree is a sequence of element names or predefined functions separated by the character / (slash): $l_1/l_2/\ldots/l_n$. For instance, path expression `/division/about_div/member` denotes the nodes of the `member` element which are children of `about_div` elements, which are children of `division` elements. Path expressions can be *absolute* or *relative*. Absolute path expressions, prefixed by a slash character, start from the root of the document. Relative path expressions, which start with an element name, describe a path whose initial point is any element in the document.

A very interesting characteristic of path expressions which very conveniently increases the expressiveness of authorizations is the support of conditions. Conditions associated with a path expression refine the set of nodes matching the path expression. Conditions may impose constraints on element contents (i.e., the 'text' of elements) or on names and values of attributes. A condition can follow any label in a path expression and is identified as such by enclosing it between square brackets. Given a path expression $l_1/l_2/\ldots/l_n$, a condition on label l_i restricts the application of the path expressions only to those node(s) l_i for which the condition evaluates to true.

3.2. Identifying authorization subjects

A straightforward and largely used approach to refer to authorization subjects and access requesters is via *user identity* and/or the *location* from which their requests originate, where locations can be expressed via numeric IP addresses (e.g., `159.149.51.40`) or via symbolic names (e.g., `tweety.acme.com`). Our system combines all these features. Subjects requesting access are characterized by a triple `<user-id,IP-address,sym-address>`, where `user-id` is the login name with which the user connected to the server, `IP-address` is the address of the client machine and sym-address is the machine's DNS name. (Remote identities trusted by the server using a *Certification Authority*, or any other secure infrastructure can be considered as well.) Authorizations can also be specified with reference to user *groups* and/or *location patterns*. Groups are set of users defined at the server; they do not need to be disjoint and can be nested. A location pattern is an expression identifying a set of physical locations, with reference to either their symbolic names or IP addresses. Patterns are specified by using the wild-card character `*`. For instance, `159.149.*` denotes all the machines belonging to subnetwork `159.149`. Similarly, `*.edu` and `*.it`, respectively, denote all the machines in the Educational and Italy domains. A user can be seen as a singleton group, a location as a simple pattern. Groups and location patterns provide an effective way to specify authorizations holding for a large set of subjects: authorizations granted to a group with respect to some location pattern apply to all the members of the group when connected from a machine satisfying the pattern. For instance, authorizations granted to `<Employee,159.149.100.*,*>` apply to all the members of group Employee when connected from machines in subnetwork `159.149.100.*`. Authorizations granted to `<Employee,*,*.acme.com>` apply to all employees connected from the local acme network. We observe that while authorization subjects are conceptually identified by triples of the general hierarchy, relationships between address (and symbolic names) patterns can be detected straightforwardly; therefore, only the usual user-group hierarchy needs to be explicitly defined and stored at the sites (or communicated to them [7]).

It is also important to note that the consideration of user's identity and location identifiers does not rule out the possibility of partial or completely anonymous connection, to which general authorizations, specified for a group `Public` to which everybody belongs and pattern * can be applied.

4. Authorization enforcement

For each possible requester (user connected from a certain location) and document, the authorizations on the document applicable to the requester describe what information can or cannot be returned to the requester. Hence, given the request from a subject to access a document, the joint application of the DTD-level and document-level authorizations applicable to the subject will produce a custom *view* on the document, including only the information that a particular requester is entitled to see. The access control process must therefore evaluate the authorizations applicable to an access request to compute such a view. We now briefly outline this computation process which exploits the hierarchical organization of documents, by operating on their DOM tree [21]. Intuitively, the analysis of all the authorizations holding for the requester on a document produces an access decision (access or not access) on each node of the document. The process to obtain this final outcome starts with a *labeling procedure* whose output reflects the authorizations on the different nodes applicable to the subject. Since authorizations can be of different level (DTD vs. instance), type (local vs. recursive), and priority (hard vs. soft), more than one sign is associated with each node. More precisely, the process assigns to each node a label reflecting the sign (permission or denial) of authorizations, if any, existing for that node at the considered type, priority, and level. A simple representation of these labels is to associate with a node an 8-tuple (2^3, each of the three fields has two possible values). The sign of each label can be '+' (permission), '−' (denial), or 'ε' (no authorization). We note that more authorizations can exist with respect to each label. In this case a resolution policy is applied to get a unique final sign [6,8] for the label. Simple and natural conflict resolution policies include the 'most specific subject takes precedence' principle (users/subgroups are more specific than the groups to which they belong, sub-patterns are more specific than their more general form) and the 'denial takes precedence' principle [8], and are those currently supported by our prototype.

After this initial labeling, propagation is applied so that local authorizations holding for each node are propagated to its attributes, while recursive authorizations are also propagated to its sub-elements. Authorizations may be overridden as follows:

(1) Authorizations on a node take precedence over those on its ancestors.
(2) Authorizations at the document level take precedence over authorizations at the local and global DTD levels, unless they are explicitly declared as *soft*.
(3) *Hard* authorizations at the global-DTD level override authorizations at other levels.

This labeling process can be obtained by means of a preorder visit on the document's DOM tree. At the end of the tree visit a single label is associated with each node defining its final sign, if any. If no sign has been determined for a node (no authorizations have been specified nor can be derived for it), its value is set to the null value 'ε'. Value 'ε' can be interpreted either as a negation (transformed into a '−') or as a permission (transformed into a '+'), corresponding to the enforcement of a *closed* and an *open* policy, respectively [8]. In the sequel, we shall act conservatively, choosing the closed policy.

For how the labeling process has been performed, the requester is allowed to access all the elements and attributes whose label is positive. Note that, in order to preserve the structure of the document, the portion of the document visible to the requester will also include start and end tags of elements with a negative or undefined label, if the elements have a descendant with a positive label. The final view on the document can be obtained simply by pruning from the original document tree all the subtrees containing only nodes labeled negative. This pruning is performed by a procedure that executes a postorder visit on the document and removes any leaf labeled '−'. The pruned document may not be valid with respect to the DTD referenced by the original XML document. This will happen, for instance, when required attributes are deleted because the requester is not entitled to receive them. To avoid this problem, a *loosening* transformation can be applied to the DTD. In the simplest case, loosening a DTD simply means to define as optional all the elements and attributes marked as required in the original DTD. This 'naive' loosening technique is currently justified by implementation-related considerations, as there is no efficient technology for processing DTDs even remotely comparable to the one available for documents. However, as DTD processing standards such as DOM level 2 [17] come of age, more sophisticated loosening techniques can be devised by taking into account the elements that are pruned by the transformation and selectively redefining them as optional. 'Looser' DTDs also prevent users from detecting whether information was hidden by access control enforcement or was simply missing in the original document. The loosening process is aimed at the satisfaction of requirement 4 stated in Section 1.

5. Design and implementation guidelines

First of all, architectural design will be briefly discussed. Two main architectural patterns are currently used for the design of XML/XSL systems: *server side* and *client side* XSL processing (see Section 6). The former technique is common in association with translation to HTML and provides limited interaction: XML documents are translated to HTML before sending them to the client, avoiding the need for the client browser to provide XML support. The latter technique requires an XSL processor to be part of the client, in order to provide it with rendering capabilities. In our approach, access control enforcement is always performed on the server side, regardless of whether other operations, such as XSL-based rendering or translation to HTML, are performed by the server site or by the client module.

The reason for this architectural choice is twofold: first, server-side execution prevents transferring to the client information he is not allowed to see or process; second, it ensures the operation and even the presence of security checking to be completely transparent to remote clients. The main usage scenario for our system involves a user requesting a set of XML elements from a remote site, either through an HTTP request or as the result of a query [5]. Our processor takes as input the valid XML document requested by the user or computed by the query, together with an *XML Access Sheet* (XAS) listing the associated access authorizations at document level. The processor operation also involves the document's DTD and the associated XAS specifying DTD level authorizations. In our design, the processor module is a *transformer* in the framework of a complete architecture complying to the well-known *Pipes and Filters* design pattern (Fig. 4) [3]. The service's interface is locally available to Web servers components storing XML documents. This solution is aimed to satisfy requirement 2 stated in Section 1. The processor output is a valid XML document including only the information the user is allowed to access. The XML document computed by processor is then transferred to the client as the result of its original request.

5.1. Internal data model

In our system, documents and DTDs are internally represented as object trees, according to the Document Object Model (DOM) level 1 specification [16]. DOM provides an object-oriented *Application*

Fig. 4. Design pattern for the processor transformer.

Program Interface (API) for HTML and XML documents. Namely, DOM defines a set of object definitions such as `Element`, `Attr`, and `Text`, to build an object-oriented document which closely models the document structure. While DOM trees are topologically equivalent to the XML trees defined in Section 3.1, they represent element containment by means of the object-oriented *part-of* relationship. For example, an XML element is represented in DOM by an `Element` object; an element contained within another element is represented as a child `Element` object, and text contained in an element is represented as a child `Text` object. The main classes of the DOM hierarchy are `Node`, `Document`, `Element`, `Attr` and `Text`. `Node` is the generic element in an XML document and provides basic methods for insertion, deletion and editing; via inheritance, such methods are also defined for more specialized classes in the hierarchy. `Node` also provides a powerful set of navigation methods, such as `parentNode`, `firstChild` and `nextSibling`. Navigation methods allow transformer modules of the security processor to visit the DOM representation of XML documents via a sequence of calls to the interface. Specifically, the `NodeList` method, which returns in a container all the children of the current node, has been used to implement the fast labeling procedure which is the core of the access control processor. Our implementation is based on a *Secure* extension of the classes of the DOM hierarchy, like `SecureDocument` and `SecureElement`. Our extension is fully compatible with other extensions supporting element-wise digital signatures, such as DOMhash [1]. Such compatibility is a step towards satisfaction of requirement 5 stated in Section 1.

5.2. Execution phases

Our security processor computes an *on line transformation* on XML documents. Its execution cycle consists of the following four basic steps:

(1) *Parsing*. The parsing step consists in the syntax check of the requested document with respect to the associated DTD and its compilation to obtain an *object-oriented document graph* according to the DOM format. Since parsing is performed externally when the access control processor is used as a transformer in the framework of a *Pipes and Filters* system, here we do not deal with parsing issues in detail.

(2) *Tree labeling*. The labeling step involves the propagation of the labeling of the DOM tree according to the authorizations listed in the XAS associated to the document and its DTD, both at the organization and at the site level. Its implementation takes advantage of the extended DOM interface for object nodes, which provides a labeling interface. Standard DOM methods allow the transformer to follow *part-of* links from each node to its children by means of a standard method call. The authorizations relevant for the user are analyzed and applied to the nodes.

(3) *Transformation*. The transformation phase is a pruning of the DOM tree according to its labeling, based on the transformation presented in Section 4. Such a pruning is computed by means of a standard preorder visit to the labeled DOM tree. This pruning preserves the validity of the document with respect to the *loosened version* of its original DTD.

(4) *Unparsing*. Finally, the fourth step is the generation of a valid XML document in text format, simply by unparsing (again, by means of a standard component) the pruned DOM tree computed by the previous step. Once again, this step is performed externally when the access control process is executed as a transformer module in the framework of a *Pipes and Filters* system

The resulting XML document, together with the loosened DTD, can then be transmitted to the user who requested access to the document.

5.3. Performance and caching

In a complex server environment, performance and memory usage are critical issues. Moreover, the processing requirement for XML parsing, transformation, document processing and formatting are particularly heavy (Fig. 5). For this reason, a special cache system is needed, in order to cache dynamically created pages. Caches of this kind are already available for XSLT processors which store their stylesheets in a pre-parsed form [12]. A cache for labeled documents is an important part of our system. When the request comes, the cache is searched. If an instance of the requested docu-

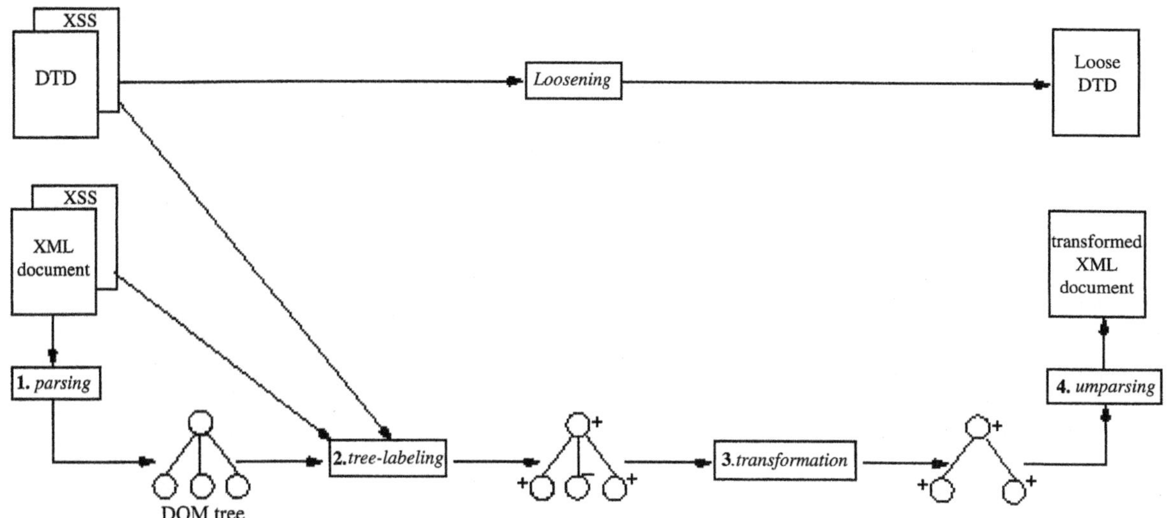

Fig. 5. Document transformations by the security processor.

ment for the same subject is found in the cache, then the cache copy is served. Otherwise, the document is parsed, labeled, transformed, unparsed and sent to the client; also, the transformed document is stored into the cache. Whenever authorizations are changed the whole cache is emptied. This technique allows dynamically generated pages (for example, XML documents created by querying a database) to be transformed and cached. Assuming that the frequency of requests is higher than that of resource changes, the cache may greatly reduce the total server load. The efficiency gain is particularly relevant when authorizations are specified with respect to a limited number of groups, as it may be the case for Internet-based servers. Moreover, the cache system can be based on a persistent object storage system which is able to save stored objects in a persistent state that outlives the module execution. This technique can be effectively used for pages that are very expensive to generate and last very long without changes, such as compiled server pages.

6. Related work

Conventional HTML tagging is aimed at defining page rendering and is seldom if ever related to information granulation. For this reason, access control mechanisms currently available for Web sites tend to be coarse-grained. For instance, the **Apache Web**[4] server allows the specification of access control lists via a configuration file (access.conf) containing a list of users, hosts (IP addresses), or host/user pairs, which must be allowed/forbidden connection to the server. Users are identified by user- and group-names and passwords, to be specified via Unix-style password files. By specifying a different configuration file for each directory on the Web server's disk, it is possible to define authorizations on a directory basis; files belonging to the same directory are subject to the same authorizations. The specification of authorizations at the level of single file (i.e., Web pages) is quite awkward, while it is not possible to specify authorizations on portions of files. This limitation forces protection requirements to affect data organization at the file system level. Recent proposals addressing authorization enforcement in the Web, addressing topics such as certificate management [9] and support of groups and roles [10] are not thought for XML, and therefore consider whole documents as granule of protection. The proposal in [14] specifies authorizations at a fine granularity providing a model for referencing portions of a file. However, again, no semantic context simi-

[4] http://www.apache.org

lar to that provided by XML can be supported and the model remains limited. Other approaches, such as the **EIT SHTTP**[5] scheme, explicitly represent authorizations within the documents by using security-related HTML tagging. Every document may have associated security (meta)tags describing its access authorizations. However, due to HTML fundamental limitations, even this proposal cannot take into full consideration the information structure and semantics.

6.1. The role of encryption

Since the advancement of public-key cryptography has solved most of the security problems in communication, it is interesting to explore the authentication and encryption role in providing fine-grained security to XML documents. Indeed, some commercial products are becoming available (e.g., AlphaWorks' XML Security Suite [1]) providing fine-grained security features, such as element-wise encryption and digital signatures. A rather coarser solution has been proposed by DataChannel, whose **DataChannel**[6] server links XML authentication to existing directory systems, supporting both Windows NT and Lightweight Directory Access Protocol 3 directories. DataChannel servers map each XML document to the requesting user's ID and then to the file system access control. Thanks to authentication, an encryption-based XML server knows what information can be sent to a user based on that user's access level, and employs element-wise encryption to prevent users without appropriate decryption keys to access the parts of the documents containing private information. However, encryption-based approaches unequally split security responsibilities between the connection protocol, the XML content, and the application processing the document, while the need for a standardization of access control is becoming well recognized for XML data. Moreover, some encryption-based techniques leave encrypted private information in the hands of unauthorized users, a design choice which may well prove unwise in the long run.

[5] http://www.ietf.org/rfc/rfc2660.txt

[6] http://www.datachannel.com

6.2. Server-side XML/XSL processing

Much work has been done recently on server-side XML/XSL processing, and several design and implementation techniques have been proposed to obtain efficient, scalable systems based on DOM representation. *Cocoon* [12] is a Web publishing system for the Apache Web server whose engine is loosely based on the *reactor* design pattern [3]. It deals with server-side *requests*, obtained processing client's requests and augmenting them with all the information needed by the processing engine. The request indicates what client generated the request, what URI is being requested and what producer should handle the request. Producer modules handle the requested URI and produce XML documents. Since producers are pluggable, they work like subservlets for this framework, allowing site designers to define and implement their own producers. It is up to the producer implementation to define the function that produces the document from the request object. Our access control processor is designed to be smoothlessly integrated in server-side architectures like Cocoon's.

7. An example

We now illustrate an example of authorization specification and document transformation.

7.1. Data organization: DTD and documents

We consider the case of an organization maintaining information regarding its departments, members, and projects. Each department is composed of one or more divisions and is responsible to create an XML document for each of them. To provide a uniform representation of this information, these XML documents must be valid with respect to a DTD defined by the organization. We consider DTD http://www.acme.com/dtd.xml reported in Fig. 6. According to the DTD, each division is characterized by general information about it (`about_div` element), its current research activities (`res_activity` element), and `seminars`. The `about_div` element includes information about the division `members` and how to contact the division (`contact` element). The `res_activity` element contains the topic of the re-

```
<!ELEMENT division (about_div,res_activity*,seminar*)>
<!ELEMENT about_div (member+,contact)>
<!ELEMENT member (name,position,e-mail?)>
<!ELEMENT e-mail (#PCDATA)>
<!ELEMENT contact (#PCDATA)>
<!ELEMENT res_activity (topic,description,project*)>
<!ELEMENT topic (#PCDATA)*>
<!ELEMENT description (#PCDATA)>
<!ELEMENT project (name,report*,fund*)>
<!ELEMENT fund (sponsor,amount)>
<!ELEMENT sponsor (#PCDATA)*>
<!ELEMENT amount (#PCDATA)*>
<!ELEMENT report (title,author+,text)>
<!ELEMENT title (#PCDATA)*>
<!ELEMENT author (#PCDATA)*>
<!ELEMENT seminar (date,title,speaker+)>
<!ELEMENT text (#PCDATA)*>
<!ATTLIST division  name CDATA #REQUIRED>
<!ATTLIST seminar  category (public|internal) #REQUIRED>
<!ATTLIST project  domain (public|private) #REQUIRED>
<!ATTLIST report  code ID #REQUIRED>
```

Fig. 6. An example of DTD.

search, a `description`, and a set, possibly empty, of related `projects`. Seminars, which can be open to everybody or restricted to the division members, are characterized by a `date`, `title`, and one or more `speaker` elements. Each member of the division has a `name`, `position`, and `e-mail` address. Projects are described by a `name`, the `fund` to which the project expenses must be charged, and by zero or more `report` elements with `title` and `author` elements belonging to them. Funds are characterized by `sponsor` and `amount` elements. Attributes of elements are defined in the attribute list declarations. Element `division` has a `name` identifying the division. Element `seminar` has a `category` attribute used to make a distinction between seminars open to all (i.e., `category` = 'public') and seminars restricted to the division members (i.e., `category` = 'internal'). Element `project` has a required attribute `domain` representing the project visibility (public vs. private). Finally, element `report` has an attribute `code` used as an identifier for the report.

Among the departments of the organizations is the CS Department which includes division `Security`. The information about this division is represented in the XML document http://www.acme.com/sec.xml illustrated in Fig. 7.

7.2. Authorization specification

We now discuss some protection requirements that the acme organization and the CS department may need to express and illustrate how they are translated into authorizations of the form considered by our system. In the following, for the sake of simplicity, relative URIs (http://www.acme.com is the base URI) are used in the authorizations.

Organization's policy: specified at the DTD level — applicable to all the divisions of all departments of the organization.

(1) Information about the name of members of any division in any department is publicly accessible; unless otherwise stated by the specific departments.
`<<Public,*,*>,dtd.xml:/division/about_div/member/name,read,+,local,_>`
(2) Information about the name of public projects *must* be publicly accessible.
`<<Public,*,*>,dtd.xml:/division/res_activity/project[./@domain="public"]/name,read,+,local,hard>`
(3) Information about report of public projects *must* be publicly accessible.
`<<Public,*,*>,dtd.xml:/division/res_`

```
<division name = "Security">
  <about_div>
    <member>
      <name>Bob</name>
      <position>Computer Scientist</position>
      <e-mail>bob@acme.com</e-mail>
    </member>
    <member>
      <name>Tom</name>
      <position>Software Engineering</position>
      <e-mail>tom@acme.com</e-mail>
    </member>
    <contact>
      Security Div. - 180 Lane St. - 81231 New Park
    </contact>
  </about_div>
  <res_activity>
    <topic> Web security </topic>
    <description>The purpose of ... </description>
    <project domain = "private">
      <name>Access Control</name>
      <fund>
        <sponsor>IT</sponsor>
        <amount>10000</amount>
      </fund>
      <report code ="R1-99">
        <title>A new access control model</title>
        <author>Sam</author>
        <author>Ron</author>
        <text>......</text>
      </report>
    </project>
    <project domain = "public">
      <name>Cryptography</name>
      <report code ="R2-99">
        <title>The study of encryption</title>
        <author>Steve</author>
        <text>......</text>
      </report>
    </project>
  </res_activity>
  <seminar category="internal">
    <date>Tues., June 8</date>
    <title>Safe statistics</title>
    <speaker>Jan</speaker>
  </seminar>
  <seminar category="public">
    <date>Thurs., July 15</date>
    <title>UML</title>
    <speaker>Karen</speaker>
  </seminar>
</division>
```

Fig. 7. An example of XML document valid with respect to the DTD in Fig. 6.

```
activity/project[./@domain="public"]
/report,read,+,recursive,hard>
```

Computer Science department's policy: specified at the DTD level and instance level to complement or override the organization's policy.

(4) Information about members of any division in the department is accessible to all members of the organization (`OrgMembers` group) unless otherwise stated by the organization.

```
<<OrgMembers,*,*>,dtd.xml:/division/
about_div/member,read,+,recursive,
soft>
```

(5) Information on funds of any division is accessible only to the members of `Admin` group connected from network `145.*`.

```
<<Admin,145.*,*>,dtd.xml:/division//
fund,read,+,recursive,_>
<<Public,*,*>,dtd.xml:/division//
fund,read,-,recursive,_>
```

(6) Information about public seminars of any division is publicly accessible.

```
<<Public,*,*>,dtd.xml:/division/
seminar[./@category="public"],read,
+,recursive,_>
```

(7) Information about seminars of the `Security` division is accessible only to users connected from network 145.*.

```
<<Public,145.100.*,*>,sec.xml:/divi
sion/seminar,read,+,recursive,_>
<<Public,*,*>,sec.xml:/division/
seminar,read,-,recursive,_>
```

(8) Topics and description of research activities of the `Security` division are publicly accessible.

```
<<Public,*,*>,sec.xml:/division/res_
activity/topic,read,+,recursive,_>
<<Public,*,*>,sec.xml:/division/
```

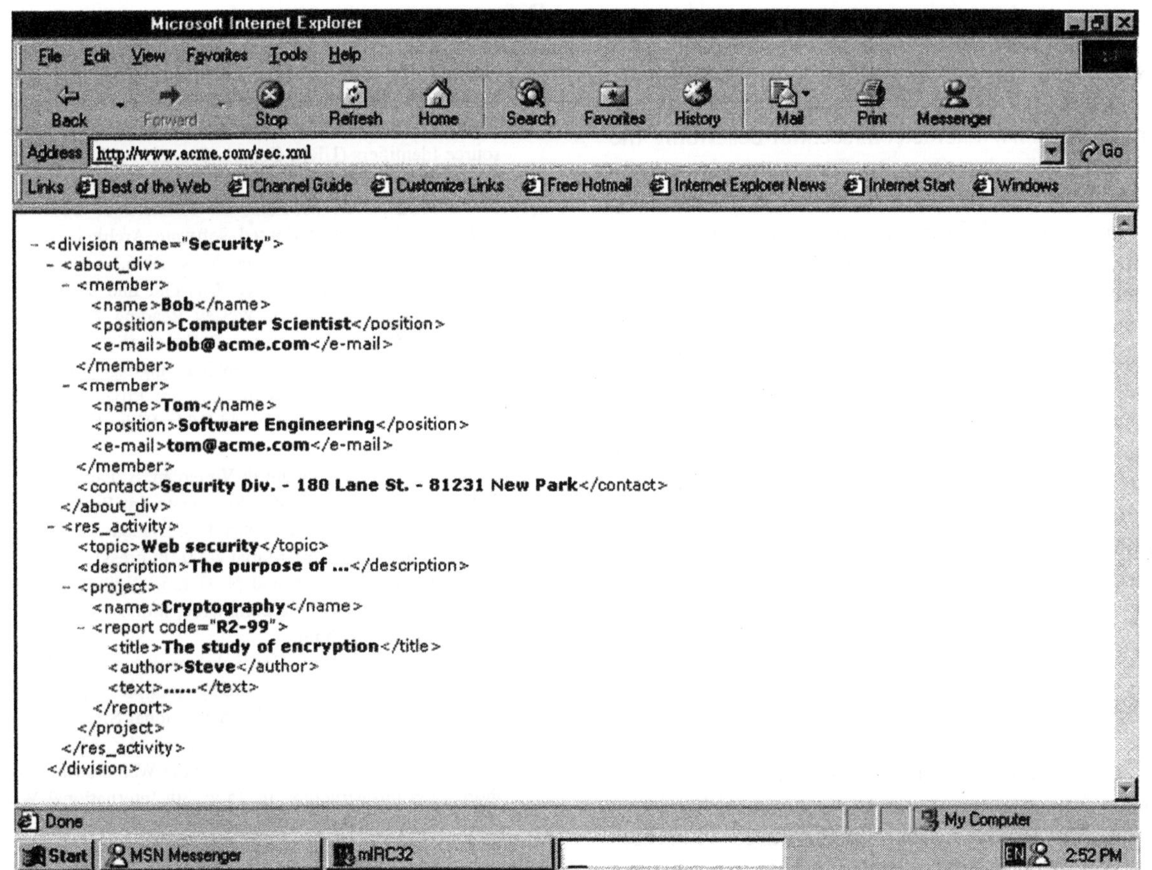

Fig. 8. An example of view on the document in Fig. 7.

```
res_activity/description,read,+,
recursive,_>
```

(9) Contact information about the `Security` division is publicly accessible unless otherwise stated by the organization.

```
<<Public},*,*>,sec.xml:/division/
about_div/contact,read,+,local,
soft>
```

(10) `Bob` cannot access information about the `Security` division projects.

```
<<Bob,*,*>,sec.xml:/division//
project,read,-,recursive,_>
```

(11) Information about projects can be accessed by members of the `Security` division when connected from hosts in the domain `*.com`.

```
<<Security,*,*.com>,sec.xml:divi
sion//project,read,+,recursive,_>
```

7.3. Document view

We now illustrate an example of document view visible to a requester in obedience to the authorizations specified. Consider a request to read the document http://www.acme.com/sec.xml describing the `Security` division (Fig. 7). The request is submitted by user `Bob`, who is a member of the `Security` group, connected from machine cslab.uniacme.edu with numeric IP 150.100.80.3. According to DTD-level authorizations 1 and 4, `Bob` can access information about the members of the division. According to document-level authorization 10, `Bob` cannot access information on projects. However, for public projects, this denial is overridden by hard authorizations 2 and 3 stated by the organization. Finally, `Bob` cannot access seminars information, since this is visible only to connections from network `145.*` (authorizations 7). The resulting view on the document of Fig. 7 as returned to `Bob` is illustrated in Fig. 8.

8. Conclusions

We have presented an access control system providing fine-grained access control for XML documents. The approach proposed is focused on enforcing and resolving fine-grained authorizations with respect to the data model and semantics. Although presented in association with a specific approach to authorization specification and subject identification, as supported in the current prototype, its operation is independent from such approaches and could then be applied in combination with different administrative policies. For instance, it can be combined with the treatment of roles [15,21] and of authentication/authorization certificates [7,9]. We are currently exploring such extensions.

Acknowledgements

The work presented in this paper has been supported by Esprit Project 'W3I3', Esprit Project 'FASTER', MURST Project 'Data-X' and by the HP Internet Philanthropic Initiative.

References

[1] AlphaWorks, XML Security Suite, April 1999, http://www.alphaWorks.ibm.com/tech/xmlsecuritysuite.

[2] T. Berners-Lee, R. Fielding and L. Masinter, Uniform Resource Identifiers (URI): Generic Syntax, 1998, http://www.isi.edu/in-notes/rfc2396.txt.

[3] F. Buschmann, R. Meunier, H. Rohnert, P. Sommerlad and M. Stal, Pattern-Oriented Software Architecture — A System of Patterns, Wiley, New York, 1996.

[4] S. Castano, M.G. Fugini, G. Martella and P. Samarati, Database Security, Addison-Wesley, Reading, MA, 1995.

[5] S. Ceri, S. Comai, E. Damiani, P. Fraternali, S. Paraboschi and L. Tanca, XML-GL: A graphical language for querying and restructuring XML documents, in: Proc. 8th International Conference on the World Wide Web, Toronto, May 1999.

[6] E. Damiani, S. De Capitani di Vimercati, S. Paraboschi and P. Samarati, Securing XML documents, in: Proc. 2000 International Conference on Extending Database Technology (EDBT2000), Konstanz, March 2000 (in press).

[7] B. Gladman, C. Ellison and N. Bohm, Digital signatures, certificates and electronic commerce, http://www.clark.net/pub/cme/html/spki.html.

[8] S. Jajodia, P. Samarati, V.S. Subramanian and E. Bertino, A unified framework for enforcing multiple access control policies, in: Proc. 1997 ACM International SIGMOD Conference on Management of Data, Tucson, AZ, May 1997.

[9] J. Kahan, WDAI: a simple World Wide Web distributed authorization infrastructure, in: Proc. 8th International World Wide Web Conference, May 1999.

[10] S. Lewontin and M.E. Zurko, The DCE project: providing authorizations and other distributed services to the World Wide Web, in: Proc. 2nd World Wide Web Conference,

October 1994, http://www.ncsa.uiuc.edu/SDG/IT94/Proceedings/Security/lewontin/Web_DCE_Conf_94.html.

[11] T.F. Lunt, Access control policies for database systems, in: C.E. Landwehr (Ed.), Database Security, II: Status and Prospects, North-Holland, Amsterdam, 1989, pp. 41–52.

[12] S. Mazzocchi, Cocoon User Manual, http://xml.apache.org/cocoon.

[13] J.D. Moffett and M. Sloman, Policies hierarchies for distributed systems management, IEEE Journal of Selected Areas in Communications 11 (9) (1993) 1404–1414.

[14] P. Samarati, E. Bertino and S. Jajodia, An authorization model for a distributed hypertext system, IEEE Transactions on Knowledge and Data Engineering 8 (4) (1996) 555–562.

[15] Youman, Role-based access control models, IEEE Computer 29 (2) (1996) 38–47.

[16] World Wide Web Consortium (W3C), Document Object Model (DOM) Level 1 Specification Version 1.0, October 1998, http://www.w3.org/TR/REC-DOM-Level-1.

[17] World Wide Web Consortium (W3C), Document Object Model (DOM) Level 2 Specification Version 1.0., September Working Draft 1999, http://www.w3.org/TR/WD-DOM-Level-2.

[18] World Wide Web Consortium (W3C). Extensible Stylesheet Language (XSL) Specification, April 1999, http://www.w3.org/TR/WD-xsl.

[19] World Wide Web Consortium (W3C), Resource Description Framework (RDF) Model and Syntax Specification, February 1999, http://www.w3.org/TR/REC-rdf-syntax.

[20] World Wide Web Consortium (W3C), XML Path Language (XPath), November 1999, http://www.w3.org/TR/xpath.

[21] M.E. Zurko, R. Simon and T. Sanfilippo, A user-centered, modular authorization service built on an RBAC foundation, in: Proc. 20th IEEE Symposium on Security and Privacy, Oakland, May 1999, pp. 57–71.

Ernesto Damiani holds a laurea degree in ingegneria elettronica from the University of Pavia and a PhD degree in computer science from the University of Milano. He is currently an assistant professor at the campus located in Crema of the University of Milano. His research interests include distributed and object-oriented systems, semi-structured information processing and soft computing.

Sabrina De Capitani di Vimercati is an assistant professor at Dipartimento di Elettronica per l' Automazione of the University of Brescia. Her research interests are in the area of information security, databases, and information systems. She has been an international fellow in the Computer Science Laboratory at SRI, CA (USA). She is co-recipient of the ACM-PODS'99 Best Newcomer Paper Award.

Stefano Paraboschi is an associate professor at the Dipartimento di Elettronica e Informazione of Politecnico di Milano. He received the laurea degree in ingegneria elettronica in 1990, and a PhD in ingegneria informatica in 1994, both from Politecnico di Milano. His main research interests are in the area of databases, with a focus on active databases, data warehouses, and the construction of data-intensive Web sites. He is the author, together with Paolo Atzeni, Stefano Ceri, and Riccardo Torlone, of the book 'Database Systems: Concepts, Languages and Architectures' (McGraw-Hill, 1999).

Pierangela Samarati is an associate professor at the Department of Computer Science of the University of Milan. Her main research interests are in data and application security. She has been computer scientist in the Computer Science Laboratory at SRI, CA (USA). She has been a visiting researcher at the Computer Science Department of Stanford University, CA (USA), and at the ISSE Department of George Mason University, VA (USA). She is co-author of the book 'Database Security', Addison-Wesley, 1995. She is co-recipient of the ACM-PODS'99 Best Newcomer Paper Award.

Supporting reconfigurable security policies for mobile programs

B. Hashii [*,1], S. Malabarba [1], R. Pandey [1], M. Bishop [1]

Parallel and Distributed Computing Laboratory, Computer Science Department, University of California, Davis, CA 95616, USA

Abstract

Programming models that support code migration have gained prominence, mainly due to a widespread shift from stand-alone to distributed applications. Although appealing in terms of system design and extensibility, mobile programs are a security risk and require strong access control. Further, the mobile code environment is fluid, i.e. the programs and resources located on a host may change rapidly, necessitating an extensible security model. In this paper, we present the design and implementation of a security infrastructure. The model is built around an event/response mechanism, in which a response is executed when a security-related event occurs. We support a fine-grained, conditional access control language, and enforce policies by instrumenting the bytecode of protected classes. This method enhances efficiency and promotes separation of concerns between security policy and program specification. This infrastructure also allows security policies to change at runtime, adapting to varying system state, intrusion, and other events.

Keywords: Mobile code; Java; Adaptive security policy; Access control; Dynamic classes

1. Introduction

The exponential growth of the Internet has precipitated a shift in popular computing, from stand-alone to distributed applications. In response, programming models that support code migration, such as remote evaluation [31] or mobile programs [5,33], have gained prominence. These models provide run-time systems that can load and execute externally defined user programs. Although appealing in terms of system design and extensibility [6], mobile programs are a security risk. They can maliciously disrupt the execution of programs on a host by unauthorized or improper use of local resources. To maintain security, a host must regulate a mobile program's use of local resources by enforcing an *access control policy* (ACP). The idea is not new; many operating systems limit access to their resources [1]. For example, in the UNIX operating system, users can control access to files they own.

Mobile code environments, however, have two important characteristics: (1) They are *dynamic*, i.e., mobile programs come and go rapidly, and the resources present on a host may change. (2) They are also *unpredictable*, i.e. administrators might not know ahead of time the source, behavior, or requirements of the programs that migrate to their host. There is no fixed set of resources that a host administers. Further, because the different components of resources and mobile programs may require different levels of protection [20], security models must support fine-grained access control.

Several techniques [3,11,13,15,17,19,20,29,35,36]

* Corresponding author.

[1] E-mail: {hashii, malabarb, pandey, bishop}@cs.ucdavis.edu

have been proposed for defining and enforcing access control for mobile programs. The primary focus in most of these approaches has been on supporting flexibility, expressibility, and efficiency. While the above approaches encompass a wide range of security policy specification and enforcement techniques [18], there is very little or no support for building security environments in which security policies can be changed and reconfigured dynamically in order to adapt to changes in operating conditions.

Dynamic reconfiguration of security policies is needed in several instances, especially in complex and large distributed systems. Consider the following cases.

- Unanticipated changes in the security environment of a system may require that its security policies change. For instance, software bugs may appear that compromise the security of the entire system; exploits exist for recently discovered bugs in such critical components as `imapd` and `ftpd`[2]. Further, spies, covert channels and Trojan horses may lurk in application code. Upon discovering such unanticipated security holes, the system administrator should be able to add policies that revoke a previously trusted program's access rights.
- Security policies may evolve due to the changes in operating conditions and organizational goals. For instance, changes in environmental factors, such as company policy or the law, may result in a different set of access rights. Consider the introduction of privacy laws, which can prohibit the collection and distribution of user-specific information. Also, coalitions are often formed by several companies to pursue common projects. A company may establish security policies that are static while a coalition exists, but change after it dissolves.
- Security policies may vary depending on the state of the system. A computer system under attack may need stricter security polices than during normal operations. For instance, a distributed intrusion detection system may respond to attacks on several sites by establishing new policies based on the attack patterns. Further, in many cases, security policy checks may become unnecessary if trust levels can be established on the basis of a program's past behavior. For example, a system may monitor a program's accesses and, on the basis of past behavior, decide to remove all restrictions on access to specific resources.

It is possible to represent many of these security policies using static security policy mechanisms. However, to do so may require that the user anticipate and specify all possible situations. In addition, the representations may be awkward and incur undesirable overhead. What is needed is support for security policies that can be reconfigured at runtime to adapt to changes in the security needs of a site.

In this paper, we present the design and implementation of a security infrastructure that supports dynamic policies. The infrastructure uses a declarative policy language to specify access constraints. It enforces these constraints by performing binary editing on programs and resources [26]. In addition, the infrastructure provides a runtime meta-interface by representing ACPs as first class objects. The user can inspect, add, delete, and modify security policies at runtime. This mechanism supports dynamic security environments that adapt to unanticipated operating condition changes and system evolution. For example, the meta-interface is useful in large distributed systems, where the local policies in individual clusters must be discovered in order to construct and enforce global policies, and to verify consistency among the different local policies. When policies change, the runtime system instruments the protected classes, using dynamic classes [23], to enforce the new policy.

The remainder of this paper is organized as follows. In Section 2, we describe the declarative security policy language and the meta-policy model. We describe the implementation of the security infrastructure in Section 3. We present a performance analysis of the implementation in Section 4. We compare related work in Section 5. Finally, in Section 6, we discuss future work and conclude.

2. The extensible security infrastructure

We begin discussion of the security infrastructure by motivating our approach. We then present our abstract security model, which defines principals,

[2] For full details see http://www.cert.org/advisories.

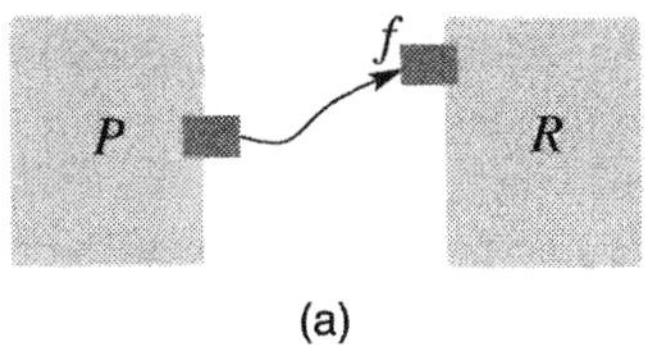

(a)

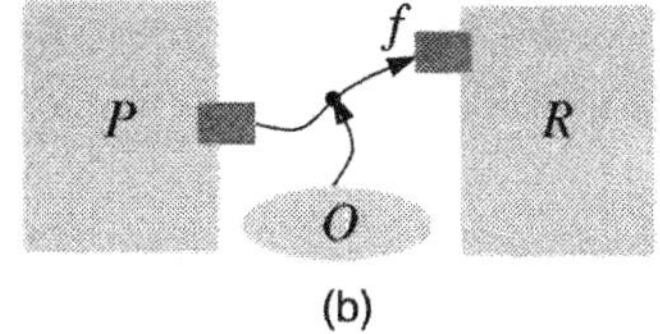

(b)

Fig. 1. Method invocation semantics. (a) Default method invocation semantics. (b) Security constraints on method invocations.

resources, and the relationships between them. Finally, we describe the domain-specific language and runtime meta-interface used to specify policies.

A program accesses a resource by invoking resource methods. In Fig. 1a, we show a program P that migrates to a host and accesses R by invoking f. During P's execution, control jumps to f, executes f, and returns back to P once f terminates. The Java compiler implements a simple access semantics in which there are no constraints on access to R through f.

In many cases, a host may wish to impose constraints on P's accesses to R. Our approach is to allow the host to make the access relationship between P and R *conditional*. For instance, in Fig. 1b, the host binds an access constraint, O, over the access relationship between P and R. Thus, P can access R if it satisfies O.

There are two notable aspects of our security mechanism. First, the access constraint, O, is defined separately from both P and f. The infrastructure enforces constraints by integrating interposition code within P and R before they are loaded in the Java virtual machine. Second, O can change at runtime, allowing the security policies of a host to evolve dynamically.

2.1. The event/response model

An access control policy is specified by a three-tuple: (1) specific access relationships that the security infrastructure should monitor, (2) conditions under which security-sensitive accesses warrant a response, and (3) the associated responses.

A security policy defines an access relationship between a principal and a resource. First, we define the notions of resource and principal, and then we show how they are used in our security model to specify policies.

2.1.1. Resource

Both hosts and mobile programs may define services or data structures that they wish to protect from unauthorized access. In keeping with the fine-grained access control model, a resource may represent any software component. Thus, a resource is defined as any method, class, or set of classes that is protected by an ACP. Conceptual resources, such as databases, and hardware resources, such as printers and the disk, must be wrapped by a Java class or method to be protected by an ACP.

2.1.2. Principal

The basis for authorization in a security model is the principal. In traditional systems, a program runs on behalf of a principal who is given certain access rights. Once the program attains these rights, it retains them during its execution. In a mobile code environment, however, a mobile program is typically composed of components that may be loaded from different hosts. A host may, thus, assign different components different rights and privileges, possibly on the basis of their origin. The level of granularity at which access rights must be checked and enforced is much finer in such an environment. The principle of least privilege [30] states that a principal should not have access to resources that are not needed to complete its job. This means that granularity of access control should be at the method level.

A principal in our security infrastructure can, thus, represent a method, an entire class, or a group of classes. For instance, `www.sun.com` denotes a principal comprising all classes loaded from this host; these classes all acquire the privileges assigned to the host. The infrastructure allows a principal to be defined as a group of classes by either enumerating the different classes or providing a filter function that determines if a class belongs to a principal. A site can use the filter function to define principals on the basis of specific characteristics such as signature, code source, or possible behavioral pattern. For example, the following class defines a filter function:

```
class GroupFunction {
 boolean static RogueSite(Class ncl) {
  URL u=ncl.getClassLoader().getURL();
  String name = u.toString();
  return
    name.equals("http://
                    www.roguesite.com");
 }
}
```

This function is executed whenever the system loads a class. The class is given to the function, and if it returns `true` then the class is added to an associated group. We will see in Example 1 how this function is used to define a policy.

It is important that sites define principals carefully so that mobile programs are unable to spoof definitions of principals, and thereby attain privileges that they should not have. For instance, principals based on simple class names can be easily spoofed. Note that we consider the problem of authenticating mobile programs orthogonal to the problem of access control discussed in this paper.

2.1.3. Event

An event occurs when a principal P accesses a resource R. We use the symbol `->` to denote a principal accessing a resource. Hence, the expression

```
-> File.Open()
```

denotes an event associated with the invocation of `Open` on an instance of a `File` resource.

An event may contain a condition, defined in terms of object, program, global, system or security states as well as the value of method parameters. For instance, the expression

```
-> File.Open() and
     (File.GetName() == "secretfile")
```

denotes only those `File.Open()` events for which the associated boolean condition is true.

2.1.4. Response

A response describes the action performed before and/or after a selected event has occurred. The infrastructure supports several predefined responses, such as `DenyResponse`, `AuditResponse`, and `ChangePolicyResponse`. `DenyResponse` denies access to a principal by throwing a security exception. `AuditResponse` logs any access to a protected resource. `ChangePolicyResponse` responds to an access attempt by changing the security policy. In addition, users can define their own responses and associate them with specific events.

Our security infrastructure provides two mechanisms for specifying policies: a *policy specification language* and a *meta-interface*. The high-level policy language permits rapid and flexible policy specification. Users may write policy files, containing series of statements, and load these files into the system. The statements are then translated into policy objects. The meta-interface provides language support for creation, management, and enforcement of policy objects at runtime.

2.2. The policy language

Fig. 2 lists the grammar for our policy language, which evolved from previous work [26] to include new constructs. Terminals in the EBNF, such as `ClassName` or `MethodName`, correspond to actual Java classes and methods, as described below. The language semantics allow for the use of either built-in event and response classes or user-defined classes. Policies are specified as a list of statements in policy files. The default policy file is loaded when an application starts, and new or modified files may be loaded during runtime via the interface described in Section 2.3.

A host uses this language to specify ACPs. As the grammar illustrates, our language is tailored to this task. It defines event/response relationships and allows entities to be grouped for ease of expression.

In addition to the access constraints, we support an `enable` statement that is used to override access constraints. This is needed when a host wants to override the default principle of least privilege. For example, assume that a security policy specifies that an applet cannot access the file system. The security infrastructure implements the default policy of least privilege, which ensures that the applet cannot access the file system directly or indirectly by calling other methods that access the file system. However,

```
Policy             ::= { PolicyStatements | Definitions }
PolicyStatements   ::= { Constraint | AddStatement | EnableStatement }
Definitions        ::= { PolicyGroup | GroupStatement }
Constraint         ::= before Event do Response | after Event do Response
AddStatement       ::= add Type Name to ClassName
EnableStatement    ::= enable Event
Response           ::= ResponseName '(' ParameterList ')'
Event              ::= [Entity] Invocation Entity [and Condition]
Invocation         ::= ↦
Entity             ::= class ClassName | method MethodName '(' ParameterList ')' | group GroupName
Condition          ::= BooleanExpression
PolicyGroup        ::= policy PolicyName '{' PolicyStatements ';' { PolicyStatements } '}'
GroupStatement     ::= group GroupName '{' Entity ';' { Entity } '}'
                       | define group GroupName '{' FunctionName '(' Parameters ')' '}'
```

Fig. 2. Access control policy language.

in many cases, this may not be desirable [36]. For instance, suppose the applet can write to the screen using the font files stored on the disk. In this instance, we want to enable the display manager to access the font files, regardless of the calling program. The `enable` statement allows one to override the default policy. This is similar to the `enablePrivileged` command in the JDK 1.2 security model [17].

2.3. *The meta-policy model*

The infrastructure represents security policies and their components as first class objects. Privileged programs can use the meta-interface to examine, add, delete and modify policy objects. Below, we describe policy objects and the meta-interface in detail.

2.3.1. *Access control policy objects*

Policy objects represent all policy statements, including constraints and groups. The class hierarchy of policy classes corresponds to the non-terminals in the policy language grammar. The security infrastructure represents policies in terms of three kinds of objects: event, response, and constraint.

Event objects. An event object consists of a subject, an invocation target, and, optionally, a boolean condition. An event may be trapped, and any bound responses executed, before or after the invocation. Creating a new event object is similar to specifying it in the policy language. For example, one can create an `Event` object to protect the password file in the following manner:

```
EventObject ev = new Event(
  "FileInputStream.
                FileInputStream(File f)",
  "f.getName() == /etc/passwd");
```

This event is trapped by an invocation of the `FileInputStream` constructor in which the file name is '/etc/passwd'. The parameters to the constructor are parsed in the same way as the language to create the same objects.

Response objects. A response object is an abstract class that users extend in order to customize responses. `ResponseObject` contains a `DoResponse` method that is invoked whenever the associated event occurs. A host redefines the `DoResponse` method to define any kind of response. An example of this is the `DenyResponse` class.

```
class DenyResponse
extends ResponseObject {
  public void DoResponse() {
  throw new SecurityException();
  }
}
```

Users may then create response objects by instantiating these classes. For example:

```
ResponseObject response = new
      DenyResponse();
```

Constraint objects. A constraint object represents an access constraint, and includes an event object and an associated response object.

```
class PolicyLoader {
      public PolicyObject get(String policyName);
      public void add(PolicyObject policy, String policyName);
      public void remove(PolicyObject policy);
      public void remove(String policyName);
      public void replace(PolicyObject oldP, PolicyObject newP);
      public void loadFromFile(String fileName);
      public void removeAllPolicies();
       ...
}
```

Fig. 3. PolicyLoader interface.

2.3.2. The policy loader

The core of the meta-interface is a module called the *policy loader*, which manages and enforces policy objects. The interface to the class `PolicyLoader` is shown in Fig. 3. It includes methods for adding, removing and examining policy objects, and loading policy files. Policy files, written in the specification language, may be loaded from disk or other sources, such as the network. `PolicyLoader` parses the policy file, translates the statements into corresponding policy objects, and adds the new objects to the overall system policy.

Users can extend `PolicyLoader` to add functionality. For example, one might redefine `PolicyLoader.loadFromFile()` to load policy files from a URL as part of a distributed security management scheme.

A `PolicyLoader` object is associated with a class loader, and, thus, enforces policies over a given namespace. We discuss this further in Section 3.4.1, and provide more implementation details on policy maintenance and enforcement in Section 3.2.

2.4. Examples

We now present four examples that illustrate how a system administrator can define and modify policies dynamically using the policy language and the meta-interface.

Example 1 (File auditing). In the first example, we illustrate how we can define principals, events and responses, and bind them together to define an access policy.

Assume that we want to audit all file accesses by programs that arrive from `www.roguesite.com`. We use the basic default audit response class, `AuditResponse`, to perform auditing. To enforce the policy, we create a `ReadFile` group that encapsulates the resources that we want to protect, and a `RogueSite` group that defines the principal using the group filter described in Section 2.1.

```
group ReadFile {
  class FileInputStream;
  class FileOutputStream;
  ...
}
group RogueSite {
    GroupFunction.RogueSite(Class
    newclass);
}
after group RogueSite ->
    group ReadFile do AuditResponse()
```

Example 2 (Protecting a resource). In this example, we show how the meta-interface can be used to define and enforce security policies in unanticipated security situations.

Assume that a host allows an external program from `www.roguesite.com` to access a public database server, `DBS`. However, the host discovers that the program is a Trojan horse that is able to exploit a bug in the database server to gain access to a protected section of the database, `PDBS`. As a result, the host wants to change the policy to prevent access to the restricted part of the database without shutting down the site. The host can enforce this new policy by constructing it and loading it using the policy loader:

```
PolicyLoader pl = getClass().getClassLoader().getPolicyLoader();
                                                // find the policy loader
Group gp = new FilterGroup ("GroupFunction.RogueSite"); // create principal
Event ev = new Event(gp, "PDBS.query"); // specify access
Response newResp = new DenyResponse(); // create a deny response
ConstraintClass newPol = new ConstraintClass(ev, newResp); // create a constraint
pl.add(newPol, "DBSquery"); // prevent access
```

Example 3 (File or network access). In this example, we demonstrate how access control policies can be changed in response to a security-related event. We implement a commonly employed security policy that allows access to either the file system or the network, but not both. This policy could be part of a larger security policy that prevents the flow of information from disk to the rest of the world. Suppose the network is accessed as in Example 4, and the file system is accessed as in Example 1. We provide a basic default change policy response class as shown below:

```
class ChangePolicyResponse extends ResponseObject {
    public void DoResponse(String oldPolicy, String newPolicy) {
        PolicyLoader pl = getClass().getClassLoader().getPolicyLoader();
        if (oldPolicy!= null) pl.remove(oldPolicy);
        if (newPolicy!= null) pl.loadFromFile(String newPolicy);
    }
}
```

This response takes as parameters the name of a policy to remove, and the name of a policy file from which to load a new policy. We then specify four policies with the names `"FileChange"`, `"NetworkChange"`, `"DenyFile"` and `"DenyNetwork"`. The deny policies prevent access to files and the network, respectively. For example:

```
define policy DenyNetwork {
  before -> Socket.Open()
    do DenyResponse();
}
```

Likewise, the change policies replace themselves with the appropriate deny policy. The `"FileChange"` policy is:

```
define policy FileChange {
 before ReadFile do
  ChangePolicy("NetworkChange",
               "DenyNetwork")
 before ReadFile do
  ChangePolicy("FileChange",null)
}
```

We can similarly implement `"DenyFile"` and `"NetworkChange"`. Thus, when a file is read, the file's change policy is invoked, which in turn removes both the file's and network's change policy and adds a policy that prevents access to the network. The new access control policy no longer checks if reads are allowed. This provides a more efficient implementation of the above policy that a similar static policy would.

Example 4 (Control over the number of accesses). Suppose we want to implement the constraint that an object `p` can open a socket connection using `Socket.Open(Host hostId, int Socketid)` at most ten times.

We create a new field of `p`, `SecurityState`, of type `SecState`. This class keeps track of the number of times `p` calls `Socket.Open`. Let method `SecState.CheckCount(int x)` be defined in the following manner:

```
public boolean CheckCount(int x) {
  if (count < x) {
    UpdateCount();
                    // increment the counter
  return(false);
  } else return(true);
}
```

The following policy statements add the new object to `p` and specify that `p` can invoke `Open` at most ten times.

```
define policy CountSockets {
 add SecState SecurityState to p
 before p -> Socket.Open()
  and p.SecurityState.CheckCount(10) do
  ChangePolicyResponse("CountSockets",
                       "DenySockets")
}

define policy DenySockets {
 before p -> Socket.Open()
 do DenyResponse()
}
```

After a socket has been opened ten times, the condition is always true. When this occurs, the policy is changed to always deny access.

The previous two examples highlight the fact that the reconfigurable policy mechanism can be used to eliminate access checks in several cases. For instance, consider a security policy: an applet can access a resource only if the condition B is true. Assume that B has the property that once it becomes true, it remains true. Clearly, checks for B can be eliminated once B becomes true. Using the dynamic security mechanism, a site can specify a policy that dynamically removes checks for B once B becomes true.

3. Implementation

In this section, we describe the implementation of our security model. We focus on two primary elements: the separation of security policy specification from resource definitions, and the ability to modify security policies during execution. We implement the first by generating binary code for each security policy on the fly, and integrating this code directly into the protected resource. We support the latter using dynamic classes, which allow the system to generate *new* interposition code and add it to previously instrumented classes.

First, we provide some background on dynamic Java classes. We then describe how our implementation enforces security policies, and how they can be modified. Finally, we present an analysis of our model and implementation. We describe potential weaknesses and their solutions, and include a general discussion of our approach's effectiveness.

3.1. Background: dynamic classes

Our implementation relies on *dynamic classes* to change policies. Using dynamic classes, we can instrument classes at runtime, and update their instances if needed. This is necessary to enforce policy changes. A previous paper [23] contains a full account of dynamic classes. In this section, we briefly outline the design and implementation, focusing on semantic and technical issues.

We wished to extend, not replace or weaken, Java's type and dynamic linking systems. We designed the semantics and interface for dynamic classes with this goal in mind. Thus, we define the semantics of a class change as follows: (1) a class change cannot cause any type violations, (2) all subclasses of the target class must change to reflect their new superclass, and (3) all existing instances of the target class must be updated to reflect the new definition. Under these conditions, the runtime state of the system remains consistent across class changes, and Java's type safety characteristics remain intact.

The JVM uses the class loader mechanism [22] for dynamic linking. We extended the class loader to provide a convenient interface for class changes. We use runtime system support for dynamic classes, modifying the JVM in Sun's JDK 1.2 to create a dynamic classes-capable virtual machine. We chose this approach over library-based support for reasons of efficiency and effectiveness.

3.2. Policy enforcement

The security system enforces an ACP by placing interposition code between the code requesting a resource and the resource itself. This interposition code checks if the specific access is allowed. A set of tools generates this interposition code and integrates it into mobile programs and resources before they are loaded.

Fig. 4 provides an overview of the components of the security infrastructure and their interaction. P denotes a mobile Java program, which migrates

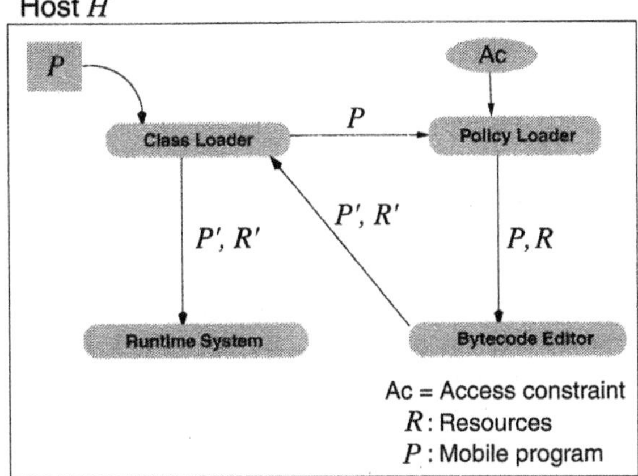

Fig. 4. Security policy enforcement.

to a host denoted H. A PolicyLoader is associated with a dynamic class loader, which defines the namespace that H provides to mobile programs. This PolicyLoader is then responsible for specifying and enforcing ACPs over all classes defined in its namespace. Upon application startup, a dynamic class loader initializes its policy loader. The policy loader parses a policy file and creates the specified policy objects. Then, the dynamic class loader loads application classes. During class name resolution and dynamic linking the class loader retrieves the resources R and passes them to the policy loader. The policy loader then generates the interposition code for enforcing the security policies and integrates it into the resource code.

The nature of the interposition code depends on the type of policy that the policy loader is trying to enforce. For instance, suppose the policy loader is implementing a constraint containing an event/response pair, named `event` and `response`, respectively. In addition, event is a triple defined by `<subject, target, condition>`. This policy is enforced by inserting the following code into `event.target`:

```
if (caller == event.subject
    && event.condition)
    response.doResponse();
```

The caller is identified by stack inspection, as described in Section 3.4.1. Details of the generated code and how it is integrated into the class definitions are beyond the scope of this paper; see [26].

After receiving the modified mobile programs and resources (P' and R'), the class loader loads the classes into the JVM, replacing any existing versions. In addition, the class loader caches copies, as raw bytecode, of the current and original versions of all loaded classes. The policy loader uses this cached data to re-integrate the interposition code when security policies affecting a class are modified.

3.3. Dynamic policy changes

PolicyLoader maintains a list of all policy objects active within its namespace. The union of the ACPs specified by these objects may be considered the system ACP for that namespace. The host can dynamically change a system ACP by adding or removing policy objects, or by loading a new policy file.

3.3.1. Adding policy objects

A system ACP may by extended via `PolicyLoader.add()` or `PolicyLoader.loadFromFile()`. The policy loader adds the new policy objects to its internal list and enforces them. It first identifies all entities affected by the change. This information is stored within the policy objects. If a group is among these, it expands the policy object to a list of objects, each replicating the policy, but applied to one class within the group. Next, the policy loader retrieves the raw bytecode version of each affected class from the dynamic class loader, and edits the bytecode according to the new policy object. Finally, it invokes the dynamic class loader to replace the existing class definition with the new, modified version. In the event that one of the classes referred to by a new policy object has not yet been loaded into the system, `PolicyLoader` stores the object and edits the class when it is loaded.

3.3.2. Removing policy objects

This requires the removal of any bytecode inserted when enforcing the target policy. First, the policy loader removes the policy object from its policy list. Then, as with addition, all affected classes are identified. For each loaded class, the policy loader retrieves the *original*, unedited, bytecode from the dynamic class loader and re-enforces all remaining policy objects.

3.3.3. Modifying the system policy

The system policy as a whole can be modified by adding and removing policy objects as described above. Alternatively, a host can modify the policy file and use the methods `removeAllPolicies()` and `loadFromFile()`. Both methods empty the policy list and retrieve the original definitions of all affected classes. `loadFromFile()` reloads the policy from the specified location, enforces each policy object, and replaces each class definition with the new version. `removeAllPolicies()` empties the policy list, retrieves the original definitions of all affected classes, and replaces the current definitions with the original versions. Therefore, calling `removeAllPolicies()` and `loadFromFile()` in sequence effectively refreshes the system policy to reflect a new or updated policy file.

3.4. Analysis

In this section, we analyze our security infrastructure and implementation. We identify techniques an attacker might use to circumvent security, and discuss the solutions.

3.4.1. Protecting against unauthorized dynamic modifications

First, we consider the security problems that arise due to the ability to dynamically change the behavior of a system, either directly, through the dynamic class loader, or indirectly, through the policy loader.

As we described in the previous section, the dynamic class loader provides a user or an applet with the ability to modify a class dynamically. A malicious applet, thus, can use this ability to modify a protected resource, and thereby bypass the access control policies associated with the resource. Consider the following security policy: applet A is granted read, but not write, access to a file class, F. So, A can invoke *F.read*, but not *F.write*. This constraint is enforced by inserting checks into *F.write* whenever F is loaded or modified. A could compromise security by adding a new method *F.Awrite*, which is identical to *F.write*, but is *not* protected by an ACP. A may then invoke *F.Awrite* and compromise file system integrity.

The problem arises because both protected resources and external mobile programs reside within the same namespace. Thus, we resolve the problem with strict namespace partitioning, as supported by Java 1.2 [21]. We associate different trust levels with the components of a program. Components with different trust levels are located within different namespaces. That is, they are loaded and managed by a different dynamic class loader and policy loader. Thus, untrusted mobile programs, local resources, and system classes are partitioned into separate namespaces. Now, applets cannot directly modify protected resources, since the dynamic class loader does not allow programs to change classes in different namespaces.

While the above separation does restrict an applet's ability to modify resources directly, the applet can still change policies through policy loaders. Since a policy loader controls all security policies within its namespace, it is vital that the policy loader itself be well protected from untrusted code, which might otherwise circumvent the entire security mechanism. Continuing with the prior example, we have ensured that A cannot modify F. However, A can get a handle to the policy loader in the resource namespace, and simply remove the ACP protecting *F.write*. Therefore, we impose the dynamic class loader's namespace constraint on the policy loader; policy loaders cannot be directly accessed across namespaces. To enforce these constraints, `PolicyLoader` includes native methods for stack inspection [37]. All methods that change policies include code that checks the previous frame on the current thread's call stack. If the corresponding method is not defined within the current namespace, then a security exception is thrown.

However, an applet may invoke the resource policy loader indirectly, via a resource. This should not be completely forbidden, since a user may specify a security policy in which resources initiate changes in the policy when accessed. The solution is to protect all resources and critical components with an ACP. Assuming that these ACPs are correctly specified, all resources are safe from unauthorized access.

3.4.2. Resolving policy conflicts

In Section 2 we described the `enable` policy statement. A policy such as `enable Fonts -> File` allows the `Fonts` class to access the `File` class regardless of what other methods are on the stack. This option introduces the possibility of policy conflicts and security holes. For example, a malicious applet can create a policy `enable BadApp -> File`, which could potentially grant file permissions. We define the semantics of `enable` to resolve conflicts and prevent security violations.

Consider a system using namespace partitioning, as described above. Such a system might have a hierarchy of namespaces, with a System namespace being the lowest and an Applet namespace being the highest. Note also that there is an implicit trust relationship between these levels; high levels need to trust lower levels. Security violations occur when objects in a higher level try to override the security policy of a lower level. Thus, whenever there is a possible conflict between an enable and a constraint, the lower level policy takes precedence.

For instance, a policy conflict would occur if the following two policies were encountered: (1) `before -> File do DenyResponse` and (2) `enable R1 -> File`. If the two policies are defined in the same namespace, then `enable` takes precedence. On the other hand, if (1) were defined in the system namespace, and (2) in the resource namespace, then (1) would take precedence.

Namespace partitioning relies on the assumption that a principal is trusted within its own namespace. Given this assumption, `enable` cannot be used by a malicious applet to circumvent an ACP protecting a resource. An `enable` policy enacted in the applet namespace is overridden by any conflicting policy in the resource namespace.

3.4.3. Reflection attacks

Reflection can be used to defeat some security mechanisms that rely on namespace partitioning [36]. This type of attack assumes that interposition code takes the form of proxy or wrapper classes that hide the protected class. A malicious applet can use reflection to discover the actual name of the protected class and invoke its methods manually, thus bypassing the proxy. Our system is immune to this sort of attack, since there are no proxy classes. Interposition code is placed directly in the protected method, and cannot be circumvented.

3.4.4. Synchronization attacks

Multithreaded systems present the attacker with the opportunity to exploit race conditions. Consider Example 4: if the `CheckCount` method was not atomic, an attacker could potentially violate the access constraint by exploiting a race condition between when the access count is checked, and when it is incremented. To prevent this sort of attack, and any synchronization-related bugs, all interposition code is synchronized. Whenever the bytecode editor encounters an object reference, it places a `monitorenter` instruction that locks the object. It then places all `monitorexit` instructions at the end of the instrumented method.

4. Performance analysis

In this section, we examine the performance behavior of our security infrastructure. The primary goal of the analysis is to evaluate the cost of providing an extensible security infrastructure. In our previous research, we evaluated the performance behavior of the binary-editing-based security infrastructure for static policies [26] and the JVM that supports dynamic classes [23]. To summarize these results:

- In many cases binary-editing-based approaches perform better than reference monitor-based approaches, such as the JDK security model, because interposition code is inlined, as opposed to involving several procedure calls.
- The overhead of implementing dynamic class is moderate, approximately six percent.

Therefore, in this section we focus primarily on the overhead required to implement reconfigurable policies. We performed all experiments on a 266 MHz Pentium II running SunOS 5.6.

One advantage of reconfigurable security is that frequently the number of security checks can be reduced. Recall Example 3. We want to prevent access to either the file system or the network. If a file is accessed, we set a policy to prevent network access. Further file accesses are not monitored. If a static security mechanism is used, a program would have to perform n security checks, where n is the number of times a file is accessed. Each check would consult a database to determine if the network has been accessed, say this takes time c. Our approach only needs to change policies once. Thus, our approach is valid whenever the time to change the policy, p, is less than $n \times c$.

Table 1
Policy modification results, recorded in seconds

Add policy	0.060
Remove policy	0.015
Loading a class (w/o policy)	0.018
Loading a class (w policy)	0.051
Invoking a method (w/o policy)	0.000070
Invoking a method (w policy)	0.00092

4.1. Microbenchmarks

In order to determine *p*, we measured the time to add or remove a simple policy using the meta-interface. The policy we used for these microbenchmarks is:

```
before -> method NoApp. run()V do
    NoResponseObject
```

The NoApp class is a subclass of Thread and redefines the run method. Both the protected method and the response are empty and do nothing. The result of each of these experiments is the average of 100 runs. It takes about 0.060 seconds to add a policy when the protected class has already been loaded. This includes the time to modify and replace the class. It takes about 0.015 seconds to remove a policy, including the time to unmodify and replace the class. Table 1 summarizes the results. For comparison, we have also included the time to load a class, with and without a relevant policy already installed, as well as the time to run the modified and unmodified methods.

4.2. Application benchmarks

We ran a second set of experiments to examine the overhead of enforcing security policies on applications. In particular, we used the SPECjvm '98 benchmark suite [32].[3] We specified a simple security policy that prints a warning message when writing more than a given number of bytes. The policy is defined as follows:

```
before -> class spec.io.FileOutputStream
 and spec.io.FileOutputStream.byteCount
    >1000000
 do AlertResponseObject
```

We also did a control run with no policy specified. Table 2 summarizes our results; the performance penalty in most cases was around 7%. The variation in overhead is partly due to the amount of times the restricted resource is used. The `jack` benchmark, for example, is very IO-intensive, resulting in a 25.7% overhead. We expect that in most cases the overhead will be minimal. In the case of `jack`, the higher overhead is due to policy enforcement. We are currently looking at optimization techniques in order to reduce this cost.

5. Related work

We have divided this section into two parts. The first compares approaches for providing access control for mobile code. The second compares security policy languages.

5.1. Access control mechanisms

We evaluate and compare several proposed access control mechanisms with our mechanism. We focus on the power, flexibility, and dynamism of each approach, as compared to our work.

A mechanism for controlling access is a wrapper [34]. A wrapper is a code that encapsulates a resource. It may change the resource's behavior by running interposition code. Thus, a wrapper could be used to add access control checks to a resource by inlining the interposition code, as in [35], or by calling a wrapper which then calls the original code, as in [13]. A technique operating at the system call level [15] uses a loadable kernel module to intercept and wrap system calls. On the other hand, type hiding [36] modifies the dynamic linking process in Java to hide or replace classes seen by an applet. It allows a class to be replaced by a proxy class that checks the arguments of the invoked method and conditionally throws an exception or call their original methods. The problem with using wrappers to implement extensible security can be seen in Naccio [13]. Naccio provides a framework for specifying resource hooks, state maintenance code, and safety policies. Pro-

[3] We used a SPECjvm problem size of 100. These results are not SPEC compliant, and are suitable for internal comparison only.

Table 2
SpecJVM results, recorded in seconds

Benchmark	Standard JVM (T_o)	Active policy (T_p)	$(T_p - T_o)/T_p$
check	1.06	1.497	0.292
mtrt	1709.399	1845.753	0.0739
jess	1420.888	1532.356	0.0727
compress	7966.578	8219.17	0.0307
db	2675.772	2963.061	0.0970
mpegaudio	6383.705	6746.463	0.0538
jack	2083.441	2804.971	0.257
javac	1682.285	1820.105	0.0757

grams are transformed to use wrappers instead of the original library code. However, in order for Naccio to support extensible security policies, it must recompile policy definitions, recreate library wrappers and re-modify programs to use the new wrappers.

As an alternative mechanism, a resource monitor [2] intercepts and validates resource accesses. Our approach uses an extensible resource manager which is essentially created and modified at runtime. Most approaches, however, use a static resource monitor. While a user can change what a static resource monitor does — denying access or not — fairly easily, it is more difficult to change the set of monitored resources. In order to support policies over any resource, all resources must be monitored, and this can be very inefficient. As a result, most existing systems do not do this. Systems such as Java and Safe-Tcl define a subset of operations which are security-relevant and check only those references. Likewise, the monitors in [20] intercept and authorize all IPC calls.

Another approach that inlines resource monitor code is used in Security Automata SFI Implementation (SASI) developed at Cornell University [12]. The main differences between SASI and our work is the way in which policies are specified, and that SASI has an implementation for x86 assembly code. The advantage of x86 assembly code is limited in that it is difficult to extract application level resources from low-level code. There is also a SASI implementation for Java which is similar to this work. However, it does not support dynamic policy changes.

In Java's security model [17], each resource has a permission class associated with it, for instance java.io.FilePermission. A policy file specifies which principals have which permissions. The java.security.Policy object contains the policies that are currently in effect. A policy can be changed by either setting a new policy object or by calling its refresh method and reloading its policy. However, this form of extensible security is limited. For example, it is possible to write resources that do not call the access controller. Protecting such resources would require rewriting the resource class. Our approach can handle this by automatically modifying the resource. Furthermore, access control decisions are based on the protection domain of the code. It is not clear how to base decisions on environmental or historical conditions.

Deeds [11] is a history-based access control mechanism built on top of Java 1.1's security mechanism. In this system, a security event is a call to the security manager. The security manager will, in turn, call the handlers for the particular event. Policies can be modified by changing these handlers. However, like other static resource monitor approaches, it is unclear how to modify policies over resources that do not use Java's security manager.

Riechmann and Hauck [29] use meta-objects to implement security policies. A number of meta-objects can be attached to an object reference. They are invoked whenever the object is accessed. This is an alternate method of applying extensible security to objects, with the limitation that anyone can attach meta-objects, but only the meta-object can remove itself.

The Distributed Trusted Operating System (DTOS) [4] provides adaptable security by using security servers. When a request for a resource is made to the kernel or other program, a resource monitor checks with a policy server that determines if the access is allowed. Policies can be changed by either reinitializing the server or changing the active server. However, switching between different kinds of policies is difficult. For example, if a Unix style security policy is in place, the context information that the server needs consists of subjects, objects, and actions. Switching to an MLS policy requires changing the context information to labels.

Another alternate mechanism is a capability [9], an unforgeable reference to an object and a set of access rights. Possession of the capability authorizes the holder to perform the associated accesses on the object. Capabilities also have a notion of revocation and delegation. For example, the J-Kernel project [19] extends Java's security model by implementing a capability system within the language. On the other hand, Cherubim's [27,28] active capabilities provide extensible security policies by containing user-defined scripts that are run when received by a host. The limitation with generic capability systems is that they cannot usually prevent a program from leaking a reference to an untrusted object. Our approach solves this problem by protecting the resource itself, and not just its references.

Domain Type Enforcement (DTE) [3] is Trusted Information System's (TIS's) access control project, in which subjects are grouped into domains and objects are grouped into domains. There is also a language (DTEL) that specifies which domains can perform certain operations on which types and how threads can change domains by executing certain specified programs. DTEL operates on the level of files and programs, whereas our language operates at a finer granularity. Fraser and Badge [14] provide a way of maintaining general security properties across policy changes. The idea is that the addition of new policies should not invalidate the access relationships of the previous policies. They can prove that adherence to policy representing predicates during DTE's policy loading process maintains these properties. While we do not provide any such guarantees, we are currently researching the area of policy reasoning and composition.

5.2. *Policy languages*

Mechanisms for specifying and enforcing security are also a focus in security policy language research. Security policy languages have been considered as the basis for verification of secure systems design. Various considerations have been given to policy languages for doing general enforcement.

In access control matrices (ACM) [1], a two-dimensional matrix captures the access rights of subjects and objects. Entries in a cell determine the list of access rights that a subject has over an object. The ACM is primarily a theoretical tool, and is not used in practice. Its implementations, capability lists and access control lists, are cumbersome to work with when the subjects and objects involved are not known in advance.

Miller and Baldwin [24] describe a method of access control based on boolean expression evaluation. The idea is that each subject and object is given a set of attributes. In addition, there is also a set of rules that link a subject, an object, and an action. These rules can be based on any number of attributes. Since these attributes can be anything, including security level, group membership or time of day, they can be used to implement most security policies. Our approach is similar in that we capture the various attributes in terms of boolean expressions.

Goguen and Meseguer [16] use an algebraic specification approach to specify security policies. Their particular approach expresses security policies as a set of non-interference assertions about a system. Cholvy and Cuppens [7] and Cuppens and Saurel [8] use a form of deontic logic to express policies. In addition to specifying what actions an agent is permitted or forbidden to perform, it allows statements that say what actions an agent is obliged to perform. They use deontic logic to find consistency problems among policies. These policy languages are much more expressive than the one proposed in this paper. We plan to close this gap in the future. Our initial focus has been to develop a simple language for access control that can be implemented easily and efficiently.

The DIAMOND [25] security model provides an alternative model for inheriting security policies in object-oriented systems. It extends the MLS security model described by Denning [10] to object oriented databases. The innovation is that security levels, and hence policies, are not inherited from a class's superclass. Instead, they are derived from its instances. This allows a particular instance of a subclass to have a higher security level than its superclass. DI-

AMOND works strictly with MLS policies, whereas our scheme works for arbitrary models.

6. Conclusion

The mobile code environment is inherently dynamic, unpredictable, and dangerous. We have presented an extensible security infrastructure that supports fine-grained security policies that can be modified dynamically to suit the underlying operating conditions. The security infrastructure enables sites to respond to unanticipated changes in the security environment of a system, and changes in operating conditions and organizational goals. Further, sites can use the dynamic capability to eliminate unnecessary security checks. We have implemented the infrastructure in Java using a dynamic class mechanism.

Our future work involves enhancements and optimizations of our implementation. We are currently using the infrastructure to develop distributed policy discovery and management systems. Further, we plan to integrate the infrastructure into a distributed intrusion detection system.

Acknowledgements

This work is supported by the Defense Advanced Research Project Agency (DARPA) and Rome Laboratory, Air Force Materiel Command, USAF, under agreement number F30602-97-1-0221. The U.S. Government is authorized to reproduce and distribute reprints for Governmental purposes notwithstanding any copyright annotation thereon. The views and conclusions contained herein are those of the authors and should not be interpreted as necessarily representing the official policies or endorsements, either expressed or implied, of the Defense Advanced Research Project Agency (DARPA), Rome Laboratory, or the U.S. Government. We thank Jeff Gragg for help and support in implementing the infrastructure. We also thank Fritz Barnes, Earl Barr and the anonymous reviewers for their excellent comments and help in writing this paper.

References

[1] E. Amoroso, Fundamentals of Computer Security Technology, P T R Prentice-Hall, Englewood Cliffs, NJ, 1994.

[2] J.P. Anderson, Computer security technology planning study, Technical Report ESD-TR-73-51, Vol. II, Electronic Systems Division, Air Force Systems Command, Hanscom AFB, Bedford, MA 01731, October 1972, [NTIS AD-758 206].

[3] L. Badger, D.F. Sterne, D.L. Sherman, K.M. Walker and S.A. Haghighat, Practical domain and type enforcement for UNIX, in: Proc. of the 1995 IEEE Symposium on Security and Privacy, Oakland, CA, May 1995, IEEE Comput. Soc. Press, pp. 66–77.

[4] M. Carney and B. Loe, A comparison of methods for implementing adaptive security policies, in: Proc. of the Seventh USENIX UNIX Security Symposium, San Antonio, TX, January 1998, pp. 1–14.

[5] D. Chess, B. Grosof, C. Harrison, D. Levine, C. Parris, and G. Tsudik, Itinerant agents for mobile computing, IEEE Personal Communications, October 1995, pp. 34–49.

[6] D. Chess, C. Harrison and A. Kershenbaum, Mobile agents: are they a good idea? in: J. Vitek and C. Tschudin (Eds.), Mobile Object Systems. Towards the Programmable Internet, Second International Workshop, MOS '96, Linz, number 1222 in Lecture Notes in Computer Science, July 1997, Springer, New York, pp. 25–47, Also available at http://www.research.ibm.com/massdist/mobag.ps.

[7] L. Cholvy and F. Cuppens, Analyzing consistency of security policies, in: 1997 IEEE Symposium on Security and Privacy, Oakland, CA, IEEE, pp. 103–112.

[8] F. Cuppens and C. Saurel, Specifying a security policy: a case study, in: 9th IEEE Computer Security Foundations Workshop, Kenmare, June 1996, IEEE Comput. Soc. Press, pp. 123–134.

[9] D. Denning, Cryptography and Data Security, Addison-Wesley, Reading, MA, 1983.

[10] D. Denning and P.J. Denning, Certification of programs for secure information flow, Communications of the ACM 20 (7) (1977) 504–513.

[11] G. Edjlali, A. Acharya and V. Chaudhary, History-based access control for mobile code, in: Proc. of the 5th ACM Conference on Computer and Communications Security, San Francisco, CA, November 1998, pp. 38–48.

[12] Ú. Erlingsson and F. Schneider, SASI enforcement of security policies: a retrospective, in: DISCEX'00, Proc. DARPA Information Survivability Conference and Exposition, Hilton Head, SC, January 2000, pp. 287–295.

[13] D. Evans and A. Twyman, Flexible policy-directed code safety, in: Proc. of the 1999 IEEE Symposium on Security and Privacy, Oakland, CA, May 1999, pp. 32–45.

[14] T. Fraser and L. Badger, Ensuring continuity during dynamic security policy reconfiguration in DTE, in: Proceedings of the 1998 IEEE Symposium on Security and Privacy, Oakland, CA, May 1998, pp. 15–26.

[15] T. Fraser, L. Badger and M. Feldman, Hardening COTS software with generic software wrappers, in: Proc. of the

1999 IEEE Symposium on Security and Privacy, May 1999, pp. 2–16.

[16] J.A. Goguen and J. Meseguer, Security policies and security models, in: Proc. of the 1982 Symposium on Security and Privacy, pp. 11–20.

[17] L. Gong, M. Mueller, H. Prafullchandra and R. Schemers, Going beyond the sandbox: an overview of the new security architecture in the Java Development Kit 1.2, in: Proc. of the USENIX Symposium on Internet Technologies and Systems, Monterey, California, December 1997, pp. 103–112.

[18] B. Hashii, M. Lal, S. Samorodin and R. Pandey, Securing systems against external programs, IEEE Internet Computing, Nov./Dec. 1998, pp. 35–45.

[19] C. Hawblitzel, C. Chang, G. Czajkowski, D. Hu and T. von Eicken, Implementing multiple protection domains in Java, Technical Report 97-1160, Cornell University, 1997.

[20] T. Jaeger, J. Liedtke and N. Islam, Operating system protection for fine-grained programs, in: Proc. of the 7th USENIX Security Symposium, San Antonio, TX, Jan. 1998, pp. 143–157.

[21] JavaSoft, JDK 1.2 Documentation.

[22] S. Liang and G. Bracha, Dynamic class loading in the Java virtual machine, ACM SIGPLAN Notices 33 (10) (1998) 36–44.

[23] S. Malabarba, R. Pandey, J. Gragg, E. Barr and F. Barnes, Runtime support for type-safe dynamic Java classes, in: Proc. of the European Conference on Object-Oriented Programming, Sophia Antipolis and Cannes, June 2000, Springer, To appear, Currently available at http://pdclab.cs.ucdavis.edu.

[24] D.V. Miller and R.W. Baldwin, Access control by boolean expression evaluation, in: Fifth Annual Computer Security Applications Conference, Tucson, AZ, 1990, IEEE Comput. Soc. Press, pp. 131–139.

[25] L.M. Null and J. Wong, The DIAMOND security policy for object-oriented databases, in: 1992 ACM Computer Science Conference, Communications Proceedings, Kansas City, MO, pp. 49–56.

[26] R. Pandey and B. Hashii, Providing fine-grained access control for Java programs, in: 13th Conference on Object-Oriented Programming, ECOOP'99, Lecture Notes in Computer Science, Lisbon, June 1999, Springer, New York.

[27] T. Qian, Active capability: an application specific security and protection model, Technical report, University of Illinois at Urbana-Champaign, December 1996.

[28] T. Qian, Cherubim agent based dynamic security architecture, Technical report, University of Illinois at Urbana-Champaign, June 1998.

[29] T. Riechmann and F.J. Hauck, Meta objects for access control: extending capability-based security, in: New Security Paradigms Workshop, Langdale, 1997, pp. 17–22.

[30] J.H. Saltzer and M.D. Schroeder, The protection of information in computer systems, Proceedings of the IEEE 63 (9) (1975) 1278–1308.

[31] J.W. Stamos and D.K. Gifford, Remote evaluation, ACM Transactions on Programming Languages and Systems 12 (4) (1990) 537–565.

[32] Standard Performance Evaluation Corporation, SPECjvm98 Documentation, 1.01 edition, August 1998, http://www.spec.org/osg/jvm98/.

[33] T. Thorn, Programming languages for mobile code, ACM Computing Surveys 29 (3) (1997) 213–239.

[34] W. Venema, TCP Wrapper: network monitoring, access control, and booby traps, in: UNIX Security Symposium III Proceedings, Baltimore, MD, September 1992, USENIX Assoc., pp. 85–92.

[35] R. Wahbe, S. Lucco, T.E. Anderson and S.L. Graham, Efficient software-based fault isolation, in: 14th ACM Symposium on Operating Systems Principles, ACM, December 1993, pp. 203–216.

[36] D.S. Wallach, D. Balfanz, D. Dean and E.W. Felten, Extensible security architecture for Java, in: 16th ACM Symposium on Operating Systems Principles, Saint Malo, Oct. 1997, Operating System Review 31 (5), pp. 116–128.

[37] D.S. Wallach and E.W. Felton, Understanding Java stack inspection, in: 1998 IEEE Symposium on Security and Privacy, Oakland, CA, May 1998, IEEE Comput. Soc., pp. 52–63.

Brant Hashii is a PhD student in the Department of Computer Science at UC Davis. His research interests include computer security, security policies, auditing, and mobile programming. Currently, he is exploring ways to apply access constraints to mobile programming systems. He is a member of IEEE and the ACM.

Scott Malabarba is an MS student in the Department of Computer Science at UC Davis. His research interests include dynamic software evolution, extensible runtime systems, and distributed computing.

Raju Pandey is an assistant professor in the Department of Computer Science at UC Davis. His research interests include Web-based computing, parallel and distributed programming, operating systems, and software engineering. He leads the Ariel project, which is developing novel techniques for supporting secure and efficient mobile-program execution. Pandey received a PhD from the University of Texas at Austin. He is a member of the IEEE and the ACM.

Matt Bishop received his PhD in computer science from Purdue University, where he specialized in computer security, in 1984. He was a research scientist at the Research Institute of Advanced Computer Science and was on the faculty at Dartmouth College before joining the Department of Computer Science at the University of California at Davis. His research areas include computer and network security, especially analysis of vulnerabilities, building tools to detect vulnerabilities, and ameliorating or eliminating them. He also teaches software engineering, machine architecture, operating systems, and (of course) computer security. He has chaired sessions and presented talks and tutorials at numerous conferences, organized and chaired the first two UNIX Security Workshops, and has been on numerous program committees. He is a charter member of the National Colloquium on Information System Security Education.

Squeal: a structured query language for the Web

Ellen Spertus [a,*], Lynn Andrea Stein [b,1]

[a] *Department of Mathematics and Computer Science, Mills College, Oakland, CA, USA*
[b] *MIT Artificial Intelligence Laboratory, Massachusetts Institute of Technology, Cambridge, MA, USA*

Abstract

The Web contains an abundance of useful semi-structured information that can and should be mined. Types of structure include hyperlinks between pages, structure within hypertext pages, and structure within URLs. We have implemented a programming language, Squeal, that facilitates structure-based queries. Specifically, the Squeal user can query the Web as if it were in a standard relational database. We describe Squeal and show the ease of writing structure-based information tools in Squeal.

Keywords: Web; Structure; Semi-structured information; Hyperlinks; Hypertext; Relational databases; SQL; Recommender systems

1. Introduction

The success of the Web is a testament to the importance of structure. Web pages consist not only of text but also of intra-document structure (via annotations indicating headers, lists, and formatting directives) and inter-document structure (hyperlinks). Even the uniform resource locator (URL) identifying a page is structured: typically a host name followed by a location in the file hierarchy or a set of query keywords and values. All of these types of information are used automatically by human readers (through browser software) but have been awkward for programmers to make use of in their search tools. Some examples of structure-based queries are:

- What pages are pointed to by both Yahoo and Netscape Netcenter?
- What are the titles of pages that point to my home page?
- What are the most linked-to pages containing the phrase "java development kit"?
- What pages have the same text as my home page but appear on a different server?

We designed Squeal to allow programmers to easily express these types of queries.

Rather than invent a new query language for structured information, we decided to build on the most popular query language for databases: Structured Query Language (SQL). Benefits of this decision include:

- Anyone who knows SQL can program in Squeal.
- Implementations of Squeal can (and do) build on existing SQL implementations.
- Users can combine references to the Web with references to their own relational databases.
- GUIs and other tools built for SQL can be used with Squeal.

In the next section, we will present Squeal. In

* Corresponding author. E-mail: spertus@mills.edu
[1] E-mail: las@ai.mit.edu

the following section, we will demonstrate the ease of writing structural queries in Squeal. We will conclude with a discussion of the implications and a comparison to other database-inspired languages for querying the Web.

2. Squeal

Squeal provides users with the illusion that the Web is stored and organized in a relational database. Squeal consists of two parts: (1) a schema describing the Web and (2) an implementation that answers queries about the schema (even though the entire Web is not really in a database).

2.1. Schema

A *schema* describes the structure of a relational database, i.e., the tables, fields, and the relationships between them. For example, the schema for an employee database might include a table **employee** with fields *first_name*, *last_name*, and *social_security_number*, where each employee has a distinct *social_security_number*, but different employees may have the same *first_name* or *last_name*.

The following description of the Squeal schema is a slight oversimplification. (The real tables are more normalized and have additional fields.) For full information on the Squeal schema, see [20].

The **page** table, which describes a Web page, has the following fields:

- *url*: the page's URL
- *contents*: the text on the page
- *bytes*: the size of the page
- *when*: the date and time when the page was last retrieved

The following are examples of legal queries (with SQL keywords in capital letters and comments preceded by slashes):

```
// What text is on the page "http://www9.org"?
SELECT contents
FROM page
WHERE url="http://www9.org";
```

```
// What pages contain "hypertext" and have fewer
// than 1000 bytes?
SELECT url
FROM page
WHERE contents LIKE "%hypertext%"
AND bytes <1000;
```

The **tag** table, which describes each html tag on a page, has the following fields:

- *url*: the page's URL;
- *tag_id*: a unique number identifying this tag instance;
- *name*: the text of this tag string (e.g., "H1" or "IMG");
- *startOffset*: the offset within the page at which the tag begins;
- *endOffset*: the offset within the page at which the tag ends.

Some legal queries are:

```
// What pages contain the word "hypertext" and
// contain a picture?
SELECT url
FROM page p, tag t
WHERE p.contents LIKE "%hypertext%"
AND t.url = p.url
AND t.name = "IMG";
```

```
// What tags appear on the page "http://www9.org"?
SELECT name
FROM tag
WHERE url="http://www9.org";
```

The **att** table contains information about the attribute names and values associated with each tag. (For example, consider the hypertext "`<IMG SRC=foo.gif ALIGN=center>`". The tag value is "IMG", the first attribute The fields of the **att** table are:

- *tag_id*: a reference to the corresponding **tag**;
- *name*: the attribute name, e.g., "SRC";
- *value*: the attribute value, e.g., "foo.gif".

Some legal queries are:

```
// What are the values of the SRC attributes
// associated with IMG tags on "http://www9.org"?
SELECT a.value
FROM att a, tag t
WHERE t.url = "http://www9.org"
AND t.name = "IMG"
AND a.tag_id = t.tag_id
AND a.name = "SRC";
```

// What pages are pointed to by “http://www9.org”?

```
SELECT a.value
FROM att a, tag t
WHERE t.url = "http://www9.org"
AND t.name = "A"
AND a.tag_id = t.tag_id
AND a.name = "HREF";
```

While it is possible to inquire about hyperlinks with the **tag** and **att** table, we also provide a more convenient **link** table with the following fields:

- *source_url*: the page on which the link occurs;
- *anchor*: the anchor text for the link;
- *destination_url*: the target of the link;
- *hstruct*: information about under what headers within the page the link appears (e.g., “after the second H1 header and a subsequent H2 header”);
- *lstruct*: information about within what lists within the page the link appears (e.g., “in the second doubly-nested list”).

Some legal queries are:

// What pages are pointed to by “http://www9.org”?

```
SELECT destination_url
FROM link
WHERE source_url="http://www9.org";
```

// What pages point to “http://www9.org”?

```
SELECT source_url
FROM link
WHERE destination_url =
    "http://www9.org";
```

// What pages are pointed to via hyperlinks with
// anchor text “Web conference”?

```
SELECT destination_url
FROM link
WHERE anchor = "Web conference";
```

The utility of the *hstruct* and *lstruct* fields will be shown later.

The **parse** table describes the structure of a URL. It has the following fields:

- *url_value*: the URL string;
- *component*, one of the following, specifying the type of data that appears in the *value* field:
  - “host”: the host portion of the URL;
  - “port”: the port number of the URL;
  - “path”: the path components (directory names) and file name;
  - “ref”: the URL’s reference field (the portion after a pound sign (#));
- *value*: the value of the item specified by the *component* field;
- *depth*: for file names, 0; for directory names, how close to the file name.

For example, the URL `"http://www.ai.mit.edu:80/people/index.html#S"` would appear in the parse table as follows:

component	value	depth
host	www.ai.mit.edu	–
port	80	–
path	index.html	1
path	people	2
ref	S	–

We are planning to also add support for parsing parameterized arguments.

2.1.1. Summary

We have presented the highlights of the Squeal schema and shown some SQL queries that can be made on it. Note that all of the queries shown are standard SQL, thus the user need only learn our schema (just as one would to access any database) and not a new query language.

2.2. Implementation

The Squeal interpreter provides the illusion that the Web is in a relational database, with certain limitations because it is impractical (if not impossible [1]) to determine complete information about the Web. Squeal responds to user queries by querying search engines and fetching and parsing Web pages, which it puts into a small local off-the-shelf relational database. Once the interpreter has caused the relevant information to be placed in the local database, it passes through the user query and returns the response. Because information is put into the database only when demanded, we call this a “just-in-time database” [21].

Let us look at how one of our sample queries would be interpreted:

// What pages are pointed to by “http://www9.org”?

```
SELECT destination_url
FROM link
WHERE source_url="http://www9.org";
```

The Squeal interpreter would respond as follows:

(1) Fetch the page “http://www9.org” from the Web.

(2) Insert information about the page and the URL into the **page** and **parse** tables in the small local database.

(3) Parse the page and store information about it into the **tag**, **att**, and **link** tables.

(4) Pass the original query (`SELECT destination_url FROM link WHERE source_url = "http://www9.org"`) to the local database server, which has a SQL interpreter. It returns a list of URLs, which the Squeal interpreter returns to the user.

Let us look at another query:

// What pages point to “http://www9.org”?

```
SELECT source_url
FROM link
WHERE destination_url =
    "http://www9.org";
```

The Squeal interpreter would respond as follows:

(1) Ask a search engine (e.g., AltaVista) what pages point to “http://www9.org”.

(2) Fetch from the Web all of the pages returned by the search engine, entering information about each page into the **page**, **parse**, **tag**, and **att** tables in the local database.

(3) Pass the original query (`SELECT source_url FROM link WHERE destination_url = "http://www9.org"`) to the local database server, which will return a list of URLs, which the Squeal interpreter returns to the user.

The interpreter is described in more detail elsewhere [20,21].

3. Applications

We call Squeal applications *ParaSites* because they exploit information on the Web in a manner unintended by the information’s authors. Our goal is not to argue that these are the best possible applications but to show the variety of useful structural queries and the ease with which they can be implemented in Squeal. Full details about the applications, including evaluations, can be found in [20].

3.1. Recommender system

One useful class of information retrieval applications is recommender systems [13], where a program recommends new Web pages (or some other resource) judged likely to be of interest to a user, based on the user’s initial set of seed pages P. The standard text-based technique for recommender systems, used by the **Excite search service**[2], is extracting keywords that appear on the seed pages and returning pages that contain these keywords. Note that this technique is based purely on the text of a page, independent of any inter- or intra-document structure.

Another technique for making recommendations is collaborative filtering [17], where pages are recommended that were liked by other people who liked P. This is based on the observation that items thought valuable/similar by one user are likely to by another user. As collaborative filtering was currently practiced, users explicitly rated pages to indicate their recommendations. This inconvenient and expensive step can be eliminated through data mining by interpreting the act of creating hyperlinks to a page as being an implicit recommendation. In other words, if a person links to pages Q and R, we can guess that people who like Q may like R, especially if the links to Q and R appear near each other on the referencing page (such as within the same list). This mines intra-document structural information.

Accordingly, if a user requests a page similar to a set of pages $\{P1, \ldots, Pn\}$, the system can find (e.g., through AltaVista) pages R that point to a maximal subset of these pages and then return to the user what other pages are referenced by R. Note that the ParaSite does not have to understand what the pages have in common. It just needs to find a list that includes the pages and can infer that whatever trait they have in common is also exemplified by other pages they point to.

For example, the first page returned from AltaVista that pointed to both Electronic Privacy In-

[2] www.excite.com

Table 1
Results for seed pages www.now.org and www.feminist.org

URL	Count	Description
www.aauw.org	4	American Assoc. of University Women
www.aclu.org	4	American Civil Liberties Union
www.feminist.org/gateway/womenorg.html#top	4	Directory of Women's Organizations
www.cs.cmu.edu/afs/cs.cmu.edu/user/mmbt/www/women/writers.html	3	A Celebration of Women Writers
www.democrats.org	3	Democratic National Committee
www.igc.org/igc/womensnet	3	WomensNet
www.pfaw.org	3	People for the American Way

formation Center ("www.epic.org") and Computer Professionals for Social Responsibility ("www.cpsr.org/home.html") was a list of organizations fighting the Communications Decency Act; links included the Electronic Frontier Foundation ("www.eff.org") and other related organizations.

We are not the only ones to use this technique, which derives from citation indexing [6,18], and many people have applied this technique to the Web [3,7,14]. What is novel is the ease with which such heuristics can be written and tested.

We use the following algorithm to find pages similar to $P1$ and $P2$:

(1) Generate a list of pages R that point to $P1$ and $P2$.
(2) List the pages most commonly pointed to by pages within R in order of number of occurrences.

The corresponding Squeal code is:

```
SELECT link3.destination_url,
    COUNT(*)
FROM link link1, link2, link3
WHERE link1.destination_url = p1
AND link2.destination_url = p2
AND link1.source_url =
     link2.source_url
AND link2.source_url =
     link3.source_url
GROUP BY link3.destination_url
ORDER BY COUNT(*) DESC;
```

Some heuristics for improving precision are:

(1) Only return target pages that include a keyword specified by the user.
(2) Return the names of hosts frequently referenced.
(3) Only return target pages that point to one or both of $P1$ and $P2$.
(4) Only follow links that appear in the same list and under the same header as the links to $P1$ and $P2$.

This last heuristic was motivated by the observation that some pages contains hundreds or thousands of links and that the most similar pairs of links are likely to be within the same list or under the same header. It makes use of the *hstruct* and *lstruct* fields described above.

The Squeal code for the recommender system, including the requirement that links occur within the same list, is:

```
SELECT link3.destination_url,
    COUNT(*)
FROM link link1, link2, link3
WHERE link1.destination_url = p1
AND link2.destination_url = p2
AND link1.source_url =
     link2.source_url
AND link2.source_url =
     link3.source_url
AND link1.lstruct = link2.lstruct
AND link2.lstruct = link3.lstruct
GROUP BY link3.destination_url
ORDER BY COUNT(*) DESC;
```

While the syntax may be confusing to people not familiar with SQL, note the relative size of the code and the English description. We know of no other computer language where this query of the Web can be expressed more concisely.

When we ran this program with seed pages www.now.org (National Organization for Women) and www.feminist.org (The Feminist Majority Foundation), we got the results in Table 1.

3.2. Home page finder

A new type of application made necessary by the Web is a tool to find users' personal home pages, given their name and perhaps an affiliation. Like many information classification tasks, determining whether a given page is a specific person's home page is an easier problem for a person to solve than for a computer. Consequently, our ParaSite's primary strategy is not determining directly if a page 'looks like' a home page but finding pages that human beings have labeled as being someone's home page. While there is no single stereotypical title for home pages, there is for the anchor text of hyperlinks to them: the author's name. This can be done in Squeal for the name "Pattie Maes" as follows:

```
// Create a table to store candidate pages
CREATE TABLE candidate (url
VARCHAR(1024));
// Populate table with destinations of links with
// anchor text "Pattie Maes"
INSERT INTO candidate (url)
SELECT destination_url
FROM link
WHERE anchor = "Pattie Maes";
```

Observe that this takes advantage of inter-document structure. In contrast, the Ahoy! home page finder [16] generates candidates by searching for the name anywhere in a document.

Once we have the candidate pages, we can make use of intra-document information to rank them. For example, while it is promising if the name appears anywhere on the page, it is most promising if the name appears in the title field or a header field:

```
// Create a table to store ranked results
CREATE TABLE result (url VARCHAR(1024),
score INT);
// Give a page 5 points if it contains the name
// anywhere
INSERT INTO result (url, score)
SELECT destination_url, 5
FROM candidate c, page p
WHERE p.url = c.url
AND p.contents LIKE "%Pattie Maes%";
// Give a page 10 points if it contains the name in the
// title
INSERT INTO result (url, score)
SELECT destination_url, 10
FROM candidate c, tag t, att a
WHERE t.url = c.url
AND t.name = "TITLE"
AND a.tag_id = t.tag_id
AND a.name = "anchor"
AND a.value LIKE "%Pattie Maes%";
```

The structure of the URL can also be used. The URL of Pattie Maes's home page is: "http://pattie.www.media.mit.edu/people/pattie/". This is easily recognized as a likely home page because:

(1) The file name is the empty string. (Other stereotypical file names for home pages are "index.html" and "home.html".)
(2) The final directory name is the user's email alias.
(3) The penultimate directory name is "people". (Other common penultimate directory names for home pages are "home" and "homes".)

The last heuristic would be added to the code as follows:

```
// Give a page 10 points if the penultimate directory
// is "home[s]" or "people".
INSERT INTO result (url, score)
SELECT destination_url, 10
FROM candidate c, parse p
WHERE p.url_value = c.url
AND p.component = "path"
AND p.depth = 2
AND (p.value = "people" OR p.value =
    "homes" OR p.value = "home");
```

The Squeal code to display the resulting URLs and their total number of points is simply:

```
SELECT url, SUM(*)
FROM result
GROUP BY url ORDER BY SUM(*) DESC;
```

Other heuristics, with their Squeal encodings, are provided in [20]. The top results for the full version are:

url	SUM(*)
pattie.www.media.mit.edu/people/pattie/	33
lcs.www.media.mit.edu/people/pattie/	23
www.media.mit.edu/~pattie	16

We implemented a simple variant of the program encodes and returns reasons for each decision [20].

Table 2

score	reason
10	File name is the empty string
10	Penultimate directory is: "people"
2	Anchor from "http://lcs.www.media.mit.edu/groups/agents/papers.html" is the full name: "Pattie Maes"
2	Anchor from "http://nif.www.media.mit.edu/" is the full name: "Pattie Maes'
1	Anchor from "http://aries.www.media.mit.edu/people/aries/home-page.html" includes the full name: "Prof. Pattie Maes"

(The code is not shown here because we wish to emphasize what is unique about Squeal and not the power of SQL.) Some of the reasons the system provided for its top decision are in Table 2.

3.3. Moved page finder

Users frequently encounter 'broken links' (obsolete URLs) while searching and browsing. In 1997, the Web Characterization Group found that 5–8% of file requests were for broken links [12]. We provide two structure-based techniques for tracking down moved pages.

Consider the following blurb, returned by **HotBot** [3] in response to the query "Lenore Blum 1943":

Lenore Blum

Lenore Blum 1943– Written by Lisa Hayes, Class of 1998 (Agnes Scott College)
Lenore Blum was a bright and artistic child who loved math, art, and music from her original introductions to them. Blum finished high school at the age of 16, after which ...

http://www.scottlan.edu/lriddle/women/BLUM.HTM, 5359 bytes, 27Apr97

The goal of a moved-page finder is to find the new URL U_{new} given the information in an out-of-date blurb, i.e., the invalid URL U_{bad} and the title of the page. In this example, U_{bad} is "www.scottlan.edu/lriddle/women/BLUM.HTM", and the title is "Lenore Blum".

3.3.1. Technique 1: climbing the directory hierarchy

We can create URL U_{base} by removing directory levels from U_{bad} until we obtain a valid URL. We can then crawl from U_{base} in search of a page with the given title. This is based on the intuition that someone who cared enough about the page to house it in the past is likely to at least link to the page now. In this example, the page was quickly found; its new name was "http://www.scottlan.edu/lriddle/women/blum.htm".

3.3.2. Technique 2: checking with pages that referenced the old URL

People who pointed to a URL U_{bad} in the past are some of the most likely people to point to U_{new} now, either because they were informed of the page movement or took the trouble to find the new location themselves. Here is a heuristic based on that observation:

(1) Find a set of pages P that pointed to U_{bad} at some point in the past.
(2) Let $P0$ be the elements of P that no longer point to U_{bad} anymore.
(3) See if any of the pages pointed to from elements of $P0$ is the page we are seeking.

A question is how to recognize when we've found the target page. We do this by looking for the known title text or letting the user specify a key phrase. The code to implement both of these techniques appears in [20].

4. Conclusions

4.1. Summary

Because the Web contains useful structural information, it is important to be able to make structure-based queries. We built such a system, Squeal, on top of the most popular structured query language, SQL. By making use of our schema and implementation, any person familiar with SQL can use Squeal to make powerful queries on the Web.

[3] www.hotbot.com

We described three applications that make use of the Web's structural information and showed or sketched their Squeal implementations. Our point was not to argue that these are the best possible such applications (although evaluations have been encouraging [20]) but to give an idea of the structure-based queries one might want to make and to show how easy it is to do so in Squeal.

4.2. Related work

An extractor developed within the TSIMMIS project uses user-specified wrappers to convert Web pages into database objects, which can then be queried [5]. Specifically, hypertext pages are treated as text, from which site-specific information (such as a table of weather information) is extracted in the form of a database object. This is in contrast to our system, where each page is converted into a set of database relations according to the same schema.

This work is influenced by WebSQL, a language that allows queries about hyperlink paths among Web pages, with limited access to the text and internal structure of pages and URLs [2,10,11]. In the default configuration, hyperlinks are divided into three categories, internal links (within a page), local links (within a site), and global links. It is also possible to define new link types based on anchor text; for example, links with anchor text "next". All of these facilities can be implemented in our system, although WebSQL's syntax is more concise. While it is possible to access a region of a document based on text delimiters in WebSQL, one cannot do so on the basis of structure. Some queries we can express but not expressible in WebSQL are:

(1) How many lists appear on a page?
(2) What is the second item of each list?
(3) Do any headings on a page consist of the same text as the title?

W3QL is another language for accessing the Web as a database, treating Web pages as the fundamental units [8]. Information one can obtain about Web pages includes:

(1) The hyperlink structure connecting Web pages;
(2) The title, contents, and links on a page;
(3) Whether they are indices ('forms') and how to access them.

For example, it is possible to request that a specific value be entered into a form and to follow all links that are returned, giving the user the titles of the pages. It is not possible for the user to specify forms in our system (or in WebSQL), access to a few search engines being hardcoded. Access to the internal structure of a page is more restricted than with our system. In W3QL, one cannot specify all hyperlinks originating within a list, for example.

An additional way in which Squeal differs from all of the other systems is in providing a data model guaranteeing that data is saved from one query to the next and (consequently) containing information about the time at which data was retrieved or interpreted. Because the data is written to a SQL database, it can be accessed by other applications. Another way our system is unique is in providing equal access to all tags and attributes, unlike WebSQL and W3QL, which can only refer to certain attributes of links and provide no access to attributes of other tags. Furthermore, Squeal is the only system that is built on genuine SQL, with the full power of that language.

Some powerful query systems have been built for Extensible Markup Language (XML), including Ozone [9] and XML-QL [4], both of which are influenced by relational and object-oriented databases. Because XML tags are customized and pages more structured than in SQL, these systems are able to support queries that focus more on semantics than syntax. Despite the different domain, the XML and Ozone work suggests that Squeal would benefit from support for object-oriented queries.

4.3. Status

We are in the process of creating:

- A public release of our Just-In-Time Database [21] implementation, written in Java.
- A pre-computed database containing the most popular sites on the Web in database form so it can be queried by any client.
- A forms-based text interface.
- A graphical user interface to make Squeal accessible to people who do not know SQL [15].

For the latest information about our project, see http://parasite.mills.edu

Acknowledgements

We were assisted in this research by Oren Etzioni, Keith Golden, Tom Knight, and Pattie Maes. We also benefited from interaction with Alberto Mendelzon's WebSQL group and with Alexa Internet. This paper was improved by comments from anonymous reviewers. Ellen Spertus is partially supported by a National Science Foundation Career Grant.

References

[1] S. Abiteboul and V. Vianu, Queries and computation on the Web, in: The Sixth International Conference on Database Theory (ICDT), Delphi, Greece, January 1997.

[2] G.O. Arocena, A.O. Mendelzon and G.A. Mihaila, Applications of a Web query language, in: Proc. of the Sixth International World Wide Web Conference, Santa Cruz, CA, Elsevier, Amsterdam, 1997.

[3] J. Dean and M. Henzinger, Finding related Web pages in the World Wide Web, in: Proc. of the Eighth International World Wide Web Conference, Elsevier, Amsterdam, 1999.

[4] A. Deutsch, M. Fernandez, D. Florescu, A. Levy and D. Suciu, A query language for XML, in: Proc. of the Eighth International World Wide Web Conference, Elsevier, Amsterdam, 1999.

[5] J. Hammer, H. Garcia-Molina, J. Cho, R. Aranha and A. Crespo, Extracting semi-structured information from the Web, in: Proc. of the Workshop on Management of Semistructured Data, Tucson, Arizona, 1997.

[6] M.M. Kessler, Bibliographic coupling between scientific papers, American Documentation, 14, 10-25.

[7] J. Kleinberg, Authoritative sources in a hyperlinked environment, in: Proc. 9th ACM–SIAM Symposium on Discrete Algorithms, 1998.

[8] D. Konopnicki and O. Shmueli, WWW information gathering: the W3QL query language and the W3QS system, ACM Trans. Database Syst. (1998).

[9] T. Lahiri, S. Abiteboul and J. Widom, Ozone: integrating structured and semistructured data, Technical Report, 1998.

[10] A. Mendelzon, G. Mihaila and T. Milo, Querying the World Wide Web, J. Digital Libr. 1 (1) (1997) 68–88.

[11] G.A. Mihaila, WebSQL — an SQL-like query language for the World Wide Web, Master's Thesis, University of Toronto, 1996.

[12] J.E. Pitkow, Summary of WWW characterizations, World Wide Web 2 (1–2) (1999).

[13] P. Resnick and H.R. Varian, Recommender systems (introduction to special section), Commun. ACM 40 (3) (1997) 56–58.

[14] R. Rousseau, Sitations: an exploratory study, Cybermetrics 1 (1) (1997).

[15] D. Sengupta, A visual interface for Internet information retrieval via ParaSite, MA Thesis proposal, Department of Mathematics and Computer Science, Mills College, 1999.

[16] J. Shakes, M. Langheinrich and O. Etzioni, Dynamic reference sifting: a case study in the homepage domain, in: Proc. of the Sixth International World Wide Web Conference, Elsevier, Amsterdam, 1997.

[17] U. Shardanand and P. Maes, Social information filtering: algorithms for automating 'word of mouth', in: Computer–Human Interaction (CHI), 1995.

[18] H. Small, Co-citation in the scientific literature: a new measure of the relationship between two documents, J. Am. Soc. Inf. Sci. 24 (1973) 265–269.

[19] E. Spertus, ParaSite: mining structural information on the Web, in: Proc. of the Sixth International World Wide Web Conference, Elsevier, Amsterdam, 1997.

[20] E. Spertus, ParaSite: mining the structural information on the World-Wide Web, Ph.D. Thesis, Department of EECS, MIT, Cambridge, MA, 1998.

[21] E. Spertus and L.A. Stein, Just-in-time databases and the World-Wide Web, in: Proc. of the Seventh International ACM Conference on Information and Knowledge Management, 1998.

Ellen Spertus is an assistant professor in the Department of Mathematics and Computer Science at Mills College in Oakland, California. She received her S.B. (1990), S.M. (1992), and Ph.D. (1998) in computer science from MIT, where she worked with Prof. Lynn Andrea Stein in information retrieval and Prof. William J. Dally in computer architecture. She has also worked at Microsoft Research and been a visiting scholar at the University of Washington.

Lynn Andrea Stein is an associate professor in the Department of Electrical Engineering and Computer Science and a member of the Artificial Intelligence Laboratory and the Laboratory for Computer Science at MIT. She received the A.B. degree in computer science from Harvard and Radcliffe Colleges in 1986 and the Sc.M. (1987) and Ph.D. (1990) from the Department of Computer Science at Brown University. Her research and teaching center on nontraditional computational architectures supporting interaction among programs and users.

Robust intra-document locations

Thomas A. Phelps *, Robert Wilensky [1]

University of California, Berkeley, CA, USA

Abstract

Several types of existing and next-generation hypertext functionality, including external hyperlinks, annotations, and transclusions, rely on references to locations within another resource. If the document domain cannot guarantee referential integrity, but rather is more like the World Wide Web, in which documents change regularly and without notification, potentially invalidating internal location references, it is crucial to build robustness into the intra-document location resolution mechanism, so that locations continue to function even as documents change chaotically. This paper aims to begin a process to evolve a standard for (normative) robust location descriptors and (non-normative) reattachment algorithms. We discuss criteria for evaluating the robustness of an intra-document location mechanism. Then we describe *robust locations*, an approach we believe meets these criteria. Robust locations include a standard minimal location descriptor and a recommended reattachment algorithm. We also suggest what can be done when the changes are so great that location resolution is problematic. Finally, we describe the implementation of robust locations within the Multivalent Document system.

Keywords: Robust; Location; Annotation; Multivalent; Hyperlink

1. Introduction

Hypertext research has long been concerned with the problem of the persistence of hyperlinks, that is, of dealing with problems that arise when one endpoint of a link, especially the destination, is unresolvable, because it was deleted, renamed, moved, or otherwise changed. A number of solutions have been proposed to deal with this problem when the reference is to a resource as a whole, including Handles [7], PURLs [11], URNs [17], ignoring it or requiring synchronous updates [4], W3Objects [5], Web page tracking [9], agents [8], a 'self-configuring information navigation infrastructure' [2] and Robust Hyperlinks [15]. This paper does not consider links between documents or 'resources'.

In contrast, this paper concerns 'sub-resources', that is, fragments or locations within a target resource. 'Location' is used in the sense that people use it, in terms of a 'semantic' location that, after editing, can be recovered by scanning for the area of the document that most closely resembles the old content, as opposed to a definition based on geometric distances or character/word/paragraph counts. For example, in the World Wide Web, a URL can refer to a named anchor within an HTML document, and the XML Pointer Language (XPointer [19]) provides a general scheme for addressing internal XML document structures. However, in contrast to inter-document links, the issue of robust intra-document locations has received less attention. For example,

* Corresponding author. E-mail: phelps@cs.berkeley.edu

[1] E-mail: wilensky@cs.berkeley.edu

most HTML browsers silently fail if they can locate the document but not the fragment within the document given by the URL.

We suggest that robust intra-document locations will become increasingly important: As the Web develops as an increasingly sophisticated hypertext platform, many types of advanced functionality will emerge that gainfully exploit intra-document locations. For example, Nelson's transclusions [10] extract a *portion* of one document for display within another. Likewise, 'stand-off' (or 'out-of-line' or 'out-of-band') annotation, in which annotations are stored separately from the annotated document, has numerous advantages over embedded annotation. Also, multimedia formats tend to come into existence independently from Web authoring, and hence, any structuring must be imposed upon them externally, hence mandating sub-resource referencing.

At the same time as the need for intra-document location increases, the openness of the Web will allow resources and locations to continue to change independently and chaotically. It is probably the case that resources will be modified with some frequency, even as the resource persists, hence creating the possibility that fragile sub-resource locations will fail to persist even if the persistence of resources is achieved.

2. Robustness criteria

Fortunately, it is possible to make intra-document locations 'robust' in uncontrolled, distributed environments, even when the target resource is not cooperating. By robust we mean that one should be able to make an intra-document reference to a location within an arbitrary resource, save this description, and then re-establish the location in the future, after a document has undergone some class of mutations.

We use the term 'location' as the object within a resource in need of positioning. We define locations as *indices into document content*. For example, for an HTML, XML, or plain text document, a location might be the point between two particular adjacent characters. If the document data format allows some other media element with addressable subcomponents, then the location might be the point before or after such a component, as for example the point between two frames of video. More complex locations may be built up out of primitive locations; for example, a span is the document fragment between two locations. (We do not consider locations of structural document objects, such as XML elements, per se, although we believe extension to such locations can be accommodated in a number of ways.)

To achieve robustness, two elements are needed: a *location descriptor*, which describes a location, and a *reattachment algorithm*, which attempts to reposition the descriptor within a possibly mutated target resource. We suggest that intra-document location descriptors and their associated robustness algorithms should provide a mechanism which is:

- *Robust to common changes in the referenced document.* Obviously this is the foremost requirement, without which the rest would be moot.
- *Gracefully degrading in the face of increasing change to the document.* Reattachment should proceed only if the computed location is likely to be the same location semantically as before the mutation. Hence minor changes should not pose much threat to reattachment; larger changes should cause reattachment to fail proportionally to the degree of change; if the change is too great, reattachment should fail. In information retrieval terms, the robustness algorithms need to minimize false positives, even at the cost of losing a small amount of accuracy (missing real, if greatly changed, positives). Thus, the reattachment algorithms should measure the likely quality of matches, and have a means to report failures to the user.
- *Based on document content.* For documents that change infrequently, and which have a fixed layout format, for example those based on scanned page images, and perhaps Adobe's PDF [1], it might be acceptable to rely upon geometric positions to indicate locations (although even here, if the document is expected to undergo editing in the future, it would be useful to anchor annotations to document content). Such an approach is certainly unsatisfactory for 'flowed' document types, such as HTML and XML, because the page geometry depends on window size, font size, font family, and other factors that vary widely from viewer to viewer. (One annotation system that does work on Web documents, Hot Off the Web

[6], fixes the document dimensions, thus violating any number of usability guidelines.) Basing locations on document content gives a basis for robustness. Locations based on content will be resolvable independent of presentation characteristics. Moreover, if a document changes, reattachment algorithms based on finding 'similar' content have some chance of finding the intended location even if a unrelated parts of the document change dramatically, and if relevant parts change only modestly.

- *Work with uncooperative servers.* A cooperative server could track and report all changes to its document collection, and notify interested parties when changes happen. Ideally, every server on the Web would be cooperative, and speak the same versioning protocol. An even more cooperative server would manage reattachment as well: accepting references to its contents, storing them, and revising them whenever needed. Given that it is unlikely that even a small fraction of servers on the Web will behave this way, a successful robustness strategy will need to husband all the data needed for the robustness algorithms within itself. On the other hand, once this requirement is met, the strategy will immediately operate on the universe of servers.
- *Extensible, to multimedia and various document types.* Documents can contain multimedia elements, such as images and video, and new document types are developed regularly. A robust location mechanism should extend naturally to accommodate these and new varied types in the future, without breaking existing locations.
- *Work with existing documents, servers, and clients.* Ideally, a solution would silently improve the existing world, but obviously any implementation has to involve at least servers or clients. At one extreme, the location descriptor could contain a complete edit trail of every character insertion and deletion, with timestamps, as in Nelson's Xanadu [10]. Or the descriptor could be a versioning history of edits in larger chunks and time periods. However, such descriptors would not be available even for all cooperating servers. It has been suggested [12] that each unit of a document can be made robustly addressable by giving each element a unique ID. However, we think it is unlikely that such IDs will soon become universal even within document types that support them. Even then, one could not use such a scheme to robustly identify locations within non-trivial media elements, such as spans of text, much less within media types not supporting this particular addressing scheme.
- *Straightforward to implement.* We want robust locations to be widely supported, which is to say, implemented by many people on many computing platforms in many computer languages. We believe that simplicity and ease of implementation are important in this regard, as the widespread deployment of XML over the more complex SGML suggests.
- *Relatively small.* To be practical, locations should be a manageable size, relative to documents, thus ruling out schemes that exploit complete edit trails, and so on, even if such were readily available.

Note that we have not added any criteria with respect to usability. This is because we expect that, to be effective, location descriptors will have to be automatically generated by clients, rather than hand-crafted by humans. Moreover, the details of the location descriptor should not concern most users.

3. Robust locations

We now describe a strategy, called *robust locations*, to meet the above criteria. The core of the strategy is to (i) provide automatically generated location descriptors, which comprise multiple descriptions of a location, each of which captures different aspects of the document, and (ii) use heuristics when a descriptor does not resolve directly to a location to hypothesize the intended location, along with a measure of the degree of confidence in the hypothesized location.

Robust locations rely on the presumption of a document object model against which location descriptors are interpreted. We call this model the 'simple, general document object model', or SGDOM. SGDOM is much simpler and more general than the XML or HTML DOM, in that it is meant to accommodate common aspects of a very wide class of possible document types. It is straightforward to map the primary structures of the XML or HTML documents onto this model, so clients specializing in these formats can create and interpret robust locations as well.

Briefly, the SGDOM describes a document as a tree of typed internal nodes (such as named XML elements), with terminal nodes being 'media elements'. The node types and the media elements are determined by the document type, according to a (hopefully well-defined) canonicalization process. Media elements are presumed to have a simple scalar index, whose meaning is determined by that media type.

For example, to interpret an HTML document according to the SGDOM for HTML, one follows the HTML parse tree, but splices out markup tags that merely serve to associated properties with spans of text, rather than truly structure content. That is, tags such as B, A, and SPAN are ignored for purposes of the model. In addition, nodes are added for text media types (so that an index into a text media element indicates the place before or after a character position).

The SGDOM allows nodes to have unique IDs, à la SGML/XML ID attribute types. However, there is no formal notion of attributes per se (or of processing instructions, or declarations, or other SGML/XML features) in the model.

3.1. Multiple location methods

Robust location descriptors describe locations redundantly, using a number of different data records. Each record type provides different quality-of-reattachment and robustness characteristics. Taken together, they provide considerable resilience.

Here we propose a core set of location descriptor records that are easy to generate, simple to understand and implement, and appear to work well in practice. Implementors are free to supplement these records with addition records, as described below.

(1) A *unique identifier (UID)* is a name unique within the document, as per ID attributes in SGML/XML. These survive the most violent document changes, except its own deletion. As noted above, such identifiers will be available only through the foresight of the document author, and even then, only for locations corresponding to document elements, but not sub-element or non-element content.

(2) A *tree walk* describes the path from the root of the document, through internal structural nodes, to a point within media content at a leaf. In practice, tree walks are the central component of robust locations. Since tree walks incrementally refine the structural position in the document as the walk proceeds from root to leaf, they are robust to deletions of content that defeat unique ID and context locations. Thus, tree walks are especially helpful for documents such as those that transclude dynamic content, as with stock quotes, where the content itself changes while the structural position remains constant. We describe tree walks with a sequence of node child numbers and associated node tags (generic identifiers), terminating with an offset into a media element. This is both a simpler, less expressive, and more redundant, representation than is allowed by XPointer. For example, consider the following tree walk into a particular HTML document:

```
21/Professor/8 0/<TEXT>0/ADDRESS
  1/H3 0/BODY0/HTML
```

Reading from right to left, the example can be decoded as starting at the root, taking its 0th child element, which should be labelled 'HTML', then taking that node's first child (numbered zero) to a node named 'BODY', taking its second child, a node named 'H3', taking its first child, 'ADDRESS', then taking its first element, which should be a media leaf element labelled with its type, here '<TEXT>'. The final portion of the descriptor, here 21/Professor/8, is always medium-specific. We propose that TEXT can profitably be divided into words, as this provides robustness to any editing within other words. Thus, here the 21/Professor portion follows the pattern of the tree walk in implicitly treating its words as child nodes, such that the 22nd word should be 'Professor'. The 8 is then an offset eight characters into this word, resolving to the point between the 'o' and 'r'.

(3) *Context* is a small amount of previous and following information from the document tree. We propose a context record containing a sequence of document content prior to the location, and a sequence of document content following the location. For example, for the location described by the tree walk above, let us suppose the word 'Professor' was found in a sentence fragment that reads 'congratula-

tions on her promotion to Professor in the Computer Science Division'. The context descriptor could be:

```
her+promotion+to+Professor+
  in+the+Computer+Science
```

with the previous and following context separated by a space, and metacharacters, including space, encoded with the same method as URL metacharacters. The amount of context to be saved can be arbitrarily large. (Here we use up 25 characters, which may be truncated at text element boundaries.) Context records work well for short documents, which can be searched quickly. Moreover, in event of a failure, the saved context can be reported to the user as a facsimile of the former location. Without supporting location methods, however, simple context can easily be confused by the same pattern of words elsewhere in the document, a danger that grows larger the longer the document.

4. The robust location reattachment algorithm

Algorithms that exploit the multiple location descriptors can detect and correctly reattach many otherwise unresolvable references in the presence of a large class of changes. Here we present a 'basic' reattachment algorithm, which reflects how we designed location descriptions to be used, and which we believe exploits them well. We do not claim this to be an optimal reattachment algorithm — many sensible variations of this algorithm, not to mention altogether different algorithms, are certainly possible, and determining the best algorithm requires empirical data we have yet to collect. Note, though, that the robust reference scheme does not require that user agents all implement the same reattachment algorithm.

Our algorithm first uses the unique identifier, then the tree walk descriptor, and then the context descriptor, continuing only if the previously tried methods are ineffective. We describe the details of each submethod below.

4.1. Unique ID submethod

First, if the location has a UID, and the same UID is located in the document, the location is presumed to be resolved. This is because UIDs will presumably be used so as to not change their meaning via editing. Moreover, they will generally survive normal editing operations, unless the element itself is deleted. However, we presume that UIDs will generally only be available at key points in a document. (In theory, UIDs could be mechanically generated for every position, but this would only be possible for document formats that support them, SGML/XML but not ASCII or scanned images, and only if the source document can be modified. Moreover, automatic generation of UIDs would vitiate any useful semantic value that makes them privileged referrers in the first place.)

Failure to reattach via UID (that is, when there is no UID in the location, or the UID in the document has been deleted) causes control to yield to the tree walk submethod.

4.2. Tree walk submethod

In practice, the tree walk submethod is the workhorse reattachment method, due to the usual absence of a UID and the fact that its strong robustness properties are quite successful in resolving locations.

As shown in Fig. 1, the tree walk exhibits strong natural robustness. In resolving the walk from root to leaf, changes of any magnitude within following sibling subtrees are safely contained. The walk is also invariant with non-structural changes to previous sibling trees.

However, it is affected by structural changes to them. For example, introducing a new previous sibling, or removing one, can invalidate the walk. Tree walks can be made much more robust with heuristics that repair broken paths. We check that a walk is valid by checking each node name, which is redundantly recorded in a robust location; for media indices, the general algorithm only checks that the indexed element can be found, after which control is passed to a medium-specific model that may have its own robustness methods.

Suppose that matching a tree walk of a robust location against the actual runtime tree fails at the exact saved offset (that is, that the walk is matched successfully up to the leaf, but that the leaf is of the wrong type, or that the index of the media element is

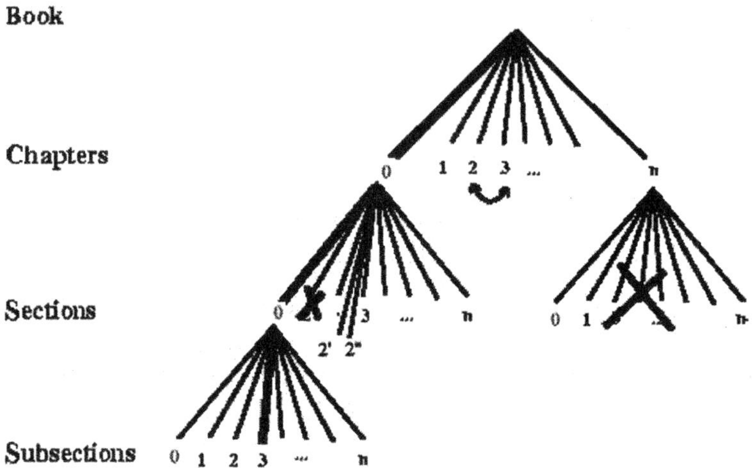

Fig. 1. The tree walk method exhibits strong natural robustness. Areas that have been deleted, inserted, or interchanged in other subtrees may not even affect the desired tree path if the changed subtrees would be examined after the desired path in a depth-first traversal. Those at or after such modifications may be recovered by the algorithm.

invalid). Then matching is tried, first, on the following sibling node, then on the previous sibling, then on the second following, the second previous and so on until the node names match. If the match fails previously, the same strategy is employed, with the proviso that the rest of the walk succeeds (possibly with additional approximations to exact matches). If no match can be found, we hypothesize that a new level of hierarchy was introduced, and skip a level of the tree. If still no match is found, we hypothesize that a level of hierarchy was removed, and skip the current location node/offset descriptor pair. If none of these attempts yields a match, the match attempt fails.

Each level of departure from the original description adds a weighted value to an overall 'unreliability' factor for the match thus far. Moving to the following or previous sibling adds a small amount of uncertainty, with increasingly larger amounts as the siblings tested grow farther away, and skipping or assuming a level of hierarchy adds a larger amount. If the factor exceeds a client-defined bound, the tree walk match attempt fails.

This algorithm makes saved tree paths robust against any number and combination of sibling insertions, deletions and reorderings at any or numerous levels of the document tree. The search pattern prefers siblings closest to the saved location, rather than, say, searching from the parent's first child to its last, reasoning that the closest match is most likely the best match. This search tactic has the desirable algorithmic property that the first match found is also the closest.

There are a number of circumstances in which the tree walk submethod will perform a questionable realignment. For example, it may happen that a numerical offset now refers to a new node of exactly the same name as the original, in which case a match would be reported at that point. However, it is likely that such a coincidence will not occur for the remainder of the subtree rooted at that node, and this false match will be caught, and another match attempted. (If the entirely new tree is identical to the original, the match will succeed without any penalty, a situation which some may consider as a flaw, however unlikely this is in practice.)

Media elements may marshall their own robustness tactics. For example, as noted above, we segment textual media elements into words, and a tree walk locator may refer to a point between characters within a word. For the purposes of resolving such references, we can treat the words just as if they are element names, and just continue to apply the same tree walk resolution method. For example, suppose one attempts to resolve such a location in a situation in which the word prior to the one containing the location has been deleted. Assuming that the word following the original target word was not the same, the tree walk now becomes invalidated, because the word asserted to be in a given position is not the same as the one that is there. However, the progressively widening searching heuristic will quickly find the target word in its new position.

4.3. Context submethod

If the structural document tree has been changed too much for the tree walk's tactics to recover — perhaps a sentence has been cut from one chapter and pasted into another far away — re-registration is attempted using the context data record.

As with the tree walk, the closest match to the original position is the preferred one. A search is done forward and backward, with the nearer match chosen. If neither direction matches, more and more of the context is shed until a match is found, or until the length of the string used for the search drops below a threshold.

The initial search position is set from the furthest extent that the tree walk described above could be resolved. This sets a restricted domain within which to search, which benefits proximity matching and performance. If no match is found within a subtree, the search climbs up the tree by one node and tries again within that subtree until a match is found or it has climbed to the root. Within a subtree, leaves are searched left to right.

As with tree walk matching, an overall unreliability factor for the match is maintained. As the search examines ever larger subtrees, the unreliability is increased. If some but not all of the context is matched, unreliability is increased.

Approximate string matching, while not presently implemented, should prove invaluable in matching context, as it is robust to the small changes typically found in spelling corrections.

4.4. Match outcomes

At the end of the match, several results are possible: the match may succeed without the use of reattachment heuristics; it may succeed using the heuristics, with a small unreliability factor; it may succeed with a large unreliability factor; or, it may fail (that is, the reliability factor is too large — infinite if there is no match at all).

Where reattachment fails, we require that clients present this fact to users. Clients may have different policies for handling the other cases. For instance, a client may not inform the user at all of what it considers to be minor reattachements; it may flag reattachments considered somewhat unreliable, perhaps asking the user to verify the repositioned object.

4.5. Meeting the robustness criteria

Robustness is achieved within and among the submethods of unique ID, tree walk, and context. The methods elaborated above provide for graceful degrading in performance with increasing change to the document. (We describe some limited empirical experience below.) Also, robust locations are based on document content, as required.

Although the implementation details of digital document systems differ in the ease of implementation of different location types, the three given are probably among the easiest across a range of systems. Within HTML/XML clients, unique IDs are in principle already available, as some variation is used for intra-document anchors. With increasing support for the Document Object Model (DOM) [19], tree walks are available to scripts in various programming languages. If tree navigation is available, then context is available with a search.

Location descriptors are self contained, needing nothing from a server beyond the document to which it refers. Their records can easily be stored separately from the document to which they refer.

Locations can be managed entirely at the client, and an implementation there would immediately bring the benefits to all existing documents and servers.

As the example below shows, an individual location record, which concatenates these three subtypes, is small; in the current implementation, each generally costs about 50–100 bytes.

Although the location descriptor has not been extended to many multimedia data types, this need has been prepared for. A tree walk should be successful to the degree to which the new data type is structured. If nothing else, the final element in the walk is the offset into the leaf. Text uses it as a character offset, but other media types could encode medium-specific internal coordinates.

As well as new media types, the system is open to new location submethods, as for instance the 'minimal unique string' method used by the ComMentor annotation system [16]. While too complicated to mandate for a minimal standard, this system uses a Patricia tree data structure to identify locations with the smallest unique string in the document, and although it seems that the addition of a single character could render this location non-unique, when coupled with an initial character offset, it reportedly works well in practice. This method could be added in parallel to the unique ID, tree walk and context methods, or perhaps as the way context is computed, with the mandate that systems must ignore methods they do not understand, just as Web browsers ignore tags they do not recognize.

5. Implementation

We have implemented robust locations within the Multivalent Document system [14,18]. Our implementation lacks application to a variety of media types and testing by a large user community, but otherwise has proven robust beyond expectation.

5.1. Example

Below is an example containing a number of robust locations. In the Multivalent system, a hub document describes a number of *layers* and *behaviors* which the client assembles into a document. One of the layers is a base layer, from which the primary document representation is constructed. The other layers and behaviors may provide arbitrary functionality, including, but not restricted to, various forms of annotation. Since the layers and behaviors are all potentially separate resources, a hub document may be used to describe stand-off annotations on a document.

Such is the case in our example, Fig. 2, which is presented by a Multivalent client. In this example, three annotations appear on an HTML page: a PostIt-style note, a 'REPLACEMENT' copyedit annotation on the main document text, and 'COMMENT' copyedit annotation on the text in the note. Each of the annotations is separate from the HTML page, and so the two copyedit annotations refer to their targets via robust locations. In particular, each of these is an instance of a large class of 'span' annotations, each of which has a starting and ending location. So, each of these annotations uses a pair of robust locations. (The note is positioned geometrically, and so does not use robust locations. However, one could attach a note, or some non-span annotation, to some base document text, in which case robust locations could also be used.)

The presentation is created by the Multivalent client from the following hub document (Fig. 3). The hub is itself an XML document. Of the 'Span' elements each describes one of the two copyeditor annotations. Each Span has a 'Start' and an 'End' element, each of which contains a robust location. Each location data item component is encoded by a separate attribute, namely, UID, TREE, and CONTEXT, which are shown in italics. (There are no UIDs in the example, as there were none in the target document, as is typical.)

Note that the spans have augmented the robust locations by adding a CONTENT attribute that contains the textual content along the extent of the span. If

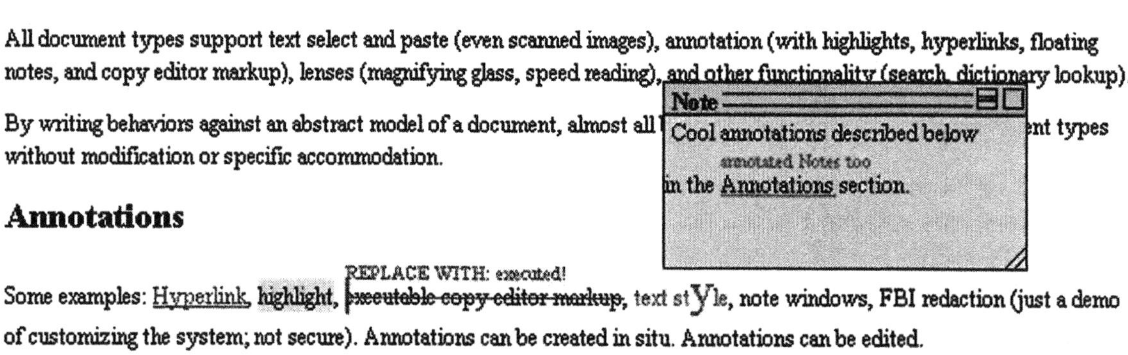

All document types support text select and paste (even scanned images), annotation (with highlights, hyperlinks, floating notes, and copy editor markup), lenses (magnifying glass, speed reading), and other functionality (search, dictionary lookup).

By writing behaviors against an abstract model of a document, almost all [...]nt types without modification or specific accommodation.

Note

Cool annotations described below

annotated Notes too

in the Annotations section.

Annotations

REPLACE WITH: executed!

Some examples: Hyperlink, highlight, ~~executable copy editor markup~~, text style, note windows, FBI redaction (just a demo of customizing the system; not secure). Annotations can be created in situ. Annotations can be edited.

Fig. 2. Some stand-off annotations on an HTML document.

```
<MULTIVALENT URL="systemresource:/sys/splash/Multivalent.html"
 SEARCHNB="ON" GENRE="HTML">

<Layer NAME="Personal" BEHAVIOR="multivalent.Layer" URL="inline">

<Span BEHAVIOR="multivalent.std.span.ReplaceWithSpan" CREATEDAT="942341857100"
 NB="COPYEDNB" CONTENT="executable+copy+editormarkup" LENGTH="29"
 INSERT="executed">
<Start BEHAVIOR="multivalent.Location"
 TREE="4/executable/0 0/<TEXT> 11/P 2/BODY 0/HTML" CONTEXT="highlight+executable+copy">
</Start>
<End BEHAVIOR="multivalent.Location"
 TREE="7/markup/6 0/<TEXT> 11/P 2/BODY 0/HTML" CONTEXT="editor+markup text>
</End>
</Span>

<Note NAME="NOTE1011000469" BEHAVIOR="Note" X="300" Y="100" WIDTH="193" HEIGHT="98"
 POSTED="TRUE">
 Cool annotations described below in the Annotations section.</Note>

<Span BEHAVIOR="multivalent.std.span.AwkSpan" CREATEDAT="942342203130"
 CONTENT="AnnotationsAnnotations" NB="COPYEDNB" LENGTH="12"
 COMMENT="annotated+Notes+too" ROOT="NOTE1011000469">
<Start BEHAVIOR="multivalent.Location"
 TREE="10/Annotations/0 0/<TEXT> 0/LINE 0/NOTE 0/CONTENT" CONTEXT="the Annotation+section.">
</Start>
<End BEHAVIOR="multivalent.Location"
 TREE="10/Annotations/11 0/<TEXT> 0/LINE 0/NOTE 0/CONTENT"
 CONTEXT="the+Annotations section.">
</End>
</Span>

</Layer>
</MULTIVALENT>
```

Fig. 3. A 'hub' document, which persistently captures some annotations and their corresponding robust location descriptors.

a failure happens in one of its endpoints, the other can be estimated by taking an offset the length of the CONTENT from the successful one. In addition, the second span augments the basic location resolution mechanism by anchoring to a secondary tree root, that for the Post-it note.

This hub document was itself generated by the user first opening some document, initially the underlying base document, and then using a Multivalent client to create annotations. The hub document is generated upon saving. Thus, the entire hub document, including the robust locations, was generated automatically.

5.2. Failed reattachments

The screen dump in Fig. 4 shows one strategy we have implemented for handling failed reattachments. It presents to the user a floating note listing unattachable spans, which have been reconstituted within the note from the saved context, to which the locations, here paired in a span annotation, are placed.

The screen dump in Fig. 5 shows an associated user interface we have implemented to allow the user to manually reposition an un-attachable span. The user first makes a selection, of which the end points will serve as the new start and end points of the annotation, moves the cursor into the unattachable span in the note, clicks the mouse, and finally, chooses `Morph to Current Selection` to move the reconstituted span to its new location.

5.3. Testing

Properly testing robust locations requires real use by a user community. Our Multivalent client is still

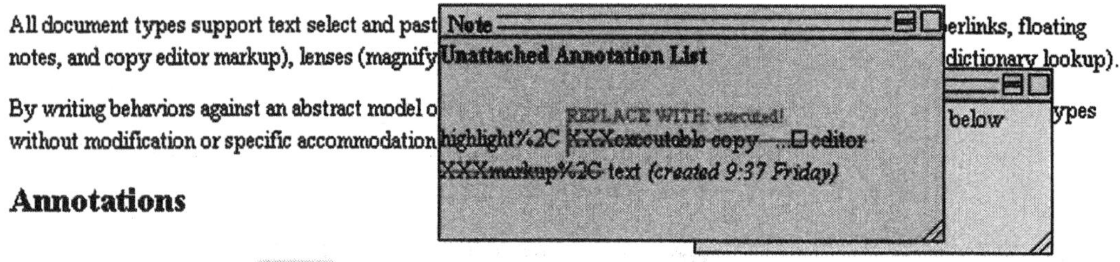

Fig. 4. In the Multivalent system, locations that cannot be reattached manually, here paired in a span annotation, are represented to the user, reconstituted with the CONTEXT text and carrying the same annotation.

a prototype, so such studies have not yet been undertaken. We offer the following relevant pieces of evidence that the algorithm will work well in practice, acknowledging that they are no substitute for actual measurement.

We collected some data using a prototype, less sophisticated implementation of robust locations in TkMan [13], a browser for UNIX manual pages that has been in use by a sizeable community for some time. Specifically, of 754 annotations that needed repositioning because the referenced Man pages underwent change out of control of the annotator, 742 annotations were automatically repositioned, leaving 12 to be reapplied by the user. In most of the latter cases, the associated position had in fact been deleted entirely.

We tested the implementation described here by creating a number of robust locations for some documents we manage, and then mutating the documents in various ways. The algorithm performed extremely well. Indeed, to generate the example of unattachable links shown above, we tried to make the algorithm fail by repeated modifications of the base document, but gave up in frustration, as a different robustness submethod would continually correctly identify the proper location. Instead, we eventually broke the location descriptor itself manually.

Perhaps more compelling is our use of this robust location implementation on a number of documents which were not under our control. In one case, we posted some annotations on the DARPA home page, which we left unchanged for over one year. During this time, each annotation reattached correctly through many alterations of the page, including one in which the page was apparently imported into an HTML authoring tool, which placed the entire document content into cells of a newly introduced table. (The location finally broke when a major Website redesign using frames rendered the location to the page completely meaningless.)

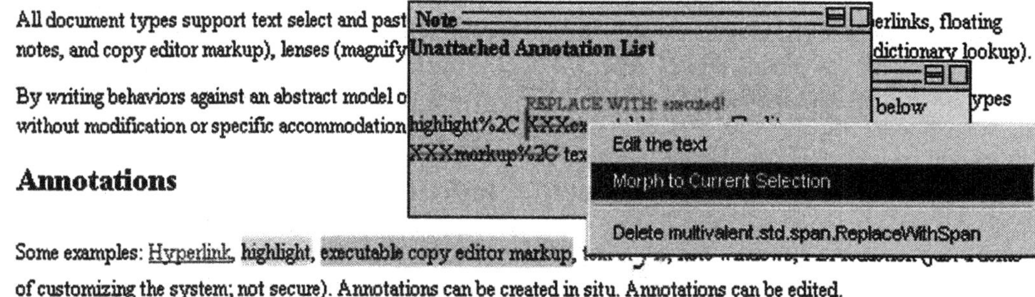

Fig. 5. The user can reassociate a span annotation by selecting the correct location and making a choice from a pop-up context menu in the reconstituted span.

6. Related work

6.1. Webvise

Webvise [3] is an open hypermedia service that provides a variety of services including "the ability for users collaboratively to create links from parts of HTML Web pages they do not own and support for creating links to parts of Web pages without writing HTML target tag" and "supports certain repairs of links that break due to modified Web pages".

Webvise proposes location specifications ('locSpecs') for a variety of media, and redundantly stores locSpecs. For instance, for a span of text, the locSpec attributes are:

- Reference: a bookmark ID or a HTML target name.
- Selection: the text of the span to search for.
- Selection context: some surrounding text.
- Axis: a position, such as start position, and length of span on a character axis.

Thus, Webvise and our robust location proposal share some goals and approaches. Webvise describes locSpecs for several media types, such as database records, not considered here.

The present work adds to the Webvise work a tree walk location method. As suggested above, the tree walk is essential for live transclusions, and has the desirable properties of working with any structured media type, working on partially constructed trees (subtrees can be faulted in on demand), being robust to user actions that can produce large changes in the document such as swapping chapters, and, even when it does fail, providing a more focussed domain for a context search. We also introduce a set reattachment algorithms, with an explicit relationship among them, and the use of an internal measure of the amount of divergence from the saved specification. Finally, the present work proposes a user interface for dealing felicitously with locations that could not be reattached automatically.

6.2. ComMentor

ComMentor [16], which annotates HTML pages, records the shortest unique substring (based on string position trees, implemented as Patricia trees) and redundant context.

Evaluated against our criteria, ComMentor has a number of drawbacks. The computation of the Patricia tree data structure is complex, at least compared to the proposed methods. The computation does not scale up, as the entire document must be processed to guarantee uniqueness, whereas, for example, the tree walk need not even instantiate a subtree that it does not traverse, perhaps faulting in that subtree on demand. If locations are made on documents in progress, such as those used by annotations on documents being collaboratively written, unique strings may be relatively short when the document is short, but then lose their uniqueness as the document grows, leading to failure. If the reattachment fails, degradation is not graceful, as there is no way to choose among possible matches. It is not easy to see how Patricia trees generalize to multimedia content.

6.3. XPointer/XLink

The task of marking a location and then recovering it in the future in the face of change seems to be outside the domain of XPointer [19]. Given that XLink [19] uses XPointer as its locator mechanism, out-of-line XLink links are not robust.

XPointer describes many means for traversing a document tree, including node position, and ID and attribute values. If a program knows where it is going, it can get there with an appropriate means. However, XPointer leaves to the client the choice of what to do if a previously stored tree path is no longer available in the current runtime tree. In fact, XPointer and the present work do not conflict: XPointer concerns tree traversal, and the present work monitors the traversal for correctness and takes recovery action when the path diverges from what is expected.

6.4. Microcosm

The Microcosm system [4] can piggyback on top of other systems, such as Microsoft Word, and augment it with new or improved hypertext functionality.

The authors of Microcosm suggest that, although the "editing problem" (as they call it) "is probably a major flaw in the Microcosm model when it comes to scaling up to deal with globally distributed documents", in their experience, documents do not change frequently enough that the lack of a solution is debilitating. According to their analysis (p. 90):

- Typically, around 50% of all links have source anchors which are generic [queries] or local. Documents containing such links may be freely edited without causing any problems.
- Typically about 50% of destination anchors are the 'top of the document' [geometric]. Again, such documents may be edited without causing problems.
- Documents consisting of bitmapped pictures, videos and sound are very rarely edited, and even when they are, it is very rarely in such a way as to alter offsets of objects within them.
- Documents such as object drawing and spreadsheets, which use the name of an object [a unique ID] rather than some offset to identify an anchor, are not subject to editing problems, so long as the edit does not change the object's name.

Nevertheless, some documents are problematic, and Microcosm does not offer good solutions for handling them. One of their proposed approach prevents mutable documents from participating in links, and the other approach requires that documents be editing together with all their links.

7. Future work

The proposed mechanisms seem to work well in limited use, but they need to be tested with a wider public. Some refinement of the heuristic weightings requires measurement of the typical kinds of locations needed by users in everyday work, and measurement of the changes documents undergo. For example, short context strings worked well in our limited experimentation, but we suspect that longer strings would be better in extended applications, and increasing the amount of context can be done inexpensively.

The proposed mechanisms have not been tested on multimedia data types very much. Microcosm argues that non-text types do not change frequently. Webvise seems to have made a good start at defining location methods for a number of diverse media types.

Many alternative reattachment algorithms are possible, ranging from variations of the one we propose (for example, using approximate string matching rather than exact string match) to entirely different mechanisms. Comparisons of such algorithms would be most useful.

Here we encoded robust locations as a set of element attributes. It might be useful to include robust intra-document locations in URLs as well. To do so, one could device a syntax to allow robust locations to extend URLs, as per XPointer (perhaps by extending XPointer syntax). Alternatively, one could shoehorn robust locations into the current URL syntax, analogously to the way we propose doing so for robust URLs in [15].

8. Conclusion

The examples of Webvise, Microcosm, ComMentor, XLink, Multivalent Documents, and others suggest an increasing need for robust intra-document locations. There appears to be incipient agreement in some areas: a unique ID is a good primary descriptor, if it exists. Several authors have found a context fragment to be useful. We make the case for adding tree walks, and for algorithms that combine all these sources.

Therefore, we think it appropriate that the next step be a Web working draft that defines the robust location specification so that makers of Web browsers and tools can begin generating robust location descriptors. We believe this process should prove relatively straightforward, even if robustness algorithms may take more time to perfect and implement.

Acknowledgements

This research was supported by Digital Libraries Initiative, under grant NSF CA98-17353.

Appendix A. Comparison of Algorithms

The following table summarizes the types of robustness of locations.

Method	Type	Robust to change type	Backoff tactic	Quality of reattachment
Unique identifier	Core method	any except deletion of itself	n/a	Perfect
		deletion	none	n/a
Tree path	Core method	insert/delete/reorder siblings	search siblings of decreasing propinquity	gracefully degrades
		add/remove level of hierarchy	skip or pseudo match level	
Context	Core method	location moved anywhere	search within matched tree path, prefer closest	gracefully degrades
		move and context changed	match less contest, increasing unreliability	
		move and context changed	fuzzy/approximate string match (unimplemented)	
(Failure)	Implementation dependent	n/a	Manual reattachment	n/a
Span (built on top of base types)	Extension	loss of one endpoint	Attach missing endpoint at fixed offset from the other	gracefully degrades
(Media-specific extensions)	Extensions	(medium-specific)	(medium-specific)	(medium specific)

References

[1] Adobe Systems, Acrobat 4.0, http://www.adobe.com/products/acrobat/main.html.

[2] P. Francis, T. Kambayashi, S. Sato and S. Shimizu, Ingrid: a self-configuring information navigation infrastructure, December 11–14, 1995, http://www.ingrid.org/francis/www4/Overview.html.

[3] K. Grønbæk, L. Sloth and P. Ørbæk, Webvise: browser and proxy support for open hypermedia structuring mechanisms on the WWW, in: Proc. Eighth World Wide Web Conference 1999, Toronto, Canada, http://www8.org/w8-papers/3a-search-query/webvise/webvise.html.

[4] W. Hall, H. Davis and G. Hutchings, Rethinking Hypertext: A Microcosm Approach, Kluwer, Dordrecht, 1996.

[5] D. Ingham, S. Caughey and M. Little, Fixing the 'broken-link' problem: the W3Objects approach, Comp. Networks ISDN Syst. 28 (7–11) (1996) 1255–1268, Proc. Fifth International World Wide Web Conference, Paris, France, 6–10 May 1996, http://arjuna.ncl.ac.uk/group/papers/p050.html.

[6] Insight Development, Hot off the Web software, http://www.hotofftheweb.com/.

[7] R. Kahn and R. Wilensky, A framework for distributed digital object services, cnri.dlib/tn95-01, May 13, 1995, http://www.cnri.reston.va.us/k-w.html.

[8] S. Macskassy and L. Shklar, Maintaining information resources, in: Proc. Third International Workshop on Next Generation Information Technologies (NGITS'97), June 30–July 3, 1997, Neve Ilan, Israel, http://www.cs.rutgers.edu/~shklar/papers/ngits97/.

[9] Mind-it, http://www.netmind.com/html/individual.html.

[10] T.H. Nelson, Computer Lib/Dream Machines, 1974, also see the Xanadu home page, http://www.xanadu.net/.

[11] OCLC PURL Service, http://www.purl.org.

[12] F. Olken, private communication.

[13] T.A. Phelps, TkMan: a man born again, X Resource 1 (10) (1994) 33–46.

[14] T.A. Phelps, Multivalent Documents: Anytime, Anywhere, Any Type, Every Way User-Improvable Digital Documents and Systems, Ph.D. Dissertation, University of California, Berkeley, UC Berkeley Division of Computer Science Technical Report No. UCB/CSD-98-1026, December 1998, also see the general and technical home pages, http://www.cs.berkeley.edu/~phelps/papers/dissertation-abstract.html, http://www.cs.berkeley.edu/~wilensky/MVD.html, http://www.cs.berkeley.edu/~phelps/Multivalent/.

[15] T.A. Phelps and R. Wilensky, Robust hyperlinks cost just five words each, University of California, Berkeley Computer Science Technical Report, CSD-00-1091, 2000, http://www.cs.berkeley.edu/~wilensky/robust-hyperlinks.html.

[16] M. Roscheisen, C. Mogensen and T. Winograd, Beyond browsing: shared comments, SOAPs, trails, and on-line communities, in: Proc. Third World Wide Web Conference: Technology, Tools and Applications, Darmstadt, April 1995.

[17] K. Sollins and L. Masinter, Functional requirements for uniform resource names, Network Working Group Request for Comments 1737, December 1994, http://www.w3.org/Addressing/rfc1737.txt.

[18] R. Wilensky and T.A. Phelps, Multivalent documents: a new model for digital documents, University of California, Berkeley Computer Science Technical Report, CSD-98-999, March 13, 1998, http://www.cs.berkeley.edu/~phelps/papers/techrep98-abstract.html.

[19] World Wide Web Consortium, Structured Vector Graphics (SVG), XPointer, XLink, Document Object Model (DOM), http://www.w3.org.

Tom Phelps earned his Ph.D. in computer science in 1998 from the University of California, Berkeley.

Robert Wilensky is a Professor at the University of California, Berkeley. He is Principal Investigator of UC Berkeley's Digital Library Initiative Project.

Integrating keyword search into XML query processing

Daniela Florescu [a,*,1], Donald Kossmann [b,2], Ioana Manolescu [a,1]

[a] *INRIA, Rocquencourt, BP 105, 78153 Le Chesnay, France*
[b] *Lehrstuhl für Dialogorientierte Systeme, University of Passau, D-94030 Passau, Germany*

Abstract

Due to the popularity of the XML data format, several query languages for XML have been proposed, specially devised to handle data of which the structure is unknown, loose, or absent. While these languages are rich enough to allow for querying the content and structure of an XML document, a varying or unknown structure can make formulating queries a very difficult task. We propose an extension to XML query languages that enables *keyword search* at the granularity of XML elements, that helps novice users formulate queries, and also yields new optimization opportunities for the query processor. We present an implementation of this extension on top of a commercial RDBMS; we then discuss implementation choices and performance results. © 2000 Published by Elsevier Science B.V. All rights reserved.

Keywords: XML query processing; Full-text index

1. Introduction

There is no doubt that XML is rapidly becoming one of the most important data formats. It is already used for scientific data (e.g., DNA sequences), in linguistics (e.g., the Treebank database at the University of Pennsylvania), to annotate large documents (e.g., Shakespeare's work), or for data exchange on the Internet (e.g., for electronic commerce). Furthermore, large software vendors, including IBM, Microsoft, and Oracle, as well as a large number of new start-ups are developing tools to manage XML data and applications which are based on XML.

One of the strengths of XML is that it can be used to represent *structured data* (i.e., records) as well as *unstructured data* (i.e., text). For example, XML can be used in a hospital to represent (structured) information about patients (e.g., name, address, birth date) and (unstructured) observations from doctors. To take advantage of this strength, however, it is important to have tools that can work effectively with both kinds of data; it is in particular important to have XML query languages which *select* records from the structured part of an XML document and *search* for information in text. For instance, it should be possible to pose one query that finds all patients that are older than 45 years and have some specific symptoms.

Keyword search is also important to query XML data with a regular structure, if the user does not know the structure or only knows the structure partially. Such a situation arises frequently on the Web; a user visits an (XML) Web site, but does not know (and does not want to know) how the data are stored at that Web site. For instance, a user who wants to buy a car on the Internet might not know how exactly

* Corresponding author.
[1] E-mail: {Daniela.Florescu,Ioana.Manolescu}@inria.fr
[2] E-mail: kossmann@db.fmi.uni-passau.de

the price and category of a car are represented at the dealer's Web site; rather than looking at the DTD, the user would prefer to directly ask for all cars with *price* $< \$1000$; this query involves a keyword search for *price* and the evaluation of a predicate on the value of *price*.

A third reason to integrate keyword search into XML query processing is to query several XML documents at the same time. Again, a user might be interested in buying a cheap car on the Internet; this time, however, the user wants to get information from several car dealers at once. The car dealers may store their data in different ways, but all car dealers that the user is interested in will somehow specify a *price* for each car. The user query will be the same as in the previous paragraph, i.e., the query will involve keyword search on *price* even if the user knows exactly how each car dealer stores his/her data.

Both regular (structured) XML query processing and keyword search have been studied extensively in previous work. (We will give an overview of related work in Section 6.) To date, however, nobody has ever shown how both features can be combined. Extending an XML query language for keyword search and showing how such an extended query language can be implemented is the purpose of this paper.

1.1. The role of relational database systems

Obviously, there are many alternative ways to process XML queries with keyword search. In this work, we propose to exploit a standard, off-the-shelf relational database system (RDBMS) as much as possible. Examples of popular RDBMS products are IBM DB2, Microsoft SQL Server, or Oracle 8. Using an RDBMS has several advantages. First, as we will see, it is very easy to build an extended XML query processor that integrates keyword search on top of an RDBMS; it already provides most of the functionality that is required. Second, RDBMSs are universally available. Most organizations have an RDBMS installed so that no additional costs are incurred. Third, RDBMSs allow to mix XML data and other (relational) data. Not all the data in the world are XML yet! Fourth, RDBMSs show very good performance for this purpose. More than twenty years of research and development have been invested into making RDBMSs the best possible general-purpose query processors and the RDBMS vendors are continuously improving their products. In particular, RDBMSs are capable of storing and processing large volumes of data (up to terabytes).

Relational databases can be used in different ways for our purposes. In this paper, we consider two scenarios. In the first scenario the whole XML data is replicated (or initially stored) in the relational database. This scenario provides the best performance. In this scenario, the XML query including keyword search can be entirely executed by the RDBMS, thereby taking full advantage of the powerful query processing capabilities of the RDBMS and interleaving keyword search with the other operations of an XML query in the best possible way. Also, no data are moved through the network and no process boundaries need to be crossed to execute queries in this scenario. In effect, this scenario shows how an RDBMS can be used as a *data warehouse* for XML data.

Unfortunately, it is not always possible or cost-effective to build a data warehouse. In the long run, for instance, it will not be viable for technical and legal reasons to replicate all the XML data on the Web. Therefore, we describe a second scenario in which query processing is carried out in a distributed way. In this scenario, XML documents are stored by individual data sources. An RDBMS is used to store indices which can be used to execute keyword searches and to find all relevant XML data sources for a query. In fact, the XML data sources could again be powered by an RDBMS; however, the data sources could also be implemented on top of a simple file system.

The techniques developed in this work are also applicable if an object-oriented database system (OODBMS) is used instead of an RDBMS. To some extent, our approaches are also applicable if a special-purpose XML query processor like Tamino [14] or Excelon [5] is used. The current generation of OODBMSs and special-purpose XML query processors, however, is not mature enough to process large amounts of data so we focus on the use of RDBMSs throughout this paper. Furthermore, we will not exploit any 'object-relational' features which are currently built into many RDBMSs because these features are not useful for our needs.

1.2. Contribution and overview of this paper

In a nutshell, the goal of our work is to integrate keyword search into XML query processing and make use of existing (relational) database systems as much as possible. In the remainder of this paper, we will report on the following developments.

(1) We will show how to extend an existing XML query language in order to support keyword search. This will make it possible to query XML data without structure (i.e., text), help users to query XML documents with structure, if the users do not know the structure, and help to query multiple XML documents with the same ontology, but different DTDs.
(2) We will present an extension of inverted files in order to support keyword search. Furthermore, we show how such extended inverted files can be stored in a relational database.
(3) We will show how XML queries that involve keyword search and other operations can be entirely processed using an RDBMS, if the XML data are replicated in one relational database.
(4) We will also show how XML queries with keyword search can be executed, if the XML data cannot be stored in a relational database.
(5) We will present performance experiments that demonstrate the overheads of our approach (size of indices, etc.) and give a feeling for the cost of extended XML query processing with keyword search.

Section 2 describes the data model and query language used in this work. Section 3 presents the proposed indices for keyword search (i.e., inverted files). Section 4 discusses the role of RDBMSs in query processing in more detail. Section 5 contains performance experiments. Section 6 gives an overview of related work. Section 7 concludes this paper with suggestions for future work.

2. Data model and query language

Abundant work recently addressed the problem of finding a formal data model and a query language for XML data. Since this still remains an open problem (no common agreement has been reached yet), we describe in this section the data model and query language that are the basis for our work. However, our data model and query language are similar in spirit to the other proposals so that the results presented in this paper can be easily adapted to those other formalisms. Assuming that the final standard will have the same characteristics and functionalities as the current proposals, our work will also be applicable to the future standard XML query language.

In this work we extend the XML-QL query language with keyword-based search capabilities. We start this section by describing our XML data model and we continue by describing the syntax and the semantics of the current language, and of our extension.

2.1. Data model

A relevant question is whether an XML query is evaluated on a single XML document, on a set of XML documents or on a set of XML elements. Concerning this subtle point, we make the following assumption: we query (and therefore model) sets of XML documents. We will call such a set of documents an XML *data set*. XML elements in a data set can be partitioned according to their *types*: an XML element that has the form *<tag_name>* ... *<tag_name>* is said to be of type *tag_name*. Therefore, an XML data set can contain multiple elements of type *document*.

We model an XML data set D as a graph (noted G_D) as follows:

- For each element e in the XML data set, there is an internal node N_e in the graph G. Each such internal node N_e is labeled with a distinct system generated element ID, *elID*.
- For each data value v in the XML data set there is a corresponding leaf V_v. Each such leaf node V_v is labeled with the value v.
- The graph G_D contains two types of edges: attribute edges and content edges. They are built as follows:
  - If the element e_2 is directly nested within the element e_1, then graph G_D contains a content edge from node N_{e_1} to node N_{e_2}. This edge is labeled with the type of the element e_2.

- If the value v is directly contained in the element e, then graph G_D contains a content edge from node N_e to node V_v. The edge is labeled with the empty string.
- If the value v is the value of an attribute of the element e, then graph G_D contains an attribute edge between node N_e and node V_v. The edge is labeled with the attribute name.

Moreover, two types of data models can be considered: an *unordered* data model or an *ordered* data model. The ordered model enforces an additional total order on the set of outgoing content edges of each internal node, according to the order of the components of each element in the original XML file. For the sake of simplicity, we will consider only the unordered data model in this paper; in this data model the order of elements is ignored. If not stated otherwise, we will also ignore IDREFs. In our data model, IDREFs would be represented by an additional type of edges. Most of the techniques presented in this paper are not affected by the presence of IDREFs.

2.1.1. Example XML data

We use the following XML data set from the bibliographical domain to exemplify the proposed data model. It consists of three article elements in one XML document, called 'bib.xml'. The three article elements contain similar types of information (e.g., authors, title, year of publication of the article) but this information is organized differently in each case.

```
<document>
<article id="1"
  <author><name>
    Adam Dingle</name></author>
  <author><name>
    Peter Sturmh</name></author>
  <author><name>
    Li Zhang</name></author>
  <title>Analysis and Characterization
    of Large-Scale Web Server Access
    Patterns and Performance</title>
  <year>1999</year>
  <booktitle>World Wide Web
    Journal</booktitle>
</article>
<article id="2" year="1999">
  <author name="A. Dingle" ></author>
  <author name="E. Levy" ></author>
  <author name="J. Song" ></author>
  <author name="D. Dias" ></author>
  <title>Design and Performance of
    a Web Server Accelerator</title>
  <booktitle> Proceedings of IEEE
    INFOCOM </booktitle>
</article>
<article id="3">
  @inproceedings{IMN97,
  author="Adam Dingle and Ed MacNair
    and Thao Nguyen",
  title="An Analysis of Web Server
    Performance",
  booktitle="Proceedings of the IEEE
    Global Telecommunications
    Conference (GLOBECOM)", year=1999}
</article>
</document
```

The graph modeling this XML data set is depicted in Fig. 1. The attribute edges are marked in dashed lines; system-generated elIDs for internal nodes are shown in bold italic.

2.2. The XML-QL query language

XML-QL queries specify declaratively the selection of data from multiple XML data inputs and the creation of an XML data output. A simple query in XML-QL has the following form:

where (*XML-pattern* [*ELEMENT_AS* $*elem_var*])*
IN *fileName*, (predicate)*
construct *XML-pattern* | *variable*

The **where** clause specifies how to filter data from the input XML data set; the *construct* clause specifies how to assemble the query results in XML. Syntactically, the **where** clause is composed of a set of XML patterns and a set of predicates. An XML-pattern is an XML element in which some of the items (tag names, data content, attribute names or attribute values) are eventually replaced with variables. A variable name is prefixed with a $ in order to distinguish it from a string value.

Similarly to an XML element, an XML-pattern can be modeled by a graph, with the major difference that some of the labels in the graph are now variables

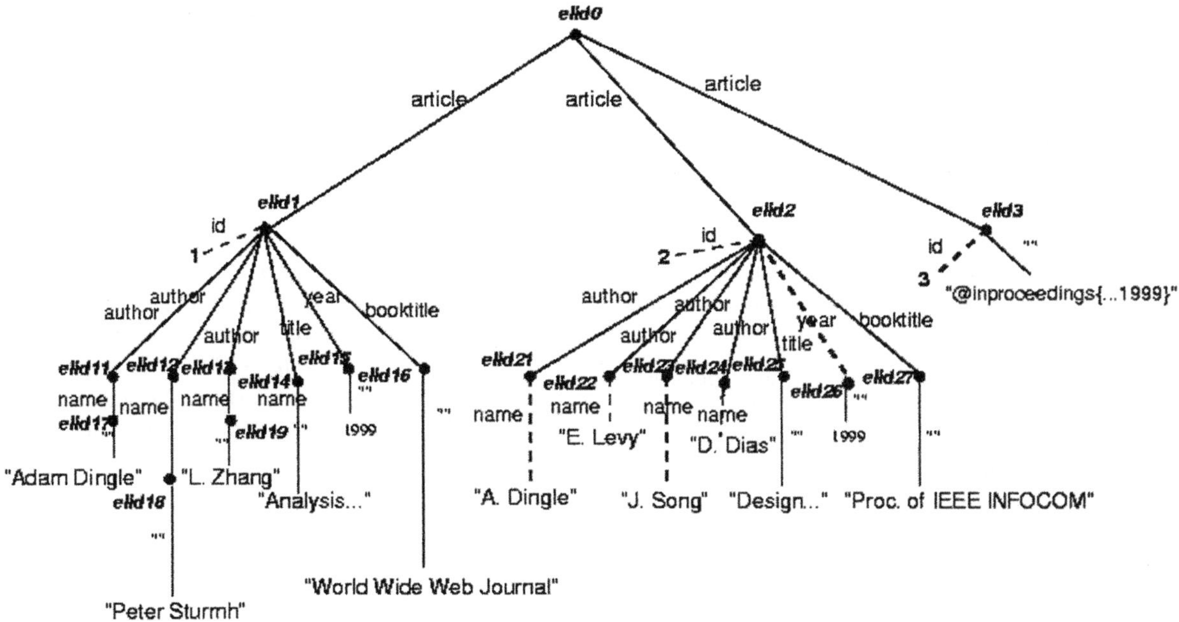

Fig. 1. Data model corresponding to the XML example data.

instead of constants. Let us denote as G_q the graph modeling the set of all XML-patterns in a query q.

Given an XML data set D, the result of the evaluation of an XML-QL query q on the input D is defined as follows. Each mapping from the graph G_q to the graph G_D which preserves the constant labels from the query induces a substitution of the variables in the query q on the set of constant values in the data graph G_D. For each such substitution which also satisfies the additional predicates, a new element, created by the instantiation of the XML-pattern in the **construct** clause, is added to the result.

An XML-pattern can be eventually followed by an *ELEMENT_AS $elem_var* clause. In this case, a mapping from the pattern's graph to the data graph will also define a substitution of the variable *$elem_var* on the set of internal nodes in the data graph (corresponding to elements in the original XML file). This variable can be projected in the *construct* clause; the result will then include the corresponding XML element.

Example 1. Let us consider the following query: 'retrieve all articles written by Mr. Dingle in 1999 about the Web'.

```
where
  <article>
    <author><name>$N</name></author>
    <title>$T</title><year>1999</year>
  </article> ELEMENT_AS $E IN
  "bib.xml", $N like *Dingle*,
  $T like *web*
construct $E
```

There are three 'query-to-data' mappings preserving the constants. These three mappings define the following substitutions:

{$N/"Adam ***Dingle****", $T/"Analysis and Characterization ...* ***Web*** *... Performance", $E/elID1 }*
{$N/"Peter Sturmh", $T/"Analysis and Characterization ... ***Web*** *... Performance", $E/elID1 }*
{$N/"Li Zhang", $T/"Analysis and Characterization ... ***Web*** *... Performance", $E/elID1 }*

Of these three substitutions, only the first one matches the additional predicates. We note that in XML-QL the *like* predicate has the same semantics as in SQL, i.e., it tests if a certain string value matches a particular string regular path expressions. Hence, according to the semantics of the query language, the first XML element in our example is projected out in the result.

2.3. Extending XML-QL with keyword search

XML-QL provides a good solution to query XML data, assuming that a reasonable amount of knowledge about the structure of the data is given. In order to facilitate the case when no or limited knowledge about the structure of the data is given, XML-QL proposes (as all the other XML query languages) the use of regular path expressions. Unfortunately, regular path expressions are not the panacea for this problem, as the following example demonstrates.

Example 2. Let us assume that the user does not know if *'name'* is the name of a tag of one of the subelements of the author element or if it is the name of an attribute of this element; moreover, in the first case, the user might not know at which depth the tag *name* appears. The query is expressed in XML-QL as follows:

```
/* search for "name" as a subelement,
   at any depth */
where
  <article>
    <author><*><name>$N</name></*>
    </author>
    <title>$T</title><year>1999</year>
  </article> ELEMENT_AS $E IN
  "bib.xml", $N like *Dingle*,
  $T like *web*
construct $E
union
/* search for "name" as an attribute
   name, at any depth */
where
  <article>
    <author><*><_ name=>$N></_></*>
    </author> <title>$T</title>
    <year>1999</year>
  </article> ELEMENT_AS $E IN
  "bib.xml", $N like *Dingle*,
  $T like *web*
construct $E
```

It is easy to imagine the complexity of the query in the absence of *any* knowledge about the usage and the potential nesting of *article*, *title*, *year*, *name* and *author*. Such queries are both hard to write and expensive to evaluate.

To solve this problem, we propose to add a special predicate called *contains* to the XML-QL query language. The *contains* predicate tests the existence of a given word within an XML element. The *contains* predicate has four arguments: an *XML element variable*, a *word*, an integer expression limiting the *depth* at which the word is found within the element and a Boolean expression over the set of constants *{tag_name, attribute_name, content, attribute_value}* imposing a constraint on the *location* of the word within the given element.

Given a data set D and a substitution of the variable $\$E$ into the set of internal nodes of the graph G_D, the predicate *contains*$(w, \$E, d, loc)$ evaluates to *true* iff w appears as a 'word' in the set of strings labeling the edges and the leaves of the subtree of depth d rooted at $\$E$ in the graph G_D. Moreover, the occurrence of the word w within $\$E$ has to obey to the specified location (e.g., *tag_name* or *attribute_name*).

Example 3. The XML-QL query in the previous example can be simplified using a *contains* predicate. Formally, the idea is to search for all elements of type *article* having an *author* subelement and containing the strings 'Dingle' below the *author* subelement and '1999' below the article itself. We limit the search to subtrees of depth 3 and we are interested in any kind of occurrences (i.e., the word can appear within a tag, an attribute name, within the content of an XML element or finally within the value to an attribute).

```
where
  <article><author></author>
  ELEMENT_AS $A, <title>$T</title>
  </article> ELEMENT_AS $E IN
"bib.xml",
  contains($A,"Dingle", 3, any),
  $T like *web*,
  contains($E,"1999", 3, any)
construct $E
```

In this example we used *any* as an alias for the expression *tag_name* OR *attribute_name* OR *content* OR *attribute_value*. According to the semantics of the *contains* predicate, the result of the evaluation of this query on the data set given previously contains the elements 1 and 2.

A relevant question is what is a 'word' in this context. Intuitively, a word is a substring of a string value, with a separate identity and carrying a separate meaning. For example, a text document can be reasonably split into English words with separate meaning. However, in a more general context, it can be very difficult to define the notion of a 'word'. If the content of an XML element is not a fragment of text, but a string encoding some application domain information (e.g., the *bibtex* entry in the third article), the methodology of splitting PCDATA values into independent, meaningful 'words' is application-dependent, too. In this example, the characters '@', '{' and ',' can be used as separators. In our work, we assume that such application-dependent procedures are given to the system. Another interesting question is whether there are normalization procedures (e.g., transform capital letters to non-capital letters) that can be applied to string values in order to increase the probability of matching the string constants in the query to values in the data. Again, if there are such application-specific procedures, we assume that they are given to us. A related field of work for application-dependent splitting and normalization procedures is the domain of data cleaning; a framework describing the integration of such external procedures in the process of data cleaning is described in [9].

To better illustrate keyword-based search capabilities, we will give another example.

Example 4. Assume that we want to ask the same query, but in the absence of *any* knowledge of the structure of the XML data. In this case, we are looking for all article elements containing the words 'Dingle', 'web' and '1999' in subtrees of depth 3. In our extension of XML-QL this would be expressed as:

```
where
  <article></article>
  ELEMENT_AS $E IN "bib.xml",
  contains($E,"Dingle", 3, any),
  contains($E,"1999", 3, any),
  contains($E,"web", 3, any)
construct $E
```

This last query returns all three XML elements of our XML data set.

We conclude the section with the following remarks. First, keyword-based search is a necessity in multiple situations: (a) if the XML data do not have structure (e.g., as in our third article example); (b) if the structure is unknown to the user; and (c) if multiple heterogeneous XML sources need to be queried. Second, in order to be able to express all ranges of queries, from fully structured ones to completely unstructured ones, and in order to allow a *global* optimization process of such queries, it is essential to support the two capabilities within the same query formalism.

3. Relational support for full-text indexing

In this section we describe an extension of inverted files for full-text indexing. An extended inverted file can be used to implement keyword search (i.e., the *contains* predicates) and to find relevant XML data sources or XML elements in a distributed environment. Furthermore, we will show how inverted files can be stored in a relational database and discuss variants. How inverted files are used during query processing is detailed in Section 4.

3.1. Inverted files

The classic index structure for keyword search is the inverted file [6]. In the simplest form, an inverted file contains records of the following form:

<word, document>

meaning that the *word* can be found in the *document*. For our purposes, we need to extend this structure in the following ways:

(1) We need to keep information in the granularity of elements rather than documents. For example, the word 'Analysis' appears in a *title* element and in an *article* element in the example of Section 2.1.
(2) We need to record whether a keyword is the name of a tag (e.g., *article*), the name of an attribute (e.g., *id*), a word in the value of an attribute, or a word in the element's data content. In a traditional information retrieval system, such a distinction is not required because such systems work in the granularity of documents; these systems are not geared towards XML, and they do not support *contains* predicates that need this information.

(3) We need to record the *depth* at which the word appears for the first time within an element in order to execute *contains* predicates that limit the depth. Again, traditional IR systems do not record this information because they ignore the structure of a document.

As a result, we propose to use inverted files that have records with the following structure:

<elID, word, depth, location>

where *word*, *depth* and *location* have the natural meaning. For the example of Section 2, the inverted file would contain, among others, the following records:

```
<"article", elID1, 0, tag>
<"id", elID1, 1, attr>
...
<"name", elID1, 2, tag>
<"Adam", elID1, 2, value>
...
```

Note that it is possible to have multiple distinct records for the same word and elID. For example, the word 'year' might appear as a tag name at depth 1 within an article and as a value at depth 2 within an article with the title 'The Year 2000 Bug'.

A relevant question is how elIDs of elements are modeled and efficiently stored. In our system we model each elID as a record containing the URL of the belonging XML document, the starting and ending positions of the element within this document, and the *type* of the element. Furthermore, if the DTD of the document specifies that the element has an attribute that uniquely identifies that element (e.g., the *id* uniquely identifies an *article*), then the value of that attribute is also stored in an elID record. Rather than manipulating such complex elIDs, each elID record is given an internal key number and all the information of the element is stored in a separate table called the *elements* table. This way, we can work internally with much smaller elIDs and query processing becomes significantly faster. Similarly, we propose to store all information concerning individual XML documents (e.g., URL and information about the DTD) in a separate *documents* table. As a result, we obtain the following relational schema to store element elIDs and document information (keys are represented in bold face):

*elements(**elID**, docid, start_pos, end_pos, type, id_val)*
*documents(**docid**, URL,...)*

3.2. Storing inverted files in a relational database

Inverted files can be implemented in many different ways. For our work, we chose to use a relational database system (RDBMS) because RDBMSs can handle large amounts of data, and inverted lists obviously tend to become very large — larger in fact than the original data. In addition, as we will see, an RDBMS can also be used to execute the other parts of an XML-QL query so that a whole XML-QL query with keyword search can be processed by a single RDBMS without crossing process boundaries.

The natural way to store an inverted file in an RDBMS is to establish one table that stores the whole inverted file; this table would have four columns: *elID*, *word*, *depth*, and *location* as described in the previous subsection. Such a table, however, would be huge and this whole, huge table would have to be inspected for each query that involves a keyword search. It is therefore desirable to partition this table into several smaller tables so that each query can be processed by looking at a few small tables only. There are many ways to partition this table and the best way depends on the query workload and characteristics of the XML data. In this work, we propose the following heuristics which have proven to be quite effective in all our experiments.

- First, we partition by *word*. That is, for each keyword w, a separate table w is established with three attributes: *elID, depth, location.* To find all elements that contain the words 'title' and 'analysis' only the *title* and *analysis* tables would have to be inspected. Partitioning an inverted file in this way is not a novel idea; this is done by virtually all IR systems today [6].
- Second, we further partition the individual *word* tables by the *type* of the elIDs. For instance, we would record all *article* elements that contain the keyword 'Dingle' in a *Dingle-Article* table and all *author* elements that contain the keyword 'name' in a separate *Name-Author* table. This partitioning is very useful for queries that specify the *scope* of the answer; an example is the second query of

Section 2 which looks for all articles that have 'Dingle' as one of the authors. To execute this query, we only need to inspect the *Dingle-Article* table. Partitioning the data in this way is novel and specific to our particular goal of processing XML queries and retrieving individual elements rather than whole documents.

As a result, we obtain the following relational schema to store inverted files: for each type (i.e., tag name) and for each word in the XML data set store a table

word-type(elID, depth, location)

Given the high number of possible *word-type* pairs, the inverted file will be stored in thousands, if not tens of thousands, of tables, but current RDBMSs are very well capable of managing such a large number of tables. If the number of tables is a concern, the partitioning can be limited to popular words; e.g., words that occur in more than 1000 elements.

We propose to store all tables sorted by elID (i.e., the number that internally represents the elID). Again, this will speed up query processing because finding all elements that contain two specific keywords can be achieved by *merging* the relevant tables for the two keywords. In most RDBMSs, such a sorting can be achieved by creating a clustered index on the elID column of the table. Furthermore, we propose to establish indices on the *docid* and *type* columns of the *elements* table and on the *docid* and *URL* columns of the *documents* table.

3.3. Variants

As mentioned in the previous subsection, there are many different ways to partition the information of the inverted file in a relational database. For example, an alternative to our proposed scheme would be to partition by *word* and by *docid.* This scheme would be beneficial if most queries retrieve information from specific documents, rather than considering *all* documents. Ultimately, the best partitioning scheme depends on the query workload. However, we have had no problems with the partitioning scheme described in the previous section.

One way to speed up query processing is to materialize the intersection (or join) of two tables. For instance, many queries will ask for *articles* and involve the keywords 'name,' 'author,' and 'title.' As a consequence, it is beneficial to materialize the join of the corresponding *Name-Article, Author-Article*, and *Title-Article* tables into a *Name | Author | Title-Article.* Now, bibliographic queries can be processed directly using such a *Name | Author | Title-Article* table instead of the individual tables. The resulting relational schema is as follows:

Name | Author | Title-Article(elID, depth_Name, loc_Name, depth_Author, loc_Author, depth_Title, loc_Title)

All elIDs in this table refer to *article* elements. Note that, say, the word 'name' may also appear in different contexts so that this materialization is indeed a useful prefiltering for bibliographic queries. For other queries, it might be useful to materialize the join of the *Name-Emp* and *Salary-Emp* tables. What exactly to materialize depends on the query workload.

A popular approach in the IR community is to ignore so-called *Stop* words in the inverted file. Stop words are words that appear very frequently in *all* or most documents; examples are the words 'the' or 'is'. Stop words can be ignored in IR systems because IR systems try to find the most relevant documents that match a query and Stop words are not important in order to determine the relevance of a document. For our purposes, however, Stop words must not be ignored. For instance, words like 'name' are likely to appear very frequently as element tags and they carry important information for the elements they appear in. Furthermore, we are interested in *all* answers that *fully* match a query, whereas IR systems are geared towards giving the ten or hundred documents that *best* match the query. For instance, counting the number of citations of works by Donald Knuth in all Computer Science papers is a valid query and involves finding *all* citations even if thousands exist.

Other approaches to improve query processing performance include the use of bitmaps and compression techniques [6]. Principally, these techniques can be exploited in our context as well; however, so far we were not able to implement these techniques as part of our work since we relied on the capabilities of standard, off-the-shelf RDBMSs. Bitmap indexing techniques and database compression techniques are currently being integrated into several relational database systems [10,11,15]; therefore, it should be possible to explore the usefulness of these features in future work.

4. Extended XML-QL query processing

We will now turn to a discussion of how XML-QL queries with *contains* predicates can be processed. We will first describe query processing in the first scenario of the introduction, in which the inverted file and all the XML data are stored or replicated in an RDBMS. After that, we will discuss the second scenario of the introduction.

4.1. Replicating the XML data in an RDBMS

4.1.1. XML-QL query processing with an RDBMS

We will first revisit how XML-QL queries *without* keyword search can be implemented using an RDBMS. We will then describe the necessary extensions to integrate keyword search.

There are many different ways to store XML data in an RDBMS and to execute XML queries using an RDBMS; see, e.g., [4,7,13]. In this work, we will only consider the *binary table* approach which was presented in [7] because this approach shows good and robust performance. (Any other approach, however, could be used just as well for our purposes.) The basic idea of this approach is to establish a *binary table* for each *type* (i.e., tag name) that appears in the XML data. Each entry of a binary table `t` contains two elIDs, `source` and `target`. Such an entry denotes that `target` is a subelement of `source` (at depth 0) and that `target` is of type `t`. Alternatively, such an entry can denote that `source` has an attribute or subelement `t` which contains an IDREF to `target`. In this way the binary tables represent the structure of an XML document. Base values such as PCDATA or integers can be stored within the binary tables or in separate value tables. In this work, we stored values within the binary tables so that the binary table for all *articles* would have the following structure: (Here and in the following, we represent binary tables and their attributes by typewriter font so that they are not confused with the tables and attributes that store the inverted file. The attributes that build the key of the table are again represented in bold face.)

```
article(source, target, value)
```

`source` is an elID that references an *article*, **`target`** is an elID that references a subelement of an *article*; **`target`** is *null* if an `article` has no subelements. `value` is some (text) value which is part of the *article* (not part of a subelement); `value` is *null* if an *article* has no text value.

Details of the whole binary approach can be found in [7]. In particular, [7] explains how any kind of XML-QL query can be translated into an equivalent SQL query; including complex XML-QL queries that involve regular path expressions and/or wild cards. To give an example, Fig. 2 shows some binary tables for the XML data set of Section 2.1. The first XML-QL query of Section 2.2 could be executed by the following SQL query:

```
select art.source
from article art, author aut, name n,
     title t, year y
where art.target=aut.sources and
      art.target=t.source and
      art.target=y.source and
      aut.target=n.source and
      y.value=1999 and
      t.value like "web" and
      n.value like "Dingle"
```

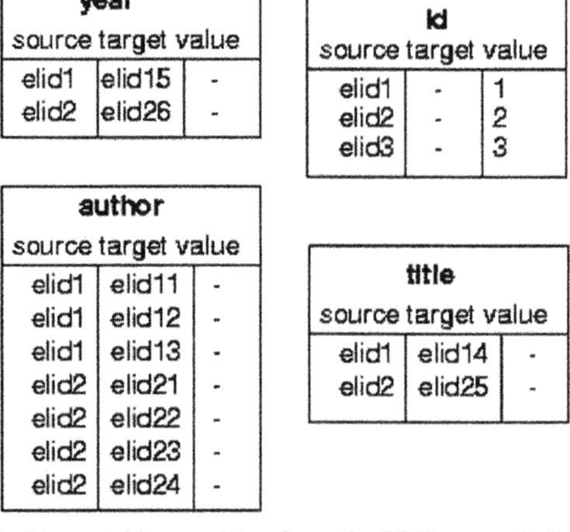

year

source	target	value
elid1	elid15	-
elid2	elid26	-

id

source	target	value
elid1	-	1
elid2	-	2
elid3	-	3

author

source	target	value
elid1	elid11	-
elid1	elid12	-
elid1	elid13	-
elid2	elid21	-
elid2	elid22	-
elid2	elid23	-
elid2	elid24	-

title

source	target	value
elid1	elid14	-
elid2	elid25	-

Fig. 2. Binary tables resulting from the XML example in Section 2.1.1.

4.1.2. Keyword search with an RDBMS

If the inverted file is stored by the same RDBMS that also stores the inverted file, then keyword search can be integrated in a straightforward way. If the query involves a *contains* predicate for a specific keyword, then the tables that store the entries of the inverted file for that keyword need to be joined as part of processing the whole query. This approach can again be best demonstrated by the means of examples.

Let us consider a simple query searching for elements of type *article* which mention the word 'Dingle'. This query can be expressed in our extension of XML-QL as follows:

```
where <article> </article> ELEMENT_AS
$E IN "bib.xml",
  contains($E,"Dingle", 3, any)
construct $E
```

To execute this query, our extended XML-QL query processor would translate it into the following simple SQL query:

select elID
from Dingle-article;

As another example, consider a query that asks for the names of all authors that have written a paper in 1999 mentioning the word 'Web'. This example demonstrates how keyword search and 'structured' XML query processing coexist. In XML-QL, this query could be formulated as follows:

```
where
  <article>
    <year>1999</year>
    <author> $A </author>
  </article> ELEMENT_AS $E IN
"bib.xml",
  contains($E,"Web", 4, any)
construct $A
```

This XML-QL query would be translated into the following SQL query:

```
select aut.target
from article art, year y, author aut,
     web-article c
where art.target=year.source and
      art.target=aut.source and
      art.target=c.elID and
      year.value="1999" and c.depth<=4
```

To execute this SQL query, the optimizer of the RDBMS would find a good order in which to join the individual tables. From a different point of view, the RDBMS interleaves keyword search (joins with the *web-article* table) with regular XML-QL query processing using the binary approach (joins with the `article`, `year`, and `author` tables). Of course, the RDBMS is not aware that it is doing keyword search and XML-QL query processing.

Keyword search and an inverted file might even be helpful in order to execute XML-QL queries without *contains* predicates. In particular, if the join of several tables that store the inverted file is materialized, this materialized join can be used as a prefilter in order to speed up the execution of the query. For instance, the last query can be rewritten into the equivalent query involving a *year | author | web-article* table (as a prefilter for the structured part) as follows:

```
select aut.target
from article art, year y, author a,
     web-article c,
     year | author | web-article A
where art.target=year.source and
      art.target=aut.source and
      art.target=c.elID and
      year.value="1999" and
      c.depth<=4 and A.elID=art.target
```

Again, the optimizer of the RDBMS will decide when to carry out the join with the *year | author | web-article* table. If this table is small, then it is a good prefilter and the RDBMS will consider it early. Otherwise, it is a poor prefilter and the optimizer will not consider it until the end; in fact, the use of this table will increase the cost of the query in this case. Therefore, this kind of prefilter should only be used with care.

4.2. Distributed XML query processing

We now turn to a discussion of how to process XML-QL queries if the XML data can be indexed using an RDBMS, but the data cannot be stored in the RDBMS. Such a situation could arise on the Web, for example, if the owners of a Web site give permission to index the content, but users must visit the Web site in order to retrieve the data. In such a scenario the inverted file stored in the RDBMS is used to locate relevant XML data sources. The full query result must be computed by a mediator. The mediator uses the RDBMS to query the inverted file and accesses the XML data sources to compute the full query results. We differentiate two cases: (1) the data sources have no query capabilities; and (2) the data sources have some query capabilities.

4.2.1. XML data sources without query capabilities

If the data sources have no query capabilities, then XML-QL queries are executed in the following way:

(1) *Prefilter:* use the inverted file stored in the RDBMS to find the relevant documents and/or elIDs.
(2) *Retrieve:* get the relevant documents (or elements) from the data sources.
(3) *Execute:* extract the query results from the retrieved documents (or elements).

Prefiltering is the most interesting step. It tries to narrow down the search as much as possible by considering all tag names, attribute names, and keywords that appear in the query. For prefiltering, the inverted file stored in the RDBMS is useful even if the query does not involve any *contains* predicates. How prefiltering works can again best be explained by looking at an example.

Let us consider a query that asks for the names of all authors of a article with the keyword 'analysis' in the title. In XML-QL, this query can be written as follows:

```
where <article>
         <author> <name> $n </name>
         </author>
         <title> $t </title>
      </article> IN "bib.xml",
                 $t like *analysis*
construct $n
```

We can use the inverted file to get the following information:

- get the elIDs of all *article* elements that have an 'author' subelement at depth 1;
- get the elIDs of all *article* elements that have a 'name' subelement at depth 2;
- get the elIDs of all *article* elements that have a 'title' subelement at depth 1;
- get the elIDs of all *article* elements that contain the word 'analysis' at depth at most 2.

Clearly, we are only interested in articles that meet all four criteria; let us call this set of *articles* *C*. *C* contains all *articles* which are relevant, but it might also contain some *articles* that do not match the query; for instance, an article that contains the word 'analysis' somewhere, but not in its *title*. To narrow down the search even further, we can use the inverted file to get all *interesting title* and *author* elements, i.e.,

- get the elIDs of all *author* elements that have a 'name' subelement at depth 1;
- get the elIDs of all *title* elements that contain the word 'analysis' at depth 1.
- from the start and end positions of the elIDs stored in the *elements* table, we can now infer which of the *article* elements of *C* have *title* and *author* subelements belonging to the previous sets; this is the result of prefiltering.

The whole prefiltering can be done with a single SQL query. We do not show this query for brevity. In this example, prefiltering proves to be very good. That is, prefiltering will only return the elIDs of *article* elements which match the query. In general, prefiltering is not always perfect. For example, predicates like *price* < 1000 cannot be evaluated using the inverted file. Furthermore, prefiltering with an inverted file cannot be perfect, if the XML data contains IDREFs. In this case, the subelement test with the start and end positions stored in the *elements* tables is not applicable and prefiltering must stop after the first step and return the elIDs of all *article* elements in *C*. Another situation in which prefiltering is not perfect is if traditional inverted files or inverted files with less information are used instead of the full-fledged, extended inverted files proposed in Section 3. In any case, it is important that prefiltering finds a *superset* of all elements that match the query.

Independent of the quality of the prefiltering step, the mediator must access the XML data sources. In our example, for instance, the mediator must access the data sources in order to construct the names of the authors. The implementation of the retrieval step depends on the interfaces of the XML data sources.

If the data sources support the retrieval of individual elements and their subelements, then this feature should be exploited. Otherwise, the entire documents that contain relevant elements must be retrieved.

The query results can be produced in the mediator in a straightforward way: while parsing the retrieved documents (or elements), the mediator can check whether they match the query (if prefiltering is not perfect) and construct the query results. If the query is complex, many large documents are retrieved, and matching is complicated, the documents can also be (temporarily) loaded into the RDBMS as described in Section 4.1; in this case, it is also possible to use the inverted file stored by the RDBMS in order to evaluate *contains* predicates. If the retrieved XML data contains IDREFs, the mediator might need to follow these IDREFs and retrieve further documents as part of query execution.

4.2.2. XML data sources with query capabilities

As an alternative to retrieving and generating query results in the mediator, it is also possible to push parts of the query down to the data sources, if the data sources have query capabilities. In this case, query processing is carried out in the following three steps.

(1) *Prefiltering:* find all relevant documents and elIDs as described in the previous subsection.
(2) *Push Down:* pass elIDs to the data sources and let the data sources execute the whole or parts of the query on these elIDs.
(3) *Refinement:* refine the results returned by the data sources if the data sources could not execute the whole query.

Step 2 can be executed in many different ways; in the database literature this step has been called *bind* or *dependent join* and it has been studied extensively. We will not go into details here and refer the interested reader to the relevant database literature; e.g., [8].

5. Experiments

We implemented a prototype XML-QL query processor with keyword search on top of an off-the-shelf RDBMS. In this section, we will present the results of initial performance experiments conducted with our prototype. We will only report on experiments performed in a scenario in which all the XML data (in addition to the inverted file) is replicated in the RDBMS.

5.1. Experimental environment

We constructed a database with all of Shakespeare's plays in XML format. The DTD and the XML representation of the plays are available from the **Oasis Web site**[1]. We also experimented with synthetic XML documents (a random XML generator) and various kinds of DTDs, but we will not present the results of these experiments for brevity.

All our test programs were written in Java, using JDK1.2. The RDBMS server was Oracle8i running on a PC with WindowsNT and a 2 Gb disk. The client programs ran on a separate PC, equipped with a Pentium at 400 MHz, running under Redhat Linux 6.2. We used the XML4J parser available at www.alphaworks.ibm.com, version 2.0.15. This is a DOM parser that constructs an in-memory parse tree for the whole document. For the Shakespeare data which consist of fairly small documents that fit into main memory, this parser worked very well. If large documents whose size exceeds the main memory need to be parsed, an event-based parser would work better.

5.2. Generating the inverted file and relational database

The indexing process proceeds in several steps.

(1) We parse the XML document into an in-memory structure, as described in the previous subsection.
(2) From the parse tree, we construct records of the inverted file. We store these records in a (temporary) file on the file system.
(3) We bulkload the file with the records of the inverted file into one big 'contains' table of the RDBMS.
(4) We partition the 'contains' table into tables for each *word* and *type* of elID using SQL queries, as described in Section 3.

The most expensive step is the second step. In this step, we need to check each word (or attribute

[1] http://www.oasis.org

Table 1
Size and loading time of Shakespeare's plays

Size of original XML file (Mb)	7.7
Number of distinct words	30468
Size of relational database (Mb)	90
Loading time (min)	27

or tag name) of the XML document and generate zero, one, or several records. First, we need to check whether the word already exists in the inverted file or is a *new* keyword which requires special handling. Then, we need to check whether this word is the first occurrence of this word in the current element (and its father element, grandfather element, etc.); only if it is the first occurrence, a record is generated. Table 1 summarizes the size and loading time of all of Shakespeare's plays with our prototype.

We note that the size of the relational database (including *binary tables*, *inverted file*, and database indices) is about ten times the size of the original XML. The main reason for this is that we construct inverted files in the granularity of XML elements, rather than documents. Building inverted files in such a fine granularity is a must for combined keyword search and XML query processing — there is nothing we can do about that. We are aware, however, that such an explosion in the data volume might be unacceptable for some applications. We therefore plan to investigate special database compression techniques and the use of *approximate inverted files* as one very important avenue for future work.

The total loading time is also quite high. Roughly half of this time is spent writing the document content into temporary files. The rest of the processing time is spent loading the data into the RDBMS and constructing the appropriate indices. We believe that by fine-tuning the DBMS and by judicious distribution of processing between the DBMS and the file system, this time can still be reduced.

5.3. Query performance

We studied two different queries. The first query asks for all *lines* by the *speaker Iago* which contain the word *love*. The second query asks for all *scenes* that contain the word *the*. We implement each query in three different variants.

- *Structured.* The query exploits the full XML structure; i.e., the query involves no *contains* predicate. This variant simulates an expert user.
- *Partially structured.* The query exploits some structure; i.e., plays have scenes and scenes *somehow* involve lines and speakers. This variant models a user who has partial knowledge of the structure of the data.
- *Unstructured.* The query has no structure; it is entirely composed of *contains* predicates. This models a user with absolutely no knowledge of the structure of the data.

The first query is expressed in the three variants as follows.

1. *Structured query:*

```
where
  <play><act><scene>
    <speaker> Iago </speaker>
    <line> $L </line> ELEMENT_AS
    $E IN "bib.xml",
  </scene></act></play,>
  $L like *love*
construct $E;
```

2. *Partially structured query:*

```
where
  <play><act>
    <scene></scene> ELEMENT_AS
    $E IN "bib.xml",
  </act> </play,>
  contains($E, "love", 5, content),
  contains($E,"Iago", 5, content),
  contains($E, "speaker", 5, tag_name),
  contains($E, "line", 5, tag_name)
construct $E;
```

3. *Unstructured query:*

```
where
  <_></_> ELEMENT_AS $E IN "bib.xml",
  contains($E, "love", 7, content),
  contains($E,"Iago", 7, content),
  contains($E, "speaker", 7, any),
  contains($E, "line", 7, any),
  contains($E, "play", 7, tag_name),
  contains($E, "act", 7, any)
construct $E;
```

Table 2
Running times and query results produced by each variant

	Query 1		Query 2	
	Running time	Query result	Running time	Query result
Structured	3 s	28 lines	7 s	208 scenes
Partially structured	1.5 s	19 scenes	2.5 s	1108 scenes
Unstructured	4 s	56 elements	10 s	10909 elements

Table 2 shows the running times and the query results produced by each variant. We observe that each query can be executed within seconds. The *partially structured* variants are somewhat faster than the *structured* variants which in turn are faster than the *unstructured* variants. The *precisest* query results can obviously be achieved with the *structured* variant. For the *partially structured* and *unstructured* variants, the user must issue further (more structured) queries in order to get the right results. For example, the *partially structured* variant of the first query returns results in the granularity of *scenes*; to get the right *lines* within these scenes, the user must refine the query, thereby considering the structure of the *scenes* returned in the first, partially structured attempt.

To conclude, the best results can of course be achieved by expert users that fully know the structure of the data. In these experiments, however, *contains* predicates are very useful to support novice users. (As mentioned in the introduction, there are also reasons for experts to use *contains* predicates.) Novice users will refine their queries stepwise, add structure, and thus get more specific results. This approach is very well doable because each step only takes seconds on a simple PC (subseconds on a powerful multi-processor machine). Of course, we do not expect novice users to be able to speak XML-QL (or any other XML query language); users will be able to use graphical query interfaces that generate XML-QL queries with *contains* predicates.

6. Related work

Both 'structured queries' and 'keyword search' have extensively been studied in the database and information retrieval literature. Specific work on XML query processing is reported in [4,13,16], and information retrieval techniques such as those used in current Web search engines can be used for XML just as well as for HTML or any other text data. What makes our work different is that we show how keyword search can be integrated into (structured) query processing and why this works particularly well for XML.

As a starting point, we used the XML-QL query language [3], and extended it to integrate keyword search. Many other query languages for XML exist; e.g., XQL [19] or XGL [2]. Most proposals for XML query languages have been presented in [12]. Also, XSL has simple query capabilities [20]. Furthermore, several languages for semi-structured data have been developed; e.g., StruQL [1]. All of these languages support features like regular path expressions in order to search for patterns and structures from XML data; keyword search, however, is not supported. One exception is Lorel [16], which has recently been extended by this feature in a similar way as we propose for XML-QL.

There are a number of companies that have products for storing and querying XML; examples are Excelon [5], Oracle's XML Developer's Kit [17], and Tamino [14]. None of these products, however, supports keyword search. Oracle's XDK allows for full-text indexing of XML documents if they are stored as flat text, i.e., there is no way of using *both* a structured query language and the text index. Recently, a few start-ups have started working on query processing and keyword search for XML. One example is XMLIndex [18], a branch of Sequoia Software. These companies, however, have not yet launched any products for this purpose and neither have they published details of their approaches.

7. Conclusion

We showed how an existing XML query language can be extended in order to support keyword search. Furthermore, we described how such an extended XML query language can be implemented. The most important data structure needed for keyword search is the inverted file. We gave the necessary extensions of inverted files for XML query processing and showed how inverted files can be stored and queried using a relational database system. The techniques described in this paper can easily be implemented; the implementation becomes even easier if in addition to the inverted files, the XML data itself can be replicated in the relational database system.

Combining keyword search and regular (structured) query processing is definitely useful. Among others, a system that supports both allows users that have no or only partial knowledge of the structure of the XML data to ask and refine queries. Our experiments showed that keyword search and overall XML query processing can be carried out very efficiently. Typically, the more structure is known, the faster a query of a user will be executed; however, totally unstructured queries can be executed very fast, too. Also, the more structure is known, the higher is the quality of the query results. If little structure is known too many results will be produced (high recall, low precision), but again, the first results returned by a completely unstructured query can be used to refine the query in order to get better results.

The flip side of our proposed approach is that extended inverted files can become very large; it is not unusual that they are a factor of ten or even more larger than the original data. As a consequence, our most important goal for future work is to investigate variants of inverted files which are significantly smaller and show (almost) as good performance.

References

[1] P. Buneman, S.B. Davidson, G.G. Hillebrand and D. Suciu, A query language and optimization techniques for unstructured data (electronic version), in: Proc. of ACM SIGMOD Conf. on Management of Data, 1996, pp. 505–516.

[2] S. Ceri, S. Comai, E. Damiani, P. Fraternali, S. Paraboschi and L. Tanca, XML-GL: a graphical language for querying and restructuring XML documents (electronic version), in: Proc. of the Int. World Wide Web Conference (WWW8), Comput. Networks ISDN Syst. 31 (11–16) (1999) 1171–1187.

[3] A. Deutsch, M.F. Fernandez, D. Florescu, A.Y. Levy and D. Suciu, A query language for XML (electronic version), in: Proc. of the Int. World Wide Web Conference (WWW8), Comput. Networks ISDN Syst. 31 (11–16) (1999) 1155–1169.

[4] A. Deutsch, M.F. Fernandez and D. Suciu, Storing semistructured data with STORED (electronic version), in: Proc. of ACM SIGMOD Conf. on Management of Data, 1999, pp. 431–442.

[5] Excelon from ODI: http://www.odi.com/excelon.

[6] W.B. Frakes and R.A. Baeza-Yates (Eds.), Information Retrieval: Data Structures and Algorithms, Prentice-Hall, Englewood Cliffs, NJ, 1992.

[7] D. Florescu and D. Kossmann, Storing and querying XML data using an RDBMS (extended version), IEEE Data Eng. Bull. 22 (3) (1999) 27–34.

[8] D. Florescu, A. Levy, I. Manolescu and D. Suciu, Query optimization in the presence of limited access patterns (electronic version), in: Proc. of ACM SIGMOD Conf. on Management of Data, 1999, pp. 311–322.

[9] H. Galhardas, D. Florescu, D. Shasha and E. Simon, AJAX: an extensible data cleaning tool (electronic version), in: Proc. of ACM SIGMOD Conf. on Management of Data, 2000.

[10] B.R. Iyer and D. Wilhite, Data compression support in databases, in: J.B. Bocca, M. Jarke and C. Zaniolo (Eds.), Proc. of the Int. Conf. on Very Large Data Bases (VLDB), 1994, pp. 695–704.

[11] T. Johnson, Performance measurements of compressed bitmap indices, in: Proc. of the Int. Conf. on Very Large Data Bases (VLDB), 1999, pp. 278–289.

[12] Query Languages — position papers: http://www.w3.org/TandS/QL/QL98/pp. html.

[13] J. Shanmugasundaram, H. Gang, K. Tufte, C. Zhang, D. J. DeWitt and J.F. Naughton, Relational databases for querying XML documents: limitations and opportunities (electronic version), in: Proc. of the Int. Conf. on Very Large Data Bases (VLDB), 1999, pp. 302–314.

[14] Tamino from SoftwareAG: http://www.softwareag.com/tamino.

[15] T. Westmann, D. Kossmann, S. Helmer and G. Moerkotte, The implementation and performance of compressed databases, Nov. 1998, Submitted for publication.

[16] J. Widom, Data management for XML: research directions (electronic version), IEEE Data Eng. Bull. 22 (3) (1999) 44–52.

[17] XDK, Oracle's XML Development Kit.

[18] XML Index: http://www.xmlindex.com/index.html.

[19] XQL query language: http://www.w3.org/TandS/QL/QL98/pp/xql.html.

[20] XSL, The Extensible Stylesheet Language: http://www.w3.org/Style/XSL.

Daniela Florescu received her Ph.D. in 1996, on 'Search Spaces for object oriented query optimization'. She is now a researcher at INRIA Rocquencourt, in the Caravel project. Dr. Florescu is among the authors of the XML-QL query language and the main designer of the Strudel Web-site management system. Her current research interests include XML technologies (query languages, storage, query optimization), static query optimization, data-intensive Web-site management, and data cleaning. Daniela Florescu is also a member of the W3C working group on XML query languages (*homepage*).

Donald Kossmann received BSc and MSc degrees in 1989 and 1991 from the University of Passau (Germany) and a Ph.D. in Computer Science in 1995 from the Technical University of Aachen (Germany). From 1995 to 1996, he was a Research Associate at the University Maryland, College Park. Since 1996, he is an Assistant Professor for Computer Science at the University of Passau (Germany). His research is focussed on distributed and object-oriented database systems (*homepage*).

Ioana Manolescu received her MSc in 1998, from Ecole Normale Supérieure, in Paris, and is now a Ph.D. student at INRIA Rocquencourt, in the Caravel project; her topic is 'Query Optimization for Semistructured Data'. She is also interested in XML schema extraction for storage optimization, and query optimization for data integration systems. Together with Daniela Florescu and Donald Kossmann, she is currently working on a new system that allows a relational data integration engine to seamlessly integrate XML documents (*homepage*).

Web Modeling Language (WebML): a modeling language for designing Web sites

Stefano Ceri *,[1], Piero Fraternali [1], Aldo Bongio [2]

Dipartimento di Elettronica e Informazione, Politecnico di Milano, Piazza Leonardo da Vinci 32, 20133 Milano, Italy

Abstract

Designing and maintaining Web applications is one of the major challenges for the software industry of the year 2000. In this paper we present Web Modeling Language (WebML), a notation for specifying complex Web sites at the conceptual level. WebML enables the high-level description of a Web site under distinct orthogonal dimensions: its data content (structural model), the pages that compose it (composition model), the topology of links between pages (navigation model), the layout and graphic requirements for page rendering (presentation model), and the customization features for one-to-one content delivery (personalization model). All the concepts of WebML are associated with a graphic notation and a textual XML syntax. WebML specifications are independent of both the client-side language used for delivering the application to users, and of the server-side platform used to bind data to pages, but they can be effectively used to produce a site implementation in a specific technological setting. WebML guarantees a model-driven approach to Web site development, which is a key factor for defining a novel generation of CASE tools for the construction of complex sites, supporting advanced features like multi-device access, personalization, and evolution management. The WebML language and its accompanying design method are fully implemented in a pre-competitive Web design tool suite, called ToriiSoft.

Keywords: Hypermedia design methodologies; Navigation; Design tools; XML

1. Introduction

In the early stage of Web development, it was current practice to approach Web applications by simply 'building the solution', with little emphasis on the development process. However, many companies are now experiencing severe problems in the management of Web sites, as these grow in size and complexity, need to inter-operate with other applications, and exhibit requirements that change over time.

State-of-the-practice Web development tools help simplify the generation and deployment of data-intensive Web applications by means of page generators, such as Microsoft's Active Server Pages or JavaSoft's Java Server Pages, whose primary function is to dynamically extract content from data sources and include it into user-programmed page templates. Even if these systems are very productive implementation tools, they offer scarce support to bridge the gap between requirements collection and the subsequent phases of the development process. We have directly experienced that many companies building Web applications deeply need design methods, formalisms, languages, and tools, which could

* Corresponding author.

[1] {ceri,fraterna}@elet.polimi.it

[2] bongio@fusberta.elet.polimi.it

complement current Web technology in an effective way, covering all the aspects of the design process.

In response to this need, the W3I3 Project (funded by the European Community under the Fourth Framework Program) is focusing on 'Intelligent Information Infrastructure' for data-intensive Web applications. The project, driven by the requirements of two major Web developers (Otto-Versand from Germany, specialized in e-commerce, and the Dutch PTT (KPN), involved in Web-hosting services) has produced a novel Web modeling language, called WebML, and a supporting CASE environment, called **Toriisoft** [3]. WebML addresses the high-level, platform-independent specification of data-intensive Web applications and targets Web sites that require such advanced features as the one-to-one personalization of content and the delivery of information on multiple devices, like PCs, PDAs, digital televisions, and WAP phones. Toriisoft is a suite of design tools, which covers the entire life cycle of Web applications and follows a model-driven approach to Web design, centered on the use of WebML.

In this paper, we focus on the presentation of WebML, and in particular on its composition and navigation modeling primitives. More information on the W3I3 Project and on the ToriiSoft tool suite can be found at http://www.toriisoft. com and http://www.txt.it/w3i3.

1.1. WebML in a nutshell

WebML enables designers to express the core features of a site at a high level, without committing to detailed architectural details. WebML concepts are associated with an intuitive graphic representation, which can be easily supported by CASE tools and effectively communicated to the non-technical members of the site development team (e.g., with the graphic designers and the content producers). WebML also supports an XML syntax, which instead can be fed to software generators for automatically producing the implementation of a Web site. The specification of a site in WebML consists of four orthogonal perspectives.

[3] http://www.toriisoft.com

(1) *Structural Model*, expresses the data content of the site, in terms of the relevant entities and relationships (see Fig. 1). WebML does not propose yet another language for data modeling, but is compatible with classical notations like the E/R model [9], the ODMG object-oriented model [5], and UML class diagrams [4]. To cope with the requirement of expressing redundant and calculated information, the structural model also offers a simplified, OQL-like query language, by which it is possible to specify derived information.

(2) *Hypertext Model*, describes one or more hypertexts that can be published in the site. Each different hypertext defines a so-called site view (see Fig. 2). Site view descriptions in turn consist of two sub-models.
   - *Composition Model*, specifies which pages compose the hypertext, and which content units make up a page. Six types of content units can be used to compose pages: data, multi-data, index, filter, scroller and direct units. Data units are used to publish the information of a single object (e.g., a music album), whereas the remaining types of units represent alternative ways to browse a set of objects (e.g., the set of tracks of an album). Composition units are defined on top of the structure schema of the site; the designer dictates the underlying entity or relationship on which the content of each unit is based. For example, the AlbumInfo data unit showing the information on an album in Fig. 2 refers to the Album entity specified in the structure schema of Fig. 1.
   - *Navigation Model*, expresses how pages and content units are linked to form the hypertext. Links are either non-contextual, when they connect semantically independent pages (e.g., the page of an artist to the home page of the site), or contextual, when the content of the destination unit of the link depends on the content of the source unit. For example, the page showing an artist's data is linked by a contextual link to the page showing the index of reviews of that specific artist. Contextual links are based on the structure schema, because they connect content units whose underlying entities are associated by relationships in the structure schema.

(3) *Presentation Model*, expresses the layout and graphic appearance of pages, independently of the output device and of the rendition language, by means of an abstract XML syntax. Presentation specifications are either page-specific or generic. In the former case they dictate the presentation of a specific page and include explicit references to page content (e.g., they dictate the layout and the graphic appearance of the title and cover data of albums); in the latter, they are based on predefined models independent of the specific content of the page and include references to generic content elements (for instance, they dictate the layout and graphic appearance of all attributes of a generic object included in the page).

(4) *Personalization Model*, models explicitly users and user groups in the structure schema in the form of predefined entities called User and Group. The features of these entities can be used for storing group-specific or individual content, like shopping suggestions, list of favorites, and resources for graphic customization. Then, OQL-like declarative expressions can be added to the structure schema, which define derived content based on the profile data stored in the User and Group entities. This personalized content can be used both in the composition of units or in the definition of presentation specifications. Moreover, high-level business rules, written using a simple XML syntax, can be defined for reacting to site-related events, like user clicks and content updates. Business rules typically produce new user-related information (e.g., shopping histories) or update the site content (e.g., inserting new offers matching users' preferences). Queries and business rules provide two alternative paradigms (a declarative and a procedural one) for effectively expressing and managing personalization requirements.

In the ToriiSoft tool suite, WebML specifications are given as input to a code generator, which translates them into some concrete markup language (e.g., HTML or WML) for rendering the composition, navigation and presentation, and maps the abstract references to content elements inside pages into concrete data retrieval instructions in some server-side scripting language (e.g., JSP or ASP).

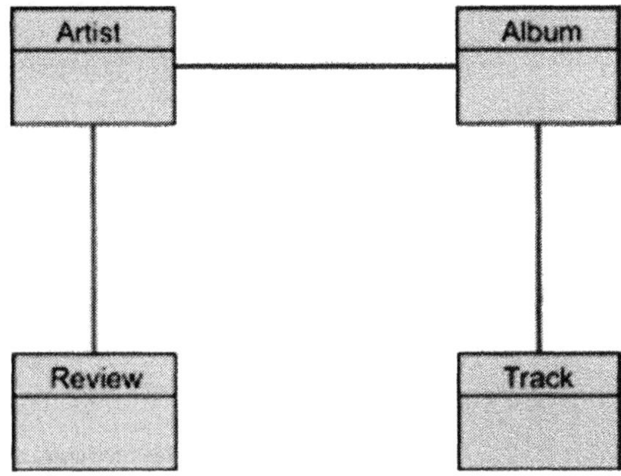

Fig. 1. Example of structure schema.

1.2. WebML by example

Fig. 1 shows a simple structure schema for the publication of albums and artists information. Artists publish albums composed of tracks, and have biographic information and reviews of their work. To publish this information as a hypertext on the Web, it is necessary to specify criteria for composition and navigation, i.e., to define a site view. Fig. 2 shows an excerpt from a site view specification, using WebML graphical language. The hypertext consists of three pages, shown as dashed rectangles. Each page encloses a set of units (shown as solid rectangles with different icons) to be displayed together in the site. For example, page AlbumPage collects information on an album and its artist. It contains a data unit (AlbumInfo) showing the information on the album, an index unit (TrackIndex) showing the list of the album's tracks, and another data unit (ArtistInfo) containing the essential information on the album's artist. The AlbumInfo unit is connected to the ArtistInfo unit by an intermediate direct unit (ToArtist), meaning that the AlbumInfo refers to the (single) artist who composed the album shown in the page. The ArtistInfo unit has one outgoing link leading to a separate page containing the list of review, and one link to a direct unit pointing to the artist's biographic data, shown on a separate page. Note that changing the hypertext topology is extremely simple: for example, if the ReviewIndex data unit is specified inside the AlbumPage instead of on a separate page, then the index of reviews is kept together with the album and artist info. Alternatively,

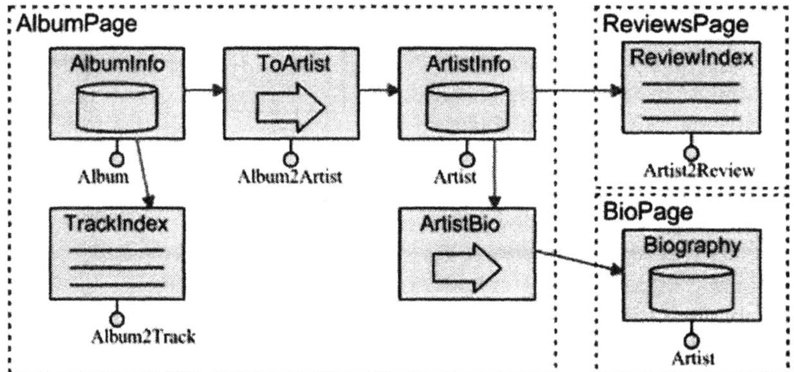

Fig. 2. Example of WebML composition and navigation specification.

if the ReviewIndex unit is defined as a multi-data unit, instead of an index unit, all reviews (and not only their titles) are shown in the ReviewsPage. A possible HTML rendition of the AlbumPage page of Fig. 2 (with some additional features omitted for simplicity in the example of Fig. 2) can be seen by accessing the site www.cdnow.com and then entering the page of any album.

1.3. Design process in WebML

Web application development is a multi-facet activity involving different players with different skills and goals. Therefore, separation of concerns is a key requirement for any Web modeling language. WebML addresses this issue and assumes a development process where different kinds of specialists play distinct roles: (1) the data expert designs the structural model; (2) the application architect designs pages and the navigation between them; (3) the style architect designs the presentation styles of pages; (4) the site administrator designs users and personalization options, including business rules.

A typical design process using WebML proceeds by iterating the following steps for each design cycle.

- *Requirements Collection.* Application requirements are gathered, which include the main objectives of the site, its target audience, examples of content, style guidelines, required personalization and constraints due to legacy data.
- *Data Design.* The data expert designs the structural model, possibly by reverse-engineering the existing logical schemas of legacy data sources.
- *Hypertext Design 'in the large'.* The Web application architect defines the structure 'in the large' of the hypertext, by identifying pages and units, linking them, and mapping units to the main entities and relationships of the structure schema. In this way, he develops a 'skeleton' site view, and then iteratively improves it. To support this phase, WebML-based tools must enable the production of fast prototypes to get immediate feedback on all design decisions.
- *Hypertext Design 'in the small'.* The Web application architect concentrates next in the design 'in the small' of the hypertext, by considering each page and unit individually. At this stage, he may add non-contextual links between pages, consolidate the attributes that should be included within a unit, and introduce novel pages or units for special requirements (e.g., alternative index pages to locate objects, filters to search the desired information, and so on). During page design in the small, the Web application architect may discover that a page requires additional information, present in another concept semantically related to the one of the page currently being designed. Then, he may use the derivation language, to add ad hoc redundant data to the structure schema and include it in the proper units.
- *Presentation Design.* Once all pages are sufficiently stable, the Web style architect adds to each page a presentation style.
- *User and Group Design.* The Web administrator defines the features of user profiles, based on personalization requirements. Potential users and user groups are mapped to WebML users and groups, and possibly a different site view is created for

each group. The design cycle is next iterated for each of the identified site views. 'Copy-and-paste' of already designed site view pages and links may greatly speed up the generation of other site views.

- *Customization Design.* The Web administrator identifies profile-driven data derivations and business rules, which may guarantee an effective personalization of the site.

Some of the above stages can be skipped in the case of development of a simple Web application. In particular, defaults help at all stages the production of simplified solutions. At one extreme, it is possible to develop a default initial site view directly from the structural schema, skipping all of the above stages except the first one (see Section 4.4).

2. The structural model

The fundamental elements of WebML structure model are entities, which are containers of data elements, and relationships, which enable the semantic connection of entities. Entities have named attributes, with an associated type; properties with multiple occurrences can be organized by means of multi-valued components, which corresponds to the classical part-of relationship. Entities can be organized in generalization hierarchies. Relationships may be given cardinality constraints and role names. As an example, the following XML code represents the WebML specification of the structural schema illustrated in Fig. 1.

```
<DOMAIN id="SupportType" values="CD Tape Vinyl">

<ENTITY id="Album">
  <ATTRIBUTE id="title" type="String"/>
  <ATTRIBUTE id="cover" type="Image"/>
  <ATTRIBUTE id="year" type="Integer"/>
  <COMPONENT id="Support" minCard="1" maxCard="N">
    <ATTRIBUTE id="type" userType="SupportType"/>
    <ATTRIBUTE id="listPrice" type="Float"/>
    <ATTRIBUTE id="discountPercentage" type="Integer"/>
    <ATTRIBUTE id="currentPrice" type="Float" value="Self.listPrice *
                (1 - (Self.discountPercentage / 100))"/>
  </COMPONENT>
  <RELATIONSHIP id="Album2Artist" to="Artist" inverse="ArtistToAlbum"
                minCard="1" maxCard="1"/>
  <RELATIONSHIP id="Album2Track to="Track" inverse="Track2Album"
                minCard="1" maxCard="N"/>
</ENTITY>

<ENTITY id="Artist">
  <ATTRIBUTE id="firstName" type="String"/>
  <ATTRIBUTE id="lastName" type="String"/>
  <ATTRIBUTE id="birthDate" type="Date"/>
  <ATTRIBUTE id="birthPlace" type="String"/>
  <ATTRIBUTE id="photo" type="Image"/>
  <ATTRIBUTE id="biographicInfo" type="Text"/>
  <RELATIONSHIP id="Artist2Album" to="Album" inverse="Album2Artist"
                minCard="1" maxCard="N"/>
  <RELATIONSHIP id="Artist2Review" to="Review" inverse="Review2Artist"
                minCard="0" maxCard="N"/>
</ENTITY>
```

```
<ENTITY id="Track">
  <ATTRIBUTE id="number" type="Integer"/>
  <ATTRIBUTE id="title" type="String"/>
  <ATTRIBUTE id="mpeg" type="URL"/>
  <ATTRIBUTE id="hqMpeg" type="URL"/>
  <RELATIONSHIP id="Track2Album" to="Album" inverse="Album2Track"
                minCard="1" maxCard="1"/>
</ENTITY>

<ENTITY id="Review">
  <ATTRIBUTE id="text" type="Text"/>
  <ATTRIBUTE id="author" type="String/>
  <RELATIONSHIP id="Review2Artist" to="Artist" inverse="Artist2Review"
                minCard="1" maxCard="1"/>
</ENTITY>
```

The structural schema consists of four entities (Artist, Album, Review and Track) and three relationships (Artist2Album, Artist2Review, Album2-track). Entity Album has a multi-valued property represented by the Support component, which specifies the various issues of the album on vinyl, CD, and tape. Note that each issue has a discounted price, whose value is computed by applying a discount percentage to the list price, by means of a derivation query. Derivation is briefly discussed in Section 5.1.

3. The composition model

The purpose of composition modeling is to define which nodes make up the hypertext contained in the Web site. More precisely, composition modeling specifies content units (units for short), i.e., the atomic information elements that may appear in the Web site, and pages, i.e., containers by means of which information is actually clustered for delivery to the user. In a concrete setting, e.g., an HTML or WML implementation of a WebML site, pages and units are mapped to suitable constructs in the delivery language, e.g., units may map to HTML files and pages to HTML frames organizing such files on the screen.

WebML supports six types of unit to compose an hypertext:

- *data units*, show information about a single object, e.g., an instance of an entity or of a component;
- *multidata units*, show information about a set of objects, e.g., all the instances of an entity or all the sub-components of a composite object;
- *index units*, show a list of objects (entity or component instances), without presenting the detailed information of each object;
- *scroller units*, show commands for accessing the elements of an ordered set of objects (the first, last, previous, next, *i*th);
- *filter units*, show edit fields for inputting values used for searching within a set of object(s) those ones that meet a condition;
- *direct units*, do not display information, but are used to denote the connection to a single object that is semantically related to another object.

Data and multidata units present the actual content of the objects they refer to, whereas the remaining types of units permit one to locate objects. Data units refer to a single object. Multidata, index, filter, and scroller refer to a set of objects. Therefore, they are collectively called container units.

3.1. Data units

Data units are defined to select a mix of information, which provides a meaningful view of a given concept of the structure schema. More than one unit can be defined for the same entity or component, to offer alternative points of view (e.g., a short or long, textual or multimedia version of the object).

The definition of a data unit requires (1) the indication of the concept (entity or component) to which the unit refers, and (2) the selection of the attributes to include in the unit. Syntactically, data units are de-

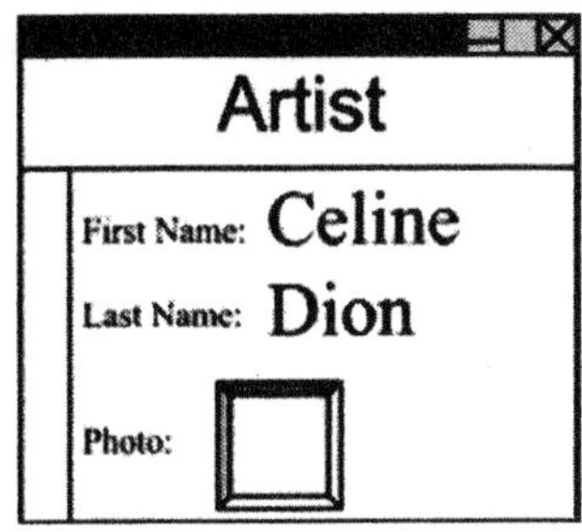

Fig. 3. WebML graphic notation for data units, and a possible rendition in HTML.

Fig. 4. WebML graphic notation for multidata units, and a possible rendition in HTML.

fined using the DATAUNIT element, which provides tags and attributes for the various aspects of unit definition. The selective inclusion of content in a unit is specified using the element INCLUDE. Included attributes must be chosen among those declared in the structure schema for the entity or component. The INCLUDEALL element can be used to specify that all attributes are included. For example, the following definitions introduce two units for presenting the Artist entity. The goal of these definitions is to provide a short view of artists (limited to the first name, last name, and photo) and a complete view, including all data.

```
<DATAUNIT id="ShortArtist"
          entity="Artist">
  <INCLUDE attribute="firstName"/>
  <INCLUDE attribute="lastName"/>
  <INCLUDE attribute="photo"/>
</DATAUNIT>

<DATAUNIT id="BiographyUnit"
          entity="Artist">
  <INCLUDEALL/>
</DATAUNIT>
```

Fig. 3 shows the WebML graphic notation for representing a data unit and its underlying entity, and a possible rendition of the ShortArtist data unit in an HTML-based implementation.

3.2. Multi-data units

Multi-data units present multiple instances of an entity or component together, by repeating the presentation of several, identical data units. Therefore, a multi-data unit specification has two parts: (1) the container which includes the instances to be displayed, which may refer to an entity, relationship, or component; (2) the data unit used for the presentation of each instance. Syntactically, a multi-data unit is represented by a MULTIDATAUNIT element, which includes a nested DATAUNIT element. The container is an argument of the external MULTIDATAUNIT element. The following example shows how all albums can be shown in the same multidata unit, by displaying all attributes of each individual album.

```
<MULTIDATAUNIT id="MultiAlbumUnit"
               entity="Album">
  <DATAUNIT id="AlbumUnit"
            entity="Album">
    <INCLUDEALL/>
  </DATAUNIT>
</MULTIDATAUNIT>
```

Fig. 4 shows the WebML graphic notation for representing a multidata unit and a possible rendition of the multidata unit in an HTML-based implementation.

3.3. Index units

Index units present multiple instances of an entity or component as a list, by denoting each object as an entry in the list. An index unit specification has two main parts: (1) the container which includes the instances to be displayed, which may be an entity, relationship, or component; (2) the attributes used as index key. Syntactically, an INDEXUNIT element is used, which includes a nested DESCRIPTION element. The following example shows how all albums can be shown in a list, by displaying only the title of each individual album. Fig. 5 shows the WebML graphic notation for representing an index unit and a possible

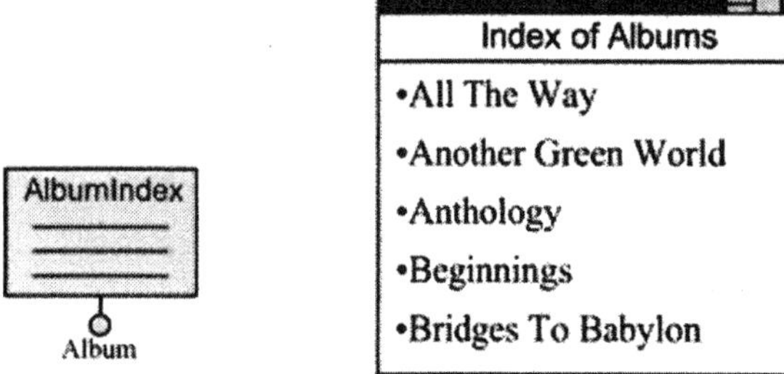

Fig. 5. WebML graphic notation for index units, and a possible rendition in HTML.

Fig. 6. WebML graphic notation for scroller units, and a possible rendition in HTML.

rendition of the index unit in an HTML-based implementation.

```
<INDEXUNIT id="AlbumIndex"
           entity="Album">
  <DESCRIPTION Key="title"/>
</INDEXUNIT>
```

3.4. Scroller units

Scroller units provide commands to scroll through the objects in a container, e.g., all the instances of an entity or all the objects associated to another object via a relationship. A scroller unit is normally used in conjunction with a data unit, which represents the currently visualized element of the container. Syntactically, the `SCROLLERUNIT` element is used, which specifies the container (entity, relationship, or component) providing the set of objects to scroll, and suitable attributes to express which scrolling commands to use. For example, the following declaration introduces a unit for moving along the set of reviews of an artist, whereby it is possible to move to the first, previous, next and last review.

```
<SCROLLERUNIT id="AlbumScroll"
        entity="Album" first="yes"
        last="yes" previous="yes"
        next="yes"/>
```

Fig. 6 shows the WebML graphic notation for representing a scroller unit and a possible rendition in an HTML-based implementation.

3.5. Filter units

Filter units provide input fields to search the objects in a container, e.g., all the instances of an entity whose attributes contain a given string. A filter unit is normally used in conjunction with an index or multidata unit, which present object matching the search condition. Syntactically, the `FILTERUNIT` element is used, which specifies the container (entity, relationship, or component) providing the set of objects to search. Inside the `FILTERUNIT` element, the `SEARCHATTRIBUTE` element is used to specify a search predicate on the value of a specific attribute. This element tells the attribute on which the search has to be performed and the comparison operator to use. In the following example, the AlbumFilter unit specifies a search form over the set of all albums. The form includes two input fields: the former for inputting a string to be located in the album's title, the latter for inputting the publication time interval of the album.

```
<FILTERUNIT id="AlbumFilter"
            entity="Album"/>
  </SEARCHATTRIBUTE name="title"
                    predicate="like">
  </SEARCHATTRIBUTE name="year"
                    predicate="between">
</FILTERUNIT>
```

Fig. 7 shows the WebML graphic notation for representing a filter unit and a possible rendition in an HTML-based implementation.

3.6. Direct units

Direct units are a syntactic convenience to express a particular kind of index, which always contains a single object associated to another object by a one-to-one relationship. Differently from index units, direct units are not displayed, but merely support the speci-

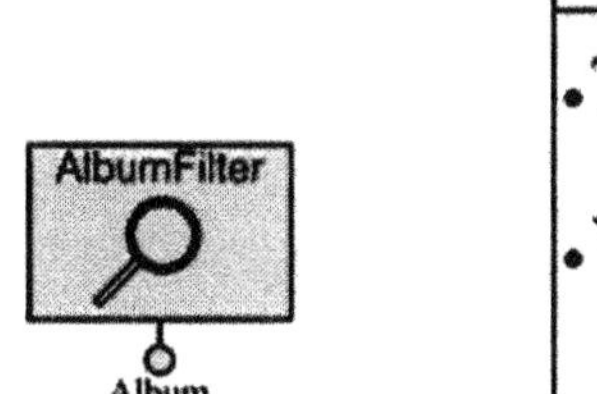

Fig. 7. WebML graphic notation for filter units, and a possible rendition in HTML.

fication of the relationship that associates the two related objects. Syntactically, direct units are expressed with the DIRECTUNIT element, as shown in the following example, which expresses the connection between an album and its unique artist:

```
<DIRECTUNIT id="ToArtist"
            relation="Album2Artist"/>
```

Fig. 2 includes two direct units. The former (ToArtist) connects each album to its (single) artist; the latter (ArtistBio) connects two data units over the same artist, one showing only a short presentation, the other including all biographic information.

3.7. Pages

The granularity of units may be too fine for the composition requirements of an application, which normally demand that the information contained in several units be delivered together (e.g., the data of an artist and the index of the albums he has published). To cope with this requirement, WebML provides a notion of page. A page is the abstraction of a self-contained region of the screen, which is treated as an independent interface block (e.g., it is delivered to the user independently and in one shot). Examples of concrete implementations of the abstract concept of page in specific languages may be a frame in HTML or a card in WML.

Pages may be internally organized into units and/or recursively other pages. In the latter case, sub-pages of a container page are treated as independent presentation blocks (similarly to the notion of frames within frame sets in HTML). Nested sibling sub-pages may be in conjunctive form (i.e., displayed together) or in disjunctive form (i.e., the display of one sub-page is alternative to the display of another sibling sub-page).

AND/OR sub-pages permit one to represent many complex page structures occurring in practice. The simplest case occurs when a portion of a page is kept fixed (e.g., the left frame in an HTML page), and another portion may display variable information based on user commands (e.g., the information in the right frame may be replaced by different data after a user's click in the left frame).

Syntactically, the organization of units into pages is specified using the PAGE element, as shown in the XML fragment of Fig. 8a, where a page portion (the sub-page named 'leftmost') contains the indexes of past and recent issues, and the remaining portion (the sub-page named 'rightmost') displays album information.

The graphic notation and possible HTML rendition of this XML specification is also illustrated in Fig. 8a. Note that the pages are shown as dashed boxes around their enclosed units and/or sub-pages.

```
<PAGE id="outermost">
<PAGE id="leftmost">
     <UNIT id="pastIndex"/>
     <UNIT id="thisYearIndex"/></PAGE>
<PAGE id="rightmost">
     <UNIT id="AlbumInfo"/></PAGE>
</PAGE>
```

Suppose now that we want a page to include the index of albums and artists, together with the information of either the album or the artist. This requires the introduction of alternative sub-pages, which is done in WebML using the ALTERNATIVE element. The XML specification in Fig. 8b describes the needed page structure. Note that since the page composition (and not only the object to display) changes, if we select an artist or an album from the indexes, the ALTERNATIVE element is required to specify which alternative sub-pages should be used to display artist and album information. The graphic notation and possible HTML rendition of the XML specification are also shown in Fig. 8b.

```
<PAGE id="outermost">
 <PAGE id="leftmost">
     <UNIT id="artistIndex"/>
     <UNIT id="albumIndex"/> </PAGE>
```

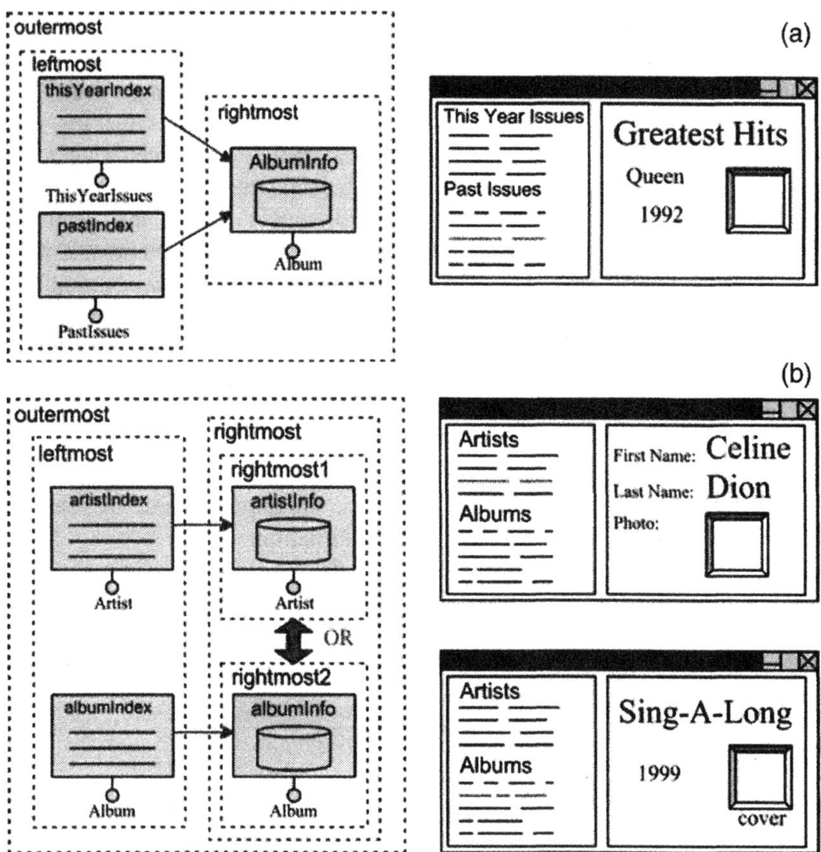

Fig. 8. (a) WebML textual and graphic notation for nested AND pages. (b) WebML graphic notation nested AND/OR pages, and a possible rendition in HTML.

```
 <PAGE id="rightmost">
   <ALTERNATIVE>
    <PAGE id="rightmost1">
        <UNIT id="artistInfo"/> </PAGE>
    <PAGE id="rightmost2">
        <UNIT id="albumInfo"/> </PAGE>
   </ALTERNATIVE>
 </PAGE>
</PAGE>
```

4. The navigation model

Units and pages do not exist in isolation, but must be connected to form a hypertext structure. The purpose of navigation modeling is to specify the way in which the units and pages are linked to form a hypertext. To this purpose, WebML provides the notion of link. There are two variants of links.

(1) *Contextual links*, connect units in a way coherent to the semantics expressed by the structure schema of the application. A contextual link carries some information (called context) from the source unit to the destination unit. Context is used to determine the actual object or set of objects to be shown in the destination unit.
(2) *Non-contextual links*, connect pages in a totally free way, i.e., independently of the units they contain and of the semantic relations between the structural concepts included in those units. Syntactically, contextual and non-contextual links are denoted by element INFOLINK and HYPERLINK, respectively nested within units and pages.

The following example demonstrates the use of contextual links, by showing a piece of hypertext composed of three linked units: a data unit showing an artist's data, an index unit showing albums, and a data unit showing album's data.

```
<DATAUNIT id="ArtistUnit"
          entity="Artist">
  <INCLUDEALL/>
  <INFOLINK id="link1"
            to="AlbumIndex"/>
</DATAUNIT>
```

```
<INDEXUNIT id="AlbumIndex"
           relation="Artist2Album">
  <DESCRIPTION key="title"/>
  <INFOLINK id="link2" to="AlbumUnit"/>
</INDEXUNIT>
```

```
<DATAUNIT id="AlbumUnit"
          entity="Album">
  <INCLUDEALL/>
</DATAUNIT>
```

The ArtistUnit data unit, based on entity Artist, is linked via an INFOLINK to the index unit, which is based on the relationship ArtistToAlbum. Such index unit in turn is linked by a second INFOLINK to the AlbumUnit data unit, based on entity Album. The semantics of the above contextual links is that:

- due to the first link (link1) a navigation anchor is added inside the artist's data unit by means of which the user can navigate to the index unit listing all the albums of a specific artist;
- due to the second link (link2), a set of navigation anchors (one per each entry in the index) is added to the index unit by means of which the user can navigate to one of the listed albums.

Context information flows along both links. The identifier of the artist whose albums are to be listed in the index unit flows from the source to the destination of the former link (link1). The identifier of the selected album flows from the source to the destination of the second link (link2), to determine the object shown in the data unit. Fig. 9a shows the WebML graphic notation for representing the above contextual links and a possible rendition of such piece of hypertext in an HTML-based implementation. In this example, each unit is placed in a separate page; therefore, three distinct HTML pages are generated. Grouping units within pages and establishing contextual links are two orthogonal design primitives, as demonstrated by Fig. 9b, where units ArtistUnit and AlbumIndex are kept on the same page. By linking data units and container units it is possible to obtain a variety of navigation modes, as shown in Fig. 9c,d where the index and album data unit are replaced by a multidata unit showing all albums of an artist together, both on the same page of the artist (case c), and in a separate page (case d).

The following rules summarize the context information that flows out of a unit through a contextual link.

- *Data units*, the identifier of the object currently shown in the unit;
- *Index units*, the key value selected from the index list;
- *Scroller units*, the identifier of the object selected by using the scrolling commands;
- *Filter unit*, the attribute values given in input by the user in the data entry form;
- *Direct units*, the key value of a single object;
- *Multidata unit*, the context information associated with the data units nested within the multidata unit.

Non-contextual links are demonstrated by the example of Fig. 10, where the page of an artist is linked to a separate, unrelated page, which contains the index of all albums. In this case, no context information flows along the link, because the content of the unit in the destination page (AllAlbums) is totally independent of the source page of the navigation. Note that, to underline the absence of context flow between units, non-contextual links are drawn between pages.

```
<DATAUNIT id="ArtistUnit"
          entity="Artist">
  <INCLUDEALL/>
</DATAUNIT>
<INDEXUNIT id="AllAlbums"
           entity="Album">
  <DESCRIPTION key="title"/>
</INDEXUNIT>
```

```
<PAGE id="ArtistPage">
  <UNIT id="ArtistUnit"/>
  <HYPERLINK id="link1"
             to="AllAlbumsPage"/>
</PAGE>
<PAGE id="AllAlbumsPage">
  <UNIT id="AllAlbums"/>
</PAGE>
```

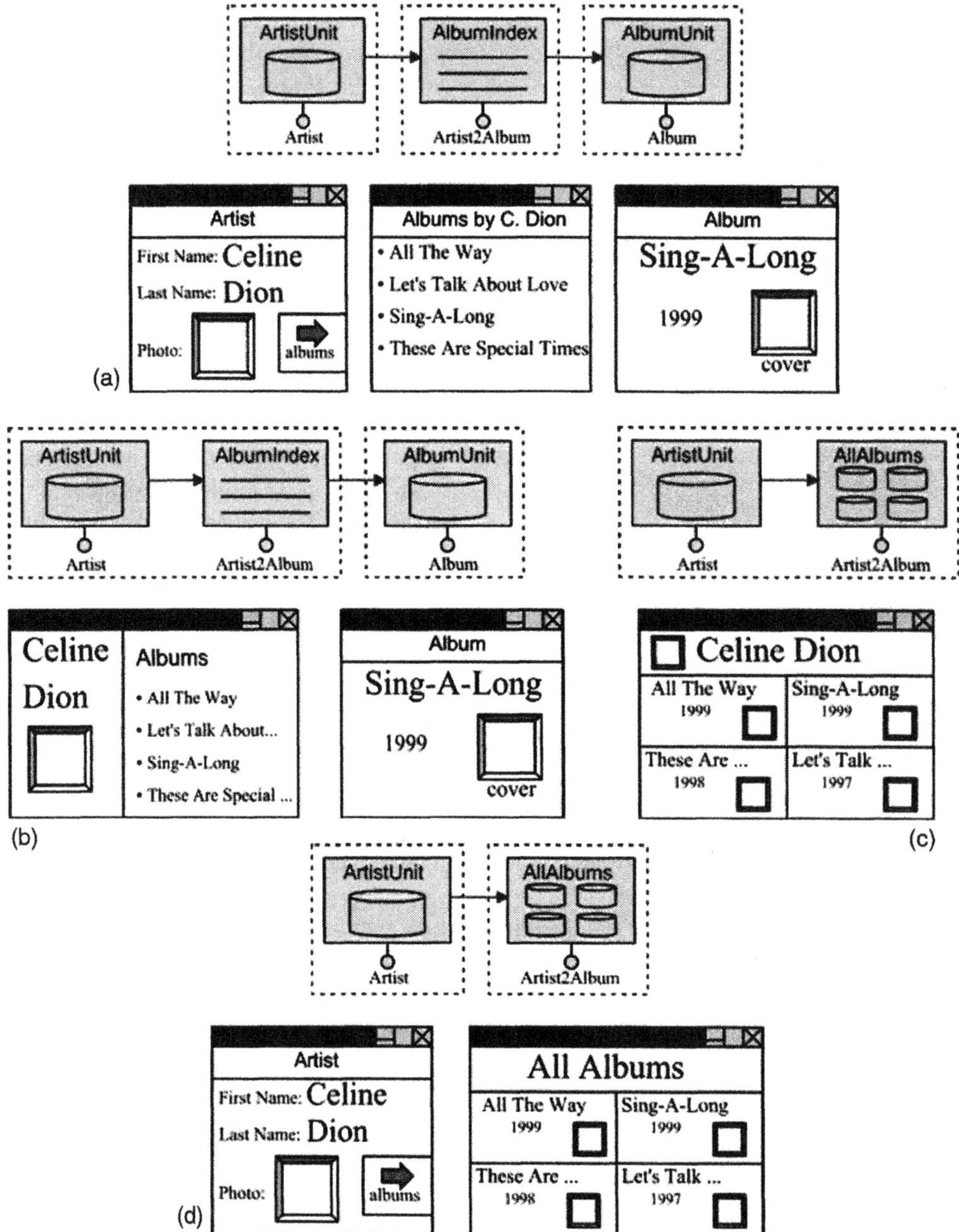

Fig. 9. (a) Index-based navigation (index in a separate page), and a possible rendition in HTML. (b) Index-based navigation (index in the source page), and a possible rendition in HTML. (c) Composite page including one data and one related multidata unit. (d) Separating the page including the artist data unit and the page including the multidata unit showing all the artist's albums.

4.1. Hidden navigation

In many sites, the interaction between the user and the application is proactive in two senses: not only the user chooses what content to see by clicking on hyperlinks, but sometimes also the system autonomously determines which page to show, by 'anticipating' the effect of some user clicks. This

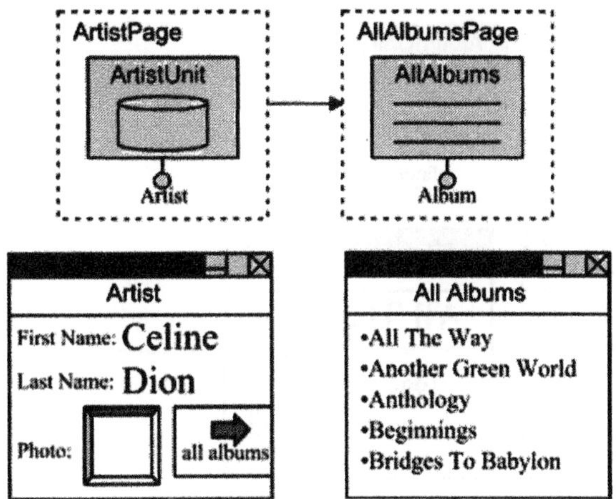

Fig. 10. WebML notation for non-contextual links.

feature can be modeled in WebML, by expressing the 'filling semantics' of pages containing multiple units. For example, the user may access a page, which contains two units: an index unit over an entity pointing to a data unit on that entity. In this case, the content of the pointed data unit is 'pending', i.e., it depends on the user's choice of one element in the preceding index unit. WebML offers three alternatives to cope with pending units.

(1) Leaving the pending unit empty, so that the user must explicitly perform a selection in one or more preceding units to display the content of the pending unit.
(2) Filling the pending unit with a predefined default value (e.g., the first element chosen from a preceding index unit).
(3) Filling the pending unit with a default value expressed by means of a declarative query (e.g., the object of a preceding index unit that satisfies a given predicate).

Syntactically, the treatment of a pending unit is specified by choosing one of the above three options as the value of an ad hoc filling attribute, located in the 'pointing' unit. If no value is specified, the pending unit is left empty.

4.2. Navigation chains and 'Web patterns'

The typical configuration of a structured hypertext alternates data units, showing information on objects, with units that support the navigation from one object to another related object. Fig. 9 shows two elementary forms of such a configuration, where an index unit and a multidata unit are used to move from an Artist to his/her Albums. WebML units and links can be composed to express more complex navigation structures, where multiple intermediate pages support the navigation towards a data unit; we call these configurations 'navigation chains'. Frequently used navigation chains are sometimes referred to as 'Web patterns' (see Section 6 and [3,13,16,17]). In this section, we briefly present a selection of representative examples of navigation chains, to show how WebML concepts can be composed to formally describe a wide variety of situations occurring in practice.

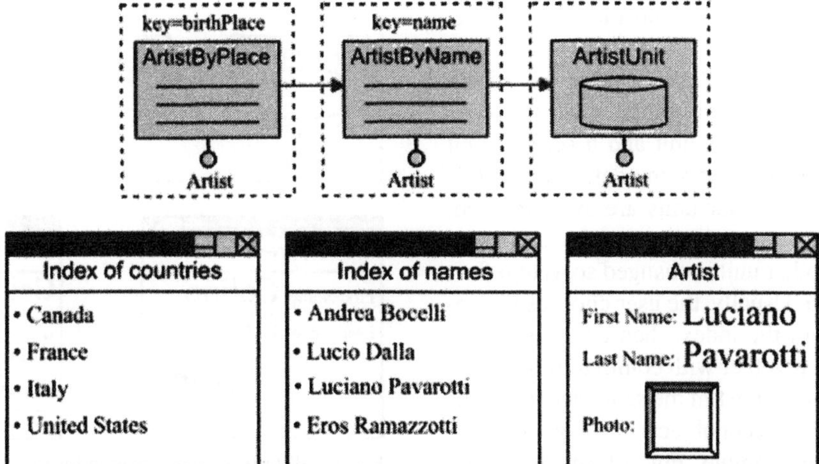

Fig. 11. WebML graphic notation for multi-step index, and a possible rendition in HTML.

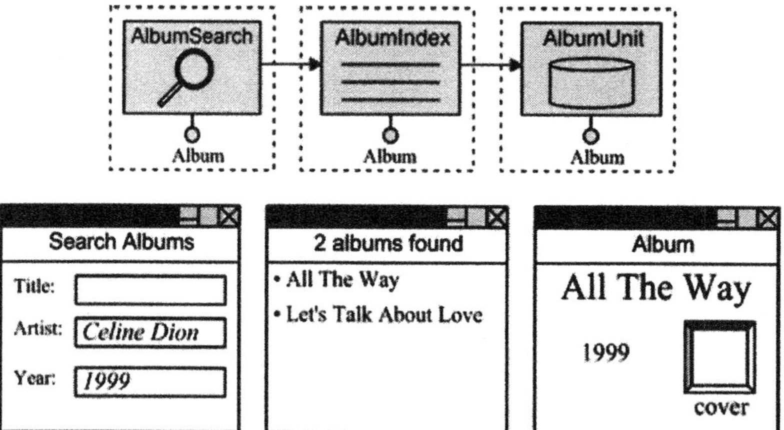

Fig. 12. WebML graphic notation for filtered index, and a possible rendition in HTML.

Fig. 11 shows an example of a navigation chain called multi-step index. A sequence of index units is defined over a given entity, such that each index unit specifies as its description key one of the attributes forming the key of the destination object. As shown in the figure, the semantics of this pattern is a hierarchical index, where the final object is located by means of a multi-step selection of its key value.

Fig. 12 shows an example of a navigation chain configuration called filtered index. A sequence formed by a filter unit followed by an index unit is defined over a given entity. As shown in the figure, the semantics of this pattern is a three-step selection. First, the user provides input values to use as a search condition, then the objects matching such condition are presented in an index and, finally, the user may choose his object of interest from the (smaller) set shown in the index.

Fig. 13 shows an example of a navigation chain configuration called indexed guided tour. The configuration includes an index unit and a scroller unit which both are linked to the same data unit; in this case, the index and scroller units are synchronized: when the user performs a selection on either of them, the context of the other unit is changed so as to reflect the user's selection. Usually, the user chooses his object of interest from the index, then he is presented the selected object together with commands to access the first, last, previous, next in the sequence, and thus he can explore the adjacent objects of the given one.

As a conclusive example, Fig. 14 shows a ring. In this configuration, two data units are linked via a

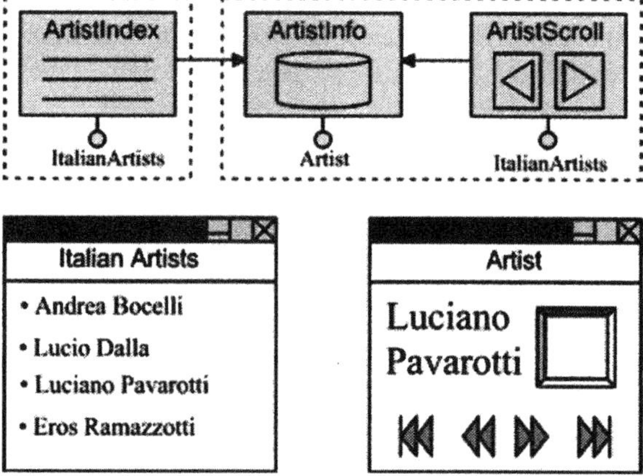

Fig. 13. WebML graphic notation for indexed guided tour, and a possible rendition in HTML.

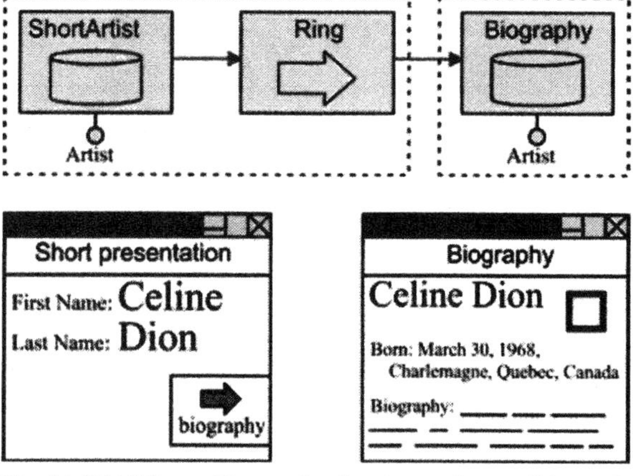

Fig. 14. WebML graphic notation for ring, and a possible rendition in HTML.

direct unit defined over the identity relationship (i.e., the predefined relationship linking each object to itself). The two data units show different attributes of the same object (e.g., a long and a short presentation) thus enabling multiple views of the same item with variable details.

4.3. Site views

The separation between the structure model and the hypertext model advocated by WebML enables the definition of multiple views of the same data, which can be tuned to meet complex access requirements. For instance, different site views can be designed for alternative access devices or for distinct user groups. A WebML site view comprises a set of pages and links, with associated presentation styles, all reachable from a designated home page. All the site views of a given Web application share the same structural schema, which represents at high level the data sources underlying the site. The structural schema, in turn, is mapped to one or more data sources, possibly embodied within legacy systems.

4.4. Default hypertext

To enable fast prototyping, WebML includes several shortcuts to obtain a running application from incomplete specifications. In particular, given the structural model, WebML supports the notion of default hypertext, automatically generated according to the following rules.

- For each entity, a data unit is generated which includes all attributes.
- For each one-to-many or many-to-many relationship R between an entity A and an entity B, an index unit P is provided over the relationship R, based on the primary key of the entity B; two contextual links are established from the data unit of A to P and from P to the data unit of B.
- For each one-to-one or many-to-one relationship R between an entity A and an entity B, a direct unit P is provided over relationship R; two contextual links are established from the data unit of A to P and from P to the data unit of B.
- For each component C of an entity A, a multi-data unit P is provided over component C, and a contextual link is established from the data unit of A to P.
- For each entity, an index unit is created on the entity's primary key, which includes the list of all instances of the entity.

The default hypertext maps every concept of the structural model into exactly one unit and provides default indexes over all the defined entities. Given the default hypertext, a default site view is defined by associating units to pages as follows.

- Data unit over entities and index pages over relationships are put in distinct pages.
- Component multi-data units are kept in the same page as the data unit of the entity or component that encloses them.
- Index units over entities are put in distinct pages. An empty page is created as the home page, and connected by means of non-contextual links to the all these pages.

Fig. 15 illustrates the default site view for the structure schema of Fig. 1.

4.5. Validity of WebML hypertexts

Not all the WebML specifications obtained by linking units and by clustering them into pages correspond to conceptually correct and practically implementable Web sites. First, we give a collection of rules for the progressive construction of correct logical hypertexts (units connected by contextual links) and then rules for verifying physical hypertexts (how units are clustered into pages).

A valid logical hypertext is defined by the following constructive rules.

(1) A logical hypertext constituted by a navigation chain over an entity followed by a data unit on such entity is valid.
(2) The logical hypertext obtained by adding a linked sequence of container units over a relationship or component of the structural schema, from a data unit of a valid hypertext to another data unit (an existing one or a new one) is valid.

Fig. 16 illustrates an invalid logical hypertext, made of a contextual link between two data units upon the entities Artist and Album; the hypertext is invalid because the album to be shown following the link is undefined.

A second notion of correctness is based on the definition of valid physical hypertext and checks that the aggregation of units into pages produces applica-

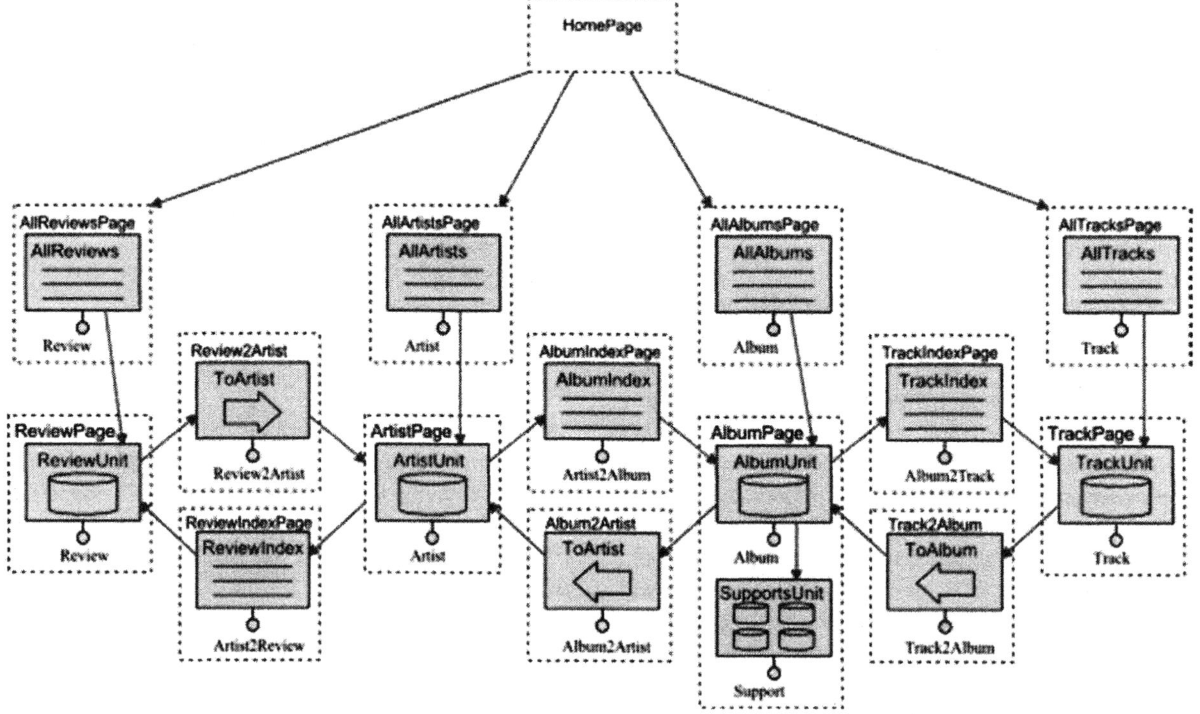

Fig. 15. A default site view.

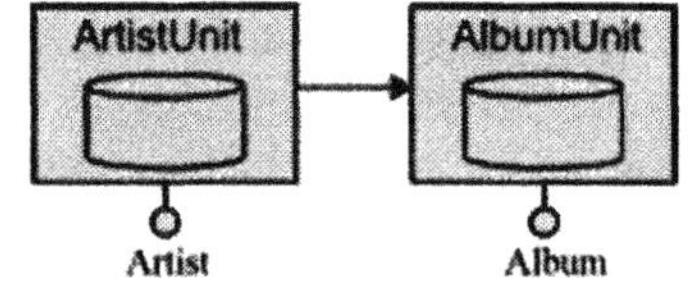

Fig. 16. Example of invalid logical hypertext.

tion screens whose content is well defined. Given a valid logical hypertext, a valid physical hypertext is obtained by grouping units within pages and adding non-contextual links between pages according to the following rules.

(1) *Reachability*: there must be no pages (with the exception of the home page) without any incoming link (contextual or non-contextual).
(2) *Context flow*: if a page contains a unit that needs context information, then such context information must be supplied by a contextual link. There are two sub-cases:
    (a) the unit may receive context from another unit in the same page that does not require context information (e.g., an index unit over an entity);
    (b) if the above case does not hold, the unit must receive its context from all the entry units in the same page, where an entry unit is any unit which is the destination of contextual links coming from outside the page.
(3) *Uniqueness of context*: if a unit in the page has more than one path from which it receives context information from another unit inside the same page, then only for one such path the initial filling option should be enabled.

Note that physical hypertext validity does not restrict the presence of non-contextual links between pages. These can be placed at will, without hampering the site correctness.

Fig. 17 (left part) illustrates an invalid physical hypertext: the Album page includes the ArtistInfo unit, which requires context information to determine the album to display, but is not linked to any other unit. On accessing the page by means of the link into the AlbumInfo unit, the content of the TrackIndex unit is well defined, but the content of the ArtistInfo unit is not, because this unit has no incoming contextual link supplying the identifier of the

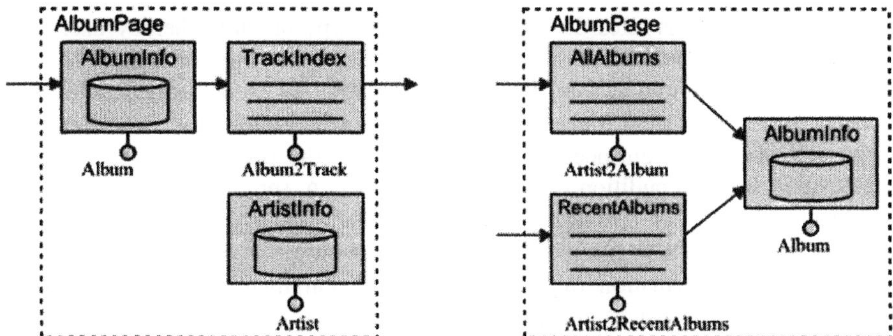

Fig. 17. Two examples of invalid physical hypertext.

artist to show. Fig. 17 (right part) illustrates a second potentially invalid physical hypertext, in which the AlbumInfo unit has two incoming contextual links, one from the index unit showing all albums of an artist, the other one from the index unit showing only this year's albums. If both indexes specify a non-empty initial filling option, the content of the destination data unit may be not uniquely defined upon accessing the page.

5. Other features of WebML

We next present briefly the other features of WebML; for greater detail, we refer the reader to [7] and to the W3I3 project's documentation available at the site http://www.toriisoft.com.

5.1. Derivation

Derivation is the process of adding redundant information to the structure schema, in order to augment its expressiveness. Derivation in WebML is expressed in a formal query language, which is a restricted version of OQL [5]; it is possible to derive entities, attributes, components, and relationships. An example of derivation is in the definition of the attribute currentPrice of the component Support shown in Section 2.

5.2. User modeling

In order to support personalization, WebML includes an explicit notion of group and user. Groups describe sets of users with common characteristics, whereas users denote individuals. Users always belong to at least one group, possibly the default one (called everyone). Users may belong to more than one group, but in this case they are required to provide a default group or to indicate one preferred group when accessing the site. Each user or group is described by means of specific properties (collectively called profile), modeled as special type of entities in the structure schema. As the normal entities, user and group profiles may be internally sub-structured into attributes and components, classified by means of inheritance, semantically related to other entities, and used for writing derivation queries. Typically, profiles include user- or group-specific data (e.g., the most frequently or recently visited objects, the list of the last purchases), whose content is progressively modified during the Web site evolution as a result of user's actions.

5.3. Declarative and procedural personalization

Personalization is the definition of content or presentation style based on user profile data. In WebML, units, pages, their presentation styles, and site views can be defined so as to take user- or group-specific data into account. This can be done in two complementary ways.

- *Declarative personalization.* The designer defines derived concepts (e.g., entities, attributes, multi-valued components) whose definition depends on user-specific data. In this way, customization is specified declaratively; the system fills in the information relative to each user when computing the content of units.
- *Procedural personalization.* WebML includes an

XML syntax for writing business rules that compute and store user-specific information. A business rule is a triple event–condition–action, which specifies the event to be monitored, the precondition to be checked when the event occurs, and the action to be taken when the condition is found true. Typical tasks performed by business rules are the assignment of users to user groups based on dynamically collected information (e.g., the purchase history, or the access device), the notification of messages to users upon the update of the information base (push technology), the logging of user actions into user-specific data structures (user tracking), and so on.

As an example of declarative personalization, the computation of an album's discounted price could be based on personalized discounts, associated with users or user groups. As an example of procedural personalization, a business rule could assign a customer to the 'best buyer' group, based on his/her purchase history. WebML declarative and procedural personalization are discussed in greater details in [7].

5.4. Presentation model

Presentation modeling is concerned with the actual look and feel of the pages identified by composition modeling. WebML pages are rendered according to a style sheet. A style sheet dictates the layout of pages and the content elements to be inserted into such layout, and is independent of the actual language used for page rendition. For better reusability, two categories of style sheets are provided: untyped style sheets (also called models) describe the page layout independently of its content, and thus can be applied regardless of the mapping of the page to a given concept; typed style sheets are specified at a finer granularity and thus apply only to pages describing specific concepts.

5.5. Updates and operations

WebML is currently being extended to support a new type of pages for performing operations and updating the site content. Write access modeling is achieved by extending the current set of WebML concepts with the introduction of operation units, a novel type of unit whereby users can invoke operations on the site. An operation unit specifies the operation to be performed, and is linked to other units, which may show the alternative results of performing the operation (e.g., in case of success or failure). A set of generic update operations (such as insert, delete, modify for entities, and drop, add for relationships) are predefined and need not be declared. Parameters needed to perform the operation either come from the context flowing to the operation unit via an incoming link, or are supplied by the user via forms. Operation units generalize the notion of filter units, which can be regarded as a particular operation unit associated to a search operation over a set of objects. Thanks to the orthogonal nature of WebML, operation units can be freely combined with the other types of units to compose complex pages, mixing information to be presented to the user and interfaces to perform operations on the site. Operation units are currently being designed by looking at trolleys and online purchase procedures used in the most sophisticated e-commerce sites.

6. Previous related work

WebML builds on several previous proposals for hypermedia and Web design language, including HDM, HDM-lite, RMM, OOHDM, and Araneus. Its design principles are stated in [6]; WebML as presented in this paper is a (quite radical) evolution of an earlier version presented in [7].

HDM [14] pioneered the model-driven design of hypermedia applications and influenced several subsequent proposals like HDM-lite [12], a Web-specific version of HDM, RMM [15], Strudel [11], and OOHDM [18]. All these methods offer powerful built-in navigation constructs, as opposed to WebML, which includes simple, yet orthogonal, composition and navigation primitives. Araneus [2] is a recent proposal for Web design and reverse-engineering, in which the data structure is described by means of the Entity Relationship Model and navigation is specified using the Navigation Conceptual Model (NCM). Conceptual modeling is followed by logical design, using the relational model for the structural part, and the Araneus Data Model (ADM) for the navigation aspects. Araneus also includes predefined navigation primitives and does not model presentation at an abstract level.

The relevance of using conceptual modeling techniques in the context of the Web was addressed in a specific workshop [8]. In particular, [18] describes an evolution of OOHDM (Object-Oriented Hypermedia Design Method), a methodology for designing hypertexts that shares with WebML the vision of orthogonal design dimensions; specifically, OOHDM is concerned with the conceptual modeling, navigation design, interface design, and implementation. Navigational contexts in OOHDM provide a rich repertoire of fixed navigation options.

Given that Web applications are, after all, software artifacts, it is not surprising that several proposals exist for using UML [4] for their specification. In particular, [10] shows how the architecture of Web applications can be modeled in UML. Web pages are modeled as UML components, distinguishing among their 'server side aspects' (i.e., their relationship with middle tiers, databases, and other resources) and their 'client side aspects' (i.e., their relationships with browsers, Java applets, ActiveX controls and so on). This distinction of roles and the use of stereotypes enables a quite effective modeling of Web applications using standard UML notations; however, the article does not show Web-specific evolutions of the notation, which are described as ongoing and traceable on the UML and Rose sections of http://www.rational.com.

A closer approach to WebML is described in [1]; the article presents UIML, a user interface language designed for abstracting from appliance-specific details while designing the user interface of a Web application. UIML designers model all aspects of a user interface in XML, so that only a portion of the specification (the style section) is appliance-dependent. Although WebML approaches the broader context of Web conceptual modeling, UIML and WebML's presentation model share the goal of obtaining independence of specifications from output devices and the use of XML as a vehicle to achieve this goal.

Recent articles have shown increasing interest on model-driven design of Web applications. In particular, several authors have addressed the importance of using patterns for describing navigation across Web sites [3,13,16,17]. Several examples in Section 4.2 show how the design patterns described in [14,17] can be formally described, and indeed WebML is a very effective description language for Web patterns.

7. Conclusions

In this paper, we have presented the core of WebML, a high-level specification language for designing data-intensive Web applications. With respect to previous proposals, WebML (1) stresses the definition of orthogonal navigation and composition primitives, which the designer can arbitrarily compose to model complex requirements, (2) includes an explicit notion of site view, whereby the same information can be structured in different ways to meet the interests of different user groups or to obtain a granularity optimized for users approaching the site with different access devices, (3) covers advanced aspects of Web site modeling, including presentation, user modeling, and personalization.

WebML is the backbone of Toriisoft, an environment for the computer-aided design of Web sites currently in an advanced development state. In particular, the Toriisoft tool suite comprises (1) Site Designer, for editing the WebML specifications of the structural, hypertext, and personalization models, (2) Presentation Designer, for visually defining presentation style sheets, (3) Site Manager, for site administration and evolution. The architecture is completed by a Template Generator, which transforms WebML specifications into Microsoft's Active Server Page (ASP) templates running on top of relational DBMSs for data storage. Code generation is based on standard XML technology (XSL) and therefore Toriisoft can be easily extended to support template generation in more than one markup language and for multiple server-side scripting engines. Work is ongoing on the translation of WebML specifications into WML-based ASP templates, thereby providing evidence that the model-driven approach of WebML is particularly effective in supporting multi-device Web sites.

Acknowledgements

WebML is the result of research work done in the context of the W3I3 Esprit Project sponsored by the

European Community. We wish to thank all W3I3 participants for the helpful feedback on the definition of the various WebML constructs. In particular, thanks to David Langley, Petra Oldengarm, Wim Timmerman, Mika Uusitalo, Stefano Gevinti, Ingo Klapper, Stefan Liesem, Marco De Michele, Fabio Gurgone, Alessandro Agustoni, Simone Avogadro, Marco Brioschi, and the innumerable POLI students who spent their time in the project.

References

[1] M. Abrams, C. Phanoriou et al., UIML: an appliance-independent XML user interface language, in: Proc. WWW8, Elsevier, Amsterdam, pp. 617–630.

[2] P. Atzeni, G. Mecca and P. Merialdo, Design and maintenance of data-intensive Web sites, in: Proc. EDBT 1998, pp. 436–450.

[3] M. Bernstein, Patterns of hypertexts, in: Proc. ACM Int. Conf. on Hypertext 1998, ACM Press, pp. 21–29.

[4] G. Booch, I. Jacobson and J. Rumbaugh, The Unified Modeling Language User Guide, The Addison-Wesley Object Technology Series, 1998.

[5] R.G.G. Cattell, D.K. Barry and D. Bartels (Eds.), The Object Database Standard: ODMG 2.0, Morgan Kaufmann Series in Data Management Systems, 1997.

[6] S. Ceri, P. Fraternali and S. Paraboschi, Design principles for data-intensive Web sites, ACM Sigmod Record 27 (4) (1998) 74–80.

[7] S. Ceri, P. Fraternali and S. Paraboschi, Data-driven, one-to-one Web site generation for data-intensive applications, in: Proc. VLDB 1999, pp. 615–626.

[8] P.P. Chen, D.W. Embley and S.W. Liddle (Eds.), Proc. Int. Workshop on the World Wide Web and Conceptual Modeling, Paris, Oct. 1999, Springer, New York, LNCS 1727.

[9] P.P. Chen, The entity-relationship model, towards a unified view of data, ACM Transactions on Database Systems 1 (1) (1976) 9–36.

[10] J. Conallen, Modeling Web application architectures with UML, Communications of the ACM 42 (10) (1999) 63–70.

[11] M.F. Fernandez, D. Florescu, J. Kang, A.Y. Levy and D. Suciu, Catching the boat with Strudel: experiences with a Web-site management system, in: Proc. ACM–SIGMOD Conf. 1998, pp. 414–425.

[12] P. Fraternali and P. Paolini, A conceptual model and a tool environment for developing more scalable, dynamic, and customizable Web applications, in: Proc. EDBT 1998, pp. 421–435.

[13] F. Garzotto, P. Paolini, D. Bolchini and S. Valenti, 'Modeling by patterns' of Web applications, in: P.P. Chen, D.W. Embley and S.W. Liddle (Eds.), Proc. Int. Workshop on the World Wide Web and Conceptual Modeling, Paris, Oct. 1999, Springer, New York, LNCS 1727, pp. 293–306.

[14] F. Garzotto, P. Paolini and D. Schwabe, HDM — a model-based approach to hypertext application design, TOIS 11 (1) (1993) 1–26.

[15] T. Isakowitz, E. Stohr and P. Balasubramanian, RMM: a methodology for structured hypermedia design, CACM 38 (8) (1995) 34–44.

[16] M. Nanard, J. Nanard and P. Kahn, Pushing reuse in hypertext applications development, in: Proc. ACM Int. Conf. on Hypertext 1998, ACM Press, pp. 11–20.

[17] G. Rossi, D. Schwabe and F. Lyardet, Improving Web information systems with navigational patterns, in: Proc. WWW8, Elsevier, Amsterdam, pp. 589–600.

[18] G. Rossi, D. Schwabe and F. Lyardet, Web application models are more than conceptual models, in: P.P. Chen, D.W. Embley and S.W. Liddle (Eds.), Proc. Int. Workshop on the World Wide Web and Conceptual Modeling, Paris, Oct. 1999, Springer, New York, LNCS 1727, pp. 239–252.

Stefano Ceri is full professor of Database Systems at the Dipartimento di Elettronica e Informazione, Politecnico di Milano; he has been a Visiting Professor at the Computer Science Department of Stanford University between 1983 and 1990. His research interests are focused on: data distribution, deductive and active rules, object-orientation and design methods for data-intensive Web sites. He is responsible for several projects at Politecnico di Milano, including W3I3: 'Web-Based Intelligent Information Infrastructures' (1998–2000). He was Associate Editor of ACM Transactions on Database Systems (1989–1992) and he is currently an associated editor of several international journals, including IEEE Transactions on Software Engineering. He is author of several articles in International Journals and Conference Proceedings, and is co-author of the books: Distributed Databases: Principles and Systems (McGraw-Hill, 1984); Logic Programming and Databases (Springer-Verlag, 1990); Conceptual Database Design: an Entity-Relationship Approach (Benjamin Cummings, 1992); Active Database Systems (Morgan Kaufmann, 1995); Advanced Database Systems (Morgan Kaufmann, 1997); The Art and Craft of Computing (Addison-Wesley, 1997); Designing Database Applications with Objects and Rules: the IDEA Methodology (Addison-Wesley, 1997); Database Systems: Concepts, Languages, and Architecture (McGraw-Hill, 1999).

Piero Fraternali is associate professor of Software Engineering at the Dipartimento di Elettronica e Informazione, Politecnico di Milano. His research interests are focused on: active rules, object-orientation, design methods for data-intensive Web sites, CASE tools for automatic Web site production, and wireless applications. He is author of several articles on International Journals and Conference Proceedings, and is co-author of the book: Designing Database Applications with Objects and Rules: the IDEA Methodology (Addison-Wesley, 1997). He is the technical manager of the W3I3 Project: 'Web-Based Intelligent Information Infrastructures' (1998–2000).

Aldo Bongio graduated at Politecnico di Milano in 1999, where he presently coordinates the development of the ToriiSoft Web Site Design Tool Suite. His research interests include XML, Web modeling languages, and Web design patterns.

JavaML: a markup language for Java source code

Greg J. Badros *

Department of Computer Science and Engineering, University of Washington, Box 352350, Seattle, WA 98195-2350, USA

Abstract

The classical plain-text representation of source code is convenient for programmers but requires parsing to uncover the deep structure of the program. While sophisticated software tools parse source code to gain access to the program's structure, many lightweight programming aids such as `grep` rely instead on only the lexical structure of source code. I describe a new XML application that provides an alternative representation of Java source code. This XML-based representation, called JavaML, is more natural for tools and permits easy specification of numerous software-engineering analyses by leveraging the abundance of XML tools and techniques. A robust converter built with the Jikes Java compiler framework translates from the classical Java source code representation to JavaML, and an XSLT stylesheet converts from JavaML back into the classical textual form.

Keywords: Java; XML; Abstract syntax tree representation; Software-engineering analysis; Jikes compiler

1. Introduction

Since the first computer programming languages, programmers have used a text representation as the medium for encoding software structure and computation. Over the years, techniques have been developed that largely mechanize the front-end of compilers; i.e., the part that performs the lexical analysis and parsing necessary to uncover the structure of programming language constructs represented as plain text. Tools such as Lex/Flex and Yacc/Bison [42] automate these tedious tasks by using well-founded concepts of regular expressions and grammars. Regular expressions describe how individual characters combine to form tokens, and the grammar enumerates how higher-level constructs are composed recursively of other constructs and primitive tokens. Together, these procedures convert a sequence of characters into a data structure called an *abstract syntax tree* (AST) which more directly reflects the structure of the program.

The textual representation of source code has several nice properties. It is fairly concise and is similar to natural languages, often making it easy to read. Text is a universal data format thus making source code easy to exchange and manipulate using a wide variety of tools including text editors, version control systems, and command pipeline utilities such as `grep`, `awk`, and `wc`.

Nevertheless, the classical source representation has numerous problems. The syntax of popular contemporary languages such as C++ and Perl push the limits of parsing capabilities. Constructing a front-end for such languages is difficult despite the support from tools. Perhaps more disconcerting is that evolving the syntax of the language often requires manipulating a fragile grammar. This limitation complicates handling an evolving language.

* E-mail: gjb@cs.washington.edu

1.1. Text representation and software tools

The most significant limitation of the classical source representation is that the structure of the program is made manifest only after parsing. This shortcoming forces language-specific parsing functionality to be duplicated in every tool that needs to reason about the program beyond its lexical nature. Compilers, by necessity, must work with the AST, and numerous other software-engineering tools would benefit from access to a structured representation of the source code. Unfortunately, many software-engineering tools do not embed a parser and thus are limited to lexical tasks.

There are several reasons why tool developers often avoid embedding a parser in tools. As mentioned previously, building a complete front-end is challenging for syntactically complex languages. Although re-use (e.g., of the grammar definition) simplifies the implementation, the resulting AST is not always intuitive. An AST typically reflects quirky artifacts of the grammar rather than representing the programming-level constructs directly. Additionally, embedding the front-end of a compiler may be deemed overkill when targeting a simple analysis that can do 'well enough' with lexical information.

Other complications arise if a transformation of the source code is desired: a change in the AST must ultimately be reflected in the classical source representation because that is the primary long-term storage format. Recreating a text representation from an AST is most straightforwardly done using an unparsing approach that can create undesired lexical side effects (e.g., changes in indentation or whitespace). Such changes can confuse the other lexical tools that a developer relies upon. For example, a version control system is unable to disambiguate between a meaningful change and a gratuitous one effected unintentionally.

Finally, using a parser in a tool necessarily targets that tool to a specific language, thus reducing its applicability and generality. Worse, because there is no standard structured external representation of a source program, supporting inter-operability of independent tools even targeting the same programming language is very difficult.

The end result of these complications is that developers often use simple, lexically oriented tools such as `grep` or search-and-replace within an editor. This approach sacrifices accuracy: imagine wanting to rename a local variable from `result` to `answer`. With simple search-and-replace, all occurrences of the word will be changed, even if they refer to characters inside comments, literal strings, or an unrelated instance field.

An alternate route taken by some developers is to rely instead on a fixed set of tools provided within an integrated development environment (IDE) that has access to the structure of their source program via an integrated language-specific parser. This approach sacrifices flexibility. IDEs generally provide only a limited set of capabilities and extending those is hard. Additionally, analyses and transformation on source code are often hard to automate or perform in batch using existing interactive environments. Some more advanced IDEs, such as IBM VisualAge for C++ [48], expose an application programming interface to the representation of the program. Although an improvement, this technique still suffers from an inability to separate simple tools from a complex environment and additionally creates a dependency on proprietary technology that may be undesirable.

1.2. A solution

One of the fundamental issues underlying the above problems is the lack of a canonical structured representation of the source code. We need a universal format for directly representing program structure that software tools can easily analyze and manipulate. The key observation is that XML, the eXtensible Markup Language [9], provides exactly this capability and is an incredibly empowering complementary representation for source code.

In this paper, I introduce the Java Markup Language, JavaML, an XML application for describing Java source programs. The JavaML document type definition (DTD) specifies the various elements of a valid JavaML document and how they may be combined. There is a natural correspondence between the elements and their attributes and the programming language constructs that they model. The structure of the source program is reflected in the nesting of elements in the JavaML document. With this representation, we can then leverage the wealth of tools for manipulating and querying XML and SGML documents to provide a rich, open infrastructure for software-engineering transformations and analyses on Java source code.

JavaML is well-suited to be used as a canonical representation of Java source code for tools. It shares most of the strengths of the classical representation and overcomes many weaknesses. The next section describes relevant features of Java and XML and Section 3 details the markup language and the implementations of converters between the classical representation and JavaML. Section 4 gives numerous examples of how existing XML and SGML tools can be exploited to perform source code analyses and transformations on the richer representation provided by JavaML. Sections 5 and 6 describe related work and suggest avenues for exciting future work, and Section 7 concludes. The full document type definition (DTD) for JavaML appears in Appendix A and further examples of converted source code are available from the author's JavaML Web page [4].

2. Background

The Java Markup Language is influenced by and benefits from numerous features of the two technologies it builds a bridge between: Java and XML.

2.1. Java

Although the XML-based representation of programming language constructs is language-independent, Java is an excellent candidate for experimenting with these ideas and techniques.

Java is a popular object-oriented programming language developed by Sun Microsystems in the mid-1990s [3,25]. It features a platform-independent execution model based on the Java Virtual Machine (JVM) and owes its quick acceptance to its use as a programming language for World Wide Web applications. Java combines a simple object model reminiscent of Smalltalk [26] with Algol block structure, a C++-like [49] syntax, a static type system, and a package system inspired by Modula-2 [10].

As in most other object-oriented (OO) languages, the primary unit of decomposition in Java is a *class* which specifies the behavior of a set of objects. Each class can define several *methods*, or behaviors, similar to functions or procedures. A class can also define *fields*, or state variables, that are associated with *instances* of the class called *objects*. Classes can inherit behavior and state from *superclasses*, thus forming a hierarchy of inter-related classes that permits factoring related code into classes at the top of the hierarchy, and encourages re-use. Behaviors are invoked by sending a *message* to a target receiver object that is a request to execute a method defined for that class. Choosing what method to execute in response to a message is called *dynamic dispatch* and is based on the run-time class of the object receiving the message. For example, an instance of the `ColoredBall` class may respond to the `draw` message differently than an instance of a `Ball` class. This ability to behave differently upon receipt of the same message is largely responsible for the extensibility benefits touted by the OO community.

Java is being widely used both in industry and in education, and it remains popular as a programming language on the Web. Unlike C++, a Java class definition exists in a single, self-contained file. There are no separate header files and implementation files, and Java is largely free from order-dependencies of definitions. A method body (when present) is always defined immediately following the declaration of the method signature. Additionally, Java lacks an integrated preprocessor. These features combine to make Java source programs syntactically very clean and make Java an ideal language for representing using XML. (The applicability of this approach to other languages is discussed further in Section 6.)

2.2. XML: eXtensible Markup Language

XML is a standardized eXtensible Markup Language [9] that is a subset of SGML, the Standard Generalized Markup Language [37]. The World Wide Web Consortium (W3C) designed XML to be lightweight and simple, while retaining compatibility with SGML. Although HTML (HyperText Markup Language) is currently the standard Web document language, the W3C is positioning XML to be its replacement. While HTML permits authors to use only a pre-determined fixed set of tags in marking up their document, XML allows easy specification of user-defined markup tags adapted to the document and data at hand [27,28].

An XML document consists simply of text marked up with tags enclosed in angle braces. A simple example is:

```
<?xml version="1.0"?>
<!DOCTYPE email SYSTEM "email.dtd">
<email>
  <head>
    <to>Mom</to>
    <to>Dad</to>
    <from>Greg</from>
    <subject>My trip</subject>
  </head>
  <body encoding="ascii">
   The weather is terrific!
  </body>
</email>
```

The `<email>` is an open tag for the `email` element. The `</email>` at the end of the example is the corresponding close tag. Text and other nested tags can appear between the open and close constructs. Empty elements are allowed and can be abbreviated with a specialized form that combines the open and close tags: <*tag-name*/>. In the above document, the `email` element contains two immediate children elements: a `head` and a `body`. Additionally, an XML open tag can associate attribute/value pairs with an element. For example, the `body` element above has the value `ascii` for its `encoding` attribute. For an XML document to be *well-formed*, the document must simply conform to the numerous syntactic rules required of XML documents (e.g., tags must be balanced and properly nested, attribute values must be of the proper form and enclosed in quotes, etc.).

A more stringent characterization of an XML document is *validity*. An XML document is valid if and only if it both is well-formed and adheres to its specified *document type definition*, or *DTD*. A document type definition is a formal description of the grammar of the specific language to be used by a class of XML documents. It defines all the permitted element names and describes the attributes that each kind of element may possess. It also restricts the structure of the nesting within a valid XML document. The preceding XML example is valid with respect to the following DTD:

```
<!-- email DTD -->
<!ENTITY % encoding-attribute
   "encoding (ascii|mime) #REQUIRED">
<!ELEMENT email (head,body)>
<!ELEMENT head (to+,from,subject?)>
<!ELEMENT to (#PCDATA)>
<!ELEMENT from (#PCDATA)>
<!ELEMENT subject (#PCDATA)>
<!ELEMENT body (#PCDATA)>
<!ATTLIST body
   encrypted (yes|no) #IMPLIED
   %encoding-attribute;>
```

According to this DTD, there are six element types. The `email` element must contain exactly one `head` followed by exactly one `body` element. The `head`, in turn, must contain one or more `to` elements and then a `from` element, followed by an optional `subject` element. The order of the elements must be as specified. Each of those elements may contain text (also know as *parsed character data* or PCDATA). The single `ATTLIST` declaration in the DTD specifies that the `body` element *may* specify a value for the `encrypted` attribute, and *must* specify either `ascii` or `mime` for the `encoding` attribute. The `ENTITY` declaration of the `encoding-attribute` (at the top of the DTD) is a simple way to factor out redundant text; the text given between the quotes is substituted as is into the following `ATTLIST` declaration (and, importantly, can be used in multiple `ATTLIST`s).

An XML document that is declared to adhere to this DTD is not valid if any of the above criteria are not met. For example, if the `from` element is missing from an `email` document, that document is not valid, though it may still be well-formed.

When modeling data in XML, a primary design decision is choosing whether to nest elements or to use attributes. In the above example, we could have folded all of the information contained in the `head` into attributes of the `email` element if we chose. There are several important differences between using attributes and nesting elements:

- attributes/value pairs are unordered, while nested children have a specific order;
- values for attributes may contain only character data, and may not include other markup, while nested children can arbitrarily nest further; and

- only one value for an attribute can be given, while multiple elements of the same class can be included by a parent element (e.g., we can have multiple `to` elements contained by the `head`).

Although the above distinctions sometimes mandate using one technique or the other, the decision is often initially a matter of taste. However, later experiences using the resulting documents may suggest revisiting the decision in order to facilitate or simplify some desired manipulation of the document.

Another useful data modeling feature of XML is the ability to attach unique identifiers to elements via an `id` attribute. These elements can then be referred to by `idref` attributes of other elements. A well-formed XML document must have every `idref` value match an `id` given in the document. The `id`–`idref` links describe edges that enable XML to represent generalized directed graphs, not just trees.

XML, in part due to its SGML heritage, is very well supported by tools such as Emacs editing modes, structure-based editors, DTD parsers and editors, validation utilities, querying systems, transformation and style languages, and many more tools. Numerous other W3C recommendations relate to XML including Cascading Style Sheets [8], XSL (Extensible Stylesheet Language) [19], XSLT (XSL for Transformations) [14], XPath [16], and DOM (Document Object Model) [2].

3. Java Markup Language (JavaML)

The Java Markup Language provides a complete self-describing representation of Java source code. Unlike the conventional character-based representation of programs, JavaML reflects the structure of the software artifact directly in the nesting of elements in the XML-based syntax. Additionally, it represents extra edges in the program graph using the `id` and `idref` linking capabilities of XML.

Because XML is a text-based representation, many of the advantages of the classical source representation remain. Because JavaML is an XML application, it is easy to parse, and all existing tools for working with XML can be applied to Java source code in its JavaML representation. JavaML tools can leverage the existing infrastructure and exploit the canonical representation to improve their inter-operability.

3.1. Possible approaches

Although the basic approach of using an XML application to model source code is fairly straightforward, there is a large design space for possible markup languages. The most obvious possibility is to simply use XML as a textual dump format of a typical abstract syntax tree derived from parsing source code. Consider the simple Java program:

```
import java.applet.*;
import java.awt.*;

public class FirstApplet
                     extends Applet {
  public void paint(Graphics g) {
    g.drawString("FirstApplet", 25, 50);
  }
}
```

Performing the obvious (but very unsatisfying) translation from the AST of the above might result in the below XML *for just the first line of code*:

```
<compilation-unit>
 <ImportDeclarationsopt>
  <ImportDeclarations>
   <ImportDeclaration>
    <TypeImportOnDemandDeclaration>
     import
     <Name>
      <QualifiedName>
       <Name>
        <SimpleName>java</SimpleName>
       </Name>
       .
       <Name>
        <SimpleName>applet</SimpleName>
       </Name>
      <QualifiedName>
     </Name>
     . *;
    </TypeImportOnDemandDeclaration>
   </ImportDeclaration>
  </ImportDeclarations>
 </ImportDeclarationsopt>
...
</compilation-unit>
```

Certainly this translation is far from ideal: it is unacceptably verbose and exposes numerous uninteresting details of the underlying grammar that was used to parse the classical source representation.

An alternate possibility is to literally mark-up the Java source program without changing the text of the program (i.e., to only add tags). This approach might convert the `FirstApplet.java` implementation to:

```
<java-source-program>
<import-declaration>import java.applet.*;
   </import-declaration>
<import-declaration>import java.awt.*;
   </import-declaration>
<class-declaration>

<modifiers>public</modifiers> class
   <class-name>FirstApplet</class-name>
    extends
     <superclass>Applet</superclass> {
  <method-definition>
   <modifiers>public</modifiers>
       <return-type>void</return-type>
    <method-name>paint</method-name>
     (<formal-arguments>
        <type>Graphics</type>
        <name>g</name>
      </formal-arguments>)
    <statements>{
    g.drawString("FirstApplet", 25, 50);
  } </statements>
 </method-definition>
}
</class-declaration>
</java-source-program>
```

This format is a huge step towards a more useful markup language. We have definitely added value to the source code and it is trivial to convert back to the classical representation: we simply remove all tags and leave the content of the elements behind (this removal of markup is exactly what the `stripsgml` [31] utility does). Although this representation seems useful for many tasks, it still has some problems. First, many of the details of the code are included in the textual content of elements. If we want to determine what packages are being imported, our XML query would need to lexically analyze the content of the import-declaration elements. Such analysis is inconvenient and does not take advantage of the capabilities that XML provides. Perhaps more significantly, the above XML representation retains artifacts from the classical source code that another representation might permit us to abstract away from and free ourselves of those syntactic burdens altogether.

3.2. The chosen representation

The prototype JavaML representation I have chosen aims to model the programming language constructs of Java (and, indeed, similar object-oriented programming languages) independently of the specific syntax of the language. One can easily imagine a SmalltalkML that would be very similar, and even an OOML that could be converted into both classical Java source code or Smalltalk file-out format. With this goal in mind, JavaML was designed from first principles of the constructs and then iteratively refined to improve the usefulness and readability of the resulting markup language.

JavaML is defined by the document type definition (DTD) in Appendix A, but is best illustrated by example. For the `FirstApplet.java` source code listed above, we represent the program in JavaML as shown in Fig. 1.

In JavaML, concepts such as methods, superclasses, message sends, and literal numbers are all directly represented in the elements and attributes of the document contents. The representation reflects the structure of the programming language in the nesting of the elements. For example, the literal string `"FirstApplet"` is a part of the message send, thus the `literal-string` element is nested inside the `send` element. This nesting is even more apparent when presented visually as in Fig. 2. See the author's JavaML Web page [4] for further examples.

The careful reader will observe that the JavaML representation is about three times longer than the classical source code. That expansion is a fundamental tradeoff of moving to a self-describing data format such as XML. It is important that the terse classical representation can be employed by programmers in certain tasks including ordinary development and program editing (though perhaps JavaML may be the underlying representation). JavaML is complementary to classical source code and is especially

```
1   <?xml version="1.0" encoding="UTF-8"?>
2   <!DOCTYPE java-source-program SYSTEM "java-ml.dtd">
3
4   <java-source-program name="FirstApplet.java">
5     <import module="java.applet.*"/>
6     <import module="java.awt.*"/>
7     <class name="FirstApplet" visibility="public">
8       <superclass class="Applet"/>
9       <method name="paint" visibility="public" id="meth-15">
10        <type name="void" primitive="true"/>
11        <formal-arguments>
12            <formal-argument name="g" id="frmarg-13">
13                <type name="Graphics"/></formal-argument>
14        </formal-arguments>
15        <block>
16          <send message="drawString">
17            <target><var-ref name="g" idref="frmarg-13"/></target>
18              <arguments>
19                <literal-string value="FirstApplet"/>
20                <literal-number kind="integer" value="25"/>
21                <literal-number kind="integer" value="50"/>
22              </arguments>
23           </send>
24        </block>
25      </method>
26    </class>
27  </java-source-program>
```

Fig. 1. FirstApplet.java converted to JavaML.

appropriate for tools while remaining accessible to and directly readable by developers.

3.3. Design decisions

JavaML provides more than just the structure of the source program. In Fig. 1, notice the use of the formal-argument `g` in line 17 as the target of the message send. The `idref` attribute of that `var-ref` tag points back at the referenced `formal-argument` element (through its `id` attribute). (The `id` value chosen for a to-be-referenced element must be unique within a document so each identifier is branded with an integer to keep the values distinct.) This linking is standard XML, thus XML tools are able to trace from a variable use to its definition to, e.g., obtain the type of the variable. Similar linking is done for local (block-declared) variables, and more could be done for other edges in the program structure graph. Although a single `var-use` tag would suffice for denoting any mention of a variable, JavaML instead disambiguates between references to variable values and variables used as lvalues: `var-ref` elements are used for the former, `var-set` for the latter.

Throughout JavaML, attributes of elements are used whenever the structure of the value can never be more complex than a simple text string. Attributes are used for modifiers such as `synchronized` and `final` and for visibility settings such as `public` or `private`. Attributes are not used for properties such as types because types have some structure: a type can consist of a base name and a number of dimensions, and it could also reference the definition of the class that implements the type, if desired. If, say, a return type were just the value of an attribute on the method element, the end user would unacceptably have to do string processing on the attribute's value `"int[][]"` to determine that the base type of that two-dimensional array was the primitive type `int`. Instead, types are modeled as explicit child elements such as `<type name="int" dimensions="2">`.

JavaML generalizes related concepts to simplify some analyses but also preserves distinctions that

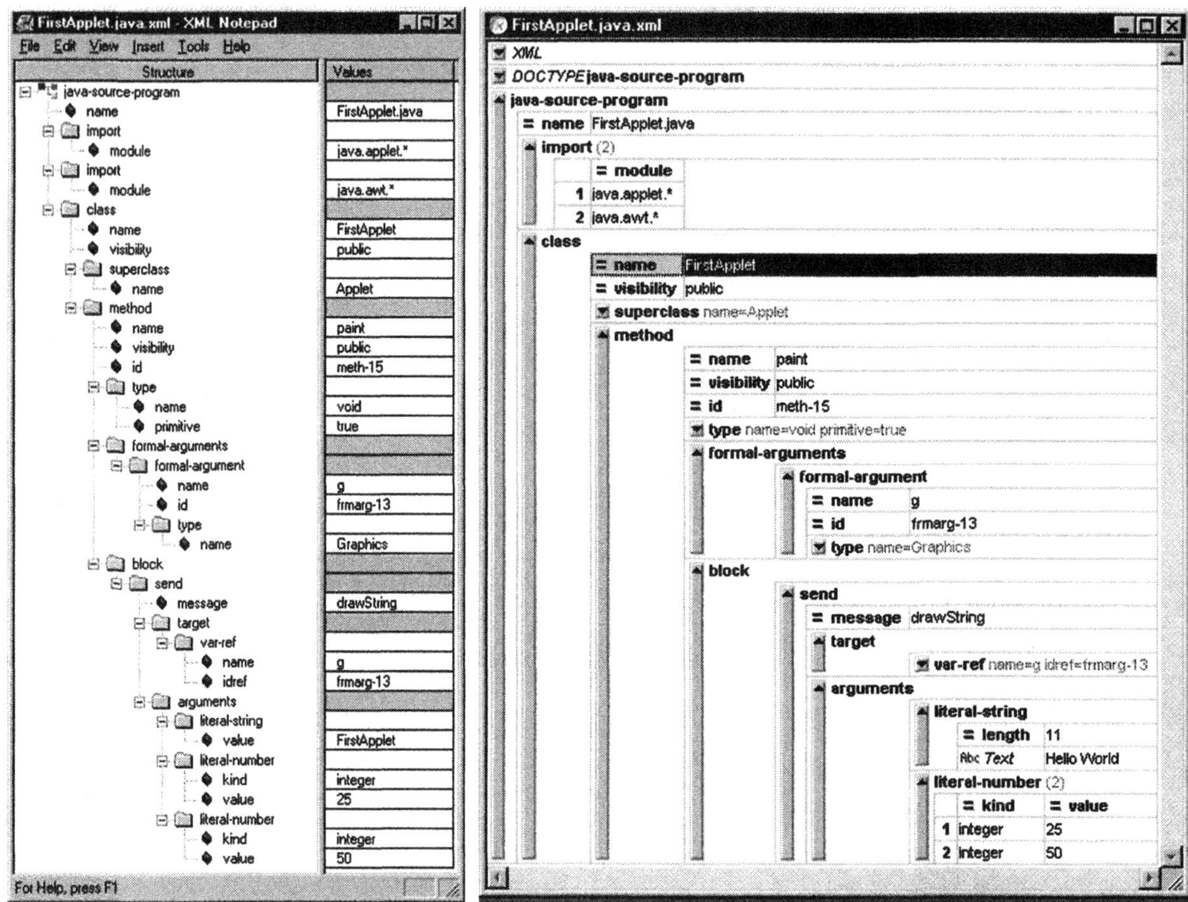

Fig. 2. Tree views of the JavaML representation of the `FirstApplet` example as displayed by the XML Notepad utility [44] (on the left/above) and XML Spy [36] (on the right/below).

may be needed for other tasks. For example, `45` and `1.9` are represented as: `<literal-number kind="integer" value="45">` and `<literal-number kind="float" value="1.9">`, respectively. An alternate possible markup is: `<literal-integer value="45">` and `<literal-float value="1.9">` but using separate element classes eliminates the tight relationship that both values are numbers and can complicate using the representation. Instead, we use a single element tag and disambiguate these literals based on a `kind` attribute. Thus, we can still tell the difference between a floating point literal and an integer literal, but in the common case we gain the same flexibility of numeric types that the Java language has.

Another place where JavaML generalizes language constructs is loops. Both `for` and `while` loops can be viewed as general looping constructs with 0 or more initializers, a guarding test that occurs before each iteration, 0 or more update operations, and a body of statements that comprise the looped-over instructions. Thus, instead of using two classes of elements, `for-loop` and `while-loop`, JavaML uses a single `loop` element that has a `kind` attribute with value either `for` or `while`. When a `while` loop is converted, it will have neither `initializer` nor `update` children, yet a `for` loop could potentially contain many of each. In contrast, distinct `do-loop` elements are used for `do` loops because they have their test performed at the end of the loop, instead of at the start.

As yet another example, we represent both instance and class (i.e., static) fields as `field` elements with a `static` attribute used to disambiguate.

Although there are more substantial differences between these two concepts than between `while` and `for` loops, it still seems beneficial to use a single kind of element for both kinds of fields.

Local variable declarations provide a syntactic shorthand that raises an interesting question about their underlying representation. The code segment `int dx, dy;` defines two variables both of type `int`, but with perhaps a subtle additional intention: that the two variables have the same type. For contrast, consider `int weight, i;`. Here, there probably is *not* the implicit desire that the two variables have the same type, but instead the shorthand syntax is being used simply for brevity. Because it is hard to automate distinguishing these cases, JavaML simply preserves this syntactic feature by using a `continued="true"` attribute on variable declarations that exploit this shorthand.

Comments in source code are especially troublesome to deal with in JavaML. At present, the DTD permits certain 'important' elements (including `class`, `anonymous-class`, `interface`, `method`, `field`, `block`, `loop`) to specify a `comment` attribute. Determining which comments to attach to which elements is challenging; the current implementation simply queues up comments and includes all that appear since the last 'important' element in the `comment` attribute of the current such element.

An alternate possibility for comments is to just insert them in the JavaML representation as parsed character data interspersed with the normal structure, thus leaving the semantic inference problem to another tool. Unfortunately, this would force various elements to have 'mixed content' which reduces the validation capabilities when checking for DTD conformance. Using XML Schema [51] instead of DTDs may make this approach more useful.

3.4. Implementation of converter

To experiment with the design of JavaML and gain experience in using the representation, it was essential to implement a converter from the Java classical source representation to JavaML. Within the IBM Jikes Java compiler framework [32], I added an `XMLUnparse` method to each of the AST nodes. This change, along with some small additional code for managing the options to request the XML output, results in a robust and fast JavaML converter. In total, I added about 1650 non-comment-non-blank lines of C++ code to the Jikes framework to support JavaML.

The converter has been tested by converting 15,000 lines of numerous sample programs including the 4300 line Cassowary Constraint Solving Toolkit [5] and over 20 diverse applets [50]. Each of the files converted was then validated with respect to the JavaML DTD using James Clark's Jade package's `nsgmls` tool [12]. The processing of the entire regression test takes only about twelve seconds on the author's RedHat6-based dual Pentium III-450 machine.

Also implemented is an XSLT stylesheet that outputs the classical source representation given the JavaML representation. The stylesheet consists of 65 template rules and just under 600 lines of code. It was tested (using both Saxon [39] and XT [15]) on numerous programs by processing a file to JavaML, back-converting it, and then re-converting to JavaML: no differences should exist between the result and the originally converted JavaML file.

All of the source code is available from the JavaML home page [4].

4. Leveraging XML

JavaML uses XML as an alternate, structured representation of a Java source program. Although the abstraction away from syntactic details of Java is convenient, the more important benefit is that JavaML enables the use of the rich infrastructure developed to support SGML and XML. Instead of building analysis and transformation tools from scratch to work on a proprietary binary structured format for a program, existing SGML and XML tools can be used, combined, and extended. XML tools encompass a broad range of features that include querying and transformation, document differencing and merging [33], and simple APIs for working with the document directly. In this paper, I will (for space reasons) limit discussion to uses of only three tool groups:

- the XML toolbox (ltxml) from Edinburgh University [52] which contains `sgcount`, `sgrpg`, `sggrep`, and more;

- XSLT [14] processors (e.g., XT [15] and Saxon [39]) and the XML parser XP [13];
- the Perl XML::DOM package [20] which exposes a DOM level 1 [2] interface to an XML tree.

These are just a very small subset of the tools that prove useful when working with JavaML. In the following examples, we will query `Hangman.java.xml`, the JavaML representation of the Hangman applet available at Sun Microsystems' applet page [50] and also at the JavaML home page [4]. Although these examples are small by real-world standards, XML and SGML tools target documents ranging up through lengthy books so the implementations are designed to scale well.

One common software-engineering task (for better or for worse) is to accumulate metrics about a source code artifact. With JavaML, the SGML utility `sgcount` does an excellent job of summarizing the constructs in a Java program (the output of commands has been pruned and slightly edited for presentation):

```
% sgcount Hangman.java.xml
```

outputs:

```
arguments               103
array-initializer       4
assignment-expr         60
catch                   3
class                   1
if                      27
true-case               27
false-case              7
field                   28
field-access            18
import                  5
java-source-program     1
literal-char            5
literal-boolean         5
literal-null            5
literal-number          127
literal-string          61
local-variable          23
loop                    13
method                  18
new                     4
new-array               5
return                  5
send                    99
type                    96
var-ref                 262
var-set                 52
...
```

In the above output, each row lists an element class and the number of times that that element appeared in the document. Thus, we can easily see that there are 18 `method` elements, thus there are 18 method definitions. Similarly, we can see that there is 1 class definition, 262 variable references, 99 message sends, and 61 string literals. This summary is far more indicative of the content of a program than a typical lexical measure such as the number of lines of code.

Suppose we wish to see all the string literals that a program contains. We can do this trivially using `sggrep` on the JavaML representation of the program:

```
% sggrep '.*/literal-string' \
          < Hangman.java.xml
```

outputs:

```
<literal-string
   value='audio/dance.au'/>
<literal-string
   value='img/dancing-duke/T'/>
<literal-string value='.gif'/>
<literal-string
   value='img/hanging-duke/h'/>
<literal-string value='.gif'/>
<literal-string value='Courier'/>
<literal-string value='Courier'/>
...
```

Notice that the output of `sggrep` is also a (not necessarily valid nor even well-formed) XML document. Thus we can string together SGML and XML tools in a Unix pipeline to combine tools in novel and useful ways. For example, it is sometimes worthwhile to convert results back into ordinary Java source representation to aid the human software-engineer. We can do this using `results-to-plain-source` which is a wrapper around an XSLT stylesheet that converts JavaML back into plain source code:

```
% sggrep '.*/literal-string' \
      < Hangman.java.xml \
      | results-to-plain-source
```

outputs:

```
"audio/dance.au"
"img/dancing-duke/T"
".gif"
"img/hanging-duke/h"
".gif"
"Courier"
"Courier"
...
```

We can also query the JavaML source for elements based on values of their attributes. For example, if we wish to find all sends of the message `setFont` we can do so easily and precisely:

```
% sggrep '.*/send[message=setFont]' \
                        < Hangman.java.xml
```

outputs:

```
<send message='setFont'>
  <target>
    <var-ref name='g'
             idref='frmarg-212'/>
  </target>
  <arguments>
    <var-ref name='font'
             idref='locvar-611'/>
  </arguments>
</send>
<send message='setFont'>
  <target>
    <var-ref name='g'
             idref='frmarg-212'/>
  </target>
  <arguments>
    <var-ref name='wordFont'/>
  </arguments>
</send>
```

Because of the structural markup, places where the seven characters 'setFont' appear in a comment, a literal string, or a variable name will *not* be reported by this query. A similar attempt to retrieve this information using lexical tools would likely contain those false positives. Imagine trying to find all type cast expressions using only lexical tools; the over-use of parentheses in Java expressions make that task very difficult, while it is trivial with JavaML thanks to the `cast-expr` element.

Another class of common analyses is the semantic checks done by the compiler prior to translation. For example, in Java code, only abstract classes may have abstract methods. When compiling, a semantic error will be flagged if this rule is violated. We can query a JavaML document for concrete (i.e., not abstract) classes that contain an abstract method:

```
% sggrep -q '.*/class[abstract!=true]/\
             method[abstract=true]' \
                < Hangman.java.xml
```

and the output will be empty because this semantic restriction is not violated in our target document (i.e., the analyzed program).

A common error for novice Java programmers is to accidentally use the assignment operator, `=`, instead of using the equality test operator, `==`. Although the Java type checker will catch most of these errors at compile time, it will miss the problem if the assigned-to variable is a `boolean`. If we wish to find these questionable constructs, `sggrep` makes this analysis trivial thanks to the JavaML representation:

```
% sggrep -q \
        '.*/if/test/assignment-expr' \
                < Hangman.java.xml
```

The `sgrpg` (SGML RePort Generator) program permits combining a top-level query with a restriction on the children and an output format for the results (a common paradigm for querying tools [24]). For example:

```
% sgrpg '.*/method' \
        '.*/send[message=drawLine]' \
        '' '%s %s
' visibility name < Hangman.java.xml
```

outputs:

```
public paint
```

searches for method definitions that contain message sends of the message `drawLine`. It then outputs the `visibility` and `name` attributes of the matched elements as shown above, confirming our intuition that the `paint()` method is the only function that invoked `drawLine`.

A wide variety of analyses are possible just using the querying capabilities provided by standard XML tools. Other things we can find are returns from inside for loops, all definitions of integer variables, string variables that do not conform to our project's naming convention, and much more.

The preceding queries illustrate a shortcoming of current XML querying tools: most respond only with the matched elements, they do not provide any context information about where in the document the results were found. Although this behavior is appropriate when treating an XML file strictly as a database, the software engineer may want to know where the results were in the JavaML file to then map them back into positions in the source document for editing or viewing by hand. I address this difficulty in JavaML by attaching information about the original source-code location of constructs as attributes of various elements. The location information includes the starting and ending line and column numbers of the construct (the filename is found in the ancestor `java-class-file` element).

In addition to queries, transformations on source code are very useful when modifying and evolving software artifacts. Querying tools generally only prune elements from the source document or combine elements from multiple documents. More powerful transformations are possible using XSLT [14], DSSSL [38], or directly manipulating the document using a DOM (Document Object Model) [2] interface accessible from numerous languages including Perl, Python, Java, and C++. For example, we can rename all methods named `isBall` to `FIsBall` using a straightforward XSLT stylesheet:

```
<xsl:stylesheet......>

<xsl:param name="oldname"/>
<xsl:param name="newname"/>

<!-- mostly do an identity transform -->
<xsl:template match="*|@*|text()">
 <xsl:copy>
  <xsl:apply-templates
       select="*|@*|text()"/>
 </xsl:copy>
</xsl:template>

<xsl:template
     match="method[@name=$oldname]">
 <method name="{$newname}">
  <xsl:apply-templates/>
 </method>
</xsl:template>

<xsl:template
     match="send[@message=$oldname]">
 <send message="{$newname}">
  <xsl:apply-templates/>
 </send>
</xsl:template>

</xsl:stylesheet>
```

and executing it like so:

```
xt source.java.xml method-rename.xsl \
      oldname=isBall newname=FIsBall
```

While a similar textual transformation could be performed using a text editor or Sed, those tools will over-aggressively change all occurrences of the six-character sequence `isBall`. Variable names, literal strings, comments, and packages might incorrectly be affected by the text-based transformation. This is a key benefit of the JavaML representation: we have more fine-grained, semantically based control over the affected constructs.

Other possibilities for transformations include using a stylesheet to output a browse-able HTML representation of the program (see Fig. 3) or syntax-highlighted PostScript. Adding debug or instrumentation code at entry and exit to and from functions is also straightforward (see Fig. 4).

5. Related work

A key benefit of JavaML is its ability to leverage the growing infrastructure of SGML and XML related tools and techniques as described in the previous section. Various researchers have similarly approached the problem of improving software engineering and development tools with varying degrees of success.

TAWK [29] extends the AWK [21] paradigm by matching patterns in the AST of a C program. Numerous XML querying tools provide this same functionality for JavaML, and the event-action frame-

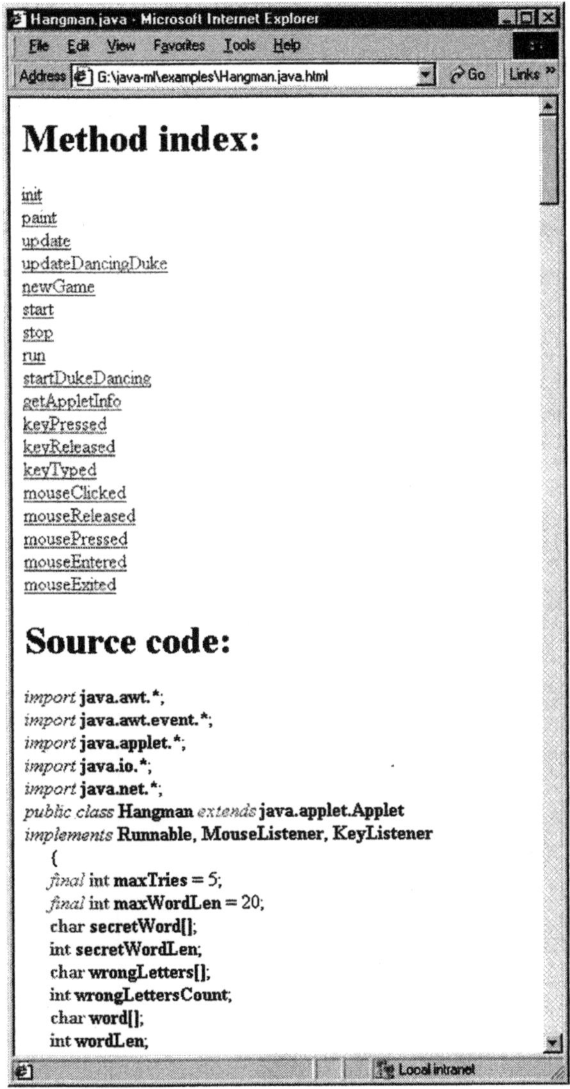

Fig. 3. A view of Hangman.java.xml processed by an XSLT HTML pretty-printer and indexer. The method index links to the start of the definition of each method, and syntax highlighting is done using color-coding and italics.

work is similar to that used by SAX (Simple API for XML) [43].

ASTLog [18] extends the Prolog [17] logic programming language with the ability to reason about an external database that models the AST. Unlike Prolog, ASTLog statements are evaluated with respect to a current object. The approach that Crew uses may be interesting to apply to the XML world, but the numerous XML tools already provide comparable functionality through a more conventional (if perhaps less convenient) framework.

GRAS [40] is a graph-oriented database system for software-engineering environments. Front-ends are available for integrating source code from ordinary representation of C, Modula-3, and Modula-2 into the database. The database approach may prove useful for storing XML, especially in the context of the software-engineering applications for which JavaML is designed.

The Software Development Foundation [46] is an open architecture based on XML designed for developing tools for programming environments. An XML database format called CSF — code structure format — stores relationships, but includes no details about the computation performed. Chava [41] takes a similar approach, but is based on the C Program Database [11]. Chava also permits interrogating Java code via reverse engineering the byte codes.

CCEL [22] provides a metalanguage for expressing non-linguistic intentions (i.e., ones that cannot be expressed in the language) about software artifacts written in C++. JavaML can provide a similar capability by simply writing queries that search for violations of the intended invariants and reporting them as part of the edit, build, or regression-test procedure throughout the development cycle.

Microsoft's Intentional Programming group [47] has long been working on a more abstract representation of computation that is syntax-independent. Their goal appears to be to permit developers to describe new abstractions along with techniques to reduce those abstractions down to known primitives. In essence, they are interested in permitting the developer to grow a domain-specific language as they build their software. JavaML is especially exciting as a representation for this approach. We can view new abstractions as incremental extensions to DTDs. In order for the new document type, call it Java++ML, to still be compilable by a stock Java compiler, the developer must simply write a transformation from Java++ML to JavaML. Because DTDs are exceptionally easy to extend, this approach is tenable and likely a fruitful avenue for future work. There are several utilities for documenting and comparing DTDs (e.g., `dtd2html` and `dtddiff` of the perlSGML package [31]) that would be helpful when applying this technique.

```
#!/usr/bin/perl -w
use XML::DOM;
use IO::Handle;

my $filename = shift @ARGV;

my $parser = new XML::DOM::Parser;
my $doc = $parser->parsefile ($filename);

my $nodes = $doc->getElementsByTagName("method");

for (my $i = 0; $i < $nodes->getLength(); $i++) {
   my $method = $nodes->item($i);
   my $block = $method->getElementsByTagName("block")->item(0);
   my $name = $method->getAttribute("name");

   my $start_code = SendMessageBlock($doc,"Tracer","StartMethod",$name);
   my $exit_code = SendMessageBlock($doc,"Tracer","ExitMethod",$name);

   $block->insertBefore($start_code, $block->getFirstChild());
   $block->appendChild($exit_code);
}
print $doc->toString;

sub SendMessageBlock {
  my ($doc,$target_var,$method_name,$data) = (@_);
  # insert, e.g: Tracer.StartMethod("paint");
  return parseXMLFragment($doc,<<"__END_FRAGMENT__"
<send message="$method_name">
  <target><var-ref name="$target_var"/></target>
  <arguments>
    <literal-string value="$data"/>
  </arguments>
</send>
__END_FRAGMENT__
 );
}

sub parseXMLFragment {
  my ($doc,$code) = (@_);
  my $newdoc = $parser->parse($code);
  my $subtree = $newdoc->getDocumentElement();
  $newdoc->removeChild($subtree);
  $subtree->setOwnerDocument($doc);
  return $subtree;
}
```

Fig. 4. Perl program to instrument every method of a Java class with invocations of `Tracer.StartMethod` (*method_name*) and `Tracer.ExitMethod` (*method_name*). The program uses the Document Object Model (DOM) [2] Perl module [20].

6. Future work

Although this paper has presented a markup language for Java, the same basic approach can be applied to other programming languages, or even to translate among languages. To the extent that the representation abstracts away syntax, JavaML may also prove useful in permitting the import of visual representations such as Unified Modeling Language diagrams [1,35]. Certainly, generating visual representations of important properties of software artifacts is on the immediate horizon given the capabilities of XSL and DSSSL.

One significant complication in applying this approach to C++, another popular conventional object-oriented-programming language, is the C preprocessor. The C preprocessor provides a first pass of textual processing to permit abstractions that cannot otherwise be expressed in the core C++ language. These abstractions are often very important to the understandability and maintainability of the code, but do not interact well with parsing techniques [6,23].

A useful extension to the current transformation system is to do more cross-linking of elements. Type elements could reference their defining classes in other JavaML documents. Import declarations could reference the top-level documentation for the imported package. Many more possibilities are feasible.

The current converter that translates back from JavaML to the classical source representation is based on XSLT. Adding a Jikes front-end would permit the compiler to read JavaML directly. Such an implementation would use an XML parser (e.g., XML4C++ [34]) to construct the XML DOM from the JavaML source, then simply recursively build the Jikes internal AST using the DOM API. Back-conversion to the plain source code could then be done using Jikes's pre-existing conventional unparser.

Using JavaML as the primary source representation has the potential to simplify the compiler beyond just eliminating its classical front-end. Some semantic analyses can be removed from the compiler once it knows that the input is a valid JavaML document. It will be useful to characterize which semantic errors are provably impossible to encounter given that precondition. Because XML Schema [7,51] provide an even finer-grained specification of validity for XML documents, it is likely beneficial to migrate JavaML to use them instead of a DTD after the working drafts are finalized. Additionally, more semantic analyses can be moved into the editing environment reasonably painlessly in the form of straightforward queries (such as some of those described earlier in Section 4).

Because the concise textual representation of source code is nicely suited to human programmers, it is unlikely that they will be interested in discarding their favorite text editor anytime soon. We must investigate better ways to convert interactively and incrementally between the classical source representation and JavaML. The capabilities could then be used to transparently support interactive editing of XML representations using plain-text format to which human engineers are accustomed. The considerable work on structured text editors [30,45] is highly relevant and may finally achieve acceptance give the incredible resources that will now be thrown at the problem given the growing commercial importance of XML technology.

7. Conclusion

JavaML is an alternate representation of Java source programs that is based on XML. Unlike the classical textual source representation, the JavaML representation makes it easy for software tools to reason about programming-level constructs in a Java program. This benefit results from the ability of JavaML to more directly represent the structure of the program.

Given JavaML, the wealth of pre-existing XML and SGML tools can perform numerous interesting and useful analyses and transformations of Java source programs. XML tools are improving continually to support the growing infrastructure of XML-based documents. Ultimately, JavaML could replace the classical source representation of Java programs as the storage format for programs, relegating text-parsing to just one of many possible ways of interacting directly with the structured representation of the software artifact throughout the development process.

Acknowledgements

I enthusiastically thank Zack Ives for his comments, discussion, and input. I thank Corin Anderson and Alan Borning for much-appreciated comments on a draft of this paper. I also thank Miguel Figueroa, Karl-Trygve Kalleberg, Craig Kaplan, Todd Millstein, Stig E. Sandø, and Stefan Bjarni Sigurdsson for their helpful discussions. Thanks to IBM for constructing the Jikes compiler framework, and for making it publicly available, and thanks to Mike Ernst for helpful pointers on using it. This work was supported by the University of Washington Computer Science and Engineering Wilma Bradley fellowship and by NSF Grant No. IIS-9975990.

Appendix A. JavaML DTD

```
<!-- java-ml.dtd 0.96 -->

<!-- Copyright (C) 2000, Greg J. Badros
     <gjb@cs.washington.edu> -->
<!-- A DTD for JavaML, an XML
     representation of Java Source Code -->
<!-- http://www.cs.washington.edu/homes/
     gjb/papers/javaml/javaml.html -->


<!ENTITY % visibility-attribute
    "visibility (public|private|\
     protected) #IMPLIED">
<!ENTITY % interface-visibility-attribute
    "visibility (public) #IMPLIED">
<!ENTITY % kind-attribute
    "kind (integer|long|float|\
     double) #IMPLIED">
<!ENTITY % mod-final
    "final CDATA #IMPLIED">
<!ENTITY % mod-static
    "static CDATA #IMPLIED">
<!ENTITY % mod-volatile
    "volatile CDATA #IMPLIED">
<!ENTITY % mod-transient
    "transient CDATA #IMPLIED">
<!ENTITY % mod-native
    "native CDATA #IMPLIED">
<!ENTITY % mod-abstract
    "abstract CDATA #IMPLIED">
<!ENTITY % mod-synchronized
    "synchronized CDATA #IMPLIED">
<!ENTITY % location-info
"line CDATA #IMPLIED col CDATA #IMPLIED
        end-line CDATA #IMPLIED end-col CD
     ATA #IMPLIED
 comment CDATA #IMPLIED">
<!ENTITY % expr-elems
    "send|new|new-array|var-ref|\
     field-access|array-ref|paren|\
     assignment-expr|conditional-expr|\
     binary-expr|unary-expr|cast-expr|\
     instanceof-test|literal-number|\
     literal-string|literal-char|\
     literal-boolean|literal-null|this|\
     super">
<!ENTITY % stmt-elems
    "block|local-variable|try|throw|if|\
     switch|loop|do-loop|return|continue|\
     break|synchronized|%expr-elems;">

<!ELEMENT code-fragment ANY>
<!ELEMENT result ANY>
<!ELEMENT java-source-program
    (java-class-file+)>
<!ELEMENT java-class-file
    (package-decl?,import*,
     (class|interface)+)>
<!ATTLIST java-class-file
    name CDATA #IMPLIED
    version CDATA #IMPLIED>
<!ELEMENT import EMPTY>
<!ATTLIST import
    module CDATA #REQUIRED>
<!ELEMENT class
    (superclass?, implement*,
      (class|interface|constructor|method|\
     field|static-initializer|\
     instance-initializer)*)>
<!ATTLIST class
    name CDATA #REQUIRED
    %visibility-attribute;
    %mod-static;
    %mod-abstract;
    %mod-final;
    %mod-synchronized;
    %location-info;>
<!ELEMENT anonymous-class
    (superclass?, implement*,
      (constructor|method|field|\
     instance-initializer)*)>
<!ATTLIST anonymous-class
    %mod-abstract;
    %mod-final;
    %mod-synchronized;
    %location-info;>
<!ELEMENT superclass EMPTY>
<!ATTLIST superclass
    name CDATA #REQUIRED>
<!ELEMENT interface
    (extend*, (method|field)*)>
<!ATTLIST interface
    name CDATA #REQUIRED
    %interface-visibility-attribute;
    %location-info;>
<!ELEMENT implement EMPTY>
<!ATTLIST implement
    interface CDATA #REQUIRED>
<!ELEMENT extend EMPTY>
<!ATTLIST extend
    interface CDATA #REQUIRED>
<!ELEMENT field
    (type,
     (array-initializer|%expr-elems;)?)>
<!ATTLIST field
```

```
    name CDATA #REQUIRED
    %visibility-attribute;
    %mod-final;
    %mod-static;
    %mod-volatile;
    %mod-transient;
    %location-info;>
<!ELEMENT constructor
    (formal-arguments,throws*,
     (super-call|this-call)?,
     (%stmt-elems;)?)>
<!ATTLIST constructor
    name CDATA #REQUIRED
    id ID #REQUIRED
    %visibility-attribute;
    %mod-final;
    %mod-static;
    %mod-synchronized;
    %mod-volatile;
    %mod-transient;
    %mod-native;
    %location-info;>
<!ELEMENT method
    (type,formal-arguments,throws*,
     (%stmt-elems;)?)>
<!ATTLIST method
    name CDATA #REQUIRED
    id ID #REQUIRED
    %visibility-attribute;
    %mod-abstract;
    %mod-final;
    %mod-static;
    %mod-synchronized;
    %mod-volatile;
    %mod-transient;
    %mod-native;
    %location-info;>
<!ELEMENT formal-arguments
    (formal-argument)*>
<!ELEMENT formal-argument (type)>
<!ATTLIST formal-argument
    name CDATA #REQUIRED
    id ID #REQUIRED
    %mod-final;>
<!ELEMENT send (target?,arguments)>
<!ATTLIST send
    message CDATA #REQUIRED
    idref IDREF #IMPLIED>
<!ELEMENT block (label*,(%stmt-elems;)*)>
<!ATTLIST block
    %location-info;>
<!ELEMENT label EMPTY>
<!ATTLIST label
    name CDATA #REQUIRED>
<!ELEMENT target (%expr-elems;)>
<!ELEMENT return (%expr-elems;)?>
<!ELEMENT throw (%expr-elems;)>
```

```
<!ELEMENT throws EMPTY>
<!ATTLIST throws
    exception CDATA #REQUIRED>
<!ELEMENT new
    (type,arguments,anonymous-class?)>
<!ELEMENT type EMPTY>
<!ATTLIST type
    primitive CDATA #IMPLIED
    name CDATA #REQUIRED
    dimensions CDATA #IMPLIED
    idref IDREF #IMPLIED>
<!ELEMENT new-array
    (type,dim-expr*,array-initializer?)>
<!ATTLIST new-array
    dimensions CDATA #REQUIRED>
<!ELEMENT dim-expr (%expr-elems;)>
<!ELEMENT local-variable
    (type,
     (static-initializer|array-initializer|\
     %expr-elems;)?)>
<!ATTLIST local-variable
    name CDATA #REQUIRED
    id ID #REQUIRED
    continued CDATA #IMPLIED
    %mod-final;>
<!ELEMENT array-initializer
    (array-initializer|%expr-elems;)*>
<!ATTLIST array-initializer
    length CDATA #REQUIRED>
<!ELEMENT arguments (%expr-elems;)*>
<!ELEMENT literal-string EMPTY>
<!ATTLIST literal-string
    value CDATA #REQUIRED>
<!ELEMENT literal-char EMPTY>
<!ATTLIST literal-char
    value CDATA #REQUIRED>
<!ELEMENT literal-number EMPTY>
<!ATTLIST literal-number
    value CDATA #REQUIRED
    %kind-attribute;
    base CDATA "10">
<!ELEMENT var-ref EMPTY>
<!ATTLIST var-ref
    name CDATA #REQUIRED
    idref IDREF #IMPLIED>
<!ELEMENT field-access (%expr-elems;)>
<!ATTLIST field-access
    field CDATA #REQUIRED>
<!ELEMENT var-set EMPTY>
<!ATTLIST var-set
    name CDATA #REQUIRED>
<!ELEMENT field-set (%expr-elems;)>
<!ATTLIST field-set
    field CDATA #REQUIRED>
<!ELEMENT package-decl EMPTY>
<!ATTLIST package-decl
    name CDATA #REQUIRED>
```

```
<!ELEMENT assignment-expr
    (lvalue,(%expr-elems;))>
<!ATTLIST assignment-expr
    op CDATA #REQUIRED>
<!ELEMENT lvalue
    (var-set|field-set|%expr-elems;)>
<!ELEMENT instanceof-test
    ((%expr-elems;),type)>
<!ELEMENT binary-expr
    ((%expr-elems;),(%expr-elems;))>
<!ATTLIST binary-expr
    op CDATA #REQUIRED>
<!ELEMENT paren (%expr-elems;)>
<!ELEMENT unary-expr (%expr-elems;)>
<!ATTLIST unary-expr
    op CDATA #REQUIRED
    post (true|false) #IMPLIED>
<!ELEMENT cast-expr (type,(%expr-elems;))>
<!ELEMENT literal-boolean EMPTY>
<!ATTLIST literal-boolean
    value (true|false) #REQUIRED>
<!ELEMENT literal-null EMPTY>
<!ELEMENT synchronized (expr,block)>
<!ELEMENT expr (%expr-elems;)>
<!ELEMENT if (test,true-case,false-case?)>
<!ELEMENT test (%expr-elems;)>
<!ELEMENT true-case (%stmt-elems;)?>
<!ELEMENT false-case (%stmt-elems;)?>
<!ELEMENT array-ref (base,offset)>
<!ELEMENT base (%expr-elems;)>
<!ELEMENT offset (%expr-elems;)>
<!ELEMENT static-initializer
    (%stmt-elems;)*>
<!ELEMENT instance-initializer
    (%stmt-elems;)*>
<!ELEMENT super-call (arguments)>
<!ELEMENT this-call (arguments)>
<!ELEMENT super EMPTY>
<!ELEMENT this EMPTY>
<!ELEMENT loop
    (init*,test?,update*,(%stmt-elems;)?)>
<!ATTLIST loop
    kind (for|while) #IMPLIED
    %location-info;>
<!ELEMENT init
    (local-variable|%expr-elems;)*>
<!ELEMENT update (%expr-elems;)>
<!ELEMENT do-loop ((%stmt-elems;)?,test?)>
<!ELEMENT try
    ((%stmt-elems;),catch*,finally?)>
<!ELEMENT catch
    (formal-argument,(%stmt-elems;)?)>
<!ELEMENT finally (%stmt-elems;)>
<!ELEMENT continue EMPTY>
<!ATTLIST continue
    targetname CDATA #IMPLIED>
<!ELEMENT break EMPTY>
<!ATTLIST break
    targetname CDATA #IMPLIED>
<!ELEMENT conditional-expr
    ((%expr-elems;),(%expr-elems;),
     (%expr-elems;))>
<!ELEMENT switch
    ((%expr-elems;),switch-block+)>
<!ELEMENT switch-block
    ((case|default-case)+,
     (%stmt-elems;)*)>
<!ELEMENT case (%expr-elems;)>
<!ELEMENT default-case EMPTY>
```

References

[1] S.S. Alhir, UML in a Nutshell, O'Reilly and Associates, Sebastopol, CA, 1998.

[2] V. Apparao, S. Byrne, M. Champion, S. Isaacs, I. Jacobs, A.L. Hors, G. Nicol, J. Robie, R. Sutor, C. Wilson and L. Wood, Document Object Model (DOM) level 1, W3C Recommendation, October 1998, http://www.w3.org/TR/REC-DOM-Level-1

[3] K. Arnold and J. Gosling, The Java Programming Language, Addison-Wesley, Reading, MA, 1998.

[4] G.J. Badros, JavaML Home Page, http://www.cs.washington.edu/homes/gjb/JavaML

[5] G.J. Badros and A. Borning, The Cassowary linear arithmetic constraint solving algorithm: Interface and implementation, Technical Report UW-CSE-98-06-04, University of Washington, Seattle, Washington, June 1998, http://www.cs.washington.edu/research/constraints/cassowary/cassowary-tr.pdf

[6] G.J. Badros and D. Notkin, A framework for preprocessor-aware C source code analyses, Software — Practice and Experience, in press.

[7] P.V. Biron and A. Malhotra, XML scheme part 2: Datatypes, W3C Working Draft, November 1999, http://www.w3.org/TR/xmlschema-2

[8] B. Bos, H.W. Lie, C. Lilley and I. Jacobs, Cascading style sheets, level 2, W3C Working Draft, Jan. 1998, http://www.w3.org/TR/WD-css2/

[9] T. Bray, J. Paoli and C.M. Sperberg-McQueen, Extensible markup language (XML) 1.0, W3C Recommendation, February 1998, http://www.w3.org/TR/REC-xml

[10] British Standards Institution, Modula-2 draft international standard, iso-94, June 1994.

[11] Y.-F. Chen, The C program database and its applications, in: Proc. Summer 1989 USENIX Conf., Baltimore, 1989, pp. 157–171.

[12] J. Clark, James' DSSSL engine (JADE), http://www.jclark.com/jade

[13] J. Clark, XP version 0.5, 1998, http://www.jclark.com/xml/xp

[14] J. Clark, XSL transformations, W3C Recommendation, November 1999, http://www.w3.org/TR/xslt

[15] J. Clark, XT version 19991105, November 1999, http://www.jclark.com/xml/xt.html
[16] J. Clark and S. DeRose, XML path language (xpath) version 1.0, W3C Recommendation, November 1999, http://www.w3.org/TR/xpath
[17] W.F. Clocksin and C.S. Mellish, Programming in Prolog, Springer, Berlin, 4th edition, 1994.
[18] R.F. Crew, ASTLOG: A language for examining abstract syntax trees, in: Proc. USENIX Conf. on Domain-Specific Languages, Santa Barbara, CA, October 1997.
[19] S. Deach, Extensible stylesheet language (xsl) specification, W3C Working Draft, January 2000, http://www.w3.org/TR/WD-xsl
[20] E. Derksen and C. Cooper, Perl XML::DOM module, http://users.erols.com/enno/dom
[21] D. Dougherty, Sed and Awk, O'Reilly and Associates, Sebastopol, CA, 1990.
[22] C.K. Duby, S. Meyers and S.P. Reiss, CCEL: A metalanguage for C++, in: Proc. USENIX 1992 C++ Conf., Portland, OR, August 1992.
[23] M. Ernst, G.J. Badros and D. Notkin, An empirical analysis of C preprocessor use, IEEE Transactions on Software Engineering, in press.
[24] M. Fernandez, J. Siméon and P. Wadler, XML query language: Experiences and exemplars, 1999, http://www-db.research.bell-labs.com/user/simeon/xquery.html
[25] D. Flanagan, Java in a Nutshell, O'Reilly and Associates, Sebastopol, CA, 2nd edition, 1997.
[26] A. Goldberg and D. Robson, Smalltalk-80: The Language, Addison-Wesley, Reading, MA, 1989.
[27] C.F. Goldfarb and P. Prescod, The XML Handbook, Prentice-Hall PTR, Englewood Cliffs, NJ, 1998.
[28] M. Goosens and S. Rahtz, The LaTeX Web Companion, Addison-Wesley, Reading, MA, 1999.
[29] W.G. Griswold, D.C. Atkinson and C. McCurdy, Fast, flexible syntactic pattern matching and processing, in: Proc. IEEE 1996 Workshop on Program Comprehension, March 1996.
[30] A.N. Habermann and D. Notkin, Gandalf: Software development environments, IEEE Transactions on Software Engineering (1986) 1117–1127.
[31] E. Hood, perlSGML library, http://www.oac.uci.edu/indiv/ehood/perlSGML.html
[32] IBM, Jikes java compiler, http://www.alphaworks.ibm.com/tech/Jikes
[33] IBM AlphaWorks, XML diff and merge tool, http://www.alphaworks.ibm.com/tech/xmldiffmerge
[34] IBM AlphaWorks, XML for C++, http://www.alphaworks.ibm.com/tech/xml4c
[35] IBM AlphaWorks, XML metadata interchange (XMI) toolkit, http://www.alphaworks.ibm.com/tech/xmitoolkit
[36] Icon I.S., XML spy 3.0beta2, http://www.xmlspy.com
[37] ISO, Standard generalized markup language (SGML), ISO 8879, 1986, http://www.iso.ch/cate/d16387.html
[38] ISO/IEC, Document style semantics and specification language (DSSSL), ISO/IEC 10179, 1996.
[39] M.H. Kay, SAXON, http://users.iclway.co.uk/mhkay/saxon/
[40] N. Kiesel, A. Schürr and B. Westfechtel, GRAS, a graph-oriented (software) engineering database system, Information Systems 20 (1) (1995) 21–52.
[41] J. Korn, Y. Chen and E. Koutsofios, Chava: Reverse engineering and tracking of java applets, in: Proc. 6th Working Conf. on Reverse Engineering, October 1999, pp. 314–325.
[42] J.R. Levine, Lex and Yacc, O'Reilly and Associates, Sebastopol, CA, 2nd edition, 1992.
[43] Megginson Technologies, SAX 1.0: The simple API for XML, Web document, 1999, http://www.megginson.com/SAX
[44] Microsoft, XML Notepad Beta 1.5, http://msdn.microsoft.com/xml/notepad
[45] R.C. Miller and B.A. Myers, Lightweight structured text processing, in: Proc. USENIX 1999, Monterey, CA, 1999.
[46] S.E. Sandø and K.-T. Kalleberg, Software development foundation, February 2000, http://sds.yi.org
[47] C. Simonyi, Intentional programming — innovation in the legacy age, International Federation for Information Processing WG 2.1 Meeting, June 1996.
[48] D. Soroker, M. Karasick, J. Barton and D. Streeter, Extension mechanisms in Montana, in: Proc. 8th Israeli Conf. on Computer-Based Systems and Software Engineering, June 1997.
[49] B. Stroustrup, The C++ Programming Language, Addison-Wesley, Reading, MA, 3rd edition, 1997.
[50] Sun Microsystems, Applet resources, February 2000, http://java.sun.com/applets/
[51] H.S. Thompson, D. Beech, M. Maloney and N. Mendelsohn, XML scheme part 1: Structures, W3C Working Draft, November 1999, http://www.w3.org/TR/xmlschema-1
[52] University of Edinburgh Language Technology Group, LT XML version 1.1, http://www.ltg.ed.ac.uk/software/xml

Greg J. Badros is a final-year Ph.D. candidate at the University of Washington in Seattle, Washington where he earned his M.Sc. degree in 1998. He graduated magna cum laude with a B.S. degree in Mathematics and Computer Science from Duke University in 1995. He is the primary author of the Scheme Constraints Window Manager and the Cassowary Constraint Solving Toolkit. His research interests include constraint technology, software engineering, languages, and the Internet.

An interchange format for cross-media personalized publishing

Patrick van Amstel, Pim van der Eijk *, Evert Haasdijk, David Kuilman

Cap Gemini Nederland BV, Daltonlaan 400, P.O. Box 2575, 3500 GN Utrecht, Netherlands

Abstract

Web sites are rapidly becoming the medium of choice for one-to-one marketing, communication and commerce. Many commercial solutions in this area have the following drawbacks: they force companies to implement systems within a single framework that is highly vendor-specific and that does not allow them to reuse content for other media. In this paper, we introduce *i*Doc*, a simple XML interchange format for content-level conditionalization based on a variant of the MIL-PRF-87269 standard for classes IV–V IETMs. This format can serve as integration format in multi-vendor CRM solutions and offers consistent cross-media publishing to multiple lower-level delivery channels such as direct mail, ASP, JSP, and WML. Personalization is determined by *properties* that can be bound to intelligent external systems and determined dynamically. As a showcase for *i*Doc*, we have developed a demonstrator of an on-line wine shop, where *i*Doc* serves to transport information between a database of product descriptions and generated ASP pages. The Web site is highly dynamic, as its behavior is controlled by properties that are re-computed using predictive models generated by the OMEGA predictive data mining (PDM) system. The use of *i*Doc* allows content to be rapidly retargeted towards other Web delivery platforms, such as JSP, direct mail or mobile Internet.

Keywords: Customer relationship management (CRM); Electronic commerce; Extensible markup language (XML); Interactive electronic technical manuals (IETM); Personalization; Predictive data mining (PDM)

1. Introduction

Customer relationship management (CRM) concerns acquiring, establishing and retaining a mutual business relationship based on knowledge the company has acquired from customer behavior, preferences and response. Coupling knowledge of company processes to the insight of customer behavior is a key factor for establishing effective communication, transaction and processing of customer sessions. Knowing, on the basis of data mining techniques and predictive modeling, how a customer wants to be treated and what triggers interest, is an important ingredient of CRM. Making connections to back-office sales strategies and content repositories completes the opportunity to build a true one-to-one experience with the customer.

The World Wide Web is rapidly becoming a medium of choice to achieve personalized marketing and commerce. Within a company, one-to-one communication affects many departments and is being addressed at many organizational levels, ranging from strategic sales, marketing analysis and decision making down to implementing their implications for back-end information systems and front-end Web engineering.

A range of commercial products are positioned as frameworks for development of one-to-one Web

* Corresponding author. E-mail: pim.vander.eijk@capgemini.nl

communication solutions. In Section 3, we will provide a brief overview of the technical approach shared by some of these products, and will argue that they have several important drawbacks.

Reaching the users of tomorrow will not only be restricted to the means we know today, but more likely to different media that will be used transparently in the situation the user is in. One could argue that communication will be driven by the *requirements* of the customer, not by the *means* of communication. Ideally, information interchange will adapt to the needs of the user, even if the person is not even aware of this fact.

As an attempt to provide for this concept, we have developed *i*Doc*, an XML-based format that encodes a snapshot of a company's portfolio and marketing strategy. *i*Doc* is heavily based on approaches developed for interactive electronic technical manuals (IETM), as discussed in Section 4. In contrast to existing approaches, *i*Doc* is neither a marketing data management solution nor a delivery format but an interchange format. Delivery formats like Microsoft Active Server Pages (ASP) or JavaServer pages (JSP) can be generated in fully automatic fashion, thus offering significant flexibility in deployment options at potentially lower cost. As an XML-based interchange format, *i*Doc* offers a simple interface to integrate information systems. Finally, *i*Doc* offers simple integration to intelligent external customer modeling systems. As a particularly relevant example of this, we discuss the OMEGA predictive data mining system [9], which can be used to generate intelligent models for customer behavior.

To demonstrate the capabilities of *i*Doc*, we have developed a sample E-commerce site that demonstrates on-line personalized wine selling. In Section 5, we will discuss the motivation of this showcase, and discuss how *i*Doc* content is generated from a wine product database, transformed to ASP using an *i*Doc* compiler, and combined with OMEGA-derived models to offer intelligent personalization.

2. CRM and content management

Key to provide the conditions necessary to meet the high and diverse demands we are putting on information, is *control*. Content management (CM) is often mentioned in this context to scope the functional domain of managing information in chunks (or components), irrespective of its purpose or use in a later (IT-) life-cycle. Bridging the gap between customer expectation and business response to individual needs and circumstances can only be properly addressed with the following prerequisites:

- content management system enabling control on arbitrary fine-grained information units (CM);
- user profiling through real-time feedback and off-line feedback (e.g. through predictive data mining);
- defining business rules that capture supply and demand mechanisms (e.g. a customer profile will match if a product has the right pricing);
- modeling user interaction in a framework that makes profiling, coupling of business rules and content collation possible in a consistent manner.

What is needed is the capability to automate the process of collecting and collating information from all the operational systems that manage interaction with the customer, such as front-office sales automation systems, call centers (including telesales and telemarketing), order processing, customer support, shipping, etc. A standard to define the relationships and enable interchange between systems is of paramount importance. XML seems like the most likely contender to address this need [3]. A content management system based on XML offers the environment to maintain information components on an arbitrary fine-grained level that makes addressing, querying and retrieval of components possible to 'fuse' with business rules. Dynamics and user-driven communication can be further extended with the use of predictive data mining (PDM). Results of interaction are constantly updated through the CRM life-cycle (knowing, targeting, selling and designing) and are stored or routed to business logic rules. One can argue that modeling of business rules and content matter on the component-level constitutes the required business intelligence and technological basis for CRM.

This paper will argue that it is necessary to encode both business rules, objects, logic and content in one platform-independent format: XML. Fig. 1 shows how one-to-one marketing is enabled by acquiring

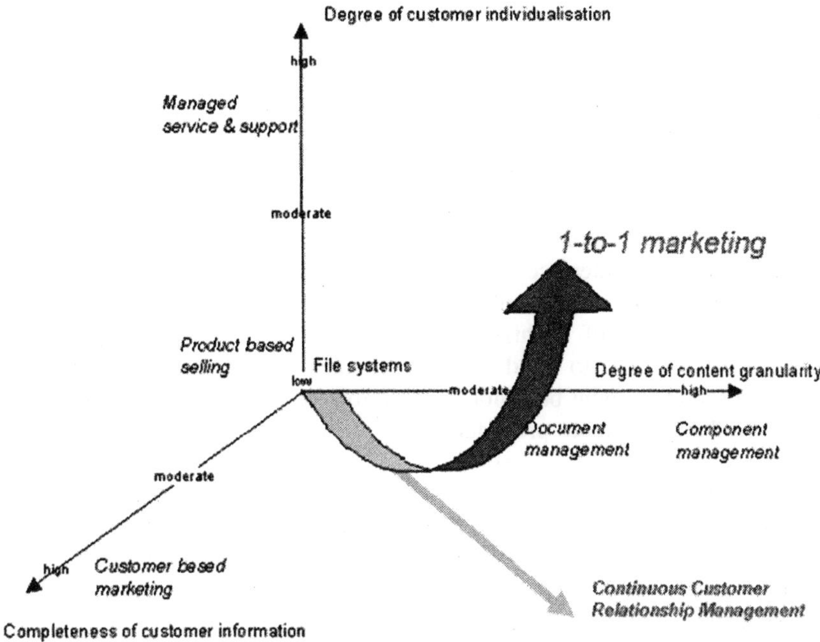

Fig. 1. Pre-requisites for one-to-one marketing.

knowledge about customers and managing content as *components*, that can be assembled according to the profile of the individual customer.

3. Current approaches

Systems that are engineered to establish a one-to-one relation with customers are usually based on application areas such as the Web, call-centers, direct mail, etc. The type of media dictates the mix of ingredients and underlying architecture used within the CRM-system. Databases are used for storing customer profiles, data-mining techniques are applied to detect patterns in customer behavior, filtering techniques for information dissemination and scripting languages to connect different information sources. There are also more monolithic systems that attempt to do all or most of these things. What is lacking is a consistent approach that is independent of application area, and can be transposed in multiple application environments such as the Web, WAP and direct mail simultaneously.

3.1. *Scope of personalized publishing*

A number of personalization techniques can be used and related to business logic rules. These techniques have varying effectiveness depending on situation and purpose in mind. The following list gives an idea of possible personalization techniques:

- rules-based matching (club members, frequent visitors, Gold-card owners, etc.);
- matching agents (established profile can be matched with other profiles displaying similar purchasing behavior);
- feedback and learning (fields of interest);
- community ratings (others help define good from bad);
- attribute searches (all books with reduced prices);
- full-text search;
- collaborative filtering (feedback on products and services defines groups of individuals with similar interests).

Encoding the above techniques can be achieved in many ways, usually based on dedicated application software working on content fragments that supply transformed and converted content elements on the fly. Within the context of this discussion, we have decided to handle these techniques as external procedures that convey values to the core variables within an *i*Doc* (see Section 4.5).

3.2. Web-oriented systems

Today's Web-oriented systems are tools that extend functionality of Web server applications. Site management systems offer the interface between server-based repositories to controlled client Web delivery. Depending on the level of sophistication of the tool, site-developers are able to build server-side applications that respond to client behavior and implement the calling of these 'remote procedures' from client Web pages. ASP and JSP technologies are widely used to encode intelligence within Web pages to deliver a personalized experience. Tools like *BroadVision One-to-One* [8] and *Vignette StoryServer* are examples of commercial products based on this concept. The approach both applications share is the separation of business rules and content and the invocation of these rules from Web pages. Fig. 2 gives an example of such code embedded in a Web page.

Business rules are encoded as methods that use relational table definitions as parameters. Usually, a GUI generates a creation-script, as shown in Fig. 3. The supplied scripting language can manipulate objects that have been defined in the 'Business Manager' workbench. These objects are user-defined entities that map to database records and fields. Setting business rules on business objects is handled in a proprietary fashion: constraints are defined describing boundaries that determine delivered content to the user (or community). Matching agents use the rules (or sets of rules) to fill HTML-templates for one-to-one publishing. Agents are implemented as server-side methods that are invoked from function-calls that reside in Web templates.

Within templates, ASP-scripting (or JSP) is commonly used for arithmetic functions and iteration on stored objects. Direct access to services on the server makes this approach very efficient but also very dependent on the implementation of the data and application layers.

Two seemingly distinct sets of information, business rules and content components, are still tied

```
<p>Some CD's you might want to check out:</p>
<table>
<tr>Artist</td>
<td>Title</td>
<td>Label</td>
</tr>
<%
content = matchObject.matchContent("match_rule", "MusicAdvice", "CDS", visitor,
      Session.Profile,100);
if (content!= null and and content.length >0)
{
  var x;
  for (x=0;x<content.length;x++)
  {
    var item = content.get(x);
    Response.write("<tr><td>" + item.get("TITLE") + "</td>");
    Response.write("<td>" + item.get("ARTIST") + "</td>");
    Response.write("<td>" + item.get("LABEL") + "</td></tr>");
  }
}
else
{
  Response.write("<tr><td>No content available!</td></tr>");
}
%></table>
```

Fig. 2. Example of BroadVision invocation of a business rule for personalized music advice.

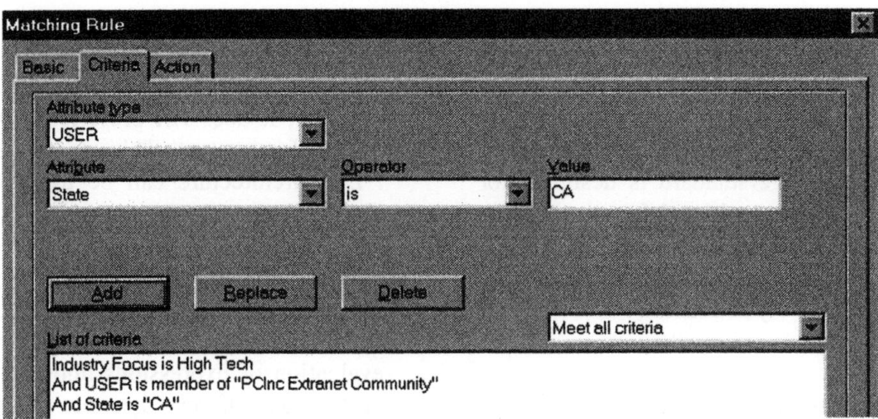

Fig. 3. A GUI enables the specification of business rules.

together by using application logic that maps directly into the tables of the business rules. In this sense, controlled content delivery is a matter of delivering templates with proprietary application logic that execute matching agents. If a certain business rule is changed, this would require editing of all occurrences of the code throughout the site.

Control on information is set on a level corresponding to the granularity of the database-schemas. However, in real-world applications more control is required such as 'tone-of-voice' and conditional texts. Creating support for these features in a relational database scheme would prove untractable. Deeply nested recursive structures do not map well on the relational paradigm.

The Web-orientation implies the maintenance of a format that is at the end of its life-cycle. In order to adapt to future market-change and communicate across media, it will be necessary to abstract from low-level access on information components, and switch to a more generic format for defining business intelligence.

Another issue is the limited distinction between content, lay-out and business information in the aforementioned tools. Cascading style sheets (CSS) provide a clear separation of lay-out information and content elements, but have the limitation that stylesheet information can only be bound to elements within an Internet environment.

Current personalized Web delivery tools can therefore be considered as low-level tools that rely on trained staff to make changes to the system when business or market demands this.

3.3. Conclusion

We have seen that within current approaches conditionalization is accounted for at a level of HTML templates rather than at the level of content, causing high maintenance cost and no cross-medium publishing capabilities. Second, systems integration is product-specific and costly. Third, customer modeling is largely based on static, handmade profiles rather than on dynamic models derived by mining the company's warehouse of historical sales data.

The challenge we are faced with is devising a format that can integrate multiple sources and serve multiple purposes in a uniform way. The format must also support extensibility: user-behavior and tracking must be fuelled back in the system enabling a more knowledgeable communication with the customer.

The systems we discussed still rely on dedicated, proprietary architectures that make it difficult to leverage the effort in building a one-to-one system and re-using that effort in multiple, future environments and applications. The eminent WAP-revolution is a good example of the requirement to maintain business information and customer communication on a higher level for cross-media purposes. The *i*Doc*-format proposes to capture and implement business rules on this level.

The ability to use a higher-level vocabulary (e.g. *isLoyalCustomer*, *likesNewWorldWine*) and a higher-level abstraction on data sources (e.g. *CustomerDatabase*, *LegalSite*, *PredictiveModelingTool*, *AccountStatements*) are vital to make sure that content can be re-purposed to meet future business demands. Business rules, objects, application logic and related content should be made independent of technical issues to meet today's and tomorrow's fast growing demands on information delivery.

The XML interchange standard is designed for text-encoding at any required level for generic purposes and can therefore be considered the choice technology for encoding information for multi-purpose, cross-media delivery of content.

4. The *i*Doc* document format

4.1. Objectives

Our interest in working on *i*Doc* is to improve development of intelligent Web-based systems that offer one-to-one communication and commerce to support CRM. The use of an XML-based interchange format allows us to avoid some of the shortcomings of existing systems as identified in Section 3, specified below.

- CRM applications typically require *integration* of multiple existing back-end systems for managing content, inventory, marketing and customer data. *i*Doc* is an interchange format that can integrate information from multiple sources in a uniform and consistent way.
- *i*Doc* is based on XML. This means that standard XML interfaces like DOM [4] and SAX [22] can be used to develop software interfaces with back-end systems and publishing systems, and that *i*Doc* content can be converted using generic (license-free) XML transformation languages like Omnimark [26] or XSLT [11].
- Conditionalized constructs can be nested and can apply to any level of granularity, ranging from top-level elements down to individual characters in running text.
- Declarative specification of conditionalization offers flexibility in choice of delivery platform. Using XML transformation tools, both conditional constructs and content can be transformed automatically to multiple delivery formats like HTML, ASP, JSP or WML, or used to control a more traditional hardcopy-based direct mail distribution channel. This enables companies to communicate consistently with their customers irrespective of channel.
- *i*Doc* only standardizes a *conditionalization* vocabulary, it does not prescribe any standard encoding for content. This means that a common *i*Doc* architecture can be used for vastly different types of content, provided that content is expressed in an XML format.
- Conditionalization information is encoded using an expression language that references *properties* associated with customers. On-demand, run-time evaluation of expressions allows personalization on the basis of very dynamic properties, such as user navigation history.
- Reference to properties in the *i*Doc* expression language is separated cleanly from binding of properties to external systems. This means that simple *i*Doc*-based systems that are based on relatively simple, fixed profiles can evolve into more complex systems where properties are (re-)computed dynamically by external intelligent systems, without the need to change *i*Doc* content.

In Section 5, we illustrate the use of *i*Doc* in a simple demonstrator system that features properties determined dynamically by an advanced predictive data mining system. A production system might keep track of hundreds of properties, many of which are customer-specific, and a significant subset of which are dynamically (re)computed using intelligent external systems.

4.2. Interactive electronic technical manuals

The *i*Doc* concept is heavily based on results of developments in the context of interactive electronic technical manuals (IETM). IETM is a concept developed at the U.S. Department of Defense to support operation and maintenance of complex technical systems [17]. The DoD uses a scale of five classes of IETM systems to distinguish various levels of functionality offered. Classes I to III are basic electronically viewable documents, ranging from page-based display (class I), via electronically scrolling documents (class II), to linearly structured IETMs (III). Common delivery platforms for these are PDF or TIFF viewers for class-I IETMs (often scanned legacy documents), and HTML viewers for class-II and class-III IETMs (the latter with extensive use of frames and limited scrolling).

Classes IV–V IETMs offer high end-functionality described in the DoD MIL-PRF-87269 standard document. These classes require the use of SGML [19] as source format, use of databases for storage, and support for context-sensitive navigation and content delivery. In the IETM context, context-sensitivity is important for various reasons. One application is to support situations where different system versions or configurations require different maintenance procedures. Another application is support for different types of users. Some IETMs offer multiple versions of particular information components for novice and expert users. The description for novice users may provide more details, introductory information, and instructions when to call in expert help. The description for expert users can be more succinct or even be limited to a check list, and may describe alternative actions that require special expert skills. Via a user interface control, expert users can switch down to the detailed description, but novice users cannot switch up to the expert view.

While the novice/expert distinction is often the only way to segment the user base of an IETM, the personalization mechanisms for context filtering as offered in MIL-PRF-87269 are very generic. *i*Doc* applies these concepts to Web site personalization.

*4.3. Building morphing Web sites using i*Doc*

As a metaphor, *morphing* illustrates a process where content adapts dynamically to the individual who accesses the site, thus reducing the need to use hyperlink traversal or search engines to access relevant content and increasing the commercial interest of the site. The *i*Doc*-format is intended to act as a flexible data format to encode content for morphing Web sites. Technically, the requirements on content for class IV–V IETMs are very similar to the requirements for morphing Web sites.

We have been using the term *i*Doc* to refer to the use of content encoded using an XML version of MIL-PRF-87269 content in combination with intelligent external systems. Apart from adapting the SGML specification to XML, *i*Doc* makes explicit use of three-valued logic and uses namespaces to merge content from multiple sources. The format also supports definition of access to ODBC [25] and external COM [24] objects.

The *i*Doc* format is a declarative XML-based vocabulary to express conditional content. As opposed to HTML, *i*Doc* only standardizes a markup *sub*language, as in itself it provides only the limited set of constructs that express conditionalization. These elements need to be complemented with content-bearing elements. The distribution of *i*Doc* tags is governed by the *i*Doc* document type definition (DTD). This schema is a simplified version derived from the MIL-PRF-87269 IETM standard. Distribution of content elements is governed by application-specific content DTDs. *i*Doc* can be used with both higher-level content DTDs like DocBook [12] or lower-level DTDs like HTML [18,32] or WML [31]. Content and conditionalization can be separated cleanly using the *namespace* mechanism [7].

In Fig. 4 an example is shown of an *i*Doc* frame, as it might be displayed graphically in a (hypothetical) marketeer's workbench. The *i*Doc* notation is shown in Fig. 6.

4.4. The MIL-PRF-87269 language

MIL-PRF-87269 offers a standard language to express conditional *context filtering* [13,15]. It offers data structures corresponding to standard programming language constructs using an SGML-based syntax (in this paper converted to XML syntax for consistency). In this subsection, we will briefly summarize (a simplified variant of) this language. Expressions can reference *properties* that can be typed as integers, strings or booleans. Constants can be defined and referenced using the elements `<integer>`, `<string>`, and `<boolean>`. Operators can be used to test property values or to construct complex expressions. There are integer operators like `<gt/>` (greater than) and `<lt/>` (less than) that yield boolean values. Boolean operators can be combined using `<and/>` and `<or/>` operators. String-valued properties can be tested for equality.

Fig. 5 displays an example from a hypothetical IETM that tests whether a property *SerialCode* is less than *16230*. This test might conditionalize content that only relates to the first instances of a particular product (that may suffer from a defect that has

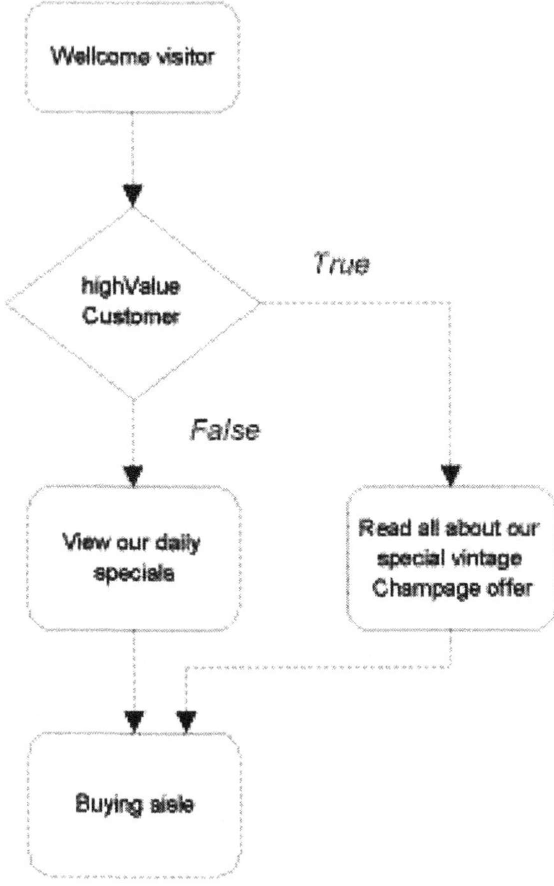

Fig. 4. An *i*Doc* flow-diagram.

been remedied for later releases). Note that in this example no namespace prefixes are used.

These expressions can be used within IETM content to conditionalize document sections. MIL-PRF-87269 contains the following constructs that express conditions.

```
<expression>
  <expression>
    <property>SerialCode</property>
  </expression>
  <lt/>
  <expression>
    <integer>16230</integer>
  </expression>
</expression>
```

Fig. 5. Example of MIL-PRF-87269 expression of the condition 'SerialCode' < 16230.

- An `<ifNode>` consists of an expression and two container elements for the 'true' and 'false' branches. Our work extends MIL-PRF-87269 in allowing explicitly for a *third* branch that is taken when expression evaluation is stalled because property values are unknown.
- A `<nodeAlts>` consists of a number of container elements that must contain a `<precond>` daughter node containing `<expression>` content. This is similar to a 'switch' or 'case' programming language construct. It resolves to the container element that contains a `<precond>` that evaluates to boolean 'true'.

The element `<Node>` can be used inside a conditional element as a generic container for content. It contains an optional first daughter node *precond.* A *precond* element contains an expression that, when evaluated at run-time, should return boolean 'true' (unless the node is contained in a *NodeAlts*). Nodes can be referenced via unique identification attributes. The *i*Doc* compiler used in Section 5 can generate separate output units (HTML pages, WML decks) for various nodes and convert *ID*/*IDREF* cross-references to hypertext links.

Fig. 6 shows the use of namespaces to differentiate *i*Doc* elements from content elements, in this case elements from the XHTML DTD [32]. The example shows an `<ifNode>` that limits access to a special offer to high-value customers. This is done by only displaying a hyperlink to users that have the boolean property *highValueCustomer* set to the value *true*. This corresponds to the graphical representation shown in Fig. 4.

The MIL-PRF-87269 standard assumes a run-time interpreter that has knowledge of the syntax and semantics of the expression language, or compilation to a format that provides equivalent functionality. The interpreter should validate the conditions on `<nodeAlts>` elements, and evaluate the `<expression>`s contained in `<ifNode>`s. It should also maintain a lookup table associating properties with values. All properties have global scope and need not be initialized.

Properties can obtain values in one of several ways. First, a value can be asserted in an `<assertion>` statement in a `<postcond>` in a node. This is shown in Fig. 7 with an example that might be used in an on-line shopping site such as the wine site

```
<idoc:ifNode>
  <idoc:expression>
    <idoc:expression>
      <idoc:property>highValueCustomer</idoc:property></idoc:expression>
    <idoc:eq/>
    <idoc:expression>
      <idoc:boolean>true</idoc:boolean>
    </idoc:expression>
  </idoc:expression>
  <idoc:node>
    <xhtml:a href="specialOffer">Read all about our special vintage Champage
      offer</xhtml:a>
  </idoc:node>
  <idoc:node>
    <xhtml:a href="dailySpecials">View our daily specials</xhtml:a>
  </idoc:node>
</idoc:ifNode>
```

Fig. 6. Conditional hyperlinks to nodes 'specialOffer' or 'dailySpecials.

discussed in Section 5. This assertion records that a customer has visited a particular page containing a Champagne offer. This illustrates a simple way to selectively record user navigation, which might subsequently be used to generate content (such as related offers) sensitive to site navigation patterns.

In IETMs, a second way a property value can be set is through user-interaction. The run-time interpreter is required to detect reference to properties that are not assigned values. In MIL-PRF-87269, a `<property>` can have a *dialogRef* attribute, which references a `<dialog>` element. At run-time, when the property value is undefined, a class-IV IETM can use this element to create a dialog box, with a request to the user to supply a value for the property. In a Web site context, `<dialog>`s could be rendered as forms. However, in an E-commerce application,

```
<postcond>
  <assertion>
    <property>champagneOfferVisited
    </property>
    <expression>
      <boolean>true</boolean>
    </expression>
  </assertion>
</postcond>
```

Fig. 7. The property 'champagneOfferVisited' is set to the value 'true'.

interaction with customers should be as specific and unintrusive as possible. The number of links to follow or forms to fill out before a user obtains relevant data has to be minimized, because each additional barrier between entry point and data means that a percentage of visitors will drop out.

Information-seeking dialogs to deal with unknown property values must also be avoided for another reason. They may reveal sensitive competitive information about a company's marketing strategy or about the type of information a company maintains about its customers. As a result, we have adopted an alternative strategy for the run-time system based on explicit three-valued logic [6]. To account for this at the content level, we have modified the MIL-PRF-87269 `<ifNode>` to takes four arguments: a condition, a 'true'-clause, a 'false'-clause, and an 'unknown'-clause, which is taken if the `<expression>` evaluates to 'unknown'. *i*Doc* authors (or tools generating *i*Doc* content) can therefore explicitly specify what content should be delivered in these cases.

Apart from assertions and by dialogs, properties can be bound to external processes. A class-V IETM is an integrated system. Values for properties may be supplied by external, intelligent systems, and need not be user-supplied (as in a class-IV IETM). In the IETM context, such systems might be data acquisition applications or expert systems. To reference such external systems, the IETM content may define

```
<process id="selectCustomerValue" type="odbc" dsn="CustomerDB" tableOrView="Customer">
  <parameter type="in">
    <property>userID</property><field>ID</field></parameter>
  <parameter type="out">
    <property>highValueCustomer</property><field>Value</field></parameter>
</process>
```

Fig. 8. Process definition and parameter specification.

`<process>` elements that define such external processes and the `<parameter>`s they take. In class-V IETMs, the *dialogRef* attribute can also reference a `<process>` element.

The demonstrator described in Section 5 was built using an implementation that supports two types of process invocations in *i*Doc*, viz. ODBC database access and COM binding. The (simplified) example given in Fig. 8 shows a simple XML notation that expresses that the value for the property *highValueCustomer* can be determined by looking up the field *Value* in a row with value of field *ID* identical to the value of property *userID* in the table *Customer* in an ODBC-accessible database named *CustomerDB*.

Note that *binding* of properties is separate from *reference to* properties in *i*Doc* content. For example, the definition of the `<process>` can be changed if the value is no longer stored statically as a database field but computed dynamically by an external predictive model. This change can be made without any changes to *i*Doc* content containing expressions that reference the property *highValueCustomer*. *i*Doc* also allows properties that are set by assertions to be marked as persistent (stored across various sessions) or only relevant to particular sessions (and thus re-set after session time-out). Apart from customer-specific properties, properties might be used to encode product availability (bindings to inventory management systems), or even to reflect time- or weather-related information.

4.5. *Associating i*Doc to predictive models*

For one-to-one marketing to be feasible, it is necessary to have an accurate picture of a customer's preferences, i.e. it is not enough to know with *whom* you are communicating, but more importantly, to know *what* that person is interested in and how that should be presented. Predictive models provide this ability and thus complement the matching techniques offered by existing CRM-solutions. Predictive models can be used to identify customers or prospects that offer cross- or up-selling opportunities, are at risk of leaving, are likely to grow or become more (or less) profitable, to name but a few possibilities. Having such predictions available greatly enhances the set of functionalities available to customize customer contact.

Predictive data mining (PDM) aims to develop such models on the basis of historical examples of customer behavior: given a set of customer data (e.g. age or level of income) and observed behavior (e.g. did or did not respond favorably to an offer for some product), models or rules are developed that map known data to predicted behavior [14, 16]. Techniques employed by predictive data-mining systems range from linear regression and decision trees to neural networks and genetic algorithms. The PDM system used in the demonstrator is OMEGA, a system that employs a combination of statistical methods and genetic programming [9].

Obviously, the predictions offered by these models need to be available at the time of customer contact. This can be achieved by appending the model results to the available data sources (off-line), but a much better alternative is to assess each case at real-time. The latter option ensures that up-to-date information is used and allows for the use of information entered by the user during the session. OMEGA-developed models can be exported to a run-time interpreter that can be incorporated into CRM systems.

*i*Doc*s use OMEGA models as external procedures that are triggered by means of a function call. Within *i*Doc* the data source and data type are insignificant. Auxiliary processing of function definitions binds the required information of the physical location of the data sources and the appropriate data handles. The models can be used both as a stand-alone application or as a module within a real-time environment. By making external function calls, *i*Doc*s remain independent of the back-office systems and the issues related to the implementation of the PDM system.

5. The Wine Online showcase

5.1. Wine Online

As a showcase of *i*Doc* technology, a prototype E-commerce site offering personalized wine offers has been developed. The wine trade is typical for businesses that feature a very broad and diverse range of products, a diversity of parameters that determine an individual customer's preference including cost, regional provenance, grape variety, ability to age or to match with food. Customer communication also needs to keep track of interest levels (novice versus professional buyers) and of opportunities for cross-selling (similar or complementary offerings) and affinity networks (other luxury goods, wine travels).

Sites like the Wine Online demonstrator generally offer free access, but require users to register to have access to (parts of) the site. User registration for the demonstrator involves specification of interest level, gender, age, regional and grape varietal interests, and of average prices of products purchased. When logging in, users are presented with a customized product offering. Advertisements are generated on the basis of similar criteria as product offerings. Interest level determines tone of voice: descriptions using wine jargon are avoided with novice users. The site features special offers of limited-edition products for its premium customers.

In a production environment, product sales history can be tracked in a data warehouse to perform trend analysis and to predict customer interest. Provided sufficient data, data-mining software might detect subtle, seemingly unrelated micro-trends, such as 'Customers that previously bought Chilean Merlot and Australian Chardonnay and now buy Argentine Malbec are likely to be interested in New Zealand Cabernet Sauvignon.' This allows the site to offer added value.

*5.2. i*Doc in Wine Online*

In Wine Online, *i*Doc*s are used as content transport format. Wine descriptions are stored using a commercial relational database. For each product, the following information is available: *ProducerName, ProducerRating, ProductName, PriceClass, Price, ProductRating, Vintage, Color, Grape, Continent, Country, Region, InformalDescription, FormalDescription*. The demonstrator contains sample content taken from a professional wine buyer's guide [27].

The *i*Doc* generator is an ad hoc XML generator (developed using the ODBC and XML libraries in Perl) that essentially produces a database dump, with wine product descriptions (the *content*) grouped according to various selection criteria, expressed as *ifNode*s and *nodeAlts* (the *marketing*). The XML generated follows a hypothetical markup language for wine descriptions corresponding to database field names. XML elements for *i*Doc* and content-encoding XML are distinguished using namespace prefixes. When registering, users indicate the average price of wines they buy as well as their interest level (novice or professional). Fig. 9 shows an XML fragment that orders products according to these properties.

Products are grouped in *Nodes* by *priceClass*. Note that there is an embedded conditional section within the *Product* that selects either the *InformalDescription* or the *FormalDescription* database field content as source for the `<wdml:Description>` element. This shows that nesting of conditional sections is straightforward and enables personalization at various levels of granularity.

To publish this *i*Doc* fragment as a Web site, two transformations are needed. First of all, the wine description *content* elements need to be mapped to an HTML presentation. The Wine Online HTML front end was developed by a graphics designer using a commercial HTML editor and incorporated as XHTML output in an XSLT stylesheet. Fig. 10 shows a personalized HTML page generated using this template from *i*Doc* content. This stylesheet replaces all content elements with XHTML but leaves all conditional elements in place. This step of the process is specific for the XML content matter and for HTML servers as publishing systems and would need to be rewritten for other XML languages and for non-HTML channels.

```
<idoc:nodeAlts>
  <idoc:node><idoc:precond>
  <idoc:expression>
    <idoc:expression>
      <idoc:property>priceClass</idoc:property>
    </idoc:expression>
    <idoc:eq/>
    <idoc:expression>
      <idoc:string>A</idoc:string>
    </idoc:expression>
    </idoc:expression></idoc:precond>
  <wdml:Product>
    <wdml:ProducerName>J.B. Adam</wdml:ProducerName>
    <wdml:ProductRating>87</wdml:ProductRating>
    <idoc:ifNode>
      <idoc:expression>
        <idoc:expression><property>interestLevel</property></idoc:expression>
        <eq/>
        <idoc:expression><string>novice</string></idoc:expression>
      </idoc:expression>
      <idoc:node>
        <wdml:Description>This fresh, dry... </wdml:Description></idoc:node>
      <idoc:node>
        <wdml:Description>... Professional wine description featuring wine trade jargon...
          </wdml:Description></idoc:node>
    </idoc:ifNode>
    <!-... other information about this product... ->
  </wdml:Product>
  <!-... other products in price class "A"... ->
  </idoc:node>
  <!-... other nodes for other price classes... ->
</idoc:nodeAlts>
```

Fig. 9. Sample *i*Doc* content for on-line wine shop.

Next, personalization semantics need to be applied to the various *conditional* constructs. After initial experiments with server-side interpretation of *i*Doc*, the demonstrator was built by compilation of the XHTML-based *i*Doc* content to ASP (Active Server Pages [23]) to benefit from standard facilities for session management and for access to ODBC and COM data sources in commodity Web servers. This step is independent of XML content matter (now replaced by XHTML) but specific to the ASP presentation engine.

5.3. *Publishing i*Doc as Active Server Pages*

For reasons of implementation efficiency, it proved useful to reuse and build on top of the Microsoft Active Server Pages [23] architecture as a delivery platform for *i*Doc* content, to benefit from built-in ASP features like session management and database connectivity. A compiler has been built to deliver *i*Doc* content for the following reasons:

- a lookahead is required when creating ASP;
- determining and resolving used data types;
- determine if properties are session-based or persistent;
- chunking *i*Doc*-fragments in multiple units for HTML-rendering;
- efficiency for scoping and accessing variables;
- translating from a three-valued logic to a two-valued logic.

The actual compilation is done in two passes. In a first pass, properties used in the *i*Doc* content are collected and proper variable initialization code

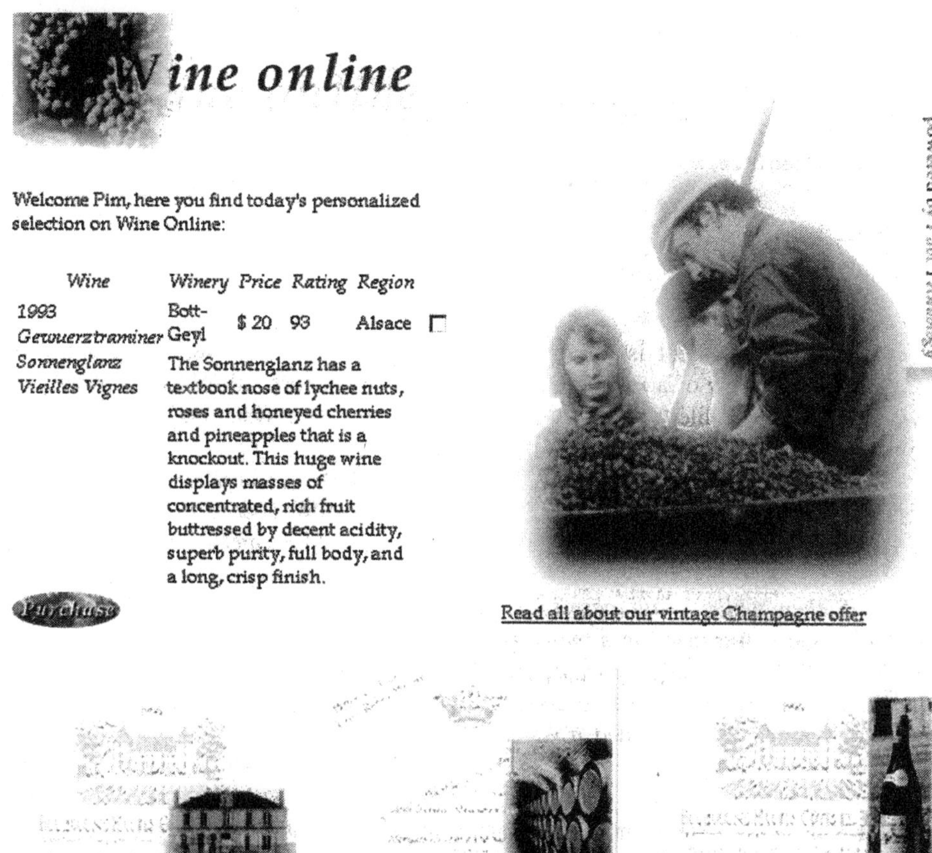

Fig. 10. Personalized Web page generated by Wine Online.

is generated. The ASP/HTML is generated in the second pass.

After an initial prototype, built using Omnimark [26], the *i*Doc* compiler is currently written in Java using the SAX API [22]. SAX offers an interface to parser *events*, such as 'element start' and 'element end'. SAX classes are written to handle these events for all *i*Doc* elements. Fig. 11 shows the interface for the `<idoc:property>` element. The string value of the property can be retrieved using the *data* interface. Content other than *i*Doc* elements is passed unchanged.

In an Internet environment, the presentable unit is the Web page. The *i*Doc* author (or generating

```
public void start (String name, AttributeList atts)
{
  m_f.m_expressionBuild.Property();
}
public void data(String pcdata){}
public void end(String name){}
```

Fig. 11. SAX interfaces for *Property*.

```
<% if (highValueCustomer <> "")) then %>
<% if (((highValueCustomer)=("TRUE"))) then %>
<A HREF='specialOffer.asp'>Read all about our special vintage champagne offer</A>
<% else %>
<A HREF='dailySpecials.asp'>View our daily specials</A>
<% end if %>
<% end if %>
```

Fig. 12. ASP code for Champagne offer.

application) can specify that content is to be rendered as separate pages. Content of a *node* with attribute *id='value'* is written to a file '*value*.asp', and *idref*-based cross-references are converted similarly.

The three-valued logic (*true, false, unknown*) requires additional programming because VBSCRIPT (the scripting language of ASP) does not support this. Therefore, when *i*Doc*'s conditional constructs are compiled into *if...then, while...wend, case* statements, three-valued logic is translated in a two-valued logic (*true, false*). An *ifNode* can be translated to an *if* statement that checks if the boolean expression in it is undefined. If defined, an embedded *if* statement checks if the expression is *true* or *false*. The *nodeAlts* element is converted similarly. In Fig. 12 this is illustrated for the *i*Doc* fragment shown in Fig. 6.

By default, Web pages are stateless. In ASP there is a solution for this problem using session variables. This approach does not solve the problem for properties that have to be saved across sessions (thus keeping a history of the interaction of a site and a particular user). The compiler makes the distinction between session and user variables and will store the user variables per user in a persistent *i*Doc*-property store.

Evaluating expressions within *i*Doc* content is easily achieved by transforming `<plus/>`, `<divide/>`, `<eq/>`, `<lt/>`, `<and/>`, etc. to the corresponding ASP control structures.

Consultation of databases can be easily generated for ASP because of its support for ODBC [25]. Appropriate bindings are generated according to the *i*Doc* `<process>` element (see Fig. 8). Retrieving values from external sources requires an additional functional component within a Web page such as a COM object [24]. This dedicated application serves as an API to a server application. Within *i*Doc* the COM object is invoked using a function call. As a matter of fact, all external processes that have to be bound to *i*Doc*-constructs are implemented as functions.

The Java subclassing mechanism is used to separate the ASP code generation from generic *i*Doc* processing. This means that the compiler can be easily re-targeted towards other publishing mechanisms, such as JavaServer pages [28].

6. Related work

One-to-one communication and personalization are actively researched topics. They have been studied in the context of areas as diverse as information filtering [1], recommender systems [30], targeted advertising [21] and personalized newspapers [20,29]. Systems integration and user interface generation are 'engineering' issues peripheral to the core research issues in these areas and therefore much less actively researched.

The concepts behind MIL-PRF-87269 have been further developed in the MID ('Metafile for Interactive Documents') project [2]. MID offers a more general language for portable IETM *view packages*. This approach is further being developed for ISMID, an upcoming ISO 'interchange standard for modifiable interactive documents' [10].

Finally, the market for Web-based CRM products and solutions is very competitive and support for XML technology is increasing in recent and upcoming product releases. While we are unaware of pure, declarative interchange formats like *i*Doc* that emphasize a strict separation from 'output channels' like HTML sites, a product like Art Technology Group's *Dynamo* improves integration with back-end content management systems using 'Open Content

Adapters' interfaces [5], and also offers some XML support. It would seem to be relatively easy to add *i*Doc* support to such a product.

7. Discussion and future work

*i*Doc* is an interchange format for conditionalized content. An *i*Doc* document instance can be seen as a snapshot of a company's marketing strategy at a particular point in time, as it contains commercial product information ('what do we sell') plus market segmentation information ('which categories of customers do we sell this to'). In a complete solution, *i*Doc*s would be intermediate data structures that are assembled from separate systems for product information and customer information.

In the Wine Online demonstrator, the marketing logic (encoded as *nodeAlts* and *ifNode* elements) is fixed in the script that maps database records to *i*Doc* XML content. In a more realistic setting, a graphical *i*Doc authoring* environment would be needed to allow marketeers to create and update this logic, possibly using intuitive lay-outs as the one shown in Fig. 4. Our limited experimentation with XML editors so far did not confirm our initial idea that these tools might be a good platform to develop such an environment. Workbenches for *i*Doc* would also need *simulation* tools to answer questions like 'How would this site present itself to this category of customers?' and 'How many of my customers will this special offer be displayed to?'. Commercial CRM systems like BroadVision and ATG offer extensive support in this area.

Another issue is the issue of *business rules.* In *i*Doc*, properties can currently be set by assertions, retrieved from database fields, or computed by models in external systems. Apart from this, there is a clear need to allow marketeers to specify rules (functional dependencies) that derive values for properties based on other properties. We are currently working on a *Business Rule Markup Language* in which such rules can be expressed and exchanged. Operationally, business rules would be evaluated dynamically using forward chaining so that values of additional relevant properties are computed before interpreting *i*Doc* fragments. Commercial CRM systems typically offer support for business rule specification, but store these in proprietary (and sometimes non-transparent) formats.

Several potential extensions to *i*Doc* are conceivable to improve its usefulness as representation format, in particular when used to transport tabular information stored as database records. The *i*Doc* content for the wine demonstrator was generated by a simple database dump program and therefore combines conditional elements and static wine product descriptions. In realistic situations, *i*Doc* content would be combined at the authoring level with elements that represent (results of) database queries, rather than being generated by a database dump program. In *i*Doc*, properties can only be bound to the simple data types number, string and boolean. When used with database query elements, there is a potential need to be able to bind properties to *collections*, to have ways to query them (such as finding out their cardinality) and to perform operations on them (such as union, intersection, duplicate removal). Another use for collection-valued properties would be to reference and represent the contents of a user's shopping basket. For instance, there might be an `<ifNode>` in *i*Doc* that shows specific content in case the number of items in the basket is three or higher. Finally, there is a need for a generic type system for properties.

Although *i*Doc* is still very much a research topic, the authors are actively evaluating the applicability of *i*Doc* and looking into its use for commercial projects to deliver personalized content and commerce. This is done in collaboration with business partners and customers of Cap Gemini.

Acknowledgements

We thank Annette Nijenbanning for designing the online wine shop.

References

[1] ACM, Special Issue on Information Filtering, Communications of the ACM 35 (12) (1992), http://www.acm.org/pubs/contents/journals/cacm/1992-35/#12

[2] M. Anderson (Ed.), The Metafile for Interactive Documents, Application Guide and Draft Performance Specification for the Encoding of Interactive Documents, MID-2,

Naval Surface Warfare Center, Carderock Division, Maryland, 1996.
[3] R. Anderson, 'Customer Relationship Management (CRM): perspective', Gartner DataPro, June 1999, pp. 1–9.
[4] V. Apparao et al., Document Object Model (DOM) Level 1 Specification, W3C Recommendation, http://www.w3.org/TR/REC-DOM-Level-1/
[5] Art Technology Group, http://www.atg.com/
[6] J. van Benthem, A Manual of Intensional Logic, Center for the Study of Language and Information (CSLI), Stanford, 1988.
[7] T. Bray, D. Hollander and A. Layman, Namespaces in XML, http://www.w3.org/TR/1999/REC-xml-names-19990114, W3C recommendation.
[8] Broadvision One-to-One, http://www.broadvision.com/
[9] Cap Gemini, KiQ, Oracle and Sun Microsystems, OMEGA+ Predictive Data Mining, White paper, http://www.kiq.com/content/Overview/html/omega.html
[10] N. Chenard and D. Cooper (Eds.), Interchange Standard for Modifiable Interactive Documents, http://www.ornl.gov/sgml/wg8/document/1974.htm
[11] J. Clark, XSL Transformations (XSLT) Version 1.0, http://www.w3.org/TR/xslt, W3C recommendation.
[12] DavenPort Group, DocBook 3 DTD, http://www.oasis-open.org/docbook/index.html
[13] Department of Defense standard MIL-PRF-87269, http://navycals.dt.navy.mil/dtdfosi/reposdtd.html#87269
[14] A.E. Eiben, A.E. Koudijs, F. Slisser, Genetic modelling of customer retention, Proc. EuroGP 98, http://link.springer.de/link/service/series/0558/bibs/1391/13910178.htm
[15] R. Fye, N.E. Montgomery, G.S. Weiss, An object-oriented approach to developing MIL-87269 conforming ETM, ICW, and IETM Content Data models and instances, Proc. of SGML/XML '97, pp. 501–510.
[16] E.W. Haasdijk, R.F. Walker, D. Barrow and M.C. Gerrets, Genetic Algorithms in Business, in: J. Stender, E. Hillebrand, J. Kingdon (Eds.), Genetic Algorithms in Optimisation, Simulation and Modelling, IOS Press, Amsterdam, 1994, pp. 157–184.
[17] B. Harvey, Interactive Electronic Technical Manuals, Paper presented at the ISO STEP Conference, Chester, 1997.
[18] HTML 4.01 Specification, http://www.w3.org/TR/html401/, W3C recommendation.
[19] International Standardization Organization, Standard Generalized Markup Language, ISO-standard, Information processing, Text and Office Systems, 8879:1986.
[20] T. Kamba, K. Bharat and M.C. Albers, The Krakatoa Chronicle — An interactive, personalized, newspaper on the Web, Proc. of WWW4, http://www.w3.org/Conferences/WWW4/Papers/93/
[21] M. Langheinrich et al., Unintrusive customization techniques for Web advertising, Proc. of WWW8, http://www8.org/w8-papers/2b-customizing/unintrusive/unintrusive.html
[22] D. Megginson et al., Simple API for XML, http://www.megginson.com/SAX/index.html
[23] Microsoft Corporation, Active Server Pages, http://msdn.microsoft.com/library/tools/aspdoc/iiwawelc.htm
[24] Microsoft Corporation and Digital Equipment Corporation, The Component Object Model Specification, http://msdn.microsoft.com/library/specs/s1d137.htm
[25] Microsoft Corporation, Microsoft ODBC, http://www.microsoft.com/data/odbc/default.htm
[26] Omnimark Technologies Corporation, Guide to Omnimark 5, http://www.omnimark.com/develop/om5/doc/
[27] R.M. Parker Jr., Parker's Wine Buyer's Guide, Simon and Schuster, New York, 1995.
[28] E. Pelegri-Llopart and L. Cable, JavaServer Pages Specification, Sun Microsystems, http://www.java.sun.com/products/jsp/index.html
[29] H. Sakagami et al., Effective personalization of push-type systems — visualizing information freshness, Proc. of WWW7, http://www7.scu.edu.au/programme/fullpapers/1871/com1871.htm
[30] I. Soboroff, Ch. Nicholas and M. Pazzani, Workshop on Recommender Systems: Algorithms and Evaluation, SIGIR Forum, Fall 1999, http://www.acm.org/sigir/forum/F99/Soboroff.html
[31] Wireless Application Forum, Wireless Markup Language Specification, http://www.wapforum.org/
[32] World Wide Web Consortium, The Extensible HyperText Markup Language (XHTML), http://www.w3.org/TR/1999/PR-xhtml1-19990824, W3C Proposed Recommendation.

Patrick van Amstel studied Technical Computer Science at the Den Haag Polytechnic. After his study he worked for a publishing and printing company. He is currently working for Cap Gemini Nederland at the R&D department.

Pim van der Eijk received an M.S. degree in Romance Linguistics from the University of Utrecht in 1988, where he subsequently worked as a researcher in Computational Linguistics. Since then he has held various R&D and consultancy positions with Digital Equipment Corporation and Cap Gemini. His interests include language technology, information retrieval, SGML/XML technology and the Web.

Evert Haasdijk received his M.S. degree in Computer Science at the University of Amsterdam in 1993. He has been working on machine learning, (predictive) data mining and CRM and is currently working as an R&D consultant at Cap Gemini. His research interests include machine learning and business intelligence.

David Kuilman received his M.S. degree in Computational Linguistics from the University of Amsterdam in 1993. He has been actively working with SGML/XML technologies in the past 6 years. Currently, he is a Content Manager working for Wolters Kluwer in The Netherlands.

Annotation-based Web content transcoding

Masahiro Hori [a,*,1], Goh Kondoh [a,1], Kouichi Ono [a,1], Shin-ichi Hirose [a,1], Sandeep Singhal [b,2]

[a] *IBM Tokyo Research Laboratory, 1623-14 Shimo-tsuruma, Yamato, Kanagawa 242-8502, Japan*
[b] *IBM Pervasive Computing Division, P.O. Box 12195, Research Triangle Park, NC 27709-2195, USA*

Abstract

Users are increasingly accessing the Internet from information appliances such as PDAs, cell phones, and set-top boxes. Since these devices do not have the same rendering capabilities as desktop computers, it is necessary for Web content to be adapted, or transcoded, for proper presentation on a variety of client devices. In this paper, we propose an annotation-based system for Web content transcoding. First, we introduce a framework of external annotation, in which existing Web documents are associated with content adaptation hints as separate annotation files. We then explain an annotation-based transcoding system with particular focus on the authoring-time integration between a WYSIWYG annotation tool and a transcoding module. Finally, after giving an example of content adaptation using a page fragmentation module for small-screen devices, we compare our approach with related work.

Keywords: Content adaptation; Annotation; Intermediary; Authoring system

1. Introduction

As more and more Web-enabled personal devices are becoming available for connecting to the Internet, the same Web content needs to be rendered differently on client devices, taking account of their physical and performance constraints such as screen size, memory size, and connection bandwidth. For example, a large full-color image may be reduced with regard to size and color depth, removing unimportant portions of the content. Such content adaptation, also called *transcoding*, is exploited for either an individual element or a set of consecutive elements in a Web document, and results in better presentation and faster delivery to the client device. Content adaptation is thus crucial for transparent Web access under different conditions, which may depend on client capabilities, network connectivity, or user preferences [4,8,15].

Although most existing HTML [9] documents are created to be displayed on desktop computers, they can be augmented with meta-information to facilitate adaptation of their contents to other types of client device. It is important to note here that the result of applying an annotation to a document depends on the transcoding policy. The role of annotations is to provide hints that enable a transcoding engine to make better decisions on the content adaptation. To put it another way, annotation plays the role of a mediating representation, which provides semantics to be shared between meta-content authors and a content adaptation engine. A potential advantage

* Corresponding author.
[1] E-mail: {horim,gkondo,onono,hiroses}@jp.ibm.com
[2] E-mail: singhal@us.ibm.com

of an annotation-based transcoding approach is the possibility of content adaptation based on semantics. This cannot be achieved with existing commercial products, which adapt contents on the basis of Web document syntax [11].

Annotations can range from simple to complex descriptions. A simple annotation, for example, specifies an importance value for a document element, and an element with lower importance may be ignored when display space is limited. In a complex case, an annotation may consist of alternative image contents for different device types and perhaps for different user preferences. It is possible for such an annotation to be embedded into an HTML document, as the value of an extra attribute that would be a proprietary extension of an HTML tag. Web content transcoding, however, usually results in the adaptation of content presentation to device capabilities. Therefore, mixing of contents and adaptation hints would not be acceptable according to the design consideration that separates content from presentation [18].

Markup languages such as HTML embed annotations into documents. For example, an `<ol>` tag indicates the start of an ordered list, and a paragraph begins with a `<p>` tag. On the other hand, annotations can be *external*, residing in a file separate from the original document. It would be impractical to incorporate meta-information for content adaptation into each of the existing HTML documents, in terms of both the difficulty of changing the established HTML specification and the need to modify a huge amount of the existing documents. External annotation is thus a key to adaptation of Web documents to various constraints stemming from user preferences, client devices, media types, and so on. Although making annotations external may require additional bookkeeping tasks, it has the substantial advantage of not requiring any modification of existing Web documents that are already published as HTML or XML files.

Various demands for content annotation are emerging, such as Web accessibility [22], speech-enabled applications on the Internet [21], language translation, and document summarization. In this paper, we focus on page fragmentation for small-screen devices. In the following sections, we elaborate a framework for external annotation. We then introduce an annotation-based transcoding system developed on top of a programmable proxy server [2], and explain the integration between a WYSIWYG annotation tool and a transcoding module at the time of content authoring. Finally, after giving an example of content adaptation using a page fragmentation module, we compare our approach with related work.

2. Annotation framework

This section describes an external annotation framework that prescribes a scheme for representing annotation files and a way of associating original documents with external annotations. The role of annotation is to characterize ways of content adaptation rather than to describe individual contents themselves. Therefore, the framework needs to specify a vocabulary for constraining the possibilities for decomposition, combination, and partial replacement of contents. The annotation vocabulary is briefly introduced in the following subsection. The basic ideas behind this annotation framework are twofold. One is that new elements and/or attributes should not be introduced into a document-type definition of annotated documents. The other is that annotations need to be created for arbitrary parts of annotated documents.

This framework is motivated by the requirements of rendering already-published HTML documents on various types of Web-enabled personal devices. Although external annotation is a general concept that has many potential applications, we focus on annotations of HTML documents that facilitate contents adaptation for personal computing devices. Fig. 1 depicts several paths from an original HTML document to different client devices. An HTML document, which is provided for desktop computers (path 1), is analyzed and annotated with a separate file by using an annotation tool (path 2). The annotated document must be viewable in a normal browser on a desktop computer (path 3). Furthermore, such an annotated document can also be authored by using a stand-alone editor (path 4). Upon receiving a request from a personal device, a proxy server may adapt the document on the basis of associated annotations (path 5). The rendered document is then

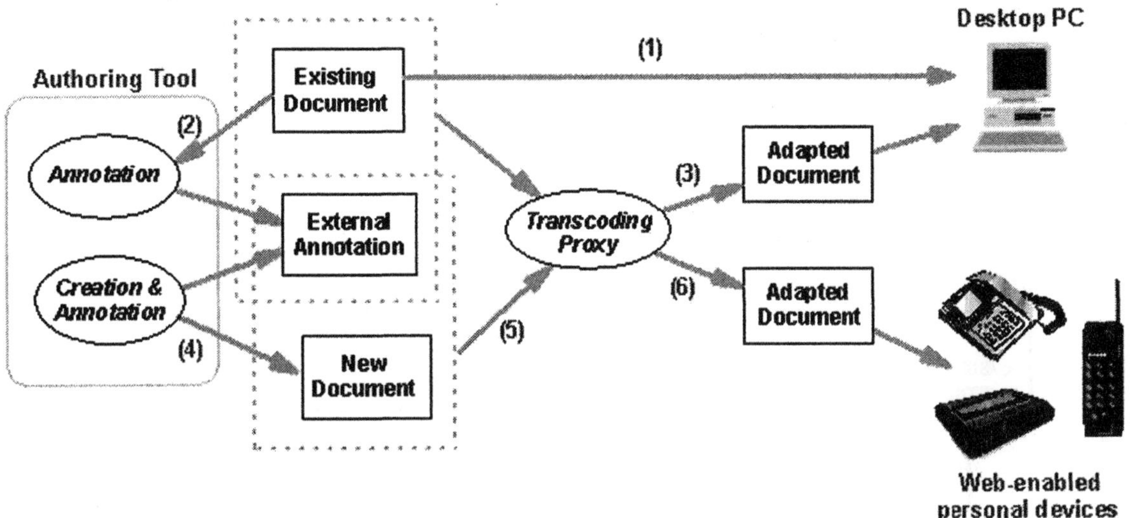

Fig. 1. Adaptation of HTML documents for personal computing devices.

downloaded to a client device with a small display (path 6).

External annotation files contain hints associated with elements in an original document. The Resource Description Framework (RDF) [14] is used as the syntax of annotation files. An annotation file, which is an XML document, therefore consists of a set of RDF descriptions. The RDF data model defines a simple model for describing relations among resources in terms of named properties and values. In the process of document transcoding, it is necessary to exploit user preferences and device capabilities for content adaptation. Such information profiles can be described by using Composite Capability/Preference Profiles (CC/PP) [5]. By using the RDF data model, CC/PP specifies client-side profiles, which can be delivered to a proxy server over HTTP [6]. Furthermore, there is current investigation into ways of describing document profiles so that requirements for desired rendering can be clarified [24], and RDF is being employed for encoding the conformance profiles. Taking account of these standardization activities, it is reasonable for annotation vocabularies to be encoded in RDF, so that comprehensive content adaptation mechanisms can be pursued.

In addition, XPath [26] and XPointer [27] are used for associating annotated portions of a document with annotating descriptions. Fig. 2 illustrates a way of associating an external description with a portion of an existing document. An annotation file refers to portions of an annotated document. A reference may point to a single element (e.g., an `IMG` element), or a range of elements (e.g., an `H2` element and the following paragraphs). For example, `/HTML/BODY/P[3]` points to the third `P` element of the `BODY` element of the annotated document. If a target element has an `id` attribute, the attribute can be used for direct addressing without the need for a long path expression. In contrast to XPath, which allows to select particular parts of a tree derived from elements or markup constructs of an XML document, XPointer makes it possible to select a range of elements by using the range expression.

When annotation files are stored in a repository, an appropriate annotation file for a Web document needs to be selected dynamically from the repository either implicitly by means of a structural analysis of the subject document or explicitly by means of a reference contained in the subject document or some other association database. An annotation file can be associated with a single document file, but the relation is not limited to one-to-one. It is possible for multiple annotation files to be associated with a single document file, when each annotation file contains descriptions related to different portions of an annotated document. On the other hand, a single annotation file may contain meta-information to be shared among multiple document files. This type of

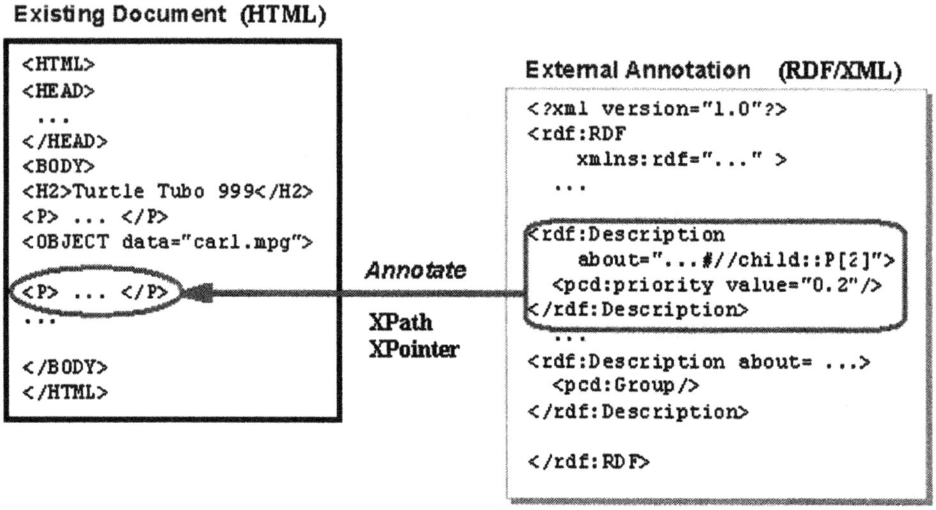

Existing Document (HTML)

```
<HTML>
<HEAD>
 ...
</HEAD>
<BODY>
<H2>Turtle Tubo 999</H2>
<P> ... </P>
<OBJECT data="carl.mpg">
<P> ... </P>
...
</BODY>
</HTML>
```

Annotate

XPath
XPointer

External Annotation (RDF/XML)

```
<?xml version="1.0"?>
<rdf:RDF
   xmlns:rdf="..." >
  ...
<rdf:Description
   about="...#//child::P[2]">
 <pcd:priority value="0.2"/>
</rdf:Description>
 ...
<rdf:Description about= ...>
 <pcd:Group/>
</rdf:Description>

</rdf:RDF>
```

Fig. 2. Framework of external annotation.

annotation would be useful when it is necessary to annotate common parts of Web documents, such as a page header, a company logo image, and a side bar menu.

2.1. Annotation vocabulary for transcoding

The above framework prescribes a skeletal structure of annotation, without regard to the ways in which concrete adaptation hints are described. This section briefly explains an annotation vocabulary that is used for adaptation hints on rendering HTML documents for personal computing devices. The vocabulary includes three types of annotation: *alternatives, splitting hints* and *selection criteria.* A namespace [25] prefix, `pcd`, is used for the transcoding vocabulary. Further details on this vocabulary can be found in [1].

2.1.1. Alternatives

Alternative representations of a document or any set of its elements can be provided. For example, a color image may have a gray-scale image as an alternative for clients with monochrome displays. A transcoding proxy selects the one alternative that best suits the capabilities of the requested client device. Elements in the annotated document can then be altered either by replacement or by on-demand conversion. The `<pcd:Alternatives>` tag specifies a list of alternative representations for an annotated element. The `<rdf:Alt>` tag provided by the RDF data model is used to specify alternatives to be included in the `pcd:Alternatives` element. Each item in the RDF containers (`rdf:Alt`, `rdf:Bag` and `rdf:Seq`) may include a `pcd:Replace` element.

2.1.2. Splitting hints

An HTML file, which can be shown as a single page on a normal desktop computer, may be divided into multiple pages on clients with smaller display screens. The `<pcd:Group>` tag specifies a set of elements to be considered as a logical unit. Another use for the `pcd:Group` element is to provide hints for determining appropriate page break points. Alternatives may be provided for the group as a whole. For example, a news headline may be associated with an alternative for a news story that consists of paragraphs of text and some images. In the following example, the range of elements from the second occurrence of an `H2` element through the second occurrence of a `P` element is annotated as a group.

```
<rdf:Description
        about = 'http://foo.com/catalog.
                html#xpointer(//H2[2] to
                //P[3])' >
    <pcd:Group />
</rdf:Description>
```

2.1.3. Selection criteria

An annotation may contain information to help a transcoding proxy select from several alternative representations the one that best suits the client device. The selection criteria include the following information.

- Client device capability expected for an alternative resource.
- Resource requirements of an alternative representation.
- Fidelity of an alternative representation in relation to an original item.
- Role of an annotated element.
- Importance of an annotated element.

The `<pcd:role>` tag, for example, specifies the role of an annotated element. A transcoder may use this meta-information in order to make decisions on the allocation of client resources (display area, data volume for transmission, etc.). This role tag is provided with a `value` attribute, which may be specified as either *proper content, advertisement, decoration, or icon,* for example. The `<pcd:importance>` tag specifies the priority of an annotated element relative to the other elements in the page. When the importance of an element is low, for example, it will be ignored or displayed in a very small font. The importance value is a real number ranging from −1 (lowest priority) to 1 (highest priority). The default importance value is 0. When an importance is specified with a value outside the range, the default value, namely, 0 is used. By referring to this importance value, a transcoding proxy can make decisions on the allocation of client resources for each element. For example, an element may not be sent to a lightweight client, when the element is provided with a decoration role and a low importance value such as −0.2. The RDF description of such annotations is given as follows.

```
<rdf:Description
       about = 'http://foo.com/catalog.
                            html#//IMG[1]' >
     <pcd:role value ='decoration' />
     <pcd:importance value = '-0.2' />
</rdf:Description>
```

3. Annotation-based transcoding system

Since content adaptation can be done on either a content server, a proxy, or a client terminal, a transcoding engine should not be forced to reside in any particular location. In order to resolve this limitation, a proxy-based approach has been adopted for content adaptation [16]. Computational entities stay along the Web transaction path are called *intermediaries* [3], and existing approaches to annotation systems confirm to a common abstract architecture based on intermediaries [29].

3.1. Transcoding architecture

As shown in Fig. 3, intermediaries are entities that reside along the paths of information streams, and facilitate an approach to making ordinary information streams into smart streams that enhance the quality of communication [3]. An intermediary processor or a transcoding proxy can operate on a document to be delivered, and transform the contents with reference to associated annotation files. From a computational perspective, the use of an intermediary architecture is an approach to providing pluggable services between

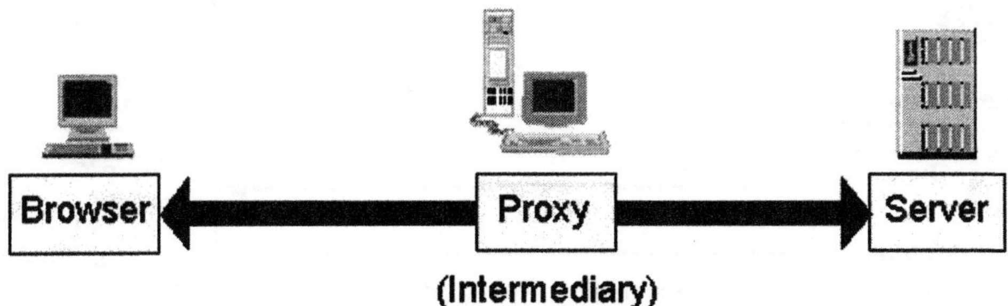

Fig. 3. Intermediary between client and server.

a Web client and server [19]. To put it another way, intermediaries provide special-purpose proxy servers for protocol extension, document caching, Web personalization, content adaptation, and so on [2]. This intermediary-based approach is suitable for realizing annotation-based content adaptation, because it allows us to provide a transcoding module as an intermediary without modifying Web browsers or content servers in any way.

As a transcoding platform, we use a programmable proxy server called Web Intermediaries (WBI) [23]. WBI is a programmable processor for HTTP requests and responses. It receives an HTTP request from a client such as a Web browser, and produces an HTTP response to be returned to the client. The processing in between is controlled by modules or plugins available at an intermediary processor. WBI's plugin is constructed from three fundamental building blocks: monitors, editors, and generators [2]. Monitors observe transactions without affecting them. Editors modify outgoing requests or incoming documents. Generators produce documents in response to requests.

We realized a page-splitting module as a WBI plugin that adapts a requested document to the capabilities of a particular client (Fig. 4). Adaptation hints are expressed by using the aforementioned transcoding vocabulary. The execution sequence of the page-splitting module for the first access to a Web document can be briefly described as follows.

(1) Upon receipt of the request from a client browser, an original page is retrieved for the first time from a content server.
(2) The editor component of the plugin tries to find the locations of annotation files.
   - If it is specified in a `link` element in an HTML header section, retrieve the designated annotation file.
   - Lookup in a table for the mapping between an URL of the original page and that of an annotation. If it is found, retrieve the designated annotation file.
   - Otherwise, the original page is returned as it is and the session is terminated.
(3) The generator component of the plugin generates a current page to be returned.
   - Taking account of client capabilities included in an HTML request header, the generator extracts a portion of a document object tree and returns a sub-tree to the client.

Note that it is determined with reference to an URL and a session identifier whether an HTTP request is for the first access or not. Each anchor

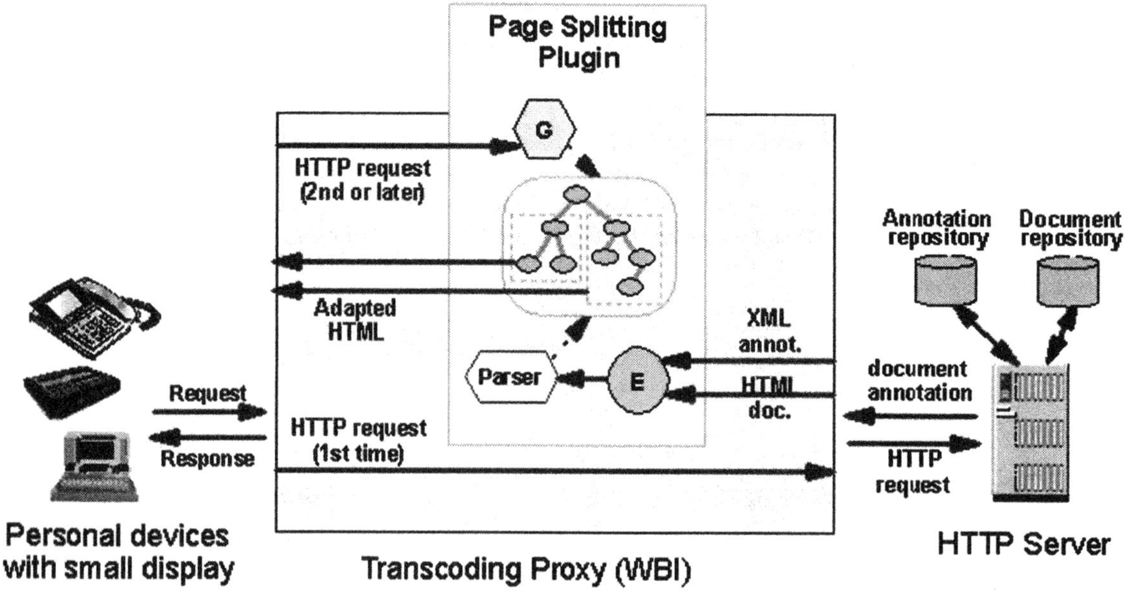

Fig. 4. Annotation-based transcoding by a page-splitting plugin.

element linking to a fragmented page is provided with an `href` attribute value, in which a corresponding session identifier is included. Currently, a single annotation file is retrieved, but it can be extended with the capability of multiple annotation.

3.2. Authoring-time transcoding

Annotation descriptions could be too complicated for a simple source tag editor to maintain, because addressing by XPath/XPointer follows a hierarchy of document elements from the root to a focal element, and alternative contents are structured as a hierarchy of conjunctive/disjunctive elements for replacement. Therefore, it is crucial to provide an annotation tool for the external annotation approach. We have developed such a tool [10] by extending an existing HTML authoring tool [20]. The high-level design of the annotation tool is depicted in Fig. 5. It consists of a WYSIWYG editor, a source tag editor, and a previewer. The WYSIWYG editor is used not only to modify a subject HTML document but also to specify a portion of the HTML document to be annotated. When the previewer is invoked, a transcoding proxy is called over HTTP and the corresponding annotation is applied to the subject document. An adapted document is then sent back to the previewer, in which the result is displayed. In this way, the annotation tool is fully integrated with the transcoding proxy, so that tool users can see the results of content adaptation and revise annotations on the fly.

Fig. 6 show a screen copy of the annotation tool. The child window in the upper half is for WYSIWYG editing of HTML contents. When an element is selected in the WYSIWYG editor (Fig. 6a), a user can pop up a dialog window for annotation (Fig. 6b). After the completion of annotation input, a DOM [7] for an XML annotation is internally modified or created for the first time. The region highlighted in reverse video in the lower-half child window (Fig. 6c) is an RDF description that annotates the role and importance of the header text 'Information on TRL' found in the WYSIWYG editor.

4. Page fragmentation for small-screen devices

This section shows the results of applying the page-splitting plugin to real-life Web contents. The Web page used as an example is a news page from a corporate Web site (Fig. 7). Use of tables for page layout is inappropriate not only as regards a

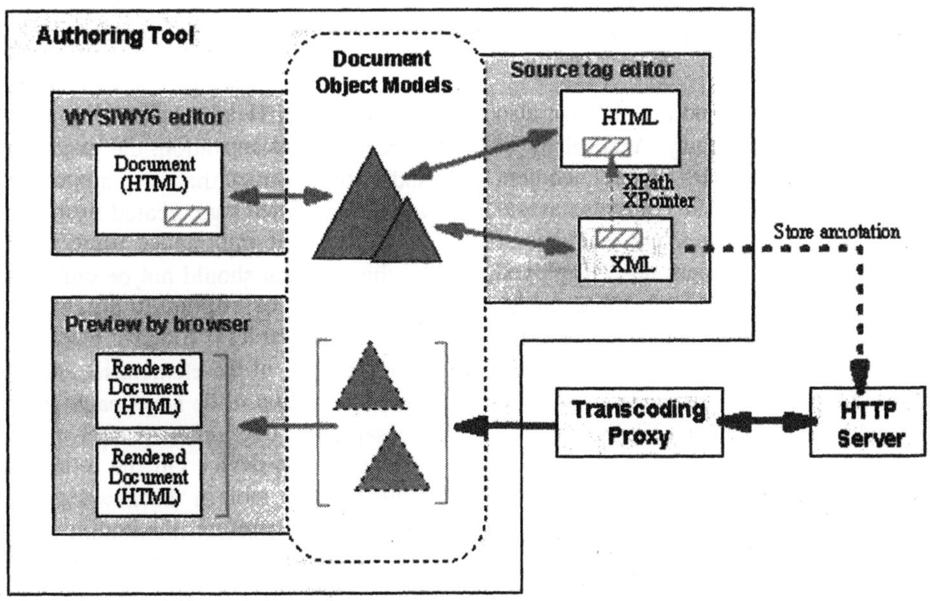

Fig. 5. Annotation tool configuration for authoring-time transcoding.

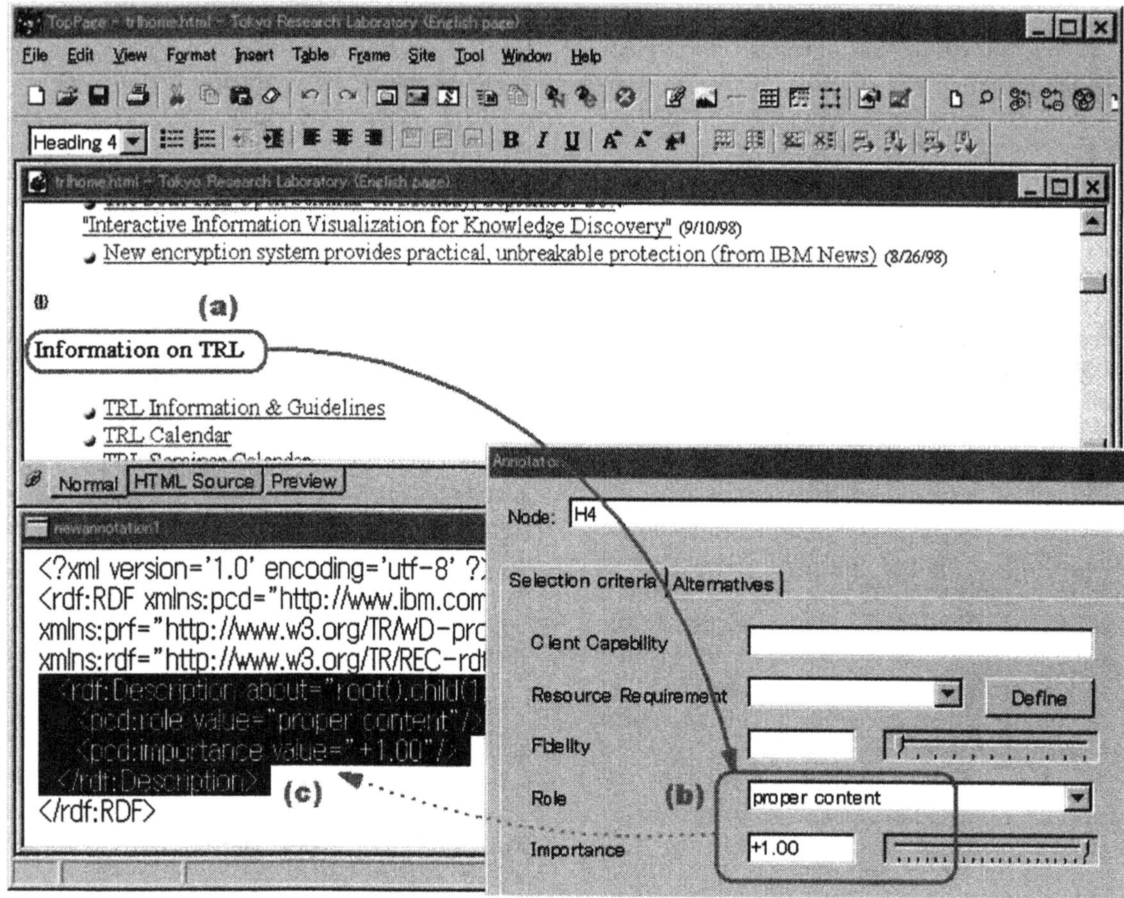

Fig. 6. Screen copy of a WYSIWYG annotation tool.

clear distinction between style and content, but also as regards Web content accessibility. According to the accessibility guidelines 12 to 14 [22], content developers are encouraged to make contents navigable. In reality, however, there are a large number of Web pages in which table elements are employed for layouting. The news page consists of three tables stacked from top to bottom as depicted in the right in Fig. 7. The top and middle tables correspond, respectively, to a header menu and a search form. The bottom table [labeled as 'Layouter (3)' in Fig. 7], however, is used for layouting.

Fig. 8 shows a portion of an annotation file to be associated with the news page mentioned above. The annotation contains RDF descriptions specifying the roles of the tables. For example, the first description in the figure is related to the top table, for a header menu ['Header (1)' in Fig. 7]. According to the header role annotation, the page-splitting plugin handles the element that is to appear as a header of every fragmented page created from this news page. In addition, the importance value '+1.00' indicates that this element should not be omitted in any case. The last RDF description in Fig. 8 concerns the left menu bar on the left ['Side bar menu (31)' in Fig. 7]. Since the role of this element is annotated as auxiliary, this portion of the news page will be presented as a separate page upon receipt of a request from a small-screen device. On the other hand, the role of the bottom table in the news page is annotated as layouter. Therefore, the bottom table will not be retained in the display for small-screen devices.

Fig. 9 illustrates how the news page will be fragmented in a small display. According to the

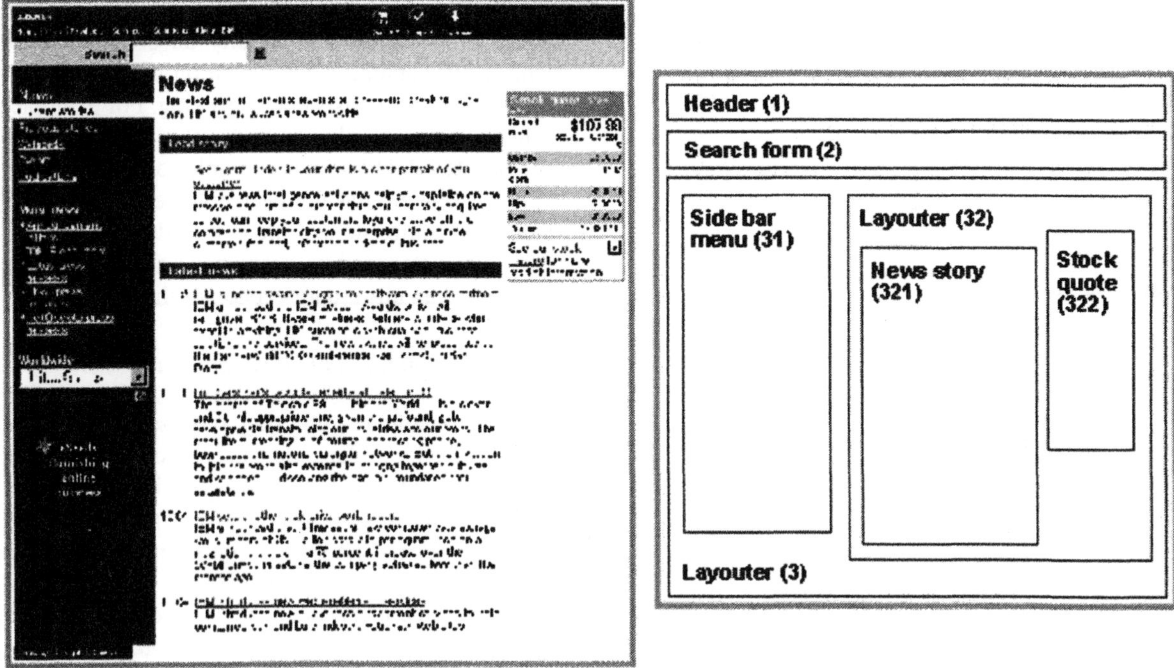

Fig. 7. Nested table elements in an actual news page.

capability for authoring-time transcoding, users of the annotation tool can check the result of page fragmentation on the fly, by simply switching to the previewer (Fig. 10). A user can also change the size of the display area by clicking the button at the bottom right. According to the header role of the top table, the same header appears in the previewer as in the original page. The 'Side bar' anchor in the center is created in accordance with the auxiliary role of the vertical side bar menu. In contrast, because the importance value is '−1.00,' the search form table in the original page is omitted. The main news content then starts after the 'Side bar' anchor, and allows users to access the primary content of the page directly.

Fig. 11 shows the contents displayed in a PalmOS and an HTML browser [13]. Fig. 11a shows the news page without fragmentation, presenting only the top one-ninth of the original content. In contrast, Fig. 11b shows the result of fragmentation by the page-splitting plugin. It is important to note here that the page splitting not only reduces the content to be delivered, but also places the primary content near the top of the fragmented page that is provided with navigational features. This result of adaptation follows the design guidelines for reducing scrolling during interaction with small screens ([11], p. 58):

- placing navigational features (menu bars, etc.) near the top of pages;
- placing key information at the top of pages;
- reducing the amount of information on the page.

Small screens force users to employ frequent scrolling activities that may affect the accessibility of contents as well as the usability of devices. It has been reported that users with small screens were 50% less effective than those with large screens in completing retrieval tasks [11]. Therefore, page fragmentation based on semantic annotation will be more appropriate than page transformation done by solely syntactic information, such as removing white spaces, shrinking or removing images, and so on. Semantic rearrangement is one of the critical limitations of the syntactic transformation approach. The navigational features achieved by this semantic annotation are noteworthy from the perspective of Web content accessibility.

```
<?xml version='1.0' ?>

<rdf:RDF
  xmlns:pcd="http://www.ibm.com/annot/pcd"
  xmlns:rdf="http://www.w3.org/TR/REC-rdf-syntax">

<rdf:Description
       about="pcd:shared#/HTML/BODY/TABLE[1]">
  <!-- header -->
  <pcd:role value="header"/>
  <pcd:importance value="+1.00"/>
</rdf:Description>

<rdf:Description
       about="pcd:shared#/HTML/BODY/TABLE[2]">
  <!-- serach form -->
  <pcd:importance value="-1.00"/>
</rdf:Description>

<rdf:Description
       about="pcd:shared#/HTML/BODY/TABLE[3]">
  <!-- main table -->
  <pcd:role value="layout"/>
</rdf:Description>

<rdf:Description
       about="pcd:shared#/HTML/BODY/TABLE[3]
              /TBODY[1]/TR[1]/TD[1]">
  <!-- Left side vertical menu -->
  <pcd:role value="auxiliary"/>
  <pcd:importance value="+1.00"/>
</rdf:Description>

<!-- More descriptions are included ... -->

</rdf:RDF>
```

Fig. 8. Portion of an annotation file for a news page.

5. Discussion

5.1. Consistency between an original document and its annotation

Since external annotations must be updated whenever a subject document is revised, it is necessary to provide a way of keeping them synchronized. Our annotation tool is especially helpful when an annotated document can be revised in parallel with a corresponding annotation. If an element is removed from or added to the document during WYSIWYG editing, the annotation file is re-created and automatically adjusted for the revision of the corresponding annotating description and for the differences in the XPath specification. This consistency is achieved because annotation source tags are updated whenever a user switches to the source tag editor or previewer in the annotation tool. Annotation source tags are re-created from internal DOMs [7] for XML annotation by referring to annotating portions of a subject HTML document. In contrast, when an annotation author is not allowed to modify an original document at all, content synchronization can be weakly implemented for consistency checking. For example, by using a digest value (a hash value such as MD5 [12] or SHA-1 [17]), it is possible to ensure that a subject document has not been changed. If the MD5 value of an entire subject file is included in an annotation file, a transcoding proxy can check whether a given file is an up-to-date version of the subject file.

5.2. Annotation for content adaptation

An automatic re-authoring process has be proposed for device-independent access to Web contents [4]. The re-authoring is conducted by a heuristic planner, which searches a document transformation space and selects the most promising state with the smallest display area. It is reported, however, that in the worst case the planner produces 80 versions of the document during the search process. If the planner is provided with meta-information (namely, an annotation), the search space will be pruned more effectively. To put it another way, it is not an issue of whether meta-information is embedded or external. The important point is that meta-information must be provided explicitly rather than implicitly in an adaptation procedure.

Meta-information is used in a multimedia presentation system [15], which creates a customized view of the presentation. In particular, a vocabulary of meta-information is defined there for synchronized multimedia content adaptation. The vocabulary provides ways of representing alternative contents, content descriptions, and content predicates. By using that vocabulary, meta-information can be associated with a subject document in two ways: as short inline descriptions or as RDF-like embedded descriptions. However, the vocabulary is defined as proprietary extensions to the HTML specification. In contrast, our external annotation approach allows such application-specific meta-information to be specified separately from the HTML specification.

5.3. Extensibility issue

Finally, we remark on the extensibility issue related to the employment of meta-information for

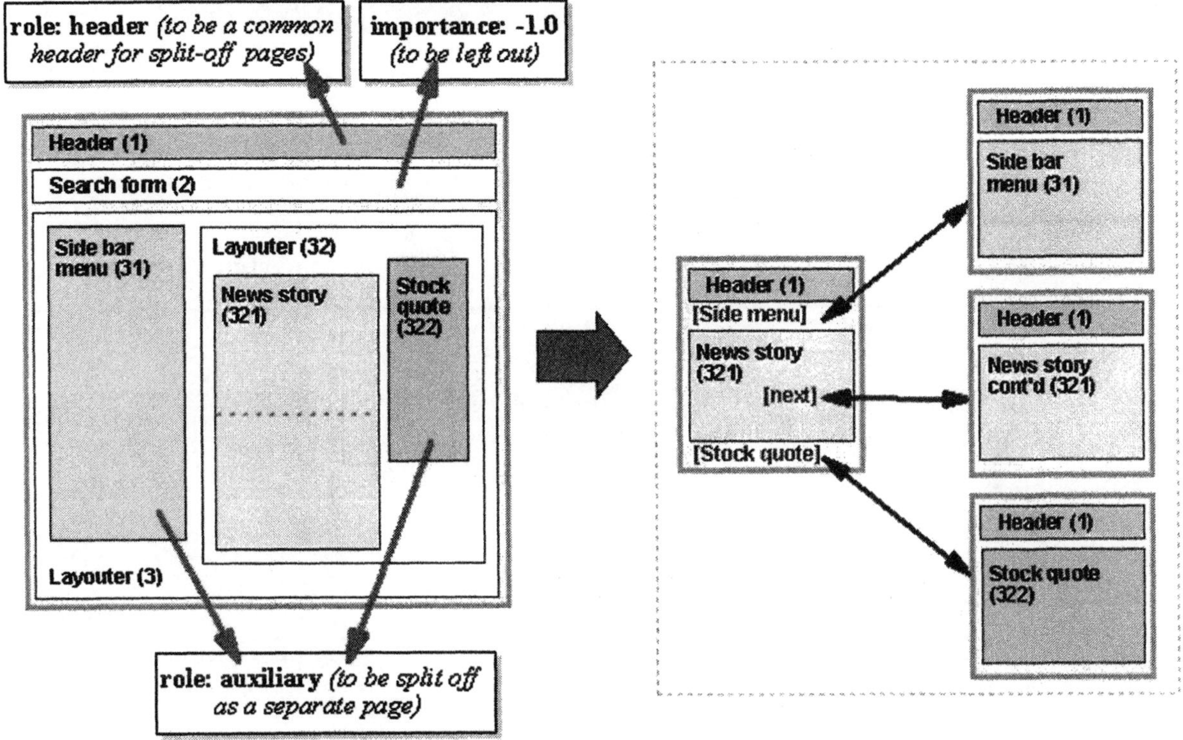

Fig. 9. Annotation for fragmentation of an actual news page.

content adaptation. Annotation-based transcoding is a way of realizing content adaptation, and a transcoding module employs external annotations, which are described in a markup language rather than a procedural programming language. On the basis of the same intermediary-based transcoding platform, it is possible to think about the other approaches. One is to provide a custom-tailored transcoding module that runs without any external meta-information. Another approach could be the case of using a general-purpose transformation engine, such as XSLT [28], which employs externally provided transformation rules, or XSL style sheets.

Fig. 12 illustrates the three approaches mentioned above. Although these three are not exhaustive, they represent major design decisions necessary for the realization of a content adaptation system. The custom-tailored module relies on heuristics or empirical knowledge of the content to be adapted (Fig. 12a). It can be applied without additional customization of the transcoding module. However, the scope of application must be carefully selected, because it will suffer a steep performance degradation when applied to domains that are not well suited to the system's purpose. In addition, modification using a conventional programming language requires considerably more effort than authoring in a markup language. Although it is possible to remedy the limitations of this approach by parameterizing the possibilities of customization, the scope of applicability is still limited. Bickmore's above-mentioned system falls into this category. In contrast to a custom-tailored module, a general-purpose transformation engine can be used so that contents can be adapted in various ways by means of application-specific transformation rules (Fig. 12c). The transformation rules are assumed to be written in a markup language, and the rule that authors rely on the solid basis of a generic transformation engine. The advantage of this approach lies in the clear distinction between the roles of those responsible for the development of a run-time module (namely, a generic transformation engine) and those responsible for the application-specific programming in a markup language.

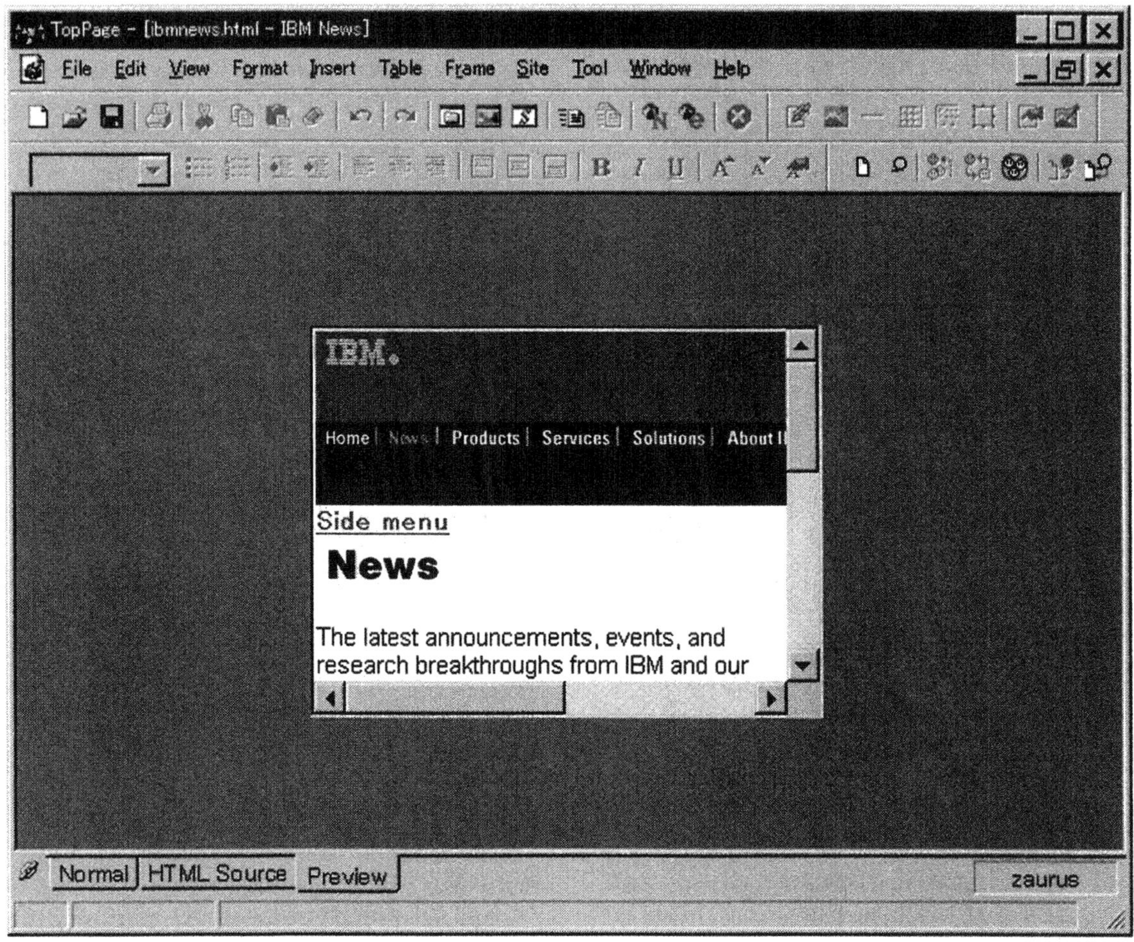

Fig. 10. Screen copy of a small display preview on an authoring tool.

The annotation-based approach discussed in this paper relies on a task-specific transcoding module, such as a page-splitting plugin, and employs declarative meta-information supplied externally (Fig. 12b). The advantage of this task-specific approach over the use of a custom-tailored module lies in the extent of the customizability achieved by programming in a markup language without any modification of the task-specific module. On the other hand, the task-specific approach is relatively limited as regards customization using a markup language. However, its advantage over the approach of using a generic transformation engine is that the semantics are made explicit according to the features of the task at hand. At the same time, this design decision involves trading the scope of applicability in the generic approach for articulated semantics in the specification of the meta-information. In the case of the page-splitting plugin, roles such as *header, auxiliary*, and *layouter* supplement semantics that cannot be fully prescribed in the definitions of Web documents. In this sense, the importance of external annotation lies in the role of the mediating representation, which articulates the semantics to be shared between meta-content authors and a content adaptation engine.

Acknowledgements

We thank the following people who have contributed to the elaboration of the annotation frame-

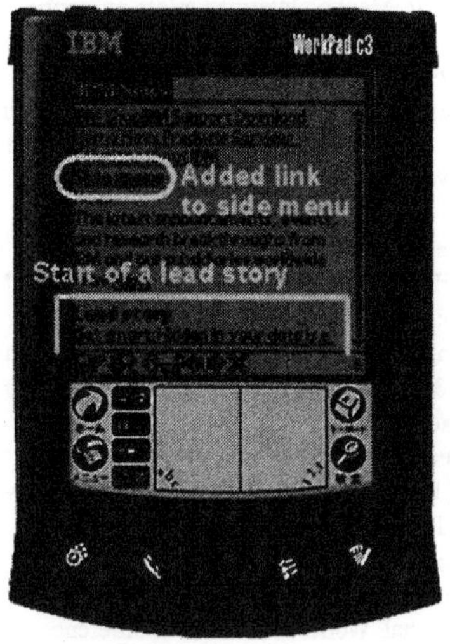

Note: display by an HTML browser.

Fig. 11. Comparison of display contents on a small-screen device.

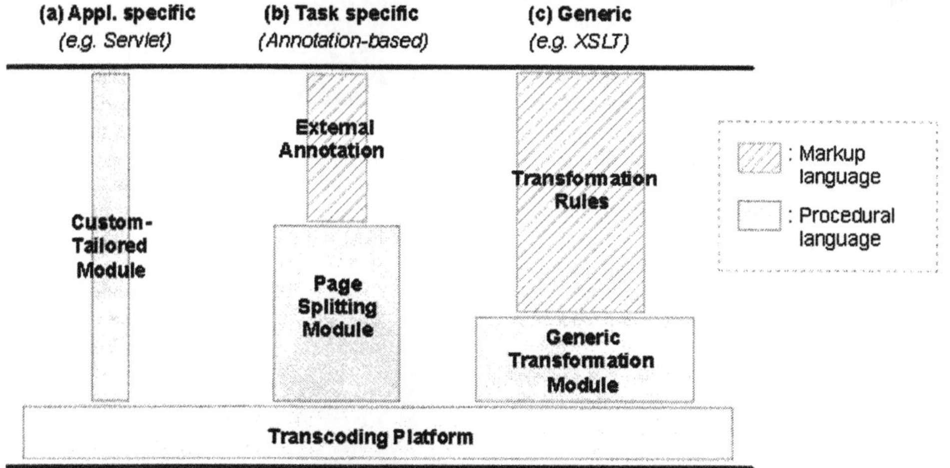

Fig. 12. Comparison of transcoding approaches in terms of extensibility.

work and the transcoding vocabulary: David Fallside, Kazushi Kuse, Chung-Sheng Li, Hiroshi Maruyama, Rakesh Mohan, Bob Schloss, John R. Smith, and Naohiko Uramoto.

References

[1] Annotation of Web content for transcoding, W3C Note (07/1999), http://www.w3.org/TR/annot/.

[2] R. Barrett and P.P. Maglio, Intermediaries: new places for producing and manipulating Web content, Proc. of the 7th International World Wide Web Conference, Brisbane, 1998.
[3] R. Barrett and P.P. Maglio, Intermediaries: an approach to manipulating information streams, IBM Systems Journal 38(4) (1999) 629–641.
[4] T.W. Bickmore and B.N. Schilit, Digestor: device-independent access to the World Wide Web, Proc. of the 6th International World Wide Web Conference, Santa Clara, CA, 1997.
[5] Composite Capability/Preference Profiles (CC/PP): a user side framework for content negotiation, W3C Note (07/1999), http://www.w3.org/TR/NOTE-CCPP/.
[6] CC/PP exchange protocol based on HTTP Extension Framework, W3C Note (06/1999), http://www.w3.org/TR/NOTE-CCPPexchange.
[7] Document Object Model (DOM) Level 1 Specification Version 1.0, W3C Recommendation, (10/1998), http://www.w3.org/TR/REC-DOM-Level-1/.
[8] A. Fox and E.A. Brewer, Reducing WWW latency and bandwidth requirements by real-time distillation, Proc. of the 5th International World Wide Web Conference, Paris, 1996.
[9] HTML 4.0 Specification, W3C Recommendation (04/1998), http://www.w3.org/TR/REC-html40/.
[10] M. Hori, K. Ono, G. Kondoh and S. Singhal, Authoring tool for Web content transcoding, Proc. of Markup Technologies '99, Philadelphia, PA, 1999, pp. 77–85.
[11] M. Jones, G. Marsden, N.M. Nasir, K. Boone and G. Buchanam, Improving Web interaction on small displays, Proc. of the 8th International World Wide Web Conference, Toronto, 1999.
[12] MD5 Message-Digest Algorithm, IETF Network Working Group RFC1321 (04/1992), http://www.ietf.org/rfc/rfc1321.txt.
[13] Palmscape Homepage (1999), http://palmscape.ilinx.co..jp/.
[14] Resource Description Framework (RDF) Model and Syntax Specification, W3C Recommendation (02/1999), http://www.w3.org/TR/REC-rdf-syntax/.
[15] F. Rousseau, J.A.G. Macias, J.V. de Lima and A. Duda, User adaptable multimedia presentations for the World Wide Web, Proc. of the 8th International World Wide Web Conference, Toronto, 1999.
[16] M.A. Schickler, M.S. Mazer and C. Brooks, Pan-Browser support for annotations and other meta-information on the World Wide Web, Proc. of the 5th International World Wide Web Conference, Paris, 1996.
[17] SHA1 Secure Hash Algorithm — Version 1.0 (10/1997), http://www.w3.org/PICS/DSig/SHA1_1_0.html.
[18] Style Sheets Activity Statement, W3C User Interface Domain Activity Statement (11/1999), http://www.w3.org/Style/Activity.
[19] C. Thompson, P. Pazandak, V. Vasudevan, F. Manola, M. Palmer, G. Hansen and T. Bannon, Intermediary architecture: interposing middleware object services between Web client and server, ACM Computing Surveys (to appear).
[20] TopPage, IBM NetObject (1999), http://www.jp.ibm.com/esbu/E/toppage/.
[21] VoiceXML Forum Version 0.9 Specification, VoiceXML Forum (08/1999), http://www.vxml.org/specs/VoiceXML-0.9-19990817.pdf.
[22] Web Content Accessibility Guidelines 1.0, W3C Recommendation (05/1999), http://www.w3.org/TR/WAI-WEBCONTENT/.
[23] Web Intermediaries (WBI) (1999), http://www.almaden.ibm.com/cs/wbi/.
[24] XHTMLTM Document Profile Requirements, W3C Working Draft (09/1999), http://www.w3.org/TR/xhtml-prof-req/.
[25] XML, Namespaces in, W3C Recommendation (01/1999), http://www.w3.org/TR/REC-xml-names/.
[26] XML Path Language (XPath) Version 1.0, W3C Recommendation (11/1999), http://www.w3.org/TR/xpath.
[27] XML Pointer Language (XPointer), W3C Working Draft (12/1999), http://www.w3.org/TR/WD-xptr.
[28] XSL Transformations (XSLT) Version 1.0, W3C Recommendation (11/1999), http://www.w3.org/TR/xslt.
[29] R. Zohar, Web annotation: an overview (02/1999), http://www-ee.technion.ac.il/~ronz/annotation/.

Masahiro Hori is an advisory researcher at IBM Tokyo Research Laboratory. He received his B.E. in Biophysical Engineering, M.E. and Ph.D. in computer science from Osaka University. His research interests include knowledge engineering methodologies, object-oriented software reuse, and Web content authoring and adaptation. Dr. Hori is a member of Industrial Advisory Board of the IBROW project conducted under the IST program of the European Commission. He received the Research Awards in 1992 and 1997 from the Japanese Society for Artificial Intelligence (JSAI). He is a member of JSAI and the Information Processing Society of Japan.

Goh Kondoh received his B.S. in mathematics and M.E. in computer science from Keio University in 1996 and 1998, respectively. His research interests include Web application development framework and tools. He is currently working at the IBM Tokyo Research Laboratory. He is a member of the Information Processing Society of Japan, and the Japan Society for Software Science and Technology.

Kouichi Ono received his B.S.E. and M.S.E. degrees, both in electronics from Waseda University, Japan in 1987 and 1989, respectively. From 1990 to 1992, he was an assistant at the university. His research interests include formal development methods, object-oriented analysis/design, software development tools, and mobile agent programming. He is currently working at the IBM Tokyo Research Laboratory. He is a member of the IEEE Computer Society.

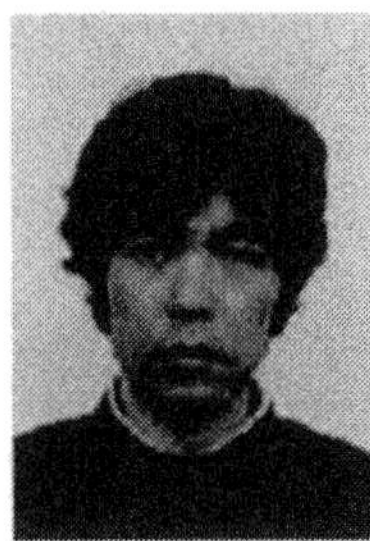

Shin-ichi Hirose is an advisory researcher at the IBM Tokyo Research Laboratory. He received his B.S. and M.S. in information science from Tokyo University. His research interests include object-oriented systems, software components, and knowledge-based systems. He is a member of the Information Processing Society of Japan, and the Japan Society for Software Science and Technology.

Sandeep Singhal is a senior technical staff member at IBM and Senior Architect at IBM's Pervasive Computing Division. He is responsible for middleware, server, and tools architecture, product definition, and technology development to enable information access from non-PC devices. He is also an adjunct assistant professor at the graduate faculty of the North Carolina State University in Raleigh, North Carolina. He holds M.S. and Ph.D. degrees in computer science from Stanford University, as well as B.S. degrees in computer science and in mathematical sciences and a B.A. in mathematics from Johns Hopkins University.

Focused Web searching with PDAs

Orkut Buyukkokten [*,1], Hector Garcia-Molina [1], Andreas Paepcke [1]

Digital Libraries Lab (InfoLab), Stanford University, Stanford, CA 94305, USA

Abstract

The Stanford Power Browser project addresses the problems of interacting with the World Wide Web through wirelessly connected Personal Digital Assistants (PDAs). These problems include bandwidth limitations, screen real-estate shortage, battery capacity, and the time costs of pen-based search keyword input. As a way to address bandwidth and battery life limitations, we provide local site search facilities for all sites. We incrementally index Web sites in real time as the PDA user visits them. These indexes have narrow scope at first, and improve as the user dwells on the site, or as more users visit the site over time. We address the keyword input problem by providing site specific keyword completion, and indications of keyword selectivity within sites. The system is implemented on the Palm Pilot platform, using a Metricom radio link. We describe the user level experience, and then present the analyses that informed our technical decisions. © 2000 Published by Elsevier Science B.V. All rights reserved.

Keywords: Personal digital assistants; Handheld computers; Mobile computing; Palm Pilot

1. Introduction

The benefits of the World Wide Web can be enhanced enormously if Web content can be made available on handheld Personal Digital Assistants (PDAs) by way of radio links. Frequently, information is needed most when a desktop machine is not available, or long boot times would be disruptive to the task at hand. Examples are information needs that arise while traveling, during business meetings, or in the course of conversations that are awkward to interrupt.

Unfortunately, the advantages in portability and instant availability of PDAs are compromised by the difficulties that arise from bandwidth and screen real-estate limitations. Radio links to PDAs carry nowhere near the volume that other World Wide Web users enjoy on wired Internet facilities. Our link, for example, performs at an average observed throughput of 1.5 KB/s. Screen sizes, like the Palm Pilot's 160×160 pixels on a 6×6 cm surface, pose a tremendous challenge to fruitful exploration of Web resources.

Input facilities are another formidable obstacle in the way of PDA usage on the Web. Typical modern PDAs employ pen-based input with optical character recognition. Even for skilled operators, text entry is a time consuming and error prone activity.

Two basic approaches have been employed to tackle the problems of bandwidth limitations and screen real-estate for PDAs on the Web. The first approach prepares Web pages specifically for use on PDAs. Two closely related examples are the Wireless Markup Language (WML), and the Handheld Device Markup Language (HDML) that are used to prepare

* Corresponding author.

[1] E-mail: {orkut,hector,paepcke}@db.stanford.edu

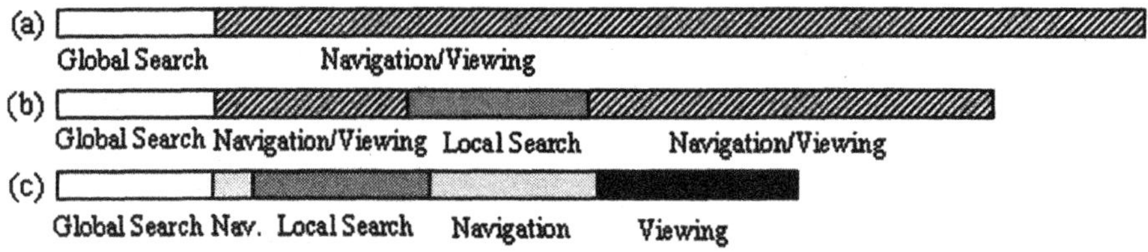

Fig. 1. Browsing patterns.

content for mobile clients. Another example is the subset of HTML that is used with Palm VII PDAs [10].

The second approach is to convert regular HTML content automatically for use on PDAs. Systems that implement this approach attempt to present the pages as faithfully as possible. This may involve, for example, sophisticated transformations of images in preparation for display on PDA screens. Examples of systems using this approach are PalmScape [9], HandWeb [12], Top Gun WingMan [4], ProxiWeb [11] and SnakeEyes [13].

The first approach has the drawback that it limits the amount of available content, and bears the danger of creating two parallel World Wide Webs. Such duplicate effort could seriously tax human and machine resources.

The second approach does not sufficiently consider the fundamental differences in user interactions when small screens are involved. Every scrolling action becomes significant. Users on small screen do not see the overall information context that is available at a glance to users of large screens, where entire pages can be displayed. Small screens show only a tiny fraction of the information that HTML content designers intend users to absorb at once. In addition to associated costs in time, the consequently required scrolling activities within pages can be very disorienting.

Neither approach addresses the issue of expensive information input modalities. For example, the entry of keywords when accessing Web search engines consumes a significant portion of user-machine interactions on PDAs. In fact, input activity may end up dominating the interaction, and constituting the critical path to completing information intensive tasks. Masui [8] reports on using word completion techniques for accelerating word input on PDAs. But his technique relies on a locally stored dictionary, and is thus not a feasible approach for Web searching.

1.1. Power Browser

Our Power Browser provides an alternative set of techniques for interacting with the Web through PDAs. These techniques are of two categories. The first supports browsing. The second helps users search more effectively. Fig. 1 shows how our techniques combine to shorten the time for finding relevant pages.

Fig. 1a shows the typical search pattern on the Web. Users consult a search engine to perform a global search of the Web. Once they receive result sets, they enter into a navigation and viewing phase, which continues until the proper page has been located. Of course, this process might require iterations, which are not represented in the figure. The horizontal axis represents time, although the chart is intended purely for qualitative illustration.

Fig. 1b shows an improvement that is available when dealing with some Web sites. The process again begins with a global search, followed by some combined navigation and viewing activity. If the target site provides a site search option, the subsequent local search can shorten the 'final approach' to the correct page. The overall time required in scenario 1b is thus shortened.

Unfortunately, not all sites provide site search, which makes the scenario of Fig. 1b a luxury users cannot always count on. Also, the local search option still does not address the cumbersome requirement for entering search keywords on the PDA. Fig. 1c shows the pattern our Power Browser attempts to afford. The system shortens the overall interaction time by making the following three main contributions. (The main focus of this paper is contributions two and three, but we include a brief description of the first contribution here for completeness.)

Link navigation: The first contribution is that the system provides facilities for navigating without having to view full pages. The navigation and viewing

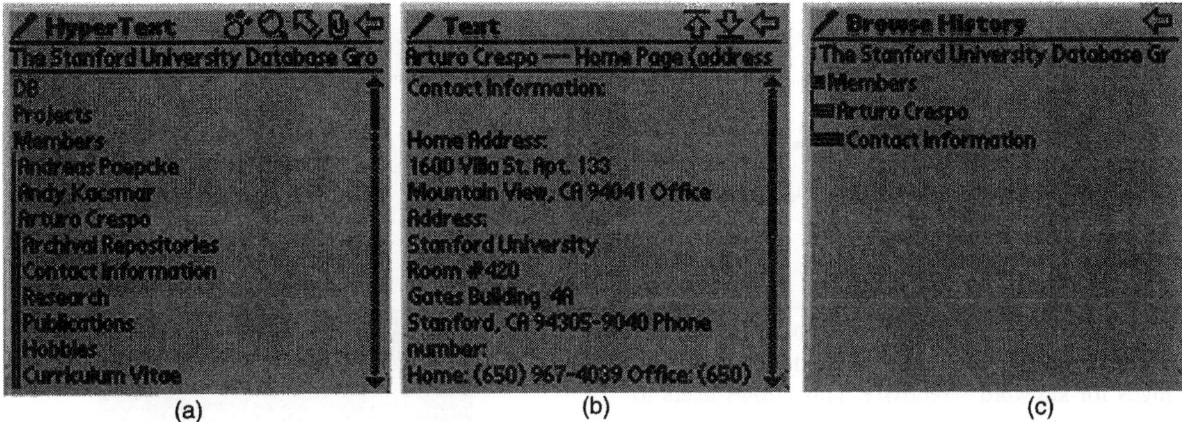

Fig. 2. Power Browser screen shots.

phases are therefore shown separately in Fig. 1c. This separation is important because the transmission and examination of pages is so expensive. It is therefore wasteful to view content simply to find that one needs to navigate on to the next page.

We accomplish this separation by extracting informative link information from pages. Instead of displaying each page the user requests during the navigation phase, we first show a page summary that presents the links contained on the page. The links are arranged in a tree widget, similar to file folders in a file browser. Users navigate by expanding and contracting nodes. This approach frequently allows users to recognize the page they need to move to next on their way to a final destination. Once they are reasonably confident that they have found the desired page, they switch from the link view to a text view. The text view shows as much as possible of the actual page text.

Fig. 2 shows example screen shots. Fig. 2a is a link view of the *Stanford Database Group*. Each left justified entry is the description of a link on that root page. The Members link has been expanded to show the links on the Members sub-page. The link to Arturo Crespo's home page has been further expanded. Fig. 2b is a text view, showing salient information on Arturo's page. Fig. 2c finally, provides an overview of the navigation levels. This is useful when operating at deep nesting levels. The details of the Power Browser's navigation facilities are documented in [3].

Local site search: The Power Browser's second contribution is that we provide automated, focused site search even for sites that do not offer such local search facilities. Our site search support is created in real time, and improves with the amount of time users spend on a site. If a user dwells on a site for a long time, or if enough users visit the site over time, the site search facility will eventually be complete.

Local search is an important improvement to the overall search activity, because users often already know which site the desired page resides on, and can thereby eliminate the global search phase altogether, if local search is available. For instance, if users wish to find the latest sports scores, they are likely to start at the Web site of some mass audience newspaper. Similarly, when looking for the academic calendar of MIT, that university's root page is the place to start.

Traditional search engines (TSEs) which specialize on covering a wide selection of sites are not a replacement for local search facilities. Their breadth of coverage prevents them from indexing deeply into most sites. Desired pages located within sites may therefore not be found at all when using a TSE. Even when a deeply nested page is indexed, TSE ranking algorithms often place them far down on their hit list, because major root pages are ranked higher. The consequent scrolling and transmission time requirements are too costly on PDAs. Finally, TSEs cannot keep indexes very fresh. Instead of building voluminous, broad-coverage indexes, we partition indices by site. While this would, of course, make broad-area searches inefficient, this approach allows us to often refresh indexes of frequently visited sites.

Keyword entry support: As its third contribution,

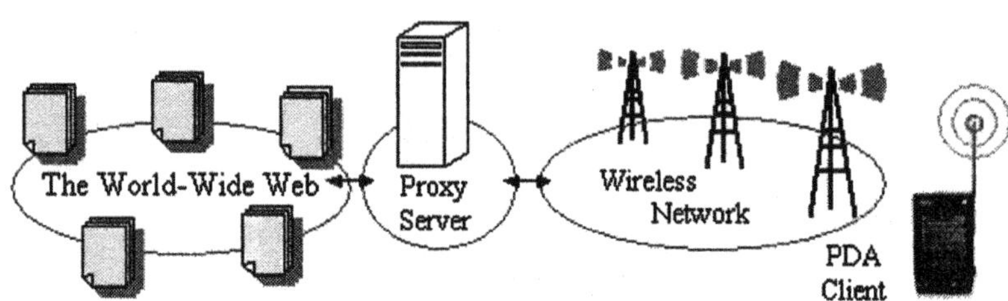

Fig. 3. Browsing through a proxy server.

the Power Browser provides site specific keyword completion to save pen entry time, and approximate gauges for keyword selectivity. This allows users to enter even long keywords by writing just two or three characters on their PDA. As users enter successive keywords, the system informs them in real time of how many matching pages to expect. Users submit their searches for execution only when the keywords they entered have improved the selectivity enough.

Fig. 3 shows the top level architecture of the system. PDAs communicate through a wireless network with a proxy server. That server provides the interface to the Web. All compute-intensive activities occur in that server.

As mentioned earlier, in this paper we focus on contributions two and three: *local site search*, and *keyword entry support*. Section 2 walks through an example interaction. Section 3 details the technical challenges posed by our approach, and explains the tradeoffs we made. Section 4 summarizes how the components introduced in the paper fit into the overall Power Browser architecture. Section 5 concludes the paper and presents some of the perspectives for the future work on the Power Browser.

2. Example interaction

2.1. Initiating the browsing process

For explanatory purposes, we present an example here to illustrate how the Power Browser works. Suppose our task is to find the academic calendar for the Spring Quarter at Stanford University. Intuitively, we expect to find this information on the Stanford Web site. Three keywords related to this task are *academic*, *calendar* and *spring*.

The browsing process is initiated through one of three facilities. The user may manually enter a URL by writing on the screen with the pen. Alternatively, the user may select a bookmark (from the box in the bottom half of the screen) or use a search engine to find the URL. In Fig. 4, the user wrote "Stanford University" and then tapped on the Search button to activate a global search engine. The search engine can be selected from the *With* pull-down list. In this example, the user chose Google [5]. The Power Browser displays the search engine results as a set of link descriptions (Fig. 5a). The user can tap on any of these link descriptions to retrieve the corresponding page. The link *Stanford Home Page: Welcome to . . .* is the Web site we are looking for. So we tap on the site search button (magnifying glass icon at the top) and then tap on this link to activate the *Site Search* command.

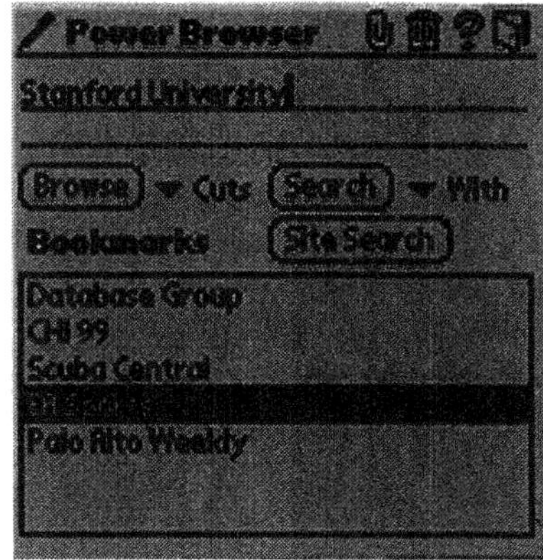

Fig. 4. Starting browsing.

2.2. Word completion

The utility of any site search is limited by the expense of two factors. The first one is the time required to enter the keywords on the PDA. The

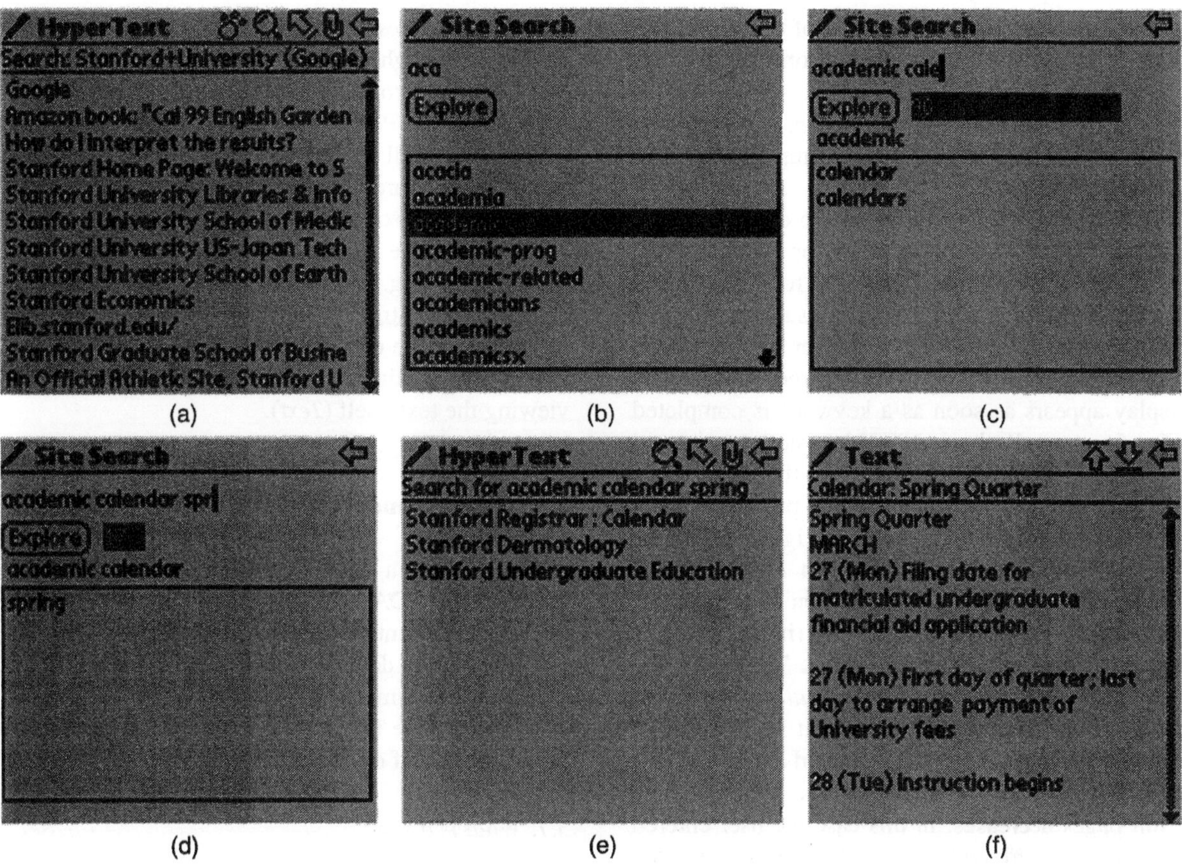

Fig. 5. Example interaction.

second factor is the time of evaluating the selectivity of chosen keywords without the expense of retrieving and examining the result lists.

Once the user selects the *Site Search* command, a message is sent to the proxy server to get ready for searching. If the Web site was previously indexed, the proxy server loads the index. Then it starts to update this index by visiting pages that were not visited before. This way, the sites that are visited frequently by the Power Browser users get a more and more complete index. If the index is not available (i.e., the site was not visited before), it is created from scratch.

The user can enter the search words on the text field provided at the top of the display (Fig. 5b,c,d). Once the user starts entering the characters, the Power Browser offers the option of completing the word immediately with *word completion*. Word completion is done in three phases:

Retrieval: After the user enters the first characters of the word, a request is sent to the proxy server to retrieve all the words in the Web site that start with those characters. The result is then displayed in a list widget. In this example, after the user entered *aca* in the search field, all the words that start with *aca* on the Stanford site are displayed in the list at the bottom of the screen. If the list is too long to display on a single screen, a scroll button is provided (Fig. 5b).

Pruning: Once the list is retrieved, the user can write more characters and decrease the number of words. Each additional character entered will decrease the number of words that begin with those characters. Therefore the list will start shrinking. This process is done on the PDA since the new list is a subset of the words we obtained in the first phase. After each additional character is entered, all the words in the list that do not start with the given input are removed. The user can use one of the words as a search keyword simply by tapping on that word on the screen. This causes the input to be completed. For example, after the user wrote *aca*, s/he can simply tap on the item *academic* to complete the word in the search field.

Refinement: The user also has the option to enter multiple keywords. This is useful for improving the selectivity of the query. In order for the user to evaluate whether additional keywords are needed, the PDA displays a count of the number of Web pages that contain all the keywords entered so far. This display appears as soon as a keyword is completed (Fig. 5c, top). If the last word is not yet entered completely (e.g., *cale* in Fig. 5c), the page count includes pages that contain all the previous words (the partially entered characters are ignored). In our example, when the user tapped on *academic*, the number 90 appeared on the screen showing that there are 90 words on the Web site (indexed so far) that have the word *academic* in it. Then the user started entering the second word (*cale*). In Fig. 5c, the list consists of all the words that start with *cale* and also occur together with the word *academic* on a page. As the user writes more words, the number of result pages decreases. In this case the user entered the second word *calendar* (either by writing the whole word or tapping on *calendar* on the list). The number 90 drops to 17 (Fig. 5d). Similarly, it goes down to 3 when the last keyword *spring* was entered (this screenshot is not shown since it is similar to the previous ones).

2.3. Search results

The user can decide to start looking at the search results when s/he thinks that the result set will be small enough. In our example the user decided that 3 results were reasonably few. Notice that until this point no pages were transmitted to the PDA. The retrieval of the titles of all matching pages is initiated by tapping on the *Explore* button. This action activates the Web browser. The browser displays the titles of the pages. While indexing the Web site, the title information is stored together with the index. For example, in Fig. 5e we see the titles of the pages that contain all the given keywords. The links are ordered according to the number of keyword occurrences on the page. The user views or navigates through the promising pages. This process is the same as browsing the results of a global search engine on the Power Browser (Fig. 5a) with the exception that all the links on the root page are guaranteed to be search results. The user can drill down into pages by expanding/collapsing the tree nodes and viewing the pages by selecting the titles/link descriptions. Fig. 5f shows the result of tapping on 'Stanford Registrar: Calendar' in Fig. 5e. The title at the top of the display informs us whether we are looking at the link descriptions (*HyperText*) or are viewing the text itself (*Text*).

3. Challenges and solutions

Fig. 6 shows a summary of the messages that pass between the PDA and the proxy server to realize the site search interactions shown above. There are, however, many details to consider in the design of the overall system. In this section we will go through the obstacles we faced, our solution approaches and the evaluation of our system.

3.1. What is a site?

The quality of a site search depends on the semantic or organizational coherence of the site. We expect the pages that are considered to be in the same site to have a common topic or to belong to the same entity (i.e. organization, company). However it might be impossible to externally determine what makes up a Web site. Multiple groups may share a single Web server, but they might be partitioned into separate directories and use different access control schemes. In other cases, a group may maintain a single logical site that happens to span multiple Web servers. We also cannot determine what Web pages are produced by a particular entity.

There are several different approaches that can be used to approximate the semantic or organizational coherence of a Web site. In all of the following approaches, the perception of a site is a logical notion since the files might be accessed over a series of IP addresses.

- *Same domain:* All the pages reachable from a given root Web page at the same domain are

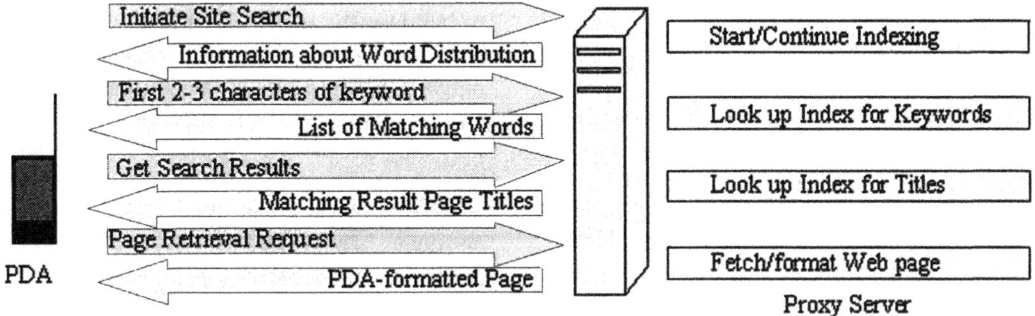

Fig. 6. Messages between PDA and proxy server.

viewed as a Web site. The Web site is identified by the domain name of the root page. For instance, if we take http://www.stanford.edu/ as the root page, all the pages that are reachable from this page and are in the www.stanford.edu domain will be considered to be within the same site. Sites like www-db.stanford.edu or cs.stanford.edu are considered to be in different domains.

- *Same neighborhood:* Another approach is to start with an initial page and to consider all the pages that are in close proximity. For instance, we can regard all the pages that are at most three links away to be within qualifying close neighborhood. The associated indexing process is complicated since indices of Web-sites may overlap. Solutions to this problem are not discussed here.
- *Same sub-domain:* In defining a site, we can also take advantage of the hierarchy of domain names. For instance www.stanford.edu and cs.stanford.edu both belong to the stanford.edu sub-domain. In this approach, we consider pages that are close in the domain hierarchy (e.g., cs.stanford.edu, www.stanford.edu, www-db.stanford.edu) to be in the same site. That is, we would regard all the pages in the domains cs.stanford.edu and www-db.stanford.edu to be in the stanford.edu site.
- *Hybrid:* Finally, we can apply a hybrid approach where we assign weights to domains. When we initiate our search by www.stanford.edu we can give less priority to the pages in www-cs.stanford.edu while indexing. This would cause more pages in the www.stanford.edu domain to be indexed compared to other pages that are considered to be in the same sub-domain.

	Stanford	Yahoo	NY Times Magazine
Pages in same domain	41.1%	24.8%	7.8%
Pages in sub-domain	18.5%	27.6%	20.4%
Remaining pages	40.4%	47.6%	71.8%

Fig. 7. Statistics of pages indexed.

In order to understand the implications of the various logical site notions, we examined the content of several sites. Fig. 7 shows the data for three of these sites: Stanford, Yahoo, and New York Times Magazine. Starting at the root page of each site, we classified the URLs found into ones pointing to the same domain, into a sub-domain (but not same domain), and outside the site. We then visited the URLs pointing to the same domain, in a breadth-first fashion, continuing to examine and classify links. The process stopped when 1000 links had been examined at a site.

Looking at Fig. 7, we see that 41% of the Stanford links identify pages in the www.stanford.edu domain. About 18% of the links point to pages in Stanford sub-domains, such as cs.stanford.edu. The remaining 40% go outside Stanford. This is very different from, say the NY Times Magazine, where over 72% of the sampled links go outside the site.

The 'same domain' site definition may be appropriate for sites like Stanford, where a substantial percentage of the content is local. However, such a definition may be inadequate for a site like Yahoo, where only 25% of the links are in the same domain. Here a 'same sub-domain' definition may work better, since it would cover about 52% of the links. For a site like the NY Times Magazine, a 'same neighborhood' definition may be more useful, so that more content could be indexed. However, there is a cost associated with the broader definitions. When we crawl pages outside a domain, the number of links to be visited increases tremendously. This results in fewer levels of pages being indexed within the same domain and causes pages that might be completely irrelevant to be indexed. Because of these concerns, in our prototype we initially implemented the *Same domain* approach, although we plan to experiment with other approaches in the near future.

3.2. Implementing site search

As mentioned in the introduction, traditional search engines (TSEs) like AltaVista and Google, have shortcomings when it comes to helping PDA users find pages within a site of interest. In particular, they may not provide thorough enough and up-to-date enough indices. Furthermore, since they index the entire Web, they often return too many hits that are not relevant to a site search.

We have therefore built our own search facility specifically targeted to the needs of PDAs. This facility has three important features: *site-specific indices*, *on-demand crawling* and *incremental index updates*.

Site-specific indices: For each Web site visited, a separate index is created (using the 'same domain' site definition). Keeping separate, partitioned indices has many advantages in our context. First, since each index is site-specific, built using the appropriate logical definition of a site, all results returned match the search context. In addition, the entire site index can be read into the proxy's memory, can be accessed efficiently, and can easily be updated incrementally, as we will see below. Finally, all the vocabulary associated with each site (needed for word completion) can be accessed efficiently since it is in the same index.

On-demand crawling: Our crawler visits pages at a site only when a user is accessing that site. The more users examine the site, or the longer they stay at the site, the more pages are crawled. This means that the resulting index will be more thorough for popular sites, and will dynamically adjust as popularities shift. When a site is visited for the first time, the crawler rapidly visits pages at that site in order to build up the index. Of course, search results will not be comprehensive unless the user waits, but the longer s/he waits, the more comprehensive the index will become. From the point of view of Web sites, they only get visited when real users are examining the site, so it is to their advantage to provide information quickly to meet the demands of a 'potential customer'. This is in contrast to traditional crawlers, which may place high loads on Web sites, requesting pages that might never be searched.

Incremental indexing: In our system indices are incrementally updated, as new pages are crawled. Users can concurrently access the index, as more data is collected for the visited site. When the user closes his/her session, or starts searching another site, the index is automatically saved for future retrieval. Next time, when a user makes a search on the same Web site, the pre-stored index is used. After loading an index, the crawling process is resumed and the index is again updated incrementally.

Associated with each Web site index, there are three pieces of information. The first one is the *Found Set*. This is a set of links that have been encountered so far in the site. The second one is the *Pending List*, which contains the Web pages that are waiting to be visited and indexed. Finally, there is the *Inverted Index* that contains the vocabulary used in the Web site. It maps words to pages, and records the number of occurrences of each word on each page. The Found Set and the Inverted Index are implemented using hash tables. This data structure provides access in constant time. The Found Set contains the URL of each page and its title. The Inverted Index contains all the distinct words occurring in the Web site crawled so far.

One of the major challenges of our approach is providing good response time to users. (With traditional crawling and indexing, all pages are collected and indexed off-line, before the user makes a request.) For a stored index, we require that it can be loaded into memory in about 3 to 5 seconds. This is the fastest any user will be able to react to the initial search form and enter a few characters for the search. Our system has no problem meeting this lower bound.

If the index does not exist, the crawling speed becomes a key factor. Choosing the order in which to crawl is an important parameter for this process.

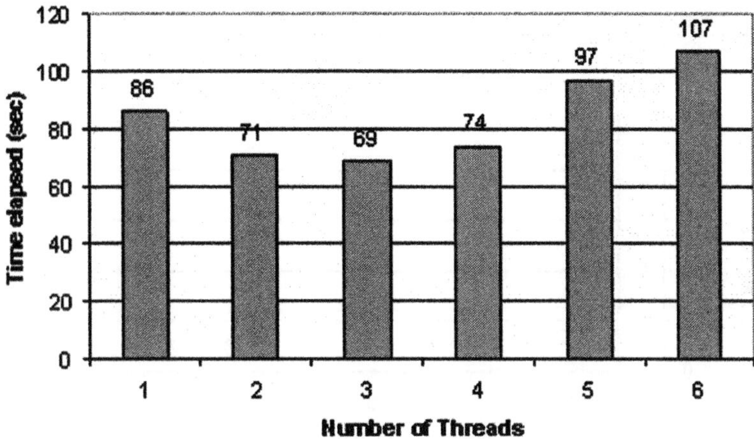

Fig. 8. Indexing speed.

The *Incremental Crawler* uses a breadth-first search approach to index Web pages. That is, pages that are reachable through fewer links are indexed first. Fortunately, many sites make important pages reachable from the root via few links, so our breadth-first strategy works well. With our 'same domain' site definition, remote links are ignored by the crawler, speeding up the local traversal.

Multithreaded programming can increase the crawling speed tremendously since it allows the indexer to parse and index multiple pages at the same time. However, in order to keep the database consistent, mutual exclusion must be enforced while updating the indices. This puts a limitation on crawling since more threads will cause more collisions to occur on the indices. To determine the best number of concurrent threads, we tested different strategies, summarized in Fig. 8. The figure shows the time it takes to index 100 pages as a function of the number of threads for the Stanford Web site. Based on these results, our system uses 3 concurrent crawling threads. Note that this number is only for a single Web site. There can be multiple crawlers running for each user that accesses different Web sites.

Notice that the maximum crawling speed should only be used for popular Web sites. The small request interval caused by fast crawling can be very resource consuming for small Web sites. The proxy server adjusts the request interval by looking at the popularity of the Web site's root page, using page rank (Section 4). For small sites it uses a 5 second interval between requests.

Since indexes for the various sites are constructed and maintained as disjoint data sets, multiple browsing sessions are supported easily. This helps with issues of scalability. In order to take advantage of locality, we plan to investigate optimal routing of user browsing requests to proxies that have already started indexing the respective target site.

3.3. Implementing word completion

The Power Browser provides keyword completion to reduce pen entry time and effort. After the user writes the first characters of a search term, all the words at that site that start with the characters are displayed. We call the set of words displayed the *matching word list*, and an entry in this list is a *matching word.*

As the user enters characters, the PDA needs to decide at what point (i.e., after how many characters) to request the matching word list from the proxy server. On the one hand, the sooner the PDA requests the matching word list, the sooner it will be able to assist the user. On the other hand, if the PDA requests the list too early, there can be two problems: First, the list of words may be too long. Suppose that the list widget can display 8 items at a time. If 120 items are returned in the list, the user would need to scroll 7 times on the average. This would not be acceptable, and in many cases the scrolling could take longer than entering the word itself (if the word is short). Second, the delay waiting for the proxy to send the matching word list could be too long. If the

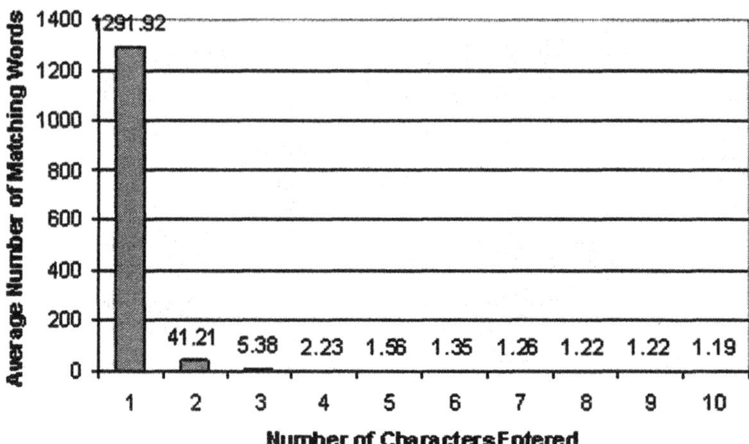

Fig. 9. Number of words in matching words list.

list is too long, or the words have many characters, the transmission time could be unacceptably high. Thus, the PDA's decision procedure needs to balance these conflicting factors.

As a first step in determining a good decision procedure, we measured the transmission speed of our wireless connection. We observed that the time (in milliseconds) to transmit a message is approximately $500 + 0.65n$, where n is the number of bytes in the message. We use this formula below, in estimating response time given the number of words in a list and their lengths.

In the best case, entering a single character with the pen requires a single gesture. But the user needs to concentrate on the task and, depending on skill, several corrections must be made if the character recognition fails. In contrast, selecting a list item requires multiple pen-taps; scrolling the list and selecting the item. However, the error rate is much lower, and the actions are more mechanical and comfortable to carry out. In order to make word completion beneficial, the user must expend less effort to select the item from the list than entering an additional character. In our studies, we found that 4 taps (3 for scrolling, one for selection) is a reasonable bound on word list interaction. Since the list widget in our system contains 8 items, this translates into a word length limit of 56 words. (With a 56 word list, 8 words can be seen with 0 scrolling taps, 8 others with 1 tap, and so on, for an average of 3 scrolling taps.)

We initially tested word completion on the Stanford University Web site. We then extended our experiments and analyses to other sample sites. We started crawling the Stanford site at the root page, and crawled and indexed 1000 pages in breadth-first order. These pages contained 32,962 distinct words. Fig. 9 shows the average number of words that begin with character sequences of varying lengths.

As we can see from this graph, when given just one character, there are too many matching words (1291.92 on the average). Therefore, transmitting the results takes too long (over 7 seconds), and looking at the list to locate a word is too expensive (80 taps on the average). When the user enters the second character, the average number of matching words drops to 41.21. When the user enters three characters, the average size of the matching word list drops down sharply to 5.38.

On the average, therefore, entering two characters discriminates sufficiently to pare the resulting word list to practical proportions. However, in order to design the system to work in all cases, we must understand the distribution of words in more detail. Fig. 10 shows the number of words that begin with each three character combination, again using the 1000 pages of the Stanford Web site. (The x-axis labels of this and several following graphs list just a small subset of the total set of prefixes.) We see that for all cases, the number of words is acceptably below 56. However, Fig. 11 shows a similar graph for the two character case. The variance is much

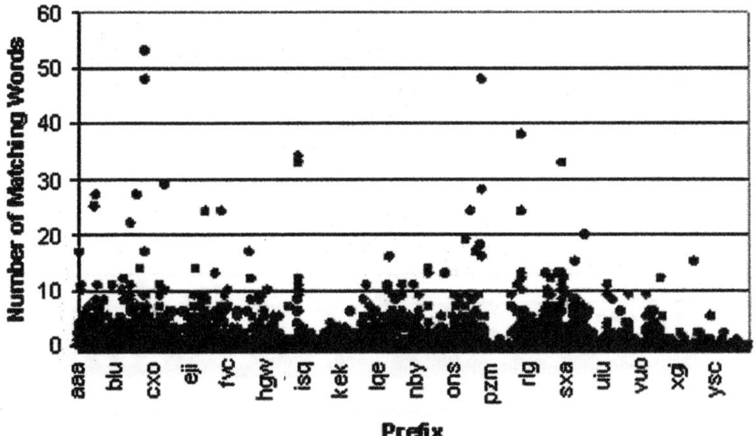

Fig. 10. Number of matching words for 3 characters.

more significant, with *co* producing 844 words, and *re* producing 715, although a large number of cases are still below 56.

Of course, the number of words to be transmitted is not the only factor that must be considered when deciding on the lists to transmit. The average length and consequent transmission time is another factor. Fig. 12 shows the time required to transmit the various word lists for prefixes of length two. Not surprisingly, the transmission time for *co* is more than five seconds, which is too long. We determined that the average word length of each word list never exceeded 12 characters. If we limit the word list length to 56 words, the transmission time would therefore not exceed 1 second (based on the transmission time formula introduced earlier).

In summary, for many cases it is sufficient if the user enters just two characters. The resulting word list is short enough to be transmitted quickly, and the scrolling effort for the user is acceptable. In some cases, however, the system should wait for three characters, before a matching word list is retrieved from the proxy server. There are three main approaches that can be used to decide when to wait for three characters. The decision in all these cases is based on the prefix distribution (i.e., the number of words that match the first two characters). In the remainder of this section we will go through these approaches and discuss the tradeoffs.

Resolution through inquiry: One option is for the PDA to request the matching word list immediately after the user enters 2 characters. If the list is short,

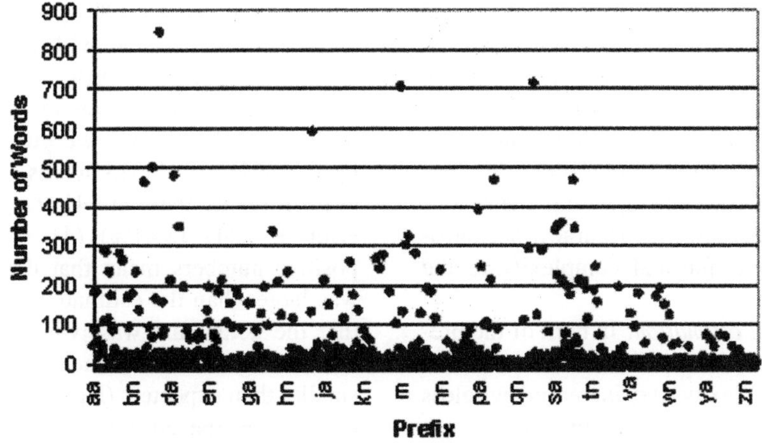

Fig. 11. Number of matching words for 2 characters.

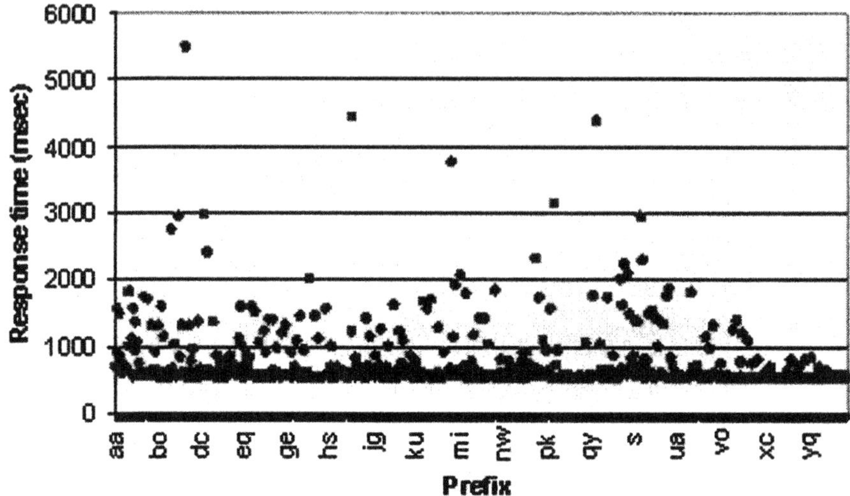

Fig. 12. Response time for transmitting words starting with each combination of 2 characters.

the proxy server sends it immediately. Otherwise, the server just sends a *negative acknowledgment* and the PDA requests the list again after the third character. There are two main problems with this approach. First, it will result in an unnecessary round trip delay when the list is too long. Second, the approach results in additional message traffic (which drains client side batteries due to radio transmissions).

Resolution through feedback: Immediately after the PDA initiates a site search, it receives the word distribution from the proxy server. The proxy can either compute the distribution on the fly, or it can have a precomputed distribution that is incrementally updated as the index changes. On-the-fly computation may be too slow, since the full site index must be read from disk before the PDA is given the distribution. In either case, if an unindexed site is visited, there will be no distribution to rely on, which can be a problem. We also need to decide if the PDA should be notified of changes to the initial distribution it received. Incrementally updating the PDA's cached distribution increases its accuracy, but introduces more wireless traffic and complexity to the protocol.

Resolution through estimation: In both of the previous approaches the exact distribution of words was used. Given the complexity and increased wireless traffic of those solutions, an alternative is to use a 'canonical' distribution that approximates the actual distributions. If we can find such a distribution, then most of the decision making could shift to the client. (As we will see, this is the approach we have initially implemented in our prototype.)

We first study if we can use a single word distribution, that is not updated as the index grows, to make decisions for a given site. For example, say the client earlier has received the distribution for the Stanford site, when 1000 pages were indexed. Say the site index now has 2000 pages. Can the client still use the older distribution?

Fig. 13 shows the relative error induced if the old distribution (1000 pages indexed) is used to 'guess' how many words have a given prefix when 2000 Stanford pages are indexed. For example, consider the prefix *il*. When 1000 pages are indexed, there are 20 words that start with that prefix, or 0.061% of the total 32962 words. When 2000 pages are indexed, there are a total of 44518 words, so using the old distribution we guess that prefix *il* will have 0.061% of 44518 words, or 27 words. However, in reality there are 41 *il* words, so the relative error is 0.341 (3.41%) $(41 - 27/41)$. In Fig. 13 positive numbers mean that the actual word count was larger than the estimate. (A value of 0.5 means that the actual list was twice the size of the estimate.) Negative values mean that the actual list was smaller than expected. (Note that there are many prefixes where the error is -0.351. These correspond to cases where both distributions have exactly the

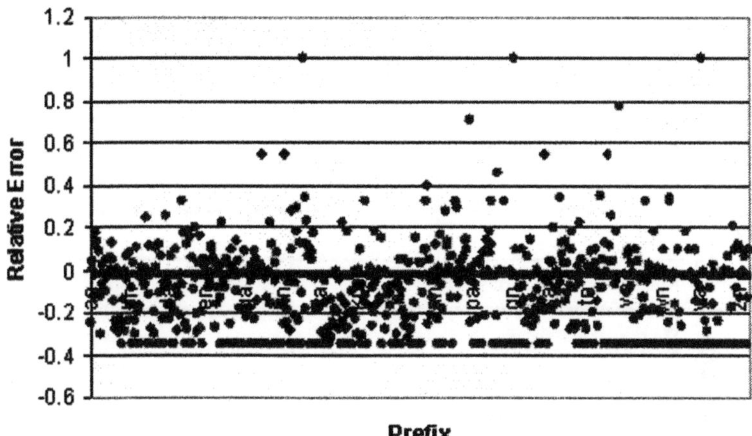

Fig. 13. Relative errors when using 1000 page distribution for 2000 page index (Stanford site).

same number of words. Thus, we overestimate by the ratio of the total vocabularies, (32962 – 44518)/ 32962.)

Fig. 13 shows that the errors can be quite large. However, surprisingly we can still make relatively good decisions using the out-of-date distribution. Recall that our goal is not to guess exactly how many words have a given prefix, but simply to decide if the list has more than our threshold 56 entries. Fig. 14 shows the actual penalty we pay for underestimating or overestimating the word list, when we use the 1000 page distribution to make decisions when 2000 pages are indexed. For example, as discussed earlier, for prefix *il* we guessed 27, but the actual list has 41 entries. However, in this case both values are less than our threshold of 56, so we did not make a mistake! There is no penalty since even if we knew the correct length, we would have still requested the list after the user entered 2 characters. Thus the figure shows no penalty in this case.

For prefix *gl*, however, our estimate is 55, while the actual list has 61 entries, above the threshold. Thus, we make a mistake and request a list that has 5 (61 – 56) entries in excess of our limit. For the negative values shown in Fig. 14 we overestimate the list length, and do not request a list after 2 characters, even though the list was actually below the threshold. The actual magnitude of the error is not significant in this case, since no list is transmitted.

Fig. 14 shows that the actual penalty paid for

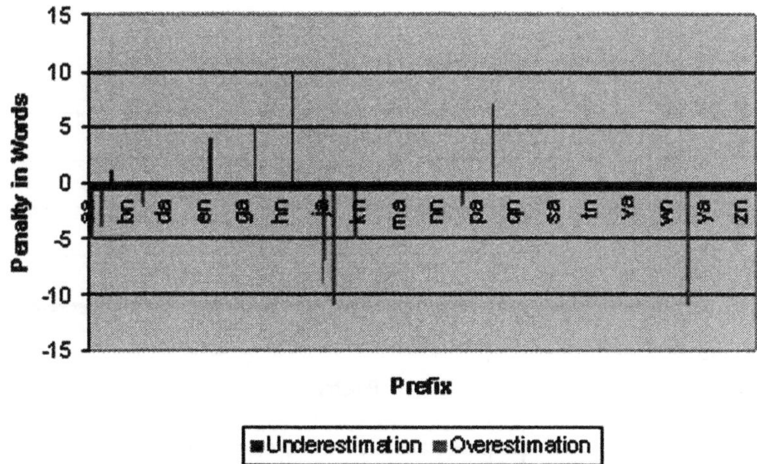

Fig. 14. Penalty for using 1000 page distribution with 2000 page index (Stanford site).

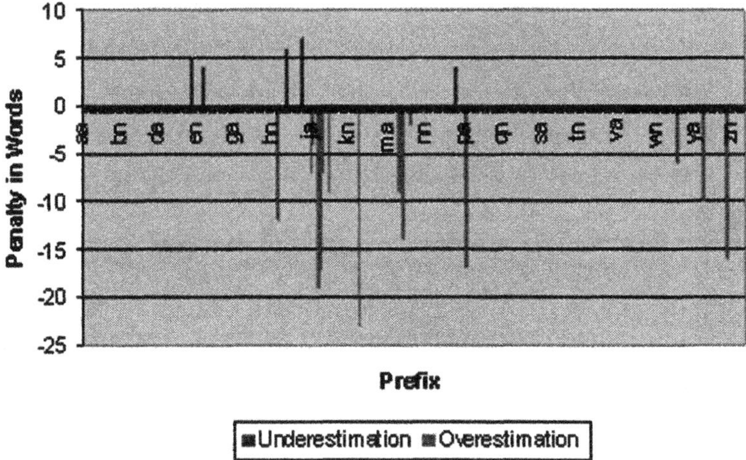

Fig. 15. Penalty for using 1000 page distribution with 4000 page index (Stanford site).

using an obsolete word distribution is quite low. A penalty is paid (a list is requested too early or too late) for only 2.07% of the prefixes (14 out of 676 prefixes). Fig. 15 shows that penalties are still low when the 1000 page distribution is used for a 4000 page index. For 4000 pages, there were 21 errors (3.11% of the cases), compared to the 14 errors in the earlier case.

We conclude that a single distribution can be used for relatively good decision making at a single site, for wide ranges of index sizes. Could we go a step further and use a single distribution, say from the Stanford site, to make decisions at other sites? If words are distributed across prefixes in a similar fashion across sites, then a single 'canonical' distribution could indeed be used.

Our experiments show that word distributions vary considerably across sites (analogous to what Fig. 13 shows for changing index sizes). However, a distribution from a foreign site can still be used to make decisions effectively. To illustrate, Fig. 16 shows the penalty for using the Stanford distribution at the NY Times Magazine site (both indexes have 1000 pages). An error is made in only 6 cases (0.89%). The worst penalty was for the prefix *wa*, where we estimated 48 words, but in reality there were 84 words (a penalty of 28 words above threshold).

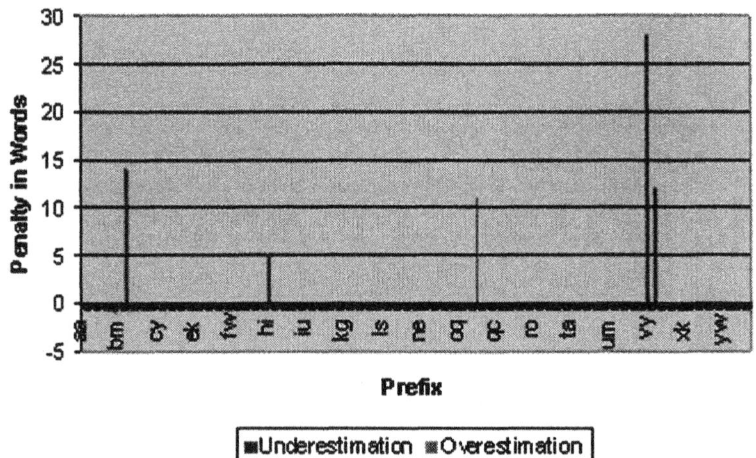

Fig. 16. Penalty for using Stanford distribution for NY Times Magazine.

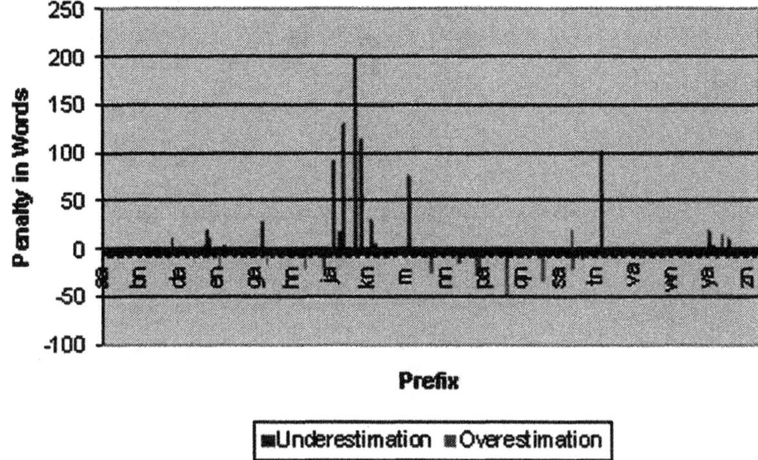

Fig. 17. Penalty for using OED distribution for Stanford site.

We also studied if the word distribution from the Oxford English Dictionary (OED) could be used for decision making. Fig. 17 shows the penalty of using the 112,334 word distribution from the OED to make decisions at the Stanford site. For example, for the prefix *jo*, we estimated 47 words but received 185 words; the penalty is 129 words. Similarly, for the prefix *os* we estimated 59 words, the actual list was 30 words; the penalty is 26 words. We see that the OED is adequate for making decisions. Overall, an error was made in only 39 cases out of 676 (5.77%).

In summary, our results show that a canonical distribution can be used to decide when to request a word completion list from the proxy, with acceptable errors. The overall procedure, implemented on our prototype, works as follows. The PDA stores the normalized distribution of the Stanford dictionary (our canonical distribution). After the PDA initiates the site-search, it receives the number of words at the site. When the user types in two characters, the PDA estimates the number of matching words using the canonical distribution. If this number is greater than 56, the PDA waits for a third input character. Otherwise, it requests the matching word list from the proxy. If desired, when the number of indexed words changes, the proxy can send the new number, so that the PDA can have more accurate information. When the server notices that the size of the matching word list requested by the PDA is too long, it can send the new number of indexed words together with the word list and thus avoid an extra message.

4. Implementation

The architecture of the system is summarized in Fig. 18. The user browses the Web through an HTTP Proxy server (large dashed box). The proxy server fetches Web pages on the PDA's behalf, dynamically generates summary views of Web pages, and manages the site search facility. The connection between the PDA and the Power Browser Proxy Server is established through a wireless modem.

The components of the proxy server are as follows:

- *User Manager:* The User Manager is responsible for keeping track of the connected users, and for answering user requests. The Manager opens a new session for each PDA and maintains browsing information about the user's activities for the duration of the session (*User Profiles*). The session terminates when the connection between the PDA and the proxy is closed. If the user is browsing or viewing pages, the User Manager initiates the Browse Manager to retrieve the Web page formatted explicitly for the PDA. If the request involves a site search, the results are retrieved through the Search Manager. For each user, a separate Browse Manager and Search Manager process is invoked.
- *Browse Manager:* This component fetches and formats Web pages explicitly for the PDA.
  Fetching: When any module needs to fetch a Web page, it sends a request to the Browse Manager. If

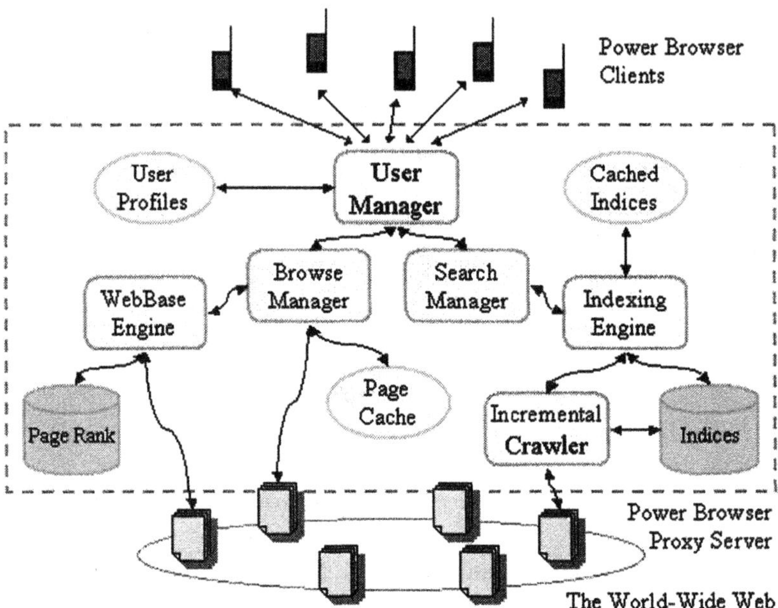

Fig. 18. The Power Browser architecture.

the page was already retrieved during the session, the Browse Manager returns the cached version of the result (*Page Cache*). Otherwise it downloads and parses the requested Web document.

Formatting Pages: In order to reduce the size of the Web pages on the PDA display, white space is avoided as much as possible. The *Browse Manager* collapses sequences of paragraphs or line-breaks. Lists and tables are re-formatted into simple text blocks. Many attributes within the pages, like color, size, font, alignment are ignored.

Formatting Links: The choice of good link descriptions for each link is made heuristically as follows. If the link has 'meaningful' anchor text, we use that text. (Anchor text is what a browser underlines to indicate the presence of a link.) We consider the anchor text to be meaningless (for our purposes) if it is one of the popular content-free expressions such as 'click here' or 'next'. If there was no meaningful anchor text, we instead consider the URL associated with the link. If it points to a directory, we use only the right-most element of the URL. If the URL ends in a file name, we remove the extension, and use the file name.

Additional Services: The Browse Manager also makes use of our *WebBase* facility. WebBase can provide the page rank of a Web page. The page rank of page p takes into account the number of Web pages that point to p, and in a sense reflects the 'importance' of the page on the Web [2]. The *Power Browser* gives the user the option to order the links of a given page using this ranking. This way, links to 'important' pages will appear first, potentially reducing the amount of scrolling needed to find links of interest. The list of links can be further improved using different algorithms besides *Page Rank* ([7]).

- *Search Manager:* The Search Manager is in charge of answering site queries. The Indexing Engine and Incremental Crawler work independently. This allows the system to answer queries even if the index is still being updated.
- *Incremental Crawler:* The crawler fetches Web pages needed by the Indexing Engine. The crawler uses and manages the *Found Set* and the *Pending List*, as described in Section 3.2.
- *Indexing Engine:* The *Indexing Engine* is responsible for answering site queries and providing word completion using the indices. When a site search is initiated through the Search Manager, the indexing engine loads the index if it is available. Then it sends a request to the *Incremental Crawler* to update the index. The Indexing Engine uses the *Inverted Index* to return search results.

5. Conclusion

Web access from radio linked PDAs is an exciting prospect. Innovation in several areas is, however, needed if the use of the Web on PDAs is to be effective. The problems of bandwidth limitations, screen real-estate, and the slow speed of pen-based input stand out among the challenges that must be addressed.

Our Power Browser supports both browsing and focused search activities on PDAs. In this paper we focused on the browser's support for one particular phase of Web-based information retrieval: the exploration of single sites. We described the following related features:

- *A search facility over individual Web sites.* As PDA users visit sites, on-demand crawlers build indices over those sites. The indices grow, as users dwell on the corresponding sites, or as more users come to visit. We explained tradeoffs between different crawling strategies, and presented experimental results to illustrate these tradeoffs.
- *Search word completion.* In addition to supporting search, the site indices are used to help users avoid time consuming pen-based input of search keywords. Once users have entered two or three characters of a promising search word, the Power Browser transmits a list of the keywords that occur on the site to be searched, and that begin with the given characters. We showed through experiments why two, or at most three characters constitute sufficient user input to make the resulting keyword list short enough to transmit and display on the PDA.
- *Selectivity estimates.* As users enter keywords, the Power Browser displays the number of hits that would be retrieved, if the search were to be launched with these keywords. Users can thereby gauge whether more keywords are needed to make the result set manageable, without having to incur the cost of actually launching the search, and examining the result.

This combination of user support mechanisms adds up to significant improvements in Web access through PDAs, especially if combined with the related browsing facilities that were described in [3]. Informal, preliminary user testing has highlighted several scenarios where our facilities are particularly useful.

One example arises when users know the beginnings of a keyword, but do not know the precise spelling. They can just enter the first two or three characters, and can then examine the list of matching keywords to identify the keyword they had in mind.

In a second scenario the user benefits from the selectivity measure. When using relatively generic keywords, such as 'color printer' on a site like Hewlett-Packard, the selectivity measures can quickly help users decide whether more terms, such as 'inkjet', might be needed to pare down the result set.

A third scenario occurs when Web sites suddenly spring up. For example, Web sites are now often established to disseminate information about highly publicized, sudden events, such as plane crashes or political scandals. Search engines that focus on covering large portions of the Web will not have indexed such 'flash sites' when the demand arises. The on-demand crawling that underlies the Power Browser offers much quicker response time.

Of course, there are many improvements we plan to introduce in future versions of the browser. One area to pursue is our definition of 'Web site'. Recall that we currently crawl pages within the same domain as the root page chosen by the user. This approach favors organizational coherence: most pages are likely to be managed by the same institution or company. We plan to explore whether other approaches, like the same neighborhood strategy, are better for some information tasks. In particular, it would be very useful to identify crawling strategies that provide better semantic coherence than our same domain approach sometimes affords.

One problem that occurs with neighborhood crawling approaches is that as crawls from different root pages are launched, their resulting indexes are no longer disjoint as they are in our current system. This can, of course, be wasteful in storage. We will need to explore new storage strategies to manage this issue.

Another enhancement to our system would distribute our proxy server across multiple machines to avoid bottleneck problems as usage grows. A consequence of such distribution would be that indexes for different sites would be stored on different servers. Clients would therefore need to be routed to the correct place. We could use a hash based approach, in which a hash of the root page's partial URL would identify the proper server. However, this approach would not guarantee effective load balancing, as the sizes of logical Web sites vary. We will need to explore appropriate distribution strategies that satisfy these requirements.

Existing techniques used to improve general Web navigation could also be applied to the wireless scenario [1,6].

Searching and browsing the Web from PDAs bears a potential for important productivity gains in how mobile users perform information intensive tasks. The Power Browser introduced in this paper takes one step towards realizing this potential.

References

[1] Alexa Internet, Alexa, http://www.alexa.com/.

[2] S. Brin and L. Page, The anatomy of a large-scale hypertextual Web search engine, in: Proc. of the Seventh World Wide Web Conference, Elsevier, Amsterdam, 1998.

[3] O. Buyukkokten, H. Garcia Molina, A. Paepcke and T. Winograd, Power Browser: efficient Web browsing for PDAs, in: Proc. of the Conference on Human Factors in Computing Systems, 2000.

[4] A. Fox, I. Goldberg, S.D. Gribble and D.C. Lee, Experience with Top Gun Wingman: a proxy-based graphical Web browser for the 3Com PalmPilot, in: Proc. of Middleware '98, 1998.

[5] Google Inc., Google, http://www.google.com/.

[6] H. Lieberman, Letizia: an agent that assists Web browsing, in: C.S. Mellish (Ed.), Proc. of 14th International Joint Conference on Artificial Intelligence, 1995.

[7] M. Marchiori, The quest for correct information on the Web: hyper search engines, in: Proc. of the Sixth World Wide Web Conference, Elsevier, Amsterdam, 1997, pp. 265–276.

[8] T. Masui, An efficient text input method for pen-based computers, in: Proc. of the Conference on Human Factors in Computing Systems, 1998, pp. 328–335.

[9] K. Oku, Palmscape, http://palmscape.ilinx.co.jp/.

[10] Palm Inc., Web Clipping development, http://www.palm.com/devzone/webclipping/.

[11] ProxiNet, ProxiWeb, http://www.proxinet.com/.

[12] Smartcode Software, HandWeb, http://www.smartcodesoft.com/.

[13] Snakefeet, SnakeEyes, http://www.snakefeet.com/.

Orkut Buyukkokten is a Ph.D. student in the Department of Computer Science at Stanford University, Stanford, CA. He is currently working on the Digital Library project and is doing research on Web Browsing and Searching for personal digital assistants.

Hector Garcia-Molina is a professor in the Departments of Computer Science and Electrical Engineering at Stanford University, Stanford, CA. From August 1994 to December 1997 he was the Director of the Computer Systems Laboratory at Stanford. From 1979 to 1991 he was on the faculty of the Computer Science Department at Princeton University, Princeton, NJ. His research interests include distributed computing systems and database systems. He received a B.S. in electrical engineering from the Instituto Tecnologico de Monterrey, Mexico, in 1974. From Stanford University, Stanford, CA, he received in 1975 a M.S. in electrical engineering and a Ph.D. in computer science in 1979.

Andreas Paepcke is a senior research scientist and director of the Digital Library project at Stanford University. For several years he has been using object-oriented technology to address interoperability problems, most recently in the context of distributed digital library services. His second interest is the exploration of user interface and systems technologies for accessing digital libraries from small, handheld devices (PDAs). Dr. Paepcke received B.S. and M.S. degrees in applied mathematics from Harvard University, and a Ph.D. in computer science from the University of Karlsruhe, Germany. Previously, he worked as a researcher at Hewlett-Packard Laboratory, and as a research consultant at Xerox PARC.

Two approaches to bringing Internet services to WAP devices

Eija Kaasinen [a,*,1], Matti Aaltonen [a,1], Juha Kolari [a,1], Suvi Melakoski [a,1], Timo Laakko [b,1]

[a] *VTT Information Technology, Sinitaival 6, P.O. Box 1206, FIN-33101 Tampere, Finland*
[b] *VTT Information Technology, Tekniikantie 4 B, P.O. Box 1203, FIN-02044 Espoo, Finland*

Abstract

The next big challenge of the Internet is mobile access. More and more information is available on the Internet and intranets and mobile users will also need access to it. Wireless Application Protocol (WAP) based devices make it possible to access Wireless Markup Language (WML) based services with mobile browsers. The first WAP compliant devices have already been released on the market and more are to come. In the future there will be a need for Web services that are specially targeted for mobile users. We have studied this mobile-aware approach to service design by implementing a WML application and evaluating it on three different WAP platforms. Based on our evaluation results, we recognize challenges for future WAP devices and mobile-aware services. We have also studied if it would be possible to access the already existing Internet information with WAP devices. We have developed an HTML/WML conversion proxy server, which converts HTML-based Web contents automatically and on-line to WML. This approach gives the mobile users transparent access to their familiar Web pages from their mobile phones and other mobile devices. Our study indicates that if HTML-based Web services follow certain guidelines, they can be converted automatically to WML and adapted to the client device. In principle these guidelines already exist as World Wide Web Consortium (W3C) Content Accessibility Guidelines and W3C Note for HTML 4.0 Guidelines for Mobile Access.

Keywords: WAP; Mobile access; HTML/WML conversion; Usability; Evaluation

1. Introduction

The rapid growth of Web services has led to a situation where companies and individuals rely more and more on material that is available on the Internet and intranets. An increasing number of people use Web services both at work and at home. The next step is to gain access to Web services for mobile users too. Already before WAP some simple interactive services have been available on mobile phones. These services are based on the GSM short message service (SMS) and include schedules, news, sport results, weather forecasts and so on. Although the available SMS-based services are quite awkward to use, they have become very popular. This indicates a need for additional mobile Web services. Access itself will probably be the killer application for the mobile Internet [5].

Wireless Application Protocol (WAP) together with Wireless Markup Language (WML) constitute an open architecture for mobile Web services. They make it possible to provide markup-language based services for different mobile devices equipped with WAP browsers. The selection of WAP devices is expected to range from mobile phones to palmtop

* Corresponding author.
[1] E-mail: {eija.kaasinen, matti.aaltonen, juha.kolari, timo.laakko}@vtt.fi

computers. The international specification work on WAP is still going on (February 2000) in the WAP Forum and several details must still be worked out [12]. The first WAP-compliant devices were introduced to the market during the fall of 1999. The WAP services currently available are not generic but they have been tailored to specific WAP devices.

How should the service providers create services to the growing variety of mobile clients? Simultaneously with the ongoing international specification work of WAP, we have studied two different approaches to bringing Internet services to WAP phones and other mobile devices. The mobile-aware approach is to design and implement totally new services that are specially designed for mobile users. A more generic approach is to develop techniques with which current Internet services can be converted transparently and in real time suitable for mobile users. We have implemented and evaluated both kinds of solutions. As an example of a mobile-aware application, we have implemented a Business Card Search Service (BCSS). Our mobile-transparent solution is an HTML/WML conversion proxy server. Through the proxy server, the users can in principle access exactly the same Web services as from their desktops. If it is possible to convert services transparently to mobile users, the service providers will save a lot in implementation and maintenance costs. However, we assumed that this mobile-transparent approach would not produce results as good as services designed specially for the mobile clients.

In this paper we first describe our technical framework as well as the implementation of the mobile-aware application and HTML/WML conversion. Then we describe our iterative design approach, evaluation methods and results. Finally, we analyze the evaluation results and recognize possibilities and challenges for future WAP devices and applications. We also point out recommendations for Web page design.

2. The technical framework

2.1. WAP devices

Symbian has classified future mobile devices into three categories: communicators, smartphones and feature phones. The classification is based on input methods and display size. Display sizes vary from 48 $\times$ 48 pixels in a feature phone to full VGA in certain communicators. The main input method for communicators is a QWERTY keyboard or an emulated keyboard on the screen. A keypad is recommended for smartphones [8].

WAP devices will include all of Symbian's categories. In addition to the display and input methods, future WAP devices will also vary by accepted content types and network connections. During the fall of 1999, WAP devices began to appear on the market, the first two being the Ericsson MC218 palmtop computer with a WAP-browser and the Nokia 7110 WAP phone.

Because the variation of WAP devices will be very wide, the services have to take into account the capabilities of the mobile clients. The WAP specification defines the User Agent Profile (UAProf), which will be used to transmit information about the client. It includes device hardware and software characteristics as well as application and user preferences. The UAProf specification was not published until November 1999 in the WAP Forum [11]. That is why we could not yet utilize it in our design.

2.2. Development environment

The contents of the WAP services are implemented in Wireless Markup Language (WML) and WMLScript. XML (eXtensible Markup Language) is a metalanguage for describing other markup languages. As a metalanguage XML makes it possible to define customized markup languages for different purposes [6]. WML is an XML-based markup language designed for low-end devices and slow, unreliable networks. WML provides basic means for document formatting and user interaction but presupposes little of how they are actually implemented. Developers of WAP services only design the interaction logic in the application. Each client device then implements these interactions in its own way [12,13].

As an example of a mobile-aware application, we have implemented a Business Card Search Service (BCSS) in WML. Our mobile-transparent solution is an HTML/WML conversion proxy server. Through the proxy server, the users can in principle access

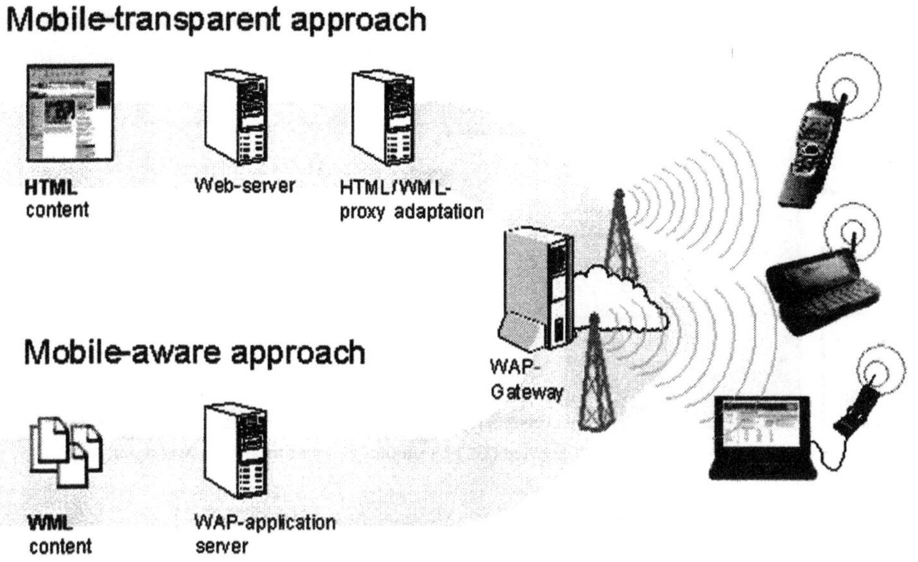

Mobile-transparent approach

HTML content

Web-server

HTML/WML-proxy adaptation

WAP-Gateway

Mobile-aware approach

WML content

WAP-application server

Fig. 1. Mobile-transparent and mobile-aware approaches to Internet access.

exactly the same Web services as from their desktops. These two design approaches are illustrated in Fig. 1.

As test platforms, we have been using three WAP device simulators. The UP.Simulator 3.1 (UP) by **Phone.com**[2], Nokia WAP SDK 1.01 and Nokia WAP Toolkit 1.1 (**Nokia**[3]) offer WAP phone simulators. Wireless Application Reader by Dynamical Research Systems Ltd. (**DSR**[4]) simulates a palmtop-computer-like device with a resizable display window. All the simulated browsers run on the Windows operating system and handle WML version 1.0 or 1.1. The test platforms can be seen in Fig. 2.

3. Business Card Search Service (BCSS)

With our Business Card Search Service (BCSS) the user can search contact information by making queries to a business card database. We could not utilize User Agent Profile (UAProf) specification yet but we studied how the same WML code would work on different devices.

3.1. Functionality

The Business Card Search Service (BCSS) offers three different query forms. The so-called simple search form uses only last and first name as search criteria. The extended search form includes additional search possibilities for title, organization, etc. With the free text search the user can search a string from any of the business card fields.

The search results are displayed as a list of names. The user can set the application up to show either organizational, phone, email or address information in addition to the name in the result list. If several persons meet the query criteria the user may decide to make a new, more refined search or browse through the list to find the correct person. When the user finds the right person she/he can get the full business card information by following the corresponding link in the result list. The user can also browse the business cards or the included photos without returning to the result list.

3.2. Implementation

The structure of WML is based on deck/card metaphor. A WAP application may consist of one or several WML decks. A WML deck is divided into cards. A deck is sent from the server in one

[2] http://www.phone.com

[3] http://www.nokia.com

[4] http://www.wap.net

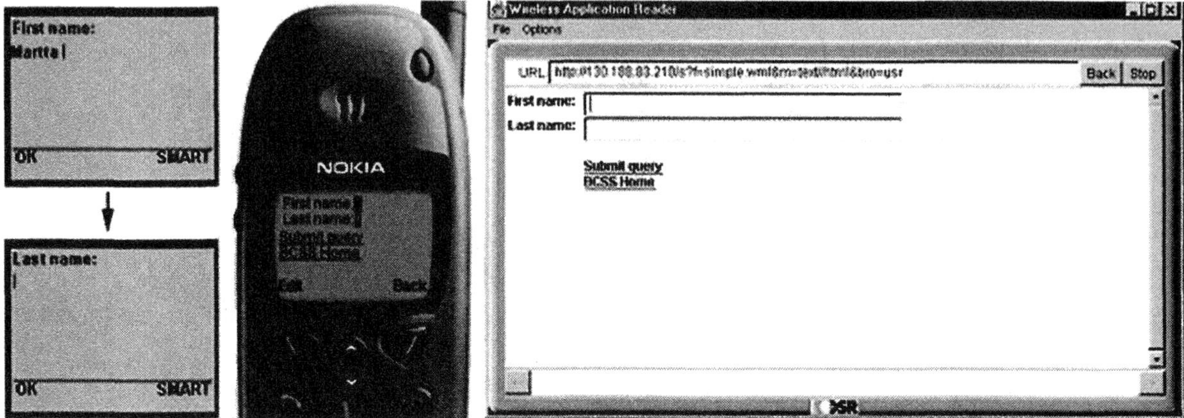

Fig. 2. Business Card Search Service (BCSS) on the test platforms: UP, Nokia and DSR.

transaction but the browser usually shows only one card at a time. Typically all the contents of a card do not fit on the screen of a WAP phone so the user has to scroll the screen to see the card in full [13].

The Business Card Search Service consists of an LDAP (Lightweight Directory Access Protocol) database, WML and WMLScript document templates, and server software written in Java. The content format of the business cards is based on vCard defined by the Internet Mail Consortium (IMC) [9]. The server fills in WML document templates with data extracted from the business card database.

3.3. Implementation issues

During our Business Card Search Service development process the specification work of Wireless Application Protocol (WAP) and Wireless Markup Language (WML) was still going on. The three browsers that we used in our tests each used a different content type for WML documents. The image format was a problem too. In the beginning of the implementation none of the WAP device simulators accepted the WAP bitmap (WBMP) format. The UP simulator handled only the BMP format and the DSR Wireless Application Reader accepted only GIF images.

In the Nokia simulator, the application could not redefine the texts for the soft keys. That is why we decided to avoid soft keys and used links instead.

In our initial design we divided the result deck into three cards. The first card contained the business-related items and the second contained more personal information like home phone number and a photo. The third card of the result deck was a pre-filled query form to be used as a template for making a new query. Only the DSR simulator supported navigation between WML cards. The links to the following cards required several user actions on the other two browsers. Our expert evaluation suggested that a single scrollable card would be easier to use. So we rejected our initial design and implemented the business card as a single WML card.

4. HTML/WML conversion

4.1. Implementation

Web environment may include separate specialized proxy servers that perform different tasks of conversion, caching and content adaptation. Proxies may support the adaptation of Web application content to different terminal and network environments. A proxy server can for instance try to minimize the information flow over low/medium speed wireless links. The proxy server may filter out some content types of HTTP streams (e.g., images, Java script or Java Applets). It can also modify the content (e.g., image depth and size) based on the user's preferences and channel throughput [7].

Our HTML/WML conversion has been implemented into a proxy server (Fig. 1). In addition to the conversion, the proxy server includes both caching

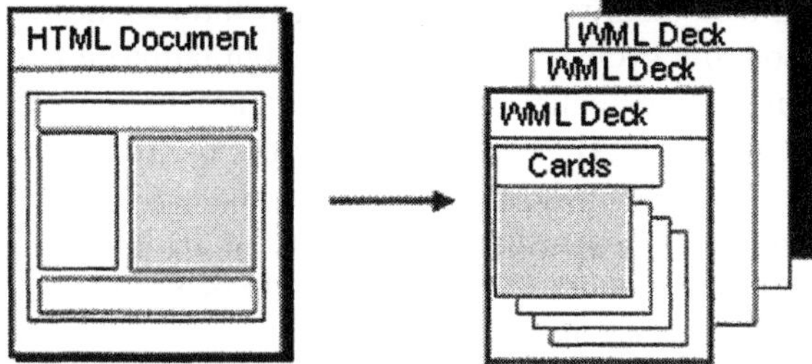

Fig. 3. HTML/WML conversion.

and content adaptation. WML devices access HTML services through the proxy and thus get transparent access to the HTML services. The conversion first checks and validates the HTML document. Then, the server parses the document, converts the contents and rearranges the contents as WML decks and cards (Fig. 3).

In addition, the conversion proxy aims to format the document according to the capabilities and preferences of the mobile client. Without the User Agent Profile (UAProf) [11] we could only adapt to the User Agent type (the browser in the client device).

The parsing breaks the HTML data into its logical elements, such as start- and end-tags, attributes and text. The parser also checks the document against the given Document Type Definition (DTD) and it corrects errors. When converting from HTML to WML, some data is inevitably lost. The terminal adaptation phase may work optimally only if it has access to all information in the original HTML, so it is reasonable to integrate adaptation to the document type conversion. The document type conversion is done by a script. During the conversion an intermediate tree structure (which corresponds to the resulting WML decks) is created. Then, the tree is manipulated according to adaptation rules, which utilize information about the capabilities of the requesting user agent, configuration parameters (such as force conversion of HTML table items to separate WML cards) and the user's preferences. After the whole document has been processed, the tree structure is converted to one or more WML decks. Each deck includes a hierarchical group of WML cards. Each child card has a link back to its immediate ancestor card and to the next child card (if any). The depth of the hierarchy is not limited.

4.2. Conversion rules

For HTML tables we have three different conversion methods, which convert the original table to a WML table, to an indexed sub-tree or to a list. The method is chosen according to the size of the table and user agent capabilities. WML (since version 1.1) supports tables that are in many ways similar to HTML tables. However, the presentation is complicated because user agents with small screens have to figure out how to present a large table in an understandable manner. Moreover, the WML 1.1 tables may not be nested. The indexed sub-tree is a two-level tree, where the root card is an index of links to the leaf cards. Each leaf card presents the content of a single table cell. This conversion method works well when converting layout tables. The simplest way to convert tables is to convert them to lists. We concatenate the contents of the table cells to form a list that produces compact and clear output, but dismisses with the table structure. This method is similar to the one that the Lynx browser uses.

HTML forms contain a group of user input elements. All essential HTML user-input elements can be converted relatively easily to WML controls. However, the graphical layout and most of the grouping of the user input elements are inevitably lost in conversion. User input elements on a form are converted to a single card, where they appear in the same order as in the original HTML code.

Each HTML frame of a frame set is converted to one or more WML decks. Frame sets are converted into decks that provide indices to WML decks that correspond with individual frames.

Images are currently presented as short text entries using either the included meta data or the image source file name. However, in the near future, we aim to adapt and convert image files according to available UAProf information. The image map is converted to a list of links. Lists are converted to a set of paragraphs, each starting a new line.

One HTML document typically produces several WML decks.

4.3. Implementation issues

The problem in creating indices is to find informative labels to the links. HTML 4.0 includes many possibilities to include the meta data but unfortunately these possibilities are seldom used. If the meta data was not present, we inferred the labels from the text or other content of the element.

Tables are common elements on Web sites. They are used either to generate page layout or to organize information. In the automatic conversion, it is difficult to define the purpose of the table. That is why we had to decide the conversion method based only on the size of the table and user agent type.

'Submit' buttons often caused problems when filling in and submitting forms. Often the button was not a standard HTML button but an image. Our conversion was not able to cope with image buttons. Logging into sites is often based on login scripts, which could not be converted. Preformatted text also was a problem because the formatting does not function on a small screen.

Often there was so much material on the Web pages that even if we managed to make the conversion, it was difficult to access the resulting WML decks and cards with a small display. Our conversion was not able to judge the importance of individual information elements.

5. Evaluation

5.1. The design process

Our human-centered design process employed four kinds of activities as described in the ISO standard 13407 'Human-centred design processes for interactive systems' [3]:

- understand and specify the context of use;
- specify the user and organizational requirements;
- produce design solutions;
- evaluate designs against requirements.

In the design process we used three different points of view: the technology itself, the mobile user and the service provider. Service providers, device manufacturers and end users have actively participated in our design process.

Our initial user requirements and context of use analysis were based on a literature survey of current research results, analysis of corresponding products and scenarios of typical usage situations. Our design process allowed us to identify new user requirements and feed them back into the process throughout the whole life cycle of the project. Design rationale has been very essential in this kind of design process where the WAP specification work is still going on. We need to keep track of the changes in user requirements as well as the changes in the technical possibilities and how we responded to these [4].

Evaluation has been a continuous activity throughout the design process. The aim of the evaluation was to find usability problems, to understand the reasons for the problems and to give feedback and new ideas to the design. In this way we could assure that our design was going in the right direction.

The main evaluation method has been the design walkthrough. This means meetings, where the users, application field experts, designers and usability experts together go through design solutions to get feedback and to generate new ideas. We also had small-scale user trials as well as expert evaluations throughout the project. In the end of the project we had a more thorough user evaluation for both the Business Card Search Service and the HTML/WML conversion.

5.2. User evaluation

The Business Card Search Service was evaluated with six test users, aged 13–52 years (Table 1). The experience of the users with mobile phones varied from modest to expert. All but one had a personal mobile phone. The Internet experience of the users was moderate or better.

We evaluated the application with each user in a separate two-hour session. Each user tested the application on at least two platforms. The order of the devices was changed for each user, so that half of the users started with the PDA type device and the other half with a phone. The phone simulators were run on a PC with a touch screen so that the users could press the keys of the phone. The test set-up is illustrated in Fig. 4. The simulated PDA device was run on a PC and operated with a mouse. We had two sets of test tasks so that the user would try each available search method. The task sets were identical except for the given search information.

The HTML/WML conversion proxy was evaluated with four test users, who were all familiar with mobile phones, the Internet and computers (Table 2).

Table 1
The test users of the Business Card Search Service (1 = modest skills, 6 = expert)

	Sex	Age	Computer skills	WWW search service skills	Versatility of mobile phone skills	Knowledge of mobile phone functions	Knowledge of mobile phone services
A	M	42	4	4	1	5	4
B	F	33	5	4	1	3	4
C	F	13	4	5	3	–[a]	–[a]
D	M	33	6	6	4	6	6
E	M	21	6	6	5	6	4
F	F	52	6	6	1	4	2

[a] User C did not own a mobile phone and did not answer questions regarding phone services and functions.

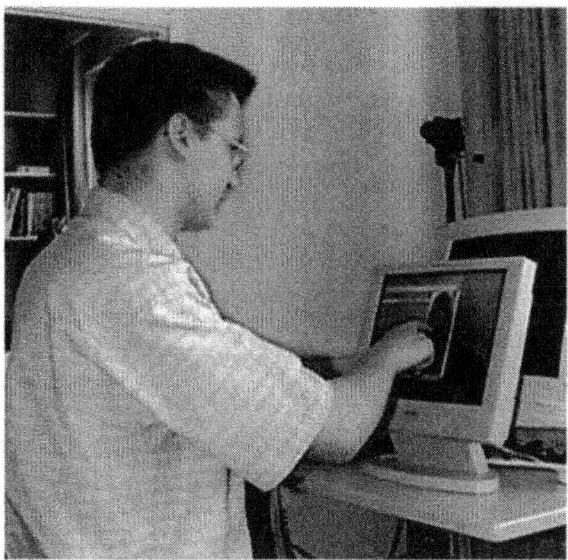

Fig. 4. The test set-up.

However, the users were not very versatile in their mobile phone skills. The attitude towards new mobile phone services was positive, except for that of one of the users who wanted to restrict his phone for only speaking purposes.

The system was evaluated with each user in a separate one-hour session. All tests were carried out with the Nokia WAP simulator, which ran on a PC and was operated with a mouse. The test session included filling in background forms, explaining to the users the basic idea of the HTML/WML conversion, doing four test tasks and conducting a final interview. The themes of the evaluation were general impression, ease of use, navigation and usefulness.

The test tasks included both familiar and unfamiliar Web pages. The test tasks included navigation, browsing, using frames and menus, editing text, etc. The users could also try the conversion with their favorite sites.

5.3. *Analysis of the evaluation results*

All the evaluation results were analyzed in the project group. We identified new or revised user requirements, classified them and decided how to respond to the requirements. Most feedback of the evaluation led to changes in our software. We also faced requirements that we could not respond to: features that could not be implemented, bugs in the simulators, requirements for the WAP devices and requirements for Web page designers.

We concluded the results with challenges for

Table 2
The test users of the HTML/WML conversion (1 = modest skills, 6 = expert)

	Sex	Age	Computer skills	WWW search service skills	Versatility of mobile phone skills	Knowledge of mobile phone functions	Knowledge of mobile phone services
A	M	24	6	6	1	5	5
B	M	24	6	6	1	6	5
C	M	22	6	6	2	6	4
D	F	25	5	4	2	4	3

WAP devices, possibilities and challenges for future mobile-aware services and recommendations for Web page design.

6. Evaluation results

Although we evaluated the Business Card Search Service application and the HTML/WML conversion proxy separately and with different users, the results include similar issues. Below, we present first similar issues like platform-related results and usability problems in scrolling, navigation and using forms. After that we describe the results that are specific to the design approach: mobile-aware Business Card Search Service or mobile-transparent HTML/WML conversion.

6.1. Platform-related results

The WML application could only utilize the soft keys and navigation keys of the phones. There seems to be a need to utilize the keypad more. All users suggested that shortcut keys would be useful. On the Nokia simulator most test users tried to start the search by pressing the green phone key. The users would also have liked to have had a shortcut key for returning to the home page of the site. Both predefined shortcuts like the green phone and user-defined personal shortcuts would be useful.

After pressing 'Back' the browsers did not return to the section on the previous page where the user had followed the link. This was frustrating, especially since scrolling a long Web page is a slow process. Another useful feature would be the possibility of scrolling the page so that the user could go straight from the top of the page to the bottom and vice versa.

6.2. Scrolling

Scrolling was difficult for most test users: the UP simulator gave no hint that more text was available than seen on the screen. The Nokia simulator had a scrollbar to indicate that there was more text available above and/or below. Most users did not, however, notice the scrollbar. The users who were most experienced in using the Internet tried more actively to find whether there was more text below. In Fig. 5 there are screen views of scrolling down the query form of the Business Card Search Service.

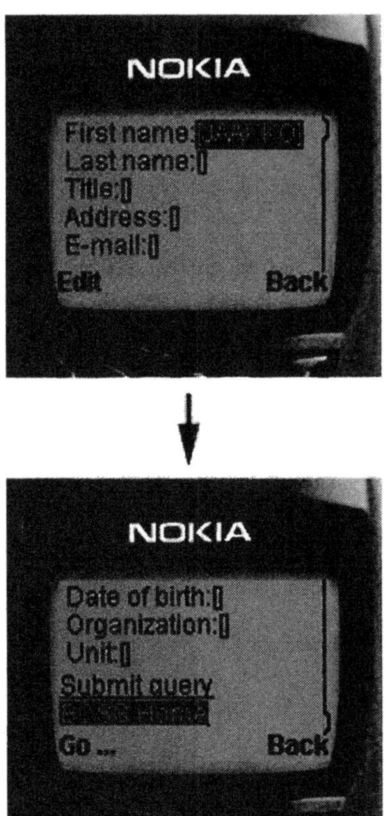

Fig. 5. Scrolling the search form of the Business Card Search Service.

With the small screen of a phone it was difficult to form a mental map of the structure of the Web page or the application. Even a few lines of text on a regular Web page requires quite an amount of scrolling on a small screen. Often the test users quit halfway through and returned back to the beginning of the page. Only a few users tried to scroll immediately just to see if there was something more outside the visible screen. The scrollbar of the Nokia simulator went unnoticed even by those test users who owned Nokia 5110 or 6110 mobile phones with a similar scrollbar.

In task two of the conversion proxy user evaluation, one of the users stated: "I expected the result to be the first thing on the page, not somewhere down there". He found the page that displayed the e-mail address requested but did not scroll far enough to find it.

One of the users suggested that scrolling would not need to proceed only row by row. After the cursor reaches the bottom row, the browser could present the whole new screen of text. Only one row of the previous screen would need to be left visible to preserve the continuity. A find function would also be useful in browsing through the information on long pages.

In the WAP phone simulators, navigation arrows were used for scrolling. Scrolling may be easier with a phone that has a scrolling wheel like Navi Roller on Nokia 7110.

6.3. Navigation

The users seemed to scroll more boldly on a familiar page, knowing it contained the links they were looking for. All users agreed that browsing through familiar pages was easier and required less mental strain than unfamiliar pages. The users claimed that they did not use the mental image they had about the page. They seemed to simply search for the link that they knew would be on the page and followed a familiar path from there. The appearance of the page was not the most relevant thing as long as the navigation path remained intact.

In the Business Card Search Service tests the users who had seen more of the page on the DSR simulator remembered quite well which information was left outside the visible screen. This encouraged them to scroll down the screen.

6.4. Forms

In the WAP phones, the visualization of the forms was quite different. The UP simulator represented each field in a separate window, whereas Nokia represented all fields on the same screen. With the UP simulator, the user could input text to the input field immediately but was forced to go through all the fields of the form. The users often thought that they had to fill in each form in the search. The situation is illustrated in Fig. 6.

In the Nokia simulator the user could select which fields to edit. The fields looked like the user could input text directly into the field on the form. It was confusing that the input fields could not be edited on the form screen but the user had to select the field first. The input operation was quite complicated, as illustrated in Fig. 7. After (a) identifying the search field the user had to (b) select the field to be edited, (c) edit the field text and finally (d) submit the field.

The users sometimes had difficulties in identify-

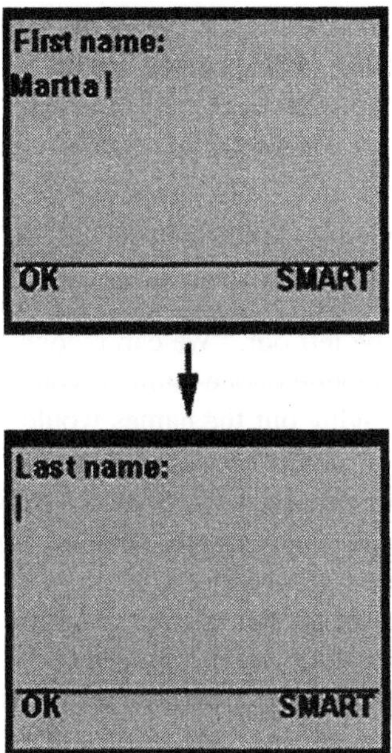

Fig. 6. Filling in a form in the UP simulator.

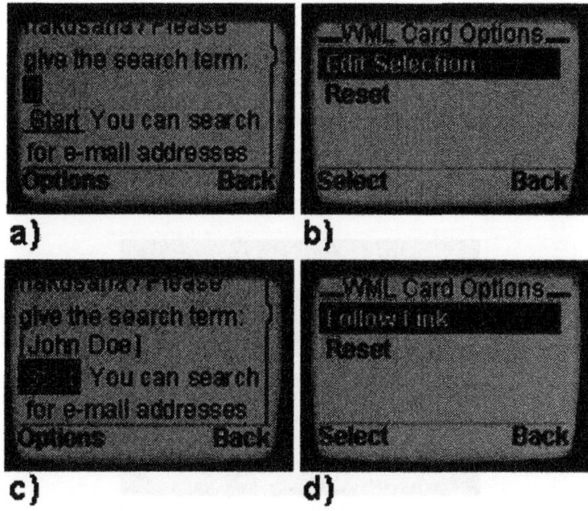

Fig. 7. Filling in a form in the Nokia simulator.

ing input fields, which on the Nokia simulator were not very visible. When searching for an input field, the users often passed the field several times while scrolling up and down without identifying it.

6.5. Business Card Search Service related results

The test users suggested that the names of the fields could be left out. "We can recognize an email address or a mobile phone number, you don't have to name it!" Leaving out the names would not work in all cases, e.g., you cannot always say if a name is a name of a person or a name of a city. However, often the texts could be replaced with descriptive icons to save screen space. Unfortunately we could not try this because of the problems with the graphics support in the WAP device simulators.

In the search results list, we presented the name of the person and his/her organization on a single line. This text was a link to the business card of the person. When all this text was shown underlined and highlighted as a selected link, the screen became too cluttered (Fig. 8). We decided to add extra line breaks to the results in order to avoid this cluttering on the small screen. Trying to improve the readability of the results on the phone screen, we could not utilize the wider screen on the PDA type device.

During the test and in the final interview, the users suggested some improvements to the application. The user has to be able to suspend a search when needed. The users pointed out personal preferences for the order of the information on a business card. It is essential to get the most important information first because scrolling takes time. In different contexts of use, the users need different search fields. It would be useful to let the user set up which fields of the business cards she/he needs and in which order.

Fig. 8. Search results with links to business cards.

Also, personally set shortcut keys would improve the efficiency, especially for frequent users. From email addresses and phone numbers there should be links to send email or to make a phone call.

Our test application did not include the possibility of storing the business cards. In practice, the users will probably have a personal database of business cards on their phones. It would be useful to get an automatic update and notice when a person's business card has changed.

6.6. HTML/WML conversion related results

Our conversion worked quite well with frames. Often, however, the frames had strange names like 'menu1.htm'. When the titles were not descriptive enough, the users had to use a trial and error approach to browse the contents. The users did not feel comfortable selecting a link named as a file name. Some test users selected these links only after trying everything else first. In Fig. 9 there is an example of converting frames. The frames are converted well to a list of links but the conversion could not find meaningful names to the links.

A layout table is often used as an alternative to frames. On this kind of a page, menu links are in the left column and the contents in the right column. When the page was converted to a WAP phone, the user saw first the list of menu items and then the contents. When the user selected a menu item, a new page was loaded. The part of the page that was visible on the screen of the phone remained unchanged because it still presented the menu links. The user got the impression that she/he came back to the same page from where she/he just left. All the test users had problems with layout tables. Fig. 10 illustrates the situation. The user has to browse through the list of menu items before getting to the contents. Each time after selecting a menu item, she/he has to browse through the same list again before getting to the actual contents.

Missing line breaks on the pages caused confusion in layout and navigation. In Fig. 11 there is a view of a news service. The number of a news item acts as a link but it is difficult to identify if the title of the news is before or after the number.

One test user suggested a variable font size so that he could browse through the contents without

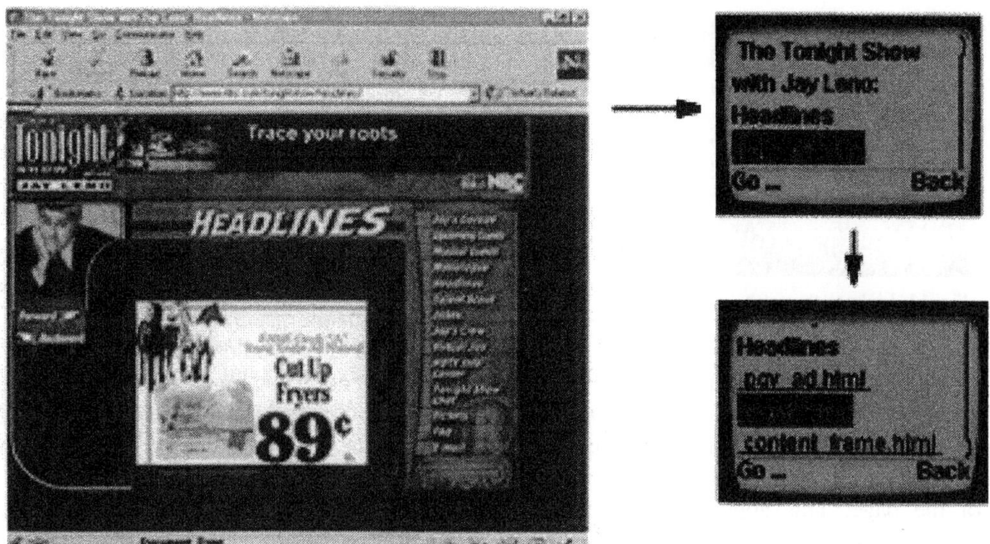

Fig. 9. Conversion of a frame set.

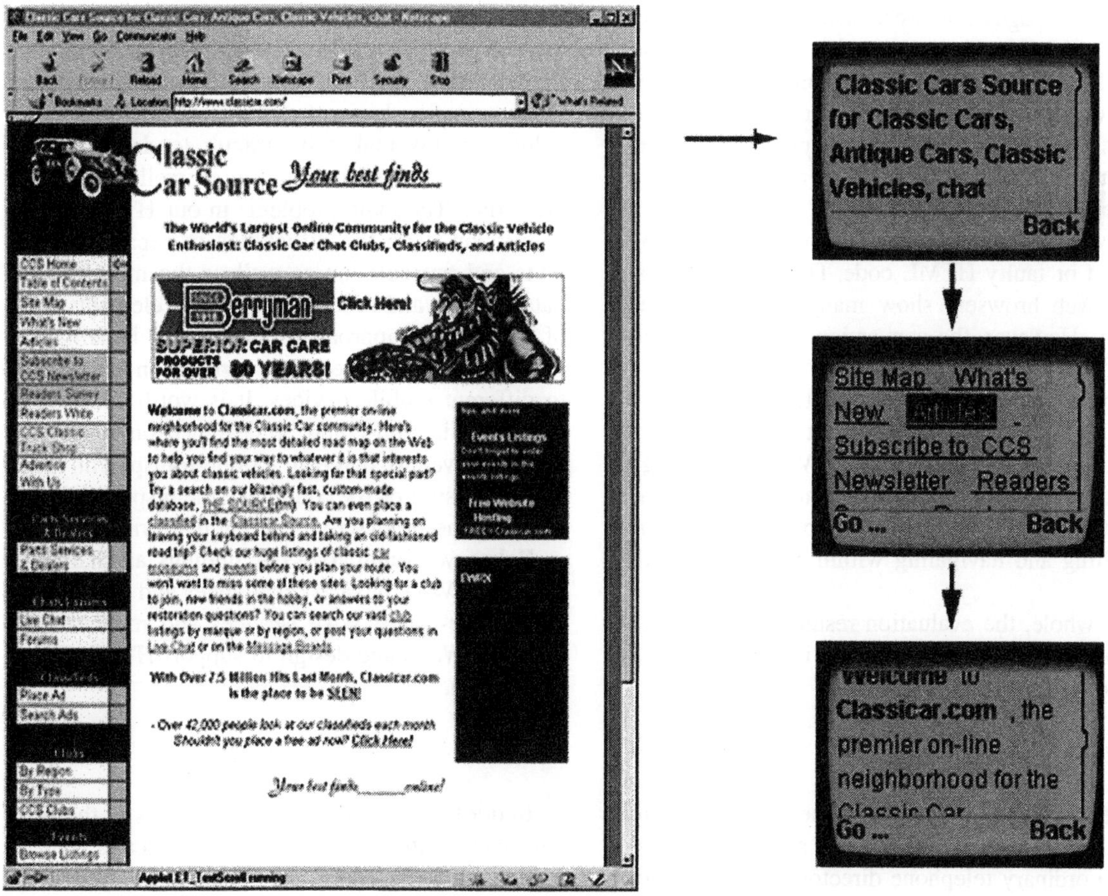

Fig. 10. Conversion of a layout table.

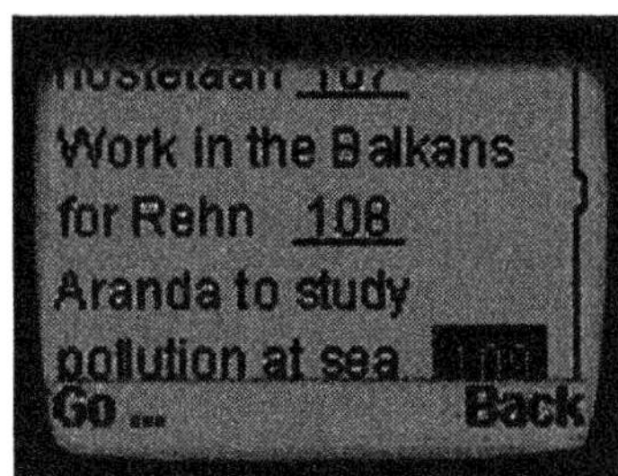

Fig. 11. Links to the news.

actually reading it yet, and then select a piece of the page to be read in larger font. Lars Holmquist has studied this kind of approach [1]. In his approach the 'small font' is actually graphics, which presents the structure of the page. This approach requires transmitting images, which is not very fast. If the WAP phones would support small fonts, the zoomed out content could still be sent as text.

Often the pages that we considered informative, such as timetables, news, opening hours, etc., did not work well with the conversion proxy. Timetables could not be found due to error messages or could not be shown properly due to problems with preformatted text and tables. News pages required logging in, which was also prone to errors.

Many of the error messages seem to be caused by imperfect or faulty HTML code. Despite the faults, regular Web browsers show many of these pages correctly. However, the conversion often turned out to be difficult or impossible.

Even if the conversion succeeds technically, there is still a problem with the amount of information. Mobile users would benefit from a Web-page design where the most often needed information is on the top of the page. Another need is better facilitation of scrolling and navigating within a page on WAP phones.

As a whole, the evaluation results indicated that even complex-looking and visually impressive pages could be converted in a useful way.

6.7. Utility

All the test users considered the Business Card Search Service useful. This kind of system could replace an ordinary telephone directory or a directory inquiry service. The users mentioned several other mobile phone services that they would like to use, e.g., banking, sport pools, bus and train schedules, a postal charge service, information searches like Yahoo! and AltaVista, chat, a weather service, service catalogues, tourist information and a dictionary.

The test users of the HTML/WML conversion said that they could use the conversion to find small bits of information, such as timetables, TV schedules, movies, price lists, happenings, addresses and news. Although the users could describe what kind of information they would like to access with their phones, they could not imagine many situations in which they would need the information on the phone. "We do have the Internet at work and at home, maybe at a bus stop to check the schedule."

7. Analysis of the results

The implementation of the Business Card Search Service revealed many challenges in designing and implementing this kind of mobile-aware application. The interaction logic of the mobile browsers varies a lot and this makes it difficult to design a user interface that as such would work well on different platforms. The main problems in our HTML/WML conversion were the difficulties in separating contents and presentation as well as the missing meta data to name and describe the HTML elements. Both of the design approaches have their benefits and problems. The mobile-aware application has to adapt to different mobile devices. It is worth considering if the application could be designed on a bit more general level to make it mobile-transparent. Then the conversion proxy could take the responsibility of adapting the service for different platforms.

Below we summarize our findings as challenges for future WAP devices, challenges and possibilities for mobile-aware WAP services and recommendations for Web-page design to support HTML/WML conversion.

7.1. Challenges for future WAP devices

In our tests we used the first versions of the WAP device simulators by Nokia, Phone.com and Dynamical Systems Research Ltd. There were some bugs in the simulators and they were sometimes a bit unstable and slow. The main problems were varying support for graphics, missing support for soft keys, implementation of the forms and problems with navigation arrows. Many of these problems still exist with the first WAP devices that are commercially available. Hopefully the problems will be solved in forthcoming WAP devices.

Two of the devices did not support the visualization of WML decks and cards. That is why we did not use this metaphor in our WML application. We replaced the deck cards with a single scrollable card. If future devices support the deck/card metaphor, the applications could be designed accordingly.

Scrolling was a problem with WAP applications. The users gave up easily if they had to scroll down to find a piece of information. The contents of the applications should be designed so that the key information is on the first screen. WAP devices like Nokia 7110 include a scrolling wheel (Nokia Navi Roller) for faster scrolling. In addition to this, the device or browser could support scrolling e.g., with an adaptive scrolling speed, an illustrative scrollbar and a find function.

It would also be useful if pressing the Back key would return the application to the section of the previous page where the user followed the link. Scrolling could be avoided by facilitating zooming in and out to the contents of a page. It was especially difficult to navigate in tables. More studies should be done on how to visualize tables on a small screen.

Filling in forms was quite a complicated process in both WAP phone simulators. The same problems seem to exist with the first WAP devices. Hopefully in future devices the forms will become easier to use.

Shortcut keys would also be useful; for instance, the users found the 'Green phone' key of the Nokia simulator as an obvious 'Accept' key. The efficiency of the services could be improved if the applications could utilize the keypad of the phone better. Shortcut keys could also be user programmable.

7.2. Challenges and possibilities for mobile-aware services

WAP specification work did not progress as fast as we expected in the beginning of the project. That is why we could not utilize User Agent Profiles in our application. In future versions the adaptation of the service must be based on the attributes of the User Agent Profile. In our study with the Business Card Search Service, the usability of the service was improved by letting the users select which business card fields they wanted to see and in which order. This kind of content and presentation adaptability would probably be useful in other services too.

In our project, the support for graphics was quite modest in the simulated WAP devices. Using descriptive icons instead of texts, where possible, could save valuable screen space in future services.

Network connections with mobile systems are often less stable than fixed connections. That is why it is important for users to be able to trace and cancel selected operations.

Future applications should be able to utilize links to e-mail addresses and telephone numbers to send e-mail or to make phone calls.

In real applications, often part of the information is stored on the user's own device and part on the server. There should be means to update and maintain the information automatically.

7.3. Recommendations for Web-page design

In future versions of the conversion proxy, even graphics and other media could be converted. The user should be informed of the existence of different elements, even if the conversion cannot convert them. However, it would be useful to recognize and skip some less important elements.

Sites that are navigable and readable with the conversion proxy are usually sites with a simple structure and few tables. Use of descriptive file names and the 'alt' attribute for images and frames is important. Also, the closer the code is to the HTML standard, the easier it is to develop the conversion rules.

Familiar pages were easier for users to navigate. This suggests that if an already existing Web service is provided to WAP users as a separate application, it would be a good idea to maintain the basic structure of the site.

Frames were easy to convert and the result was easy to use. We could not convert layout tables so that the result would be usable. It was difficult to distinguish layout tables from other tables in the conversion.

Some elements turned out to be problematic in

the conversion. Image buttons should have textual alternatives. Login scripts cannot be converted; there should be alternatives for them. Preformatted text does not work on the small and variable-size screens. Missing line breaks create confusing layout or even navigational errors. Line breaks should be used to enforce the visual structure of the page by grouping data. Style sheets for different screen sizes should be provided instead of preformatted text.

Many Web sites were loaded with a lot of textual information. The main pages should be kept simple and the extra material should be put on additional pages for those who need it and are able to access it. Anchor links within a page are very useful because they reduce the need for scrolling.

The World Wide Web Consortium, W3C, has recently published two guidelines for improving Web accessibility. The work on HTML 4.0 Guidelines for Mobile Access is still going on but a Note for Discussion was released in March 1999 [2]. This planned guideline will include instructions on how to make a Web site available to users with slow mobile network connections and/or small devices. Web content Accessibility Guidelines version 1.0 was released in May 1999 as a W3C recommendation [10]. These guidelines give instructions on how to make a Web site accessible to users with disabilities and to people using text or voice based browsers, slow networks or small screens. The guidelines point out that everybody can have accessibility problems depending on his/her context of use and the available terminal. The duty of the designer of a Web service is to assure that the accessibility problems can be overcome.

The recommendations of the W3C Accessibility Guidelines include the following:

- Provide alternatives to auditory and visual content;
- Don't rely on color alone;
- Control presentation with style sheets;
- Use tables only for tabular information;
- Ensure that pages featuring new technologies transform;
- Ensure user control of time-sensitive content changes;
- Design for device-independence;
- Use interim solutions (until user agents address these issues);
- Provide context and orientation information;
- Provide clear navigation mechanisms;
- Ensure that documents are clear and simple.

The W3C guidelines have not been designed especially for conversion proxies in mind. In spite of that, we found out that most of our conversion problems could have been avoided if the Web sites that we were using in our tests would have followed W3C Accessibility Guidelines. The Mobile Access Guidelines Note was even a bit too strict for our purposes. However, by following it, the designer of a Web site can almost be sure that the page can be automatically converted to WML. When the designers of Web sites start to follow these guidelines, their sites will be available for a variety of devices, browsers and networks. Because the amount of the different mobile devices is growing all the time, this kind of approach should be very appealing to the site designers.

8. Conclusions and future work

The information content and number of services on the Internet is growing rapidly. At the same time the number of users and the variety of their devices is growing. Service providers face a big challenge in how to respond to the growing demand. Users want to use the same services with different devices depending on their current context of use. The services have to adapt their contents and presentation according to the user's personal and device characteristics and the context of use.

Our experience shows that it is possible to make Web services that adapt to different terminals, both desktop and mobile, without diminishing the site's visual appeal. To support the conversion, the Web-page designer has to follow certain guidelines. In principle, these guidelines already exist as W3C Accessibility and Mobile Access guidelines. The guidelines do not restrict the visual design of the service but rather recommend alternative formats and proper use of meta data. When designing a service for both mobile and desktop users, this approach is worth considering.

There will still be a need for mobile-aware applications designed and tailored to the exact needs of mobile clients. In these applications usability can be improved by using descriptive icons instead of texts and adapting contents and presentation to user needs.

In WAP devices, better support will be needed for navigation and scrolling. Forms should be easier to use and it should be possible to define and use shortcut keys.

Our future plans include more studies on the adaptivity of the services. The WAP Forum is still working on the specification of the User Agent Profile. We will study user needs for adaptivity more thoroughly. We will also study how the User Agent Profile could be utilized both in mobile-aware applications and in the HTML/WML conversion. We believe that when providing services to the growing variety of mobile devices, service adaptivity is the key issue.

Our research project was carried out with the financial support of the National Technology Agency of Finland (Tekes). Our work was also supported both financially and technically by companies Ericsson, Radiolinja and Teamware. The authors would like to thank these partners for the fruitful co-operation.

References

[1] L. Holmquist, Will baby faces ever grow up? in: H.-J. Bullinger and J. Ziegler (Eds.), Human–Computer Interaction: Ergonomics and User Interfaces, Proc. of the 8th International Conference on Human–Computer Interaction, vol. 1, 1999, pp. 706–709.

[2] HTML 4.0 Guidelines for Mobile Access, W3C Note, 15 March 1999, http://www.w3.org/.

[3] International Standard ISO 13407:1999, Human-centred design processes for interactive systems, The International Organization for Standardization, 1999.

[4] E. Kaasinen, M. Aaltonen and T. Laakko, Defining user requirements for WAP services, in: H.-J. Bullinger and J. Ziegler (Eds.), Human–Computer Interaction: Ergonomics and User Interfaces, Proc. of the 8th International Conference on Human–Computer Interaction, vol. 2, 1999, pp. 33–37.

[5] M. Kylänpää and T. Laakko, Adapting content to mobile terminals: examining two approaches, Third Generation Mobile Systems in Europe, London, 25–27 January 1999.

[6] M. Leventhal, D. Lewis and M. Fuchs, Designing XML Internet Applications, Prentice-Hall, Englewood Cliffs, NJ, 1998.

[7] A. Luotonen, Web Proxy Servers, Prentice-Hall, Englewood Cliffs, NJ, 1998.

[8] Symbian home page, http://www.symbian.com/.

[9] vCard, The Business Card, Version 2.1, A Versit Consortium Specification, 1996.

[10] Web Content Accessibility Guidelines 1.0, W3C Recommendation, 5 May 1999, http://www.w3.org/.

[11] Wireless Application Group, User agent profile specification, Version 10 November 1999, available at http://www.wapforum.org/what/technical.htm.

[12] Wireless Application Protocol, Wireless application environment overview, Version 04 November 1999, available at http://www.wapforum.org/what/technical.htm.

[13] Wireless Markup Language Specification, Version 1.1, 16 June 1999, available at http://www.wapforum.org/what/technical.htm.

Eija Kaasinen, M.Sc. in Software Engineering, is a Group Manager at VTT Information Technology, Human-Centered Design Research Group. Her research interests include methods for human-centred design, intelligent and adaptive user interfaces and usability issues in mobile applications. Eija Kaasinen is currently in charge of usability design and evaluation activities within different research projects dealing with mobile applications and services.

Matti J. Aaltonen received his M.Sc. in Technical Mathematics in 1984 from the Technical University of Tampere. Following completion of the M.Sc. degree, he spent five years at the Technical University of Tampereworking at the Department of Mathematics. From 1989 he has been working at the Technical Research Centre of Finland as a Research Scientist. His main research interests are in user interface and graphics programming.

Juha Kolari, M.Sc. in Psychology, is working at VTT Information Technology as Research Scientist. His research interests include usability design and evaluation as well as usability issues with mobile services.

Suvi Melakoski is studying software engineering at Tampere University of Technology. She was working at VTT Information Technology as a usability research assistant in 1999.

Timo Laakko is a research professor at VTT Information Technology, Service Platforms Research Group. He received a D.Tech. in 1994 from the Helsinki University of Technology in information processing science. His research interests include wireless Internet, multimedia applications and communication and product models. He is currently the project manager of two research projects, both of which are related to the development of application environments and platforms for Wireless Application Protocol (WAP).

The Term Vector Database: fast access to indexing terms for Web pages

Raymie Stata [a,*], Krishna Bharat [a,b], Farzin Maghoul [c]

[a] *Compaq Systems Research Center, 130 Lytton Avenue, Palo Alto, CA 94301, USA*
[b] *Google Inc., 2400 Bayshore Parkway, Mountain View, CA 94043, USA*
[c] *AltaVista Corporation, 1825 S. Grant Street, San Mateo, CA 94402, USA*

Abstract

We have built a database that provides term vector information for large numbers of pages (hundreds of millions). The basic operation of the database is to take URLs and return term vectors. Compared to computing vectors by downloading pages via HTTP, the Term Vector Database is several orders of magnitude faster, enabling a large class of applications that would be impractical without such a database. This paper describes the Term Vector Database in detail. It also reports on two applications built on top of the database. The first application is an optimization of connectivity-based topic distillation. The second application is a Web page classifier used to annotate results returned by a Web search engine.

Keywords: Page classification; Term vectors; Topic distillation; Web connectivity; Web search

1. Introduction

In the vector space model of information retrieval [8], documents are modeled as vectors in a high-dimensional space of many thousands of terms. The terms are derived from words and phrases in the document and are weighted by their importance within the document and within the corpus of documents. Each document's vector seeks to represent the document in a 'vector space', allowing comparison with vectors derived from other sources, for example, queries or other documents. This model has had a long and distinguished history, having been used as the basis of successful algorithms for document ranking, document filtering, document clustering, and relevance feedback (see [2,10]).

Despite its usefulness, term vector information for Web pages is not readily available. One could, of course, compute vectors on demand by downloading pages over HTTP, but the amount of time required by this approach rules out all but the simplest experiments. Even in companies that run Web search engines, term vector information is typically stored in inverted form; that is, given a term, one can find the vectors containing it, but not the other way around. While this inverted form is useful for some applications (including, of course, serving queries), many other applications need to retrieve vectors based on a page identifier.

To support such applications, we have built the *Term Vector Database*. We have populated it with term vectors for all the pages in the AltaVista index. Unlike search engines, which map from terms to page ids, our database maps from page ids to terms. Compared to retrieving pages over the Web, our database is many orders of magnitude faster.

* Corresponding author. E-mail: stata@pa.dec.com

One must note that the selection of indexing terms for documents has been standard practice in library science even before information retrieval came into existence as a discipline. Librarians would select a small set of semantically representative, discriminatory keywords to represent each document. This is essentially what we do in our database, but on the scale of the Web, which makes it a challenging engineering problem.

The Term Vector Database is especially useful in conjunction with another tool that we created, the *Connectivity Server* [3]. The Connectivity Server provides fast access to the connectivity graph of the Web. Given an URL or a set of URLs, the server rapidly computes a graph of pages and links surrounding the input URLs. A task-specific agent can use this graph to walk the Web or mine information from the graph structure. This can be done many orders of magnitude faster than crawling actual pages on the Web. Unfortunately, the connectivity server lacks content information. The Term Vector Database provides a complementary service that addresses this problem. It provides rapid access to *content information* for most pages in the Connectivity Server database, thus allowing more intelligent and selective computation on the World Wide Web's structure.

In addition to adding value to the Connectivity Server, the Term Vector Database supports other applications, including classifying pages, finding representative passages within pages, identifying the language in which a page is written, and helping to filter spam and pornography. In Section 3, we describe two applications that we have implemented using the database: topic distillation and page classification. But first, Section 2 gives an overview of the system.

2. System overview

This section describes the Term Vector Database. Section 2.1 gives a precise definition of the data stored in the database, that is, a definition of exactly what a 'term vector' is in our context. The following subsection (Section 2.2) describes the primary operation exported by the database, which is to retrieve vectors given URLs. Section 2.3 describes the internal organization of the data in the database. The final subsection (Section 2.4) describes the software modules that make up the database.

2.1. Definition of term vectors

A term vector is a sequence of term-weight pairs. The design of a term vector database must answer the following questions: What exactly is a term? Which terms are to be included in a page's term vector? How are the term weights stored in vectors computed?

In our system, we answer these questions as follows.

- *Terms*. The terms of an HTML page are sequences of non-space characters found by filtering and normalizing the page's *term candidates*. The term candidates of an HTML page are sequences of non-space characters found either outside HTML tags or inside HTML `meta` tags, excluding such sequences found between `script` tags. A page's term candidates are filtered by a lexicon (discussed below) and then normalized by conversion to lower case and application of the Porter stemming algorithm [7]. (Our use of Porter stemming means that our system currently works only for English pages.)

  The lexicon used for the Term Vector Database is built by taking the 'middle third' terms from the AltaVista index minus a few dozen terms from a stop list. That is, we start with the terms in the AltaVista index and eliminate the most frequent third and least frequent third. Our reason for eliminating the most frequent third is standard: such terms provide little discrimination across vectors. (Given that we throw out frequent terms, one might wonder why we need a stop list. The answer is that the index does not normalize terms, so some variants of frequent terms, such as `THE`, appear in the middle third.)

  We eliminate the least frequent third because they are noisy and do not provide a good basis for measuring semantic similarity. For example, one such term is `hte`, a misspelling of `the`. This term appears in a handful of pages that are completely unrelated semantically. However, because this term is so infrequent, its appearance in term vectors makes those vectors appear to be quite closely related.

- *Term selection.* We select terms for inclusion in a page's vector by the usual Salton TF-IDF methodology (see, for example, [2]). That is, we weight a term in the page by dividing the number of times it appears in the page by the number of times it appears in the collection. For a given page, we select the 50 terms with the greatest weight according to this formula.
- *Weights.* Although we use the usual TF-IDF weighting to select terms for vectors, we do not store these weights in vectors. Instead, we store just the term frequency, that is, the number of times the term appears in the page. A number of weighting schemes have been proposed over the years (see, for example, [9]), and we did not know what weighting scheme would be best for our applications. Instead of choosing a weighting scheme a priori, we allow applications to implement their own weighting schemes by providing them with the raw data needed by most weighting schemes. In addition to the term counts themselves, these raw data include the lengths of pages, both in bytes and in terms. (An additional benefit of storing term counts is that they compress well.)

2.2. API

The main function in the API takes a set of page identifiers and returns a set of vectors:

```
tv_lookup(int n,
          const conn_id_t *pages,
          /*out*/tv_t *vectors);
```

This function retrieves vectors for a set of URLs rather than a single one. Taking a set encourages a batch-oriented style of use, which potentially amortizes the cost of disk IOs over the retrieval of multiple vectors.

The type `conn_id_t` is a *page identifier* assigned to pages by our Connectivity Server [3]. As mentioned earlier, the Connectivity Server provides fast access to connectivity data for the Web: given an URL, it returns the pages that point to and are pointed to by the URL. Rather than deal directly with URLs, the Connectivity Server uses a set of densely packed integers to identify pages. Functions in the Connectivity Server convert between these integers and text URLs. In our work with the Connectivity Server, these identifiers have proven more convenient to handle in code than text URLs. By adopting them in the Term Vector Database, we not only gain this convenience, but we also gain easy interoperation with the Connectivity Server, supporting interesting applications (see, for example, Section 3.3).

The type `tv_t` is defined as follows:

```
typedef struct tv_pair_s {
      int tid; /* Term identifier. */
      float weight;
} tv_pair_t;

typedef struct tv_s {
      conn_id_t pageid;
      int len; /* Number of pairs in
                  vector */
      tv_pair_t e[TV_MAX_VECTOR_LEN];
} tv_t;
```

Notice the use of integers to represent terms; as with page ids in the Connectivity Server, we find these to be more convenient to manipulate than text strings. Notice the use of `float` for weights. As mentioned earlier, term vectors in the database use simple counts as weights, so these vectors always have integral counts. However, applications often normalize vectors or combine them in ways that produce non-integral weights.

2.3. Data representation

An instance of the Term Vector Database is stored as a single file. This file is split into four sections: the header section which contains assorted database-wide information, the index section which maps from page ids to physical locations of vector data, the term vectors section which stores the vector data in a compressed format, and the term text section which maps from term identifiers to the actual term text.

The rest of this subsection describes the implementation details of the vector and index data. Readers not interested in this level of detail may want to skip to the next subsection.

The main section of a Term Vector Database file is the term vectors section, which contains the actual term vector data. This section is a sequence of fixed-length (128-byte) records in the following format.

- The page id of the vector is stored in the first 4 bytes of the vector's record.
- The terms in the vector are stored as a sequence of integer identifiers. The term ids are stored in a variable-length format consisting of a two-bit field giving the length `L` of the integer plus `L` bits giving the actual integer. The two-bit length field is actually an index into a table of bit counts stored in the header section of the database file.
- The counts of terms are stored in the bytes following the term identifiers. These are stored as count/run-length pairs because many counts appear many times within a vector (terms within a vector are sorted by count to maximize these run lengths).

  In most cases, a count/run-length pair is stored as a single byte consisting of a prefix code for the count in the high-order bits plus the run length stored in the low-order bits. Like the term id length code, this prefix code is stored in the header of the database file.

  There are some cases where the count/run-length may require two or even three bytes of storage. First, the prefix code has an escape code for infrequent counts. In this case, the count is stored in an extra byte. Second, run lengths do not always fit in the low-order bits allotted to them. When such an overflow occurs, a run length of '0' is packed into the first byte and the run length is given in an extra byte. If both special cases apply (that is, the escape code is needed and the run length does not fit into the first byte), then the escape code and a run length of '0' are packed into the first byte, the count is given in the second byte, and the run length is given in the third.

This format provides good compression for vector data. However, even with compression, vectors sometimes do not fit into 128 bits. In this case, terms are removed from it (starting from the least frequent) until it will fit.

Recall that page identifiers are a dense set of integers. Given this and the fact that vector records are of fixed size, one might think we could simply use page identifiers as indices into the vector section. However, the Connectivity Server has more page identifiers than the Term Vector Database has vectors. This is because the Connectivity Server has page identifiers for many pages on the frontier of the crawl, that is, pages discovered by the crawler but not yet downloaded. To avoid wasting space, we pack vector records densely. To quickly find the vector for a particular identifier, we use the index section.

The index section contains an index for mapping page identifiers to indices of vector records. The index consists of a sequence of 64-byte entries, each providing a mapping for 480 page ids. The first 4-byte integer in an index entry is a base index for the entry. The next 60 bytes of an index entry is a vector of 480 bits indicating whether or not there is a term vector for a given id. To compute the offset of the vector data for page id `P`, one can proceed as follows. Divide `P` by 480 to find the appropriate index entry. The remainder of that division is the bit for `P` within that entry. Check that this bit is set. If so, let `L` be the number of bits that are set between the start of the index entry and the bit for `P`, that is, the number of vectors present in the database before `P` mapped by the same entry as `P`. Add `L` to the base index for the index entry, and one has the index for `P`.

2.4. *Software components*

The Term Vector Database consists of three main software components, illustrated in Fig. 1.

The page filter implements the policy described in Section 2.1 to convert pages to vectors. The output of the filter is stored in a 'raw format' that is about twice as big as the ultimate format. The Term Vector Database builder converts these raw vectors into the file representation described in Section 2.3; in addition to compressing the vectors, the builder sorts them according to page identifier. The final piece of software is the implementation of the API described in Section 2.2.

3. Experience

The Term Vector Database has been used in a variety of research projects. This section describes our experience so far. First, we describe the build process and give some quantitative data. Next, we

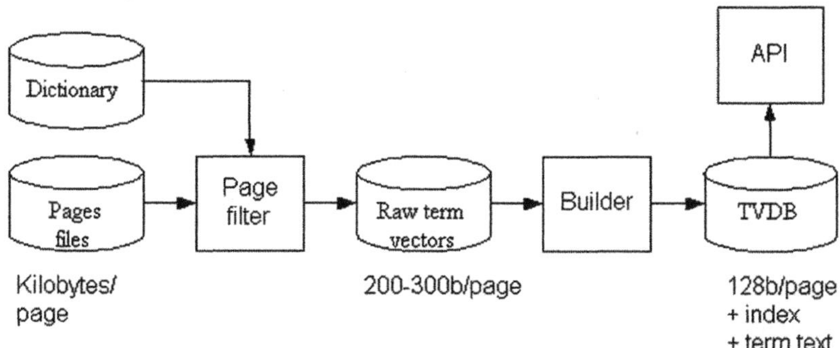

Fig. 1. Software components.

describe two projects built on top of the Term Vector Database: topic distillation and page classification.

3.1. Builds of the Term Vector Database

We have built the Term Vector Database on three different crawls of the Web performed by AltaVista. The page filter (the first box in Fig. 1) is run as part of a proprietary process. Once the raw vectors are produced, the builder is run to produce a database file. The most recent build of the Term Vector Database contains 272 M vectors and requires 33 GB of storage (32.5 GB for the term vectors section, 0.5 GB for the term text section, and a relatively small amount for the index and header sections). It took 11 hours to build this database on a 16 GB AlphaServer ES-40 with four 500-MHz processors. As described in Section 2.3, the build process may drop terms when the data for a vector cannot be compressed into 128 bytes. This build dropped terms from 5 M vectors, a little under 2%; in these 5 M vectors, an average of about 4 terms were dropped per vector.

Fig. 2 gives some histograms of our vector data. The plot on the left gives a histogram of vector sizes; the big jump at '50' occurs because the page filter clips all larger vectors to 50 terms. The plot on the right gives a histogram of term counts. Clearly, small counts dominate: 45% of terms in a vector have a count of 1; 99% of terms in a vector have a count of at most 31.

On an AlphaServer 4100, after the index section of the database file has been preloaded into the system's file cache, it takes 17 ms to access a random vector (approximately the cost of reading a random disk block).

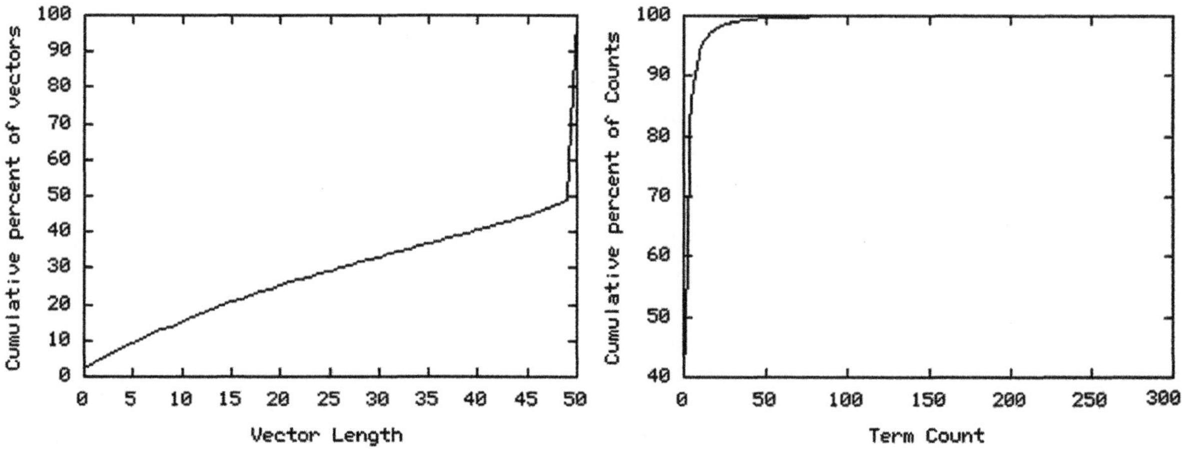

Fig. 2. Term vector statistics.

3.2. Topic distillation

Our first application of the Term Vector Database — indeed, the motivation for building it — was topic distillation. Topic distillation is a technique of using hyperlink connectivity to improve ranking of Web search results (see [1,3,4,6] for specific instances of topic distillation algorithms). These algorithms work on the assumption that some of the best pages on a query topic are highly connected pages in a subgraph of the Web that is relevant to the topic. A simple mechanism for constructing this query-specific subgraph is to seed the subgraph with top-ranked pages from a standard search engine and then expand this set with other pages in the vicinity of the seed set [6]. However, this expanded set sometimes includes highly connected pages that are not relevant to the query topic, reducing the precision of the final result. Bharat et al. [4] identify this problem as *topic drift*.

Bharat et al. [4] show that topic drift can be avoided by using *topic vectors* to filter the expanded subgraph. A topic vector is a term vector computed from the text of pages in the seed set. A page is allowed to remain in the expanded graph only if its term vector is a good match to this topic vector. Specifically, the inner product of the two vectors is compared to a suitable relevance threshold, and pages below the threshold are expunged from the expanded graph.

In the past, we computed term vectors and topic vectors by downloading pages from the Web after computing the initial subgraph. Downloading pages to compute vectors proved to be a significant bottleneck. We eliminated this bottleneck by re-implementing the algorithm on top of the Term Vector Database. The dramatic performance improvement provided by the Term Vector Database allows us to increase the size of our seed sets and expanded subgraphs while still reducing the overall time it takes to perform topic distillation.

This example illustrates how the Connectivity Server and Term Vector Database can be combined to produce interesting applications. Thus, it is beneficial to use page identifiers from the Connectivity Server as keys to the Term Vector Database. In the case of topic distillation, for example, the expanded subgraph is computed using the Connectivity Server, which means that the result is expressed in terms of Connectivity Server page identifiers. These identifiers are then given directly to the Term Vector Database without any translation.

3.3. Classifying Web pages

Perhaps one of the most interesting applications we have built so far is page classification.

Page classification is the process of categorizing pages as belonging to one of a number of a priori topics. We use a bayesian classifier implemented by term vector matching (see [5] for details). For categories, we use the 12 top-level categories in the *Yahoo* directory. For each of these categories, a *category vector* of 10,000 terms was precomputed from a training set of roughly 30,000 pages from Yahoo per category. A page is classified by retrieving its term vector from the Term Vector Database and matching it against each of the category vectors. The category with the highest resulting match score is selected as the category for the page. We only allow one category per page; ambiguous pages whose vectors are not definitively closer to one category over all other categories are not classified. For efficiency, the category vectors are combined into a sparse matrix implemented as an inverted index of terms.

We used this classification engine to build a cgi-proxy that augments AltaVista search results with *category tags*, text strings that indicate the dominant topic of the result page. For example, if a page predominately contains sports-related information, the tag `Recreation_or_Sports` is used to inform the user of this fact. These tags serve the same purpose as showing titles and abstracts with search results: they allow users to understand the topic of a result page without actually fetching it.

Fig. 3 is a screen shot of the results returned by our proxy given the ambiguous query 'bulls take over'

These results are annotated with tags such as `Business_and_Economy` and `Recreation_or_Sports` that indicate the general topic of the page.

The 'More on this topic' link lets users refine queries according to topic. In Fig. 3, when the user clicks on the 'More on this topic' link associated with the second result labeled `Recreation_or_Sports`, the user gets the refined result given in Fig. 4.

Mark **1. Bulls take over Wall St. - Jan. 5, 1999** Business_and_Economy *More on this topic*
Bulls take over Wall St. Optimistic investors push the Nasdaq Composite and S&P 500 to records How stocks in Canada performed today How other markets in...
URL: www.cnnfn.com/markets/9901/05/marketwrap/
Last modified 8-Jun-99 - page size 12K - in English [Translate]

Mark **2. The Triangle: Spectator - CitySearch** Recreation_or_Sports *More on this topic*
College, High School, Professional, Baseball/ Softball, Basketball, Fencing, Football, Golf, Gymnastics, Ice Sports/ Hockey...
URL: triangle.citysearch.com/The_Triangle/Spo...oors/Spectator/
Last modified 26-May-99 - page size 27K - in English [Translate]

Fig. 3. Example of categorized results.

The 'More on this topic' link leads to a result page devoted to the activities of the Chicago Bulls basketball team rather than activities on the stock market. (Northern Light's *custom folders* are a different user interface to the same refinement functionality. Our UI provides the users with information about the predominant topic of items in a result list; Northern Light's UI allows users to refine their search according to a given topic even if a page belonging to that topic is not in the current list of search results.)

For our 12-category configuration, the inverted term index is small enough to keep in memory, so we are able to tag result pages dynamically as they come through the proxy without noticeable overhead. If

1. CyberSight: The Bulls Take Five!
Take Five! by Justin (age 15) STARTING LINE-UP. The Bulls have taken all days, the Bulls took their fifth championship...
http://www.lincolnnet.net/cybersight/bulls-jay.html 3207

2. Augusta Georgia: sports@ugusta: Bulls take 5th title in 7 years 6/14/97
sports@ugusta -- Augusta, Georgia: Metro news and information from T daily and as news happens....
http://augustachronicle.com/stories/061497/spo_nba.html 2

3. Bulls take the fight out of Knicks
Download the new Microsoft Explorer browser right here! SportsFlash S Sports | Little League Kids Soccer | Golf Guide Sports on..
http://www.greatlinks.com/knicks/stories/1210bulls.html 1

4. WashingtonPost.com: Bulls Take Jazz by the Horn, 97-85
More information on the Chicago Bulls and the Utah Jazz is available in NBA Finals Section. Go to NBA Section. Go to Sports...
http://www.washingtonpost.com/wp-srv/sports/nba/longterm/ 11323 11-Jun-99

5. Bulls refuse to take a seat
Saturday June 6, 1998 SALT LAKE CITY. Reply RELATED SECTIONS: S sports. Home | Top stories | Contents | Help. Bulls...
http://www.spokane.net/stories/1998/Jun/6/S402252.asp 965

Fig. 4. Refined results.

the overhead is unacceptable, or if a larger set of category vectors needs to be matched, an alternative would be to classify and tag pages in advance.

4. Future work

We will continue using the database to build new applications. However, based on our experience so far, we also plan to make improvements to the Term Vector Database itself.

The biggest area of change will be in the definition of term vectors. We will look for term candidates in more places, such as `alt` text in tags and link text on incoming links. We will be supporting multi-word terms. We will be switching to a table-based stemmer, which will both improve performance and allow support for multiple languages. We will explore weights for terms that are influenced by markup (for example, give higher weightings to terms in titles), and we will explore alternative lexicons.

Another area of fruitful research would be in improvements to the compression of vectors. We would like to cut the storage requirements of the database in half, which would allow it to fit in a reasonable amount of RAM, either on a single large machine or partitioned across multiple, smaller machines. Our current compression techniques work mostly by eliminating redundancy from within individual vectors; we are unlikely to achieve another factor of two by continuing down that path. The next path to explore is eliminating redundancy across vectors.

5. Conclusions

Term vectors have proven themselves to be a robust and useful data structure for information retrieval. Our work has shown that a database that quickly maps from page identifiers to term vectors enables a variety of Web information retrieval applications. We believe this database will be especially interesting when combined with other Web-specific sources of information such as the Connectivity Server.

References

[1] S. Chakrabarti, B. Dom, D. Gibson, J. Kleinberg, P. Raghavan and S. Rajagopalan, Automatic resource list compilation by analyzing hyperlink structure and associated text, in: Proc. 7th International World Wide Web Conference, 1998.

[2] R. Baeza-Yates and B. Ribeiro-Neto, Modern Information Retrieval, Addison-Wesley/ACM Press, 1999.

[3] K. Bharat, A. Broder, M. Henzinger, P. Kumar and S. Venkatasubramanian, The Connectivity Server: fast access to linkage information on the Web, in: Proc. 7th International World Wide Web Conference, August 1998, pp. 104–111.

[4] K. Bharat and M. Henzinger, Improved algorithms for topic distillation in a hyperlinked environment, in: Proc. 21st International ACM SIGIR Conference on Research and Development in Information Retrieval, August 1998, pp. 104–111.

[5] T. Kalt and W.B. Croft, A new probabilistic model of text classification and retrieval, University of Massachusetts, 1996, http://ciir.cs.umass.edu/info/psfiles/irpubs/ir-78.ps.gz.

[6] J. Kleinberg, Authoritative sources in a hyperlinked environment, in: Proc. 9th ACM-SIAM Symposium on Discrete Algorithms, 1998, Also appeared as IBM Research Report RJ 10076, May 1997.

[7] M.F. Porter, An algorithm for suffix stripping, Program 14(3) (1980) 130–137.

[8] G. Salton, The SMART Retrieval System — Experiments in Automatic Document Processing, Prentice-Hall, Englewood Cliffs, NJ, 1971.

[9] G. Salton and C. Buckley, Term weighting approaches in automatic text retrieval, Information Processing and Management 24(5) (1988) 513–523.

[10] K. Sparck Jones and P. Willet (Eds.), Readings in Information Retrieval, Morgan Kaufmann, San Mateo, CA, 1997.

Raymie Stata received his Ph.D. from the Massachusetts Institute of Technology in 1996. Afterwards, he joined the Systems Research Center as a member of the research staff. He is interested in a broad spectrum of Web-related issues, including: Web information retrieval, extraction and mining; Web security; Web servers; and the creation of new Web applications.

Krishna Bharat is a member of the research staff at Google Inc. in Mountain View, California. Formerly he was at Compaq Computer Corporation's Systems Research Center, which is where the research described here was done. His research interests include Web content discovery and retrieval, user interface issues in Web search and task automation, and relevance assessments on the Web. He received his Ph.D. in Computer Science from Georgia Institute of Technology in 1996, where he worked on tool and infrastructure support for building distributed user interface applications.

Farzin Maghoul is a member of the engineering staff at AltaVista Corporation. His research interests include relevance and ranking, semantic topic clusters, and text summarization. He received his MS in Computer Science from Indiana University in 1977.

How dynamic is the Web? ☆

Brian E. Brewington [1], George Cybenko [1]

Thayer School of Engineering, Dartmouth College, Hanover, NH 03755-8000, USA

Abstract

Recent experiments and analysis suggest that there are about 800 million publicly-indexable Web pages. However, unlike books in a traditional library, Web pages continue to change even after they are initially published by their authors and indexed by search engines. This paper describes preliminary data on and statistical analysis of the frequency and nature of Web page modifications. Using empirical models and a novel analytic metric of 'up-to-dateness', we estimate the rate at which Web search engines must re-index the Web to remain current.

Keywords: Web dynamics; Monitoring; Document management

1. Introduction

Since its inception scarcely a decade ago, the World Wide Web has become a popular vehicle for disseminating scientific, commercial and personal information. The Web consists of individual pages linked to and from other pages through Hyper Text Markup Language (HTML) constructs. The Web is patently decentralized. Web pages are created, maintained and modified at random times by thousands, perhaps millions, of users around the world.

Search engines are the indexes of the Web, playing the role of traditional library catalogs. However, a book or magazine does not change once it is published, whereas Web pages typically do. Therefore, Web search engines must occasionally re-visit pages and re-index them to stay current. This is a constant challenge considering that recent empirical studies by Lawrence and Giles [8] have estimated the size of the publicly-indexable Web to be at least 800 million pages (and climbing). The size of the Web is only one factor in the re-indexing problem; the rate at which pages change is equally important.

This paper starts with a description of our observational data on the rates of change for a large sample of Web pages. Based on this data, we develop an exponential probabilistic model for the times between individual Web page changes. We further develop a model for the distribution of the change rates defining those exponential distributions. These two estimates can be combined to answer questions about how fast a search engine must re-index the Web to remain 'current' with respect to a novel definition of currency. We introduce the concept of (α, β)-currency which defines our notion of being up-to-

☆ This research was partially supported by AFOSR grant F49620-97-1-0382, DARPA grant F30602-98-2-0107 and NSF grant CCR-9813744. Any opinions, findings, and conclusions are those of the authors and do not necessarily reflect the views of the above agencies.

[1] E-mail: {brian.e.brewington,george.cybenko}@dartmouth.edu

date by using a probability, α, that a search engine is current, relative to a grace period, β, for a randomly selected Web page.

Our observational data is based on statistics gathered from over two million Web pages specified by over 25,000 users of a Web clipping service [5]. We have observed pages at a rate of about 100,000 pages per day, for a period of over seven months, recording how and when these pages have changed. The data indicate that the time between modifications of a typical Web page can be modeled by an exponential distribution, which is parameterized by the rate of changes for the page. Our data further indicate that the reciprocal of that parameter, which is the expected time between changes, is well-modeled by a Weibull distribution across pages.

As a measure of how up-to-date a search engine is, we develop the precise concept of (α, β)-currency of a search engine with respect to a changing collection of Web pages. Loosely speaking, the search engine data for a given Web page is said to be β-current if the page has not changed between the last time it was indexed and β time units ago. In this context, β is the 'grace period' for allowing unobserved changes to a Web page. A search engine for a collection of pages is then said to be (α, β)-current if a randomly (according to some specified probability distribution) chosen page in the collection has a search engine entry that is β-current with probability at least α.

To get an intuitive feeling for this concept, we might say that a daily newspaper is (0.90, 1 day)-current when it is printed, meaning that the newspaper has at least 0.9 probability of containing 1 day current information on topics of interest to its readers (this reader interest is the specified probability distribution). Here 1 day current means that events that have happened within the last day, namely the grace period, are not expected to be reported and we 'forgive' the newspaper for not reporting them. Similarly, hourly television news would be (0.95, 1 hour)-current and so on. The idea is that we are willing to 'forgive' an index or source if it is not completely up-to-date with respect to the grace period, but we have a high expectation that it is up-to-date with respect to that time.

Our empirical analysis of Web page changes is combined with existing estimates of the Web's size to estimate how many pages a search engine must re-index daily to maintain (α, β)-currency of the entire indexable Web. Using 800 million documents [8] as the size of the Web, we show that a (0.95, 1 week)-current search engine must download and index at least 45 million pages a day, which would require a bandwidth of around 50 megabits/second (using an average page size of approximately 12 kilobytes and assuming uniform processing). A (0.95, 1 day)-current search engine must re-index at the rate of at least 94 million pages daily, or 104 megabits/second. Our results allow estimation of re-indexing rates in order to maintain general (α, β)-currency of a Web index.

Previous work on Web page change rates has addressed the effect changing pages have on cache consistency [2]. The metrics used there focus on the effect of dynamics on Web caching, rather than on the Web page change dynamics themselves. For example, [2] uses a Web page 'change ratio', defined as the number of accesses to a changed page divided by the total number of accesses.

Our work also concerns the performance of a search engine in maintaining a Web index. In [1], a formal proof is given for the optimal sample period for monitoring a collection of pages that change memorylessly, under certain sampling conditions. Optimality is measured by a sum of total time out-of-date for pages in the index, where each term is weighted by expected time between page changes. Our measures are similar in spirit, but introduce a temporal and probabilistic relaxation of what it means to be up-to-date, namely the concept of (α, β)-currency.

2. Collecting Web page change data

Since early 1996, we have maintained a Web clipping service called **The Informant**[2] that downloads and processes on the order of 100,000 Web pages daily. The service monitors specific URLs for changes, and also runs standing user queries against one of four search engines[3] at specified intervals. Any of three events trigger a notification of a user by email.

[2] http.//informant.dartmouth.edu.

[3] AltaVista, Excite, Infoseek, and Lycos.

The user is notified by email if (1) a monitored URL changes, (2) new results appear in the top results returned by a search engine in response to a standing query, or (3) any of the current top search results shows a change. A change, for our purposes, is any alteration of the Web page, no matter how minor.

Beginning in March 1999, we started archiving HTML page summary information for all downloads. As of this writing, this has involved the download and processing of over 200 gigabytes of HTML data. The archived information includes the last-modified time stamp (if given), the time of observation (using the remote server's time stamp if possible), and stylistic information (number of images, tables, links and similar data). The Informant selects and monitors Web pages in a very specific way, so conclusions from the data must be interpreted only after knowing our sampling methods.

Since the Informant makes repeated observations of only those pages ranked high by search engines, this biases against those pages which are not relevant to our users' standing queries. Our sample is also biased towards the individual user-selected URLs which have been deemed worth monitoring. While neither of these is crippling, they do color our results by being slanted towards those pages that our users wish to monitor. We do not claim that this bias is a popularity bias, since our users' queries are not necessarily the same as those which are of general interest.

Another important consideration is the sample rate. Standing queries are run no more often than once every three days for any single user, and some users' queries are run once every seven days or more. Therefore, the only way a page is observed more than once every three days is if it is needed by a different user on each of those days. A number of popular sites (news sites, shareware distributors, proficient 'keyword spammers') fall into this category. Moreover, to keep our service from annoying providers of popular content, we cache pages (and delete the cache prior to gathering each day's results), so no more than one observation is made of a single page per day. In addition, since we run our queries periodically and only at night, sample times for any given page are correlated.

Many monitored sites exhibit a partial overlap between users, resulting in observations being made at irregular intervals. For extremely fast-changing pages, it is quite possible that many changes will occur between observations, making direct observation of all such changes impossible. When `LAST-MODIFIED` information is given in the `HTTP` header, we can work around this by estimating change rates from ages. This will be discussed in greater detail in later sections.

While `LAST-MODIFIED` information is available for around 65% of our observations, the absence of such information does seem to indicate a more volatile resource. Specifically, not having this timestamp makes an observation of any given resource about twice as likely to show a modification. Therefore, estimates of change rates based solely on pages that provide a timestamp are lower bounds (slowest estimate). Timestamps also show, indirectly, that most Web pages are modified during the span of US working hours (between around 8 AM and 8 PM, Eastern time). This is shown in Fig. 1. This is where any assumption of stationarity in change probability will break down; modifications are less likely during the low times on this plot.

Not surprisingly, there is a correlation between the style of a Web page and its age. For example, in Fig. 2, we show how the distribution of content-lengths and number of images depends upon age. Each plot shows two distributions, one using data from pages last modified between 6/94 and 6/95, and the other using pages between 6/98 and 6/99, to show how newer pages are frequently longer and have more images. Both distributions in the figure argue for the importance of space-saving technology (such as compression techniques written into the HTTP-1.1 standard, cascading style sheets (CSS), and use of Extended Markup Language (XML) where appropriate). Similar trends, sometimes much more pronounced, are seen in the usage of second-generation tags, such as the `<TABLE>` and `<FORM>` tags. While it might be feasible to use stylistic cues to estimate ages for pages which do not provide a timestamp, a far better solution is for content providers to include one along with an estimated expiration time. This potentially has many benefits, including better cache performance and fewer wasted observations by search engines (if honesty in expiration estimation is enforced).

A popular question regarding our data is, "What about dynamically-generated pages?" We can deter-

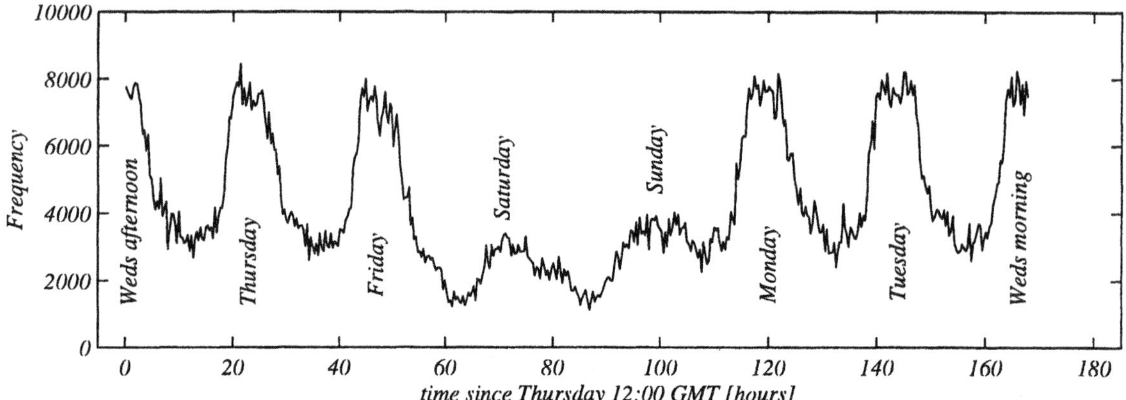

Fig. 1. Histogram: last-modified times (GMT), mod 24 × 7 hours. Peaks in modification frequency are clearly visible during US working hours, and diminish on weekends. Assumptions of stationarity in page alteration probability will break down at this scale.

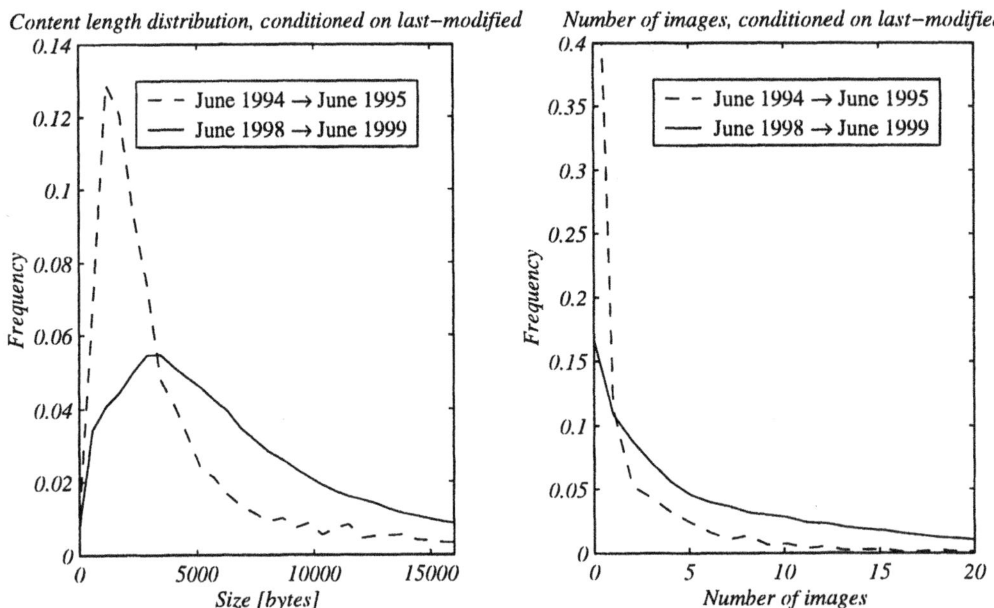

Fig. 2. Stylistic clues to Web page age. On the left, we show two distributions of content-length, or the number of bytes in a Web page. One is for pages dated between 6/94 and 6/95, and the other is for pages last modified between 6/98 and 6/99. Widespread use of space-intensive scripting languages and stylistic elements (<FONT> tags, precise table and image sizing, and so forth) has driven the content length upwards. On the right, a similar trend is seen in the number of images, often used in more recently modified pages to make a more visually appealing presentation. Much of this reflects the shift from an academic-centric Web to a commercial-centric one.

mine an upper bound on what percentage of pages are dynamic by looking at how many pages change on every repeat observation. Following [2], we can plot a cumulative distribution function of 'change ratios' as in Fig. 3. As mentioned in the introduction, a change ratio is defined by the number of changes observed, divided by the number of repeat accesses made. Obviously, this statistic depends heavily upon the sample rate, but it does give a feeling for the distribution of change rates. We have plotted change ratios corresponding to pages which had been observed six times or more. A unit ratio indicates a

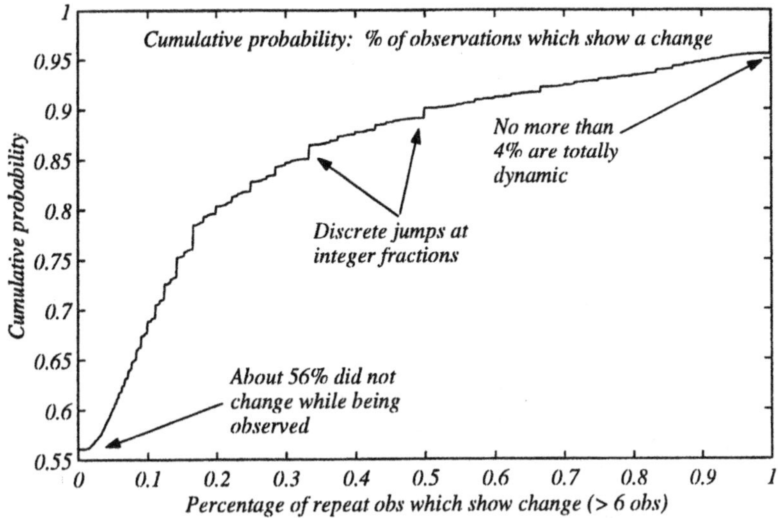

Fig. 3. Cumulative distribution of change ratios. The 'change ratio' for a page is defined as the number of changes observed divided by the number of repeat accesses. We have plotted the cumulative distribution of this statistic for pages which have been observed six times or more. This shows that no more than 4% of these pages are totally dynamic, while we have never observed any sort of change for 56% of pages. These values are very dependent upon the sampling scheme and are therefore not comparable to numbers taken from Web cache-based studies.

resource that always changes faster than the sample rate, meaning it may be totally dynamic, although it may just change very quickly. The plot shows that 4% of pages changed on every repeat observation (70% of these pages did not give a timestamp), while no change was observed for 56% of pages. The average page is observed 12 times over an average of 37 days, so this portion of pages that did not change would be much smaller if the monitoring was over a longer timespan.

The difference between a downloaded page's last-modified timestamp and the time at downloading is defined as the page's *age*. Recording the ages of the pages in the Informant database allows us to make several inferences about how those ages are distributed.

Estimates of the cumulative distribution function (CDF) and the probability density function (PDF) of page age are shown in Fig. 4. A few observations about these plots give insight into the distribution of document ages. About one page in five is younger than eleven days. The median age is around 100 days, so about half of the Web's content is younger than three months. The older half has a very long tail: about one page in four is older than one year and sometimes much older than that. In a few rare cases, server clocks are set incorrectly, making the timestamp inaccurate. The oldest pages that appear to have correct timestamps are from around 1992, some of which are 'archaeologically' interesting[4]. Our data on page age is similar to that found in an earlier study [2]; when the histograms in Fig. 4 are altered so that the bins have the same size as in [2], our distribution matches their data for 'infrequently-accessed' HTML pages.

Typical age observations are shown in Figs. 5 and 6. Since pages are only observed for as long as they remain in any user's search results, many single pages are only monitored for a limited time. As such, no alterations are ever observed on about 56% of the pages we have monitored[5]. This type of behavior is often appears like the examples shown in Fig. 5. When Web pages are more dynamic, their age samples look more like the examples in Fig. 6, where the pages have progressed through many changes and

[4] These may not be around for long; before they disappear, see http://www.w3.org/Out-Of-Date/... hypertext/DataSources/WWW/servers.html (a listing of Web servers from 1992) or http://www.hcc.hawaii.edu/guide/... www.guide.html (a Web guide from 1993).

[5] This statistic obviously depends upon the length of time we monitor a Web page.

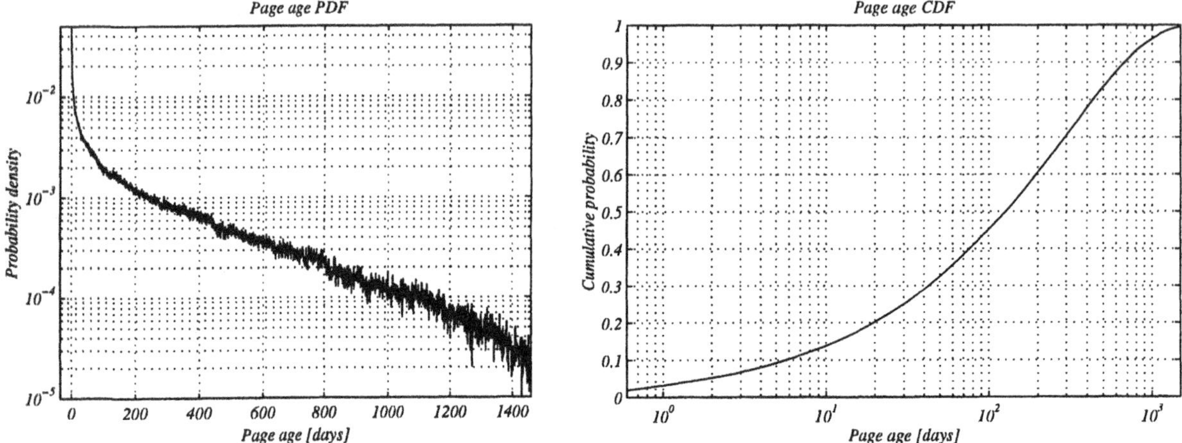

Fig. 4. Estimated distribution of Web page ages. Here we show estimates of the probability density function (PDF) and cumulative distribution function (CDF) of Web page age. On the left, we estimate the PDF using a rescaled histogram of Web page ages, using only one age observation per page. On the right, the corresponding CDF is formed by integrating the estimate of the PDF.

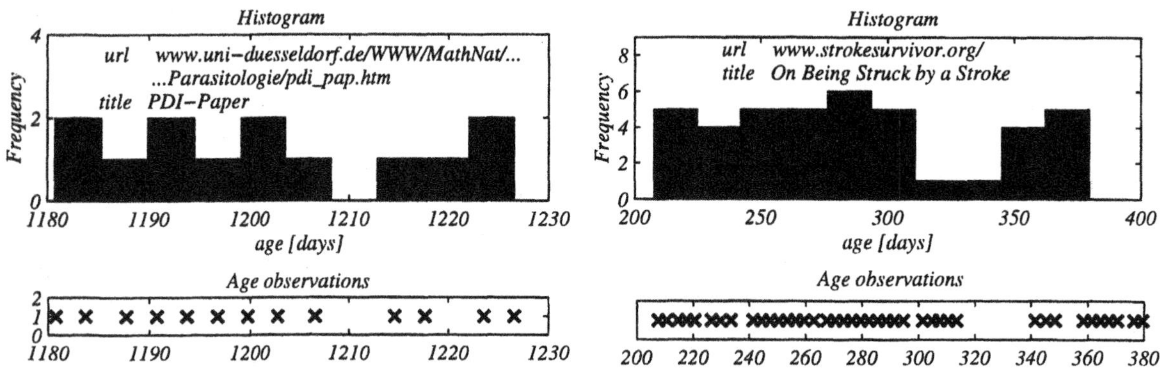

Fig. 5. Example age observations for relatively static pages. Many of the pages we monitor do not change during the time they are observed, like the examples shown here. The upper plots are histograms, and the lower plots show the raw data. These examples show that many of the pages are quite old, and for some of them, the only change they will ever experience is their eventual disappearance.

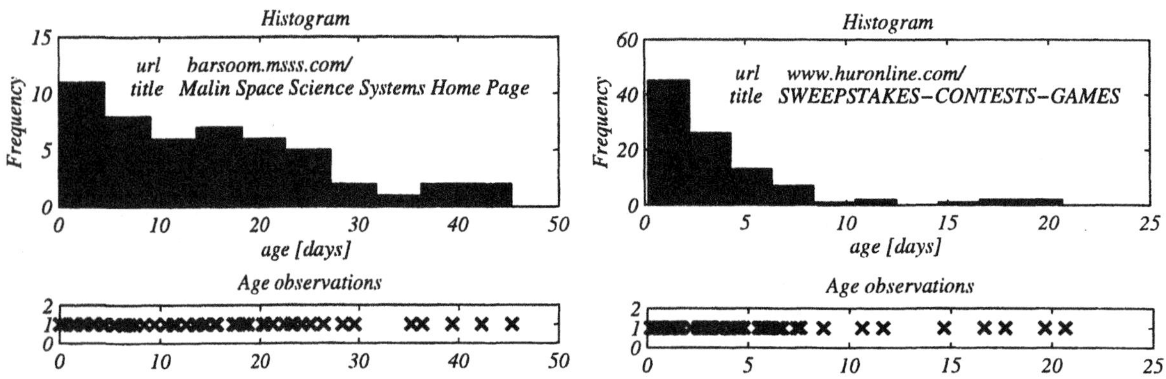

Fig. 6. Example age observations for changing Web pages. For some of our pages, we have observed a number of changes over a long timespan. The distribution of ages over this time is often approximately exponential, as can be seen in the histograms. The raw data is shown in the lower plots.

we have observed the ages over that time span. This usually produces distributions close to an exponential PDF. Some rapidly changing pages appear to be periodic, though the period is rarely larger than one day. Periodicity can be inferred from age distributions that appear to be approximately uniform. Still other pages are entirely dynamic, generated anew with each access, but these are not more than 4% of our collection.

3. Modeling the changes in a single page

To make further analysis possible, we model the changes in a single Web page as a renewal process [10]. A good example and analogy is a system of replacement parts. Imagine a light fixture into which we place a lightbulb. Whenever that bulb burns out, it is replaced immediately. We speak of the time between lightbulb failures as the 'lifetime' of a bulb. At a specific instant, we define the time since the present lifetime began to be the 'age' of the bulb. The analogy to Web page changes is that a page's lifetime is the time between changes (where change is arbitrarily but unambiguously defined). The age is the time between a given instant and the most recent change prior to that instant. We diagram these concepts in Fig. 7.

In this initial study, we assume that individual lifetimes are independent and identically distributed, and that the lifetime distribution of a particular page does not change over time (the distribution is stationary). Not surprisingly, the lifetime probability density, $f(t)$, is closely related to the age probability density, $g(t)$. The act of observing "the age is t units" is the same as knowing "the lifetime is no smaller than t units". Intuitively, this indicates that the PDF $g(t)$ should be proportional to the probability $1 - F(t)$ of a given lifetime exceeding t units, where $F(t)$ is the CDF corresponding to $f(t)$. To make $g(t)$ a proper probability distribution, the constant of proportionality is chosen so that $g(t)$ is normalized. This intuition proves correct and formal methods [10] show that:

$$g(t) = \frac{1 - F(t)}{\displaystyle\int_0^{\infty} [1 - F(t)]\,\mathrm{d}t}. \tag{1}$$

Some examples of this relationship are shown in Fig. 8.

Establishing the relationship of age to lifetime is useful, since it is difficult to sample the distribution $f(t)$ directly. Rather, it can be easier to estimate change rates using samples from the age distribution $g(t)$ and then use (1) to estimate $F(t)$ and then $f(t)$. Aliasing of $f(t)$ may happen when a page change is observed, since an observer can only conclude that one *or more* changes have occurred since the previous observation. In observing ages, there is no such difficulty. Avoiding the aliasing problem is not magic; we are merely making proper use of the fact that the file systems on which the pages reside have sampled much faster than we can. Clearly, observation of a Web page age requires the availability of the LAST-MODIFIED information, which restricts our analysis to a smaller sample.

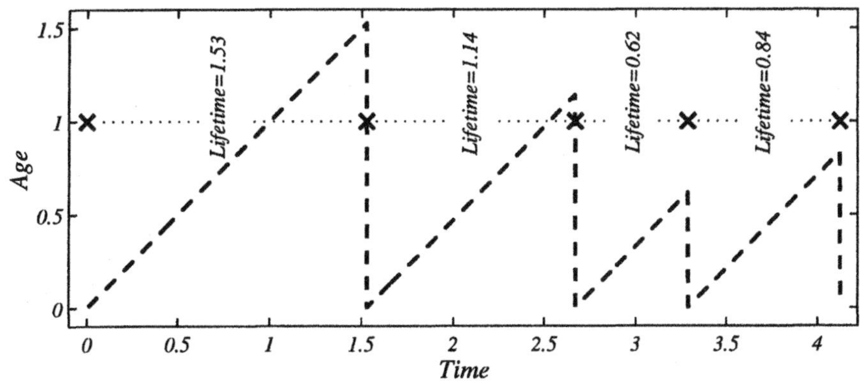

Fig. 7. Lifetimes vs. ages. A single lifetime is represented by the time separating changes, which are denoted by ×'s in the graph. For each lifetime, the age (shown as a dashed line) increases linearly from 0 to the lifetime, then resets to 0 as the next lifetime begins.

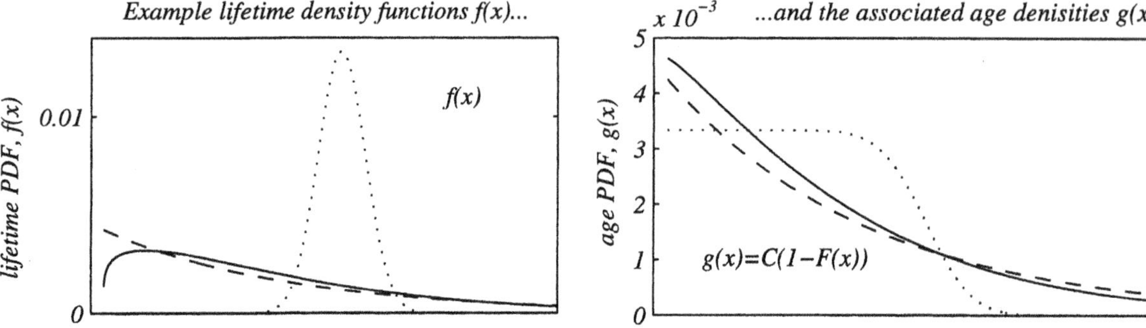

Fig. 8. Relationship between lifetime and age distributions. On the left, we show three hypothetical lifetime distributions; a Gaussian (dotted), Weibull (solid), and an exponential (dashed). On the right, we show the corresponding age distributions. For the Gaussian, the age distribution is a renormalized and shifted complementary error function (erfc). For the exponential, the age and lifetime distributions are identical. The age distribution for the Weibull has a more general shape. Note that periodic lifetimes imply uniform age distributions.

The simplest possible page lifetime model, and a good one to use for this initial investigation, is one in which pages change memorylessly. Intuitively, this means that the probability of a page being altered in some short time interval is independent of how much time has elapsed since the last change was made. This is a common model used in queuing systems and statistical reliability theory [10]. For such pages, $f(t)$ is an exponential distribution with parameter λ. This distribution is a good choice, since much of our data on page changes show behavior like that shown in Fig. 6. As for the more slowly-changing content, like the examples shown in Fig. 5, it is certainly possible that these pages are not at all dynamic or that they change at a very low rate. We proceed with the assumption that all pages are dynamic, even if the only change they will ever experience is their disappearance. For these longer lifetimes, the best we can do is to obtain several (dependent) samples of the age distribution. Pages for which $f(t)$ is an exponential distribution also have exponentially distributed ages $g(t)$, since:

$$\begin{aligned}1 - F_c(t) &= 1 - (1 - e^{-\lambda t}) \\ &= e^{-\lambda t}\end{aligned}$$

implies

$$g(t) = \frac{1 - F_c(t)}{\int_0^\infty [1 - F_c(t)]\,dt} = \frac{e^{-\lambda t}}{\int_0^\infty e^{-\lambda t}} = \lambda e^{-\lambda t}. \qquad (2)$$

This means we can estimate a page's lifetime PDF, assuming an exponential distribution, using only page age observations which we easily obtain from the data.

4. Dealing with a growing Web

It is clear from the empirical page age distribution shown in Fig. 4 that the majority of Web pages are young. What is less clear is why. Different explanations can give rise to the same observed age distribution. One the one hand, a fixed population of pages whose change times are governed by identical exponential PDF's will produce an exponential age distribution when sampled collectively, as in (2). At the other extreme, an exponentially growing population of Web pages in which changes are rare or even nonexistent will be skewed towards youth as well — there will be exponentially more pages in one generation relative to the previous generation.

The middle ground is an exponentially growing Web in which each page changes at time intervals determined by an exponential. Such a model will also yield an exponential distribution of page ages when sampled.

Consider two very different models for the Web. First, an exponentially-growing population of completely static Web pages will produce an exponential distribution of observed page ages. To see this, note that the population at time t is given by an expression of the form where P_0 is the initial population and is the exponential growth rate parameter. An age distribution at time can be formed by reversing the sense of time, and normalizing by the population size:

$$g_{\text{growing}}(t,\tau) = \begin{cases} \dfrac{\xi e^{-\xi t}}{1 - e^{-\xi \tau}}, & t \in [0,\tau], \\ 0, & t \notin [0,\tau]. \end{cases} \tag{3}$$

This distribution will approach an exponential density with parameter ξ as τ gets large.

But an exponential distribution of page ages can arise for completely different reasons. Consider a fixed-size group of identical pages, each of which changes at time intervals governed by an exponential distribution. Each page undergoes many changes, with each change returning that page to age zero. Such a population also gives rise to essentially an exponential age distribution (see 2). In particular, the age distribution for such a population is:

$$g_{\text{dynamic}}(t,\tau) = \begin{cases} \lambda e^{-\lambda t}, & t \in (0,\tau), \\ (e^{-\lambda \tau})\delta(t-\tau), & t = \tau, \\ 0, & t \notin [0,\tau]. \end{cases} \tag{4}$$

As the time since the population's birth, τ, becomes large, the distribution of observed page ages will also approach an exponential distribution and will be hard to distinguish from that of a growing population of unchanging Web pages. The hybrid model we use in this paper represents the middle ground — the Web is growing *and* pages change according to exponential time distributions. These are reasonable working assumptions.

We now combine the effects of Web growth and page change dynamics. The Web has been growing for several years so that the time since creation of Web pages is distributed approximately exponentially:

$$h(t_c) = \xi e^{-\xi t_c}$$

where ξ is the growth rate and t_c is the time since creation of a page. We emphasize that t_c is not to be confused with our definition of the page's age, since age refers to the time since the last modification.

For an exponentially-growing population of dynamic pages, each of which has an exponential age distribution as described by (4), the aggregate age distribution $g(t,\lambda)$ will be a weighted average over time since creation, weighted by the number of pages created at the same time. Specifically:

$$g(t,\lambda) = \int_0^\infty g(t,\lambda,t_c)h(t_c)\,dt_c, \tag{6}$$

$$g(t,\lambda) = \int_0^\infty \xi e^{-\xi t_c} e^{-\lambda t_c}\delta(t-t_c)\,dt_c + \int_0^\infty \xi e^{-\xi t_c}[U(t) - U(t-t_c)]\lambda e^{-\lambda t}\,dt_c, \tag{7}$$

$$g(t,\lambda) = \xi e^{-(\xi+\lambda)t} + \int_0^\infty \xi e^{-\xi t_c}\lambda e^{-\lambda t}\,dt_c - \int_0^t \xi e^{-\xi t_c}\lambda e^{-\lambda t}\,dt_c,$$

$$g(t,\lambda) = \xi e^{-(\xi+\lambda)t} + \lambda e^{-\lambda t} - \lambda e^{-\lambda t}(1 - e^{-\xi t}),$$

$$g(t,\lambda) = (\xi + \lambda)e^{-(\xi+\lambda)t}. \tag{8}$$

This means that the age distribution of an exponentially growing population of objects with (identical) exponential age distributions remains exponential, with parameter given by the sum of the population growth and page change rate constants.

The age distribution for the entire population (namely the whole Web) is yet another mixture, in which we take expectation of (8) with respect to a joint distribution of growth rate ξ and change rate λ. For simplicity we use the same growth rate for all change rates. Using a distribution over the inverse rate $\lambda = 1/x$, with this uniform growth rate ξ, we express the mixture as:

$$g(t) = \int_0^\infty \left(\xi + \frac{1}{x}\right) e^{(\xi+1/x)t} w(x)\,dx. \tag{9}$$

The only factor remaining before this distribution can be matched to the data is the shape of the distribution $w(x)$ of inverse change rates. In our initial development, we use a generalized exponential (Weibull) distribution over the inverse change rate (which is also the mean change time), such that:

$$w(t) = \frac{\sigma}{\delta}\left(\frac{t}{\delta}\right)^{\sigma-1} e^{-(t/\delta)^\sigma} \tag{10}$$

where δ is a scale parameter and σ is a shape parameter. See [9] for a discussion of Weibull distributions, as well as a more general discussion of this family of exponential distributions in [3]. The shape parameter can be varied to change the shape from a very sharply-peaked distribution (for $\sigma < 1$) to an exponential (for $\sigma = 1$), to a unimodal distribution with maximum at some positive t (for $\sigma > 1$). The scale parameter δ adjusts the mean of the distribution.

To determine what values of ξ, σ, and δ best model the observations, we numerically evaluate (9) at a number of ages t. This is used to estimate the cumulative age distribution $G(t)$ at N points t_i. These estimates, $\hat{G}(t)$, are compared with samples from the empirical distribution $G(t)$ (as diagrammed in the left half of Fig. 4) at points t_i. A sum of the squared error over all sample times t_i provides a scalar error function of the vector (ξ, σ, δ). This error function can be minimized:

$$SE_{\mathrm{age}}(\xi, \sigma, \delta) = \frac{1}{N} \sum_{i=1}^{N} (\hat{G}(\xi, \sigma, \delta, t_i) - G(t_i))^2. \tag{11}$$

When this minimization is carried out numerically, the optimal values are found to be $\xi = 0.00176$, $\sigma = 0.78$, and $\delta = 651.1$. The fitted age distribution is shown in Fig. 9. These parameters imply a steeper-than-exponential age distribution (since $\sigma = 0.78$) and a growth rate that implies a doubling time of around 390 days. This is not unreasonable, as [7] estimated a lower bound size of 320 million pages in December 1997, which increased in [8] to 800 million pages by February 1999. This would imply a growth constant over the 14 months of $\xi = 0.0022$, or a doubling time of 318 days. The difference in these estimates tells us to proceed with caution, understanding that estimates based on these results are somewhat uncertain. Moreover, the assumption of exponential growth in the number of *documents* is based on assertions of exponential growth in the number of Web *hosts* (as in [4,6], for example). Growth rates have slowed appreciably, especially in the last year; other estimation methods prove more reliable.

5. Estimating the change rate distribution using lifetimes

As mentioned previously, inferring change rates from observed lifetimes is somewhat tricky, since an observed change may only be the most recent

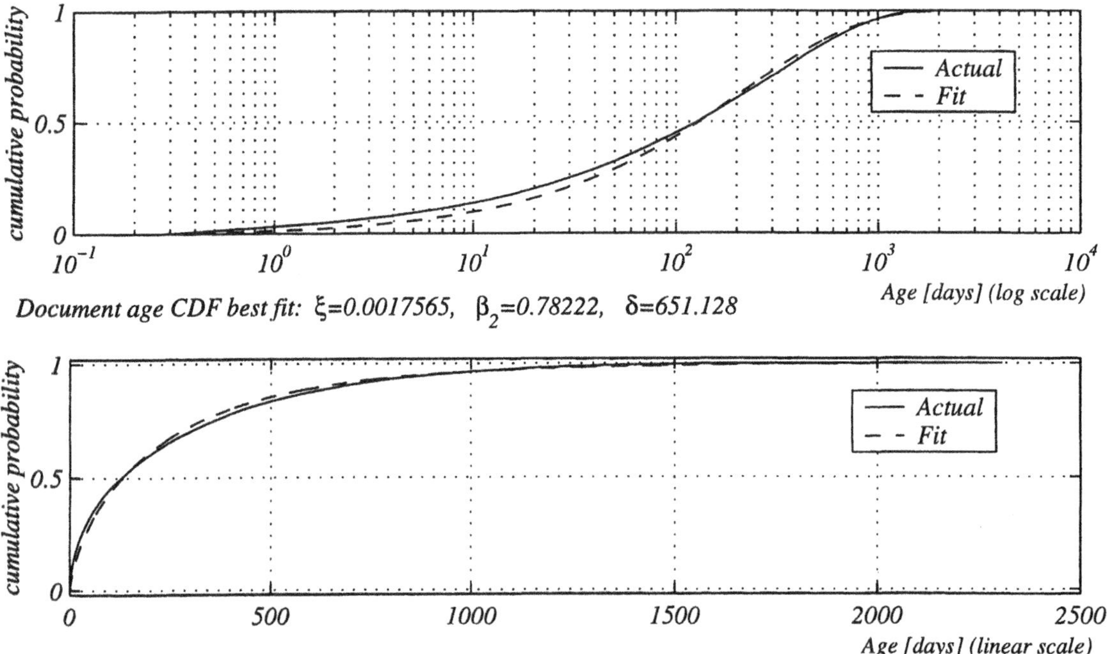

Fig. 9. Best-fit age CDF. These plots show the distribution which results from a numerical optimization of (11), yielding the values $\xi = 0.00176$ (growth rate), $\sigma = 0.78$ (shape parameter), and $\delta = 651.1$ (scale parameter). The top plot uses a log scale to show the deviations in the fit for small age. The minimization was carried out using linearly-spaced points.

of many changes that took place since the last observation. Moreover, changes that take a long time to happen are inherently more difficult to catch. For example, if one were to watch a calendar for three consecutive days, waiting for the month to change, there is a good chance that this event will not be observed. However, as the timespan gets longer it becomes more probable that a change will be seen. In the same way, it is necessary to account for the probability of observing a change, given the timespan of observation.

For a page which changes exponentially at rate λ, the probability that at least one change will be observed within a timespan τ is:

$$\Pr(\text{change observed} \mid \tau, \lambda) = 1 - e^{-\lambda\tau}. \tag{12}$$

The pages in our collection are observed over many different timespans τ. Therefore, to determine the probability of observing changes for pages having change rate λ, we assume that change rate and timespan are independent and weight (12) with respect to the probability of all possible observation timespans t_i (discretized):

$$\Pr(\text{change observed} \mid \lambda) = Z_{\text{bias}}(1/\lambda)$$

$$= \sum_{i=1}^{i=N} \Pr(\tau_i)(1 - e^{-\lambda\tau_i}). \tag{13}$$

Possible timespans t_i are distributed as shown in Fig. 10. Combining this data with (13) allows us to compute Z_{bias} weighting each mean lifetime's probability of being among the observed data. The

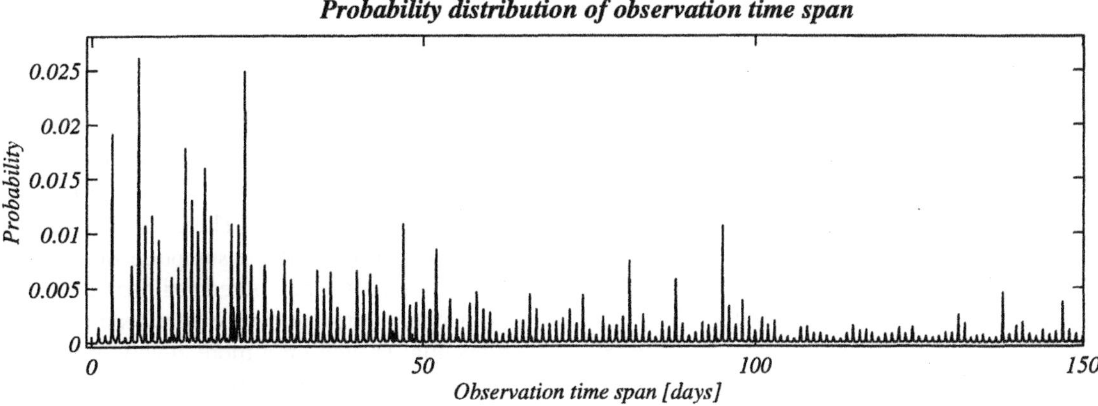

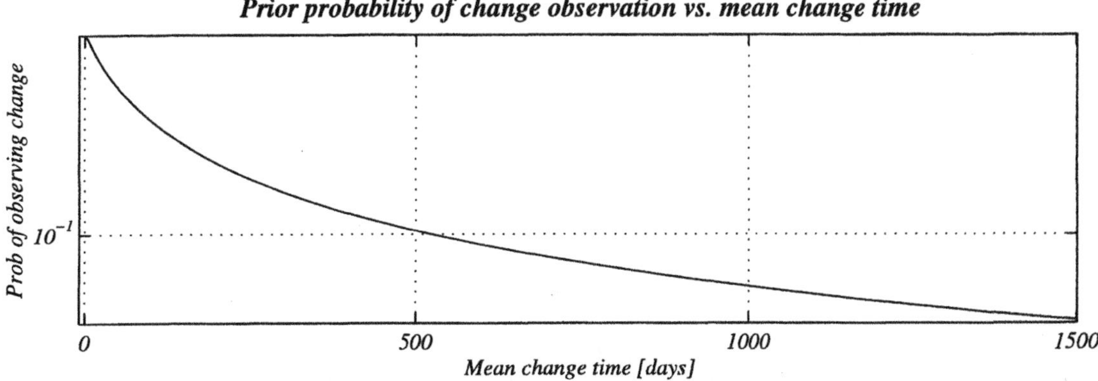

Fig. 10. Observation time distribution and induced finite time span bias. The top plot shows the distribution of observation time spans, or the time difference between the first and last observation timestamps for individual pages. The spikes appear in this graph because we only run our checks at night, so timespans tend to cluster around 24-hour intervals. Using (13), these timespans translate into the probability of any mean change time being represented among our observed Web page changes.

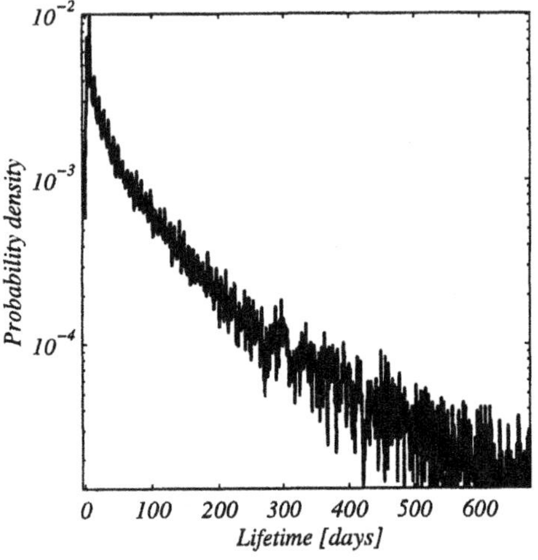

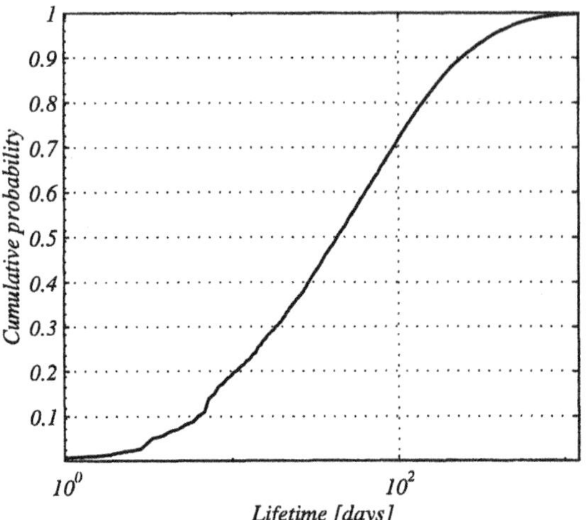

Fig. 11. PDF and CDF of observed lifetimes. On the left, a rescaled histogram approximates the PDF of observed lifetimes, or differences in successive modification timestamps. On the right, we show the corresponding CDF.

distribution of change rates sampled in our experiment is not the true rate distribution, but rather one that is weighted by (13). If the *actual* density of mean lifetimes is $f_{\text{mean}}(t)$, then the *observed* density of mean lifetimes is:

$$f'_{\text{mean}}(t) = \frac{f_{\text{mean}}(t) Z_{\text{bias}}(t)}{\displaystyle\int_0^{\infty} f_{\text{mean}}(t) Z_{\text{bias}}(t)\,\mathrm{d}t}. \tag{14}$$

These mean lifetimes are only seen through a mixture of exponential distributions, so the observed lifetimes should approximate the probability density:

$$f_{\text{observed}}(t) = \int_0^{\infty} \lambda \mathrm{e}^{-\lambda t} f'_{\text{mean}}(1/\lambda)\,\mathrm{d}(1/\lambda). \tag{15}$$

As with the age-based estimates, we can form a mean squared-error function like (11) and fit the CDF corresponding to (15) to the observed lifetime distribution. We show the distribution of observed lifetimes in Fig. 11. Using $F(t)$ as the cumulative lifetime distribution, and $\hat{F}(\alpha, \delta, t)$ as the estimator, the error function is:

$$SE_{\text{lifetime}}(\alpha, \delta) = \frac{1}{N} \sum_{i=1}^{N} (\hat{F}(\sigma, \delta, t_i) - F(t_i))^2. \tag{16}$$

As before, we use a Weibull density (10) for the distribution of inverse rates (mean times) $\bar{t}$. This results in an error surface having a minimum at ($\sigma = 1.4$, $\sigma = 152.2$). An intensity plot of (16) is shown in Fig. 12. The CDF and its estimator are overlaid in Fig. 13, and the error in this fit is magnified in Fig. 14. Using our estimates, the *mean* lifetime PDF and CDF are shown in Fig. 15.

The lifetime-based estimates differ substantially from the age-based estimates, but are also more trustworthy, as can been seen by comparing the quality of the fit in Figs. 13 and 9. There are two reasons for the difference. First, the assumption of exponential growth used for the age-based estimation is probably a poor one, as true growth is much slower. Forcing exponential growth on a more slowly growing population forces the dynamics to be under-represented, driving our estimates away from their true value. The lifetime-based estimation is not perfect either, as change rates may not be independent of observation timespan. A change in a page might very well push it into or out of a user's set of search results. We count on the fact that in observing faster than the search engines, we can observe changes before these force a result from the top of the list. It is difficult to justify an assumption of any particular dependence, since this relationship is controlled by many unknown factors (re-indexing time for search engines used and result ranking strategy, for example).

6. How fast do search engines need to work

We now interpret our model of the constantly changing Web in terms of Web search engine perfor-

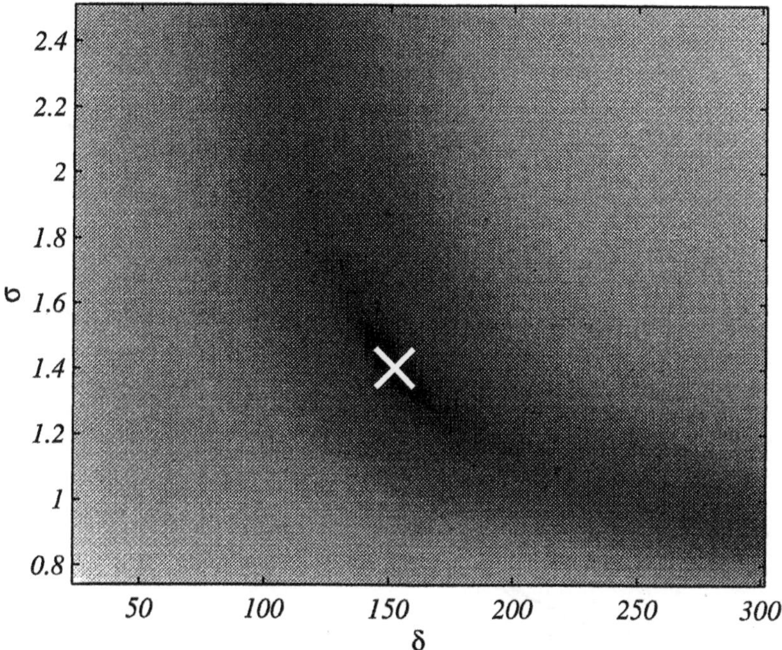

Fig. 12. Intensity plot of mean squared-error. The minimum of (16) in the space of shape parameters σ and scale parameters δ is marked by a white '×' in the center of the dark patch, at ($\sigma = 1.4$, $\delta = 152.2$). The error function appears to be unimodal.

mance. Our measure of performance is based on the intuitive concept of (α, β)-currency that we define below. Our Web model and this new performance measure will allow us to estimate the speed at which pages must be re-indexed in order to maintain a given level of currency.

Recall from Section 1 that a Web page's index entry in a search engine is β-current if the Web page has not changed since the last time the page was re-indexed and β time units ago. We are willing to forgive changes that have occurred within β time of the present. The grace period, β, relaxes the temporal aspect of what it means to be current. The smaller β is, the more 'current' our information about the page is. See Fig. 16 for a graphical depiction of the concept.

To determine whether or not an index entry for a Web page is β-current, we need to know the most recent time t_Δ at which the page changed. Assume that the page was last observed at time t_0. With this notation, the index entry corresponding to a page is β-current at time t_n if the page did not change between the last observation (at time t_0) and β units before the present, or time $t_n - \beta$ (assuming $t_0 \le t_n - \beta$). For $t_0 > t_n - \beta$, the entry is by definition β-current because the most recent unobserved page change can occur either within the grace period or before we observed the page at t_0, but this includes all past time.

Combining these two cases, the probability that the search engine entry for a page is β-current at time $t_n > t_0 + \beta$ is:

$$\begin{aligned} &\Pr(\text{a fixed Web page is } \beta\text{-current} \mid t_0, t_n) \\ &\quad = 1 - \Pr(t_0 \le t_\Delta \le t_n - \beta) \end{aligned} \tag{17}$$

where these probabilities are understood to be for a fixed, given Web page. We now compute the probability that the search engine index entry for a randomly (according to some probability distribution) selected Web page is β-current.

The above expression (17) for a single Web page is stated in terms of a conditional probability. Given a prior distribution on the variables t_0 and t_n, we can use Bayes' Theorem or the total probability theorem to eliminate them.

In our model, each Web page has a change rate λ and an associated distribution of re-indexing times T

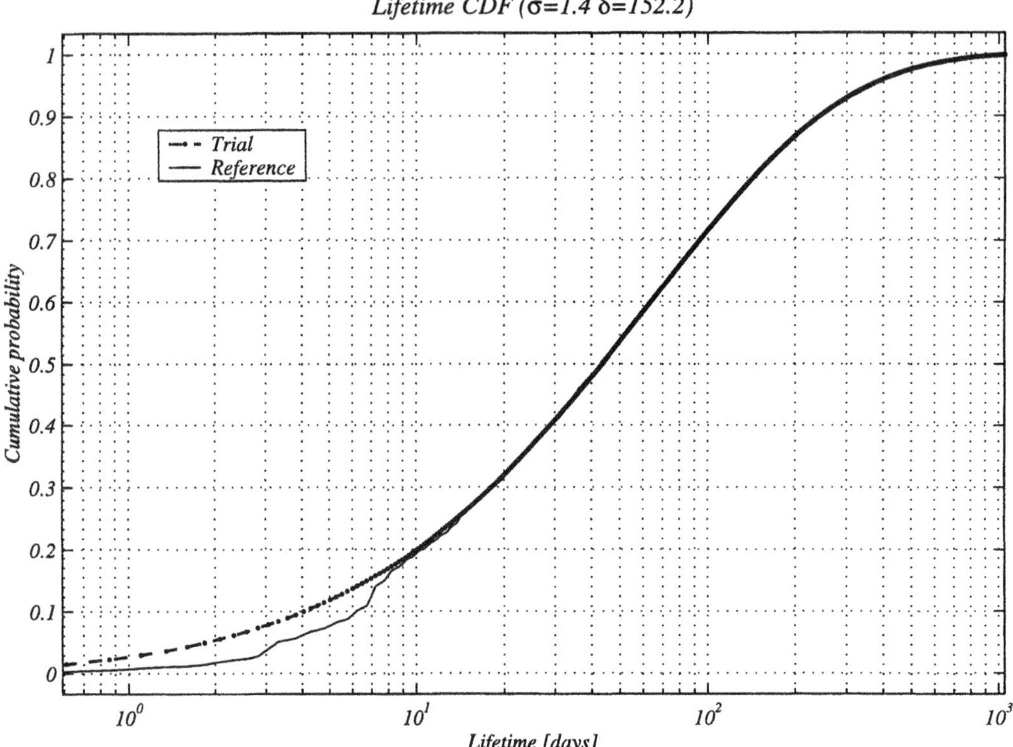

Fig. 13. Overlay of model lifetime CDF and observed CDF. The minimum error distribution (marked *Trial* above) found by minimizing (16) is shown along with the observed lifetime distribution (marked *Reference*). Errors in the fit below around 8 days are due to aliasing, where multiple changes are masked and treated as a single, larger lifetime. Our estimates are only extrapolations in this region and may be inaccurate. The region above 8 days is an extremely precise fit; the two curves are nearly identical.

(a periodic re-indexing system will have a single constant T_0). These parameters determine density functions which, together with the grace period β, specify the probability α of being β-current. First, define the probability Pr (a page is β-current | λ, T, β, t_n) to be the probability the of a single index entry being β-current given λ, T, β, and the time t_n at which the index is examined. Second, define the density $h(\lambda, T)$ to be the joint probability density for (λ, T). We assume that $h(\lambda, T)$ is independent of the time t_n, which is distributed according to a density $x(t_n)$. Using these densities and Bayes' Theorem, the probability α that the system is β-current is:

$$\begin{aligned}\alpha &= \Pr(\text{The search engine } \beta\text{-current}) \\ &= \iiint \Big[\Pr(\text{a single page is } \beta\text{-current} \mid \lambda, T, t_n) \\ &\qquad \times x(t_n)\,\mathrm{d}t_n\Big] h(\lambda, T)\,\mathrm{d}\lambda\,\mathrm{d}T. \qquad (18)\end{aligned}$$

The integral is restricted to the first octant since no negative times or rates are allowed. In some settings, it is reasonable to assume a dependence between T and λ, since different re-visitation periods are desirable for sources with different change rates.

We will now evaluate (18) for a single, memorylessly-changing page. As before, this page has a change rate λ, and is observed periodically (every T time units). The probability that the next page change occurs in the time interval $[t_1, t_2]$, where the last observation or change (whichever occurred most recently) was at time $t_0 \le t_1 < t_2$, is:

$$\int_{t_1-t_0}^{t_2-t_0} \lambda \mathrm{e}^{-\lambda t}\mathrm{d}t = \mathrm{e}^{-\lambda(t_1-t_0)} - \mathrm{e}^{-\lambda(t_2-t_0)}.$$

If $t_1 = t_0$, this reduces to $1 - \mathrm{e}^{\lambda(t_2-t_0)}$ so that the probability that a page change *did not occur* in the interval $[t_o, t_2]$ is the complement, $1-(1-\mathrm{e}^{\lambda(t_2-t_0)}) = \mathrm{e}^{\lambda(t_2-t_0)}$.

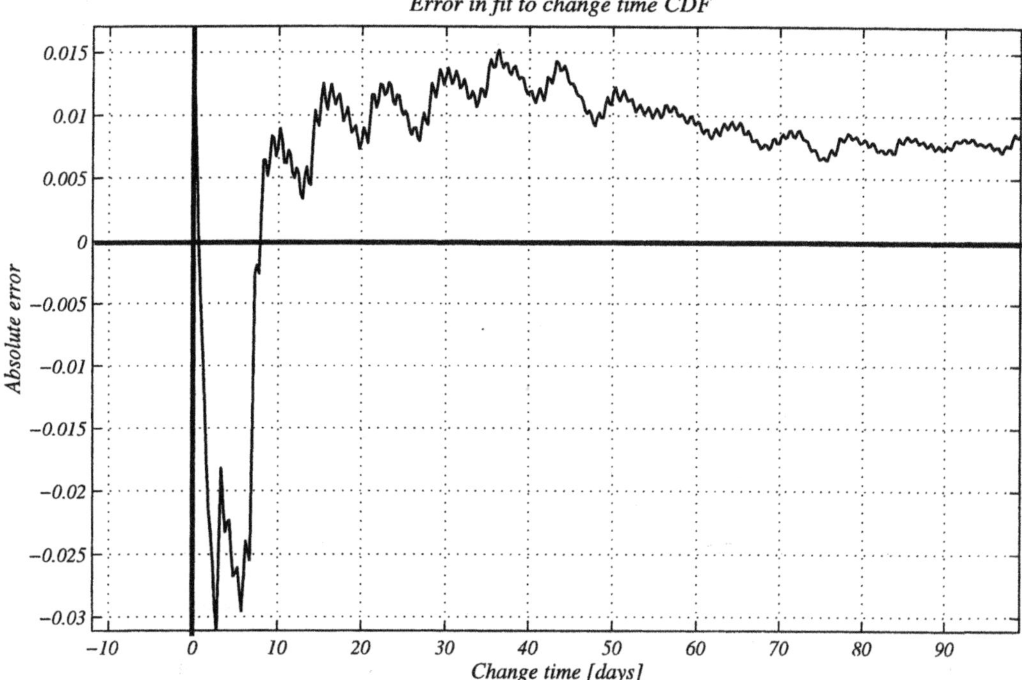

Fig. 14. Absolute error $\hat{F} - F$ vs. lifetime. These are the errors in the fit shown in Fig. 13; we have used a linear scale and just show the leftmost region. Note the large errors below around 8 days due to aliasing. The effect of diurnal and weekly trends, as plotted in Fig. 1, is clearly visible in the long and short period ripples above 8 days. Slight improvements in our estimates could be had if we restricted the fit to samples above 8 days.

To evaluate (18) we need to specify the function $h(\lambda, t)$ as well as the distribution of times $x(t_n)$ over which we average the β-currency of the index. First, we consider the limits on the inner integral over t_n. Assuming as we have that all the Web pages change memorylessly, it is sufficient to evaluate the inner integral in (18) over a single observation period T, since adding additional periods would only replicate the integral over one period.

For convenience, we choose an interval starting at $t_0 = 0$, at which time an observation was last made, and extends until the time T at which the next observation occurs. Using this interval, the probability that the page does not change between $t_0 = 0$ and $t = t_n - \beta$, and is therefore β-current, is by the above discussion:

$$\Pr(\beta\text{-current} \mid \lambda, T, t_n) = \mathrm{e}^{-\lambda(t_n - \beta)} \text{ for } \beta < t_n < T. \tag{19}$$

Further, note that the page is β-current with probability one in the interval $[t_n - \beta, t_n]$. Specifically:

$$\Pr(\beta\text{-current} \mid \lambda, T, t_n) = 1 \text{ for } 0 < t_n < \beta. \tag{20}$$

Combining these, the expected probability of a single page being β-current over all values of the observation time t_n, using a uniform density $x(t_n) = 1/T$, is just an average value of the piecewise-defined $\Pr(\beta\text{-current} \mid \lambda, T, t_n)$ on the interval $t_n \in [0, T]$. This gives:

$$\Pr(\beta\text{-current} \mid \lambda, T, B)$$

$$= \int_0^\beta \frac{\mathrm{d}t_n}{T} + \int_\beta^T \frac{1}{T}\mathrm{e}^{-\lambda(t_n - \beta)}\,\mathrm{d}t_n \tag{21}$$

$$= \frac{\beta}{T} + \frac{1 - \mathrm{e}^{-\lambda(T-\beta)}}{\lambda T}. \tag{22}$$

In the first integral of (21), the probability of being β-current is one when $t_n \in [0, \beta]$, since this would force any change to be within β units of the present. We can clean up (22) by expressing β as a fraction υ of T (that is, $\beta = \upsilon T$) and setting $z = \lambda T$.

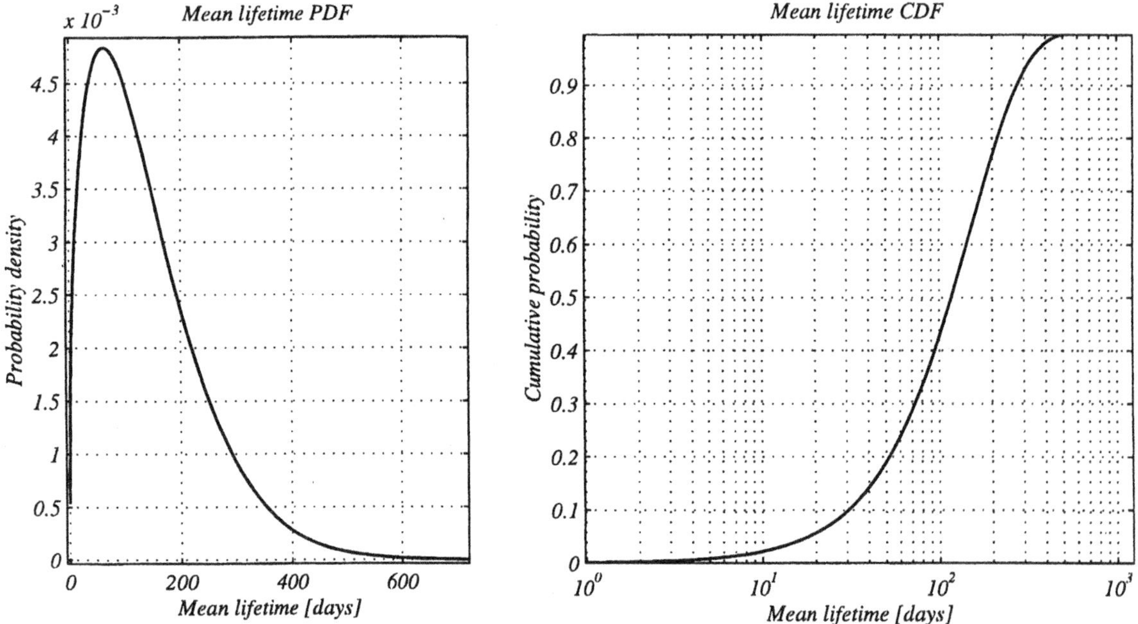

Fig. 15. Mean lifetime ($1/\lambda$) estimated PDF and CDF. Our lifetime-based population parameter estimation implies these distributions of mean lifetimes for the documents observed by the Informant. Note that these mean values are to be distinguished from the distribution of *observed* lifetimes. The average is around 138 days, the most likely value is 62 days, and the median is 117 days.

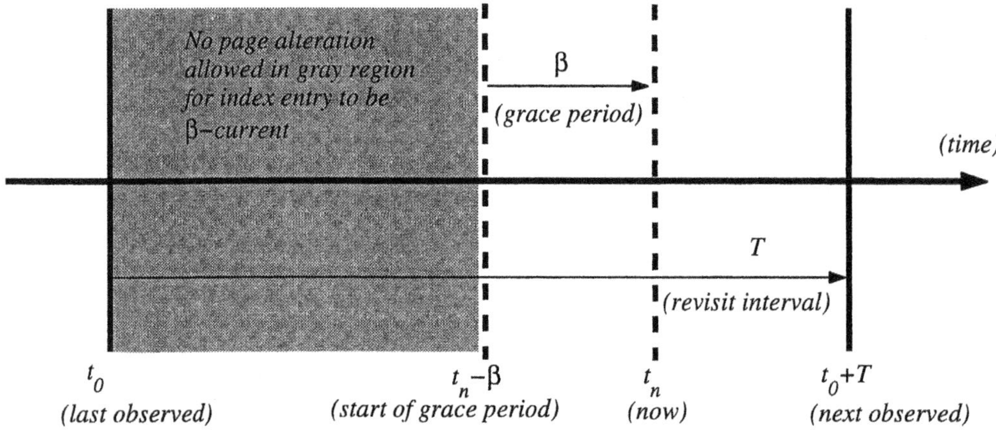

Fig. 16. Definition of *β-current*. This diagram shows what is meant when we say that an index entry is current with respect to a grace period, β. In order to be β-current, no modification can go unobserved up to β time units before the present.

With these changes, (22) becomes a function of the dimensionless relative rate, z, and the ratio of the grace period to the observation period, υ. When $z > 1$, a source is expected to change once or more prior to T, whereas $z < 1$ suggests fewer than one change expected before T. What fraction of these changes fall within the grace period β is loosely described by the parameter υ; some curves are shown for different choices of υ in Fig. 17.

We note in passing some properties of the curves in Fig. 17 that verify our intuition. First, note that the probability of being β-current goes to υ as the relative rate λT approaches infinity. High relative rate implies a Web page which is observed much

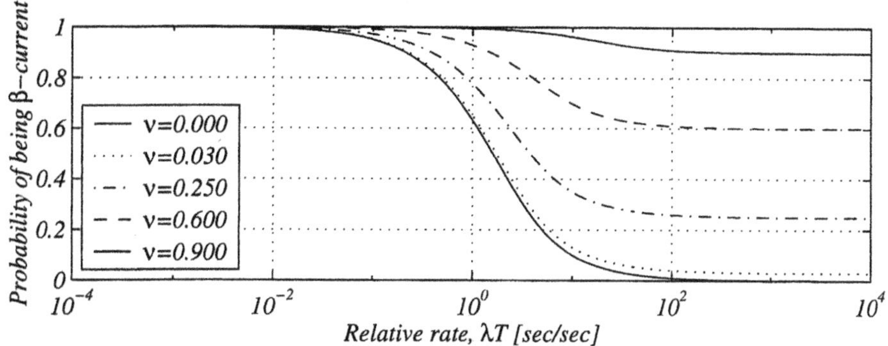

Fig. 17. Probability of β-currency vs. relative rate. Expected value of Pr (β-current | (λ, T, υ)) as a function of relative rate $z = \lambda T$ and grace period percentage $\upsilon = \beta / T$.

too slowly; the page changes many times between observations. As such, in the high rate limit, υ simply represents the percentage of these changes that occur during the grace period. For the case of low relative rate, where pages are sampled much faster than they change, the probability of a page being β-current approaches one, regardless of the grace period fraction υ.

Choosing a random Web page to which we apply (22) is equivalent to selecting a value for λ. In our collections, as discussed earlier, we have observed that the mean time $\bar{t}$ between changes roughly follows a Weibull distribution, (10), which is given by:

$$w(\bar{t}) = \frac{\sigma}{\delta}\left(\frac{\bar{t}}{\delta}\right)^{\sigma-1} \mathrm{e}^{-(\bar{t}/\delta)^{\sigma}}. \tag{23}$$

The change rate λ is the inverse of the mean time between changes, so we can replace λ in the integral with the change rate $1/\bar{t}$.

Using (23), along with the parameter values that resulted from our numerical optimization, we can determine the expected value of (22) over λ for our collection. This calculation for other collections or other demand distributions depends only on finding the distribution $w(\bar{t})$ of mean change times for those collections. Our analysis uses a simple periodic, round-robin re-indexing schedule, where the revisitation time T is the same for all sources. Since we propose visiting each page every T time units, an accurate model for a real engine would need to account for the growth of the collection over time.

For this preliminary analysis, we assume a constant Web size to avoid this difficulty. Using the Weibull distribution for inverse change rates, the expected probability that a uniformly randomly selected page will be β-current in the search engine index is:

$$\alpha = \int_0^{\infty} \left[\frac{\sigma}{\delta}\left(\frac{t}{\delta}\right)^{\sigma-1} \mathrm{e}^{-(t/\delta)^{\sigma}}\right] \times \left[\frac{\beta}{T_0} + \frac{1-\mathrm{e}^{-(1/t)(T_0-\beta)}}{(1/t)T_0}\right] \mathrm{d}t. \tag{24}$$

The integral (24) can only be evaluated in closed form when the Weibull shape parameter σ is 1;

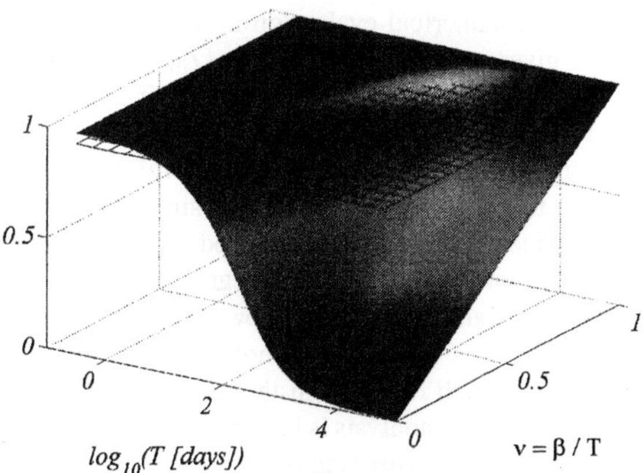

Fig. 18. Probability α as a function of υ and T_0. Here, we plot the probability surface α as a function of the grace period fraction $\upsilon = \beta / T_0$ and fixed re-indexing period T_0. This surface results from using the more accurate lifetime-based population parameters, although this surface could be constructed for any population. The plane at $\alpha = 0.95$ intersects the surface in a level set, which is plotted in Fig. 19 (with β values used instead of percentages υ).

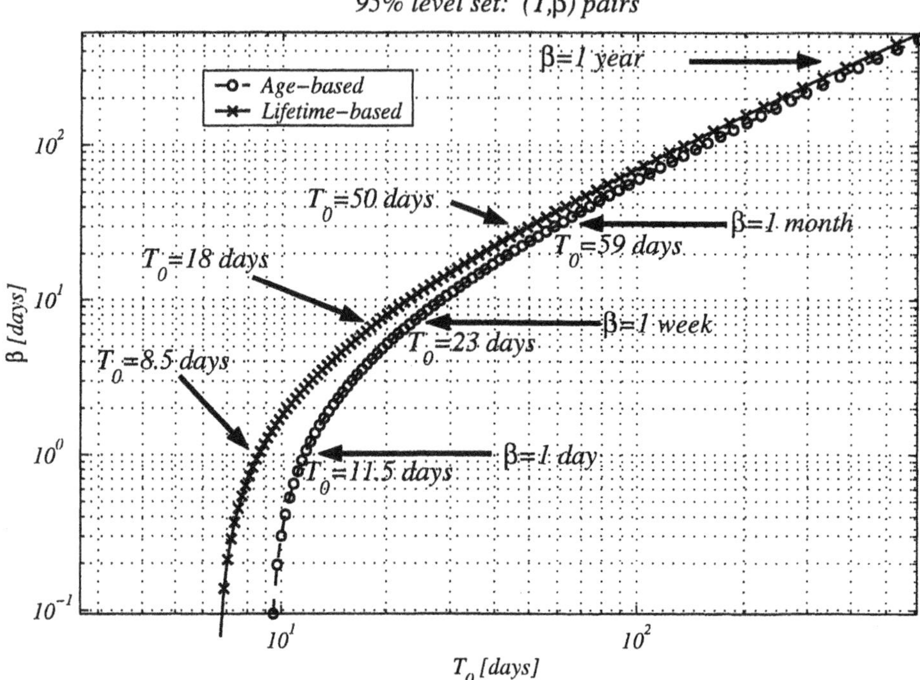

Fig. 19. Relating β and T_0: $\alpha = 95\%$ level set. Here we have plotted two level sets of pairs (T_0, β) which yield a probability $\alpha = 0.95$ of being β-current. The two curves are derived from two different estimation methods, minimizing (11) or (16). The lifetime-based estimates are much more accurate. Regardless of the size of the collection, this data can be used to estimate how current an engine is when the indexing period T_0 takes on a value (in days) along the horizontal axis. As T_0 becomes large, the relative check rate is too slow, and β approaches 95% $\times$ T_0.

otherwise, numerical evaluation is required. The integral gives an σ for every pair (T_0, β), defining a search engine 'performance surface'. This surface can be interpreted in a number of ways. For example, we can choose a probability and determine all pairs (T_0, β) that give that probability. Using our parameter choices from the lifetime-based optimization of (16), we have evaluated the integral and plotted it in Figs. 18 and 19, which show the level set for $\alpha = 95\%$. It is important to note that the revisitation times which result from this analysis are upper bounds since our analysis is based on the less volatile pages that provide timestamps.

From that plot, we can see that in order to maintain (0.95, 1 day)-current search engine, a re-indexing period of 8.5 days is necessary. For (0.95, 1 week)-currency, a re-indexing period of 18 days is necessary. Notice that these figures do not depend upon the number of documents in an index, so a re-indexing period defines a set of pairs (α, β), regardless of changes in the size of the index. Alternatively, we can estimate effective bandwidth requirements to maintain a given level of currency for a uniform index of a given size. By 'uniform' we mean that no documents are given any sort of preference; all are re-indexed at the same rate. The effective bandwidth is not to be confused with the link bandwidth, it simply describes the overall processing rate, including download and analysis.

For example, a (0.95, 1 day) index of the entire Web, using the estimate of 800 million pages from [8], would require a total effective bandwidth of (approximately):

$$\frac{800 \times 10^6 \text{ pages}}{8.5 \text{ days}} \times \frac{12 \text{ kilobytes}}{1 \text{ page}} = \frac{104 \text{ Mbits}}{\text{s}}$$

for 0.95, 1 day currency of index of the entire Web.

A more modest index, slightly closer to those actually in use, might have 150 million documents at (0.95, 1 week)-currency, requiring an effective bandwidth of around:

$$\frac{150 \times 10^6 \text{ pages}}{18 \text{ days}} \times \frac{12 \text{ kilobytes}}{1 \text{ pages}} = \frac{9.4 \text{ Mbits}}{\text{s}}$$

for (0.95, 1 week) currency of index of around 1/5 of the Web.

Clearly, other re-indexing schemes exist where T is not constant but is a function of λ; see [1] for some good discussion on possible schemes. When T is a function of λ, the integral (24) is modified by substituting in the function $T(1/\bar{t})$ and evaluating along the appropriate line in the $(T, \bar{t})$-plane. Additional modifications to this development might include the addition of a noise term to the observation period β and choosing the grace period as a function of the change rate λ.

7. Summary

This paper describes our efforts at estimating how fast the Web is changing, using a combination of empirical data and analytic modeling. From here, we can begin to consider the 'dynamics' of information, and how best to deal with observation of changing information sources over limited-bandwidth channels. Much work remains to be done. With a reasonable model of how the Web is growing and how fast pages change, we can start to formulate scheduling problems for search engines. These scheduling problems will depend on what objective we are trying to optimize. This work has used a simple, deterministic periodic revisiting strategy. By allowing different revisit intervals for different pages, we can formulate a variety of scheduling problems, holding two of α, β and the communication resources (that is, server bandwidth) fixed for example. We have not gone into any detail about which changes are 'important' and which changes are not, nor have we delved into the reliability and popularity of the Web pages in question. These clearly bear heavily on a user's perception of how good a search engine performs. While we have such data available to us in our empirical database, we have not yet addressed this. How can we estimate the currency, in our formal terms of (α, β)-currency, of commercial search engines that only allow external probes? How do the different search engines compare in this sense? Indeed, the fast-changing and fast-growing Web may soon force increased reliance on specialty search engines for the most volatile information sources.

References

[1] E.G. Coffman, Z. Liu and R.R. Weber, Optimal robot scheduling for Web search engines, J. Scheduling (1997), available at http://www.inria.fr/mistral/personnel/Zhen.Liu/

[2] F. Douglis, A. Feldmann, B. Krishnamurthy and J. Mogul, Rate of change and other metrics: A live study of the World Wide Web, in: Proc. of the USENIX Symposium on Internetworking Technologies and Systems, 1997, available from http://www.research.att.com/~anja/feldmann/papers.html.

[3] W. Feller, An Introduction to Probability Theory and Its Applications, volume 2, 2nd edition, Wiley, New York, 1971.

[4] M. Gray, Internet growth summary, http://www.mit.edu/people/mkgray/net/internet-growth-raw-data.html, 1997.

[5] Informant, 1995, http://informant.dartmouth.edu/.

[6] ISC, 1999, Internet Software Consortium; http://www.isc.org/.

[7] S. Lawrence and C.L. Giles, Searching the World Wide Web, Science 28 (1998) 98–100, available by request at http://www.neci.nj.nec.com/homepages/lawrence/.

[8] S. Lawrence and C.L. Giles, Accessibility of information on the Web, Nature (1999).

[9] D.C. Montgomery and G.C. Runger, Applied Statistics and Probability for Engineers, Wiley, New York, 1994.

[10] A. Papoulis, Probability, Random Variables and Stochastic Processes, McGraw-Hill, New York, 2nd edition, 1984.

Brian Brewington received a B.S. in Engineering and Applied Science from the California Institute of Technology in 1995. He began his doctoral research at the Thayer School of Engineering, Dartmouth College, with Professor George Cybenko in the fall of 1995. He will complete the program by late spring 2000. His academic interests include distributed information retrieval and signal processing, and he enjoys time away from work hiking and playing *ultimate frisbee*.

George Cybenko is the Dorothy and Walter Gramm Professor of Engineering at Dartmouth College. He has done pioneering work on several topics including load balancing for distributed computing, function approximation by neural networks and advanced algorithms for statistical signal processing. Cybenko's current areas of research include distributed information and computing systems, signal processing and mobile computing. In addition to serving on advisory and review boards at Argonne National Laboratory, the Minnesota Supercomputer Institute and the Institute for Mathematics and its Applications, he is the founding Editor-in-Chief of *Computing in Science and Engineering*, jointly published by the IEEE Computer Society and the American Institute of Physics. Cybenko has B.Sc. (University of Toronto, 1974) and Ph.D. (Princeton, 1978) degrees in Mathematics. Prior to joining Dartmouth, Cybenko was Professor of Electrical and Computer Engineering and Computer Science at the University of Illinois at Urbana-Champaign and Associate Director of the Center for Supercomputer Research and Development. In 1996, he was the Kloosterman Distinguished Visiting Professor at Leiden University, the Netherlands. Cybenko is a Fellow of the IEEE.

ELSEVIER

WebBase: a repository of Web pages

Jun Hirai [a,1,2], Sriram Raghavan [b,*,3], Hector Garcia-Molina [b,3], Andreas Paepcke [b,3]

[a] *System Integration Technology Center, Toshiba Corporation, 3-22 Katamachi, Fuchu, Tokyo 183-8512, Japan*
[b] *Computer Science Department, Stanford University, Stanford, CA 94305, USA*

Abstract

In this paper, we study the problem of constructing and maintaining a large shared repository of Web pages. We discuss the unique characteristics of such a repository, propose an architecture, and identify its functional modules. We focus on the storage manager module, and illustrate how traditional techniques for storage and indexing can be tailored to meet the requirements of a Web repository. To evaluate design alternatives, we also present experimental results from a prototype repository called *WebBase*, that is currently being developed at Stanford University.

Keywords: Repository; WebBase; Architecture; Storage management

1. Introduction

A number of important applications require local access to substantial portions of the Web. Examples include traditional *text search engines* [2,9], *related page* services [1,9], and *topic-based search and categorization* services [18]. Such applications typically access, mine or index a local cache or *repository* of Web pages, since performing their analyses directly on the Web would be too slow. For example, the Google search engine [9] computes the PageRank [3] of every Web page by recursively analyzing the Web's link structure. The repository receives Web pages from a *crawler*, which is the component responsible for mechanically finding new or modified pages on the Web. At the same time, the repository offers applications an access interface (API) so that they may efficiently access large numbers of up-to-date Web pages.

In this paper, we study the design of a large shared repository of Web pages. We present an architecture for such a repository, we consider and evaluate various implementation alternatives, and we describe a prototype repository that is being developed as part of the *WebBase* project at Stanford University. The prototype already has a collection of around 40 million Web pages and is being used as a testbed to study different storage, indexing, and data mining techniques. An earlier version of the prototype was used as the back-end storage system of the Google search engine. The new prototype is intended to offer parallelism across multiple storage computers, and support for a wider variety of applications (as opposed to just text-search engines). The prototype does not currently implement all the features and components that we present in this paper, but the

* Corresponding author.
[1] jun.hirai@toshiba.co.jp
[2] This work was performed while Jun Hirai was a visiting scholar in the Computer Science Department at Stanford University.
[3] {rsram, hector, paepcke}@db.stanford.edu

most important functions and services are already in place.

A Web repository stores and manages a large collection of data 'objects', in this case Web pages. It is conceptually not that different from other systems that store data objects, such as file systems, database management systems, or information retrieval systems. However, a Web repository does not need to provide a lot of the functionality that the other systems provide, such as transactions, or a general directory naming structure. Thus, the Web repository can be optimized to provide just the essential services, and to provide them in a scalable and very efficient way. In particular, a Web repository needs to be tuned or targeted to provide:

Scalability: Given the size and the growth of the Web [12], it is paramount that the repository scale to very large numbers of objects. The ability to seamlessly distribute the repository across a cluster of computers and disks is essential. Of particular interest to us is the use of *network disks* [14] to hold the repository. A network disk is a disk, containing a processor, and a network interface that allows it to be connected directly to a network. Network disks provide a simple and inexpensive way to construct large data storage arrays, and may therefore be very appropriate for Web repositories.

Streams: While the repository needs to provide access to individual stored Web pages, the most demanding access will be in bulk, to large collections of pages, for indexing or data mining. Thus the repository must support *stream* access, where for instance the entire collection is scanned and fed to a client for analysis. Eventually, the repository may need to support ordered streams, where pages can be returned at high speed in some order. (For instance, a data mining application may wish to examine pages by increasing modified date, or in decreasing page rank.)

Large updates: The Web changes rapidly [7,12,16]. Therefore, the repository needs to handle a high rate of modifications. As new versions of Web pages arrive, the space occupied by old versions must be reclaimed (unless a history is maintained, which we do not consider here). This means that there will be substantially more space compaction or reorganization than in most file or data systems. The repository must have a good strategy to avoid excessive conflicts between the update process and the applications accessing pages.

Expunging pages: In most file or data systems, objects are explicitly deleted when no longer needed. However, when a Web page is removed from a Web site, the repository is not notified. Thus, the repository must have a mechanism for detecting obsolete pages and removing them. This is akin to 'garbage collection' except that it is not based on reference counting.

In this paper we study how to build a Web repository that can meet these requirements. In particular,

- We propose a repository architecture that supports the required functionality and high performance. This architecture is amenable to the use of, but does not require, network disks [14].
- We present alternatives for distributing Web pages across computers and disks. We also consider different mechanisms for staging the new pages provided by the crawler, as they are applied to the repository.
- We consider ways in which the crawler and the repository can interact, including through batch updates, or incremental updates.
- We study strategies for organizing the Web pages within a 'node' or computer in the system. We consider how space compaction or reorganization can be performed under each scheme.
- We present experimental results from our prototype, as well as simulated comparisons between some of the approaches. This sheds light on the available design options and illustrates how the nature of the workload (in terms of crawling speed, streaming rate, etc.) determines the appropriate design choices.

Our goal is to cover a wide variety of techniques, but to keep within space limitations, we are forced to make some restrictions in scope. In particular, we do make the following assumptions about the operations of the crawler and the repository. Other alternatives are interesting and important, but simply not covered here.

- We assume that the crawler is *incremental* [4] and does not visit the entire Web each time it runs. Rather, the crawler merely visits those pages that it believes have changed or been created since the last run. Such crawlers scale better as the Web grows.

- The repository does not maintain a temporal history (or multiple versions) of the Web. In other words, only the latest version of each Web page is retained in the repository.
- The repository stores only standard HTML pages. All other media and document types are ignored by the crawler.
- Finally, indexes are constructed using a snapshot view of the contents of the repository. In other words, the indexes represent the state of the repository between two successive crawler runs. They are updated only at the end of each crawler run and not incrementally.

The rest of this paper is organized as follows. In Section 2, we present an architectural description of the various components of the repository, while in Section 3 we concentrate on one of the fundamental components of the architecture — namely the *storage manager*. In Section 4 we present results from experiments conducted to evaluate various options for the design of the storage manager, while in Section 5 we survey some related work. Finally, we conclude in Section 6.

2. Architecture

Fig. 1 depicts the architecture of the WebBase system in terms of the main functional modules and their interactions. It shows the five main modules — the crawler, the storage manager, the metadata and indexing module, the multicast module, and the query engine. The connections between these modules represent exchange of information in the indicated directions.

The crawler module is responsible for retrieving pages from the Web and handing them to the storage management module. The crawler periodically goes out to the Web to retrieve fresh copies of pages already existing in the repository, as well as pages that have not been crawled before. The storage module performs various critical functions that include assignment of pages to storage devices, handling updates from the crawler after every fresh crawl, and scheduling and servicing various types of requests for pages. Our focus in this paper will be on the storage module, but in this section we provide an overview of all the components.

The metadata and indexing module is responsible for extracting metadata from the collected pages, and for indexing both the pages and the metadata. The metadata represents information extracted from the Web pages, for example, their title, creation date, or set of outgoing URLs. It may also include information obtained by analyzing the entire collection. For instance, the number of incoming links for each page (coming from other pages), or citation count, can be computed and included as metadata. The module also generates indexes for the metadata and for the Web pages. The indexes may include traditional

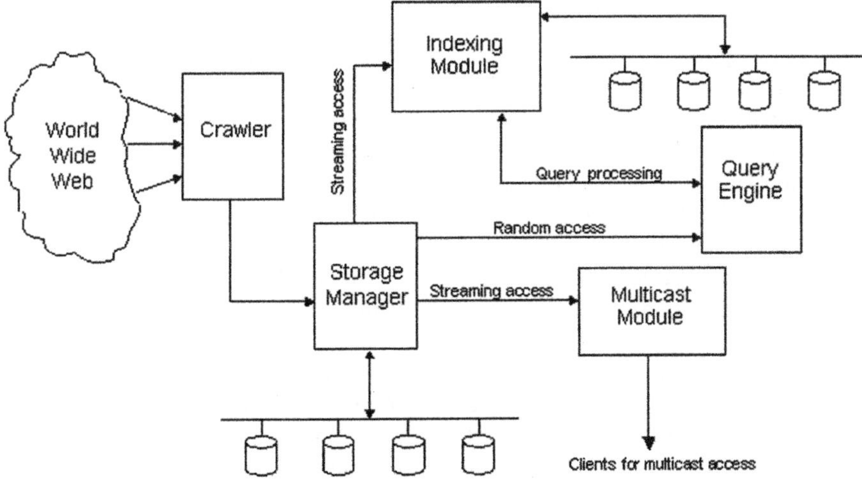

Fig. 1. WebBase architecture.

full text indexes, as well as indexes on metadata attributes. For example, an index on citation count can be used to quickly locate all Web pages having more than say 100 incoming links. The metadata and indexes are stored on separate devices from the main Web page collection, in order to minimize access conflict between page retrieval and query processing. In our prototype implementation simple metadata attributes are stored and indexed using a relational database.

The query engine and the multicast module together provide access to the content stored in the repository. Their roles are described in the following subsection.

2.1. Access modes

The repository supports three major access modes for retrieving pages:

- Random access
- Query-based access
- Streaming access

Random access: In this mode, a specific page is retrieved from the repository by specifying the URL (or some other unique identifier) associated with that page.

Query-based access: In this mode, requests for a set of pages are specified by queries that characterize the pages to be retrieved. These queries may refer to metadata attributes, or to the textual content of the Web pages. For example, suppose the indexing module maintains one index on the words present in the title of a Web page and another index on the hypertext links pointing out of a given page. These indexes could together be used to respond to a query such as: "Retrieve the URLs of all pages which contain the word Stanford in the title and which point to http://www-db.stanford.edu/". The query engine (shown in Fig. 1) is responsible for handling all such query-based accesses to the repository.

Streaming access: Finally, in the streaming access mode, all, or at least a substantial portion, of the pages in the repository are retrieved and delivered in the form of a data stream directed to the requesting client application. This access mode is unique to a Web repository and is important for applications that need to deal with a large set of pages. For example, many of the search applications mentioned in Section 1 require access to millions of pages to build their indexes or perform their analysis. In particular, within the WebBase system, the streaming interface is used by the indexing module to retrieve all the pages from the repository and build the necessary indexes.

The multicast module in Fig. 1 is responsible for handling all external requests for streaming mode access. In particular, multiple clients may make concurrent stream requests. Therefore, if the streams are organized properly, several clients may share the transmitted pages. Our goal for the WebBase repository is to make the streams available not just locally, but also to remote applications at other institutions. This would make it unnecessary for other sites to crawl and store the Web themselves. We believe it will be much more efficient to multicast streams out of a single repository over the Internet, as opposed to having multiple applications do their own crawling, hitting the same Web sites, and on many occasions requesting copies of the same pages.

Initially, WebBase supports stream requests for the entire collection of Web pages, in an arbitrary order that best suits the repository. WebBase also supports *restartable streams* that give a client the ability to pause and resume a stream at will. This requires that state information about a given stream be continuously maintained and stored at either the repository or the client, so that pages are not missed or delivered multiple times. Stream requests will be extended to include requests for subsets of pages (e.g., get all pages in the '.edu' domain) in arbitrary order. Eventually, we plan to introduce order control, so that applications may request particular delivery orders (e.g., pages in increasing page rank). We are currently investigating strategies for combining stream requests of different granularities and orders, in order to improve data sharing across clients.

2.2. Page identifier

Since a Web page is the fundamental logical unit being managed by the repository, it is important to have a well-defined mechanism that all modules can use to uniquely refer to a specific page. In the WebBase system, a page identifier is constructed by computing a signature (e.g., checksum or cyclic redundancy check) of the URL associated with that page. However, a given URL can have multiple text string representations. For example, *http://www.stanford.edu:80/* and *http://www.stanford.edu* both represent the same Web page but would give rise to different signatures. To avoid this problem, we first *normalize* the URL string and derive a *canonical representation*. We then compute the page identifier as a signature of this canonical representation. The details are as follows:

- *Normalization:* A URL string is normalized by executing the following steps:
  - Removal of the protocol prefix (*http://*) if present;
  - Removal of a *:80* port number specification if present (However, non-standard port number specifications are retained);
  - Conversion of the server name to lower case;
  - Removal of all trailing slashes ('/').

  The resulting text string is *hashed* using a signature computation to yield a 64-bit page identifier.

The use of a hashing function implies that there is a non-zero collision probability. Nevertheless, a good hash function along with a large space of hashes makes this a very unlikely occurrence. For example, with 64 bit identifiers and 100 million pages in the repository, the probability of collision is 0.0003. That is, 3 out of 10,000 repositories would have a collision. With 128 bit identifiers and a 10 billion page collection, the probability of collision is 10^{-18}. See [5] for more discussion and a derivation of a general formula for estimating collisions.

3. Storage manager

In this section we discuss the design of the storage manager. This module stores the Web pages on local disks, and provides facilities for accessing and updating the stored pages. The storage manager stores the latest version of every page retrieved by the crawler. Its goal is to store *only* the latest version (not a history) of any given page. However, two issues require consideration:

- *Consistency of indexes:* A page that is being referenced by one or more indexes must not be removed from the repository even if a later version of the same page has been retrieved by the crawler. For all such pages, two versions might need to temporarily co-exist until the indexes can be modified. This requirement impacts the functioning of the various update schemes and we defer a discussion of this issue to Section 3.3.
- *Expunging pages:* The storage manager is free to expunge pages that no longer exist on the Web. Since the crawler does not explicitly indicate what pages have been removed from Web sites, it is the responsibility of the storage manager to ensure that old copies of non-existent pages are periodically expunged.

Traditional garbage collection algorithms [17] reclaim space by discarding objects that are no longer referenced. The inherent assumption is that all data objects are available for testing, so that non-referenced objects can be identified. This differs from our situation, where the aim is to detect, as soon as possible, whether an object has been deleted in a remote location (a Web site) so that it can be similarly deleted from a local copy (the repository). To do this cleanup, the storage manager associates two numerical values with each page in the repository — *allowed lifetime* and *lifetime count*. Allowed lifetime represents the time a page can remain in the repository without being refreshed or replaced. When a page is crawled for the first time, or when a new version of the page is received from the crawler, the page's lifetime count is set to the *allowed lifetime*. Otherwise, the lifetime count of all pages is regularly decremented to reflect the amount of time for which they have been in the repository. Periodically, the storage manager runs a background process that constructs a list of URLs corresponding to all those pages whose lifetime count is about to reach 0. It forwards the list to the crawler, which attempts to visit each one of those URLs during the next crawling cycle. Those URLs in the list for which no pages are received from the crawler during the next update cycle are removed from the repository. If the crawler indicates that it was unable to verify the existence of a certain page, possibly because of network problems, then that page is not expunged. Instead, its lifetime count is set to a very small value to ensure that it will be included in the list next time around.

Note that the crawler has its own parameters [4] for deciding the periodicity with which individual pages are to be crawled. The list provided by the storage manager is only in addition to the pages that the crawler already intends to visit.

For scalability, the storage manager must be distributed across a collection of *storage nodes*, each equipped with a processor, one or more disks, and the ability to connect to a high-speed communication network. (For WebBase, each node can either be a network disk, or a regular computer.) To coordinate the nodes, the storage manager employs a central *node management server*. This server maintains a table of parameters describing the current state of each storage node. The parameters include:

- Total storage capacity, occupied space, and free space on each node;
- Extent of fragmentation on each storage device;
- Current state of the node — possible states include *down*, *idling*, *streaming*, and *storing* (the significance of each of these states will become clear once the update operations are presented);
- Number of outstanding requests for page retrieval and their types (random access, query-based, or streaming mode).

Based on this information, the node management server allocates storage nodes to service requests for stream accesses. It also schedules and controls the integration of freshly crawled pages into the repository. In the remainder of this section we discuss the following design issues for the storage manager:

- *Distribution of pages* among the storage nodes (Section 3.1);
- *Organization of pages* on each storage device for maximum efficiency during streaming and random access (Section 3.2);
- *Update mechanism* to integrate freshly crawled pages into the system (Section 3.3).

3.1. Page distribution across nodes

We consider two policies for distributing pages across multiple storage nodes.

- *Uniform distribution:* All storage nodes are treated identically; any page can be assigned to any of the nodes in the system.
- *Hash distribution:* The page identifier (computed as the signature of the URL as described in Section 2.2) is used to decide the allocation of pages to storage nodes. Each storage node is associated with a range of identifiers and contains all the pages whose identifiers fall within that range.

The hash distribution policy requires only a very sparse global index to locate the node in which a page with a given identifier would be located. This global index could in fact be implicit, if we interpret some portion (say the high order n bits) of the page identifier as denoting the number of the storage node to which the page belongs. In comparison, the uniform distribution policy requires a dense global index that maps each page identifier to the node containing the page. On the other hand, by imposing no fixed relationships between page identifiers and nodes, the uniform distribution policy simplifies the addition of new storage nodes into the system. With hash-based distribution, this would require some form of 'extensible hashing'. For the same reason, the uniform distribution policy is also more robust to failures. Failure of one of the nodes, when the crawler is providing new pages, can be handled by allocating all new incoming pages to the remaining nodes. With hashing, if an incoming page falls within a failed node, special recovery measures will be called for.

3.2. Organization of pages on disk

Each storage node must be capable of efficiently supporting three operations: page addition, high-speed streaming, and random page access. In this subsection we describe three ways to organize the data within a node to support these operations: *hash-based organization*, *log-structured organization*, and *hashed-log organization*. We defer an analysis of the pros and cons of these methods to a later section where we describe experiments that aid in the comparison.

3.2.1. Hash-based organization

Hash-based organization treats each disk as a collection of hash buckets. Each bucket is small enough to be read into memory, processed, and written back to disk. Each bucket stores pages that are allocated to that node and whose identifiers fall within the bucket's range. Note that this range is different from the range of page identifiers allocated to the storage node as a whole according to the hash distribution policy of Section 3.1. Buckets that are associated with successive ranges of identifiers are also assumed to be physically continuous on disk (excluding overflow buckets if any). Also, we assume that within each bucket, pages are stored in increasing order of their identifiers. Note that at any given time, only a portion of the space allocated to a hash bucket will be occupied by pages — the rest will be free space.

Clearly, this organization is very efficient for random page access since there is no need for a local index to map a page identifier to the physical location on disk. Streaming can also be supported efficiently by sequentially reading the buckets from disk in the order of their physical locations. The effective streaming rate will be some fraction of the maximum disk transfer rate, with the fraction being the average space utilization of the hash buckets.

The performance of hash-based organization during page addition depends on the order in which the pages are received. If new pages are received in a purely random order, then each page addition will require one read of the relevant bucket, followed by an in-memory update, and then a disk write to flush the modified bucket back to disk. Space used by old, unwanted pages can be reclaimed as part of this process. Note that buffering is unlikely to be very useful here since the probability that two buffered pages hash to the same bucket will be very low, given the size and number of hash buckets on a typical disk.

On the other hand, if pages are received in the *order* of their page identifiers, a more efficient method is possible. In particular, as each bucket is read from disk, a batch of new pages can be added, and then written to disk. (The in-memory addition is simple since the incoming and the stored pages are in order.) As a result, buffering of pages is guaranteed to be much more effective than in the unsorted case. If main memory is available, more than one bucket can be read into memory and merged with the incoming pages, allowing each disk operation to be amortized among even more pages (cf. Scenario 2 of Section 3.3.1).

3.2.2. *Log-structured organization*

The log-structured page organization is based on the same principles as the Log-structured File System (LFS) described in [15]. New pages received by the node are simply appended to the end of a log, making the process very efficient. To be more specific, the storage node maintains either two or three objects on each disk:

- A large *log* that occupies most of the space available on disk and which includes all the pages allocated to that disk as a single continuous chunk
- A *catalog* that contains one entry corresponding to each page present in the log. A typical catalog entry includes the following information:
  - Identifier of the page in question;
  - Pointer to the physical location of the page within the log;
  - Size of the page;
  - Status of the page (*valid* or *deleted* — the semantics of these states will be clear once the update strategies are discussed);
  - Timestamp denoting the time when the page was added to the repository;

  If random access to a page is required, then a local *B-tree index* that maps a given page identifier to the corresponding location of the page, is also maintained.

For typical network or PC disk sizes and average Web page sizes, the number of pages in the log is small enough that only the leaves of the B-tree need to reside on disk. Therefore, from now on, we will assume that only one disk access is required to retrieve an entry from the B-tree index.

New pages are appended to the end of the log. If we assume that the catalog and B-tree do not necessarily have to be kept continuously up to date on disk, then batch mode page addition is extremely efficient since it involves successively writing to contiguous portions of the disk. The required modifications to the catalog are buffered in memory and periodically flushed to disk. Log space must eventually be compacted, to remove old, unwanted pages. Also, once page addition completes, the B-tree index must be updated.

Random page access requires two disk accesses, one to read the appropriate B-tree index block and retrieve the physical position of the page, and another to retrieve the actual page.

Streaming, with no restrictions on stream order, is very efficient since it merely involves a sequential read of the log. Note that this assumes that all the pages in the log at the time of streaming are 'valid'. For batch-update systems that perform disk compaction (cf. Section 3.3.1), this assumption is guaranteed to be true. For systems that cannot make the same guarantee, additional disk accesses will be needed to examine the catalog and discard pages whose status flag is not set to 'valid'.

3.2.3. Hashed-log organization

As the name suggests, the hashed-log organization is a hybrid of the above two organization methods. In this scheme, a disk contains a number of large logs (and their associated catalogs) each similar in structure, but smaller, than the single log used in the pure log-structured organization. Each of these individual logs is typically about 8–10 MB in size. Like hash buckets, each log file is associated with a range of hash values and stores all pages that are assigned to that node and whose page identifier falls within that range. However, there are two major differences between hash buckets and the logs used in the hashed-log organization. First, the logs are much bigger than hash buckets and are therefore expensive to read into memory for each random page access. Second, the pages are not stored in sorted order within each log. As a result, efficient random access in a hashed-log node requires a B-tree index. Page addition in a hashed-log node involves buffering pages in memory, to the extent possible, and appending them to the appropriate logs based on their identifiers. However, the most important feature of this organization (for our purposes) is the ability to stream out pages in sorted order. To accomplish this, logs are read into memory in the order of their associated hash range values, sorted in memory, and then transmitted. Note that we assume that the logs, though much bigger than hash buckets, are still small enough to fit completely in memory. The motivation for such an organization is discussed in Section 4.2.1.

3.3. Update schemes

We assume that updates proceed in cycles. The crawler collects a set of new pages, these are incorporated into the repository, the metadata indexes are built for the new snapshot, and a new cycle begins. Under this model, there is a period of time, between the end of a crawl and the completion of index rebuilding, when older versions of pages (that are being referenced by the existing index) need to be retained. This will ensure that ongoing page retrieval requests, either through query-based access or streaming mode access, are not disrupted. Thus, we classify all pages in the repository as:

- *Class A:* Old versions of pages (referenced by the current active indexes) whose newer versions already exist in the repository.
- *Class B:* Unchanged pages — those pages for which only one version exists because they were not crawled between the time the index was last built and the time the latest crawl was executed.
- *Class C:* These include pages not seen before, as well as new versions of pages whose older versions already exist as class A pages. In other words, all the pages received from the crawler during a crawling cycle are class C pages.

Thus, the update process consists of the following steps:

- Receive class C pages from the crawler and add them to the repository.
- Rebuild all the indexes using the class B and class C pages.
- Delete the class A pages.

If the system does not accept random or query-based page access requests until the entire update operation is complete, it is possible to exchange the order of execution of the last two steps. In that case, the class A pages need not be retained until the indexes are rebuilt. The batch update method described in Section 3.3.1 operates in this manner. Besides the batch update scheme, we also briefly describe an incremental update scheme in Section 3.3.2. There are additional options beyond these two. For example, one could have two full copies of the repository, and alternate between them when one copy is updated. We do not discuss these other strategies here.

3.3.1. Batch update scheme

In this update scheme, the storage nodes in the system are partitioned into two sets — *update nodes* and *read nodes*. The freshly crawled class C pages are stored on the update nodes whereas class B and class A pages are stored on the read nodes. By definition, the active index set (before rebuilding) references only class A and class B pages — therefore all requests for page retrieval will involve only the read nodes. Analogously, only the update nodes will be involved in receiving and storing pages retrieved by the crawler. Fig. 2 illustrates the flow of

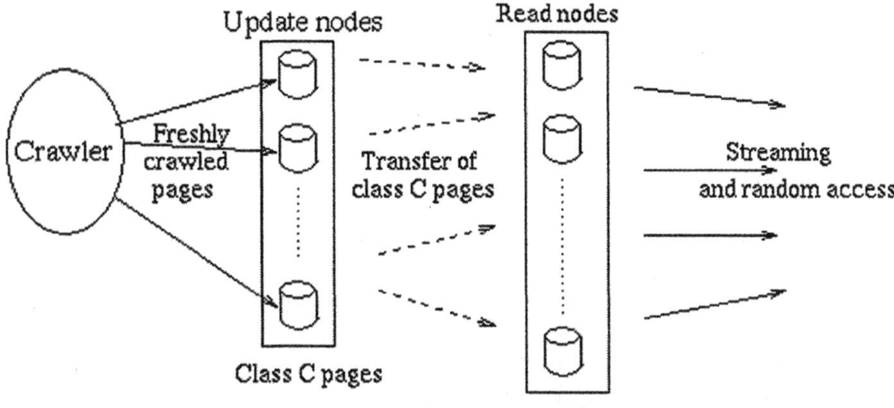

Fig. 2. Batch update strategy.

data between the crawler and the two sets of nodes during the batch update process. The steps for a batch update are as follows:

(1) *System isolation:*
   (a) The multicast module stops accepting new stream requests.
   (b) The crawler finishes adding class C pages to the update disks.
   (c) Queries are suspended, and the system waits for ongoing stream transfers to complete.

(2) *Page transfer:* Class C pages are transferred from the update nodes to the read nodes, and class A pages are removed from the read nodes. The details of these operations depend on both the page organization scheme and the page distribution policy. We discuss some examples of page transfer at the end of this section.

(3) *System restart:*
   (a) The class C pages stored in the update nodes are removed. If needed, the crawler can be restarted to start populating the update nodes once more.
   (b) All the pages from the read nodes are streamed out to the indexing module to enable index reconstruction. External requests for streaming access can be accepted provided they do not involve access to one or more indexes.
   (c) Once the indexes have been rebuilt, the read nodes start accepting random and query-based requests.

The exact mechanism for the transfer of pages between update and read nodes depends on the page organization and distribution policy used in each set of nodes (both the organization and the policy could be different for the two sets). In what follows, we illustrate two possible scenarios for the transfer.

Scenario 1: Log-structured organization and hash distribution policy on both sets: For illustration, let us assume there are 4 update nodes and 12 read nodes. The crawler computes the identifier of each new page it obtains. Pages in the first quarter of the identifier range are stored in update node 1, the pages in the second quarter go to node 2, and so on. When the crawl cycle ends, update node 1 will sub-partition its allocated identifier range into 3 subranges, and will send its pages to the first three read disks. Similarly, update disk 2 will partition its pages to read disks 4, 5 and 6, and so on. Thus, each read disk receives pages from only one update disk. The sequence of steps for transferring pages to the read nodes is as follows:

(1) Each update node i constructs lists $L_{i,j}$. List $L_{i,j}$ contains the identifiers of class C pages that are currently in i and which are destined for read node j.
(2) Suppose read node j receives a list of pages from the update node i. It then computes $L'_{i,j} = \mathit{Intersection}(L_{i,j}, R_j)$ where R_j denotes the list of identifiers corresponding to pages currently

stored in j (note that R_j is directly available by a scan of the catalog).

(3) By definition, $L'_{i,j}$ represents the set of class A pages at read node j. The catalog entries for these pages are located and their status flags are modified to indicate that they have been 'deleted'.

(4) Next, the read nodes go into compaction mode to reclaim space created by the deletion of these class A pages.

(5) Finally, each update node begins transmitting streams of class C pages to the corresponding read nodes. Each stream contains exactly the pages that are destined for the receiving read node.

(6) Once all the pages have been received, each read node, if necessary, builds a local B-tree index to support random access.

Scenario 2: Hash-based organization and hash distribution policy on both sets: The use of a hash-based node organization allows for certain optimizations while transferring pages to the read nodes. For one, since corresponding class A and class C pages are guaranteed to be present in the same hash bucket, deletion of class A pages does not occupy a separate step, but is performed in conjunction with the addition of class C pages. The steps are as follows:

(1) Each update node reads the hash buckets into memory in the order of their physical locations on disk. As a result (Section 3.2.1), the pages are read in the increasing order of their identifiers.

(2) For each page retrieved from disk, the update nodes determine the read node to which the page is to be forwarded, and transmit the page accordingly.

(3) Each read node begins to receive a sorted stream of pages from one of the update nodes.

(4) The read nodes read their hash buckets into memory in the order of their physical locations on disk. They then execute a 'merge sort' that involves both the incoming sorted stream as well the pages that they read from disk. As part of the merge sort, if a page arriving on the stream has the same identifier as one of the pages retrieved from disk, then the former is preferred and the latter is discarded. (This corresponds to replacing a class A page by the corresponding class C page). The resulting merged output is written out to disk as the modified hash buckets. Fig. 3 illustrates how the merge sort is executed.

Advantages of the batch update scheme: The most attractive characteristic of the batch update scheme is the lack of conflict between the various operations being executed on the repository. A single storage node does not ever have to deal with both page addition and page retrieval concurrently. Another useful property is that the physical locations of pages on the read nodes do not change between updates. (This is because the compaction operation, which could potentially change the physical location, is part of the update). This helps to greatly simplify the state information required to support restartable streams as described in Section 2.1. For a given restartable stream, the state information merely consists of a

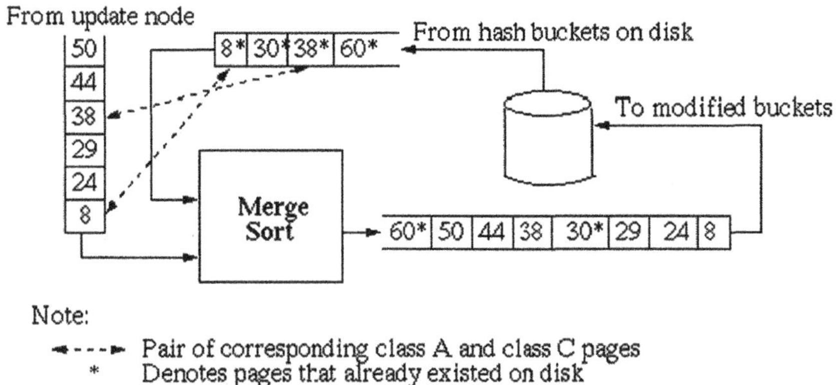

Fig. 3. Addition of new pages using merge sort.

pair of values *(Node-id, Page-id)* where, *Node-id* represents some unique identifier for the storage node that contained the last page transmitted to the client before the interruption, and *Page-id* represents the identifier for that last page.

3.3.2. Incremental update scheme

In the incremental update scheme, there is no division of work between read and update nodes. All nodes are equally responsible for supporting both update and access simultaneously. The crawler is allowed to place the freshly crawled pages on any of the nodes in the system as long as it conforms to the page distribution policy. Analogously, requests for pages through any of the three access modes may involve any of the nodes present in the system. The extraction of metadata and construction of indexes are undertaken periodically, independent of the ingestion of new pages into the repository.

As a result, the incremental update scheme is capable of providing continuous service. Unlike in the batch update scheme, there is no need to isolate the system during update. The addition of new pages into the repository is a continuous process that takes place in conjunction with streaming and random access. Further, this scheme makes it possible to provide even very recently crawled pages to the clients through the streaming or random access modes (though the metadata and indexes associated with these pages may not yet be available). However, such continuous service does have its drawbacks:

Performance penalty: Performance may suffer because of conflicts between multiple simultaneous read and update operations. This performance penalty can be alleviated, to some extent, by employing the uniform distribution policy and having the node management server try to balance the loads. For example, when the node management server detects that a set of nodes are very busy responding to a number of high-speed streaming requests, it can ensure that addition of new pages from the crawler does not take place at these nodes. All such page addition requests can be redirected to other more lightly loaded nodes.

Requires dynamically maintained local index: Consider the case when the incremental update scheme is employed in conjunction with log-structured page organization. Holes created by the removal of class A pages are reclaimed through compaction which has the effect of altering the physical location of the stored pages. This makes it necessary to dynamically maintain a local index to map a given page identifier to its current physical address. This was not necessary in the batch update scheme since the physical location of all the pages in the read nodes was unaltered between two successive updates.

Restartable streams are more complicated: When incremental update is used in conjunction with hash-based page organization, the state information required to support restartable streams gets complicated, since the physical locations of pages are not preserved when there are bucket overflows. However, it turns out that in the case of log-structured organization, it is possible to execute compaction in such a way that despite incremental update, the simple state information used by the batch-update system suffices. The extended version of this paper [10] discusses these issues in further detail.

4. Experiments

We conducted experiments to compare the performance of some of the design choices that we have presented. In this section we will describe selected results of these experiments and discuss how various system parameters influence the 'best' configuration (in terms of the update strategy, page distribution policy, and page organization method) for the storage manager.

4.1. Experimental setup

Our WebBase prototype includes an implementation of the storage manager with the following configuration:

- Update strategy: batch update;
- Page distribution policy for both update and read nodes: hash distribution;
- Page organization method used in both sets of nodes: log-structured organization.

The storage manager is fed pages by an incremental crawler that retrieves pages at the rate of approximately 50–100 pages/second. The WebBase storage manager can run on network disks or on conventional PCs. For the experiments we report here, we used a cluster of PCs connected by a 100 Mbps Ethernet LAN, since debugging and data collection are easier on PCs. In addition to the repository, we have also implemented a *client module* and a *crawler emulator*. The client module sends requests for random or streaming mode accesses to the repository, and receives pages from the read nodes in response. The crawler emulator retrieves stored Web pages from an earlier version of the repository and transmits it to the update nodes at a controllable rate. Using such an emulator instead of the actual crawler provided us with the necessary flexibility to control the crawling speed, without interacting with the actual Web sites.

For ease of implementation, the storage manager has been implemented on top of the standard Linux file system. In order to conform to the operating system limit on maximum file size, the log-structured organization has been approximated by creating a collection of individual log files, each approximately 512 MB in size, on each node.

To compare different page distribution and node organization alternatives, we conducted extensive simulation experiments. The simulation hardware parameters were selected to match our prototype hardware. This allowed us to verify the simulation results with our prototype, at least for the scenario that our prototype implements (batch updates, hash page distribution, log-structured nodes). For other scenarios, the simulator allows us to predict how our prototype would have performed, had we chosen other strategies. All of the performance results in this section are from the simulator, except for those in Table 3 and Fig. 4, which report the performance of the actual prototype.

We used the following performance metrics for comparing different system configurations (all are expressed in terms of number of pages/second/node):

- *Page addition rate:* This is the maximum rate at which the system is able to receive new pages and add them to the repository.
- *Random page access rate:* Random page access refers to the retrieval of a certain page from the repository by specifying the identifier associated with that page. Random page access rate is the maximum rate at which such requests can be serviced by the system.
- *Streaming rate:* refers to the rate at which all the pages in the system can be retrieved and transmitted without imposing any specific transmission order.

Note that all our performance metrics are on a per-node basis. This enables us to present results that are independent of the number of nodes in the actual system. For systems using batch-update, the inherent parallelism in the operations implies that the overall page addition rate of the system (random page access rate) is simply the per-node value multiplied by the number of update nodes (number of read nodes) if we assume that the network is not a bottleneck. For incremental update systems, the scale up is not perfectly linear because of conflict between operations. For batch update systems, an additional performance metric is the *batch update time*. This is the time during which the repository is isolated and does not provide page access services.

We present some selected experimental results below. The first set of results include a comparison of the three different page organization methods described in Section 3.2, as well as a comparison of different system configurations. The second set of results measure the performance of our implemented prototype. Additional experiments and discussions, that illustrate the optimization process that can be carried out to tune the nodes to handle Web data, are included in an extended version of this paper [10].

4.2. Comparing different systems

In this section we present some selected results from our simulator. For simplicity we do not consider network performance, i.e., we assume that the network is always capable of handling any traffic. Performance is solely determined by the disk characteristics and the disk access pattern associated with the system configuration. The architecture of the simulator and the details of the simulation process are described in an extended version of this paper [10].

4.2.1. Comparing page organization methods

In this section, we use Table 1 to analyze the three page organization methods presented in Section 3.2. Note that Table 1 only deals with the performance characteristics of a single node. Overall system per-

Table 1
Comparing page organization methods on a single node (from simulation)

Performance metric	Log-structured	Hash-based	Hashed-log
Streaming rate and ordering	6300 pages/s unsorted	3900 pages/s sorted	6300 pages/s sorted
Random page access rate	35 pages/s	51 pages/s	35 pages/s
Page addition rate (random order, no buffering)	6100 pages/s	23 pages/s	53 pages/s
Page addition rate (random order, 10 MB buffer)	6100 pages/s	35 pages/s	660 pages/s
Page addition rate (sorted order, 10 MB buffer)	6100 pages/s	1300 pages/s	1300 pages/s

Hash-based uses 1 million 64 KB buckets with 60% average occupancy.

formance, though dependent on the performance of an individual node, is also influenced by other factors such as the page distribution policy and the update strategy. These are discussed in the succeeding sections.

Performance characteristics: Table 1 compares these organizations based on their performance characteristics.

- *Streaming:* Since pages are more tightly packed in a log, a log-structured node can stream out pages 62% faster than a hash-based node. A hashed-log node not only matches the high streaming rate of the log-structured organization but also generates a sorted stream.
- *Random read:* Since the hash-based node does not have to use a local index for random reads, it is able to read pages at a higher rate (46% higher) than a log-structured node.
- *Page addition (random):* A log-structured node can clearly append new pages at a much higher rate than a hash-based node. Increasing the available memory to 10 MB improves the add rate for the hash-based node from 23 to 35 pages/s, still way under the performance of the log-structured node. (The observed improvement is merely because buffering allows the use of a single disk sweep (the 'elevator algorithm') to update all the hash buckets.) Since a hashed-log node must distribute pages to multiple logs, its page addition rate is only about 10% that of the log-structured organization. However, this is still almost 20 times better than the page addition rate possible with the hash-based organization.
- *Page addition (sorted):* On the other hand, if pages are received in sorted order (by identifier), then the merging technique of Section 3.2.1 can improve the page addition performance of the hash-based organization by almost two orders of magnitude.

Space usage: The log-structured organization requires space to maintain catalog information. In our experience, the catalog typically contributes an additional space overhead of only 1.2% which implies an effective space utilization of almost 99%. For the hash-based organization, disk space utilization is a function of how empty or full the hash buckets are. Analysis using sample data from our repository indicates that average space utilization for this organization is typically around 60% [10].

Motivation for hashed-log: The results of Table 1 suggest that in a batch system, update nodes should be log-structured to support a large throughput from the crawler, while read nodes should be hash-based to support high random read traffic. However, to achieve good performance at the read nodes during update, pages transferred to them from the update nodes should arrive in sorted order. The log-structured organization is not capable of providing such a sorted stream. However, the hashed-log organization provides exactly such a facility in conjunction with a reasonably high page addition rate.

4.2.2. *Comparing different configurations*

To compare different system configurations, we require a notation to easily refer to a specific configuration. We adopt the following convention:

- Incr$[p, o]$: denotes a system that uses the incremental update scheme, policy p for distributing pages across nodes, and organization method o to organize pages within each node. Here, p can be either 'hash' or 'uniform' and o can be either 'hash' or 'log'.
- Batch$[U(p1, o1), R(p2, o2)]$: denotes a system that uses the batch update scheme, uses policy $p1$

Table 2
Sample performance results for different configurations (from simulation)

System configuration	Page addition rate (pages/s/node)	Batch update time [a] (s)
Batch[U(hash, log), R(hash, hash)]	6100	11700
Batch[U(hash, hash), R(hash, hash)]	35	1260
Batch[U(hash, hashed-log), R(hash, hash)]	660	1260

[a] Update ratio = 0.25.

and organization method $o1$ on the update nodes, and policy $p2$ and organization method $o2$ on the read nodes.

For example, the system configuration for our prototype (as discussed in Section 4.1) can be represented as Batch[U(hash, log), R(hash, log)].

Table 2 presents some sample performance results for three different system configurations that use the batch update method, employ the hash distribution policy, and use hash-based page organization at the update nodes. For this experiment we assume that 25% of the pages on the read nodes are replaced by newer versions during the update process. We call this an *update ratio* of 0.25. The three configurations differ in the organization method that they employ at the update nodes. The center column gives the page addition rate supported by a single update node (derived earlier). If we multiply these entries by the number of update nodes we get the total rate at which the crawler can deliver pages. The third column gives the total time to perform a batch update of the read disks, and represents the time the repository would be unavailable to clients. The last configuration, which uses a hashed-log organization at the update nodes, provides the best balance between page addition rate and a reasonable batch update time. Note that because of the parallelism available in the batch update systems, the update time does not depend on the number of nodes but is purely determined by the update ratio.

4.3. Experiments on overall system performance

Table 3 summarizes the results of experiments conducted directly on our prototype. Since our prototype employs a log-structured organization on both sets of nodes, it exhibits impressive performance for both streaming and page addition. Note that the results of Table 3 include network delays, and hence the numbers are lower than those predicted by Table 1. In particular, the streaming rate is measured at our client module, and the page addition rate is what the emulated crawler sees.

Table 3
Performance of prototype (from actual measurements)

Performance metric	Observed value
Streaming rate	2800 pages/s (per read node)
Page addition rate	3200 pages/s (per update node)
Batch update time	2451 s (for update ratio = 0.25)
Random page access rate	33 pages/s (per read node)

Fig. 4 plots the variation of batch update time with *update ratio* for our prototype. As before, the update ratio refers to the fraction of pages on the read nodes that are replaced by newer versions. Our prototype system uses a batch update process with stages corresponding to Scenario 1 of Section 3.3.1. Fig. 4 shows how each stage contributes to the overall batch update time. (Note that the y-axis in Fig. 4

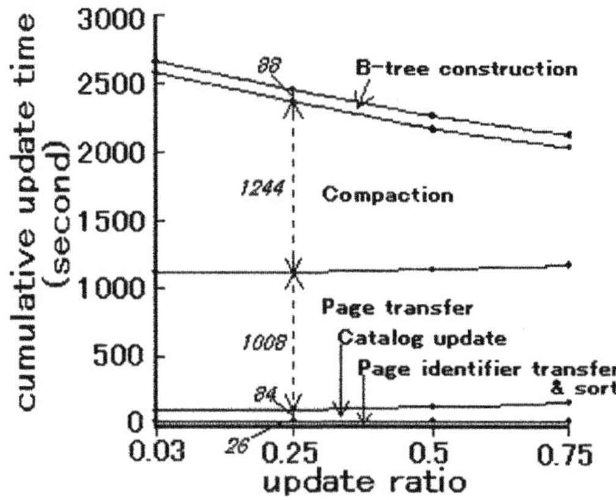

Fig. 4. Batch update time of prototype.

is cumulative, i.e., each curve includes the sum of the contributions of all the stages represented below it). For example, for an update ratio of 0.25, we see that catalog update, page identifier transfer, and B-tree construction require only 26, 84, and 88 seconds respectively. However, compaction requires 1244 seconds whereas page transfer requires 1008 seconds. The domination of compaction and page transfer holds at all update ratios. In addition, the figure shows that the time for page transfer remains almost constant, independent of the update ratio. This is because an increase in update ratio requires a corresponding increase in the number of update nodes to accommodate the larger number of pages being received from the crawler. Since page transfer is an operation that each update node executes independently and simultaneously, we are able to achieve perfect parallelism and keep the page transfer time constant. Compaction, on the other hand, exhibits a marked decrease with increase in update ratio. This is reasonable, since at higher update ratios, more class A pages are deleted, thereby leaving behind a smaller set of class B pages to be moved around on the read nodes during compaction.

4.4. Summary

There is a wide spectrum of system configurations for a Web repository, each with different strengths and weaknesses. The choice of an appropriate configuration is influenced by the deployment environment, the anticipated workload, and the functional requirements. Some of the factors that influence this choice are crawling speed, required random page access performance, required streaming performance, node computing power and storage space, and the importance of continuous service. For example, in an environment that includes a high-speed crawler, configurations that perform poorly on page addition, such as Incr[hash, hash] or Batch[U(hash, hash), $R(*, *)$], are not suitable. Similarly, if continuous service is essential in a certain environment, then none of the batch update based schemes presented in this paper would be applicable. Table 4 presents a summary of the relative performance of some of the more useful system configurations. In that table, the symbols ++, +, +−, −, and − − represent, in that order, a spectrum of values from the most favorable to the least favorable for a given performance metric.

5. Related work

From the nature of their services, one can infer that all Web search engines either construct, or have access to, a Web repository. However, these are proprietary and often specific to the search application. In this paper, we have attempted to discuss, in an application-independent manner, the functions and features that would be useful in a Web repository, and have proposed an architecture that provides these functions efficiently.

A number of Web-based services have used Web repositories as part of their system architecture. However, often the repositories have been constructed on a much smaller scale and for a restricted purpose. For example, the WebGUIDE system [6] allows users to explore changes to the World Wide Web and Web structure by supporting recursive document comparison. It tracks changes to a user-specified set of Web pages using the AT&T Difference Engine (AIDE) [8] and provides a graphical visualization tool on top of AIDE. The AIDE version

Table 4
Relative performance of different system configurations

System configuration	Streaming	Random page access	Page addition	Update time
Incr [hash, log]	+	−	− −	inapplicable
Incr [uniform, log]	+	− −	+	inapplicable
Incr [hash, hash]	+	+	−	inapplicable
Batch[U(hash, log),R(hash, log)]	++	−	++	+−
Batch[U(hash, log),R(hash, hash)]	+	+	++	− −
Batch[U(hash, hash),R(hash, hash)]	+	+	−	+
Batch[U(hashed-log, hash),R(hash, hash)]	+	+	+−	+

repository retrieves and stores only pages that have explicitly been requested by users. As such, the size of the repository is typically much smaller than the sizes targeted by WebBase. Similarly, GlimpseHTTP (now called WebGlimpse) [13] provides text-indexing and 'neighborhood-based' search facilities on existing repositories of Web pages. Here again, the emphasis is more on the actual indexing facility and much less on the construction and maintenance of the repository.

The Internet Archive [11] project aims to build a digital library for long-term preservation of Web-published information. The focus of that project is on addressing issues relevant to archiving and preservation. Their target client population consists of scientists, sociologists, journalists, historians, and others who might want to use this information in the future for research purposes. On the other hand, our focus with WebBase has been on designing a Web repository in such a way that it can be kept relatively fresh, and be able to act as an immediate and current source of Web information for a large number of existing applications.

The use of log-structured organization in our storage manager is based on the work on log-structured file systems described in [15]. However, there are two essential differences between the two systems. The first is the use of multiple disks in WebBase, that enables us to separate the read and update operations across disjoint sets of nodes. The second difference is the need for WebBase to support high-speed streaming, an operation that is not part of the anticipated workload in the design of LFS.

6. Conclusion

In this paper we proposed an architecture for structuring a large shared repository of Web pages. We argued that the construction of such a repository calls for judicious application of new and existing techniques. We discussed the design of the storage manager in detail and presented qualitative and experimental analysis to evaluate the various options at every stage in the design.

Our WebBase prototype is currently being developed based on the architecture of Section 2. Currently, working implementations of an incremental crawler, the storage manager, the indexing module, and a query engine are available. Most of the low-level networking and file-system operations have been implemented in C/C++ whereas the query interface has been implemented in Java.

For the future, we plan to implement and experiment with some of the more advanced system configurations that we presented in Section 4.2.2. We also plan to develop advanced streaming facilities, as discussed in Section 2.1, to provide more client control over streams. Eventually, we plan to enhance WebBase so that it can maintain a history of Web pages and provide temporal information.

Acknowledgements

We wish to thank all members of the Stanford WebBase project for their contributions to the design and implementation of the WebBase prototype. We also wish to thank Quantum Inc. for donating the network disks that were used to build our prototype.

References

[1] Alexa Incorporated, http://www.alexa.com

[2] Altavista Incorporated, http://www.altavista.com

[3] S. Brin and L. Page, The anatomy of a large-scale hypertextual Web search engine, in: Proc. 7th Int. World Wide Web Conf., April 14–18, 1998.

[4] J. Cho and H. Garcia-Molina, Incremental crawler and evolution of the Web, Technical Report, Department of Computer Science, Stanford University, available at http://www-db.stanford.edu/ ~cho/papers/cho-incre.ps

[5] A. Crespo and H. Garcia-Molina, Archival storage for digital libraries, in: 3rd ACM Conf. on Digital Libraries, June 23–26, 1998.

[6] F. Douglis, T. Ball, Y.-F. Chen and E. Koutsofios, WebGUIDE: Querying and navigating changes in Web repositories, in: Proc. 5th Int. World Wide Web Conf., May 6–10, 1996.

[7] F. Douglis, A. Feldmann, B. Krishnamurthy and J. Mogul, Rate of change and other metrics: a live study of the World Wide Web, in: USENIX Symp. on Internet Technology and Systems, December 1997.

[8] F. Douglis, T. Ball, Y.-F. Chen and E. Koutsofios, The AT&T Internet Difference Engine: Tracking and viewing changes on the Web, World Wide Web 1 (1) (1998).

[9] Google Incorporated, http://www.google.com

[10] J. Hirai, S. Raghavan, H. Garcia-Molina and A. Paepcke, WebBase: A repository of Web pages, Stanford Digital

Libraries Project Technical Report SIDL-WP-1999-0124, Computer Science Dept., Stanford University, Nov. 1999, available at http://www-diglib.stanford.edu/diglib/WP/PUBLIC/DOC319.html

[11] Internet Archive, http://www.archive.org

[12] S. Lawrence and C.L. Giles, Accessibility of information on the Web, Nature 400, July 8, 1999.

[13] U. Manber, M. Smith and B. Gopal, WebGlimpse — Combining browsing and searching, in: Proc. 1997 USENIX Technical Conf., Jan. 6–10, 1997.

[14] National Storage Industry Consortium — NASD Project, http://www.nsic.org/nasd/

[15] M. Rosenblum and J.K. Ousterhoust, The design and implementation of a log-structured file system, in: Proc. 13th ACM Symp. on Operating Systems Principles, Oct. 1991, pp. 1–15.

[16] C.E. Wills and M. Mikhailov, Towards a better understanding of Web resources and server responses for improved caching, in: Proc. 8th Int. World Wide Web Conf., May 1999.

[17] P.R. Wilson, Uniprocessor garbage collection techniques, in: Proc. Int. Workshop on Memory Management, September 1992, pp. 1–42.

[18] Yahoo Incorporated, http://www.yahoo.com

Jun Hirai received his B.E. and M.E in Electrical and Electronic Engineering from the University of Tokyo, Japan, in 1986 and 1988, respectively. He joined Toshiba Corporation in 1988 and was engaged in research and development in the area of network management and telecommunication technology. He was a visiting scholar in the Computer Science Department at Stanford University from 1998 to 2000. His current interests include information management issues on various scales ranging from the personal level to the World Wide Web, and Internet-related technologies.

Sriram Raghavan is currently a Ph.D. student in the Computer Science department at Stanford University, Stanford, California. He received a Bachelor of Technology degree in Computer Science and Engineering from the Indian Institute of Technology, Chennai, India in 1998. His research interests include information management on the Web, large-scale searching and indexing, database and IR systems integration, and query processing.

Hector Garcia-Molina is the Leonard Bosack and Sandra Lerner Professor in the Departments of Computer Science and Electrical Engineering at Stanford University, Stanford, California. From August 1994 to December 1997 he was the Director of the Computer Systems Laboratory at Stanford. From 1979 to 1991 he was on the faculty of the Computer Science Department at Princeton University, Princeton, New Jersey. His research interests include distributed computing systems and database systems. He received a B.S. in Electrical Engineering from the Instituto Tecnologico de Monterrey, Mexico, in 1974. From Stanford University, Stanford, California, he received in 1975 a M.S. in Electrical Engineering and a Ph.D. in Computer Science in 1979. Garcia-Molina is a Fellow of the ACM, received the 1999 ACM SIGMOD Innovations Award, and is a member of the President's Information Technology Advisory Committee (PITAC).

Andreas Paepcke is a senior research scientist and director of the Digital Library project at Stanford University. For several years he has been using object-oriented technology to address interoperability problems, most recently in the context of distributed digital library services. His second interest is the exploration of user interface and systems technologies for accessing digital libraries from small, handheld devices (PDAs). Dr. Paepcke received B.S. and M.S. degrees in Applied Mathematics from Harvard University, and a Ph.D. in Computer Science from the University of Karlsruhe, Germany. Previously, he worked as a researcher at Hewlett-Packard Laboratory, and as a research consultant at Xerox PARC.

ELSEVIER

On near-uniform URL sampling

Monika R. Henzinger [a,*], Allan Heydon [b], Michael Mitzenmacher [c], Marc Najork [b]

[a] *Google, Inc. 2400 Bayshore Parkway, Mountain View, CA 94043, USA*
[b] *Compaq Systems Research Center, 130 Lytton Avenue, Palo Alto, CA 94301, USA*
[c] *Harvard University, Division of Engineering and Applied Sciences, Boston, MA, USA*

Abstract

We consider the problem of sampling URLs uniformly at random from the Web. A tool for sampling URLs uniformly can be used to estimate various properties of Web pages, such as the fraction of pages in various Internet domains or written in various languages. Moreover, uniform URL sampling can be used to determine the sizes of various search engines relative to the entire Web. In this paper, we consider sampling approaches based on random walks of the Web graph. In particular, we suggest ways of improving sampling based on random walks to make the samples closer to uniform. We suggest a natural test bed based on random graphs for testing the effectiveness of our procedures. We then use our sampling approach to estimate the distribution of pages over various Internet domains and to estimate the coverage of various search engine indexes.

Keywords: URL sampling; Random walks; Internet domain distribution; Search engine size

1. Introduction

Suppose that we could choose a URL uniformly at random from the Web. Such a tool would allow us to answer questions about the composition of the Web using standard statistical methods based on sampling. For example, we could use random URLs to estimate the distribution of the length of Web pages, the fraction of documents in various Internet domains, or the fraction of documents written in various languages. We could also determine the fraction of Web pages indexed by various search engines by testing for the presence of pages chosen uniformly at random. However, so far, no methodology for sampling URLs uniformly, or even near-uniformly, at random from the Web has been discovered.

The contributions of this paper are threefold. First, we consider several sampling approaches, including natural approaches based on random walks. Intuitively, the problem with using a random walk in order to sample URLs from the Web is that pages that are more highly connected tend to be chosen more often. We suggest an improvement to the standard random walk technique that mitigates this effect, leading to a more uniform sample. Second, we describe a test bed for validating our technique. In particular, we apply our improved sampling approach to a synthetic random graph whose connectivity was designed to resemble that of the Web, and then analyze the distribution of these samples. This test bed may prove useful for testing other similar techniques. Finally, we apply our sampling technique to three sizable random walks of the actual Web. We then use these samples to estimate the distribution

* Corresponding author.

of pages over Internet domains, and to estimate the coverage of various search engine indexes.

1.1. Prior work

For the purposes of this paper, the size of a search engine is the number of pages indexed by the search engine. Similarly, the size of the Web corresponds to the number of publicly accessible, static Web pages, although, as we describe in Section 4, this is not a complete or clear definition.

The question of understanding the size of the Web and the relative sizes of search engines has been studied previously, most notably by Lawrence and Giles [14,15] and Bharat and Broder [2]. Part of the reason for the interest in the area is historical: when search engines first appeared, they were often compared by the number of pages they claimed to index. The question of whether size is an appropriate gauge of search engine utility, however, remains a subject of debate [19]. Another reason to study size is to learn more about the growth of the Web, so that appropriate predictions can be made and future trends can be spotted early.

In 1995, Bray simply created (in an undisclosed way) a start set of about 40,000 Web pages and crawled the Web from them [3]. He estimated the size of the Web to be the number of unique URLs the crawl encountered.

The initial work by Lawrence and Giles used a sampling approach based on the results of queries chosen from the NEC query logs to compare relative sizes of search engines [14]. Based on published size figures, the authors estimated the size of the Web. The approach of sampling from NEC query logs leaves questions as to the statistical appropriateness of the sample, as well as questions about the repeatability of the test by other researchers. In contrast, we seek tests that are repeatable by others (with sufficient resources).

Further work by Lawrence and Giles used an approach based on random testing of IP addresses to determine characteristics of hosts and pages found on the Web, as well as to estimate the Web's size [15]. This technique appears to be a useful approach for determining characteristics of Web hosts. Given the high variance in the number of pages per host, however, and the difficulties in accessing pages from hosts by this approach, it is not clear that this technique provides a general methodology to accurately determine the size of the Web. In particular, the scalability of this approach is uncertain for future 128 bit IP-v6 addresses.

Bharat and Broder, with motivation similar to ours, suggested a methodology for finding a page near-uniformly at random from a search engine index [2]. Their approach is based on determining queries using random words, according to their frequency. For example, in one experiment, they chose queries that were conjunctions of words, with the goal of finding a single page (or a small number of pages) in the search engine index containing that set of words. They also introduced useful techniques for determining whether a page exists in a search engine index. This problem is not as obvious as it might appear, as pages can be duplicated at mirror sites with varying URLs, pages might change over time, etc. Although Bharat and Broder used their techniques to find the relative overlap of various search engines, the authors admit that their techniques are subject to various biases. For example, longer pages (with more words) are more likely to be selected by their query approach than short pages.

This paper is also related to a previous paper of ours [9], in which we used random walks to gauge the *weight* of various search engine indexes. The weight of an index is a generalization of the notion of its size. Each page can be assigned a weight, which corresponds to its importance. The weight of a search engine index is then defined to be the sum of the weights of the pages it contains. If all pages have an equal weight, the weight of an index is proportional to its size. Another natural weight measure is, for example, the PageRank measure (described below). We used the standard model of the Web as a directed graph, where the pages are nodes and links between pages represent directed edges in the natural way. With this interpretation, we used random walks on the Web graph and search-engine probing techniques proposed by Bharat and Broder [2] to determine the weight of an index when the weight measure is given by the PageRank measure. The random walks are used to generate random URLs according to a distribution that is nearly equal to the PageRank distribution. This paper extends that approach to generate URLs according to a more uniform distribution.

1.2. Random walks and PageRank

We first provide some background on random walks. Let $X = \{s_1, s_2, \ldots, s_n\}$ be a set of states. A *random walk* on X corresponds to a sequence of states, one for each step of the walk. At each step, the walk switches from its current state to a new state or remains at the current state. Random walks are usually *Markovian*, which means that the transition at each step is independent of the previous steps and depends only on the current state.

For example, consider the following standard Markovian random walk on the integers over the range $\{0 \ldots j\}$ that models a simple gambling game, such as blackjack, where a player bets the same amount on each hand (i.e., step). We assume that if the player ever reaches 0, they have lost all their money and stop, and if they reach j, they have won enough money and stop. Hence the process will stop whenever 0 or j is reached. Otherwise, at each step, one moves from state i (where i is not 0 or j) to $i+1$ with probability p (the probability of winning the game), to $i-1$ with probability q (the probability of losing the game), and stays at the same state with probability $1 - p - q$ (the probability of a draw).

The PageRank is a measure of a page suggested by Brin and Page [4] that is fundamental to our sampling approach. Intuitively, the PageRank measure of a page is similar to its in-degree, which is a possible measure of the importance of a page. The PageRank of a page is high if it is linked to by many pages with a high PageRank, and a page containing few outgoing links contributes more weight to the pages it links to than a page containing many outgoing links. The PageRank of a page can be easily expressed mathematically. Suppose there are T total pages on the Web. We choose a parameter d such that $0 < d < 1$; a typical value of d might lie in the range $0.1 < d < 0.15$. Let pages $p_1, p_2, \ldots, p_k$ link to page p. Let $R(p)$ be the PageRank of p and $C(p)$ be the number of links out of p. Then the PageRank $R(p)$ of a page is defined to satisfy:

$$R(p) = d/T + (1-d)\sum_{i=1}^{k} R(p_i)/C(p_i).$$

This equation defines $R(p)$ uniquely, modulo a constant scaling factor. If we scale $R(p)$ so that the PageRanks of all pages sum to 1, $R(p)$ can be thought of as a probability distribution over pages.

The PageRank distribution has a simple interpretation in terms of a random walk. Imagine a Web surfer who wanders the Web. If the surfer visits page p, the random walk is in state p. At each step, the Web surfer either jumps to a page on the Web chosen uniformly at random, or the Web surfer follows a link chosen uniformly at random from those on the current page. The former occurs with probability d, the latter with probability $1 - d$. The equilibrium probability that such a surfer is at page p is simply $R(p)$. An alternative way to say this is that the average fraction of the steps that a walk spends at page p is $R(p)$ over sufficiently long walks. This means that pages with high PageRank are more likely to be visited than pages with low PageRank.

2. Sampling-based approaches

We motivate our approach for sampling a random page from the Web by considering and improving on a sequence of approaches that clearly fail. Our approach also has potential flaws, which we discuss.

2.1. Deterministic approaches

One natural approach would be to simply try to crawl the entire Web, keeping track of all unique pages. The size of the Web prevents this approach from being effective.

Instead, one may consider crawling only a part of the Web. If one obtains a large enough subset of the Web, then perhaps a uniform sample from this subset would be sufficient, depending on the application. The question is how to obtain this sample. Notice that crawling the Web in some fixed, deterministic manner is problematic, since then one obtains a fixed subset of the Web. One goal of a random sampling approach is *variability*; that is, one should be able to repeat the sampling procedure and obtain different random samples for different experiments. A sampling procedure based on a deterministic crawl of the Web would simply be taking uniform samples from a fixed subset of the Web, making repeated experiments problematic. Moreover, it is not clear how to argue that a sufficiently large subset of the Web is representative. (Of course, the Web might change, leading to different results in different deterministic experiments, but one should not count on changes over which one has no control, and whose effect is unclear.)

2.2. *Random walks with Mercator*

Because of the problems with the deterministic crawling procedure, it is natural to consider randomized crawling procedures. For example, one may imagine a crawler that performs a random walk, following a random link from the current page. In the case where there are no links from a page, the walk can restart from some page in its history. Similarly, restarts can be performed to prevent the walk from becoming trapped in a cycle.

Before explaining our sampling approach, we describe our tool for performing PageRank-like random walks. We use Mercator, an extensible, multi-threaded Web crawler written in Java [10,17]. We configure Mercator to use one hundred crawling threads, so it actually performs one hundred random walks in parallel, each walk running in a separate thread of control. The crawl is seeded with a set of 10,000 initial starting points chosen from a previous crawl. Each thread begins from a randomly chosen starting point. Recall that walks either proceed along a random link with probability $1 - d$, or perform a random jump with probability d (and in the case where the out-degree is 0). When a walk randomly jumps to a random page instead of following a link, it chooses a page at random from all pages visited by any thread so far (including the initial seeds).

Note that the random jumps our walk performs are different from the random jumps for the Web surfer interpretation of PageRank. For PageRank, the random Web surfer is supposed to jump to a page chosen uniformly at random from the entire Web. We cannot, however, choose a page uniformly at random; indeed, if we could do that, there would be no need for this paper! Hence we approximate this behavior by choosing a random page visited by Mercator thus far (including the seed set). Because we use a relatively large seed set, this limitation does not mean that our walks tend to remain near a single initial starting point (see Section 6 below). For this reason, we feel that this necessary approximation has a reasonably small effect.

3. Mathematical underpinnings

A problem with using the pages discovered by a random walk is that certain pages are more likely to be visited during the course of a random walk than other pages. For example, the site www.microsoft.com/ie is very likely to appear even during the course of a very short walk, because so many other pages point to it. We must account for this discrepancy in determining how to sample pages visited in the course of our random walk.

More concretely, consider a sampling technique in which we perform a random walk in order to crawl a portion of the Web, and we then sample pages from the crawled portion in order to obtain a near-uniform sample. For any page X,

$$\Pr(X \text{ is sampled}) = \Pr(X \text{ is crawled}) \cdot \Pr(X \text{ is sampled} \mid X \text{ is crawled}). \tag{1}$$

We first concentrate on finding an approximation for the first term on the right hand side. Consider the following argument. As we have already stated, the fraction of the time that each page is visited in equilibrium is proportional to its PageRank. Hence, for sufficiently long walks,

$$E(\text{number of times } X \text{ is visited}) \approx L \cdot R(X), \tag{2}$$

where L is the length of the walk.

Unfortunately, we cannot count on being able to do long walks (say, on the order of the number of pages), for the same reason we cannot simply crawl the entire Web: the graph is too large. Let us consider a page to be *well-connected* if it can be reached by almost every other page through several possible short paths. Under the assumption that the Web graph consists primarily of well-connected pages, approximation (2) is true for relatively short walks as well. (Here, by a *short walk*, we will mean about $O(\sqrt{n})$ steps, where n is the number of pages in the Web graph; see Section 4 below regarding more about this assumption.) This is because a random walk in a well-connected graph rapidly loses the memory of where it started, so the short-term behavior is like its long-term behavior in this regard.

Now, for short walks, on the order of $O(\sqrt{n})$ steps, we would expect most pages to appear at most once. This is similar in intuition to the birthday paradox, which states that if everyone has a random ID from a set of n IDs, you need roughly $\sqrt{n}$ people in a room before you find two people who share the same ID. Hence, for short walks,

$$\Pr(X \text{ is crawled}) \approx E(\text{number of times } X \text{ is visited}). \tag{3}$$

Combining approximations (2) and (3), we have

$$\Pr(X \text{ is crawled}) \approx L \cdot R(X). \tag{4}$$

Our mathematical analysis therefore suggests that $\Pr(X \text{ is crawled})$ is proportional to its PageRank. Under this assumption, by equation (1) we will obtain a uniform sampling if we sample pages from the crawled subset so that $\Pr(X \text{ is sampled} \mid X \text{ is crawled})$ is inversely proportional to the PageRank of X. This is the main point, mathematically speaking, of our approach: we can obtain more nearly uniform samples from the history of our random walk if we sample visited pages with a skewed probability distribution, namely by sampling inversely to each page's PageRank.

The question therefore arises of how best to find the PageRank of a page from the information obtained during the random walk. Our random walk provides us with two possible ways of estimating the PageRank. The first is to estimate $R(X)$ by what we call the *visit ratio* of the page, or $VR(X)$, which is simply the fraction of times the page was visited during the walk. That is,

$$VR(X) = \frac{\text{number of appearances of } X \text{ in the walk}}{\text{length of the walk}}.$$

Our intuition for using the visit ratio is that if we run the walk for an arbitrarily long time, the visit ratio will approach the PageRank. If the graph consists of well-connected pages, we might expect the visit ratio to be close to the PageRank over small intervals as well.

We also suggest a second possible means of estimating the PageRank of a page. Consider the graph consisting of all pages visited by the walk, along with all edges traversed during the course of the walk. We may estimate the PageRank $R(X)$ of a page by the sample PageRank $R'(X)$ computed on this sample graph. Intuitively, the dominant factor in the value $R'(X)$ is the in-degree, which is at least the number of times the page was visited. We would not expect the in-degree to be significantly larger than the number of times the page was visited, since this would require the random walks to cross the same edge several times. Hence $R'(X)$ should be closely related to $VR(X)$. However, the link information used in computing $R'(X)$ appears to be useful in obtaining a better prediction. Note that calculating the values $R'(X)$ requires storing a significant amount of information during the course of the walk. In particular, it requires storing much more information than required to calculate the visit ratio, since all the traversed edges must also be recorded. It is therefore not clear that in all cases computing $R'(X)$ will be feasible or desirable.

4. Limitations

In this section, we consider the limitations in our analysis and framework given above. In particular, we consider biases that may impact the accuracy of our approach.

It is first important to emphasize that our use of random walks as described above limits the pages that can be obtained as samples. Hence, we must clarify the set of Web pages from which our approach is meant to sample. Properly defining which pages constitute the Web is a challenging prospect in its own right. Many Web pages lie behind corporate firewalls, and are hence inaccessible to the general public. Also, pages can be dynamically created in response to user queries and actions, yielding an infinite number of potential but not truly extant Web pages.

Our crawl-based approach finds pages that are accessible only through some sequence of links from our initial seed set. We describe this part of the Web as the *publicly accessible Web*. Implicitly, we are assuming that the bulk of the Web lies in a giant component reachable from major sites such as Yahoo. Furthermore, we avoid crawling dynamic content by stripping the query component from discovered URLs, and we log only those pages whose content type is text/html.

Finally, because our random walk involves jumping to random locations frequently, it is very difficult for our random walk to discover pages only accessible though long chains of pages. For example, if the only way to reach a page N is though a sequence of links $A \rightarrow B \rightarrow \ldots \rightarrow N$, such that the only link to B is from A, and so on, then N will almost never be discovered. Hence, our technique is implicitly biased against pages that are not well-connected. If we assume that the giant component of publicly accessible pages is well-connected, then this is not a severe problem. Recent results, however, suggest that the graph structure of the Web may be more complex, with several pages reachable only by long chains of links and a large component of pages that are not reachable from the remainder of the Web [5].

We therefore reiterate that our random walk approach is meant to sample from the publicly accessible, static, and well-connected Web.

We now consider limitations that stem from the mathematical framework developed in Section 3. The mathematical argument is only approximate, for several reasons that we outline here.

- *Initial bias*. There is an initial bias based on the starting point. This bias is mitigated by choosing a large, diverse set of initial starting points for our crawl.
- *Dependence*. More generally, there is a dependence between pages in our random walk. Given a page on the walk, that page affects the probability that another page is visited. Therefore we cannot treat pages independently, as the above analysis appears to suggest.
- *Short cycles*. This is a specific problem raised by the dependence problem. Some pages that lie in closed short cycles may have the property that if they are visited, they tend to be visited again very soon. For these pages, our argument does not hold, since there is a strong dependence in the short term memory of the walk: if we see the page we are likely to see it again. In particular, this implies that approximation (3) is inaccurate for these pages; however, we expect the approximation to be off by only a small constant factor, corresponding to the number of times we are likely to visit the page in a short interval given we have visited it.
- *Large PageRanks*. Approximation (3) is inappropriate for long walks and pages with very high PageRank. For a page with very high PageRank, the probability that the page is visited is close to one, the upper bound. Approximation (4) will therefore *overestimate* the probability that a high PageRank page is crawled, since the right hand side can be larger than 1.
- *Random jumps*. As previously mentioned, our random walk approximates the behavior of a random Web surfer by jumping to a random page visited previously, rather than a completely random page. This leads to another bias in our argument, since it increases the likelihood that a page will be visited two or more times during a crawl. This bias is similar to the initial bias.

Despite these problems, we feel that for most Web pages X, our approximation (4) for $\Pr(X \text{ is crawled})$ will be reasonably accurate. However, approximation (4) does not guarantee uniform samples, since there are other possible sources of error in using the visit ratio to estimate the PageRank of a page. In particular, the visit ratio yields poor approximations for pages with very small PageRank. This is because the visit ratio is discrete and has large jumps compared to the smallest PageRank values.

To see this more clearly, consider the following related example. Suppose that we have two bins, one containing red balls and the other containing blue balls, representing pages with small and large PageRanks, respectively. The balls have unique IDs and can therefore be identified. There are one million red balls and one hundred blue balls. We 'sample' balls in the following manner: we flip a fair coin to choose a bin, and we then choose a ball independently and uniformly at random from the selected bin. Suppose we collect ten thousand samples in this manner.

Let us treat this sampling process as a random walk. (Note that there are no links; however, this is a random process that gives us a sequence of balls, which we may treat just like the sequence of pages visited during a random walk.) Suppose we use the visit ratio as an approximation for the long-term sample distribution. Our approximation will be quite good for the blue balls, as we take sufficient samples that the visit ratio gives a fair approximation. For any red balls we choose, however, the visit ratio will be (at it smallest) 1 in 10,000, which is much too large, since we expect to sample each red ball once in every 2,000,000 samples.

The problem is that rarely visited pages (i.e., pages with small PageRank) cannot be properly accounted for, since over a short walk we have no chance to see the multitude of such pages. Hence, our estimate for the PageRank of pages with small PageRank is too large, and hence our estimate for the inverse of the PageRank (which we use as $\Pr(X \text{ is sampled} \mid X \text{ is crawled})$ in Eq. 1) is too small. The effect is that such pages will still be somewhat under-sampled by our sampling process. Computing $R'(X)$ in place of $VR(X)$ does not solve this problem; an analogous argument shows that pages with small PageRank are also under-sampled if this estimate is used.

The best we can hope for is that this sampling procedure provides a more uniform distribution of pages. In what follows, we describe the experiments we performed to test the behavior of our sampling procedure on a random graph model, as well as the results from random walks on the Web.

5. A random test bed

In order to test our random walk approach, it is worthwhile to have a test bed in which we can gauge its performance. We suggest a test bed based on a class of random graphs, designed to share important properties with the Web.

It has been well-documented that the graph represented by the Web has a distinguishing structure. For example, the in-degrees and out-degrees of the nodes appear to have a power-law (or Zipf-like) distribution [13]. A random variable X is said to have a power-law distribution if

$$\Pr(X = k) \sim \frac{1}{k^{\alpha}}$$

for some real number α and some range of k. One explanation for this phenomenon is that the Web graph can be thought of as a dynamic structure, where new pages tend to copy the links of other pages.

For our test bed, we therefore choose random graphs with in-degrees and out-degrees governed by power-law distributions. The in-degrees and out-degrees are chosen at random from a suitable distribution, subject to the restriction that the total in-degree and out-degree must match. Random connections are then made from out links to in links via a random permutation. This model does not capture some of the richer structure of the Web. However, we are primarily interested in whether our sampling technique corrects for the variety of the PageRanks for the nodes. This model provides a suitable variety of PageRanks as well as in-degrees and out-degrees, making it a useful test case.

We present results for a test graph. The probability of having out-degree k was set to be proportional to $1/k^{2.38}$, for k in the range five to twenty. The probability of having in-degree k was set to be proportional to $1/k^{2.1}$. The range of the in-degrees were therefore set to lie between five and eighteen, so that the total in-degree would be close to the total out-degree. (There are a few nodes with smaller in-degree, due to the restriction that the total in-degree and out-degree must match.) The exponents 2.38 and 2.1 were chosen based on experimental results [13]. Our final graph has 10,000,000 nodes and 82,086,395 edges. Note that we chose a relatively high minimum in-degree and out-degree to ensure that with high probability our graph is strongly connected. That is, there are no small isolated components, and every page can reach every other page through some path.

To crawl this graph, we wrote a program that reads a description of the graph and acts as a Web server that returns synthetic pages whose links correspond to those of the graph. We then used Mercator to perform a random walk on this server, just as we would run Mercator on the real Web. The walk visited 848,836 distinct nodes, or approximately 8.5% of the total graph. Three sets of two thousand samples each were chosen from the visited nodes, using three different sampling techniques. A *PR sample* was obtained by sampling a crawled page X with probability inversely proportional to its apparent PageRank $R'(X)$. Similarly, a *VR sample* was obtained by sampling a crawled page X with probability inversely proportional to its visit ratio $VR(X)$. Finally, a *random sample* was obtained by simply choosing 2000 of the crawled pages independently and uniformly at random.

One way to test the efficacy of our sampling technique is to test if the sampled nodes are uniformly distributed according to certain graph attributes that may affect which nodes we sample. In particular, it seems likely that a node's out-degree, in-degree,

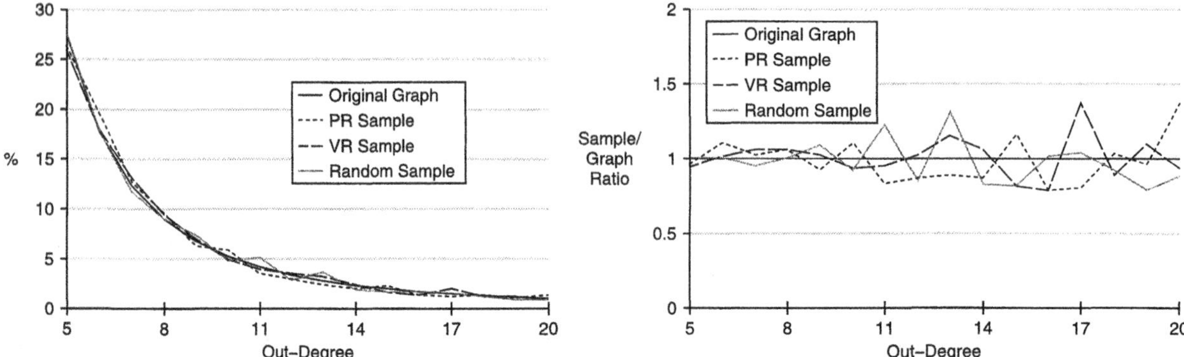

Fig. 1. Out-degree distributions for the original graph and for nodes obtained by three different sampling techniques.

and PageRank might affect how likely it is to be sampled. For example, since a node's PageRank is so closely tied to the likelihood that we crawl it, there is a good chance that the node's PageRank will be somewhat correlated with the probability that our sampling technique samples it, while this will of course not be the case if our sampling technique is truly uniform. We therefore compared the proportions of the in-degrees, out-degrees, and PageRanks of our samples with their proportions in the original graph.

For example, we consider first the out-degrees, shown in Fig. 1. The graph on the left shows the distributions of node out-degrees for the original graph and nodes collected by three sampling techniques. The graph on the right hand side normalizes these distributions against the percentages from the original graph (shown as a horizontal solid line with value 1). In both graphs, sample curves closer to the graph curve (shown in solid black) are better. Although the distributions for the samples differ somewhat from that of the original graph, the differences are minor, and are due to the variation inherent in any probabilistic experiment. As might be expected, there does not appear to be any systematic bias against nodes with high or low out-degree in our sampling process.

In contrast, when we compare our samples to the original graph in terms of the in-degree and PageRank, as shown in Figs. 2 and 3, there does appear to be a systematic bias against pages with low in-degree and low PageRank. (Note that in Fig. 3, the PageRank values are scaled as multiples of the average PageRank, namely 10^{-6}, the inverse of the number of nodes in the graph. For example, the percentage of pages in the PageRank range 1.0–1.2 corresponds to the percentage of pages whose PageRanks lie between 1.0 and 1.2 times the average.) This systematic bias against pages with low in-degree or PageRank is naturally understood from our previous discussion in Section 4. Our random walk tends to

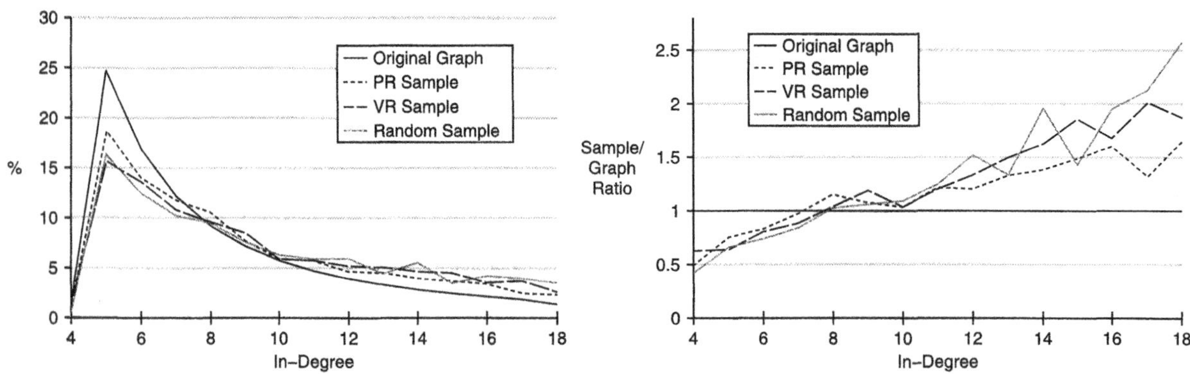

Fig. 2. In-degree distributions for the original graph and for nodes obtained by three different sampling techniques.

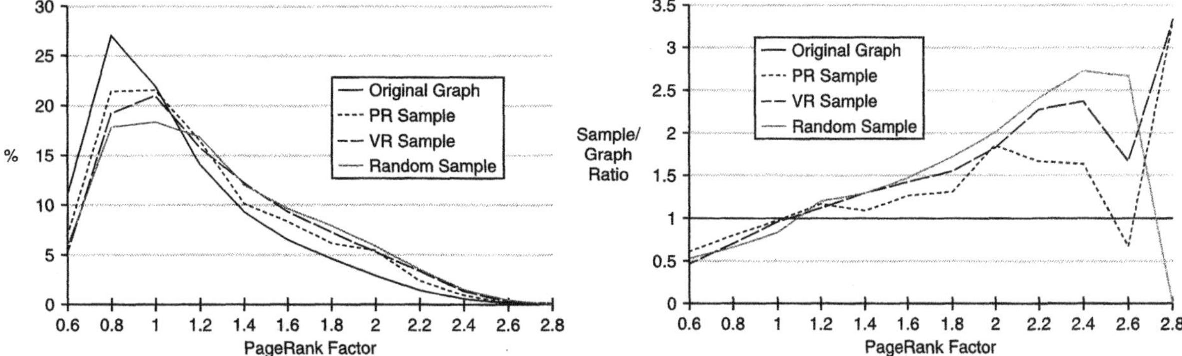

Fig. 3. PageRank distributions for the original graph and for nodes obtained by three different sampling techniques.

discover pages with higher PageRank. Our skewed sampling is supposed to ameliorate this effect but cannot completely correct for it. Our results verify this high-level analysis.

As can be seen from the right-hand graphs in Figs. 2 and 3, the most biased results for in-degree and PageRank appear in the random samples. In other words, both PR and VR sampling produces a net sampling that is more uniform than naive random sampling of the visited sub-graph.

We have similarly experimented with random graphs with broader ranges of in- and out-degrees, more similar to those found on the Web. A potential problem with such experiments is that random graphs constructed with small in- and out-degrees might contain disjoint pieces that are never sampled, or long trails that are not well-connected. Hence graphs constructed in this way are not guaranteed to have all nodes publicly accessible or well-connected. In such graphs we again find that using the values $VR(X)$ or $R'(X)$ to re-scale sampling probabilities makes the resulting sample appear more uniform. However, the results are not exactly uniform, as can be seen by comparing the distribution of in-degrees and PageRanks of the samples with those of the original graph.

6. Sampling random walks of the Web

To collect URLs for sampling, we performed three random walks of the Web that lasted one day each. All walks were started from a seed set containing 10,258 URLs discovered by a previous, long-running Web crawl. From the logs of each walk, we then constructed a graph representation that included only those visited pages whose content type was text/html. Finally, we collected PR, VR, and uniformly random samples for each walk using the algorithms described above.

Various attributes of these walks are shown in Table 1. For each walk, we give the walk's start date, the total number of downloaded HTML pages (some of which were fetched multiple times), as well as the number of nodes and (non-dangling) edges in the graph of the downloaded pages. Note that *Walk 3* downloaded pages at roughly twice the rate of the other two walks; we attribute this to the variability inherent in network bandwidth and DNS resolution.

Given any two random walks starting from the same seed set, one would hope that the intersection of the sets of URLs discovered by each walk would be small. To check how well our random walks live up to this goal, we examined the overlaps between the sets of URLs discovered by the three walks. Fig. 4 shows a Venn diagram representing this overlap. The three differently hatched regions represent the sets of URLs encountered by Walks 1, 2, and 3, respectively. The values in each region denote the

Table 1
Attributes of our three random Web walks

Name	Date	Downloads	Nodes	Edges
Walk 1	11/15/99	2,702,939	990,251	6,865,567
Walk 2	11/17/99	2,507,004	921,114	6,438,577
Walk 3	11/18/99	5,006,745	1,655,799	12,050,411

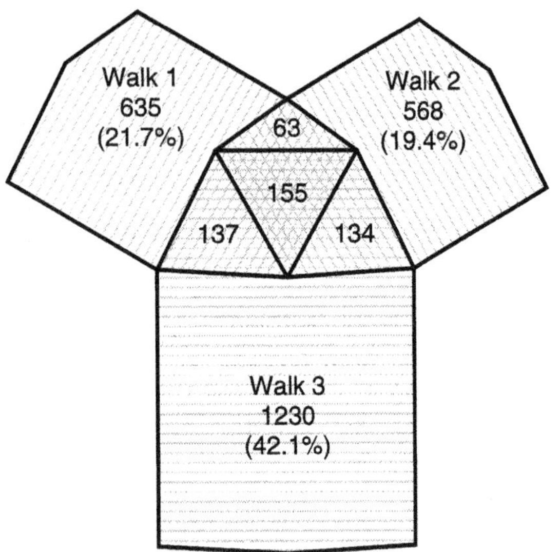

Fig. 4. Overlap of the URLs (in thousands) visited during the three walks.

number of URLs (in thousands), and the areas accurately reflect those values. The main conclusion to be drawn from this figure is that 83.2% of all visited URLs were visited by only one walk. Hence, our walks seem to disperse well, and therefore stand a good chance of discovering new corners of the Web.

7. Applications

Having a set of near-uniformly sampled URLs enables a host of applications. Many of these applications measure properties of the Web, and can be broadly divided into two groups: those that determine characteristics of the URLs themselves, and those that determine characteristics of the documents referred to by the URLs. Examples of the former group include measuring distributions of the following URL properties: length, number of arcs, port numbers, filename extensions, and top-level Internet domains. Examples of the latter group include measuring distributions of the following document properties: length, character set, language, number of out-links, and number of embedded images. In addition to measuring characteristics of the Web itself, uniformly sampled URLs can also be used to measure the fraction of all Web pages indexed by a search engine. In this section we report on two such applications, top-level domain distribution and search engine coverage.

7.1. Estimating the top-level domain distribution

We analyzed the distribution of URL host components across top-level Internet domains, and compared the results to the distribution we discovered during a much longer deterministic Web crawl that downloaded 80 million documents. Table 2 shows for each walk and each sampling method (using 10,000 URLs) the percentage of pages in the most popular Internet domains.

Note that the results are quite consistent over the three walks that are sampled in the same way. Also, as the size of the domain becomes smaller, the variance in percentages increases, as is to be expected by our earlier discussion.

There appears to be a relatively small difference between the various sampling techniques in this exercise. Although this may be in part because our skewed sampling does not sufficiently discount high PageRank pages, it also appears to be because the PageRank distributions across domains are sufficiently similar that we would expect little difference between sampling techniques here. We have found in our samples, for example, that the average sample PageRank and visit ratio are very close (within 10%) across a wide range of domains.

7.2. Search engine coverage

This section describes how we have used URL samples (using 2,000 pages) to estimate search engine coverage. For each of the URL samples produced as described in Section 6 above, we attempt to determine if the URL has been indexed by various search engines. If our samples were truly uniform over the set of all URLs, this would give an unbiased estimator of the fraction of all pages indexed by each search engine.

To test whether a URL is indexed by a search engine, we adopt the approach used by Bharat and Broder [2]. Using a list of words that appear in Web documents and an approximate measure of their frequency, we find the r rarest words that appear in each document. We then query the search engine using a conjunction of these r rarest words and check

Table 2
Percentage of sampled URLs in each top-level domain

Domain	Deterministic crawl	Uniform sample Walk 1	Uniform sample Walk 2	Uniform sample Walk 3	PR sample Walk 1	PR sample Walk 2	PR sample Walk 3	VR sample Walk 1	VR sample Walk 2	VR sample Walk 3
com	47.03	46.79	46.48	47.02	46.59	46.77	47.53	45.62	46.01	45.42
edu	10.25	9.01	9.02	8.90	9.31	9.36	9.13	9.84	9.08	9.96
org	8.38	8.51	8.82	8.99	8.66	8.74	8.38	9.12	8.91	8.65
net	6.41	4.80	4.52	4.39	4.96	4.63	4.62	4.74	4.50	4.52
jp	3.99	3.83	3.74	3.41	3.70	3.22	3.61	3.87	3.62	3.62
gov	2.75	2.97	3.04	2.74	3.13	3.09	2.53	3.42	3.53	2.89
uk	2.53	2.46	2.65	2.70	2.73	2.77	2.76	2.59	3.08	2.83
us	2.44	1.73	1.86	1.53	1.65	1.73	1.62	1.77	1.52	1.80
de	2.14	3.24	2.93	3.29	3.21	3.25	3.06	3.26	3.13	3.52
ca	1.93	2.07	2.31	1.94	2.13	1.85	1.86	2.05	1.89	2.07
au	1.51	1.85	1.87	1.64	1.75	1.66	1.66	1.74	1.49	1.71
fr	0.80	0.96	1.04	0.99	0.84	0.69	0.89	0.99	1.01	0.90
se	0.72	0.81	1.33	1.04	0.86	1.27	1.06	0.84	1.10	1.05
it	0.54	0.65	0.63	0.80	0.91	0.82	0.70	0.82	0.82	0.83
ch	0.37	0.87	0.71	0.99	0.64	0.71	0.87	0.92	0.72	0.89
Other	8.21	9.45	9.05	9.63	8.93	9.44	9.72	8.41	9.59	9.34

for the appropriate URL. In our tests, we use $r = 10$. Following their terminology, we call such a query a *strong query*, as the query is designed to strongly identify the page.

In practice, strong queries do not always uniquely identify a page. First, some sampled pages contain few rare words; therefore, even a strong query may produce thousands of hits. Second, mirror sites, duplicates or near-duplicates of the page, or other spurious matches can create difficulties. Third, some search engines (e.g., Northern Light) can return pages that do not contain *all* of the words in the query, despite the fact that a conjunctive query was used.

To deal with some of these difficulties, we adopt an approach similar to one suggested by Bharat and Broder [2]. In trying to match a URL with results from a search engine, all URLs are normalized by converting to lowercase, removing optional extensions such as `index.htm[l]` and `home.htm[l]`, inserting defaulted port numbers if necessary, and removing relative references of the form '#...'. We also use multiple matching criteria. A match is *exact* if the search engine returns a URL that, when normalized, exactly matches the normalized target URL. A *host* match occurs if a search engine returns a URL whose host component matches that of the target URL. Finally, a *non-zero* match occurs if a search engine returns any URL as a result of the strong query. Non-zero matches will overestimate the number of actual matches; however, the number of exact matches may be an underestimate if a search engine removes duplicate pages or if the location of a Web page has changed.

To measure the coverage of several popular search engines, we fetched the 12,000 pages corresponding to the URLs in the PR and VR samples of the three walks described in Section 6. We then determined the 10 rarest words in each fetched page, and performed queries on the following eight search engines: AltaVista [1], Excite [6], FAST Search [7], Google [8], HotBot [11], Infoseek [12], Lycos [16], and Northern Light [18].

The results of these experiments are shown in Figs. 5–7, which show the exact, host, and non-zero match percentages, respectively. Note that the results are quite consistent over the three walks and the two sampling methods.

An issue worth remarking on is that Google appears to perform better than one might expect from reported results on search engine size [19]. One possible reason for the discrepancy is that Google sometimes returns pages that it has not indexed based on key words in the anchor text pointing to the page. A second possibility is that Google's index may contain pages with higher PageRank than other

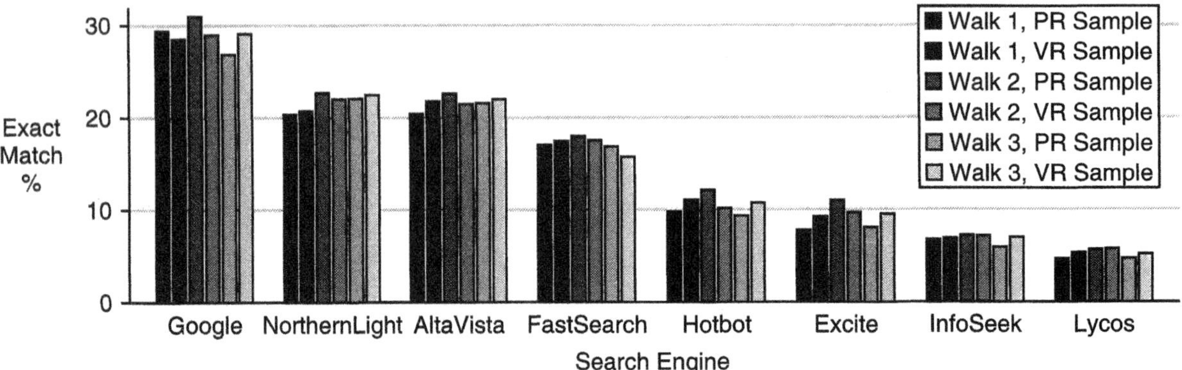

Fig. 5. Exact matches for the three walks.

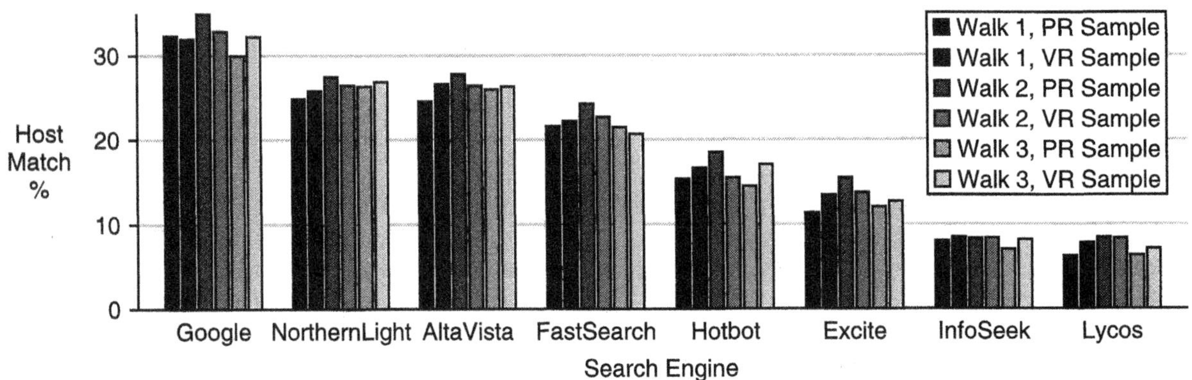

Fig. 6. Host matches for the three walks.

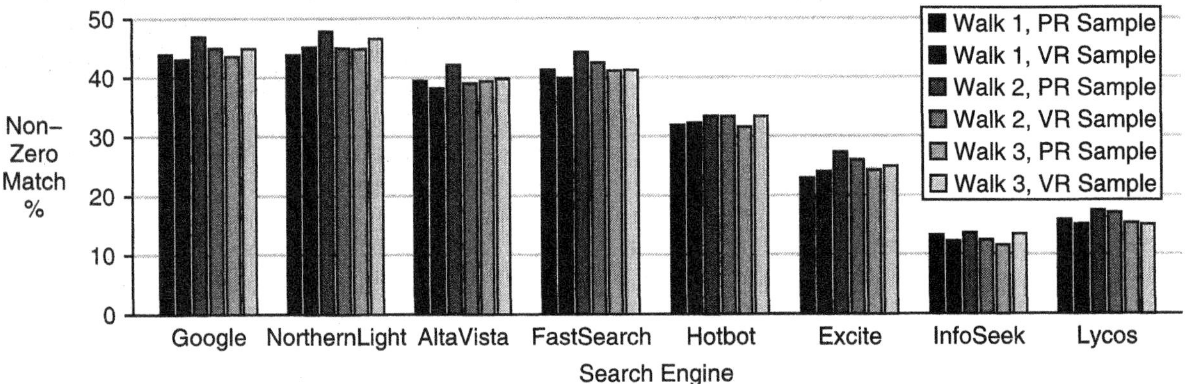

Fig. 7. Non-zero matches for the three walks.

search engines, and the biases of our approach in favor of such pages may therefore be significant. These possibilities underscore the difficulties in performing accurate measurements of search engine coverage.

8. Conclusions

We have described a method for generating a near-uniform sample of URLs by sampling URLs discovered during a random walk of the Web. It is known that random walks tend to over-sample URLs with higher connectivity, or PageRank. To ameliorate that effect, we have described how additional information obtained by the walk can be used to skew the sampling probability against pages with high PageRank. In particular, we use the visit ratio or the PageRanks determined by the graph of the pages visited during the walk.

In order to test our ideas, we have implemented a simple test bed based on random graphs with Zipfian degree distributions. Testing on these graphs shows that our samples based on skewed sampling probabilities yield samples that are more uniform over the entire graph than the samples obtained by sampling uniformly over pages visited during the random walk. Our samples, however, are still not uniform.

Currently, we have focused attention on making our approach universal, in that we do not take advantage of additional knowledge we may have about the Web. Using additional knowledge could significantly improve our performance, in terms of making our samples closer to uniform. For example, we could modify our sampling technique to more significantly lower the probability of sampling pages with apparently high PageRank from our random walk, and similarly we could significantly increase the probability of sampling pages with apparently low PageRank from our random walk. Our sampling probabilities could be based on information such as the distribution of in-degrees and out-degrees on the Web. However, such an approach might incur other problems; for example, the changing nature of the Web makes it unclear whether additional information used for sampling can be trusted to remain accurate over time.

References

[1] AltaVista, http://www.altavista.com/.

[2] K. Bharat and A. Broder, A technique for measuring the relative size and overlap of public Web search engines, in: Proc. of the 7th International World Wide Web Conference, Brisbane, Australia, Elsevier, Amsterdam, 1998, pp. 379–388.

[3] T. Bray, Measuring the Web, World Wide Web J. 1 (3) (1996).

[4] S. Brin and L. Page, The anatomy of a large-scale hypertextual Web search engine, in: Proc. of the 7th International World Wide Web Conference, Brisbane, Australia, Elsevier, Amsterdam, 1998, pp. 107–117.

[5] A. Broder, R. Kumar, F. Maghoul, P. Raghavan, S. Rajagopalan, R. Stata, A. Tomkins and J. Wiener, Graph structure in the Web, Comput. Networks 33 (2000) 309–320, this volume.

[6] Excite, http://www.excite.com/.

[7] FAST Search, http://www.alltheweb.com/.

[8] Google, http://www.google.com/.

[9] M. Henzinger, A. Heydon, M. Mitzenmacher and M. Najork, Measuring search engine quality using random walks on the Web, in: Proc. of the Eighth International World Wide Web Conference, Elsevier, Amsterdam, 1999, pp. 213–225.

[10] A. Heydon and M. Najork, Mercator: a scalable, extensible Web crawler, World Wide Web 2 (4) (1999) 219–229.

[11] HotBot, http://www.hotbot.com/.

[12] Infoseek, http://www.infoseek.com/.

[13] S.R. Kumar, P. Raghavan, S. Rajagopalan and A. Tomkins, Extracting large scale knowledge bases from the Web, in: IEEE International Conference on Very Large Databases (VLDB), Edinburgh, Scotland, September 1999, pp. 639–650.

[14] S. Lawrence and C.L. Giles, Searching the World Wide Web, Science 280 (536) (1998) 98.

[15] S. Lawrence and C.L. Giles, Accessibility of information on the Web, Nature 400 (1999) 107–109.

[16] Lycos, http://www.lycos.com/.

[17] Mercator Home Page, http://www.research.digital.com/SRC/mercator/.

[18] Northern Light, http://www.northernlight.com/.

[19] Search Engine Watch, http://www.searchenginewatch.com/reports/sizes.html.

Monika R. Henzinger received her Ph.D. from Princeton University in 1993 under the supervision of Robert E. Tarjan. Afterwards, she was an assistant professor in Computer Science at Cornell University. She joined the Digital Systems Research Center (now Compaq Computer Corporation's Systems Research Center) in 1996. Since September 1999 she is the Director of Research at Google, Inc. Her current research interests are information retrieval on the World Wide Web and algorithmic problems arising in this context.

Allan Heydon received his Ph.D. in Computer Science from Carnegie Mellon University, where he designed and implemented a system for processing visual specifications of file system security. In addition to his recent work on Web crawling, he has also worked on the Vesta software configuration management system, the Juno-2 constraint-based drawing editor, and algorithm animation. He is a senior member of the research staff at Compaq Computer Corporation's Systems Research Center.

Michael Mitzenmacher received his Ph.D. in Computer Science from the University of California at Berkeley in 1996. He then joined the research staff of the Compaq Computer Corporation's

Systems Research Center. Currently he is an assistant professor at Harvard University. His research interests focus on algorithms and random processes. Current interests include error-correcting codes, the Web, and distributed systems.

Marc Najork is a senior member of the research staff at Compaq Computer Corporation's Systems Research Center. His current research focuses on 3D animation, information visualization, algorithm animation, and the Web. He received his Ph.D. in Computer Science from the University of Illinois at Urbana-Champaign in 1994, where he developed Cube, a three-dimensional visual programming language.

Graph structure in the Web

Andrei Broder [a], Ravi Kumar [b,*], Farzin Maghoul [a], Prabhakar Raghavan [b], Sridhar Rajagopalan [b], Raymie Stata [c], Andrew Tomkins [b], Janet Wiener [c]

[a] *AltaVista Company, San Mateo, CA, USA*
[b] *IBM Almaden Research Center, San Jose, CA, USA*
[c] *Compaq Systems Research Center, Palo Alto, CA, USA*

Abstract

The study of the Web as a graph is not only fascinating in its own right, but also yields valuable insight into Web algorithms for crawling, searching and community discovery, and the sociological phenomena which characterize its evolution. We report on experiments on local and global properties of the Web graph using two AltaVista crawls each with over 200 million pages and 1.5 billion links. Our study indicates that the macroscopic structure of the Web is considerably more intricate than suggested by earlier experiments on a smaller scale.

Keywords: Graph structure; Diameter; Web measurement

1. Introduction

Consider the directed graph whose nodes correspond to static pages on the Web, and whose arcs correspond to links between these pages. We study various properties of this graph including its diameter, degree distributions, connected components, and macroscopic structure. There are several reasons for developing an understanding of this graph.

(1) Designing crawl strategies on the Web [15].
(2) Understanding of the sociology of content creation on the Web.
(3) Analyzing the behavior of Web algorithms that make use of link information [9–11,20,26]. To take just one example, what can be said of the distribution and evolution of PageRank [9] values on graphs like the Web?
(4) Predicting the evolution of Web structures such as bipartite cores [21] and Webrings, and developing better algorithms for discovering and organizing them.
(5) Predicting the emergence of important new phenomena in the Web graph.

We detail a number of experiments on a Web crawl of approximately 200 million pages and 1.5 billion links; the scale of this experiment is thus five times larger than the previous biggest study [21] of structural properties of the Web graph, which used a pruned data set from 1997 containing about 40 million pages. Recent work ([21] on the 1997 crawl, and [5] on the approximately 325 thousand node nd.edu subset of the Web) has suggested that the distribution of degrees (especially in-degrees, i.e., the number of links to a page) follows a *power law.*

The power law for in-degree: the probability

* Corresponding author. E-mail: ravi@almaden.ibm.com

that a node has in-degree i is proportional to $1/i^x$, for some $x > 1$.

We verify the power law phenomenon in current (considerably larger) Web crawls, confirming it as a basic Web property.

In other recent work, [4] report the intriguing finding that most pairs of pages on the Web are separated by a handful of links, almost always under 20, and suggest that this number will grow logarithmically with the size of the Web. This is viewed by some as a 'small world' phenomenon. Our experimental evidence reveals a rather more detailed and subtle picture: most ordered pairs of pages cannot be bridged at all and there are significant numbers of pairs that can be bridged, but only using paths going through hundreds of intermediate pages. Thus, the Web is not the ball of highly connected spaghetti we believed it to be; rather, the connectivity is strongly limited by a high-level global structure.

1.1. Our main results

We performed three sets of experiments on Web crawls from May 1999 and October 1999. Unless otherwise stated, all results described below are for the May 1999 crawl, but all conclusions have been validated for the October 1999 crawl as well. First, we generated the in- and out-degree distributions, confirming previous reports on power laws; for instance, the fraction of Web pages with i in-links is proportional to $1/i^{2.1}$. The constant 2.1 is in remarkable agreement with earlier studies at varying scales [5,21]. In our second set of experiments we studied the directed and undirected connected components of the Web. We show that power laws also arise in the distribution of *sizes* of these connected components. Finally, in our third set of experiments, we performed a number of breadth-first searches from randomly chosen start nodes. We detail these experiments in Section 2.

Our analysis reveals an interesting picture (Fig. 9) of the Web's macroscopic structure. Most (over 90%) of the approximately 203 million nodes in our May 1999 crawl form a single connected component if links are treated as *undirected* edges. This connected Web breaks naturally into four pieces. The first piece is a central core, all of whose pages can reach one another along directed links; this 'giant strongly connected component' (*SCC*) is at the heart of the Web. The second and third pieces are called *IN* and *OUT*. *IN* consists of pages that can reach the *SCC*, but cannot be reached from it; possibly new sites that people have not yet discovered and linked to. *OUT* consists of pages that are accessible from the *SCC*, but do not link back to it, such as corporate Websites that contain only internal links. Finally, the *TENDRILS* contain pages that cannot reach the *SCC*, and cannot be reached from the *SCC*. Perhaps the most surprising fact is that the size of the *SCC* is relatively small; it comprises about 56 million pages. Each of the other three sets contain about 44 million pages, thus, all four sets have roughly the same size.

We show that the diameter of the central core (*SCC*) is at least 28, and that the diameter of the graph as a whole is over 500 (see Section 1.3 for definitions of diameter). We show that for randomly chosen source and destination pages, the probability that any path exists from the source to the destination is only 24%. We also show that, if a directed path exists, its average length will be about 16. Likewise, if an undirected path exists (i.e., links can be followed forwards or backwards), its average length will be about 6. These analyses appear in the Section 3. These results are remarkably consistent across two different, large AltaVista crawls. This suggests that our results are relatively insensitive to the particular crawl we use, provided it is large enough. We will say more about crawl effects in Section 3.4.

In a sense the Web is much like a complicated organism, in which the local structure at a microscopic scale looks very regular like a biological cell, but the global structure exhibits interesting morphological structure (body and limbs) that are not obviously evident in the local structure. Therefore, while it might be tempting to draw conclusions about the structure of the Web graph from a local picture of it, such conclusions may be misleading.

1.2. Related prior work

Broadly speaking, related prior work can be classified into two groups: (1) observations of the power law distributions on the Web; and (2) work on applying graph theoretic methods to the Web.

1.2.1. Zipf–Pareto–Yule and power laws

Distributions with an inverse polynomial tail have been observed in a number of contexts. The earliest observations are due to Pareto [27] in the context of economic models. Subsequently, these statistical behaviors have been observed in the context of literary vocabulary [32], sociological models [33], and even oligonucleotide sequences [24] among others. Our focus is on the closely related power law distributions, defined on the positive integers, with the probability of the value i being proportional to $1/i^k$ for a small positive number k. Perhaps the first rigorous effort to define and analyze a model for power law distributions is due to Simon [30].

More recently, power law distributions have been observed in various aspects of the Web. Two lines of work are of particular interest to us. First, power laws have been found to characterize user behavior on the Web in two related but dual forms:

(1) access statistics for Web pages, which can be easily obtained from server logs (but for caching effects); see [1,2,17,19];
(2) numbers of times users at a single site access particular pages, as verified by instrumenting and inspecting logs from Web caches, proxies, and clients (see [6] and references therein, as well as [23]).

Second, and more relevant to our immediate context, is the distribution of degrees on the Web graph. In this context, recent work (see [5,21]) suggests that both the in- and the out-degrees of vertices on the Web graph have power laws. The difference in scope in these two experiments is noteworthy. The first [21] examines a Web crawl from 1997 due to Alexa, Inc., with a total of over 40 million nodes. The second [5], examines Web pages from the University of Notre Dame domain, *.nd.edu, as well as a portion of the Web reachable from three other URLs. In this paper, we verify these power laws on more recent (and considerably larger) Web crawls. This collection of findings reveals an almost fractal-like quality for the power law in-degree and out-degree distributions, in that it appears both as a macroscopic phenomenon on the entire Web, as a microscopic phenomenon at the level of a single university Website, and at intermediate levels between these two.

There is no evidence that users' browsing behavior, access statistics and the linkage statistics on the Web graph are related in any fundamental way, although it is very tempting to conjecture that this is indeed the case. It is usually the case, though not always so, that pages with high in-degree will also have high PageRank [9]. Indeed, one way of viewing PageRank is that it puts a number on how easy (or difficult) it is to find particular pages by a browsing-like activity. Consequently, it is plausible that the in-degree distributions induce a similar distribution on browsing activity and consequently, on access statistics.

Faloutsos et al. [16] observe Zipf–Pareto distributions (power law distributions on the *ranks* of values) on the Internet network topology using a graph of the network obtained from the routing tables of a backbone BGP router.

1.2.2. Graph theoretic methods

Much recent work has addressed the Web as a graph and applied algorithmic methods from graph theory in addressing a slew of search, retrieval, and mining problems on the Web. The efficacy of these methods was already evident even in early local expansion techniques [10]. Since then, the increasing sophistication of the techniques used, the incorporation of graph theoretical methods with both classical and new methods which examine context and content, and richer browsing paradigms have enhanced and validated the study and use of such methods. Following Butafogo and Schneiderman [10], the view that connected and strongly connected components represent meaningful entities has become accepted. Pirolli et al. [28] augment graph theoretic analysis to include document content, as well as usage statistics, resulting in a rich understanding of domain structure and a taxonomy of roles played by Web pages.

Graph theoretic methods have been used for search [8,9,12,13,20], browsing and information foraging [10,11,14,28,29], and Web mining [21,22,25, 26]. We expect that a better structural characterization of the Web will have much to say in each of these contexts.

In this section we formalize our view of the Web as a graph; in this view we ignore the text and other content in pages, focusing instead on the links between pages. Adopting the terminology of graph theory [18], we refer to pages as *nodes*, and to links as *arcs*. In this framework, the Web becomes a large graph containing several hundred million nodes, and a few billion arcs. We will refer to this graph as the *Web graph*, and our goal in this paper is to understand some of its properties. Before presenting our model for Web-like graphs, we begin with a brief primer on graph theory, and a discussion of graph models in general.

1.3. A brief primer on graphs and terminology

The reader familiar with basic notions from graph theory may skip this primer.

A *directed graph* consists of a set of *nodes,* denoted V and a set of *arcs,* denoted E. Each arc is an ordered pair of nodes (u, v) representing a directed connection from u to v. The *out-degree* of a node u is the number of distinct arcs $(u, v_1)\ldots(u, v_k)$ (i.e., the number of links from u), and the *in-degree* is the number of distinct arcs $(v_1, u)\ldots(v_k, u)$ (i.e., the number of links to u). A path from node u to node v is a sequence of arcs $(u, u_1), (u_1, u_2), \ldots (u_k, v)$. One can follow such a sequence of arcs to 'walk' through the graph from u to v. Note that a path from u to v does not imply a path from v to u. The *distance* from u to v is one more than the smallest k for which such a path exists. If no path exists, the distance from u to v is defined to be infinity. If (u, v) is an arc, then the distance from u to v is 1.

Given a directed graph, a *strongly connected component* (strong component for brevity) of this graph is a set of nodes such that for any pair of nodes u and v in the set there is a path from u to v. In general, a directed graph may have one or many strong components. The strong components of a graph consist of disjoint sets of nodes. One focus of our studies will be in understanding the distribution of the sizes of strong components on the Web graph.

An *undirected graph* consists of a set of nodes and a set of *edges*, each of which is an unordered pair $\{u, v\}$ of nodes. In our context, we say there is an edge between u and v if there is a link between u and v, without regard to whether the link points from u to v or the other way around. The *degree* of a node u is the number of edges incident to u. A path is defined as for directed graphs, except that now the existence of a path from u to v implies a path from v to u. A *component* of an undirected graph is a set of nodes such that for any pair of nodes u and v in the set there is a path from u to v. We refer to the components of the undirected graph obtained from a directed graph by ignoring the directions of its arcs as the *weak components* of the directed graph. Thus two nodes on the Web may be in the same weak component even though there is no *directed* path between them (consider, for instance, a node u that points to two other nodes v and w; then v and w are in the same weak component even though there may be no sequence of links leading from v to w or vice versa). The interplay of strong and weak components on the (directed) Web graph turns out to reveal some unexpected properties of the Web's connectivity.

A *breadth-first search* (BFS) on a directed graph begins at a node u of the graph, and proceeds to build up the set of nodes reachable from u in a series of layers. Layer 1 consists of all nodes that are pointed to by an arc from u. Layer k consists of all nodes to which there is an arc from some vertex in layer $k - 1$, but are not in any earlier layer. Notice that by definition, layers are disjoint. The distance of any node from u can be read out of the breadth-first search. The shortest path from u to v is the index of the layer v belongs in, i.e., if there is such a layer. On the other hand, note that a node that cannot be reached from u does not belong in any layer, and thus we define the distance to be infinity. A BFS on an undirected graph is defined analogously.

Finally, we must take a moment to describe the exact notions of diameter we study, since several have been discussed informally in the context of the Web. Traditionally, the *diameter* of a graph, directed or undirected, is the maximum over all ordered pairs (u, v) of the shortest path from u to v. Some researchers have proposed studying the *average distance* of a graph, defined to be the length of the shortest path from u to v, averaged over all ordered pairs (u, v); this is referred to as diameter in [4]. The difficulty with this notion is that even a single pair (u, v) with no path from u to v results in an infinite average distance. In fact, as we show from our experiments below, the Web is rife with such pairs (thus it is not merely a matter of discarding a few outliers before taking this average). This motivates the following revised definition: let P be the set of all ordered pairs (u, v) such that there is a path from u to v. The *average connected distance* is the expected length of the shortest path, where the expectation is over uniform choices from P.

2. Experiments and results

2.1. Infrastructure

All experiments were run using the Connectivity Server 2 (CS2) software built at Compaq Systems Research Center using data provided by AltaVista. CS2 provides fast access to linkage information on the Web. A build of CS2 takes a Web crawl as input and creates a representation of the entire Web graph induced by the pages in the crawl, in the form of a database that consists of all URLs that were crawled together with all in-links and out-links among those URLs. In addition, the graph is extended with those URLs referenced at least five times by the crawled pages. (Experimentally, we have determined that the vast majority of URLs encountered fewer than five times but not crawled turn out to be invalid URLs.)

CS2 improves on the original connectivity server (CS1) described in [7] in two important ways. First, it significantly increases the compression of the URLs and the links to data structures. In CS1, each compressed URL is, on average, 16 bytes. In CS2, each URL is stored in 10 bytes. In CS1, each link requires 8 bytes to store as both an in-link and out-link; in CS2, an average of only 3.4 bytes are used. Second, CS2 provides additional functionality in the form of a host database. For example, in CS2, it is easy to get all the in-links for a given node, or just the in-links from remote hosts.

Like CS1, CS2 is designed to give high-performance access to all this data on a high-end machine with enough RAM to store the database in memory. On a 465 MHz Compaq AlphaServer 4100 with 12 GB of RAM, it takes 70–80 μs to convert an URL into an internal id or vice versa, and then only 0.15 μs/link to retrieve each in-link or out-link. On a uniprocessor machine, a BFS that reaches 100 million nodes takes about 4 minutes; on a 2-processor machine we were able complete a BFS every 2 minutes.

In the experiments reported in this paper, CS2 was built from a crawl performed at AltaVista in May, 1999. The CS2 database contains 203 million URLs and 1466 million links (all of which fit in 9.5 GB of storage). Some of our experiments were repeated on a more recent crawl from October, 1999 containing 271 million URLs and 2130 million links.

In general, the AltaVista crawl is based on a large set of starting points accumulated over time from various sources, including voluntary submissions. The crawl proceeds in roughly a BFS manner, but is subject to various rules designed to avoid overloading Web servers, avoid robot traps (artificial infinite paths), avoid and/or detect spam (page flooding), deal with connection time outs, etc. Each build of the AltaVista index is based on the crawl data after further filtering and processing designed to remove duplicates and near duplicates, eliminate spam pages, etc. Then the index evolves continuously as various processes delete dead links, add new pages, update pages, etc. The secondary filtering and the later deletions and additions are not reflected in the connectivity server. But overall, CS2's database can be viewed as a superset of all pages stored in the index at one point in time. Note that due to the multiple starting points, it is possible for the resulting graph to have many connected components.

2.2. Experimental data

The following basic algorithms were implemented using CS2: (1) a BFS algorithm that performs a breadth-first traversal; (2) a WCC algorithm that finds the weak components; and (3) an SCC algorithm that finds the strongly connected components. Recall that both WCC and SCC are simple generalizations of the BFS algorithm. Using these three basic algorithms, we ran several interesting experiments on the Web graph.

2.2.1. Degree distributions

The first experiment we ran was to verify earlier observations that the in- and out-degree distributions on the Web are distributed according to power laws. We ran the experiment on both the May and October crawls of the Web. The results, shown in Figs. 1 and 3, show remarkable agreement with each other, and with similar experiments from data that is over two years old [21]. Indeed, in the case of in-degree, the exponent of the power law is consistently around 2.1, a number reported in [5,21]. The anomalous bump at 120 on the x-axis is due to a large clique formed by a single spammer. In all our log–log plots, straight lines are linear regressions for the best power law fit.

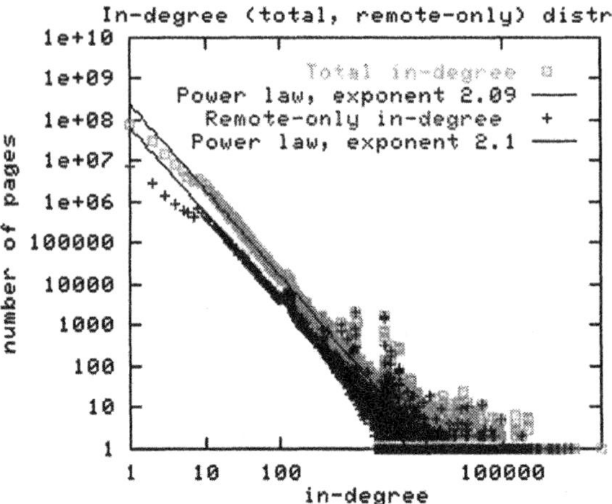

Fig. 1. In-degree distributions subscribe to the power law. The law also holds if only off-site (or 'remote-only') edges are considered.

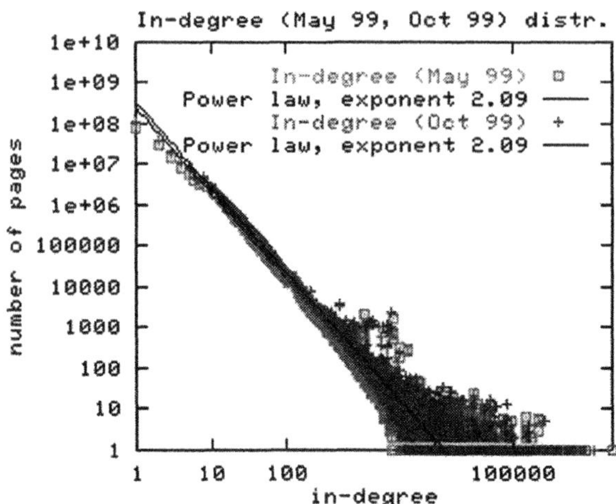

Fig. 3. In-degree distributions show a remarkable similarity over two crawls, run in May and October 1999. Each crawl counts well over 1 billion distinct edges of the Web graph.

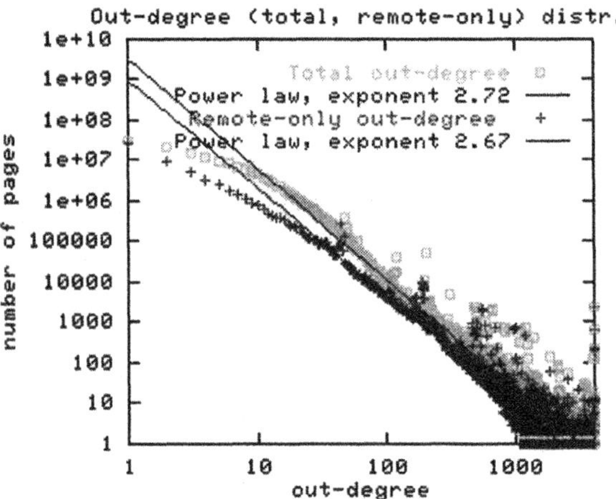

Fig. 2. Out-degree distributions subscribe to the power law. The law also holds if only off-site (or 'remote-only') edges are considered.

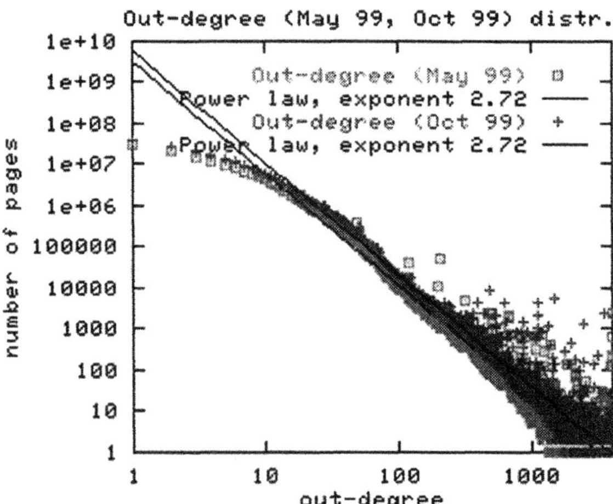

Fig. 4. Out-degree distributions show a remarkable similarity over two crawls, run in May and October 1999. Each crawl counts well over 1 billion distinct edges of the Web graph.

Out-degree distributions also exhibit a power law, although the exponent is 2.72, as can be seen in Figs. 2 and 4. It is interesting to note that the initial segment of the out-degree distribution deviates significantly from the power law, suggesting that pages with low out-degree follow a different (possibly Poisson or a combination of Poisson and power law, as suggested by the concavity of the deviation) distribution. Further research is needed to understand this combination better.

2.2.2. *Undirected connected components*

In the next set of experiments we treat the Web graph as an undirected graph and find the sizes of the undirected components. We find a giant component of 186 million nodes in which fully 91% of the nodes in our crawl are reachable from one another by following either forward or backward links. This is done by running the WCC algorithm which simply finds all connected components in the undirected Web graph. Thus, if one could browse along both

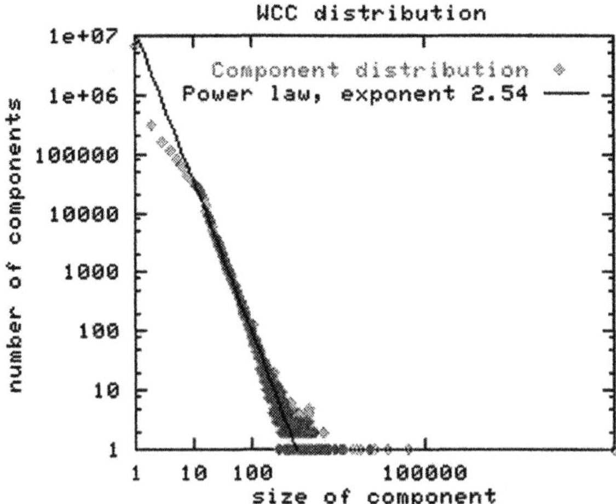

Fig. 5. Distribution of weakly connected components on the Web. The sizes of these components also follow a power law.

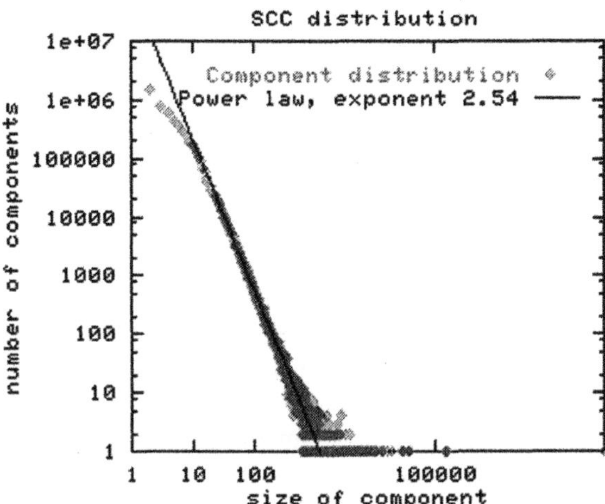

Fig. 6. Distribution of strongly connected components on the Web. The sizes of these components also follow a power law.

forward and backward directed links, the Web is a very well connected graph. Surprisingly, even the distribution of the sizes of WCCs exhibits a power law with exponent roughly 2.5 (Fig. 5).

Does this widespread connectivity result from a few nodes of large in-degree acting as 'junctions'? Surprisingly, this turns out not to be the case. Indeed, even if all links to pages with in-degree 5 or higher are removed (certainly including links to every well-known page on the Web), the graph still contains a giant weak component of size 59 million (see Table 1). This provides us with two interesting and useful insights. First, the connectivity of the Web graph as an undirected graph is extremely resilient and does not depend on the existence of nodes of high in-degree. Second, such nodes, which are very useful and tend to include nodes with high PageRank or nodes that are considered good hubs and authorities, are embedded in a graph that is well connected without them. This last fact may help understand why algorithms such as HITS [20] converge quickly.

Table 1
Size of the largest surviving weak component when links to pages with in-degree at least k are removed from the graph.

k	1000	100	10	5	4	3
Size (millions)	177	167	105	59	41	15

2.2.3. Strongly connected components

Motivated in part by the intriguing prediction of [4] that the average distance (referred to in their paper as diameter) of the Web is 19 (and thus it should be possible to get from any page to any other in a small number of clicks), we turned to the strongly connected components of the Web as a directed graph. By running the strongly connected component algorithm, we find that there is a single large SCC consisting of about 56 million pages, all other components are significantly smaller in size. This amounts to barely 28% of all the pages in our crawl. One may now ask: where have all the other pages gone? The answer to this question reveals some fascinating detailed structure in the Web graph; to expose this and to further study the issues of the diameter and average distance, we conducted a further series of experiments. Note that the distribution of the sizes of SCCs also obeys a power law (Fig. 6).

2.2.4. Random-start BFS

We ran the BFS algorithm twice from each of 570 randomly chosen starting nodes: once in the *forward* direction, following arcs of the Web graph as a browser would, and once *backward* following links in the reverse direction. Each of these BFS traversals (whether forward or backward) exhibited a sharp bimodal behavior: it would either 'die out' after reaching a small set of nodes (90% of the time this set has fewer than 90 nodes; in extreme cases it has a few hundred thousand), or it would 'explode' to cover about 100 million nodes (but never the entire 186 million). Further, for a fraction of the starting nodes, both the forward and the backward BFS runs would 'explode', each covering about 100 million nodes (though not the same 100 million in the two runs). As we show below, these are the starting points that lie in the SCC.

The cumulative distributions of the nodes covered in these BFS runs are summarized in Fig. 7. They reveal that the true structure of the Web graph must be somewhat subtler than a 'small world' phenomenon in which a browser can pass from any Web page to any other with a few clicks. We explicate this structure in Section 3.

2.2.5. *Zipf distributions vs power law distributions*

The *Zipf distribution* is an inverse polynomial function of *ranks* rather than magnitudes; for example, if only in-degrees 1, 4, and 5 occurred then a power law would be inversely polynomial in those values, whereas a Zipf distribution would be inversely polynomial in the ranks of those values: i.e., inversely polynomial in 1, 2, and 3. The in-degree distribution in our data shows a striking fit with a Zipf (more so than the power law) distribution; Fig. 8 shows the in-degrees of pages from the May 1999 crawl plotted against both ranks and magnitudes (corresponding to the Zipf and power law cases). The plot against ranks is virtually a straight line in the log–log plot, without the flare-out noticeable in the plot against magnitudes.

3. Interpretation and further work

Let us now put together the results of the connected component experiments with the results of the random-start BFS experiments. Given that the set SCC contains only 56 million of the 186 million nodes in our giant weak component, we use the BFS runs to estimate the positions of the remaining nodes. The

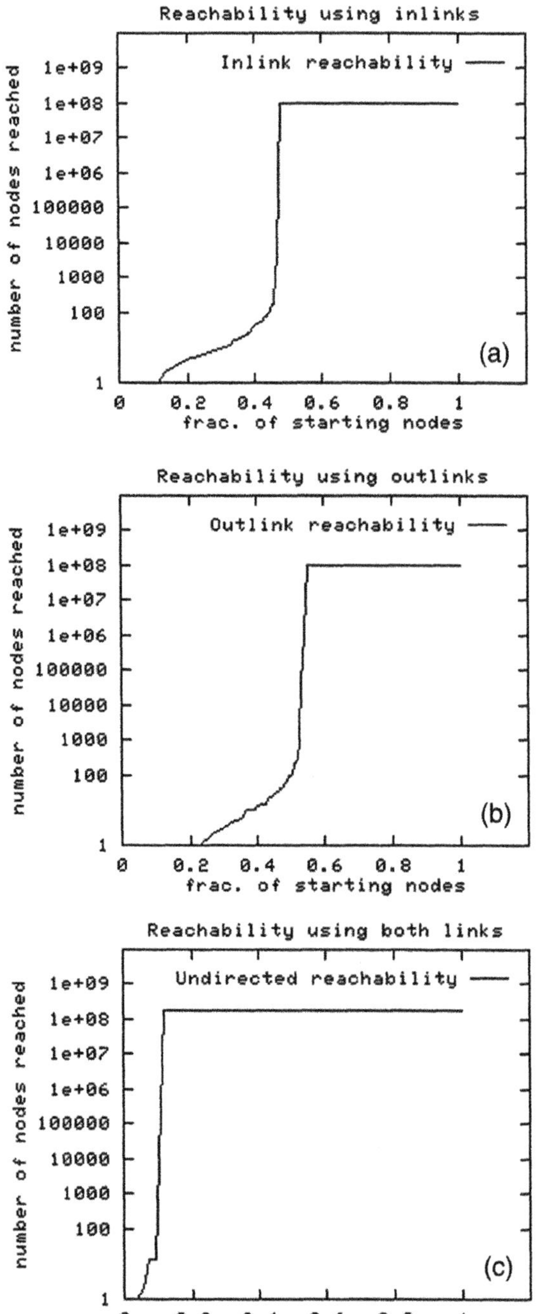

Fig. 7. Cumulative distribution on the number of nodes reached when BFS is started from a random node: (a) follows in-links, (b) follows out-links, and (c) follows both in- and out-links. Notice that there are two distinct regions of growth, one at the beginning and an 'explosion' in 50% of the start nodes in the case of in- and out-links, and for 90% of the nodes in the undirected case. These experiments form the basis of our structural analysis.

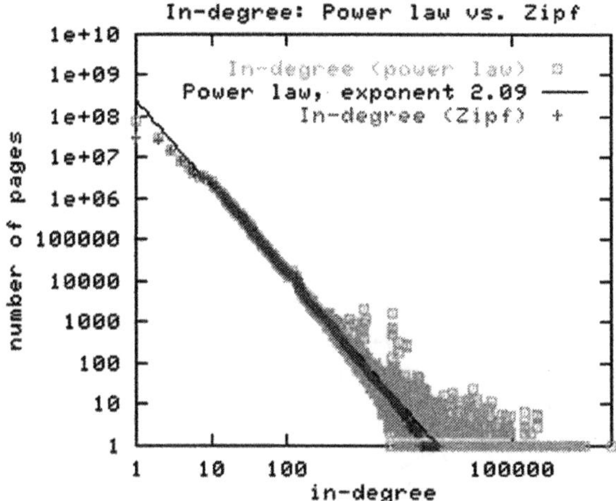

Fig. 8. In-degree distributions plotted as a power law and as a Zipf distribution.

starting points for which the forward BFS 'explodes' are either in SCC, or in a set we call IN, that has the following property: there is a directed path from each node of IN to (all the nodes of) SCC. Symmetrically, there is a set we call OUT containing all starting points for which the backward BFS 'explodes'; there is a directed path from any node in the SCC to every node in OUT. Thus a forward BFS from any node in either the SCC or IN will explode, as will a backward BFS from any node in either the SCC or OUT. By analyzing forward and backward BFS from 570 random starting points, we can compute the number of nodes that are in SCC, IN, OUT or none of these. Fig. 9 shows the situation as we can now infer it.

We now give a more detailed description of the structure in Fig. 9. The sizes of the various components are as follows:

Region	SCC	IN	OUT
Size	56,463,993	43,343,168	43,166,185
Region	TENDRILS	DISC.	Total
Size	43,797,944	16,777,756	203,549,046

These sizes were determined as follows. We know the total number of nodes in our crawl, so by subtracting the size of the giant weak component we determine the size of DISCONNECTED. Then our strong-component algorithm gives us the size of SCC. We turn to our breadth-first search data. As noted, searching from a particular start node following a particular type of edges (in-edges or out-edges) would either terminate quickly, or grow the search to about 100 million nodes. We say that a node *explodes* if it falls into the latter group. Thus, if a node explodes following in-links, and also explodes following out-links, it must be a member of a strong component of size at least $100 + 100 - 186 = 14$ million. Since the second largest strong component is of size 150 thousand, we infer that SCC is the unique strong component that contains all nodes exploding following in- as well as out-links. In fact, this observation contains two corroborating pieces of evidence for the structure in the table above: first, it turns out that the fraction of our randomly chosen BFS start nodes that explode under in- and out-links is the same as the fraction of nodes in the SCC as returned by our SCC algorithm. Second, every BFS start node in the SCC reaches exactly the same number of nodes under in-link expansion; this number is 99,807,161. Likewise, under out-link expansion every node of SCC reaches exactly 99,630,178 nodes.

Thus, we know that SCC + IN = 99,807,161, and similarly SCC + OUT = 99,630,178. Having already found the size of SCC, we can solve for IN and OUT. Finally, since we know the size of the giant weak component, we can subtract SCC, IN, and OUT to get TENDRILS. We now discuss each region in turn.

3.1. TENDRILS and DISCONNECTED

We had 172 samples from TENDRILS and DISCONNECTED; our BFS measurements cannot be used to differentiate between these two regions. By following out-links from a start point in this region, we encounter an average of 20 nodes before the exploration stops. Likewise, by following in-links we encounter an average of 52 nodes.

3.2. IN and OUT

Our sample contains 128 nodes from IN and 134 from OUT. We ask: when following out-links from nodes in OUT, or in-links from nodes in IN, how many nodes do we encounter before the BFS terminates? That is, how large a neighborhood do points in these

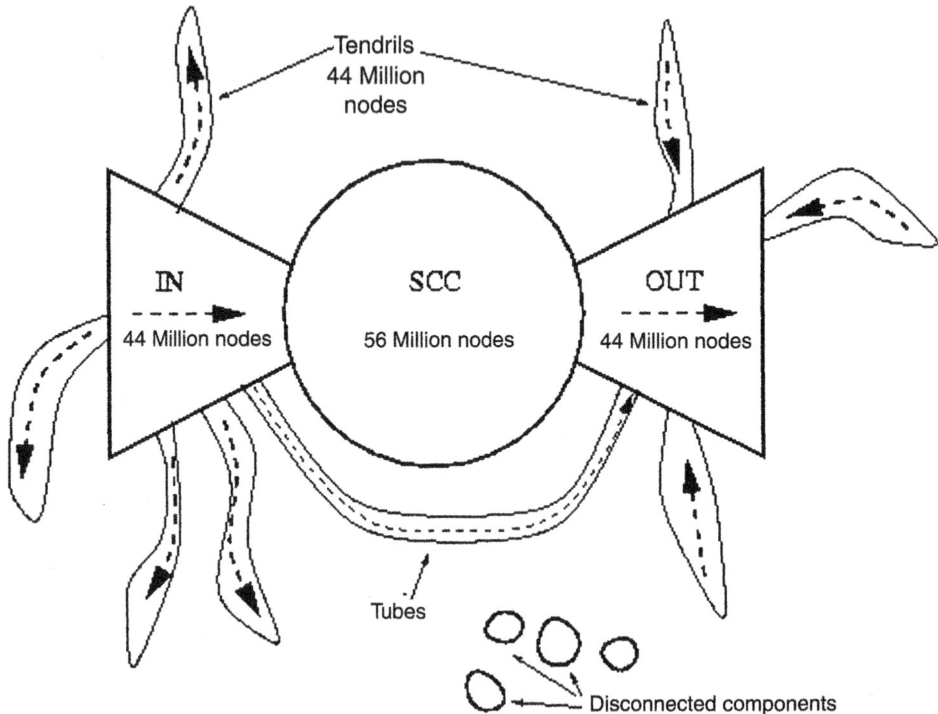

Fig. 9. Connectivity of the Web: one can pass from any node of IN through SCC to any node of OUT. Hanging off IN and OUT are TENDRILS containing nodes that are reachable from portions of IN, or that can reach portions of OUT, without passage through SCC. It is possible for a TENDRIL hanging off from IN to be hooked into a TENDRIL leading into OUT, forming a TUBE: i.e., a passage from a portion of IN to a portion of OUT without touching SCC.

regions have, if we explore in the direction ‘away’ from the center? The results are shown below in the row labeled ‘exploring outward – all nodes’.

Similarly, we know that if we explore in-links from a node in OUT, or out-links from a node in IN, we will encounter about 100 million other nodes in the BFS. Nonetheless, it is reasonable to ask: how many other nodes will we encounter? That is, starting from OUT (or IN), and following in-links (or out-links), how many nodes of TENDRILS and OUT (or IN) will we encounter? The results are shown below in the row labeled ‘exploring inwards – unexpected nodes’. Note that the numbers in the table represent averages over our sample nodes.

Starting point	OUT	IN
Exploring outwards – all nodes	3093	171
Exploring inwards – unexpected nodes	3367	173

As the table shows, OUT tends to encounter larger neighborhoods. For example, the second largest strong component in the graph has size approximately 150 thousand, and two nodes of OUT encounter neighborhoods a few nodes larger than this, suggesting that this component lies within OUT. In fact, considering that (for instance) almost every corporate Website not appearing in SCC will appear in OUT, it is no surprise that the neighborhood sizes are larger.

3.3. SCC

Our sample contains 136 nodes from the SCC. To determine other properties of SCC, we require a useful property of IN and OUT: each contains a few long paths such that, once the BFS proceeds beyond a certain depth, only a few paths are being explored, and the last path is much longer than any of the others. We can therefore explore the radius at which the BFS completes, confident that the last long path will be the same no matter which node of SCC we start from. The following table shows the depth at which the BFS terminates in each direction (following in-links or out-links) for nodes in the SCC.

Measure	Minimum depth	Average depth	Maximum depth
In-links	475	482	503
Out-links	430	434	444

As the table shows, from some nodes in the SCC it is possible to complete the search at distance 475, while from other nodes distance 503 is required. This allows us to conclude that the directed diameter of SCC is at least 28.

3.4. Other observations

As noted above, the (min, average, max) depths at which the BFS from SCC terminates following in-links are (475, 482, 503). For IN, we can perform the same analysis, and the values are: (476, 482, 495). These values, especially the average, are so similar that nodes of IN appear to be quite close to SCC.

Likewise, for SCC the (min, average, max) depths for termination under out-links are (430, 434, 444). For OUT, the values are (430, 434, 444).

Now, consider the probability that an ordered pair (u, v) has a path from u to v. By noting that the average in-size of nodes in IN is very small (171) and likewise the average out-size of nodes in OUT is very small (3093), the pair has a path with non-negligible probability if and only if u is in SCC + IN, and v is in SCC + OUT. The probability of this event for node pairs drawn uniformly from our crawl is only 24%; for node pairs drawn from the weak component it is only 28%. This leads to the somewhat surprising conclusion that, given a random start and finish page on the Web, one can get from the start page to the finish page by traversing links barely a quarter of the time.

The structure that is now unfolding tells us that it is relatively insensitive to the particular large crawl we use. For instance, if AltaVista's crawler fails to include some links whose inclusion would add one of the tendrils to the SCC, we know that the resulting change in the sizes of SCC and TENDRIL will be small (since any individual tendril is small). Likewise, our experiments in which we found that large components survived the deletion of nodes of large in-degree show that the connectivity of the Web is resilient to the removal of significant portions.

3.5. Diameter and average connected distance

As we discussed above, the directed diameter of the SCC is at least 28. Likewise, the maximum finite shortest path length is at least 503, but is probably substantially more than this: unless a short tube connects the most distant page of IN to the most distant page of OUT without passing through the SCC, the maximum finite shortest path length is likely to be close to $475 + 430 = 905$.

We can estimate the average connected distance using our 570 BFS start points, under both in-links and out-links. The values are shown below; the column headed 'Undirected' corresponds to the average undirected distance.

Edge type	In-links (directed)	Out-links (directed)	Undirected
Average connected distance	16.12	16.18	6.83

These results are in interesting contrast to those of [4], who predict an average distance of 19 for the Web based on their crawl of the nd.edu site; it is unclear whether their calculations consider directed or undirected distances. Our results on the other hand show that over 75% of time there is no directed path from a random start node to a random finish node; when there *is* a path, the figure is roughly 16. However, if links can be traversed in either direction, the distance between random pairs of nodes can be much smaller, around 7, on average.

4. Further work

Further work can be divided into three broad classes.

(1) More experiments aimed at exposing further details of the structures of *SCC, IN, OUT,* and the *TENDRILS*. Would this basic structure, and the relative fractions of the components, remain stable over time?

(2) Mathematical models for evolving graphs, motivated in part by the structure of the Web; in addition, one may consider the applicability of such models to other large directed graphs such as the phone-call graph, purchase/transaction graphs, etc. [3].
(3) What notions of connectivity (besides weak and strong) might be appropriate for the Web graph? For instance, what is the structure of the undirected graph induced by the co-citation relation or by bibliographic coupling [31].

Acknowledgements

We thank Keith Randall for his insights into our SCC algorithm and implementation.

References

[1] L. Adamic and B. Huberman, The nature of markets on the World Wide Web, Xerox PARC Technical Report, 1999.
[2] L. Adamic and B. Huberman, Scaling behavior on the World Wide Web, Technical comment on [5].
[3] W. Aiello, F. Chung and L. Lu, A random graph model for massive graphs, ACM Symposium on the Theory and Computing, 2000.
[4] R. Albert, H. Jeong and A.-L. Barabasi, Diameter of the World Wide Web, Nature 401 (1999) 130–131.
[5] A. Barabasi and R. Albert, Emergence of scaling in random networks, Science 286 (509) (1999).
[6] P. Barford, A. Bestavros, A. Bradley and M.E. Crovella, Changes in Web client access patterns: characteristics and caching implications, World Wide Web, Special Issue on Characterization and Performance Evaluation, 2 (1999) 15–28.
[7] K. Bharat, A. Broder, M. Henzinger, P. Kumar and S. Venkatasubramanian, The connectivity server: fast access to linkage information on the web, in: Proc. 7th WWW, 1998.
[8] K. Bharat and M. Henzinger, Improved algorithms for topic distillation in hyperlinked environments, in: Proc. 21st SIGIR, 1998.
[9] S. Brin and L. Page, The anatomy of a large scale hypertextual web search engine, in: Proc. 7th WWW, 1998.
[10] R.A. Butafogo and B. Schneiderman, Identifying aggregates in hypertext structures, in: Proc. 3rd ACM Conference on Hypertext, 1991.
[11] J. Carriere and R. Kazman, WebQuery: searching and visualizing the Web through connectivity, in: Proc. 6th WWW, 1997.
[12] S. Chakrabarti, B. Dom, D. Gibson, J. Kleinberg, P. Raghavan and S. Rajagopalan, Automatic resource compilation by analyzing hyperlink structure and associated text, in: Proc. 7th WWW, 1998.
[13] S. Chakrabarti, B. Dom, D. Gibson, S. Ravi Kumar, P. Raghavan, S. Rajagopalan and A. Tomkins, Experiments in topic distillation, in: Proc. ACM SIGIR Workshop on Hypertext Information Retrieval on the Web, 1998.
[14] S. Chakrabarti, D. Gibson and K. McCurley, Surfing the Web backwards, in: Proc. 8th WWW, 1999.
[15] J. Cho, H. Garcia-Molina, Synchronizing a database to improve freshness, To appear in 2000 ACM International Conference on Management of Data (SIGMOD), May 2000.
[16] M. Faloutsos, P. Faloutsos and C. Faloutsos, On power law relationships of the internet topology, ACM SIGCOMM, 1999.
[17] S. Glassman, A caching relay for the world wide web, in: Proc. 1st WWW, 1994.
[18] F. Harary, Graph Theory, Addison-Wesley, Reading, MA, 1975.
[19] B. Huberman, P. Pirolli, J. Pitkow and R. Lukose, Strong regularities in World Wide Web surfing, Science 280 (1998) 95–97.
[20] J. Kleinberg, Authoritative sources in a hyperlinked environment, in: Proc. 9th ACM–SIAM SODA, 1998.
[21] R. Kumar, P. Raghavan, S. Rajagopalan and A. Tomkins, Trawling the Web for cyber communities, in: Proc. 8th WWW, April 1999.
[22] R. Kumar, P. Raghavan, S. Rajagopalan and A. Tomkins, Extracting large scale knowledge bases from the Web, in: Proc. VLDB, July 1999.
[23] R.M. Lukose and B. Huberman, Surfing as a real option, in: Proc. 1st International Conference on Information and Computation Economies, 1998.
[24] C. Martindale and A.K. Konopka, Oligonucleotide frequencies in DNA follow a Yule distribution, Computer and Chemistry 20 (1) (1996) 35–38.
[25] A. Mendelzon, G. Mihaila and T. Milo, Querying the World Wide Web, Journal of Digital Libraries 1 (1) (1997) 68–88.
[26] A. Mendelzon and P. Wood, Finding regular simple paths in graph databases, SIAM J. Comp. 24 (6) (1995) 1235–1258.
[27] V. Pareto, Cours d'économie politique, Rouge, Lausanne et Paris, 1897.
[28] P. Pirolli, J. Pitkow and R. Rao, Silk from a sow's ear: extracting usable structures from the Web, in: Proc. ACM SIGCHI, 1996.
[29] J. Pitkow and P. Pirolli, Life, death, and lawfulness on the electronic frontier, in: Proc. ACM SIGCHI, 1997.
[30] H.A. Simon, On a class of stew distribution functions, Biometrika 42 (1955) 425–440.
[31] H.D. White and K.W. McCain, Bibliometrics, in: Annual Review of Information Science and Technology, Vol. 24, Elsevier, Amsterdam, 1989, pp. 119–186.
[32] G.U. Yule, Statistical Study of Literary Vocabulary, Cambridge University Press, New York, 1944.
[33] G.K. Zipf, Human Behavior and the Principle of Least Effort, Addison-Wesley, Reading, MA, 1949.

BLT: Bi-layer Tracing of HTTP and TCP/IP ☆

Anja Feldmann [1]

Universität des Saarlandes, Saarbrücken, Germany

Abstract

We describe BLT, a tool for extracting full HTTP level as well as TCP level traces via packet monitoring. This paper presents the software architecture that allows us to collect traces continuously, online, and at any point in the network. The software has been used to extract extensive traces within AT&T WorldNet since spring 1997 as well as at AT&T Labs-Research. BLT offers a much richer alternative to Web proxy logs, client logs, and Web server logs due to the accuracy of the timestamps, the level of details available by considering several protocol layers (TCP/IP and HTTP events), and its non intrusive way of gathering data. Traces gathered using BLT have provided the foundation of several Web performance studies. © 2000 Published by Elsevier Science B.V. All rights reserved.

Keywords: Trace collection; Web; HTTP; TCP; Packet traces

1. Introduction

To improve the performance of the network and the network protocol, it is important to characterize the dominant applications [7,12,13,18,28,31,32]. Only by utilizing data about all events initiated by the Web (including TCP and HTTP events) can one hope to understand the chain of performance problems that current Web users face. Due to the popularity of the Web it is crucial to understand how usage relates to the performance of the network, the servers, and the clients. Such comprehensive information is only available via packet monitoring. Unfortunately, extracting HTTP information from packet sniffer data is non-trivial due to the huge volume of data, the line speed of the monitored links, the need for continuous monitoring, the need to preserve privacy, and the need to be able to monitor at any point in the network. These needs translate into requirements for online processing and online extraction of the relevant data, the topic of this paper.

The software described in this paper runs on the PacketScope monitor developed by AT&T Labs [1]. PacketScope is deployed at several different locations within AT&T WorldNet, a production IP network, and at AT&T Labs-Research. One PacketScope monitors T3 backbone links, another PacketScope may monitor traffic generated by a large set of modems on a FDDI ring or traffic on other FDDI rings, another PacketScope monitors traffic between AT&T Labs-Research and the Internet. First deployed in spring 1997, the software has run without interruption for weeks at a time collecting and reconstructing detailed logs of millions of Web downloads with less than a worst case packet loss of 0.3%.

The rest of this paper is organized as follows. Section 2 discusses the advantages of packet sniffing

☆ An earlier version of this paper was presented as a position paper at the W3C Web Characterisation Workshop, November 1998, Cambridge, MA.

[1] E-mail: anja@cs.uni-sb.de

and Section 3 outlines some of the difficulties of extracting HTTP data from packet traces. The overall software architecture is described in Section 4. Our solution (including the logfile format) is presented in Sections 5–7. In Section 8 we revisit some of the studies based upon data collected by BLT and point out how each study benefited from the data. Finally, Section 9 briefly summarizes some of the lessons learned.

2. Strength of packet monitoring

There are many ways of gaining access to information about user accesses to the Web:

- from users running modified Web browsers
- from Web content provider logging information about which data are retrieved from their Web server
- from Web proxies logging information about which data are requested by the users of the Web proxy
- from the wire via packet monitoring.

While each of these methods has its advantages, most have severe limitations regarding the detail of information that can be logged. Distributing modified Web browsers to a representative sample of consumers and having them agree to monitor their browsing behavior is problematic, especially since Microsoft Internet Explorer and Netscape's browser became more popular than Mosaic and Lynx. The source code to Microsoft Internet Explorer is not available and the source code to Netscape has just recently become available. Some studies such as Crovella et al. [12] clearly show the benefit of such data sources. Yet, to evaluate changes in Web client access patterns between 1995 and 1999 [6] the same authors augmented a proxy instead of modifying the client.

While the logfiles from Web servers are extremely useful to scale the performance of the specific Web server they are not necessarily representative of the overall Web. The access pattern from users to specific files are heavily influenced by what content the Web server is offering [14,27]. Therefore a lot of Web server logs have to be analyzed in order to generalize to the overall Web. While possible [3,11,27], this is non trivial. Another aspect is that currently the standard log files generated by Web servers do not include sufficient detail regarding timing of all possible aspects of data retrieval.

Using the Web proxy for logging information can be suboptimal especially if either not all users are encouraged/forced to use the Web proxy, or it is impossible to instrument the Web proxy, or if insufficient detail is available in the logged information. The work of Mogul and co-authors [25,30] shows how useful Web proxy traces can be. One benefit of data from packet traces over proxy traces is very precise timestamps.

The information gathered from packet monitoring includes the full HTTP header information plus detailed timestamps of HTTP and TCP events. This may, e.g., include the timestamp for when a GET request was issued, when the corresponding HTTP response was sent, when the first/last data packet was sent, etc. In addition full IP packet headers can be collected. The advantages of monitoring on the wire via packet sniffing include that this monitoring methodology is passive and therefore oblivious to the user. It does not impact the performance of the network. The amount of detail that can be gathered is sufficient to capture TCP and HTTP interactions. If desired and allowed BLT has the potential to collect the actual downloaded Web page (including results from CGI scripts). Having this detail available has enabled such studies as the effectiveness of delta-encoding and compression [28], the rate of change of Web pages [14], Web cache coherency schemes [24], the benefit of Web caching for heterogeneous bandwidth environments [8,16], and the characterization of IP-flows for WWW traffic [18].

Three other projects have used packet level data to extract Web data. A group from IBM augmented their Web server logs with partial packet level data for the collection of the traces during the Olympics. These data allow TCP level performance characterization and analysis [5]. Still, while it is possible to glean information about the access patterns within a site it is impossible to learn cross-site effects. A group at Berkeley used a packet sniffer on the HomeIP network at the University of California at Berkeley [20]. They wrote their own set of software to continuously extract HTTP information on top of the Internet Protocol Scanning Engine ISPE [19]. Their user-level HTTP module is sitting on top of the TCP module and mainly logs HTTP level information. Since the main interest of the authors at the time of the sniffer code development was focused on HTTP traces they currently do not log full HTTP headers nor the full set of timestamp for TCP events. If studying things like Web caching and the burstiness of the arrival pattern of Web requests [8,16,17,20] these missing details can lead to misleading predictions. A group at Virginia Tech have developed HTTPDump [34] to extract HTTP headers from tcpdump traces [21]. The performance of their general tool is not sufficient to collect continuous traces on an 10Mbit/s Ethernet. The simpler perl version [35] that only parses the first packet of the first HTTP request/response on a TCP connection promises good performance but is severely limited in its generality.

Other applications of accessing Web data from packet level data are layer 5 switching [2] and content-based request distribution schemas [4]. Both redirect HTTP request towards different servers based upon the content of the HTTP request by either moving the TCP state or rewriting the TCP sequence numbers or a combination of the two methods. Layer 5 switching is easier than layer 5 information extraction because the switch is in the data path and it is close to the Web server. Therefore it can throttle the server and it should see both sides of the packet stream.

The work most closely related to ours in terms of being able to collect 24 × 7–24 hours, 7 days a week, around the clock passive measurements at key locations in the network is Windmill [26]. Windmill offers an extensible experimental platform in which application modules can process the subsets of the packet stream that they need. Our software design is driven by the desire to collect an extensive TCP/IP and HTTP level traces. As such we have identified the key events to log for Web performance studies, and since more than 70% of the traffic is Web traffic, we have designed the system for maximal throughput and minimal interaction between data collection and data processing.

3. Challenges of HTTP reconstruction

Adding support for Web trace extraction goes well beyond the basic idea of packet sniffers like tcpdump [21] that any packet can be processed in isolation. Indeed, the extraction software has to almost run a TCP and a full HTTP stack in order to demultiplex the packets and extract the content. The software has to go from packets to TCP connections, from TCP connections to individual HTTP transactions (there may be more than one), from individual HTTP transactions to HTTP requests and HTTP responses and the transferred data. While this is hard enough to implement correctly on an end system it is even harder in this case because the software is incapable of throttling the end system, cannot make any assumptions about the compliance of either the clients nor the servers with the TCP and HTTP specifications [22], nor may it see both halves of the TCP connection. Even worse, due to packet by packet load balancing it may only see every other packet for some, currently small fraction, of the transfers. On the other hand the software has the advantage that it does not have to be perfect. It is our desire to gather continuous traces without downtime on a high-speed transmission medium such as FDDI or multiple T3's with capacities greater than 100 Mbit/s. In such an setting it is almost impossible to not lose some small fraction of the HTTP transactions due to packet losses at the sniffer. It is possible to keep packet losses small (e.g., by running the sniffer at higher priority) but it is impossible to guarantee that no packet will ever be lost. Therefore the resulting trace data should only be used for such analysis that are statistically robust against losing a very small fraction of the transactions.

To get a better flavor for the problems that need to be addressed consider the following subproblems: assumptions about how Web pages and their meta information are fragmented into packets, assumptions about how TCP connections are used by HTTP, demultiplexing (including reordering and loss) of TCP packets to HTTP transactions, and sanity checking of the extracted information.

Web pages and their meta information are often fragmented into TCP packets in an unexpected fashion:

- A single HTTP request or response header can be almost arbitrarily long. Sizes of greater than 5000 bytes are not too uncommon (as such, they are certainly longer than the typical 1500 bytes per packet).
- A single HTTP header (even if less than 500 bytes) can easily be split among multiple packets.

(It is not too uncommon to see each line of an HTTP request or response being transmitted in a single packet.)

- Retransmitted data may have a completely different fragmentation, e.g., the original HTTP request and first 300 bytes of data might have been transmitted in 5 separate packets; the end-system thinking that the packets got lost may retransmit all of the data in a single packet.

HTTP uses TCP as its underlying transport protocol leading to the following issues:

- A TCP connection may be terminated at any point.
- On abort some HTTP clients will close the connection via RST, others will send a FIN.
- Even in HTTP/1.0 one TCP connection can be used to transfer multiple HTTP requests and responses.
- Within a single TCP connection, determining when a transfer has completed and the new meta information starts, is non trivial because there is nothing marking the data transfer as completed.
- HTTP header information does not always start at the beginning of a packet.
- Even an HTTP GET request may contain data.
- Multiple HTTP requests can be pipelined on a TCP connection.

Demultiplexing of the TCP packets into HTTP transactions implies dealing with lost packets, retransmitted packets, and reordered packets:

- The packet sniffer may lose any packet (even the ones containing the TCP open connection or close connection events). Therefore using a TCP connection as the demultiplexing unit is problematic.
- The sniffer may lose the packet containing the HTTP header or response information and therefore has to ignore the data associated with the request.
- Even packets containing the newline separating the HTTP response from the HTTP data can get lost, making it tricky to decide when the HTTP meta data end and when the real data begin.
- The packet containing the Web page data may not always arrive at the sniffer location before the packet containing the HTTP response.
- A packet containing the HTTP request may be received after the packet for the HTTP response for the HTTP request is received. (This is possible since the source might have thought that the packet got lost and retransmitted the packet.)

While it seems easy to debug HTTP extraction software, not all bugs may be bugs:

- The HTTP response content length is not always accurate.
- The HTTP header field can contain wrong/misleading information, e.g., bogus last modified times.
- Requests to the same Web page do not need to yield the same results (some sites return customized data (e.g., depending on the browser type).

All of the above indicate that one needs a sophisticated tool to extract HTTP information from packet level data and that just inspecting the first x bytes of each Web TCP connection is insufficient.

4. Packet monitoring software

The hardware and software design for the monitoring system was driven by the desire to gather continuous traces without downtime on a high-speed transmission medium. If there is a collection machine that is capable of capturing packets on a medium than it should be possible to run BLT. The software should be deployable even on backbone links. Due to the asymmetric routing, common in today's Internet, backbone links may only see packets of one direction of a TCP connection.

Hardware design. The hardware of the AT&T Packetscope [1] consists of standard hardware components, a Dec Alpha 500 MHz Workstation with a 8 Gigabyte Raid disk array and a 7 tape DLT tape robot. For more details on the hardware architecture, see Fig. 1. Several security precautions have been taken, including using no IP addresses and using read only device drivers. The Dec Alpha platform was chosen because of the kernel performance optimizations to support packet sniffing by Mogul and Ramakrishnan [29].

Software design, online vs. offline extraction. Given that HTTP headers can easily be larger than 1500 bytes and will span multiple packets we had no choice but to collect full packet traces of the wire. At speeds of 100 Mbit/s this implies that the processing

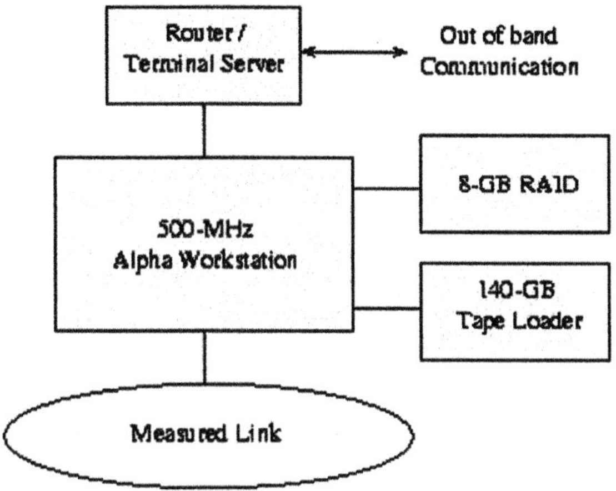

Fig. 1. AT&T PacketScope architecture.

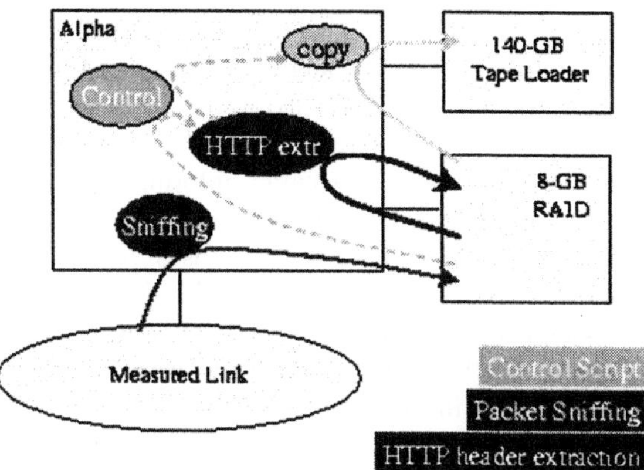

Fig. 2. Control flow of HTTP header extraction software.

of the data into the log format has to be done on the monitoring machine itself. No current DLT tape technology can transfer data to tape at a rate anywhere close the 100 Mbit/s. Neither does the disk system allow storage of more than a few hours of data. Besides, processing the logs offline would introduce serious privacy concerns with respect to the data content of the packets. Since the PacketScope, due to the placement in the network, may only see packets either directed to the Web server or to the Web client, no matching of HTTP requests with their HTTP responses is done online. Rather, where possible, this is done offline.

Software design, partitioning of the software. Packet sniffing involves having the packets pass through at least some part of the protocol stack on the monitoring machine at interrupt level. At line rate even pure packet sniffing can already stress even such powerful machines as the DEC Alphas [29]. The amount of processing per packet for HTTP header extraction is variable and potentially quite large. E.g., one can imagine collecting all packets of a TCP connection and extracting the HTTP information upon receiving a packet with a FIN flag. In this case the processing time for the packet with the FIN flag would be much larger than the processing time for any of the other packets of the same TCP connection. Only when receiving a packet with a FIN flag would the much more involved HTTP extraction be executed. Due to variable processing time we separated the processing priorities of the tasks — high priority for the packet sniffing; lower priorities for the packet extraction and any other software. To avoid interference between the HTTP extraction software and packet sniffing, the extraction software should avoid processing at interrupt level. Splitting the software into two stages introduces the need to pipeline the processing. We choose to use files as buffers between the collection and the processing stages.

We decompose the overall task into four components: packet sniffing, a control script, HTTP header extraction, and HTTP header matching. Fig. 2 shows how the first three interact with each other:

- *Packet sniffling*: software based on tcpdump [21] that will copy a fixed number of bytes from each packet to a file. Once it has processed some number of packets, this software will close the current file, move the file to a different directory, and open a new file. In addition all IP addresses are encrypted as they come of the wire before saving them to disk. This process runs at normal priority.
- *Control script*: a perl [33] script that controls the pipeline. It monitors a directory and will start the HTTP header extraction software for each file that the packet sniffing software generates. Once the header extraction software is done it will copy the logfiles to tape and clean up the disk. Besides controlling the copying of files the control script also needs to monitor the tape usage, switch tapes on the tape robot, and allow for personnel at the PacketScope locations to change tape sets at any point in time.

- *HTTP header extraction*: software that will process files generated by tcpdump (containing packets with full data content) and extracts logfiles containing full HTTP request and response headers and relevant timestamp information, TCP timestamps and data summarizing the data portion of the HTTP requests/responses. In addition the software creates pure packet header tcpdump files for the observed traffic. The software extends tcpdump [21] to reconstruct HTTP sessions and is run niced to the maximum possible level.
- *HTTP header matching*: offline post-processing software that will match HTTP request information with HTTP response information where applicable. The match is based upon either a match between sequence numbers and acknowledgment numbers or additional heuristics.

The benefit of building most of the software on top of tcpdump is that we can take full advantage of the filtering mechanism, and the built-in knowledge about the IP/TCP protocol stack. Using the filtering mechanism is especially useful if BLT is run in an environment where the capturing hardware is at its limits. In this case using a more restrictive filter may provide BLT with the cycles. (Note, that not all Web traffic is using port 80.) Adding the support for multiple files for the packet sniffing software is a trivial extension of tcpdump. Next, we give more detail on the HTTP header extraction (Section 5), the logfile format (Section 6), and the HTTP header matching software (Section 7).

5. Implementation of HTTP header extraction

The software is built along the following lines:

(1) Demultiplexing packets according to 'Web pages', using 'IP-flows'.
(2) Reordering packets according to TCP sequence numbers.
(3) Eliminating duplicate packets (due to retransmissions).
(4) Identifying missing packets (due to loss in monitor, or due to packet per packet multiplexing).
(5) Extracting the HTTP protocol header information and the HTTP body part and timestamp information from the data content of the TCP packets.
(6) Extracting relevant TCP timestamp information.
(7) Computing the HTTP protocol information and summarizing information about the HTTP data part, such as the length of the data content, and starting and ending sequence numbers.
(8) Unless the policy of the collection location allows the storage of the HTTP data part, it is discarded immediately and should never leave the monitoring machine.

To not impede the packet sniffing effort it is crucial to avoid unnecessary file I/O and therefore the software should stay memory resident. This makes it impossible to follow the above recipe step by step while continuously monitoring packets. Alone the memory requirements for storing about 200,000 packets each of size 1500 bytes exceeds the memory of our monitoring machine. Therefore it is necessary to split the steps outlined above into substages. Whenever all packets have been received for one HTTP transaction its information is extracted. Unfortunately, a single transaction can involve thousands of packets; therefore even this step has to be staged. Whenever a sufficient number of packets is received for one HTTP transaction its partial information is extracted. The clean-up step controls this staging.

5.1. Data structure

Instead of using TCP connections we use IP-flows [10,18] to demultiplex packets. This accounts for the possibility of losing packets with TCP flags, monitoring only packets from one side of a TCP connection, and fragmentation of Web pages and their meta information. An IP-flow is a set of packets that are close in time and that have the same IP addresses and the same TCP port numbers of both the source and the destination. Our definition of close in time is somewhat looser than the definition used in [18] by using a 10-min (a compile time constant) timeout value. For the most part, all packets in an IP-flow correspond to a single unidirectional TCP connection, and all packets in a single unidirectional TCP connection correspond to a single flow. The main data structure is a per flow list of packets and a list of partial information extracted from this flow. The desire is to append any new incoming packet to the correct list of packets and then, at the appropriate time intervals, extract the HTTP information. Fig. 3

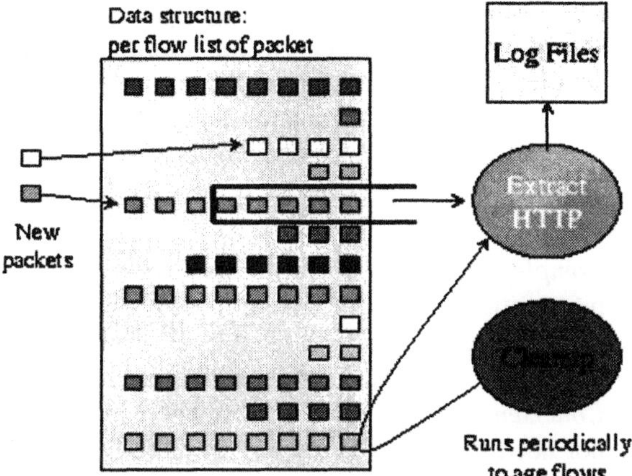

Fig. 3. HTTP header extraction.

shows a schematic of how the various steps are done on the per flow data structure.

If every TCP connection would contain exactly one HTTP transaction, the key for indexing the per flow data structure would correspond to a single HTTP request or response. Unfortunately the use of persistent connections [30] is common enough, even in HTTP/1.0, that the key is not sufficient. Instead, the offline matching of HTTP requests and HTTP responses is done by matching the sequence numbers with the acknowledgments. Indeed there may not be a match because not all HTTP requests will generate a HTTP response message. Given the complications of finding the match between HTTP requests and HTTP responses and the fact that it is separable from the information extraction, this step is done during offline post-processing.

5.2. Extraction

The extraction stage performs the steps outlined at the beginning of the section on a single, sufficiently long, list of packets. This means that the packets are ordered according to their sequence numbers. (The sorting is efficient since most packets are only slightly or not at all out of order. The chosen sorting routine handles sequence number overflows correctly.) Next, either all or an initial subset of the packets will be used to extract the TCP/HTTP timing and HTTP request/response information. If no packet has been received for an IP-flow within the last 10 min all packets will be processed. If the list contains more than 300 packets, the first say 200 packets (both numbers are compile time constants) within the list are processed. By processing only about 2/3 of the packet list current gaps in the later part of the list are likely to be filled by packets that are still in transit. (The TCP window size is limited.) In contrast processing all packets would lead to many more missing packets and a much more incomplete logfile.

Due to persistent connections an HTTP header can start at any point during an IP-flow. The HTTP header information is found by looking for one of the following patterns. (For simplicity we are denoting the patterns using perl the number of tcp connection notation even though the implementation is in C.)

```
/GET \w+ HTTP\/\d+\.\d+\n/
/HEAD \w+ HTTP\/\d+\.\d+\n/
/POST \w+ HTTP\/\d+\.\d+\n/
/HTTP\d+\.\d+ \d+ \w+\n/
```

Here `\n` may be the UNIX or the MSDOS newline character. The end of the HTTP header is found by looking for two CRLF or when running out of a preset limit of 50,000 bytes. This limit is necessary in case the packet containing the newline is lost. Whenever a gap in the sequence numbers is discovered, the flag GAP is set in the logfile and the data should be disregarded in further analysis. In general the packet loss is well below 0.3% and very few HTTP transactions are affected by losses.

To support partial processing of packets, our software keeps a state machine for any active flow. The state machine records

- the number of TCP connections using this flowid since the flowid was started
- the number of HTTP requests within the TCP connection
- timestamp of the packet with the first sequence number
- file containing the extracted data content (only at appropriate trace locations)
- flag indicating partial HTTP data extraction yes/no
- size of partially extracted data content
- the next sequence number.

It is necessary to record the number of TCP connections that are using a flowid although it is very unlikely that the same customer may reuse a given flowid for a different TCP connection. Still in modem environments this is more likely since a given IP address can be reassigned to different customers and those may use the same port number to visit for example the same Web server. (Port numbers on newly rebooted machines usually start at a fixed port number 1024.)

Since persistent connections can use a given TCP connection for more than one HTTP request the index of an HTTP request within a TCP connection leads to a useful heuristics for the matching of HTTP requests and responses. The next field keeps track of information extracted from each HTTP body, the timestamp of the first packet containing data and the filename containing the partially reassembled body (where appropriate). The remaining fields store the flow state once a partial list of packets has been processed. The state consists of a bit to indicate if the software is currently extracting an HTTP body, the size of the body extracted so far, and the next sequence number. This state is sufficient under the assumption that partial processing never ends within an HTTP header. To keep this invariant, partial processing is continued beyond the first 200 packets of the current list of packets if an HTTP header is reconstructed. (While HTTP headers can be spread among many packets, we have not yet found an HTTP header spread among more than 50 packets.) As soon as some complete information, e.g., about a TCP event or about an HTTP header, has been retrieved from the packets this information is written to the logfile.

5.3. Clean-up

This stage is used to age flows. It triggers the extraction stages for an IP-flow if either the list of its packets is larger than 300 packets or if no packet has been received for this flow for the timeout of 10 min. Finding the time intervals for scheduling the clean-up stage is complicated by the desire to balance processing overheads versus memory. Currently, the clean-up stage is executed after processing 50,000 packets (another compile-time constant).

6. Logfile format

Finding an appropriate logfile format for BLT is crucial since the online processing paradigm makes it impossible to go back in time and augment the logfile with additional information. The other motivation for a detailed discussion of the logfile format is that it shows the breath of information that is available by tracing across multiple protocol layers. Our choice of logfile format for BLT was guided by the following concerns.

- *Completeness*: We want to distill all essential information from the traces; this includes full HTTP headers information, full IP/TCP header information, and TCP connection information.
- *Conciseness*: Most Web performance studies do not need the full IP/TCP header information but they gain significantly from accurate timestamp information about HTTP events.
- *Bi-protocol*: Web performance studies also gain from knowledge of lower layer events such as, e.g., TCP connection establishment timestamps. These timestamps have a natural equivalent in the application and supply crucial timing information.
- *Privacy*: The HTTP header information may contain fields that reveal information about the source or destination of the HTTP request. Privacy concerns demand that one separates this information from IP address information.

To meet our goals the HTTP header extraction software splits the information into three different files:

- *Packet header*: IP/TCP packet headers of all observed traffic stored in tcpdump file format.
- *Flow*: information about every unidirectional IP flow [18].
- *HTTP/TCP*: TCP events and HTTP events; the logfile includes the raw text of every HTTP request/response.

In terms of size the packet header logs are by far the largest. The next smaller ones are the HTTP/TCP logs while the per flow files are the smallest ones. By separating IP/TCP packet headers from HTTP level information we address the conciseness problem. Yet, by keeping strategic TCP events and HTTP events together with the HTTP header information we ensure a level of completeness sufficient for most Web performance studies. In case this level of detail is insufficient, the packet header information is structured to allow an easy join of the datasets. This level of detail is sometimes necessary to verify assumptions and simplifications made using timing in-

Table 1
Format of the event and header logfile

f_id	unique flow identifier from the other logfile
f_count	number of TCP connections seen using the connection f_id
f_http	number of HTTP requests or responses seen on flow identified by f_id and f_count
information	the information field can be one of the following: • TCP event, DATA, REQUEST, magic number

formation available at the higher levels. For example, we used the packet level information to estimate the impact of slow start on the time savings yielded by first applying delta encoding or compression before transferring the data [28]. By keeping TCP events and HTTP events in the same file it becomes natural to consider cross-protocol effects. We keep full HTTP header information since the HTTP protocol is still under development, subject to customization, e.g., cookies, and subject to use by other applications as their transport protocol. (Ignoring any such header can potentially lead to misleading number, e.g., ignoring cookies may lead to much higher cache hit rates for Web caching [16]). For privacy reasons it is necessary to separate the per flow information from the HTTP header information since the per flow information contains encrypted IP addresses and the HTTP header may, e.g., contain the hostname of the contacted host. (There is not always a one-to-one correspondence between IP address and hostname.) By keeping the information separate we lessen the impact.

In general the file formats where chosen to facilitate easy processing by scripting languages such as awk and perl. The per flow files contain the encrypted source and destination IP addresses and port numbers, and each entry contains a unique identifier for each flow that is used to cross-reference with the HTTP/TCP logfile. We need this cross-reference ability in order to match HTTP requests with HTTP responses.

The file format of the HTTP/TCP file is more complicated in part because it needs to record different kinds of information such as TCP events, HTTP events, and HTTP request/response headers. But more importantly the reconstruction procedure may create information for a particular request at any time. We can identify the parts that are associated with the same HTTP transfer by taking advantage of the per flow state. One can identify all TCP events associated with the TCP connection that is used by a particular HTTP transfer by locating all of the TCP events with the same flow identifier and flow count. A TCP connection identified via flow identifier and flow count is a persistent connection if it has more than one HTTP request with the same index.

The file format of the HTTP/TCP file consists of two parts. The first part consist of the basic flow information including flow identifier, number of TCP connections seen on this flow identifier and the number of HTTP requests seen on this flow identifier (see Table 1). Each of these numbers is initialized to 0 in the beginning. The second part consists of a string identifying what kind of record to expect followed by the record-specific information. We distinguish four kinds of records: TCP, DATA, REQUEST, and HTTP headers.

TCP events are identified by the TCP flag they use: SYN, FIN, RST. In addition we differentiate between the first instance of such an event and additional instances. Most analyses are only concerned about when the first such event happened, yet others (e.g., those that track error conditions) care about repeated TCP signaling and therefore about repeated SYNs, FINs, RSTs. By labeling them differently these are easier to find or eliminate. The specific information is just the timestamp of the packet with the TCP flag.

DATA events summarize the information about an HTTP body, the time of the first packet of the body, the time of the last packet of the body, the length of the body and potentially the filename that contains the data. In addition the information contains a flag that indicates if BLT suspects a missing packet might have created a gap in the data content.

REQUEST events and HTTP headers occur together. The first contain the information if BLT encountered a potential gap and the timestamp information of the first and last packet contributing

Table 2
Content of the HTTP header logfile

TCP event	one of the SYNi, FINi, RSTi $i = 0$ marks the first time a packet with flag X is seen $i = 1$ records additional times a packet with flag X is seen
timestamp	timestamp of event
DATA	line summarizing the characteristic of the data received for this flow f_id, f_count and f_http
gap	missing packet for this HTTP event
time_start	timestamp of the packet containing the first part of the data
time_end	timestamp of the packet containing the last part of the data
length	number of bytes for this Web page
filename	if reasonable filename that contains the Web page
REQUEST	an HTTP request/response on this flow f_id, f_count and f_http
gap	is there any packet missing for this connection
time_start	timestamp of the packet containing the first part of the HTTP request
time_end	timestamp of the packet containing the last part of the HTTP request
0xa1b2c3d4	more information about the HTTP request/response
header_length	length of the HTTP request header
ignore	ignore
start_seq	sequence number of the first packet of the request
end_seq	sequence number of the last packet of the request
start_ack	acknowledgment number of the first packet
end_ack	acknowledgment number of the last packet
HTTP_request	actual text of the HTTP request/response (multiple line entry)
0xb1b2c3d4	end of entry

Table 3
Sample entry from a log file

211	1	0	SYN0	870839085.884436 3871951
211	1	1	REQUEST	0 870839086.513424 870839086.513424
211	1	1	0xa1b2c3d4	285 1 3871952 3872237 68743 68743

HTTP/1.0 200 OK
Date: Wed, 06 Aug 1997 03:40:57 GMT
Server: Apache/1.1.1 BSDI 2.1
Content-type: text/html
Set-Cookie: Apache = 207203958723565857752; path=/
Content-length: 56298
Last-modified: Wed, 06 Aug 1997 00:26:36 GMT
Connection: Keep-Alive
Keep-Alive: timeout = 15, max = 5

0xb1b2c3d4

to this HTTP header. We delimit the raw text of the HTTP header fields with two 'random' magic numbers to simplify post-processing of the log files. The HTTP header field starts with the magic number 0xa1b2c3d4 and ends with the magic number 0xb1b2c3d4 on a separate line. In between those two magic numbers we store the header length, the start and end sequence number and the start and end acknowledgment numbers and the actual content of the HTTP header fields. Table 2 summarizes the file format of the per HTTP event tables while Table 3 shows a sample entry from one of the logfiles.

This means that for flow 211 and the first TCP connection on this flow the first SYN was observed at time 870839085.884436. The first HTTP request on flow 211 1 starting at time 870839086.513424 and ending at time 870839086.513424. The actual HTTP request header was 285 bytes in size, started at sequence number 3871952 and ended at sequence number 3872237. The acknowledgments were for sequence numbers 68743 and the actual text of the requests is: HTTP/1.0 200 OK Date: Wed, 06 Aug 1997 03:40:57 GMT etc.

7. Matching requests and responses

Most Internet service providers (ISP) use hot potato routing to hand traffic off to other ISPs as early as possible, creating lots of asymmetric routes in the Internet. Therefore it is very unlikely that a packet monitor will see the HTTP response that is generated by an HTTP request unless the packet monitor is deployed close to either the Web clients or the Web servers. Close here means that there is exactly one pass from the Web clients or the Web servers to the rest of the Internet and that the packet monitor is on this pass. Since our goal is to be able to deploy BLT at any point in the network, we match HTTP requests with HTTP responses in a separate offline step. This has the additional advantage of reducing processing overheads on the monitoring machine itself. The timeline in the left of Fig. 4 shows the the basic steps in a Web transfer. In the simplest possible case each line corresponds to a single packet. For the purpose of matching HTTP requests and HTTP responses we would like to point out that the HTTP response is the first data being sent back to the client and acknowledging the last byte of the HTTP request. Consequently the sequence number of the last byte of the HTTP request should be equal to the acknowledge number from the HTTP request. In addition the first sequence number of the HTTP response should be equal to the acknowledge number of the request. This reasoning holds even if the client and server use persistent TCP connections as long as no HTTP requests are pipelined. If HTTP requests are pipelined (see right timeline in Fig. 4), detectable by finding more HTTP requests than HTTP responses during a time interval, the above equalities become inequalities. In this case we need additional information; the logfile contains the information about the index of each HTTP request/response on a given TCP connection. Missing HTTP requests/responses are detected by monitoring the inequalities on the sequence numbers and acknowledgment numbers and timing information. Any inconsistencies are handled by adding/subtracting an offset to the request index number. The matching of requests with responses both for non-pipelined as well as for pipelined requests/responses is using the same information that we would have used if the matching had been done online. But for pipelined requests the matching may incorrectly

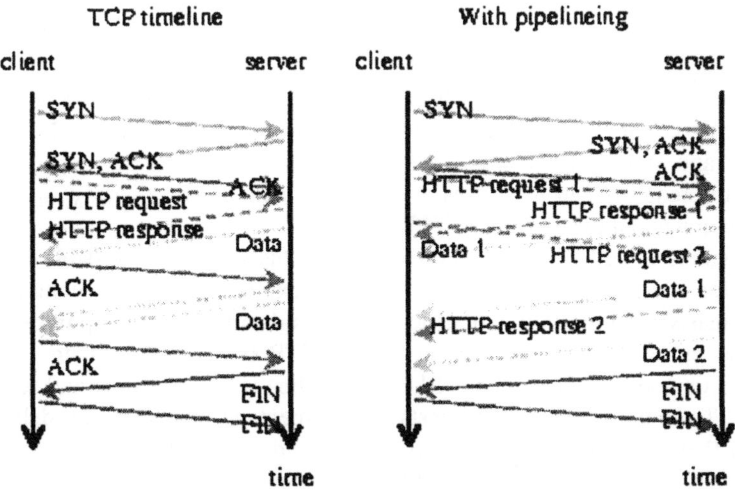

Fig. 4. Timeline of a Web transfer.

match a request with a response. In matching requests and responses that were collected at different places in the network one has to be especially careful with regards to the clock synchronization of the monitoring machines.

Besides matching the HTTP requests and responses the HTTP header matching software (written in C) produces a second logfile that contains HTTP request/response pair information. The design of this second logfile format is significantly simpler than the design of the original logfile format (Section 6) since it can be recomputed from the initial logfile format. The choice of logfile format was guided by the following concerns.

- *Index:* there is a logfile entry for every HTTP request/response pair. Therefore the request/response pair provides a good index for this log file.
- *Completeness:* relevant information about each HTTP request/response pair should be included. This includes timing information from both the HTTP as well as the TCP events.
- *Simplicity:* not every program using this log file should need to parse the full HTTP headers and HTTP responses.
- *Privacy:* customer privacy needs to be protected.

To meet these goals the traces that are extracted in an online fashion are processed on a file by file basis. (Requests/response pairs that span more than one file are not matched.) While processing the file the software creates an index of all events and parses the HTTP requests and response headers. Any HTTP header that is questionable (e.g., because of a missing packet or a miss-parsing of the HTTP header pattern) is rejected. While parsing the HTTP headers the presence of certain header fields and their values is noted and stored. Once all events have been processed the requests and responses are matched. Next information about the associated TCP events and DATA transfers is added to the records and a log entry is written.

A logfile entry consists of information that describes the events and entries that make post processing simpler, e.g., a unique index for each HTTP request/response pair. To be able to sort all requests in the order in which they were issued, the first element of the log entry is the timestamp of the first packet of the HTTP request. A flag field is added to flag those request/response pairs whose transfers where affected by a packet loss. The per HTTP request information includes the type of request (one of GET, HEAD, POST), the URL, the referrer field, and the size of the HTTP request header. The per HTTP response information includes the response timestamp, the response code, the number of bytes in the response header, the number of bytes of the data that were received, the content-length and type from the HTTP response header, and where appropriate the filename of the file that stores the reassembled content. Additional timestamps are the SYN|FIN|RST timestamps from the sender and receivers, the timestamp of the first DATA packet and the timestamp of the last data packet. The header fields that are extracted from the HTTP headers include pragma, cache, authorization, authentication, refresh, cookie, set-cookie, expire time, if-modified-since, last-modified, and cache-last-checked directives.

A simple indexing schema for our logfile uses the unique flow identifier and the timestamp of the request. Studies [14,16,28] have shown that the logfile contains relevant timing and HTTP header information and as such is fairly complete but also concise and simple. Privacy is achieved by eliminating any reference to even the scrambled IP addresses. The flow identifier still allows the identification of the same source/destination IP addresses.

8. Studies enabled by BLT

Data collected by BLT and its predecessors have been used for various Web performance analysis studies. In this section we will point out what part of BLT has enabled each study.

8.1. Benefits of compression and delta encoding [28]

This study was possible because BLT is capable of extracting the full content of the HTTP body plus detailed timestamp information. We needed the HTTP bodies to evaluate (1) what percent of all bodies is compressible and to what degree, (2) what percentage of bodies can delta-encoding be applied to and to what degree. We used the body of the HTTP responses to estimate the byte savings achieved by delta encoding and compression and we used the detailed timestamp information, HTTP request time, HTTP response time, timestamp of first data packet and last data packet to evaluate the latency savings that could be gained by deploying compression and delta encoding. In addition we used the TCP/IP timestamp information to evaluate the impact of neglecting slow start and per packet dynamics.

8.2. Rate of change [14]

Besides providing us with a precise timestamp and a checksum of the HTTP body associated with an HTTP request BLT extracts information from the HTTP headers such as the last-modified timestamp, the age of the resource, etc. These data were used to evaluate the frequency with which different resources are requested, how often they change, what the distribution of the Web page ages is, etc.

8.3. Policies for web traffic over flow-switched networks [18]

The main emphasis of this paper is on the analysis of the TCP/IP traces. Still the availability of the across level traces from BLT enabled us to correlate the statistical results about IP-flow distributions with the actual events in the network, such as number of requests with response code 304. This allowed us to explain the observed phenomena in terms of an application and to identify traffic invariants. Datasets extracted by BLT were used in a similar way to reason about traffic invariants in scaling phenomena [17].

8.4. Performance of web proxy caching [16]

This study considers the impact of cookies, aborted connections, persistent connections on the performance of Web caching in terms of memory usage and latency savings. It would not have been possible without the level of detail provided by BLT about TCP as well as HTTP events.

8.5. Piggyback cache validation [23]/server invalidation [24]

Both of these studies address the problem of maintaining cache coherency for proxy caches. At AT&T Labs-Research nobody is required to use a proxy to browse the Web. Since modifying the clients was not a possibility, BLT provided the only way to extract Web client traces necessary to perform Web proxy studies at AT&T Labs-Research. The study took advantage of the time of request field, the last modified time, the status information, the size information and the flow identifier that identifies the clientid and the server.

In addition to the studies mentioned above the data collected by BLT have been used to derive various statistics about the popularity of Web sites, the usage of HTTP header fields [15], the behavior of consumers and researchers browsing the Web.

Yet another use for BLT involves augmenting active measurements by passive measurements, e.g., to measure what the performance of retrieving a Web page is from a Web server. The level of detail, available via BLT, allows us to distinguish DNS delay, from TCP connection setup delay, from delay to process the HTTP request, from delay to send the data. The biggest benefit of using BLT to augment active measurements is that one does not need to use a specially instrumented client. Rather one can use a standard Web client such as Netscape and control it via the remote control features. This approach enables one to separate delays due to rendering at the client from delays due to the network or Web server.

9. Summary

BLT has been designed to allow continuous collection of real world traces at many different locations in the Internet. It has been used to collect several months of real world traces from AT&T WorldNet, a consumer-based ISP, and from AT&T Labs-Research in Florham Park. BLT is unique in giving us access to HTTP and TCP level traces at the same time. The collected datasets are novel (1) in the degree of detailed information they provide, (2) in presenting us with a client side view of the Web and (3) in the duration of the traces. The latter both challenges and benefits any analysis driven by data collected by BLT. Without datasets such as those collected by BLT, one can only speculate about the Web or construct artificial datasets with all their pitfalls. The richness of the datasets and their completeness have motivated and enabled several studies.

The most important lesson we learned from writing BLT is: expect the unexpected and respect the challenges to the HTTP header reconstruction as discussed in Section 3. Once data about multiple layers in the networking stack are available it provides a playground for many analyses. To avoid preempting these analyses it is important to create well documented, precise, yet complete logfiles (e.g., include the full HTTP headers). In extracting the information it is crucial to avoid assumption about how well-behaved either the clients or the servers or the network might be [22]. They are not. Other common lessons from the implementation include: do not try to do too much processing in the time-critical steps of the logfile extraction; simplify wherever sensible and reasonable; reduce memory use and disk I/O. But in the end the most crucial lesson was to never expect a perfect logfile. There will always be one more exception or one more misbehaved client/server. Therefore, the matching software and any analysis program should test whatever assumption the data have to satisfy and eliminate any data that violate the assumption. With enough care the number of requests that are discarded by each step is small.

It is currently possible to monitor links up to 100 Mbits using of the shelf computer components. As link speeds grow, the memory and CPU performance of these systems become bottlenecks. In this case the processing of the data could to be pushed closer to the link, e.g., onto the interface cards. Alternatively one could develop special purpose hardware or restrict the observed traffic to the specific subset of interest. There are two options for the later approach, select a subset and perform the same computation or select all and perform a simpler computation that approximates the full computation. The experience collected with tools like BLT are crucial to judge the quality of the resulting datasets.

The software needs to undergo continuous evolution. Even as we are outlining the current design of BLT the next generation is being developed. The new version incorporates, among others, the following significant improvements. (1) There is no notion of files and requests, responses pairs will be properly matched. (2) It is not necessary to parse the data content since the new tool can determine the length of the HTTP content from the HTTP header information unless a RST is encountered. (3) This enables a direct split of the HTTP content from the HTTP header information and has the potential to reduce the overhead of protocol information extraction significantly. (4) The linked list of packets is replaced with a modified splay tree routine that will automatically account for retransmitted packets and/or gaps. Another avenue of future work is to extent the protocol awareness to other protocols such as RTSP. Such protocols add the complication of using dynamically assigned UDP ports for exchanging media data. mmdump [9] is a tool that allows users to monitor such multimedia traffic.

Acknowledgements

I acknowledge all my colleagues at AT&T Labs that are involved in the measurement effort and their help in developing the software architecture. Special thanks go to A. Greenberg, R. Caceres, N. Duffield, P. Mishra, C. Kalmanek, K.K. Ramakrishnan, and J. Rexford. Many thanks to everyone in WorldNet that made the deployment of the PacketScopes possible.

I am very grateful to J. Rexford and B. Krishnamurthy for many discussions and constructive criticism on the presentation of the material. Many thanks to G. Glass for writing the HTTP header matching software.

References

[1] N. Anerousis, R. Cáceres, N. Duffield, A. Feldmann, A. Greenberg, C. Kalmanek, P. Mishra, K.K. Ramakrishnan and J. Rexford, Using the AT&T Labs PacketScope for Internet Measurement, Design, and Performance Analysis, AT&T Labs-Research Internal TM, 1997.

[2] G. Apostolopoulos, V. Peris, P. Pradhan and D. Saha, A self-learning layer 5 switch, IBM Research Report, 1999.

[3] M.F. Arlitt and C.L. Williamson, Internet Web servers: workload characterization and implications, IEEE/ACM Transactions Networking 5 (5) (1997) 631–644.

[4] M. Aron, P. Druschel and W. Zwaenepoel, Efficient support for P-HTTP in cluster-based Web servers, in: Proc. USENIX 1999 Annual Technical Conf., 1999.

[5] H. Balakrishnan, V.N. Padmanabhan, S. Seshan, M. Stemm and R.H. Katz, TCP behavior of a busy Internet server: Analysis and improvements, in: Proc. IEEE INFOCOM, April 1998.

[6] P. Barford, A. Bestavros, A. Bradley and M.E. Crovella, Changes in Web client access patterns: characteristics and caching implications, World Wide Web, Special Issue on Characterization and Performance Evaluation, 1999.

[7] P. Barford and M.E. Crovella, Generating representative Web workloads for network and server performance evaluation, in: Proc. ACM SIGMETRICS, June 1998.

[8] R. Caceres, F. Douglis, A. Feldmann, G. Glass and M. Rabinovich, Web proxy caching: the devil is in the details, in: Proc. Workshop on Internet Server Performance, June 1998.

[9] R. Caceres, C.J. Sreenan and J.E. van der Merwe, mmdump — a tool for monitoring multimedia usage on the Internet, 1999.

[10] K.C. Claffy, H.-W. Braun and G.C. Polyzos, A parameterizable methodology for Internet traffic flow profiling, IEEE Journal on Selected Areas in Communications 13 (8) (1995) 1481–1494.

[11] E. Cohen, B. Krishnamurthy and J. Rexford, Improving end-to-end performance of the Web using server volumes and proxy filters, in: Proc. ACM SIGCOMM, September 1998.

[12] M.E. Crovella and A. Bestavros, Self-similarity in World Wide Web traffic: Evidence and causes, in: Proc. ACM SIGMETRICS, May 1996, pp. 160–169.

[13] P.B. Danzig, S. Jamin, R. Cáceres, D.J. Mitzel and D. Estrin, An empirical workload model for driving wide-area TCP/IP network simulations, Internetworking: Research and Experience 3 (1) (1992) 1–26.

[14] F. Douglis, A. Feldmann, B. Krishnamurthy and J.C. Mogul, Rate of change and other metrics: a live study of the World Wide Web, in: Proc. USENIX Symp. on Internet Technologies and Systems, December 1997, pp. 147–158.

[15] A. Feldmann, Popularity of HTTP header fields, December 1998, www.research.att.com/~anja/w3c_webchar/

[16] A. Feldmann, R. Caceres, F. Douglis, G. Glass and M. Rabinovich, Performance of Web proxy caching in heterogeneous bandwidth environments, in: Proc. IEEE INFOCOM, 1999.

[17] A. Feldmann, A.C. Gilbert, W. Willinger and T.G. Kurtz, The changing nature of network traffic: scaling phenomena, ACM Computer Communication Review 28 (2) (1998).

[18] A. Feldmann, J. Rexford and R. Caceres, Reducing overhead in flow-switched networks: an empirical study of Web traffic, in: Proc. IEEE INFOCOM, April 1998.

[19] S.D. Gribble, System Design Issues for Internet Middleware Services: Deductions from a Large Client Trace, Master's thesis, U.C. Berkeley, 1997.

[20] S.D. Gribble and E.A. Brewer, System design issues for Internet middleware services: deductions from a large client trace, in: Proc. USENIX Symp. on Internet Technologies and Systems, December 1997.

[21] V. Jacobson, C. Leres and S. McCanne, tcpdump, available at ftp://ftp.ee.lbl.gov, June 1989.

[22] B. Krishnamurthy and M. Arlitt, Pro-cow: Protocol compliance on the Web, July 1999 (submitted).

[23] B. Krishnamurthy and C.E. Wills, Study of piggyback cache validation for proxy caches in the World Wide Web, in: Proc. USENIX Symp. on Internet Technologies and Systems, December 1997, pp. 1–12.

[24] B. Krishnamurthy and C.E. Wills, Piggyback server invalidation for proxy cache coherency, in: Proc. World Wide Web Conf., April 1998.

[25] T.M. Kroeger, D.E. Long and J.C. Mogul, Exploring the bounds of Web latency reduction from caching and prefetching, in: Proc. USENIX Symposium on Internet Technologies and Systems, December 1997, pp. 13–22.

[26] G.R. Mallan and F. Jahanian, An extensible probe architecture for network protocol performance measurement, in: Proc. ACM SIGCOMM, 1999.

[27] S. Manley and M. Seltzer, Web facts and fantasy, in: Proc. USENIX Symp. on Internet Technologies and Systems, December 1997, pp. 125–133.

[28] J.C. Mogul, F. Douglis, A. Feldmann and B. Krishnamurthy, Potential benefits of delta encoding and data compression for HTTP, in: Proc. ACM SIGCOMM, September 1997, pp. 181–194.

[29] J.C. Mogul and K.K. Ramakrishnan, Eliminating receive livelock in an interrupt-driven kernel, in: Proc. Winter 1996 USENIX Conf., USENIX Association, January 1996.

[30] V.N. Padmanabhan and J.C. Mogul, Improving HTTP latency, Computer Networks and ISDN Systems 28 (1/2) (1995) 25–35.

[31] V. Paxson and S. Floyd, Wide-area traffic: the failure of Poisson modeling, IEEE/ACM Transactions Networking 3 (3) (1995) 226–255.

[32] K. Thompson, G.J. Miller and R. Wilder, Wide-area internet traffic patterns and characteristics, IEEE Network Magazine 11 (6) (1997) 10–23.

[33] L. Wall and R.L. Schwartz, Programming Perl, O'Reilly and Associates, Sebastopol, CA, 1991.

[34] R. Wooster, S. Williams and P. Brooks, HTTPDUMP: a network HTTP packet snooper, 1996.

[35] R. Wooster, S. Williams and P. Brooks, HTTPDUMP, http://www.cs.vt.edu/chitra/httpdump/, 1998.

Anja Feldmann is currently a professor for computer networking in the Computer Science department at the University des Saarlandes, Saarbrücken, Germany. From 1995 to 1999 she was a member of the Networking and Distributed Systems Center at AT&T Labs – Research in Florham Park, New Jersey. Her current research interests include Internet measurement, traffic engineering and traffic characterization, network performance debugging, and improving Web performance. She received a M.S. degree in Computer Science from the University of Paderborn, Paderborn, Germany, in 1990 and M.S. and Ph.D. degrees in Computer Science from Carnegie Mellon University in Pittsburgh, USA, in 1991 and 1995, respectively. She can be reached via electronic mail to anja@cs.uni-sb.de, and on the Web at http://www.research.att.com/~anja/

Web search behavior of Internet experts and newbies

Christoph Hölscher [*,1], Gerhard Strube [1]

Center for Cognitive Science, Institute for Computer Science and Social Research, University of Freiburg, Freiburg, Germany

Abstract

Searching for relevant information on the World Wide Web is often a laborious and frustrating task for casual and experienced users. To help improve searching on the Web based on a better understanding of user characteristics, we investigate what types of knowledge are relevant for Web-based information seeking, and which knowledge structures and strategies are involved. Two experimental studies are presented, which address these questions from different angles and with different methodologies. In the first experiment, 12 established Internet experts are first interviewed about search strategies and then perform a series of realistic search tasks on the World Wide Web. From this study a model of information seeking on the World Wide Web is derived and then tested in a second study. In the second experiment two types of potentially relevant types of knowledge are compared directly. Effects of Web experience and domain-specific background knowledge are investigated with a series of search tasks in an economics-related domain (introduction of the Euro currency). We find differential and combined effects of both Web experience and domain knowledge: while successful search performance requires the combination of the two types of expertise, specific strategies directly related to Web experience or domain knowledge can be identified.

Keywords: Expertise; Information retrieval; Internet search engines; Logfile analysis

1. Introduction

The accelerated growth of the World Wide Web has turned the Internet into an immense information space with diverse and often poorly organized content. Online users are confronted with rapidly increasing amounts of information as epitomized by the buzzword 'information overload'. While skills necessary for browsing individual Web sites seem to be available to users after only minimal training [7], considerably more experience is required for query-based searching [13] and intersite navigation.

The underlying question of the research presented in this paper is what types of knowledge are relevant for Web-based information seeking, and which knowledge structures and strategies are involved. Two experimental studies are presented, which address these questions from different angles and with different methodologies.

Search engines such as AltaVista or Excite are a central part of information seeking on the Internet. Their efficient use requires sophisticated knowledge. Since experienced users make use of search engines regularly for diverse information needs, i.e., using them quite often, it is reasonable to assume that they will develop particular expert knowledge in mastering these more complex services. Thus the research presented here is focused on interactions

* Corresponding author.

[1] E-mail: {hoelsch,strube}@cognition.iig.uni-freiburg.de

with search engines and related services. In addition, query-based searching allows for comparisons with research on search behavior of end-users in traditional IR systems.

Investigations on the search behavior of both expert and novice Web users have several practical applications. First and foremost, a model of search behavior can serve as the basis for improving interfaces and functionality of existing search systems. The varied needs of experts and novices can be identified and considered by more sophisticated future systems. Also, help systems and Internet education (e.g., courses and tutorials) can also benefit from a better understanding of users' difficulties with the search process.

1.1. Related research on Web search

The first influential studies on Web user behavior mainly investigated aspects of *Browsing* when navigating the World Wide Web [2,4,17]. Byrne et al. [1] have recently proposed a 'taxonomy of World Wide Web user tasks' that span a user's complete range of behaviors while surfing the Web, but does not have a focus on information seeking or Web search.

Choo et al. [3] have investigated the information-seeking behavior of knowledge workers over a period of 2 weeks. Combining surveys, interviews and client-side logging they were able to characterize a number of information-seeking behaviors of Web users that are summarized in a model of behavioral modes and moves.

Navarro-Prieto et al. [12] identified cognitive strategies related to Web searching. They compared Web searchers with high and low experience and concluded that expert searchers plan ahead in their searching behavior based on their knowledge about the Web, while novice searchers hardly plan at all and are rather driven by external representations (what they see on the screen).

Several researchers (e.g., [9,15]) have collected impressively large data sets derived from the logs of Internet search engines like Excite or AltaVista. Their studies give a detailed picture of how the average Web user approaches a search service, but they also have drawbacks: since the data are anonymous, we do not know anything about the context of the *individual* user, that is, we do not know what information problem he or she was trying to find or how experienced a user is with respect to the Internet in general or searching in particular. In the present study we use aggregated data from a large German search service to complement data collected from individual users.

In the User Modeling community the behavior of Web users has also attracted some attention. Lau and Horvitz [10], for example, constructed Bayesian networks to model the successive search queries issued by users of a search engine. Augmenting the search engine's logfile with manually assigned categories of presumed information goals they are able to predict query modifications. Similarly, Zukerman et al. [18] propose the use of Markov models to predict a Web user's next request based on the timing and location of past requests. Again, these studies do not address personal characteristics of the user and his level of expertise.

2. Experiment 1: exploratory investigation of expert knowledge and search behavior

The behavior of experienced Internet users and their specific knowledge has not been systematically investigated. Thus the first study is exploratory, aiming at a detailed description of Web expertise, describing typical search behavior of Web experts and constructing a descriptive model of information seeking with search engines. Comparable models for searching in electronic information systems were proposed by Marchionini et al. [11] and Shneiderman et al. [14], but did not consider, for example, the specific differences between the World Wide Web and bibliographic database systems.

We define Web expertise as a type of media competence, i.e., the knowledge and skills necessary to utilize the World Wide Web and other Internet resources successfully to solve information problems. This has to be clearly distinguished from background-knowledge related to the topic area of a specific Web search (see Experiment 2, Section 3).

Well established Internet professionals were recruited for this study. All had at least 3 years of intensive experience with this medium and a daily use of the Internet as a source of information at their workplace. Among the 12 participants — each of them participated in both parts of the expert study — were information brokers, Web masters, Internet consultants, Web content designers, librarians and authors of books about online searching. It is noteworthy that most participants had not received formal training in Internet use, they are clearly to be characterized as self-trained experts.

2.1. Phase I: interviews

First, the participants were asked to describe their experience with the available search services, their search behavior and their intentions and rationales for using certain sources and strategies. With the help of *mental walk-throughs* the process of searching for online information was then discussed step by step. To reveal those experts' conceptual structures, the interview was augmented with a specialized card-sorting task [8,16]: during the interview, relevant terminology and actions were made explicit by recording them on color-coded cards. Afterwards, the experts were asked to build a graphic structure with these cards. This structure is supposed to represent an expert's personal conceptualization of the search process. To support the participants in this task, some appropriate concept categories and relations were predefined and presented to the experts.

2.2. Phase II: experiment using Web-based information tasks

In the second phase of this expert study, a number of real-life information-seeking tasks were employed that had to be performed by the experts on the Internet. Examples: 'which finger is unaffected in RSI?' or 'Find a sound archive for the VIRUS music synthesizer'. The experts were not limited in their choices for searching the Web and could freely choose which search engines — if any — they wanted to use.

All inputs to the computer were mediated through an assistant of the experimenter who had to be orally instructed by the expert for each action. This procedure forced the expert to make every step of the interaction process verbally explicit, including those that might otherwise be missed because of rapid interaction sequences. Additionally, the experts were asked to think aloud about their search activities. The method can be categorized as being between a classic thinking-aloud and a teaching-aloud scenario [5]. All utterances were audio-taped and later transcribed for the analysis. Web-page requests and search queries were also included in the protocol.

2.3. Results of the expert study

2.3.1. Interviews

The experts reported a wealth of Internet-related knowledge, most of it highly idiosyncratic. Therefore, their statements relating to the search process were collected from the transcripts and entered into a matrix to determine which concepts, heuristics and strategies were common to the majority of the experts. Likewise, the concept-card models were inspected for interindividually common knowledge structures. The statement matrix and the card models were aggregated into an initial process model of information seeking with search engines. This model describes the search process from the experts' shared perspective.

2.3.2. Web-based information-seeking tasks

We distinguish two levels of data analysis, the level of information-seeking steps, and the level of individual search queries. For the analysis of information-seeking steps, a set of rules was derived from the experts' process model for segmentation and categorization of the protocol into action units. A total of 56 information problems were tackled by the subjects, two thirds of these successfully. A total of 1956 action units were identified, each corresponding to a step in the process model. The matrix of transition probabilities between all steps of the model was computed, allowing for an analysis of interaction sequences. The main results are summarized below.

Fig. 1 shows the experts' information-seeking behavior on a global level of browsing and searching. In two thirds of the search tasks, the experts initially choose to use a search engine. Only in one third of the cases did they opt for browsing as the initial strategy. Finding potentially relevant documents with a search engine led to browsing episodes of varying length in about 47% of the cases. Once the searchers were in 'browsing mode' they continued browsing for several clicks, hence the 0.73 probability of one browsing move leading to the next. Such browsing episodes could lead directly to a solution, but often

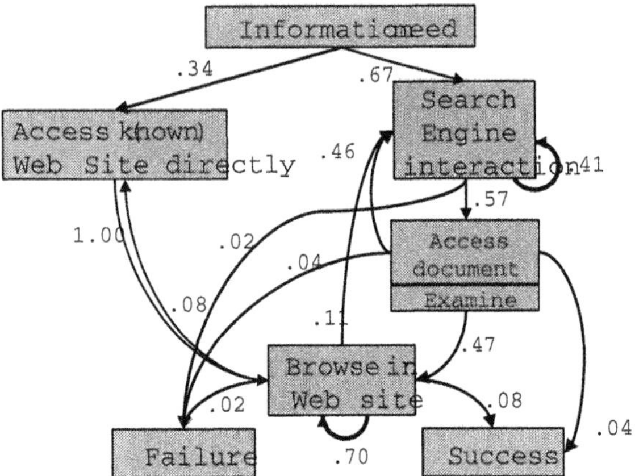

Fig. 1. Global level of the process model of information seeking in Experiment 1: browsing vs. searching. (Values represent transition probabilities to the next unit. The transition probabilities going out from a given step of the model add up to 100%, but transition probabilities of 0.03 and below are omitted here to reduce visual clutter.)

enough, a return to the search engine for further queries was observed. This indicates that the experts in our study quite frequently switched back and forth between browsing and querying if necessary.

Fig. 2 shows a close-up of actions directly involved in search-engine interaction. The straight downward arrows represent the default handling of the search engine with correspondingly high transition probabilities. Additionally, the experts showed more complex behavior if no relevant documents were found, including reformulations or reformatting of existing queries, changing search engines, requesting additional result pages as well as backtracking to earlier result pages or queries. Again we observe opportunistic behavior making use of all the options a search engine provides. Flexible use of available search behaviors is a characteristic feature of expert searchers.

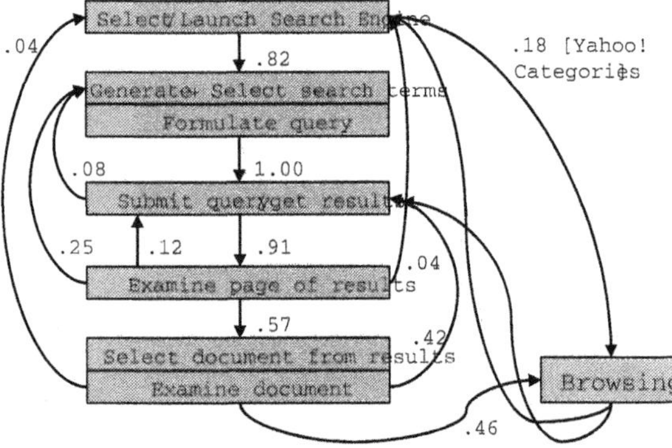

Fig. 2. Close-up of direct interaction with a search engine. (Values represent transition probabilities to the next unit. Transition probabilities of 0.03 and below are omitted to reduce visual clutter.)

Individual search queries were analyzed as well, and compared to available data on user behavior. Jansen et al. [9] report a quantitative analysis of a large sample of search requests from the Excite search engine, representing the search queries of the average Internet user. Similar data have been reported by Silverstein et al. [15] for the AltaVista search service.

A corresponding sample from German search-engine users was made available to us by the managers of the Fireball search engine, representing some 16 million queries and 27 million non-unique terms. A comparison of data sets from average users with the experts' queries in our study revealed several differences: first of all, the average length of a query in Fireball is only 1.66 words, while the experts used an average of 3.64 words, twice as many.

We also found that Web experts make use of advanced search options like Boolean operators, modifiers, phrase search, etc., much more frequently than the average user (see Table 1). A noteworthy exception is the '+' operator. It is equally popular among the general public, making it the most important query formatting tool for non-expert users.

This first expert study confirms the significance of media-specific skills of Internet users, and gives a detailed picture of Internet expertise. While IR skills were the focus of this study we found nu-

Table 1

Usage of query formatting in Experiment 1 (the expert study) and aggregated statistics from the Fireball search engine

	Experts in expert study		Fireball logfile	
	No. of queries	%	No. of queries	%
AND	56	34.57	390,272	2.40
OR	13	8.02	13,817	0.09
NOT	–	–	10,372	0.06
( )	12	7.41	15,738	0.10
+ (plus)	47	29.01	4,034,312	24.82
– (minus)	–	–	77,531	0.48
" "	40	24.69	1,401,738	8.62

merous hints of the importance of content-specific knowledge. Experts frequently complained about lacking relevant domain knowledge regarding individual search questions and were highly aware of this obstacle while being confident of their technical competence.

3. Experiment 2: the Euro study

Several authors (e.g., [6]) were able to show that technical competencies in using bibliographic database systems are necessary for successful information retrieval, but that such knowledge has to be combined with background knowledge about the topic area to be searched. This finding is in line with observations from the verbal protocols obtained in our expert study, where Web experts complained that they lacked domain-specific background knowledge for particular search tasks. The following experiment addresses these two types of knowledge that contribute to the success of searching on the Web, and how the two interact.

Experiment 2 is designed to compare directly the contributions that technical Internet skills and content-area-specific domain knowledge make to the search process. A current topic from the domain of economics — the European Monetary Union — was chosen for this laboratory experiment. The subjects were given a set of information-search problems from this domain. A 2×2 design of the independent factors *Web expertise* and *domain knowledge* results in four experimental groups. Participants with domain knowledge were recruited from students of economics. Web expertise was assessed by interview and pre-test, allowing us to clearly identify novices and advanced Web users, thereby excluding intermediate-level Web users from data analysis.

In the experiment two kinds of tasks were used, simulated search tasks and tasks that had to be performed live on the Web.

3.1. Simulated search tasks

Based on the process model developed in the expert study above, complex search tasks were broken down into sub-tasks corresponding to individual steps of the process, such as search term selection or query revision. The resulting sub-tasks allowed for a focussed investigation of the direct effects that different types of expertise have on individual steps of the model. These simulated tasks were collated in a questionnaire. The approach made sure that each participant worked on the same stimuli (words, queries, result pages), allowing for comparisons that are not readily available from observing unrestricted task performance on the Web. In 'real' searches on the Web participants follow different paths trying to solve given tasks and hardly ever face exactly the same pages of results or have to reformulate the exact same search queries as another participant.

3.2. Web-based search tasks

In the second part of the experiment, the actual Web searches, we tried to impose as few restrictions as possible, and did not employ thinking-aloud techniques. Participants were asked to solve five information problems directly via the World Wide Web. The only restriction imposed on the participants was a time limit of 10 min per task. All interactions were recorded by a proxy server (Siemens WebWasher) and a traditional observer protocol to complement the proxy log. Again, subjects could freely choose how to tackle the search tasks and which search engines to consult.

While in Experiment 1 interaction sequences and search statements were reconstructed from the audio protocol of the thinking-aloud tasks, in Experiment 2 the same measures are recorded directly with the proxy server installed on the client's computer. The proxy logfile contains most of the necessary information like the date and time of each access, the Uniform Resource Locator (URL) of each file viewed and its length. Additionally, we have the HTTP result code (indicating, e.g., if the file to be accessed was physically unavailable) and for most cases also the Referrer URL that indicates from which URL a user requests another page and this is an important tool for reconstructing the behavioral trace. The logfile data can be processed to reveal the majority of the users' interactions. Nonetheless, a traditional observer protocol was written during the experiment to complement the logfile, because certain interactions are not adequately recorded in the proxy logfile, mainly concerning navigation in Frame-Sets, use of the back-button in the browser and queries submitted via the Post method. For the analysis, the proxy log and the observer protocol were combined for categorizing the user's actions in terms of the process model developed above.

Browsing and searching behaviors which manifest in the interaction sequences during the search are compared to identify differences in information-seeking strategies and tactics.

3.3. Results of the double comparison of advanced and novice searchers

The data presented below are based on a sample of 24 participants, 6 from each cell of the 2×2 design of Web expertise (high/low) and domain knowledge (high/low). We analyzed four types of data: rate of success, action sequences (expressed as transition probabilities), time data and formal properties of search queries.

3.3.1. Rate of success

The Web-based search tasks proved to be rather difficult for all participants, resulting in low overall success rates. In 3 of the experimental groups, participants solved no more than 2 of 5 tasks on average. Only those users who could rely both on high Web expertise and high domain knowledge ('double experts') were able to solve an average of 3.2 out of the 5 tasks.

3.3.2. Action sequences

Across all experimental groups the pattern of action sequences is comparable to the data from the expert study.

One important difference is the fact that participants now obviously found less useful pages and had to reiterate their searches more frequently to find relevant information (for details see Figs. 3 and 4). This increased difficulty most likely reflects both differences in the tasks (harder) and the participants (overall lower levels of expertise, since 50% were novices) of the two studies. Please note that the coding scheme was slightly revised from the expert study to the Euro study. This accounts for differences between the studies at the process stages, *Access Web site directly* (Fig. 3) and *Select + launch search engine* (Fig. 4).

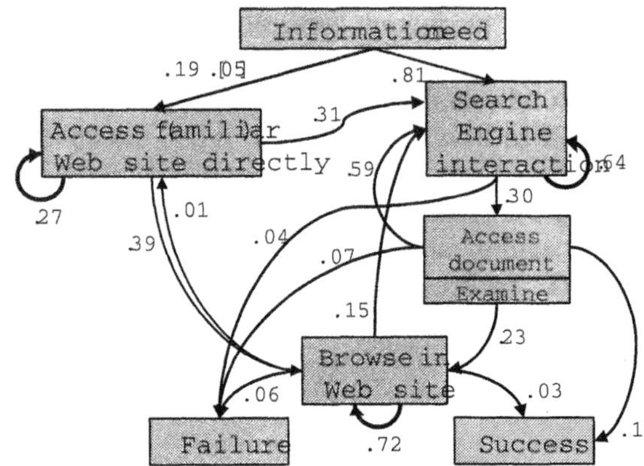

Fig. 3. Global level of the process model of information seeking: all four groups of the Euro study combined (transition probabilities).

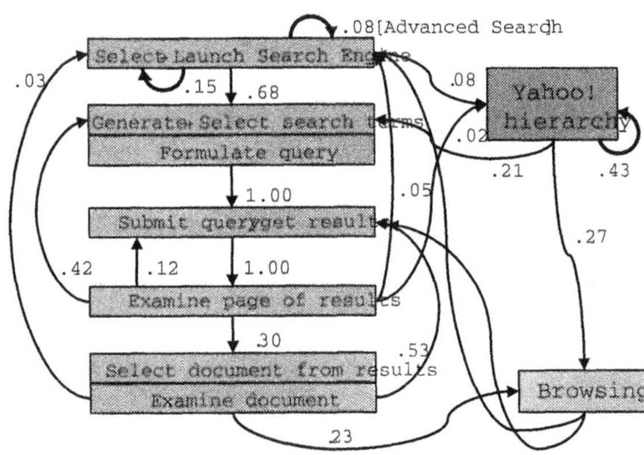

Fig. 4. Close-up of direct interaction with a search engine: all four groups (novices and experts) of the Euro study combined (transition probabilities).

3.3.3. Differences between experts and novices

Looking at the actions subjects choose as their initial behavior (Fig. 5) we find several important differences between groups. Only 'double experts' initially tried to access directly Web sites related to economics, while all others immediately accessed a search engine in one way or the other. Web experts would type in the URL of their favorite search engine, while the 'double novices' were highly inclined to simply click on the Netscape Search button (these effects — and all others discussed below — prove to be significant in Hiloglinear analysis, unless stated otherwise).

Once a Web search has led to a page of results (Fig. 6), Web experts were significantly more

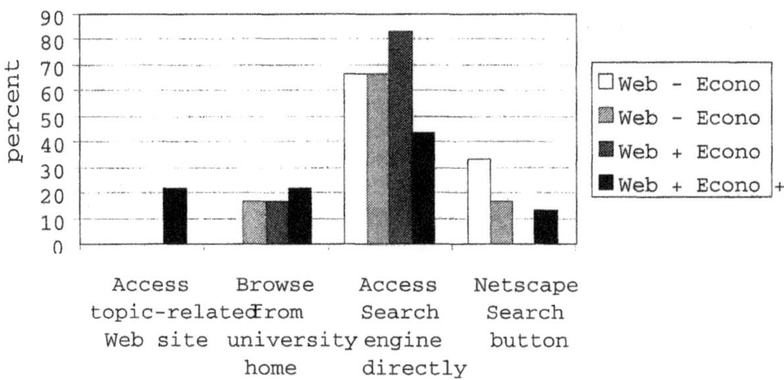

Fig. 5. Initial behavior — the first action performed after receiving a task (Web ± refers to Web expertise; Econo ± refers to domain knowledge).

likely to choose a target document for closer inspection than Web novices (35% vs. 25%), while Web novices more often reiterate their search queries. We also found significant interactions of domain knowledge and Web expertise: when Web experts had little domain knowledge, they were most likely to pick a target document (possibly for lack of clear selection criteria). Double novices showed the highest proportion of query reformulations while choosing the smallest number of target documents for closer examination, and of these documents the highest proportion turned out to be irrelevant. A qualitative inspection of the query reformulations that were issued by the double novices indicated that they often make only small and ineffective changes to their queries, forcing them to reiterate repeatedly.

Looking at browsing behavior, we can once again identify some clear patterns. Fig. 7 shows what the participants choose to do next once they have accessed a document in a browsing episode. The behavior of the double experts with technical and domain-specific knowledge can be characterized as follows: they are most likely to continue browsing (follow another link) to explore more content from a Web site or to change their strategy and use a different search engine. They are the group least likely to engage in backward-oriented behavior like clicking the back-button to browse back or return to previous search-engine results. Such backward-oriented behavior is very common for the less experienced users, with double novices showing it most often. It is not fully clear, if novices browse less useful material than the experts, but once they face a dead end their only way out is to go backwards, while experts have more flexible ways of reacting.

3.3.4. *Time data*

From the proxy logfile one can reconstruct how much time has elapsed between page transmissions. These intervals cannot be translated into steps of our

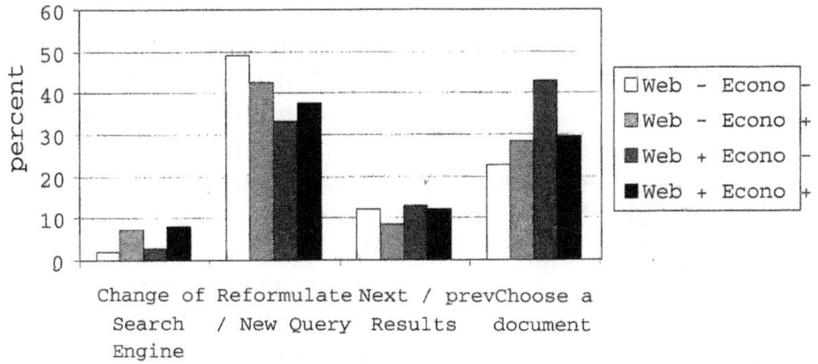

Fig. 6. Actions selected on a search-engine result page (Web ± refers to Web expertise; Econo ± refers to domain knowledge).

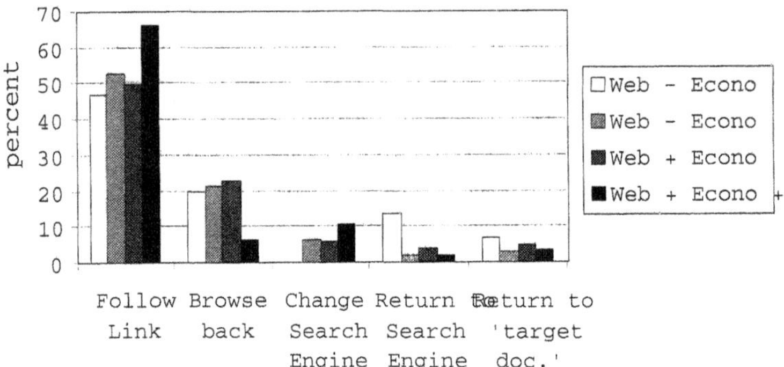

Fig. 7. Transitions while browsing (Web ± refers to Web expertise; Econo ± refers to domain knowledge).

search model equally well for all steps. For example, when a user refines an initial query, the corresponding interval between page loadings contains three steps: reviewing the initial result set, generating terms, and formatting the revised query, and submission of that query. This makes an analysis of time spent in direct search-engine interaction difficult and statistical results for these measures are not so clear.

This problem is far less pronounced for the timing of content pages. Consequently, the stronger differences could be established for the time that users spent with content pages (Fig. 8).

For the time spent with a document that was directly selected from a page of search-engine results, we find a clear independent main effect of domain knowledge (MANOVA: $F = 11.44$, $p < 0.003$). People with considerable background knowledge about the domain spend significantly less time with a document from that domain. It takes them less time to read it and make a decision about the next move. Descriptively, Web expertise also reduces the time spent in content documents, but this effect was not found to be significant.

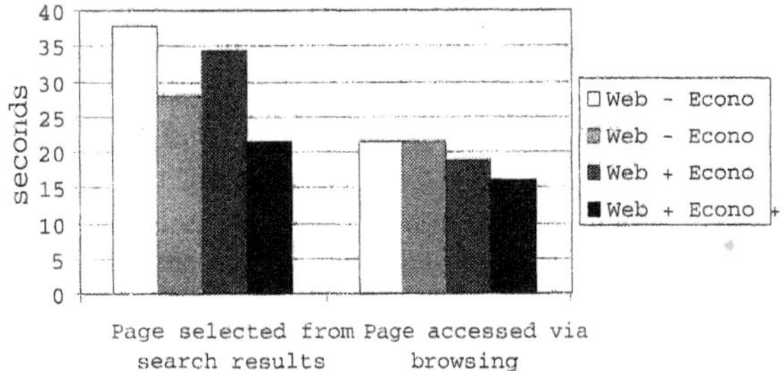

Fig. 8. Time spent with Web pages (Web ± refers to Web expertise; Econo ± refers to domain knowledge).

No significant differences between the groups were found for pages accessed during browsing episodes. Quite likely this can be attributed to the nature of pages included in this category. The category not only includes content pages relevant to the domain of economics, but also a number of function pages like navigation pages (which lead to content pages, but do not contain longer paragraphs of task-related information) and even search-engine help pages. This may have diminished the influence of domain knowledge on reading times for these kinds of documents. Descriptively, we again find shorter reading times for Web experts, but no significant effect. Thus the influence of Web expertise on the time measure is rather weak, but less dependent on whether or not a topic-related page is accessed.

3.3.5. Query properties

We found the same general pattern of query formulations for both the Web-based search and the simulated search tasks, with the data from the search simulations being somewhat more clear-cut (Table 2).

Web experts relied significantly more on query formatting tools than Web novices (87% vs. 47%), while higher domain knowledge corresponded to a lower number of Boolean operators and modifiers being used. A very clear effect of Web expertise was found for the number of queries with formatting errors (19.6% vs. 1.9%).

Effects of the experimental conditions could also be established for the number of search terms per query, and the sources of search terms, but only in the searches actually performed on the Web, not in the simulated search.

From the expert study one would have expected

Table 2
Query formatting in simulated search tasks (percent of all queries)

	Domain knowledge LOW		Domain knowledge HIGH	
	Web novice	Web expert	Web novice	Web expert
AND	4.2	25.9	–	11.1
+ (plus)	33.3	44.4	11.1	22.2
" "	20.8	22.2	18.5	37.0
Any kind of formatting	58.3	92.6	37.0	81.5
Errors	29.2	–	11.1	3.7

Web experts to use longer queries. This hypothesis was not confirmed: the queries issued by Web experts were only marginally longer than those of Web novices (2.61 vs. 2.32 words/query). Instead we found a significant effect of domain knowledge: participants with little domain knowledge made significantly longer queries (average query length: 2.96 vs. 1.97 words). Maybe domain experts know more appropriate terms and hence need fewer of them.

The analysis of query formatting (Table 2) revealed that participants who know a lot about the subject domain, but lack Web expertise are quite reluctant to use query formatting (see above). But they seem to compensate for this by showing more verbal creativity and flexibility than the other groups: they most likely used their own terminology instead of relying on the words that were already in the original task statement. Also, more often than others they used completely different terminology from one query to the next.

4. Discussion

In the expert study we investigated how Internet professional conceptualize the search process and derived a *process model of search-engine interaction.* This model was first applied to the search behavior of the same Internet professionals and we believe that it has shown its value as a tool for capturing expert searching behavior.

In the second study, the Euro study, we focus on a direct comparison of expert and novice Web searchers. It turns out that the process model can be applied to the behavior of both expert and novice searchers and that it also captures differences between these groups.

Expertise was further differentiated into technical Web expertise and domain-specific background knowledge, in this case the field of economics. The two types of expertise have shown independent and combined effects. Participants which could rely on both types of expertise were overall most successful in their search behavior. Deficits in one or the other type of expertise led to compensatory behavior, for example, domain-expert/Web-novices relying heavily on terminology and avoiding query formatting. Participants with lower levels of knowledge are less flexible in their strategies and return to previous stages of their search more often rather than trying new approaches (like changing the search engine).

The severe troubles that the 'double novices' faced when dealing with the tasks in the Euro study again point at the joint contribution that both domain knowledge and Internet expertise make to the search process.

Overall, Web-based information seeking turned out to be rather difficult for the participants of both Experiment 1 and Experiment 2. This indicates that there still is much room for improvement in Web-based searching. The behavioral differences we found between the experimental groups clearly show that search-engine users are a heterogeneous crowd and may need to be catered to differently. Novice users had severe problems with formulating a reasonable query and tools that support the query formulation process would seem desirable.

Because successful search on the Web turns out to be so difficult for novice users, learning how to use search engines efficiently should be a central part of any Internet skills training. Novices in our study were ignorant about a number of core problems of Web searching, e.g., the limited scope of individual search engines or the necessity to state a search query at an adequate level of specificity. The differences found between the Web novices and the Web experts point at specific deficiencies in the novices' knowledge and could be directly addressed in Internet skills training.

Acknowledgements

The first author is a PhD student in the Virtual PhD Program (**VGK**[2]: Knowledge Acquisition and Knowledge Exchange with New Media) and the work was funded by the German Research Council (DFG). We would like to thank Gruner + Jahr EMS, Hamburg for supporting the expert study and giving us access to the Fireball statistics reported in this paper.

References

[1] M.D. Byrne, B.E. John, N.S. Wehrle and D.C. Crow, The tangled web we wove: a taskonomy of WWW use, in: Human Factors in Computing Systems: Proc. CHI 99, Addison-Wesley, Reading, MA, 1999, pp. 544–551.

[2] L.D. Catledge and J.E. Pitkow, Characterizing browsing strategies in the World-Wide Web, Comput. Networks ISDN Syst. 27 (1995) 1065–1073.

[3] C.W. Choo, B. Detlor and D. Turnbull, Information seeking on the Web — an integrated model of browsing and searching, in: Proc. Annual Meeting of the American Society for Information Science (ASIS) [WWW document], 1999, Available at http://choo.fis.utoronto.ca/fis/respub/ais is99/

[4] A. Cockburn and S. Jones, Which way now? Analysing and easing inadequacies in WWW navigation, Int. J. Hum.–Comput. Stud. 45 (1996) 105–129.

[5] K.A. Ericsson and H.A. Simon, Protocol Analysis: Verbal Reports as Data, MIT Press, Cambridge, MA, 1993.

[6] I. Hsieh-Yee, Effects of search experience and subject knowledge on the search tactics of novice and experienced searchers, J. Am. Soc. Inf. Sci. 45(3) (1993) 161–174.

[7] J. Hurtienne and H. Wandke, Wie effektiv und effizient navigieren Benutzer im World Wide Web? Eine empirische Studie [How effectively and efficiently do users navigate in the WWW? An empirical study], in: D. Janetzko, B. Batanic, D. Schoder, M. Mattingley-Scott and G. Strube (Eds.), CAW-97: Workshop Cognition and Web, Freiburg, 1997, IIG Berichte 1/97, pp. 93–104.

[8] D. Janetzko, Card-sorting and knowledge elicitation, unpublished manuscript, 1998.

[9] B.J. Jansen, A. Spink, J. Bateman and T. Saracevic, Real life information retrieval: a study of user queries on the Web, SIGIR Forum 32(1) (1998) 5–17.

[10] T. Lau and E. Horvitz, Patterns of search: analyzing and modeling web query dynamics, in: Proc. 7th Int. Conf. User Modelling — UM99, 1999, pp. 119–128.

[11] G. Marchionini, S. Dwiggins, A. Katz and X. Lin, Information seeking in full-text end-user-oriented search systems: the roles of domain and search expertise, LISR 15 (1993) 35–69.

[12] R. Navarro-Prieto, M. Scaife and Y. Rogers, Cognitive strategies in web searching, in: Proc. 5th Conf. on Human Factors and the Web, June 1999 [WWW document], Available at http://zing.ncsl.nist.gov/hfweb/proceedings/navarro-prieto/index.html

[13] A. Pollock and A. Hockley, What's wrong with Internet searching. D-Lib Magazine, 1997 [WWW document], Available at http://www.dlib.org/dlib/march97/bt/03pollock.html

[14] B. Shneidermann, D. Byrd and W.B. Croft, Clarifying search: a user-interface framework for text searches, D-Lib Mag. 1997 [WWW document], Available at http://www.dlib.org/dlib/january97/retrieval/01shneiderman.html

[15] C. Silverstein, M. Henzinger, H. Marais and M. Moricz, Analysis of a very large Alta Vista Query Log (SRC Technical Note 1998-014), Digital Systems Research Center, Palo Alto, CA, 1998.

[16] G. Strube, D. Janetzko and M. Knauff, Cooperative construction of expert knowledge: the case of knowledge engineering, in: P.B. Baltes and U.M. Staudinger (Eds.), Interactive Minds, Cambridge University Press, Cambridge, 1996, pp. 366–393.

[17] L. Tauscher and S. Greenberg, How people revisit web pages: empirical findings and implications for the design of history systems, Int. J. Hum.–Comput. Stud. 47 (1997) 97–137.

[18] I. Zukerman, D.W. Albrecht and A.E. Nicholson, Predicting users' requests on the WWW, in: User Modeling: Proc. 7th Int. Conf., UM99, 1999, pp. 275–284.

[2] http://www.vgk.de

Extensible use of RDF in a business context

Kerstin Forsberg [a,*,1], Lars Dannstedt [b,2]

[a] *Viktoria Institute and Adera, O Hamngatan 41–43, S-411 10 Gothenburg, Sweden*
[b] *Volvo Information Technology, Web Program Center, S-405 08, Gothenburg, Sweden*

Abstract

The next generation of intranets should facilitate the structuring of information as well as the organizing of communication in networking organizations. For many organizations, one step in that direction is to structure information by adding metadata. We have encountered problems when applying Dublin Core, a metadata element set developed for discovery of existing information resources on the public Internet, on an extensive intranet. Our conclusion, argued in this paper, is that these problems are a consequence of trying to describe information resources without taking into account the context in which end users create and consume information. The next generation of intranets calls for a more contextual approach. The contribution of this paper is such an approach. We propose a framework including: (1) A model for describing three different areas of resources: business, information and communication, and integrating the resources description areas by means of generic classes, constrains and relations. (2) An extension to the model describing and integrating nodes and relations in networking organizations. (3) An extension to the model describing and organizing the communication of information in the business. The framework suggests an extensible use of RDF (Resource Description Framework) in a business context. © 2000 Published by Elsevier Science B.V. All rights reserved.

Keywords: Metadata; RDF; XML; Intranet

1. Introduction

The first generation of intranets provided easy access to large amount of information using (hyper)links. The second generation of intranets provided interaction and transaction through numerous Web enabled applications. Many intranets have become a gigantic 'mess' of information, links and applications. It has been argued that if such an intranet remains uncontrolled, it will be perceived useless and therefore users will abandon it [5]. This paper heads for *the next generation of intranets that facilitate the structuring of information, as well as the organizing of communication, in networking organizations.*

The introduction of XML (eXtensible Markup Language) will make information self-describing [2] and facilitate information discovering. At the same time the deployment of *metadata* will be required. Metadata is "... structured, encoded data that describe characteristics of information-bearing entities to aid in the identification, discovery, assessment, and management of the described entities" [1]. We prefer the phrase: *structured descriptions of resources* and have used it instead of metadata. One set of structured descriptions of information resources on Internet is recommended by the Dublin Core ini-

* Corresponding author.
[1] kerstin.forsberg@aderagroup.com
[2] it1.larsd@memo.volvo.se

tiative [6]. This recommendation includes elements such as Creator, Date, Resource Type and Coverage. Resources could be described using RDF (Resource Description Framework), proposed by W3C [14]. The RDF Schema [15] provides a machine-understandable application of XML to encode *schemas* for descriptive vocabularies like the Dublin Core.

Currently, many organizations use the Dublin Core schema [7] for information resources on the public Internet as a template for recommending schemas for intranets. Although contemporary literature has a number of references to existing metadata schema and *resource description communities*, few of them report experiences from intranets, and hardly anyone covers the process of establishing new resource description communities or the long-term managing process. One exception is the work by EU-NSF Working Group on Metadata that points out: "The definition and maintenance of metadata standards over time is a complex social process requiring negotiation, consensus-building, and iteration. Learning to manage such processes effectively and to coordinate the ever-growing activities of many disparate communities of interest is clearly a long-term research undertaking involving complex economic, technical, and social questions" [8]. In this paper we summarize problems occurring when an organization entered this 'complex social process' without paying enough attention to the context in which end users create and consume information.

The framework we propose enables resource description communities, such as business units, projects, departments and professional groups within the organization, to *set their own context*. They can extend the model and add their own structures and vocabulary for the business, information and communication resources. However, the extensions must conform to the proposed model of generic classes, constrains and relations integrating the three areas of resource descriptions. To visualize next generation of intranets, we introduce a news exchange application for an extensive intranet that shows how the framework could be applied. In the future, an extended framework could enable *context sensitive editing* for users creating information, as well as *context driven views and navigation* for users consuming information.

The framework could be seen as a *meta model for a shared information spaces*. Our approach has some similarities with the work conducted by the Advanced Intranet Collaboration (AIS) project. They use the notion of a shared information spaces (SIS): "A SIS may be considered as a background canvas, a reference frame shared by all fellow employees ... materialized as a corporate intranet" [13]. However, in our approach we extend the notion of a shared information space to become a *shared resource description space*.

The rest of the paper is structured as follows. In the next section we summarize encountered problems and in Section 3 we explore the foundations for the proposed framework. In Section 4, we introduce some examples of existing communities of descriptions of resources in each of the three areas of resource description that we propose. We highlight some of the RDF and RDF Schema concepts used in Section 5. Section 6 elaborates on the proposed news exchange application and framework implementing our approach of *Extensible use of RDF in a Business Context*. Finally, in Section 7, we summarize lessons learned and outline future directions concerning the *framework for the next generation of intranets*.

2. Problems

Currently, information masters, site owners, content providers and Web editors ask themselves how to enhance discovery of information through the use of metadata. One key question is: *what to cover in a recommended metadata element set for an intranet*? We have encountered problems when recommending structured descriptions of information resources for an extensive intranet. Our starting point was the Dublin Core recommendation [7], which is nowadays often used in industry.

- *Fail to make the assumptions made about the business explicit*. Schema recommendations developed for information resources always make assumptions about the business. However, these assumptions are rarely made explicit. For example, questions like the following are in most cases not considered: What types of entities in the business should be encoded as the metadata element Creator? What should the metadata element Coverage refer to in the business model?

- *Only takes into account communication through static Web pages.* Information resources are not just static HTML pages. Even though the Dublin Core has the ambition to cover a wider spectrum of information resources, the main interpretation of the Dublin Core information resource category is Web pages. Information resources in a modern business must be possible to communicate through many different channels, e.g., assembled as a dynamic Web page, included in a subscribed e-mail newsletter, or distributed as a short message to a wireless device.
- *Are defined using a top-down strategy which does not fit the flat organizations of today.* The recommendation is often defined top-down in the organization. Accordingly, it is based on the assumption of a hierarchical organization. However, in the flat organizations of today this kind of top-down strategies may not be suitable, as groups and local units need to control and define information resources according to their practices.
- *Are seldom used for metadata creation and validation.* The recommended set of structured descriptions of information resources is seldom used for metadata creation and validation in an effective way. This causes inconsistent and incomplete descriptions of the resources.

This list of problems is not a critique of Dublin Core. It is to be seen as a consequence of trying to describe information resources not taking into account the context in which end users create and consume information.

3. Foundations for the proposed framework

In just a few years the Internet has changed the conditions of doing business. The notion of the Web has become the metaphor for the whole Internet, as well as for intranets. The notion of the network has become the metaphor for modern organizations. Several authors have suggested the notion of *networking* (cf. [4,9]) as the metaphor for the future:

> "It is a networking society, not a network society. It is activities and actions rather than organizations and agents that make up that society. (Even when we want to use verbs, we find only nouns.) Weick (1976) therefore wanted us to study organizing rather than organizations, and Czarniawska (1997) therefore prefers to speak of 'action-nets' rather than 'actor-networks'." [9]

Accordingly, the framework for next generation of intranets that we propose, is based on the foundation that intranets should facilitate the *structuring of information*, as well as the *organizing of communication*, in *networking organizations*. Below we discuss the design principles for the proposed framework.

3.1. Structuring and integrating resource descriptions

Our point of departure is a resource-based view. Resources are assets that have a structured description, which makes them maintainable, usable, and reusable. Based on the experiences gained during the process of recommending an intranet version of the Dublin Core schema, our conclusion is that resource descriptions should be separated into three different areas of resources. In a business context we propose following areas: *business*, *information* and *communication*, each one with its own set of structured descriptions.

- *Business resources* should be described through a vocabulary that captures *what people talk about and act upon* in their everyday work: what they do, what services and products they offer, how they are organized, how they divided their responsibilities into roles and so on.
- *Communication resources* should include descriptions of available communication channels, such as e-mail, paper, Web, and mobile phone, and the specific device capabilities, as well as communication mechanisms such as subscription.
- *Information resources* should include information types that are created, maintained and communicated in business.

Obviously, the three separate areas of resource descriptions are related to each other. Information resources should be related to what they cover in the business context and how they should be communicated within the business. Business resources could be described in different ways, using different types of information resources. Communication resources are the connection between information and business. We propose that the three different areas of resource descriptions should be integrated by means of generic classes, constrains and relations. One example is that business resource can point to information resources for more information and information resources could point to business resources to capture the coverage of the information. Another example is that new types of information resources should include core properties common for all information resources.

3:2. *Descriptions of networking organizations*

In the business area an extension to the model using the concept of *nodes in the business network* could be used to describe and integrate modern networking organizations. Nodes have positions in the business network that describe relations to other nodes. Relations that not only capture the hierarchical relationship: belong-to respective contains, but also includes relations like cooperate-with, interested-in, delivers-to and so on. Nodes that encompass preferred communication channels and also direct communication to preferred destination. A department, an employee or a product, all of them nodes in the business network, could point to more information about the node on a home page or to some other type of information resource.

3.3. *Descriptions of the organizing of communication*

In the communication area an extension to the model could be used to facilitate the organizing of communication. It should enable two-way communication: both consumer-driven (subscription) and producer-driven communication (distribution). People and organization in the business context should be able to define subscription of their own views of information resources based on search criteria, sort order and preferred communication channel (pull). At the same time enable distribution of information to other nodes in the business, through the communication channel they prefer (push).

3.4. *Encoding the framework*

Resources are described using RDF (Resource Description Framework), proposed by World Wide Web Consortium (W3C) [14] and RDF Schema [15]. RDF is a common infrastructure to encode, exchange and reuse structured descriptions of resources. Throughout this paper we have used RDF to encode both the framework and the instances of resource descriptions. Of course, the instances often exist in different sources such as employee databases, service catalogues, department tables, and so on. In this paper, we have not covered the question of interfaces to databases and legacy systems. However, we think that RDF could offer a scalable approach also to data integration.

4. Three different areas of resource description

In this section we introduce some of the communities of resource description existing today. To illustrate the different areas we present one community for description of resources from each area, which we have based our model on. The examples are also used directly in our model further on.

(1) In the *information area* we describe the Dublin Core initiative.
(2) In the *communication area* we selected the W3C Mobile Access Interest Group and their Composite Capability/Preference Profiles (CC/PP).
(3) From the *business area* we use one part of the Open Information Model (OIM) from the Metadata Coalition as our example.

4.1. *Descriptions of information resources*

Lately, general specifications for structured descriptions of information resources have been developed. The Dublin Core initiative [6] is the most well known example for resources on Internet. They focus on simple resource descriptions for discovery of existing information. Their vocabulary [7] is captured in a 15-element set of descriptors in three groups: (1) Content; title, subject, description, type, source, relation and coverage, (2) Intellectual property; creator, publisher, contributor and rights, (3) Instantiation; date, format, identifier and language. Guidance concerning how to express the Dublin Core with RDF [12] has also been published and is now being discussed in the Dublin Core community.

The Dublin Core recommendation is well known and often used as a template and therefore a natural starting point for our proposed model.

4.2. Descriptions of communication resources

A community that uses RDF from the beginning to set up a mechanism to describe resources is the W3C Mobile Access Interest Group [17]. They describe communication resources; new mobile devices, such as wireless phones. A general, yet extensible framework for describing user preferences and device capabilities, called Composite Capability/Preference Profiles (CC/PP) [3], has been proposed by the group. It is intended to provide information necessary to adapt the content and the content delivery mechanisms to fit the capabilities and preferences of the user and its agents. The profile vocabulary is clustered into three groups of metadata elements: (1) User of the device; such as preferred language, sound on/off and images on/off, (2) Hardware platform, attributes; like vendor, screen size and input device, (3) Defined variables; such as application brand and version and level of WAP [18] support.

CC/PP has some interesting features that could be used for a wide range of communication devices that we find usable and therefore include it in our proposed model.

4.3. Descriptions of business resources

Business resources are a wide area of assets. In the same way as information and communication resources they have to have a structured description to make them maintainable, usable, and reusable. Business resources are described through a vocabulary that captures what people talk about and act upon in their everyday work. The descriptions of business resources have traditionally been captured using entity-relationship representations and conceptual modelling languages. In the document-centric world these models have often been overlooked. The structured document representation (à la SGML) has been favored. In these cases DTDs (Document Type Definitions) have been used to structure the documents, not the business objects and their relations.

The Metadata Coalition is a community of software vendors and users. Lately, they have launched the Open Information Model (OIM), a set of metadata specifications to facilitate sharing and reuse in the application development and data warehousing domains [10]. OIM is described in UML (Unified Modeling Language) and Metadata Coalition does not, so far, encode their models using RDF.

We have found some very usable parts of their models that we have included in our model. In particularly, the key phrase: "Business Units can be arranged into a hierarchy to reflect the structure of industries or organizations. Because they are Resources, Business Units may play specific Resource Roles in relationships to other Resources" [11]. That phrase inspired us to introduce the concept of organizational nodes in a business network.

The information description communities mentioned above, and the examples from their respective vocabulary, can be positioned in the model we elaborated in this paper (see Fig. 1).

5. Concepts used in the framework

In this section we describe the RDF [14] and RDF Schema [15] concepts used in our framework and in the proposed news exchange application. We start of with the basic RDF statement, then we describe how to use classes and subclasses and introduce a specific set of property categories, describe how to use domain and range constraints, discuss how to use property typing. We conclude the section with a general discussion regarding constrained vs. unconstrained models.

5.1. RDF statement

RDF is a framework to describe resources and their properties. The basic concept is the *RDF statement*. This is a triple, describing a resource, a property of that resource and its property value. The property value can be another resource or a literal value.

The common *namespace* for the entire Volvo group is called Volvo core (namespace prefix =

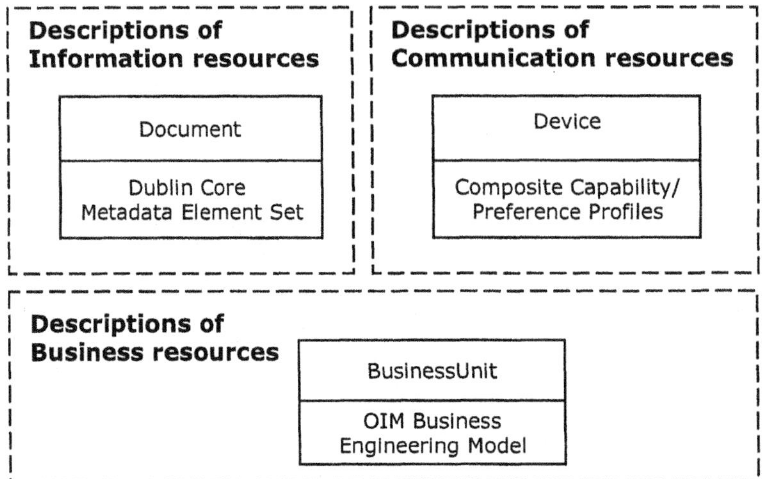

Fig. 1. The three resource description areas form the basis for the proposed model. Included are the three examples introduced above.

`vc:`). If the headline property was defined in the Volvo core namespace, the RDF statement for the example above can be seen in Appendix B, Code example A.

5.2. Classes and subclasses

Other organization units within the Volvo group can define own subclasses of a core class. All resources in our application have to be instances of a *class or subclass* that is defined in Volvo core namespace or a subordinate namespace. For example, Volvo core defines the class InfoObject with its subclass News as shown in Appendix B, Code example B.

The class `InfoObjects` and its subclasses, which are common for the entire Volvo Group, share a common namespace. `Headline` is one of the properties defined in that Information namespace (namespace prefix = `vci:`).

The news bulletin '`vits-0067`' is an instance of the class '`vci:News`' with a headline property defined in the namespace with the prefix = `vci`. In Appendix B, Code example C the RDF statement in Fig. 2 can be seen in abbreviated form.

5.3. Property categories

All properties in our application have to be categorized as one of four Volvo-core defined subproperties. The Open Information Model (OIM) [10] proposes the categorization term, facts, action and inference:

- *term* — Describes a category of properties used for definition of terms.
- *facts* — Describes a category of properties used for to give characteristics of resources.
- *action* — Describes a category of properties for supporting invocation of actions. They express triggering conditions.

An example of an action property is the property '`date`'. When used for Information Objects this property gives date of release, best before, etc. These kinds of dates will trigger distribution, removal from a site etc. A second example is the property '`moreinfo`'. It gives a link from a Business Object to an Information Object with more detailed in-house information. The property '`moreinfo`' will trigger an access control to check that the user is allowed to get the in-house details.

- *inference* — Describes a category of properties for inference or derivation of a business rule from other rules. The property value for this kind of properties will by derived dynamically instead of explicitly stored.

An example of an inference property is the property '`distributeTo`'. This property is used to give a distribution list for a published instance. It is also used in subscriptions to give the address of the subscriber. The application must create an aggregated

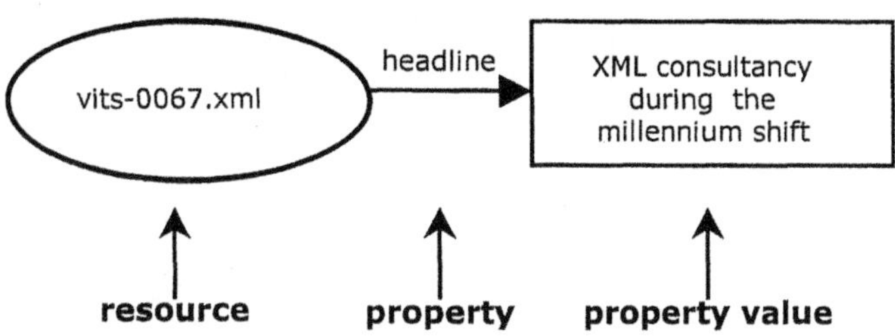

Fig. 2. RDF statement.

distribution list, removing multiple occurrences of receivers.

5.4. Domain and range constraints

Most properties are constrained by the property domain, described in the RDF Schema Specification [15]. The domain property defines the class to which the resource in the RDF statement must belong. When possible, the property values are constrained by the property range from RDF Schema Specification. The range property implies a class. Instances of that class will give the set of values that the property can be given.

The property 'headline' is defined in Volvo Information namespace (vci:) with the domain constraint. In Appendix B, the RDF code can be seen as Code example D.

5.5. Property typing

Often there is a need to further qualify a property value. The properties 'date' and 'relation' are good examples of properties that are likely to be used in different places. Different usage requires different ranges. If 'date' is used for an Information Object it gives date of creation, date of release, etc. When used for an organization node the date will give valid-from-date, valid-to-date etc. To qualify general properties for different usages we add a qualification ('typing') property. This property and its range are defined in appropriate namespaces. Table 1 shows different ranges for information (vci:), organization node (vcbo:) and employee (vcbe:).

In Appendix B, the range for the 'dateType' property in the RDF schema (namespace vci:) can be seen as Code example E.

If we add two dates to the instance in Fig. 2, we get the graphic in Fig. 3. See also RDF Schema Specification [15], Non-Binary Relations.

The RDF description related to Fig. 3 can be seen in Appendix B, Code example F.

5.6. Constrained vs. unconstrained models

Building an RDF model without any constraints will give total freedom. But, as in our case, when the model describes a business and its business rules, then the RDF model has to conform to a business model. We can still build in flexibility, but under control by corporate rules and conventions. The examples above illustrate decentralized use of subclasses and subproperties in a controlled way and

Table 1

Main property	Type property	Type property values
vc:date	vci:dateType	BestBefore Creation Obsolete Release
vc:date	vcbe:dateType	Employed Retired
vc:relation	vcbo: relationType	BelongTo Contain CooperateWith
vc:relation	vcbe: relationType	EmployedBy ResponsibleFor MemberOf

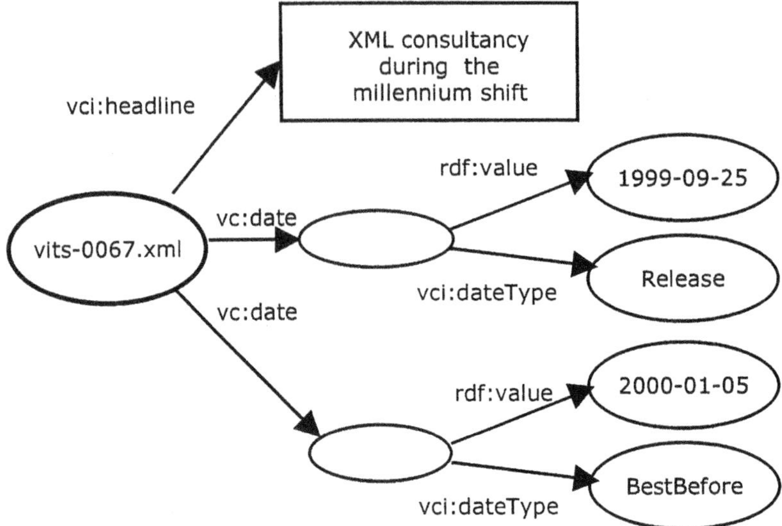

Fig. 3. Qualification (typing) of date property.

use of namespace-controlled qualification (typing). The advantages with a constrained model are:

- The RDF-model is more easily developed if the core classes and properties are defined, based on a business model. The classes serve as anchor points when new resources and properties are added. Inconsistency in the definition of resources and properties can be discovered earlier.
- An RDF knowledgeable tool can dynamically govern the editing of a resource. A list of valid properties for the actual resource could be produced. The validity of property values can be validated.

The core classification of properties indicates where business rules have to interact (action and inference properties).

6. Applying the proposed framework

We start the description of the proposed news exchange application using a scenario. In the following sections we describe the model enabling the scenario using the RDF concepts described in Section 5, and connects the proposed framework to the existing descriptions of resources earlier introduced in Section 4. See also Appendix A: Code examples from the News exchange application, including following instances:

(1) News instance (information resource);
(2) News metadata (information resource description);
(3) News aggregated distribution list (communication resource description);
(4) OrgNode description of Dept. D153 (business resource description);
(5) Subscription (communication resource description).

6.1. Scenario

To visualize the next generation of intranets, we introduce a news exchange application for an extensive intranet that shows how the framework we propose could be applied.

A department wants to inform about one of the offered services during the millennium shift. A Web based news form reached via the department's start page is used to write the news message. The form includes all data and metadata needed. The creator of the news message gets relevant values in drop-down boxes in the news form and gets error messages if data is not valid. The creator of the information can be confident that all relevant persons and organizations receive information about the news in a way that is chosen by each one. This means that the news message about the service during the millennium shift reaches all customers who use the service and col-

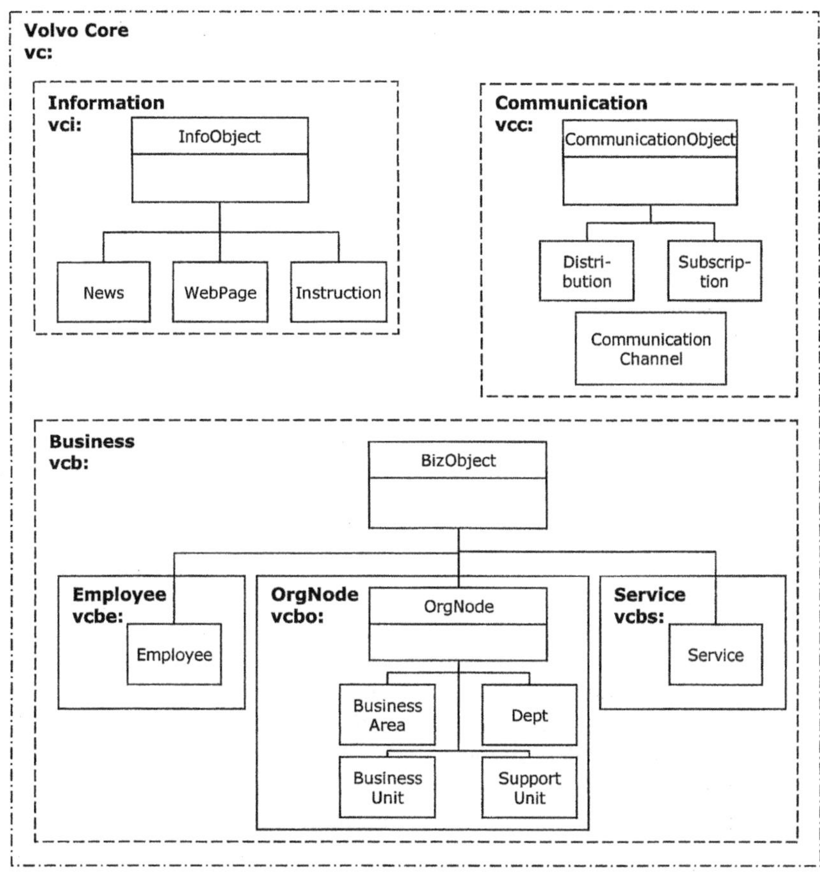

Fig. 4. Overview of the Volvo Core model: classes and namespaces.

leagues they cooperate with, as well as colleagues in the same organization. This implies both implicit and explicit receivers: implicit as a consequence of the defined network of relations in the business, explicit as a consequent of subscriptions. A complete distribution list is available for the news message afterwards.

6.2. Classes and namespaces

In the model we divide resource descriptions into three areas: business, information and communication. Each area has a top class: `BizObject`, `InfoObject` and `CommunicationObject`. All of these share a common namespace for the entire Volvo group (`vc:`). Each area (business, information and communication) also has its own unique namespace (`vcb:`, `vci:` and `vcc:`) to be able to define the vocabulary used to describe resources.

In the business area it is a appropriate to divide the namespace around the next level of subclasses: The vocabulary to describe Employees differs from the vocabularies describing Organizations and Services. Employees, Organizations and Services are the types of Business objects common to the Volvo group that we identified for the news exchange application. In the Information area the `InfoObject` has a couple of proposed subclasses: `News`, `WebPage` and `Instructions`. Fig. 4 shows an overview of the Volvo Core model applying classes and namespaces.

6.3. Properties

The Volvo Core domain also defines the property categories (term, facts, action and inference); see Table 2.

In the three areas: information, business and com-

Table 2

Volvo Core domain			
Property	Property Type	Domain	Range
date	Action		ISOdate
relation	Fact		

munication the defined properties set the basic typing and the core relationships between the classes. Together with the described typing for the Volvo Core properties date and relations the tables below gives an overview of the properties.

6.3.1. Information resource descriptions properties

In the information area we have used the Dublin Core Metadata Element Set (see Section 4) as a starting point for the proposed set of properties. We also propose a set of properties to capture the relations to other classes: `BizObject`, `Employee` and `CommunicationChannel`. An example of an information resource description, see Appendix A: Code example 2 News metadata. Table 3 describes constrains for relevant information resource descriptions properties.

6.3.2. Business resource descriptions

In the business area we have been inspired by the description of business units, proposed by Metadata Coalition (see Section 4), adding an extension to the model to be able to describe nodes and relations in networking organizations. In our proposed model each business object instantiate itself by:

- Position it in the business network, describing the relations to other nodes (using the types of relation valid for OrgNodes: `BelongTo`, `Contain`, `CooperateWith`, see above)
- How to communicate with it (`communicationChannel` and `destination`) for example via e-mail to a department's common e-mail-id or via the news section on their start page on the intranet.
- Where to find more information about it.
- What services each identified node in the organizational network offers.

An example of a business resource description, see Appendix A: Code example 4 OrgNode description of Dept. D153. Table 4 describes constrains for relevant business resource descriptions properties.

6.3.3. Communication resource descriptions

In the communication area we have been inspired by the proposed Composite Capability/Preference Profiles (CC/PP) (see Section 4) as a framework for describing properties for devices. We propose a similar framework describing different communication channels such as e-mail, Web, paper etc. with properties such as `graphicsAllowed` and `maxSize`.

We also propose a mechanism for description of organizing communications of information about the business. This gives employees, departments etc. the possibility to subscribe on different types of information using `searchString` and `sortOrder`. We suggest that these are encoded using the proposed XSLT pattern [16].

Two example of business resource descriptions, see Appendix A: Code example 3 News aggregated distribution list, and 5 Subscription. Table 5 describes constrains for relevant communication resource descriptions properties.

Table 3

Info Object domain			
Property	Property type	Domain	Range
abstract	Fact	InfoObject	
communication	Fact	InfoObject	CommunicationChannel
coverage	Fact	InfoObject	BizObject
creator	Fact	InfoObject	Employee
employeeRef	Inference	InfoObject	EmployeeRef
headline	Fact	InfoObject	
longDescr	Term	InfoObject	
shortDescr	Term	InfoObject	
uri	Term	WebPage	

Table 4

BizObject domain			
Property	Property Type	Domain	Range
communicationChannel	Fact	BizObject	CommunicationChannel
destination	Fact	BizObject	
moreinfo	Action	BizObject	InfoObject
serviceOffering	Fact	OrgNode	Service

Table 5

Communication object domain			
Property	Property type	Domain	Range
distributeTo	Inference	CommunicationObject	BizObject
elementRef	Fact	Subscription	XSLT pattern
graphicsAllowed	Fact	CommunicationChannel	YesOrNo
maxSize	Fact	CommunicationChannel	
searchString	Fact	Subscription	Literal
sortOrder	Fact	Subscription	XSLT pattern
subscriptOf	Fact	Subscription	InfoObject

6.4. Extending the model

The company Volvo IT is an instance of the class SupportUnit in the domain for Volvo Core Business Object (vcbo:). It is a service company and needs to define its own subclasses for services, information and organization nodes. Below an overview of how Volvo IT (VIT) extend the model and introduce their company wide vocabulary:

- Volvo IT specific type of organizations:
- BPU. Business Process Unit (defined in the VIT schema as: An organization node which supports a Business Process with IT services.)
- Team (defined in the VIT schema as: A number of individuals with the same role or mission, constituting a formal or informal group for a limited period of time).
- Volvo IT specific types of services: Application Service and Service Bureau.

7. Lessons learned and future directions

The work reported in this paper was initiated by the encountered problems trying to recommend a metadata schema for an extensive intranet. Although, it has been energized by the vision of *context sensitive editing* for users creating information, and gradually, also by the vision of *context driven views and navigation* for users consuming information. We wanted to explore the possibilities to develop context-sensitive content editing that uses RDF [14] and RDF schemas [15] to provide content providers with dynamic forms including relevant properties, permitted values to choose from and direct validation of data and metadata. The conclusion is that such visions could be realized, but require a consistent approach for how to set the context. In addition, a framework implementing such an approach, must take into account the constantly change of context: re-structuring of information, re-organizing of communication and re-positioning nodes in the business network.

The contribution of this paper is such a framework called: *A framework for the next generation of intranets*. The framework includes three interrelated components:

(1) A model describing three different areas of resources: business, information and communication, and integrating the resources descriptions areas by means of generic classes, constraints and relations.
(2) An extension to the model describing and integrating nodes and relations in networking organizations.

(3) An extension to the model describing and organizing the communication of information in the business.

The framework suggests an *extensible use of RDF (Resource Description Framework) in a business context.*

Our experiences are very promising. Combining subclassing and the namespace-controlled qualification (typing) gave us a robust implementation and application of the framework. However, we did found it hard to select between the RDF subclassing and instancing mechanism in a consequent way. The RDF-syntax is sometime very complex and offers several different ways of encoding for example the typing mechanism. There is an intensive debate in the RDF interest community regarding a simpler syntax. We look forward to see the implications of this debate. The ongoing discussion on the overlaps and complements between RDF Schemas and XML Schemas could also improve the encoding of the framework. We would also like to see cross discipline communities that combine lessons learned from the deployment of object orientation analysis and programming, with the scalable and non-centralized mechanisms cultivated throughout the development of Internet.

The next step will be to evaluate the different RDF parsers, RDF editors and as well as RDF spiders that we now can see being introduced on the market. We would also like to expand the scope of the framework, opening up new possibilities:

- Add *functional resource descriptions.* The proposed property categories; action and inference, could be used as anchor points for adding structured specifications of business rules in the business area.
- Add *presentational and navigational resource descriptions.* Adding structured specifications of styles and navigational patterns in the communication area. Connecting such a mechanism to the consumer-driven subscription, which defines views of information, could enable a context driven navigation.

The result of the experiments reported in this paper, will also be used in future work regarding editorial systems. Adapt the framework to a news production context, instead of a business context.

Appendix A. Code examples from the News exchange application

(1) News instance (information resource);
(2) News metadata (information resource description);
(3) News aggregated distribution list (communication resource description);
(4) OrgNode description of Dept. D153 (business resource description);
(5) Subscription (communication resource description).

Code example 1. News instance

```
<!DOCTYPE News SYSTEM "news.dtd">
<News id="vits-0067">
    <headline>Web consultancy during the millennium shift</headline>
    <abstract>Limited uptime for......</abstract>
    <fulltext>The schedule is......</fulltext>
</News>
```

Code example 2. News metadata

```
<rdf:RDF xmlns:rdf="http://www.w3.org/1999/02/22-rdf-syntax-ns#"
         xmlns:vc="http://volvo.se/vc-namespace/schema.rdf#"
         xmlns:vci="http://volvo.se/vci-namespace/schema.rdf#"
         xmlns:vcbe="http://volvo.se/vcbe-namespace/schema.rdf#">

    <vci:News rdf:about="http://vit.volvo.se/153/news/vits-0067.xml">
        <vci:headline>XML consultancy during the millennium shift
```

```
        </vci:headline>
        <vci:abstract>Limited support during......</vci:abstract>
        <vci:coverage
    rdf:resource="http://vit.volvo.se/153/service.rdf#WebConsulting"/>
        <vc:date rdf:parseType="Resource">
            <rdf:value>1999-09-25</rdf:value>
            <vci:dateType
    rdf:resource="http://volvo.se/vci-namespace/schema.rdf#Release"/>
        </vc:date>
        <vc:date rdf:parseType="Resource">
            <rdf:value>2000-01-05</rdf:value>
            <vci:dateType
    rdf:resource="http://volvo.se/vci-namespace/schema.rdf#BestBefore"/>
        </vc:date>
        <vci:creator rdf:parseType="Resource">
            <rdf:value
            rdf:resource="http://vit.volvo.se/empl.rdf#E12345"/>
                <vcbe:employeeRef
    rdf:resource="http://volvo.se/vcbe-namespace/schema.rdf#EmployeeId"/>
        </vci:creator>
    </vci:News>
</rdf:RDF>
```

Code example 3. News aggregated distribution list

```
<rdf:RDF xmlns:rdf="http://www.w3.org/1999/02/22-rdf-syntax-ns#"
        xmlns:vcc="http://volvo.se/vcc-namespace/schema.rdf#">
        <vcc:Distribution
         rdf:about="http://vit.volvo.se/153-news/vits-0067.xml">
        <vcc:distributeTo
         rdf:resource="http://vit.volvo.se/153-org.rdf"/>
        <vcc:distributeTo
         rdf:resource="http://vit.volvo.se/empl.rdf#E44180"/>
        <!-- Added by subscription S0001 -->
        <vcc:distributeTo
         rdf:resource="http://vit.volvo.se/empl.rdf#E12345"/>
        <!-- Added by subscription S0002 -->
        <vcc:distributeTo
         rdf:resource="http://vit.volvo.se/empl.rdf#E123456"/>
    </vcc:Distribution>
</rdf:RDF>
```

Code example 4. OrgNode description of Dept. D153

```
<rdf:RDF
    xmlns:rdf="http://www.w3.org/1999/02/22-rdf-syntax-ns#"
    xmlns:rdfs="http://www.w3.org/TR/1999/PR-rdf-schema-19990303#"
    xmlns:vc="http://volvo.se/vc-namespace/schema.rdf#"
    xmlns:vcb="http://volvo.se/vcb-namespace/schema.rdf#"
    xmlns:vcbo="http://volvo.se/vcbo-namespace/schema.rdf#">
    <vcbo:Dept ID="D153">
        <rdfs:label>XML/SGML Center</rdfs:label>
        <rdfs:comment>The main tasks for XML/SGML Center is..
        </rdfs:comment>
        <vcb:communicationChannel rdf:parseType="Literal">
            <rdf:value>Email</rdf:value>
            <vcb:destination>it1.jsmith@memo.volvo.se"
```

```
            </vcb:destination>
        </vcb:communicationChannel>
        <vc:relation rdf:parseType="Resource">
            <vcbo:relationType
        rdf:resource="http://volvo.se/vcbo-namespace/schema.rdf#BelongTo"/>
        <rdf:value rdf:resource="http://vit.volvo.se/org.rdf#D15"/>
        </vc:relation>
        <vc:relation rdf:parseType="Resource">
            <vcbo:relationType
        rdf:resource="http://volvo.se/vcbo-namespace/schema.rdf#CooperateWith"/>
            <rdf:value>
            <rdf:Bag>
            <rdf:li
            rdf:resource="http://volvo.se/vit-namespace/schema.rdf#BPU"/>
            <rdf:li
            rdf:resource="http://vit.volvo.se/D173-org.rdf"/>
            <rdf:li
            rdf:resource="http://vit.volvo.se/InfoMasters-org.rdf"/>
            </rdf:Bag>
            </rdf:value>
        </vc:relation>
        <vcbo:serviceOffering
        rdf:resource="http://vit.volvo.se/D153-service.rdf"/>
        <vcb:moreInfo rdf:parseType="Resource">
        <vcb:moreinfoType
            rdf:resource="http://volvo.se/schema.rdf#WebPage"/>
            <rdf:value resource="http://vit.volvo.se/D153/webpage.rdf#D153HP"/>
        </vcb:moreInfo>
    </vcbo:Dept>
</rdf:RDF>
```

Code example 5. Subscription

```
<rdf:RDF
    xmlns:rdf="http://www.w3.org/1999/02/22-rdf-syntax-ns#"
    xmlns:vci="http://volvo.se/vci-namespace/schema.rdf#"
    xmlns:vcc="http://volvo.se/vcc-namespace/schema.rdf#">
    <vcc:Subscription rdf:ID="S0001">
        <vcc:subscriptOf
            rdf:resource="http://volvo.se/vci-namespace/schema.rdf#News"/>
        <vcc:searchString rdf:parseType="Literal">
            <rdf:value>XML</rdf:value>
            <vcc:elementRef>vci:headline</vcc:elementRef>
        </vcc:searchString>
        <vcc:sortOrder>
            <rdf:Seq>
                <rdf:li>vc:date[@vci:dateType="BestBefore"]</rdf:li>
                <rdf:li>vci:headline</rdf:li>
            </rdf:Seq>
        </vcc:sortOrder>
        <vcc:distributeTo rdf:resource="http://vit volvo.se/empl.rdf#E12345"/>
    </vcc:Subscription>
</rdf:RDF>
```

Appendix B. Code examples

(A) RDF Statement;
(B) News is a subclass of InfoObject;
(C) Part of the News metadata;
(D) Definition of the headline property;
(E) Date typing of Information Objects;
(F) Dates in the News metadata.

Code example A. RDF Statement

```
<rdf:RDF xmlns:rdf="http://www.w3.org/1999/02/22-rdf-syntax-ns#"
        xmlns:vc="http://volvo.se/vc-namespace/schema.rdf#">
    <rdf:Description
     rdf:about="http://vit.volvo.se/153-news/vits-0067.xml">
        <vc:headline>XML consultancy during the millennium shift
        </vc:headline>
    <rdf:Description>
</rdf:RDF>
```

Code example B. News is a subclass of InfoObject

```
<rdfs:Class rdf:ID="InfoObject">
    <rdfs:label>Information object</rdfs:label>
    <rdfs:comment xml:lang="en">
        The InfoObject class is comprised of textual, graphical
        and video-based information objects.
        Volvo-defined subclasses of InfoObject are:
        News, WebPage, Instruction, etc.
        Example of possibly new objects are: Policy, Minute,
        Agreement, Directive, Standard, Template, Form, etc.
    </rdfs:comment>
</rdfs:Class>

<rdfs:Class rdf:ID="News">
    <rdfs:subClassOf rdf:resource="#InfoObject"/>
    <rdfs:label>News</rdfs:label>
    <rdfs:comment xml:lang="en">
        The News class is comprised of all information about
        changes or events at Volvo, like press releases, product
        launches and organizational changes.
        When needed, subclasses of News are defined by appropriate
        instances in the organization, outside Volvo core.
    </rdfs:comment>
</rdfs:Class>
```

Code example C. Part of News metadata

```
<rdf:RDF xmlns:rdf="http://www.w3.org/1999/02/22-rdf-syntax-ns#"
        xmlns:vci="http://volvo.se/vci-namespace/schema.rdf#">
     <vci:News
      rdf:about="http://vit.volvo.se/153-news/vits-0067.xml">
        <vci:headline>XML consultancy during the millennium shift
        </vci:headline>
    </vci:News>
</rdf:RDF>
```

Code example D. Definition of the headline property

```
<rdf:Property ID="headline">
    <rdfs:subPropertyOf
        rdf:resource="http://volvo.se/vc-namespace/schema.rdf#factProperty"/>
    <rdfs:domain rdf:resource="#InfoObject"/>
    <rdfs:label xml:lang="en">Headline</rdfs:label>
    <rdfs:comment xml:lang="en">
            A header, describing the content of an information object.
    </rdfs:comment>
</rdf:Property>
```

Code example E. Date typing for Information Objects

```
<!-- Valid range of property 'date' -->
<rdfs:Class rdf:ID="DateType"/>
        <DateType rdf:ID="BestBefore">
        <rdfs:label xml:lang="en">Best-before date</rdfs:label>
        <rdfs:comment xml:lang="en">Date after which the information
        may be invalid
        </rdfs:comment>
    </DateType>
        <DateType rdf:ID="Creation">
        <rdfs:label xml:lang="en">Creation date</rdfs:label>
        <rdfs:comment xml:lang="en">Date when the information
        was created
        </rdfs:comment>
    </DateType>
        <DateType rdf:ID="Obsolete">
        <rdfs:label xml:lang="en">Obsolete date</rdfs:label>
        <rdfs:comment xml:lang="en">Date after which the information
        is obsolete
        </rdfs:comment>
    </DateType>
        <DateType rdf:ID="Release">
        <rdfs:label xml:lang="en">Release date</rdfs:label>
        <rdfs:comment xml:lang="en">Date when the information
        is released
        </rdfs:comment>
    </DateType>

<!-- ****** Volvo core properties in domain InfoObject ****** -->
<rdf:Property ID="dateType">
    <rdfs:subPropertyOf
    rdf:resource="http://volvo.se/vc-namespace/schema.rdf#actionProperty"/>
    <rdfs:domain rdf:resource="#InfoObject"/>
        <rdfs:range rdf:resource="#DateType"/>
    <rdfs:label xml:lang="en">Type of date</rdfs:label>
    <rdfs:comment xml:lang="en">
        Defines the kind of date of an Information Object
    </rdfs:comment>
</rdf:Property>
```

Code example F. Dates in the news metadata

```
<rdf:RDF xmlns:rdf="http://www.w3.org/1999/02/22-rdf-syntax-ns#"
        xmlns:vc="http://volvo.se/vc-namespace/schema.rdf#"
        xmlns:vci="http://volvo.se/vci-namespace/schema.rdf#">
        <vci:News rdf:about="http://vit.volvo.se/153-news/vits-0067.xml">
        <vci:headline>XML consultancy during the millennium shift
        </vci:headline>
        <vc:date rdf:parseType="Resource">
            <rdf:value>1999-09-25</rdf:value>
            <vci:dateType
    <rdf:resource="http://volvo.se/vci-namespace/schema.rdf#Release"/>
        </vc:date>
        <vc:date rdf:parseType="Resource">
            <rdf:value>2000-01-05</rdf:value>
            <vci:dateType
    <rdf:resource="http://volvo.se/vci-namespace/schema.rdf#BestBefore"/>
        </vc:date>
    </vci:News>
</rdf:RDF>
```

References

[1] Association for Library Collections and Technical Services, Task Force on Metadata, Summary Report, June 1999, http://www.ala.org/alcts/organization/ccs/ccda/tf-meta3.html.

[2] J. Bosak and T. Bray, XML and the second-generation Web, Sci. Am., May 1999, http://www.sciam.com/1999/0599issue/0599bosak.html.

[3] Composite Capability/Preference Profiles (CC/PP), W3C Note, 27 July 1999, http://www.w3.org/TR/NOTE-CCPP/.

[4] B. Dahlbom, From infrastructure to networking, in: C. Ciborra (Ed.), From Control to Drift, Oxford University Press, Oxford, 2000.

[5] J. Damsgard and R. Scheepers, A stage model of intranet technology implementation and management, Inf. Syst. J., in press.

[6] Dublin Core Home Page, http://purl.org/DC/.

[7] Dublin Core Metadata Element Set, Version 1.1: Reference Description, Dublin Core, http://purl.oclc.org/dc/documents/rec-dces-19990702.htm.

[8] EU-NSF Working Group on Metadata, Metadata for Digital Libraries: a Research Agenda, http://www.iei.pi.cnr.it/DELOS/REPORTS/metadata.html.

[9] F. Ljungberg, Networking, Ph.D. thesis, Department of Informatics, Gothenburg University, 1998.

[10] Meta Data Coalition, Open Information Model, Version 1.0, August 1999, http://www.mdcinfo.com/OIM/OIM10.html.

[11] Meta Data Coalition, Open Information Model, Business Engineering Model Business Rules, July 15, 1999 Review draft, http://www.mdcinfo.com/OIM/models/BRM.html.

[12] E. Miller, P. Miller and D. Brickley, Guidance on expressing the Dublin Core within the Resource Description Framework (RDF), draft proposal, 1999, http://www.ukoln.ac.uk/metadata/resources/dc/datamodel/WD-dc-rdf.

[13] M.K. Natvig and O. Ohren, Modelling shared information spaces (SIS), in: Proc. of the International ACM SIGGROUP Conference on Supporting Group Work, 1999, pp. 199–208.

[14] Resource Description Framework (RDF), Model and Syntax Specification, W3C Recommendation, 22 February 1999, http://www.w3.org/TR/REC-rdf-syntax.

[15] Resource Description Framework (RDF), Schema Specification, W3C Proposed Recommendation, 3 March 1999, http://www.w3.org/TR/PR-rdf-schema/.

[16] XSL Transformations (XSLT), Version 1.0, W3C Proposed Recommendation, 8 October 1999, http://www.w3.org/TR/PR-rdf-schema/.

[17] W3C Mobile Access Interest Group, http://www.w3.org/Mobile/.

[18] WAP Forum, http://www.wapforum.org/.

Kerstin Forsberg is a consultant at Adera, Europe's first e-agency, uniting skills in marketing, communication, management and IT. She is also a Ph.D. student at the Viktoria Institute, Gothenburg, Sweden, and belongs to the Mobile Informatics research group. Her research interests include editorial processes, information structuring and mobile IT support for knowledge management.

Lars Dannstedt is a Senior Consultant at Volvo information Technology. He has promoted the use of structured information since early 1980s. Recently he joined the Web Program Center at VOLVO IT with main focus on XML-based solutions. At that position the need for robust metadata solutions has been proven.

The evolution of a manufacturing Web site

Shannon L. Fowler [1], Anne-Marie J. Novack, Michael J. Stillings *

The Boeing Company, Boeing Commercial Airplanes, Wing Responsibility Center, P.O. Box 3707 M/C 61-71, Seattle, WA 98124, USA

Abstract

The Boeing Commercial Airplanes Wing Responsibility Center (WRC) needed a way to communicate quickly and effectively between its various plant locations. An important requirement was the ability to provide a common means to update and disseminate information, such as vital organizational statistics, in a timely manner.

Several Web applications were built for the site, providing data entry and validation, charting, reporting, paging, e-mail notification, automatic detection of broken links, and the ability to build and update pages without the knowledge of HTML or a Web authoring tool. The site and its applications work daily to support the people who build the wings for Boeing airplanes.

Keywords: The Boeing Company; Wing Responsibility Center; Intranet solutions; Broken links; Content management

1. Introduction

In 1995 Boeing Commercial Airplanes (BCA), the division of The Boeing Company that builds internationally famous airliners, created responsibility centers. This was done to focus attention on major segments of the airplane by having all of the functional areas required to design, build, and service in one organization. Wings and empennage (the tail sections) constitute such a segment, and make up the Wing Responsibility Center (WRC).

The WRC is accountable for all aspects of designing, producing, and supporting wing and empennage components for BCA. In doing so, the WRC is also responsible for the quality, cost, and delivery of these products, as well as the safety and morale of its employees [2].

The customers who benefit from these products and services are the 717, 737, 747, 757, 767, and 777 airplane programs.

The WRC is located at several plants in the Seattle, Washington area and also in Toronto, Ontario, Canada. The organization consists of about 6000 employees, most of whom work directly on the factory floor.

The WRC's goal is to help the airplane programs meet their production targets. To accomplish this goal, the WRC web site was created as part of the Boeing Intranet.

2. Purpose

The original purpose of the WRC Web site was to give a comprehensive view of the factory status on a daily basis and to provide the primary means of communication between the vice-president and his management team. Later, enhancements to the site enabled all levels of management, employees, and internal suppliers to see the same information.

* Corresponding author. E-mail: michael.j.stillings@boeing.com

[1] E-mail: shannon.l.fowler@boeing.com

Additionally, it was anticipated that this manner of information sharing would reduce travel time along the 77 mile interstate highway corridor between WRC locations, as well as allow employees from the Toronto plant to participate in meetings held in the Seattle area. As a result of this site, the days of chart-lined visibility rooms and meeting attendees laden with stacks of status printouts and view foils are dwindling. In addition, WRC management can instantly post critical information to the home page when it needs to be disseminated quickly. For example, during an emergency (an injury to a worker, severe weather, a volcanic eruption, etc.) employees can look quickly to a 'panic button' link on the home page for instructions.

3. History

The site went online in the fall of 1996 as a set of static pages and was completely redesigned by the Web team in the winter of 1996 in response to new customer requests. A process has been followed to enhance the site and solve problems encountered in daily operation, for example, when content providers break links to their files on a server. When a linked file is moved, renamed, or deleted without prior coordination with the Webmaster, a broken link results. Two of the Web applications covered later in this paper were written to solve this problem. Much of the site is now interactive and uses a combination of tools the Web team has selected and assembled.

Tool selection is based on customer requirements. Table 1 details some of the requirements and the tools ultimately chosen to support them.

4. Design

Initially, the WRC Web team decided to use frames to make the navigation more consistent and the menu entries easier to update. Frames also simplify the design scheme for many of the content providers by wrapping the site navigation around their Web pages. In addition, most of the requirements for posting to the Boeing Intranet are included in the frames documents so the content providers do not have to consider them when designing a page.

The WRC home page has two menus. The menu on the left side is set up to follow the same hierarchy as the WRC organization chart. Since each WRC location has unique information, the left menu on each location's home page changes, depending on which part of the site the end-user is viewing. The second menu can be found at the top of every location's home page and always remains the same since it contains information common to all the sites.

A style guide was set up to encourage a similar look and feel across all the sites. For example, the background color, menu colors, fonts, and link colors are all covered in the style guide.

Eventually, a series of drop down boxes containing the same information found in the top and left menus was added to the home page to provide another way to navigate the Web site.

5. Current state

The WRC Web site now has over 3000 pages and averages 782 user sessions (37,229 hits) every weekday. The average user spends about 18 min on the site. The site was designed with few formal controls to allow for individual creativity. Because of the lack of constraints, the page count grew exponentially. End-users went from seeing the Intranet as a toy to using it to daily access a library of information that helps them perform their jobs.

This Web site is a vital, dynamic, working tool and provides the whole engineering to manufacturing perspective. For example, legacy applications now have Web interfaces for engineers, parts are ordered using a Web paging system, machines are monitored by an attached online system, and the factory status metrics are available 24 h a day.

6. Web applications

Several applications were developed to provide extra functionality to the WRC Web site. For example, 'Vital Measures' was the outcome of the former vice-president's desire to see real-time data on the health of the WRC; OEE (Overall Equipment Effectiveness) was developed to visually show the real-time status of factory machines; the SHEA

Table 1
Tool selection

Requirement	Tool
Create a Web page of dynamically generated thumbnail charts enabling the customer to quickly scan the health of the WRC and to drill down to a larger, more detailed chart.	Microsoft® Active Server Pages technology includes VBScript, a subset of the Visual Basic language designed to run 'in the box' on the browser without I/O capability. The similarity between the two languages, and the use of Microsoft® Access to build initial back-end databases, made it easier for our experienced Windows application developers to learn how to develop Web applications. Software F/X's ChartFX (an ActiveX control useful for producing charts from a database) had just been released as well, so we chose Microsoft® Internet Information Server (IIS) as our Web server platform.
Find a search engine that could scan the Web site and additional data repositories not linked to any Web page, and produce a catalog of all HTML, Microsoft® Office, and Adobe® Acrobat® files found.	The Web team was also interested in the possibilities offered by personalization so Microsoft® Site Server was selected as the search engine.
Provide a 'chat room' that is capable of threaded messaging so employees from different time zones and/or different work shifts can communicate with each other on a variety of topics.	After researching products available at the time, O'Reilly® WebBoard™ was chosen because of its easy administration, live chat capability, threaded messaging, archiving options, and cost.
Analyze the Web server's logs, and find and fix broken links.	WebTrends® and Tetranet's Linkbot™ were picked to help satisfy these requirements, based on product cost and features.
Provide the ability to send e-mail notifications through any Web application.	When IIS 4.0 was released, we were already using an ASP SMTP mail component, but discarded it in favor of the component now included with IIS.
Provide a menu for the site that includes a long list of links without overwhelming site visitors.	At first, a commercially available Java applet with an expandable menu listing was selected to perform this task. However, it was slow to load and sometimes would not load at all when the server was running with high processor utilization (we have not been able to determine the reason). The applet was then phased out and replaced with a new menu based on JavaScript functions.

(Safety, Health and Environmental Affairs) application implemented a WRC-wide standard process for the first time; 'Part Paging' allows a paging request to be sent over the Web to retrieve a needed part from storage; and both the 'Web Link Checker' and 'Database Grid application' were created to deal with the problem of broken links.

6.1. Vital Measures application

The vital statistics of the WRC — items such as how many wings were delivered during a given week, the number of engineering releases, and the current staffing level — give a detailed picture of our manufacturing organization's health in real time. The Vital Measures application makes it easy to see these critical statistics and includes a thumbnail view of all the measures for a quick scan of data trends, as well as the capability to drill-down to a more detailed view of the data.

Fig. 1 shows sample measures, one per row, for all of the airplane models Boeing builds in the Seattle area. The database-driven, thumbnail-size charts for Measures 1 and 2 show the trend of the latest data for each measure. Image files, colored green, yellow, or red, show the overall health of that measure for all of the models, both for the current period (usually week or month) and the previous period. The information for these database-driven measures is input through Web pages on the site.

The charts are created with the ChartFX software package listed in Table 1; ChartFX is a commer-

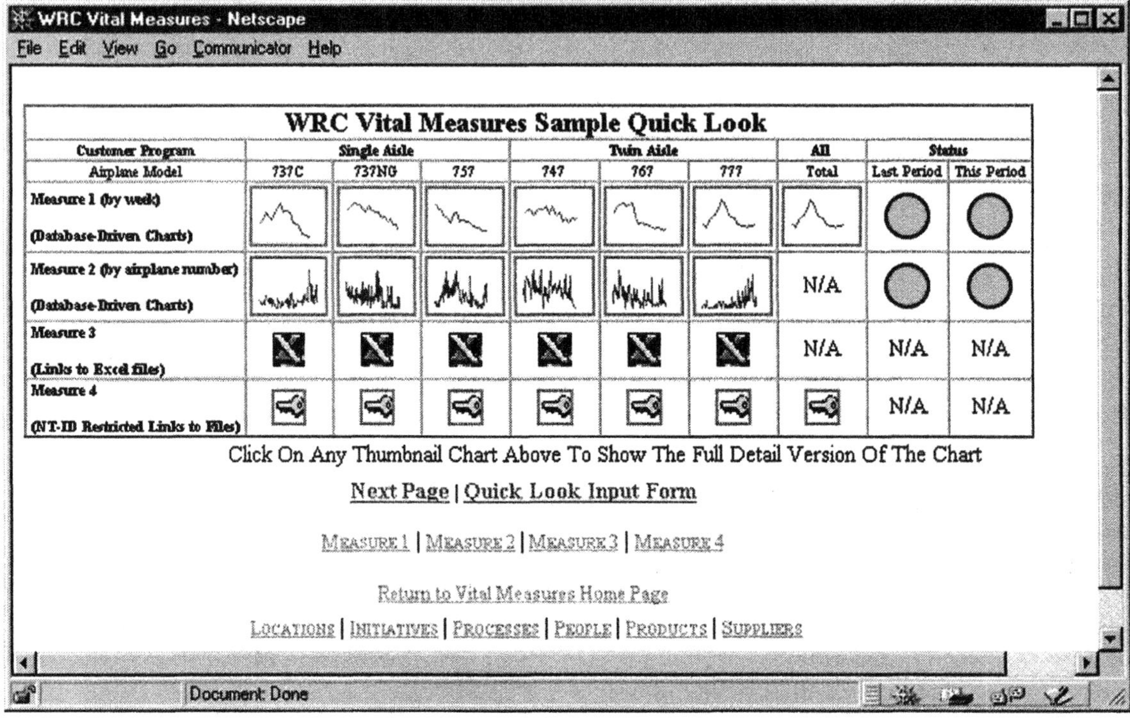

Fig. 1. WRC Vital Measures quick look page.

cially available C++ ActiveX control installed on the WRC Web server. VBScript Server Side Includes were written to set and invoke Chart FX objects, properties, and methods to create the desired charts.

Icons for Measure 3 are linked to chart files, such as Excel charts. The key icons for Measure 4 indicate that file viewing is restricted by NT ID permission to particular end-users. Clicking on Measure 1's thumbnail chart for the 757 provides more data on the 757 airplane model (Fig. 2).

The blue vertical bars in Fig. 2 show the actual Measure 1 data by week. The middle green horizontal target line indicates where the data numbers should be, showing in this case that the data numbers were originally too high but the problem has been brought under control. The top red and bottom magenta horizontal lines (above and below the green target line) show the upper and lower control limits for statistical process control purposes. The links in the first row beneath the chart access similar detailed charts for the other airplane models and totals for the single-aisle and twin-aisle airplane programs. Other rows (not shown) provide links to the pages for other WRC health measures.

6.2. OEE application

The OEE (Overall Equipment Effectiveness) system records machine set-up, run, and loss time, effectively measuring asset capacity, efficiency, availability, and quality. When combined with TAKT Time (actual customer demand for product based on planned production time), OEE can be used to determine how effectively an asset (in this case a machine tool) produces a product and the number of assets required to meet customer demand. Improving OEE results can dramatically decrease the number of assets required to meet current flow-through requirements and eliminate or reduce the need to purchase more equipment to meet future increases in customer demand [1].

The OEE machine status interface shows the real-time state of individual machines using colored circles (green = running, blue = idle, yellow = idle with a reason, red = stopped) and is automatically updated. It also provides additional information, such

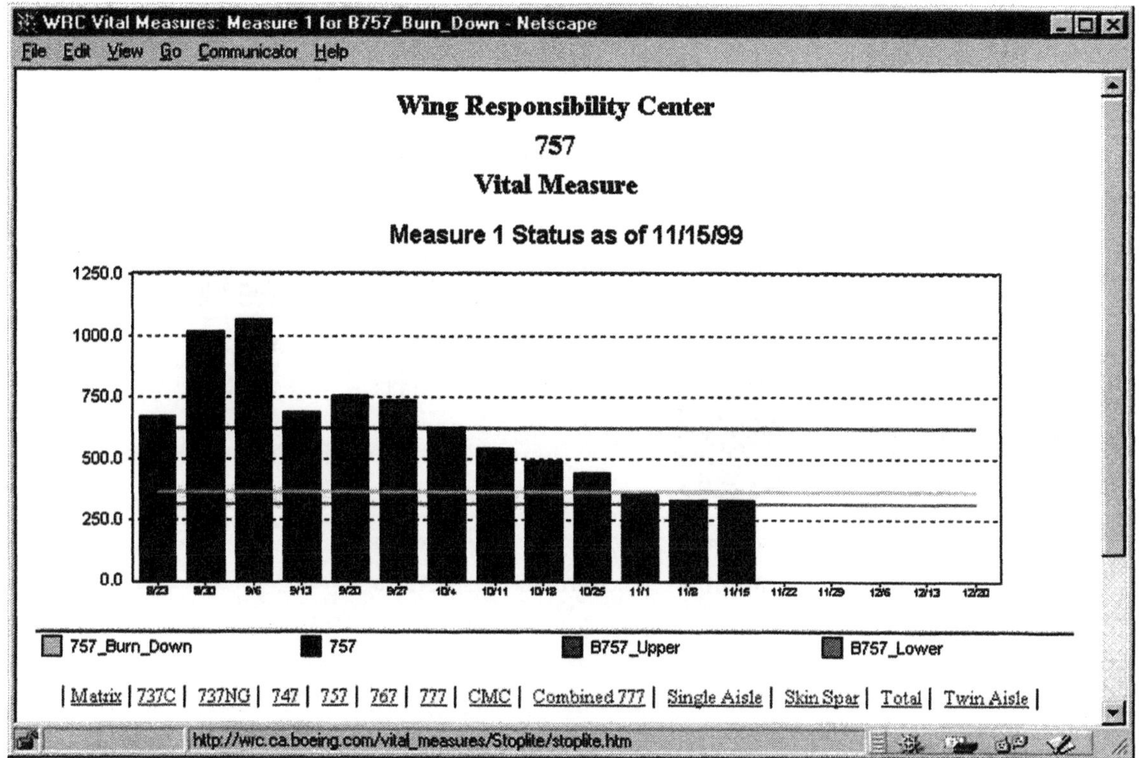

Fig. 2. Detail chart for sample Measure 1.

as time elapsed since the machine entered the current state, job and part numbers, loss code descriptions, and shift status.

Data input, capture, and analysis are for the most part done automatically, although a small amount of data is input manually. For example, the OEE system automatically records whether a machine is running or is stopped. When the machine is stopped, the operator can then input the reason using a computer on the factory floor. Depending on the setup, the operator either selects the reason from a drop down menu on the OEE interface or wands over a bar code.

Lights attached to the machines are wired into the OEE system and are used as visual aids, supplementing the status provided on the Web site.

The OEE system can page one or more people as needed. For instance, if a machine is stopped, a supervisor can be notified of a potential problem or a maintenance person can be called for repairs. Supervisors can use the system to more efficiently allocate the available resources. If one machine is stopped because no work is available for it and another machine is stopped for set up, work can be diverted to the first machine.

Using the OEE system, the machine operators can view the status of the machines around them. For instance, the operator of Machine B, which receives parts from Machine A, can check the status of Machine A and plan work accordingly.

Charts displaying the data captured are also available via a Web interface, allowing anyone with a browser to view them. Analyses of these charts point out opportunities for better capacity utilization, such as restructuring the number of employees assigned to different shifts and decreasing the set up time. Employees used to spend as much as four to six hours summing up a week's worth of data for just one machine; now it takes just five minutes [3].

Fig. 3 is a sample screen print of the OEE system.

6.3. SHEA application

Safety, Health, and Environmental Affairs (SHEA) data are tracked by safety focals at each

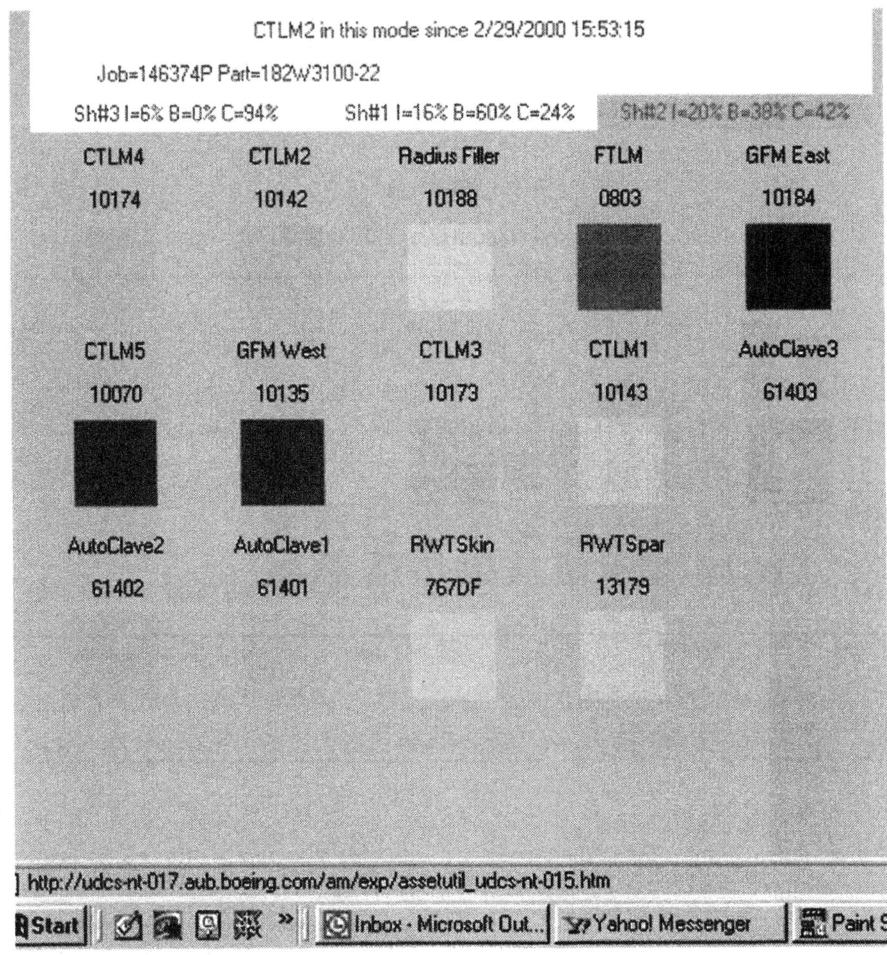

Fig. 3. Sample OEE page showing machine status.

Boeing plant location. If a SHEA-related incident occurs (e.g., a WRC factory employee becomes injured), the incident information is entered into a form using the SHEA application (Fig. 4).

Partial information about a safety-related incident can be input and stored until all the data have been gathered, at which time the incident data are submitted to the database. Then, the general supervisor listed to be notified is automatically e-mailed a message of the incident. These notification rules are also updated through the application. In addition, incident data can be searched for and revised once more accurate information is available.

The SHEA application charts data in several ways, using the Chart FX ActiveX charting tool. Many combinations of data fields can be used to produce the charts, such as factory location, injury date, control code, etc. (Fig. 5).

6.4. Part Paging application

This Web application automatically pages the appropriate workers in the factory when parts or part information is needed. Previously, workers had to manually locate the specific routing for each part and ensure that both a primary and backup person were notified of a part request. This application automatically provides the correct information and has significantly reduced flow time. Wing assembly parts or information about the parts, such as build work orders and details, replacement work orders, and Kanban (visual aid) cards, can be requested through

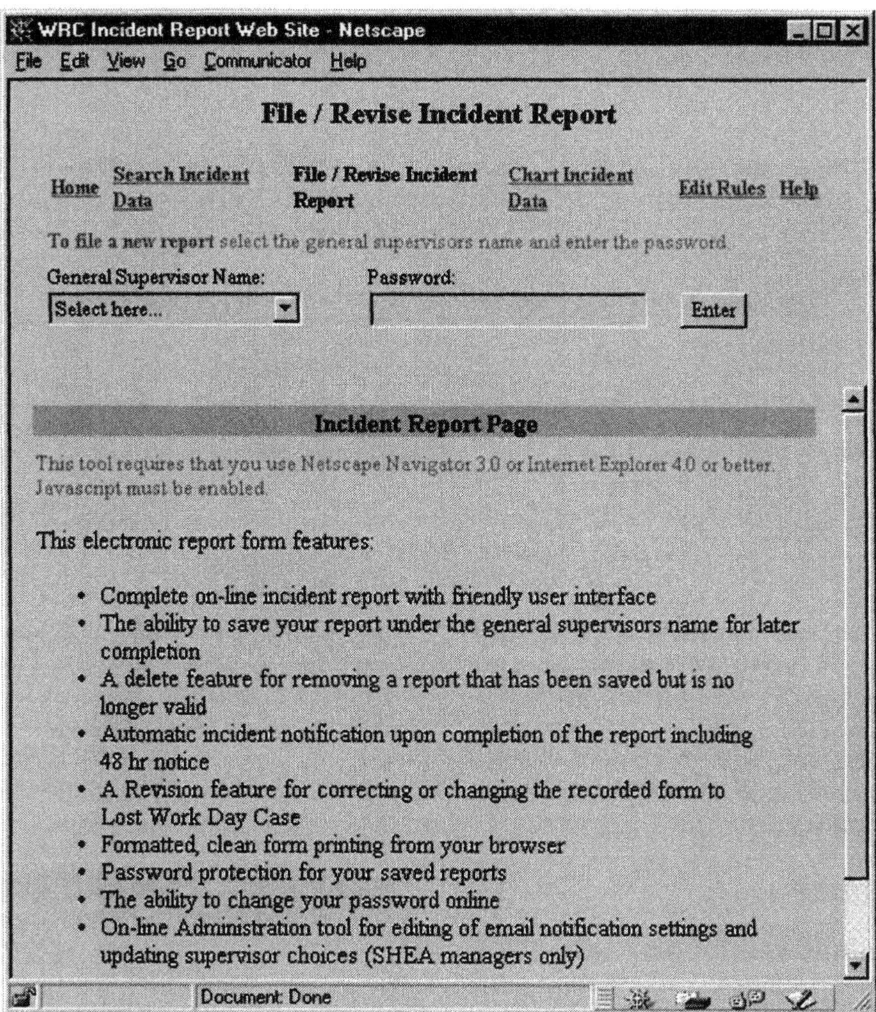

Fig. 4. SHEA application home page.

the application. When the form on the application's Web page is submitted, a message is sent to the pager of the attendant at the parts storage area. Pages sent to initiate an order process may be delivered to several individuals or queues so no more requests are lost in the mail or forgotten.

6.5. Web Link Checker application

Content providers with little knowledge of the Web or computers are often asked to post information to the WRC Web site according to documented roles and responsibilities. Unfortunately, this situation produces a major problem — broken links caused when the content provider moves, deletes, or renames a file. The Web site is so large that it is difficult for the Web team to know when broken links occur. The content providers often do not know why their actions break links or how to correct the problem.

To solve this problem, a Visual Basic application was written that checks the Web pages twice a day for broken links. If a broken link is found, e-mail notifications are automatically sent to the designated content provider and the Webmaster.

The notification includes the URL of the broken link, the URL of the Web page on which the link is located, and the name of the link as it appears on

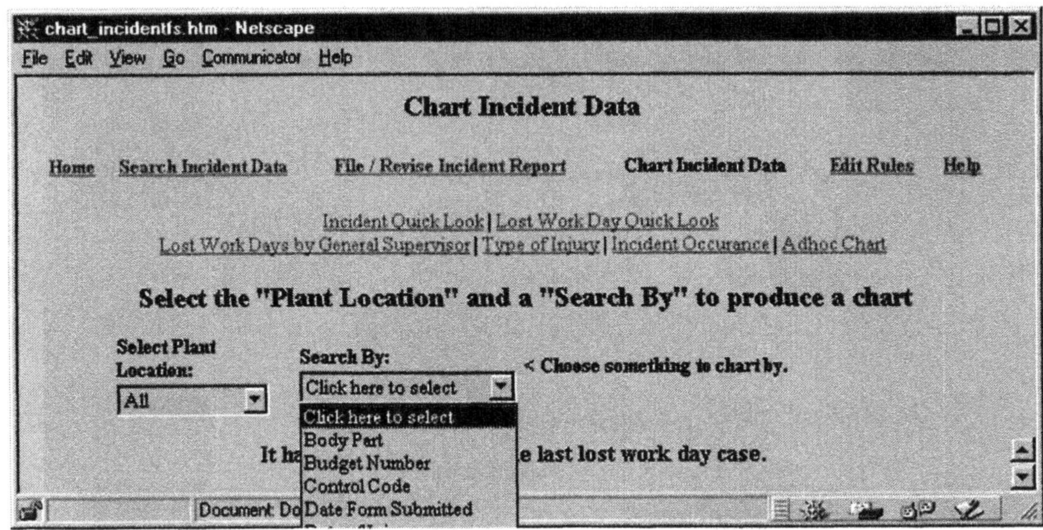

Fig. 5. SHEA application charting page using two fields.

the page. The Web Link Checker increases visibility of broken links and allows Web team members to pinpoint the source of the problem, ensuring that it is fixed quickly. Once the notification system was put in place, the Web team began work on a solution to prevent the occurrence of broken links, called the Database Grid application.

6.6. Database Grid application

This application tracks and displays a grid of links to files found on a specified NT server share. A share on any NT server in the Boeing network can be used for this application as long as the share is established as a virtual directory on the WRC Web server.

The Database Grid application allows content providers to create or update Web pages without having to know HTML or a Web page authoring tool. The content providers simply drag and drop files within a server share, eliminating the chance of breaking links by adding, deleting, or renaming folders, subfolders, or files.

The advantage this application provides over enabling directory browsing is the ability of the user to quickly see the context each file falls into among the categories and subcategories. In addition, the use of directory browsing is discouraged within the Boeing Company for security reasons.

Fig. 6 displays the files that are found within a set of folders and subfolders in a sample share ('Initiatives') on an NT server. Its folders and subfolders correspond to the rows and columns of the grid, an HTML table with cells containing 'crosshair' image files.

When a file is found in a particular subfolder, the

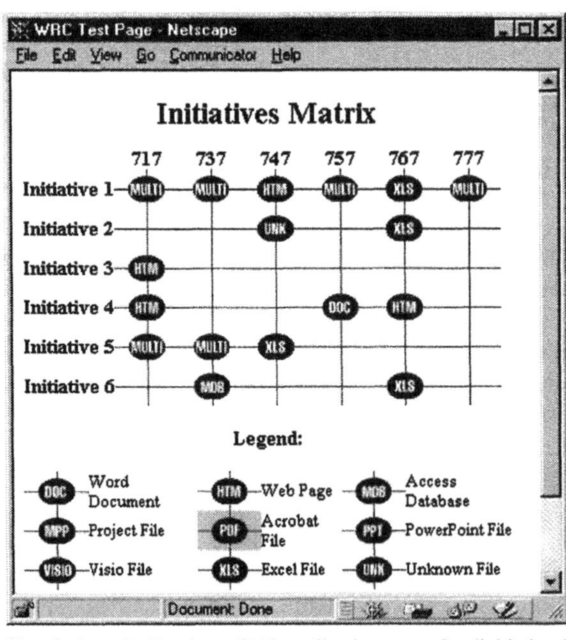

Fig. 6. Sample Database Grid application page for 'initiatives' share.

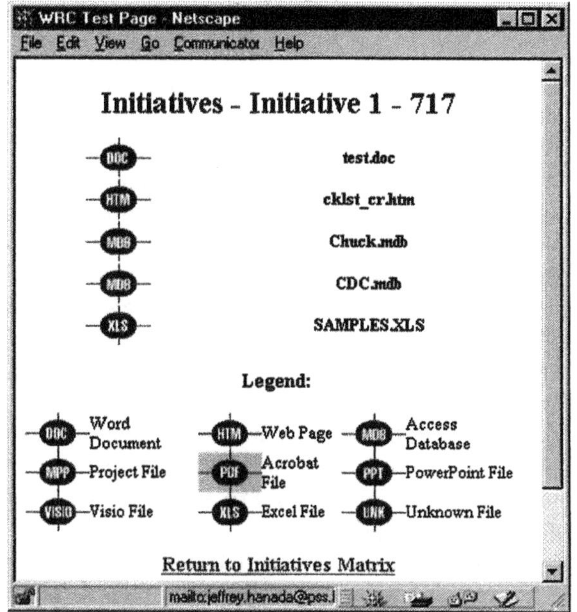

Fig. 7. Script-generated Web page for '717' subfolder of 'initiative 1' folder.

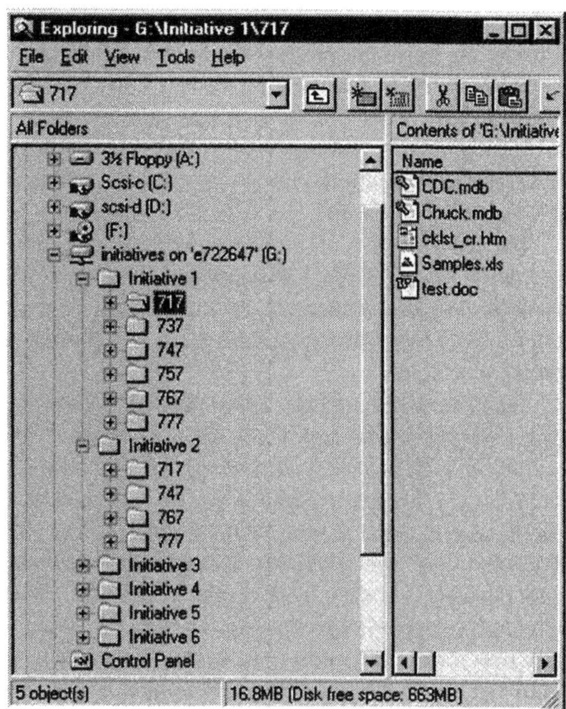

Fig. 8. Microsoft® Explorer view of 'initiatives' share.

crosshair image file corresponding to the file's extension is displayed in the table cell at the intersection of the grid row and column. The image file contains a blue oval and indicates the format of the file (e.g., DOC is a Word file, HTM is a Web page, etc.). If no file is found, an image file of only the crosshair lines is displayed.

If more than one file is found within a subfolder, an image file that says 'MULTI' is displayed in the corresponding grid table cell. A Web page listing the multiple files as links is then generated from the database.

Fig. 7 shows the Web page produced when five files are found within the '717' subfolder of the 'Initiative 1' folder. A linked crosshair image file is shown to the left of each file's name.

The only limitation on the use of the Database Grid application is that each folder must have a similar set of subfolders. For example, Fig. 8 shows the subfolders set up within the 'Initiative 1' and 'Initiative 2' folders.

The grid page is produced from a database periodically updated by a Visual Basic executable. This program runs as an automatic service on the WRC Web server. The service runs continually through a set of shares specified in the database and updates the database with the folders, subfolders, and files found on each share in each pass.

The Database Grid application code is currently being enhanced to show multiple levels of matrices through the use of a 'MATRIX' crosshair image file. This will enable the grid pages to handle multiple levels of folder and file hierarchy.

7. Tools used to accomplish Web site goals

In addition to the Web site and its applications, organizational tools were established to ensure the success of the site and promote communication. A good combination of software also contributed to the Web site's success.

7.1. Web team

The WRC is spread across six different locations, with plants in Washington and Canada. When the Web site was first launched, it focused on providing information for the executives. Because each of the current six locations produces different products, it became apparent that each needed to have its own section of the Web site. To facilitate communication with the primary customer of the Web site, employees from each location who understood the business processes were invited to be Web team members.

The WRC Web team members work toward commonality, and exchange information about ongoing projects and new technology. No one is required to attend, but people do because the work is significant, creative, and fun.

Team members include a Webmaster, a Web application developer, and a site focal from each location, as well as a project manager to organize the group, a graphic artist, and a Web server administrator. Team members determine the architecture of the Web sites and the standards that will be followed, and develop complex Web applications. The Web team members provide the data owners (who actually post and maintain the data on the Web site) with both the tools and the means of publishing to the Web, and also guidance and training.

The Web team is given high-level direction by WRC management but allowed creative license on lower-level design content. All employees are encouraged to make their line of business information and processes generally available by posting them to the Web site.

7.2. Software tool kit configuration

The software tool kit configuration is shown in Table 2.

8. Future

The spring of 1999 brought new management into the WRC and with it a new vision of how the Web site should look. Web technology has matured, providing reliable solutions to fulfill several new customer and Web team requirements, including making more information visible at the top level pages. This will reduce the number of mouse clicks needed to access the data, and give end-users insight into the information available under each menu heading. The future vision is to show a new, united WRC, with more focus on The Boeing Company.

To this end, the Web team is implementing a dynamic HTML-based home page, including numerous navigational improvements. Fig. 9 is a sample view of the new WRC home page.

The action of moving the mouse over any entry in the top or left menus loads a new page into the lower right portion of the screen. In applying this technology, we have overcome technical difficulties such as slow page loading upon a mouseover event. Mouseover-based loading was chosen as the best alternative to avoid initially loading 22 pages at the same time; however, this alternative needs work and the Web team is refining this solution.

9. Results, benefits, and lessons learned

The main result of the evolution of the WRC Intranet site has been the simplification of page creation and maintenance by end-users, and the quick detection and prevention of broken links. Valuable Web applications which save time have been created in response to customer requirements and needs. As

Table 2
Software tool kit

Adobe® Acrobat®	Microsoft® FrontPage®
Adobe® Photoshop®	Microsoft® GIF Animator
Allaire HomeSite™	Microsoft® Internet Information Server (IIS)
HTML 4.0, VBScript, Visual Basic, JavaScript	Microsoft® Office
IIS SMTP Mail Component	Microsoft® Site Server
Macromedia® Dreamweaver™	O'Reilly® WebBoard™
Macromedia® Flash™	Software FX ChartFX Internet Edition
Macromedia® FreeHand™	Tetranet Linkbot™
Microsoft® Active Server Pages	WebTrends®

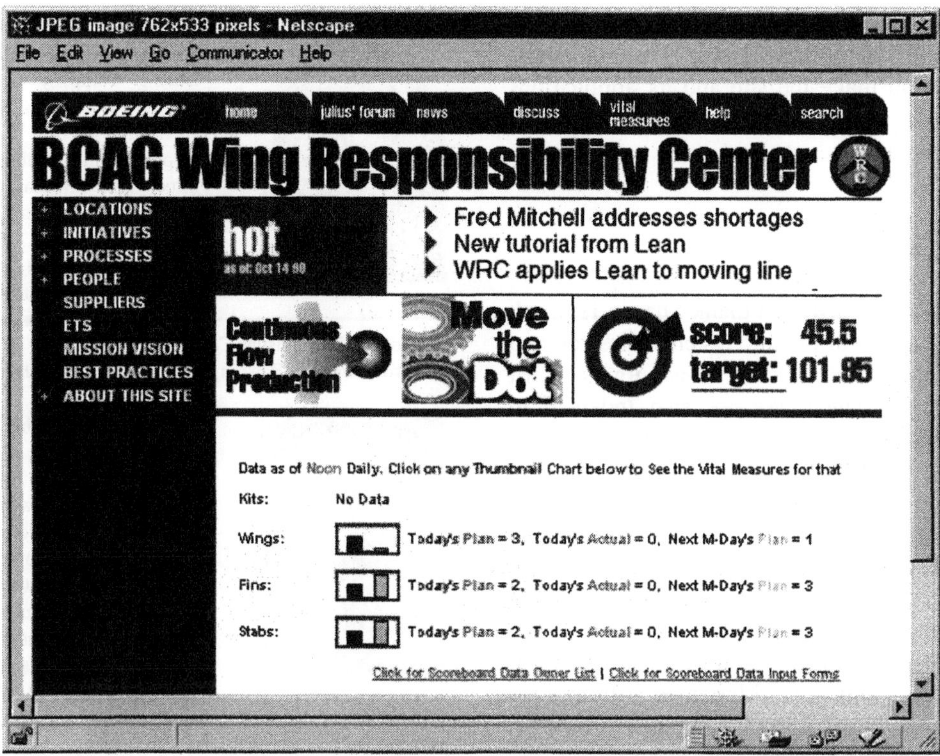

Fig. 9. New sample WRC home page.

a result of this site, much of the work of creating charts to status organizational measures has been eliminated. Now the data are available 24 hours a day, seven days a week in one easy-to-access, central location. WRC management can quickly post critical information for organization-wide dissemination.

The WRC's initial Web site successes often had to do with providing some incentives, such as a fun experience, recognition, prizes, and/or awards. In the early days it was especially important because it was difficult to get the message out that the Web site was now the primary means of communication. Several feedback forms and surveys were tried but received few responses. The Web team learned how to creatively work with content providers and end-users to 'turn them on to the Web.' When new Web products came out on the market, our Webmaster designed on-site classes for employees so they could learn the latest technology and receive company-recognized training credits. The Web team also learned that those who worked daily with the content providers had the most success getting them interested in Web work. 'Fun and familiarity' were key words to working with our customers.

An extremely popular part of the Web site, the WRC scavenger hunt, was created as part of our second survey attempt and featured a prize drawing for participants. 543 people logged on to the hunt, and 188 left their contact information to be eligible for the drawing. End-users were asked ten questions about specific areas of the Web site (each question was displayed along with the appropriate area of the Web site). Once the contestants answered all the questions, they were able to view dynamically generated pie charts comparing their score to previous contestants. This particular survey allowed the Web team to showcase new technology and introduced our end-users to different areas of the Web site.

The lessons learned include obtaining signed off customer requirements for significant site changes, keeping content up to date when providers are assigned to other duties, providing incentives for customer participation, and coordinating the content providers' changes to links and pages. The Web team's goal is to create as simple a customer interface as possible. All of these lessons have helped the WRC Web team make the site and its applications work daily to support the people who build the wings for Boeing airplanes.

Acknowledgements

The authors would like to thank Sharon Howard, the Components Information Systems director and WRC Web site owner, for her E-passionate spirit and nurturing guidance. We are also indebted to George Sickel for his creative and visionary style and 'no holds barred' leadership, and Chuck Kahler, the creator of the WRC and a Boeing Intranet 'imagineer'. The following people were valuable contributors to the WRC Web site by virtue of their leading edge skills: Gary Krieg, developer of the 'Web Link Checker'; Sidney Ly, creator and developer of the 'OEE' application; Martin Manning, customer focal for the 'OEE' application; Marianne Stillings, for her technical writing support; and Ron Stracener, developer of the 'Part Paging' application.

References

[1] Boeing Facilities Asset Mgmt, Overall Equipment Effectiveness (OEE), 1998.
[2] C. Kahler, 1998 BCAG WRC Business Plan, 1998.
[3] A. Landers, New way of tracking machine efficiency, Fabrication Division PaceSetter, August–September 1997.

Shannon Fowler is a Web design and development specialist with the Boeing Company in Seattle, WA and has worked on the Wing Responsibility Center Web site, which is part of the Boeing Intranet, for three years. She has worked in the field for nine years and previously created Web sites for other customers, including a nationwide tool company and an internationally distributed outdoor magazine. She received a B.S. in Visual Communications and a B.A. in Journalism from Western Washington University in 1992.

Mike Stillings is the lead Web application developer at the Wing Responsibility Center. He has a B.S. in Numerical Analysis from the University of Washington in Seattle. He has been a computing professional for over 20 years, at the Boeing Company and the University of Washington Academic Computer Center. His interests include the development of Web-based scientific applications and expert systems, as well as data visualization and warehousing, and the development of numerical algorithms.

Link prediction and path analysis using Markov chains ☆

Ramesh R. Sarukkai [1]

Yahoo Inc., 3420 Central Expressway, Santa Clara, CA, USA

Abstract

The enormous growth in the number of documents in the World Wide Web increases the need for improved link navigation and path analysis models. Link prediction and path analysis are important problems with a wide range of applications ranging from personalization to Web server request prediction. The sheer size of the World Wide Web coupled with the variation in users' navigation patterns makes this a very difficult sequence modelling problem. In this paper, the notion of probabilistic link prediction and path analysis using Markov chains is proposed and evaluated. Markov chains allow the system to dynamically model the URL access patterns that are observed in navigation logs based on the previous state. Furthermore, the Markov chain model can also be used in a generative mode to automatically obtain tours. The Markov transition matrix can be analysed further using eigenvector decomposition to obtain 'personalized hubs/authorities'. The utility of the Markov chain approach is demonstrated in many domains: HTTP request prediction, system-driven adaptive Web navigation, tour generation, and detection of 'personalized hubs/authorities' from user navigation profiles. The generality and power of Markov chains is a first step towards the application of powerful probabilistic models to Web path analysis and link prediction.

Keywords: Link prediction; HTTP request; Adaptive navigation; Tour generation; Hubs/authorities; Markov chains

1. Introduction

1.1. Problem description

With the rapid growth of the World Wide Web (currently estimated to be about 800 million pages [10]), it is almost impractical for individual users to navigate effectively through many of the Web documents. The most obvious and prominent methods are search engines (e.g. Google) and directory services (e.g. Yahoo!) to access information from the World Wide Web. While search tools and directories are very useful in indexing Web documents relevant to a particular topic, they are seldom efficient for the user to 'navigate' through a set of related/connected pages.

There are alternate approaches that are currently adopted to address the navigation problem [12]. The first concept is agent-assisted navigation (e.g. [3, 14]). In such a system, the system suggests links that the user can follow during the process of browsing. The second approach is that of tour generation (e.g. [7]) wherein the system generates a tour which takes the user from one link to another. Another approach is analysis of the World Wide Web structure to identify important hubs and authorities [8] which are

☆ This work was done by the author prior to his employment at Yahoo Inc.

[1] E-mail: rsarukkai@yahoo.com

important sites that the user might want to browse. The concept of Hubs/Authorities leads to the notion of a 'Web community' [6].

While the above techniques are the right direction towards solving the navigation problem, the key lies in 'personalization'. Personalization can be achieved in a variety of forms. A common example of personalization is matching of a user's profile with a set of users. The system then suggests to the user items that other users with similar interests have purchased (e.g. books on amazon.com). Another example of personalization is a configurable information filtering agent to deliver personalized news. Similarly, the notion of navigation can be personalized, and we believe that this approach will lead to a satisfactory solution to navigating the huge World Wide Web space.

While users' access to the information on the World Wide Web is an important problem, the ability of Web servers to provide this information in a rapid manner is also crucial. Link prediction may be used to prefetch documents while the user is perusing the current document. This allows the server to utilize free cycles to reduce the latencies of users' requests.

At the heart of all the above problems lies the analysis and modelling of Web link sequences. An efficient and accurate mechanism of modelling users' navigation link sequences will offer a general and extensible solution to all the above problems. Thus, this paper focuses on a probabilistic approach to the problem of Web link sequence modelling, analysis and prediction.

1.2. Our contributions

Given that the main problem is 'Web sequence modelling', the next step is the selection of an appropriate mathematical model. Probabilistic models have been applied successfully to numerous time-series prediction problems. In particular, Markov chains and hidden Markov models have been enormously successful in sequence matching/generation. In this paper, we demonstrate the utility of applying such techniques to World Wide Web link prediction and path analysis.

Markov chains have many attractive properties. They can be easily estimated statistically. Since the Markov chain model is also generative, navigation tours can be automatically derived. The Markov chain model can also be adapted on-the-fly with additional user navigation information. When used in conjunction with a Web server, the same model can be used to predict the probability of seeing a link in the future given a history of accessed links. The Markov state transition matrix can be viewed as a 'user traversal' representation of the Web space, and eigenvector decomposition techniques can be applied to generate hubs/authorities. In such a case, since the transition matrix is generated using client/user traversal data, the hubs/authorities can be viewed as 'personalized hubs/authorities'. Thus, the main contribution of our work is the notion of probabilistic link prediction and path analysis using Markov chains.

1.3. Organization of the paper

Section 2 presents the basics of Markov chains [4], and describes their utility in the context of link prediction. Section 3 describes the overall architecture of a system that utilizes the Markov chain prediction and analysis module. Section 4 summarizes four applications: HTTP server request prediction, link prediction, automatic tour generation and 'personalized' hub/authority detection. Experimental results are summarized in Section 5. Section 6 on 'related work' contrasts our work with other approaches to navigation, personalization, link prediction, and HTTP request analysis. This is followed by concluding remarks and references.

2. Markov chain models for link prediction

A discrete Markov chain model can be defined by the tuple $\langle S, \boldsymbol{A}, \lambda \rangle$. S corresponds to the state space, $\boldsymbol{A}$ is a matrix representing transition probabilities from one state to another, and λ is the initial probability distribution of the states in S. The fundamental property of the Markov model is the dependency on the previous state. If the vector $s(t)$ denotes the probability vector for all the states at time t, then:

$$\hat{s}(t) = \hat{s}(t-1)\boldsymbol{A}. \tag{1}$$

If there are n states in our Markov chain, then the matrix of transition probabilities $\boldsymbol{A}$ is of size $n \times n$.

Markov chains can be applied to Web link sequence modelling. In this formulation, a Markov state can correspond to any of the following:

- URI/URL
- HTTP request
- Action (such as a database update, or sending e-mail)

The matrix A can be estimated using many methods. Without loss of generality, the maximum likelihood principle is applied in this paper to estimate A and λ. Each element of the matrix $A[s, s']$ can be estimated as follows:

$$A(s, s') = \frac{C(s, s')}{\sum_{s''} C(s, s'')}, \tag{2}$$

$$\lambda(s) = \frac{C(s)}{\sum_{s'} C(s')}. \tag{3}$$

$C(s, s')$ is the count of the number of times s' follows s in the training data. Although Markov chains have been traditionally used to characterize asymptotic properties of random variables, we utilize the transition matrix to estimate short-term link predictions. An element of the matrix A, say $A[s, s']$ can be interpreted as the probability of transitioning from state s to s' in one step. Similarly an element of $A * A$ will denote the probability of transitioning from one state to another in two steps, and so on.

Given the 'link history' of the user $L(t-k)$, $L(t-k+1) \ldots L(t-1)$, we can represent each link as a vector with a probability 1 at that state for that time (denoted by $i(t-k), i(t-k+1) \ldots i(t-1)$). The Markov chain models estimation of the probability of being in a state at time t is shown in Eq. (4).

$$\hat{s}(t) = \hat{i}(t-1)A. \tag{4}$$

The Markovian assumption can be varied in a variety of ways. In our problem of link prediction, we have the user's history available; however, a probability distribution can be created about which of the previous links are 'good predictors' of the next link. Therefore we propose variants of the Markov process to accommodate weighting of more than one history state. In the following equations, we can see that each of the previous links are used to predict the future links and combined in a variety of ways. It is worth noting that rather than compute $A * A$ and higher powers of the transition matrix, these may be directly estimated using the training data. In practice, the state probability vector $s(t)$ can be normalized and thresholded in order to select a list of 'probable links/states' that the user will choose.

$$\hat{s}(t) = a_0\hat{i}(t-1)A + a_1\hat{i}(t-2)A^2 + a_2\hat{i}(t-3)A^3 \ldots, \tag{5}$$

$$\hat{s}(t) = \mathrm{Max}(a_0\hat{i}(t-1)A, a_1\hat{i}(t-2)A^2, a_2\hat{i}(t-3)A^3 \ldots). \tag{6}$$

3. System overview

Fig. 1 shows the overview of a typical architecture utilizing the Markov chain link prediction system. The major components of the probabilistic predictor are the following.

(a) *The Markov chain model.* The Markov Chain model consists of a (sparse) matrix (compressed to an appropriate form) of state transition probabilities, and the initial state probability vector. These are stored in the form of both counts and probabilities.

(b) *Client path buffer.* All client requests are buffered into a client buffer, and flushed once a minimum sample threshold is exceeded, or the session timeouts. Each client is assigned a separate buffer, and the sequence of client requests stored in the buffer.

(c) *Adaptation module.* This module updates the Markov chain model with user path trace information available to the system. The update is typically achieved by smoothing the default/current count matrix with the counts derived from the additional path sequences available.

(d) *Tour generator.* Given a start URL, the tour generator outputs a sequence of states (URL/URIs) which corresponds to the tour generated by the model. A tour generation algorithm is described in the next section.

(e) *Path analysis and clustering.* The path analyser currently extends the hub/authority [8] weight estimation algorithm using the Markov transition matrix. The clustering module (still under development) is used to cluster the states into 'similar

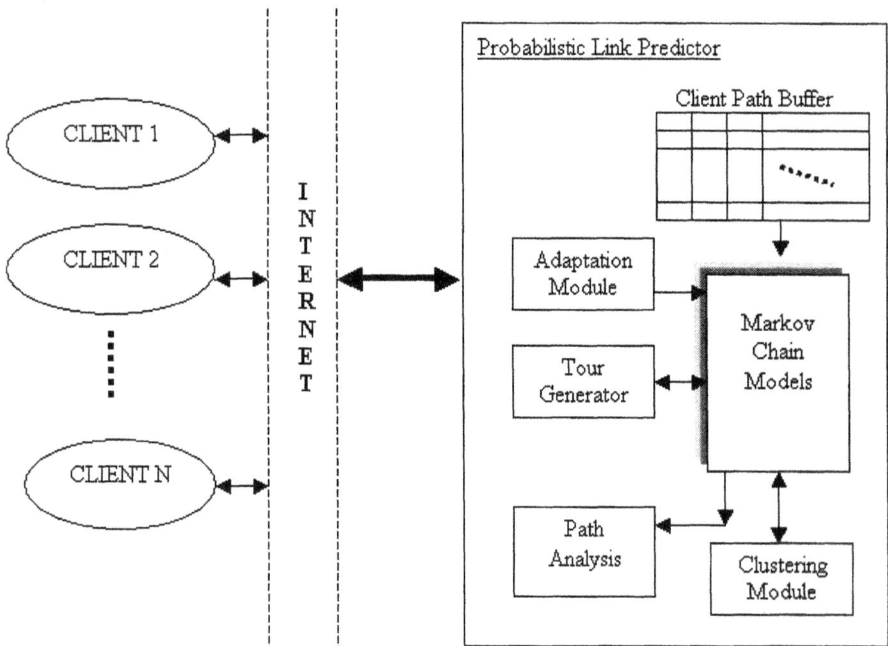

Fig. 1. Overview of the probabilistic link prediction system.

groups' in order to reduce the dimensionality of the transition matrix. A last component that is not shown in the figure is the URL table, which retains the URL (string) for each state index.

4. Applications

In this section, four applications of Markov chains to link prediction and path analysis are discussed.

4.1. Web server HTTP request prediction

The first application of the probabilistic link prediction discussed in this paper is HTTP request prediction. Extensive work (e.g. see [1]) has been done on the analysis of HTTP requests in order to enhance server performance. Most of the work involves statistical analysis of request file sizes, request patterns, and caching mechanisms. Recently, Schechter et al. [13] discuss methods of building a sequence prefix tree using path profiles and using the longest matched most-frequent sequence to predict the next request. To our knowledge, probabilistic sequence generation models such as Markov chains have not been applied to the problem of HTTP request prediction.

The incorporation of the Markov chain models and its extensions into a server or proxy is quite straightforward. The client sends a request to the Web server (or proxy) which uses the HTTP probabilistic link prediction module in order to predict the probabilities of the next requests from the same user based on the history of requests from that client. The server can also use the Markov chain model in an adaptive mode, updating the transition matrix using the sequence of requests that arrive at the Web server.

4.2. Application 2: adaptive Web navigation

The second application of the Markov chain probabilistic link predictor is system-aided Web navigation. Link prediction is used to build a navigation agent which suggests (to the user) which other sites/links would be of interest to the user based on the statistics of previous visits (either by this particular user or a collection of users). In the current framework, the predicted link does not strictly have to be a link present in the Web page currently being viewed. This is because the predicted links are based on actual user traversal sequences which can include explicit user jumps between disjoint Web sites.

If the link modelling is user-specific then the link predictor module can be resident at the client side rather than the server side. In the architecture that we have implemented, we have the link predictor as a servlet in the server side. Whenever a client clicks on a link, this information is posted to the link predictor servlet, which processes this link and suggests a list of possible links that the user can go to next. These links are ordered according to the probability of prediction (and thresholded to discard low-probability links).

4.3. Application 3: tour generation

The tour generator module is given as input the starting URL (e.g. the current document the user is browsing). The tour module generates a sequence of states (or URLs) using the Markov chain process. This is returned and displayed to the client as a tour. A simple example of such a tour is presented in the experimental section.

In order to demonstrate tour generation with Markov chains we implemented the following *Tour generation Using Markov Models* (TUMMs) algorithm. The tour generation uses the Markov model to predict a sequence of states (URLs) to visit next. Since the chain can generate a cyclic sequence of links, we can mark each state as either 'visited' or 'unvisited'. Furthermore, in the case of a tie (i.e. multiple states have the same probability), a mechanism of choosing the next state should be formulated. Lastly, if the outgoing probability of all states from the current state is below some threshold, then the facility to 'restart' should be provided. Note that this can be extended in a variety of ways including better handling of 'restarts', and tie-breaking mechanisms. In the TUMMs algorithm, ties are broken by choosing the first link with the longest matching prefix URL as the parent.

Algorithm TUMMs

(1) Set start state to be $s0$;
(2) Mark start state $s0$ as already visited. $s' = s0$
(3) While the length of tour not reached or not(Exit Criteria) do thru' step (9)
(4) For all unvisited states s:
(5) Compute $P(s' \to s)$ using the Markov chain model
(6) Choose the $\mathrm{Max}(P(s' \to s))$ and let the corresponding set of states be S
(7) If $|S| > 1$ then pick the state s'' from S, such that URL(s'') and URL(s') have the maximal URL path prefix match (further ties arbitrarily broken).
(8) If $|S| = 0$ then restart (for example: $s'' = s0$)
(9) $s' = s''$
(10) End of tour generation procedure

4.4. Application 4: personalized hub/authority

The notion of 'hubs/authorities' [8] is typically applied on the Web graph structure. Hubs refer to Web sites that are often good starting points to find information. Authority refers to Web sites that contain a lot of useful information on a particular topic. The term 'personalized' is used here (somewhat loosely) to pertain to a specific set of users, or a specific type of sites.

'Personalized hubs/authorities' extend the notion of hubs/authorities to focus on a specific group of users/sites *using the path traversal* patterns that are collected. The Markov state transition matrix is a representation of the users traversal patterns, and can be viewed as a 'traversal connectivity' matrix. Thus, the idea of iterative estimation of hub and authority weights using this Markovian transition matrix can be applied to extract the prominent 'personalized' hubs/authorities. The algorithm is similar to the one described in [8] with the important difference of initialization of the hub and authority weights using the transition probabilities specified by the Markov chain transition matrix.

5. Experimental results

In this section we report various experimental results. The first subsection describes a number of simulation experiments, followed by real-data experiments on HTTP request prediction, link prediction, and tour generation. Lastly we discuss results obtained by eigenvector decomposition of the Markov chain matrix to obtain 'personalized hubs/authorities'.

5.1. Simulations

Each simulation consists of generating a link connectivity for a specified number of states/links. The density of link connectivity was generated to be within a specified value. Two million training samples and twenty thousand test samples are generated from the same random process for each experiment. Each data point in the graphs shown corresponds to ten trials. Some trials are discarded due to zero probability link connectivity. For each test sample, the probability of being in any state at that time is computed using the various methods detailed earlier. 'Correct link' refers to the actual link chosen at the next step. The rank/depth of the correct link is measured by counting the number of links which have a probability greater than or equal to the correct link.

Fig. 2 shows the results of varying number of links on the average depth of the correct link. The link connectivity density of the set of simulations depicted in Fig. 2 is ~6.5%. It can be seen that the average depth of the correct link slightly increases with increasing dimensionality.

Next, we studied the effect of the link connectivity density on the average depth of the correct link (see Fig. 3). As expected, with increasing densities, the average depth of the correct link increases, although non-linearly.

In real-world situations, the user's navigation history is often noisy. The user may go through a few pages, then get distracted by an advertisement, and then return to his/her original navigation goal. In order to simulate such conditions, noisy state sequences are added to the test data (whose underlying probabilistic generator is the same as the training data). Experiments are conducted for different levels of noise in the test data (note that the training data is uncorrupted in these experiments). Fig. 4 shows the results of link prediction in the presence of noise. PH represents 'prediction history' as applied in Eq. (5) and the weighting coefficients a being uniform. Fig. 4 shows that for low noise data, using single history is sufficient, whereas when the data get noisier, 'voting' with probability estimates from more than one history is useful.

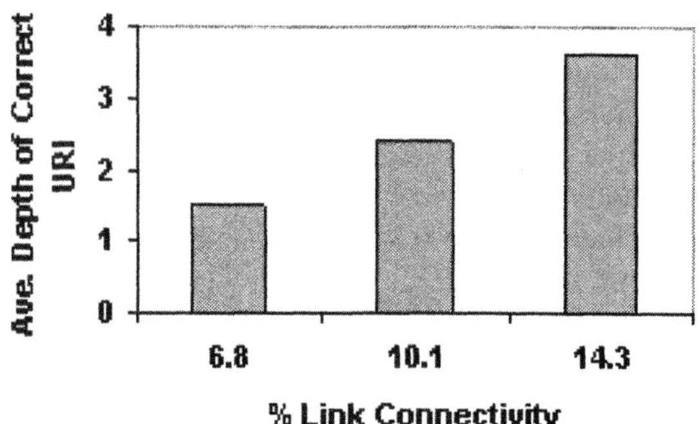

Fig. 3. Effect of linkage density on average depth of correct link.

5.2. HTTP server request prediction

Next we turn to real server log data experiments. The EPA-HTTP data server logs collected at Research Triangle Park, NC, are used in the server-log experiments (and downloadable at http://ita.ee.lbl.gov/html/traces.html). Since we are interested in applying the techniques to user-oriented patterns, the

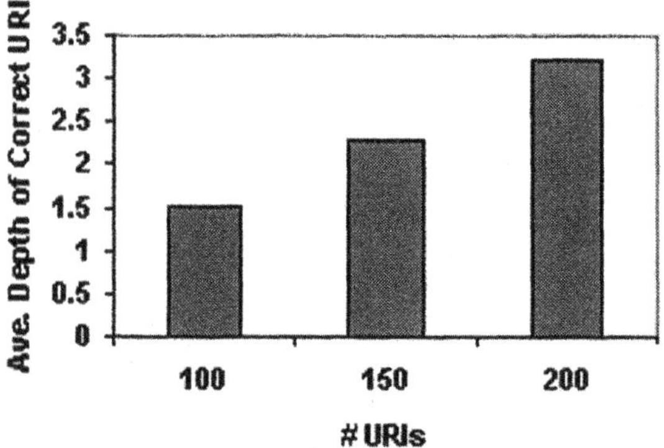

Fig. 2. Effect of dimensionality on average depth of correct link.

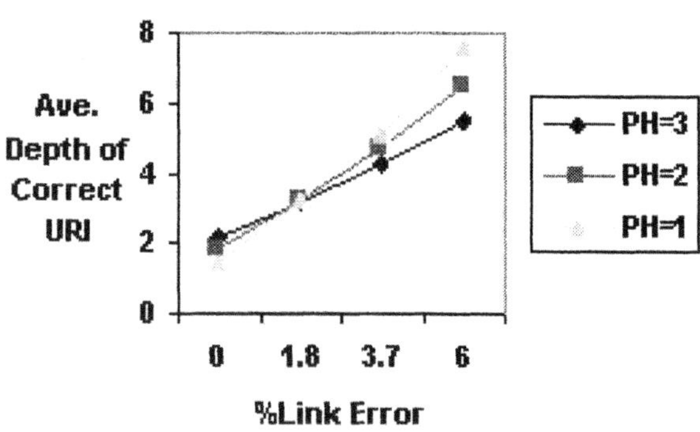

Fig. 4. Effect of noise on the probabilistic link prediction technique.

server logs are sorted according to the originating host (assuming that each session host corresponds to the same user). The total number of unique URIs (including html documents, directories, gifs, and cgi requests) is 6572. The total number of samples in the server log data is 47,751. 40,000 samples were used as training data, and the remaining as test data.

Fig. 5 shows the results of experiments on the EPA-HTTP server logs. It can be seen that using the Markov chain prediction technique, over 50% of the Web server requests can be predicted to be the state with the highest probability. Even with just the top twenty links, slightly less than 70% of the requests can be predicted with the proposed probabilistic predictor.

5.3. Link prediction

The next experiment performed with the EPA-HTTP log data is link prediction. For this experiment, the data consist of only html documents (i.e. discarded images and cgi posts). The results of such an experiment are shown in Fig. 6 ('static' columns). The test set consisted of 3576 samples, and a Markov chain ($H = 1$) was used. When compared to Fig. 5, we see that the performance of link prediction is better than generic HTTP server request prediction.

The Markov chain model can also be used in an *adaptive* manner. In this case, the (test) sequence of links that have already been evaluated are also added to the training data, and the Markov chain model dynamically adapted. This updated adapted model is used to probabilistically predict the next link. The results of such an experiment are shown in Fig. 6. It should be noted that the adaptive model results in a relative error rate reduction of 3.5% for the '<2' case in comparison to the static model.

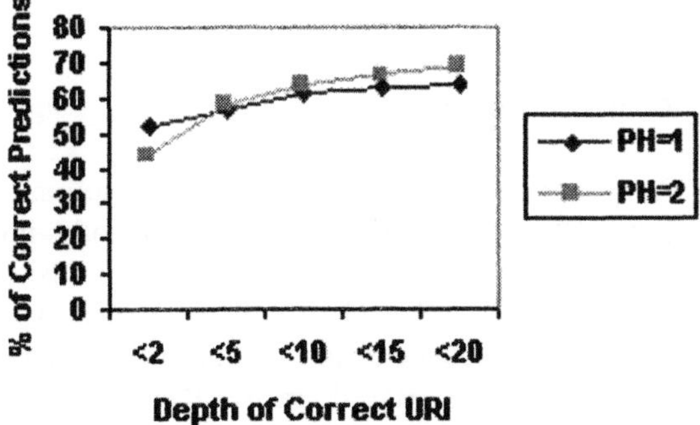

Fig. 5. Probabilistic link prediction on the EPA-HTTP server log data.

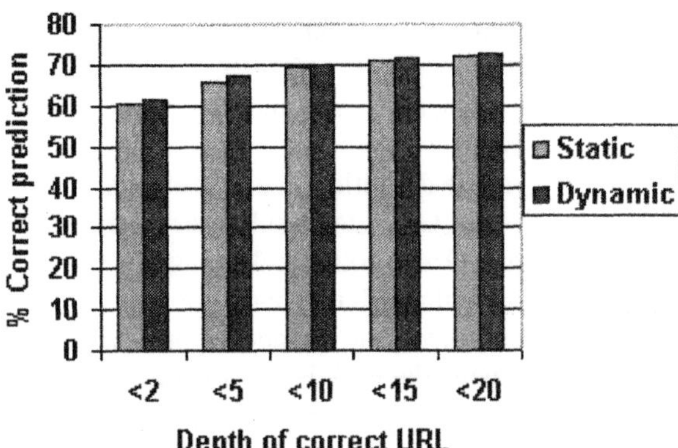

Fig. 6. Probabilistic link prediction on the EPA-HTTP server log data without gif's, cgi requests, and xbm's.

5.4. Tour generation

It is difficult to quantitatively evaluate the tours generated by the model. Some anecdotal evidence is provided to give the reader an idea of the types of tour generated. Shown below is a sample tour (limit of 20 URLs) generated using the TUMMs algorithm.

(1) /docs/ozone/index.html (Starting URL)
(2) /docs/ozone/science/science.html
(3) /docs/ozone/science/q_a.html
(4) /docs/ozone/science/process.html
(5) /docs/ozone/science/marcomp.html
(6) /docs/ozone/defns.html
(7) /docs/ozone/mbr/mbrqa.html
(8) /docs/ozone/events.html
(9) /docs/ozone/othlinks.html
(10) /docs/GCDOAR/OAR-APPD.html
(11) /docs/GCDOAR/gcd-goal.html
(12) /docs/GCDOAR/EnergyStar.html
(13) /docs/GCDOAR/esrp.html
(14) /docs/GCDOAR/homes.html
(15) /docs/GCDOAR/geothermal.html
(16) /docs/ozone/index.html
(17) /docs/ozone/olaw/olaw.html
(18) /docs/ozone/olaw/olawlet.html
(19) /docs/ozone/index.html
(20) /docs/ozone/olaw/consumer.html

The above tour can be summarized as follows.
(a) Start at the index pages on Ozone.
(b) Go to the science section, and the question and answer section.
(c) Later stop at the definitions, current events.
(d) Examine the GCDOAR subpages (which is reached from the Ozone 'other links' page).
(e) Finally browse through the law section.

It should be noted that the above tour has been generated just using the EPA-HTTP logging done for a short period. Thus, the tour reflects the browsing patterns for the duration of the EPA-HTTP logging. Furthermore, we did not include session markers (sessions were not explicitly marked in these data) between sessions of different users, and that could account for the topic drift. Another advantage of the Markov chain approach to tour generation is the ability to start a tour from any URL (which has been traversed before).

5.5. Personalized hubs/authorities

The hub/authority iterative algorithm described in [8] is applied using the Markov transition matrix obtained using the EPA-HTTP server logs (no images/cgi requests). The important difference is in the initialization of the hub and authority weights. Typically, the Web graph connectivity structure is used to determine the hub and authority weights. In our case, the initial authority weight of a state is initialized to be the sum of the transition probabilities of all other states into that state as determined by the Markov chain transition matrix. Similarly, the hub weight for a state is initialized to be the sum of the transition probabilities of all the states that are reachable from that state. Note that this is entirely based on the user traversal patterns, and not the static structure of the Web linkage.

Table 1 lists a few of the top hubs and authorities selected by the application of the modified hub/authority algorithm on the Markov chain transition matrix extracted using EPA-HTTP client requests.

Table 1
Identified hubs and authorities using path analysis

Hub	Authority
/	/
/Rules.html	/Rules.html
/docs/CSO.html	/docs/WhatsHot.html
/Access/	/Info.html
/docs/WhatsNew.html	/Software.html
/docs/titlesearch.html	/Offices.html
/docs/WhatsHot.html	/docs/Access
/Research.html	/docs/WhatsNew.html
/Information.html	/PIC.html
/Software.html	/Research.html
/Standards.html	/News.html
/docs/Welcome/EPA.html	/docs/Contacts

6. Limitations of the current approach

The Markov chain approach has the following limitations.

(a) *Amount of training data.* Since the approach is statistical, by definition, the goodness of the model is dependent on the amount of data available. This is usually not a problem when modelling a particular site with high visitation, but becomes more difficult when multi-site analysis with low visitations are required.

(b) *Dimensionality.* The second problem is one of dimensionality. The Markov chain matrix is typically very large ($N \times N$ for N URIs). This is clearly not scalable for very large numbers of sites. Such a dimensionality problem may be addressed by modelling site-specific transition models and within-site transition models. Another approach would be to cluster sites based on their access patterns before applying the Markov chain analysis. Finally, the Markov chain matrix is usually very, very sparse for high-dimensional matrices, and sparse matrix storage representations can reduce the memory requirements.

7. Related work

Perkowitz and Etzioni [11] discuss the notion of adaptive Web sites which semi-automatically improve their organization by learning from visitor access patterns. The PageGather algorithm uses page co-occurrence frequencies to find clusters of related but unlinked pages. Based on the PageGather algorithm, index pages are created for easier navigation.

In [18], data mining and data warehousing techniques are used to analyse Web log records. The Web log miner is implemented through the following phases: (a) data cleaning and transformation, (b) a multi-dimensional Web data cube is constructed, (c) OLAP (Online Analytical Processing) operations are performed on this data cube. [2] is also an earlier application of data mining approaches to Web path analysis.

Shahabi et al. [14] describe a remote Java agent that captures client's selected links and page orders, accurate page viewing time, and cache references. Link path sequences are enumerated and clustering in this path space is done using the cosine angle distance metric. While the link sequence information is used in this model, the link prediction is not probabilistically based on the frequency of user navigation profiles.

Intelligent agents that detect topics of interest to the users are described in [3]. The Web pages visited by users are analysed and topic spotting performed. This enables suggesting Web documents based on the topic of interest demonstrated by the user's navigation.

In [17], each user session is represented as an N-dimensional vector capturing the frequency of access to different documents within the site. These collections of vectors are clustered based on users' interests and the clusters used to determine which pages are most interesting to the particular set of users. Sequence information is ignored in this analysis.

Wexelblat and Maes [15] describe the footprint system which provides a metaphor of travellers creating footpaths which other travellers can use. The Web site map that is displayed is adapted through a modified Boltzmann algorithm "which works by computing attraction and repulsion forces among objects" [16].

A Web tour guide is described in [7] where the agent guides the user along an appropriate path of links based on the user's interests. WebWatcher also uses words from the document to detect the topics of interest to the user, and estimates link probabilities using TF-IDF heuristic using the extracted keywords. A second approach used by WebWatcher is based on reinforcement learning where each link is represented as a state in the reinforcement learning state space, and the rewards correspond to the TF-IDF measures.

Numerous approaches to Web client access modelling have been done in relation to server caching modelling. Notably many researchers have found that the Web access follows a Zipf distribution. Various statistical properties are extracted using server logs including file sizes of transferred data, relative document popularity etc. Researchers have studied performance of various caching strategies in light of these statistical properties of server requests (e.g. [1]).

Schechter et al. [13] present a mechanism of constructing path profile maximal prefix trees using client HTTP requests. However, there is no probabilistic weighting of the paths: the maximal matching most-frequent prefix is used to predict the next request. Kraiss and Weikum [9] apply continuous Markov chains to influence caching priorities between primary, secondary and tertiary storages, and report experimental results on synthetic workloads.

All the above techniques do not directly try to capture the sequence of link traversal in a probabilistic manner. The novelty of our approach stems from the application of probabilistic link sequence modelling using maximum likelihood estimation of Markov models and robust extensions. Furthermore, the estimation is purely data-driven and statistical in nature, techniques commonly used in various other sequence modelling applications such as speech recognition.

8. Conclusion

The rapid growth of the World Wide Web makes good models for link prediction and path analysis absolutely crucial. Markov chain models lend themselves as viable models for Web sequence modelling. Markov chain models can be estimated statistically, adaptively, and are generative. This facilitates the application of Markov chains to HTTP server request prediction, link prediction, tour generation and identification of 'personalized' hubs/authorities.

The experimental results obtained by applying Markov chains to the above problems are very promising. Web server requests can be predicted correctly, using the highest probability state, over

50% of the time on the EPA-HTTP data. Links can be predicted correctly with the highest state probability over 60% of the time, and over 70% of the correct links are in the top 20 scoring states. A novel algorithm for tour generation (TUMMs) using Markov chains is presented and anecdotal experimental results presented. Finally, the state transition matrix of the Markov chain model can be viewed as a 'weighted traversal' representation of the user's model of the World Wide Web, and further analysis can be done on this matrix. We demonstrated the application of the hub/authority weight estimation procedure in order to generate 'personalized' hubs/authorities from client navigation profiles. The results suggest that Markov chains are useful tools for Web link sequence modelling and path analysis.

Acknowledgements

We thank Prof. S.K. Rangarajan for useful discussions on Markov chains. We are also grateful to Prof. Mark Crovella and Dr. Barford of Boston University for pointing us to the server log data. We also thank Dr. Sekhar Sarukkai of HP Labs for many useful discussions on server performance issues. The EPA-HTTP logs were collected by Laura Bottomley of Duke University.

References

[1] P. Barford, A. Bestavros, A. Bradley and M. Crovella, Changes in web client access patterns: characteristics and caching implications, to appear in World Wide Web, special issue on Characterization and Performance Evaluation.

[2] M.S. Chen, J.S. Park and P.S. Yu, Data mining for path traversal in a web environment, in: Proc. 16th International Conference on Distributed Computing Systems, Hong Kong, May 1996.

[3] D.W. Chueng, B. Kao and J.W. Lee, Discovering user access patterns on the World-Wide Web, in: Proc. First Pacific–Asia Conference on Knowledge Discovery and Data Mining (PAKDD-97).

[4] W. Feller, Introduction to Probability Theory and Its Applications, Vols. 1 and 2, Wiley, New York, 1971.

[5] J. Garofalakis, P. Kappos and D. Mourloukos, Web site optimization using page popularity, IEEE Internet Computing, July–August 1999, pp. 22–29.

[6] D. Gibson, J. Kleinberg and P. Raghavan, Inferring web communities from link topology, in: Proc. 9th ACM conference on Hypertext and Hypermedia, 1998.

[7] T. Joachims, D. Freitag and T. Mitchell, WebWatcher: a tour guide for the World Wide Web, IJCAI'97.

[8] J. Kleinberg, Authoritative sources in a hyperlinked environment, in: Proc. 9th ACM-SIAM Symposium on Discrete Algorithms, 1998.

[9] A. Kraiss and G. Weikum, Integrated document caching and prefetching in storage hierarchies based on Markov-chain predictions, The VLDB Journal 7 (7) (1998) 141–162.

[10] S. Lawrence and C.L. Giles, Accessibility of information on the Web, Nature 400 (1999) 107–109.

[11] M. Perkowitz and O. Etzioni, Towards adaptive Web sites: conceptual framework and case study, WWW8, Toronto, 1999.

[12] R.R. Sarukkai, Fundamentals of Internet Technology, book proposal in progress.

[13] S. Schechter, M. Krishnan and M.D. Smith, Using path profiles to predict HTTP requests, WWW7, 1998.

[14] C. Shahabi, A.M. Zarkesh, J. Adibi and V. Shah, Kowledge discovery from users Web-page navigation, IEEE RIDE 1997.

[15] A. Wexelblat and P. Maes, Footprints: history-rich tools for information foraging, CHI'99.

[16] A. Wexelblat and P. Maes, Visualizing histories for web browsing, RIAO'97, Computer Assisted Information Retrieval on the Internet, Montreal, 1997.

[17] T.W. Yan, M. Jacobsen, H. Garcia-Molina and U. Dayal, From user access patterns to dynamic hypertext linking, 5th International World Wide Web Conference, May 1996.

[18] O.R. Zaiane, M. Xin and J. Han, Discovering Web access patterns and trends by applying OLAP and data mining technology on Web logs, in: Proc. Advances in Digital Libraries Conf. (ADL'98), Santa Barbara, CA, 1998, pp. 19–29.

Ramesh Sarukkai received his MS and PhD degrees in computer science from the University of Rochester, NY. Prior to his current position at Yahoo! Inc., Dr. Sarukkai spent two summers at IBM Watson Research Center and was a senior scientist at L& H. His research interests range from Internet applications, agents, Web information retrieval to speech technology and machine learning. He holds an Internet patent, and many publications in the above areas. He is also a member of the World Wide Web Consortium (W3C) Working group on Voice Browsers.

The stochastic approach for link-structure analysis (SALSA) and the TKC effect ☆

R. Lempel *, S. Moran [1]

Department of Computer Science, The Technion, Haifa 32000, Israel

Abstract

Today, when searching for information on the World Wide Web, one usually performs a query through a term-based search engine. These engines return, as the query's result, a list of Web sites whose contents match the query. For broad topic queries, such searches often result in a huge set of retrieved documents, many of which are irrelevant to the user. However, much information is contained in the link-structure of the World Wide Web. Information such as which pages are linked to others can be used to augment search algorithms. In this context, Jon Kleinberg introduced the notion of two distinct types of Web sites: *hubs* and *authorities*. Kleinberg argued that hubs and authorities exhibit a *mutually reinforcing relationship*: a good hub will point to many authorities, and a good authority will be pointed at by many hubs. In light of this, he devised an algorithm aimed at finding authoritative sites. We present SALSA, a new stochastic approach for link structure analysis, which examines random walks on graphs derived from the link structure. We show that both SALSA and Kleinberg's mutual reinforcement approach employ the same meta-algorithm. We then prove that SALSA is equivalent to a weighted in-degree analysis of the link-structure of World Wide Web subgraphs, making it computationally more efficient than the mutual reinforcement approach. We compare the results of applying SALSA to the results derived through Kleinberg's approach. These comparisons reveal a topological phenomenon called the *TKC effect* (Tightly Knit Community) which, in certain cases, prevents the mutual reinforcement approach from identifying meaningful authorities.

Keywords: Information retrieval; Link structure analysis; Hubs and authorities; Random walks; SALSA

1. Introduction

Searching the World Wide Web — the challenge. The World Wide Web is a rapidly expanding hyperlinked collection of unstructured information. The lack of structure and the enormous volume of the World Wide Web pose tremendous challenges on the World Wide Web information retrieval systems called search engines. These search engines are presented with queries, and return a list of Web sites which are deemed (by the engine) to pertain to the query.

When considering the difficulties which World Wide Web search engines face, we distinguish between narrow-topic queries and broad-topic queries. This distinction pertains to the presence which the query's topic has on the Web. Narrow topic queries are queries for which very few resources exist on the Web, and which present a 'needle in the haystack' challenge for search engines. An example for such a

☆ Abridged version

* Corresponding author. E-mail: rlempel@cs.technion.ac.il

[1] E-mail: moran@cs.technion.ac.il

query is an attempt to locate the lyrics of a specific song, by quoting a line from it ('We all live in a yellow submarine'). Search engines encounter a *recall* challenge when handling such queries: finding the few resources which pertain to the query.

On the other hand, broad-topic queries pertain to topics for which there is an abundance of information on the Web, sometimes as many as millions of relevant resources (with varying degrees of relevance). The vast majority of users are not interested in retrieving the entire huge set of resources. Most users will be quite satisfied with a few *authoritative* results: Web sites which are highly relevant to the topic of the query, significantly more than most other sites. The challenge which search engines face here is one of *precision*: retrieving only the most relevant resources to the query.

This work focuses on finding authoritative resources which pertain to broad-topic queries.

Term-based search engines. Term-based search engines face both classical problems in information retrieval, as well as problems specific to the World Wide Web setting, when handling broad-topic queries. The classic problems include the following issues [4,20]:

- Synonymy — retrieving documents containing the term 'car' when given the query 'automobile'.
- Polysemy/ambiguity — when given the query 'Jordan', should the engine retrieve pages pertaining to the Hashemite Kingdom of Jordan, or pages pertaining to basketball legend Michael Jordan?
- Authorship styles — this is a generalization of the synonymy issue. Two documents, which pertain to the same topic, can sometimes use very different vocabularies and figures of speech when written by different authors (as an example, the styles of two documents, one written in British English and the other in American English, might differ considerably).

In addition to the classical issues in information retrieval, there is a Web-specific obstacle which search engines must overcome, called *search engine persuasion* [19]. There may be millions of sites pertaining in some manner to broad-topic queries, but most users will only browse through the first ten results returned by their favorite search facility. With the growing economic impact of the World Wide Web, and the growth of e-commerce, it is crucial for businesses to have their sites ranked high by the major search engines. There are quite a few companies who sell this kind of expertise. They design Web sites which are tailored to rank high with specific queries on the major search engines. These companies research the ranking algorithms and heuristics of term-based engines, and know how many keywords to place (and where) in a Web page so as to improve the page's ranking (which directly impacts the page's visibility). A less sophisticated technique, used by some site creators, is called *keyword spamming* [4]. Here, the authors repeat certain terms (some of which are only remotely connected to their site's context), in order to 'lure' search engines into ranking them highly for many queries.

Informative link structure — the answer? The World Wide Web is a hyperlinked collection. In addition to the textual content of the individual pages, the link structure of such collections contains information which can, and should, be tapped when searching for authoritative sources. Consider the significance of a link $p \to q$: with such a link p suggests, or even recommends, that surfers visiting p follow the link and visit q. This may reflect the fact that pages p and q share a common topic of interest, and that the author of p thinks highly of q's contents. Such a link, called an *informative link,* is p's way to confer authority on q [16]. Note that informative links provide a positive critical assessment of q's contents which originates from outside the control of the author of q (as opposed to assessments based on q's textual content, which is under complete control of q's author). This makes the information extracted from informative links less vulnerable to manipulative techniques such as spamming.

Unfortunately, not all links are informative. There are many kinds of links which confer little or no authority [4], such as intra-domain (inner) links (whose purpose is to provide navigational aid in a complex Web site of some organization), commercial/sponsor links, and links which result from link-exchange agreements. A crucial task which should be completed prior to analyzing the link structure of a given collection, is to filter out as many of the non-informative links as possible.

Related work on link structures. Prior to the World Wide Web age, link structures were studied in the area of bibliometrics, which studies the citation structure of written documents [15,23]. Many works in this area were aimed at finding high-impact papers published in scientific journals [10], and at clustering related documents [1].

Some works have studied the Web's link structure, in addition to the textual content of the pages, as means to visualize areas thought to contain good resources [3]. Other works used link structures for categorizing pages and clustering them [21,24].

Marchiori [19] uses the link-structure of the Web to enhance search results of term-based search engines. This is done by considering the potential hyper-information contained in each Web page: the information that can be found when following hyperlinks which originate in the page.

This work is motivated by the approach introduced by Jon Kleinberg [16]. In an attempt to impose some structure on the chaotic World Wide Web, Kleinberg distinguished between two types of Web sites which pertain to a certain topic. The first are *authoritative* pages in the sense described previously. The second type of sites are *hub* pages. Hubs are resource lists. They do not directly contain information pertaining to the topic, but rather point to many authoritative sites. According to this model, hubs and authorities exhibit a *mutually reinforcing relationship*: good hubs point to many good authorities, and good authorities are pointed at by many good hubs.

In light of the mutually reinforcing relationship, hubs and authorities should form communities, which can be pictured as dense bipartite portions of the Web, where the hubs link densely to the authorities. The most prominent community in a World Wide Web subgraph is called the *principal community* of the collection. Kleinberg suggested an algorithm to identify these communities, which is described in detail in Section 2.

Researchers from IBM's Almaden Research Center have implemented Kleinberg's algorithm in various projects. The first was *HITS*, which is described in [11], and offers some enlightening practical remarks. The *ARC* system, described in [7], augments Kleinberg's link-structure analysis by considering also the anchor text, the text which surrounds the hyperlink in the pointing page. The reasoning behind this is that many times, the pointing page describes the destination page's contents around the hyperlink, and thus the authority conferred by the links can be better assessed. These projects were extended by the *CLEVER* project [14]. Researchers from outside IBM, such as Henzinger and Brahat, have also studied Kleinberg's approach and have proposed improvements to it [13].

Anchor text has also been used by Brin and Page in [2]. Another major feature of their work on the *Google* search engine [12] is a link-structure based site ranking approach called *PageRank*, which can be interpreted as a stochastic analysis of some random-walk behavior through the entire World Wide Web.

In [18], the authors use the links surrounding a small set of same-topic sites to assemble a larger collection of neighboring pages which should contain many authoritative resources on the initial topic. The textual content of the collection is then analyzed in ranking the relevancy of its individual pages.

This work. While preserving the theme that Web sites pertaining to a given topic should be split to hubs and authorities, we replace Kleinberg's mutual reinforcement approach [16] by a new stochastic approach (SALSA), in which the coupling between hubs and authorities is less tight. The intuition behind our approach is the following. Consider a bipartite graph G, whose two parts correspond to hubs and authorities, where an edge between hub r and authority s means that there is an informative link from r to s. Then, authorities and hubs pertaining to the dominant topic of the sites in G should be highly visible (reachable) from many sites in G. Thus, we will attempt to identify these sites by examining certain random walks in G, under the proviso that such random walks will tend to visit these highly visible sites more frequently than other, less connected sites. We show that in finding the principal communities of hubs and authorities, both Kleinberg's mutual reinforcement approach and our stochastic approach employ the same meta-algorithm on different representations of the input graph. We then compare the results of applying SALSA to the results derived by Kleinberg's approach. Through these comparisons, we isolate a particular topological phenomenon which we call the *Tightly Knit Community (TKC) effect*. In certain scenarios, this effect hampers the ability of the mutual reinforcement approach to identify meaningful authorities. We demonstrate that SALSA is less vulnerable to the TKC effect, and can find meaningful authorities in collections where the mutual reinforcement approach fails to do so.

After demonstrating some results achieved by means of SALSA, we prove that the ranking of sites in the stochastic approach may be calculated by examining the weighted in/out degrees of the sites in G. This result yields that SALSA is computationally lighter than the mutual reinforcement approach. We also discuss the reason for our success with analyzing weighted in/out degrees of sites, which previous work has claimed to be unsatisfactory for identifying authoritative sites.

The rest of the paper is organized as follows. Section 2 recounts Kleinberg's mutual reinforcement approach. In Section 3 we view Kleinberg's approach from a higher level, and define a meta-algorithm for link structure analysis. Section 4 presents our new approach, SALSA. In Section 5 we compare the two approaches by considering their outputs on the World Wide Web and on artificial topologies. Then, in Section 6 we prove the connection between SALSA and weighted in/out degree rankings of sites. Our conclusions and ideas for future work are brought in Section 7. The paper uses basic results from the theory of stochastic processes, which are brought in the full version. The main contribution of the paper can be grasped without following the full mathematical analysis.

2. Kleinberg's mutual reinforcement approach

The mutual reinforcement approach [16] starts by assembling a collection $\mathcal{C}$ of Web sites, which should contain communities of hubs and authorities pertaining to a given topic t. It then analyzes the link structure induced by that collection, in order to find the authoritative sites on topic t.

Denote by q a term-based search query to which sites in our topic of interest t are deemed to be relevant. The collection $\mathcal{C}$ is assembled in the following manner.

- A *root set* S of sites is obtained by applying a term-based search engine, such as AltaVista [8], to the query q. This is the only step in which the lexical content of the Web sites is examined.
- From S we derive a *base set* $\mathcal{C}$ which consists of (a) sites in the root set S, (b) sites which point to a site in S, and (c) sites which are pointed to by a site in S. In order to obtain (b), we must again use a search engine. Many search engines store linkage information, and support queries such as 'which sites point to [a given URL]'.

The collection $\mathcal{C}$ and its link structure induce the following directed graph G: G's nodes are the sites in $\mathcal{C}$, and for all $i, j \in \mathcal{C}$ the directed edge $i \to j$ appears in G if and only if site i contains a hyperlink to site j. Let W denote the $|\mathcal{C}| \times |\mathcal{C}|$ adjacency matrix of G.

Each site $s \in \mathcal{C}$ is now assigned a pair of weights, a hub weight $h(s)$ and an authority weight $a(s)$, based on the following two principles:

- The quality of a hub is determined by the quality of the authorities it points at. Specifically, a site's hub weight should be proportional to the sum of the authority weights of the sites it points at.
- 'Authority lies in the eyes of the beholder(s)': a site is authoritative only if good hubs deem it as such. Hence, a site's authority weight is proportional to the sum of the hub weights of the sites pointing at it.

The top ranking sites, according to both kinds of weights, form the mutually reinforcing communities of hubs and authorities. In order to assign such weights, Kleinberg uses the following iterative algorithm:

(1) Initialize $a(s) \leftarrow 1$, $h(s) \leftarrow 1$ for all sites $s \in \mathcal{C}$.

(2) Repeat the following three operations until convergence:

- Update the authority weight of each site s (the $\mathcal{I}$ operation):

$$a(s) \leftarrow \sum_{x \mid x \text{ points to } s} h(x)$$

- Update the hub weight of each site s (the $\mathcal{O}$ operation):

$$h(s) \leftarrow \sum_{x \mid s \text{ points to } x} a(x)$$

- Normalize the authority weights and the hub weights.

Note that applying the $\mathcal{I}$ operation is equivalent to assigning authority weights according to the result of multiplying the vector of all hub weights by the matrix W^T. The $\mathcal{O}$ operation is equivalent to assigning hub weights according to the result of multiplying the vector of all authority weights by the matrix W.

Kleinberg showed that this algorithm converges, and that the resulting authority weights [hub weights] are the coordinates of the normalized principal eigenvector[2] of W^TW [of WW^T]. W^TW and WW^T are well known matrices in the field of bibliometrics:

(1) $A \triangleq W^TW$ is the *co-citation matrix* [23] of the collection. $[A]_{i,j}$ is the number of sites which jointly point at (cite) pages i and j. Kleinberg's iterative algorithm converges to authority weights which correspond to the entries of the (unique, normalized) principal eigenvector of A.

(2) $H \triangleq WW^T$ is the *bibliographic coupling matrix* [15] of the collection. $[H]_{i,j}$ is the number of sites jointly referred to (pointed at) by pages i and j. Kleinberg's iterative algorithm converges to hub weights which correspond to the entries of H's (unique, normalized) principal eigenvector.

3. A meta-algorithm for link structure analysis

Examining the mutual reinforcement approach from a higher level, we can identify a general framework, or meta-algorithm, for finding hubs and authorities by link structure analysis. This meta-algorithm is a version of the spectral filtering method, presented in [6].

- Given a topic t, construct a site collection $\mathcal{C}$ which should contain many t-hubs and t-authorities, but should not contain many hubs or authorities for any other topic t'. Let $n = |\mathcal{C}|$.
- Derive, from $\mathcal{C}$ and the link structure induced by it, two $n \times n$ association matrices: a *hub matrix* H and an *authority matrix* A. Association matrices are widely used in classification algorithms [22] and will be used here in order to classify the Web sites into communities of hubs/authorities. The association matrices which are used by the meta-algorithm will have the following algebraic property (let M denote such a matrix). M will have a unique real positive eigenvalue $\mu(M)$ of multiplicity 1, such that for any other eigenvalue μ' of M, $\mu(M) > |\mu'(M)|$. Denote by $v_{\mu(M)}$ the (unique) unit eigenvector which corresponds to $\mu(M)$ whose first non-zero coordinate is positive. $v_{\mu(M)}$ will actually be a positive vector, and will be referred to as the *principal eigenvector* of M.
- The sites that correspond to the largest coordinates of $v_{\mu(A)}$ will form the *principal algebraic community of authorities* in $\mathcal{C}$, and the sites that correspond to the largest coordinates of $v_{\mu(H)}$ will form the *principal algebraic community of hubs* in $\mathcal{C}$.

For the meta-algorithm to be useful, the algebraic principal communities of hubs and authorities should reflect the true authorities and hubs in $\mathcal{C}$.

The two degrees of freedom which the meta-algorithm allows, are the method for obtaining the collection, and the definition of the association matrices. Given a specific collection, the algebraic communities produced by the meta-algorithm are determined solely by the definition of the association matrices.

4. SALSA: analyzing a random walk on the Web

In this section we introduce the *stochastic approach for link structure analysis* (SALSA). The approach is based upon the theory of Markov chains, and relies on the stochastic properties of random walks performed on our collection of sites. It follows the meta-algorithm described in Section 3, and differs from the mutual reinforcement approach in the manner in which the association matrices are defined.

The input to our scheme consists of a collection of sites $\mathcal{C}$ which is built around a topic t in the manner described in Section 2. Intuition suggests that authoritative sites on topic t should be visible from many sites in the subgraph induced by scC. Thus, a random walk on this subgraph will visit t-authorities with high probability.

We combine the theory of random walks with the notion of the two distinct types of Web sites, hubs and authorities, and actually analyze two different Markov chains: a chain of hubs and a chain of authorities. Unlike 'conventional' random walks on graphs, state transitions in these chains are generated by traversing *two* World Wide Web links in a row,

[2] The eigenvector which corresponds to the eigenvalue of highest magnitude of the matrix.

one link forward and one link backwards (or vice versa). Analyzing both chains allows our approach to give each Web site two distinct scores, a hub score and an authority score.

The idea of ranking Web sites using random walks is not new. The search engine *Google* [2,12] incorporates stochastic information into its ranking of pages. The *PageRank* component of the search engine examines a *single* random walk on the *entire* World Wide Web. Hence, the ranking of Web sites in *Google* is independent of the search query (a global ranking), and no distinction is made between hubs and authorities.

Let us build a bipartite undirected graph $\tilde{G} = (V_h, V_a, E)$ from our site collection C and its link structure:

- $V_h = s_h | s \in C$ and *out-degree(s)* >0 (the *hub side* of $\tilde{G}$).
- $V_a = s_a | s \in C$ and *in-degree(s)* >0 (the *authority side* of $\tilde{G}$).
- $E = (s_h, r_a) | s \to r$ in C.

Each non-isolated site $s \in C$ is represented by two nodes of $\tilde{G}$, s_h and s_a. Each World Wide Web link $s \to r$ is represented by an undirected edge connecting s_h and r_a.

On this bipartite graph we will perform two distinct random walks. Each walk will only visit nodes from one of the two sides of the graph, by traversing paths consisting of two $\tilde{G}$-edges in each step. Since each edge crosses sides of $\tilde{G}$, each walk is confined to just one of the graph's sides, and the two walks will naturally start off from different sides of $\tilde{G}$. Note also that every path of length 2 in $\tilde{G}$ represents a traversal of one World Wide Web link in the proper direction (when passing from the hub side of $\tilde{G}$ to the authority side), and a retreat along a World Wide Web link (when crossing in the other direction). Since the hubs and authorities of topic t should be highly visible in $\tilde{G}$ (reachable from many nodes by either a direct edge or by short paths), we may expect that the t-authorities will be amongst the nodes most frequently visited by the random walk on V_a, and that the t-hubs will be amongst the nodes most frequently visited by the random walk on V_h.

We will examine the two different Markov chains which correspond to these random walks: the chain of the visits to the authority side of $\tilde{G}$ (the *authority chain*), and the chain of visits to the hub side of $\tilde{G}$. Analyzing these chains separately naturally distinguishes between the two aspects of each site.

We now define two stochastic matrices, which are the transition matrices of the two Markov chains at interest.

(1) *The hub matrix* $\tilde{H}$, defined as follows:

$$\tilde{h}_{i,j} = \sum_{k|(i_h,k_a),(j_h,k_a)\in\tilde{G}} \frac{1}{\deg(i_h)} \times \frac{1}{\deg(k_a)}.$$

(2) *The authority matrix* $\tilde{A}$, defined as follows:

$$\tilde{a}_{i,j} = \sum_{k|(k_h,i_a),(k_h,j_a)\in\tilde{G}} \frac{1}{\deg(i_a)} \times \frac{1}{\deg(k_h)}.$$

A positive transition probability $\tilde{a}_{i,j} > 0$ implies that a certain page h points to both pages i and j, and hence page j is reachable from page i by two steps: retracting along the link $h \to i$ and then following the link $h \to j$.

Alternatively, the matrices $\tilde{H}$ and $\tilde{A}$ can be defined as follows. Let W be the adjacency matrix of the directed graph defined by C and its link structure. Denote by W_r the matrix which results by dividing each non-zero entry of W by the sum of the entries in its row, and by W_c the matrix which results by dividing each non-zero element of W by the sum of the entries in its column. (Obviously, the sums of rows/columns which contain non-zero elements are greater than zero.) Then $\tilde{H}$ consists of the non-zero rows and columns of $W_r W_c^{\mathrm{T}}$, and $\tilde{A}$ consists of the non-zero rows and columns of $W_c^{\mathrm{T}} W_r$. We ignore the rows and columns of $\tilde{A}$, $\tilde{H}$ which consist entirely of zeros, since (by definition) all the nodes of $\tilde{G}$ have at least one incident edge. The matrices $\tilde{A}$ and $\tilde{H}$ serve as the association matrices required by the meta-algorithm for identifying the authorities and hubs. Recall that the mutual reinforcement approach uses the association matrices $A \triangleq W^{\mathrm{T}}W$ and $H \triangleq WW^{\mathrm{T}}$.

We shall assume that $\tilde{G}$ is connected, causing both stochastic matrices $\tilde{A}$ and $\tilde{H}$ to be *irreducible.* This assumption does not form a limiting factor, since when $\tilde{G}$ is not connected, we may use our technique on each connected component separately. Section 6.1 further elaborates on the case when $\tilde{A}$ and $\tilde{H}$ have multiple irreducible components.

Some properties of $\tilde{H}$ and $\tilde{A}$:

- Both matrices are primitive, since the Markov chains which they represent are aperiodic: when visiting any authority (hub), there is a positive probability to revisit it on the next entry to the authority (hub) side of the bipartite graph (since all the nodes are non-isolated). Hence, every state (= site) in each of the chains has a self-loop, causing the chains to be aperiodic.

- The adjacency matrix of the support graph of $\tilde{A}$ is symmetric, since $\tilde{a}_{i,j} > 0$implies $\tilde{a}_{j,i} > 0$. Furthermore, $\tilde{a}_{i,j} > 0 \Leftrightarrow [W^{\mathrm{T}}W]_{i,j} > 0$ (and the same is also true of $\tilde{H}$ and WW^{T}).

Following the framework of the meta-algorithm, the principal community of authorities (hubs) found by the SALSA will be composed of the sites whose entries in the principal eigenvector of $\tilde{A}$ ($\tilde{H}$) are the highest. By the ergodic theorem [9], the principal eigenvector of an irreducible, aperiodic stochastic matrix is actually the stationary distribution of the underlying Markov chain, and its high entries correspond to sites most frequently visited by the (infinite) random walk.

5. Results

5.1. *The tightly knit community (TKC) effect*

A tightly knit community is a small but highly interconnected set of sites. Roughly speaking, the TKC effect occurs when such a community scores high in link-analyzing algorithms, even though the sites in the TKC are not authoritative on the topic, or pertain to just one aspect of the topic. Our study indicates that the mutual reinforcement approach is vulnerable to this effect, and will sometimes rank the sites of a TKC in unjustified high positions.

As an example, consider a collection C which contains the following two communities: a community y, with a small number of hubs and authorities, in which every hub points to most of the authorities, and a much larger community z, in which each hub points to a smaller part of the authorities. The topic covered by z is the dominant topic of the collection, and is probably of wider interest on the World Wide Web. Since there are many z-authoritative sites, the hubs do not link to all of them, whereas the smaller y community is densely interconnected. The TKC effect occurs when the sites of y are ranked higher than those of z.

In the full paper we provide a combinatorial construction, which demonstrates such (artificial) communities y and z, where the mutual reinforcement approach scores y higher than z, and the stochastic approach scores z higher. This bias of the mutual reinforcement approach towards tightly knit communities will be demonstrated on World Wide Web queries in the next section.

5.2. *The World Wide Web*

We tested the different approaches on broad-topic World Wide Web queries (both single-topic queries and multi-topic queries). We obtained a collection of sites for each query, and then derived the principal community of authorities with both approaches. Two of these queries ('Java', 'abortion') were used by Kleinberg in [16], and are brought here for the sake of comparison. All collections were assembled during February, 1999. The root sets were compiled using AltaVista [8], which also provided the linkage information needed for building the base sets.

When expanding the root set to the entire collection, we filtered the links pointing to and from Web sites. Following [16], we ignored intra-domain links (since these links tend to be navigational aids inside an intranet, and do not confer authority on the link's destination). We also ignored links to *cgi scripts*, and tried to identify ad-links and ignore them as well. Overall, 38% of the links we examined were ignored. The collections themselves turn out to be relatively sparse graphs, with the number of edges never exceeding three times the number of nodes. We note that a recent work by Kleinberg et al. [17] has examined some other connectivity characteristics of such collections.

For each query, we list the top authorities which were returned by the two approaches. The results are displayed in tables containing four columns:

(1) The URL.
(2) The title of the URL.
(3) The category of the URL: (a) for a member of the root set, (b) for a site pointing into the root set, and (c) for a site pointed at by a member of the root set.
(4) The value of the coordinate of this URL in the principal eigenvector of the authority matrix.

Table 1
Authorities for World Wide Web query 'Java' (size of root size = 160, size of collection = 2810)

URL	Title	Cat.	Weight
Principal community, mutual reinforcement approach			
http://www.jars.com/	EarthWeb's JARS.COM Java Review Service	(3)	0.334102
http://www.gamelan.com/	Gamelan — The Official Java Directory	(3)	0.303624
http://www.javascripts.com/	Javascripts.com — Welcome	(3)	0.255254
http://www.datamation.com/	EarthWeb's Datamation.com	(3)	0.251379
http://www.roadcoders.com/	Handheld Software Development@RoadCoders	(3)	0.250816
http://www.earthweb.com/	EarthWeb	(3)	0.249373
http://www.earthwebdirect.com/	Welcome to Earthweb Direct	(3)	0.247467
http://www.itknowledge.com/	ITKnowledge	(3)	0.246874
http://www.intranetjournal.com/	intranetjournal.com	(3)	0.24518
http://www.javagoodies.com/	Java Goodies JavaScript Repository	(3)	0.238793
Principal community, SALSA			
http://java.sun.com/	Java(tm) Technology Home Page	(3)	0.365264
http://www.gamelan.com/	Gamelan — The Official Java Directory	(3)	0.36369
http://www.jars.com/	EarthWeb's JARS.COM Java Review Service	(3)	0.303862
http://www.javaworld.com/	IDG's magazine for the Java community	(3)	0.217269
http://www.yahoo.com/	Yahoo!	(3)	0.21412
http://www.javasoft.com/	Java(tm) Technology Home Page	(3)	0.203099
http://www.sun.com/	Sun Microsystems	(3)	0.187355
http://www.javascripts.com/	Javascripts.com — Welcome	(3)	0.138548
http://www.htmlgoodies.com/	htmlgoodies.com — Home	(3)	0.130676
http://javaboutique.internet.com/	The Ultimate Java Applet Resource	(1)	0.118081

5.2.1. Single-topic query: Java

The results for this query, with our first example of the TKC effect, are shown in Table 1. All of the top ten mutual reinforcement authorities are part of the EarthWeb Inc. network. They are interconnected, but since the domain names of the sites are different, the interconnecting links were not filtered out. Some of the sites are highly relevant to the query (and have many incoming links from sites outside the EarthWeb net), but most appear in the principal community only because of their EarthWeb affiliation. With SALSA, only the top three mutual reinforcement authorities are retained, and the other seven are replaced by other authorities, some of which are clearly more related to the query.

5.2.2. Single-topic query: movies

This query demonstrates the TKC effect in a most striking fashion on the World Wide Web. First, consider the mutual reinforcement principal community of authorities, presented in Table 2.

The top 30 authorities returned by the mutual reinforcement approach were all *go.msn.com* sites. All but the first received the exact same weight, 0.167202. Recall that we do not allow same-domain links in our collection, hence none of the top authorities was pointed at by a *go.msn.com* site. To understand how these sites scored so well, we turn to the principal community of hubs, shown in Table 3.

These innocent looking hubs are all part of the *Microsoft Network (msn)*, but when building the ba-

Table 2
Mutual reinforcement authorities for World Wide Web query 'movies' (size of root size = 175, size of collection = 4539)

URL	Title	Cat	Weight
http://go.msn.com/npl/msnt.asp	MSN.COM	(3)	0.167332
http://go.msn.com/bql/whitepages.asp	White Pages — msn.com	(3)	0.167202
http://go.msn.com/bsl/webevents.asp	Web Events	(3)	0.167202
http://go.msn.com/bql/scoreboards.asp	MSN Sports scores	(3)	0.167202

Table 3
Mutual reinforcement hubs for World Wide Web query 'movies'

URL	Title	Cat	Weight
http://denver.sidewalk.com/movies	movies: denver.sidewalk	(1)	0.169197
http://boston.sidewalk.com/movies	movies:boston.sidewalk	(1)	0.169061
http://twincities.sidewalk.com/movies	movies: twincities.sidewalk	(1)	0.1688
http://newyork.sidewalk.com/movies	movies: newyork.sidewalk	(1)	0.168537

sic set we did not identify them as such. All these hubs point, almost without exception, to the entire set of authorities found by the MR approach (hence the equal weights which the authorities exhibit). However, the vast majority of the sites in the collection were not part of this 'conspiracy', and almost never pointed to any of the *go.msn.com* sites. Therefore, the authorities returned by the stochastic approach (Table 4) contain none of those *go.msn.com* sites, and are much more relevant to the query.

A similar community is obtained by the mutual reinforcement approach, after deleting the rows and columns which correspond to the top 30 authorities from the matrix $W^{T}W$. This deletion dissolves the *msn.com* community, and allows a community similar to the one obtained by SALSA to manifest itself.

5.2.3. Multi-topic query: abortion

This topic is highly polarized, with different cyber communities supporting pro-life and pro-choice views. In Table 5, we bring the top 10 authorities, as determined by the two approaches.

All 10 top authorities found by the mutual reinforcement approach are pro-life resources, while the top 10 SALSA authorities are split, with 6 pro-choice sites and 4 pro-life sites (which are the same top 4 pro-life sites found by the mutual reinforcement approach). Again, we see the TKC effect: the mutual reinforcement approach ranks highly authorities on only one aspect of the query, while SALSA blends authorities from both aspects into its principal community.

5.2.4. Multi-topic query: genetics

This query is especially ambiguous in the World Wide Web: it can be in the context of genetic engineering, genetic algorithms, or in the context of health issues and the human genome.

As in the 'abortion' query, SALSA brings a diverse principal community, with authorities on the various contexts of the query, while the mutual reinforcement approach is focussed on one context (genetic algorithms, in this case). Both principal communities are shown in Table 6.

6. SALSA and the in/out degrees of sites

In the previous sections we have presented the stochastic approach as an alternative method for link-structure analysis, and have shown a few encouraging results obtained by it, as compared with the mutual reinforcement approach. We have also presented the TKC effect, a topological phenomenon which sometimes derails the MR approach and prevents it from converging to a useful community of authoritative sites.

Table 4
Stochastic authorities for World Wide Web query 'movies'

URL	Title	Cat	Weight
http://us.imdb.com/	The Internet Movie Database	(3)	0.253333
http://www.mrshowbiz.com/	Mr Showbiz	(3)	0.22335
http://www.disney.com/	Disney.com — The Web Site for Families	(3)	0.22003
http://www.hollywood.com/	Hollywood Online: ...all about movies	(3)	0.213355
http://www.imdb.com/	The Internet Movie Database	(3)	0.199987
http://www.paramount.com/	Welcome to Paramount Pictures	(3)	0.196682
http://www.mca.com/	Universal Studios	(3)	0.180021

Table 5
Authorities for World Wide Web query 'abortion' (size of root size = 160, size of collection = 1693)

URL	Title	Cat	Weight
Principal community, mutual reinforcement approach			
http://www.nrlc.org/	National Right To Life	(3)	0.420832
http://www.prolife.org/ultimate/	The Ultimate Pro-Life Resource List	(3)	0.316564
http://www.all.org/	What's new at American Life League	(3)	0.251506
http://www.hli.org/	Human Life International	(3)	0.212931
http://www.prolife.org/cpcs-online/	Crisis Pregnancy Centers Online	(3)	0.187707
http://www.ohiolife.org/	Ohio Right to Life	(3)	0.182076
http://www.rtl.org/	Abortion, adoption assisted-suicide, Information at Right to Life...	(1)	0.17943
http://www.bethany.org/	Bethany Christian Services	(3)	0.161359
http://www.ldi.org/	Abortion malpractice litigation	(1)	0.140076
http://www.serve.com/fem4life/	Feminists for Life of America	(3)	0.122106
Principal community, SALSA			
http://www.nrlc.org/	National Right To Life	(3)	0.344029
http://www.prolife.org/ultimate/	The Ultimate Pro-Life Resource List	(3)	0.284714
http://www.naral.org/	NARAL Choice for America	(3)	0.240227
http://www.feminist.org/	Feminist Majority Foundation	(3)	0.186843
http://www.now.org/	National Organization for Women	(3)	0.177946
http://www.cais.com/agm/main/index.html	The Abortion Rights Activist	(1)	0.166083
http://www.gynpages.com/	Abortion Clinics Online	(3)	0.163117
http://www.plannedparenthood.org/	Planned Parenthood Federation	(3)	0.157186
http://www.all.org/	What's new at American Life League	(3)	0.142357
http://www.hli.org/	Human Life International	(3)	0.142357

Table 6
Authorities for World Wide Web query 'genetic' (size of root size = 120, size of collection = 2952

URL	Title	Cat	Weight
Principal community, mutual reinforcement approach			
http://www.aic.nrl.navy.mil/galist/	The Genetic Algorithms Archive	(3)	0.27848
http://alife.santafe.edu/	Artificial Life Online	(3)	0.276159
http://www.yahoo.com/	Yahoo!	(3)	0.273599
http://www.geneticprogramming.com/	The Genetic Programming Notebook	(1)	0.25588
http://gal4.ge.uiuc.edu/illigal.home.html	illiGAL Home Page	(3)	0.235717
http://www.cs.gmu.edu/research/gag/	The Genetic Algorithms Group...	(3)	0.201237
http://www.scs.carleton.ca/ csgs/resources/gaal.html	Genetic Algorithms and Artificial Life Resources	(1)	0.181315
http://lancet.mit.edu/ga/	GAlib: Matthew's Genetic Algorithms Library	(3)	0.181157
Principal community, SALSA			
http://www.ncbi.nlm.nih.gov/	The National Center for Biotechnology Information	(3)	0.250012
http://www.yahoo.com/	Yahoo!	(3)	0.227782
http://www.aic.nrl.navy.mil/galist/	The Genetic Algorithms Archive	(3)	0.223191
http://www.nih.gov/	National Institute of Health (NIH)	(3)	0.194688
http://gdbwww.gdb.org/	The Genome Database	(3)	0.177001
http://alife.santafe.edu/	Artificial Life Online	(3)	0.172383
http://www.genengnews.com/	Genetic Engineering News (GEN)	(1)	0.141617
http://gal4.ge.uiuc.edu/illigal.home.html	illiGAL Home Page	(3)	0.13259

The sample results shown so far have all been produced on unweighted collections, in which all informative links have received unit weight. Both approaches can produce better rankings when applied on weighted collections, in which each informative link receives a weight which reflects the amount of authority that the pointing site confers to the pointed site. Possible factors which may contribute to a link's weight include the following:

- Anchor text which is relevant to the query. Such text around a link heightens our confidence that the pointed site discusses the topic at hand [7].
- One of the link's endpoints being designated by the user as highly relevant to the search topic. When a site points to one of a small set of predefined authorities, it seems reasonable to raise the weights of other links which originate from that site. Similarly, when a site is known to be a good hub, it seems reasonable to assign high weights to its outgoing links. This approach has been recently applied in [5]. We coin it the *anchor sites* approach, since it uses user-designated sites as anchors in the collection, around which the communities of hubs and authorities are grown.
- The link's placement in the pointing page. Many search engines consider the text at the top of a page as more reflective of its contents than text further down the page. The same line of thought can be applied to the links which appear in a page, with the links which are closer to the top of the page receiving more weight than links appearing at the bottom of the page.

6.1. Analysis of the stochastic ranking

We now prove a general result about the ranking produced by SALSA in weighted collections, for which some basic background in stochastic processes is assumed.

Let $G = (H; A; E)$ be a positively weighted, directed bipartite graph with no isolated nodes, and let all edges be directed from sites in H to sites in A. We will use the following notations:

- The weighted in-degree of site $i \in A$:

$$d_{\text{in}}(i) \triangleq \sum_{k \in H | k \to i} w(k \to i).$$

- The weighted out-degree of site $k \in H$:

$$d_{\text{out}}(k) \triangleq \sum_{i \in A | k \to i} w(k \to i).$$

- The sum of edge weights:

$$\mathcal{W} = \sum_{i \in A} d_{\text{in}}(i) = \sum_{k \in H} d_{\text{out}}(k).$$

Let M_A be a Markov chain whose states are the set A of vertices, with the following transition probabilities between every two states $i, j \in A$:

$$P_A(i, j) = \sum_{k \in H | k \to i, k \to i} \frac{w(k \to i)}{d_{\text{in}}(i)} \times \frac{w(k \to j)}{d_{\text{out}}(k)}.$$

Similarly, let M_H be a Markov chain whose states are the set H of vertices, with the following transition probabilities between every two states $k, l \in H$:

$$P_H(k, l) = \sum_{i \in A | k \to i, l \to i)} \frac{w(k \to i)}{d_{\text{out}}(k)} \times \frac{w(l \to i)}{d_{\text{in}}(i)}.$$

Consider the following binary relation on the vertices of A (states of M_A):

$$R_A = (i, j) | P_A(i, j) > 0.$$

It is not hard to show (and is shown in the full paper) that R_A is an equivalence relation on A (similar arguments can be made concerning M_H). This implies that all the states of M_A are recurrent (none are transient). The equivalence classes of R_A are the irreducible components of M_A. We first deal with the case where R_A consists of one equivalence class (i.e., M_A is irreducible).

Proposition 1. *Whenever M_A is an irreducible chain (has a single irreducible component), it has a unique stationary distribution $\pi = (\pi_1, \ldots, \pi_{|A|})$ satisfying:*

$$\pi_i = \frac{d_{\text{in}}(i)}{\mathcal{W}} \quad \textit{for all } i \in A.$$

Similarly, whenever M_H is an irreducible chain, its unique stationary distribution $\pi = (\pi_1, \ldots, \pi_{|H|})$ satisfies:

$$\pi_k = \frac{d_{\text{out}}(k)}{\mathcal{W}} \quad \textit{for all } k \in H.$$

Proof. We will prove the proposition for M_A. The proof for M_H is similar.

By the ergodic theorem [9], any irreducible, aperiodic Markov chain has a unique stationary distribution vector. It will therefore suffice to show that the vector π with the properties claimed in the proposition is indeed a stationary distribution vector of M_A.

- π is a distribution vector: its entries are non-negative, and their sum equals one.

$$\sum_{i \in A} \pi_i = \sum_{i \in A} \frac{d_{\text{in}}(i)}{\mathcal{W}} = \frac{1}{\mathcal{W}} \sum_{i \in A} d_{\text{in}}(i) = 1.$$

- π is a stationary distribution vector of M_A. Here we need to show the equality $\pi P_A = \pi$:

$$
\begin{aligned}
[\pi P_A]_i &= \sum_{j\in A} \pi_j P_A(j,i) \\
&= \sum_{j\in A} \frac{d_{\text{in}}(j)}{\mathcal{W}} \sum_{k\in H|k\to i,k\to j} \frac{w(k\to j)}{d_{\text{in}}(j)} \frac{w(k\to i)}{d_{\text{out}}(k)} \\
&= \frac{1}{\mathcal{W}} \sum_{j\in A} \sum_{k\in H|k\to i,k\to j} \frac{w(k\to j)w(k\to i)}{d_{\text{out}}(k)} \\
&= \frac{1}{\mathcal{W}} \sum_{k\in H|k\to i} \sum_{j\in A|k\to j} \frac{w(k\to j)w(k\to i)}{d_{\text{out}}(k)} \\
&= \frac{1}{\mathcal{W}} \sum_{k\in H|k\to i} \frac{w(k\to i)}{d_{\text{out}}(k)} \sum_{j\in A|k\to j} w(k\to j) \\
&= \frac{1}{\mathcal{W}} \sum_{k\in H|k\to i} w(k\to i) \\
&= \frac{d_{\text{in}}(i)}{\mathcal{W}} \\
&= \pi_i
\end{aligned}
$$

□

Thus, when the (undirected) support graph of G is connected, SALSA assigns each site an authority weight which is proportional to the sum of weights of its incoming edges. The hub weight of each site is proportional to the sum of weights of its outgoing edges. In unweighted collections (with all edges having unit weight), each site's stochastic authority (hub) weight is simply proportional to the in-(out-)degree of the site.

This mathematical analysis, in addition to providing insight about the ranking that is produced by SALSA, also suggests a very simple algorithm for calculating the stochastic ranking: simply calculate, for all sites, the sum of weights on their incoming (outgoing) edges, and normalize these two vectors. There is no need to apply any resource-consuming iterative method to approximate the principal eigenvector of the transition matrix of the Markov chain.

Markov chains with multiple irreducible components. Consider the case in which the authority chain M_A consists of multiple irreducible components. Denote these (pairwise disjoint) components by $A_1, A_2, \ldots, A_k$ where $A_i \subset A$, $1 \le i \le k$. What will be the outcome of a random walk performed on the set of states A according to the transition matrix P_A? To answer this question, we will need some notations:

- Let e denote the $|A|$-dimensional distribution vector, all whose entries equal $1/|A|$.
- For all vertices $j \in A$, denote by $c(j)$ the irreducible component (equivalence class of R_A) to which J belongs: $c(j) = l \Leftrightarrow j \in A_l$.
- Let $\pi^1, \pi^2, \ldots, \pi^k$ be the unique stationary distributions of the (irreducible) Markov chains induced by $A_1, \ldots, A_k$.
- Denote by $\pi^{c(j)_j}$ the entry which corresponds to j in $\pi^{c(j)}$ (the stationary distribution of j's irreducible component, $A_{c(j)}$).

Proposition 2. *The random walk on A, governed by the transition matrix P_A and started from all states with equal probability, will converge to a stationary distribution as follows:*

$$\lim_{n\to\infty} eP_A^n = \tilde{\pi} \quad \textit{where} \quad \tilde{\pi}_j = \frac{|A_{c(j)}|}{|A|}\pi^{c(j)_j}$$

Proof. Denote by p_i^n, $1 \le i \le k$ the probability of being in a site belonging to A_i after the nth step of the random walk. This probability is determined by the distribution vector eP_A^n. Clearly,

$$p_i^0 = \sum_{j\in A_i} e_j = \frac{|A_i|}{|A|}$$

Since the transition probability between any two sites (states) which belong to different irreducible components is zero, $p_i^n = p_i^0$ for all n (probability does not shift from one component to another). Inside each irreducible component the ergodic theorem holds, thus the probabilities which correspond to the sites of A_i in $\lim_{n\to\infty} eP_A^n$ will be proportional to π^i, and the proposition follows. □

This proposition points out a natural way to compare the authoritativeness of sites from different irreducible components: simply multiply each site's authority score by the normalized size of the irreducible component to which it belongs. We do not claim that this is in any way optimal, as very small irreducible components should be trimmed from the graph altogether. But the underlying principle is important: consider the size of the community when evaluating the quality of the top sites in that community. The budget which the Mayor of New York City controls is much larger than that of the Mayor of Osh Kosh, Wisconsin.

It is this combination of a site's intra-community authority score and its community's size that allows the stochastic approach to blend authorities from different aspects of a multi-topic query, and which reduces its vulnerability to the TKC effect.

6.2. In-degree as a measure of authority (revisited)

Extensive research in link-structure analysis has been conducted in recent years under the premise that considering the in-degree of sites as a sole measure of their authority does not produce satisfying results. Kleinberg, as a motivation to the mutual reinforcement approach, showed some examples of the inadequacy of a simple in-degree ranking [16]. Our results in Section 5.2 seem to contradict this premise: the stochastic rankings seem quite satisfactory there, and since those collections were unweighted, the stochastic rankings are equivalent to simple in-degree counts (normalized by the size of the connected component which each site belongs to). To gain more perspective on this apparent contradiction, let us elaborate on the first stage of the meta-algorithm for link-structure analysis (from Section 3), in which the graph to be analyzed is assembled:

(1) Given a query, assemble a collection of Web sites which should contain many hubs and authorities pertaining to the query, and few hubs and authorities for any particular unrelated topic.
(2) Filter out non-informative links connecting sites in the collection.
(3) Assign weights to all non-filtered links. These weights should reflect the information conveyed by the link.

It is only after these steps that the weighted, directed graph is analyzed and the rankings of hubs and authorities are produced. The analysis of the graph, however important, is just the second stage in the meta-algorithm, and the steps involved in the first stage are crucial to the success of the entire algorithm.

Considerable research efforts have been invested in improving the quality of the assembled graphs. The current state of the art techniques for these steps is now such that in many cases, simple (and efficient) algorithms and heuristics produce quite satisfying results on the assembled graphs.

It is important to keep in mind the main goal of broad-topic World Wide Web searches, which is to enhance the precision at 10 of the results, not to rank the entire collection of sites correctly. It is entirely irrelevant if the site in place 98 is really better than the site in place 216. The stochastic ranking, which turns out to be equivalent to a weighted in-degree ranking, discovers the most authoritative sites quite effectively (and very efficiently) in many (carefully assembled) collections. No claim is made on the quality of its ranking on the rest of the sites (which constitute the vast majority of the collection).

7. Conclusions

We have developed a new approach for finding hubs and authorities, which we call SALSA: the stochastic approach for link structure analysis. SALSA examines random walks on two different Markov chains which are derived from the link structure of the World Wide Web: the authority chain and the hub chain. The principal community of authorities (hubs) corresponds to the sites that are most frequently visited by the random walk defined by the authority (hub) Markov chain. SALSA and Kleinberg's mutual reinforcement approach are both in the framework of the same meta-algorithm.

We have shown that the ranking produced by SALSA is equivalent to a weighted in/out-degree ranking (with the sizes of irreducible components also playing a part). This makes SALSA computationally lighter than the mutual reinforcement approach.

Both approaches were tested on the World Wide Web, where SALSA appears to compare well with the mutual reinforcement approach. These tests, as well as analytical work, have revealed a topological phenomenon on the Web called the TKC effect. This effect sometimes derails the mutual reinforcement approach, and prevents it from finding relevant authoritative sites (or from finding authorities on all meanings/aspects of the query):

(1) In multi-topic collections, the principal community of authorities found by the mutual reinforcement approach tends to pertain to only one of the topics in the collection.

(2) In single-topic collections, the TKC effect sometimes results in the mutual reinforcement approach ranking many irrelevant sites as authorities.

We note that SALSA is less vulnerable to the TKC effect, and produces good results in many cases where the mutual reinforcement approach fails to do so.

The following issues are left for future research:

(1) In collections with many connected components, we have studied one manner in which to combine the inner-component authority score with the size of the component. There may be better ways to combine these two factors into a single score.

(2) We have found a simple property of the stochastic ranking, which enables us to compute this ranking without the need to approximate the principal eigenvector of the stochastic matrix which defines the random walk. Is there some simple property which will allow us to calculate the mutual reinforcement ranking without approximating the principal eigenvector of $W^{T}W$? If not, can we alter the graph G in some simple manner (for instance, by changing some weights on the edges) so that the stochastic ranking on the modified graph will be approximately equal to the mutual reinforcement ranking on the original graph?

Acknowledgements

The second author would like to thank Udi Manber for introducing him to the search problems studied in this paper, and Udi Manber and Toni Pitassi for delightful and interesting discussions at the early stages of this research.

References

[1] J.G. Auguston and J. Minker, An analysis of some graph theoretical cluster techniques, J. ACM 17 (4) (1970) 571–588.

[2] S. Brin and L. Page, The anatomy of a large-scale hypertextual Web search engine, Proc. 7th Int. WWW Conf., 1998.

[3] J. Carrière and R. Kazman, Webquery: searching and visualizing the web through connectivity, Proc. 6th Int. WWW Conf., 1997.

[4] S. Chakrabarti, B. Dom, D. Gibson, J. Kleinberg, S.R. Kumar, P. Raghavan, S. Rajagopalan and A. Tomkins, Hypersearching the Web, Sci. Am., June 1999.

[5] S. Chakrabarti, B. Dom, D. Gibson, J. Kleinberg, S.R. Kumar, P. Raghavan, S. Rajagopalan and A. Tomkins, Mining the Web's link structure, IEEE Comp., August 1999.

[6] S. Chakrabarti, B. Dom, D. Gibson, S.R. Kumar, P. Raghavan, S. Rajagopalan and A. Tomkins, Spectral filtering for resource discovery, ACM SIGIR Workshop on Hypertext Information Retrieval on the Web, 1998.

[7] S. Chakrabarti, B. Dom, D. Gibson, J.M. Kleinberg, P. Raghavan and S. Rajagopalan, Automatic resource list compilation by analyzing hyperlink structure and associated text, Proc. 7th Int. WWW Conf., 1998.

[8] Compaq Computer Corporation, Altavista Net Guide, http://www.altavista.com/.

[9] R.G. Gallager, Discrete Stochastic Processes, Kluwer, Dordrecht, 1996.

[10] E. Garfield, Citation analysis as a tool in journal evaluation, Science 178 (1972) 471–479.

[11] D. Gibson, J.M. Kleinberg and P. Raghavan, Inferring Web communities from link topology, Proc. 9th ACM Conf. on Hypertext and Hypermedia, 1998.

[12] Google Inc., Google Search Engine, http://www.google.com/.

[13] M.R. Henzinger and K. Bharat, Improved algorithms for topic distillation in a hyperlinked environment, Proc. 21st Int. ACM SIGIR Conf. on Research and Development in IR, August 1998.

[14] IBM Corporation Almaden Research Center, Clever, http://www.almaden.ibm.com/cs/k53/clever.html.

[15] M.M. Kessler, Bibliographic coupling between scientific papers, American Documentation 14 (1963) 10–25.

[16] J.M. Kleinberg, Authoritative sources in a hyperlinked environment, Proc. 9th ACM–SIAM Symp. on Discrete Algorithms, 1998.

[17] J.M. Kleinberg, R. Kumar, P. Raghavan, S. Rajagopalan and A.S. Tomkins, The Web as a graph: measurements, models and methods, Proc. 5th Int. Computing and Combinatorics Conf., 1999.

[18] K. Law, T. Tong and A. Wong, Automatic categorization based on link structure, Stanford University, Stanford, 1999.

[19] M. Marchiori, The quest for correct information on the web: hyper search engines, Proc. 6th Int. WWW Conf., 1997.

[20] C.H. Papadimitriou, P. Raghavan, H. Tamaki and S. Vempala, Latent semantic indexing: a probabilistic analysis, Preliminary version appeared in PODS 98, pp. 159–168.

[21] P. Pirolli, J. Pitkow and R. Rao, Silk from a sow's ear: extracting usable structures from the Web, Proc. ACM SIGCHI Conf. on Human Factors in Computing, 1996.

[22] H. Small, Co-citation in the scientific literature: a new measure of the relationship between two documents, Journal of the American Society for Information Science 24 (1973) 265–269.

[23] C.J. van Rijsbergen, Information Retrieval, Butterworths, 1979.

[24] R. Weiss, B. Vélez, M. Sheldon, C. Namprempre, P. Szilagyi, A. Duda and D. Gifford, Hypursuit: a hierarchical net-

work search engine that exploits content-link hypertext clustering, Proc. 7th ACM Conf. on Hypertext, 1996.

Ronny Lempel is a Ph.D. student in the Department of Computer Science, Technion, Haifa, Israel, focusing on World Wide Web link-structure analysis. He received his B.Sc. and M.Sc. from the same department in 1997 and 1999, respectively.

Shlomo Moran received his BSc and DSc degrees in mathematics from the Technion, in 1975 and 1979, respectively. Since 1981 he is a faculty member in the Computer Science Department in the Technion, where he is now a Professor and Chairman. His current research interests include communication in high speed networks, exact communication complexity of distributed tasks, confidentiality protection in medical records, and search methods in the Internet.

Concepts for improved visualization of Web link attributes

Harald Weinreich *,1, Winfried Lamersdorf 2

Distributed Systems Group, Computer Science Department, University of Hamburg, Hamburg, Germany

Abstract

This paper discusses methods to generate and display automatically additional hyperlink information to the users of the World Wide Web. Current Web browsers make it hard to predict what will happen if a link is followed: users get different information than they expect, a new window may be opened, a download starts, or the destination object is just not available. Instead of giving an appropriate notification in advance, users have to follow a link, check whether the document contains the expected information, get back, try another link etc. However, usually it is possible to obtain additional hyperlink information from several sources like link anchor tags, the user's history and Web servers. Furthermore, with little enhancements, Web servers may include even more additional information to the hyperlinks in Web documents. These can be displayed before users select a link to improve navigation and reduce the cognitive overhead. In this paper several types of Web hyperlink information are listed, potential methods to present these facts are compared, the prototype implementation of the proposed concept — called by us *HyperScout* — is presented, and further developments are discussed.

Keywords: Hypertext; Navigation; Links; Typed links; Usability

1. Introduction

New users to the World Wide Web are usually impressed by the amount and richness of contents accessible on the Web. Soon after, they unfortunately have to discover that finding the right information is a challenging task, as search engines and hyperlinks often do not lead them to the information they expect.

The tremendous number of documents is only one of the reasons for usability problems of the Web. Nielsen discovered in a field study that users can even lose their orientation in a small hypertext system, if no orientation clues are given ([22], p. 133). Several reasons have been identified why users often do not know where they are, what they did and what way to choose next.

Hypertext systems like the Web can be seen as a space, where readers can move directly from one place to another. The concepts of *orientation* and *navigation* refer to this travel metaphor. Unlike in the real world, getting an overview of the *hyperspace* is nearly impossible, as only one object is displayed at a time, which is an insignificantly small part of the overall space. Furthermore, hyperlinks often do not carry enough information to predict the referenced object, what makes it demanding to select the right way.

The *cognitive overhead* associated with choosing whether to follow a link or not has long been realized. Regarding hypertext navigation, already Conklin ([9], p. 40) characterized cognitive overhead as

* Corresponding author.

1 E-mail: harald@weinreichs.de

2 E-mail: lamersd@informatik.uni-hamburg.de

"the additional effort and concentration necessary to maintain several tasks or trails at one time". Different solutions were suggested to reduce this cognitive overhead. Two key aspects of these solutions are tools to allow an overview about the hyperspace and the enhancement of link capabilities.

Some hypertext systems provide additional hyperlink *overview maps* like the Guide System [35], or an extra *hierarchy browser* for structural navigation like HyperWave's former client Harmony [10]. Unfortunately, Web clients do neither of the above. In fact the present concept of the Web does not inherently provide any kind of structural information (except of the file-system folder structure represented in the URL). Links are embedded in the HTML documents and have to be extracted first to create overview maps. While local overviews are still possible and several tools are available, comparable global navigation tools are not supported.

The second solution to reduce cognitive overhead in hypertext navigation is to improve the substance of links. Hypertext systems like MUCH [38] and Sepia [35] enforce the author to set a link type and add link titles. This information is shown to the user before he selects a link, and he can get a more precise impression about the referenced document. In fact HTML 4.0 [27]a also supports link types and titles, but hardly any author uses them.

The main reason for this shortcoming is probably the poor support for these features by Web browsers and editors. But hypertext research did also show that setting link types is not easy. This was discovered by Wang and Rada [38] in a two-year field study with over 200 users of the MUCH hypertext system. When writing documents and setting hyperlinks, the users rarely bothered to select link types or assigned link names other than the default ones. If a link type was chosen, the choice was often inconsistent with the way other authors would categorize the link. As a result it was recommended to make specifying the link type as easy as possible.

2. Concept

Web usage studies by Catledge and Pitkow [7] or Tauscher and Greenberg [34] indicate that about half the navigation actions of users are open URL events. The GVU Survey [12] indicates that users see hyperlinks from Web pages as the most important way to find new World Wide Web pages.

These findings show that links are the Web's most important navigation facility. However, the user interface for hyperlinks is quite abstract: the only information a user gets about a link destination is the *link anchor text* and the *referenced URL* displayed in the status bar of browsers, like Netscape Communicator or Microsoft Internet Explorer.

Usability studies by Spool et al. [31] bore out that Web links are usually not sufficient for the user to predict the referenced document. Especially embedded hyperlinks, only one or two words long, are often too generic. Users were more certain about what link to choose when the links were displayed in a separate line and explained with an extra description. However, this is rarely available.

Missing link information has the consequence that users try to help themselves by interpreting the only additional information they have: the URL. We noticed in *thinking-aloud tests* [3] with our campus wide information system that more experienced users learn to interpret some of the information included in the URL [39]. It was apparent from the users' comments that the URL was often an important element for the users' orientation and navigation actions. A study on how people make link selections was conducted by Stanyer and Procter [32]. It confirmed that users are often forced to fall back on heuristics drawn from past experience and interpret the URL before selecting a link. The address was used to predict different aspects of the referenced object, like their contents, the expected download time, and the destination Web site.

However, the readability of URLs for humans is poor as they are primarily technical addresses. Particularly less experienced users are unable to understand URLs and do not know how to interpret the different parts. Consequently, several projects aim to make URLs avoidable, like **RealNames** [4], a service that maps key phrases to Web pages. Since

[3] This method from cognitive psychology was first used for software evaluation by Lewis in 1982 [17].

[4] The RealNames Corporation can be found at http://www.centraal.com/. Their 'Internet Keyword Concept' has been integrated in some search engines and browsers like the Microsoft Internet Explorer 5.

the location of a Web object is defined by the URL, it will not become obsolete in the near future. We could still try to make it less important, also by providing the user a better link interface.

If we want to make URLs less considerable, more meaningful information has to be provided. However, hypertext research did show that authors often have problems adding useful information to hyperlinks, and actually in the Web they are rarely offered (see introduction). Therefore it might be reasonable to display that piece of information to users which is already available and might be extracted automatically.

There are several sources the browser could use to give Web links additional information. Link anchors and the referenced URLs are two of them. Like experienced users know how to interpret URLs, the browser might decode this data and present it in a more legible way. This would reduce cognitive overhead and avoid the need of the users to observe the address in the status bar when looking for information on the Web.

Another prosperous source is the user's history. By maintaining a considerably comprehensive log of the user's visited documents and offering better history tools, retrieving information could be made much easier. Moreover the user's history could be integrated more seamlessly into the navigation. Facts like the last visit to a Web page or the title of a document could be displayed to a link.

The fourth source of additional hyperlink information could be Web servers. By regularly gathering information about all local and directly referenced external documents into a database, this information could be used to add new attributes to link tags.

Since the user interface for links has hardly changed from the first versions of NCSA's Mosaic and as many users complain that they have significant problems finding things on the Web [12], there is a big potential for improvements, and we should give the users all the help we can. We try to go one step in this direction with our tool *HyperScout*.

3. Methods to display additional link information

To determine how to display additional link information most appropriately, we compared different methods introduced by earlier hypertext systems. This paragraph will give a short survey of the most promising ways to present supplementary link type data.

3.1. Overview map

Some hypertext systems with typed links, such as SEPIA [35] and MacWeb [20], display the link information as labels within an overview diagram of the hyperspace. Labels appear next to the arrow representing the link. The advantage of this method is an improved overview of the structure and the document relations.

However, if the user wants to consider this information, he has to keep two areas in view, and the overview map needs certain additional screen space.

3.2. Reserved area

The most popular Web browsers display the referenced URL of a link in the browser's status bar at the bottom of the window. *Hyperties* uses the last screen line to show a short description when the cursor touches a hyperlink [19,29].

If a system shall put more link information on view than a single line of text, an extra window, or frame can be used. For example, the hypermedia version of the papers of the August 1995 issue of *Communications of the ACM* displays additional link data in an extra frame.

Though, placing the comment that far away from its associated anchor makes it difficult to compare them. It forces the reader to make large visual saccades in order to read the comment and then return to the anchor's text.

3.3. Next to the links

Web links sometimes provide a short supplementary information next to the anchor text. Web design guidelines recommend this for links to objects with considerable properties [16,18]. For instance, authors put the size of the referenced object in brackets after the link, if the file is reasonably big. It is also possible to use small icons to envision some kinds of link types.

However, adding such kind of data by the browser or a navigation tool automatically can cause problems with some Web documents, as even little changes can mess up the layout of the page. The Web browser tool 'Traffic-Lights', which adds little colored bars before and behind every link anchor, demonstrates this [6].

3.4. Link color

Already the first graphical Web Browser Mosaic used two different colors for the link anchor text to distinguish between links to unknown documents and links to recently visited documents. HyperWave's former client Harmony additionally utilizes different anchor text background colors to make multiple link destinations in one anchor visible.

The color of a link is an important navigation aid for Web users. Unfortunately the complexity and number of the displayed link properties is quite low. Furthermore it does only work with text link anchors, and it requires that Web designers do not change the standard colors of the documents.

3.5. Mouse pointer

Another method to make different link attributes apparent is utilizing different mouse pointers. The pointer changes according to the link type if it is moved over a link. For example, the Guide system uses this method ([23], p. 57).

This method allows to display link attributes instantly if a the pointer hovers over a link. Since it is completely independent of the screen layout, different mouse pointers may be an interesting option for Web clients, too. The only drawback is that the complexity of the displayed properties is limited, e.g. no text may be displayed.

3.6. Popup

Popups or *rollovers* are small floating windows which appear next to the mouse cursor if it is moved over an active object. Recent versions of Microsoft's Internet Explorer display the *title* attribute of anchor tags in a little popup. Jakob Nielsen strongly recommends to use these titles as they "are one of the first enhancements to the Web that actually help people navigate (as opposed to simply making pages look more fancy)" [24]. Unfortunately, they can rarely be found.

Popup information is also used in most current GUI systems. For instance, they appear if the mouse pointer floats over icons and control elements. That makes them quite common to users.

Nevertheless, there is a well-known disadvantage: popups can cover some important information as they obstruct objects near to the link anchor. This problem is reduced by letting them appear only on demand when a user points the mouse over an active object for a certain time.

We chose popups as the method for our project HyperScout in order to display additional link information. They seem to be best applicable to the Web and appear most advantageous. In particular, they do not interfere with the page layout, and they even can be used together with image-maps, which hold several links in one graphic. Furthermore, they appear next to the focus of attention and can show a flexible amount of information.

4. Characteristics of hyperlinks in the World Wide Web

On the first view Web hyperlinks might seem simple compared to the typed links of other hypertext systems. Looking closer, there are several new features that make the use of the Web even more challenging than other hyperdocuments. Additional aspects regarding Web links may be identified, like a local versus an external link. Furthermore, a lot of unexpected things can happen if a user clicks on a link: World Wide Web clients incorporate different protocols, like news and ftp, links can control the contents of other frames or windows, or the user may be requested to write an e-mail. It also occurs that users return to pages they visited before but afterwards cannot remember their former actions.

This section describes the most important characteristics of Web hyperlinks and explains which information we think should not be hidden from users any more.

4.1. Semantics

A link between two documents sets them in a semantic relationship. Web authors try to express this relationship and give an impression of the target by selecting an appropriate link anchor text or graphic. However, in many cases this is not sufficient. Therefore semantic information like link titles and link types were introduced [4].

Thüring, Hannemann and Haake list *semantic link information* as their first principle of useful hypermedia system design [35]. Already in HTML 2.0 additional anchor attributes were defined to express the relationship between source and destination more precisely [3]. Web authors can set a link *title* and use the two attributes *rel* and *rev* to set a forward and backward relationship type. HTML 4.0 identifies several relationship types as useful like 'contents', 'subsection', or 'alternate' [27]b. The approach for the prospective XLink [11] is similar, but even the HTML attributes are hardly considered in today's browsers. Only the latest versions of the Internet Explorer display the link title in a popup window.

Until these attributes are applied by more authors, semantic information about the target document, like its title or author, is a useful source (Fig. 1). This information can either be extracted from the user's history or be transferred from the server as will be shown later.

4.2. Navigation direction

Direction is an essential aspect of hypertext navigation. From the user's view, it can be distinguished between forward and backward navigation. Forward navigation occurs if a user is looking for new information, whereas backward navigation occurs when he tries to regain information obtained before [35]. The most important tool for backward navigation is the back button, followed by the Bookmarks (also called Favorites or Hotlist) and the History [7,34].

Another aspect of backward navigation is the revisit of Web pages. In a 6 weeks' study with 23 users Tauscher and Greenberg found that about 60% of all pages an individual visits are pages he has visited before [34]. Given these statistics, we believe that Web browsers should regard a user's history better in his active navigation. Contemporary Web browsers consider the user's history only in a very unsatisfactory way: links change their color; links to pages that have not been seen by the user are blue, links to previously seen pages are purple.

This was perhaps appropriate for the first Web browser, but it is not any more. Today many link anchors are graphics, so this information is not displayed at all. In other cases Web authors change the link colors for design purposes. Even if none of this is done, users cannot see exactly when they visited a destination object before. Furthermore the link color returns to blue after a certain time.

Bookmarks are a further aspect of backward navigation that is not considered either. A user cannot see if he has a bookmark to a document, or if a link leads to a page he has already bookmarked. Seeing that many users have more than 100 bookmarks [1,12] it is unlikely that they are aware of all of them.

By displaying the information gathered from the user's history (Fig. 1), we want to seamlessly integrate the user's navigation direction into active Web operation.

4.3. Access time

System response time is a crucial factor for the usability of interactive systems ([30], p. 297). User studies with one of the first hypertext systems, the ZOG system of the Carnegie Mellon University, indicated that a maximum response time of 2 s should not be exceeded ([28], pp. 31).

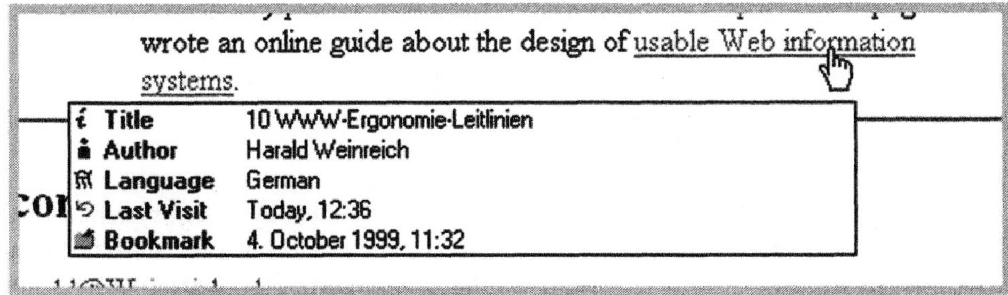

Fig. 1. Link to a page the user visited before. He has also bookmarked that URL.

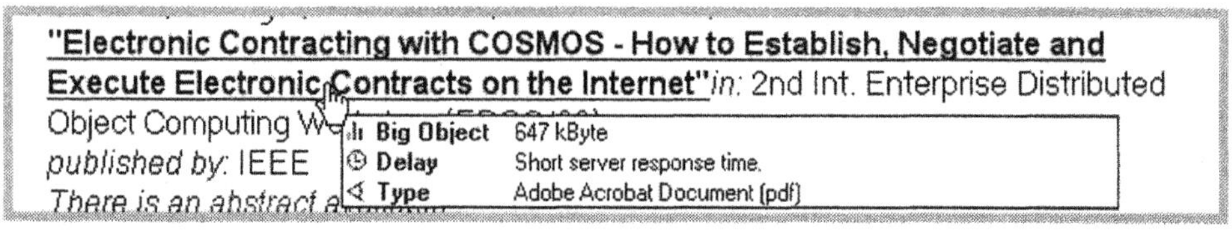

"Electronic Contracting with COSMOS - How to Establish, Negotiate and Execute Electronic Contracts on the Internet" *in:* 2nd Int. Enterprise Distributed Object Computing W... *published by:* IEEE *There is an abstract a...*

Big Object 647 kByte
Delay Short server response time.
Type Adobe Acrobat Document (pdf)

Fig. 2. Link to a large pdf-file.

Unfortunately a comparable response time cannot be guaranteed to the Web user. The access time to different Web objects varies quite a lot. Johnson argued that the value of an information is dependent on the access time [13], and usability test showed that a lot of users quit the transfer and return to the last object if the download takes too long [31]. Slow access time interrupts the user's task solving process, and leads to more cognitive burden and lower productivity.

The predictability of a system's response time of a link can help users to choose whether it may be worth to follow a link or not. The already mentioned Web browser tool 'Traffic-Lights' uses small red, yellow and green bars next to the link anchors to give the user an idea of the anticipated transfer time. It is estimated by requesting the head of a referenced server's homepage. A user evaluation showed that this concept was beneficial for users and helped them to find suitable documents to a topic more quickly [6].

Unfortunately the access time to a Web object cannot really be predicted as there is no quality of service support in the current TCP/IP implementation. However, a big file size or a slow server response can give a good impression about the probable response speed and should be displayed to the user (Fig. 2).

4.4. *Type of referenced object*

Although HTML is still the primary language for documents on the Web, hyperlinks may also lead to documents in other formats. Graphics, Adobe Acrobat documents, VRML worlds and XML documents are only a selection of what can be found. Some of these types do not provide hyperlinks, others require a special plug-in or viewer. This can apparently set hurdles to the user.

Web design guidelines like [16] or [18] advise one to make this somehow visible to the user. This is not always followed. Fortunately the document type can often be extracted from the extension of the referenced object (Fig. 2). Nevertheless Web browsers do not make this fracture in navigation clear. The users have to look at the URL in the status bar and to learn a lot about different file types.

4.5. *Link action*

Regarding the Web, hyperlinks behave in different ways. The most frequent ones are *replacement links* where the destination document replaces the source object. *Reference links* lead to another position in a Web document ([22], pp. 96). This information can still be extracted by the experienced user from the link URL, but Web links can also lead to more unpredictable actions. Some links open a new browser window, control the contents of another frame or start a new client, like an e-mail program. Some of these link actions are defined more precisely in XLink with the two new attributes *show* and *acutate*, nevertheless, the presentation of these characteristics is not defined.

Design guidelines recommend to make these aspects apparent in the link anchor or next to it. Some Web authors follow these recommendations, others do not. Anyway there is no standard.

Most of this information can be extracted just by analyzing the parameters of the anchor tag, however, no common browser does this. HyperScout makes use of this information and displays it in popups (Fig. 3).

4.6. *Local, remote*

Unlike a local hypertext system, hyperlinks in the Web can lead to an object from another provider than the referrer. These external links normally have another signification than internal links. Usability

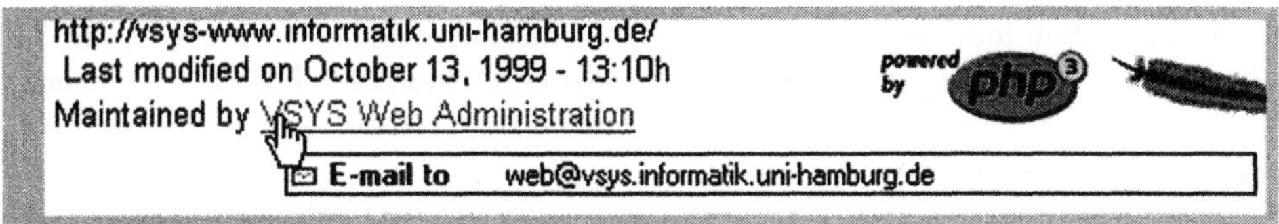

Fig. 3. A 'mailto:' URL.

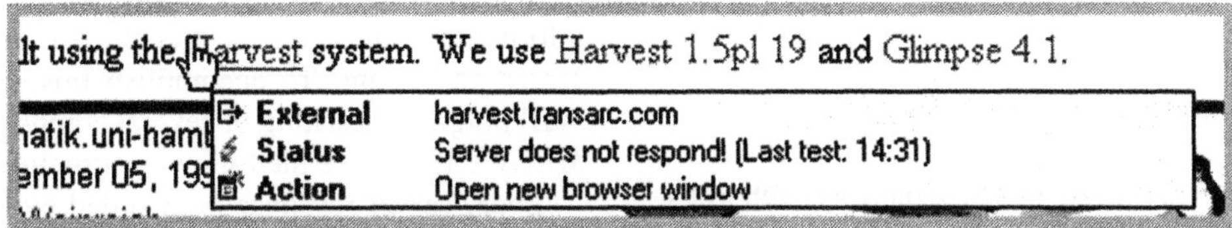

Fig. 4. An external link that opens a new window. The server is down.

studies conducted by Spool et al. ([31], pp. 45) pointed out that users do not expect that a link leads to a different site, if this is not illustrated. However, to the user this information is only apparent if he compares the current URL with the referenced object's address.

This cognitive overhead could easily be avoided, if Web clients would qualify external links adequately [25]. Therefore we included this attribute in our tool (Fig. 4).

4.7. Link status

Users consider dangling hyperlinks as one of the most serious usability problems of the Web [12]. A recent survey showed that nearly 6% of all Web links are broken [33]. Advanced systems like HyperWave [14] or the Atlas Link Service [26] incorporate concepts to avoid broken hyperlinks, even for a distributed hypertext, by removing them immediately when detected by the server.

However, this may lead to a new usability problem. We noticed during user tests with a prototype Web information system that users sometimes expected hyperlinks in titles of menus and in graphics that were not linked yet. Although some of those objects did not even appear like hyperlinks, the participants tried to click on them and got confused as nothing happened.

In these cases it would be more advantageous if non available links could be clearly distinguished from working links before clicking on them. If Web servers did contain a component that frequently checks all links and saves the data in a database, they could easily add this information to the transferred document's link anchor tags. Browsers could display the link status to the user and help him to find another destination until the author fixes the problem.

HyperScout has two mechanisms to check the status automatically. One works on server side and regularly checks the existence of referenced objects, the other operates along with the browser and checks servers to see if they are responding. This information is presented to the user before he is clicking on a link (Fig. 4).

4.8. Further meta information

There are several further aspects of Web links that might be presented to users. A document's language, its popularity, or its last update time can users help to decide if to follow a link or not.

Although Web guidelines recommend one to make the most important and unexpected link characteristics apparent with the link anchor text, authors often do not follow this. The exact user group of a Web server can hardly be identified, therefore a Web author can only vaguely predict what may be important clues for the user and what not.

Specifying link attributes is an additional and demanding work for hypertext authors. At least it could be reduced to some extend if Web server and browser technology would be more advanced. Especially user specific adaptable navigation tools seem promising. They have a better capability to present the user just the link information he needs. At the same time, to avoid information overload, they should only display the important data being available. This requires a configurable and situation-adaptive tool. HyperScout does not reach this objective completely yet, but it is a step in this direction.

5. Implementation

We had two options to enhance the way Web links are being displayed to the user without changing the documents on the server. Either an open-source Web browser like **Mozilla**[5] can be used and modified in the desired way, or a proxy can be used to alter the documents when they are transferred from server to client. Although the former method gives better control over the link presentation, the latter seemed more appropriate for our needs. First of all such a proxy technology can be used on client and on server side. The client proxy is used to let the browser display user specific or even group specific link information. The server side proxy is used to append additional information to the links on server side, like the status, avoiding that the client needs to pre-fetch information about the referenced documents. Furthermore the client proxy concept can be collaboratively used in a work group.

Another reason for this decision was, that we primarily wanted to implement and evaluate a proof of concept prototype, and this method seemed less complicated. The capabilities of Dynamic HTML are sufficient for our concept as will be described later.

For the implementation we used an expandable proxy framework by IBM alphaworks called WBI (Web Browser Intelligence). Barrett and Maglio describe this technology as a new approach to programming Web applications [2]. They call the concept *intermediary*, a new place for producing and manipulation Web data in several ways. **WBI**[6] is freely available in Java for researchers.

To parse, analyze and modify the documents in the intermediary we used Arthur Do's **HTML-StreamTokenzer**[7]. For persistent data storage the relational database system **MySQL**[8] was employed.

5.1. Client side implementation

The client side proxy has three tasks: to record the browsing history of the user, generate additional link information, and alter the transferred data between server and client. To accomplish this, we wrote a WBI *plug-in* consisting of several components called *MEGs*[9]. They have the following structure and tasks:

Every server response is recorded by the monitor (Fig. 5). It gathers status, attributes and links of every requested document. This data is stored into the database to track the user's navigation.

Meanwhile 'document editor 1' adds commands to the head of the document, which tell the browser to request[10] a short CSS definition and some JavaScript functions from the intermediary's 'generator 1' (Fig. 5). This code is needed to display the popups. This generator just transfers files from the hard disk of the intermediary.

Subsequently 'document editor 2' parses the body of the document and adds JavaScript event commands to all anchor and image map tags (`<A>`- and `<AREA>`-tags). These events call the JavaScript functions of the header when the mouse pointer floats over a link. At the end of the document another line is inserted by 'document editor 2' which requests data from the intermediary's second generator. 'Generator 2' produces Dynamic HTML code on the fly. It consists of as many popup elements as distinct links are in the document. These elements contain the additional link information (see Figs. 5 and 6).

Appending the code for the popups at the end

[5] http://www.mozilla.org/

[6] The WBI Development Kit for Java is available from: http://www.alphaworks.ibm.com/tech/wbidk

[7] The HtmlStreamTokenizer can be downloaded as Java source code from Arthur Do's site, http://www.do.org/products/parser/

[8] http://www.mysql.org/

[9] MEG stands for Monitor, Editor, Generator. These are the main concepts for WBI plug-in components [2].

[10] Current Web browsers recognize commands to insert other objects into a document. This concept is related to Ted Nelson's transclusions [21]. For a CSS-definition the `<LINK rel="stylesheet" type="text css" href="popup.css">` tag is used and for JavaScript `<SCRIPT Language="JavaScript1.1" SRC="popup.js">`.

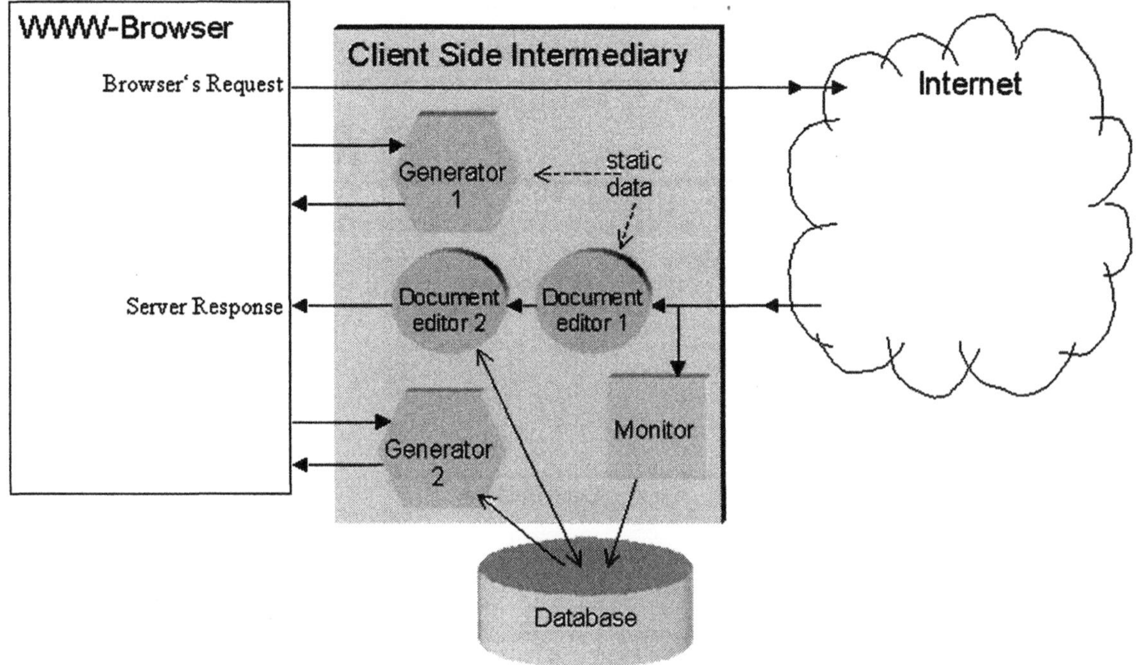

Fig. 5. The architecture of the HyperScout plug-in.

of the document has the advantage that the page can be displayed by the browser before the popups are generated. This decelerates browsing the Web as little as possible.

The Dynamic HTML code concept consists of the following components: the Document Object Model (DOM) is used to address the popups, which consist of a HTML division (`<div>`-tag) including a table. Cascading Style Sheets control the appearance, visibility and position of these divisions [5,36]. Via JavaScript the browser reacts on the user's mouse movements [11]. If the mouse pointer hovers over a link for more than 1.2 s the additional link information is displayed next to it. After leaving the link it disappears instantly. Moving the pointer over another link within 0.4 s, a new label appears instantly. Like this popups appear only 'on demand'.

The monitor of the HyperScout plugin has the further function, to the contact the external servers that are referred within the actual page, to estimate their response time. Another tool parses the bookmark file and adds the URLs to the database (not depicted).

5.2. Server side implementation

If the browser shall display additional link information about referenced objects, that data can be taken from the user's history if he visited the documents before. Otherwise it would normally be necessary to pre-fetch all referenced objects (at least their headers) to get data on the link status, or the document size and title. However, the present situation of the Internet does not make this seem advisable as pre-loading increases the amount of transferred data significantly and therefore slows down Web usage.

We developed a solution that avoids this problem. Our concept proposes a second intermediary at the Web server. This intermediary has a database with meta information on all the documents offered by the Web server. It contains also data on all directly referenced external objects.

When a document is requested, the intermediary adds new attributes to all anchor-tags, like the title of the referenced document, its size, language, and the links status (Fig. 7). For this purpose we used

[11] Although the models used by Netscape's Communicator and Microsoft's Internet Explorer to address and control HTML objects are dissimilar, it is possible to make JavaScript functions work with both browsers as of version 4.

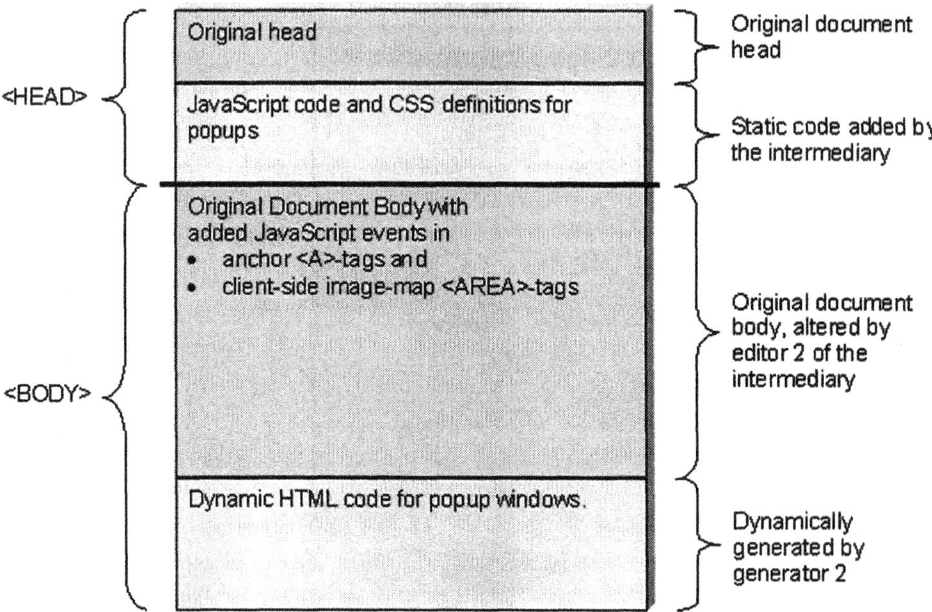

Fig. 6. Document after the modification by HyperScout.

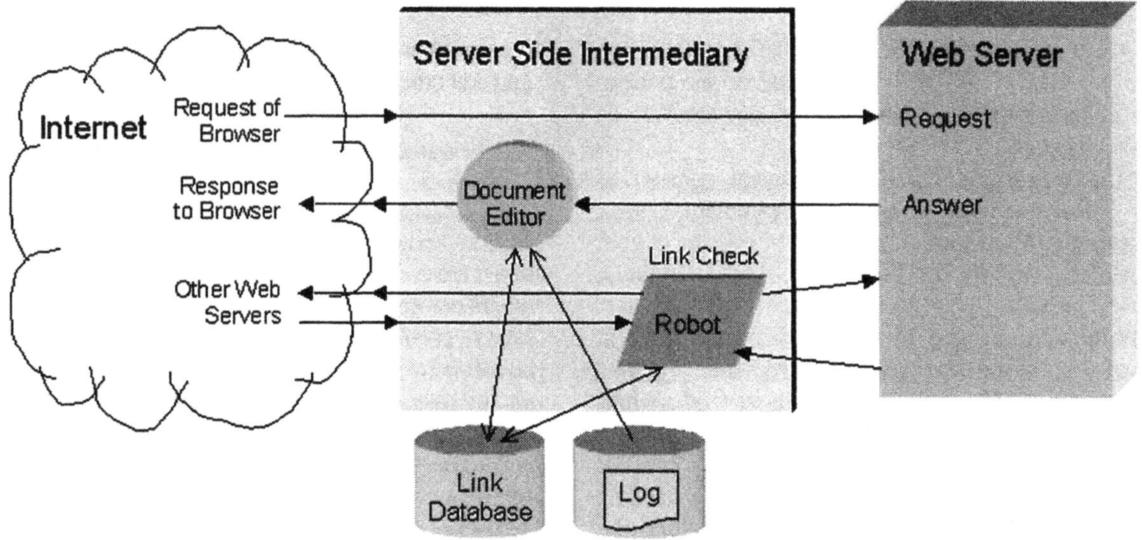

Fig. 7. The structure of the server side intermediary.

XHTML 1.0 to define additional tags to the anchor tag [37]. We called these attributes `hreftitle`, `hrefsize`, `hreflang`[12] etc.

To check all documents and their internal and external links, a robot of the intermediary is started regularly, for instance once a week. By this means, the intermediary does not always have consistent data, but most of the time; much more steadily than usual for the Web. The information is in a state of *weak consistency*.

Doubtlessly, systems which keep all documents

[12] In fact the attribute `hreflang` of the anchor tag was defined in HTML 4.0 [27]c.

and links in a database (e.g. HyperWave) are more advanced than ordinary Web servers. They can guarantee consistent meta and link data and could add it directly to the link tags. However, the concept we propose can also be used with any current Web server without the need of major modification to its documents or the programmed dynamic pages (like servlets). Therefore we think it is more likely that it might be used with current Web services.

5.3. Limitations

It is a disadvantage of this implementation that the inserted Dynamic HTML code occasionally interferes with the code of the original document. However, this could be avoided with a more sophisticated implementation. More often we had problems with HTML frames that left only insufficient space for the popups.

Another weakness of the prototype is the deceleration of the page transfer. Java seems to be still too slow for this kind of application. But we can still recommend WBI for prototyping.

After all, this implementation of HyperScout is primarily an example. The listed problems speak for a direct implementation of these concepts into browser and server.

6. Future work

The next step we will accomplish is a usability evaluation of our concept. First of all we need to know if these enhancements really help to find information faster and easier. A result could be that users follow wrong links less often and therefore need to *undo* their operation by pressing the back-button more rarely.

Several aspects of this link interface concept are new and need further research. In particular we are afraid that the dynamic character of the popups might be confusing. It is possible that beginners would prefer popups displaying information on the same attributes for every link.

We are thinking of further enhancements to HyperScout. They will provide information on a user's own navigation habits and help him to find and regain information easier. Moreover, we want to offer strategic information on the actions of other users of a Web service, which can for instance be extracted from the server log (Fig. 7). Traces left by other users can help current users to find and understand information easier [40].

Furthermore, additional hyperspace information, like link traversal statistics and incoming links to a document [13], could be added to the documents by the server's intermediary and displayed on demand. Readers can find out how other users came to a page and discover along these lines newer documents about a subject, that link to the actual page [8].

7. Related work

This paper refers to several preceding projects. This sections lists three recent projects with related activities.

A novel technique to display link information was presented by Zellweger, Chang and Mackinlay [41]. The concept is called *fluid links*, as the document adjusts dynamically and makes space for a 'gloss', i.e., additional information to a link. The advantage of this technique is that the original document is not covered by a popup window. However, applying this technique to today's Web pages will be quite unfeasible as little changes to HTML-documents can already mess up the entire page layout.

A prototype system presented by Kopetzky and Mühlhäuser uses a similar proxy technology to display *thumbnail* previews of the referenced documents [15]. This concept probably helps users to remember navigation paths easier as they might be able to recognize a page visited earlier. Nevertheless, this vision has disadvantages: Reduced previews of a page usually do not allow to read any of its information. Besides most sites nowadays use the corporate identity of an organization what makes the thumbnails of all pages look alike. Moreover the data transfer necessary to generate the previews would slow down the use of the World Wide Web significantly as all referenced pages including graphics would have to be pre-loaded with a document.

[13] Most Web clients transfer the URL of the preceding document (referrer) of a requested object to the Web server. This information can be stored and obtained later from the server log.

The project '*Link Lens*' deals with link information previews as well. Stanyer and Procter propose a tool that displays additional link information if the tool is moved over a Web link. The Link Lens pre-fetches additional data about the referenced document on demand and displays it in a kind of magnifying glass [32].

8. Conclusion

Previous hypertext research did show that additional link information helps users to get a better idea of the target of a link. Like opening every door and peering inside before entering, this can help to avoid unnecessary navigational operations and therefore reduce the cognitive overhead.

HyperScout's automatically generated additional link information can adaptively point out the most important available facts, and popups display them on demand before a user follows a link. If the frequency may be reduced that Web users select a wrong link, they could save a lot of time and find required documents earlier.

The proposed methods are also an approach to make URLs for Web navigation less important. Furthermore, the history of the user is more seamlessly integrated into his navigation, and the fight against broken links has come one step ahead.

The HyperScout concept combines novel ideas with desired features of previous approaches: additional link information is generated automatically, intermediaries monitor and enrich the transferred information, and popups are used to display this information to the user.

Our prototype implementation proves that the ideas work. Several advantages can be identified: the implementation is lightweight and almost platform independent. It works with the most popular Web clients and on any platform that supports Java. It can also be used with the majority of Web servers without the effort of Web authors to change current or future documents.

Still a lot of work has to be accomplished to improve the usability and the abilities of HyperScout.

More information on the project and a prototype is available at: http://vsys-www.informatik.uni-hamburg.de/projects/hyperscout/.

Acknowledgements

Special thanks go to Volkert Jürgens and Matthias Mayer for their support in developing and implementing these concepts.

References

[1] D. Abrams, R. Baecker and M. Chignell, Information archiving with bookmarks: personal Web space construction and organization, in: Proc. of CHI '98 Human Factors in Computer Systems, Los Angeles, ACM, New York, 1998, pp. 41–48.

[2] R. Barrett and P. Maglio, Intermediaries: new places for producing and manipulating Web content, in: Proc. of the 7th World Wide Web Conference, Comput. Networks ISDN Syst. 30 (1998) 509–518.

[3] T. Berners-Lee and D. Connolly (Eds.), HTML 2.0 specification: The anchor-element, World Wide Web Consortium, 1995, available at: http://www.w3.org/MarkUp/html-spec/html-spec_5.html#SEC5.7.3.

[4] M. Biber, F. Vitali, H. Ashman, V. Balasubramanian and H. Oinas-Kukkonen, Fourth generation hypermedia: some missing links for the World Wide Web, in: Special issue on World Wide Web Usability, Int. J. Human-Comput. Stud. 47 (1) (1997) 31–65.

[5] B. Bos (Ed.), Cascading style sheets, World Wide Web Consortium, 1999, available at: http://www.w3.org/Style/css/.

[6] C. Campbell and P. Maglio, Facilitating navigation in information spaces: road-signs on the World Wide Web, Int. J. Human-Comput. Stud. 50 (1999) 309–327.

[7] L. Catledge and J. Pitkow, Characterizing browsing strategies in the World Wide Web, in: Proc. of the 3rd International World Wide Web Conference, Darmstadt, Germany, Comput. Networks ISDN Syst. 27 (1995) 1065–1073.

[8] S. Chakrabarti, D. Gibson and K. McCurley, Surfing the Web backwards, in: A. Mendelzon et al. (Eds.), Proc. of the 8th International World Wide Web Conference, Toronto, Comput. Networks 31 (1999) 1679–1693.

[9] J. Conklin, Hypertext: an introduction and survey, IEEE Comput. 20 (9) (1987) 17–40.

[10] W. Dalitz and G. Heyer, Hyper-G: Das Internet-Informationssystem der 2. Generation, dpunkt-Verlag, Heidelberg, 1995.

[11] S. DeRose, E. Maler, D. Orchard and B. Trafford (Eds.), XML linking language (XLink), World Wide Web Consortium XLink Working Group, 2000, available at: http://www.w3.org/TR/xlink.

[12] Graphic, Visualization, and Usability Center's (GVU) 10th World Wide Web User Survey, available at: http://www.cc.gatech.edu/gvu/user_surveys/survey-1998-10/.

[13] C. Johnson, What's the Web worth? The impact of retrieval delays on the value of distributed information, Workshop on Time and the Web, Staffordshire University, 1997.

[14] F. Kappe, A scalable architecture for maintaining referential integrity in distributed information systems, IICM Graz University of Technology, Austria, 1994.

[15] T. Kopetzky and M. Mühlhäuser, Visual preview for link traversal on the WWW, in: A. Mendelzon et al. (Eds.), Proc. of the 8th International World Wide Web Conference, Toronto, Comput. Networks 31 (1999) 1525–1532.

[16] R. Levine, Guide to Web style, Sun Microsystems, 1996, available at: http://www.sun.com/styleguide/.

[17] C. Lewis, Using the 'thinking-aloud' method in cognitive interface design, IBM Research Report RC 9265, IBM Watson Research Center, Yorktown Heights, New York, 1982.

[18] P. Lynch and S. Horton, Web Style Guide: Basic Design Principles for Creating Web Sites, Yale University Press, 1999, available at: http://info.med.yale.edu/caim/manual/.

[19] G. Marchionini and B. Shneiderman, Finding facts vs. browsing knowledge in hypertext systems, IEEE Comput. 21 (1) (1988) 70–80.

[20] J. Nanard and M. Nanard, Hypertext design environments and the hypertext design process, Commun. ACM 38 (8) (1995) 49–56.

[21] T. Nelson, Literary Machines, Mindful Press, Sausalito, CA, 1987.

[22] J. Nielsen, Hypertext and Hypermedia, Academic Press, New York, 1993.

[23] J. Nielsen, Multimedia and Hypertext: The Internet and Beyond, Academic Press, New York, 1995.

[24] J. Nielsen, Using link titles to help users predict where they are going, Jakob Nielsen's Alertbox, 11 January 1998, available at: http://www.useit.com/alertbox/980111.html.

[25] J. Nielsen, Designing Web Usability: The Practice of Simplicity, New Riders Publishing, Indianapolis, 2000.

[26] J. Pitkow and R.K. Jones, Supporting the Web: a distributed hyperlink database system, in: Proc. of 5th International World Wide Web Conference, Paris, France, Comput. Networks ISDN Syst. 28 (1996) 981–991.

[27] D. Raggett, A. Le Hors and I. Jacobs (Eds.), HTML 4.0 specification, World Wide Web Consortium, 1998, (a) Available at: http://www.w3.org/TR/REC-html40, (b) HTML Link Types: http://www.w3.org/TR/REC-html40/types.html#type-links, (c) The A Element: http://www.w3.org/TR/REC-html40/struct/links.html#edef-A.

[28] G. Robertson, D. McCracken and A. Newell, The ZOG approach to man-machine communication, Department of Computer Science, Carnagie Mellon University, Pittsburgh, 1979.

[29] B. Shneiderman and G. Kearsley, Hypertext Hands-On: An Introduction to a New Way of Organizing and Accessing Information, Addison-Wesley, Reading, MA, 1989.

[30] B. Shneiderman, Designing the User Interface: Strategies for Effective Human–Computer Interaction, 2nd edition, Addison-Wesley, Reading, MA, 1992.

[31] J. Spool, T. Scanlon, W. Schroeder, C. Snyder and T. DeAngelo, Web Site Usability: A Designer's Guide, Morgan Kaufmann, Los Altos, CA, 1999.

[32] D. Stanyer and R. Procter, Improving Web usability with the Link Lens, in: A. Mendelzon et al. (Eds.), Proc. of the 8th International World Wide Web Conference, Toronto, Comput. Networks 31 (1999) 455–466.

[33] T. Sullivan, 'All Things Web', May 1999, available at: http://www.pantos.org/atw/35654.html.

[34] L. Tauscher and S. Greenberg, How people revisit Web pages: empirical findings and implications for the design of history systems, Int. J. Human-Comput. Stud. 47 (1) (1997) 97–138.

[35] M. Thüring, J. Hannemann and J. Haake, Hypermedia and cognition: designing for comprehension, Commun. ACM 38 (8) (1995) 57–66.

[36] W3C DOM Working Group, Document Object Model Level 1, 1999, available at: http://www.w3.org/DOM/.

[37] W3C HTML Working Group, XTHML 1.0: The Extensible HyperText Markup Language, 1999, available at: http://www.w3.org/TR/xhtml1/.

[38] W. Wang and R. Rada, Experiences with semantic net based hypermedia, Int. J. Human-Comput. Stud. 43 (1995) 419–439.

[39] H. Weinreich, Ergonomie von Hypertext-Systemen und das World Wide Web: Evaluation und Überarbeitung des WWW-Informationssystems des Fachbereiches Informatik, Diploma Thesis at the Computer Science Department of the University of Hamburg, 1997.

[40] A. Wexelblat, History-based tools for navigation, in: Proc. of the Hawai'i International Conference on System Sciences, IEEE Press, 1999.

[41] P. Zellweger, B.-W. Chang and J. Mackinlay, Fluid links for informed and incremental link transitions, in: Proc. of ACM Hypertext '98, Pittsburgh, 1998, pp. 50–57.

Harald W.R. Weinreich studied computer science at the University of Hamburg (Germany) and the University of Limerick (Ireland). After obtaining his diploma degree in 1998, he became a research assistant and Ph.D. student at the Research Group on Distributed Systems (VSYS) of the Computer Science Department of the University of Hamburg. His research interests are distributed information systems, hypertext systems, Web usability, e-commerce and usability engineering.

Winfried Lamersdorf holds a full professorship in the Department of Computer Science of the University of Hamburg and leads the Research Group on Distributed Systems. Areas of his current research include application-layer communication, system support for open distributed systems, open distributed software architectures and applications, distributed co-ordination and co-operation, and specific distributed application areas, such as electronic libraries and electronic commerce. Since 1986, he has been involved actively in various national and international standards bodies in the area of open systems and applications. He organized and led various national and international research projects.

Query routing for Web search engines: architecture and experiments

Atsushi Sugiura [a,*], Oren Etzioni [b,1]

[a] *Human Media Research Laboratories, NEC Corporation, Japan*
[b] *Department of Computer Science and Engineering, University of Washington, Seattle, WA, USA*

Abstract

General-purpose search engines such as AltaVista and Lycos are notorious for returning irrelevant results in response to user queries. Consequently, thousands of specialized, topic-specific search engines (from VacationSpot.com to KidsHealth.org) have proliferated on the Web. Typically, topic-specific engines return far better results for 'on topic' queries as compared with standard Web search engines. However, it is difficult for the casual user to identify the appropriate specialized engine for any given search. It is more natural for a user to issue queries at a particular Web site, and have these queries automatically *routed* to the appropriate search engine(s). This paper describes an automatic query routing system called *Q-Pilot*. Q-Pilot has an off-line component that creates an approximate model of each specialized search engine's topic. On line, Q-Pilot attempts to dynamically route each user query to the appropriate specialized search engines. In our experiments, Q-Pilot was able to identify the appropriate query category 70% of the time. In addition, Q-Pilot picked the best search engine for the query, as one of the top three picks out of its repository of 144 engines, about 40% of the time. This paper reports on Q-Pilot's architecture, the query expansion and clustering algorithms it relies on, and the results of our preliminary experiments.

Keywords: Web search; Query routing; Query expansion; Search engines

1. Introduction

Search engines, such as Yahoo! [20] and AltaVista [2], are useful for finding information on the World Wide Web. However, these *general-purpose* search engines are subject to low precision and/or low coverage. Manually-generated directories such as Yahoo! provide high-quality references, but cannot keep up with the Web's explosive growth. Although crawler-based search engines, like AltaVista, cover a larger fraction of the Web, their automatic indexing mechanisms often cause search results to be imprecise. It is thus difficult for a single search engine to offer both high coverage *and* high precision. This problem is exacerbated by the growth in Web size and by the increasing number of naive users of the Web who typically issue short (often, single word) queries to search engines.

The recent growth in both the number and variety of specialized *topic-specific* search engines, from VacationSpot.com [16] to KidsHealth.org [10] or epicurious.com [5], suggests a possible approach to this problem: search topic-specific engines. Topic-specific search engines often return higher-quality references than broad, general-purpose search engines for several reasons. First, specialized engines are often a front-end to a database of authoritative

* Corresponding author. E-mail: sugiura@hml.cl.nec.co.jp
[1] E-mail: etzioni@cs.washington.edu

information that search engine spiders, which index the Web's HTML pages, cannot access. Second, specialized search engines often reflect the efforts of organizations, communities, or individual fanatics that are committed to providing and updating high-quality information. Third, because of their narrow focus and smaller size, word-sense ambiguities and other linguistic obstacles to high-precision search are ameliorated.

The main stumbling block for a user who wants to utilize topic-specific search engines is: How do I find the appropriate specialized engine for any given query? Search.com offers a directory of specialized search engines, but it is up to the user to navigate the directory and choose the appropriate engine. A search engine of search engines is required. To build such an engine two questions have to be addressed: How can we build an index of high-quality, specialized search engines? And, given a query and a set of engines, how do we find the best engine for that query? In this paper, we focus on the latter problem, which is often referred to as the *query routing* problem.

Although many query routing systems [4,8,12] have been developed, few of them are aimed at the topic-specific search engines provided on the Web. To automate the query routing process, conventional query-routing systems need to access the complete internal database associated with each engine. Yet most of the specialized search engines on the Web, do not permit such access to their internal databases.

This paper presents a novel query routing method, called *topic-centric* query routing, which compensates for lack of unfettered access to search engine databases by using two key techniques:

- *Neighborhood-based topic identification:* a technique for collecting the abstract topic terms relevant to a search engine from existing Web documents.
- *Query expansion:* a technique for obtaining the terms relevant to a query. For the purpose of topic-centric query routing, it is used mainly for evaluating the relevance of a query to the identified topic terms of search engines.

While conventional query routing techniques compare a user query with all the documents or terms contained in search engines' databases, our method compares a query with a relatively small number of abstract topic terms. In this sense, we call the proposed method *topic-centric* query routing. It is implemented in a query routing system called *Q-Pilot*.

The rest of this paper first describes related work to clarify the position of our research and then describe the topic-centric query routing method and Q-Pilot in detail. It also presents the results of experiments using Q-Pilot.

2. Related work

Conventional query routing systems and services (some of them are currently available on the Web) can be classified into three groups.

Manual query routing services. Some query routing services has recently become available on the Web. However, each has some aspect of query routing performed manually by the user. AllSearch Engines.com [1], SEARCH.COM [14], Invisible Web.com [9] and The Search Broker [13] provide a categorized list of specialized search engines, but these services basically require the users themselves to choose engines from the list. Although they provide keyword search interfaces to find desired search engines, the terms that can be accepted as the keywords are limited to the abstract category names (such as "sports"). The users are required to map from their specific queries (such as "Michael Jordan") to the related categories in their mind.

Automated query routing systems based on centroids. Some systems perform automated query routing. A centroid-based technique is widely used by these kinds of systems. Namely, it generates 'centroids' (summaries) of databases, each of which typically consists of a complete list of terms in that database and their frequencies, and decides which databases are relevant to a user query by comparing the query with each centroid. CORI [4] is a centroid-based system. GlOSS [8] is also based on the same kind of the idea, although it does not explicitly generate the centroid. STARTS [7] and WHOIS++ [18] propose standard architectures and protocols for the distributed information retrieval using centroids provided by information sources.

An advantage of the centroid-based technique is to be able to handle a wide variety of search keywords by using the large number of the terms obtained from databases. However, this technique cannot be applied to most of the topic-specific search engines provided on the Web because of the restricted access to their internal databases, as we mentioned in Section 1.

Automated query routing systems without centroids. There are some automated query routing systems that do not generate centroids. However, these systems have strict limitations on acceptable search keywords. Query routing in Discover [15] relies on short texts, associated with WAIS databases, to explain the contents of databases given by service providers. Discover can operate only when some of the search keywords are contained in the short texts. Although Discover helps users refine their queries so that it can select topic-specific search engines, this effort is insufficient for handling a wide variety of search keywords. Profusion [6] routes queries in thirteen predefined categories to six search engines. It posts sample queries from each category to the search engines and examines which engine is good for that category by checking relevance of the returned documents. Profusion has a dictionary to determine which categories the given user queries are relevant to. Since, however, this dictionary is created by looking at newsgroups' names (a term "movie" can be categorized into a recreation category from "rec.movie.reviews"), as a result Profusion can accept only limited types of queries.

One exceptional system that cannot be classified into any of these three groups is Ask Jeeves [3], which performs automated routing of queries to a limited set of Web sites that contain "answers" to user "questions." Since Ask Jeeves is a proprietary commercial system, little is known about its internal routing algorithm, its degree of automation, or its ability to scale.

3. Q-Pilot: a topic-centric query routing system

3.1. Overview

Q-Pilot is an automated query routing system, which does not generate centroids, composed of an off-line pre-processing component and an on-line interface (Fig. 1). Off-line, Q-Pilot takes as input a set of search engines' URLs and creates, for each engine, an approximate textual model of that engine's content or scope. We experimented with several methods for approximating an engine's scope and found that the *neighborhood-based topic identification* technique, which collects terms representing the scope from Web pages in the 'neighborhood' of the search engine's home page, is surprisingly effective. Q-Pilot stores the collected terms and their frequency into the search engine selection index.

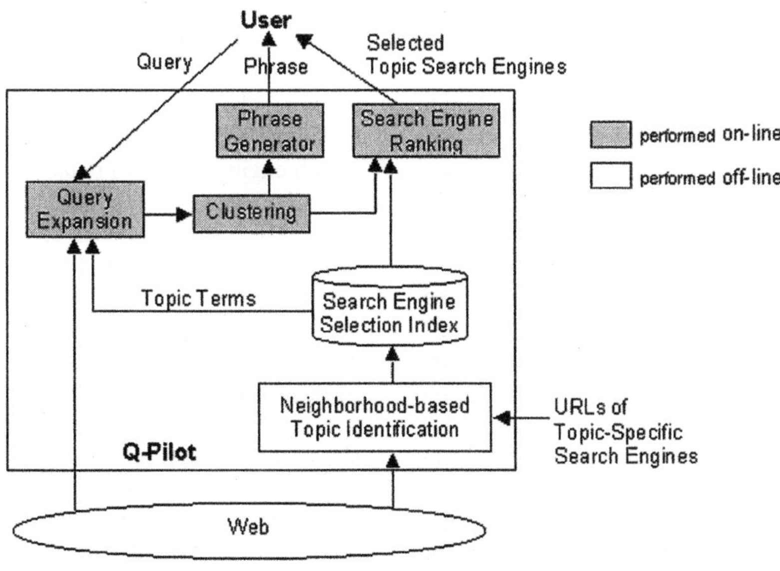

Fig. 1. System architecture of Q-Pilot.

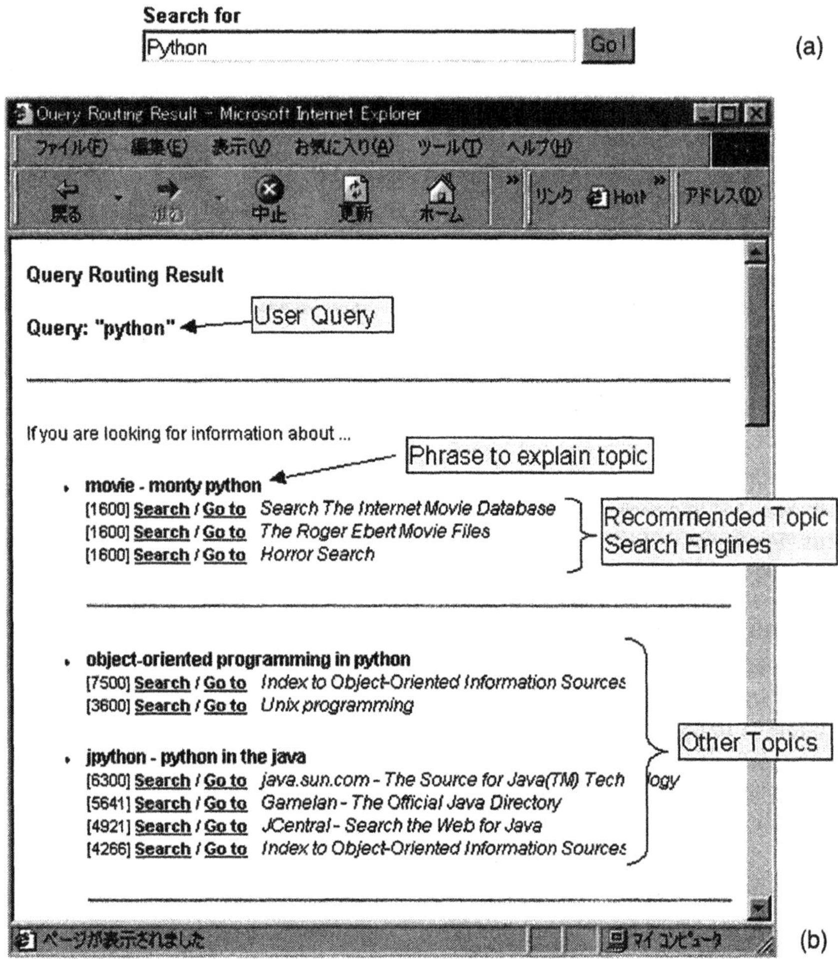

Fig. 2. Screen snapshots of Q-Pilot. (a) A query form. (b) An example of query routing results.

On-line, Q-Pilot takes a user query as input, applies a novel query expansion technique to the query and then clusters the output of query expansion to suggest multiple topics that the user may be interested in investigating. Each topic is associated with a set of search engines, for the query to be routed to, and a phrase that characterizes the topic (Fig. 2b). For example, for the query "Python" Q-Pilot enables the user to choose between movie-related search engines under the heading "movie — monty python" and software-oriented resources under the headings "objected-oriented programming in python" and "jpython — python in Java".

An important key point in the Q-Pilot design is to use the neighborhood-based identification of search engines' topics in combination with query expansion. The neighborhood-based method does not collect terms relevant to search engine's topics from search engine's internal databases, but collects them from the limited 'neighborhood' Web pages. Therefore, only a small number of abstract terms (some of them representing the topics of a search engine) can be obtained. On the other hand, user queries are likely to be short (only two or three search keywords, usually), and no topic term is specified in many cases. Query expansion bridges a gap between the short query and the small number of terms about search engines' topics. The query expansion technique used in Q-Pilot is specially tailored for the query-routing purpose to identify the topics implicit in the query. Thereby Q-Pilot can make the topic-level mapping from queries to search engines.

Another important benefit of the query expansion process is the ability to automatically obtain terms relevant to a query from the Web, which is an immense corpus. This allows Q-Pilot to identify topics of any kinds of queries without having to maintain a massive dictionary or database of terms in a wide range of fields.

Note that Q-Pilot obtains all the information necessary in query routing from the Web. That is, the topics of search engines are identified using the existing neighborhood Web documents, and the terms relevant to the query are also obtained from Web documents. In a sense, Q-Pilot is an intelligent agent that uses the Web as its knowledge base and autonomously learns what it does not know.

Computer security search engine (www.securityfocus.com)		Hotel search engine (hotel search under www.travelweb.com)	
security	1.00	*hotel*	1.00
bug	0.89	travel	0.57
bugtraq	0.44	airline	0.57
unix	0.39	reservation	0.43
exploit	0.28	restaurants	0.29
attack	0.28	map	0.29
password	0.22	book	0.29
mail	0.17	flights	0.29
holes	0.17	availability	0.29
nt	0.17	points	0.29

Fig. 3. Terms collected by the back-link method. (Italic fonts designate topic terms and frequencies are normalized).

3.2. User interface

Q-Pilot provides a simple keyword search interface (Fig. 2a) and outputs the query routing result for the given query (Fig. 2b). As shown in Fig. 2b, when the query is related to multiple topics, Q-Pilot selects search engines for each different topic and gives phrases explaining the topics. The user can choose the search engine to be queried by clicking a "Search" link or a "Go to" link. With the "Search" link, the user's original query is forwarded to the corresponding topic-specific search engine and the search results from that engine are displayed. The "Go to" link leads the user to a search form page of the topic-specific search engine, where the user has to submit the query again.

Some query routing systems forward the query directly to the selected search engines, skipping the intermediate step shown in Fig. 2b, and subsequently merge the search results into a unified format. The current version of Q-Pilot, however, does not perform such merging.

3.3. Neighborhood-based identification of search engine's topics

We propose two methods for neighborhood-based topic identification, which collect terms relevant to a search engine from existing, static Web documents:

- *The front-page method.* Every search engine has a page providing a query interface (we call this page a *front page*), and the front page usually contains terms explaining a topic of that search engine. In the front-page method, all terms in the front page [1] and their frequencies are registered to a search engine selection index.
- *The back-link method.* Web pages that have links pointing to a search engine's front page (we call these pages *back-link pages*) often contain good explanations of that search engine. The back-link method first finds multiple back-link pages for a target search engine e_i,[2] next extracts from all the back-link pages only the terms that are in the lines of the links to e_i, and stores into the search engine selection index all the extracted terms and their document frequencies.

We call high-frequency terms, which appear in the search engine selection index, *topic terms*. Specifically, a set of topic terms $TOPIC_i$ for the search engine e_i is defined as follows:

$$TOPIC_i = \{w_{ij} \mid f_{ij} > f_{\max} * 0.8\}$$

where w_{ij} $(1 \le j \le m)$ is a term in the index for e_i, f_{ij} is its frequency, and $f_{\max}$ is the highest frequency observed in the index. Fig. 3 shows examples of terms obtained by the back-link method. The abstract general terms would usually be topic terms.

For comparison in the experiments described later, we also implemented a method that collects terms from the search engine's database.

[1] Stop words are excluded.

[2] Q-Pilot finds back-link pages by using the link search function of AltaVista, querying "*link:URL_of_engine*".

(1) Get a document set D_0 relevant to a user query Q_0, where search keywords are $w_{01}, \ldots, w_{0n}$, by sending Q_0 to a general search engine.
(2) Count co-occurrences of search keywords and other terms in the document set D_0.
(3) Let WH_0 and WL_0 be a set of terms whose co-occurrences exceed a certain threshold and a set of the other terms, respectively. WH_0 is considered relevant to the query Q_0 and will be a part of the query expansion result.
(4) Pick up at most four topic terms wt_1–wt_4 from WL_0.
(5) Formulate four queries QT_1–QT_4 by combining wt_1–wt_4 with Q_0 (for example, QT_1 = "$w_{01} \ldots w_{0n} wt_1$").
(6) Clustering all terms in D_0 to at most three clusters: $W_1 = \{w_{11}, \ldots, w_{1m}\}$, $W_2 = \{w_{21}, \ldots, w_{2k}\}$ and $W_3 = \{w_{31}, \ldots, w_{3j}\}$.
(7) Formulate three queries Q_1–Q_3 by combining W_1–W_3 with Q_0 (for example, Q_1 = "$w_{01} \ldots w_{0n} w_{11} \ldots w_{1m}$").
(8) Get document sets DT_1–DT_4 and D_1–D_3 by sending QT_1–QT_4 and Q_1–Q_3 independently to a general search engine.
(9) Count co-occurrences in DT_1–DT_4 and D_1–D_3. Sets of high co-occurrence terms WTH_1–WTH_4 and WH_1–WH_3, as well as WH_0 in step 3, are query expansion results.

Fig. 4. Query expansion procedure.

- *The database sampling method.* A database sampling method obtains a part of a database and generates a kind of an incomplete centroid. That is, it submits training queries to the search engine and stores in the search engine selection index all the terms in the returned documents and frequencies of those terms. A similar method has been proposed by Xu [19].

Due to the nature of the sources used for the term collection, most of the terms collected by the front-page and back-link methods are abstract general terms like "hotel" and "travel." Relatively few specific terms, such as the proper noun "Hilton", are obtained. In contract, the database sampling method is quite successful at collecting specific terms.

3.4. Query expansion

Query expansion is a technique, widely used in information retrieval, for obtaining additional terms relevant to a given query (search keywords). It is usually used to help information searchers express their intentions more accurately and increase the precision of search results. In Q-Pilot, however, its main purpose is to evaluate the relevance of search keywords to the topic terms stored in the search engine selection index. Fig. 4 shows a query expansion algorithm in Q-Pilot. Its general framework is as follows:

- *Getting relevant terms from the Web dynamically.* Q-Pilot does not use any special dictionaries for query expansion, but it uses the Web (the existing Web documents) as the source of relevant terms. As shown in step 1 of Fig. 4, it finds the Web documents relevant to the user query dynamically by submitting that query to a general Web search engine [3]. The relevant terms are extracted from those documents. Since there is an immense corpus on the Web, terms relevant to any kind of search keywords can be obtained, even peculiar proper nouns, technical terms, etc. In thesaurus-based query expansion [17], covering any terms of any fields is difficult.
- *Co-occurrence-based evaluation of term relevance.* The mutual relevance of terms is evaluated on the basis of their co-occurrence in the documents. In steps 2 and 3, the co-occurrences of the search keywords and other terms are counted in 30 documents retrieved by the general search engine in step 1. That is, the system lists all distinct terms contained in 30 documents, and counts for each term the number of documents that contain both the search keyword and that term. To reduce the computational time, Q-Pilot handles a pair of

[3] Q-Pilot currently uses MetaCrawler, a meta-search engine, in Step 1 so that it can collect a variety of terms from many information sources. Step 8 uses AltaVista because of its short response time.

a page title and a snippet in the search result as a single document and does not download the actual documents.

- *Using a pseudo-feedback technique.* It is difficult to determine the term relevance from only the results of a single document search on the general search engine. Even closely relevant terms often have few co-occurrences in the 30 documents of the first search. Q-Pilot, therefore, re-evaluates such low co-occurrence terms: selecting terms to be re-evaluated from the first search results (steps 4 and 6), formulating new queries by adding the selected terms to the original query (steps 5 and 7), and performing the co-occurrence-based evaluation again for each formulated query (steps 8 and 9). Such automatic query refinement is called pseudo-feedback [11].

The pseudo-feedback process treats topic terms as follows. First, as shown in step 4, low co-occurrence topic terms in the first search results are selected for re-evaluation prior to other non-topic terms.

Steps 6 and 7 are also important for topic terms. In these steps, non-topic terms are added to the original user query for the pseudo-feedback. However, the main purpose of this is to get new topic terms that were not obtained through the first search rather than to re-evaluate the added non-topic terms. As found in earlier query expansion experiments, search results can be improved in many cases by using additional terms. The improved search results are more likely to contain good terms like topic terms.

The clustering in step 6 (explained in the next subsection) is expected to contribute effectively to finding new topic terms. Suppose, for example, that the non-topic terms "Monty", "scripting", and "language" are obtained by the first search when the user query is "Python". The topic terms like "comedy" and "programming" are more likely to be obtained in the pseudo-feedback process by clustering non-topic terms and querying "Python Monty" and "Python language scripting" independently rather than by querying "Python Monty language scripting" without clustering.

Both the topic terms and the non-topic terms obtained through query expansion are used in the ranking of topic-specific search engines and the extraction of phrases to explain topics of the selected search engines.

In the pseudo-feedback process, seven queries are posted to the general search engine in parallel and the total processing time for query expansion is about four seconds currently.

3.5. Clustering

As shown in Fig. 4, the terms in the document set D_0 retrieved in response to the original user query Q_0 are clustered for the preparation of the pseudo-feedback process (step 6). Since Q-Pilot spends a lot of time (about four seconds) on query expansion, it uses a simple, ad hoc method for the clustering in order to reduce the total computational time. The clustering algorithm in Q-Pilot generates at most only three clusters that are mutually exclusive, such as one about the comedy group Monty Python, one about the programming language Python, and one about the snake python. The algorithm is as follows:

(1) Pick up the term $wmax_1$ with the highest co-occurrence in the document set D_0 obtained in step 1 of the query expansion algorithm in Fig. 4. Let D_{01} be a set of documents containing $wmax_1$.
(2) Pick up the highest co-occurrence term $wmax_2$ in a set of documents not containing $wmax_1$. Let D_{02} be a set of documents containing $wmax_2$ and not containing $wmax_1$.
(3) Let D_{03} be a set of the other documents.
(4) Terms that appear in D_{01}, D_{02}, and D_{03} would be the clusters of terms W_1, W_2, and W_3 in step 6 of Fig. 4, respectively.

For the user query "python", for example, "Monty" and "programming" would typically be $wmax_1$ and $wmax_2$, respectively, and "snake" would be contained in D_{03}.

After the query expansion process, there are at most eight clusters of terms: WH_0 (step 3), WTH_1–WTH_4, and WH_1–WH_3 (step 9). Since, however, different clusters are often related to the same topic, Q-Pilot merges them to eliminate the duplicates. Basically, it merges clusters that contain the same topic term. It also merges clusters that have many common terms. In future work, we plan to compare the performance of this ad hoc method with that of standard, linear-time clustering algorithms such as buckshot or fractionation.

3.6. Ranking topic-specific search engines

Q-Pilot calculates the *goodness* of each topic-specific search engine for the given query by comparing the terms obtained through query expansion with the terms stored in the search engine selection index. Using the calculated *goodness*, it generates a ranked list of the search engines and selects the top three as query routing results. If there are multiple clusters of query expansion terms, the search engines are ranked for each cluster. Therefore, $3 \times n$ search engines are selected for n clusters.

The *goodness* of a search engine e for a given set $W = \{w_1, w_2, \ldots\}$ of query expansion terms is calculated as follows:

$$goodness(e, W) = \sum_{w_i \in W} f_i * c_i$$

where c_i is the number of co-occurrences of w_i counted in query expansion process and f_i is the frequency of term w_i in the search engine selection index for e ($f_i = 0$ if there is no w_i in the index). Note that not only topic terms but also non-topic terms are used in the calculation of *goodness*.

3.7. Extracting phrases to explain topics

As shown in Fig. 2b, Q-Pilot gives a phrase to explain a topic representing the content of each cluster. The phrase is extracted from the document sets $D_0 - D_3$ and $DT_1 - DT_4$ obtained in the query expansion process. In extracting a phrase for a cluster of terms $W = \{w_1, w_2, \ldots\}$, Q-Pilot first finds in those document sets all phrases (sequence of terms), each of which contains only $w_i \in W$, prepositions, and articles. Using some heuristics, it then selects the best one. Basically, a phrase that contains topic terms and many high co-occurrence terms is selected.

For example, if $W =$ {"python", "object", "programming", "scripts", "oriented"} is obtained by query expansion, "object oriented programming with python" and "scripts of python" would be extracted and the first phrase that has the topic term "programming" would be selected.

STC [21], a linear-time document clustering algorithm, which also extracts phrases that represent document clusters from the classified documents. In STC, cluster choice is a function of phrase length and the number of documents in a cluster. However, the phrase extraction process of Q-Pilot is more sensitive to the relevance of the phrases, search keywords, and topic terms, and it would be expected that Q-Pilot extract more appropriate phrases. A detailed comparison between STC and Q-Pilot's clustering algorithm is a direction for future work.

4. Experiments

To evaluate the proposed topic-centric query routing method, we conducted several experiments. The questions here are:

- How do three methods for topic identification (the front-page, the back-link and database the sampling methods) affect the routing accuracy?
- To what extent do query expansion and clustering improve accuracy?
- How does the number of routing-target topic-specific search engines impact accuracy?
- Is the topic-centric method practical for routing queries to topic-specific search engines on the Web?

In the rest of this section, we will describe a data set used in the experiments, the accuracy measure, an experimental setup and results.

4.1. Experimental data and performance measure

As the experimental data, we used a query log given by actual users to The Search Broker [13], which is a query routing system using about 400 topic-specific search engines classified into 25 categories, such as Computer, Travel, and Entertainment.

The Search Broker has a table, created manually, mapping a specific topic term t_i to a specific search engine e_i and it can select the engine only when the user describes the topic term at the top of the submitted list of search keywords. Therefore, every query in the Search Broker's query log $Q = \{q_1, q_2, \ldots, q_N\}$ has the following format:

$$q_i = \text{"}t_i w_{i1} w_{i2} \ldots w_{im}\text{"}$$

In the experiments, we fed to Q-Pilot the query $qb_i = \text{"}w_{i1} w_{i2} \ldots w_{im}\text{"}$ (q_i minus the topic term t_i) and examined whether Q-Pilot could select the search engine e_i corresponding to t_i. More precisely, since Q-Pilot returns a ranked list of search engines, we examined whether e_i was contained in the top d elements in that ranking. Given a set of test queries Q, the accuracy of query routing is calculated as follows:

$$Accuracy(Q, d) = \sum_{q_i \in Q} F(R(d, qb_i), e_i)/|Q|$$

where $R(d, qb_i)$ is a set of search engines that Q-Pilot ranks within the top d for qb_i, and F returns 1 if $e_i \in R$ and otherwise returns 0.

Note that this measure of accuracy is conservative for two reasons. First, human users of the Search Broker can make inappropriate engine choices, but when Q-Pilot fails to match these, its accuracy measure is penalized. Second, there may be more than one appropriate engine choice per query. Again, when Q-Pilot fails to match the choice made by the human — its accuracy is penalized.

4.2. Experimental setup

Before the measurement of accuracy, it is necessary to create the search engine selection indices for each topic identification method. To create the indices, we used 50 back-link pages for the back-link method and used 600 training queries for the database sampling method. This is because, as shown in Fig. 5a,b, the most important parts of two indices (the 20 terms with the highest frequencies) are rarely changed after the learning by the 50 back-link pages and the learning of the 600 training queries. The 600 training queries were randomly selected from the Search Broker's query log and they were distinct from the set of test queries used in the later experiments.

4.3. Experimental results

4.3.1. Comparison of three topic identification methods and evaluation of the effectiveness of query expansion

We first measured, for each of the three topic identification methods, the *Accuracy* in routing 150 test queries to 27 topic-specific search engines in the Computer and Travel categories of the Search Broker. There are originally 52 engines of those two categories in the Search Broker. However, only 27 of them (15 in the Computer category and 12 in the Travel category) allow a Web page collection robot to access their databases. So, we used the 27 engines to which the database sampling method is applicable.

Table 1 lists the results obtained when *Accuracy* was calculated with $d = 3$ (the correct engine is within the top three). The Simple_QR denotes the results obtained without query expansion and clustering. The QR + QE denotes the results ob-

Table 1
Accuracy (%) by three topic identification methods ($d = 3$, 27 topic-specific search engines, 150 test queries)

	Simple_QR	QR + QE
Front-page method	9.2	32.2
Back-link method	13.5	54.2
Database sampling method	43.2	55.4

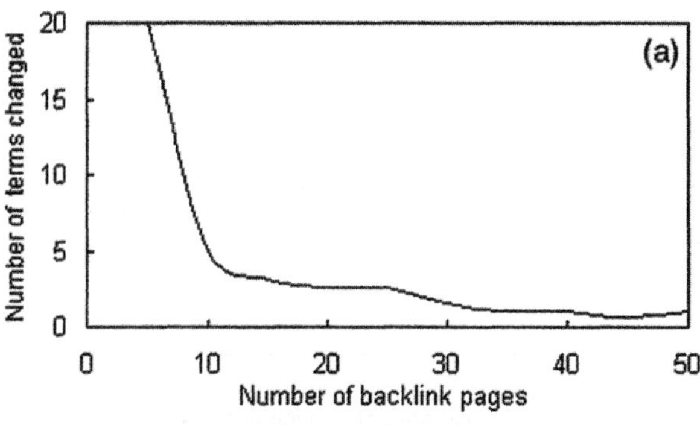

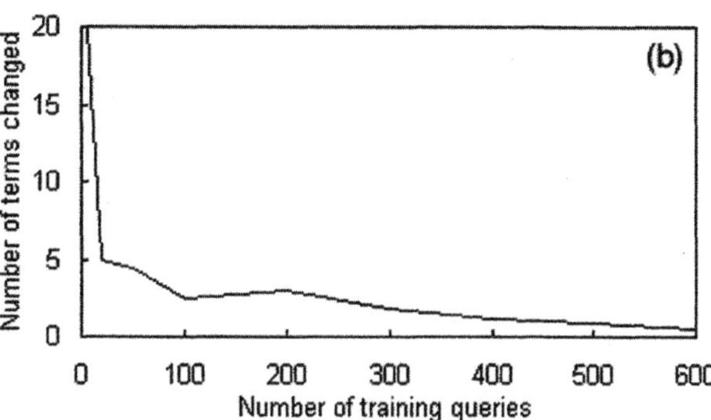

Fig. 5. Changes of terms with the 20 highest frequencies when creating the search engine selection index. (a) Back-link method. (b) Database sampling method.

tained with query expansion (but without clustering).

In the Simple_QR, the database sampling method performed best because of its ability to collect terms relevant to search engines. As we mentioned, the neighborhood-based methods (the front-page and the back-link methods) can collect only a small number of abstract terms. Therefore, in many cases, the search keywords did not match any terms in the search engine selection index and could not be mapped to any search engine.

Query expansion improved the performance of all three topic identification methods, especially, that of the back-link method. Its accuracy was improved by about 40% to almost the same level as that of the database sampling method. This result shows that the proposed query expansion technique can find topics of given queries well enough to compensate for the lack of term collection capability of the back-link method.

The poor performance of the front-page method is due to the difficulty of identifying topic terms by using only the front page. That is, there can be no big difference in term frequencies when the terms are collected from only that page. When multiple back-link pages are used, however, the back-link method can identify the topic terms more precisely.

Learning curves for the back-link method and the database sampling method are shown in Fig. 6. At 50 back-link pages and 600 training queries, the learning curves of both are saturated in terms of QR + QE. These results show that 50 back-link pages and 600 training queries are reasonable sizes as the learning data sets needed to create search engine selection indices.

Table 2
Accuracy (%) when using clustering (27 topic-specific search engines, 150 test queries)

	QR + QE ($d = 5$)	QR + QE + clustering ($d = 3$)
Front-page method	32.2	46.1
Back-link method	63.5	61.5
Database sampling method	66.9	63.8

4.3.2. Effectiveness of clustering

When performing both query expansion and clustering on the 150 test queries, an average of 1.6 clusters of terms was generated. Since three engines are selected for each cluster, a total of 4.8 engines are selected. To be fair, we compared the accuracy in selecting the top five engines without clustering ($d = 5$) with the accuracy in selecting the top three engines for each cluster with clustering ($d = 3$). As shown in Table 2, the performances were not improved by clustering in the back-link and the database sampling methods.

Although the clustering did not greatly improve of the query routing performance, it is important from a point of view of the user interface. Suppose, for example, that the system displays the search engines about programming languages together with those about comedies without clustering when the user query is "Python". A user who is searching for the comedy group Monty Python and does not know about the programming language Python would be likely to mistrust the performance of the system. Clustering and giving phrases to explain the clusters would be expected to make the user more confident of the query routing results.

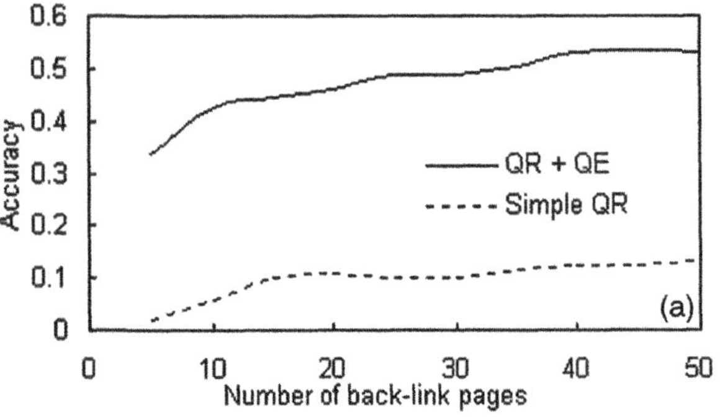

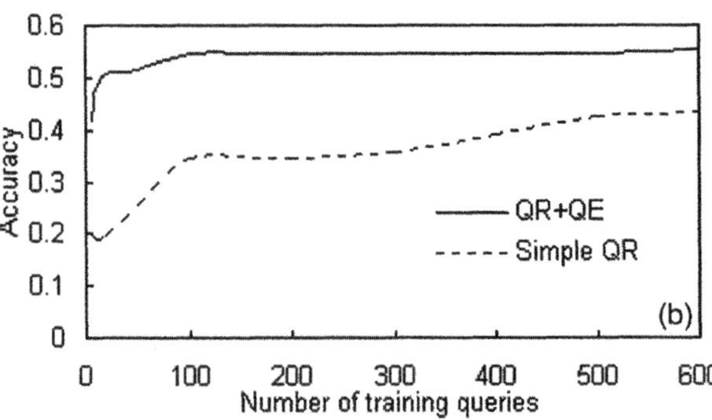

Fig. 6. Learning curves ($d = 3$, 27 topic-specific search engines, 150 test queries). (a) Back-link method. (b) Database sampling method.

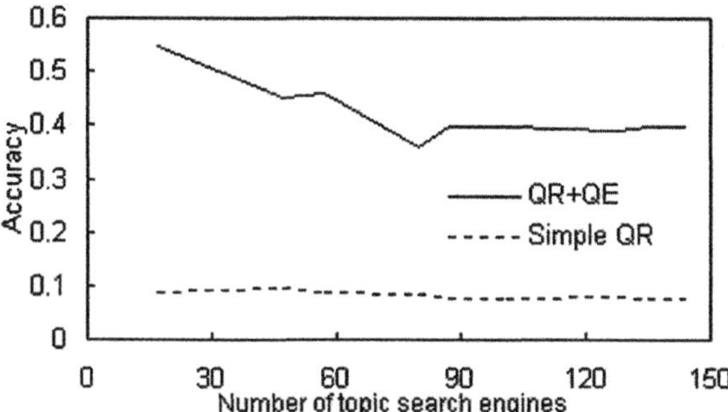

Fig. 7. Performance for 144 engines in back-link method (d = 3, 144 topic-specific search engines in 9 categories, 800 test queries).

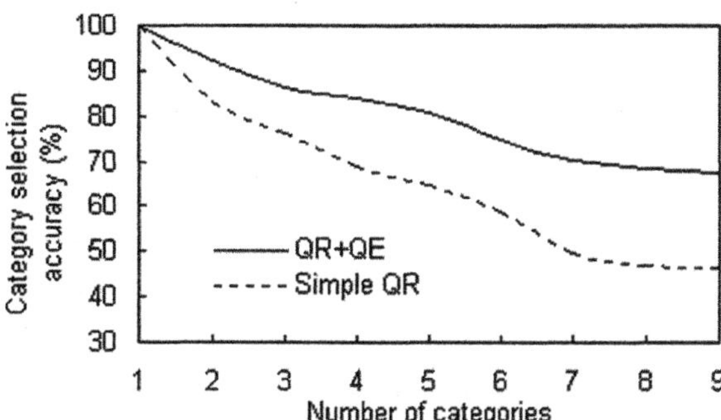

Fig. 8. Category selection accuracy (d = 3, 144 topic-specific search engines in 9 categories, 800 test queries).

4.3.3. Scalability against the number of topic-specific search engines

We measured the performance in routing 800 test queries to 144 topic-specific search engines belonging to nine categories: Animal, Entertainment, Computer, Food, Music, Medical, US Government, Travel and Sport. The database sampling method could not be applied to many of the 144 search engines in our experimental set because these engines forbid robots. In addition, we did not believe that the front-page method would perform well. As a result, our experiments below relied exclusively on the back-link method.

The results are shown in Fig. 7. *Accuracy* naturally decreased as the number of search engines increased, but it was still high, about 40%, even on 144 engines. Also, It was almost constant from 90 engines. One of the reasons for this high accuracy is that the nine categories of the 144 engines are not closely related to each other conceptually. In such a set of routing-target search engines, it would be expected that the topic-centric query routing method could operate well even when routing to the larger number of topic-specific search engines.

This experiment, using 144 topic-specific search engines in nine categories, also demonstrated that the proposed query expansion technique that obtains from the Web terms relevant to queries could operate well for a wide variety of queries.

4.3.4. Possibility of practical use

The most important aspect with regard to practical use of the proposed topic-centric query routing method is of course its accuracy. We consider that, as an automated query routing method, the performance of Q-Pilot is good as demonstrated by the experiments conducted in the Sections 4.3.1, 4.3.2 and 4.3.3. However, about 40% accuracy on the 144 search engines might not be high enough for practical Web services. But, even when the wrong engines were selected, most of them were in the same category of the correct engines and were somewhat relevant to the queries. This is supported by other experimental results shown in Fig. 8 and Table 3.

Fig. 8 shows the category selection accuracy when routing the 800 queries to the 144 topic-specific search engines. The category selection accuracy was calculated for the search engines ranked within the top three by Q-Pilot and it denotes the percentage of engines that were in the correct engines' category. As shown in Fig. 8, the category selection accuracy was very high: about 70% when using nine categories.

Table 3 shows the percentage of that topic-specific search engines ranked within the top three by Q-Pilot

Table 3
Percentage of search engines actually having data records relevant to queries (d = 3, 27 topic-specific search engines, 150 test queries)

	QR + QE
Front-page method	68.5
Back-link method	78.6
Database sampling method	83.5 [a]

[a] The index created by the database sampling method consists of terms that the search engine's database actually contains. Therefore, in the Simple_QR, this value will be 100%. In the QR + QE, however, terms obtained through query expansion match the terms in the index and it is not 100%.

actually possess the data records and/or documents relevant to the query. We submitted qb_i (excluded a topic term from the original query q_i) to the selected search engines and examined whether those search engines returned at least one reference. This experiment was conducted on the 27 routing-target engines used in the experiments presented in Sections 4.3.1 and 4.3.2. As shown in Table 3, about 80% of the engines, selected when the back-link method was used, had information relevant to the queries.

It is important to note that 'accuracy' in this paper is defined by the level to which variants of Q-Pilot match the judgements of human users as captured in the Search Broker logs. However, in Table 3 we use a different measure of accuracy (did the engine return results in response to the query?) with higher accuracy figures. Probably, the measurement in Table 3 is overly liberal — just because an engine returned some results doesn't mean that they are actually relevant to the query, so the 'true' accuracy is probably somewhere in the middle between Tables 3 and 1.

Although these results were encouraging, the query routing accuracy depends on the set of topic-specific search engines. If the system would know higher-quality topic-specific search engines, the percentages listed in Table 3 could be better. As for the scalability, if we carefully choose routing-target topic-specific search engines that are independent of each other, both the engine selection accuracy and the category selection accuracy could be still high even when the number of the topic-specific search engines increases. So, in the practical use of the proposed method, how we choose a set of routing-target topic-specific search engines is critical.

Another important aspect is the response time. Current response time of Q-Pilot is 6–7 seconds, not short enough for practical use. The main reason of this long response time is its query expansion process referring the general search engine that can be used only through the Web. If we use a crawler and generate in local storage the index of the Web documents necessary for query expansion, the response time could be shorter. Further reduction of the response time would be possible by performing query expansion in advance for keywords frequently specified by users and making a cache of the query expansion results.

5. Conclusion and future work

This paper presented an automated query routing system Q-Pilot, which routes queries to topic-specific search engines available only through the World Wide Web. Q-Pilot learns topics of the search engines from the existing Web documents and identifies topics of given queries dynamically by query expansion.

Our preliminary experimental results show that the combination of the back-link method and the query expansion technique can yield performance that matches that of conventional query routing techniques, which are based on analyzing the contents of internal databases. We also found that Q-Pilot performs well even when routing queries to the large number (144) of topic-specific search engines. Finally, we showed that the proposed query expansion technique correctly identify the topics of a wide variety of queries. Our results offer a baseline for future research on query routing on the Web.

One direction for future research is the further improvement of the accuracy of query routing. One way to do this is to use user feedback given through the operations of the users who select their intended search engines on the query routing results like those in Fig. 2b. It is expected that the search engine selection index can be optimized by adjusting the weights of the terms contained in the search keywords according to the engines that the user selected.

Another way to improve the accuracy is to rank topic-specific search engines by using collocations. In the case of a query "white paper of …", for example, the current Q-Pilot might give a top rank to the White House search engine, although it should be ranked at the top only when both "white" and "house" are adjacent in a query. Such cases could be avoided by using collocation information when ranking search engines.

Several more experiments should be carried out. The most important one is to examine the performance of Q-Pilot on a substantially larger number of topic-specific search engines. Although the current version of Q-Pilot handles only 144 engines in 9 categories, far more engines are needed to cover all categories and topics. We need to verify that our query routing architecture scales to several thousands of engines, and identify methods of enhancing its accuracy. Also, as mentioned, we should compare the performance of our clustering and phrase extraction methods with that of the standard clustering algorithms and STC algorithm.

Acknowledgements

The authors express their appreciation to Erik Selberg and Liang Sun, who helped develop the system, and to Udi Manber, who kindly provided the experimental data from the Search Broker query log. Thanks are due to Dan Weld and Cody Kwok for discussions on related topics. This research was funded in part by Office of Naval Research grant 98-1-0177, and by National Science Foundation grants IRI-9357772 and DL-9874759.

References

[1] AllSearchEngines.com, http://www.allsearchengines.com/
[2] AltaVista, http://www.altavista.com/
[3] Ask Jeeves, http://www.ask.com/
[4] J.P. Callan, Z. Lu and W.B. Croft, Searching distributed collections with inference networks, in: Proc. SIGIR'95, 1995, pp. 21–29.
[5] Epicurious.com, http://epicurious.com/
[6] S. Gauch, G. Wang and M. Gomez, ProFusion: intelligent fusion from multiple, distributed search engines, J. Univers. Comp. 2 (9) (1996).
[7] L. Gravano, K. Chang, H. Garcia-Molina, C. Lagoze and A. Paepcke, Stanford protocol proposal for Internet search and retrieval, http://www-db.stanford.edu/~gravano/starts.html
[8] L. Gravano, H. Garcia-Molina and A. Tomasic, GlOSS: text-source discovery over the Internet, ACM Trans. Database Syst. (1999).
[9] InvisibleWeb, http://www.invisibleweb.com/
[10] KidsHealth.org, http://www.kidshealth.org/
[11] K.L. Kwok and M. Chan, Improving two-stage ad-hoc retrieval for short queries, in: Proc. SIGIR'98, 1998, pp. 250–256.
[12] L. Liu, Query routing in large-scale digital library systems, Proc. of ICDE'99, 1999.
[13] U. Manber and P.A. Bigot, The Search Broker, in: Proc. 1st Usenix Symp. on Internet Technologies and Systems, 1997.
[14] Search.com, http://www.search.com/
[15] M.A. Sheldon, A. Duda, R. Weiss and D.K. Gifford, Discover: a resource discovery system based on content routing, in: Proc. 3rd Int. World Wide Web Conf., Comp. Networks ISDN Syst. 27 (1995) 953–972.
[16] VacationSpot.com, http://www.vacationspot.com/
[17] Voorhees and M. Ellen, Expanding query vectors with lexically related words, in: Harman (Ed.), 1994, pp. 223–231.
[18] C. Weider, J. Fullton and S. Spero, Architecture of the Whois++ Index Service, RFC1913, 1996.
[19] J. Xu and J. Callan, Effective retrieval with distributed collections, in: Proc. 21st Annual Int. ACM SIGIR Conf. on Research and Development in Information Retrieval, 1998, pp. 112–120.
[20] Yahoo!, http://www.yahoo.com/
[21] O. Zamir and O. Etzioni, Grouper: A dynamic clustering interface to Web search results, in: Proc. 8th Int. World Wide Web Conf., Comp. Networks 31 (1999) 1361–1374.

Atsushi Sugiura received B.E. and M.E. degrees in electric engineering from the University of Osaka in 1988 and 1990. He then joined NEC Corporation, where he is currently an assistant research manager at the C & C Media Research Laboratories. From 1998 to 1999 he was a visiting scientist at Department of Computer Science and Engineering, the University of Washington. His research interests include human computer interactions, visual programming, programming by demonstration, and intelligent software agents.

Oren Etzioni is an associate professor in the Department of Computer Science and Engineering at the University of Washington. He received his Ph.D. from Carnegie Mellon University in 1991. After joining the University of Washington he launched the Internet Softbot project. He received an NSF Young Investigator Award in 1993. His research interests include software agents, Web navigation and search technology, and human–computer interaction. See http://www.cs.washington.edu/homes/etzioni

ADMIRE: an adaptive data model for meta search engines

Lieming Huang [*,1], Matthias Hemmje [1], Erich J. Neuhold [1]

GMD-IPSI, Dolivostraße 15, D-64293 Darmstadt, Germany

Abstract

Considering the diversity among search engines, efficient integration of them is an important but difficult job. It is essential to provide a data model that can provide a detailed description of the query capabilities of heterogeneous search engines. By means of this model, the meta-searcher can map users' queries into specific sources more accurately, and it can achieve good precision and recall. Moreover, it will benefit the selection of target source and computing priority. Because new search engines emerge frequently and old ones are updated when their function and content change, the data model needs good adaptivity and scalability to keep in step with the rapidly developing World Wide Web. This paper gives a formal description of the query capabilities of heterogeneous search engines and an algorithm for mapping a query from a general mediator format into the specific wrapper format of a specific search engine. Compared with related work, the special features of our work are that we focus more on the constraint of/between the terms, attribute order, and the impact of logical operator restraints. The contribution of our work is that we offer a data model that is both expressive enough to meticulously describe the query capabilities of current World Wide Web search engines and flexible enough to integrate them efficiently.

Keywords: Meta search engine; Data model; Wrapper; Mediator; Query capability mapping

1. Introduction

Meta search engines and other agent-based search tools provide a uniform query interface for Internet users to search for information. Depending on users' needs, they select relevant sources and map user queries into the target search engines, subsequently merging the results. However, considering the great diversity in schematic, semantic, interface, and domain aspects, it is very important but quite difficult to make full use of the functions of specific search engines. It is essential to provide a data model that can elaborately describe the query capabilities of World Wide Web search engines. Based on such a data model, a meta search engine can achieve several advantages: (1) it will present to users a more sophisticated query interface rather than a 'Least-Common-Denominator' or mixed interface; (2) it will make the translation of queries from mediators to selected wrappers more accurate; (3) it will let users get more complete and precise results; (4) it will improve source selection and running priority decisions. However, providing a detailed data model means that a more complicated algorithm is needed to cope with the constraints of or between query terms and the restraints of logical operators when translating queries from mediators to specific wrappers.

New search engines appear frequently. Old search engines are updated when their function or content changes. In order to keep up with the rapidly developing Internet, the data model must have good

* Corresponding author.
[1] E-mail: {lhuang, hemmje, Neuhold}@darmstadt.gmd.de

adaptivity and scalability. Designing a good data model is undoubtedly a challenging job.

We have built a meta search engine for users to search for scientific publications in the Internet. This meta search engine employs a 'Mediator–Wrapper' architecture that has been used by many information integration systems. The mediator [28] provides users with integrated access to multiple heterogeneous data sources, while each wrapper represents access to a specific data source. Users formulate queries in line with the mediator's global view that is combined schemas [24] of all sources. Mediators deliver user queries to some relevant wrappers. Each selected wrapper translates user queries into source-specific queries, accesses the data source, and translates the results of the data source into information that can be understood by the mediator. The mediator then merges all results and displays them to users.

ADMIRE (Adaptive Data Model for Integration of seaRch Engines) is a data model that we use to describe the query capabilities of heterogeneous search engines. This kind of information has been extracted from the query interfaces of search engines instead of the schemas of them because most of such internal information cannot be achieved by meta search engines.

This paper is organized as follows. We start by briefly introducing some related work. In Section 3 we first give a formal description of the query input interface of heterogeneous search engines; then we model the query capabilities of three concrete search engines and a corresponding mediator. In Section 4, based on this data model, we describe some problems regarding query mapping, and an algorithm for mapping queries from a general mediator format into the specific wrapper format of a specific search engine. Finally, Section 5 concludes this paper and suggests some future work.

2. Related work

In the Internet there are a lot of meta search engines like **SavvySearch**[2], **Dogpile**[3], **ProFusion®**[4] **Ask Jeeves**[5], **Highway 61**[6], **Cyber411**[7], **Internet Sleuth**[8], **MetaFind**[9], **ONESEEK**[10], **MetaCrawler**[11], **I.SEE**[12], etc. Although they integrate a lot of World Wide Web search engines, most of their user interfaces are too simple. They only use a 'Least-Common-Denominator' user interface and discard some of the rich functionalities of specific search engines. It is difficult for users to input complicated queries and retrieve specific information. This weakness is especially obvious when users want to search for scientific publications or specialized information. 'From the users' perspective the integration of different services is complete only if they are usable without loss of functionality compared to the single services and without handling difficulties when switching from one service to another'[13]. In order to avoid losing important functions of search engines, both generality and particularity should be considered when designing a data model for a meta search engine. Some other meta search engines display the searching controls of all search engines on one page or on several hierarchically organized pages, e.g. **All-in-One**[14] displays many original query interfaces on a single page.

Some systems deal with the description of source query capability. Information Manifold [22] uses capability records that specify five tuples of information with regard to each source (input set, outputs of the source, the selections the source can apply, the minimum and maximum number of inputs allowed), and it gives an algorithm for query planning. Yerneni et al. [29] give five attribute adornments 'f' (for free), 'u' (for unspecifiable), 'b' (for bound), 'c[S]' (for constant), 'o[S]' (for optional) to describe the query capabilities of wrappers and mediators and present algorithms to compute the set of mediator-supported queries based on the capability limitations of its sources. Adali et al. [2] use 'Search Support Spec-

[2] http://www.savvysearch.com
[3] http://www.dogpile.com
[4] http://www.profusion.com
[5] http://www.askjeeves.com
[6] http://www.highway61.com
[7] http://cyber411.com
[8] http://isleuth.com/
[9] http://www.metafind.com
[10] http://www.oneseek.com
[11] http://www.go2net.com/search.html
[12] http://www.cs.rpi.edu/research/isee/
[13] http://www.tu-darmstadt.de/iuk/global-info/sfm-7/
[14] http://www.allonesearch.com

ification' to describe the capabilities of the search engines and discuss query relaxation and transformation. Adali and Bufi [1] use Church–Rosser systems to characterize the query capabilities of information sources. Chang et al. [10] give a detailed description of rewriting predicates like 'contains' and word patterns, 'equals' and phrase patterns, proximity operators. Chang et al. [9] and Chidlovskii et al. [11] introduce algorithms for generating the supported subsuming queries and filters. Tukwila [17] uses adaptive query operators to produce answers quickly, and dynamic collectors to organize access to redundant and overlapping information sources. Chang and Garcia-Molina [8] apply user-defined mapping rules to translate query constraints from the mediator to specific sources and discuss the converting methods between CNF and DNF. Vassalos and Papakonstantinou [27] uses the p-Datalog Language to describe sources and to answer queries. Ariadne [3] uses the LOOM knowledge representation system for modeling data. Other projects (such as Disco [26], MeDoc [6], UniCats [12], METALICA [25], etc.) also make contributions on integrating information from multiple data sources. All these methods more or less address the problems discussed in this paper in certain respects. Some results are very useful for constructing a meta search engine. But they do not consider the following problem: 'the translation of a query will be limited not only by the constraints of some attribute modifiers, but also by the order of terms and the restraints of logical operators'. This problem needs to be considered more elaborately; otherwise, fully exploiting the functions of heterogeneous search engines will be impossible. Because they do not deal with subtle differences comprehensively, most current methods use post-processing to refine the results. On the one hand post-processing costs a lot of CPU time, on the other hand in most cases it is impossible because the meta-searcher cannot acquire the relevant information. Therefore, we should try to make use of the functions of heterogeneous search engines as much as possible. Only thus can we improve the processing speed and achieve more accurate and complete results. This is exactly what meta search engines should do.

Of course, if there are protocols or standardization for query models and interfaces of all search engines and for document construction, perfect realization of meta search engines will be as easy as falling off a log. Although there are a lot of efforts towards laying down all kinds of standards (such as Z39.50 [30], **Dublin Core**[15], GILS [23], STARTS [15], XML, RDF, etc.), for a number of reasons (e.g. a large amount of legacy information, authors unwilling to write articles complying with strict rules, great differences from one domain to another, etc.), these standards are not being applied extensively. With the emergence of XML, some systems are using it to model information sources. MIX (Mediation of Information using XML) [7] uses XML as data model for semi-structured data and exploits the structuring information provided by XML DTDs. Goldman et al. [14] also provides an XML-based data model. Just like Alon Levy [21] points out: "XML without agreed upon DTDs does nothing to support integration at the semantic level. The names and meanings of the tags used in XML documents are arbitrary. As a result, the emergence of XML is fueling activity in various communities to agree on DTDs". Nicholas Kushmerick [19] also says that: "Data-exchange standards such as XML will simplify the information extraction, but they are not widely used. Furthermore, they do not entirely solve the problem, since they force the data consumer to accept the producer's ontological decisions." Such problems will require meta-searchers to translate between different DTDs. We can build our meta search engine based on some attribute sets (such as the metadata elements of Dublin Core, Z39.50-1995 Bib-1 and GILS attribute set), standards of query languages (e.g. the type-101 query of the Z39.50-1995 standards, STARTS protocol) and some information formats (e.g. Harvest SOIFs).

3. Query capability description

There are some commonalities among search engines. At the same time, many differences exist between them. Current meta search engines use these common features to build the integrated query interface and cast away the discrepancies. This will inevitably cause the loss of many important functions. They will spend a lot of time in post-processing the results or simply display all results to users, thus in-

[15] http://purl.oclc.org/dc/

creasing the users' cognitive load. Making full use of the specific functions of search engines will alleviate such weaknesses. In order to accommodate for the frequent emerging of new search engines and updating of old ones, we also demand that our data model be adaptive and scalable enough. In this section, we provide a data model to formally describe the query capabilities of search engines. First, we would like to introduce some basic definitions. Then, we use these definitions to model three concrete examples. Finally, we will present the integrated interface of our mediator.

3.1. General definitions

In the following, we show the query pages of three typical scientific search engines with quite different query capabilities: ACM-Digital Library (see Fig. 1), NCSTRL (Networked Computer Science Technical Reference Library, see Fig. 2) and IDEAL® (International Digital Electronic Access Library, see Fig. 3).

A query expression is constructed using a number of basic elements such as terms, operators and attribute constraints. In the following, we use a 'bottom-up' strategy to introduce 12 definitions, which describe the query elements successively. The first six definitions (Terms, Fields, Qualifiers, Logical Operators, Constant Tree and Constant Set) are directly derived from the query interfaces. They correspond to the basic controls of the query pages like Input box, Check box, Radio box, Pull-down menu, List box, etc. The last six definitions are constructed based on the first six basic definitions.

Definition 1 *(Terms)* . A Term is the content keyed into an input box on the query interface of a search engine. For example, users can key in a single keyword, a phrase, or a Boolean expression in order to search for relevant information. In some cases, the input term may support wildcards, truncation, stemming, it may be case-sensitive, and might drop stop-words, hyphens, diacritics and special characters. This definition is different from the usual meaning of 'term'. This means that even if an input box can be filled with a complex query expression, we still call it a term.

$T = \{T_i\}$

where $1 \leq i \leq N_t$, N_t is the number of terms in which users can input keywords.

Example 1. From Fig. 1, we can see that ACM-DL has six terms in which users can input keywords. Fig. 2 shows that NCSTRL provides four terms; the first term and the other three terms, respectively, belong to two separate forms. In addition, in Fig. 3 we see that IDEAL® Search provides three terms.

Definition 2 *(Fields).* A field limits the scope of a term, i.e. it requires that the provided term has to be contained in the appointed part of the result. 'Fielded search' usually means that keywords provided by users should be found in certain parts of a publication.

$F = \{F_i\}$

where $1 \leq i \leq N_f$, N_f is the number of fields.

Example 2. F = {<Title>, <Full-Text>, <Review>, <Article Keywords>, <Abstract>, <Author>, <Affiliation>, <Date>, <ISBN>, <ISSN>, <Journal Title>, <Citation>, <Editor>, <Anywhere>}.

In Fig. 1 we can see that the first four terms can be limited by arbitrary fields (subset of {<Title>, <Full-Text>, <Review>, <Article Keywords>, <Abstract>}), while the fifth term and the sixth term can only be modified by the <Author> field. In Fig. 2, in the first querying form, the term can be limited by several fields, while in the second form, each term of NCSTRL can only be limited by a certain field. Fig. 3 shows that each term of IDEAL® Search can be limited by one of {<Title>, <Abstract>, <Author>, <Affiliation>, <Date>} or all these five fields. It cannot be limited by a subset of all terms, while ACM-DL can.

Definition 3 *(Qualifiers).* A qualifier is used to describe the quality and form of the term input by users.

$Q = \{Q_i\}$

where $1 \leq i \leq N_q$, N_q is the number of qualifiers.

Example 3. Q = {<Exactly Like>, <Multiple Words>, <Using Stem Expansion>, <Phrase>, <Expression>, <Sound Like>, <Spelled Like>, <Natural Language>}.

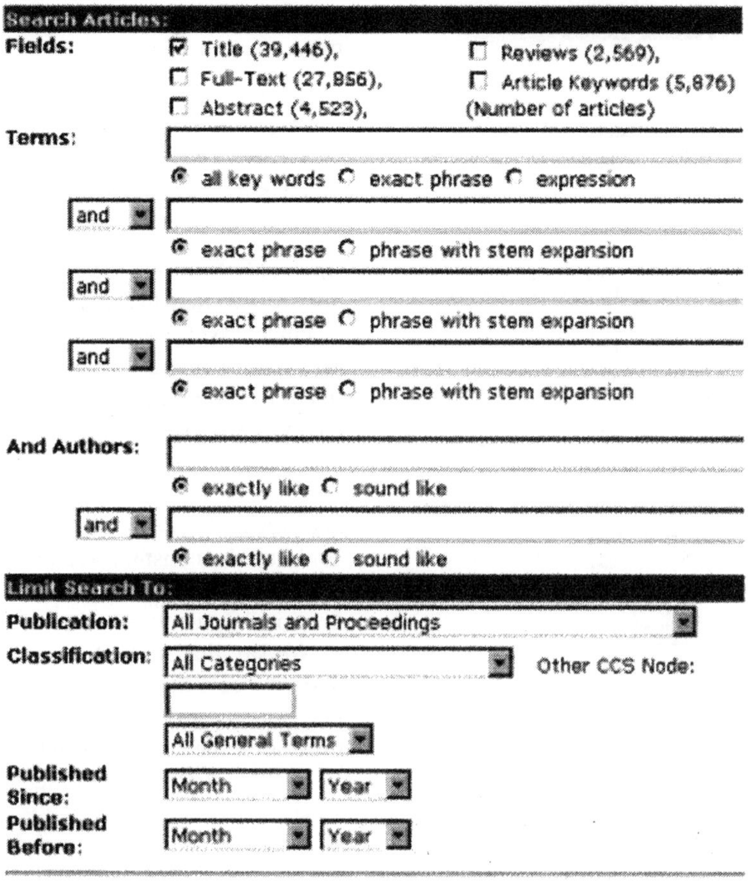

Fig. 1. The query page of ACM-DL.

For ACM-DL, users can select qualifiers from the query page. The first term has three possible qualifiers {<Multiple Words>, <Phrase>, <Expression>}, while each of the other five terms has two qualifiers. For NCSTRL and IDEAL® Search, there are no qualifier controls for users to select. However, from the help files we know that the functions of qualifiers can be embodied in the terms. For example, the phrase qualifier can be applied by using quotation marks (""); wildcard signs like '*' and '?' can be used to express stemming expansion. We can define some rules in specific wrappers for translating query expressions. For some search engines, the qualifiers of some terms can be <Expression>. At first, it seems that query mapping is easy. Unfortunately, each term will be limited by 'Fields', and in the meantime, the expression in a term will be limited by the same 'Fields'. The mapping problem for this case will be discussed in Section 4. In Chang et al. [10], there is a deep-going discussion about the conversion of qualifiers and qualified terms. However, it does not consider the constraints imposed by 'Fields'.

Definition 4 *(Logical Operators).* A Logical Operator is used to combine logically two terms to perform a search, the results of which are then evaluated for relevance.

$L = \{L_i\}$

where $1 \leq i \leq N_l$, N_l is the number of logical operators.

Example 4. $L = \{\wedge, \vee, \neg, \sim\}$, where $\wedge$ means AND, $\vee$ means OR, $\neg$ means NOT, $\sim$ means NEAR.

Each logical operator has its own 'sphere of action'; it can only join two terms. Some search en-

Fig. 2. The query page of NCSTRL.

gines have stricter restrictions for logical operators. For example, the two logical operators of NCSTRL must have the same value and can only be 'AND' or 'OR'. This will greatly hinder the query mapping process. We must decompose the original query expression into equivalent sub-query expressions or minimal subsuming query sub-expressions. In Chang et al. [9], there is a detailed discussion about the general transformation of the users' queries into a subsuming query by the conversion of DNF and CNF. It does not cope with the constraints of fields and qualifiers on the terms.

Definition 5 *(Constant Trees)*. A constant tree is a hierarchical classification of constant attributes that cannot be modified by users. Users can only select one or some of them to limit the search results. The constant tree is often implemented by using a list box with multiple items.

$$\text{ConstTree} = \{\text{Node}_i\}$$

where $1 \leq i \leq N_{\text{ConstTree}}$, $N_{\text{ConstTree}}$ is the number of attributes in this tree.

The following is a BNF definition of constant tree:

ConstTree ::= Node SubTree
SubTree ::= {IncludeOrNot, ConstTree
(, ConstTree)* }|ε
IncludeOrNot ::= +|−
Node ::= attribute

'IncludeOrNot=+' means that the parent node of a current sub-tree has a value that is not null, while 'IncludeOrNot=−' means that the parent node has no value. For example, NCSTRL only contains publications from the fields of computer science and technology, so it does not contain the parent node 'All categories' (the root node in this case). It can be denoted as '<All Categories> {-,<Computer Science and Technology> {+,<Software>,<Hardware>...}}'. Building the constant tree in such a way will benefit the integration of information and query mapping. In Section 3.3, we will further discuss it.

We say that node A is an ancestor of node B if node A has a higher position than node B and there is a direct path (not passing through a node higher than or on the same level with node A) from node A to B. Node B is called a descendant of node A.

Example 5. ConstTree = {Category ConstTree, Publication ConstTree}; Fig. 4 displays an example of a Category ConstTree.

Definition 6 *(Constant Sets)*. A constant set is a one-dimensional set consisting of some attributes that cannot be modified by users. A constant set is often implemented by using check boxes, radio boxes, or pull-down menus.

$$\text{ConstSet} = \{\text{Element}_i\}$$

where $1 \leq i \leq N_{\text{ConstSet}}$, N_{ConstSet} is the number of elements in this set. ConstSet is a special case of ConstTree.

Example 6. ConstSet = {Sorting Criteria ConstSet, Grouping Size ConstSet}.
Sorting Criteria ConstSet = {<Relevance ranking>, <Author>, <Date>, <Institution>, <Title>, <Journal>}.
Grouping Size ConstSet = {<10>,<20>,<30>,<50>, <100>}.

1 Select Collection:

◉ IDEAL®

○ PubMed™ (Medline)

2 Limit Your Search:

Select IDEAL Category:

(All Categories)

Categories only apply to IDEAL

Select Journal:

(All Journals)

Choosing a journal overrides the Category selection

IDEAL® Search Help

3 Select Fields, Terms, Operators, and Output Options:

Field(s) to Search: Enter Search Term(s):

Search All fields for and

All fields for and

All fields for

Display in groups of: 10 Sort by: Relevance

4 Submit:

Search

Reset

Fig. 3. The query page of IDEAL® Search.

As for the <Relevance ranking> in Sorting Criteria ConstSet, because each search engine has its own algorithm for computing relevance, we cannot rearrange all items when merging results from various search engines. Gravano and Garcia-Molina [16] provide a detailed discussion of the merging of ranked result lists from heterogeneous sources. With regard to Grouping Site ConstSet, if a wrapper does not have the same value, we can use a nearest value and finally use buffer technology to satisfy user demands.

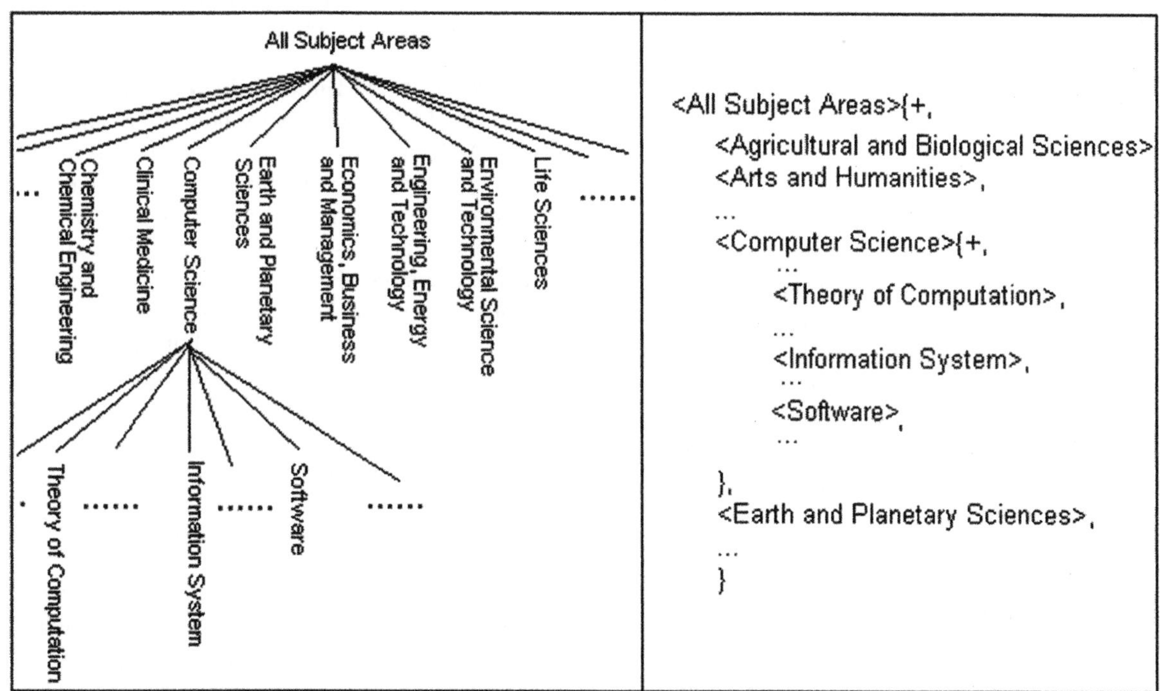

Fig. 4. Example of category ConstTree.

Definition 7 *(Constant Terms).* A Constant Term is a term that cannot be modified but only selected by users. This constant term can be a Constant Tree or a Constant Set:

ConstTerm = ConstTree | ConstSet

Definition 8 *(Logical Expressions).* A Logical Expression $\overline{\text{Exp}}_i$ is constructed by one or more Terms T_j (in some special cases it can also be a Constant Term, ConstTerm_k) combined by logical operators L. $\overline{\text{Exp}}_i = T_1\theta_1 T_2 \ldots \theta_{k-1} T_k$, where $k \geq 1$; Field $(T_i) \subseteq F$; Qualifier $(T_i) \in Q$; $1 \leq i \leq k$; $\theta_j \in L$; $1 \leq j \leq (k-1)$.

Definition 9 *(Sequential Boolean Expressions).* Some search engines interpret the logical expression $\overline{\text{Exp}}_i$ by order. If $\overline{\text{Exp}}_i = T_1\theta_1 T_2 \ldots \theta_{k-1} T_k = ((\ldots(T_1\theta_1 T_2)\theta_2 T_3) \ldots \theta_{k-1} T_k)$, we call the logical expression $\overline{\text{Exp}}_i$ a *Sequential Boolean Expression* denoted by $\textbf{SEQ}(\overline{\text{Exp}}_i)$.

Definition 10 *(Priority Operators).* We use the $\prec$ sign as a priority operator, and $\alpha \prec \beta$ denotes that α has a higher priority than β. We also use the following signs to denote all other kinds of priority operators accordingly: $\succ, \preceq, \succeq, \not\prec, \not\succ$.

Definition 11 *(Priority Boolean Expressions).* Some search engines compute a logical expression $\overline{\text{Exp}}_i$ by some stipulated priority rules, such as $\wedge \prec \vee$, $\neg \prec \vee$, $\sim\prec \vee$, $\wedge \not\prec \neg$, etc. In this case we call the logical expression $(\overline{\text{Exp}}_i)$ a *Priority Boolean Expression* denoted by $\textbf{PRI}(\overline{\text{Exp}}_i)$.

Many search engines interpret the query expression sequentially. Our mediator has the choice of interpreting the query expression by priority or sequentially. If the query expression is based on priority, we will transform the query expression into disjunctive form; each sub-expression is a conjunctive expression or a single term. We will further discuss it in Section 4.

Definition 12 *(Query Expressions).* A *Query Expression* $\overline{Q}$ is a conjunction of logical expressions or Constant Terms:

$$\overline{Q}\left\{\sum_{i=1}^{n}(\Phi_i(\overline{\text{Exp}}_i(T_{i_1}\theta_{i_1}\ldots\theta_{i_{k-1}}T_{i_k}))), \sum_{j=1}^{m}\text{ConstTerm}_j\right\}$$

where $n \geq 1, m \geq 0$; $i_k \geq 1$.

- $\Phi_i \in \{\textbf{SEQ}, \textbf{PRI}\}$, $1 \leq i \leq n$; Field $(T_{i_l}) \subseteq F$, $1 \leq i_l \leq i_k$, C_F;
- Qualifier $(T_{i_l}) \in Q$, $1 \leq i_l \leq i_k$, C_Q; $\theta_{i_l} \in L$, $1 \leq i_l \leq i_{k-1}$, C_θ;
- $\text{ConstTerm}_j \in \text{ConstTerm}$.

Here C_F, C_Q, C_θ mean some special constraints for each adornment. They alter along with the changes of various wrappers. For example, from Fig. 2, C_θ is "$\theta_1 = \theta_2$". $\overline{Q}$ can also be denoted as a tuple

$$\overline{Q} = \overline{Q}(\overline{\text{Exp}}_1, \ldots, \overline{\text{Exp}}_n, \text{ConstTerm}_1, \ldots, \text{ConstTerm}_m).$$

3.2. Wrapper modeling for some examples

Many institutions provide search engines for Internet users to search through publication information, for example ACM-DL, NCSTRL, IDEAL®, Kluwer, Elsevier, etc. Each search engine collects its own publications. Perhaps there are some overlapping publications, for example: ACM-DL and NCSTRL.

In the following, we provide a description of some publication search engines. We let Fields F be as in Example 2; Qualifiers Q as in Example 3; Logical Operators L as in Example 4.

Example 7. ACM Digital Library[16], see Fig. 1.

The ACM Digital Library now offers about 95% of all ACM articles and proceedings back to 1991. A query expression is built through the combination of terms (the specified words or phrases, wildcards '%'), search options (Contains phrase/Exactly Like, Stem expansion, Fuzzy expansion/Spelled Like, Sounds Like) and Logical Operators (AND, OR, NOT, NEAR). A query can be limited through the selection of the various categories presented. The refinement of a query is performed to further narrow down the result set obtained from a previous query. This result set is used as the scope within which the new query will run. A query can continue to be refined until the desired result is achieved.

$$\overline{Q}^{w}_{\text{acm}} = \{\textbf{PRI}(\overline{\text{Exp}}_1(T_{1_1}T_{1_1}Q_{1_1}T_{1_2}Q_{1_2}T_{1_3}Q_{1_3}T_{1_4})), \textbf{PRI}(\overline{\text{Exp}}_2(T_{2_1}Q_2T_{2_2})), T_3, \text{Publication ConstTree}, \text{Classification ConstTree}\}$$

[16] http://www.acm.org/dl/newsearch.html

where

- Field (T_{1_i}) $\subseteq$ {<Title>, <Full-Text>, <Review>, <Article Keywords>, <Abstract>}, $1 \le i \le 4$;
  Field (T_{2_i}) = <Author>, $1 \le i \le 2$;
  Field (T_3) = <Date>;
- Qualifier (T_{1_1}) $\in$ {<Multiple Words>, <Phrase>, <Expression>};
  Qualifier (T_{1_i}) $\in$ {<Using Stem Expansion>, <Phrase>}, $2 \le i \le 4$;
  Qualifier (T_{2_1}) $\in$ {<Exactly Like>, <Sounds Like>}, $1 \le i \le 2$;
- $\theta_{1_i} \in L, 1 \le i \le 3; \theta_2 \in \{\wedge, \vee\}$;
- Publication ConstTree = <All Publications> {-,<All Journals and Proceedings of the ACM> {+,<Communications of the ACM>, <Computing Surveys>, ...}}
- Classification ConstTree = <All Categories> {-,<Computer Science & Technology> {+,<Software>,<Theory of Computation>, ...}}

Here term T_3 is limited by the <Date> field. However, from Fig. 1, we can see that there are four pull-down menus (two for 'Month ConstSet', two for 'Year ConstSet') for this term. The translation will be carried out by human-defined rules in a wrapper. The field modifier of term T_{1_i} can be a subset of all fields. This is the characteristic which distinguishes ACM-DL the most from other scientific search engines.

Example 8. NCSTRL[17], see Fig. 2.

NCSTRL (Networked Computer Science Technical Reference Library) is an international collection of computer science research reports and papers made available for non-commercial use from a number of participating institutions and archives. NCSTRL is based on Dienst [20], which is a protocol and server that provides distributed document libraries over the World Wide Web. Dienst is based on a document model that incorporates unique document names, multiple document formats, and multiple document decompositions.

$$\overline{Q}^{w}_{\mathrm{ncstrl},1} = \{T_1, \text{Sorting ConstSet}, \text{Category ConstTree}\}$$

where

- Field (T_1) $\subseteq$ {<Author>, <Title>, <Abstract>}.

$$\overline{Q}^{w}_{\mathrm{ncstrl},2} = \{\mathbf{SEQ}(\overline{\mathrm{Exp}}(T_2\theta_1 T_3\theta_2 T_4)), \text{Sorting ConstSet}, \text{Category ConstTree}\}$$

where

- Field (T_2) = <Author>; Field (T_3) = <Title>; Field (T_4) = <Abstract>;
- Qualifier (T_i) $\in$ {<Exactly Like>, <Multiple Words>, <Using Stem Expansion>, <Phrase>}, $2 \le i \le 4$;
- $\theta_i \in \{\wedge, \vee\}, 1 \le i \le 2, \theta_1 = \theta_2$;
- Sorting ConstSet = {<Rank>, <Author>, <Date>, <Institution>, <Title>};
- Category ConstTree = <Computer Science & Technology>.

Each of the search engines of ACM-DL and IDEAL® has only one query form. Therefore, there is only one query expression for each of them. In NCSTRL, there are two separate query forms. The first query form allows users to search keywords in all fields, while in the second one, users must limit the keywords to a specific field.

Example 9. IDEAL® search[18], see Fig. 3.

IDEAL® (International Digital Electronic Access Library) is an online electronic library containing 174 Academic Press journals. IDEAL® covers 11 categories (Biomedical Science, Business and Law, Engineering, Social Sciences, etc.). If users find that an article in the returned results is close to what they are searching for, clicking 'More Like This' will perform a new search using the full article as the basis for the search.

$$\overline{Q}^{w}_{\mathrm{ideal}} = \{\mathbf{SEQ}(\overline{\mathrm{Exp}}(T_1\theta_1 T_2\theta_2 T_3)), \text{CategoryConstTree}, \text{JournalConstTree}, \text{Grouping ConstSet}, \text{Sorting ConstSet}\}$$

where

- Field (T_i) $\in$ {<Anywhere>, <Title>, <Abstract>, <Author>, <Affiliation>, <Date>}, $1 \le i \le 3$;
- Qualifier (T_i) $\in$ {<Exactly Like>, <Multiple Words>, <Using Stem Expansion>, <Phrase>}, $1 \le i \le 3$;
- $\theta_i \in \{\wedge, \vee, \neg\}, 1 \le i \le 2$;

[17] http://www.ncstrl.org/

[18] http://search.idealibrary.com/europe

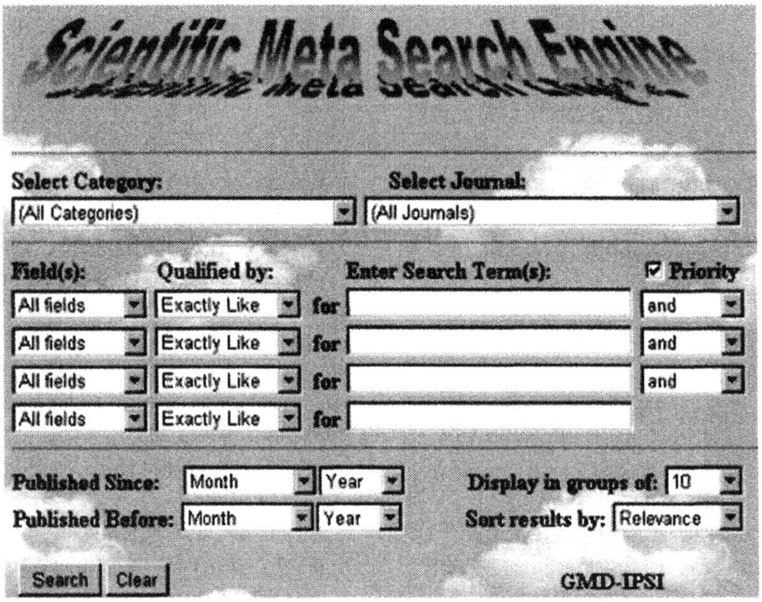

Fig. 5. The query page of a mediator.

- Category ConstTree = <All Categories> {+, <Biomedical Sciences>, <Business and Law>, <Computer Science>, <Economics and Financing>,...};
- Journal ConstTree = <All Publications> {-, <All Journals and Proceedings of the IDEAL®> {+, <Advances in Applied Mathematics>, <Animal Behavior>,...}};
- Grouping ConstSet = {10, 20, 50, 100};
- Sorting ConstSet = {<Relevance ranking>, <Date>, <Journal>}.

From the above three examples (7, 8 and 9), we know there are many common and different points between search engines. Some provide rich and complicated functions, while others have simple functions. Controls of some search engines are less limited, while controls of other search engines are limited by all kinds of constraints. Only if all these features are understood by a meta search engine can it achieve better performance.

We have used Definition 12 (Query Expression) to describe the query capabilities of search engines. The implementation described in the following will demonstrate that this data model can describe an integration of the capabilities of several search engines and that it is also efficient to be used for query mapping.

3.3. Description of the mediator's query capability

3.3.1. Mediator

Fig. 5 displays the query interface of a meta search engine for scientific publications. This mediator integrates several famous scientific search engines such as the three which are introduced in Section 3.2, Elsevier, Kluwer, etc.

In Fig. 5, there is a check box on the right in the center part of the query page. If it is checked, the query expression will be interpreted by priority; otherwise, the query expression will be interpreted sequentially. Usually, users' query expressions are in disjunctive form like ((**A** *AND* **B**) *OR* (**C** *AND* **D**)). This kind of expression can be interpreted by priority. The sequential explanation of the example is (((**A** *AND* **B**) *OR* **C**) *AND* **D**), which has a different meaning from the original expression. In some cases, users' information needs must be expressed in conjunctive form like (**A** *AND* (**B** *OR* **C** *OR* **D**)). In our mediator, this example can be expressed in the form (**B** *OR* **C** *OR* **D** *AND* **A**), which has the same meaning as the original expression if interpreted in sequential order. Because of the space limitations of a query page, users cannot express queries that are more complicated. In Section 3.3.3, we can see that the progressive query interface will solve this problem to some extent. The conjunctive expression can be transformed into a disjunctive expression and vice versa.

In a sense, a mediator can be regarded as a union of all wrappers. In each wrapper, there is almost no conflict between controls (terms, fields, qualifiers and logical operators). However, for a mediator, there will inevitably exist all kinds of conflicts. For example, the term limited by the <Date> field should not be modified by <Sounds Like> or <Using Stem Expansion>. In order to reduce users' cognitive load, the query interface of the mediator should consist of only some common controls. It is really a dilemma. If the mediator's interface is too general, it will not make full use of the specific functions of wrappers. Therefore, we must define some rules to evaluate the expression. There are two ways to control the conflicts. The first method is to embed these rules in the querying interface on the client side; when users select one of the controls on the page, these rules will check if there will be a conflict, if so, then alert users. The second method is to analyze users' queries at the server. If there are serious conflicts, the system will let the users redo them; otherwise, if there are only some small conflicts, the system will correct them.

The query expression of the mediator can be described as follows:

$$\overline{Q}_{\text{med}} = \{\Phi(\overline{\text{Exp}}(T_1\theta_1 T_2\theta_2 T_3\theta_3 T_4)),$$

CategoryConstTree, Publication ConstTree,

Grouping Size ConstSet, Sorting Criteria ConstSet}

where

- $\Phi \in$ {**PRI**, **SEQ**}; Field $(T_i) \in F$, Qualifier $(T_i) \in Q, 1 \le i \le 4; \theta_j \in L, 1 \le j \le 3$;
- MediatorConstTerm $= \bigcup_{i-1}^{n}$ WrapperConstTerm$_i$.

3.3.2. Construction of the mediator's ConstTerm

Fig. 6 depicts how to construct the corresponding ConstTree of the mediator from the ConstTrees of all wrappers. While each search engine only refers to one or more special fields, some publishing houses refer to the knowledge of almost all domains. For example, the third wrapper ConstTree in Fig. 6 is an instance of a search engine that only offers publications in the field of Artificial Intelligence. Its parent node is <Computer Science> and its grandparent node is <All Categories> (i.e. the root node). It is denoted as 'A{-, C{-, I}}'. Because search engines change easily, the ConstTrees of the mediator will adapt themselves to such changes. In the implementation, we use the B-Tree data structure to represent the ConstTree.

3.3.3. Progressive and customizable query interface

Just like most other meta search engines, at the present time we build the query interface of our mediator as a static HTML page (see Fig. 5). Although such a user interface is easy to create and maintain, it lacks flexibility and the interactive nature of an information retrieval dialogue between users and the system. The functionality offered to the users is also limited. On the one hand, we do not want to provide

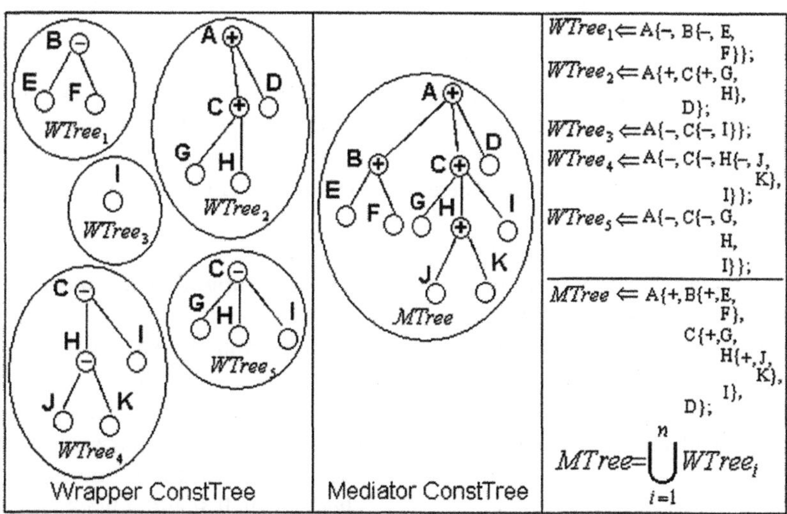

Fig. 6. Construction of the mediator's ConstTree from ConstTrees of wrappers.

the users with an unwieldy interface filled with all kinds of controls that will make the users' heads swim. On the other hand, we cannot simply extract some common attributes from most heterogeneous search engines to provide the users with a simplified interface that will not satisfy some specific information needs. During the information retrieval dialogue, the expression of the users' information needs is a self-refining process. Therefore, it is necessary to design a flexible and progressive query interface that is capable of supporting the iterative and self-refining nature of an interactive IR dialogue.

The search engine of **Elsevier Science**[19] provides such a progressive HTML query page. The start query page consists of only one input box with a pull-down menu of field modifiers (also including Category ConstTree, Publication ConstTree and Grouping Size ConstSet). Besides, there is a link 'ADD MORE FIELDS'. When users want to add additional criteria to the search, they can click this link, then the second page appears. This page has two input boxes, two field modifiers and one logical operator. If users need to add more additional criteria to the search, they can click this link many times until they have finished the query construction. In consideration of the disadvantages of the static HTML page, there are some efforts towards building graphical user interfaces for meta-searchers. In the MIX system [7], the user interface BBQ (Blended Browsing and Querying, which is driven by the mediator view DTD) allows users to define a query by clicking, dragging and dropping of visual objects. 'SenseMaker' [5], an interface for information exploration running on the **InfoBus**[20], utilizes an interactive, structure-mediated approach. It supports the context-driven evolution of a user's interests [4]. AQUA [18] provides a progressive user interface written in a Java applet.

For a progressive query interface, the starting page usually consists of some common controls just like the 'Least-Common-Denominator' interface supported by most search engines. During the user query process, the query pages change according to users' needs until the query is finished. Therefore, this kind of query interface has the advantages of both a simple and a sophisticated query interface. Sometimes users only need a simple interface to input keyword(s) without any extra controls. But sometimes users want to input complicated queries and they will complain about the lack of input controls.

A conjunctive query expression based on priority is difficult to implement in an HTML page because there is no bracket mechanism to improve the priority, e.g. '**A** *AND* (**B** *OR* **C**)' <> '**A** *AND* **B** *OR* **C**'. A progressive interface will also be good for the generation of such expressions. We can use some visual tools to help users to generate complicated priority-based query expressions. For example, users can implement it by manipulating the tree control or dragging and dropping of visual objects.

Because the users of a meta search engine come from all kinds of application areas, it is favorable for users to be able to personalize their user interface. For example, some people have interests only in the field of computer science. In this case the meta search engine has to provide users with functionality to customize the query interface, such as selecting some relevant search engines and category items of some general-purpose search engines. Users can also set up other parameters like sorting criteria, grouping size, quality of results (layout, file format, field selection, etc.). When a user customizes the interface to a certain extent, the resulting interface will be limited to some specific search engines. Therefore, the meta search engine will provide the function of customization and the possibility for users to save often-used query templates.

Both the progression support and the customization mechanism require that mediators have to become more flexible. However, no matter how the query page changes, we can use query expression (Definition 12) to describe its query capabilities.

4. Query capability mapping

In Section 3, we use the query expression to describe the capabilities of wrappers and mediator. Based on this data model, we now introduce how the meta search engine answers users' queries. When a user submits a query, the meta search engine first checks which search engines may have relevant answers to the user's query; then it maps the user's

[19] http://www.elsevier.nl/inca/search/

[20] http://www-giglib.stanford.edu/diglib/

query to wrappers for all selected sources and dispatches the transformed queries to the corresponding sources. Then it post-processes the results from each source; finally all results are merged and displayed to the user.

4.1. Source selection

When mapping a query, if a node <A> in a mediator's ConstTree is the same as or is the descendant node of a node <B> of a wrapper's ConstTree, attribute <A> will match to this wrapper.

When a user has finished the query construction and submits it, the meta search engine's mediator will judge which search engines will be used to answer the user's query. If the number of relevant search engines is large, the running priority order will also be decided. The rough description of the algorithm of source selection is shown in Table 1.

For source selection, Dreilinger and Howe [13] use a meta-index approach which is a matrix (where the number of rows is the number of terms that have been used and the number of columns is the number of search engines). The meta-index tracks the effectiveness of each search engine in responding to previous queries. The meta-index grows as new terms are encountered. This method judges if a search engine will support a keyword based on experience. But because the contents of a search engine's collection and index always change, yesterday a search engine may have found 0 hits for the term 'Artificial Intelligence', and today it may add some new papers on AI, but the meta search engine still excludes this search engine on the basis of the history records. The method of using experience can quicken source selection. For example, a search engine focusing on publications on mathematics cannot support some terms from chemistry fields. Therefore, we can build a thesaurus to record some often-used terms from various fields and map these terms to some search engines.

4.2. Query mapping algorithm

Because the conjunctive expression in sequential order can be transformed internally into a disjunctive expression fitting priority explanation, we assume the query expression of the mediator is interpreted in priority order. How can we map such a query expression to a query understood by a specific search engine? First, the query expression has to be transformed into a standard disjunctive expression where the left part consists of some sets of conjunctive sub-expressions, while the right part consists of some sets of single terms; then we map all ConstTerms to the corresponding ones of the specific wrapper. After that, we map the main part of the query expression; for each of the sub-expressions of the wrapper and each of the sub-expressions of the mediator, the meta search engine will check if they are compatible, if true then it maps this sub-expression. Otherwise the meta search engine will rearrange the order of terms or decompose the sub-expression into several smaller sub-expressions (equivalent or minimal subsuming), then continue checking the compatibility and continue the mapping. Finally, the meta search

Table 1
Rough description of the algorithm of source selection

```
SetofSource ← φ
bLimit ← FALSE
FOR (each of some important ConstTrees (such like Publication ConstTree and Category ConstTree))
    IF (a user selects items from one or more constant trees)
        FOR (each of all items the user selects)
            Check if the term that the user inputs is (or is a descendant of) a node of corresponding ConstTree of each
            source wrapper
                IF (TRUE)
                    SetofSource ← this source wrapper
                    Rearrange the order of SetofSource by computing similarity points
                bLimit ← TRUE
IF (bLimit ≡ FALSE) // This means that the user does not have any limits on search results
    SetofSource ← All source wrappers
```

engine post-processes the results. This post-processing is not merely the union of all results. It will furthermore consider the former decomposition of the query expression and users' selections that the search engine cannot support.

First we suppose the query expression of the mediator (i.e. users' query expressions) is:

$$\overline{Q}_{\text{med}} = \left\{ \mathbf{PRI}(\overline{\text{Exp}}(T_1\theta_1 \ldots \theta_{k-1}T_k)), \sum_{j=1}^{m} \text{ConstTerm}_j \right\}$$

where $k \geq 1, m \geq 0$; Field $(T_i) \in F, 1 \leq i \leq k$

- Qualifier $(T_i) \in Q$, $1 \leq i \leq k$; $\theta_i \in L$, $1 \leq i \leq k-1$; $\text{ConstTerm}_j \in$ ConstTerm

and the query expression of selected source wrapper is as Definition 12.

The following is the sketchy algorithm for translating a query expression from the mediator to a selected source wrapper. Here we ignore the coordination of conflicts from schematic, semantic and operational aspects, such as measuring and naming conventions (e.g. different expressions of date type: 19.11.1999 = 11/19/1999; different scaling methods: some systems use values between [0, 1] to denote the relevance, while some use values between [0, 100]). Some search engines can return all information about an entry in one time, while some search engines require users to visit their server more than one time, e.g. **Cora**[21] (Computer Science Research Paper Search Engine) only returns the title, authors and abstract fields and links to a Postscript file and BibTeXEntry. The meta search engine needs to revisit the Cora search engine to get the information about book title and publishing date by following the link 'BibTeXEntry'; and the URL of this 'BibTeXEntry' is determined by session number and the id of this entry found on the previous result. The following algorithm supposes that all these kinds of translations and transformations are realized inside each wrapper.

Step 1. Rewrite the mediator query expression $\overline{\text{Exp}}(T_1\theta_1 \ldots \theta_{k-1}T_k)$ as the disjunctive form:

$$\bigcup_{i=1}^{N'_m} \left(\bigcap_{j=S_p(i)}^{E_p(i)} T_j^m \right) \cdot \bigcup \cdot \bigcup_{l=k'+1}^{k} T_l^m$$

[21] http://www.cora.justresearch.com/

where

- N'_m means the number of conjunctive ($\wedge$, $\neg$, $\sim$) sub-expressions,
- $S_p(i)$ means the start position of the ith conjunctive sub-expression,
- $E_p(i)$ means the end position of the ith conjunctive sub-expression,
- $S_p(1) = 1$; $E_p(N'_m) = k'$; $S_p(i+1) = E_p(i) + 1$; $E_p(i) - S_p(i) \geq 2$

The rewritten form consists of two parts: the first part is $N'_m (\geq 0)$ conjunctive sub-expression(s); the second part is $(k - k')$ SingleTerms.

Step 2. For each of the ConstTerms in the mediator, the meta search engine will check if the user has selected one or more items. If the user has done so and the selected item(s) can be mapped into the corresponding ConstTree of the wrapper, then fill in the query parameters of the source wrapper using user-selected value or ancestor of the user's selected value; otherwise, fill in the default value (for ConstTree, it is often the value of the root node).

Step 3 (see Table 2). Considering that the constraints of field modifiers, term qualifiers and logical operators, the function MatchSubQE($\overline{\text{ME}}$, $\overline{\text{WE}}$, $*\overline{S}_i$) judges whether the sub-query expression $\overline{\text{ME}}$ can match $\overline{\text{WE}}$, or after changing the order of the elements in $\overline{\text{ME}}$ can $\overline{\text{ME}}$ match $\overline{\text{WE}}$? If so, return TRUE and $*\overline{S}_i$ is the reorganized sub-expression; else return FALSE. Table 3 shows the brief description of this function.

4.3. An example and some problems of query mapping

Example 10. Suppose that a user wants to search for publications as follows. ((Author is 'Tom Bush') AND ('Information Retrieval' in All fields) OR (Title contains 'User Interface') AND (('Metadata', 'XML') in Keywords)) in the Computer Science category, published during the period of 1997 and 1999, the results to be sorted by date.

- T_1^m = 'Tom Bush', Field(T_1^m) = <Author>, Qualifier(T_1^m) = <Exactly Like>;
- T_2^m = 'Information Retrieval', Field(T_2^m) $\in F$, Qualifier(T_2^m) = <Phrase>;

Table 2
Step 3 of the query mapping algorithm

01. int N_S = the number of the selected search engine(SE)'s sub-expressions
02. FOR ($i = 1$; $i \leq N'_m$; $i++$) /* The initial value of N'_m comes from step 1, and it may change during this cycle.*/
03. $\overline{\text{ME}} = \bigcap_{l=S_p(i)}^{E_p(i)} T_l^m$
04. BOOLEAN SendTag = FALSE
05. FOR ($j = 1$; $j \leq N_S$; $j++$)
06. $\overline{\text{WE}} = \Phi_j(\overline{\text{Exp}}_j^w(T_{j_1}\theta_{j_1}\ldots\theta_{j_{k-1}}T_{j_k}))$
07. IF (MatchSubQE($\overline{\text{ME}}$, $\overline{\text{WE}}$, $*\overline{S}_i$))
08. FOR ($n = 1$; $n \leq$ (NumberOf($\overline{\text{WE}}$) – NumberOf($\overline{S}_i$)); $n++$)
09. IF (NotEmpty(SingleTermSet) AND ($\notin$ a SingleTerm$\overline{\text{ST}} \in$ SingleTermSet and it is fit for the constraint conditions (or after relaxing them) of the slot in this SE, such as Field($\overline{\text{ST}}$) $\in / \subseteq$ Field(T_{j_n}), $\theta_{j_{n-1}}$ can be set as $\vee$, etc.))
10. Append $\overline{\text{ST}}$ to $\overline{S}_i$ ($T_{j_n} \leftarrow \overline{\text{ST}}$; Field($T_{j_n}$) $\leftarrow$ Field($\overline{\text{ST}}$; $\theta_{j_{n-1}} \leftarrow \vee$; etc.)
11. Remove $\overline{\text{ST}}$ from the SingleTermSet
12. ELSE Break FOR n
13. Dispatch this newly generated SE sub-expression $\overline{S}_i$
14. SendTag = TRUE
15. Break FOR j
16. IF (SendTag $\equiv$ FALSE)
17. $\overline{S}_i \leftarrow \emptyset$;
18. Use function Decompose($\overline{\text{ME}}$, $*p$, $**\overline{S}_i$, $*q$, $**\overline{\text{ST}}$) to decompose $\overline{\text{ME}}$ into p sub-expressions that meet the limitations of the N_S sub-expressions and q single terms; /* int $p \geq 0$; int $q \geq 0$ */
19. Append these p newly generated sub-expressions to the unchecked set of mediator sub-expressions; $N'_m += p$; /* Therefore, the FOR(i) cycle will be extended. */
20. Put these q single terms into SingleTermSet
21. IF (NotEmpty(SingleTermSet))
22. Divide these remaining single terms into h ($h \geq 1$) groups. Each group will meet the limitations (or after broadening the term's modifiers) of one of the N_S sub-expressions. Some groups each contains several single terms combined by logical operator $\vee$, other groups each contains only one single term.
23. Dispatch these h sub-expressions: $\overline{S}_{i+1}, \overline{S}_{i+2}, \ldots, \overline{S}_{i+h}$
24. Result $\Leftarrow$ Post-processing ($\sum \overline{\text{WE}}_i$)

Table 3
Brief description of the Boolean MatchSubQE($\overline{\text{ME}}$, $\overline{\text{WE}}$, $*\overline{S}_i$) function

01. Boolean tag = TRUE
02. For (int $j = 1$; $j \leq$ NumberOf($\overline{\text{ME}}$); $j++$)
03. int $k = 1$
04. While ($k \leq$ NumberOf($\overline{\text{WE}}$) && tag)
05. If ((all modifiers of T_j^m in $\overline{\text{ME}}$) $\in / \subseteq$ (the relevant modifiers of T_k^w in $\overline{\text{WE}}$))
06. If (Empty($*\overline{S}_i \cdot T_k$) && ($\theta_{k-1}^w$ can be set as θ_{j-1}^m))
07. $*\overline{S}_i \cdot T_k \leftarrow T_j^m$; Modifiers ($*\overline{S}_i \cdot T_k$) $\leftarrow$ Modifiers(T_j^m); $*\overline{S}_i \cdot \theta_{k-1} \leftarrow \theta_{j-1}^m$
08. Else if ((<Multiple Word> $\in$ Qualifier($*\overline{S}_i \cdot T_k$)) && ($*\overline{S}_i \cdot \theta_{k-1} \equiv \theta_{j-1}^m$))
09. Append T_j^m to $*\overline{S}_i \cdot T_k$
10. Else tag = FALSE
11. Else tag = FALSE
12. $k++$
13. if (!tag) return FALSE
14. return TRUE

- T_3^m = 'User Interface', Field(T_3^m) = <Title>, Qualifier(T_3^m) = <Phrase>;
- T_4^m = 'Metadata, XML', Field(T_4^m) = <Keywords>, Qualifier(T_4^m) = <Multiple Words>;
- θ_1^m = <AND>, θ_2^m = <OR> and θ_3^m = <AND>

Now we map this query expression into the wrapper of the NCSTRL search engine. By using the algorithm in Section 4.2, three query expressions will be generated conforming to NCSTRL: (1) ((Author is 'Tom Bush') AND ('Information Retrieval' in Title)); (2) ((Author is 'Tom Bush') AND ('Information Retrieval' in Abstract)); (3) (Title contains 'User Interface') AND ('Metadata', 'XML') in Keywords). After three visits to the NCSTRL search engine we get the raw results. Because NCSTRL does not provide the date selection and sorting function, the meta search engine needs to post-process the results and rearrange them in date order to meet the needs of the user.

In query mapping, if the query expression is not simple, some of the following problems maybe occur:

Relationship between Fields and Terms. In Fig. 2, each term of NCSTRL is limited only by a certain field. When translating a query, we will rearrange the order of terms without changing the logical consistency.

Relationship between Terms and Logical Operators. The two logic operators of NCSTRL must be the same and only have the values <AND> or <OR>. If the target wrapper demands that all fields be the same, we can transform the original query expression into equivalent Conjunctive or Disjunctive query expressions, e.g. (**A** *AND* (**B** *OR* **C**)) = ((**A** *AND* **B**) *OR* (**A** *AND* **C**)).

*Transforming **PRI**-Expression to **SEQ**-Expression.* If the length of one conjunctive sub-expression is larger than that of the corresponding expression of a wrapper, the sub-expression of the mediator needs to be pruned. In most cases, it is impossible to post-process the broken conjunctive expression, because we cannot get relevant information or the post-processing will cost unbearable CPU-time. The query expression of the mediator can be transformed into a disjunctive form expression, each of its sub-expressions is either a conjunctive sub-expression or a single term. When the system finds a wrapper expression corresponding to the conjunctive sub-expression, the latter will fill in the former; if there are free slots available, feasible single terms will be used to fill these slots in order to reduce the number of generated expressions and improve efficiency.

Term in Wrapper can be Expression. Some search engines allow users to input an expression in a term (an input box). Field modifiers will limit the use of expressions because all elements of the expression belong to the same field(s). We can extract sub-expressions with the same field modifier(s) to fill such term slots.

Post-processing. In some cases, the post-processing is impossible due to inaccessible information. For example, suppose that the query expression of the mediator is (**A** *AND* **B** *AND* **C** *AND* **D**) and the wrapper only supports two terms, and we decompose the original expression into two sub-expressions (**A** *AND* **B**) and (**C** *AND* **D**). If the four terms are limited to the fields of 'abstract' or 'full-text' of the publications, then we cannot intersect the two result sets from (**A** *AND* **B**) and (**C** *AND* **D**) because we cannot check whether a term is in such fields. Even if we can get such information (e.g. by analyzing the PS or PDF source file), such work is unnecessary. If the four terms are in the 'title' field of the publications, it is possible to check if each item from the two result sets contains these four terms. If the post-processing costs a lot of time, it is better to directly display the raw results to users.

When a meta search engine meets the above-mentioned problems, it will judge whether it is necessary to cost a lot of CPU time to make results more exact. For an information searcher sometimes the response time is considered first. Users are the best filters of the results.

5. Conclusions

This paper gives a formal description of the query capability of heterogeneous search engines and an algorithm for translating queries from a mediator to a specific wrapper. From the previous sections, we know that there is great diversity among search engines. Exact and efficient query mapping is a complicated and significant task. This paper only copes with the problems of the input interface. From the output page of search engines, we can get a lot of information such as long/short description, document type (technical report, paper, thesis, etc.) and formats (PS, PDF, HTML, etc.), different languages, related information. The combination of input interface modeling and output interface modeling would better satisfy users' needs. It is also important to apply the SPJ algebra to query planning of meta search engines. We think that it is also necessary to deeply research the following problems: (1) finding an efficient model of the constraints and dependence of fields, qualifiers, and logical operators; (2) coordinating the relationship between query decomposing and post-processing.

Acknowledgements

Thanks to Barbara Lutes for discussion on this work.

References

[1] S. Adali and C. Bufi, A flexible architecture for query integration and mapping, in: 3rd IFCIS Conf. on Cooperative Information Systems (CoopIS'1998), New York, August 20–22, pp. 341–353.

[2] S. Adali, C. Bufi and Y. Temtanapat, Integrated search engine, in: Proc. of the IEEE Knowledge and Data Engineering Exchange Workshop, KDEX97, Newport Beach, CA, November 4, 1997, pp. 140–147.

[3] J. Ambite, N. Ashish, G. Barish, C. Knoblock, S. Minton, P. Modi, I. Muslea, A. Philpot and S. Tejada, Ariadne: a system for constructing mediators for internet sources, in: Proc. of the ACM SIGMOD Int. Conf. on Management of Data, Seattle, WA, June 1998, pp. 561–563.

[4] M. Baldonado and T. Winograd, SenseMaker: an information-exploration interface supporting the contextual evolution of a user's interests, in: Proc. of the ACM Conf. on Human Factors in Computing Systems (CHI '97), Atlanta, GA, April 1997, pp. 11–18.

[5] M. Baldonado and T. Winograd, A GUI-based version of the SenseMaker interface for information exploration, http://cs-tr.cs.cornell.edu:80/Dienst/UI/1.0/Display/stanford.cs/CS-TN-98-67. 1998

[6] A. Barth, M. Breu, A. Endres and A. de Kemp, Digital Libraries in Computer Science: The MeDoc Approach, Springer, New York, 1998.

[7] C. Baru, A. Gupta, B. Ludaescher, R. Marciano Y, Papakonstantinou and P. Velikhov, XML-based information mediation with MIX, in: Proc. SIGMOD 99, Philadelphia, PA, June 1999, pp. 597–599.

[8] C. Chang and H. Garcia-Molina, Mind your vocabulary: query mapping across heterogeneous information sources, in: Proc. SIGMOD 99, Philadelphia, PA, June 1999, pp. 335–346.

[9] C. Chang, H. Garcia-Molina and A. Paepcke, Boolean query mapping across heterogeneous information sources, IEEE Trans. Knowledge Data Eng. 8(4) (August 1996).

[10] C. Chang, H. Garcia-Molina and A. Paepcke, Predicate rewriting for translating Boolean queries in a heterogeneous information system, ACM Trans. Inf. Syst. 17(1) (January 1999) 1–39.

[11] B. Chidlovskii, U.M. Borghoff and P.Y. Chevalier, Boolean query translation for brokerage on the Web, in: Proc. 2nd Int. Conf. EuroMedia/WEBTEC'98, Leicester, January 5–7, 1998, pp. 37–44.

[12] M. Christoffel, S. Pulkowski, B. Schmitt, P. Lockemann and C. Schütte, The UniCats approach — new management for books in the information market, in: Proc. Int. Conf. IuK99 — Dynamic Documents, 1999.

[13] D. Dreilinger and A. Howe, Experiences with selecting search engines using meta-search, ACM Trans. Inf. Syst. (1996).

[14] R. Goldman, J. McHugh and J. Widom, From semistructured data to XML: migrating the Lore data model and query language, in: Proc. 2nd Int. Workshop on the Web and Databases (WebDB '99), Philadelphia, PA, June 1999.

[15] L. Gravano, K. Chang, H. Garcia-Molina and A. Paepcke, STARTS: Stanford protocol proposal for Internet retrieval and search, in: Proc. 1997 ACM SIGMOD Conf. (Tucson, AZ, May), ACM Press, New York, 1997, pp. 126–137.

[16] L. Gravano and H. Garcia-Molina, Merging ranks from heterogeneous Internet sources, in: Proc. 23rd VLDB Conf., Athens, Greece, August 1997.

[17] Z. Ives, D. Florescu, M. Friedman, A. Levy and D. Weld, An adaptive query execution engine for data integration, in: Proc. SIGMOD Int. Conf., Philadelphia, PA, June 1999, pp. 299–310.

[18] L. Kovács, A. Micsik and B. Pataki, AQUA: an advanced user interface for the Dienst digital library system, in: The 8th DELOS Workshop on User Interfaces for Digital Libraries, Stockholm, October 1998.

[19] N. Kushmerick, Regression testing for wrapper maintenance, AAAI-99 Orlando, 1999.

[20] C. Lagoze, E. Shaw, J. Davis and D. Krafft, Dienst: Implementation Reference Manual, 1995.

[21] L. Alon, More on data management for XML, May 9th, 1999, Available at http://www.cs.washington.edu/homes/alon/widom-response.html

[22] A. Levy, A. Rajaraman and J. Ordille, Querying heterogeneous information sources using source descriptions, in: Proc. 22nd VLDB Conf., Bombay, 1996.

[23] W. Moen, E. Christian et al., Application profile for the Government Information Locator Service (GILS), 1997, http://www.gils.net/prof_v2.html

[24] B. Panchapagesan, J. Hui, G. Wiederhold, S. Erickson, L. Dean and A. Hempstead, The INEEL data integration mediation system, in: AIDA'99, Int. ICSC Symp. on Advances in Intelligent Data Analysis, Rochester, NY, June 1999.

[25] B. Schmitt and A. Schmidt, METALICA: an enhanced meta search engine for literature catalogs, in: Proc. 2nd Asian Digital Library Conferences (ADL'99), 1999.

[26] A. Tomasic, L. Raschid and P. Valduriez, A data model and query processing techniques for scaling access to distributed heterogeneous databases in Disco, Invited paper in the IEEE Trans. Comput., special issue on Distributed Computing Systems, 1997.

[27] V. Vassalos and Y. Papakonstantinou, Describing and using query capabilities of heterogeneous sources, in: Proc. 23rd VLDB Conf. Athens, pp. 256–265.

[28] G. Wiederhold, Mediators in the architecture of future information systems, IEEE Comput. 25(3) (March 1992) 38–49.

[29] R. Yerneni, C. Li, H. Garcia-Molina and J. Ullman, Computing capabilities of mediators, in: Proc. SIGMOD, Philadelphia, PA, June 1999, pp. 443–454.

[30] Z39.50 Maintenance Agency, Information retrieval (Z39.50): application service definition and protocol specification, 1995, ftp://ftp.loc.gov/pub/z3950/official

Lieming Huang, a computer scientist now is working and pursuing Ph.D. degree in GMD-IPSI. In 1994, he received a Bachelor of Science degree on computer software from the Department of Computer Science and Technology, Peking University, Beijing, P.R. China. In 1997, he received his Master of Engineering degree on computer software from the Chinese Academy of Sciences, Beijing, P.R. China, and his Master thesis is on intelligent user interface for database systems. He is interested in the research fields of meta-data, information retrieval, data management, and user interface.

Matthias Hemmje is division manager of the DELITE digital libraries research division at GMD-IPSI in Darmstadt, Germany. He holds a diploma and a Ph.D. degree from Department of Computer Science of the Technical University of Darmstadt. His research interests include information retrieval, multimedia databases, agent-based user interfaces, virtual environments, information visualization, visual interaction, multimedia, and evaluation of interactive systems. From 1987 to 1991 he worked as a Systems Engineer, Department for Computer Aided Testing at Gebr. Hofmann KG, Darmstadt, from 1991 to 1999 he worked as a research associate at GMD-IPSI in the Department for Visual Interaction Tools (VISIT) and in the research division for Open Adaptive Information Management Systems (OASYS). Matthias Hemmje is working in the context of R&D related to VRML-, MPEG-, and XML-based information retrieval and information visualization systems, such as e.g. the Internet virtual gallery project (i-VG), the Congress Online (CO) congress information system which is based on a database-supported Information Catalogue Environment enabling navigation on multimedia document collections. Matthias Hemmje is a member of the Visual Information Retrieval Interfaces (VIRI) working group founded by Bob Korfhage at the University of Pittsburgh and he is a member of the European working group on Foundations of Advanced 3D Information Visualization (FADIVA).

Erich J. Neuhold is the director of the Institute for Integrated Publication and Information Systems (IPSI) of the German National Research Center for Information Technology (GMD) and at the same time a professor of Department of Computer Science, Technical University of Darmstadt in Darmstadt, Germany. He received his M.S. in Electronics and his Ph.D. degree in Mathematics and Computer Science at the Technical University of Vienna, Austria, in 1963 and 1967, respectively. In 1986, he was appointed Director of the Institute for Integrated Publication and Information Systems of the German National Research Center for Information Technology in Darmstadt. His primary research and development interests are in heterogeneous interoperable database systems, object-oriented multimedia knowledge bases and intelligent information retrieval. He also guides research and development in user interfaces including virtual reality concepts for information visualization, computer-supported cooperative work, virtual meetings and conferences as well as integrated publication and information systems with special emphasis on multimedia hyperdocuments and on information mining in the Internet/WEB environment. National and international cooperation with research and industrial partners ensures the transfer of results into widely available prototypes and products. Since 1989 he is also Professor of Computer Science, Integrated Publication and Information Systems, at the Darmstadt University of Technology, Germany. He has published 190 papers, 4 books and 9 edited books.

An efficient algorithm to rank Web resources

Dell Zhang *, Yisheng Dong

Department of Computer Science and Engineering, Southeast University, Nanjing, 210096, China

Abstract

How to rank Web resources is critical to Web Resource Discovery (Search Engine). This paper not only points out the weakness of current approaches, but also presents in-depth analysis of the multidimensionality and subjectivity of rank algorithms. From a dynamics viewpoint, this paper abstracts a user's Web surfing action as a Markov model. Based on this model, we propose a new rank algorithm. The result of our rank algorithm, which synthesizes the relevance, authority, integrativity and novelty of each Web resource, can be computed efficiently not by iteration but through solving a group of linear equations.

Keywords: Web; Resource discovery; Search engine; Rank algorithm

1. Introduction

The World Wide Web is rapidly emerging as an important medium for the dissemination of information related to a wide range of topics [1]. There are about 300 million pages on the Web today with about 1 million being added daily. According to most predictions, the majority of human information will be available on the Web in 10 years. But, it is widely believed that 99% of the information on the Web is of no interest to 99% of the people. Looking for something valuable in this tremendous amount of information is as difficult as looking for a needle in a haystack.

Searching for valuable information on the Web is called resource discovery (RD). The IETF-RD group argues that resource discovery should provide the user a consistent, organized view of information [15]. In a typical RD procedure, the user submits a query Q, which is simply a list of keywords (with some additional operators), to the RD server (RDS), then RDS returns a set of related Web page URLs: R_1, R_2, ... R_n. There are many search engines to support RD on the Web, such as **Yahoo!** [1], **AltaVista** [2], **Excite** [3], **Hotbot** [4], **Infoseek** [5], etc. A search engine usually collects Web pages on the Internet through a robot (spider, crawler) program, then these Web pages are automatically scanned to build giant indices, so you can quickly retrieve the set of all Web pages containing the given keywords.

RD on the Web is especially difficult due to the following five characteristics of the Web data source: (1) huge and ubiquitous; (2) mostly semistructured or unstructured; (3) diverse in quality; (4) dynamic; (5) distributed and autonomous. In particular, a topic of any breadth will typically contain several thousand or

* Corresponding author. E-mail: dell.z@ieee.org

1 http://www.yahoo.com
2 http://altavista.digital.com
3 http://www.excite.com
4 http://www.hotbot.com
5 http://www.infoseek.com

million relevant Web pages. For instance, if you enter the search engine AltaVista, input 'data mining', over 50,000 Web pages will be found. Yet, a user will be willing, typically, to look at only a few of these pages.

The rank algorithm, can then help a user to select the *correct* ones (those of most value to him or her), from this sea of Web resources. Given a Web resource r and a user's query q, the rank algorithm will compute a score rank(r, q). The bigger rank(r, q) is, the more valuable r to q, i.e., the more valuable for the user. In practice, RD on the Web can be viewed as fuzzy queries driven by the rank algorithm, but not SQL-style precise queries. Moreover, a good rank algorithm is very helpful to crawl the Web more efficiently [7]. Meta-search engines also need the rank algorithm to synthesize the results from other search engines [2,10]. All in all, we argue that the rank algorithm is the core technique of a search engine, and it is critical to improve the quality of RD on the Web.

This paper is organized as follows. Section 2 points out the weakness of current approaches in ranking Web resources. Section 3 presents in-depth analysis of the multidimensionality and subjectivity of rank algorithms. Section 4 abstracts a user's Web surfing action as a Markov model and we propose a new rank algorithm based on this model. Section 5 concludes this paper and discusses future work.

2. State of the art

At the present time, most rank algorithms of Web resources are using the similarity measure based on the vector-space model, which has been well studied by the Information Retrieval (IR) community. To compute the similarities, we can view each document as an n-dimensional vector $\langle w_1, \ldots, w_n \rangle$. The term w_i in this vector represents the ith word in the vocabulary. If w_i does not appear in the document, then w_i is zero. If it does appear, w_i is set to represent the significance of the word. One common way to compute the significance w_i is TF $\times$ IDF, i.e., to multiply the number of times the ith word appears in the document (TF) by the inverse document frequency (IDF) of the ith word. The IDF factor is 1 divided by the number of times the word appears in the entire 'collection', which in this case would be the entire Web. The IDF factor corresponds to the content discriminating power of a word: a term that appears rarely in documents (e.g., 'algebra') has a high IDF, while a term that occurs in many documents (e.g., 'the') has a low IDF. The similarity between query Q and document R can then be defined as the inner product of the vectors of Q and R. Another option is to use the cosine similarity measure, which is the inner product of the normalized vectors. The w_i terms can also take into account where on a HTML page the word appears, for instance, words appearing in the title may be given a higher weight than other words in the body [6]. Along with the popularization of Web meta-data standards such as RDF, it becomes feasible to take advantage of the meta-data of Web resources, which can also improve the rank algorithm's accuracy [13].

But the rank algorithms derived from IR have lots of limitations, as they only evaluate the content, but totally neglect the quality of Web resources. So these rank algorithms can be easily cheated. Webmasters can make their sites highly ranked through inserting some irrelevant but popular words (e.g., 'Clinton', 'sex') into important places (e.g., title page) or meta-data. This phenomenon is called Search Engine Persuasion (SEP) or Web Spamming [12,14].

Recent researches in this area concentrate on mining the linkage structure of Web resources to support RD on the Web [3,5,7,12,16]. A typical one in such rank algorithms is PageRank [3], which is proposed by the Stanford University and has been applied in the famous search engine **Google** [6]. The PageRank metric, PR(P), recursively defines the importance of a page P to be the weighted sum of the back-links to it. Such a metric has been found to be very useful in ranking results of user queries. More formally, if a page has no outgoing link, we assume that it has outgoing links to every single page. Consider a page P that is pointed at by pages $T_1, T_2, \ldots, T_n$. Let $C(T_i)$ be the number of links going out of page T_i. Also, let d be a damping factor. Then, the weighted back-link count of page P is given by

$$\mathrm{PR}(P) = (1-d) + d(\mathrm{PR}(T_1)/C(T_1) + \cdots + \mathrm{PR}(T_n)/C(T_n)).$$

[6] http://www.google.com/

This leads to one equation per Web page, with an equal number of unknowns. The equations can be solved iteratively, starting with all PR values equal to 1. At each step, the new PR(P) value is computed from the old PR(T_i) values (using the equation above), until the values converge. Through the famous Perron–Frobenius Theorem [18], we can find out that this calculation corresponds to computing the principal eigenvector of the linkage matrix.

Theorem 1 (Perron–Frobenius Theorem). *If an n-dimensional matrix* $\mathbf{A}$ *is positive or non-negative irreducible, then:*

- *the spectrum radius of* $\mathbf{A}$, ρ, *is also a latent root of* $\mathbf{A}$*;*
- *there is a positive eigenvector of* $\mathbf{A}$ *corresponding to* ρ*;*
- *the eigenfunction of* $\mathbf{A}$ *has a single root* ρ, *i.e.,* $mult\rho(\mathbf{A}) = 1$,
- ……

Although the rank algorithms based on linkage structure break through the limitation of traditional IR technology, they still have some shortcomings:

- only the authority metric has been taken into account;
- the iterative computation results in bad performance;
- it is difficult to deal with the overflow or underflow problem during iteration;
- because of the 'rank sink problem', the iterative computation may not converge.

The last situation, 'rank sink problem', is illustrated in Fig. 1. Consider two Web pages that point to each other but to no other page, and suppose there is some Web page that points to one of them. During iteration, this loop will accumulate rank but never distribute any rank (since there are no outgoing edges). The loop forms a sort of trap called a 'rank sink' [3]. This problem can be analyzed more formally as follows.

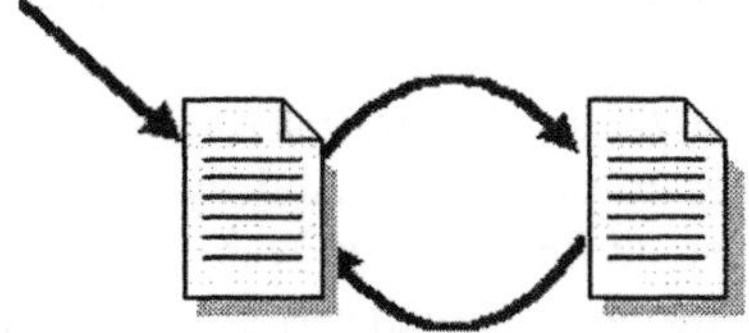

Fig. 1. The 'rank sink problem'.

Definition 1. $A = (a_{ij})_{n\times n}$ is an n-dimensional matrix, the graph, $D(\mathbf{A}) = \{(i, j) \mid a_{ij} \neq 0\}$ is named the adjoint directed graph of $\mathbf{A}$.

Theorem 2. *$\mathbf{A}$ is an n-dimensional non-negative matrix, so $\mathbf{A}$ is irreducible, if and only if, the adjoint directed graph of $\mathbf{A}$ is strongly connected (there exists a path from u to v for any node u and v in the graph) [18].*

It is obvious that the 'rank sink problem' makes the Perron–Frobenius Theorem no longer applicable, so the iteration computation method loses its foundation.

To sum up, there are still many weaknesses of current rank algorithms. Simply inheriting IR technology and merely mining the linkage structure are not enough.

3. Analysis of the rank algorithm

3.1. Definition

The rank function of Web resources can be formally defined as rank : $R \times Q \to \mathbf{R}^+ \cup \{0\}$, here R represents the set of relevant Web resources, Q represents the set user's queries. Without loss of generality, we can view R as the relevant Web pages found by the search engine. Given $\forall r \in R, \forall q \in Q$, the bigger rank$(r, q)$, the more valuable r to q, i.e., the more valuable for the user.

If the function 'rank' satisfies

(1) $\forall r \in R, \forall q \in Q,\ \ 0 < \text{rank}(r, q) < 1$,

(2) $\forall q \in Q,\ \ \sum_{r\in R} \text{rank}(r, q) = 1$,

then it is called a normal rank function. Since all rank functions can be transformed to equivalent normal rank functions, we assume all rank functions are normal in the following discussion.

3.2. Multidimensionality

In our opinion, a rational rank algorithm of Web resources should be multidimensional, at least it should include the following metrics.

- *Relevance*. The relevance metric means the distance between the content of a Web resource r and a user's query q. It is also the metric used by most search engines. The normalized relevance function can be defined as corr : $R \times Q \to [0, 1]$.

As stated in Section 2, the method to calculate relevance can be derived from IR technology, based on TF, IDF, word weight, meta-data, etc.

- *Authority*. The authority metric means how many Web resources refer to the Web resource r. Moreover, the Web resources referred to by higher-quality resources should be assigned with higher authority.
- *Integrativity*. The integrativity metric means how many Web resources are pointed by the Web resource r. Moreover, the Web resources pointed to higher-quality resources should be assigned with higher integrativity. A Web resource with high integrativity is just like a good 'survey' or 'review' style academic paper, it can lead users to valuable information.
- *Novelty*. The novelty metric means in which degree the Web resource r is different from others, i.e., provide novel information. Analysis of query logs has demonstrated that users are impatient, rarely examining more than the first page of results (usually displaying 7–12 URLs). Hence we hope that the top 30 Web resources will be very representative. Such Web resources should have few direct links between themselves, because they will act as roadmaps so that users can easily follow the links embedded in them to find other valuable resources.

3.3. Subjectivity

The value of a Web resource r depends not only on the query q, but also on the user's nation, age, gender, career, culture, hobby, etc. So there is no absolute best rank function. But we can still evaluate the rank algorithm based on the user's reaction.

Assuming 'RANK' represents the set of all possible rank functions, the user's satisfaction function can be defined as sat: $Q \times \text{RANK} \rightarrow [0,1]$, sat($q$, rank) will be proportional to the user's satisfaction of this rank function. Given the Web sources set $R = \{r_1, r_2, \dots, r_n\}$, without loss of generality, we suppose $r_1, r_2, \dots, r_n$ are decreasingly ordered by their value according to the user's judgement. Define the 'reverse order number' of the Web resource r_i under the rank function as

$$\psi(r_i) = |\{r_k \mid (r_k \in R) \wedge (1 \leq k < i) \wedge (\text{rank}(r_k) < \text{rank}(r_i))\}|$$

then

$$\text{sat}(q, \text{rank}) = \frac{\sum_{i=1}^{n} \psi(r_i)}{(n-1)(n-2)/2}.$$

Given the queries set $Q = \{q_1, q_2, \dots, q_m\}$, the average satisfaction function should be

$$\text{sat}(Q, \text{rank}) = \frac{\sum_{j=1}^{m} \text{sat}(q_j, \text{rank})}{m}.$$

4. The rank algorithm based on Markov model

The above rank algorithms of the Web resources are all from a statistic approach, but this paper presents a user-centered rank algorithm from a dynamics viewpoint. In fact, surfing on the Web can be viewed as a dynamic procedure in that a user jumps from one Web resource to another. We abstract this surfing procedure as a Markov chain.

Definition 2. Suppose $\{x_t, t \geq 0\}$ is a series of random variables on a finite state space $S = \{s_1, s_2, \dots, s_n\}$. If the state of x_{k+1} only depends on x_k, but not on $x_0, x_1, \dots, x_{k-1}$, i.e., for any $k \geq 0$ and positive integers $i_0, i_1, \dots, i_k, i_{k+1}$ the equation $P(x_{k+1} = s_{i_{k+1}} \mid x_0 = s_{i_0}, \dots, x_k = s_{i_k}) = P(x_{k+1} = s_{i_{k+1}} \mid x_k = s_{i_k})$ is always true, then $\{x_t, t \geq 0\}$ is named a finite Markov chain. $P(x_{k+1} = s_j \mid x_k = s_i)$, $p_{ij}(t)$ for short, represents the probability to transit from the state s_i to s_j in the time t. If the transition probability $p_{ij}(t)$ is independent of t, i.e., for any $s_i, s_j \in S$ and any t_1, t_2, $p_{ij}(t_1) = p_{ij}(t_2)$, then these types of Markov chains are called homogeneous ones. $\boldsymbol{P} = (p_{ij})_{n \times n}$ is the transition probability matrix of this homogeneous Markov chain, where $p_{ij} \in [0, 1]$, $1 \leq i, j \leq n$, $\sum_{j=1}^{n} p_{ij} = 1$, $1 \leq i \leq n$.

For a query q, $R = \{r_1, r_2, \dots, r_n\}$ denotes the set of related Web resources found by the search engine. We can use R as the state space (one Web resource corresponds to one state). And then we consider a virtual user surfing on the Web, in time t; he is browsing the Web resource r_i in probability $p_i(t)$, and will jump to the Web resource r_j in probability

p_{ij}. It is in this way that the user's surfing action on the Web can be abstracted as a homogeneous Markov chain. Although this modeling is rather simple and intuitive, we believe that it has grasped the spirit of the surfing procedure.

Definition 3. A finite Markov chain's distribution vector in time t is $\boldsymbol{p}(t) = (p_1(t), p_2(t), \ldots, p_n(t))$, where $p_j(t) = P(x_t = s_j)$, $p_j(t) \in [0, 1]$, $\sum_{j=1}^{n} p_j(t) = 1$.

Theorem 3. *A homogeneous Markov chain's behavior can be determined by its initial distribution vector $\boldsymbol{p}(0)$ and its transition probability matrix $\boldsymbol{P}$, $\boldsymbol{p}(t) = \boldsymbol{p}(0)\boldsymbol{P}^t$.*

Suppose in time t, the virtual user is in state r_i, i.e., browsing the Web resource r_i, then in the next time $t+1$, he may have the following choices:

- continue browsing the Web resource r_i;
- click a hyperlink in r_i and jump to a new Web resource;
- press the 'BACK' button in the browser and return to the last browsing Web resource;
- select another Web resource from the results of the search engine, R.

Facing each of the above choices, the virtual user's tendencies are measured as $\alpha \times \text{sim}(r_i, q)$, β, γ and ε separately, where $\text{corr}(r_i, q)$ is the relevance function defined in Section 2, and $\alpha, \beta, \gamma, \varepsilon$ are four constants to a specific user, which satisfy the condition $0 < \alpha, \beta, \gamma, \varepsilon < 1, \alpha + \beta + \gamma + \varepsilon = 1$.

Definition 4. The linkage structure graph of the Web resources, $G = (V, E)$, is a directed graph, where V is the set of nodes ($|V| = n$) (a node corresponds to a resource in R), and E is the set of edges, $E = \{(v_i, v_j) \mid v_i, v_j \in V \text{ and } r_i \text{ points to } r_j \text{ through hyperlink}\}$, $\text{in}(v_i) = |\{(v_k, v_i) \mid (v_k, v_i) \in E\}|$, $\text{out}(v_i) = |\{(v_i, v_k) \mid (v_i, v_k) \in E\}|$.

Definition 5. The tendency matrix for the set of related Web resources, R, is

$$U = (u_{ij})_{n \times n}, \quad u_{ij} = \begin{cases} \alpha \times \text{sim}(r_i, q) & \text{if } i = j, \\ \beta & \text{if } (v_i, v_j) \in E, \\ \gamma & \text{if } (v_j, v_i) \in E, \\ \varepsilon & \text{otherwise.} \end{cases}$$

Note that the tendency matrix here has synthesized the four metrics mentioned above (relevance, authority, integrativity and novelty).

After normalizing the tendency matrix, we get the transition probability matrix in the Markov model for user's surfing procedure on the Web.

Theorem 4. *The transition probability matrix for the set of related Web resources, R, is*

$$\boldsymbol{P} = (p_{ij})_{n \times n}, \quad p_{ij} = \frac{u_{ij}}{\sum_{j=1}^{n} u_{ij}}.$$

Through Theorems 3 and 4, the probability distribution vector at any time t can be calculated easily. Now it is obvious that $\alpha, \beta, \gamma, \varepsilon$ actually reflect the relative importance, in the user's opinion, of the relevance, authority, integrativity and novelty metrics. So we also call α the relevance parameter, β the authority parameter, γ the integrativity parameter, and ε the novelty parameter.

Definition 6. A homogeneous Markov chain, on the state space $S = \{s_1, s_2, \ldots, s_n\}$, is holomorphic, if for any $\forall s_i, s_j \in S$ there exists a positive integer k, the state can transit from s_i to s_j in a positive probability, within k steps.

Definition 7. $\boldsymbol{A} = (a_{ij})_{n \times n}$ is an n-dimensional positive matrix.

(1) $\boldsymbol{A}$ is called stochastic when $\sum_{j=1}^{n} a_{ij}(t) = 1, i = 1, 2, \ldots, n$.
(2) $\boldsymbol{A}$ is called primitive when there exists a positive integer k, $\boldsymbol{A}^k > 0$ (that is, every element in $\boldsymbol{A}^k$ is positive).

It is obvious that multiplying several stochastic matrices produces a stochastic matrix, and every positive matrix is sure to be primitive.

Theorem 5. *A homogeneous Markov chain, on the state space $S = \{s_1, s_2, \ldots, s_n\}$, is holomorphic, if and only if, its transition probability matrix $\boldsymbol{P}$ is a primitive stochastic matrix.*

Based on Theorems 4 and 5, it is easy to discover that the Markov chain corresponding to the user's surfing procedure is a holomorphic Markov chain.

Theorem 6. *A holomorphic and homogeneous Markov chain,* $\{x_t, t \geq 0\}$*, with* $S = \{s_1, s_2, \ldots, s_n\}$ *as its state space,* $\boldsymbol{P}$ *as its transition probability matrix, and* $\boldsymbol{p}(0)$ *as its initial distribution vector, will converge to a unique ultimate distribution when* $t \to \infty$*, that is*

$$\lim_{t\to\infty} \boldsymbol{p}(t) = \boldsymbol{\pi}$$

The ultimate (stable) distribution vector, $\boldsymbol{\pi} = (\pi_1, \pi_2, \ldots, \pi_n)$, is the unique solution of the equation $\boldsymbol{\pi P} = \boldsymbol{\pi}$ that satisfies $\pi_i > 0$, $\sum_{i=1}^{n} \pi_i = 1$ [8,9].

Assuming that the virtual user is rational and experienced enough, we argue that the probability of browsing the Web resource r_i should be proportional to its worthiness. In practice, we can also establish out that a user usually spends more time on the Web resources he cares for most. At first, the user has no knowledge about the value of each Web resource, he selects Web resources blindly or randomly. The user becomes more and more experienced while browsing more and more Web resources, so his judgement on the value of resources becomes more and more accurate. With time, the ultimate probability of browsing each Web resource should reflect the worthiness of each Web resource accurately. This is our main idea.

From Theorem 6, we know that the ultimate distribution vector $\boldsymbol{\pi}$ of a holomorphic Markov chain is independent of the initial distribution vector $\boldsymbol{p}(0)$, but totally determined by the transition probability matrix $\boldsymbol{P}$. So given a set of related Web resources, R, we can construct the transition probability matrix $\boldsymbol{P}$ through Theorem 4, then calculate the ultimate distribution vector based on Theorem 6. The ultimate distribution vector is just the rank of Web resources we are looking for. The group of equations in Theorem 6 can be solved using the 'Gaussian method' without any iteration. Some ad-hoc mathematical software (such as MatLab) has already provided such capability. Our initial implementation shows that the rank algorithm is efficient and scalable in practice.

The parameters in this rank algorithm $(\alpha, \beta, \gamma, \varepsilon)$ will be different for different users, and can be adjusted for particular needs. These parameters can also be automatically estimated based on the user's surfing history, which is discussed in another paper. In our experiment, the parameters are initially set as $\alpha = 0.6$, $\beta = 0.2$, $\gamma = 0.19$, $\varepsilon = 0.01$.

5. Conclusion

From a dynamics viewpoint, this paper provides a rank algorithm of Web resources based on a Markov model. The advantages of this rank algorithm are:

- several metrics (relevance, authority, integrativity and novelty) have been synthesized;
- the result can be calculated efficiently through solving a group of linear equations, without any iteration;
- the parameters can be customized and dynamically adjusted by the user.

Several researchers have pointed out that there is plenty of information buried in the user's bookmark and historic visits log [4]. Now we are investigating how to leverage this information in our rank algorithm. Classifying and clustering the Web resources automatically are also very important to RD on the Web [11,17]. We believe that the Markov model proposed in this paper can also be applied.

The Web can be viewed as a 'complex system', and nonlinear dynamics (chaos, fractal, and so on) should be very helpful to manage and make use of the Web. We believe that the World Wide Web (WWW) will eventually become an information retrieval tool whoever, whenever, wherever (WWW) you are.

References

[1] P. Bernstein, M. Brodie, S. Ceri, et al., The Asilomar Report on Database Research, Technical Report MSTR-TR-98-57, Microsoft Research, Microsoft Corporation, September 1998.

[2] K. Bharat and A. Broder, A technique for measuring the relative size and overlap of public Web search engines, Computer Networks and ISDN Systems 30 (1998) 379–388.

[3] S. Brin and L. Page, The anatomy of a large-scale hypertextual Web search engine, Computer Networks and ISDN Systems 30 (1998) 107–117.

[4] S. Chakrabarti, B. Dom, D. Gibson, J. Kleinberg, S.R. Kumar, P. Raghavan, S. Rajagopalan and A. Tomkins, Hypersearching the web, Scientific American, June 1999.

[5] S. Chakrabarti, B. Dom, P. Raghavan, S. Rajagopalan, D. Gibson and J. Kleinberg, Automatic resource compilation by analyzing hyperlinkage structure and associated text, Computer Networks and ISDN Systems 30 (1998) 65–74.

[6] Y. Chen, Web as A Data Source, Ph.D. Thesis, Department of Computer Science and Engineering, Southeast University, Nanjing, 1999.

[7] J. Cho, H. Garcia-Molina and L. Page, Efficient crawling through URL ordering, 7th International Web Conference (WWW 98), Brisbane, April 14–18, 1998.

[8] M. Iosifecu, Finite Markov Processes and Their Applications, Wiley, Chichester, 1980.

[9] Q.Y. Jiang, Mathematical Model (version 2), High Education Press, Beijing, 1993.

[10] S. Lorence and C.L. Giles, Inquirus, the NECI meta search engine, Computer Networks and ISDN Systems 30 (1998) 95–105.

[11] S.A. Macskassy, A. Banerjee, B.D. Davison, et al., Human performance on clustering Web pages: a preliminary study, in: Proc. of the 4th International Conference on Knowledge Discovery and Data Mining, New York, August 1998.

[12] M. Marchiori, The quest for correct information on the Web: hyper search engines, Computer Networks and ISDN Systems 29 (1997) 1225–1235.

[13] M. Marchiori, The limits of Web metadata, and beyond, Computer Networks and ISDN Systems 30 (1998) 1–9.

[14] G. Pringle, L. Allison and D.L. Dowe, What is a tall poppy among Web pages? Computer Networks and ISDN Systems 30 (1998) 369–377.

[15] C.M. Rowman, Scalable Internet resource discovery: research problems and approaches, Communications of the ACM 37 (8) (1994) 98–107.

[16] E. Spertus, ParaSite: mining structural information on the Web, Computer Networks and ISDN Systems 29 (1997) 1205–1215.

[17] M.R. Wulfekuhler and W.F. Punch, Finding salient feature for personal Web page categories, Computer Networks and ISDN Systems 29 (1997) 1147–1156.

[18] D.Y. Zhu, Mathematical Modeling Cases, Southeast University Press, Nanjing, 1999.

Dell Zhang was born in July 1976 in Yangzhou, China. He received his bachelor's degree in Computer Science from Southeast University, China, and is now a Ph.D. candidate in Computer Science there. He is a member of ACM and IEEE Computer Society. His main research interests are data mining, information retrieval, and evolutionary computing.

Yisheng Dong is a full professor of Computer Science, and also the dean of the Department of Computer Science and Engineering at Southeast University, China. He graduated in 1965, from Nanjing Institute of Technology, China. His research domain includes databases, software engineering and information systems.

WTMS: a system for collecting and analyzing topic-specific Web information

Sougata Mukherjea [1]

C&C Research Laboratories, NEC USA Inc., San Jose, CA, USA

Abstract

With the explosive growth of the World Wide Web, it is becoming increasingly difficult for users to collect and analyze Web pages that are relevant to a particular topic. To address this problem we are developing WTMS, a system for Web topic management. In this paper we explain how the WTMS crawler efficiently collects Web pages for a topic. We also introduce the user interface of the system that integrates several techniques for analyzing the collection. Moreover, we present the various views of the interface that allow navigation through the information space. We highlight several examples to show how the system enables the user to gain useful insights about the collection. © 2000 Published by Elsevier Science B.V. All rights reserved.

Keywords: World Wide Web; Topic management; Focussed crawling; Information visualization; Graph algorithms; Hubs; Authorities

1. Introduction

The World Wide Web is undoubtedly the best source for getting information on any topic. Therefore, more and more people use the Web for *topic management* [1], the task of gathering, evaluating and organizing information resources on the Web. Users may investigate topics both for professional or personal interests.

Generally the popular portals or search engines like Yahoo and Alta Vista are used for gathering information on the World Wide Web. However, with the explosive growth of the Web, topic management is becoming an increasingly difficult task. On the one hand this leads to a large number of documents being retrieved for most queries. The results are presented as pages of scrolled lists. Going through these pages to retrieve the relevant information is tedious. Moreover, the Web has over 350 million pages and continues to grow rapidly at a million pages per day [4]. Such growth and flux pose basic limits of scale for today's generic search engines. Thus, many relevant information may not have been gathered and some information may not be up-to-date.

Because of these problems, recently there is much awareness that for serious Web users, focussed *portholes* are more useful than generic portals [9]. Therefore, systems that allow the user to collect and organize the information related to a particular topic and allow easy navigation through this information space is becoming essential. Such a Web topic management system should have several features to be really useful:

- *Focussed crawler:* A crawler that allows the collection of resources from the World Wide Web that relates to a user-specified topic is an essential

[1] E-mail: sougata@icarian.com

requirement of the system. An effective crawler should have high precision (all the retrieved Web pages should belong to the topic) and recall (most of the relevant information available on the topic should be gathered). Moreover the crawler should be efficient; the relevant information should be collected in the least amount of time possible.

- *Viewing information at various levels of abstraction:* A search engine generally shows the relevant Web pages as the result of a user's query. However, sometimes authors organize the information as a collection of pages; in these cases presenting the collection may be more useful for the reader. In fact, if a Web site has many relevant pages, presenting the Web site itself may be better. Furthermore, if there are many Web sites for a particular topic, grouping similar Web sites may be more convenient. Therefore, an effective topic management system should be able to present the information at various levels of abstraction depending on the user's focus.
- *Integrate querying and browsing:* The two major ways to access information in the Web are querying and browsing. Querying is appropriate when the user has a well-defined understanding of what information is needed and how to formulate a query. However, in many cases the user is not certain of exactly what information is desired and needs to learn more about the content of the information space. In these cases browsing is an ideal navigational strategy. Browsing can also be combined with querying when the result of the query is too large for the user to comprehend (by letting the user browse through the results) or too small (by showing the user other related information). An effective topic management system should allow the user to smoothly integrate querying and browsing to retrieve the relevant information.
- *Beyond keyword-based querying:* For advanced analysis of a topic, the keyword-based queries that are provided by the search engines may not be adequate. More sophisticated querying techniques based on the contents as well as the structure of the information space are essential. For example, the user should be able to group together related information and filter out unimportant information.
- *Allow easy sharing of the gathered information* Once the collection for a particular topic has been gathered and organized, different users with interest in the topic should be able to share the information.

We are building a Web topic management system (WTMS) to allow the collection and analysis of information on the Web related to a particular topic. This paper discusses the various features of the system. Section 2 cites related work. Section 3 explains how the focussed crawler of WTMS allows the collection of information from the World Wide Web relevant to a topic. Section 4 presents the various views of the system that allow the user to navigate through the information space. Several graph algorithm based techniques to analyze the collection are introduced in Section 5. Finally, Section 6 is the conclusion.

2. Related work

2.1. Visualizing the World Wide Web

Several systems for visualizing World Wide Web sites have been developed. Examples include Navigational View Builder [17], Harmony Internet Browser [2] and Narcissus [11]. Visualization techniques for World Wide Web search results are also being developed. For example, the WebQuery system [7] visualizes the results of a search query along with all pages that link to or are linked to by any page in the original result set. Another example is WebBook [6], which potentially allows the results of the search to be organized and manipulated in various ways in a 3D space. In this paper our emphasis is on developing views that allow navigation through Web pages about a particular topic and gain useful insights about the collection.

2.2. World Wide Web topic management

In recent times there has been much interest in collecting Web pages related to a particular topic. The shark-search algorithm for collecting topic-specific pages is presented in [12]. Another focussed crawler is presented in [9]. The crawler used in WTMS is similar to these systems. However, it uses several heuristics to improve performance.

Another interesting problem is determining the important pages in a collection. Kleinberg defines the HITS algorithm to identify *authority* and *hub* pages in a collection [13]. Authority pages are authorities on a topic and hubs point to many pages relevant to the topic. Therefore, pages with many in-links, specially from hubs, are considered to be good authorities. On the other hand, pages with many out-links, specially from authorities, are considered to be good hubs. The algorithm has been refined in CLEVER [8] and Topic Distillation [5]. We feel that this algorithm is very important for a Web topic management system. However, we also believe that determining the hub and authority sites for a topic are more useful than determining the hub and authority pages.

Mapuccino (formerly WebCutter) [3,12,15] and TopicShop [1,20] are two systems that have been developed for World Wide Web topic management. Both systems use a crawler for collecting Web pages related to a topic and use various types of visualization to allow the user to navigate through the resultant information space. While Mapuccino presents the information as a collection of Web pages, TopicShop presents the information as a collection of Web sites. As emphasized in the introduction, we believe that it is more effective to present the information at various levels of abstraction depending on the user's focus. Moreover, a topic management system should allow the user to use several techniques to analyze the information space.

3. Crawling

The architecture of the Web topic management system is discussed in [16]. The system uses a focussed crawler to collect Web pages related to a user-specified topic. In this section we will discuss the basic strategy for focussed crawling and how we can improve performance by using some heuristics.

3.1. Basic focussed crawling technique

For collecting World Wide Web pages related to a particular topic the user has to first specify some *seed URLs* relevant to the topic. Alternatively, the user can specify the keywords for the topic and the crawler issues a query with the specified keywords to a popular Web search engine and uses the results as the seed URLs. The WTMS crawler downloads the seed URLs and creates a *representative document vector (RDV)* based on the frequently occurring keywords in these URLs.

The crawler then downloads the pages that are referenced from the seed URLs and calculates their similarity to the RDV using the vector space model [19]. If the similarity is above a threshold, the pages are indexed by a text search engine and the links from the pages are added to a queue. The crawler continues to follow the out-links until the queue is empty or a user-specified limit is reached.

The crawler also determines the pages pointing to the seed URLs. (A query *link:u* to search engines like AltaVista and Google returns all pages pointing to URL *u*.) These pages are downloaded and if their similarity to the RDV is greater than a threshold, they are indexed and the URLs pointing to these pages are added to the queue. The crawler continues to follow the in-links until the queue is empty or a user-specified limit is reached.

After crawling, the collection consists of the seed URLs as well as all pages similar to these seed URLs that have paths to or from the seeds. We believe that this collection is a good source of information available on the World Wide Web for the user-specified topic. It should be noted that the crawler has a *stop URL list* to avoid downloading some popular pages (like Yahoo's and Netscape's Home pages) as part of the collection.

This focussed crawling strategy is similar to the techniques described in [12] and [9]. Most focussed crawlers start with some seed URLs and follow the out-links (sometimes in-links also). Pages that are relevant to the topic of interest are indexed and the links from these pages are also followed. The relevancy can be determined by various techniques like the vector space model (as in [12]) or using a classifier (for example in [9]).

3.2. Using heuristics to improve performance

The main bottleneck of a crawler is the time spent in downloading Web pages. Besides network congestion, a crawler needs to follow the convention of issuing one download request to a site per 30 seconds.

Therefore, downloading many pages from a single site may take a long time. For a focussed crawler only Web pages relevant to the topic are important. So many of the downloaded pages may have to be discarded. In fact, using our basic focussed crawler for topics as diverse as *World Cup Soccer*, *Information Visualization* and *Titanic* we found that less than 50% of the downloaded pages were found to be relevant. If we could determine that a page will be irrelevant without examining the contents of the page, we can avoid downloading the page, thereby improving performance. We use two heuristics for the purpose.

3.2.1. Nearness of the current page to the linked page

If a Web site has information related to several topics, a page in the Web site for one of the topics may have links to pages relating to the other topics or to the main page of the site for ease of navigation. For example, the page *http://www.discovery.com/area/science/titanic/weblinks.html*, a page relevant to *Titanic*, has a link to *http://www.discovery.com/online.html*, the main page of Discovery online, a page not related to the topic. However, since most Web sites are well organized, pages that are dissimilar do not occur near each other in the directory hierarchy.

Therefore, when we are examining the pages linked to or linked from a Web page, we need to download the linked page only if it is **near** the current page. The determination of nearness will be an optimization between the number of irrelevant downloads and the number of relevant pages that are not downloaded. If we use a strict criterion to determine the nearness between two pages, the number of downloads will be lower, but we may miss some relevant pages. On the other hand, a lenient criterion to determine nearness will retrieve all the relevant pages but at the cost of increasing the number of downloads.

Fig. 1 shows how nearness is determined by the WTMS crawler. Suppose a page in the directory A/B is the current page. Then pages in the same Web site are considered to be near (and therefore downloaded) if and only if they belong to the directories shown in the figure. Thus pages in the parent directory (*A*) as well as any children directories (*C, D*) are considered to be near. Sections of sibling directories (*E, F, G*) are also downloaded. After crawling several Web sites, we found that this definition of nearness gives the optimal result. It should be noted that if a page has a link to or from a page in another Web site, we have to download the page (unless it is in the stop URL list). Also note that if an URL contains any of the topic keywords, the page will be always downloaded. So all pages from *http://www.titanicmovie.com* will be downloaded for the *Titanic* collection.

3.2.2. Irrelevant directories

Because Web sites are well organized, generally most pages in the same directory have similar themes. Thus all pages in *http://www.murthy.com/txlaw/* talk about tax laws. One of these pages, *http://www.murthy.com/txlaw/txwomsoc.html* was retrieved by a query to Google with the keywords *World Cup Soccer* since it talks about visa issuance to the Women's World Cup Soccer tournament. However, none of the other pages of the directory are relevant to the collection on *World Cup Soccer*. However, in the basic crawler all these pages were downloaded, only to be discarded after determining the similarity to RDV.

To avoid this problem, during crawling, we keep a count on the number of pages that have been indexed and ignored for each directory. If more than 25 pages of a directory are downloaded and 90% of those pages are ignored, we do not download any more pages from that directory.

3.3. Evaluation

Table 1 shows the comparison between the basic crawler and the enhanced crawlers for three collec-

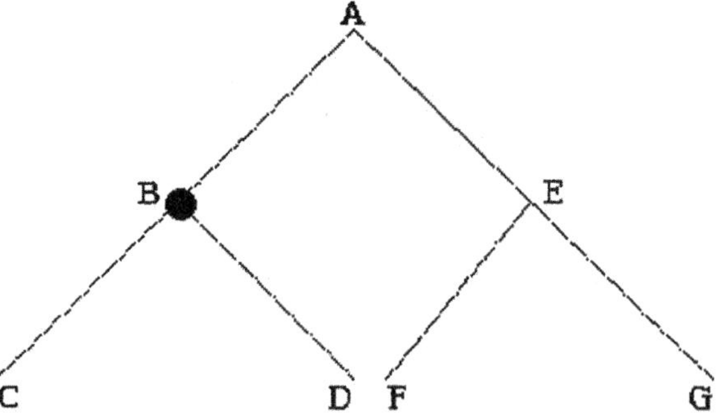

Fig. 1. Determining the nearness of two pages in the directory hierarchy.

Table 1
Effectiveness of the heuristics in improving crawling performance

Collections:	Information Visualization	World Cup Soccer	Titanic
% Download	73.54	66.27	77.4
% Nearness	21.9	27.59	15.7
% Rejected directories	4.56	6.14	6.9
% Relevant pages missed	4.26	4.04	2.56
Average score pages missed	0.261	0.279	0.254

tions, *Information Visualization*, *World Cup Soccer* and *Titanic*. The following statistics are shown:

- *% Download* = 100 × (Number of pages downloaded by enhanced crawler)/(Number of pages downloaded by basic crawler). For all the three collections there is a significant decrease in the number of URLs that were downloaded. Besides reducing the network overhead, the amount of time needed to wait between successive requests to the same server is also decreased.
- *% Nearness* is the number of pages not downloaded because the linked page was not near the original page. A significant number of pages were not downloaded using this heuristic.
- *% Rejected directories* is the number of pages not downloaded because a significant number of pages from the directory the page belonged to, were already rejected after downloading. Unfortunately, only a small number of pages were ignored using this criterion. Maybe extending the criteria to determine irrelevant sites instead of irrelevant directories may be more useful.
- *% Relevant pages missed* = 100 × (Number of relevant pages indexed by the basic crawler but ignored by the enhanced crawler)/(Total number of pages indexed by the basic crawler). This statistic shows the number of relevant pages that were ignored by the enhanced crawler. It indicates that most of the pages that were not downloaded by the enhanced crawler were not relevant to the topic and were not indexed by the basic crawler also.
- *Average score pages missed* is the average score of the relevant pages indexed by the basic crawler but ignored by the enhanced crawler. Even if the enhanced crawler misses some relevant pages, for the crawler to be acceptable, none of these pages should be very important to the collection. To measure the importance of the missed pages, we calculate the average similarity scores of these pages. In our crawler all pages whose similarity to the representative document vector is greater than 0.25 are indexed (we use a vector space model where the similarity of a page is a number between 0 and 1). Since the average score of the missed pages is close to 0.25, it shows that these pages were not the most important pages of the collection.

Thus, our enhancements were able to significantly reduce the download time without missing many relevant pages of the collection.

4. Interfaces for topic management

After the information about a particular topic has been crawled and indexed, a WTMS server is initialized. Any user can access the WTMS server from a Web browser. The WTMS user interface is opened in the client browser as a Java (*Swing*) applet. Since most users will require all the collected information, the applet initially loads only a minimal amount of information. Based on user interactions, the applet can request further information from the WTMS server. XML is used for information exchange between the WTMS server and clients.

The WTMS interface provides various types of views to allow navigation through the gathered information space. This section gives a brief description of the WTMS interface applet.

4.1. Tabular overview

In WTMS the collected information is organized into an abstraction hierarchy as discussed in [16]. The Web pages relevant to a topic downloaded by the crawler are considered to be the smallest unit of information in the system. The pages can be grouped into their respective *physical domains*; for example all pages in *www.cnn.com* can be grouped together. Many large corporations use several Web servers based on functionality or geographic location. For example, *www.nec.com* and *www.nec.co.jp* are the Web sites of NEC Corporation in US and Japan, respectively. Similarly, *shopping.yahoo.com* is the shopping component of the Yahoo *www.yahoo.com* portal. Therefore, we group together related physical domains into *logical Web sites* by analyzing the URLs. (In other cases we may need to break down the domains into smaller logical Web sites. For example, for corporations like Geocities and Tripod who provide free home pages, the Web sites *www.geocities.com* and *members.tripod.com* are actually a collection of home pages with minimal relationship among each other. However, this technique has not yet been incorporated into WTMS.)

Most HTML authors organize the information into a series of HTML pages for ease of navigation. Moreover, readers generally want to know what is available on a given site, not on a single page. Therefore, logical Web sites are the basic unit of information in WTMS. Thus, for calculating the hub and authority scores, we apply the algorithm introduced in [13] to logical sites instead of individual Web pages.

Fig. 2 shows the initial view of the WTMS interface for a collection on *World Cup Soccer*. It shows a table containing various information about the logical Web sites that were discovered for the topic. Besides the URL and the number of pages, it shows

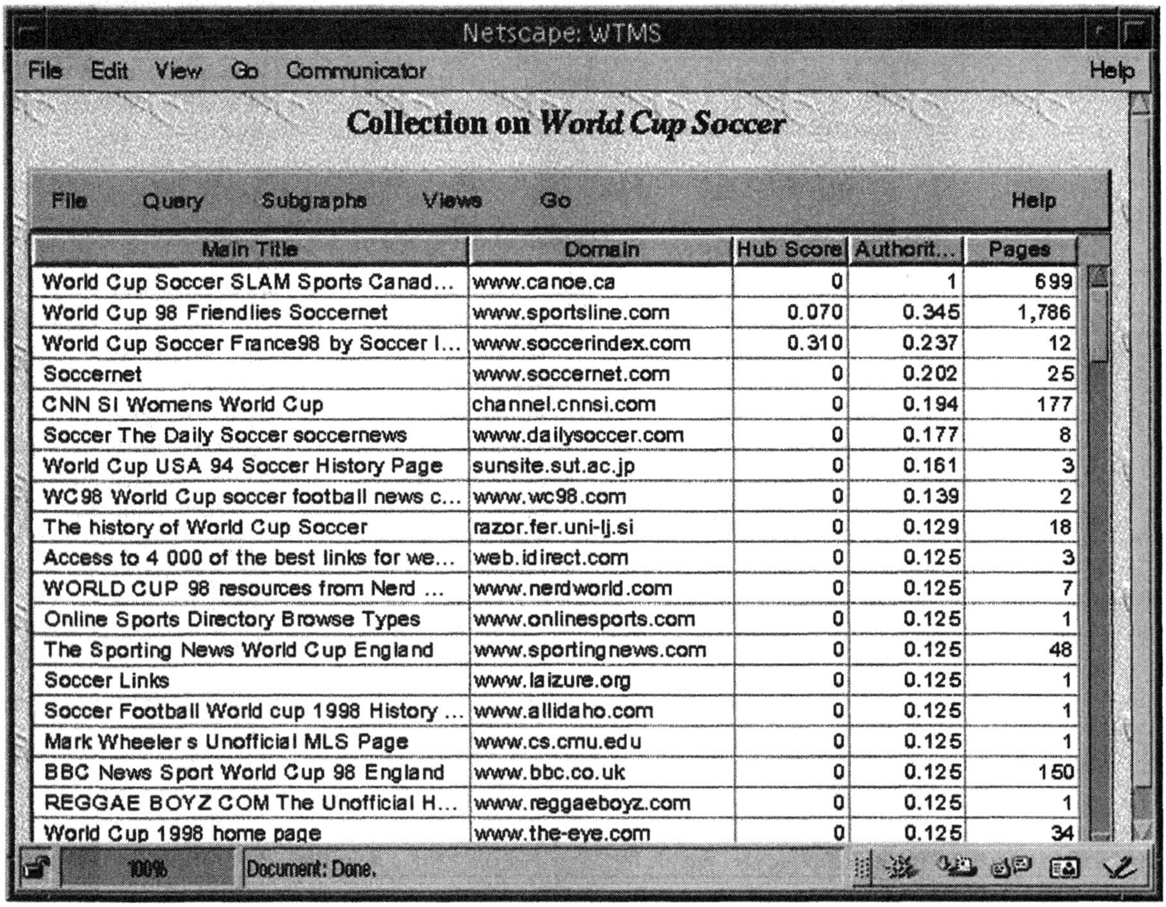

Netscape: WTMS

File Edit View Go Communicator Help

Collection on *World Cup Soccer*

File Query Subgraphs Views Go Help

Main Title	Domain	Hub Score	Authorit...	Pages
World Cup Soccer SLAM Sports Canad...	www.canoe.ca	0	1	699
World Cup 98 Friendlies Soccernet	www.sportsline.com	0.070	0.345	1,786
World Cup Soccer France98 by Soccer I...	www.soccerindex.com	0.310	0.237	12
Soccernet	www.soccernet.com	0	0.202	25
CNN SI Womens World Cup	channel.cnnsi.com	0	0.194	177
Soccer The Daily Soccer soccernews	www.dailysoccer.com	0	0.177	8
World Cup USA 94 Soccer History Page	sunsite.sut.ac.jp	0	0.161	3
WC98 World Cup soccer football news c...	www.wc98.com	0	0.139	2
The history of World Cup Soccer	razor.fer.uni-lj.si	0	0.129	18
Access to 4 000 of the best links for we...	web.idirect.com	0	0.125	3
WORLD CUP 98 resources from Nerd ...	www.nerdworld.com	0	0.125	7
Online Sports Directory Browse Types	www.onlinesports.com	0	0.125	1
The Sporting News World Cup England	www.sportingnews.com	0	0.125	48
Soccer Links	www.laizure.org	0	0.125	1
Soccer Football World cup 1998 History ...	www.allidaho.com	0	0.125	1
Mark Wheeler s Unofficial MLS Page	www.cs.cmu.edu	0	0.125	1
BBC News Sport World Cup 98 England	www.bbc.co.uk	0	0.125	150
REGGAE BOYZ COM The Unofficial H...	www.reggaeboyz.com	0	0.125	1
World Cup 1998 home page	www.the-eye.com	0	0.125	34

100% Document: Done.

Fig. 2. A table showing the logical sites relevant to a collection on *World Cup Soccer* sorted by the authority scores.

the hub and authority scores. (These scores have values between 0 and 1.) The table also shows the title of the main page of the sites. The main page is determined by the connectivity and the depth of the page in the site hierarchy as discussed in [18]. Note that generally while calculating the hub and authority scores, intra-site links are ignored [5]. Assuming that all Web pages within a site are by the same author, this removes the author's judgment while determining the global importance of a page within the overall collection. However, while determining the local importance of a page within a site, the author's judgment is also important. So the intra-site links are not ignored while determining the main page of a site.

The table gives a good overview about the collection. Clicking on the labels on the top the user can sort the table by that particular statistic. For example, in Fig. 2, it is sorted by the authority scores. Some authorities for information on World Cup Soccer are shown at the top.

4.2. *Visualizing information at various levels of abstraction*

A logical site has several physical domains. The domains consist of directories and each directory has several Web pages and sub-directories. WTMS allows the users to view the information about a collection at various levels of abstraction depending on their focus. We discuss some of these visualizations in this subsection. Note that WTMS also allows the user to group related sites as discussed in Section 5.

4.2.1. *Site level views*

Fig. 3 shows the details of the site *seawifs.gsfc. nasa.gov*, the highest authority for the collection on *Titanic*. In Fig. 3a the logical site itself is selected. The constituents of the site as well as sites having links to and from the selected site are shown as *glyphs* (graphical elements). The figure shows that the logical site has several physical domains like *rsd. gsfc.nasa.gov* and *seawifs.gsfc.nasa.gov*. Notice that if a physical domain has just one directory or site (for example *daac.gsfc.nasa.gov*) then the glyph for that directory or page is shown. The brightness of a glyph is proportional to the last modification time of the freshest page in the group. Thus, bright red glyphs indicate groups which contain very fresh pages (for example, *www.dimensional.com*) and black glyphs indicate old pages (for example, *www.nationalgeo graphic.com*).

The view also shows the links to and from the currently selected site. If another site has a link to the site, it has an arrow pointing out. Similarly, if a site has a link from the selected site, it has an arrow pointing in. Thus, Fig. 3a shows that *www.marine museum.org* has both links to and from *seawifs.gsfc. nasa.gov*. The arrows to and from the children of the selected site, give an indication of their connectivity. For example, the figure shows that the domain *rsd. gsfc.nasa.gov* has only out-links while *seawifs. gsfc.nasa.gov* has both in-links and out-links. The thickness of the arrow is proportional to the number of links. On the other hand, the color of the arrows indicates whether the link is inter-site or intra-site. Green indicates inter-site links. Thus all links from pages in the domain *rsd.gsfc.nasa.gov* are to other pages within the same logical site. On the other hand, blue indicates inter-site links. Thus all links from the other sites are blue. A combination of inter-site and intra-site links is indicated by cyan. Thus *seawifs. gsfc.nasa.gov* has both inter-site and intra-site in-links and out-links.

The user can click on a glyph with the right mouse button to see more details. For example, in Fig. 3b the user has navigated further down the hierarchy and selected the directory *seawifs.gsfc.nasa.gov/ OCEAN_PLANET/HTML*. The relevant Web pages in the directory are shown. The directory has a page with a large number of in-links and out-links, *tita nic.html*. Note that the glyph is a circle for a Web page and rectangle for the groups. Further, the label of the currently selected node is highlighted and the rectangles representing the currently selected path is not filled.

4.2.2. *Page level views*

Clicking on a glyph with the left mouse button shows information about the corresponding page or site. Thus, Fig. 4 shows information about the *Georgia Tech Graphics, Visualization and Usability Center Home Page*, a page in the *Information Visualization* collection. This dialog box allows the user to visit the page, see the links to and from the page

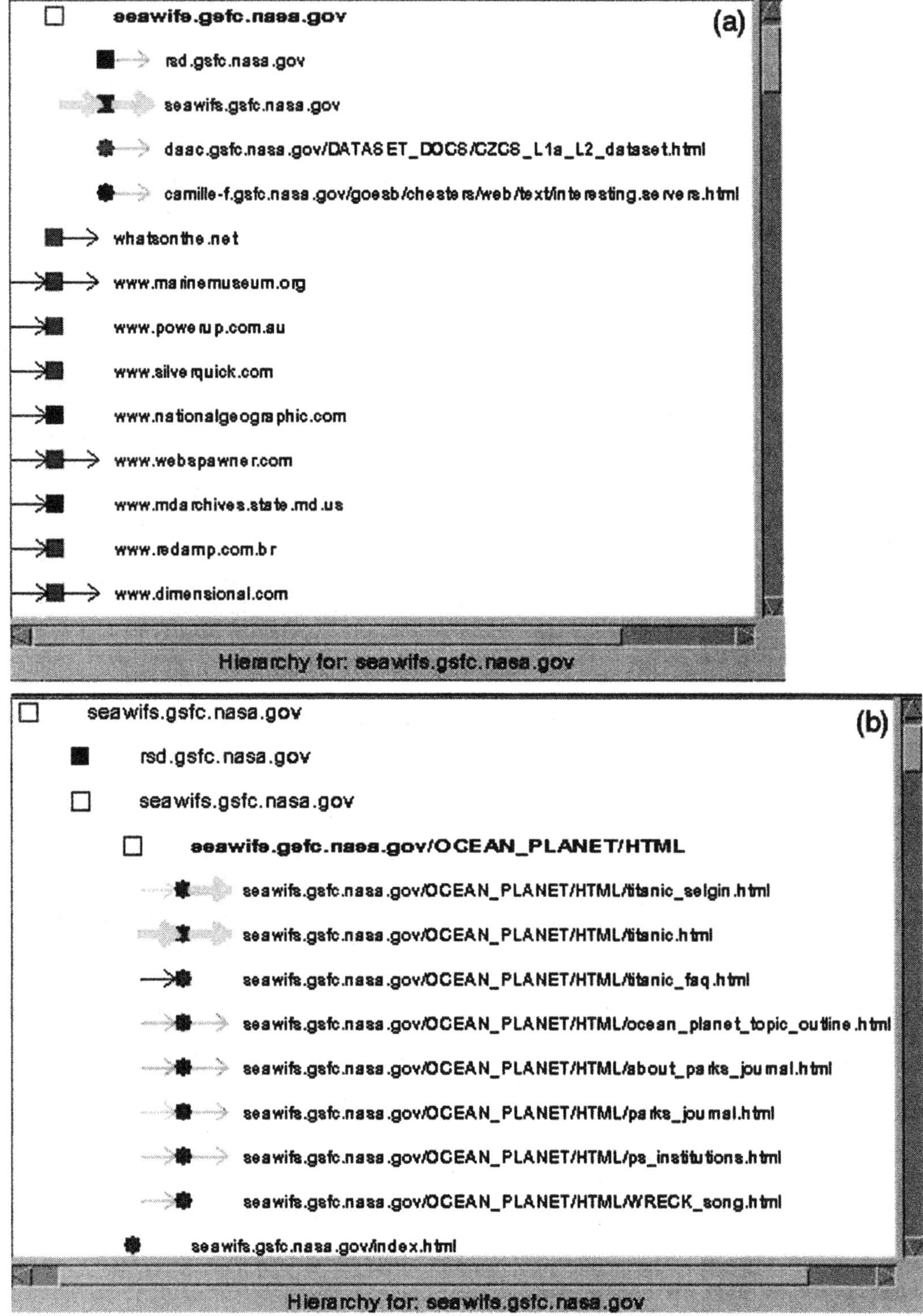

Fig. 3. Visualizing the details of a logical site. (a) The logical Web site is selected. (b) A directory within the site is selected.

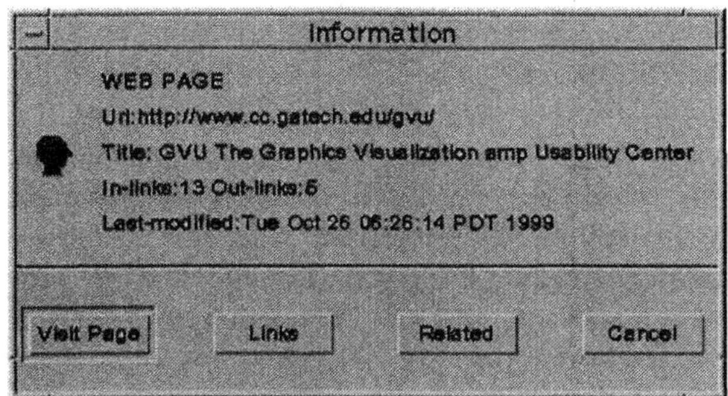

Fig. 4. Information about the Web page *www.cc.gatech.edu/gvu.*

or see the related pages. For example, Fig. 5 shows the URL, title as well as the structural and semantic similarity values of pages related to the above page. The table is sorted by the semantic similarity of a page to the selected page which is determined by the vector space model [19]. The structural similarity of a page is determined by the links of the page with respect to the selected page and is calculated as follows:

- For each direct link to and from any page *B* to *A*, the structural similarity score of *B* is increased by 1.0.
- For each indirect link between pages *B* and *A*, the structural similarity score is increased by 0.5. There can be 3 types of indirect links: (1) transitive, *B* links to *C* and *C* links to *A* or vice versa; (2) social filtering, both *A* and *B* point to *C*; (3) co-citation: *C* points to both *A* and *B*.
- The scores are normalized to determine the structural similarity.

5. Analyzing the site graph

The WTMS interface allows the user to filter the information space based on various criteria. For example, the user can see only pages modified before or after a particular date. Moreover, in the table of related pages (Fig. 5), the user can see only pages that are co-cited or directly linked to the selected page. Another useful technique is to specify keywords to determine relevant Web pages or sites. For keyword queries, as well as for determining the similar pages to a selected page, the WTMS interface sends a query to the WTMS server. The results from the server are used in the visualizations.

To make a Web topic management system more useful, it should provide analysis beyond traditional keyword- or attribute-based querying. At present WTMS provides various techniques based on graph algorithms to analyze the topic-specific collection. The algorithms are applied on the *site graph* which is a directed graph with the logical sites as the nodes. If a page in site *a* has a link to a page in site *b*, then an edge is created from node *a* to *b* in the site graph. It should be emphasized that our analysis techniques are not very complex and thus applicable to collections with a large number of Web sites in real time.

WTMS

Select View Go Help

Title	Url	Structural	Semantic
GVU Alphabetical Listing of Research Grou...	http://www.cc.gatech.edu/...	0.05	0.41
GVU Center Frequently Asked Questions	http://www.cc.gatech.edu/...	0.45	0.23
GVU Center Research	http://www.cc.gatech.edu/...	1	0.22
GVU Related Conferences	http://www.cc.gatech.edu/...	0.1	0.21
Readings in Information Visualization	http://www.cs.umd.edu/hcil...	0	0.2
UNB s HCI Lab Projects	http://www.omg.unb.ca/hci...	0	0.2
No element of the R amp D enterprise is as...	http://www.house.gov/scie...	0	0.19
Information Visualization research at GVU	http://www.cc.gatech.edu/...	0.2	0.18
Information Visualization research at GVU	http://www.cc.gatech.edu/...	0	0.18
GVU Cognitive Approaches	http://www.cc.gatech.edu/...	0.1	0.17

Related Urls for: www.cc.gatech.edu/gvu/

Fig. 5. Related Web pages for *www.cc.gatech.edu/gvu.*

5.1. Connected components

One useful technique is to consider the site graph as an undirected graph and determine the connected components [10]. Nodes in the same connected component are connected by paths of one or more links and can thus be considered to be related.

Fig. 6 shows the connected components that were discovered for the collections *World Cup Soccer* and *Titanic*. If some connected component contained only one site, the site itself is shown (for example, *www.iranian.com* in Fig. 6a). Each component is represented by a glyph whose size is proportional to the number of Web pages the group contains. The glyphs are ordered by the maximum authority score among the sites in the group. Thus the group containing *seawifs.gsfc.nasa.gov* is at the top for the *Titanic* collection. The label of a connected component is determined by the site with the highest authority score it contains. The user can click on a glyph to see the logical sites and web pages of the corresponding component. For example, in Fig. 6a, the user is seeing the details of a connected component containing the site *www.ee.umd.edu*.

Fig. 6 shows that for both the collections only a few connected components were formed (even though the collections had thousands of pages). Thus the connected components are a useful mechanism to group the logical sites into meaningful clusters. The major information about the topic can be found in the top few components. The isolated sites found later in the view generally contain information different from the main theme of the collection. For example, as seen from Fig. 6a, we see that the *Electrical Department of the University of Maryland* is in the collection on *World Cup Soccer*. On examining the main page of the site (for this collection) *www.ee.umd.edu/~dstewart/pinball/PAPA6/*, we found that the page talks about the 1998 World Pinball Championship. The search engine retrieved the page, since one of the participating teams was named *World Cup Soccer*! Similarly, as discussed in Section 3.2.2, the site *www.murthy.com* which talks about tax laws, is in the collection since one of its *page* talks about visa issuance to the Women's World Cup Soccer tournament. Further, for the *Titanic* collection shown in Fig. 6b, we found an isolated site for a *casino named Titanic*. Thus, it is evident that *the connected components are effective in isolating pages that are in the fringes of the collection.*

5.2. Strongly connected components

Considering the site graph as a directed graph we can also determine the strongly connected components [10]. Each pair of nodes of a strongly connected component have bi-directional links between them. Fig. 7 shows a strongly connected component for the *Information Visualization* collection. All the sites shown in the figure are reachable from

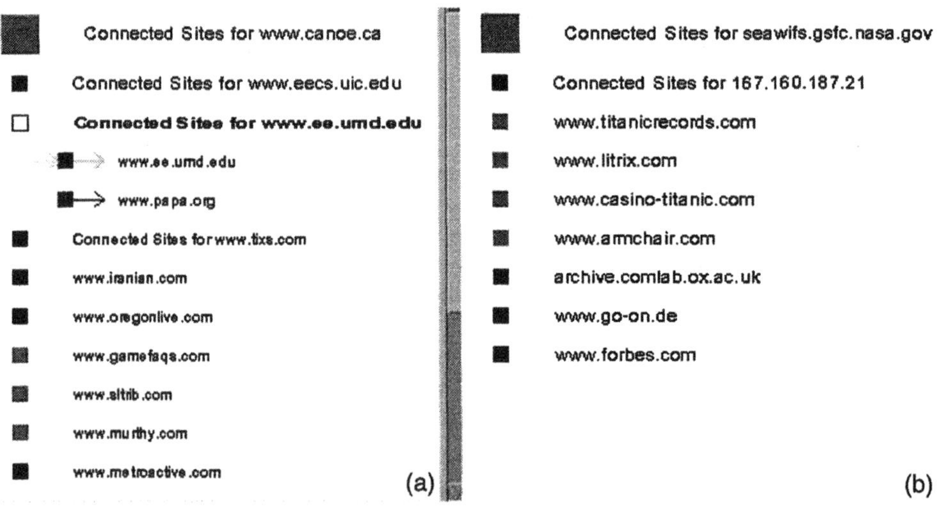

Fig. 6. The connected components of collections. (a) World Cup Soccer. (b) Titanic.

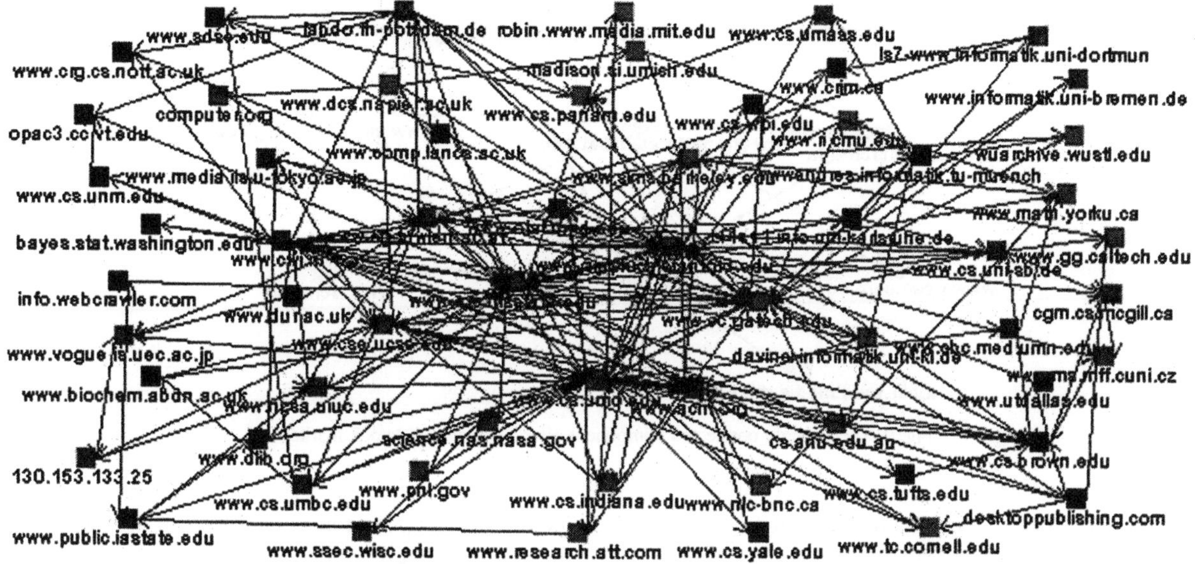

Fig. 7. A strongly connected component in the *Information Visualization* collection.

each other. For a strongly connected component with a large number of nodes and links, the graph is too complex for the user to understand. Therefore WTMS allows various ways to filter the graph:

- The user can see the paths to or from a selected node to all other nodes in the graph. For example, Fig. 8 shows the paths from the site *www-graphics.stanford.edu*, one of the best hubs on the topic.
- We also allow the integration of keyword queries with structure-based analysis. For example, Fig. 9 shows the same strongly connected component after a query with the keywords 'stock market'. Sites relevant to visualization of stock markets are only shown. Notice that the site *computer.org* is

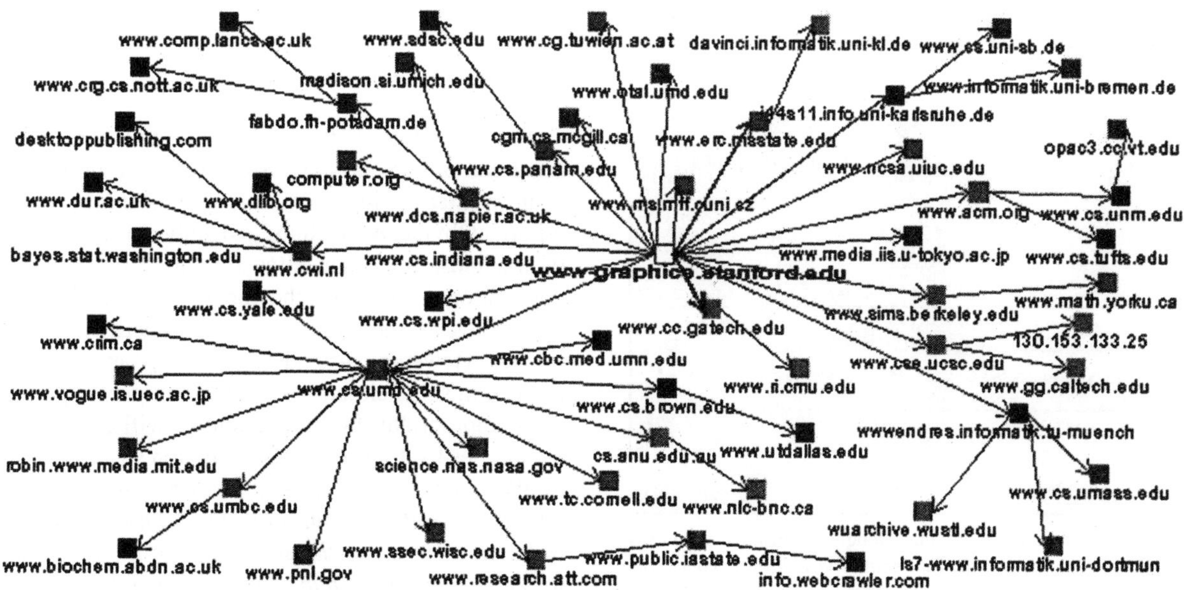

Fig. 8. Showing the paths from *www-graphics.stanford.edu* in the strongly connected component.

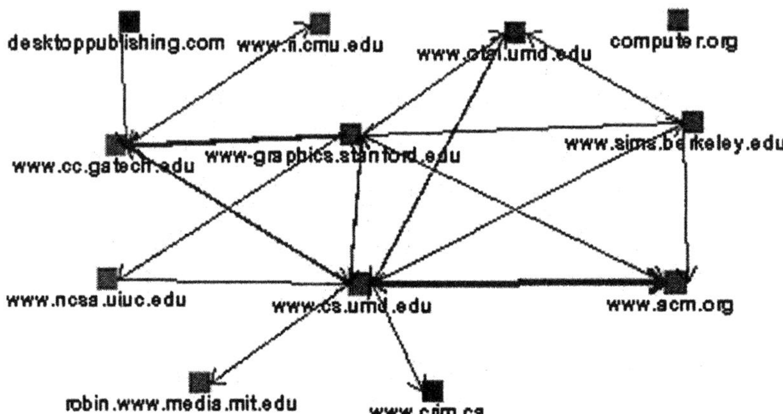

Fig. 9. The strongly connected component after a query with 'stock market'.

isolated since the sites connecting it to the other sites were filtered out by the query.

The dialog box shown in Fig. 10 gives an indication about the strongly connected components of a collection. The figure shows that for an academic topic like *Information Visualization* more sites are grouped into strongly connected components (20%) than for a topic of more general interest like *World Cup Soccer* (only 3.5%). On analyzing the collections using the WTMS interface, we determined that this is because the *Information Visualization* collection mainly consists of Web sites of research communities which sometimes cross-reference each other. On the other hand, the *World Cup Soccer* collection consists of several commercial Web sites on the topic as well as personal pages of people interested in the topic. The personal pages may point to some commercial sites but not vice versa and of course there is hardly any cyclical referencing among competing commercial sites. Thus, *the number of sites that belong to a strongly connected component gives an indication about whether the collection is competitive or collaborative.* In a collaborative collection, unlike a competitive collection, there will be several Web sites referencing each other; therefore these sites will be grouped into strongly connected components.

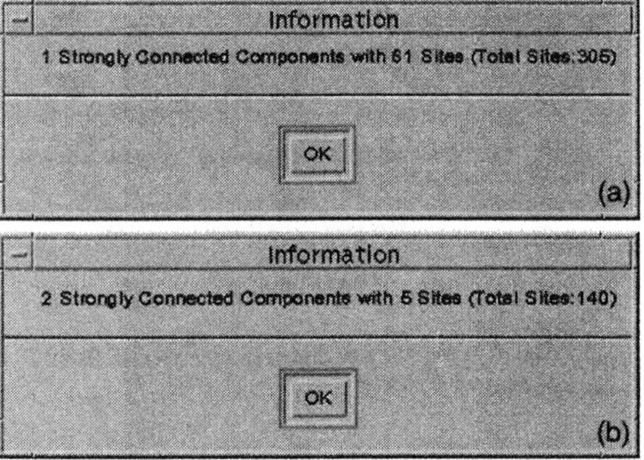

Fig. 10. Information about the strongly collected components for a collection. (a) For the *Information Visualization* collection, 20% of the sites reference each other. (b) For the *World Cup Soccer* collection, 3.5% of the sites reference each other.

5.3. Optimum hub/authority covers

For most topics, the collections will consist of hundreds of logical sites. Sometimes the user may want to filter the information space based on various criteria. Obviously, the hubs and authorities are some of the most important sites for the collection. So one option is to show the top n or $n\%$ hubs and authorities as the important sites, where n is any integer. However, instead of choosing an arbitrary integer, in some situations other techniques might be more appropriate. In this section we will define two techniques for filtering the information space.

We define *a hub cover for a site graph with* V *sites and* E *links as a subset* V_h *of* V*, such that for all links* (u, v) *in* E*,* u *(the source of the link) belongs to* V_h*. An optimum hub cover is the hub cover of the smallest size for the given graph.* That is, the

Table 2
Statistics for determining approximate optimum hub and authority covers

Collections:	Information Visualization	World Cup Soccer	Titanic
Number of sites	305	140	528
Size of approximate optimal hub cover	35	20	52
Size of approximate optimal authority cover	28	18	68

optimum hub cover of a collection is the smallest number of sites that have links to all the sites of the collection. Filtering the collection by showing only the optimum hub cover is useful, because from these sites the user can reach all the sites of the collection.

On the other hand, *the authority cover for a site graph with V sites and E links is a subset V_a of V, such that for all links (u, v) in E, v (the destination of the link) belongs to V_a. The optimum authority cover is the authority cover with the smallest size in the site graph.* That is, the optimum authority cover of a collection is the smallest number of sites that have links from all the sites of the collection. Obviously, filtering the collection by the optimum authority cover is also useful.

Determining the optimum hub and authority covers for a site graph is similar to the *vertex cover problem* [10]. The vertex cover problem for an undirected graph $G = (V, E)$ is to determine the smallest possible subset V' of V such that if (u, v) is in E, then at least one of u or v is in V'. Unfortunately, the vertex cover problem is *NP-complete* [10].

In WTMS we determine the *approximate optimum hub and authority covers*. The algorithm to determine the approximate optimum hub cover is as follows:

- Let $G = (V, E)$ be the site graph
- $V_h = ()$
- Let V_s be the nodes of the graph sorted by their increasing in-degrees
- Remove from V_s all nodes with no incoming links
- While V_s is not empty,
  - Let v be the next node of V_s
  - Let u be the node with the highest hub score among the nodes that have links to v
  - Add u to V_h
  - Remove from V_s, u as well as all nodes that have links from u
- Return to V_h as the approximate optimum hub cover

The algorithm examines the nodes of the graph sorted by their increasing in-degrees. For nodes having just one in-link, the source of the link has to be added to the hub cover. For nodes having more than one link, the algorithm adds to the hub cover the link source with the highest hub score. Whenever a node is added to the hub cover, all nodes that have links from that node can be ignored.

Notice that even though we remove the sites with no in-links before the while loop in the above algorithm, these sites can still be in a hub cover. However, sites with both no in-links and out-links will be ignored by the algorithm. Since these sites are in the fringes of the collection (as discussed in Section 5.1), they should not be considered important to the collection.

The approximate optimum authority cover can be determined by a similar algorithm. We can also determine the hub and authority covers for the Web pages by applying the algorithms on the original graph of the collection.

Table 2 shows the size of the approximate optimal hub and authority covers that were discovered for the collections. In all cases we could discover a few sites, significantly smaller than the total number of sites, which have links to/from all the sites of the collections.

Fig. 11a shows the approximate optimal hub cover for the *World Cup Soccer* collection, sorted by the hub scores. Similarly, Fig. 11b shows the approximate optimal authority cover sorted by the authority scores. These views are useful because starting from these sites the user can visit all the sites of the collection. Clicking on one of the sites in the *hub cover* view shows the sites that can be directly reached from the selected site. Thus, Fig. 11c shows the sites with links from the main hub for the *World Cup Soccer* collection *www.anancyweb.com*. Similarly, clicking on a site in the *authority cover* view shows the sites that have links to the selected site.

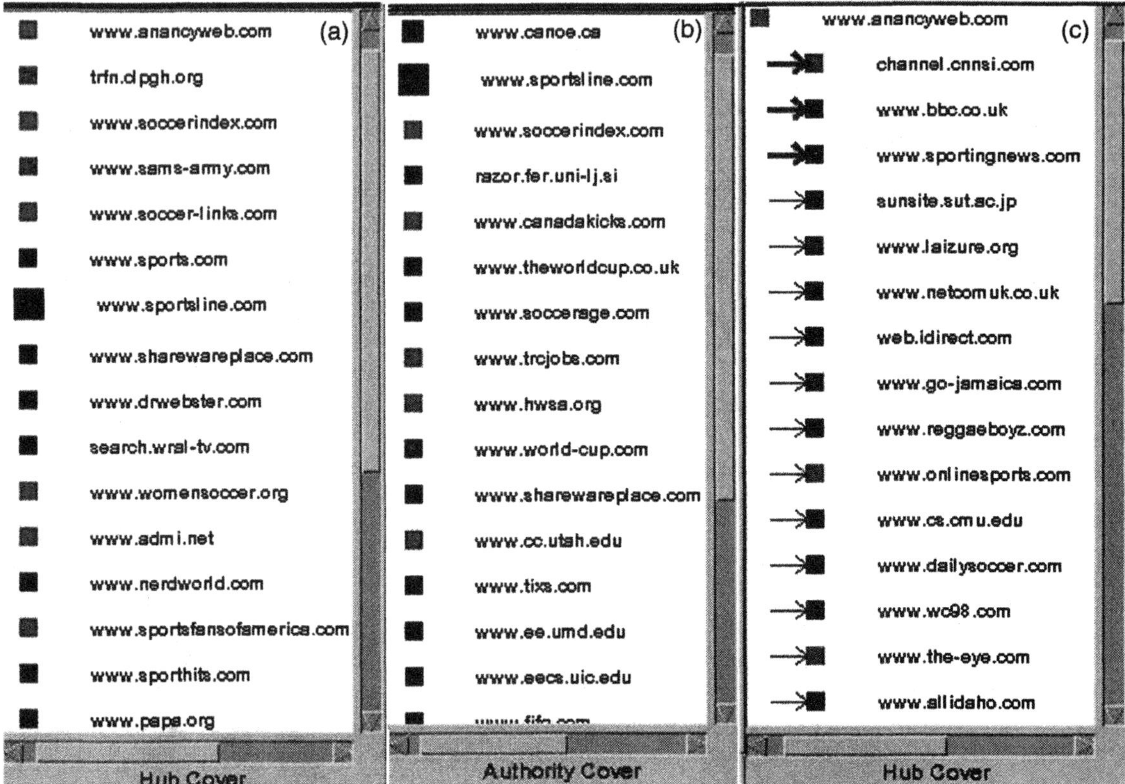

Fig. 11. The hub and authority covers for the *World Cup Soccer* collection. (a) Hub cover. (b) Authority cover. (c) Nodes directly reachable from the main hub *www.anancyweb.com*

6. Conclusion

In this paper, we have presented a Web topic management system, WTMS. WTMS uses a crawler to gather information related to a particular topic from the World Wide Web. The enhancements to the crawler have resulted in improved performance by reducing the number of pages that need to be downloaded by more than 20% while missing only a few insignificant pages.

The WTMS interface provides various visualizations to navigate through the information space at different levels of abstraction. For example, the user can see the details of a logical site or a Web page. The system allows the user to integrate searching and browsing. Besides traditional keyword-based search, structural analysis techniques are provided which allow the user to gain several useful insights about the collection. This kind of analysis is not easy using traditional search engines or the previous systems for topic management. We have also introduced the concept of optimum hub and authority covers as a technique to filter the information space. The example scenarios presented in the paper indicate the usefulness of the system for Web topic management. Future work is planned along various directions:

(1) *Incorporating other analysis techniques*. We need to integrate other techniques of analysis to enable the users to understand the information space from different perspectives. For example, we may determine the cores or bi-partite sub-graphs in the site graph to understand the communities within the collection as discussed in [14]. Techniques that examine the contents of the collection are also required.

(2) *Allowing collaboration*. We plan to allow distributed users to collaborate over the Internet while navigating through the same information space. For example, colleagues can collaborate while performing a literature survey on a particular topic. Our

client–server architecture will facilitate such a collaborative environment.

(3) *Usability studies*. Although the initial reactions to the system have been positive, more formal user studies are required to determine the effectiveness of the WTMS for analyzing information about a particular topic. Such feedback will help us to improve the system.

We believe that as the World Wide Web grows bigger, systems like the WTMS will become essential for retrieving useful information.

References

[1] B. Amento, W. Hill, L. Terveen, D. Hix and P. Ju, An empirical evaluation of user interfaces for topic management of Web sites, in: Proc. ACM SIGCHI '99 Conf. on Human Factors in Computing Systems, Pittsburgh, PA, May 1999, pp. 552–559.

[2] K. Andrews, Visualizing cyberspace: information visualization in the Harmony Internet Browser, in: Proc. of the 1995 Information Visualization Symposium, Atlanta, GA, 1995, pp. 97–104.

[3] I. Ben-Shaul, M. Hersovici, M. Jacovi, Y. Maarek, D. Pelleg, M. Shtalheim, V. Soroka and S. Ur, Adding support for dynamic and focussed search with Fetuccino, in: Proc. 8th Int. World Wide Web Conf., Toronto, Ont., May 1999, pp. 575–588.

[4] K. Bharat and A. Broder, A technique for measuring the relative size and overlap of public Web search engines, Computer Networks and ISDN Systems, Special Issue on the 7th Int. World-Wide Web Conf., Brisbane, 30(1–7) (1998).

[5] K. Bharat and M. Henzinger, Improved algorithms for topic distillation in a hyperlinked environment, in: Proc. ACM SIGIR '98 Conf. on Research and Development in Information Retrieval, Melbourne, August 1998, pp. 104–111.

[6] S. Card, G. Robertson and W. York, The WebBook and the Web Forager: an information workspace for the World-Wide Web, in: Proc. ACM SIGCHI '96 Conf. on Human Factors in Computing Systems, Vancouver, April 1996, pp. 112–117.

[7] J. Carriere and R. Kazman, Searching and visualizing the Web through connectivity, in: Proc. 6th Int. World-Wide Web Conf., Santa Clara, CA, April 1997, pp. 701–711.

[8] S. Chakrabarti, B. Dom, D. Gibson, J. Kleinberg, P. Raghavan and S. Rajagopalan, Automatic resource compilation by analyzing hyperlink structure and associated text, Computer Networks and ISDN Systems, Special Issue on the 7th Int. World-Wide Web Conf., Brisbane, 30(1–7) (1998).

[9] S. Chakrabarti, M. van den Berg and B. Dom, Focussed crawling: a new approach to topic-specific Web resource discovery, in: Proc. 8th Int. World-Wide Web Conf., Toronto, Ont., May 1999, pp. 545–562.

[10] T. Cormen, C. Leiserson and R. Rivest, Introduction to Algorithms, The MIT Press, Cambridge, MA, 1992.

[11] R. Hendley, N. Drew, A. Wood and R. Beale, Narcissus: visualizing information, in: Proc. of the 1995 Information Visualization Symposium, Atlanta, GA, 1995, pp. 90–96.

[12] M. Hersovici, M. Jacovi, Y. Maarek, D. Pelleg, M. Shtalheim and S. Ur, The shark-search algorithm — an application: tailored Web site mapping, Computer Networks and ISDN Systems, Special Issue on the 7th Int. World-Wide Web Conf., Brisbane, 30(1–7) (1998).

[13] J. Kleinberg, Authoritative sources in a hyperlinked environment, in: Proc. 9th ACM–SIAM Symp. on Discrete Algorithms, May 1998.

[14] R. Kumar, P. Raghavan, S. Rajagopalan and A. Tomkins, Trawling the Web for emerging cyber-communities, in: Proc. 8th Int. World-Wide Web Conf., Toronto, Ont., May 1999, pp. 403–415.

[15] Y. Maarek and I. Shaul, WebCutter: a system for dynamic and tailorable site mapping, in: Proc. 6th Int. World-Wide Web Conf., Santa Clara, CA, April 1997, pp. 713–722.

[16] S. Mukherjea, Organizing topic-specific Web information, to appear in: Proc. 11th ACM Conf. on Hypertext, San Antonio, TX, May 2000.

[17] S. Mukherjea and J. Foley, Visualizing the World-Wide Web with the navigational view builder, Computer Networks and ISDN Systems. Special Issue on the 3rd Int. World-Wide Web Conf., Darmstadt, 27(6) (1995) 1075–1087.

[18] S. Mukherjea and Y. Hara, Focus+Context views of World-Wide Web nodes, in: Proc. 8th ACM Conf. on Hypertext, Southampton, April 1997, pp. 187–196.

[19] G. Salton and M. McGill, Introduction to Modern Information Retrieval, McGraw-Hill, New York, 1983.

[20] L. Terveen and H. Will, Finding and visualizing inter-site clan graphs, in: Proc. ACM SIGCHI '98 Conf. on Human Factors in Computing Systems, Los Angeles, CA, April 1998, pp. 448–455.

Sougata Mukherjea received his bachelor degree in computer science and engineering from Jadavpur University, Calcutta, India in 1988 and MS in computer science from Northeastern University, Boston, MA in 1991. He then obtained his Ph.D. in Computer Science from Georgia Institute of Technology, Atlanta, Ga in 1995. Till 1999 he was working at NEC's C&C Research Laboratories in San Jose, CA. Presently he is working for Icarian, a start-up company in Sunnyvale, CA. His main research interests are in Web technologies like crawling and link analysis, information retrieval and information visualization. He can be reached by e-mail at *sougata@icarian.com* or *sougata_m@yahoo.com*.

Semantic community Web portals

S. Staab [a,b,*,2], J. Angele [b,2], S. Decker [a,b,2], M. Erdmann [a,1], A. Hotho [a,1], A. Maedche [a,1], H.-P. Schnurr [a,b,2], R. Studer [a,b,2], Y. Sure [a,1]

[a] *Institute AIFB, University of Karlsruhe, 76128 Karlsruhe, Germany*
[b] *Ontoprise GmbH, Hermann-Loens-Weg 19, 76275 Ettlingen, Germany*

Abstract

Community Web portals serve as portals for the information needs of particular communities on the Web. We here discuss how a comprehensive and flexible strategy for building and maintaining a high-value community Web portal has been conceived and implemented. The strategy includes collaborative information provisioning by the community members. It is based on an ontology as a semantic backbone for accessing information on the portal, for contributing information, as well as for developing and maintaining the portal. We have also implemented a set of ontology-based tools that have facilitated the construction of our show case — the community Web portal of the knowledge acquisition community.

Keywords: Web portal; Collaboration; Ontology; Web site management; Information integration

1. Introduction

One of the major strengths of the Web is that virtually everyone who owns a computer may contribute high-value information — the real challenge is to make valuable information be found. Obviously, this challenge cannot only be achieved by centralized services, since the coverage of even the most powerful crawling and indexing machines has shrunk in the last few years in terms of percentage of the number of Web pages available on the Web. This means that a proper solution to this dilemma should rather be sought along a principle paradigm of the World Wide Web, viz. self-organization.

Self-organization does not necessarily mean automatic, machine-driven organization. Rather, from the very beginning communities of interest have formed on the Web that covered what they deemed to be of interest to their group of users in, what we here call, *community Web portals*. Community Web portals are similar to Yahoo and its likes by their goal of presenting a structured view onto the Web; however, they are dissimilar by the way knowledge is provided in a collaborative process with only few resources (manpower, money) for maintaining and editing the portal. Another major distinction is that community Web portals count in the millions, since a large percentage, if not the majority, of Web or intranet sites is not maintained by a central department, but rather by a community of users. Strangely enough, technology for supporting communities of interest has not quite kept up with the complexity of the tasks of managing community Web portals. A few years ago such a community of interest would have comparatively few sources of information to consider. Hence, the overall complexity of managing

* Corresponding author.
[1] http://www.aifb.uni-karlsruhe.de/WBS/
[2] http://www.ontoprise.de

this task was low. Now, with so many more people participating a community portal of only modest size may easily reach the point where it appears to be more of a jungle of interest rather than a convenient portal to start from.

This problem gave us reason to reconsider the techniques for managing community Web portals. We observed that a successful Web portal would weave loose pieces of information into a coherent presentation adequate for sharing knowledge with the user. On the conceptual, knowledge-sharing, level we have found that Davenport and Prusak's maxime [6], "people can't share knowledge if they don't speak a common language", is utterly crucial for the case of community Web portals. The only difference with Davenport and Prusak's thoughts derives from the fact that knowledge need not only be shared between people, but also between people and machines.

At this point, ontologies and intelligent reasoning come in as key technologies that allow knowledge sharing at a conceptually concise and elaborate level. These AI techniques support core concerns of the 'Semantic Web' (cf. [3]). In this view, information on the Web is not restricted to HTML only, but information may also be formal and, thus, machine understandable. The combination may be accounted for by an explicit model of knowledge structures in an *ontology*. The ontology formally represents common knowledge and interests that people share within their community. It is used to support the major tasks of a portal, viz. *accessing* the portal through manifold, dynamic, conceptually plausible views on the information of interest in a particular community, and *providing* information in a number of ways that reflect different types of information resources held by the individuals.

Following these principles when putting the semantic community Web portal into practice, incurs a range of subtasks that must be accounted for and requires a set of tools that support the accomplishment of these tasks. In Section 2 we discuss requirements that we have derived from a particular application scenario, the KA2 portal, that also serves as our testbed for development. Section 3 describes how ontologies are created and used for structuring information and, thus, appears as the conceptual cornerstone of our community Web portal. We proceed with the actual application of ontologies for the purposes of accessing the KA2 portal by navigating and querying explicit and implicit information through conceptual views on and rules in the ontology (Section 4). Section 5 covers the information-provisioning part for the community Web portal considering problems like information gathering and integration. Then, we describe the engineering process for our approach (Section 6) and present the overall architecture of our system (Section 7). Before we conclude with a tie-up of experiences and further work, we compare our work with related approaches (Section 8).

2. Requirements for a community Web portal — the KA2 example

Examples for community Web portals abound. In fact, one finds portals that very well succeed regarding some of the requirements we describe in this section. For instance, **MathNet**[3] introduces knowledge sharing through a database relying on Dublin Core metadata. Another example, RiboWeb [1], offers means to navigate a knowledge base about ribosomes. However, these approaches lack an integrated concept covering all phases of a community Web portal, viz. information accessing, information providing, and portal development and maintenance. We pursue a system that goes beyond isolated components towards a comprehensive solution for managing community Web portals.

2.1. Portal access by users

Navigating through a community Web portal that is unknown is a rather difficult task in general. Information retrieval may facilitate the finding of pieces of texts, but its usage is not sufficient in order to provide novice users with the right means for exploring unknown terrain. This turns out to be a problem particularly when the user does not know much about the domain and does not know what terms to search for. In such cases it is usually more helpful for the user to *explore* the portal by browsing, given that the portal is well and comprehensively structured. Simple tree-structured portals may be easy to maintain, but the chance is extremely high that

[3] http://www.math-net.de/

an inexperienced user looking for information gets stuck in a dead-end road. Here, we must face the trade-off between resources used for structuring the portal (money, man-power) and the extent to which a comprehensive navigation structure may be provided. Since information in the community portal will be continually amended by users, richly interrelated presentation of information would usually require extensive editing, such as is done, e.g., for Yahoo. In contrast, most community Web portals require that comprehensive structuring of information for presentation comes virtually for free.

There has been interesting research (e.g. [13] or [15]) that demonstrates that authoring, as well as reading and understanding of Web sites, profits from conceptual models underlying document structures 'in the large', i.e. the interlinking between documents, as well as document structures 'in the small', i.e., the contents of a particular document. Rather naturally, once a common conceptual model for the community exists and is made explicit, it is easier for the individual to access a particular site. Hence, in addition to rich interlinking between document structures 'in the large', comprehensive surveys and indices of contents and a large number of different views onto the contents of the portal, we require that the semantic structure of the portal is made explicit at some point. The following sections will show that this stipulation does not raise a conflict with other requirements, but that it fits well with the requirements that arise from provisioning of information and maintenance of the portal. Section 4 will elaborate on how such a conceptual level is exploited for a complex Web site with extensive browsing and querying capabilities.

2.2. Information provisioning through community members

An essential feature of a community Web portal is the contribution of information from all (or at least many) members of the community. Though they share some common understanding of their community, the information they want to contribute comes in many different (legacy) formats. Still, presentations of and queries for information contents must be allowed in many ways that need to be rather independent from the way by which that information was provided originally. The Web portal must remain adaptable to the information sources contributed by its members — and not vice versa. This requirement precludes the application of database-oriented approaches (e.g., [21]), since they presume that a uniform mode of storage exists that allows for the structuring of information at a particular conceptual level, such as a relational database scheme. In real-world settings, one must neither assume that a uniform mode for information storage exists nor that only one particular conceptual level is adequate for structuring information of a particular community. In fact, even more sophisticated approaches such as XML-based techniques that separate content from layout and allow for multiple modes of presentation appear insufficient, because their underlying transformation mechanisms (e.g., XSLT or XQL [9,24]) are too inconvenient for integration and presentation of various formats at different conceptual levels. The reason is that they do not provide the semantic underpinning required for proper integration of information.

In order to integrate diverse information, we require another layer besides the common distinction into document content and layout, viz. explicit knowledge structures that may structure *all* the information in different formats for a community at various levels of granularity. Different information formats need to be captured and related to the common ontology:

(1) several types of metadata such as available on Web pages (e.g., HTML META-tags),
(2) manual provision of data to the knowledge base, and
(3) a range of different wrappers that encapsulate structured and semi-structured information sources (e.g., databases or HTML documents).

Section 5 will address exactly these issues. The question now remains as to *how* this kind of semantic community Web portal is put into practice.

2.3. Development and maintenance

A community Web portal as we have stipulated constitutes a complex system. Hence, the developers and editors will need comprehensive tool support for presenting contents through views and links, and for maintaining consistency in the system, as well as guidelines that describe the procedures for actually building such a portal. Indeed, some of our first experiences with the example portal described in Section 2.4 was that even users who were well acquainted with all the principles hated to acquire detailed, technical knowledge in order to provide information or maintain 'their' information in the portal. Thus, we need a comprehensive concept that integrates tools and methods for building the portal, capturing information, and presenting its contents to the community. While some of the tools will be touched upon in subsequent sections, development and maintenance issues in general will be dealt with in Section 6.

2.4. The example

The example that we draw from in the rest of this paper is the portal for the *Knowledge Annotation initiative of the Knowledge Acquisition community* (KA2; cf. [2]). The KA2 initiative has been conceived for semantic knowledge retrieval from the Web building on knowledge created in the KA community. To structure knowledge, an ontology has been built in an international collaboration of researchers. The ontology constitutes the basis to annotate World Wide Web documents of the knowledge acquisition community in order to enable intelligent access to these documents and to infer implicit knowledge from explicitly stated facts and rules from the ontology. Though KA2 has provided much of the background knowledge we now want to exploit, it lacked much of the ease for accessing and providing community knowledge that we aim at with the KA2 community Web portal.

Given this basic scenario, which may be easily transferred towards other settings for community Web portals, we have investigated the techniques and built the tools that we describe in the rest of this paper. Nevertheless the reader may note that we have not yet achieved a complete integration of all tools and neither have we exploited all our technical capabilities in our up and running demonstration portal (http://ka2portal.aifb.uni-karlsruhe.de).

3. Structuring the community Web

Let us now summarize the principal stipulations we have found so far. We need:

- a conceptual structure for presenting information to the user,
- support for integrating information from different granularities stored in various formats,
- comprehensive tool support for providing information, developing and maintaining the portal
- a methodology for implementing the portal.

In particular, we need an explicit structuring mechanism that pervades the portal and reaches from development and maintenance, over provisioning to presentation of information. For this purpose, we use an ontology as the conceptual backbone of our community Web portal.

3.1. The role of ontologies

An *ontology* is an explicit specification of a shared conceptualization [14]. Their usefulness for information presentation (e.g. [13]), information integration (e.g. [30]) and system development (e.g. [2]) has been demonstrated recently. We introduce another application area, viz. the use of ontologies for intranet management or, more specific in our example, for community portal management. The role of ontologies is the capturing of domain knowledge in a generic way and the provision of a commonly agreed understanding of a domain, which may be reused and shared within communities or applications. Though only few communities have explicitly modeled their knowledge structures yet (examples are [1,26]), practically all share a common understanding of their particular domain.

Hence, our strategy is to use an ontology as a backbone of our community Web portal. In fact, we even allow the usage of multiple views that reflect diverging standards of understanding and usage of terminology in different subcommunities or for different groups of users (e.g., novice vs. expert). Rules may then be used to translate between different views such that one may view the information contributed from another subcommunity.

3.2. Modeling

The KA2 ontology consists of (i) concepts defining and structuring important terms, (ii) their attributes specifying properties and relations, and (iii) rules allowing inferences and the generation of new

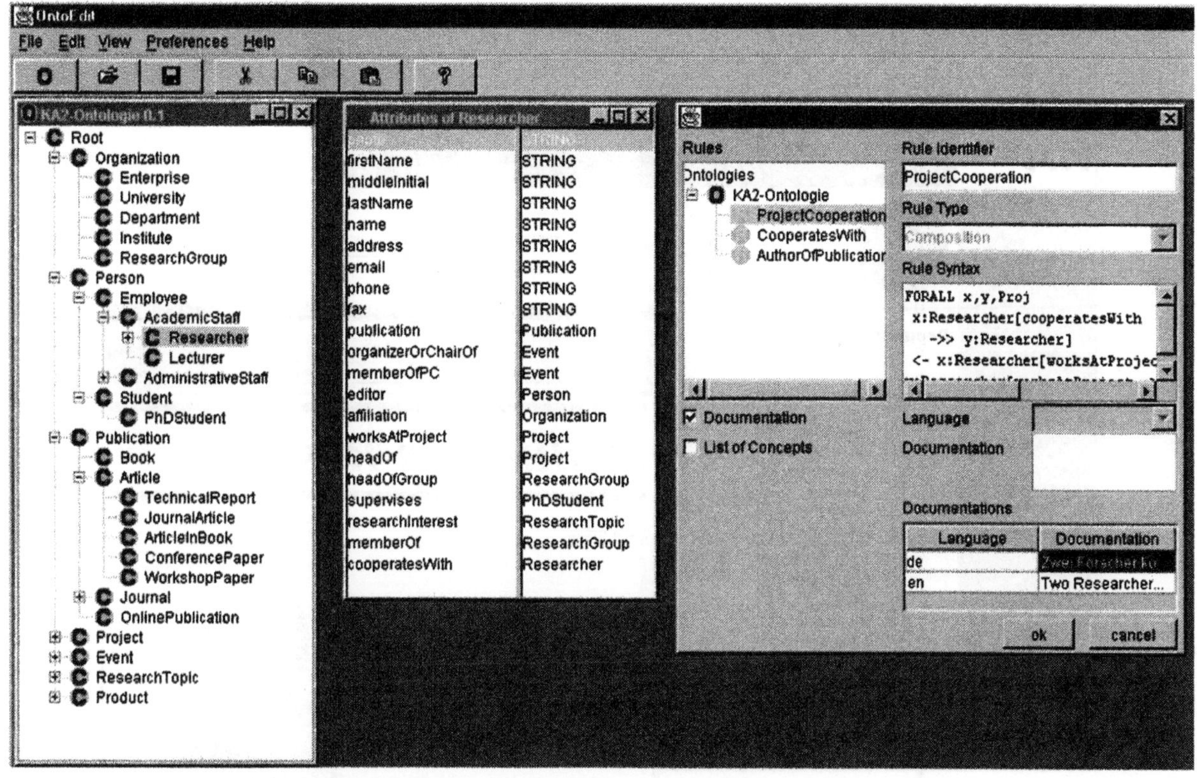

Fig. 1. Part of the KA2 ontology in an OntoEdit screenshot.

knowledge. Our representation language for defining the ontology is F-Logic [16], which provides adequate modeling primitives integrated into a logical framework.

To illustrate the structure of the ontology, the screenshot in Fig. 1 depicts part of the KA2 ontology as it is seen in the ontology development environment *OntoEdit* (cf. Section 6.2). The leftmost window shows the is-a-relationship that structures the concepts of the domain in a (possibly multiple) taxonomy. Attributes and relations of concepts are inherited by subconcepts. Multiple inheritance is allowed as a concept may fit into different branches of the taxonomy. In Fig. 2, attributes and relations of the concept Researcher appear in the middle window. Some of these attributes, like FIRSTNAME and LASTNAME are inherited from the superordinate concept Person. Relations refer to other concepts, like WORKSATPROJECT denoting a relation between Researcher and Project.

We use the KA2 ontology to manage and structure the community portal. The structure of concepts with its attributes and relations supports user navigation through the domain as detailed in Section 4. Beyond simple structuring we model rules allowing inferencing and by that means the generation of new knowledge. The rightmost window in Fig. 1 shows some rules of our KA2 ontology. One of them, the *ProjectCooperation* rule, describes the cooperation of two researchers working in the same project. The rule states that two researchers cooperate, if a Researcher X works at a Project $Proj$ and if a Researcher Y works at the same Project $Proj$ and X is another person than Y. The rule is formulated in an F-Logic representation:

(1) FORALL $X, Y, Proj$
X:Researcher
[COOPERATESWITH $\twoheadrightarrow$ Y:Researcher]
$\leftarrow$ X:Researcher
[WORKSATPROJEKT $\twoheadrightarrow$ $Proj$:Project]
AND Y:Researcher
[WORKSATPROJEKT $\twoheadrightarrow$ $Proj$:Project]
AND NOT equal(X, Y).

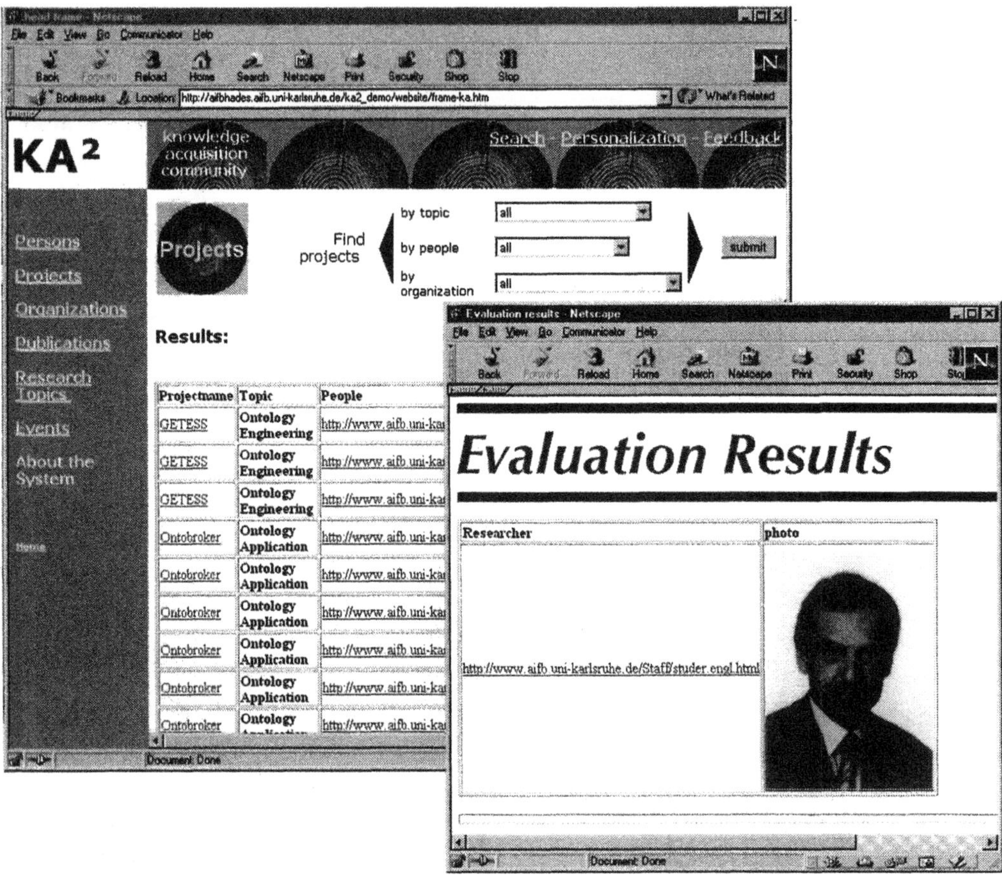

Fig. 2. Accessing the community Web portal.

With this rule, we may infer that researcher X cooperates with researcher Y due to the fact that they work in the same project, even, if there is no *explicit* fact that they cooperate.

4. Accessing the community Web portal

A major requirement from Section 2 has been that navigation and querying of the community Web portal need to be conceptually founded, because only then a structured, richly interwoven presentation may be compiled on the fly. In fact, we elaborate in this section how a semantic underpinning, like the KA2 ontology described above, lets us define a multitude of views that dynamically arrange information. Thus, our system may provide the rich interlinking that is most adequate for the individual user and her navigation and querying of the community Web portal that we have aimed at in the beginning. We start with a description of the query capabilities of our representation framework. The framework builds on the very same F-Logic mechanism for querying as it did for ontology representation and, thus, it may also exploit the ontological background knowledge. Through this semantic level we achieve the independence from the original, syntactically proprietary information sources that we stipulated earlier. Nevertheless, F-Logic is as poorly suited for presentation to naive users as any other query language. Hence, its use is mostly disguised in various easy-to-use mechanisms that more properly serve the needs of the common user (cf. Section 4.2), while it still gives the editor all the power of the principal F-Logic representation and query capabilities. Finally in this section, we touch upon some very mission-critical issues of the actual inference engine that answers queries and derives new facts by combining facts with structures and rules from the ontology.

4.1. Query capabilities

Though information may be provided in a number of different formats our underlying language for representation and querying is F-Logic. For instance, using a concrete example from our showcase the following query asks for all publications of the researcher 'Studer'.

(2) FORALL *Pub*
   ← EXISTS *ResID ResID*:Researcher
      [LASTNAME ↠ "Studer";
      PUBLICATION ↠ *Pub*].

The substitutions for the variable *Pub* constitute the publications queried by this expression. The expressiveness and usability of such queries is improved by the possibility to use a simple form of information retrieval using regular expressions within queries. For instance the following query asks for abstracts that contain the word 'portal':

(3) FORALL *Abstr*
   ← EXISTS *Pub*, *X*
      Pub:Publication [ABSTRACT ↠ *Abstr*] AND
      regexp ("[p|P]ortal", *Abstr*, *X*).

The substitutions for the variable *Abstr* are the abstracts of publications which contain the word 'portal'. In addition, the query capabilities allow to make implicit information explicit. They use the background knowledge expressed in the KA2 ontology including rules as introduced in Section 3.2. If we have a look at Web pages about research projects, information about the researchers (e.g. their names, their affiliation, ...) involved in the projects is often explicitly stated in HTML. However, the fact that researchers who are working together in projects are cooperating is not explicitly given. A question might be: "Which researchers are cooperating with other researchers?" Querying for cooperating researchers, the implicit information about project cooperation of researchers is exploited. The query may be formulated by:

(4) FORALL *ResID1*, *ResID2*
   ← *ResID1*:Researcher
      [COOPERATESWITH ↠ *ResID2*].

The result set includes explicit information about a researchers cooperation relationships, which are stored in the *knowledge warehouse*, and also implicit information about project cooperation between researchers derived using the project-cooperation rule, which is modeled in the ontology.

4.2. Navigating and querying the portal

Usually, it is too inconvenient for users to query the portal using F-Logic. Therefore we offer a range of techniques that allow for navigating and querying the community Web:

- A *hypertext link* may contain a query which is dynamically evaluated when one clicks on the link. Browsing is made possible through the definition of views onto top-level concepts of the KA2 ontology, such as *Persons*, *Projects*, *Organizations*, *Publications*, *Research Topics* and *Events*. Each of these topics can be browsed using predefined views. For example, a click on the *Projects* hyperlink results in a query for all projects known at the portal. The query is evaluated and the results are presented to the user in a table.
- A choice of concepts, instances, or combinations of both may be issued to the user in *HTML forms*. Choice options may be selected through check boxes, selection lists or radio buttons. For instance, clicking on the *Projects* link (cf. upper part of Fig. 2) an F-Logic query is evaluated and all projects contained in the portal are retrieved. The results can be restricted using topic-specific attributes contained in the KA2 ontology for projects, such as topics of a project, people involved etc. The selection list (e.g. for all people involved in projects) is generated dynamically from the information contained in the knowledge warehouse (cf. Section 5.4). Using the form's contents a query may be compiled and evaluated.
- A query may also be generated by using the hyperbolic view interface (cf. Fig. 3). The hyperbolic view visualizes the ontology as a hierarchy of concepts. The presentation is based on hyperbolic geometry (cf. [18]) where nodes in the center are depicted with a large circle, whereas nodes at the border of the surrounding circle are only marked with a small circle. This visualization technique allows a survey over all concepts, a

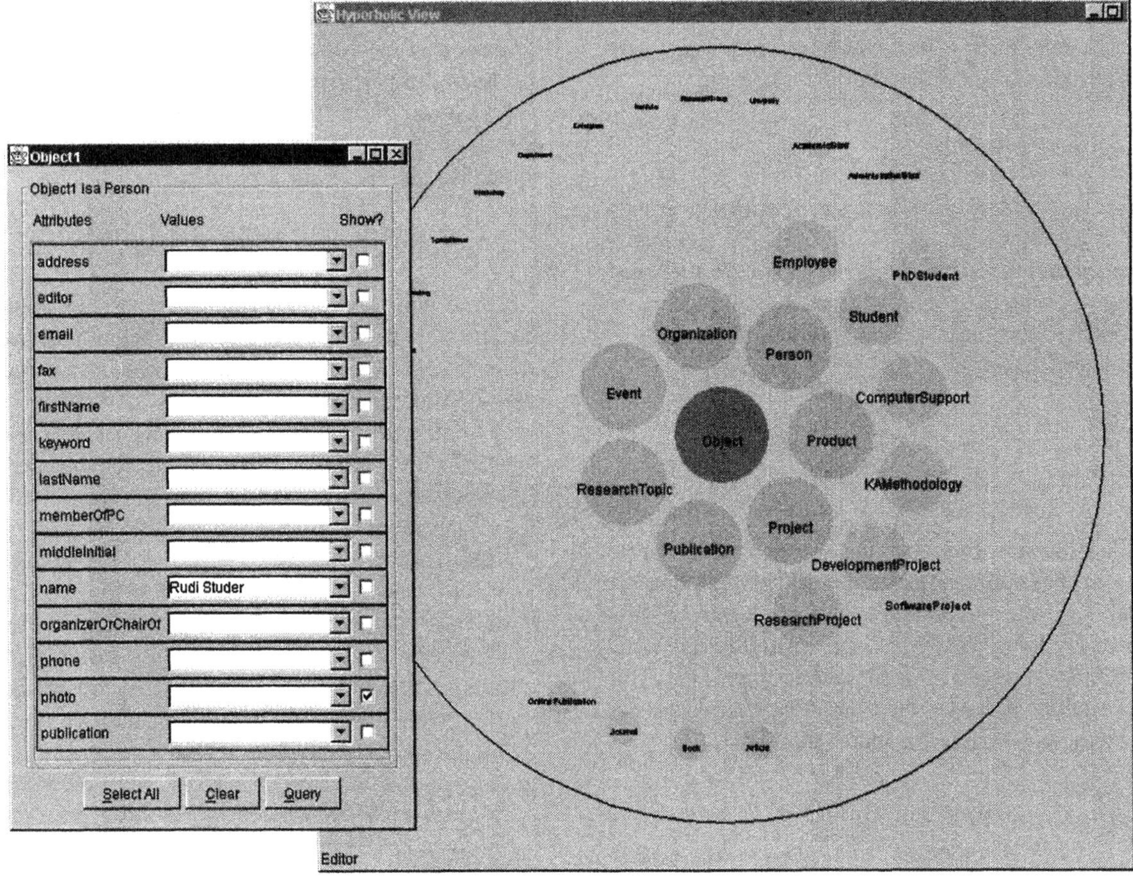

Fig. 3. Hyperbolic view interface.

quick navigation to nodes far away from the center, as well as a closer examination of nodes and their vicinity. When a user selects a node from the hyperbolic view, a form is presented which allows the user to select attributes or to insert values for the attributes. An example is shown in Fig. 4. The user is searching for the community member 'Studer' and his photo. Based on the selected node and the corresponding attributes, a query is compiled. The query result is shown in the right part of Fig. 2.

- Furthermore, queries created by the hyperbolic view interface may be stored using the personalization feature. Queries are personalized for the different users and are available for the user in a selection list. The stored queries can be considered as *semantic bookmarks*. By selecting a previously created bookmark, the underlying query is evaluated and the updated results are presented to the user. By this way, every user may create a personalized view on the portal.
- Finally, we offer an expert mode. The most technical (but also most powerful and flexible) way for querying the portal requires that F-Logic is typed in by the user. This way is only appropriate for users who are very familiar with F-Logic and the KA2 ontology.

4.3. The inference engine

The inference engine answers queries and it performs derivations of new knowledge by an intelligent combination of facts with an ontology denoted in F-Logic like the examples described above. While the expressiveness of F-Logic and its Java-powered realization in our inference engine constitute two

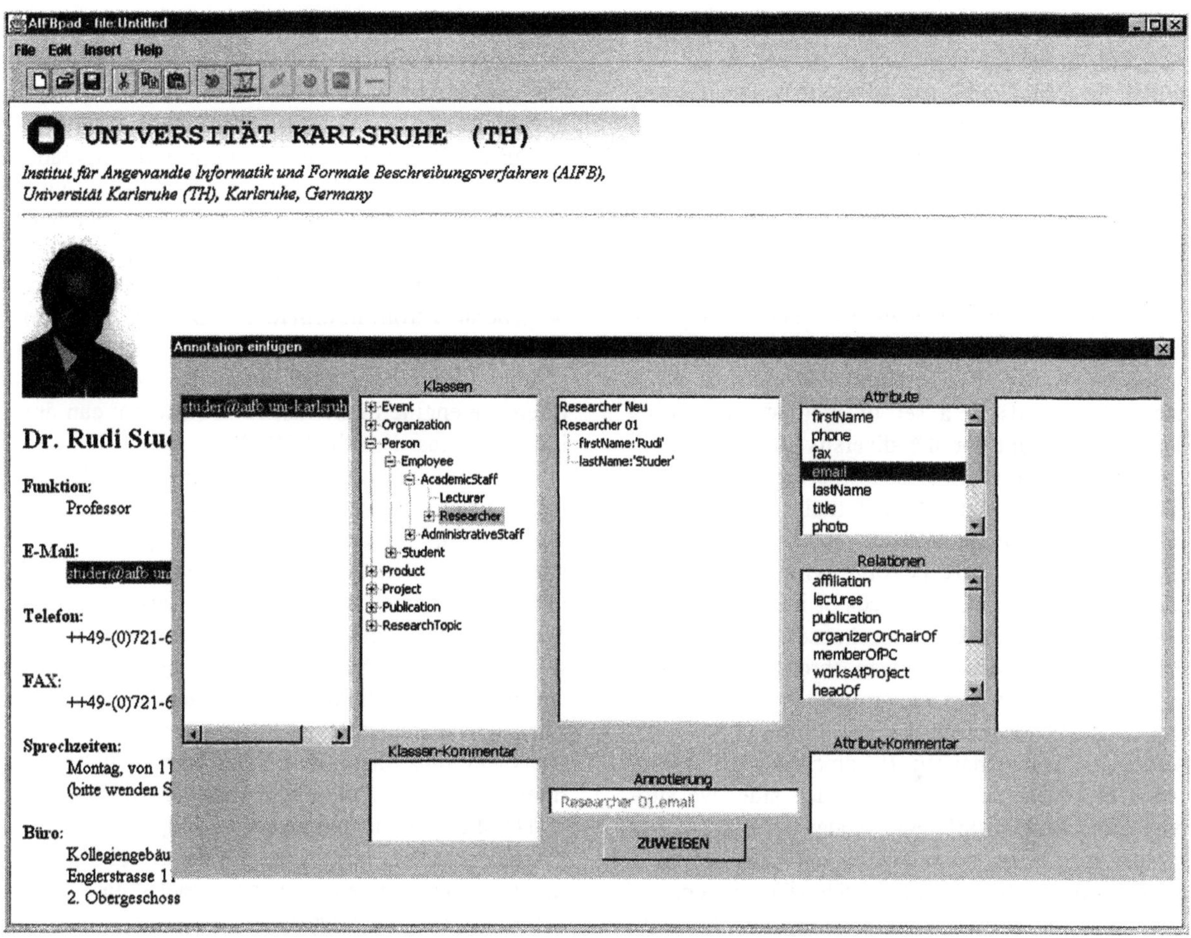

Fig. 4. OntoPad — providing semantics in HTML documents using HTML-A.

major arguments for using it in a semantic community Web portal, wide acceptance of a service like this also depends on *prima facie* unexciting features like speed of service. The principal problem we encounter here is that there exist worst case situations (not always recognizable as such by the user) where a very large set of facts must be derived by the inference engine in order to solve a particular query. While we cannot guarantee for extremely fast response times, unless we drastically cut back on the expressiveness of our representation formalism, we provide several strategies to cope with performance problems:

- The inference engine may be configured to subsequently deliver answers to the query instead of waiting for the entire set of answers before these answers are presented to the user. Thus, answers that are directly available as facts may be presented immediately, while other answers that have to be derived using rules are presented later.
- The inference engine caches all facts and intermediate facts derived from earlier queries. Thus, similar queries or queries that build on previously derived facts may be answered fast.
- Finally, we allow the inference engine to be split into several inference engines that execute in parallel. Every engine may run on a different processor or even a different computer. Every inference engine administers a subset of the rules and facts. A master engine coordinates user queries and distributes subqueries to the slave engines. These slave engines either answer these subqueries directly or distribute incoming subqueries to other inference engines.

The reader may note that though we have provided all the technical means to pursue one or several of these strategies, our showcase has not reached yet the amount of facts that really necessitates any performance enhancing strategies.

5. Providing information

'One method fits all' does not meet the requirements we have sketched above for the information-provisioning part of community Web portals. What one rather needs is a set of methods and tools that may account for the diversity of information sources of potential interest to the community portal. While these methods and tools need to obey different syntactic mechanisms, coherent integration of information is only possible with a conceptual basis that may sort loose pieces of information into a well-defined knowledge warehouse. In our setting, the conceptual basis is given through the ontology that provides the background knowledge and that supports the presentation of information by semantic, i.e. rule-enhanced, F-Logic queries. Talking about the syntactic and/or interface side, we support three major, different, modes of information provisioning. First, we handle *metadata-based information sources* that explicitly describe contents of documents on a semantic basis. Second, we align regularities found in documents or data structures with the corresponding semantic background knowledge in *wrapper-based* approaches. Thus, we may create a common conceptual denominator for previously unrelated pieces of information. Finally, we allow the direct provisioning of facts through our *fact editor*. All the information is brought together in a knowledge warehouse that stores data and metadata alike. Thus, it mediates between the original information sources and the navigating and querying needs discussed in the previous section.

5.1. Metadata-based information

Metadata-based information enriches documents with semantic information by explicitly adding metadata to the information sources. Over the last years several metadata languages have been proposed which can be used to annotate information sources. In our approach the specified ontology constitutes the conceptual backbone for the different syntactic mechanisms.

Current Web standards for representing metadata like RDF [28] or XML [27] can be handled within our semantic Web portal approach. On the one hand, RDF facts serve as direct input for the knowledge warehouse, while on the other hand, RDF facts can be generated from information contained in the portal knowledge warehouse. We have developed *SiLRI* (Simple Logic-based RDF Interpreter), a logic-based inference engine implemented in Java that can draw inferences based on the RDF data model [7].

XML provides the chance to get metadata for free, i.e. as a side product of defining the document structure. For this reason, we have developed a method and a tool called *DTDMaker* for generating DTDs out of ontologies [10]. DTDMaker derives an XML document type definition from a given ontology in F-Logic, so that XML instances can be linked to an ontology. The linkage has the advantage that the document structure is grounded on a true semantic basis and, thus, facts from XML documents may be directly integrated into the knowledge warehouse.

HTML-A, early proposed by [11], is an HTML extension which adds annotations to HTML documents using an ontology as a metadata schema. HTML-A has the advantage to smoothly integrate semantic annotations into HTML and prevents the duplication of information. An example is an HTML page that states that the text string 'Rudi Studer' is the name of a researcher where the URL of his homepage is used as his object identifier. Using HTML-A, this could be realized by:

```
<HTML>
  <BODY>
    <A onto="page:Researcher"/>
    <H1> HomePage of
      <A onto="page[firstName=body]">
        Rudi</A>
      <A onto="page[lastName=body]">
        Studer</A>
    </H1>
    ...
  </BODY>
</HTML>
```

The keyword page refers to the Webpage that contains the ontological mark-up. The first annotation denotes an object of type Researcher that represents the homepage of Rudi Studer. Subsequent annotations define the FIRSTNAME and the LASTNAME attributes of this object by relating to the values from the body of the corresponding anchor-tags. To facilitate the annotation of HTML, we have developed an HTML-A annotation tool called *OntoPad*. An example annotation of an *e-mail* of the Researcher Rudi Studer using OntoPad is illustrated in Fig. 4. Similarly to HTML-A, it is possible to enrich documents generated with Microsoft Office applications with metadata by using our plug-ins *Word-A* and *Excel-A*.

5.2. Wrapper-based information

In general, annotating information sources by hand is a time-consuming task. Often, however, annotation may be automated when one finds regularities in a larger number of documents. The principal idea behind wrapper-based information is that there are large information collections that have a similar structure. We here distinguish between semi-structured information sources (e.g. HTML) and structured information sources (e.g. relational databases).

5.2.1. Semi-structured sources

In recent years several approaches have been proposed for wrapping semi-structured documents, such as HTML documents. Wrapper factories (cf. [25]) and wrapper induction (cf. [17]) have considerably facilitated the task of wrapper construction. In order to wrap directly into our knowledge warehouse we are currently developing our own wrapper approach that directly aligns regularities in semi-structured documents with their corresponding ontological meaning.

5.2.2. Structured sources

Though, in the KA2 community Web there are no existing information systems, we would like to emphasize that existing databases and other legacy-systems may contain valuable information for building a community Web portal. Ontologies have shown their usefulness in the area of intelligent database integration. They act as information mediators (cf. [30]) between distributed and heterogeneous information sources and the applications that use these information sources. Existing entities in legacy systems are mapped onto concepts and attributes defined in the ontology. Thus, existing information may be pumped into the knowledge warehouse by a batch process or it may be accessed on the fly.

5.3. Fact Editor

The process of providing new facts into the knowledge warehouse should be as easy as possible. For this reason the hyperbolic interface tool (cf. Fig. 3) which may be used as a *Fact Editor*. In this mode its forms are not used to ask for values, but to insert values for attributes of instances of corresponding concepts from the ontology. The Fact Editor is also used for maintaining the portal, viz. to add, modify, or delete facts.

5.4. Knowledge warehouse

The different methods and tools we have just described feed directly into the knowledge warehouse or indirectly when they are triggered by a Web crawl. The warehouse itself hosts the ontology, i.e. the metadata level, as well as the data proper. The knowledge warehouse is indirectly accessed, through a user query or a query by an inference engine such as described in Section 4. Hence, one may take full advantage of the distribution capabilities of the inference engine and, likewise, separate the knowledge warehouse into several knowledge bases or knowledge marts. Facts and concepts are stored in a relational database; however, they are stored in a *reified* format that treats relations and concepts as first-order objects and that is therefore very flexible with regard to changes and amendments of the ontology.

6. Development of Web portals

6.1. The development and maintenance process

Even with the methodological and tool support we have described so far, developing a Web portal for a community of non-trivial size remains a complex

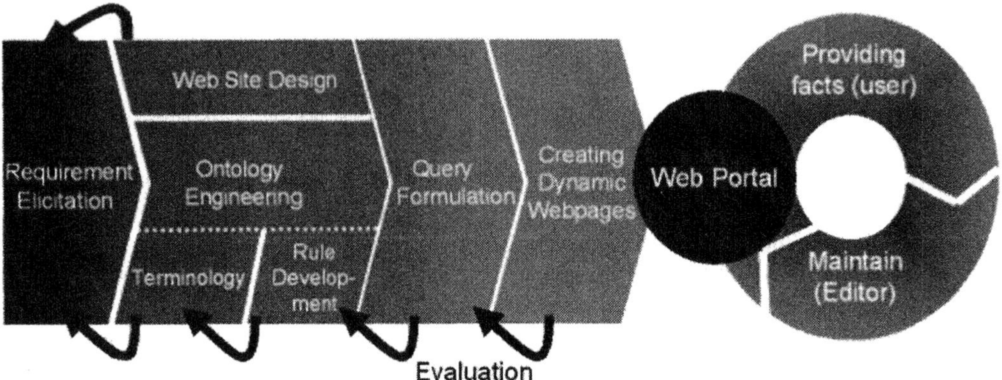

Fig. 5. The development process of the community Web portal.

task. Strictly ad-hoc rapid prototyping approaches easily doom the construction to fail or they easily lead up to unsatisfactory results. Hence, we have thought about a more principled approach towards the development process that serves as means for documenting development, as well as for communicating principal structures to co-developers and editors of the Web portal. We distinguish different phases in the development process that are illustrated in Fig. 5. For the main part this model is a sequential one. Nevertheless, at each stage there is an evaluation as to whether and as to how easily further development may proceed with the design decisions that have been accomplished before. The results feed back into the results of earlier stages of development. In fact, experiences gained by running the operational system often find their way back into the system.

The main stages of the development process and their key characteristics are given in the following.

- The process starts with the *elicitation* of user requirements in the requirements elicitation phase. In this phase, requirements about important and interesting topics in the domain are collected, the information goals of potential users of the portal are elicited, and preferences or expectations concerning the structure and layout of presented information are documented. Results of this very first phase constitute the input for the design of the Web site and for preliminary HTML pages and affect the formal domain model embodied in the ontology.
- The requirements determine, e.g., which views and queries are useful for users of the portal, which navigation paths they expect, how different Web pages are linked, or which functionality is provided in different areas of the portal. Requirements like these are realized in the *Web site design*. This design phase may be performed independently to a very large extent from the underlying formal structuring, i.e. the ontology. Since a mock-up version of the Web site is developed early in the development phase, one may check early whether the system to be developed really meets the users' needs.
- In parallel to the development of the structure and layout of the Web site an *ontology engineering* process is started. The first phase elicits relevant *domain terms* that need to be refined and amended in the ontology engineering phase. First, the static ontology parts, i.e. the concept hierarchy, the attributes, and relations between concepts, are formally defined. Thereafter, *rules* and constraints are developed. Rule development may necessitate a major revision of the concept hierarchy. For instance, new subconcepts may have to be introduced, attributes may have to turn into relations or into other concepts, or relations may have to become concepts. This (intra-ontology) engineering cycle must be performed until the resulting ontology remains sufficiently stable.
- In the *query formulation* step the views and queries described in one of the earlier phases are formalized. At first, their functionality is tested independently from the Web site design. To express the information needs formally, the developer has to access the ontology, whereby additional rules

or relations that define new views or ease the definition of queries may become necessary. In order to test ontology and queries, a set of test facts has to be prepared. During this process of testing, inconsistencies in the ontology may be detected, which may lead to a feed back-loop back into the ontology engineering phase.

- Finally, Web pages are *populated*, i.e. the queries and views developed during Website design, and formalized and tested during query formalization are integrated into the operational portal. Information may be accessed via the portal as soon as a sufficient amount has been made available as outlined in Section 5.

During operation of the community portal it must be *fed* and maintained:

- The user community provides facts via numerous input channels (cf. Section 5).
- These facts may contain errors or undesired contents, or the integration of different sources may lead to inconsistencies. To counter problems like these, an editor is responsible to detect these cases and act appropriately. The detection of inconsistencies is supported by the inference engine via constraints formulated in F-Logic. The editor then has to decide how to proceed. He may contact responsible authors, simply ignore conflicting information, or he may manually edit the contents.
- Changing requirements of the community must be reflected in the portal, e.g. popularity increasing in new fields of interests or technologies or viewpoints that shift may incur changes to the ontology, new queries, or even a new Web site structure. In order to meet such new requirements, the above-mentioned development process may have to be partially restarted.

6.2. *Tools for development and maintenance*

The previous subsection has described the principal steps for developing a community Web portal. For efficient development of a community Web portal, however, the process must be supported by tools. In the following, we describe the most important tools that allow us to facilitate and speed up the development and maintenance process. The tools cover the whole range from ontology engineering (OntoEdit), query formulation (Query Builder), up to the creation of dynamic Web pages with the help of HTML/JavaScript templates. We just want to note here that we also rely on common HTML editing tools for Web site design.

6.2.1. *OntoEdit*

The OntoEdit toolset has already been mentioned in Section 3.2 and a screenshot is shown in Fig. 1. OntoEdit is used during terminology engineering and rule development. It delivers a wide range of functionalities for the engineering of ontologies. As introduced in Section 3, ontology modeling, from our point of view, includes the creation of concepts, attributes, relations, rules, and general metadata. To reduce complexity and to simplify the difficult task of ontology modeling, OntoEdit offers different views on the main modeling elements, thus facilitating the complex process of ontology modeling. The modeling task is usually started with introducing new concepts and organizing them into a hierarchy (cf. left part of Fig. 1). The next step of the modeling task uses the concepts to model attributes of and relations between concepts. On the basis of these knowledge structures, OntoEdit includes a rule view enabling the user to model rules which state common legalities (e.g. the symmetry of the cooperation relationship between two persons).

6.2.2. *Query Builder*

While queries with low complexity can be expressed in F-Logic using the rule debugger alone, in other cases it is more convenient to create queries using our Query Builder tool. The hyperbolic view (cf. Section 4) interface may be configured for this tool to allow the user to generate queries instead of posing queries. Such queries may then be integrated as links into a Web page with the help of a common Web page editor by copying and pasting it into the Web editors form.

6.2.3. *HTML/JavaScript templates*

Another time consuming activity is the development of the Web pages that assemble queries from parts and that display the query results. For that purpose we have developed a *library of template pages*:

- Templates with check boxes, radio boxes, and selection lists are available. These HTML forms produce data which are used in JavaScript functions to generate queries. These queries can then be sent to the inference engine using submit buttons.

- The results of a query are fed into a template page as Javascript arrays. From these data different presentation forms may be generated (for the future, we envision that XML is returned by the inference engine and outlaid by XSL style sheets):
  - A general purpose template contains a table that presents answer tuples returned by the inference engine in a HTML table. The template provides functions to sort the table in ascending or descending order on different columns. Substitutions of certain variables may be used as URLs for other entries in the table. Different data formats are recognized and processed according to their suffixes, i.e. a '.gif' or '.jpg' suffix is interpreted as a picture and rendered as such (cf. Fig. 2 for an example).
  - Results may also be fed into selection lists, radio boxes, or check lists. Thus, query results can provide the initial setting of further HTML form fields. These forms can be used to create new queries based on the results of previous ones.
- A user can create queries using the hyperbolic view interface (cf. Section 4). As a personalization feature of our Web portal he can store these queries by assigning a personal label. All stored queries can be accessed through a selection list, to restart the query and retrieve the most up-to-date answers. This list of stored queries provides individual short cuts to often needed information.

The template pages are compatible with some standard Web editors, i.e. the Web designer is able to rearrange or redesign the elements without destroying their functionality.

7. The system architecture

This section summarizes the major components of our system. An overall view of our system is depicted in Fig. 6, which includes the core modules for accessing and maintaining a community Web portal:

- *Providing information* in our community Web portal has already been introduced in Section 5. In our approach we distinguish between metadata-based, wrapper-based and fact-based information. Metadata-based information (such as HTML-A, Word-A, Excel-A, RDF, XML) is collected from the Web using a fact crawler. Wrapper-based information means integrating semi-structured and structured information semi-automatically into the knowledge warehouse. Using the *fact editor* factual information can be directly added to the knowledge warehouse.
- The *knowledge warehouse* is the knowledge base of the community Web portal. It is structured according to the ontology. The facts contained in the knowledge warehouse and the ontology itself serve as the input for the inference engine.
- The *inference engine* uses information from the knowledge warehouse to answer queries. In addition, it uses ontological structures and rules to derive additional factual knowledge that is only implicitly provided. This inference mechanism may also be used to reduce the maintenance efforts, because facts that may be automatically derived from other facts need not be provided by some member of the community.
- *Accessing* the community Web portal means navigating and querying for information as described in Section 3. Queries embedded in the portal or formulated using the hyperbolic view interface

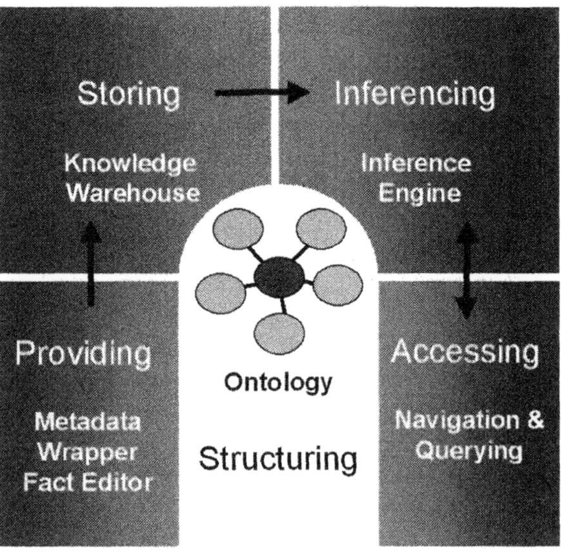

Fig. 6. System architecture.

(cf. Fig. 3) are posted to the inference engine. The results may be delivered in different forms like HTML, XML, or RDF.

8. Related work

This section positions our work in the context of existing Web portals like Yahoo and Netscape and also relates our work to other technologies that are or could be deployed for the construction of community Web portals.

One of the well-established Web portals on the Web is **Yahoo**[4], a manually maintained Web index. Yahoo allows information seekers to retrieve Web documents by navigating a tree-like taxonomy of topics. Each Web document indexed by Yahoo is classified manually according to a topic in the taxonomy. In contrast to our approach Yahoo only utilizes a very light-weight ontology that solely consists of categories arranged in a hierarchical manner. Yahoo offers keyword search (local to a selected topic or global) in addition to hierarchical navigation but is only able to retrieve complete documents, i.e. it is not able to answer queries concerning the contents of documents, not to mention to present or combine facts being found in different documents. Due to its weak ontology Yahoo cannot extend information to include facts that could be derived through ontological axioms. The mentioned points are realized in our portal that builds upon a rich ontology enabling the portal to give detailed and integrated answers to queries. Furthermore, our portal supports the active provision of information by the user community. Thus we get rid of the manual and centralized classification of documents. The portal is made by the community for the community.

A portal that is specialized for a scientific community has been built by the Math-Net project, an initiative for "setting up the technical and organizational infrastructure for efficient, inexpensive and user driven information services for mathematics" [5]. At http://www.math-net.de/ the portal for the (German) mathematics community is installed that makes distributed information from several mathematical departments available. The scope of offered information ranges from publications such as preprints and reports to information about research projects, organizations, faculty etc. All these data are accompanied by metadata according to the **Dublin Core**[5] standard [29] that makes it comparatively easy to provide structured views to the stored information. The 15 elements of Dublin Core primarily describe metadata about a resource, e.g. its title, its author, or its format. The Dublin Core element 'Subject' is used to classify resources as students, as conferences, as research groups, as preprints etc. A finer classification (e.g. via attributes) is not possible except for instances of the publication category. Here the common MSC (**Mathematical Subject Classification**[6]) is used that resembles an ontology of the field of mathematics. The pros of Math-Net lie in the "important organizational task" of "establishing a network of persons [...] dedicating their time and work to the electronic information system" [5] and in the technical task of collecting various resources and integrating them to make them uniformly accessible. The cons of Math-Net are the lack of a rich ontology that could enhance the quality of search results (esp. via inferencing), and the restriction to information in the DC format.

Parts of Math-Net are implemented on the basis of the Hyperwave system [21], an elaborated Web server that is based on databases providing information in a structured manner. Hyperwave has a lot of fancy and useful features such as external links, automatic handling of outdated pages, avoiding of dangling links, presenting different views for different users, etc. The system is a useful basis for the development of a portal, but since it does not have the notion of an ontology, the portal is restricted to the power of the underlying database. Its capabilities clearly stay behind the inferential properties of Ontobroker's inference engine.

Another community-focused portal is RiboWeb [1], an ontology-based data resource of published ribosome data and computational models that can process these data. RiboWeb exploits several types of ontologies to provide semantics for all the data and computational models that are offered. These ontologies are specified in the OKBC (Open Knowl-

[4] http://www.yahoo.com

[5] http://www.purl.org/dc

[6] http://www.ams.org/msc/

edge Base Connectivity) representation language [4]. The primary source of data is given by published scientific literature which is manually linked to the different ontologies. Both systems, RiboWeb and our community portal, rely on ontologies for offering a semantic-based access to the stored data. However, the OKBC knowledge base component of RiboWeb does not support the kind of automatic deduction that is offered by the inference engine of Ontobroker. Furthermore, RiboWeb does not include wrappers for automatically extracting information from the given published articles. On the other hand, the computational modules of RiboWeb offer processing functionalities that are not part of (but also not intended for) our community Web portal.

The Ontobroker project [8] lays the technological foundations for the KA2 portal. On top of Ontobroker the portal has been built and organizational structures for developing and maintaining it have been established. Therefore, we compare our system against approaches that are similar to Ontobroker.

The approach closest to Ontobroker is SHOE [19]. In SHOE, HTML pages are annotated via ontologies to support information retrieval based on semantic information. Besides the use of ontologies and the annotation of Web pages the underlying philosophy of both systems differs significantly: in SHOE, arbitrary extensions to ontologies can be introduced on Web pages and no central provider index is maintained. As a consequence, when specifying a query, users can not know all the ontological terms which have been used and the Web crawler will miss annotated Web pages. In contrast, Ontobroker relies on the notion of a community defining a group of Web users who share a common understanding and, thus, can agree on an ontology for a given field. Therefore, both the information providers and the clients have complete knowledge of the available ontological terms, a prerequisite for building a community Web portal. SHOE and Ontobroker also differ with respect to their inferencing capabilities. SHOE uses description logic as its basic representation formalism, but it offers only very limited inferencing capabilities. Ontobroker relies on Frame-Logic and supports complex inferencing for query answering.

WebKB [20] aims at providing intelligent access to Web documents. WebKB uses conceptual graphs for representing the semantic content of Web documents. It embeds conceptual graph statements into HTML-tags to provide metadata about the contents of HTML documents. These statements are based on an ontology defining the concepts and relations which may be used for annotating the HTML documents. WebKB pursues a rather similar approach when compared to our backbone system Ontobroker: both systems use a general representation language for representing metadata (conceptual graphs and Frame-Logic, respectively) and embed metadata within the HTML source code. However, Ontobroker (and thus our portal) provides additional means for accessing non-HTML resources, e.g. exploiting XML, RDF metadata, or using ontology-based wrappers. Furthermore, the tool environment of WebKB does not offer the methods and tools that are needed to build a community portal on top of WebKB and, thus, to make an application out of a core technology.

The STRUDEL system [12] applies concepts from database management systems to the process of building Web sites. STRUDEL uses a mediator architecture to generate such Web sites. Wrappers transform the external data sources, being either HTML pages, structured files or relational databases, into the semi-structured data model used within STRUDEL's data repository. STRUDEL then uses so-called 'site-definition queries' to create multiple views to the same Web site data. These queries are defined in STRUQL, a query language for manipulating semi-structured data. When compared to our approach, the STRUDEL system lacks the semantic level that is provided in our approach by the domain ontology and the associated inference engine.

The Observer system [23] uses a network of ontologies to provide access to distributed and heterogeneous information. Each ontology can describe the information contained in one or more information repositories. Since these ontologies are linked explicitly by so-called inter-ontology relationships (synonym, hypernym, and hyponym), the informations stored in the different resources are linked as well. A user selects an ontology (a vocabulary) to express his query. The Observer system accesses the resources described by the selected ontology to answer the query. If the answers are not satisfactory other ontologies and thus other resources can be accessed. Observer provides means to state queries but does not offer predefined or customizable views.

From our point of view, our community portal system is rather unique with respect to the collection of methods used and the functionality provided. Our approach for accessing information, providing information and maintaining the portal are more comprehensive than those found in other portals. We are able to offer this functionality since our backbone system Ontobroker and its add-ons provide more powerful techniques for, e.g., inferencing or extracting information from various sources than those offered by comparable systems. Moreover, all these methods are integrated into one uniform system environment.

9. Conclusion

We have demonstrated in this paper how a community may build a community Web portal. The portal is centered around an ontology that structures information for the purposes of presentation and provisioning of information, as well as for the development and maintenance of the portal. We have described a small-scale example, the KA portal, that illustrates some of our techniques and methods. In particular, we have developed a set of ontology-based tools that allow to present multiple views onto the same information appropriate for browsing, querying, and personalizing Web pages. Adding information in the up and running portal is possible for members of the community or the editors of the portal through a set of methods that support the integration of metadata and (semi-)structured information sources, as well as the manual manipulation of data. Also the tools that support development of the portal and maintenance by the editors are ontology-based and, thus, fit together smoothly with the overall process of running the community portal.

The concepts that we have explained are general enough to apply to many other domains. As a second application, we have constructed an intranet management application for an IT service company, the rationale being that the people in a company just form a community with common interests.

For the future, we will need to tackle some very practical issues, like improving and integrating the interfaces of our tools, adding a component for session management, or versioning of views and ontologies. A major experience so far has been that community members are only willing to contribute information if this is very easy to accomplish. We could not provide this quality of service from the start. Hence our knowledge warehouse is still rather small, but large enough to show the viability of our approach. Besides fancy interfaces, the most urgent needs will be the improvement of provisioning. There are some machine learning approaches (e.g. [22]) that may help with dedicated subtasks of the information provisioning process. Our general experience, however, is that there is no single tool or technique that fits all needs, but there is a conceptual strategy that ties up all the loose ends, viz. ontologies.

References

[1] R. Altmann, M. Bada, X. Chai, M.W. Carillo, R. Chen and N. Abernethy, RiboWeb: an ontology-based system for collaborative molecular biology, IEEE Intell. Syst. 14 (5) (1999) 68–76.

[2] R. Benjamins, D. Fensel and S. Decker, KA2: building ontologies for the Internet: a midterm report, Int. J. Human Comput. Stud. 51 (3) (1999) 687.

[3] T. Berners-Lee, Weaving the Web, Harper, New York, 1999.

[4] V. Chaudri, A. Farquhar, R. Fikes, P. Karp and J. Rice, OKBC: a programmatic foundation for knowledge base interoperability, in: Proc. 15th Nat. Conf. on Artificial Intelligence (AAAI-98), 1998, pp. 600–607.

[5] W. Dalitz, M. Grötschel and J. Lügger, Information services for mathematics in the Internet (Math-Net), in: A. Sydow (Ed.), Proc. 15th IMACS World Congress on Scientific Computation: Modelling and Applied Mathematics, Artif. Intell. Comput. Sci. 4 (1997) 773–778.

[6] T. Davenport and L. Prusak, Working Knowledge: How Organizations Manage What They Know, Harvard Business School Press, Cambridge, MA, 1998.

[7] S. Decker, D. Brickley, J. Saarela and J. Angele, A Query and Inference Service for RDF, in: Proc. W3C Query Language Workshop (QL-98), Boston, MA, December 3–4, 1998.

[8] S. Decker, M. Erdmann, D. Fensel and R. Studer, Ontobroker: ontology based access to distributed and semi-structured information, in: R. Meersman et al. (Eds.), Database Semantics: Semantic Issues in Multimedia Systems, Kluwer, Dordrecht, 1999, pp. 351–369.

[9] A. Deutsch, M. Fernandez, D. Florescu, A. Levy and D. Suciu, A query language for XML, in: Proc. 8th Int. World Wide Web Conf. (WWW'8), Toronto, May 1999, pp. 1155–1169.

[10] M. Erdmann and R. Studer, Ontologies as conceptual models for XML documents, in: Proc. 12th Int. Workshop

on Knowledge Acquisition, Modelling and Management (KAW'99), Banff, October, 1999.
[11] D. Fensel, S. Decker, M. Erdmann and R. Studer, Ontobroker: the very high idea, in: Proc. 11th Int. Flairs Conf. (FLAIRS-98), Sanibel Island, FL, May, 1998.
[12] M. Fernandez, D. Florescu, J. Kang and A. Levy, Catching the boat with Strudel: experiences with a Web-site management system, in: Proc. 1998 ACM Int. Conf. on Management of Data (SIGMOD'98), Seattle, WA, 1998, pp. 414–425.
[13] P. Fröhlich, W. Neijdl and M. Wolpers, KBS-Hyperbook — an open hyperbook system for education, in: Proc. 10th World Conf. on Educational Media and Hypermedia (EDMEDIA'98), Freiburg, 1998.
[14] T.R. Gruber, A translation approach to portable ontology specifications, Knowledge Acquisition 6 (2) (1993) 199–221.
[15] M. Kesseler, A schema based approach to HTML authoring, in: Proc. 4th Int. World Wide Web Conf. (WWW'4), Boston, MA, December 1995.
[16] M. Kifer, G. Lausen and J. Wu, Logical foundations of object-oriented and frame-based languages, J. ACM 42 (1995) 741–843.
[17] N. Kushmerick, Wrapper induction: efficiency and expressiveness, Artif. Intell. 118 (2000) 15–68.
[18] L. Lamping, R. Rao and P. Pirolli, A focus + context technique based on hyperbolic geometry for visualizing large hierarchies, in: Proc. ACM SIGCHI Conf. on Human Factors in Computing Systems, 1995, pp. 401–408.
[19] S. Luke, L. Spector, D. Rager and J. Hendler, Ontology-based Web agents, in: Proc. 1st Int. Conf. on Autonomous Agents, 1997.
[20] P. Martin and P. Eklund, Embedding knowledge in Web documents, in: Proc. 8th Int. World Wide Web Conf. (WWW'8), Toronto, May 1999, pp. 1403–1419.
[21] H. Maurer, Hyperwave. The Next Generation Web Solution, Addison-Wesley, Reading, MA, 1996.
[22] A. McCallum, K. Nigam, J. Rennie and K. Seymore, A machine learning approach to building domain-specific search engines, in: Proc. 16th Int. Joint Conf. on Artificial Intelligence (IJCAI-99), 1999, pp. 662–667.
[23] E. Mena, V. Kashyap, A. Illarramendi and A. Sheth, Domain specific ontologies for semantic information brokering on the global information infrastructure, in: N. Guarino (Ed.), Formal Ontology in Information Systems, IOS Press, Amsterdam, 1998.
[24] J. Robie, J. Lapp and D. Schach, XML Query Language (XQL), in: Proc. of the W3C Query Language Workshop (QL-98), Boston, MA, December 3–4, 1998.
[25] A. Sahuguet and F. Azavant, Wysiwyg Web Wrapper Factory (W4F), Technical report, http://db.cis.upenn.edu/DL/WWW8/index.html, 1999.
[26] UMLS, Unified Medical Language System, http://www.nlm.nih.gov/research/umls/.
[27] W3C, XML Specification, http://www.w3.org/XML/, 1997.
[28] W3C, RDFS Specification, http://www.w3.org/TR/PR-rdf-schema/, 1999.
[29] S. Weibel, J. Kunze, C. Lagoze and M. Wolf, Dublin Core Metadata for Resource Discovery, Number 2413 in IETF, The Internet Society, 1998.
[30] G. Wiederhold and M. Genesereth, The conceptual basis for mediation services, IEEE Expert/Intell. Syst. 12 (5) (1997) 1997.

Steffen Staab is assistant professor for Applied Computer Science at Karlsruhe University. He has published in the fields of computational linguistics, information extraction, knowledge representation and reasoning, knowledge management, knowledge discovery, and intelligent systems for the Web. Steffen studied computer science and computational linguistics between 1990 and 1998, earning a M.S.E. from the University of Pennsylvania during a Fulbright scholarship and a Dr. rer. nat. from Freiburg University during a scholarship with Freiburg's graduate program in cognitive science. Since then, he has also been working as a consultant for knowledge management at Fraunhofer IAO and at the start-up company Ontoprise.

Jürgen Angele received the diploma degree in Computer Science in 1985 from the University of Karlsruhe. From 1985 to 1989 he worked for the companies AEG, Konstanz, and SEMA GROUP, Ulm, Germany. From 1989 to 1994 he was a research and teaching assistant at the University of Karlsruhe. He did research on the operationalization of the knowledge acquisition language KARL, which led to a Ph.D. from the University of Karlsruhe in 1993. In 1994 he became a full professor in Applied Computer Science at the University of Applied Sciences, Braunschweig, Germany. In 1999 he cofounded the company Ontoprise together with S. Decker, H.-P. Schnurr, S. Staab, and R. Studer and has been CEO of Ontoprise since then. His interests lie in the development of knowledge management tools and systems, including innovative applications of knowledge-based systems to the World Wide Web.

Stefan Decker is working as a PostDoc at Stanfords Infolab together with Prof. Gio Wiederhold in the Scalable Knowledge Composition project on ontology articulations. He has published in the fields of ontologies, information extraction, knowledge representation and reasoning, knowledge management, problem solving methods and intelligent systems for the Web. He is one of the designers and implementers of the Ontobroker-System. Stefan Decker studied computer science and mathematics at the University of Kaiserslautern and finished his studies with the best possible result in 1995. From 1995–1999 he did his Ph.D. studies at the University of Karlsruhe, where he worked on the Ontobroker project.

Michael Erdmann gained his M.D. in Computer Science from the University of Koblenz (Germany) in 1995. Since October 1995 he has been working as a junior researcher at the University of Karlsruhe (Germany). He is a member of the Ontobroker-Project-Team and currently engaged in finishing his Ph.D. about the relationship between semantic knowledge modeling with ontologies and XML.

Andreas Hotho is a Ph.D. student at the Institute of Applied Computer Science and Formal Description Methods at Karlsruhe University. He earned his M.D. in Information Systems from the University of Braunschweig, Germany, in 1998. His research interests include the application of data mining techniques on very large databases and intelligent Web applications.

Alexander Maedche is a Ph.D. candidate at the Institute of Applied Computer Science and Formal Description Methods at Karlsruhe University. He received his diploma in Industrial Engineering (computer science, operations research) in 1999 from Karlsruhe University. His research interests include ontology engineering, machine learning, data and text mining and ontology-based applications.

Hans-Peter Schnurr is a Ph.D. candidate at the Institute of Applied Computer Science and Formal Description Methods at Karlsruhe University. He received his diploma in Industrial Engineering in 1995 from Karlsruhe University. Between 1995 and 1998, Hans-Peter was working as a researcher and practice analyst at McKinsey and Company and is co-founder of the start-up company Ontoprise, a knowledge management solutions provider. His current research interests include knowledge management methodologies and applications, ontology engineering and ontology-based applications.

Rudi Studer obtained a diploma in Computer Science at the University of Stuttgart in 1975. In 1982 he was awarded a Doctor's degree in mathematics and computer science at the University of Stuttgart, and in 1985 he obtained his Habilitation in computer science at the University of Stuttgart. From January 1977 to June 1985 he worked as a research scientist at the University of Stuttgart. From July 1985 to October 1989 he was project leader and manager at the Scientific Center of IBM Germany. Since November 1989 he has been full professor in Applied Computer Science at the University of Karlsruhe. His research interests include knowledge management, intelligent Web applications, knowledge engineering and knowledge discovery. He is co-founder and member of the scientific advisory board of the knowledge management start-up company Ontoprise.

York Sure is a Ph.D. candidate at the Institute of Applied Computer Science and Formal Description Methods at Karlsruhe University. He received his diploma in Industrial Engineering in 1999 from Karlsruhe University. His current research interests include knowledge management, ontology merging and mapping, ontology engineering and ontology-based applications.

SearchPad: explicit capture of search context to support Web search

Krishna Bharat *

Compaq Systems Research Center, 130 Lytton Avenue, Palo Alto, CA 94301, USA

Abstract

Experienced users who query search engines have a complex behavior. They explore many topics in parallel, experiment with query variations, consult multiple search engines, and gather information over many sessions. In the process they need to keep track of search context — namely useful queries and promising result links, which can be hard. We present an extension to search engines called *SearchPad* that makes it possible to keep track of 'search context' explicitly. We describe an efficient implementation of this idea deployed on four search engines: AltaVista, Excite, Google and Hotbot. Our design of *SearchPad* has several desirable properties: (i) portability across all major platforms and browsers; (ii) instant start requiring no code download or special actions on the part of the user; (iii) no server side storage; and (iv) no added client–server communication overhead. An added benefit is that it allows search services to collect valuable relevance information about the results shown to the user. In the context of each query *SearchPad* can log the actions taken by the user, and in particular record the links that were considered *relevant* by the user in the context of the query. The service was tested in a multi-platform environment with over 150 users for 4 months and found to be usable and helpful. We discovered that the ability to maintain search context explicitly seems to affect the way people search. Repeat *SearchPad* users looked at more search results than is typical on the Web, suggesting that availability of search context may partially compensate for non-relevant pages in the ranking.

Keywords: Search engines; Search context; Queries; Bookmarking; Data collection; Relevance information; JavaScript; Cookies

1. Introduction

As users gain expertise in searching on the World Wide Web they begin to make use of the wide choice in search services available online. However, as they cast a wider net to locate the information they seek, they start to employ a more elaborate and complex search process. Experienced users searching on the Web seem to have the following behavior.

(1) They search on many unrelated topics in parallel, often with many browser windows.
(2) A given search for information may extend over many sessions. They may terminate and restart the browser between sessions.
(3) For each information need they use many queries, often by a process of query refinement. Power users may employ variants of queries that worked well in other contexts.
(4) They may try the same query on many search services. (By a search service we mean search engines such as AltaVista [1] and Google [4], meta-search engines such as AskJeeves [2] and MetaCrawler [6], and resource directories such as Yahoo! [12] and Open Directory [8].)
(5) Some users may look at more than one search result page.

* Present address: Google Inc., 2400 Bayshore Parkway, Mountain View, CA 94043, USA. E-mail: krishna@google.com

(6) When they do find a useful result, they are often unsure whether the information they have found is the best available or they should search further.

The trouble with the above behavior is that the user needs to carry around a lot of contextual information over time and there is no convenient way to record it or make it explicit. Specifically, they need to remember URLs of potentially useful results as they look for more results, and remember useful queries over time. Both of these can be hard to memorize. Saving information to the browser's collection of bookmarks is one potential solution. However, there are several reasons why this is not convenient, as outlined below.

(1) Most users would be reluctant to contaminate their bookmark list with tentative leads. The list of bookmarks is intended to store high-quality Web pages that they wish to remember for a long time, and not intermediate results.
(2) To remember a query one would need to bookmark a search result page. However, this provides no way to run the same query on a different search service.
(3) As result pages and tentative results from many queries get bookmarked they become interleaved and hard to distinguish. One solution to avoid clutter would be to create bookmark folders for each information need in advance, and bookmark each result and query into the appropriate folder. However, this takes too much effort on the part of the user.

In this paper we describe an extension to the search result page called *SearchPad*, which helps users search more effectively by explicitly maintaining their 'search context'. By search context, we mean queries recently deployed by the user, along with hyperlinks of result pages the user visited and/or liked in the context of each query. *SearchPad* is very similar to a bookmarks window except that it is search-specific and maintains a relationship between queries and links the user would like to keep track of (which we call *leads*). As with bookmarks, clicking on a saved lead causes the corresponding page to be loaded in the browser. Saved queries can be replayed on other search engines.

To make *SearchPad* usable by a large audience we had two design goals which made the implementation of the system challenging.

- To appeal to the widest possible audience we wanted an implementation that was portable (i.e., worked on all browsers and platforms) and did not impose any overhead on users (loaded quickly and transparently). The rationale for the latter condition was the feeling that many users would be unwilling to use a search service which required them to first explicitly download a modified client or a plug-in. Indeed, on some platforms the delay of several tens of seconds in starting the Java Virtual Machine makes even Java a poor choice for implementation.
- A second design goal was to not impose any extra storage or communication overhead on the search service. This greatly simplifies the integration of *SearchPad* support into new search services. However, this implies that all control and storage happens at the user end.

Our implementation of *SearchPad* uses cookies and a subset of Javascript that is known to work on all platforms. It loads instantly with the first result page obtained from the search service, and communicates with the server on an *as needed* basis. To simulate the behavior of actual services providing support for *SearchPad*, we implemented a proxy that provides access to four major search engines: AltaVista, Excite, Google and HotBot. The role of the proxy was to transform result pages streaming through to make them appear as they would if they were implementing a service such as *SearchPad*. Note that other pages such as result pages are not fetched through the proxy. They are fetched directly from the World Wide Web. The role of the proxy is *only* to simulate how search engines would behave if they supported *SearchPad*.

As we shall describe, our implementation provides an additional service. It allows the search service to collect query-specific result relevance and usage data. Specifically, *SearchPad* can log for each client:

(1) queries that were issued;
(2) result pages viewed for each query;
(3) result hyperlinks considered relevant for each query;
(4) the order in which result pages were viewed;
(5) the time spent viewing the result;
(6) whether a result hyperlink considered relevant was actually viewed by the user.

Such information is valuable to search providers. It can be used to statistically compare two ranking algorithms and find out which one is better. Similarly, it can be used to compare two search services. It can also be used to discover the most relevant pages for popular queries, which in turn can be used to improved results for those queries in the future.

Collection of usage data raises concerns about privacy and the author strongly supports the privacy of users on the Web. However, the major vulnerability from the user's point of view is having search services know about their interests. Unfortunately, this is already revealed by the query. The information we collect, namely the results they viewed and found useful, reveals more about the quality of the pages returned than about the user. Thus we argue that this is not a further breach of privacy. In any case there other search companies on the Web, notably Direct Hit [3], with a business model based on collecting data on the pages that users look at. They count 'click-throughs' (i.e., the number of times users click on a particular link) received by result links for popular queries and reorder results based on perceived popularity. We believe that the information we can collect is superior to Direct Hit's data, because we discover the results people actually liked — not just the results they clicked on. Even when a query finds no useful results, users tend to click on a few results per query to understand what happened, which can contaminate the click-through log. With our scheme the data collected is purer. Also, collecting click-throughs as done previously imposes an overhead both on the server and the user. In Direct Hit's scheme click-throughs are trapped by redirecting result accesses through a Web server that logs the data and then issues a redirect to the actual result page. With our scheme all logging is done at the client without an extra HTTP access.

2. Interaction with SearchPad

We present a walk-through to illustrate the user's interaction with *SearchPad*. In our implementation, the user accesses AltaVista, Excite, Google and Hotbot through special URLs that route communication with the engines through the *SearchPad* proxy.

Fig. 1 shows an AltaVista page transformed by the proxy. The 'SearchPad' button at the top left brings up the *SearchPad* agent (Fig. 3), allowing the user access to any previously marked queries and leads. Each result on the AltaVista page has a blue 'Mark' button associated with it. Clicking on this button causes the corresponding link to be added to *SearchPad*, along with the corresponding query. If the query already exists the link is merged into the existing set of links. Links added to *SearchPad* are called 'leads'. Note that marking is a cheap operation, and involves only a local transfer of data from the result page to the *SearchPad* agent. No network communication occurs and hence no delay. This is illustrated in Figs. 2 and 3.

Fig. 2 shows the second AltaVista result for the query: genetic engineering, which has just been visited by the user. All visits to result page and time spent therein are logged by *SearchPad* as part of its data collection process. Also, on return from a result page, the blue 'Mark' button for the just-visited result link turns red as in Fig. 2 (hard to see in gray-scale). The color change is an invitation for the user to mark the link. Also, it makes the result easier to spot, increasing the likelihood of the user marking the lead if they liked it.

Fig. 3 shows the *SearchPad* window with a list of three queries bookmarked, and under each query a list of leads. *SearchPad* is merely a Web page rendered by Javascript code, and appears within an independent browser window. Each query has an *open/close* triangular toggle to control the visibility of leads under it. E.g., clicking on an *open* toggle causes it to close. The last marked query ('genetic engineering') is at the top of the *SearchPad* heap and hence most visible. Queries in *SearchPad* are maintained in a *most-recently accessed order* to keep pace with the user's varying interests. For each marked lead the title is shown, hyperlinked to the corresponding Web page. To conserve space only the hostname is shown after it. *SearchPad* is designed to have the form factor of a small notepad — small yet useful for recording essential information during a search.

Each query has a circular selector in front of it to support query selection. To send a query to a search engine the user would first select the query and click on the search engine. If they selected the most recent query, 'genetic engineering', and clicked on Google, they would get the result set shown in Fig. 4.

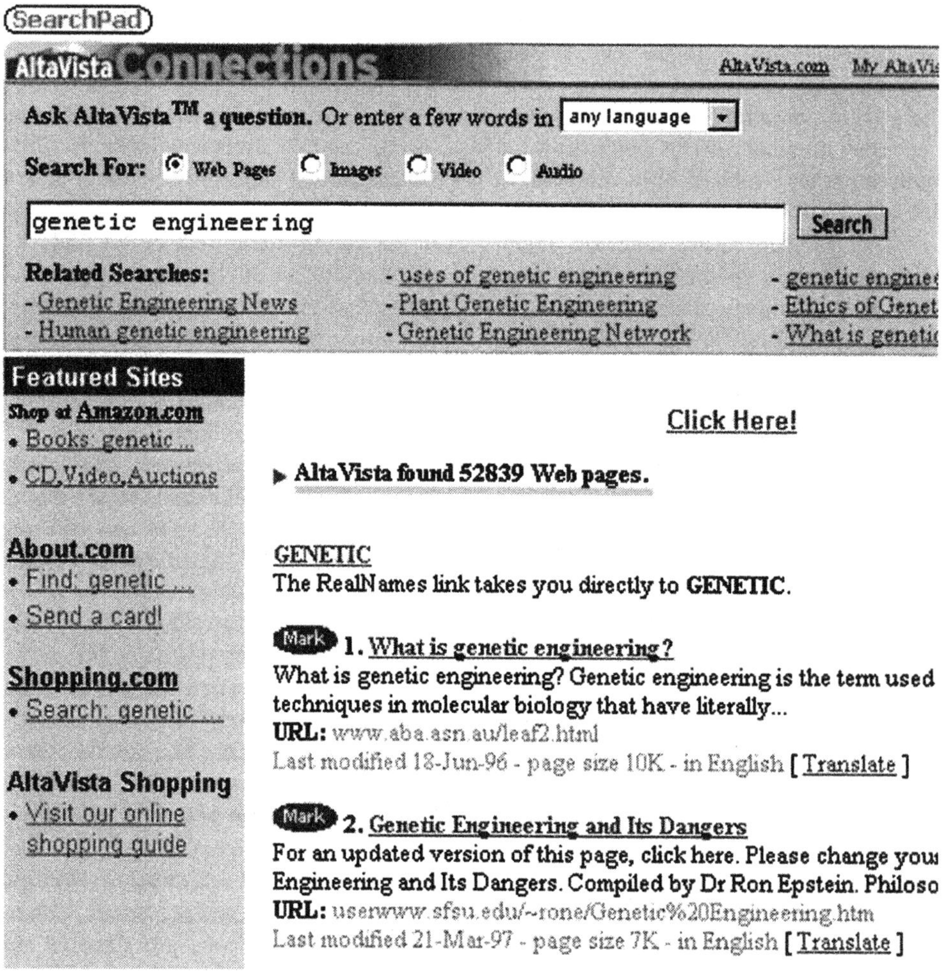

Fig. 1. An AltaVista result page extended with *SearchPad* support.

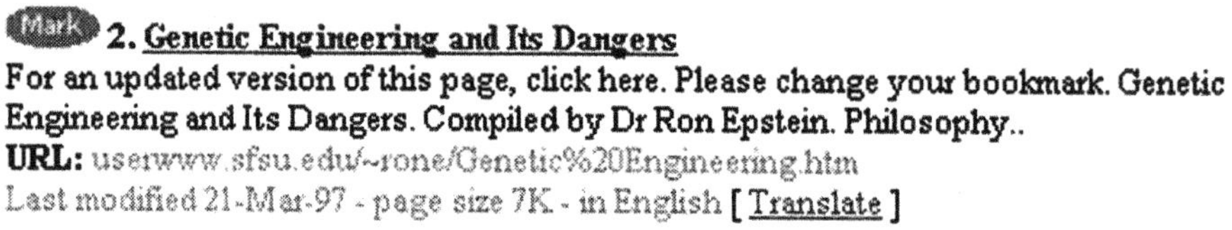

Fig. 2. Result visited by the user and then marked.

In Fig. 5 the user has subsequently marked the lead labeled 'MelissaVirus.com: The very latest Melissa Virus information' for the (repeat) query 'melissa virus'. This moves 'melissa virus' to the top of the list of *SearchPad* queries and adds the new lead to the end of the list of leads for the query.

SearchPad also has an 'Edit Mode' (see Fig. 6) to support changes to the stored data. This is because, although the browser may shutdown and the machine get rebooted, the information stored in *SearchPad* is permanent. Hence, the user may periodically want to delete some leads or queries to free up space. Also they might want to merge the leads classified under various related queries into a single meaningful

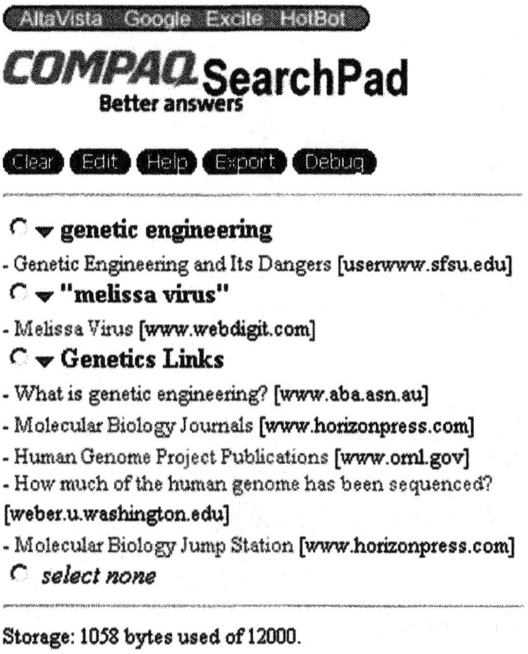

AltaVista Google Excite HotBot

COMPAQ SearchPad
Better answers

Clear Edit Help Export Debug

genetic engineering

- Genetic Engineering and Its Dangers [userwww.sfsu.edu]

"melissa virus"

- Melissa Virus [www.webdigit.com]

Genetics Links

- What is genetic engineering? [www.aba.asn.au]
- Molecular Biology Journals [www.horizonpress.com]
- Human Genome Project Publications [www.ornl.gov]
- How much of the human genome has been sequenced? [weber.u.washington.edu]
- Molecular Biology Jump Station [www.horizonpress.com]

select none

Storage: 1058 bytes used of 12000.

Fig. 3. The *SearchPad* Helper with a new query: 'genetic engineering' and a new lead.

query. In 'Edit Mode', *SearchPad* is still fully functional, except that it provides extra buttons to edit its state. The cross ('X') marks are buttons to delete the query or lead they are associated with. Queries can be renamed by clicking on 'Rename', which brings up a dialog to enter the new query. If the new query matches another existing query the leads in the two queries are merged. The old query is discarded.

3. Implementation

In this section we describe the implementation of *SearchPad*.

Since a design goal was to not require any extra storage at the server or impose any communication overhead for marking, all storage and computation is moved to the client. Consequently, we implemented *SearchPad* as an HTML document containing embedded code in Javascript [5] (VB Script [11] could have been used as well). Result pages are extended by embedding code in Javascript as well. When the user marks a link the associated scripting code communicates the link's URL and associated information to a corresponding piece of code in *SearchPad*. The code within *SearchPad* then updates its display showing the new link.

This approach is faced with the following problem. Embedded scripts are constrained by the browser both in terms of access (i.e., limited access to other windows) and storage (no access to the file system) in the normal mode of operation. In some Web browsers, the embedded scripts can request the user for more access to the Web browser's state. Nonetheless this is not useful because many users will refuse such a request, since it might represent a security risk. Thus, embedded scripts face many restrictions. We describe next how these may be overcome.

We use cookies (a mechanism for host-specific persistent client-side storage) both for communication between the result page and *SearchPad*, and for persistent storage. (See RFC 2109 [9] and Netscape's documentation on cookies [7].) A client such as Netscape's Navigator which implements RFC 2109, supports a limited amount of client-side storage in the form of cookies. Each cookie holds 4 Kb of text data, and each host a user visits will be allowed at least 20 cookies. Such cookies are persistent and save their state on the user's hard disk. This allows *SearchPad* to remember marked leads across Web browser sessions.

Javascript was ideal for our implementation because it allowed cookies to be read and written from within the browser. A restricted form of cookies sharing is possible between Javascript instances. This allows code on the result page to pass messages to code in *SearchPad*. Javascript is single-threaded across the entire browser. This gives us mutual exclusion and simplifies the design. Also, Javascript has support for timer-driven callbacks which is needed to implement polling behavior within *SearchPad*.

The search service (or a proxy server through which the search service is accessed) embeds a button (or equivalent device) within each search result to allow the user to 'mark' the result as a lead. The button links to embedded code in JavaScript. The code is invoked when the button is clicked, and causes relevant information about the link and query to be written to a log maintained in a set of cookies,

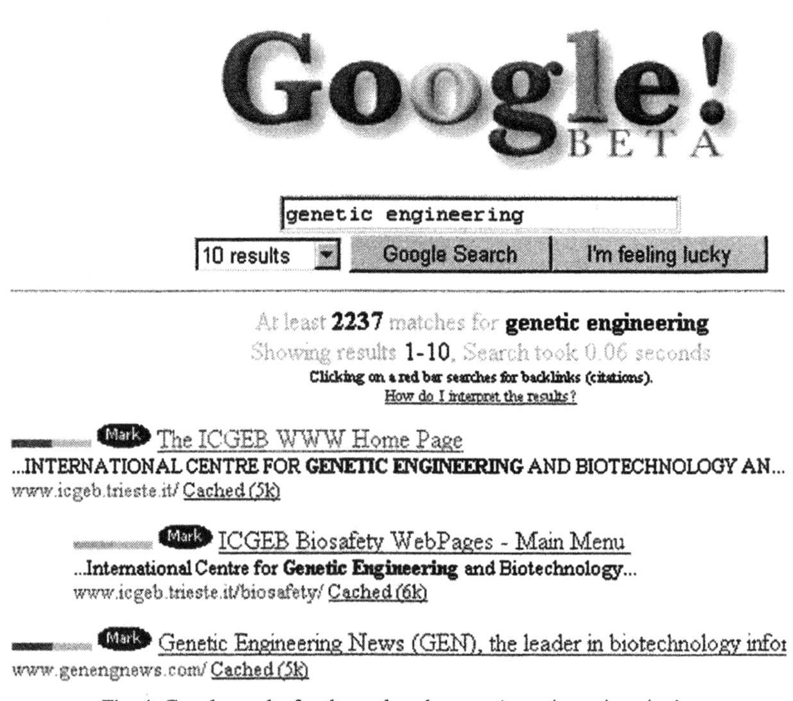

Fig. 4. Google results for the replayed query: 'genetic engineering'.

associated with the Web site (known as the access log).

For example, the following are logged for each 'mark' action:

- the query;
- the title, URL and rank of the result being marked;
- the time at which the event occurred.

Similarly, when a result's hyperlink is clicked to view the result page, we log the same type of information in association with the 'view' event. When the user returns to the page containing search results after viewing a result page, the 'return' event is logged as well, with a time-stamp. When a 'return' event follows a 'view' event, the time difference provides an estimate of the time spent viewing the result page.

All the information collected above resides in a set of cookies associated with the originating Web site, and is available to scripts executing within other pages downloaded from the same site. In particular it is visible to *SearchPad*, which is an HTML document whose contents are dynamically generated by embedded Javascript. *SearchPad* polls the access logs every few seconds in order to respond to events.

All the data needed by *SearchPad* to display marked queries and leads to the user are maintained in a cookie access log. When the cookie access log is updated due to a new event which requires a change in *SearchPad*'s display, the *SearchPad* code initiates a 'soft' reload. The soft reload operation fetches the cached Web page corresponding to *SearchPad* from the browser cache and executes the code again. At this point the Javascript reads the cookies and redraws itself to reflect the new state. To initiate a reload, either the code in the result page can signal *SearchPad* to notify that the state has changed, or *SearchPad* can periodically examine the cookie log to see if new leads have been added (as in our implementation). Changes to *SearchPad*'s display due to interaction with *SearchPad* (e.g., open/close operations and mode change operations) are handled similarly. The Javascript event handler updates the visual state of *SearchPad* represented in the cookies, and initiates a soft reload.

AltaVista Google Excite HotBot

COMPAQ SearchPad
Better answers

Clear Edit Help Export Debug

▾ "melissa virus"
- Melissa Virus [www.webdigit.com]
- MelissaVirus.com: They very latest Melissa Virus information [www.melissavirus.com]

▾ genetic engineering
- Genetic Engineering and Its Dangers [userwww.sfsu.edu]
- The ICGEB WWW Home Page [www.icgeb.trieste.it]

▾ Genetics Links
- What is genetic engineering? [www.aba.asn.au]
- Molecular Biology Journals [www.horizonpress.com]
- Human Genome Project Publications [www.ornl.gov]
- How much of the human genome has been sequenced? [weber.u.washington.edu]
- Molecular Biology Jump Station [www.horizonpress.com]

select none

Storage: 1333 bytes used of 12000.

Fig. 5. Updated *SearchPad* page.

AltaVista Google Excite HotBot

COMPAQ SearchPad
Better answers

Edit Mode: Click ✖ to delete queries and links. Click Rename to rename a query. Renaming to an existing query merges results.

▾ Genetics Links ✖ Rename
- What is genetic engineering? [www.aba.asn.au] ✖
- Molecular Biology Journals [www.horizonpress.com] ✖
- Human Genome Project Publications [www.ornl.gov] ✖
- How much of the human genome has been sequenced? [weber.u.washington.edu] ✖
- Molecular Biology Jump Station [www.horizonpress.com] ✖
- Genetic Engineering and Its Dangers [userwww.sfsu.edu] ✖
- The ICGEB WWW Home Page [www.icgeb.trieste.it] ✖

▾ "melissa virus" ✖ Rename
- Melissa Virus [www.webdigit.com] ✖
- MelissaVirus.com: They very latest Melissa Virus information [www.melissavirus.com] ✖

Storage: 1308 bytes used of 12000.

Fig. 6. Edit Mode *SearchPad* view after all Genetics related pages are merged under 'Genetic Links'.

Eventually, as events accumulate and leads are added, the storage available in the cookie access log will be exhausted. At this point either the user can be prevented from marking any more leads (unless some are deleted), or *SearchPad* can compress the data. We support a clever form of data compression to free up more space.

To compress data in the cookie access log, *SearchPad* does a 'hard' reload of itself. This causes that fresh copy of the *SearchPad* Web page is fetched from the server ignoring the cache. The cookies comprising the cookie access log are configured so that they are transmitted to the Web server every time *SearchPad* is reloaded over the net. Also, a fresh set of cookies are transmitted back from the server and overwrite the previous cookies. This is part of the standard RFC 2109 cookie exchange protocol. We use this to transfer activity log information to the server and also to reduce the data stored in *SearchPad* as follows.

(1) All data in the event log that the server needs to keep for its data collection is logged at the server. The remaining logged data is cleared in the cookies.
(2) The verbose information for each newly bookmarked lead is removed from the cookies. This is because the same information is already present at the server. Each lead is replaced by an identifier representing the URL (known as the URLID), based on the internal handle to the URL at the server.
(3) However, the URLID is not intelligible to the user and unsuitable for presentation. Hence, the server dynamically generates a new version of the *SearchPad* Web page in which the Javascript code is augmented with a lookup table mapping URLIDs to title and URL information, for all marked leads. This allows the same presentation to be given to the user as before compression. However, the bulk of the data is moved from the

cookies to the *SearchPad* Javascript code. Since the mapping from URLIDs (server internal ids) to title and URL information is assumed to be available at the server, no extra storage is needed at the server to support the user base.

To ensure timely data collection at the server, *SearchPad* is configured to periodically hard reload itself, thus logging the user's activity periodically. Further, to avoid transmitting the cookies to the server during other communications, the cookies are configured so that they will be transmitted only when *SearchPad* is reloaded and not when result pages are fetched. We do this by associating *SearchPad* with a path that extends the path of result pages, as explained in RFC 2109. This has the effect of allowing *SearchPad* to read cookies set by result pages but *not* vice versa.

4. Experience

We conducted a trial of the *SearchPad* service at our research laboratory — Compaq, Systems Research Center — from May 6 to September 3, 1999. The service was available on the company intranet, but most of the usage was by the research staff of the Systems Research Center (about 50 people), and to a smaller extent by Compaq Research as a whole (about 150 people). Logs were collected in partially shrouded format so that queries themselves were unrecognizable, but hostnames and other details were preserved. Our logs show that accesses outside the research community did not contribute significantly to usage.

Table 1 summarizes the usage statistics for the 4-month period. This does not include accesses by the author for testing. The aim of the study was to understand if people would find our service useful. Although users were invited to use the system through internal advertising, no incentive was given to make them use it. Also, assurances were given that we would protect their privacy. Hence, we did not attempt to keep track of the results that were bookmarked, since within a small community such information might reveal more than it would on the Internet at large. Also, we would need a large user base to collect a statistically significant sample of usage information to make any relevance judgements.

Table 1
Usage statistics from a 4-month trial

Number of result pages viewed:	
AltaVista	1352
Excite	148
Google	724
HotBot	57
Total	2281
Number of distinct accessing hosts	178
Number of distinct queries	1133
Average number of result pages/query	2.01
Average number of result pages/host	12.8
Percentage accesses w *SearchPad* 'docked'	8

The high usage of AltaVista may be biased by the fact that AltaVista was created by Compaq Research. The usage of the other engines can be taken to represent perceived value by our user base. In most cases each host in the log corresponds to a distinct user. We were curious to see if usage patterns would change with the *SearchPad* model of searching. For example, we were curious if users look at more pages, since they now had the option of keeping track of temporary leads? The average number of result pages per query was 2.01, which is higher than previously reported (e.g., 1.39 was reported in a previous study by Silverstein et al. [10]). Our number is somewhat diluted by the presence of casual users who used *SearchPad* marginally, possibly for test queries. Considering more seasoned users (users who used *SearchPad* to view more than 50 result pages), the number of result pages viewed per query is slightly higher = 2.15. We noticed a large number of single page views in the logs, even for seasoned users. A single result page view is often evidence of the fact that the users found the result they were looking for immediately (i.e., the ranking was good), or that they were disappointed with the query and formulated a better query. If we consider only cases in which users looked at more than one result page we find that the average page views per query is higher = 3.98. This suggests that having a tool to record search context *may* encourage users to explore result sets more deeply, and compensate for some non-relevant pages in the ranking.

The only interface design choice we tried to evaluate was the option of attaching *SearchPad* to the left of the results window, as an extra frame. This was done by clicking on the 'SearchPad' button at the top left of the result page (see Fig. 1). We call this 'docking'. Each result window could have a docked version of *SearchPad* potentially. Docking was hard to implement since it meant keeping several versions of *SearchPad* synchronized. However, the user study shows that only 8% of the users liked the docking option. This actually reduced to 5% for users with more than 50 result page views, suggesting that embedding *SearchPad* in a frame is not convenient.

SearchPad was tested on Netscape versions 3 and higher on Unix, MacOS, and Windows 95/NT, and on Internet Explorer versions 4 and higher on Windows 95/NT, and found to work reliably.

5. Conclusions

In this paper we describe an extension to search engines to explicitly maintain user search context as they look for information, on many topics, using many search engines, and over many sessions. By search context we mean queries that were previously deployed and considered useful, and promising result links associated with each query. *SearchPad* is an agent that works collaboratively with result pages, and allows users to remember queries and associated leads in a convenient helper window. Unlike bookmarks, which correspond to the user's long-term memory of information, the leads in *SearchPad* constitute the user's short-term memory and represent work in progress. They tend be less valuable than bookmarks and are maintained only as long as the user's information need is current. Hence we perceive *SearchPad* as a complement to the browser's bookmarks facility.

SearchPad is implemented as a Javascript extension to the search results page. We demonstrated the generality of our design with an implementation that works on four major search engines. Our implementation is highly portable, requires no download or start-up delay, needs no storage at the browser and does not increase the communication overhead with the server. An added benefit is that *SearchPad* can record user actions on the search result page, and also discover which results are most valuable to users in the context of specific queries. This imposes less overhead and is qualitatively more useful than the information collected using the click-through tracking strategy of search engines such as Direct Hit.

The service was tested in a multi-platform environment with over 150 users for 4 months and found to be usable and helpful. It is possible that the ability to maintain search context explicitly affects the way people search. Repeat *SearchPad* users looked at more search results than reported previously. This suggests that explicit availability of search context might partially compensate for non-relevant pages in the ranking.

References

[1] AltaVista: http://www.altavista.com/
[2] AskJeeves: http://www.ask.com/
[3] Direct Hit: The Direct Hit Technology — A White Paper, Direct Hit Inc., http://system.directhit.com/whitepaper.html
[4] Google: http://www.google.com/
[5] Javascript: Javascript Reference, Netscape, http://developer.netscape.com/docs/manuals/communicator/jsref/contents.htm
[6] MetaCrawler: http://www.metacrawler.com/
[7] NetscapeCookies: Persistent Client State — HTTP Cookies, Netscape, http://www.netscape.com/newsref/std/cookie_spec.html
[8] Open Directory: http://www.dmoz.org/
[9] RFC 2109: HTTP State Management Mechanism, http://andrew2.andrew.cmu.edu/rfc/rfc2109.html
[10] C. Silverstein, M. Henzinger, H. Marais and M. Moricz, Analysis of a very large AltaVista query log, Compaq SRC, Technical Note, 1998-014, ftp://ftp.digital.com/pub/DEC/SRC/technical-notes/SRC-1998-014.pdf
[11] VB Script: http://msdn.microsoft.com/scripting/vbscript/default.htm
[12] Yahoo: http://www.yahoo.com/

Krishna Bharat is a member of the research staff at Google Inc. in Mountain View, California. Formerly he was at Compaq Computer Corporation's Systems Research Center, which is where the research described here was done. His research interests include Web content discovery and retrieval, user interface issues in Web search and task automation, and relevance assessments on the Web. He received his Ph.D. in Computer Science from Georgia Institute of Technology in 1996, where he worked on tool and infrastructure support for building distributed user interface applications.

Automating Web navigation with the WebVCR

Vinod Anupam [1], Juliana Freire [*,1], Bharat Kumar [1], Daniel Lieuwen [1]

Bell Laboratories, 600 Mountain Ave., Murray Hill, NJ 07974, USA

Abstract

Recent developments in Web technology such as the inclusion of scripting languages, frames, and the growth of dynamic content, have made the process of retrieving Web content more complicated, and sometimes tedious. For example, Web browsers do not provide a method for a user to bookmark a frame-based Web site once the user navigates within the initial frameset. Also, some sites, such as travel sites and online classifieds, require users to go through a sequence of steps and fill out a sequence of forms in order to access their data. Using the bookmark facilities implemented in all popular browsers, often it is not possible to create a shortcut to access such data, and these steps must be manually repeated every time the data is needed. However, hard-to-reach pages are often the best candidates for a shortcut, because significantly more effort is required to reach them than to reach a standard page with a well-defined URL. The WebVCR system addresses this problem by letting users record and replay a series of browsing steps in smart bookmarks — shortcuts to Web content that require multiple steps to be retrieved. It provides a VCR-style interface to transparently record and replay users' actions. Creating and updating smart bookmarks is a simple process involving only the usual browsing actions and requiring no programming by the user. In addition to saving users time by providing shortcuts to hard-to-reach Web content, smart bookmarks can be used as building blocks for many interesting Web applications and new e-commerce services. In this paper, we describe the WebVCR and the techniques it uses to record and replay smart bookmarks, as well as our experiences in building the system. We also discuss some applications that are simplified/enabled by smart bookmarks.

Keywords: Affiliate programs; Bookmarks; Dynamic content; Electronic commerce; Notification; Personalization; Smart bookmarks; Tutorials; Web clipping; Wrappers

1. Introduction

The growing trend of making the Web more interactive and personalized, together with the explosion of dynamic content has led to the wide use of scripting languages, frames, cookies, and forms. As a result, the process of retrieving Web content has become more complicated, and can sometimes be tedious. For example, Web browsers do not provide a method for a user to bookmark a frame-based Web site once the user navigates away from the initial frameset. Also, some sites require users to go through a sequence of steps in order to access their data. For example, in order to find out the available flights and fares for a certain itinerary, one needs to login at a travel Web site (by filling out a form with login id and password), and enter the itinerary information to retrieve the available fares. These steps cause dynamic pages to be generated, often with

* Corresponding author.

[1] E-mail: {anupam,juliana,bharat,lieuwen}@research.bell-labs.com

session-ids encoded in the URL or embedded inside the page. Using the bookmark facilities implemented in all popular browsers, it is not possible to create a shortcut to the list of available flights. Consequently, in order to track the cost of a trip, these steps must be repeated multiple times. Such pages are often the best candidates for a shortcut, because significantly more effort is required to reach them than to reach a standard page which has a well-defined URL.

In order to address this shortcoming, we built the WebVCR system. WebVCR presents a VCR-style interface to record and play browsing steps. It is very simple to use: a user needs only instruct the system to start recording and go on with his usual navigation. Once he reaches the desired final page, he can stop recording and save the sequence of browsing steps in a *smart bookmark* to be replayed at a later time. Smart bookmarks are shortcuts to Web content that require multiple browsing steps to be retrieved — they may be saved in bookmark lists, or mailed to others like any other bookmark.

Example 1.1 (*Navigating travelocity.com*). Consider the following scenario. Juliana plans to attend the WWW9 conference and she is looking for flights from Newark to Amsterdam, that leave from Newark May 14th and return from Amsterdam on May 20th. She must take the following steps:

- Go to `http://www.travelocity.com`
- Choose the *Find/Book a Flight* option (Fig. 1),
- Login (Fig. 2),
- Specify details of itinerary (Fig. 3).

This series of steps produces a page with a list of alternative flights (Fig. 4) whose URL is something like:

```
http://dps1.travelocity.com:80/
  airgchoice.ctl?SEQ=94312
```

Bookmarking this URL is not useful, since once the session[2] times out, the URL can no longer be used to access the page. However, it is likely that a single visit to this page will be insufficient. It may take weeks or months to find an acceptable fare. Using the WebVCR, these steps can be saved and later replayed with a single click — saving Juliana a lot of clicking and time.

[2] The number at the right-hand side of the URL is a session id.

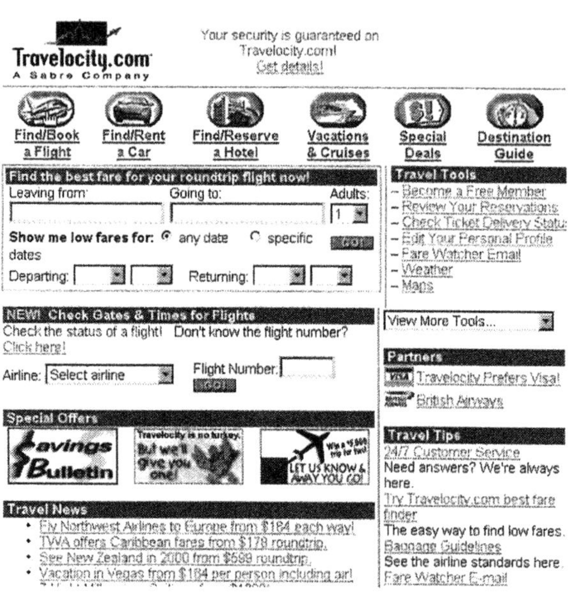

Fig. 1. Travelocity main page.

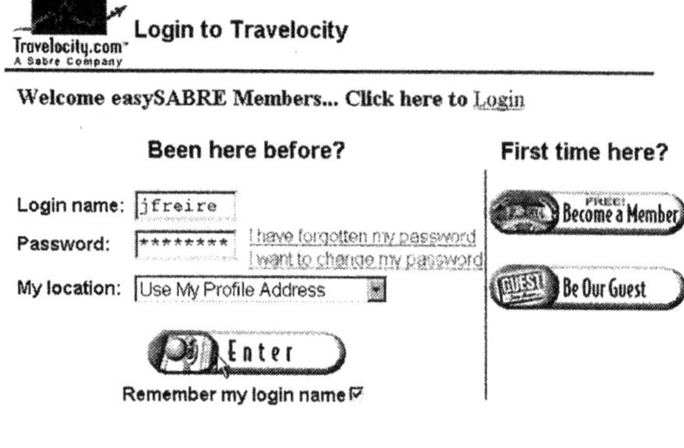

Fig. 2. Travelocity login.

Whereas the ability to create shortcuts to *hard-to-reach* Web content can be a time saver for a user, it is specially useful for applications that consume such content. Significant effort has already been invested into developing techniques to build wrappers to extract information from HTML pages (see, e.g., [2,11,15]) and more recently to query XML documents (see, e.g., [7]). However, issues involving the

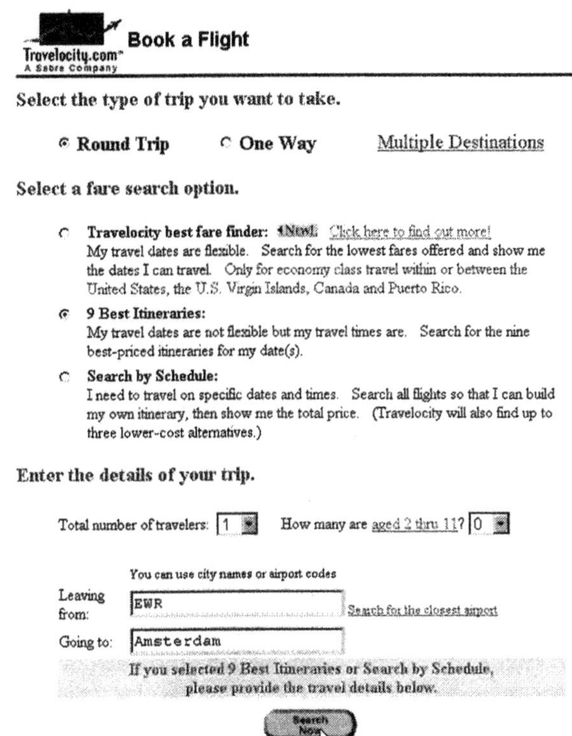

Fig. 3. Itinerary form (to specify origin, destination, dates, etc.).

Fig. 4. List of alternative flights.

actual retrieval of the data have been largely overlooked. Currently, in order to automate the retrieval process, one must write a program (an access wrapper) in general purpose languages such as Perl and Java, or more specialized languages such as WebL [11] to perform the required navigation. However, especially in the context of Web integration systems, this is not always practical. Given the rate at which Web sites change, maintaining a large number of access wrappers can be very time consuming. The WebVCR can be used to quickly create access wrappers to Web content. Creating and updating these wrappers is a simple process involving only the usual browsing actions.

As a result, a number of applications can be greatly simplified by the WebVCR. For example, casual users can easily put together *personal portals* (such as `http://my.yahoo.com`) with information retrieved from sites of their choice (e.g., their bank balance, weather report, etc.) [1]. This and other new applications enabled by WebVCR are described in Section 3.

Even though the underlying idea of the WebVCR is rather simple, there are many issues that need to be addressed for it to work properly. For example, in order to record users' actions in a transparent fashion and handle various features present in Web sites (e.g., cookies, JavaScript, etc.), we have to get around issues such as security restrictions of browsers and their limited APIs. In addition, because the structure of a Web page may change between record and replay, a major challenge is to guarantee that the smart bookmark leads to the Web page originally intended. In what follows, we will discuss these and other problems we found in detail, as well as our solutions to them.

The paper is organized as follows. In Section 2 we give an overview of the WebVCR system and its methodology. Applications simplified and/or enabled by WebVCR are described in Section 3. Implementation details and our experiences are presented in Section 4. Related work is discussed in Section 5, and we conclude in Section 6 with future directions we plan to pursue.

2. Methodology

The *record–play* facility provided by WebVCR allows users to save shortcuts to Web pages that do not have a well-defined (static) URL. In this section we describe the methodology behind WebVCR, and illustrate one of its uses: a personal WebVCR that lets casual Web users create smart bookmarks.

The main idea behind WebVCR is to *transparently* record a sequence of browsing steps that can be saved, and automatically replayed later. We break down this functionality into three coarse functions:

Notification: Tracking users' actions. In order to provide this functionality, the WebVCR requires a mechanism to keep track of all actions performed by a user while browsing, which links and buttons are clicked, what information is input in forms, etc. This can be achieved in many different ways, for example: the browser can be modified to provide notifications for each action performed (e.g., the link with DOM address `link[0]` and label *Find Flights* was clicked); a proxy can be used that rewrites each page and replaces all *hrefs* with calls to a well-known script which can then provide the notification facility; a proxy can be used to monitor all HTTP commands sent to/from the browser; JavaScript event handlers can be attached to all *active* (clickable and changeable) objects in the page. Note that multiple techniques can be combined.

Recording: Storing user's browsing information. Once notification about an action is received, enough information must be saved so that the step can be replayed later. Since a smart bookmark may visit several (static and dynamic) pages, at each page the WebVCR must be able to identify the correct action needed to retrieve the next page. Our initial implementation uses the DOM signature (e.g., `document.links[5]`, that represents the fifth link in the current document) of the active (clicked/modified) object, as well as other information available about the object (see Section 4.1 for details). Note that storing only the DOM signature of the objects is not enough. Take for example sites such as `http://amazon.com` that may display a different number of ads each time a page is visited. If the new ad contains a link (or a form), the DOM signatures of all subsequent links (or forms) change — if the selection of the object is based solely on the DOM, an incorrect object may be chosen during replay.

Playback: Replaying users' actions. Correctly replaying a series of steps is one of the major challenges for the WebVCR. Complications arise for many reasons. For example, as illustrated in Example 1.1, since URLs may have embedded session-ids, during replay simply using a recorded URL for the final page will not work. Other complicating factors include: the difficulty of determining that a page has been fully loaded, and as a result, determining when the next step should be executed during replay; changes in the structure of pages that occur between the record and replay (e.g., banner ads may be added or removed); forms with hidden attributes which encode session and other information that changes constantly; steps that encompass the execution of a JavaScript function (e.g., the `onclick` event handler of a button), or the use of a plugin or Java applet. Robustness issues and the implementation of the replay functionality are discussed in more detail in Section 4.3.

2.1. Building a WebVCR

There are many possible ways to implement a WebVCR system depending on the choice of notification system, where and how smart bookmarks are replayed, and where and how they are stored. Because of space limitations, in this paper we restrict our discussion to two different architectures, client-based and server-based. The differences and tradeoffs between these architectures are discussed in Section 2.2. We also restrict our discussion of implementation details to Netscape Navigator[3]. In what follows, we illustrate how Web traversals are recorded and replayed using a client-based implementation, the personal WebVCR.

The architecture of the personal WebVCR is

[3] Issues regarding implementation of WebVCR using Microsoft Internet Explorer are discussed in Section 4.

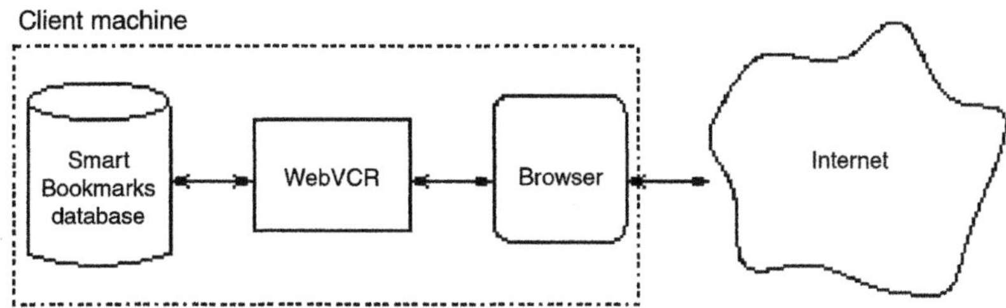

Fig. 5. Client-based architecture.

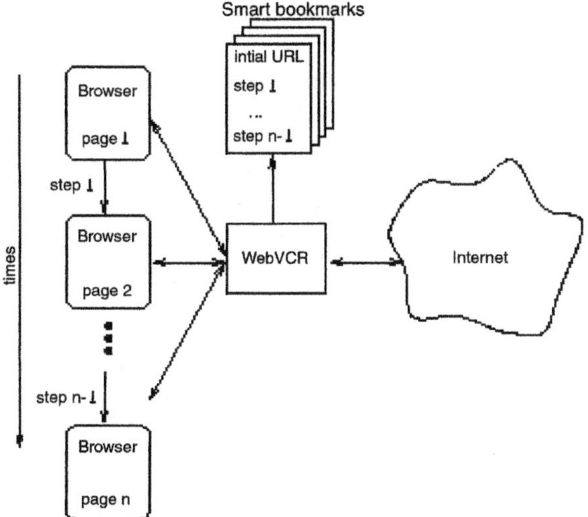

Fig. 6. Recording smart bookmarks.

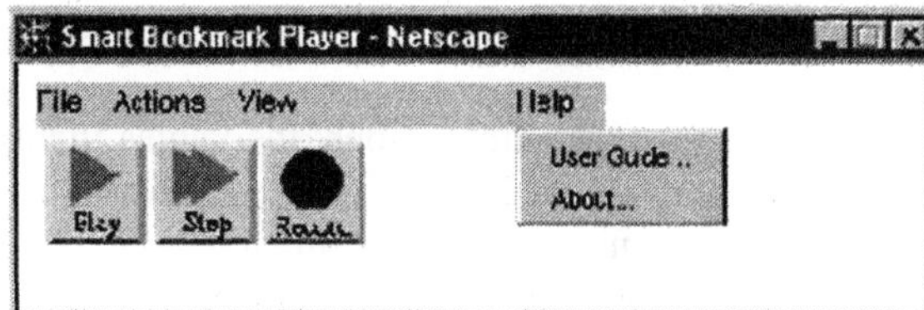

Fig. 7. Screenshot of WebVCR applet when first started up.

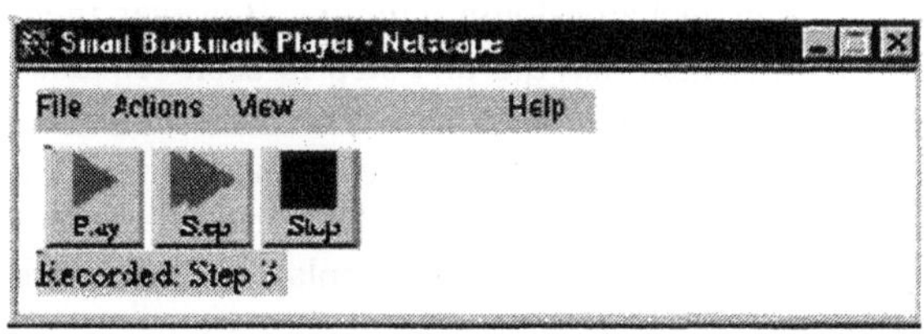

Fig. 8. Screenshot of WebVCR applet while recording steps.

shown in Fig. 5. The personal WebVCR uses a Java applet in conjunction with the user's browser to record and replay smart bookmarks. The applet can be installed on the end-user's desktop, or downloaded whenever required from a Web site hosting this applet.

The user starts the WebVCR by loading the WebVCR starting page into a browser window (*MainWindow*). The starting page opens a new browser window (*AppletWindow*) and loads an HTML page containing the WebVCR applet. The reason for loading the WebVCR applet in its own browser window is to make the applet persistent (while the user is recording/playing smart bookmarks in the MainWindow). The applet, which has standard VCR-style buttons (see Fig. 7), is then started. The recording process is depicted in Fig. 6. To record a smart bookmark, the user traverses the Web to the desired starting point for the smart bookmark and clicks on the `Record` button in the applet. Clicking on the `Record` button causes two actions to take place (which are transparent to the user): (1) the applet records the current URL as the starting location of the smart bookmark; and (2) the applet inserts event handlers on all elements in the MainWindow that the user might operate on. From then on, as the user navigates via link traversals or form submissions, each action triggers an event handler that causes the applet to record the corresponding action. Whenever a new page is loaded, the applet re-inserts the event handlers (Step 2 above). As shown in Fig. 8, the applet window keeps the user informed of his progress.

When the user finally reaches the desired page, he clicks on the `Stop` button and the applet stops recording. The user can then play or step through the recorded smart bookmark. During replay, the WebVCR applet uses the steps recorded in the smart bookmark to inform the browser which action to take in order to retrieve the next page. For example, for link traversals, the corresponding URL is loaded into

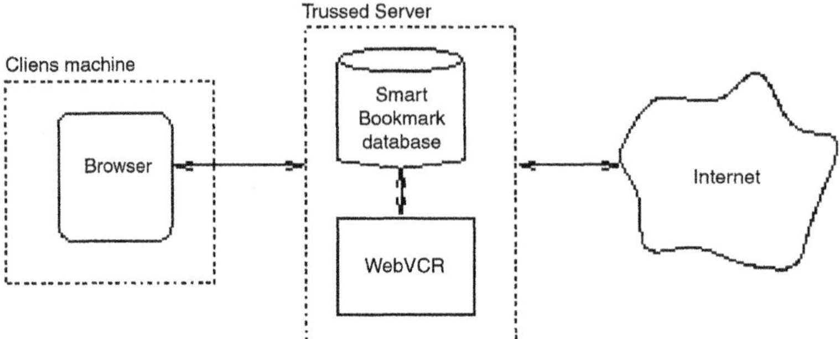

Fig. 9. Server-based architecture.

the browser; for form submissions, the values input by the user (and recorded in the smart bookmark) are used to fill the form before submitting it.

A set of smart bookmarks can be concatenated. For example, one may create a smart bookmark for login at a specific site, and a number of others to perform distinct after-login activities. However, there is a requirement that the first step in each sequence of smart bookmarks must have a well-defined URL. For example, if the user has been browsing inside a frameset such that the current URL doesn't reflect the content in the frames, then replay will not work properly.

Once a smart bookmark is recorded, the user also has the option of saving it into an HTML file that contains a representation of the smart bookmark along with a reference to the WebVCR applet. This HTML page can be bookmarked like any other Web page, and can be added to the browser's bookmark/favorites list. If the user loads that HTML page into a browser, the WebVCR applet starts and automatically replays the entire recorded smart bookmark, thus providing the user with one-click access to the final page.

2.2. *Architectural variants*

In the discussion above, we described an implementation of a client-based WebVCR that uses a WebVCR applet and browser to record and play smart bookmarks. However, for applications such as Web clipping for wireless access (see Section 3), a tool is needed that does not require the use of a full-fledged browser on the client side, and that minimizes the communication between client and server. For such an application, a server-side process that receives a request, performs the replay, and ships *only* (some section of) the final page is more appropriate.

Fig. 9 depicts a server-based architecture for the WebVCR. A central server provided by a *trusted* third party records, stores, and replays smart bookmarks[4]. Since the WebVCR does not make use of the layout of HTML pages rendered by a browser, a browser is not necessary during replay. Instead, a light-weight Web client that understands the HTTP protocol, has an HTML parser to extract the DOM information, and (possibly) has a JavaScript interpreter to handle Dynamic HTML can be used. In the scenario where multiple users simultaneously access the central server, a light-weight client is preferable to a heavyweight browser, making for a more scalable solution.

Different issues arise in the implementation of a server-based architecture. For example, JavaScript handlers are no longer a valid option for detecting browsing actions. One possible mechanism for recording user actions in this scenario is to have the WebVCR server rewrite the HTML pages before presenting them to the user, so that all link traversals and form submissions to the destination site are in fact redirected through the WebVCR server[5]. Note that the server must also simulate some of the actions performed by browser, such as the handling of cookies — since it is the WebVCR server that requests documents from the destination site, any cookies present in the user's machine are not visible. Other differences between the two architectures include:

[4] Smart bookmarks can be made available through a unique URLs generated by the server.

[5] Some notification services such as Mind-It [14] use this technique.

- *Privacy:* A WebVCR server has access to all information recorded in the smart bookmark, and that is sent to and downloaded from the destination site during record and replay. The client-based architecture in contrast, offers greater privacy to the user, since record/replay occur at the user's desktop, and the information recorded in the smart bookmark is also stored locally.
- *Implementation complexity:* In client-based architectures, since record and replay is done via the user's browser, destination sites requiring cookies or secure access (HTTPS) pose no problems. In contrast, server-based implementations must provide special support for these features.
- *Ease of use and convenience:* In server-based architectures, the user does not need to install/ download the application, but needs to access the third party's Web server every time the smart bookmarking functionality is required.
- *Security:* Because of security restrictions imposed by browsers, in client-based architectures, the WebVCR applet must be granted certain privileges. For example, `UniversalBrowserAccess` is required since the applet needs to read/modify pages downloaded from different domains, and `UniversalFileAccess` is required if the user desires to save bookmarks into HTML files for later access. It is our experience that some users are not comfortable with accepting certificates and granting such privileges to applets [6].
- *Secure connections:* In server-based architectures, HTTPS connections must be handled properly. In order to provide an end-to-end secure connection, the WebVCR server must open two distinct secure connections: one to the destination, and one to the client.
- *Handling scripting languages:* In some sites, selecting an option from a selection box causes a JavaScript event handler to fire, which in turn causes a new page to be loaded. To handle this in a server-side setting would require analyzing all such JavaScript code, and rewriting it so that all requests go through the WebVCR server.

It is worth pointing out that a hybrid architecture consisting of a combination of server-based and client-based components is also possible: a user may create a smart bookmark with a personal WebVCR on his desktop, and later replay this smart bookmark on the desktop from his personal digital assistant (PDA) using a wireless modem.

[6] Note that the `UniversalFileAccess` requirement can be relaxed if the user is willing to have the HTML dumped to the browser, and then saved to file from the browser itself.

3. Example applications: beyond smart bookmarks

Some applications of smart bookmarks are evident, for example: a user can record smart bookmarks for any task he might need to perform multiple times, such as accessing local weather information, searching used car classifieds, checking for best airfares to a particular destination, filling up an online shopping basket, etc. However, a variety of other applications can also be built using smart bookmark technology. We list some of these applications.

Web personalization and mobile access. Smart bookmarks were described in passing in our previous work on Web personalization [1], where we propose a new approach to personalization that allows users to specify the contents of a personal home page, much like in **MyYahoo** [7] but with more choices: a personal page is built from a set of general queries over information from multiple Web sites. For instance, the user can specify that an arbitrary Web page (or section thereof) be embedded in the personal home page as a frame (or layer). The specification of the content of each frame can be a URL, a smart bookmark, or a more complex query that retrieves the desired content.

The ability to easily create access wrappers makes it possible to produce highly personalized Web clipping services when combined with the ability to extract parts of pages. The ability to return only select portions of the final Web page is very desirable for mobile clients (e.g., smart phones and PDAs) that have limited bandwidth. Furthermore, this can be combined with phone browsing technology (e.g., [3,16]) to make this personalized content available via phone.

Smarter affiliate programs and permission marketing. Many sites offer affiliate programs, where

[7] http://my.yahoo.com

they give third-party sites commissions from sales originated in those sites (see e.g., [4]). Using smart bookmarks to produce complex orders, affiliate programs can be made more valuable, both to the merchant who ultimately ships the items and to the consumer who uses the service. For instance, currently, a recipe site can put a link to a merchant site selling ingredients used in the recipe or to a product on that site which is needed in the recipe. In the latter case, the user clicks on the product link and then makes a second click on the resulting page at the merchant site to add the item to the shopping cart. However, affiliate programs cannot make it really simple to order all the items in the recipe unless the merchant site has already produced such a bundle. With the WebVCR, staff of the affiliate programs can produce a smart bookmark that will load a user's shopping cart with exactly the right items for the recipe from the merchants site. The user can remove any unneeded items or add any other desired items before checking out. The increased ease of purchasing makes impulse buying of ingredients to make the recipe more likely. By producing more recipes and corresponding smart bookmarks, the affiliate site can add significant value to the merchant's offerings and gain significant revenue.

Similarly, bundles of offers, for example, clothing suggestions (possibly with ability to see tried on), party supplies, gift baskets items, can be produced by a merchant employing permission marketing and sent as email or placed on a personal Web page for individual customers. The user can easily order the items as above — the difference being that the bookmark is customized with a particular customer in mind rather than as a more general offering. Given the simplicity of producing smart bookmarks, creative bundling options are significantly easier to develop than the alternatives which require server-side programming — creating smart bookmarks requires no programming, only an intuitive VCR style interface. This makes it possible to do many more experiments on what kind of promotions really work. This is crucial in permission marketing — examples of improving response rates from 3% to 40% by repeated experimentation have been reported in [9].

Tutorials. Smart bookmarks can be used as tutorials of how to use a site. The WebVCR has a step-facility that allows users to take their time at each page encountered during a traversal. This can help them learn how the site is structured for particular kinds of use. For example, an online customer care representative for `travelocity.com` can instruct customers how to navigate the travelocity site for specific tasks (e.g., booking a flight) by remotely creating smart bookmarks and emailing it to customers (possibly including some further explanation in the email).

Web site testing. Another useful application for the WebVCR is in Web site testing. Smart bookmarks can be used not only as a test suite to test Web site functionality, but also to test how well a site responds to high volume of hits — for example, by firing multiple smart bookmarks simultaneously.

4. Implementation

In this section, we describe in detail a client-based WebVCR implementation: the personal WebVCR. Because the tool is targeted to casual Web users, important requirements must be met, most notably the tool must be easy to use and it must also be portable. In order to ensure portability, the WebVCR functionality is implemented as a combination of an applet and JavaScript that (at least in theory) runs on any browser. The applet presents an intuitive VCR-like interface that lets users record/replay smart bookmarks.

The WebVCR applet has a very small footprint, so that it is practical for users to experiment with the system without experiencing large delays for downloading the Java code. It achieves that in part by not duplicating functionality provided by the browser (e.g., instead of implementing an HTML parser, it uses the user browser's DOM API to locate page elements).

The rest of this section describes the implementation as well as issues we encountered while building the system. Certain details are omitted to simplify the presentation, for example we consider user actions to be only link traversals or form submissions, though other kinds of actions (e.g., button clicks) can also be handled.

```
<URL>http://travelocity.com</URL>
<LINK>
  <text>null</text>
  <href>http://dpsi.travelocity.com/lognlogin.ctl?trmodule=AIRG&SEQ=1</href>
  <target>null</target>
  <loc>opener.document.links[1]</loc>
</LINK>
<FORM>
  <name>nameFocusForm</name>
  <method>post</method>
  <target></target>
  <action>https://dpsi.travelocity.com:443/lognmain.ctl?SEQ=1</action>
  <loc>opener.document.forms[0]</loc>
  <ATTRS>
    <ATTR><name>es_alias</name><loc>3</loc>
    <type>text</type><prop>stored</prop>
    <val>juliana</val></ATTR>
    <ATTR><name>es_password</name><loc>4</loc>
    <type>password</type><prop>prompt</prop>
    <val></val></ATTR>
    <ATTR><name>ctry_cd</name><loc>5</loc>
    <type>select-one</type><prop>stored</prop>
    <val>null</val>
    <text>UseMyProfileAddress</text></ATTR>
  </ATTRS>
</FORM>
```

Fig. 10. Smart bookmark steps to login at `http://www.travelocity.com`.

4.1. Information stored in smart bookmarks

As mentioned earlier, the WebVCR applet tracks a user's navigation actions by adding JavaScript event handlers to Web pages during recording. These event handlers are invoked when certain user actions occur (e.g., link traversals, form submissions), which in turn cause the WebVCR applet to record the corresponding action as a smart bookmark *step*. Fig. 10 shows an excerpt of a smart bookmark file (simplified for exposition purposes) to illustrate the kind of information stored.

For *link steps*, the WebVCR records the following information: text associated with the link; URL that the link refers to; the target name[8] (if present) in which the resulting Web page should be displayed; and DOM location of the link. *Form steps* contain: name of the form; DOM location of the form; action associated with the form; method associated with the form (GET/POST); and all the elements in the form. For each *form element*, further recorded information includes: element name; index of the element in the form (e.g., 3rd element); type of element (e.g., text, password); properties of the element (see below); and type-specific properties (e.g., values for text fields, checked flag for checkboxes and radioboxes, selection index or option lists for selections).

There are different modes for storing user-specified information in smart bookmarks. For instance, the user is able to specify that password fields (e.g., Fig. 2) are either prompted for when needed during replay, or are stored encrypted in the smart bookmark, whereas fields like the origin and destination of flight (Fig. 3) can often be stored in plain text. Accordingly, each attribute has the one of the following properties to guide the WebVCR during playback: `prompt` (ask the user for the attribute value); `stored` (use the value that is stored in plain text); `encrypted` (use the value that is stored encrypted)[9].

[8] For example, if the document is to be displayed in a particular frame, the target specifies the frame.

[9] The decryption key can be entered once for each WebVCR session.

4.2. Creating smart bookmarks

The recording process is as follows. When the user presses the record button in the applet window, the applet uses LiveConnect [8] to set event handlers on all clickable elements in the page displayed in the browser (i.e., `onclick` handlers for links, `onsubmit` handlers for forms, etc.). If there are already event handlers present in the page, the new handlers are chained to the existing handlers to ensure proper replay.

When an event fires, the applet records all the necessary information for the event. It must then wait until the following page is loaded to repeat the process of adding handlers and waiting for events. The WebVCR adds `onload` handlers to each page to detect when a page has been fully loaded. However, if the page has already loaded when the `onload` handler is added, the event will never fire. Thus, in addition to `onload` handlers, the WebVCR uses a separate thread that polls the browser window to check whether the document changed.

4.3. Ensuring correct replay

The recorded steps are replayed as described in Fig. 11. Each step is executed depending on its type. For URL steps (lines 4–5), the stored href is fetched and loaded into the browser. For link traversals (lines 6–8), the recorded properties of the link (DOM location, text, URL) are used to determine the href of the page to be fetched (see below for details on the heuristics used to find the closest match). The page is displayed in the target window specified in the step. Finally, for form submissions (lines 9–11), the recorded properties of the form (name, DOM location, element names and types) are used to determine the appropriate form to be submitted. Attribute values specified as *stored* or *encrypted* are read from the smart bookmark, and the user is prompted for attribute values specified as *prompt* — these values are used to set the values of the form elements, and the form is then submitted.

During replay, the applet must also detect when a new page is loaded (line 2). The process used is similar to that used for recording. The applet inserts an `onload` handler in the Web page to detect when the page has been completely loaded. In addition, the applet *polls* the DOM structures (created by the browser) at regular intervals to check if a sufficient portion of the page has loaded. This is determined currently by checking if the link/form at the recorded DOM location is available, though more sophisticated reasoning is possible.

Since Web pages may change after a smart bookmark is recorded, special care must be taken to ensure that smart bookmarks are correctly replayed. In what follows, we describe some error-correction heuristics that are required to make the replay robust in the presence of changes to the page structure. Even though we limit our discussion to link traversals, similar techniques can be applied for other kinds of smart bookmark steps as well.

During the replay of a link step, the WebVCR first accesses the properties of the link in the currently loaded page that has the same DOM location as the recorded link. If the URL and the target of this link are the same as the recorded information, a match

```
1    for (i=0; i<smartbookmark.length; i++)
2      waituntilnewpageisloaded;
3      step=smartbookmark[i];
4      if (step.type == "URL")
5        setbrowserlocationtostep.href;
6      elseif (step.type == "link")
7        link=findClosestLink(step);
8        link.follow();
9      elseif (step.type == "form")
10       form = findClosestForm(step);
11       form.submit(step);
12     endif;
```

Fig. 11. Playing a smart bookmark.

is declared, and this link is used for the replay. However, occasionally there will not be a match. There are several reasons for this. For example:

- *The DOM location may have changed.* A Web page may have ads that appear before the link that the user has recorded. Since ads that appear in the page usually differ from one traversal to the next, the number of links embedded in the ads may also differ, and consequently, the DOM location of the recorded link may change.
- *The URL may have changed.* Some sites encode session information in the URLs. Consequently, when one logs out and then logs in, the corresponding URL will have changed, and thus, using the same URL is likely to result in a server error. However, the text associated with the link can still be used to perform the match.
- *The link text may have changed.* For example, the `cnn.com` Web page has a link pointing to the daily almanac, where the text associated with the link refers to the current date. Hence, the link text changes daily, however, the URL associated with the link remains the same.

These changes do not pose a problem to a user browsing the Web since the user can easily determine which link he wants to follow, but they do present a challenge to a system that performs automatic navigation. We use the following heuristics in order to *find the closest* match for a recorded link step (note that a number of the steps given below can be combined for efficiency):

(1) Attempt to locate a link in the last retrieved page corresponding to DOM location stored in current smart bookmark step. If the link exists, the target of the link matches the bookmark, and either the URL or text of the retrieved link match the step, then use that link.

(2) Otherwise, if there is a unique link in the page whose target, URL, and text match those of the stored link, use that link.

(3) Otherwise, if there is a unique link in the page whose target and URL match those of the stored link, use that link.

(4) Otherwise, if there is a unique link in the page whose target and text match those of the stored link, use that link.

(5) Otherwise, if the link corresponds to a CGI bin script (e.g., contains "?" in it), then find all links that match the stored URL up to the first occurrence of a "?" and store them in set of candidate links, which we denote L.

(6) Eliminate any elements of L whose parameter names do not match the stored version. For instance, if the stored URL is `http://xyz.com/script?x=10&y=12` then `http://xyz.com/script?x=20&y=32` matches, but `http://xyz.com/script?x=10&z=12` does not, since it has a parameter named `z` that does not appear in the stored version.

(7) For each parameter in the stored version whose value matches the corresponding parameter value in at least one element of L, eliminate all elements of L with a non-matching value for the same parameter.

(8) If L is a singleton set, use that element.

(9) Otherwise, the playback can either be aborted, or the link present at the recorded DOM location can be used to *try* and proceed through the playback (our implementation uses the latter). However, the playback might fail later in the sequence, or the sequence might traverse pages different from what the user had recorded.

Steps 1–4 are self explanatory. Steps 5–8 deal with the case where the link refers to a cgi-script. Step 6 eliminates the case when the same CGI-bin script is used to handle a variety of tasks, where the same set of variables is required even if there values differ because session information is encoded in them. Step 7 is used to differentiate between variables that specify the task to perform and those which encode session information. For instance, `menu=7` almost certainly implies a task to perform rather than encoding session information. Thus, if a match is found, all non-matching candidates are eliminated.

These heuristics are hard-coded in our current implementation of the WebVCR. In the future, we plan to let users manipulate them, for example, by choosing the order in which they are applied. The robustness of smart bookmarks can be further improved by letting users define their own matching rules for the various steps in smart bookmarks.

4.4. Optimizations

Certain optimizations are possible to speed up the replay. During replay, the user is usually interested in looking at the final page, hence, time can be saved by not loading figures present in the intermediate pages. This can be achieved easily since the browser exposes this functionality via JavaScript.

Also, it might be possible to skip some steps during replay. For example, if the replay is currently at step *i*, and it can be determined that a subsequent step *j* has a well-defined (static) URL, then intermediate steps between *i* and *j* can be skipped, thus *compressing* the bookmark. In Example 1.1, the *Find/Book a Flight* step can be skipped, and the WebVCR can go directly to the login page. Another example case is searching for cars in Yahoo classifieds, where some of the intermediate form submissions can be skipped as the information entered into forms in preceding steps ends up encoded in the URL, for example:

```
http://classifieds.yahoo.com/yc?
ce_mk=&ck=Toyota&za=and&ce_sl=&cc=
automobiles&cr=New+York+City&cs=
time+2&g=&cf=1
```

encodes two form submissions, one entering a zip code and one entering the car make `Toyota`.

Automatically compressing smart bookmarks is made difficult by the fact that the Web server could be maintaining (and updating) some server state during the entire interaction. However, if either no such server state is maintained, or it is not essential for the interaction, reasonable heuristics can be used for compression.

4.5. Some other issues and limitations of the WebVCR

HTTP authentication. One limitation of solely using the browser for recording smart bookmarks is that some user actions cannot be recorded in the client. For example, it is not possible to *detect* when HTTP authentication takes place, and since the values entered by the user are not available through the DOM API, such interaction cannot be recorded by the applet. One way to handle this scenario is to have a proxy that intercepts the HTTP authentication messages during recording, so that they can be recorded by the WebVCR applet. During playback, the WebVCR applet can inform the proxy to directly perform the authentication with the destination Web site (without going through the browser). In the current implementation, smart bookmarks that require HTTP authentication can be recorded, but during replay, the WebVCR blocks at the HTTP authentication stage until the user enters the proper values and clicks OK.

State information. The HTTP protocol is stateless, however, Web sites usually maintain some kind of state (e.g., session information). This is accomplished in various ways, the common ones being (1) embedding session ids in URLs, (2) encoding session information in hidden variables inside HTML forms, or (3) storing appropriate cookies on the user's machine. The first two cases are handled easily by heuristics mentioned earlier in the paper. The third case presents some interesting problems. If a user records a smart bookmark with cookies turned off, but replays it with cookies turned on (or vice versa), he might see completely different pages during record and replay. The problem is aggravated if smart bookmarks are shared among users. In the general case (if the two sets of pages are radically different), there is not much that can be done. However, there are specific, common cases that can be handled.

Many sites require users to login to the site, by entering a username and password (or some other such information), and use cookies to keep track of the user as he navigates within that site. Hence, if a user records a smart bookmark with cookies turned on, and logs on to the Web site, this information is stored on the user's machine so that if he re-visits that site (during replay), the user is not presented with the login page at all. A naive way to handle this during replay is to assume that all pages that require a password (i.e., the form submission recorded has a input field of type *password*) could be login pages, and check if one of the following steps (generally the next step) recorded in the smart bookmark can be used in the current page. If so, the login step is skipped, and replay resumes from that step.

Signed applets. During both recording and replay of smart bookmarks, WebVCR needs to access and modify the Web pages being navigated. By default, to prevent unauthorized snooping of a user's Web activity, the browser only allows such access to Web pages retrieved from the same domain as the WebVCR applet. Hence, the WebVCR code needs to be digitally signed with a certificate from a trusted third-party (e.g., Verisign), and the user needs to explicitly grant the requested privileges before WebVCR can be used.

Users might not mind granting privileges to WebVCR to access Web documents from other domains during record and replay, but might hesitate granting privileges that allow the WebVCR applet to modify their files (which is required if a user wants to save smart bookmarks). A less convenient mechanism, which doesn't require such a privilege, is to display the recorded bookmark in a browser window, and ask the user to use the browser to save the smart bookmark into an HTML file.

Automatic refresh. Accessing some sites (e.g., `cnn.com`) results in pages being retrieved which might be redirected after some time to a different URL (e.g., due to the `METATAG` with an `HTTP-EQUIV` value of "`REFRESH`"). While recording a smart bookmark, it is not possible to automatically distinguish between this case, and the case where the user simply typed in a different URL in the location bar (or pulled one from his bookmark list). However, during replay, the WebVCR must distinguish between these cases, since it must execute a step for the latter but not for the former. In our current implementation, the default is to assume that a refresh took place, and if the user wants to create a smart bookmark with *disconnected* steps, he must explicitly specify so.

Microsoft IE limitations. Even though IE 4.0 and higher purports to implement complete JavaScript and LiveConnect, we found that certain features of LiveConnect were not implemented. Also, the security model in IE 4.0 is such that there is no way for JavaScript code in a page to access an applet's methods if the applet is from a different domain than the page containing the JavaScript code. Note that this is exactly the capability that is required in a client-based implementation when recording a smart bookmark. IE 5.0 supports HTML Applications (HTAs) that relax cross-domain access restrictions, and make a client-side implementation feasible. HTAs seem to be unable to directly run applets, so part of the implementation needs to be moved to JavaScript. In addition, relaxation of cross-domain access restrictions is asymmetric. A workaround is to have the JavaScript code that is inserted into Web pages set a local page variable, and have the applet poll the page to determine if the local variable has been changed. The applet can then take whatever action is appropriate. The port of the WebVCR to IE 5.0 is currently underway.

5. Related work

Smart bookmarks were described in passing in [1] as a basic building block of a personalization platform. In this paper, we give a detailed description of the idea underlying smart bookmarks, the methodology and implementation of a system that provides the functionality.

There is a huge literature on tools and techniques to build wrappers for Web sites (e.g., [2,10,11,15]). However, the main focus of previous work is on extracting information from Web pages. While it is possible to add extraction functionality to the WebVCR, its major emphasis is to automate the retrieval of *hard-to-reach* pages.

Internet Explorer (IE) version 5 has introduced the *Intellisense Technology*, a feature built into the browser that records values of certain form elements every time a form is filled out. If the same form is later loaded in the browser, IE displays, under the elements, a list previously entered values from which the user may choose. Note that not all form elements are supported, for example, the values for elements such as radio buttons or pull-down lists are not recorded.

The automation of the process to retrieve dynamically generated Web pages was addressed in [6], where navigation maps were proposed to represent the structure, access paths, and contents of a Web site. Some of the techniques developed for WebVCR can be used in the implementation of a navigation map builder. Krulwich [12] did earlier work on automation of mundane and repetitive browsing tasks. The *LiveAgent* architecture described in [12] uses a proxy to modify/filter Web pages (similar to Mind-It [14]), and it thus has a number of limitations, for example, it is unable to record JavaScript steps.

Recently, there has been a proliferation of personalization and notification services (e.g., [5,13,14]).

The WebVCR and smart bookmarks can be used to simplify as well as extend these services. For example, Mind-It [14] is a notification service that allows users to specify pages or sections of pages that they would like monitored. When the pages change, Mind-It alerts the users. However, Mind-It is not able to track hard-to-reach pages (e.g., whose URLs contain session ids, or that are only reachable via a sequence of dynamically generated pages). Similar limitations apply to the other services that we are aware of.

6. Conclusions and future directions

In this paper, we describe the WebVCR system and the techniques it uses to create and replay *smart bookmarks* — shortcuts to Web content that require multiple browsing steps to be retrieved. The WebVCR presents a VCR-style interface to record and play browsing steps, requiring no programming by the user. Creating and updating smart bookmarks is a simple process involving only the usual browsing actions. Smart bookmarks may be saved in bookmark lists, or mailed to others like any other bookmark. They offer an easy means to *auto-navigate* the Web, thus simplifying the retrieval of hard-to-reach Web content. Besides saving users time, smart bookmarks may also be used to create a variety of new e-commerce services.

Despite our effort to make the software portable by using standard languages and APIs (e.g., DOM, JavaScript, and Java), differences between Netscape and IE have proved to be a barrier. Our initial implementation runs on Netscape 4.0 and higher, and the port to Microsoft IE 5.0 is underway.

For future work, we plan to address many of the issues described in Section 4 such as the recording of HTTP authentication steps. In addition, we plan to extend the WebVCR to support editing as well as parameterization of smart bookmarks. For example, to let users create template smart bookmarks and provide different input values at each interaction. Other future extensions include: a server-side version to enable to creation of services like Mind-It [14] and CallTheShots [5], as well as for Web site testing; and the integration of the WebVCR with existing extraction tools.

References

[1] V. Anupam, Y. Breitbart, J. Freire and B. Kumar, Personalizing the Web using site descriptions, in: DEXA — Workshop on Internet Data Management (IDM), 1999, pp. 732–738.

[2] B. Adelberg, NoDoSe — a tool for semi-automatically extracting structured and semi-structured data from text documents, in: Proc. SIGMOD, 1998, pp. 283–294.

[3] D. Atkins et al., Integrated Web and telephone service creation, Bell Labs Tech. J. 2 (1) (1997) 19–35.

[4] Amazon affiliate program, http://www.amazon.com/exec/obidos/subst/associates/join/associates.html.

[5] CallTheShots, http://www.calltheshots.com/.

[6] H. Davulcu, J. Freire, M. Kifer and I. Ramakrishnan, A layered architecture for querying dynamic Web content, in: Proc. SIGMOD, 1999, pp. 491–502.

[7] A. Deutsch, M. Fernandez, D. Florescu, A. Levy and D. Suciu, A query language for XML, in: Proc. of World Wide Web, 1999, pp. 77–91.

[8] D. Flanagan, JavaScript: The Definitive Guide, O'Reilly, Sebastopol, CA, 1998.

[9] S. Godin and D. Peppers, Permission Marketing: Turning Strangers into Friends, and Friends into Customers, Simon and Schuster, New York, 1999.

[10] J. Hammer, H. Garcia-Molina, J. Cho, A. Crespo and E. Aranha, Extracting semistructured information from the Web, in: Proc. of the Workshop on Management of Semistructured Data, 1997.

[11] T. Kistlera and H. Marais, WebL: a programming language for the Web, in: Proc. of World Wide Web, 1998, http://www.research.digital.com/SRC/WebL/index.html.

[12] B. Krulwich, Automating the Internet: agents as user surrogates, IEEE Computing, July–August 1997, http://computer.org/Internet/v1n4/krul9707.htm.

[13] Liaison Technology, http://www.liaison.com/.

[14] Mind-It, http://www.netmind.com/.

[15] A. Sahuget and F. Azavant, Building light-weight wrappers for legacy Web data-sources using W4F, in: Proc. of VLDB, 1999, pp. 738–741.

[16] VoiceXML Forum, http://www.voicexml.org/.

Vinod Anupam is a research scientist in the Systems and Software Research Center at Bell Labs, Lucent Technologies, in Murray Hill, NJ. He received a Ph.D. in computer sciences from Purdue University, USA in 1994, and a bachelor's in computer science from Birla Institute of Technology and Science, India in 1988. His research interests include collaborative computing (specifically synchronous and asynchronous multi-user Web-based interaction), Internet and Web security, and electronic commerce.

Juliana Freire is a member of the technical staff in the Database Systems Research Department at Bell Laboratories, Lucent Technologies. She received a B.S. from Federal University of Ceará (Brazil), and M.S. and Ph.D. from the University at Stony Brook, all in computer science. Her early research focussed on optimizing evaluation of Datalog programs, and recently she has been working on various issues related to integrating and querying heterogeneous data sources, such as the ones found in the Web.

Bharat Kumar is a member of the technical staff at Bell Laboratories, Lucent Technologies. His research interests are on querying and integrating information from Web sources having limited query capabilities. He is also working on tools and techniques to support easy specification and efficient execution of CRM (Customer Relationship Management) treatments, for customer contacts over different media. He has received a B.Tech. in computer and information science from the Indian Institute of Technology, Delhi (India), and M.S. and Ph.D. in computer science from The Ohio State University.

Daniel F. Lieuwen is a member of technical staff in the Database Systems Research Department at Bell Laboratories, a division of Lucent Technologies. Lieuwen attended Calvin College, Grand Rapids, Michigan where he studied mathematics and computer science (and a fair bit of German). He received the M.S. and Ph.D. degrees in Computer Science from the University of Wisconsin-Madison. He joined Bell Laboratories in 1992. His early research foci were object-oriented databases (particularly Ode), main-memory databases, and active databases. More recently, he has been working on topics related to materialized views, directory enabled networks, and the Internet.

Continuous querying in database-centric Web applications

John C. Shafer *,[1], Rakesh Agrawal [1]

IBM Almaden Research Center, 650 Harry Road, San Jose, CA 95120, USA

Abstract

Web applications are becoming increasingly database-centric. Unfortunately, the support provided by most Web sites to explore such databases is rather primitive and is based on the traditional database metaphor of submitting an SQL query and packaging the response as an HTML page. Very often, the result set is empty or contains too many records. It is up to the user to refine the query by guessing how the query constraints must be tightened or relaxed and then go through another submit/response cycle. Furthermore, once results are displayed, typically no further exploration capabilities are offered. Web applications requiring interactive exploration of databases (e.g. e-commerce) need that the above submit/response metaphor be replaced with a continuous querying metaphor that seamlessly integrates querying with result browsing. In addition to supporting queries based on predicates on attribute values, queries based on example records should also be supported. We present techniques for supporting this metaphor and discuss their implementation in a Web-based database exploration engine.

Keywords: Search; Database; Interactive

1. Introduction

Web applications are becoming increasingly database-centric. In a 1997 Forrester survey [5], respondent companies indicated that nearly 40% of the content at their Web sites originated from databases. This was expected to rise as high as 65% by 1998, and that this fraction was expected to increase. Many new Web applications require that a user be able to interactively explore these databases over the Internet or an internal network.

A common example of such interactive exploration is the task of finding products or services matching a user's requirements. While this is a widely performed task [9], the support provided by current Web sites for implementing this functionality is rather primitive. Typically, a server-side database is relied upon for all query processing. The user is presented a form for providing specifications of the desired product in terms of bounds on the values of the product attributes (e.g. a 3.3 V zero delay clock buffer in 16-pin 150-mil SOIC or TSSOP package with output skew less than 250 ps and device skew less than 750 ps having an operating range of 25–100 MHz). On submission, this information is used to construct an SQL query that is in turn submitted to a server-side database. The result is returned to the browser formatted as an HTML page. Very often, the result set is empty or contains too many records. It is up to the user to refine the query by guessing how the query constraints must be tightened or relaxed and then go through another submit/response cycle. Furthermore, once results are displayed, typi-

* Corresponding author.

[1] E-mail: {shafer, ragrawal}@almaden.ibm.com

cally no further exploration capabilities are offered. As a result, the user needs knowledge of not only the domain of interest but also the particular dataset. Further aggravating this problem is that the round-trip time between browser and the database server for each submit/response cycle is often frustratingly large.

The problem is that database query technology is targeted at reporting rather than user exploration. In traditional database applications, queries are rigid in that they are intended for asking very specific questions. The query results are interesting regardless of whether they contain zero records or ten thousand. In a sense, an individual query itself is the goal. In user exploration, the goal is not simply an individual query or its results, but rather locating particular records of interest. Rarely can this be achieved with a single query. As a result, users typically issue many related queries before they are finally satisfied.

What is needed is that this 'submit a query and wait for a response' metaphor be replaced by a new continuous querying metaphor. The user should be able to combine searching with result browsing so that the user simultaneously sees the current query and the qualifying records in a single view. As the user changes the query constraints, the user should immediately see the impact on the qualifying records in that view.

We present techniques for supporting this continuous querying metaphor. These techniques have been implemented in a database exploration engine, we call Eureka. We present in Section 2 the user interface that facilitates database exploration using the continuous querying metaphor. For this metaphor to be successful, it is imperative that as soon as a user manipulates a GUI control, the user sees its effect instantaneously, which in turn requires well-tuned data structures. In Section 3, we present the design and implementation of the Eureka engine. We conclude with a summary and some possible directions for future work in Section 4.

1.1. Related work

A large number of e-commerce sites provide parametric search capabilities in which users search for desired products by providing bounds on attribute values. Stock screens at investment sites such as **Charles Schwab** [2], travel package selection at travel sites such as **Travelocity** [3], electronic component search at semiconductor sites such as **Cypress** [4] are examples of this type of search. Some e-commerce tools (e.g. Net.Commerce [7]) provide support for implementing such searches. As stated earlier, these sites typically rely entirely on a server-side database for query processing. They are thus limited to the submit/response metaphor and suffer from the problems of long response times and too many or too few answers.

Some newer sites are providing a subset of interactive exploration capability described in this paper. For example, Microsoft's **Carpoint** [5], **Cars.com** [6] and **Wireless Dimension** [7] combine browsing with querying; as the query is changed, the user immediately sees the effect on results. These sites currently do not support querying based on example products. The details of their implementations are not available in published literature. It is doubtful that the Wireless Dimension's Javascript implementation (which uses HTML for its output) is designed to scale to large product sets, and only Carpoint (using native ActiveX code) allows users to explore datasets with more than a few hundred products.

An interesting approach to handle the problem of too many or too few answers was taken by 64K Inc. [1]. Although still an HTML form-based approach, the query pages generated by the 64K engine contain histogram information, showing how records are distributed over each attribute's range of values, as well as a count of the total number of records. This information is meant to provide hints to the user for modifying the query before resubmitting it. If a query results in too many records, rather than showing them to the user, the engine redisplays the query page updated with new histogram and count information. In the case of too few answers, the engine uses domain-specific distance metrics to relax the query and return nearby records. However, the 64K search metaphor is still the standard submit/response metaphor (although perhaps with fewer cycles and richer features).

[2] www.schwab.com
[3] www.travelocity.com
[4] www.cypress.com
[5] carpoint.msn.com
[6] www.cars.com
[7] www.wirelessdimension.com

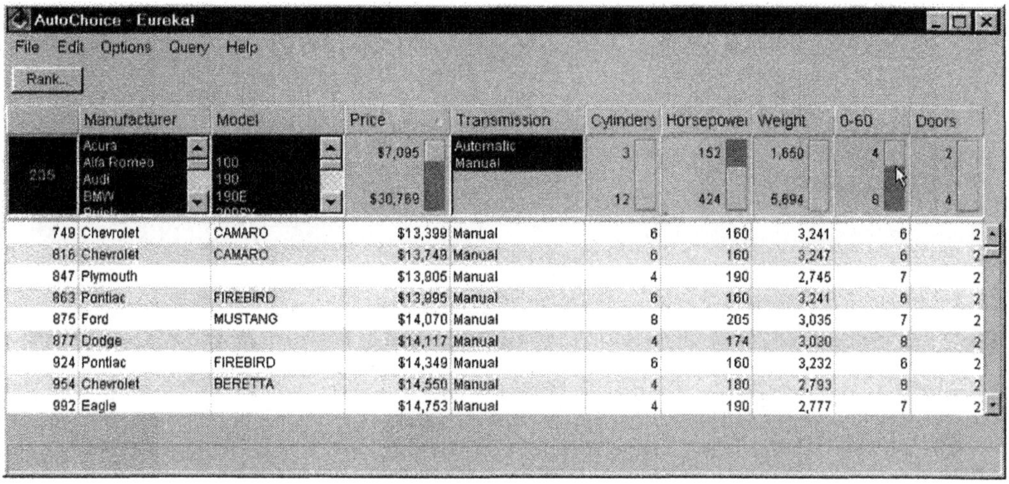

AutoChoice - Eureka!

File Edit Options Query Help

Rank...

	Manufacturer	Model	Price	Transmission	Cylinders	Horsepower	Weight	0-60	Doors
235	Acura Alfa Romeo Audi BMW	100 190 190E	$7,095 $30,769	Automatic Manual	3 12	152 424	1,650 5,694	4 8	2 4
749	Chevrolet	CAMARO	$13,399	Manual	6	160	3,241	6	2
816	Chevrolet	CAMARO	$13,749	Manual	6	160	3,247	6	2
847	Plymouth		$13,906	Manual	4	190	2,745	7	2
863	Pontiac	FIREBIRD	$13,995	Manual	6	160	3,241	6	2
875	Ford	MUSTANG	$14,070	Manual	8	205	3,036	7	2
877	Dodge		$14,117	Manual	4	174	3,030	8	2
924	Pontiac	FIREBIRD	$14,349	Manual	6	160	3,232	6	2
954	Chevrolet	BERETTA	$14,550	Manual	4	180	2,793	8	2
992	Eagle		$14,753	Manual	4	190	2,777	7	2

Fig. 1. User interface.

Another approach to handling too many answers is represented by the FOCUS application described in [10]. In this technique, the results of a query are cached and displayed in a compressed table. Further restrictions to reduce the result set are applied on the cached results. However, as the authors acknowledge, FOCUS is mainly suited for tables with up to a few hundred records and attributes. In the case of **Spotfire Pro** [8], results are presented in various graphical formats (e.g. pie charts, scatter plots, etc.) and users can manipulate sliders and list boxes to interactively search through the data. Spotfire Pro is a client-side application that must be installed locally on the user's machine. Details of their implementation are not available in the published literature.

Other related work includes the dynamic query and starfield work of [2] and [3]. Like Spotfire Pro, users can manipulate numeric sliders and other GUI controls and see the effects of these actions on result sets displayed in 2D scatter plots. This work focuses mainly on the human-interface aspect of this search metaphor and the implementation details are rather sparse.

2. User interface

Fig. 1 shows Eureka's user interface. Records are displayed in a scrollable list format with a separate column for each numeric and categorical attribute. At the top of each column is a title bar showing the name of the attribute. The names of the attributes are obtained from the database catalog. Beneath each of these titles is an 'attribute control' used for specifying attribute restrictions. Categorical attributes are represented by select lists that allow users to (de)select (un)desired values. Numeric attributes are represented by vertical sliders which may be resized and dragged to specify desired ranges. Initially, these attribute controls are maximized to include the full value range of each attribute. Immediately, a user can see how many records are available, the value range of each attribute, and actual matching records. At any stage, the user can scroll through the list of records in the result set and can instantaneously change the sort order of the record list by clicking on the title bar of any column.

Note that there is no 'submit' button. As the user adjusts the attribute controls under each column's heading, the records in the view pane are continuously updated to reflect new restrictions. The record count in the upper left is also continuously updated during these adjustments. This lets the user know immediately if the query is becoming too restrictive and whether or not the user should continue adding specifications.

Contrast this continuous querying model with the conventional form-based approach. The user would be entering her requirements into a static query page and would not know the result of her actions until

[8] www.spotfire.com

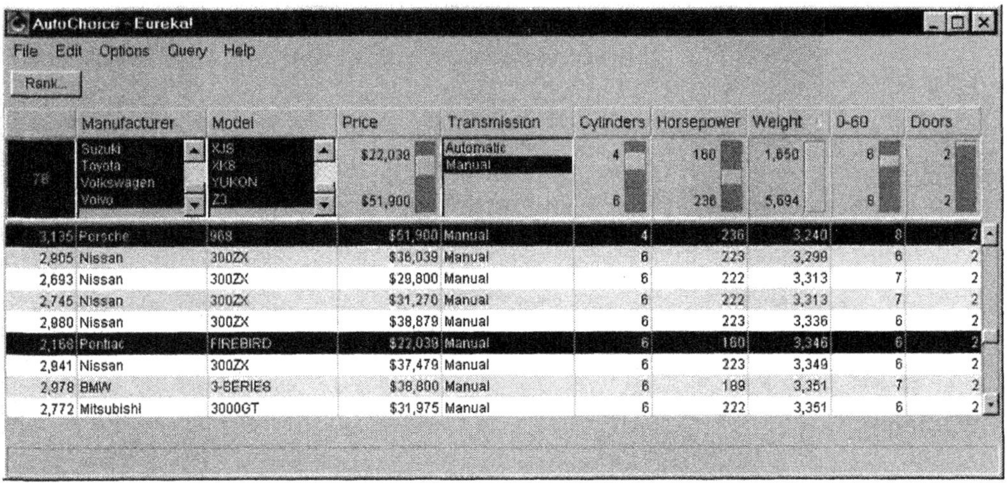

Fig. 2. Implicit restrictions.

she submitted her query and received the response. If her query is too restrictive, she would most likely be presented with a short message telling her that no records matched her criteria, and that she should try again. If the query is too loose, she would probably be shown a single large listing of all matching records, or more likely, a series of linked pages containing twenty or so matching records per page. In both cases, no information is given as to how she should relax or tighten her query, forcing her to repeat this submit/response cycle as she adjusts her requirements unaided. Each such cycle requires the attention of the Web and database servers, not to mention a round-trip through the network. In the case of continuous querying, empty result sets can be easily avoided or backed out because the user can actually see the result set change as the query is tightened or relaxed.

2.1. Exploration based on example records

Since query results are always visible in Eureka, this allows a query-by-example capability not available in most search interfaces. Rather than explicitly specifying a desired range of attribute values, a user can select example records to direct the exploration. This type of querying can be very useful in situations where the user may not be too knowledgeable about the domain, but knows of some sample records of interest. In our car example, a user who does not know about horsepower or what a 'fast' 0–60 mph time is can still search for sporty cars by selecting several known examples. These records implicitly define a query region comprising the smallest hypercube that contains all the selected data points.

As shown in Fig. 2, the user indicates the example records by highlighting the corresponding rows with the mouse (in this case, a Porche 968 and a Pontiac Firebird). The attribute space is then collapsed around those examples by holding down the control key and using the mouse to click on the headings of the columns to collapse. This action immediately results in the attribute controls being adjusted to reflect the new query space. Simultaneously, the result pane is updated to reflect the new qualifying records. The user can now continue exploration by explicitly manipulating attribute controls or she can proceed by selecting some other example records and collapsing the attribute space further.

2.2. Exploration based on similarity

In addition to querying by example, Eureka allows 'sorting by example' as well. This is essentially similarity search, except that instead of treating similarity as a separate stand-alone query like **Excite** [9] does for Web pages, it is integrated into Eureka's existing view. After selecting one or more sample records, the user can click the rank button (see Fig. 3) and sort all the records by how 'near' they

[9] www.excite.com

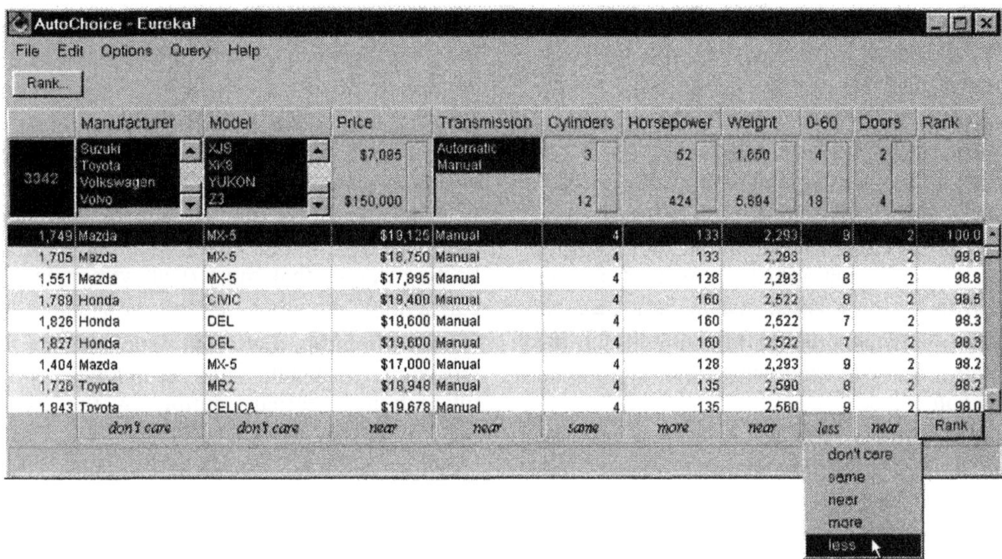

Fig. 3. Querying by similarity.

are to the selected examples. Nearness is based on a similarity model that computes the weighted sum of the normalized difference in attribute value [6,11]. The similarity scores are then displayed in a new column labeled 'Rank' which appears after the rank button is pressed.

The user can also control similarity by manipulating the select buttons that appear underneath each column. Normalized difference is represented by the 'near' option. Selecting 'don't care' removes an attribute from the similarity model entirely. The 'same' option rewards identical values with a 100% score for that attribute — all other values get 0%. For numeric attributes, we have included additional support for 'directional nearness'. As shown in Fig. 3, we can specify that larger values (the 'more' option) or smaller values (the 'less' option) should not be penalized in the scoring model. In our example, this allows us to increasingly penalize cars with 0–60 mph times larger than 9 s, but not penalize those with smaller times.

3. System design and implementation

We now describe the details of how we implement continuous querying in Eureka. In order to obtain interactive response times, we exploit several key observations. First and foremost is that we must cache data records in the local client. There is little chance of interactive response times unless the interaction between the user and data is moved off of the server and out of the network. While this does place a non-trivial memory requirement on the client, it offers an advantage beyond that of just faster access — the cache can be tailored to the user and the particular task of data exploration. An initial query representing the set of data to be explored is used to transfer data from the server-side database. This data is then cached in Eureka using special data structures for further exploration. In cases where users may with to explore data outside the current cache, techniques such as semantic data-caching described in [4] can be used.

Fortunately, while the total size of the underlying database can be huge, the scope of the data over which a user performs interactive exploration for some task at hand is often limited enough that corresponding records are able to fit in a reasonably sized cache. For example, in Web-based product exploration applications, a user will explore options within one product category at a time and not across product categories. The active set thus typically consists of records in thousands and not millions.

Eureka also takes advantage of the fact that there is always a notion of a current state. This state is represented by the current settings of the attribute controls (i.e. the 'query') and the corresponding set of matching records. Every adjustment of these controls represents a minor change to an existing query. Rather than execute the new query entirely from scratch, Eureka need only update the current results to reflect the change. This can be made extremely efficient because of another observation: there is only one mouse. The user can adjust the restrictions of only one attribute at any given instant. Since query adjustments are always effected immediately on the result set, these changes are always small and along a single attribute.

The last important observation is that, regardless of the result size or the capability of scrolling through those results, the user can only see those records currently displayed on the screen, the full result set is never completely visible. As a result, Eureka never explicitly generates a complete list of all records satisfying the current query state. In fact, the list of records Eureka does create never contains any records other than those currently being displayed.

By taking advantage of these observations, Eureka is able to exhibit extremely fast response times, even with datasets containing hundreds of attributes and hundreds of thousands of records.

3.1. Architecture

Fig. 4 gives a high-level overview of the Eureka architecture. The *DataColumn* objects represent the data cache with each DataColumn representing one column of attribute data. *DataGroup* maintains this cache and is responsible for managing statistics needed to generate the result sets. Observe that with this design, data for different attributes can be loaded and processed asynchronously. Thus, during data loading, the user can see column data appear progressively, rather than be forced to wait for the entire dataset. Furthermore, once a column of input data has been loaded and its DataColumn object created, the user may immediately begin to restrict or sort on that column, even as other columns are still being loaded.

ListRenderer represents the Eureka GUI. It is responsible for rendering the current set of matching records, as well as passing user changes in attribute restrictions to the core engine. This interaction is handled by events and explicit API calls. While the ListRenderer is not responsible for much of the engine logic, it is nevertheless an important component, as the back-end is specifically designed with assumptions about how the user will interact with the system.

The final piece labeled *Eureka* encompasses the entire design. In our Java implementation, this is the hosting applet that must deal with menus, graphical layout and other details. It is also responsible for determining what data source to use and what attributes to select. This is handled through user interaction or perhaps simply by the user clicking on an URL in a Web browser (e.g. a link labeled 'Explore mid-cap stocks in Eureka'). The *Eureka* component is also responsible for retrieving the data from the data source. It does so through a standard API called the 'DataPump API'. This design allows us to support various data sources by simply plugging in a different implementation of the DataPump API. In the particular instance shown in Fig. 4, the DataPump communicates via HTTP to a Java servlet running on a Web server. This servlet uses JDBC to communicate with the database. When *Eureka* requests data via the DataPump API, the DataPump object passes the request to the servlet,

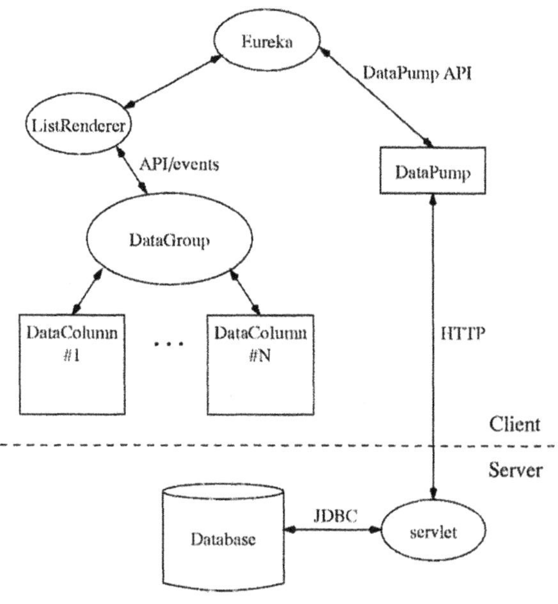

Fig. 4. Architecture overview.

which in turn issues a query to the database. Data is returned to *Eureka* from the DataPump in column-order rather than row-order using callbacks. This allows each column to be converted into DataColumn objects independently and asynchronously by using multiple threads to service the callbacks. How data is transferred between the server and the DataPump (row-order vs. column-order, synchronous vs. asynchronous) is entirely up to the DataPump implementation.

In other situations, such as intranet applications, we have incorporated the JDBC communication directly into the DataPump object. We have also built a file-based DataPump that can load data from a local comma-delimited file. Regardless of the particular DataPump implementation, it should be noted that *Eureka*, *DataPump*, *ListRenderer*, *DataGroup* and the *DataColumn* objects all reside on the client machine and not on a server. For the remainder of this discussion, we will focus on the core engine pieces consisting of the *ListRenderer* and the components underneath it.

For concreteness, we will be describing the Eureka design using the example dataset shown in Fig. 5. This dataset represents car listings and contains attribute data for the make of each car and the distance in miles between the user and seller locations. Note that this example demonstrates how the data received and cached by Eureka can be tailored for a particular user; *Distance* is a derived attribute that depends upon the user and would not exist in the server's database. Each record in this dataset is uniquely identified by an integer in the range $[0, n-1]$, called a record identifier, or *rid*. These rids are not part of the dataset and do not correspond to any database or server-side identifiers. They are simply internal IDs used in the cache, assigned sequentially as records are loaded from the server.

3.1.1. DataColumns

Each DataColumn is responsible for caching and indexing one attribute's worth of data. DataColumns consist of two basic components: an array of data values indexed by record id, and a rid-list. The rid-list contains rids sorted by their corresponding attribute value. As we shall see in Section 3.2, the rid-lists are required for performing fast attribute restrictions, but offer the additional benefit of pre-computed sorts. The DataColumn objects differ for numeric and categorical data types and so are described separately below.

Numeric DataColumns. For numeric attributes, we allocate an integer or float array and copy incoming data values into it. At the same time, we allocate an integer array for the rid-list and store the rid values in order (from 0 to $n-1$, where n is the total number of records). The rid-list is then sorted by the corresponding attribute values, resulting in a final DataColumn object like the one shown in Fig. 6.

rid	Input Data	
0	Ford	23
1	Honda	3
2	Ford	537
3	Chrysler	117
4	Honda	64
5	Honda	8
6	Chrysler	363
7	Ford	192
8	BMW	41
9	Honda	89
10	BMW	207

Fig. 5. Example dataset.

RID List	Data
1	23
5	3
0	537
8	117
4	64
9	8
3	363
7	192
10	41
6	89
2	207

Fig. 6. *Distance* DataColumn.

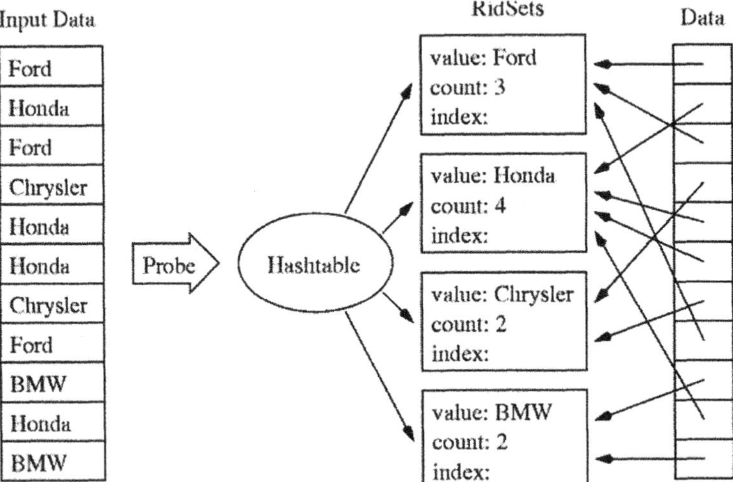

Fig. 7. *Make* DataColumn (after input scan).

Observe that *Data[RidList[i]]* gives the value of the *i*th item in the sorted list of Data values.

Categorical DataColumns. Categorical DataColumns are somewhat more involved than numeric ones. In addition to a data array and a rid-list, categorical DataColumns also require a hashtable and specialized objects called RidSets. This is due to the fact that users need to be able to add and drop arbitrary categorical values to and from the query. A RidSet object consists of three components: a categorical string value, an integer count value, and an integer index. The importance of these additional data structures in supporting fast restrictions will be explained in Section 3.2.

We first describe the creation of the categorical data array. Instead of allocating an array strings to store the data values, we allocate an array of RidSet references. We also allocate an empty hashtable. As we scan the incoming categorical attribute data, we first probe the hashtable with each string value. If the probe fails (meaning that this is the first time we have seen this categorical value), we allocate a new RidSet object. The string value is stored in the new RidSet (RidSet.value) and the RidSet count (RidSet.count) is set to one. RidSet.count will eventually indicate the number of records that share this categorical value. The new RidSet is then stored in the hashtable, indexed by the string value. If our initial probe of the hashtable does not fail, we will get back an existing RidSet whose string value is the same as the current record. In this case, we simply increment RidSet.count by one. In either situation, we then set the current record's corresponding entry in the data array to point to this new RidSet. Once the scan of the input data is finished, we will have exactly one RidSet object per unique categorical value, and a fully initialized data array consisting of pointers to these RidSets. At this point, the original categorical data can be discarded. Fig. 7 shows this state for a categorical DataColumn constructed from the *Make* attribute of our example dataset. Observe that if we now scan the data array in order and examine the string value of each referenced RidSet, the values seen will correspond exactly with the original input data.

Now we must build a sorted rid-list for this DataColumn. As a performance optimization, rather than sort an entire rid-list as is done for numeric DataColumns, we instead collect each unique string value (or *key*) and sort them in a separate array. The number of keys should be smaller than the total number of records and so will improve our sort cost. These keys can be retrieved from the RidSets, the hashtable, or collected during the data-scanning phase. In our running example, we would sort an array of four keys. Next, we allocate a temporary variable called *index* and set its value to zero. We then step through the sorted array of keys and for each key, we retrieve the corresponding RidSet object from the hashtable and

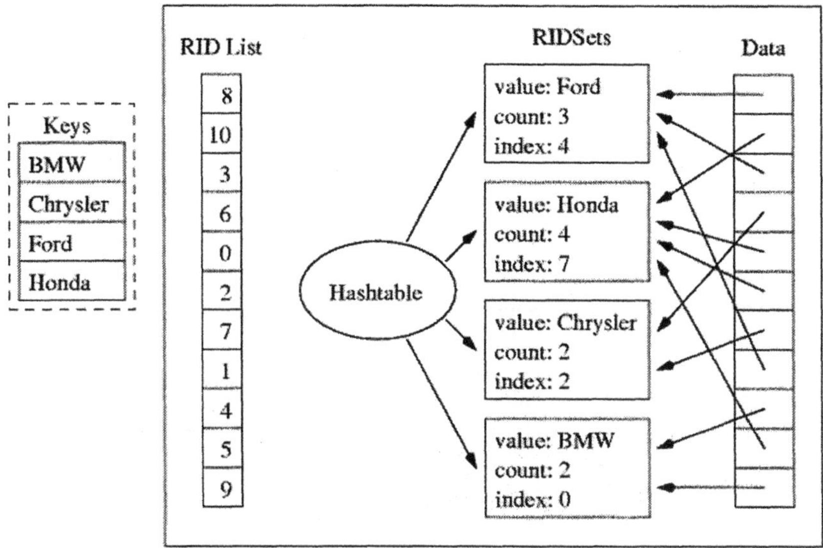

Fig. 8. Categorical DataColumn for *Make* (completed).

set RidSet.index equal to *index*. We then increment *index* by RidSet.count and then set RidSet.count equal to zero. Once this scan is completed, the index value of each RidSet will tell us where in the rid-list the rids of those records that share RidSet.value to store. At this point, the sorted list of keys can be discarded.

The rid-list is now allocated and we initiate a scan of the DataColumn's data array. For each RidSet encountered, we store the corresponding record's rid in the rid-list at the position: *RidSet.index* + *RidSet.count*. We then increment the RidSet.count by one. Fig. 8 shows the completed DataColumn after this scan has finished, along with the temporary sorted array of key values. Note that the rid-list is now in sorted order and all the RidSet.counts have been restored to their original value.

3.1.2. DataGroup

As we will see later, the DataGroup manages the DataColumn objects and is the mechanism through which the ListRenderer interacts with the data cache. It also manages two other crucial items, i.e. the *restrictions array* and the *resultSize* counter. The restrictions array is an array of integers, indexed by record id, that keeps track of the number of restrictions against each record. If a record's restriction count is zero, then that record is unrestricted and belongs to the current result set; otherwise it does not. The resultSize counter indicates the number of unrestricted records (i.e. the size of the current result set).

Initially, all the restriction counts are set to zero and resultSize is set to the total number of records. When a record is restricted along some attribute, its corresponding restriction count is incremented (even if that record is already restricted along some other attribute). Likewise, whenever a record is unrestricted along some attribute, its restriction count is decremented. Additionally, whenever a record moves out of or into the result set (i.e. its restriction count is incremented from zero or decremented to zero), the resultSize counter is decremented or incremented accordingly. Further details about this process, including illustrating examples, are given in Section 3.2 below.

3.2. Performing restrictions

We now discuss how Eureka uses the data structures just described to realize instantaneous response time for doing interactive exploration. As mentioned earlier, every change to an attribute control in the Eureka GUI represents a change in state. A state change is always a tightening or relaxation of the restriction bounds on one attribute. State changes are passed down by the ListRenderer to the DataGroup object, which in turn passes the state change down to the appropriate DataColumn object for building the cache.

3.2.1. Numeric restrictions

While the attribute controls in the GUI represent the current query state for the user, internally the current state is represented differently. The current state for numeric DataColumns is represented by two values, *lowerIndex* and *upperIndex*. These values identify a subrange in the DataColumn's rid-list. Since the rid-list is sorted by attribute value, a subrange in the rid-list corresponds to a subrange in attribute value. Initially, lowerIndex is set to 0 and upperIndex is set to $n - 1$. A state change on a numeric attribute always means that either the lowerIndex or the upperIndex may have to change.

Suppose in our car example, that all attributes are currently unrestricted, meaning that lowerIndex and upperIndex for the *Distance* DataColumn are currently set to 0 and $n - 1$, respectively. The state change *Distance* < *100* now arrives indicating that the upperIndex must be changed. This is done by initiating a scan backwards through the rid-list from the current upperIndex position. For each rid encountered, we look up its corresponding attribute value in the data array and compare it to the new upper bound of 100. If the value lies outside the new boundary, we update the restriction information in the DataGroup and continue the scan. We stop once we reach a value that lies within the new boundary. The current scan position in the rid-list becomes the new value for upperIndex. This process is illustrated in Fig. 9.

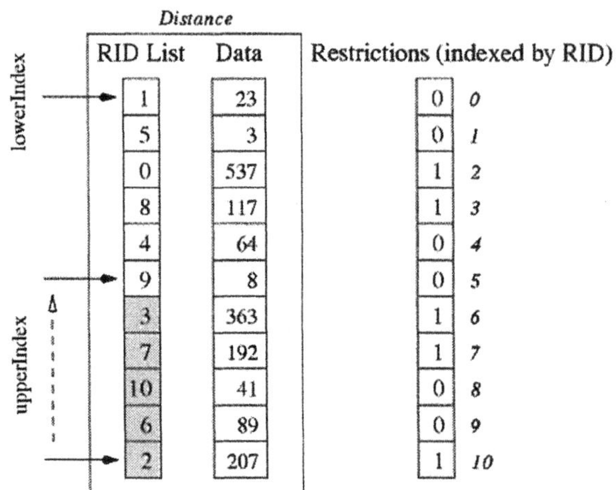

Fig. 9. Example numeric restriction (*Distance* < 100).

3.2.2. Categorical restrictions

For categorical attributes, state changes always involve a single categorical value being either restricted or unrestricted. For ease of exposition, assume that each RidSet in a DataColumn has an additional boolean flag that indicates whether or not that value is currently restricted. Together, these boolean flags represent the current state for this attribute. When a state change arrives (e.g. *Make* – *{Ford}*, i.e. *Ford* is excluded), we retrieve the corresponding RidSet from the hashtable. We then scan the portion of the rid-list marked by RidSet.index and RidSet.count and update the DataGroup statistics accordingly. We also set the boolean flag in the RidSet to indicate the new state. Fig. 10 shows how the data structures would look after performing both the restrictions *Distance* < *100* and *Make* – *{Ford}*. Note that the RidSet structures allow us to examine only those rids that are relevant to the restriction.

The processes described above are essentially identical when relaxing restrictions. The primary difference is in how the DataGroup statistics are updated and, for numeric DataColumns, in what direction the rid-list is scanned. It should be emphasized that when performing restrictions, we need only look at the data of the attribute involved. Additionally, we only examine data for those records actually affected by the restriction change. If a restriction change only affects 50 records, then we only examine those 50 records in one DataColumn, regardless of the total number of records or attributes.

3.3. Rendering the list

After a restriction change has been processed, the ListRender may be notified to update the result set information displayed in the GUI. This event is triggered whenever at least one record moves in or out of the current result set. However, as mentioned earlier, the user can only see the portion of the result set currently displayed on the screen. Thus the ListRenderer never need draw (and thereby instantiate) the entire result set. All it has to do is

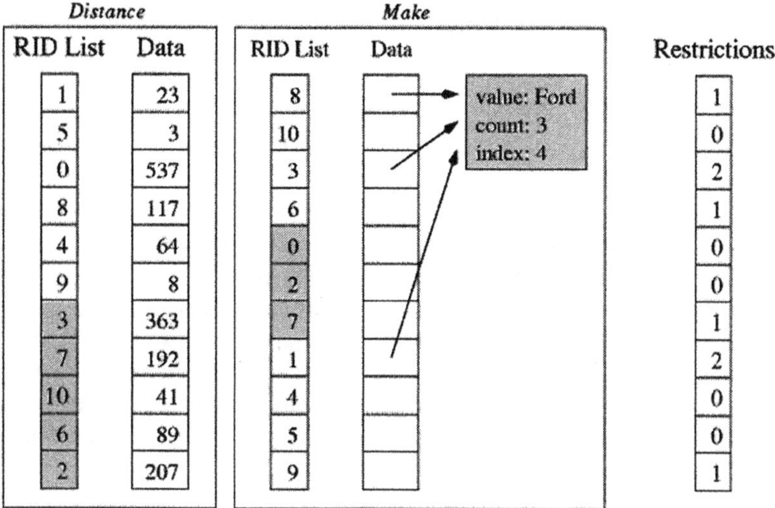

Fig. 10. Example categorical restriction (*Make* – *{Ford}*).

redraw the 20 or so records that the user will see at any given moment.

Note that what appears in the Eureka GUI to be a standard scrollable list displaying matching records is in fact a separate paintable 'canvas' and an independent scrollbar. If this component was implemented as a standard GUI list object, then we would be forced to insert every matching record from the current result set into that list. Changing sort order would also require reinserting the entire result set. While this may be satisfactory for small datasets of a few hundred records, this does not scale to datasets with thousands or tens-of-thousands of items.

To display the current visible portion of the result set, the ListRenderer needs a list of those records it is to display. Once it has a list of rids, the ListRenderer can interrogate the DataGroup object for the attribute data needed to render those records on the screen. This list of rids must reflect the current result set, the current sort order, and the current position within the result set (as indicated by the scrollbar).

Rendering begins with the ListRenderer making an API call to the DataGroup asking for N unrestricted rids, starting at position P and sorted by column C. Upon receiving this request, the DataGroup object passes it on to the corresponding DataColumn. The DataColumn initiates a scan of its rid-list, starting at the indicated position and in the appropriate direction (depending on an increasing or decreasing sort order). For each rid scanned, its restriction count is examined; if the count is zero, the rid is added to the list of rids to be returned. The scan halts when enough rids have been collected, or there are no more rids to scan. For categorical DataColumns, we perform an optimization whereby if a rid is restricted, we examine its corresponding RidSet to see if that RidSet is restricted. If so, we use its count and index information to skip that entire block of rids in the rid-list. Due to realistic limits on the size of the GUI display, the number of requested rids will likely never be larger than about 30, making this scanning process extremely fast. Note that if the GUI requests rids in record id order, then the DataGroup can handle the request itself by scanning the restrictions array directly.

In our car example, assume that we have the two restrictions illustrated in Fig. 10 and our current displayed position is at the very top of the result set. Assuming our sort column is *Distance* and the GUI is sized such that only three records are visible at any given instant, then the rid-list returned to the *ListRenderer* would be 1, 5 and 4. If our sort column is *Make*, then the rids would be 8, 1 and 4.

3.4. Memory requirements

The following formula gives the estimate of the memory requirements for the cache. In the formula, n is total number of records, f_n is the number of numeric attributes, f_c is the number of categorical attributes and v_c is the total number of unique categorical values.

$$((f_n + f_c) \times n \times (\text{data} + \text{rid})) + (f_c \times \text{hashtable}) + (v_c \times \text{ridsets}) + (n \times \text{restriction}).$$

Each data-array element in a DataColumn consumes 'data' bytes and each rid-list element consumes 'rid' bytes. From the categorical DataColumns, 'hashtable' represents the average number of bytes required for hashtables and 'ridsets' represents the average size of a RidSet (including its associated string value). Finally, 'restriction' is the number of bytes consumed by each entry in the DataGroup's restrictions array.

In our Java implementation, 'data' is 4 bytes. Depending on the value of n, 'rid' may either be 2 bytes (for up to 64 thousand records) or 4 bytes (up to 4 billion records). In virtually every situation, the restrictions array can be implemented with single byte values (for up 255 attributes), meaning that 'restriction' is 1 byte. For example, the dataset used for illustration in Section 2 contained 3342 records, with each record consisting of 9 attributes. The cache requirement for this dataset is less than 200 KB.

4. Conclusions

We presented the design of Eureka, a database exploration engine that implements continuous querying in data-centric Web applications. Eureka has extremely fast response time even when exploring hundreds of thousands of records containing hundreds of attributes. Besides predicates on attribute values, Eureka also supports searching using example records. Query borders in Eureka can also be made non-strict such that records that lie just outside the query region can still be included in the result set.

Obtaining interactive response times in Eureka is made possible by exploiting several key observations. One of the primary observations exploited is that searching is a process and not a one-step operation. As a result, users invariably issue multiple 'queries' over the data which are typically not unrelated. Each query in fact is usually some modification of a previous one. When standard database technology such as SQL is used, this fact is not exploited; although query state may be maintained in the HTML search form, each query submitted to the database is treated as a new query regardless of how small the change. By exploiting the concept of state and integrating it into the engine's data structures, Eureka is able to handle these successive queries extremely quickly.

The speed at which query changes are processed is further enhanced by processing changes immediately rather than waiting for the user to hit a submit button. This not only results in small query changes that can be effected quickly, but also offers the additional advantage of immediate feedback for the user.

The final optimization we leveraged is that Eureka is a visual tool rather than a reporting tool. As such, full result sets never need full instantiation. Since users can only view as many result records as can fit on the screen at one time, the subset of the results that Eureka does instantiate is never larger than 20 or so records.

The design we presented here for Eureka is our second iteration on building a database exploration engine. In our first implementation, we followed the conventional submit/response metaphor. However, instead of directly returning the result of the SQL query, we first examined the size of the result set. If the result set was empty, we used a query relaxation algorithm that removed one constraint at a time until we obtained a non-empty set to return to the user. On the other hand, if there were too many result records, we selected a 'representative' subset of the result set and returned only those records instead. The representative subset can be determined by clustering the result records and selecting the medoids of the clusters [8]. In practice, choosing the representatives by a random sampling of the result set worked equally well and was much faster. The user could then explore the neighborhood of a record so returned by optionally specifying in the GUI the search direction for each attribute (e.g. faster processor, more memory, etc.) These user hints were then used to generate modified SQL and the cycle was repeated.

While technically interesting, we found that the system became quite painful to use because of the delay the user encountered between two successive interactions. Some users also found it unnerving that we were only showing representative records; there was a nagging fear that they might have missed something important.

The current Eureka design addresses these concerns effectively. The user explores the neighborhood by moving attribute controls and there is instantaneous response that the user can see. Indeed, we have received very positive feedback from the users of Eureka in an internally deployed Web application.

Acknowledgements

We would like to thank Sunita Sarawagi who helped design and implement our first database exploration engine. We also thank Andreas Arning, Daniel Gruhl, Dimitrios Gunopulos, Howard Ho and Magnus Stensmo for their contributions to the discussions.

References

[1] 64K Inc., San Jose, DBGuide Introduction and Technology Overview, 1997.

[2] C. Ahlberg and B. Shneiderman, Visual information seeking: tight coupling of dynamic filters with starfield displays, in: Proc. CHI 94, Boston, 1994.

[3] C. Ahlbert, C. Williamson and B. Shneiderman, Dynamic queries for information exploration: an implementation and evaluation, in: Proc. CHI 92, May 1992.

[4] S. Dar, M.J. Franklin, B.T. Jonsson, D. Srivastava and M. Tan, Semantic data caching and replacement, in: Proc. VLDB 96, Mumbai, 1996.

[5] D.A. DePalma, J.C. McCarthy and M. Mackenzie, Interactive technology strategies: content road map, Technical Report 2 (1), Forrester, October 1997.

[6] International Business Machines, IBM Intelligent Miner User's Guide, Version 1 Release 1, SH12-6213-00 edition, June 1996.

[7] International Business Machines, IBM Net.Commerce Technologies, Version 3 Release 1, G310-0705-00 edition, June 1998.

[8] R.T. Ng and J. Han, Efficient and effective clustering methods for spatial data mining, in: Proc. VLDB Conf., Santiago, September 1994.

[9] SIGMOD Record, Special Section on Electronic Commerce, Vol. 27 No. 4 edition, December 1998.

[10] M. Spenke, C. Beilken and T. Berlage, The interactive table for product comparison and selection, in: Proc. UIST 96, Seattle, 1996.

[11] I. Vollrath, W. Wilke and R. Bergmann, Case-based reasoning support for online catalog sales, in: IEEE Internet Computing, July–August 1998.

AVoN calling: AXL for voice-enabled Web navigation

Sami Rollins [a,*], Neel Sundaresan [b,1]

[a] *Department of Computer Science, University of California at Santa Barbara, Santa Barbara, CA 93106-5110, USA*
[b] *IBM Almaden Research Center, 650 Harry Road, San Jose, CA 95120, USA*

Abstract

The World Wide Web is a rich source of information that has become a universal means of communication. XML promises to be the future of the World Wide Web. However, as HTML is replaced by its more powerful counterpart, traditional browsers are not sufficient to display the information communicated in an XML document. Today's browsers are capable of showing only a textual version of an XML document. This is limiting not only for a viewer in a traditional scenario, but is a barrier for a user who wishes to access the information without having access to a traditional keyboard, mouse, and monitor. This paper presents a framework for developing non-traditional, schema-driven, customizable interfaces used to navigate and modify XML documents that may be served over the Web. Our system, Audio XmL (AXL) focuses on developing a speech-based component within that framework. At the most basic level, we provide a Speech DOM, a spoken equivalent to the Document Object Model. Beyond that, we provide an intuitive set of commands based upon schema as well as a customization language. AXL enables voice-based Web browsing, but without requiring extra effort on the part of the Web page designer. Given any XML document, AXL allows the user to navigate, modify and traverse the structure and links of the document entirely by voice. To illustrate, we focus on how AXL can enable a user to browse the Web via a cellular phone.

Keywords: Voice browsing; Audio; Multi-modal; Accessibility; Portable devices

1. Introduction

The eXtensible Markup Language (XML) [6] is emerging as a new way to both store and communicate data. It affords the user the benefit of separating the content of information from its presentation which makes it well suited for a variety of applications. The primary application of XML is as the new language of the World Wide Web [3]. As HTML is replaced by its more powerful counterpart XML, traditional Web browsers do not provide the necessary means to display and navigate XML data [21]. Currently, the only browser support for XML provides a textual view of the XML document. This is insufficient for the user who wishes to have a graphical view of the document in her browser. Further, a user may actually wish to interact with the document using a completely different input and output mode.

As pervasive computing technology brings the Web to anyone anywhere, XML accommodates the vast and diverse types of communication that must occur. With the explosive growth of portable devices such as Palm Pilots and cellular phones, there is a growing demand for technology that will allow

* Corresponding author. E-mail: srollins@cs.ucsb.edu
[1] E-mail: neel@almaden.ibm.com

users to be connected to the Internet from anywhere through devices that are not suitable for use with a traditional keyboard, mouse, and monitor [24]. Current technology [23,29,30] allows limited access to static data extracted from Websites such as Yahoo!; however, a current goal is to find an all-purpose solution to allow access to *any* Website. Along with that goal comes the challenge of finding a way for the user to interact with the browsing system without having to have a mouse in hand.

This paper presents a fully customizable system that provides a user-specified, multi-modal view of any XML document. The system that we call the MakerFactory allows the user to select a set of rendering components as well as define an optional rule document that further specifies the rendering. Additionally, the MakerFactory defines a link traversal mechanism. Therefore, a user can navigate not only within the document, but may navigate the entire Web using our Renderer. This system eliminates many of the constraints imposed by current browsing systems. First, the user is not constrained to a visual representation of the data. In fact, the system eliminates the requirement of a monitor. Moreover, the system also eliminates the requirement of keyboard/mouse input. A further benefit of the system is that we take advantage of the XML schema model. Given a published schema, the MakerFactory generates a renderer that is unique to that schema.

The focus of our work has been to develop an auditory component for our system. We call this component Audio XmL (AXL). AXL allows a user to access any XML document without requiring special directives or alternative designs from the Web page designer's point of view. When instantiated, AXL automatically generates an aural interface to an XML document conforming to a given schema. The generated class can be used in conjunction with the MakerFactory Renderer to navigate and modify an XML document using speech.

The use of speech for input and output is inherent for the user of a cellular telephone. AXL provides a system that uses speech as both the input and output medium. As long as a document is in XML form, AXL provides a mechanism for a user to navigate and modify that document. As the Web transitions to XML, AXL provides the means to navigate the Web by voice. Even if a page has an unknown schema, AXL will provide a basic navigational mechanism. With a published schema, a user can specify a customized view of any page conforming to that schema. Moreover, unlike many of the standards that are currently being developed, AXL does not require any extra stylesheet-type specifications. All that is required is the XML document itself.

As an example, let us suppose that a business executive wishes to browse his newspaper on his way to work. AXL can be customized to allow the user to first browse all of the headlines, then choose a story to be read. Additionally, the user can stop the current story, move to the next story, return to the previous story, ask for the author, and all without taking his eyes off of the road. Furthermore, if the user reads the sections of the paper in the same order everyday, AXL can be customized to automatically browse in that order saving the user the trouble of navigating the document.

To test the usability of our system, we designed a test schema and observed user's reactions to using voice input and hearing speech output when navigating a document. The results indicate that our design supports many of the goals we set out to achieve. However, we also found that AXL needs to be extended to support features like a logical help command and more intuitive error feedback mechanisms.

In Section 2 we present a description of work done in related areas. Section 3 examines the design decisions and architecture of the MakerFactory system and of AXL in particular. Section 4 details the implementation of the system. Section 5 elaborates on one specific Web-based application and Section 6 looks at the observations we have made about our system based upon user experience. Section 7 concludes with a look at the contributions of this work and future directions of this research.

2. Related work

We first evaluate work that has been done involving audio in the human–computer interface in general. We then examine efforts to bring audio specifically to the Web. Next we survey current trends toward uniting speech and XML and conclude with a look at current work in voice browsing by phone.

2.1. Audio in the human–computer interface

Aster [20] proposed a new paradigm for users of aural interfaces. It suggests that the reader of a document can scan a page worth of information and, virtually simultaneously evaluate the content of the entire page. Based upon cues like font size and page layout, a reader can determine which part of the page is useful and which part of the page is not. The user can then choose to read one portion or another of a given page. A listener does not have that luxury. Audio by nature is serial. However, by using the semi-structured nature of LaTex [13], Aster creates a system to allow a user to 'listen to' a LaTex document in a more interactive manner.

We propose that XML provides an even greater benefit. Aster provides a static navigational mechanism. However, XML is more dynamic. Each document changes based upon the given schema. By using the knowledge of a given schema, we provide not one, but many customized aural interfaces.

Other types of systems have been constructed that look at how to use sound, speech or non-speech, to represent the structure of a document. Ref. [4] develops a set of guidelines for integrating non-speech audio into user interfaces. It presents a comprehensive look at the components of sound and how each can be used to convey information. Ref. [2] is a similar system that looks at how to design sounds to represent the types of activities performed in your application. Ref. [18] looks specifically at how sound can convey structure and location within a document. We leverage off of the results presented in this work to determine the most effective method of integrating sounds into the AXL system.

Data sonification is another related area. Ref. [31] examines what it means to represent data with sound. Similar work is detailed in [25]. The concepts defined in these bodies of work help us to define what it means to represent something visual using sound. These concepts are integral in determining the best way to generate speech-based interfaces. Our system is without benefit unless a user can actually make use of the system. The work detailed in this section helps to define the standards by which such a system can be evaluated.

2.2. Audio Web

There is a large body of work that has addressed the question of how to make the current World Wide Web accessible through a speech-based interface. Most of the work done has focused around how to make the Web accessible to users with print disabilities. By looking at previous research in this area, we generalize the concepts developed for the HTML case in order to create a system that makes XML-based documents accessible to any person who is not accessing electronic data through a traditional computer interface using a keyboard, mouse, and monitor.

Both [8] and [9] look at how to make the Web more accessible by integrating sound components like voice and pitch. This work focuses around designing useful experiments to determine how a user would best react to different aural representations. It details a thorough analysis of the parameters involved with designing an aural interface. Where this work mainly focuses on designing a set of tactics used to represent HTML structures, we want to design a more general system that takes into account these findings and examines how useful an interface we can generate automatically, in the general case.

Other work on making the Web accessible has taken a similar approach, looking at HTML in specific and determining, for example, how one should best represent an <H1> tag. Refs. [1,12,16,36,37] all look specifically at HTML. Our goal is to generalize the approach presented in this body of work.

2.3. XML and speech

A slew of different XML instances are currently being developed with the goal of making the Web voice-enabled [11,22,23,29,30]. The attention seems to be centered around developing a language in which the Website developer or voice Web service provider can specify how the user can access Web content. In other words, it is up to the developer to create an XML specification of the speech-based interaction that a user can have with the server.

VoiceXML [29] is emerging as the standard and essentially subsumes SpeechML in functionality. VoiceXML provides the programmer with the ability to specify an XML document that defines the types of commands a voice-enabled system can receive and the text that a voice-enabled system can synthesize. Similar to the Java Speech Markup Language, it allows the XML programmer to specify the attributes used to render a given excerpt of text. This may include information about parameters such as rate and volume. Beyond that, VoiceXML, VoXML, and TalkML provide the infrastructure to define dialogues between the user and the system.

Our system takes a slightly different approach and can actually incorporate these concepts at a lower level. We would like to eliminate the burden of having to specifically design a voice-enabled document. Rather, our system seeks to automatically voice-enable *any* document. Our system actually analyzes the XML schema and automatically discovers the specification that a developer would otherwise have to write. In fact, our system generates instances of SpeechML.

2.4. Voice browsing by phone

We focus on voice Web browsing as the primary application for our system. [27] is the W3C note describing necessary features of voice Web browsers. Some of the features it describes are alternative navigational mechanisms, access to forms and input fields, and error handling. Other work such as [19,28] present standards and issues related to voice-enabling the Web; however, they focus on designing systems with limited functionality. There are a limited and static set of commands that any user can give to the browser.

There is also a body of work that is specifically developing protocols for communication with cellular phones. WAP [32] looks at the network protocol itself while WML [33] is the XML-based language used to communicate on top of the WAP protocol. However, like VoiceXML, VoxML, SpeechML, and the rest, WML requires that the Web page designer provide either a manually generated WML version of a Web page, or a means of transcoding the page into WML. Both solutions require human intervention. This work does not intend to replace the standards developed in that body of work. Rather, we hope to discover a means to automatically perform the conversion from general XML to a format such as WML or VoiceXML.

Our work seeks to leverage off and generalize the concepts described in the work discussed in this section. We wanted to design a general system to provide an interface to any type of XML document, not just HTML. By doing so, we eliminate the restrictions posed by similar voice browsing systems. Furthermore, we wish to use the findings of previous auralization work to integrate sound and its different components into our generated interfaces. Given any XML document, our system provides a speech-based interface.

3. Design of the system

Existing XML editing and browsing tools are limited in their support. They produce a standard view of *all* XML documents. Every document is presented in the same way. However, we propose that we can take advantage of the knowledge of an XML schema to produce a customized rendering system that will be unique for every different type of document and possibly for every user as well. The primary goal in the design of the MakerFactory was to create a system that would automate the process of generating a usable, customizable interface for an XML document. We not only wanted to address the issue of generating an XML-based Web browsing system, we wanted to develop a system that would provide automatic generation of an interface that would allow a user to do anything that she would want to do with an XML document. This could include linking, navigation, creation, and modification of XML documents. The MakerFactory architecture supports this goal. It is completely interactive, customizable, and useful not only for the XML reader, but for the XML writer as well.

Our design considers XLink [34] as the link traversal mechanism. XLink is currently being developed as a standard for integrating linking mechanisms into XML [34,35] and will likely be the standard implemented by most XML parsers. We focus on developing a voice-enabled mechanism for traversing XML links as defined in the XLink working draft.

3.1. The MakerFactory

The MakerFactory is designed to operate in two phases. The first phase is the code-generation phase.

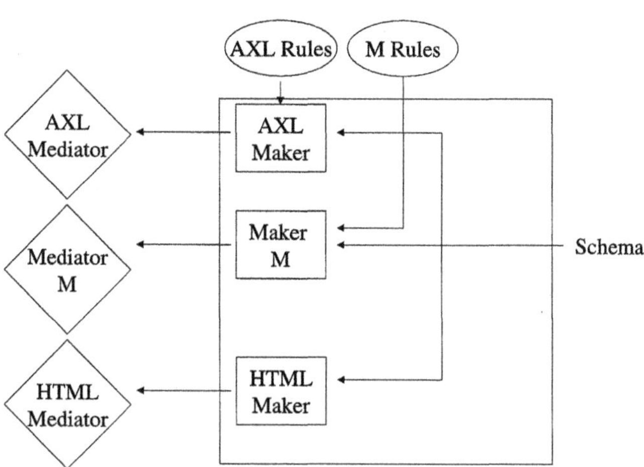

Fig. 1. An XML schema is fed into a user-selected series of Makers along with an optional set of customization rules for each type of Maker. The Maker analyzes the schema as well as the rules to produce a customized Java Mediator class for each type of Maker. Each Mediator provides the user with a different input/output mode that can be customized by the user via the optional rules. At run-time, a user-selected set of Mediators is used to mediate communication between the user and the underlying XML structure.

In this phase, the user selects a series of interface generation components from the library provided. To generate a customized interface, the user need only select those components that will be relevant to the run-time rendering scenario. Each component is responsible for *making* a specialized interface for an XML document and hence must implement our Maker interface. In addition, the user may optionally specify a set of customization rules that further define how the document will be rendered. The result of code-generation is a set of Java classes designed to *mediate* communication between the user and the synchronized tree manager. Therefore, the Maker-generated classes should minimally implement our Mediator interface. Since each Mediator is designed to be independent of the others, the user need only select to invoke the Mediators that are relevant to the current scenario and hence not incur the overhead of having to run all Mediators simultaneously.

The second phase is the run-time rendering phase. The MakerFactory provides a Renderer that is responsible for controlling synchronized rendering of the XML tree. Each Mediator acts as an intermediary between the Renderer and the user allowing its own specialized input and output mode. Specifically, AXL is designed to act as the auditory Mediator, allowing the user to navigate the XML document and traverse its links via a speech-based interface.

3.1.1. Code generation

Fig. 1 shows the architecture of the code-generation system. A given schema is analyzed and the results of the analysis are passed into a series of user-selected Maker classes. Given the schema and any optional customization rules specified by the user, the system produces a set of customized Mediator classes that can be used with the Renderer to interact with any XML document conforming to the given schema. For example, if the user specifies the AXL Maker (a component used to generate auditory input and output) and the HTML Maker (a component used to produce an HTML representation of the data), the result should be two independent Mediator classes. The AXL Mediator will listen for spoken commands from the user and provide aural output whereas the HTML Mediator may display the XML in HTML format and disallow input from the user. Additionally, if the given schema were a NEWSPAPER with a list of ARTICLES containing HEADLINE and BODY elements, the AXL Maker might determine that the AXL Mediator should render an ARTICLE by rendering the HEADLINE whereas the HTML Maker may determine that the HTML Mediator will render an ARTICLE by displaying both HEADLINE and BODY.

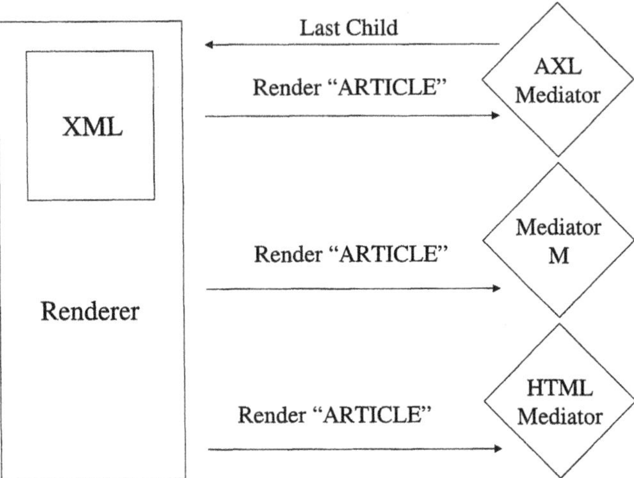

Fig. 2. The Renderer controls synchronized access to the XML tree. Each Mediator may receive input from the user in the mode supported by the Mediator. The Mediator interprets the command and issues a command to the Renderer. The Renderer changes the tree view based upon the command and updates the synchronized view for all other Mediators. Once the Mediator view changes, it may provide output to the user via the Mediator's supported mode of output.

3.1.2. Rendering

The architecture of the Renderer is shown in Fig. 2. The MakerFactory produces a set of classes that listen for user input and provide directives to the Renderer. When instantiated, the Renderer acts as the tree manager. It controls synchronized access to the tree by receiving commands from the Mediators and in turn performs the task given by each Mediator and informs all of the other Mediators of the result.

The Renderer defines the concept of a cursor. At any given point, all of the registered Mediators should be rendering the portion of the tree pointed to by the cursor. When the cursor is moved, the new view of the tree should be rendered. However, it is possible that a Mediator will have to move the cursor more than one time to achieve the desired view. This is because the methods to move the cursor are generally incremental and somewhat limited. To accommodate this situation, the Renderer implements a locking mechanism. Before calling a method that will move the cursor, the given Mediator must acquire the lock. After all movement is complete, the lock should be released. When the lock is released, all of the Mediators are notified that the cursor has changed. For example, if a Mediator directs the Renderer to move the current cursor to an ARTICLE node, the Renderer will in turn ask all of the other Mediators to render the given ARTICLE.

3.2. AXL

The primary goal in the design of AXL was to create a component that would produce a usable, voice-based interface to any XML document. There are many questions we sought to answer in conjunction with this goal. First, we wanted to produce user interfaces that would give the user as much control as possible over the navigation of the document. In the case of a large Web page, the user would likely want the ability to choose which portion of the page she wanted to hear. However, we recognized that there are situations where the user may actually wish to be the passive participant while allowing the rendering system to navigate and present the XML document. This would likely be the case in the NEWSPAPER example. Therefore, we wanted our design to allow the user the freedom to choose the level of interaction she wishes to have with the document.

3.2.1. Code generation

In the code-generation phase, the AXL Maker analyzes the schema and produces a vocabulary for interacting with a document conforming to the given schema. For example, the previously cited NEWSPAPER example might generate a vocabulary {article, body, headline}. Each word in the vocabulary

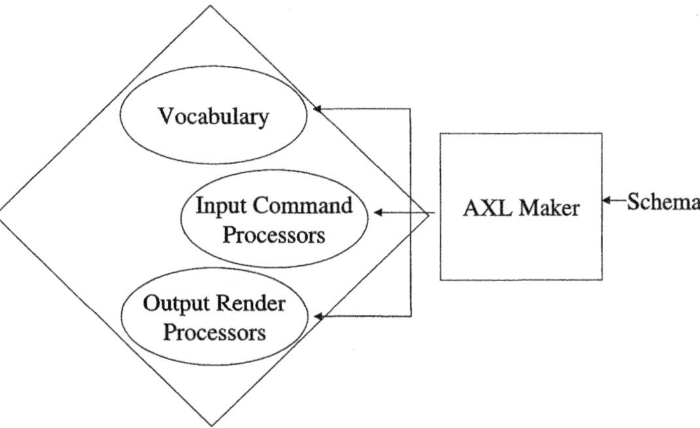

Fig. 3. The AXL Maker produces an AXL Mediator by (a) constructing a vocabulary that can be used to access the information in a document conforming to the given schema, (b) constructing a set of classes to listen for spoken commands within that vocabulary and (c) constructing a set of classes that will perform a text-to-speech conversion of the information contained in the appropriate nodes in a given XML subtree.

has a semantic meaning associated with traversing a document of the given type. The 'headline' command may mean to read the headline of the current article. Given that vocabulary, the AXL Maker generates a set of classes that process commands within the vocabulary as well as a set of classes that know how to render nodes of the given schema via a speech-synthesizing engine as shown in Fig. 3. The resulting set of classes compose the AXL Mediator.

3.2.2. Rendering

The AXL Mediator operates as shown in Fig. 4. When the Mediator is asked to render a node, AXL will determine the type of node it is being asked to render and then perform the appropriate operations. The rendering may include everything from a simple rendering of the node's tag name to performing the action defined in a pre-compiled Java class. Perhaps a HEADLINE node has two parts, one being the title of the ARTICLE and one being the subtitle. The

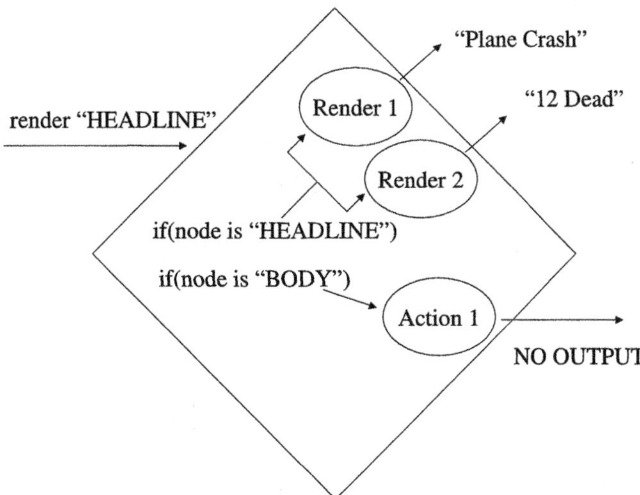

Fig. 4. The AXL Mediator receives 'render' directives from the Renderer. It determines the node type based upon the tag name and invokes the appropriate set of render and action methods. Each render or action method should provide the appropriate output to the user either by doing a text-to-speech conversion of the information in the subtree or performing a specialized action method.

rendering of a HEADLINE may indicate to render first the title and then the subtitle. Correspondingly, perhaps rendering a BODY node simply means to perform some action and provide no output to the user. This situation is depicted in Fig. 4.

3.3. Link traversal support

In order to make the MakerFactory usable as a Web browsing system, it is imperative that we support a method of link traversal. At the most basic level, we want to support the kinds of links defined in HTML using the 'A' tag and 'href' attribute. For XML, the XLink standard is being developed. Not only does XLink provide the mechanism to define HTML style links, it also has the benefit of attaching semantic meaning to the action of link traversal. We investigate how to design our system to support XLink style link traversal.

3.3.1. MakerFactory linking

In order to support a linking mechanism, the Renderer must provide a mechanism for the Mediator classes to request that a link be followed. We investigate this requirement by looking at the different attributes that may occur within the *xlink* namespace. Currently, we are looking at XLink *simple* links. Table 1 outlines XLink-defined links an their corresponding AXL interpretation.

The *href* location attribute is necessary for determining where to find the given node. The arc end attributes are not required at this time for the purposes of the MakerFactory. The behavior attributes help the MakerFactory in determining how to load the referenced resource. The resource may be appended to the current tree, replace the current tree possibly causing the system to instantiate a new set of Mediator classes, or may require that a new Renderer be instantiated. Additionally, the Renderer may automatically load the resource, or may wait for a Mediator to explicitly ask to load it. Finally, a Mediator may use the semantic attributes in its own rendering of a node.

3.3.2. AXL linking

It is the job of AXL to appropriately interpret the MakerFactory-supported commands and provide the user with a suitable method of accessing those commands via a speech-based interface. Therefore, AXL must allow the user to issue a command that *follows* a link. If the user has reached a node that is identified as a link, the user may ask to follow the link. AXL will subsequently invoke the Renderer method used to perform the traversal. The result may be a new tree which will then be rendered appropriately by all of the Mediators including AXL.

XLink provides the definition of *role* and *title* attributes. These define the link's function and provide a

Table 1
The XLink standard defines four classes of attributes. Each type of attribute can be specified in an XLink node and helps the parser to determine how to traverse and display the attribute as well as provides metadata describing the function and content of the link itself. The MakerFactory considers how to integrate all of the possible values of those attributes given the XLink definition of their functions

Conceptual classification	Attribute	Function	MakerFactory implications
Location	href	provides URI of resource	Renderer uses value to load resource
Arc End	from	defines where link originates	NONE
	to	defines where the link traverses to	NONE
Behavior	show	defines how the resource should be presented to the user	• parsed – resource is appended as child of current node • replace – resource replaces current data; new Mediators may be instantiated • new – requires a new Renderer be instantiated; see future work on *Speech Spaces*
	actuate	defines how link traversal is initiated	• user – a Mediator must request link traversal • auto – the Renderer traverses the link upon rendering the XLink node
Semantic	role	defines function of link	may be used to enhance rendering
	title	description of the link	may be used to enhance rendering

summary of the link. AXL can take advantage of both of these attributes. If the node currently being rendered is a link node, AXL will render the node by synthesizing both semantic attributes for the user. These attributes provide a built-in way for the XML writer to indicate to AXL the best rendering for the node.

4. Implementation

This section details the implementation of the MakerFactory and AXL. Many of the implementation details of the MakerFactory are more clearly illustrated by using AXL as an example.

The entire system has been implemented in Java using the IBM Speech for Java [22] implementation of the Java Speech API [11]. Furthermore, the Speech for Java implementation requires that IBM's ViaVoice be installed and used as the synthesizing and recognizing engine.

4.1. The MakerFactory

The MakerFactory is invoked using a configuration file defined by an XML DTD. The first piece of information that must be specified is the SchemaProcessor class. For each different type of schema specification (e.g. DTD, XML Schema) a class implementing our SchemaProcessor interface must be written. The appropriate class should be specified to deal with the type of schema used for the current MakerFactory invocation. The second item to be specified is the SchemaLocation. This should be the URL of the schema definition itself (e.g. the file name of the DTD file). Finally, for each different type of Maker used for a particular invocation, the Classname of the Maker as well as the location of a Rulefile must be specified.

Each Maker is instantiated and notified of each different type of element defined in the schema. Based upon this information as well as the rules defined in the Rulefile, each Maker generates a set of Java classes that implement the Mediator interface and can be invoked using the MakerFactory Renderer. The Renderer is invoked at run-time with a configuration file similar to that defined by the MakerFactory. The XMLFile to be traversed as well as the set of Mediator classes to be instantiated are specified. The Renderer traverses and modifies the XML document according to the Mediator directives and notifies each Mediator when there as been a change. Table 2 details the Renderer supported methods to be called by the Mediator classes.

All of the methods function like their org.w3c.dom.Node counterparts with the exception of the *setData* method. This method allows the user to change the tree that is being traversed. This is especially useful for link traversal where the current document changes often.

The remainder of the implementation including the rule language is best explained by examining AXL, the SpeechMaker.

4.2. AXL

At the lowest level, AXL provides an auditory version of the Document Object Model (DOM). DOM is a parsing model that parses an entire XML document into a tree structure and provides a series of methods to navigate within the XML tree. Beyond an auditory DOM, AXL provides a customized interface through schema analysis, and also via user-customization.

4.2.1. Speech DOM

At the most basic level, AXL provides a speech version of the Document Object Model [5]. At the core level, an XML tree is a collection of org.w3c.dom.Node objects. Therefore, the AXL Speech DOM provides a set of commands conforming to the org.w3c.dom.Node API.

The basic commands available are:

- Parent
- Next Sibling
- Previous Sibling
- Next Attribute
- Previous Attribute
- First Child
- Last Child
- Name
- Value
- Remove
- Insert Before
- Append
- New Text
- Set Attribute

Table 2
Methods supported by the MakerFactory Renderer, their functions, and what they return to the calling Mediator. Each Mediator should implement a mode-specific way of invoking this set of methods. Each user issued command should be transformed into a call to one or more of these methods and the result should be an update to the view held by each Mediator

Method	Behavior	Return value
appendChild(Node newChild)	appends the newChild as the last child of the current element	true if the append was successful
attribute(String attrname)	moves the current attribute cursor to the attribute of the current element with the given name	true if the move was successful
element(String eltname, int n)	moves current element cursor to nth occurrence of element 'eltname'	true if the move was successful
firstChild()	moves the current element cursor to the first child of the current element	true if the move was successful
insertBefore(Node newChild)	inserts newChild as the previous sibling of the current element node	true if the insert was successful
lastChild()	moves the current element cursor to the last child of the current element	true if the move was successful
name()	get tag name of the current element	String-tag name of the current element node
nextAttr()	moves the current attribute pointer to the next attribute of the current element	true if the move was successful
nextSibling()	moves the current element cursor to the next sibling of the current element	true if the move was successful
parent()	moves the current element cursor to the parent of the current element	true if the move was successful
previousAttr()	moves current attribute pointer to the previous attribute of current element	true if the move was successful
previousSibling()	moves the current element cursor to the previous sibling of the current element	true if the move was successful
remove()	removes the current element and moves the current element cursor to the parent	true if the remove was successful
replaceChild(Node newChild)	replaces the current element with newChild	true if the replace was successful
setAttr(String name, String value)	sets attribute name of the current element to the value	true if the set was successful
setData(Document newDoc)	replaces the XML tree with newDoc and renders the root	true if the set was successful
value()	return a cloned copy of the current element node and its children	Node-cloned copy of the current element and its children

For each command, the Mediator simply calls the corresponding method of the Renderer class (see Table 2). The only commands that warrant explanation are *Insert Before*, *Append*, *New Text*, and *Set Attribute*. Each of these commands requires more input than the command itself. *Insert Before* causes the system to beep indicating that it is waiting for more user input. It waits for the user to speak the tag name of the node to be inserted. When it hears the name it inserts the node and returns to normal operation mode. *Append* is exactly the same, except that the new element is appended as the last child of the current node rather than inserted as the current node's previous sibling. *New Text* and *Set Attribute* both require actual dictation from the user. Therefore, the *New Text* command causes the system to beep indicating that it is waiting for free dictation. It records everything the user speaks until the user issues the command *Complete*. At that point, all of the text is appended as the last child of the current node. Finally, *Set Attribute* is much like the *New Text* command. However, there are two parts to the new node, the name and the value. Therefore, *Set Attribute* puts the system in the dictation mode. The first word spoken in this mode is interpreted as the name of the attribute. The remainder of the spoken

Table 3
AXL defines a set of commands to direct the engine itself. Each command tells the engine to perform a function independent of the underlying document. This command set should not result in an update to the view of the XML structure

Command	Behavior
Complete	ends dictation mode
Pause	pauses input; engine only recognizes Resume command
Resume	ends paused state; engine listens for all commands
What can I say	lists the set of commands available at the current node
Save	saves the current XML tree
Stop	stops the rendering of the current node
Exit	performs any necessary cleanup and exits the program

phrase until the *Complete* command is issued is interpreted as the value of the attribute. For example, '*Set Attribute* [Title] [A Midsummer Night's Dream] *Complete*' would set the Title attribute of the current element to be 'A Midsummer Night's Dream'.

In addition, AXL defines a set of commands used by the engine itself. Table 3 illustrates what the user may say to direct the engine.

The AXL engine can be in one of four states as shown in Fig. 5. The *Normal* state simply waits for another command. If in the *Tag Specification* state, the engine expects a valid tag name for the given schema. The *Paused* state means that the engine will not listen to any user input except for the *Resume* command. Finally, the *Dictation* state indicates that the engine is waiting for free dictation from the user.

This basic implementation does not require a schema or user-specified rules. In fact, this interface can be created one time and used to navigate any XML document. However, it is not enough to provide a generic, low-level interface to an XML document. We would like to leverage off of the functionality provided by the Speech DOM, and build a higher-level interface on top of it to give users a more intuitive way to navigate a document. Ultimately, given an XML document conforming to one schema, we would like to interact with it in a way specific to that schema. Given another document conforming to a different schema, we would like for the user-interface to be different.

4.2.2. *A schema-driven interface*

Primarily, the DTD tells us what kind of children and attributes an element is allowed to have. The first

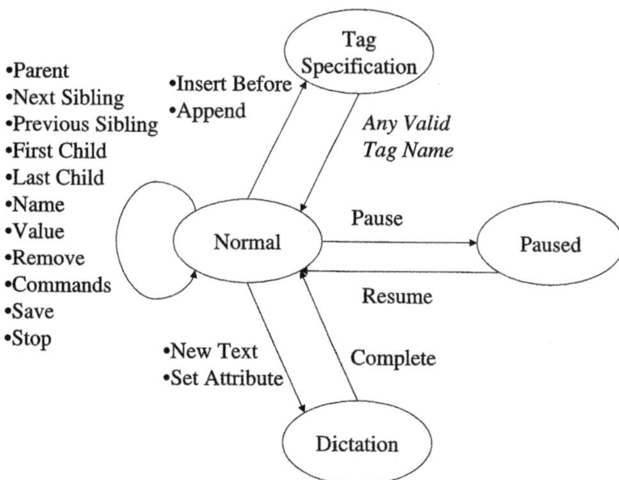

Fig. 5. The AXL Speech DOM engine can be in one of four states. The transition from one state to another is initiated by a spoken command from the user. To transition from Normal to Paused, the user speaks the command Pause. Resume returns the system to normal operation. Dictation mode is entered by speaking either the New Text or Set Attribute command. After dictation is finished, Complete returns the system to normal operating mode. Tag Specification is entered by either the Insert Before command or the Append command. Once the tag name is spoken, the system automatically returns to the Normal state. The remaining commands cause the system to perform some action which may or may not result in output to the user, however the system itself remains in the Normal state.

task is to use that information to provide a rendering of the node. For example, in addition to rendering the node by speaking the tag name, we can also speak the names of the children and attributes that the node is allowed to have. For example, the rendering of an ARTICLE node might be 'An ARTICLE is a HEADLINE and a BODY'. This provides the user with a brief overview of the structure at any given node without having to know the structure before hand.

The second task is to use the schema-derived information to produce a more intuitive vocabulary with which we can interact with the document. First, we can use the knowledge of the elements and attributes that exist in the document to develop a vocabulary. Suppose that a user wished to navigate to the BODY element of an ARTICLE. Instead of navigating all of the children using the Speech DOM vocabulary, we allow the user to actually speak the command 'BODY'. This is more intuitive for the user and also provides faster access over the iterative DOM methods. In addition, developing such a vocabulary allows us to easily disallow illegal directives. If the user asks for the NEWSPAPER node while at the BODY element, we can immediately give the user feedback indicating that no such node exists without having to actually look for the node in the subtree. This creates a more efficient system.

Even though this design allows us to query using a higher-level language, it still does not provide all of the facilities that one might desire. The user may want to have more control over how each type of node should be rendered. The automatically generated interface may not be sufficient for all different uses of an interface. In this case, user input is required.

4.2.3. User customization

There are many reasons why a user might want to specify how they would like a document to be rendered. The complete semantic definition of the structure might not be specifiable in an XML schema. Furthermore, the user may just have a different preference than that which is defined by the default AXL Maker. Therefore, AXL defines its own rule language, the Audio Browsing Language (ABL). ABL allows a user to provide input about the rendering of the element and attribute nodes in the XML tree.

The general MakerFactory architecture provides a high-level rule language that we can use to specify general customization rules that direct how rendering should occur. For each type of element or attribute, a rule can be defined that specifies the rendering of that element or attribute. Attached to each rendering is an optional condition that specifies when the rendering should be invoked. A rendering will be invoked if the condition is true or if no condition is specified. To define a condition, an implementation of a generic UnaryPredicate interface must be written as a Java class and specified as the condition in the Rulefile. The UnaryPredicate takes a single argument, in this case the node to be rendered, and returns a boolean value indicating whether or not the condition has been met. At run-time, the class is loaded and the condition is evaluated. Additionally, each different rendering specifies a depth to which the node should be rendered. The depth specifies any combination of one or more of the node, its children, and/or its attributes. For example, the value ATTRS_NODE would render the attributes of the node and then the node itself. For the attribute rules, the options are one or more of the attribute's name or its value.

Finally, the rendering rule for a node may specify an action. To specify an action, the user must specify the name of a Java class that will be instantiated and invoked if the given node type is encountered. All action classes should implement the following interface:

```
public interface Action {
  public void notify(Node node);
}
```

Like the Java event model [10], a render *event* causes the *notify* method of the Action class to be invoked. The current node to be rendered is passed as an argument. If the action modifies the node or its subtree, the Renderer should be notified of the change following the completion of the notify method.

ABL also defines its own set of rules specific to a speech-based rendering. First, because tag names are not always in an understandable format ABL allows the user to specify the output and input phrases that represent each type of tag. The rendering of a node may be defined as the tag name of that node. Similarly, to access such a node, the user may need to speak the tag name of the node. However, there may be some tags that a user simply cannot speak. Suppose the HEADLINE tag were actually specified as HDLN. The user can define how the tag should be spoken by the system as well as by the user. The user can specify that upon seeing a HDLN node, render 'HEADLINE'. Also, upon receipt of a 'HEADLINE' command, look for a HDLN node.

Another function provided by ABL is to allow the user to specify a phrase that may be spoken before and after a node, attribute, or child node. These phrases should be defined such that nodes can be connected together with a more sentence-like flow. Finally, ABL defines a way to change how the AXL default commands are spoken by the user. For example, if a user wanted the command 'this node' to retrieve the name of the current node rather than 'name', that change could be easily specified in the rule file.

5. Voice-enabling the Web using AXL

This section details AXL's application as a front-end component enabling Web browsing by voice and looks at AXL as a way to read the morning newspaper in specific. Most current voice browsing technology focuses around browsing the Web via a cellular telephone. Cellular phones are becoming ubiquitous. People use their phones while driving, shopping, even while at the movie theater. Moreover, current work looks at using technologies such as VoiceXML to extract Web content and push a static view of information such as stock quotes or the weather to the user on the other end of the wireless network.

This work seeks a more generalized view of the phone-Web. Push technology [14,30] is not sufficient for the users who want control over their own Web browsing. We want to enable a user to access any Web page and more specifically, we want to provide full interaction for the user to be able to navigate the page. By using AXL as the front-end system (Fig. 6), a user can make a request to the AXL Renderer which contacts the XML server, caches the document, and navigates it as the user directs.

5.1. The daily news

To illustrate, we use the scenario in which a person wishes to browse the morning newspaper online. AXL not only allows users to navigate the paper document, users can customize a rendering of the paper so that they hear their favorite sections in the order that they would normally read the non-electronic version. We use the following DTD influenced by [15]:

```
<!ELEMENT NEWSPAPER (ARTICLE|AD)+>
<!ELEMENT ARTICLE(HEADLINE, LEAD,
                            BODY, NOTES)>
<!ATTLIST ARTICLE
          AUTHOR CDATA #REQUIRED
```

Fig. 6. The Renderer, using AXL, caches the XML document from a given server. The user navigates the document by speaking commands and the Renderer responds by doing a text-to-speech conversion of the data in the document. If the user chooses to traverse a link, the Renderer will contact the server to cache the new document.

```
        EDITOR CDATA #IMPLIED
        DATE CDATA #IMPLIED
        EDITION CDATA #IMPLIED>
<!ELEMENT HEADLINE (#PCDATA)>
<!ELEMENT LEAD (#PCDATA)>
<!ELEMENT BODY (#PCDATA)>
<!ELEMENT NOTES (#PCDATA)>
<!ELEMENT AD EMPTY>
<!-- An AD is a link to a subtree
  containing information about the
  company being advertised. -->
<!-- The attributes of an AD are
  those link attributes detailed in
  Table 1. -->
<!ATTLIST AD
        HREF CDATA #IMPLIED
        SHOW CDATA #IMPLIED
        ACTUATE CDATA #IMPLIED
        ROLE CDATA #IMPLIED
        TITLE CDATA #IMPLIED>
```

At the most basic level, AXL would render the root NEWSPAPER node as 'Newspaper'. The user could then issue the command 'Article 1' which would move the current cursor to the first article in the paper. Similarly, the user can ask for the *n*th article and the cursor will correspondingly move to the *n*th article. Once the cursor moves, the ARTICLE node is rendered as 'Article'. At the ARTICLE node, the user has the choice of asking for the HEADLINE, LEAD, BODY, or NOTES. Similarly, the user can ask for the AUTHOR, EDITOR, DATE, or EDITION attributes. Any of these commands will result in the movement of the current cursor to the corresponding node and the system reading the tag name and contents of that node. For example, the command 'Body' will move the current cursor to the BODY element and will read the body of the article.

Additionally, AXL provides the user with the ability to traverse links. Given the plethora of advertisements that exist in traditional newspapers, it is not unrealistic to think that online newspapers will adopt the same format. Suppose that an *eNewspaper* were littered with *eAdvertisements*. In this example, the AD element is simply a link to another tree containing the body of the ad. If the user wanted to follow an AD link, the user would only have to traverse the tree to the AD node, and then issue a *Follow* command. If the SHOW attribute had the value *parsed*, the advertisement body would simply become part of the NEWSPAPER tree. However, a value of *replace* or *new* would either replace this tree or open a new document containing just the body of the ad.

AXL also holds the benefit of customization. Suppose that the user always wanted to hear all of the headlines before reading any of the paper. A simple set of rendering rules could be written that indicated that the rendering of the NEWSPAPER element included rendering the HEADLINE element of each ARTICLE. An example rule specification follows:

```
<RenderRules>
 <ElementRule elementid="NEWSPAPER">
  <ElementRendering>
   <Render depth="CHILDREN_ONLY"/>
  </ElementRendering>
 </ElementRule>
 <ElementRule elementid="ARTICLE">
  <ElementRendering>
   <Render depth="CHILDREN_ONLY"
                    cond="isHeadline"/>
  </ElementRendering>
 </ElementRule>
</RenderRules>
```

The NEWSPAPER element is rendered by rendering all of its ARTICLE children. Each ARTICLE is rendered by rendering all of its children that meet the *isHeadline* condition. It is assumed that *isHeadline* is the name of a Java class that will check the node to make sure that its tag name is 'HEADLINE'. Once the user hears the headline that she is interested in, the user issues the command 'Stop' which stops the current rendering and listens for a new command. The user then navigates to the body of the desired article.

AXL also allows the user to modify the current document. For some types of documents, it may be sufficient for the user to have read-only access. For the most part, the user does not need to modify a newspaper document. However, suppose that a user was listening to the classified ads looking for a new house and wanted to annotate a given ad. AXL would allow the user to insert a text node with an annotation indicating the given ad was appealing. Moreover, there are lots of Web pages that require user input. For example, suppose that a search engine expressed its search form in XML. The user could create a new search node with the text to use for the search and execute the search all without access to a keyboard.

6. User experience

Our main goal was to produce a system that would be usable for people with a variety of skill levels. We hoped that the command set we provided was intuitive enough to allow any user to extract information from an XML document without knowing about the underlying data representation. Further, we hoped that any user would be able to extract information from the document with a minimal learning curve. Finally, we hoped that users would be able to understand the context of the information they received from the document.

6.1. Design of the user tasks

The study we conducted asked a set of users to navigate and extract information from an XML document outlining possible travel plans. The concept was that a user could plan a vacation online by navigating such a document to find the necessary information and choose a destination, find a flight to that destination, etc.

A total of eight users participated. Our subject set included both male and female users, users who were both familiar and not familiar with XML, and users with non-American accents. First, the users were asked to read six words and two sentences as minimal training for the ViaVoice system. Then, the subjects were given a brief set of oral directions and were shown the structure shown in Fig. 7 and told that the document they would be navigating would follow the same structure.

Following the oral directions, any questions were answered and the user was given a set of written instructions that contained the commands to issue to navigate within the document. The user was then expected to execute each instruction without help from the proctor.

The first set of written directions was intended to familiarize the user with the system and the commands provided. The directions led the user down one path of the tree to a *Flight* element and investigated all of the information at the leaf level including price, destination, and airline. The users then continued to the second set of instructions which were designed to test whether or not the user could remember and apply the commands from the first section and successfully navigate the structure without explicit directions. The instructions asked the user to navigate from the root of the tree to a sibling *Flight* element and retrieve the same information retrieved in the first set of directions. The third set of directions led the user down a different path of the tree to the *Rental Car* element and tested the user's ability

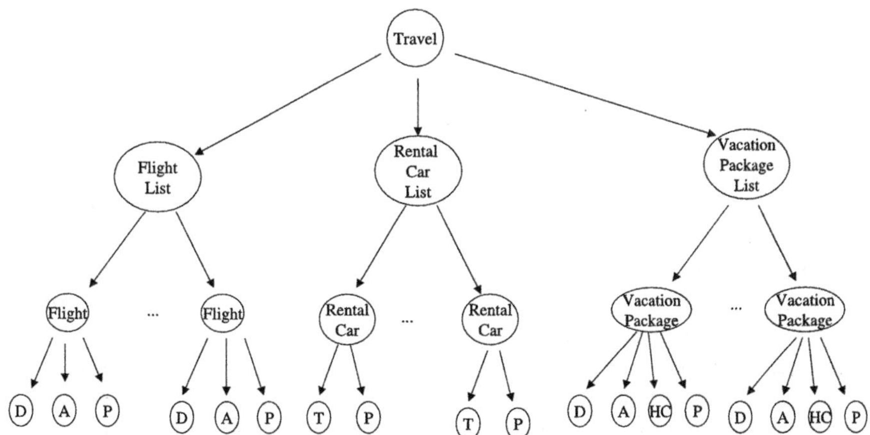

Fig. 7. The tree representation of the Travel document used in the user evaluation.

to find the price without explicit instructions on how to find the price of a *Rental Car*. The final set of instructions asked the user to navigate the tree to a *Vacation Package* element and asked them to insert a new node into the tree. The intention was to examine the user's ability and reaction to modifying the XML structure.

Finally, the users were asked a series of questions about their experience using the system. The questions involved rating and commenting on the command set provided, the appropriateness of the feedback provided by the system, and the user's prior experience including familiarity with XML.

6.2. *Observations*

We made five main observations:

- the automatic generation of a command set based upon schema yields commands considered natural by users;
- the limited vocabulary produced by schema analysis aids the ViaVoice recognition engine;
- the users' frustration with the rendering of some of the nodes facilitates the need for customization rules;
- there is a need to develop enhanced feedback mechanisms;
- there is a need to develop a better *help* command.

6.2.1. *The command set*

We observed the users' perceptions of the command set in two ways. First, the initial set of questions we asked the subjects was designed to probe the user's opinion of the commands provided. We wanted to know how natural or intuitive the commands were for the user and whether or not it was difficult to understand the function of any of the commands. Moreover, we wanted to know if the subjects felt that the command set provided was complete or if the users found themselves in want of different commands. Second, the directions provided included instructions to access information, but allowed the user the freedom to choose between a Speech DOM level command or a schema-based command. For example, the users were asked to get the price of a given flight, but were able to choose between the commands *price* and *last child*. We expected that the Speech DOM level commands would seem less natural to users and that the commands generated through schema analysis would be more natural.

We found that the users were generally pleased with the command set provided. As we had anticipated, most users indicated that the natural commands were the generated commands like *price* and *destination* while commands like *first child* and *parent* were less natural. When able to choose between a Speech DOM command and a schema-based command, most users chose the schema-based commands (i.e. *price*). However, surprisingly, one user did choose to use a Speech DOM command. We propose that those familiar with tree structures and the terminology related to them would be more inclined to use the Speech DOM commands. However, more novice users find the more natural commands most useful.

6.2.2. *Recognition accuracy*

We were somewhat skeptical of the recognition accuracy of the ViaVoice system. It has been given accuracy ratings in the 85 percent range [26], but tends to require extensive training in order to perform well. However, we were encouraged to discover that with only two sentences of training, the system was able to understand a variety of people who had a variety of accents with high accuracy. We attribute this benefit to the restricted vocabulary used by the system. Because there are only a limited number of commands a user can speak, ViaVoice performs much better than in a general dictation scenario.

There were some instances of misunderstanding, however. Background noise and misuse of the microphone (i.e. touching the microphone causing extra noise) accounted for some instances of the system not hearing or mishearing the user. In some cases, the system's complete lack of response caused the users frustration. We attribute this behavior to the speech recognition software itself.

6.2.3. *The need for customization rules*

The study itself did not provide customization rules nor did it allow the users to write their own customization rules. Therefore, the rendering of all elements was simply the rendering of the tag name or the tag name and text data if the element had the content model (PCDATA). Many users expressed frustration with the fact that when they asked for 'Flight eight', that is to say that they moved the current cursor to the eighth flight element, the response from the computer was simply 'Flight'. Many of the users wanted the computer to say 'Flight eight'. One user even suggested that when she asked for the 'Flight List' the response should be the price, destination, and airline of each flight in the list.

Despite the users' frustrations, this observation indicates that our customization language is imperative to allow users to easily specify their preferred method of rendering. By writing a simple set of customization rules using the customization language we have designed, the user could easily program the system to render each node in a more descriptive manner. A more extensive user study will evaluate the customization language in place by asking the users to write customization rules themselves.

6.2.4. System feedback

AXL attempts to provide feedback by using different sounds to convey different errors. In the initial instructions given to the users, they were told what each of the sounds meant, but most were unable to recall the meaning when they encountered the sounds while later traversing the document.

We believe that more extensive research must be done to determine which sounds are best suited for providing error feedback. In this case, one uniform beep would likely have been less confusing than the three different sounds the system emitted. However, three different sounds could be most useful if the sounds were carefully selected. Moreover, users expressed frustration in general with the feedback of the system in terms of communicating positioning within the document. Based upon this observation, we would like to undertake a more exhaustive study to examine how to aurally communicate a relative position within a document in an understandable way.

6.2.5. A help command

The only help facility provided by the system is the *command list* command which lists all possible commands at the given node including all schema-based commands as well as all Speech DOM commands. We made a couple of observations based upon the use of this command.

First, users expressed the desire for two separate help commands, one to hear the schema-based and another to hear the Speech DOM commands. Some wanted to hear only the schema-based commands, but were inundated with all of the possible commands for the system. Second, one user expressed frustration with the fact that the commands listed were all *possible* commands. She wanted to hear only the commands that were valid for the given node in the given subject tree. For example, if an optional node were absent in the subject tree, the command to access that node should not be given.

We can first conclude that a thorough help facility needs to be integrated into the system. Because the system is designed to be used by a person who cannot see the document or its structure, we need to examine how to best communicate possible navigation paths and how to access them using only auditory input and output.

However, we also anticipate that there is a steep learning curve related to AXL. If each user underwent a short period of AXL training, they would be less likely to need such a help facility. Moreover, we predict that more advanced users would be likely to use the Speech DOM level commands more often simply because they would not want to learn a new set of commands for every new schema.

We can conclude from this study that a more extensive study must be undertaken in order to fully analyze the behavior of the system and of the users. We predict that the results would change considerably if the users were given a practice document first. Moreover, we would like to examine the effects of using elements versus attributes in the structure of the document. We predict that attributes would be easier for a user to navigate since the structure is flatter.

7. Conclusions and future work

Current work on AXL focuses on integrating the system into a variety of applications. One important use of AXL is as the front-end application of the Aurora [7] project. Aurora seeks to make the Web more accessible to people with disabilities by using XML to simplify the services people access over the Web. By integrating AXL as the user interface, we can provide a comprehensive solution to allow print-disabled people easy access to Web data and services.

We are also investigating the integration of AXL and the Open eBook Standard [17]. Unlike the traditional 'book on tape' scenario, an AXL interface to an eBook document would give the user the opportunity to navigate within the book. This would eliminate the restriction posed by the serial nature of audio. Moreover, by integrating the multi-modal nature of the MakerFactory system, a user may choose to switch between listening, reading, and taking notes in her eBook.

Finally, in order to fully implement the concepts defined by XLink [34], we introduce the concept of *Speech Spaces*. If multiple Renderers exist simultaneously, the AXL Mediator classes attached to a given Renderer should only listen for user commands that fall within the scope of the given Renderer. By attaching a prefix command to any command in the grammar of a given AXL Mediator, only commands beginning with the given prefix will be processed.

XML promises to be one of the most popular ways to store and exchange data. It holds a host of benefits, not the least of which is allowing non-traditional access to the World Wide Web. As XML becomes more universal, there is a desperate need to develop tools that will allow all users to access and update XML data in traditional and non-traditional scenarios. This work provides an infrastructure to develop usable, customized ways to view and modify XML structures. Furthermore, by supporting the XLink standard, we enable users to navigate not only the current document, but to traverse across links as well. As the world becomes more and more computerized, our infrastructure can be used and extended to provide essential, non-traditional methods of human–computer interaction.

References

[1] M. Albers, Auditory cues for browsing, surfing, and navigating, in: Proc. of ICAD 1996 Conference, 1996.

[2] S. Barrass, Auditory Information Design, PhD Thesis, Department of Computer Science, Australian National University, 1997.

[3] J. Bosak, XML, Java, and the future of the Web http://metalab.unc.edu/pub/sun-info/standards/xml/why/xmlapps.htm.

[4] S. Brewster, Providing a Structured Method for Integrating Non-Speech audio into Human–Computer Interfaces, PhD Thesis, Department of Computer Science, University of York, August 1994.

[5] Document Object Model (DOM), Level 1 Specification, Version 1.0 http://www.w3.org/TR/REC-DOM-Level-1/.

[6] Extensible Markup Language (XML) 1.0 http://www.w3.org/TR/1998/REC-xml-19980210.

[7] A. Huang and N. Sundaresan, Aurora: Gateway to an accessible World Wide Web, IBM Technical Report, December 1999.

[8] F. James, Lessons from developing audio HTML interfaces, ASSETS 98, April 1998, pp. 15–17.

[9] F. James, Representing Structured Information in Audio Interfaces: A Framework for Selecting Audio Marking Techniques to Represent Document Structures, PhD Thesis, Department of Computer Science, Stanford University, Palo Alto, CA, June 1998.

[10] Java Beans Specification Document, ftp://ftp.javasoft.com/docs/beans/beans.101.pdf.

[11] Java Speech, http://java.sun.com/products/java-media/speech/.

[12] M. Krell and D. Cubranic, V-Lynx: bringing the World Wide Web to sight impaired users, ASSETS 96, Vancouver, BC, April 1998, pp. 23–26.

[13] L. Lamport, Latex: A Document Preparation System, Addison-Wesley, Reading, MA, 1986.

[14] Motorola introduces Voice Browser, http://www.speechtechmag.com/st16/motorola.htm December/January, 1999.

[15] Newspaper DTD, http://www.vervet.com/Tutorial/newspaper.dtd.

[16] T. Oogane and C. Asakawa, An interactive method for accessing tables in HTML, in: Proc. ASSETS'98, Marina del Rey, CA, April 1998, pp. 126–128.

[17] Open eBook Publication Structure 1.0, http://www.openebook.org/OEB1.html.

[18] S. Portigal, Auralization of Document Structure, MSc Thesis, Department of Computer Science, University of Guelph, Guelph, ON, 1994.

[19] Position paper — Standards for voice browsing, http://www.w3.org/Voice/1998/Workshop/ScottMcGlashan.html.

[20] T.V. Raman, Audio System for Technical Readings, PhD Thesis, Department of Computer Science, Cornell University, Ithaca, NY, May 1994.

[21] K. Sall, XML software guide: XML browsers, http://www.stars.com/Software/XML/browsers.html.

[22] SpeechML, http://www.alphaworks.ibm.com/formula/speechml.

[23] TalkML, http://www.w3.org/Voice/TalkML/.

[24] The next net craze: wireless access, http://www.businessweek.com/bwdaily/dnflash/feb1999/nf90211g.htm.

[25] The Voice: seeing with sound, http://ourworld.compuserve.com/homepages/Peter_Meijer.

[26] Voice recognition software: comparison and recommendations, http://www.io.com/~hcexres/tcm1603/acchtml/recomx7c.html.

[27] Voice browsers, http://www.w3.org/TR/NOTE-voice.
[28] Voice browsing the Web for information access, http://www.w3.org/Voice/1998/Workshop/RajeevAgarwal.html.
[29] VoiceXML, http://www.voicexml.org/.
[30] VoXML, http://www.voxml.org/.
[31] C.M. Wilson, Listen: A Data Sonification Toolkit, M.S. Thesis, Department of Computer Science, University of California at Santa Cruz, 1996.
[32] Wireless application protocol white paper, October 1999, http://www.wapforum.org/what/WAP_white_pages.pdf.
[33] Wireless application protocol wireless markup language specification version 1.2, November 1999, http://www.wapforum.org/what/technical/SPEC-WML-19991104.pdf.
[34] XML Linking Language (XLink), http://www.w3.org/TR/WD-xlink.
[35] XML Pointer Language (XPointer), http://www.w3.org/TR/1998/WD-xptr-19980303.
[36] M. Zajicek and C. Powell, Building a conceptual model of the World Wide Web for visually impaired users, in: Proc. Ergonomics Society, 1997, Annual Conference, Grantham.
[37] M. Zajicek, C. Powell and C. Reeves, A Web navigation tool for the blind, in: 3rd ACM/SIGAPH on Assistive Technologies, California, 1998.

Sami Rollins is a PhD student at the University of California at Santa Barbara in the Networking and Multimedia Systems Lab. She completed an industrial Master's thesis at the IBM Almaden Research Center on the topic of using XML to produce usable speech-based interfaces. Her previous XML related work includes a visual, schema-driven XML editing tool as well as XML to XML transcoding engine. She has also done work in the areas of global computing and multicast content scheduling. Her interests include HCI, Internet technologies, and networking.

Neel Sundaresan is a research manager of the eMerging Internet Technologies Department at the IBM Almaden Research Center. He has been with IBM since December 1995 and has pioneered several XML and Internet-related research projects. He was one of the chief architects of the Grand Central Station project at IBM Research for building XML-based search engines. He received his PhD in CS in 1995. He has done research and advanced technology work in the area of Compilers and Programming Languages, Parallel and Distributed Systems and Algorithms, Information Theory, Data Mining and Semi-structured Data, Speech Synthesis, Agent Systems, and Internet Tools and Technologies. He has over 30 research publications and has given several invited and refereed talks and tutorials at national and international conferences. He has been a member of the W3C standards effort.

Open hypermedia as user controlled meta data for the Web

Kaj Grønbæk [*,1], Lennert Sloth [1], Niels Olof Bouvin [1]

Department of Computer Science, Aarhus University, Åbogade 34, DK-8200 Aarhus, Denmark

Abstract

This paper introduces an approach to utilise open hypermedia structures such as links, annotations, collections and guided tours as meta data for Web resources. The paper introduces an XML based data format, called Open Hypermedia Interchange Format, OHIF, for such hypermedia structures. OHIF resembles XLink with respect to its representation of out-of-line links, but it goes beyond XLink with a more rich set of structuring mechanisms, including e.g. composites. Moreover OHIF includes an addressing mechanisms (LocSpecs) that goes beyond XPointer and URL in its ability to locate non-XML data segments. By means of the Webvise system, OHIF structures can be authored, imposed on Web pages, and finally linked on the Web as any ordinary Web resource. Following a link to an OHIF file automatically invokes a Webvise download of the meta data structures and the annotated Web content will be displayed in the browser. Moreover, the Webvise system provides support for users to create, manipulate, and share the OHIF structures together with custom made Web pages and MS Office 2000 documents on WebDAV servers. These Webvise facilities goes beyond earlier open hypermedia systems in that it now allows fully distributed open hypermedia linking between Web pages and WebDAV aware desktop applications. The paper describes the OHIF format and demonstrates how the Webvise system handles OHIF. Finally, it argues for better support for handling user controlled meta data, e.g. support for linking in non-XML data, integration of external linking in the Web infrastructure, and collaboration support for external structures and meta-data.

Keywords: Open hypermedia; XML; Meta data; Semantic Web; WebDAV; XLink

1. Introduction

Recently the notion of meta data has received a lot of attention in relation to the World Wide Web [1], through the introduction of standards such as XML [4] and RDF [26]. Meta data is seen as a potential means to create the 'Semantic Web' as called for by Tim Berners-Lee in his WWW8 keynote. Services such as Alexa and the Netscape 'What's related?' predates RDF. These meta data services are mainly based on author supplied or automatic generated meta data. This paper goes beyond these services and introduces a mechanism also for users or groups of users to control and generate their own meta data and structures for specific purposes.

In the digital library domain, Marshall [20] has argued that user generated annotations and structures are useful meta data for other users of a digital library collection who need to pursue research in the same territory as other colleagues have covered earlier. The Webvise system and the OHIF format discussed in this paper are aimed at supporting this kind of meta data creation by end users. The principles

* Corresponding author.
[1] E-mail: {kgronbak,les,n.o.bouvin}@daimi.au.dk

and the approach is inherited from Open Hypermedia System research.

Open Hypermedia Systems research [6,10,15, 23–25] has been working since the early 1990s on providing general support for user controlled annotations and structuring which can be kept separate to the documents containing the information content. Recently, open hypermedia systems have been developed with support for annotating and structuring Web content [3,5,12,13,17,21].

This paper describes how the Webvise [13] open hypermedia system has been extended to act as a tool for users to generate and control meta data in an XML format which can be distributed on the Web similar to the documents containing the base information. The meta data format is an XML encoding of a data model agreed upon in the Open Hypermedia Systems Working Group [25]. This in turn comes from earlier work on developing interchange formats for general hypermedia structures. Interchange formats have been a research and standardisation focus for many individual types of media, such as text and video. Within the area of hypermedia, work on interchange mainly focus on the hypermedia structures and not the contents per se. The Dexter model [14] made a proposal for a SGML-family interchange format for hypermedia structures. This proposal was used e.g. to interchange hypertexts between two quite different hypermedia systems KMS and Intermedia [18]. Later the HyTime standard [7] was introduced as a general format to cover hypermedia structures as well as synchronisation mechanisms for time based content. However, these formats have not been supported by general tools on the Web yet and they have thus not been put into widespread use. The upcoming Xlink language, however, represents a simpler and easier implementable version of HyTime-like linking mechanisms.

The Open Hypermedia Interchange Format (OHIF) that we propose in this paper is taking advantage of XML and it is thus simpler and easier to build tools for than HyTime. Currently we have two prototypes Webvise [13] and Arakne [2] that can read and generate the format. Currently the Webvise prototype can be downloaded for trial from **http://www.cit.dk/coconut** under 'Prototypes'.

Finally, we have addressed the issue of supporting collaboration on meta data and open hypermedia structures by building WebDAV [30] support into our Open Hypermedia client applications. Webvise is thus able to open and save meta data files to WebDAV servers, it takes and releases locks such that collaborating users are prevented from lost updates on the meta data and content files that are shared on the WebDAV server.

The rest of the paper is organised as follows. Section 2 provides a brief overview of current work on supporting meta data for the Web. Section 3 introduces open hypermedia structures and the OHIF format as meta data for the Web. Section 4 describes the kind of support for user controlled meta data that is provided by the Webvise system. Section 5 describes the WebDAV based collaboration support for meta data provided by Webvise. Section 6 concludes the paper.

2. Current meta data support on the Web

The amount of raw data on the Web has reached a point, where it has become difficult to find pages precisely relevant to a given topic. As it stands, the Web can be compared to a giant library with no index, no catalogue, and no librarian. Sophisticated search engines abound, but these face many problems:

- The sheer size of the Web makes it very difficult to maintain a complete and up to date index;
- Keyword spamming is quite common (i.e. the practice of manipulating a Web page's ranking in a query result by e.g. inserting superfluous keywords to fool search engines);
- Most searches result in (many) pages unrelated to the topic the user is interested in.

A natural consequence has been the proliferation of Web sites that categorise other Web sites (e.g. `www.yahoo.com` and `www.about.com`). These Web sites essentially provide information about information, or meta data. This is however mainly human readable information, difficult for computers to handle and analyse.

Meta data can take many forms. It can be information about the author of some pages, a classification of the information found on the page, the relationship between these pages and other pages, a ranking of the pages in some index, or relations between indices. A crucial element of meaningful meta data is a clear and widely adhered to standard. An example of a widely used classification standard found in libraries is the Dewey Decimal Code. A system for bibliographic information often cited in conjunction with RDF is the **Dublin Core** [2].

2.1. The Resource Description Framework (RDF) and the emergence of meta data on the Web

RDF [26] is a World Wide Web Consortium Recommendation for the description of meta data relating to data found on the Web (or more precisely anything that can be addressed with a URI). Meta data adhering to the RDF standard is usually encoded in XML, and consists generally of a series of statements. Statements are triplets of a resource (addressed with a URI), a property type (an attribute of the resource, such as 'author'), and a value (such as 'John Doe'). Statements can be resources or values for other statements. By using XML Name Spaces it is possible to mix different meta data standards in a statement.

While XML is but one representation of RDF (RDF can also be represented as graphs or 3-tuples), meta data is usually distributed as XML files. To support inter-operation between related meta data formats, name spaces as well as schemas are utilised. Protocols such as querying/searching are currently not supported, though listed as possible future activities by the RDF interest group. RDF is still a new technology and has not yet become widespread in use. One question that remains is this: who will author the meta data? Meta data is of enormous importance in the library world, where there is a well-established culture regarding the creation of meta data, and where meta data (such as an index card) can be relied on. Not so on the Web, where the `<meta>` header tag introduced in HTML has become widely misused through keyword spamming, rendering the information highly unreliable. This is most unfortunate, but a reality of the Web. Meta data is as such no silver bullet for the Web's current information overload. A likely development will be the development of Web sites concentrating on specific subject domains, within which meta data can be meaningfully defined and relied on by users, thus establishing a community of use.

[2] http://purl.oclc.org/dc

2.2. RDF and open hypermedia

RDF and (open) hypermedia are both ways of describing relations between entities. Both are externally stored outside the documents, they reflect upon, and both provide a reader with an 'added value' or a structuring mechanism. A major distinction between RDF and open hypermedia is the addressing scheme used. RDF resources are identified by a URI. The advantage is that URI is very well supported on the Web. The disadvantage is that it severely limits what can be addressed and how. URI is a coarse grained addressing scheme limited to whole documents or predefined (named) regions within. Through the use of LocSpecs [9] in open hypermedia, arbitrary selections can be addressed. This makes it easier to create a relationship (e.g. a link) between two or more statements in different documents of diverse media types. Conceivably RDF could be combined with addressing schemes such as XPointer to provide a finer granularity.

RDF and open hypermedia can work well in conjunction with each other, as they address different needs. RDF is very well-suited for making general statements about documents and their relationship to other documents. Open hypermedia on the other hand is a general structuring mechanism, and can be used to express explicit relationships between multiple statements in documents of arbitrary types.

2.3. XLink, XPointer, and XPath

Linking to and from XML documents is to be supported through the use of XLink [32] (used to describe links), XPointer [34] (used to identify regions in XML documents to link to and from), and XPath [33] (used by XPointer to identify regions in XML documents using a hierarchical scheme). As of this writing (29/2/2000) XPath 1.0 is recommended by the W3C, XLink is pending 'Last Call' for comments, and XPointer has passed the 'Last Call' for comments.

XLink is a general tool to describe navigational hypermedia, and to allow expressions of navigational hypermedia to be inserted into XML documents. While the main application of XLink is expected to be linking *in* XML documents, the standard itself is not limited to address solely XML locations, provided that appropriate locators have been defined. XLink can support the linking currently found on the Web (e.g. unidirectional 1-ary untyped links), as well as bi-directional *n*-ary typed links. Links can be stored externally ('out-of-line') of the documents, they address, or they can be in-line (as with HTML documents). Traversal of a link may result in replacing the document currently viewed (as is the standard behaviour in the context of HTML), or by inserting the target for the link in the viewed document. The traversal may be initiated by the user (e.g. by clicking on a link), or at the time of document retrieval.

XPointer is used to identify regions of interest in XML documents. XPointer allows for selection based on ids, hierarchical structure (from XPath), or an arbitrary user selection (e.g. selecting a string in the rendered XML document). This is a quite sophisticated addressing scheme that should cover most uses. XPointer can address arbitrary XML documents, but the explicit support for XPointer can also be added to a DTD. A given region may be identified using several locators, which improves reliability, as one locator might fail after a document has been edited.

XLink is designed for navigational hypermedia, which has long been the classic hypermedia application. While linking is certainly still very important in hypermedia, new structuring mechanisms have been introduced which cannot easily (or at all) be described in terms of links. This goes for composites, guided tours, spatial, or taxonomic hypermedia [24].

XLink/XPointer is more closely related to open hypermedia than is RDF. On the whole these standards address similar goals and employ similar means to achieve this. One major difference is the integration of third party applications, that is the core of open hypermedia [22]. Open hypermedia is explicit about this support, and much effort has been done in the open hypermedia community to integrate third party applications with open hypermedia systems. While XLink is general in the sense that locators can be (and have been) created to allow linking into non XML documents, the specification is vague on the behaviour of the applications that support these document types. Not all applications can be expected to be conforming to XLink, and how XLink works with such applications remains unclear.

2.4. Alexa/What's Related

A widely used service on the Web is the one provided by Alexa. Alexa is available as a stand alone tool as well as integrated with several Web browsers. By clicking a 'What's Related' button (the exact invocation depends on the Web browser) users are presented with Web sites related to the one currently shown. The result is generated on basis of the collective browsing habits of people using Alexa, which is stored centrally. Whereas the model behind open hypermedia, RDF, and XLink/XPointer is based on humans asserting relationships between entities, Alexa functions solely by relying on the relevance between consecutively visited Web sites. In practice the authors have found this to work quite well, especially for high profile Web sites. With less popular Web sites the success rate seems to be lower, which should be expected, as the 'error rate' (users consecutively visiting Web sites not related to each other) would be more significant. As a tool Alexa is well suited to give suggestions to sites that might be of interest. However as the relationship between pages is wholly statistical rather than semantic, it is of little help, when searching for an answer to a specific question. Furthermore the individual user has little control over which pages are presented. Alexa works well in conjunction with the above described technologies as a tool for gathering Web sites relevant for the task at hand; Web sites that must later be sorted by a human. In this manner Alexa is similar in use to ordinary search engines. By the nature of how it works, Alexa is restricted to relate whole Web pages to each other, which is also a marked difference between it and open hypermedia/RDF/XLink/XPointer.

2.5. Flyswat

A recent development is the **Flyswat** service [3]. The Flyswat service (through the use of an ActiveX component) highlights keywords on Web pages, so that a click on the keywords can lead to a definition of the word, the Web site associated with the term, or a page where the item may be purchased. The effectiveness of Flyswat greatly depends on whether

[3] http://www.flyswat.com

a given subject is covered by the Flyswat company or any of the associated partners. There does not seem to be any possibility of submitting links or keywords to the service, outside of becoming an associated partner with Flyswat. Thus, the system does not provide for *user* controlled meta data or hypermedia functionality.

3. Open hypermedia structures as meta data

As mentioned in the introduction, we consider relationships and annotations made by users of Web resources as potential useful meta data for other collaborating users or for the general public. An example of user annotations as meta data are the reviews made by readers of books from Amazon.com, and an example of automatically generated meta data relationships is the information that "buyers of this book also bought ... ". Amazon.com is an example of a site that provides this specific service for its visitors, based on opening up their site for adding and computing such meta data relationships.

Another example of the need for user controlled meta data is in the areas of digital libraries [19,20], where readers of a particular resource may benefit from the fact that another reader has read the material and commented on it with marginalia, similar to what is possible in paper books.

Instead of having every Web site implementing their own forms and databases for user generated meta data, we are proposing a general open hypermedia mechanism that can provide support for such meta data for arbitrary Web sites, thus reducing the cost of developing Web sites that enables dynamic exchange of information among its users.

In the following sections we will describe a meta data format and tools to help users (collaboratively) to generate and control meta data, including annotations and relationships.

3.1. The basic open hypermedia data model

In the OHS community a standard data model for open hypermedia structures has been proposed [8]. An outline of the currently agreed upon OHSWG navigational data model is depicted in Fig. 1.

From this data model, an XML DTD [4] is derived, which in turn allows OHS systems to use standard XML parsers to load the structures into OHSs, which are compliant with the standardised data model. The derived data format is called OHIF, and excerpts of the XML are shown below. Each OHIF file represents a 'context' object of the data model. A context is an (indexed) collection of other hypermedia objects. An example of a node is shown in Table 1.

OHIF links are general many-to-many relationships as supported first in the Dexter model [14] and HyTime [7]. The OHIF link is thus a collection of endpoints as shown in Table 2.

[4] See http://www.daimi.au.dk/~les/ohif/ohif.dtd

Table 1
Example of an OHIF 'node' element

```
<NODE id="ariel.xserver.2" type="NODE"
name="DOM">
   <DESCRIPTIONSET>
      <DESCRIPTION name="default">
         <VALUE>DOM Specifications</VALUE>
      </DESCRIPTION>
   </DESCRIPTIONSET>
   <CHARACTERISTICSSET></CHARACTERISTICSSET>
   <COMPUTATIONID></COMPUTATIONID>
   <CONTENTSPEC>
      <URL>http://www.w3.org/TR/REC-DOM-level-1/</URL>
      <CONTENTS></CONTENTS>
      <MIMETYPE>Text/HTML</MIMETYPE>
   </CONTENTSPEC>
</NODE>
```

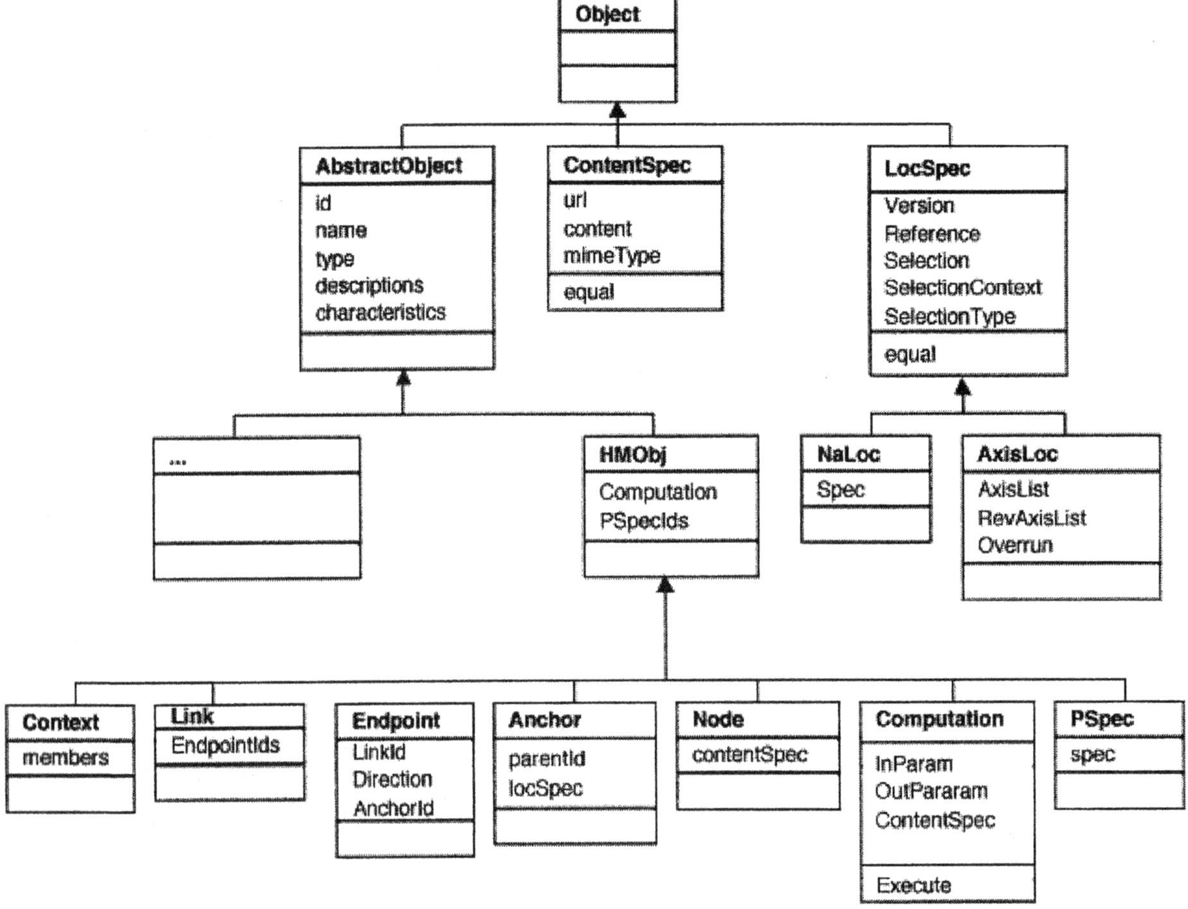

Fig. 1. Outline of OHSWG navigational data model.

Table 2
An example of an OHIF 'link' element

```
<LINK id=ariel.xserver.6 type="LINK" name="DOM relationships">
   <DESCRIPTIONSET>
      <DESCRIPTION name="default">
         <VALUE>DOM specifications</VALUE>
   </DESCRIPTIONSET>
   <CHARACTERISTICSSET></CHARACTERISTICSSET>
   <COMPUTATIONID></COMPUTATIONID>
   <ENDPOINTIDSET>
      <ID>xsite.xserver.10</ID>
      <ID>xsite.xserver.14</ID>
      <ID>xsite.xserver.20</ID>
   </ENDPOINTIDSET>
</LINK>
```

Table 3
An example of an endpoint element. This endpoint is referenced by a link with id `xsite.xserver.3`, its presentation specification is stored a `pspec` with id `xsite.xserver.7` and the location specification is stored an anchor with id `xsite.xserver.10`

```
<ENDPOINT id="ariel.xserver.9" type="ENDPOINT" name="Professor"
          linkid="xsite.xserver.3" anchorid="xsite.xserver.10"
          direction="BIDIRECTIONAL">
   <PSPECIDSET>
      <ID>xsite.xserver.7</ID>
   </PSPECIDSET>
</ENDPOINT>
```

Table 4
An example of an 'anchor' element. The anchor contains location information in a 'locspec' element. This anchor also contains the id of the shown in Table 5. The pspec designates this anchor to be presented as an annotation anchor

```
<ANCHOR id="xsite.xserver.6" type="ANCHOR" name="Information" >
   <CHARACTERISTICSSET>
      <CHARAC name="userNote">
         <VALUESET>
            <VALUE>This mobile phone is the...</VALUE>
         </VALUESET>
      </CHARAC>
   </CHARACTERISTICSSET>
   <PSPECIDSET>
      <ID>xsite.xserver.5</ID>
   </PSPECIDSET>
   <SIMPLELOC>
      <SELECTION>Information</SELECTION>
      <SELECTIONCONTEXT>Information about the Coconut project</SELECTIONCONTEXT>
   </SIMPLELOC>
</ANCHOR>
```

The OHIF link element resembles links in the upcoming XLink specification [32], and when the XLink standard is stable we may consider simply using the XLink language and name spaces for specifying the linking part of the OHIF format. However, we need support for other structuring mechanisms such as composites [14] like collections and guided tours to get the power needed to express more elaborate hypermedia structures. With respect to locating and addressing we need to go beyond the URL and XPointer specs and get support for LocSpecs to locate fragments of arbitrary non-XML based media as proposed in [9].

Endpoints are responsible for addressing the anchor which is responsible for keeping the LocSpec for a specific location inside a node's content. But endpoints also hold a presentation specification (PSpec) which allow a link to determine how the endpoint node should be presented when arrived at via this link. The PSpec may for example impose a specific stylesheet on the document as a side effect of following the link. Endpoints also hold a direction attribute, with information about whether the endpoint is considered a source, a destination or both (Table 3).

The anchor element inlines the LocSpec to locate the actual part of a node's content which constitute a source or a destination for the link (Tables 4 and 5).

Table 5
An example of a 'pspec' element. This is a pspec for an annotation anchor

```
<PSPEC id="xsite.xserver.5" type="PSPEC">
   <CHARACTERISTICSSET>
      <CHARAC name="userNoteKind">
         <VALUESET>
            <VALUE>Popup</VALUE>
         </VALUESET>
      </CHARAC>
   </CHARACTERISTICSSET>
</PSPEC>
```

Table 6
An example of a small guided tour with five vertices and two edges, as well as an example of an 'edge' element. Besides being a HMObject an edge contains the ids of the two vertices it is connecting

```
<GUIDEDTOUR id="xsite.xserver"
            type="GUIDEDTOUR"
            name="Mobile computing">
   <COMPREFIDSET>
      <ID>xsite.xserver.8</ID>
      <ID>xsite.xserver.12</ID>
      <ID>xsite.xserver.6</ID>
      <ID>xsite.xserver.10</ID>
      <ID>xsite.xserver.4</ID>
   </COMPREFIDSET>
   <EDGEIDSET>
      <ID>xsite.xserver.14</ID>
      <ID>xsite.xserver.13</ID>
   </EDGEIDSET>
</GUIDEDTOUR>
```

```
<EDGE id="xsite.xserver.14"
      type="EDGE"
      originid="xsite.xserver.10"
      destinationid="xsite.xserver.12">
</EDGE>
```

The anchor and pspec shown above implement annotations, similar to **ThirdVoice**[5] and ComMentor [27] in a specific location inside a Web document [13].

The above elements are included in the basic OHSWG data model for open hypermedia. However, the users of our prototypes are requiring several structuring mechanisms that are not yet covered in the data model. But the OHSWG data model has on purpose been specified as an extensible model, where new structures may be added without disturbing the standardised handling of the basic elements. In the next section we will show a few examples on such extensions, which have already been implemented on top of the basic model.

3.2. Example of an extension to the Core OHSWG Data model

Our open hypermedia systems, Webvise and Arakne, both support guided tours similar to the mechanisms described by [17,29]. This mechanism is not included in the basic open hypermedia data model, but since the data model is extensible, we can add this specialised data model element without interfering with the general and common data model elements. Extending the XML based DTD with this new data element will thus just cause the systems not supporting the data element to skip it in the XML parse procedure.

Table 6 shows an example of such an OHIF extension namely a guided tour, which is a composite representing a graph of nodes.

Finally, a first attempt has been made on providing semantic types for open hypermedia links which in turn can bring us closer to what Tim Berners-Lee called the 'Semantic Web' in his WWW8 keynote. The type mechanism is inspired by the hypermedia type system introduced by Trigg in his TextNet system [28]. When introducing types on links and other hypermedia objects, the need for a full-blown hierarchical type system is revealed, and it thus requires an XML representation in it self. Such a type system and an XML representation has been proposed in [16], and it is illustrated in Table 7. It has, however, not been implemented in OHIF yet.

Having introduced the OHIF meta data model and its XML format, we will in the next section illustrate how it can be utilized to provide support for users to generate, control, and manipulate meta data for arbitrary Web resources.

4. Support for open hypermedia meta data

Webvise is an application that augments Microsoft Internet Explorer with open hypermedia services. It provides structures such as contexts, links,

[5] http://www.thirdvoice.com

Table 7
Representing a hierarchical link type system as proposed by Hansen et al. [15]

```
<LINKTYPES>
   <LINKTYPE typeid="0" typename="Link Type">
      <TYPEATTRIBUTES>
         <ATTRNAME>noOfUsages</ATTRNAME>
         <ATTRVALUE>0</ATTRVALUE>
      </TYPEATTRIBUTES>
      <SUPERTYPES></SUPERTYPES>
   </LINKTYPE>
   <LINKTYPE typeid="1" typename="Quality of Source">
      <TYPEATTRIBUTES>
         <ATTRNAME>Why</ATTRNAME>
         <ATTRVALUE></ATTRVALUE>
      </TYPEATTRIBUTES>
      <SUPERTYPES>
         <TYPEID>0</TYPEID>
      </SUPERTYPES>
   </LINKTYPE>
</LINKTYPES>
```

annotations and guided tours that are stored and read from OHIF files. An OHIF file represents a context and when an OHIF file is loaded by Webvise, links and annotations are dynamically merged into existing HTML pages, and the guided tours can be displayed in graphical browsers. The Webvise service consists of a structure server and a client application. See [13] sections 3 and 4 for details about Webvise. In the following section we will describe different methods for transferring OHIF files over the Internet and for loading them into Webvise, which in turn imposes the OHIF structures on existing HTML pages.

4.1. The Webvise approach

The structures stored in a given OHIF file can be applied by loading the file into Webvise. If the OHIF file is stored locally the user can open the file using a traditional file dialogue in Webvise. If the file is stored on a HTTP server the user can open the file by clicking a URL in a Web page or by typing the URL in the address field of the Web browser. When navigating to an OHIF file residing on a HTTP server using Microsoft Internet Explorer, a handler, either a stand alone application, an ActiveX object or a plug-in, must be registered to handle the file. Only the use of stand alone applications and ActiveX objects are discussed here.

If the protocol of the URL is HTTP the action taken by Internet Explorer depends on what kind of handler that is associated with the OHIF file type. If the handler is an application, Internet Explorer downloads the OHIF file and then invokes the application with the path to the downloaded file. This might be a problem if the structure server (see [13]) used by the application handler is not running locally, since it is the structure server that must parse the OHIF file and build the open hypermedia structures and this would require that the OHIF file would be sent over the wire one more time.

One solution to this problem is to define another file type, e.g. OHL (open hypermedia locator) that only contains the URL of the 'real' OHIF file and then use URLs to OHL files instead. The handler application would then be able to send only the URL of the OHIF file to the structure server instead of the whole content of the file. This would be similar to the approach taken by **Real Media** [6], with their .ram files.

Another solution is to define a new URL protocol and then register the handler application to this protocol. This will make Internet Explorer omit downloading the file and invoke the handler application with the URL. This is one of the approaches supported by Webvise, which registers the OHTP

[6] http://www.real.com

Table 8
An example of an OHTP link embedded in a standard HTML page. 'confirmDefault' is a Java script that informs the user that he/she must have Webvise installed to be able to use the link

```
<A onclick="return confirmDefault()"
    HREF="ohtp://www.daimi.au.dk/~les/ohiffiles/www9/xanadu.ohif ">Xanadu.</A>
```

protocol when installed. An example of how to use the OHTP protocol is shown in Table 8.

A third possibility is to use an ActiveX object (an In-Proc Server) as handler. Registering the ActiveX object as the default player for the OHIF MIME type can do this. Using this approach Internet Explorer loads the ActiveX object and the URL is passed to the ActiveX object. This method is used by Webvise to handle the situations where the protocol of the URL is HTTP. The ActiveX object used in the current implementation does not have a user-interface and simply passes the URL on to the Webvise application. However, we do plan to add a user-interface and (some of) the open hypermedia functionality found in Webvise to the ActiveX object. This will allow a tighter integration with Internet Explorer and remove the need for a stand alone handler application.

Regardless of the method used to load the OHIF file, the result is that the structures stored in the OHIF file are used to augment the original HTML pages that they refer to. Links and annotations are dynamically merged into existing HTML Web pages, i.e. the locations of links and annotations are decorated similar to how ordinary Web links are shown, but with distinct colours. Composites such as guided tours and collections are displayed in graphical browsers residing in the Webvise application. The merge of meta data and content is illustrated in Fig. 2.

The Webvise approach demonstrates how meta data and out-of-line hypermedia structures can be integrated with ordinary Web content in a seamless manner, allowing meta data and structures to become first class citizens on the Web. The fact that the OHIF format is in XML also opens up for possibilities for letting the Web browsers display and utilise the data directly by means of XSL and transformations to dynamic HTML, thus not requiring a helper application for plain read access.

5. Collaborating on open hypermedia meta data

When a group of users are doing research on a common subject area they may wish to share their meta data among the group and collaboratively construct a common set of meta data for the subject area. Previous research in open hypermedia has proposed three layered architectures with servers being responsible for handling concurrency control, access control and event notifications on hyperme-

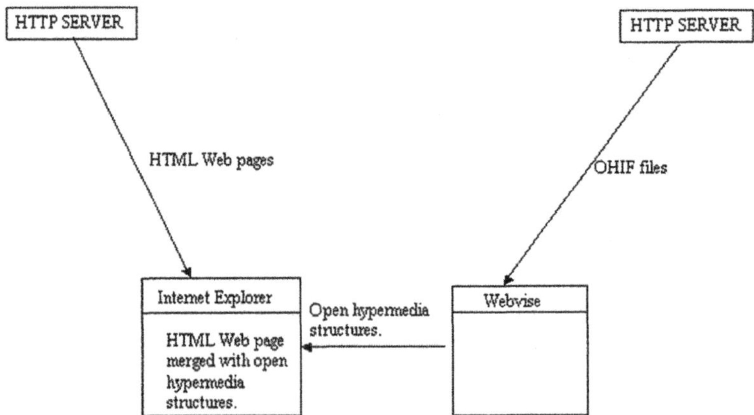

Fig. 2. HTML Web pages are augmented with open hypermedia structures stored externally from the Web pages in OHIF files.

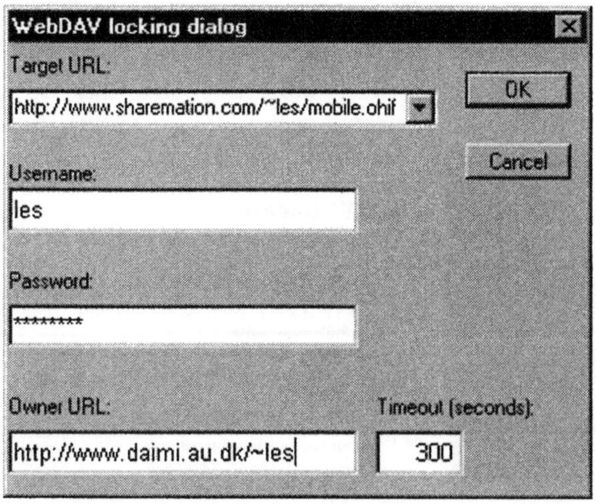

Fig. 3. The dialogue used in Webvise to lock an OHIF file on a WebDAV server. `http://www.sharemation.com/~les/demo1.ohif` is the file on which the user *les* requests a lock. The owner resource `http://www.daimi.au.dk/~les` should contain contact information for the owner of the lock. The timeout field indicates the number of seconds after which the WebDAV server automatically should remove the lock.

dia objects at runtime [11,31]. However, to support a simpler and less tightly coupled collaboration on open hypermedia structures via the World Wide Web, WebDAV client support has been added to Webvise. This enables Webvise to offer controlled sharing of OHIF files. In this section we describe the WebDAV features currently available in Webvise.

Since each OHIF file contains one context, contexts represent the level of granularity at which open hypermedia structures can be shared. The WebDAV client features implemented in Webvise are: LOCK, UNLOCK and retrieval of the `lockdiscovery` property via the PROPFIND method. Standard HTTP PUT and GET are also supported. If the user has a lock on a resource PUT requests on that resource will contain the `locktoken` in an `If`header.

To collaborate on a given context a user of Webvise must first request a lock on the OHIF file from the WebDAV compliant server on which the file is stored. The dialogue used to lock the file is depicted in Fig. 3.

If the request for the lock is successful the file is downloaded. The context can now be modified using the usual editing facilities in Webvise and at any time the user can save the context and then upload it to the WebDAV server (these operations may be bundled into a compound operation). Having uploaded the modified context the user can choose to remove the lock on the OHIF file or he/she can continue to edit the context and then perhaps upload the context again. This way the user can take a long-term lock on a context and publish changes to the context in several smaller steps.

If it is not possible to obtain a lock on a given context, the context can still be downloaded and modified. To publish the modified context it is necessary however, to store it under a different name. When WebDAV servers that support versioning become available it should be possible to store the context under the same name but as a new version.

When taking a lock users are encouraged to supply a URL to a Web page that contains contact information to enable other users to get in contact with the lock owner. Webvise users can inquire the WebDAV server for lock information to get this information.

Having integrated WebDAV support in Webvise, makes it possible to support distributed maintenance of the meta data and structure files, as well as accompanying files written in applications supporting WebDAV, e.g. Microsoft Office 2000. Apart from linking into Web pages, Webvise also support linking to and from Microsoft Word and Excel. Compared to earlier Open Hypermedia integrations with MS Office developed in Microcosm [15] and Devise Hypermedia [10] it is now for the first time possible to have fully distributed Open Hypermedia linking between MS Office documents and Web documents since we can get global URLs for the MS Office documents on the WebDAV servers (see Fig. 4). Earlier integrations only worked locally on networks that could mount shared drives and use ordinary local filesystem addressing schemes. Thus the spreading of WebDAV to Web servers world wide is an important step to achieve fully distributed open hypermedia linking between Web documents and arbitrary WebDAV aware applications.

6. Conclusion

This paper has proposed an XML based format for open hypermedia structures to be utilised for sup-

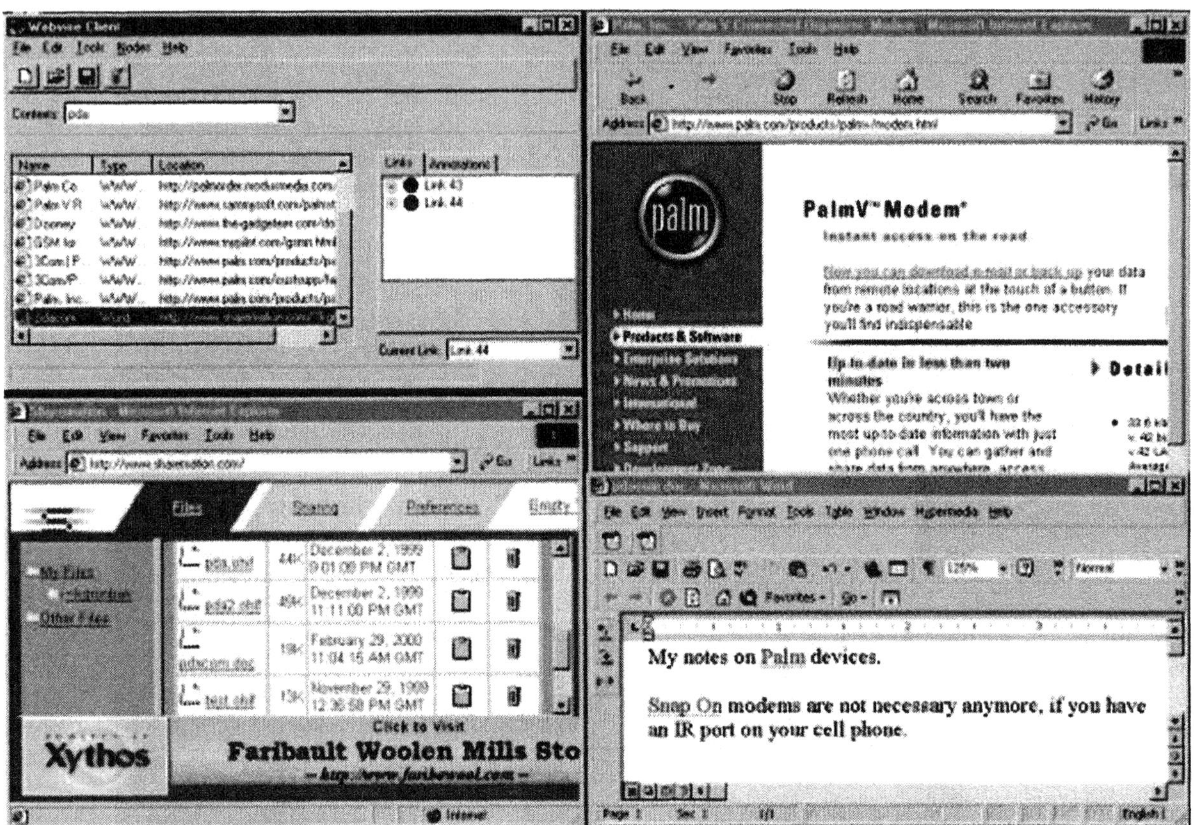

Fig. 4. A scenario, where Webvise is used by a group of users with accounts on Sharemation to link and annotate Web materials and Word files about Palm devises. The Word and OHIF files are shared on a Sharemation account, and they provide meta data for Web pages such as relevant product documentation and FAQs.

porting user controlled meta data and hypermedia structures on the Web. Moreover, it has proposed to transfer the meta data format with a new protocol prefix called 'OHTP', which can be used to start transfer of meta data (OHIF files). The transfer can be the responsibility of the Web browser per se, or a separate helper application. Currently two available helper applications Webvise and Arakne supports this OHIF format and protocol. OHIF covers some of the same territory as the proposed XLink language and the XPointer standard, but OHIF contains locating facilities for arbitrary non-XML data and a more rich set of structuring mechanisms, including composites, such as guided tours, and it would require extensions of the scope of the XLink language and XPointer to cover the full power of OHIF. It is our hope that the OHIF structuring and addressing mechanisms will become a new supplementary standard, or alternatively that the emerging standards will adopt the ideas and incorporate the mechanisms.

Acknowledgements

This project is supported by CIT — The Danish national centre for IT research grant no. 123.2 (COCONUT.2). Thanks to our colleagues in the COCONUT.2 project for their contributions to the work.

References

[1] T. Berners-Lee, R. Cailliau, J.-F. Groff and B. Pollerman, World-Wide Web: the information universe, Electron. Network. Res. Appl. Policy 1 (2) (1992).

[2] N.O. Bouvin, Unifying strategies for Web augmenting, in:

Proc. of Hypertext '99 — The Tenth ACM Conference on Hypertext and Hypermedia, Darmstadt, Germany, ACM, New York, 1999, pp. 91-100.

[3] N.O. Bouvin and R. Schade, Integrating temporal media and open hypermedia on the World Wide Web, in: Proc. of the 8th International World Wide Web Conference, Toronto, Canada, Elsevier, Amsterdam, 1999, pp. 375–387.

[4] T. Bray, J. Paoli and C.M. Sperberg-McQueen, Extensible Markup Language (XML) 1.0, W3C Recommendation 10-February-1998, http://www.w3.org/TR/1998/REC-xml-19980210

[5] L. Carr et al., The distributed link service: a tool for publishers, authors and readers, in: Fourth International World Wide Web Conference: The Web Revolution, Boston, MA, 1995.

[6] H. Davis, A. Lewis and A. Rizk, OHP: A draft proposal for a standard open hypermedia protocol, in: 2nd Workshop on Open Hypermedia Systems, Washington, DC, University of California, Irvine, 1996, pp. 27–53.

[7] S.J. DeRose and D.G. Durand, Making Hypermedia Work: A User's Guide to HyTime, Kluwer, Boston, 1994.

[8] K. Grønbæk, OHS interoperability — issues beyond the protocol, in: Proc. of OHS Workshop 4.0 held at Hypertext '98, Pittsburgh, June 20–24, 1998.

[9] K. Grønbæk and R.H. Trigg, Toward a Dexter-based model for open hypermedia: unifying embedded references and link objects, in: Hypertext '96 — Seventh ACM Conference on Hypertext, Washington, DC, ACM, New York, 1996.

[10] K. Grønbæk and R.H. Trigg, From Web to Workplace: Designing Open Hypermedia Systems, MIT Press, Boston, MA, 1999, 424 pp.

[11] K. Grønbæk, J. Hem, O.L. Madsen and L. Sloth, Cooperative hypermedia systems: a Dexter-based architecture, Commun. ACM 37 (2) (1994) 64–75.

[12] K. Grønbæk, N.O. Bouvin and L. Sloth, Designing Dexter-based hypermedia services for the World Wide Web, in: Proc. of Hypertext 97, Southampton, ACM, New York, 1997.

[13] K. Grønbæk, L. Sloth and P. Ørbæk, Webvise: Browser and Proxy support for open hypermedia structuring mechanisms on the WWW, in: Proc. of The Eighth International World Wide Web Conference, Toronto, Canada, Elsevier, Amsterdam, 1999, pp. 253–267,

[14] F. Halasz and M. Schwartz, The Dexter hypertext reference model, Commun. ACM 37 (2) (1994) 30–39.

[15] W. Hall, H. Davis and G. Hutchings, Rethinking Hypermedia: The Microcosm Approach, Kluwer, Boston, 1996.

[16] K.M. Hansen, C. Yndigegn and K. Grønbæk, Dynamic use of digital library material — supporting users with typed links in open hypermedia, in: Proc. of the European Conference on Digital Libraries, Paris, France, 1999, Springer Lecture Notes in Computer Science no. 1696, pp. 254–273.

[17] J. Jühne, A.T. Jensen and K. Grønbæk, Ariadne: a Java-based guided tour system for the WorldWide Web, in: Proc. of The Seventh International World Wide Web Conference (WWW7), Brisbane, Queensland, Australia, Elsevier, Amsterdam, 1998.

[18] R. Killough and J. Leggett, Hypertext interchange with the Dexter model: Intermedia to KMS, TAMU-HRL 90-002, Hypertext Research Lab., Texas A & M University, August 1990.

[19] C.C. Marshall, Annotation: from paper books to the digital library DL '97, in: Proc. of the 2nd ACM International Conference on Digital Libraries, Philadelphia, PA, ACM, New York, 1997, pp. 131–140.

[20] C.C. Marshall, Making metadata: a study of metadata creation for a mixed physical–digital collection DL '98, in: Proc. of the 3rd ACM International Conference on Digital Libraries, Pittsburgh, PA, 1998, pp. 162–171.

[21] H. Maurer, Hyperwave — The Next Generation Web Solution, Addison-Wesley, Harlow, UK, 1996.

[22] N. Meyrowitz, The missing link: why we're all doing hypertext wrong, in: E. Barrett (Ed.), The Society of Text: Hypertext, Hypermedia and the Social Construction of Information, MIT Press, Cambridge, MA, 1989, pp. 107–114.

[23] P.J. Nürnberg, J. Leggett, E.R. Schneider and J.L. Schnase, Hypermedia operating systems: a new paradigm for computing, in: Seventh ACM Conference on Hypertext — Hypertext '96, Washington, DC, ACM, New York, 1996.

[24] P.J. Nürnberg, J. Leggett and E.R. Schneider, As we should have thought, in: Proc. of the Hypertext '97 Conference, Southampton, UK, ACM, New York, 1997.

[25] OHSWG, Open Hypermedia Systems Working Group WWW site, 1998, http://www.ohswg.org/.

[26] Resource Description Framework (RDF), model and syntax specification, W3C Recommendation 22 February 1999, http://www.w3.org/TR/REC-rdf-syntax/.

[27] M. Röscheisen, C. Mogensen and T. Winograd, Shared Web annotations as a platform for third-party value-added information providers: architecture, protocols, and usage examples (Technical Report CSDTR/DLTR), Stanford University, Stanford Integrated Digital Library Project, Computer Science Dept.

[28] R.H. Trigg, A network-based approach to text handling for the online scientific community, Ph.D. thesis, University of Maryland, TR-1346, 1983.

[29] R.H. Trigg, Guided tours and tabletops: tools for communicating in a hypertext environment, ACM Trans. Office Inf. Syst. 6 (4) (1988) 398–414.

[30] E.J. Whitehead Jr. and Y.Y. Goland, WebDAV: a network protocol for remote collaborative authoring on the Web, in: Proc. of the Sixth European Conference of Computer Supported Cooperative Work, Copenhagen, Denmark, 1999, pp. 291–310.

[31] U.K. Wiil and J. Leggett, HyperDisco: collaborative authoring and Internet distribution, in: Hypertext '97, Southampton, England, ACM, New York, 1997, pp. 13–23.

[32] XML Linking Language (XLink), World Wide Web Consortium Working Draft, 21 February 2000, http://www.w3.org/TR/xlink.html.

[33] XML Path Language (XPath), Version 1.0, W3C Recommendation, 16 November 1999, http://www.w3.org/TR/xpath.

[34] XML Pointer Language (XPointer), W3C Working Draft, 6 December 1999, http://www.w3.org/TR/xptr.

Kaj Grønbæk is professor at the Department of Computer Science, University of Aarhus, Denmark. He finished his master's degree in 1988 and his Ph.D. in 1991 both from the Dept. of Computer Science, University of Aarhus, Denmark. His research interests are: hypermedia; multimedia; computer supported cooperative work (CSCW); cooperative design (system development with active user involvement, cooperative prototyping); user interface design; object oriented tools and techniques for system development.

Lennert Sloth is research programmer at the Department of Computer Science, University of Aarhus, Denmark. He finished his master's degree in 1992 from the Dept. of Computer Science, University of Aarhus, Denmark. His areas of interests are: design and development of hypermedia technologies, development of graphical user interface libraries.

Niels Olof Bouvin is a Ph.D. student at Department of Computer Science, University of Aarhus, Denmark. His research interests include open hypermedia systems, Web augmentation, structural computing, and collaboration on the Web. Niels Olof Bouvin received his master's degree in 1996 from Department of Computer Science, University of Aarhus, Denmark.

ELSEVIER

I-Views: a community-oriented system for sharing streaming video on the Internet

Pengkai Pan [1], Glorianna Davenport [1]

Massachusetts Institute of Technology, Room E15-435 Media Laboratory, 20 Ames Street, Cambridge, MA 02139, USA

Abstract

Streaming media is pervasive on the Internet now and is continuing to grow rapidly. Most streaming media systems have adopted the model of broadcast. Unfortunately, the nature of the broadcast-like one-to-many communication model is not able to foster interaction and collaboration among people. In this paper we discuss a community-oriented communication model for sharing streaming video and introduce a prototype, I-Views. This is a system that permits individuals to use published, communally-owned media clips in order to author narratives by assembling clips, and to build communities of similar interests based on comparison of these narratives. By offering shared authorship, tools and virtual environments, I-Views demonstrates some potential directions for 'sharable video.'

Keywords: Sharable video; Streaming media; Virtual community; Collaborative filtering; Retelling stories

1. Introduction

From the earliest civilization, news and stories have been perpetually shared and retold. Recent story technologies — movies, radio, TV — offer a one-to-many channel for broadcast of stories but lack back channels for modification or discussion of these stories by the audience. The technology separates the teller from the mass audience. Lacking an obvious channel for interchange, it is very difficult for participants to comment on news, present their own interpretations of fiction, add their own material, or share their thoughts, experiences and impressions with other audience members (Fig. 1).

The decentralized Internet infrastructure provides an efficient means for people to distribute and discuss digital content. There are at least three major reasons we believe that the adoption of sharing video-based content on the Internet will grow rapidly. First, the infrastructures are developing rapidly. According to RealNetworks, more than 70 million users have registered to use the RealPlayer [22]. By 2003, almost 26 million broadband subscribers will be connected to the Internet [9] and these connections will ease access to video material. Second, the penetration of low-cost PC cameras and digital video cameras is increasing daily. IDC's research [12] suggests that worldwide PC camera shipments will surge from 606,000 in 1997 to 9.2 million in 2002, a compound annual growth rate of 72.3%. These low-cost video cameras in combination with powerful personal computers will facilitate individual creation and publication of video stories. Third, people have used a variety of tools and systems to share text-based information. Chat Room [15], ICQ [11], Newsgroup, and Third Voice [19]

[1] E-mail: {Ppk, Gid}@media.mit.edu

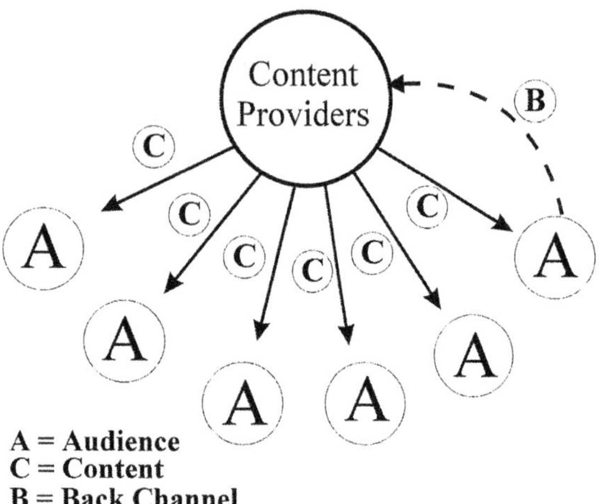

Fig. 1.

have attracted multiple millions of users to exchange information, impressions and feelings on a daily basis. Applications in the domains of training, distance learning, and entertainment also need to share video-based content on a daily basis. We imagine that, in the very near future, millions of hours of streaming video will be shot by $200 digital video cameras, edited on 5000 MHz computers and distributed over gigabyte fiber Internet connections.

Further, broadband today is ill-suited to the requirements of either learning or entertainment. Most broadband programming is fragmented by advertising and the full window interface of current cumbersome broadcast-like models [9] requires viewers to seek the narrow text-based channel of today's Internet if they wish to share their impressions or ideas. New approaches to communication suggest that the integration of interaction can help us create, learn and collaborate more effectively. Inspired by the 'intercreativity' idea [1], a term coined by Tim Berners-Lee, we have addressed the following questions. What type of interchange might be developed to encourage people to share streaming video on the Internet? Can we create easy-to-use models that facilitate sharing and reusing available content which exists or will exist on the Internet? What are the best mechanisms for people to initiate conversations around streaming video-based content? How can video foster virtual communities or sub-communities?

In the past two years, we have focused on designing a system for asynchronous sharing of streaming video on Internet-like distributed networks. We have built a prototype, called I-Views, which allows widely distributed groups of people to view, edit, compare, evaluate, and discuss streaming video material over the Internet. I-Views presents the user with two types of tools: Web-based video editing tools and virtual community-building tools. The former allows the user to view, select, save, re-sequence and publish video clips; the latter allows the user to initiate dialogues by matching common interests and assumptions and to build virtual communities around stories. In marrying these two types of communication — streaming video-based viewing/editing tools and email tools — audience members are able to create and share content. By creating active dialogues around reconfigured sequences, the audience can enjoy an entertaining and intellectual interchange (Fig. 2).

Currently, we are evaluating the prototype system of I-Views using video footage documenting the Junior Summit '98 [18], which was a cross-cultural, cross-geographical and multi-language project involving thousands of children, Junior Summit staff, volunteers, sponsors, and MIT Media Lab faculty and students. The content reflects children's think-

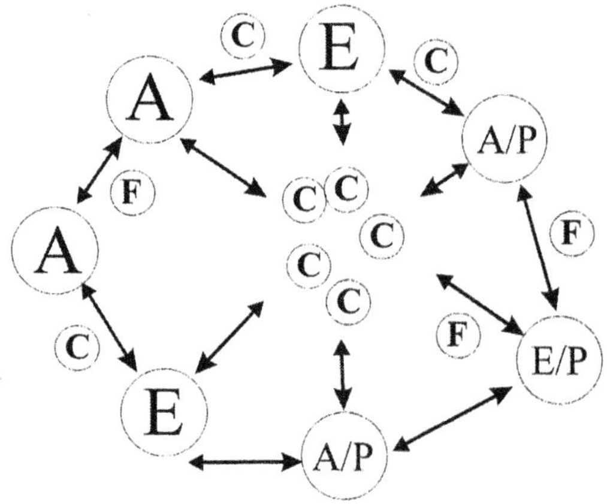

Fig. 2.

ing about world culture, child labor, kids banks, telecommunications access and environmental responsibility. Specifically, an international group of filmmakers including four junior filmmakers have contributed more than one hundred hours of footage. The current video database includes eighty streaming video clips selected and edited from the footage shot. We will use this particular example throughout this paper.

The paper is organized as follows. We first present a context section in which we discuss related work and our approach. We then describe the structure and implementation of I-Views, its client/server architecture and the tools developed for shareable video. The third section presents a preliminary evaluation. Finally, we draw conclusions about our contributions and offer future suggestions.

2. Context

In this section, we basically discuss two questions: what the participant is able to share and with whom s/he can share. We also discuss research works related to our studies.

2.1. What to share

The concept of 'Sharable Video' should not be limited to sharing video content only. We need to rethink 'Sharable Authorship' and 'Sharable Tools' on the Internet. A decade ago, Professor Glorianna Davenport developed a 'Sharable Video' project, New Orleans in Transition [6], on a UNIX workstation supported by a bank of video disc players. The purpose of the project was to give students of Urban Planning an insider view into the process of change. Students using this material could make use of an editing tool which allowed them to excerpt from the available segments, re-sequence and compile movies. These movies could then be imbedded into the systems which they developed for the class. On using the systems, first without the video and then online with the video, Professor Denis Frenchman at MIT commented that the video clips added enormously to the overall argument of the systems. Nowadays, millions of families and friends share a variety of still pictures and video. Recycling or sharing other peoples' work is more efficient than each person repeating similar work. For example, one person has shot a beautiful landscape of Paris from an eagle-eyed perspective. His or her friends traveling to Paris would like to reuse the same shot and make their own travel stories about Paris. As mentioned above, ubiquitous digital cameras and fast Internet connections will definitely produce millions of hours of video content on the Internet. Sharing video content as well as sharing authorship will be widely accepted by mutual consent.

Some related work has been developed in the Web-based editing field from varying perspectives. In VideoFarm.com [20], users can download a Java-based Premiere-like editing software, edit their footage, then upload final cuts to VideoFarm's server. VideoFarm [20] is a combination of a Web-based editing application and video content hosting service. VideoFarm is developed mainly from the content author's point of view. Mimicry [2] is a system allowing users to create links to and from temporal (video and audio) media on the Web regardless of the users' ownership of the Web pages or media clips involved. Mimicry demonstrates additional features for current media players. Unlike VideoFarm, Mimicry is created mainly from the audience's point of view.

In I-Views, we rethink the roles of the author and the audience in sharable media environments on the Internet. In these environments, the distinction between the author and the audience becomes blurred. All participants are able to share authorship, video content and on-line tools. The participants can save and edit their favorite video clips and publish their new sequences back to I-Views without applying for permission from the authors of the original clips. The sharable authorship offers each individual freedom to retell stories from different perspectives and assumptions. On the other hand, all retold sequences record the original information about the sequences, such as who the authors of the original clips are, when the clips were made, etc.

2.2. Who will share with whom?

In her doctoral dissertation, Professor Judith S. Donath comments "The problem [has been] designs for data, not people." She stated how "visitors to a site are likely to share common interests, yet they cannot communicate with each other, nor are they aware of each other's presence" [7]. The most critical mechanism lacking in current networked storytelling systems is the mechanism of initiating conversations around streaming video-based content such that it fosters the construction of virtual communities. A very real question we must ask in constructing an environment for sharing video is: Who will share video with whom?

The Junior Summit '98 generated an on-line conversation of over 2000 children; one hundred of those children later convened at the MIT Media Lab. The first night these children were given pagers for real-time messaging. Different people have different skills, interests and passions. Some children at the Summit loved playing LEGO while others focused on children's rights. Building matchmaker-like agents for their real time communications (see previous case study of ICQ) [16] was a useful approach to bringing individuals with similar interests together. In our first case-study of I-Views, we built a database of over 100 short movies representing the diverse activities of the Junior Summit. The children of the Summit were our test users. Having been at the Summit, they had an interest in the video representation of the event. Would they edit and message with it?

The question of "who will share with whom?" is informed by examples in the growth of various virtual communities, as well as by research in collaborative filtering techniques. Pascal Chesnais' Canard [4] thesis takes a constructionist approach and outlines the ASE framework, which represents the three attributes which contribute to usability within a shared technological environment: Ability, Support and Effort. Amy Bruckman's MOOSE Crossing [3] encourages interactive chats through the use of 'rooms' and 'objects' for building communities. Rooms are similar to chat channels and objects are artifacts transported from one room to others. Both studies are inspiring in terms of understanding how virtual communities emerge and grow. In I-Views, the objects are the video materials and the email messages.

Once we have a database of users, how do they find each other? The basic goal of collaborative filtering is to cluster people who have similar interests in order to grow the community itself. In I-Views, the mechanism of the comparison algorithms is able to analyze the sequence that is made by the participant and compare that sequence to all other sequences in the database. I-Views then presents the ten most similar sequences to the participant. A user might watch some of the ten sequences and decide whether or not to initiate conversations. The comparison tool is a means for participants to match their common interests and foster new communications with others. The comparison algorithms look similar to prior collaborative filtering methods [8,13,14]. However, there are a few significant differences in terms of user data retrieval, objectives, and procedures. We compare our algorithms to that used in Ringo [14]. Ringo is an on-line music recommendation system which has mechanisms to recycle word-of-mouth knowledge by matching common interests among users.

2.2.1. Data retrieval

In Ringo, users have to vote which song is good or bad. The processes to retrieve users' feedback are very time-consuming and subjective. I-Views takes a different approach. We assume that the clips that the user selects make sense to that user. Participants need not vote. The process of retrieving participants' feedback is transparent in I-Views.

2.2.2. Objectives

The objective of Ringo is to make personalized recommendations. The users expect to get accurate recommendation results. However, because of the nature of the algorithm, the method cannot work well if the user base is not large enough. In I-Views, the comparison tools offers a means for participants to find other people with whom to initiate dialogues. Our focus is on matching people. The comparison tools also work even when there are very few participants using the system.

2.2.3. Procedures

In Ringo, the procedure of recommendation is static and black-boxed. The user votes on a set of songs, then Ringo gives out a list. I-Views' comparison tools are dynamic. The participant can move the scroll bars to justify the criteria and define the similarities. The movements of thumbnails react to the changes of scroll bars simultaneously. The participant is able to perceive the interconnection among these sequences. We are still testing and improving our comparison algorithms and interface design. We believe that meaningful comparison tools can bring distributed participants closer together.

Other related work of interest includes XML and SMIL. While World Wide Web Consortium is rapidly developing new languages and standards [21], SMIL 2.0 [17] is supposed to have more compelling features than the 1.0 version [10]. Unfortunately, few features have been proposed which will facilitate collaboration. Collaboration might involve one video editor working with two composers on a soundtrack for a movie which will be shown on the Internet. The new version of SMIL should enable multiple audio tracks to be shared, synched and unsynched in a distributed exchange such that the editor can listen to a mixed track incorporating changes from both composers even while commenting on the effect. We would like to see that World Wide Web Consortium pay increased attention to the user's point of view which is different from that of the broadcaster. It is useful to remember that in interactive expression, a single person will alternate between the role of the author and the role of the audience.

3. Implementation

I-Views has evolved monthly. In this chapter, we present the version of July 1999: client and server side modules, database modules, net work architecture and data flow. We also discuss the comparison algorithms.

3.1. Modules on client side

There are seven major components on client side:
(1) User registration and login;
(2) Viewing original video clips;
(3) Editing video clips;
(4) Comparing video sequences;
(5) Finding the most popular sequences;
(6) Contributing video content;
(7) Searching for content.

In this paper, we discuss the following three components: viewing original video clips, editing video clips and comparing video sequences. For the other components, please read Pengkai's Master's thesis.

3.2. Viewing original video clips

In our test application, approximately eighty thumbnails are loaded into the Viewing applet (Fig. 3). Each thumbnail is linked to a video clip in the video database. The participant is able to move the yellow oval scroll bar to browse the images. The sizes and positions of the images change based on the movement of the scroll bar. In our first implementation, the presentation of images is random; ideally, the scroll bar would allow the user to browse the material according to certain criteria, such as chronology, subjects and characters. The participant can double-click on any thumbnail, and a Real G2 player pops up and plays the associated video clip (Fig. 4). If the participant finds any of the clips interesting, s/he can single-click on the clips and save them into her or his personal archive. The selected images have a thin yellow outline around them for ease of selection. After the participant selects his or her favorite images, s/he can click on the Next Page button and go to the editing page.

3.3. Editing video clips

This applet is a simple on-line, real time sequencing tool (Fig. 5), which allows the participant to drag and drop images into the editing box to sequence video clips into a longer assembly. The participant can modify this sequence by inserting, deleting, and switching clips. To preview the sequence, s/he clicks on the preview button and the G2 player pops up. When the participant is satisfied with the sequence, the participant gives the sequence a name and broadcasts it. To offer the on-line real time sequencing tool, we adopted SMIL language. The language is able to precisely synchronize the timing of diverse media elements as well as the presentation of these elements through a SMIL-enabled player such as a G2 player, which is also used in our environment. When the participant links some clips to make a sequence, the Java server and Perl scripts automatically generate SMIL tags and call the G2 player. The G2 player is able to play these clips seamlessly one by one according to the tags. Because of the nature of SMIL language, we will be able to add more features such as fade in/out and trimming clips later. The simplicity is the beauty of this tool.

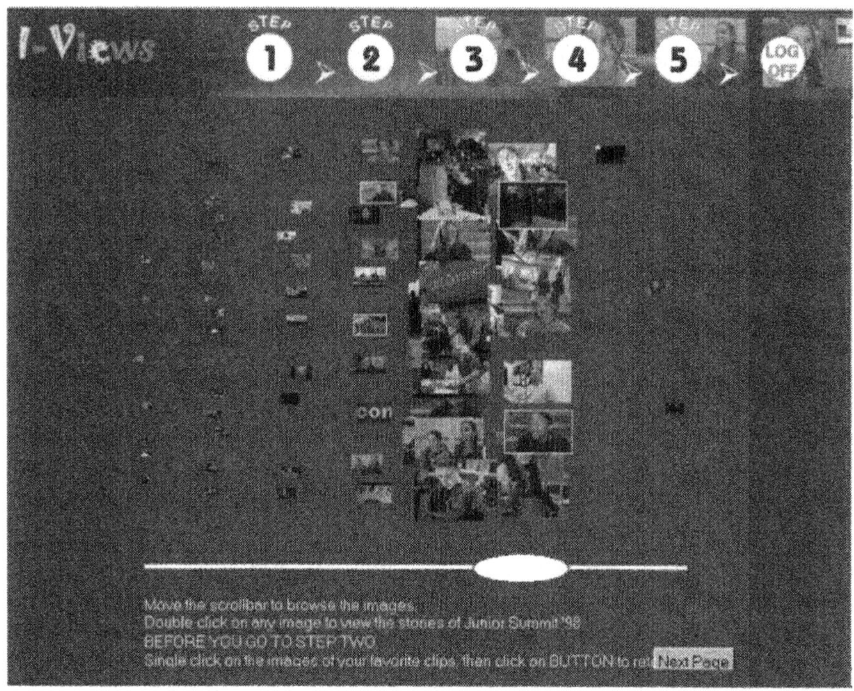
I-Views
STEP 1
STEP 2
STEP 3
STEP 4
STEP 5
LOG OFF
Move the scrollbar to browse the images.
Double click on any image to view the stories of Junior Summit '98
BEFORE YOU GO TO STEP TWO
Single click on the images of your favorite clips, then click on BUTTON to ret
Next Page
{About I-Views} {Help} {Junior Summit '98} {Contact Us} {Download G2 Player}

Fig. 3.

I-Views
STEP 1
STEP 2
STEP 3
STEP 4
STEP 5
LOG OFF
Move the scrollbar to browse the images.
Double click on any image to view the stories
BEFORE YOU GO TO STEP TWO
Single click on the images of your favorite cli
{About I-Views} {Help} {Junior Summit '98}

Fig. 4.

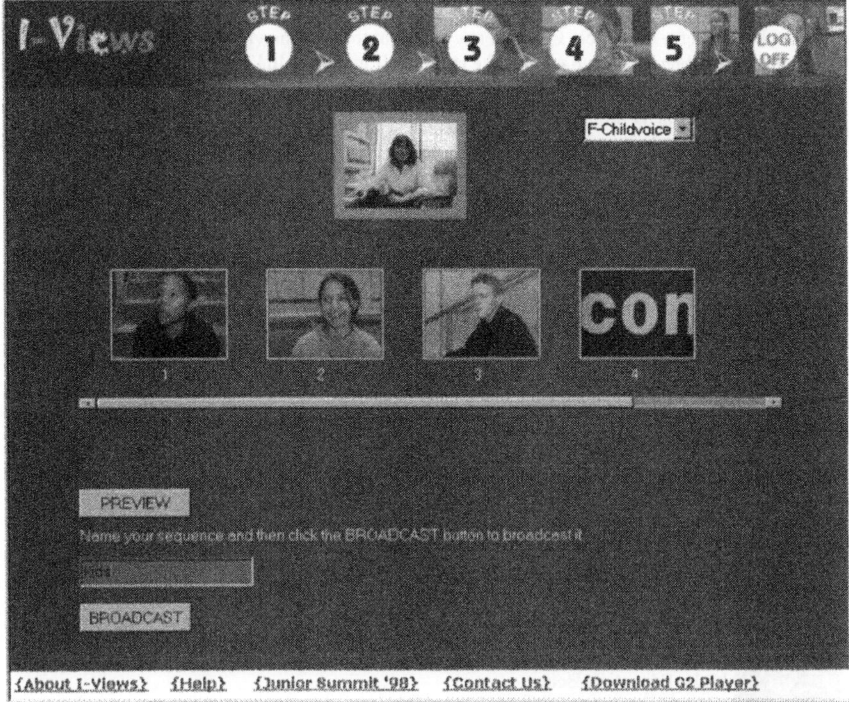
I-Views
STEP 1
STEP 2
STEP 3
STEP 4
STEP 5
LOG OFF
F-Childvoice
con
1
2
3
4
PREVIEW
Name your sequence and then click the BROADCAST button to broadcast it
kids
BROADCAST
{About I-Views} {Help} {Junior Summit '98} {Contact Us} {Download G2 Player}

Fig. 5.

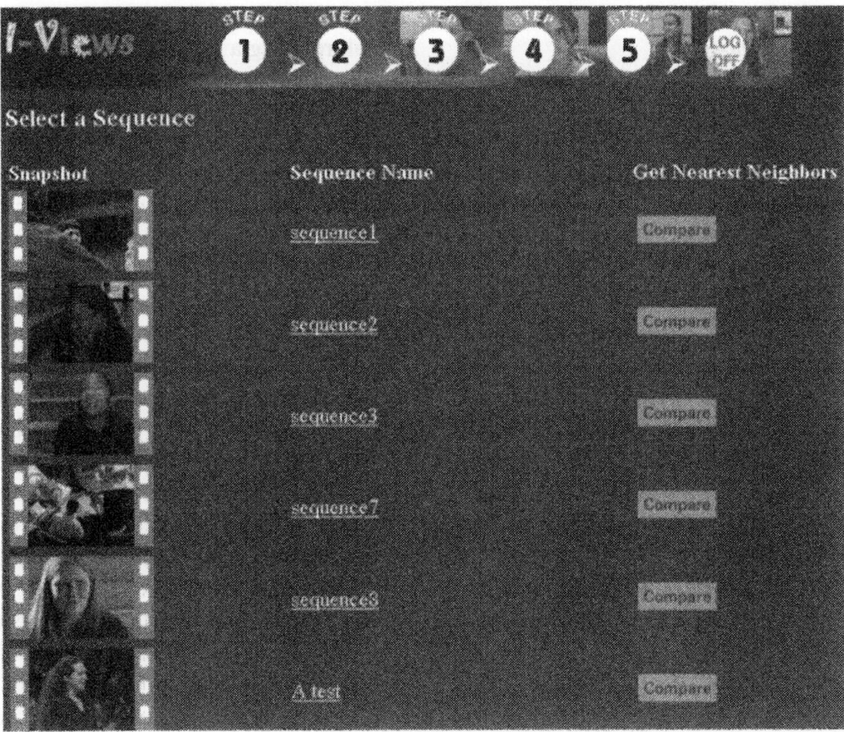
I-Views
STEP 1
STEP 2
STEP 3
STEP 4
STEP 5
LOG OFF
Select a Sequence
Snapshot
Sequence Name
Get Nearest Neighbors
sequence1
sequence2
sequence3
sequence7
sequence8
A test
Compare

Fig. 6.

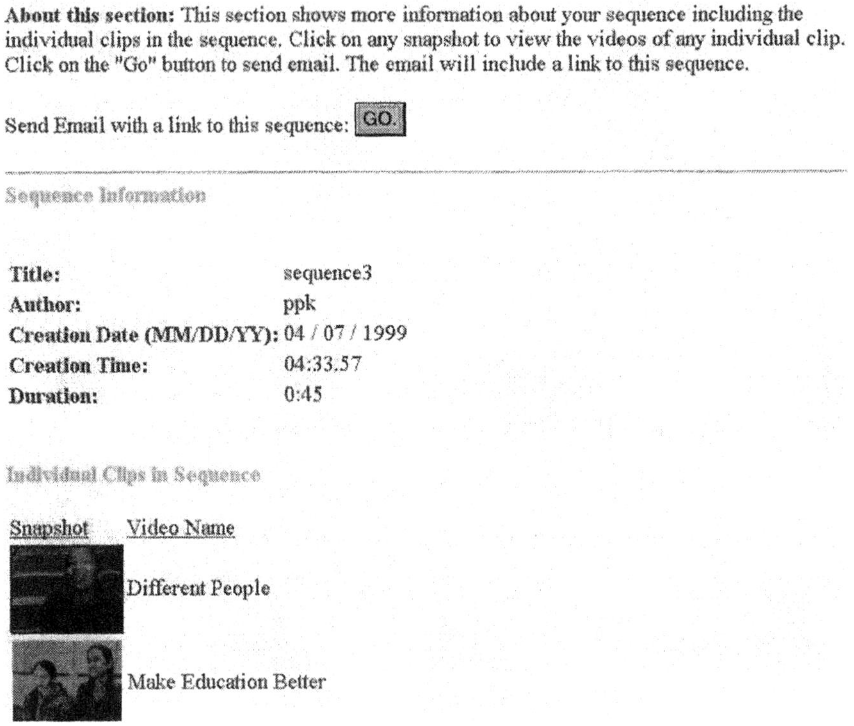

About this section: This section shows more information about your sequence including the individual clips in the sequence. Click on any snapshot to view the videos of any individual clip. Click on the "Go" button to send email. The email will include a link to this sequence.

Send Email with a link to this sequence: GO.

Sequence Information

Title:	sequence3
Author:	ppk
Creation Date (MM/DD/YY):	04 / 07 / 1999
Creation Time:	04:33.57
Duration:	0:45

Individual Clips in Sequence

Snapshot	Video Name
	Different People
	Make Education Better

Fig. 7.

3.4. Comparing video sequences

After the participant broadcasts the sequences, he or she is able to view the sequence by clicking on the STEP TWO button. There are three columns on this page: Snapshot, Sequence Name, and Comparison (Fig. 6). To view the sequence that the participant produced, the viewer clicks on the associated snapshot and a G2 player plays the video clip. To find out more information about the sequence, the viewer clicks on the name of the sequence and a new window pops up (Fig. 7). The window presents the related information: the author, the clips contained in the sequence, the date the sequence was produced, etc. To share the sequence with friends, the viewer clicks on the Go button and a message window pops out. The viewer can send out an email to his or her friends, who will receive a URL link to that sequence. By clicking on the URL, the receivers are able to view the sequence via a G2 player. We provide a comparison tool for the participant to find other participants who have similar interests. Clicking on the Compare button, the participant is able to explore using a radar-like interface. We have adopted radar as a metaphor in interface design to provide a useful means for very distributed participants to interact.

In the middle of the applet, there is the sequence that the participant selects as a metric for comparison with other sequences in the database (Fig. 8). Around the selected sequence, the ten most similar sequences are displayed. On the right side of the applet, there are four criteria: Clips, Keywords, The Beginning, and The Ending. The criteria allow the participant to determine what it means to be similar; similarity is communicated in a display where thumbnails of the movies appear nearer to or farther from the center. The distance between the selected sequence and another sequence suggests how similar the two sequences are based on different criteria. For example, if the participant wants to find out which sequences have the same beginning as the selected sequence, he or she can move the scroll bar of The Beginning to the position of one hundred percent (Fig. 9). Three sequences that have the same beginning move closer to the center. Or, the participant can use a combina-

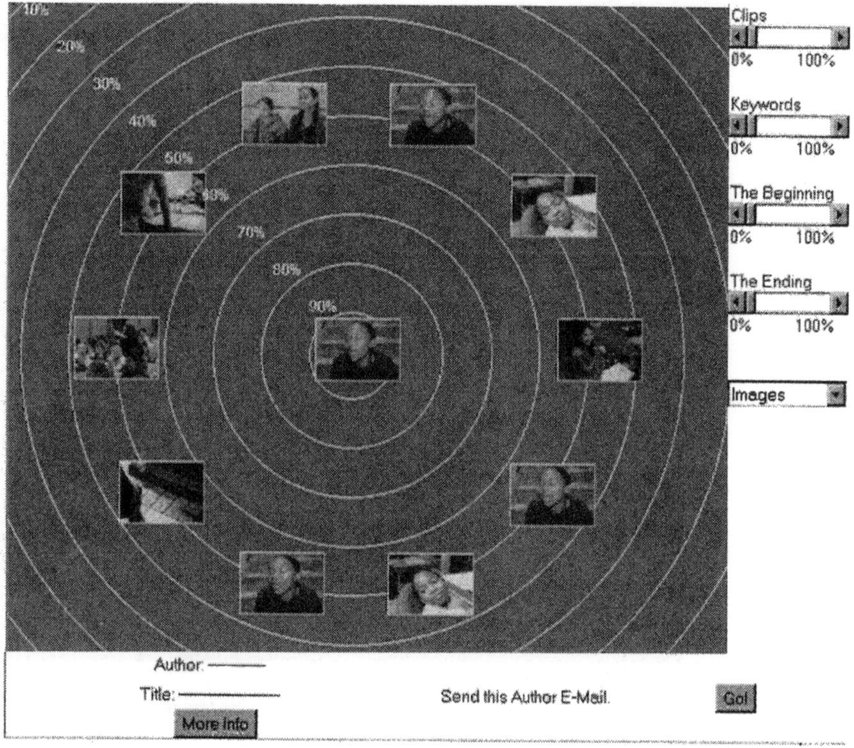

Fig. 8.

tion of the four criteria: for example, the scroll bar of Keywords can be positioned to fifty percent and the scroll bar of The Beginning to one hundred percent. Or, by setting all scroll bars to one hundred percent, the participant can easily see the movies which are most different, hence farthest away. As the participant discovers sequences that s/he is interested in, s/he clicks on the sequence to learn the author and title of the sequence. In the example (Fig. 10), the author is Vincent and the title is Interview with Nic. If a participant wants to initiate a dialogue with Vincent, s/he can click on the Go button to get a message window from which to send a message to Vincent. So far, email is the only means that we provide for participants to initiate dialogues. We are considering of designing a synchronous communication system in future versions of I-Views.

3.5. Comparison algorithms

Here, we briefly introduce the algorithms that were used to implement the comparison scale in I-Views. The comparison scale helps the participant find out which sequences are similar to the sequence that they selected as a metric. Two factors determine how similar two sequences are: the subjective factor and the objective factor. The subjective factor is determined by the percentage of a criterion; the objective factor is determined by the number of common clips or keywords between two sequences. The high level algorithm is as follows.

$$W = \sum_{j=0}^{n-1} \left(\left(\frac{1}{n} \right) * (Sf_j * Of_j) \right)$$

where W is the weight for measuring the similarity between two sequences; n is the number of criteria (in I-Views' case, there are four criteria;) Sf is the percentage of the subjective factor; Of is the percentage of the objective factor.

For example, say we have a metric Sequence A which includes Clip 1, Clip 2 and Clip 3 and two other Sequences to be compared with it: Sequence B, including Clip 1, Clip 2 and Clip 5, and Sequence

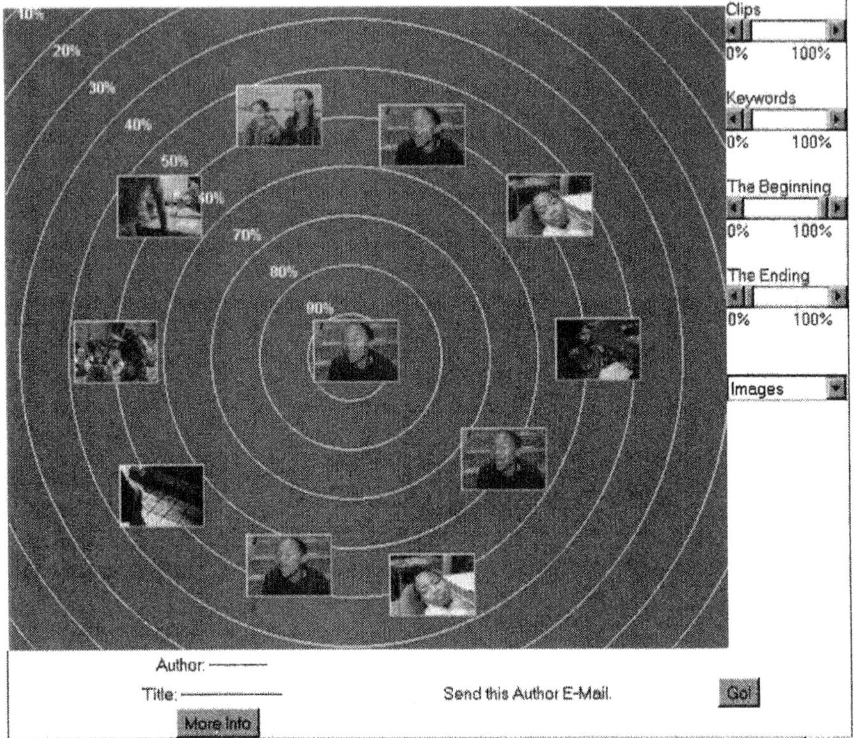

Fig. 9.

Send mail to a nearby neighbor....

Your username, and the sequence you selected will be included in the body of this message.

To: vincent [hilldrup@]
Subject: Hi

Message:

Hi Vincent,

I have watched your story and would like to talk to you.

Submit reset

Fig. 10.

C, including Clip 3, Clip 4, and Clip 6. Let's say that we only want to make the comparisons based on similar clips between two sequences. So we move the scroll bar of the Clips to one hundred percent. *Of* is a variable determined by the number of common clips between two sequences.

$$Of = \frac{\text{the number of common clips}}{\text{the number of clips in the longer sequence}}.$$

The number of Sequence B's *Of* is: $Of = 2/\text{Max}(3, 3) = 0.667$, while the number of Sequence C's *Of* is: $Of = 1/\text{Max}(3, 3) = 0.333$. Now, n is 4 and *Sf* is 100%.

The weight of Sequence B is:

$$W = (\tfrac{1}{4}) * (1 * 0.667) = 0.1667.$$

The weight of Sequence C is:

$$W = (\tfrac{1}{4}) * (1 * 0.333) = 0.0833.$$

The weight of Sequence C is smaller than the weight of Sequence B, since Sequence A and B share two of the same clips while Sequence A and C share only one. The keyword-based algorithm is the same as the one described above, while the process of matching a similar beginning is similar to the one above.

3.6. Modules on server side

I-Views is a multimedia-based multi-client/server system built on various computer languages and using a variety of tools. We took a client-oriented approach in the design of the server side modules [5]. The design and implementation of server side modules are primarily based on the client side needs. We also considered the performance of communication and computation as certain limiting hardware and software resources exist. The whole system is built on freeware, such as Linux, Java, Perl, Apache, MySQL, etc. To present the system's back-end, we discuss the system architecture, then briefly describe Perl script modules.

All modules and data exist on three machines: wwwic.media.mit.edu, fellini.media.mit.edu and Yimou.media.mit.edu. On the three machines, there are four servers running simultaneously: Web Server, Java Server, Database Server and the Real Video Server (Fig. 11). The diagram shows the locations of all servers, contents, applet classes, Perl scripts, etc. Generally speaking, the IC Web server is in charge of static HTML files and contains a mirror copy of the thumbnail images; Fellini contains Java

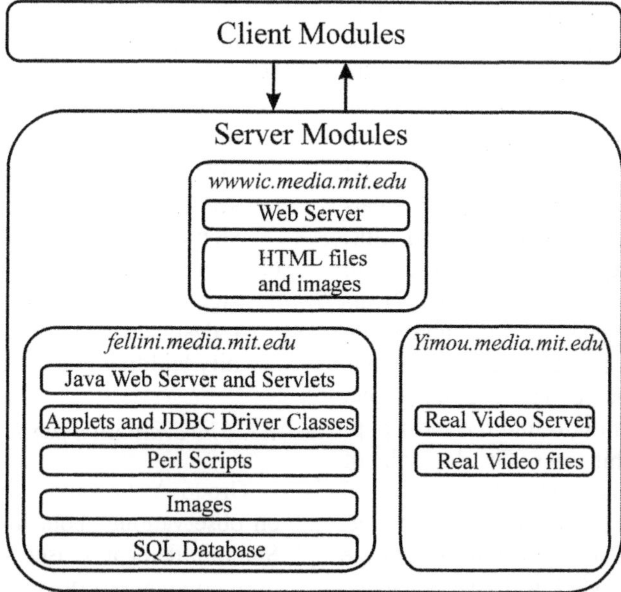

Fig. 11.

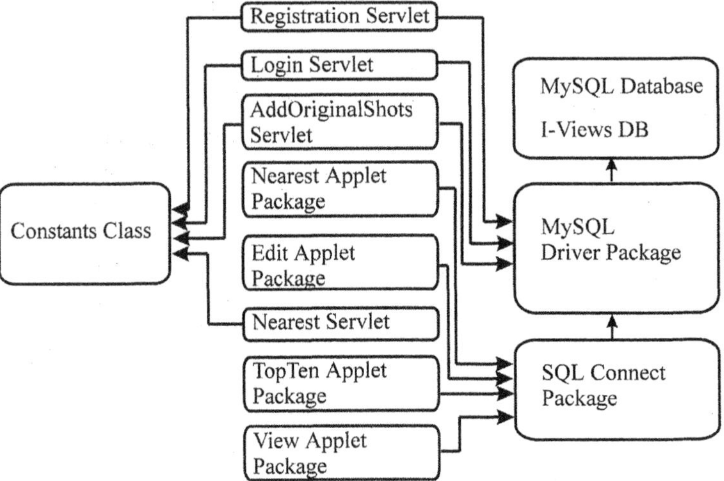

Fig. 12.

Web server, Servlets, Applets, JDBC driver classes, Perl programs, MySQL Database, etc.; Yimou is the streaming video powerhouse.

Fig. 12 represents the Applet-Servlet modules for I-Views. On the left of the diagram, there is a Java Constants class, which contains all of the URLs and pathnames in Servlet codes. In the middle of the diagram, there are eight independent Servlet and Applet modules, which have different functions. Registration Servlet handles new participants and transfers their registration information to the database. Login Servlet deals with the participant who already has registered. If the participant logs in successfully, their browser is given a cookie which includes the participant's identification number. The View Applet package contains the View applets that allow the participant to browse and watch the original video clips. The applets in the Edit Applet package deal with editing, previewing and broadcasting events. Nearest Servlet automatically generates the appropriate HTML tags, which have the Comparison applets in the Nearest Applet Package. The TopTen Applet package does the computation to find the most popular sequences based on hit rates. On the right of this diagram are the database related modules. All applet codes are associated with the JDBC driver: MySQL Driver Package. The SQLConnect Package works as an interface to the MySQL Driver Package. In I-Views, Perl scripts perform two types of jobs: generating the SMIL tags and processing supporting work such as searching keywords and sending email.

4. Evaluation

In our preliminary evaluation we engaged two small groups of users, a group of eight Junior Summit delegates who used the system remotely and a group of Media Lab students and faculty. Our evaluation focused on two objectives:

(1) Will users, who are portrayed in a particular set of observational video content, engage with that content to the point of creating their own video sequences from the set, publishing their sequences to their friends and developing discussion communities around this material?

(2) Can we improve the workflow and interface design of I-Views? Should aspects of I-Views be redesigned to better accommodate the community building objective?

4.1. The evaluation participants and methods

Group A: Our most interesting evaluation draws on observations about how a group of eight Junior Summit delegates used the system remotely. This user group was critical to evaluating our main hypothesis, that people presented with a system in which they can share, reedit and publish video will

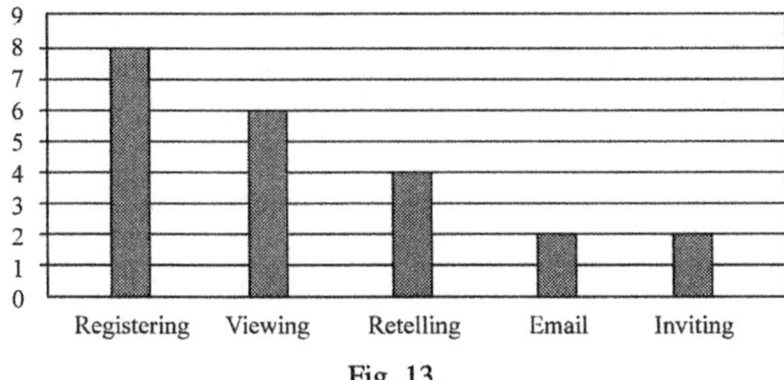

Fig. 13.

do so. All members of this group had participated in the six-month on-line forum and the one-week Media Lab Summit. They knew each other and worked together through a variety of projects, discussion groups and email lists. From June 12, 1999 to July 12, 1999, they volunteered to test I-Views. Eight of them successfully registered in I-Views and six of them were able to view video clips from I-Views. Four participants retold stories and two of them sent out email and invited other people to join in I-Views (Fig. 13). We discuss the details later.

Group B: Our second group of users, while not engaged in community building, were selected to comment on the actual design of the systems at the MIT Media Lab. During the on-site evaluation processes at Media Lab, six participants were able to register in I-Views and watch video clips. Four of them tried to retell stories. Three of them tried the email function; none of them invited other people to watch or discuss their reedited segments (Fig. 14).

Following the hands on portion of the evaluation, we talked to participants to understand more fully their engagement with the system. Our evaluation results relate to three topics: accessibility, workflow and interface design and virtual community building.

4.1.1. Accessibility

To engage with I-Views, the participant needs a fast Internet connection such as a cable modem, a DSL, ISDN or T1. The cost of Internet connection and low data rates are two major reasons why they couldn't use I-Views. For example, one participant said:

> *Sorry but I don't think I'll be able to use I-Views as I'm not allowed to pay in order to download the G2 real player. I wish I could help.* (Konstantina)

The bandwidth is a big barrier for most people experimenting with I-Views.

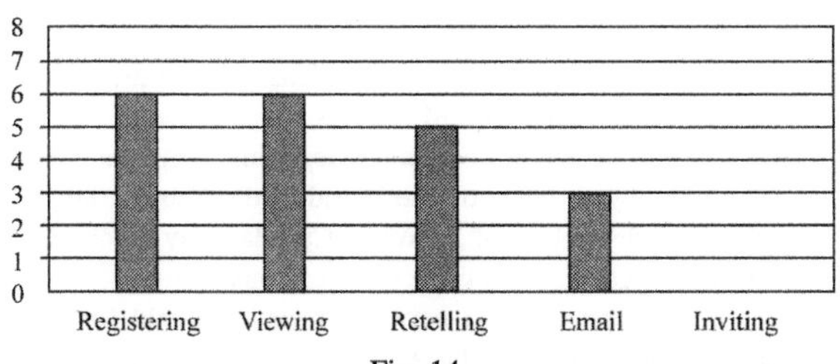

Fig. 14.

4.1.2. Workflow and interface design

We have received many valuable comments on workflow, function design and interface design. Most people like the interface design and explicit workflow design. However, some users were confused by some parts of I-Views, particularly, the View applet and the comparison tool.

> *Maybe because I was using a portable, but many were very small I'd no sooner locate one and view it and mark it then I'd lose the place where the next one for my sequence was. It was a lot like those memory games where you have to remember where the face down cards are in order to turn a pair over... As I said before, I didn't like those pictures moving around — kind of neat in the beginning to watch but very frustrating to work with. I would have preferred something more static and larger. I think that I would have then made many more sequences and sent them to people.* (Vincent, age 13, Paris)

Children of different ages respond quite differently to the comparison module. Children from 10 to 12 years old don't understand the comparison tool at all. We assume the reason is that the design of the tool is not clear and compelling enough. However, we found that the older children from 13 to 16 years are more willing to try the comparison tool, retell stories and send out messages to their friends and family than the younger children are. They also enjoy receiving the comments that their friends send back.

4.1.3. Community building

We have not had a large enough group using I-Views to comment on its ability to build community. In the Junior Summit database, participants retold stories focused on only two topics: LEGO and the international fashion show. While they did share their stories among themselves and their friends through email, the system did not encourage them to submit new materials, nor would many of them have had the means to shoot, edit and upload video. Obviously creating a system that grows community requires the right mix of content invitation and tools. Neither is sufficient on its own.

As one reader of this paper commented "aside from having discussions about the finished product, get users to collaborate and/or help each other during the production process. For example, set up a competition. Divide people into groups and have them collaborate for the competition." Competition in conjunction with a constructive environment represents a critical aspect of World Wide Web initial popularity.

Within our small user group, we observed that different participants assumed different roles. Three basic roles are: observer, builder and leader. Among eight testers, about four participants were observers, two of them were builders and two of them were leaders. We also had a few new users who were invited by the two leaders. These leaders played a key role in terms of self-organizing virtual community. For example, Vincent not only watched a lot of video clips, retold stories with extreme patience, but he also sent sequences to his moderator, Julia, and invited her to join the test of I-Views. When Julia had problems with using I-Views, he immediately sent email to us and tried to solve her problems. Since the leaders played extremely active roles in growing a community, we will in the next redesign focus on functionality to promote the leader role for building up and organizing sub-communities.

5. Conclusion

In this paper we have examined a hypothesis: Can we design and implement a distributed system for video that encourages the social use of back channel to build a sense of community? Inspired by Tim Berners-Lee's 'intercreativity,' we have built I-Views, a prototype of Sharable Video that presents the stories of a global event, the Junior Summit '98. Specifically, there are two major contributions of this aspect of the work:

(1) A democratic sharable storytelling model which enables very distributed participants to share authorship, tools, spaces, impressions and experiences around video stories on the Internet. Stories about the Junior Summit '98 were used as our video database as the children and parents who participated in this event offered an existing community of interest.
(2) A dynamic similarity scale: this tool attempts to match common interest through various metrics of similarity. By identifying common interest, such a tool can bring participants together who might like to engage in conversation around a topic. In turn, this could encourage the social use of back channel to build the sense of community.

Our hypothesis has been explored through the implementation of I-Views and on-site and remote tests and evaluation. This Sharable Video environment invites participants to use the back channel to build a community of interest. In our limited case study, we observe three types of participants: Observer, Builder and Leader. These types may prove useful in the construction of a tiered application in which complexity is matched to the type of user.

Many thanks to our undergraduate research assistants, Christina Chu, Vikas Sodhani, Alice Yang and Carmen Woo. Their creativity and diligent work built the working system, I-Views. This research would not have progressed as far and as quickly without them. We thank Prof. Walter Bender, Prof. Brian Smith, and Prof. Bruce Blumberg for excellent feedback and advice. Thanks to our Interactive Cinema colleagues: Dr. Kevin Brooks, Brian Bradley, Barbara Barry, Ricardo Torres, Paul Nemirovsky, Aisling Kelliher, James Seo, Roger Sipitakiat, Arjan Schutte and Phillip Tiongson for kindness and support. This work is supported in part by a grant from the News in the Future and Digital Life Consortia.

References

[1] T. Berners-Lee, Focus on intercreativity instead of interactivity: create things together, in: Plenary Sessions, 5th Int. World Wide Web Conf., May 1996, Paris, France.

[2] N.O. Bouvin and R. Schade, Integrating temporal media and open hypermedia on the World Wide Web, in: 8th Int. World Wide Web Conf., Toronto, Canada, May 1999.

[3] A.S. Bruckman, MOOSE crossing: construction, community, and learning in a networked virtual world for kids, Ph.D. Thesis, MIT Media Arts and Sciences, June 1997.

[4] P.R. Chesnais, A framework for designing constructionist approaches to community-centered messaging, Ph.D. Thesis, MIT Media Arts and Sciences, 1999.
[5] C. Chu, Technical architecture and implementation of I-Views: an online storytelling community, Advanced Undergraduate Project Final Report, 1999.
[6] G. Davenport, New Orleans in transition, 1983–1987: the interactive delivery of a cinematic case study, Int. Congress for Design and Planning Theory, Education Group Conf. Proc., May 1987.
[7] J. Donath, Inhabiting the virtual city: the design of social environments for electronic communities, Ph.D. Thesis, MIT Media Arts and Sciences, 1997, http://judith.www.media.mit.edu/Thesis/.
[8] D. Goldberg, D. Nichols, B. Oki and T. Douglas, Using collaborative filtering to weave an information tapestry, Commun. ACM, December 1992.
[9] M.E. Hardie, Hooked on broadband, The Forrester Report, July 1999.
[10] P. Hoschka (Ed.), Synchronized multimedia integration language, World Wide Web Consortium Recommendation, June 1998, http://www.w3.org/TR/REC-smil/.
[11] ICQ, A Net-wide instant messenger, http://www.icq.com/icqhomepage.html.
[12] IDC Research, IDC research brings PC camera market into focus – shipments to exceed 9 million in 2002, Feb. 1999, http://www.idg.com/cgi-bin/pressroom.cgi?566E3ADB8F45B1A18525672900772037.
[13] J. Konstan, B. Miller, D. Maltz, J. Herlocker, L. Gordan and J. Riedl, GroupLens: applying collaborative filtering to Usenet news, Commun. ACM, March 1997.
[14] P. Maes and U. Shardanand, Social information filtering: algorithms for automating 'Word of Mouth', CHI, 1995.
[15] J. Oikarinen and D. Reed, Internet relay chat protocol, Network Working Group Request for Comments (RFC1495), May 1993.
[16] P. Pan, I-Views, a storymaking community of, by and for the audience, P22, Master Thesis, MIT Media Arts and Sciences, 1999.
[17] L. Rutledge, J. van Ossenbruggen and L. Hardman, Anticipating SMIL 2.0: the developing cooperative infrastructure for multimedia on the Web, 8th Int. World Wide Web Conf., Toronto, Canada, May 1999.
[18] The Junior Summit '98, http://www.jrsummit.net.
[19] Third Voice, Third Voice helps people post public or personal notes on any Web Page, http://www.thirdvoice.com/products/product_features.htm.
[20] VideoFarm, http://www.videofarm.com/.
[21] XML Extensible Markup Language, http://www.w3.org/XML/.
[22] Yahoo Finance, http://biz.yahoo.com/e/l/r/mwk.html

Pengkai Pan is a Ph.D. candidate and works as a research assistant for the Interactive Cinema group at the MIT Media Lab. He earned a B.E. in industrial design and a minor degree in Computer Science with highest honors from ZheJiang University in 1994. He then joined the Department of Electrical Engineering and Computer Science as an assistant professor. In 1999 he earned a Master's degree from MIT Media Lab, where he designed I-View, an Internet-based, streaming video, story-sharing system. He continues to investigate 'sharable media', with the goal of inventing efficient and novel means for sharing visual information. He is an Interval Fellow.

Glorianna Davenport is the head of the Interactive Cinema group at the MIT Media Laboratory. Between 1988 and 1995, Davenport's graduate workshop in multimedia production was adopted by five international institutions. Her publications on subjects of responsive media, as well as several of her interactive digital prototype programs, have been included in international symposia, conferences, and film festivals. Information on some of these projects is accessible on the Web (http://ic.www.media.mit.edu/). She serves on the editorial board of IEEE Multimedia, and on the advisory board of several digital content companies and cultural organizations. Trained as a documentary filmmaker, she has achieved international recognition for her work in new media forms, content, and delivery systems. Her research explores fundamental issues related to the collaborative co-construction of digital media experiences, where the task of narration is split among authors, consumers, and computer mediators. Ms. Davenport's recent work focuses on customizable, personalizable storyteller systems that dynamically serve and adapt to a widely dispersed society of audience and on mobile media systems.

Enhancing Web accessibility via the Vox Portal and a Web-hosted dynamic HTML↔VoxML converter

Stuart Goose [a,*,1], Mike Newman [a,1], Claus Schmidt [b,2], Laurent Hue [c,3]

[a] *Multimedia Department, Siemens Corporate Research, 755 College Road East, Princeton, NJ 08540, USA*
[b] *Information and Communication Networks, Siemens AG, Schertlinstraße 8, D-81379 Munich, Germany*
[c] *Information and Telecommunication Research, Siemens AG, 3 rue Blaise Pascal, 22300 Lannion, France*

Abstract

Interactive voice browsers offer an alternative paradigm that enables both sighted and visually impaired users to access the World Wide Web. In addition to the desktop PC, voice browsers afford ubiquitous mobile access to the World Wide Web using a wide range of consumer devices. This technology can facilitate a safe, 'hands-free' browsing environment which is of importance both to car drivers and various mobile and technical professionals. By providing voice-mediated access, information providers can reach a wider audience and leverage existing investment in their World Wide Web content. In this paper we describe the Vox Portal, a scaleable VoxML client, and a World Wide Web Server-hosted dynamic HTML↔VoxML converter.

Keywords: Structure; Browsing; Accessibility; Speech; VoxML

1. Introduction and motivation

The World Wide Web has enjoyed phenomenal growth over recent years and now accounts for a significant proportion of all Internet traffic. The unmitigated success of the World Wide Web bears testimony to the previously unsatisfied need for a system able to integrate and deliver distributed information. The profile of hypermedia has been raised significantly by the World Wide Web, which has endorsed hypermedia as an appropriate technology for accessing and navigating information spaces. Users can access a wealth of information and associated services over the World Wide Web, ranging from international news to local restaurant menus.

Interactive voice browsers that make extensive use of speech synthesis and recognition, offer an alternative paradigm that enables both sighted and visually impaired users to access the World Wide Web. This technology can facilitate a safe, 'hands-free' browsing environment which is of importance both to car drivers and various mobile and technical professionals. By providing voice-mediated access, information providers can reach a wider audience and leverage existing investment in their World Wide Web content.

The interest in ubiquitous computing has escalated in recent times. Ubiquitous, or pervasive, computing is the attempt to break away from the traditional desktop interaction paradigm by distributing

* Corresponding author.
1 {sgoose,newman}@scr.siemens.com
2 claus.schmidt@icn.siemens.de
3 laurent.hue@srit.siemens.fr

computational power and resources into devices in the environment surrounding the user. The primary aim of the Vox Portal is to support ubiquitous voice-driven access to multiple information services from a range of devices. This technology has the potential to increase the global user community exponentially. Subscribers will enjoy greater convenience and flexibility by being able to access dynamic information at any time from anywhere.

VoxML [16] is a new standard markup language for specifying the dialogs of interactive voice response applications that feature speech synthesis and recognition technologies. The Vox Portal is a carrier-class VoxML client. Rather than expecting World Wide Web publishers to translate their HTML content and services to VoxML, we have built a dynamic HTML↔VoxML converter that bridges the void between the voice and World Wide Web domains. HTML forms are translated to VoxML, thus enabling the interactive input of data into the respective fields and hence requires the converter to be bi-directional to submit form data to the originating World Wide Web Server. Voice-driven interactive support for HTML form input affords the user mobile access to a variety of compelling E-commerce World Wide Web services such as financial services, on-line purchasing, arranging travel, route finding, etc.

Described in this paper is the Vox Portal that uses a World Wide Web Server-hosted dynamic HTML↔VoxML converter. A survey of the related work is discussed in Section 2. A justification of the importance of document structure is outlined in Section 3. An overview of the system architecture and operation is provided in Section 4. Section 5 proposes areas for further research and provides some concluding remarks.

2. Related work

Making extensive use of earcons [6,7], Albers et al. [2] suggests a variety of acoustic embellishments to a standard World Wide Web browser for conveying and reaffirming to the user the dynamic behavior of the browser.

Much hypermedia research has focused on the seamless integration of media within a unified framework. Due to the application scenarios and the delivery devices targeted, our emphasis is exclusively on the audio medium. In comparison with its visual counterpart, little work has been conducted on interactive audio-only hypermedia systems. The Hyperspeech system [3] was the first to demonstrate such an approach. Arons manually transcribed several recorded interviews, analyzed their structure and generated corresponding audio nodes and links. Unlike our system, HyperSpeech requires that documents be pre-recorded in audio prior to use.

To access computer-mediated information, blind people, until recently, largely relied upon Braille output devices and software known as *screen readers*. A screen reading program applies various techniques to gain access to the textual content of application software and employs speech synthesis technology to speak this information to the user. Although far from perfect, screen readers provided visually impaired people with a tool for hearing the content of the screen until graphical user interfaces (GUIs) became commonplace. The advent of the GUI made the task of screen reading more complex, thus inspiring research into GUIs for the blind [17,18]. Petrie et al. [18] have conducted preliminary evaluations on input and output schemes to identify favorable hypermedia system interfaces for blind users. As screen readers are application software-independent they can also be used to read the text displayed within a visual World Wide Web browser. In this case the screen reader extracts only the text, as it is not concerned, or aware, of the underlying HTML. As a result, the speech output generated communicates the raw content to the listener but fails to impart any information regarding the structure of the document. The importance of document structure as an aid to understanding, orientation and navigation support is elucidated upon in Section 3.

Several researchers have since attempted to address this shortcoming. Raman [19] has integrated the EmacsSpeak system with Emacs W3 to create a browser that intersperses appropriate spoken descriptions of the HTML document structure along with content. Asakawa et al. [5] explains how the Netscape browser supplies Home Page Reader data to achieve a similar result. Also designed specifically for visually impaired computer users, the pwWebSpeak browser [11] parses HTML documents in order to augment the audio rendering with structural descriptions. The car radio was selected as the interface metaphor by Wynblatt et al. [26] as the basis of the voice browser (WIRE) for providing drivers with access to E-mail and World Wide Web. These systems are for sedentary computer users, with the exception of pwWebSpeak which has support for single-user telephone access.

Goose et al. [10] describe a proxy-based interactive service (DICE) into which multiple users can simultaneously dial and use touch tones or voice commands to browse dynamically generated audio renditions of both E-mail and World Wide Web documents. The DICE audio renderings are also imbued with rich structural descriptions of the document. Web-On-Call [8] offers telephone access to World Wide Web sites rendered using audio, but this solution requires documents to be specially prepared on the server side. Since only a small proportion of sites offer this service this is not a generic solution for telephony World Wide Web browsing. WebGalaxy [14] supports natural language queries and navigation of the World Wide Web. Users can formulate rich and flexible queries, but the domains currently supported are limited to weather, air travel and tourism in Boston.

Reported by Goose et al. [9] is a voice browser that judiciously applies three-dimensional (3D) audio technology. A new 3D conceptual model of the HTML document structure and exploitation of the 'cocktail party effect' [4] facilitate a variety of novel features for improving comprehension of structure, orientation and navigation. Unfortunately, current telephone devices preclude the use of 3D audio technology.

Tim Berners-Lee is quoted as saying "The power of the Web is in its universality. Access by everyone regardless of disability is an essential aspect." In early 1997 the Web Accessibility Initiative (WAI) [23] was introduced by the W3C to promote this theme through publishing guidelines and developing associated tools. A voice-centric extension to HTML has also been proposed: Aural Cascading Style Sheets (ACSS) [1]. A Voice Browser Working Group [21] was also initiated in 1998 to reach consensus on the appropriate markup language requirements for speech technology. Work on extending accessibility principles to Java are being pursued by Sun and IBM with Java Accessibility and Microsoft with Active Accessibility. Lazzaro [15] provides a good review of accessibility issues, products and related organizations.

This literature review confirms that much progress has been made in the area of voice browsing, but to the authors' knowledge the Vox Portal is the first standards-based (VoxML) carrier-class voice-browsing system with a generic solution for dynamic HTML↔VoxML conversion to be reported. The conversion service handles HTML documents through to version 4 and includes full support for sophisticated features, such as the description of and interactive input to HTML forms, tables and the linearization of arbitrary depth HTML framesets.

3. Deriving structure from documents

The native document description language of the World Wide Web is called Hypertext Markup Language (HTML). At a quick glance, a sighted user can assimilate the document structure of a richly graphical HTML page as rendered by a visual World Wide Web browser. This is possible as much of the context is conveyed implicitly through the document structure and layout of the information. Users can then apply their understanding of the HTML document structure to aid orientation, navigation, and ultimately, the location-relevant information.

Given that structure is obviously a key aid to the comprehension of a visual document, it is of paramount importance to convey this to the user of a voice browser. It is clear that most of the context would be lost if a document were 'rendered' by simply sending the raw text of a document to a text-to-speech synthesizer. The Siemens WIRE [26] and DICE [10] voice browsers and the HTML↔VoxML converter all apply an analytical algorithm to an HTML document, or frameset, to elicit both the structure and context. This analysis also distinguishes between 'content sections' and 'navigation sections' based on a link-density metric calculation [24]. The difference is clear visually, but this technique informs the listener as to whether the section is mainly a menu of links or contains mostly text.

Although intended to represent document structure, HTML has also evolved to include constructs for visual specifications. Consequently, no clear distinction exists between the document structure and its presentation view. Many authors strive to design aesthetic and intuitive graphical HTML pages. In order to achieve this goal some authors purposefully select alternative HTML constructs to fashion a custom graphical view of the structure of the page, as opposed to employing the HTML constructs originally designated for specifying the logical structure. One typical example of this is the selection of a large font to customize the appearance of a section heading in favor of the standard HTML header construct. While entirely legitimate, algorithms that analyze the HTML document structure must attempt to identify such behavior to determine the author's logical intent. Such problems have been documented together with recommendations and guidelines for publishers [11,19,23,25].

Once analyzed, the converter generates VoxML output which is forwarded to the Vox Portal. An audio rendering is then produced which combines the use of descriptions, earcons [6,7] and the features of a speech synthesis engine, such as multiple voices, prosody, announcements and pausing, to make structural elements of the document explicit to the listener. The aesthetics of the audio rendition can simultaneously help reduce the monotony factor and enhance comprehension [12].

4. Standards-based architectural support for mobile voice browsing

VoxML proved to be an obvious candidate with which to deliver value-added services because the subscribers interact with the Vox Portal using telephones and other audio-enabled devices. This section begins with a topological overview of how such audio-enabled devices can connect and access Internet and World Wide Web services via the Vox Portal. Following this is a brief description of the Vox Portal and HTML↔VoxML converter. The operation and features of the voice browser are then explained.

4.1. Four tier architecture

Over recent years, three tier architectures have become commonplace and well integrated into the World Wide Web. A typical 3-tier architecture comprises a Client (Tier 1), a Server (Tier 2) and a Database (Tier 3). The architecture described below adds an additional tier to this model to create a Client–Agent–World Wide Web Server–Database. Fig. 1 is a context diagram that depicts (in the region labelled *Voice Client*) how various devices can connect to the Vox Portal; how the Vox Portal interacts with the VoxML–Agent (in the region labelled *Agent*), and how the VoxML–Agent communicates with World Wide Web Servers (in the region labelled *Server*).

4.2. Overview of the Vox Portal client

The client consists of three main components: a Voice Terminal, a Voice Over IP Gateway (VoIP) and a Vox Portal. The Voice Terminal is typically a device such as a traditional or cellular telephone. This terminal is connected through the appropriate native local network with the audio channel carried to the PSTN. A digital channel is then routed through a VoIP gateway. The VoIP gateway maps the circuit-switched domain to the packet-switched domain. The audio channel data is then sent through the packet-switched network (LAN/WAN) using the H.323 protocol. With the aid of an auxiliary component, called a Gatekeeper (not shown in Fig. 1), the H.323 session is routed to the Vox Portal.

The Vox Portal is a scaleable, multi-user client able to interface with the VoxML–Agent. The Vox Portal acts as a gateway that maps H.323 sessions to HTTP sessions. Although any media type can be carried by the H.323 protocol, audio is the only medium currently supported. Interactivity is facilitated by interpreting voice and/or out-of-band DTMF (Digital Tone Multiple Frequency). As alluded to earlier, the Vox Portal currently subscribes to the standard VoxML v1.1 [16] for specifying the nature of the interaction and behavior of the speech technologies. It is likely in the future that the Vox Portal will evolve to support the new standard VoiceXML [22] as promulgated by the VoiceXML Forum. The Vox Portal also includes necessary support for issues and services such as management, accounting, user profiles, and internationalization.

4.3. Web-hosted dynamic HTML↔VoxML converter

The VoxML–Agent component is responsible for retrieving HTML documents, transforming them into

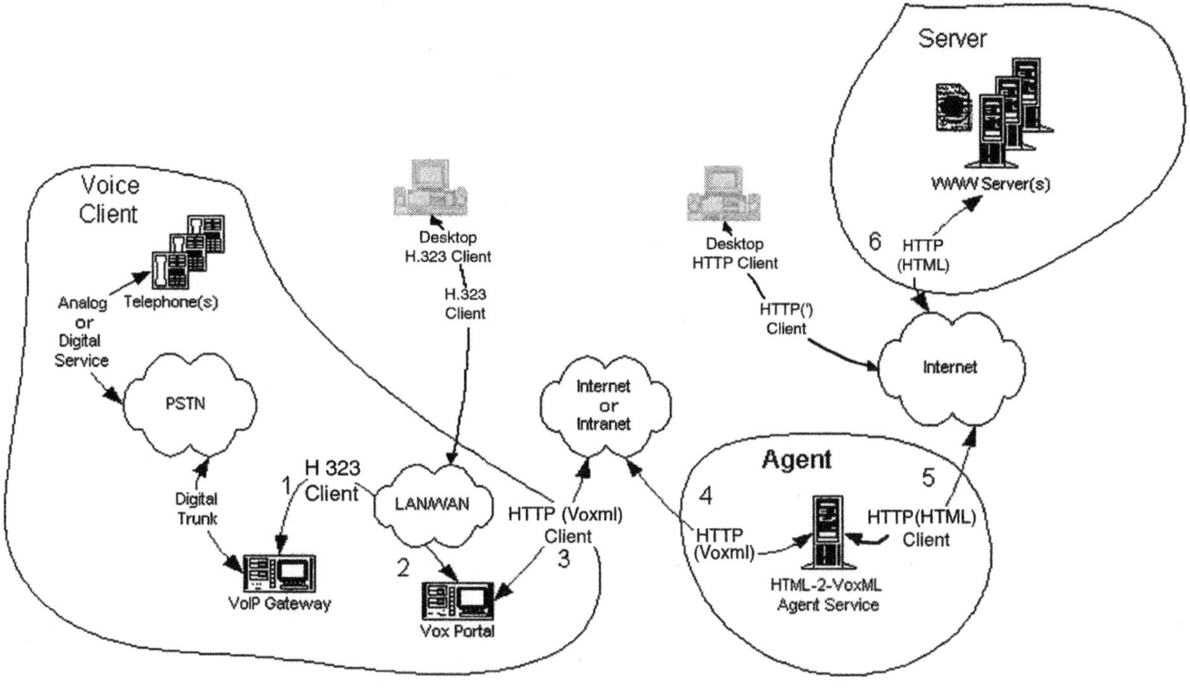

Fig. 1. Multi-tiered architecture context diagram.

VoxML documents and returning the VoxML content to the requesting HTTP(VoxML) client. Since the core functional components are hosted by a World Wide Web Server, the attributes of multi-user support, horizontal scaleability, security and administration are inherited. The VoxML–Agent component bears similarities to a Proxy Server with the major difference being that the HTML content undergoes analysis and transformation prior to being returned to the client. Additionally, Proxy Servers do not support session handling, which can be necessary when accessing some World Wide Web sites.

4.3.1. VoxML–Agent architecture

The VoxML–Agent is architected with modular and reusable components. It consists of a primary HTTP entry point, an HTTP client plus HTML parser, core HTML to VoxML transformation logic, core Form Processing logic, and various fixed documents such as the VoxML DTD. Fig. 2 depicts the high-level architecture of the VoxML–Agent and its external interfaces.

The entry point of the VoxML–Agent application is the HTTP Query Processor which interprets the request of the HTTP (VoxML) client. The HTTP Query Processor supports two query types: FetchURL and PostForm. Clearly other queries are possible, but these two cover the majority of the HTTP requests usually encountered when browsing the World Wide Web. Once the query is categorized as FetchURL or PostForm, the HTTP Query Processor delegates tasks to the appropriate modules.

The HTTP client and HTML parser module is responsible for carrying out the Agent HTTP GET or POST methods. The HTTP client supports SSL (HTTPS) and interoperability with Proxy Servers. The parsing capabilities allow this module to perform the majority of functions found in a typical World Wide Web browser, such as automatically constructing nested framesets and combining XML/XSL to produce HTML.

The HTML-2-VoxML Core is the component in which the HTML document analysis and VoxML construction functionality reside. The HTML document analysis remains independent of the VoxML document construction. The HTML document structure and content analysis is performed as outlined in Section 3. On completion of the HTML analy-

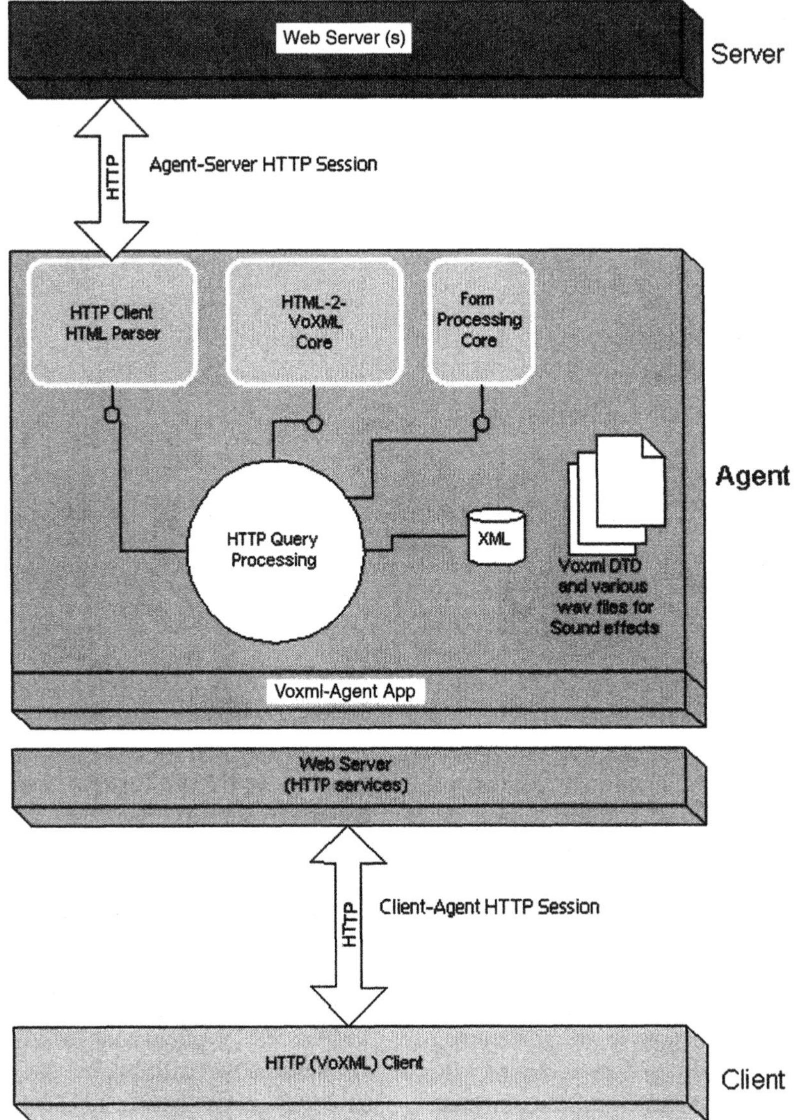

Fig. 2. VoxML–Agent high-level architecture diagram.

sis, a VoxML version of the document is generated. To ensure compliance with the VoxML standard, the VoxML XML document generated is validated against the VoxML DTD before being transferred to the Vox Portal.

The Form Processing Core is the module responsible for constructing the POST or GET data of HTML forms that were converted to VoxML and returned by the VoxML client. This module does not perform the POST or GET, it takes the information returned by a VoxML client and invokes the appropriate POST or GET method as expected by the originating World Wide Web Server that hosts the form.

4.3.2. *VoxML–Agent session control*

Since the VoxML–Agent is a multi-user (or multi-session) middle-tier component, it is responsible for keeping track of the Client–Agent HTTP session and any associated established Agent–Server HTTP session. This is achieved through the combination of session cookies and the help of the World Wide Web Server that hosts the VoxML–Agent. After the first HTTP request by the VoxML client, the VoxML–Agent's hosting World Wide Web Server inserts a session ID in the cookie field of the HTTP response header. The VoxML–Agent services can also be used without cookies; however, the Agent–Server connection may fail in situations where the requested URL resides at a World Wide Web site that employs session cookies. The use of such cookies are common on World Wide Web sites that host free E-mail, financial services and other pre-paid services.

4.3.3. Overview of converter operation

Illustrated in Fig. 3 is a simplified flow of events that transpire during a typical VoxML–Agent session. The shadowed boxes represent VoxML client states that can prompt an action, the circles represent actions performed by the VoxML–Agent and the diamonds represent basic decisions that result in the branching to different actions.

Using the flow diagram in Fig. 3 as a guide, the following example describes the process of navigating to a World Wide Web URL, completing a Form and then submitting it to the originating World Wide Web Server. Each step is labelled in the diagram from 1 to 8.

Step 1. A VoxML client (HTTP(VoxML)) performs an HTTP request to the VoxML–Agent to fetch an URL. *Step 2.* The VoxML–Agent processes the request by dynamically creating an HTTP client to fetch the designated URL. *Step 3.* The document and its constituent parts, such as frames, are downloaded. *Step 4a.* If an error 'time-out' occurs a VoxML page describing the error is generated and returned to the VoxML client. *Step 4b.* Otherwise, while the document is downloading a VoxML document describing the status is generated and returned to the VoxML client. A new status document is periodically generated and sent to the client until the successful download or the process 'times-out'. *Step 4c.* Upon successful download, the HTML document is analyzed and a VoxML representation is created. The VoxML document is then returned to the VoxML client for rendering. *Step 5.* At the time of rendition, the VoxML client will allow the user to follow links and complete forms. *Step 6.* If the user chooses to follow a link, the process described from Step 1 to Step 6 is repeated. *Step 7.* If the user completes and submits a form using the VoxML client, it is returned and handled by a process on the VoxML–Agent. *Step 8.* The Form Processor of the VoxML–Agent accepts the data returned by the VoxML client and recreates the appropriate GET or POST method expected by the originating World Wide Web Server. Starting from Step 3, the cycle is then repeated.

4.4. The browsing experience

An essential ingredient of hypermedia documents is the link, and, in the context of the World Wide Web, a link can either point to another place within the same document (intra-document link) or another document entirely (inter-document link). Petrie [18] notes that users can become disorientated during navigation without a mechanism for disambiguating these two link types. Moreover, Landow [13] advocates the use of a 'rhetoric of arrival and departure' when authoring hypermedia documents for mitigating the effects of disorientation during navigation. In order to navigate the World Wide Web a user must be cognizant of the links. Once aware of the convention, empirical tests indicated that the combination of a distinct earcon, followed by a specific synthesized voice reserved for announcing the anchor text, enabled users to identify the presence of links correctly every time. Two sonically related earcons are used for link notification thus enabling the listener to distinguish easily between the two link types.

It is a challenge to create an intuitive graphical user interface, but it is notoriously difficult to design an intuitive telephone user interface. We have implemented many of Resnick's recommendations [20] for spoken feedback and keypad mappings. To reduce complexity, we sought an interface that required minimal interaction. The activity of browsing in an audio-only environment is quite different in comparison with its visual counterpart. The serial nature of audio gives rise to a 'listen and interrupt' paradigm.

Akin to bookmarks, a number of favorites can be set in advance and accessed through the Vox Portal. Browsing commences by selecting a favorite. Once downloaded, the document is processed by the converter and rendered as previously described.

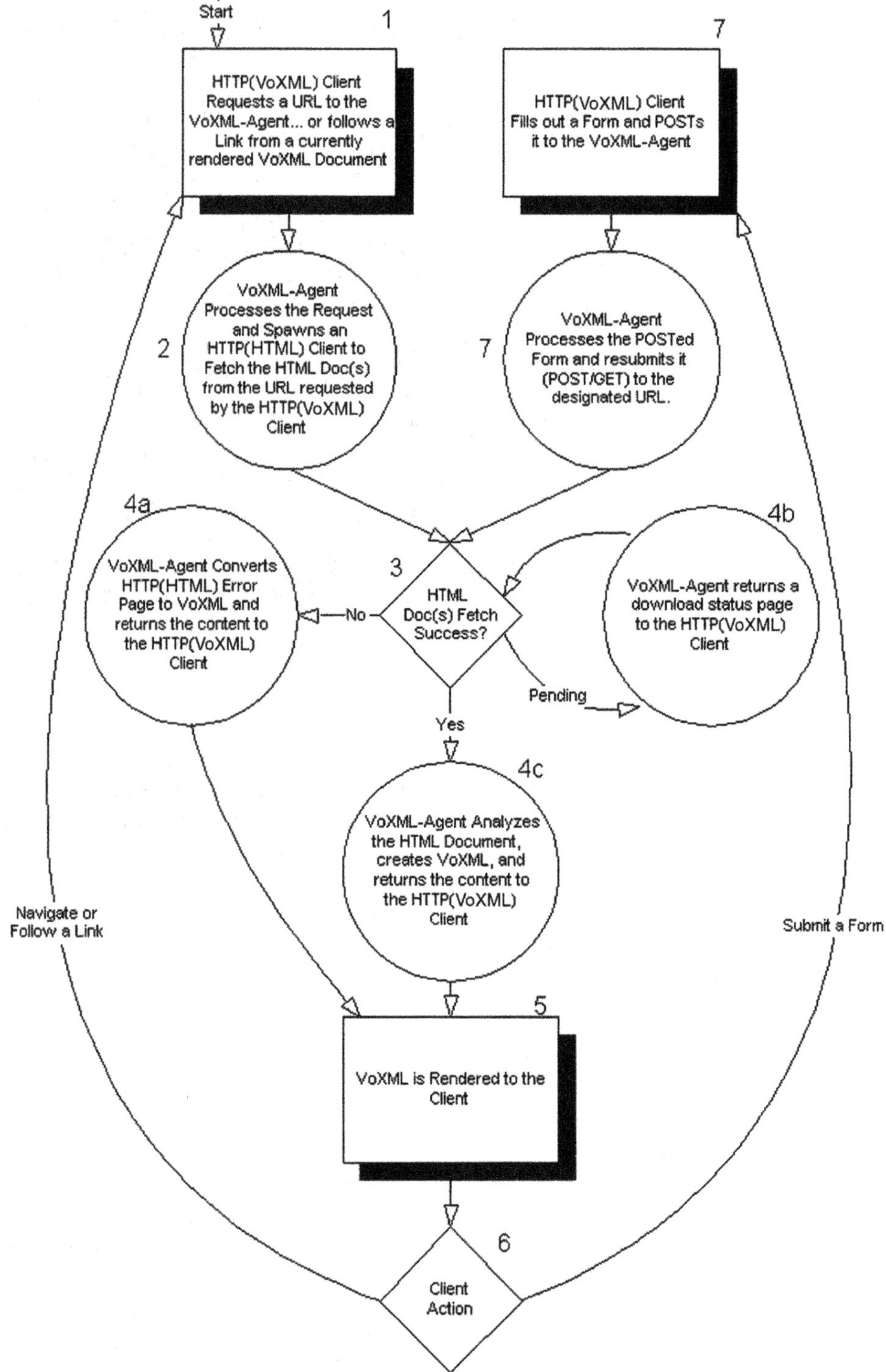

Fig. 3. VoxML–Agent interaction flow diagram.

Each link encountered is announced and becomes the active link. A link remains traversable until the next link is reached. The minimal pattern of interaction for browsing can thus be reduced to selecting favorite(s) and following the active link(s).

To alleviate the user from listening to every document in its entirety, a selection of browsing modes allow different perspectives of the document to be generated. In addition to the entire document being rendered, a second mode announces each link anchor; useful if a document is frequently used as an index to subsequent documents. A third mode announces only the sections headings; a convenient mechanism for rapidly scanning a document. A fourth mode skips over dense link clusters and renders the content. As the browsing mode can be changed dynamically, a user can combine these approaches to navigate more efficiently within and across document boundaries. In addition, a history list of the documents visited is also maintained. The user typically traverses backward or forward through the history listening to the titles being announced, and selects the desired document to revisit.

5. Future work and conclusions

Naturally, a voice browser cannot challenge a traditional World Wide Web browser in delivering a rich multimedia presentation. Hence traditional World Wide Web browsers are unlikely to be supplanted by voice-browsing technologies. However, voice browsers can provide an appropriate interface for many people in many situations. Voice-browsing technologies still face many interesting research challenges. The effectiveness of all voice browsers are compromised when faced with unsympathetically authored HTML documents [11,19,23,25] without explicit logical structure, an abundance of graphics, use of client side scripting and unclear associations between form labels and their corresponding fields. In addition, more research is necessary to take this technology beyond the current generation of voice browsers.

In this paper we described a standards-based (VoxML) carrier-class voice-browsing system called the Vox Portal and an associated generic solution for dynamic, bi-directional HTML$\leftrightarrow$VoxML conversion. This generic conversion service unites the voice and World Wide Web arenas and also relieves publishers from translating their HTML content and services to VoxML. The conversion service handles HTML documents through to version 4 and includes full support for sophisticated features, such as the description of and interactive input to HTML forms, tables and the linearization of arbitrary depth HTML framesets.

Interactive voice browsers offer an alternative paradigm that enables both sighted and visually impaired users to access the World Wide Web. In addition to the desktop PC, voice browsers afford ubiquitous mobile access to the World Wide Web using a wide range of consumer devices. This technology can facilitate a safe, 'hands-free' browsing environment which is of importance both to car drivers and various mobile and technical professionals. By providing voice-mediated access, information providers can reach a wider audience and leverage existing investment in their World Wide Web content.

Acknowledgements

Thanks are due to the following members of technical staff at SCR and SRIT who have contributed to the work described in this paper: Steffen Rusitschka, Sreedhar Kodlahalli, Denis Perraud, Laurent Strullu and Philippe Menard.

References

[1] ACSS – Aural Cascading Style Sheets, W3C Note, http://www.w3.org/Style/css/Speech/NOTE-ACSS

[2] M. Albers and M. Bergman, The audible Web: auditory enhancements for WWW browsers, Proc. 3rd Int. World Wide Web Conf., April 1995.

[3] B. Arons, Hyperspeech: navigating in speech-only hypermedia, Proc. ACM Int. Conf. on Hypertext, December 1991, pp. 133–146.

[4] B. Arons, A review of the cocktail party effect, J. Am. Voice I/O Soc. 12 (1992) 35–50.

[5] C. Asakawa and T. Itoh, User interface of a home page reader, Proc. ACM Conf. on Assistive Technologies (ASSETS), 1998.

[6] M. Blattner, D. Sumikawa and R. Greenberg, Earcons and icons: their structure and common design principles, Hum.–Comput. Interaction 4(1) (1989) 11–44.

[7] W. Gaver, Auditory icons: using sound in computer interfaces, Hum.–Comput. Interaction 2(2) (1986) 167–177.
[8] General Magic, Web-On-Call, http://www.netphonic.com
[9] S. Goose and C. Möller, A 3D audio only interactive Web browser: using spatialization to convey hypermedia document structure, Proc. ACM Int. Conf. on Multimedia, October 1999, pp. 363–371.
[10] S. Goose, M. Wynblatt and H. Mollenhauer, 1-800-hypertext: browsing hypertext with a telephone, Proc. ACM Int. Conf. on Hypertext, June 1998, pp. 287–288.
[11] M. Hakkinen, Issues in non-visual Web browser design: pwWebSpeak, Proc. 6th Int. World Wide Web Conf., April 1997.
[12] F. James, Presenting HTML structure in audio: user satisfaction with audio hypertext, Proc. Int. Conf. on Auditory Display (ICAD), November 1997, pp. 97–103.
[13] G. Landow, The Rhetoric of Hypermedia: Some Rules for Authors, Hypermedia and Literary Studies, MIT Press, Cambridge, MA, 1991.
[14] R. Lau, G. Flammia, C. Pao and V. Zue, WebGALAXY: Beyond point and click: a conversational interface to a browser, Proc. 6th Int. World Wide Web Conf., April 1997.
[15] J. Lazzaro, Helping the Web Help the Disabled, IEEE Spectrum, March 1999, pp. 54–59.
[16] Motorola, VoxML: The mark-up language for voice applications, http://www.voxml.com
[17] E. Mynatt and W. Edwards, The Mercator environment: a non-visual interface to the X Window System, Technical Report GIT-GVU-92-05, February 1992.
[18] H. Petrie, S. Morley, P. McNally, A. O'Neill and D. Majoe, Initial design and evaluation of an interface to hypermedia system for blind users, Proc. ACM Int. Conf. on Hypertext, April 1997, pp. 48–56.
[19] T.V. Raman, The audible WWW: The world in my ears, Proc. 6th Int. World Wide Web Conf., April 1997.
[20] P. Resnick and R. Virzi, Skip and scan: cleaning up telephone interfaces, Proc. CHI '92, May 1992, pp. 419–426.
[21] Voice Browser Working Group, http://www.w3.org/UI/Voice/
[22] VoiceXML Forum, VoiceXML: the Voice eXtensible Mark-up Language, http://www.voicexml.com
[23] Web Accessibility Initiative, http://www.w3.org/WAI
[24] M. Wynblatt and D. Benson, Web page caricatures: multimedia summaries for WWW documents, Proc. IEEE Int. Conf. on Multimedia and Computing Systems, June 1998.
[25] M. Wynblatt and S. Goose, Towards improving audio Web browsing, WWW Consortium (W3C) Workshop on Voice Browsers, Boston, MA, October 1998.
[26] M. Wynblatt, D. Benson and A. Hsu, Browsing the World Wide Web in a non-visual environment, Proc. Int. Conf. on Auditory Display (ICAD), November 1997, pp. 135–138.

Stuart Goose received B.Sc. (1993) and Ph.D. (1997) degrees in Computer Science from the University of Southampton, England. At Siemens he leads a research group with multiple projects exploring and applying various aspects of Internet, mobility, multimedia, hypermedia, speech and audio technologies.

Mike Newman received his B.S. Electrical Engineering (1992) from Temple University and his M.S. Computer Science (1997) from Penn State University.

Claus Schmidt received a Dipl. Informatiker degree from FH Furtwangen, Germany (1990) and a M.Sc degree in Computer Science from Leicester Polytechnic, England. He leads a group that develops next-generation voice data convergence applications for telecommunication networks. His foci are Voice-over-IP, Multimedia and Web-enabled telephony.

Laurent Hué graduated from the Ecole Nationale Supérieure des Télécommunications de Bretagne in 1992. At Siemens, he leads a service developing VoIP products, including the Vox Portal Server (SURPASS family). He worked first for Thomson in the field of signal processing (publication at GRETSI '93 and OCEAN '93). He then joined the France Telecom Research Center in 1993, where he was in charge of IP and ATM network design and ATM equipment specification. He has taken part in the standardization process of ATM equipment, as Chairman of the Q10/15 within ITU-T and as a delegate in the ETSI body. He has been awarded three European patents in the domain of the ATM access networks for mobiles.

HTTP ‘Next Generation’

Mike Spreitzer *,[1], Bill Janssen [1]

Xerox Palo Alto Research Center, 3333 Coyote Hill Road, Palo Alto, CA 94304, USA

Abstract

We report on the results of the Protocol Design Group of the W3C's HTTP ‘Next Generation’ Activity. The group produced and measured a prototype that shows that it is possible, largely using familiar engineering principles, to make simultaneous improvements in the following problem areas of HTTP/1.1: (1) the layering of other application protocols over HTTP; (2) modularity and extensibility; (3) networking performance and fairness; (4) the rigid binding between identifiers and protocol stacks; and (5) the opacity of layered traffic to firewalls. The prototype also suggests that these can be done in a way that may lead to unifying the Web with related middleware systems such as COM, CORBA, and Java RMI. © 2000 Published by Elsevier Science B.V. All rights reserved.

Keywords: HTTP-NG; Type system; Web applications; Distributed objects; RPC

1. Introduction

In mid-1997 the W3C chartered an Activity (currently only post-conclusion Web pages [18,19] are available) on HTTP-NG. The Activity consisted of two parts, one devoted to characterizing the Web and one devoted to prototyping a major revision to HTTP. The second part, known as the Protocol Design Group (PDG), ran through late 1998 and produced and measured a prototype to study the feasibility of moving the Web onto an application-independent distributed object system. The prototype showed that it is indeed possible to make improvements in a number of problem areas of HTTP/1.1 [11], and that this can be done in a way that could lead to the unification of the Web with the related middleware systems COM [6,7,25], CORBA [33], and Java RMI [24].

The group addressed the following problem areas.

* Corresponding author.

[1] E-mail: {spreitze,janssen}@parc.xerox.com

1.1. Modularity and extensibility

Although HTTP's initial success was fueled by simplicity, HTTP is no longer simple. The HTTP/1.1 specification [11] is 175 pages long. Over the years many features have been added, each for a reason. Simplicity encompasses many things, only some of which remain within the realm of possibility for HTTP. Because of the many strong demands placed on it, HTTP cannot return to being a small protocol. However, HTTP could be made much more modular.

HTTP currently addresses concerns over a wide range of levels of abstraction. These include low-level transport issues, such as persistent connections and the delimiting of messages. These also include mid-level issues, such as regular patterns for identifying methods and passing parameters, as you find in RPC (Remote Procedure Call) and messaging middleware. And there is the relatively high-level issue of defining a particular application focussed on fetching/storing documents/forms. The PDG called this application 'The Classic Web Application' (TCWA), to distinguish it from the great many other applications now using HTTP. The levels addressed by HTTP are not cleanly separated in the specification, requiring every reader to consider the whole thing. There are complex interactions between the levels. For example, there are five different ways to delimit a message, and four of them involve interactions with the higher levels (and the fifth uses TCP particularly badly). For another example, the lack of clean separation between messages and documents has a negative impact on caching (as has also been observed by Jeff Mogul [28]).

HTTP is now being used for applications other than TCWA, which causes additional problems. These other applications include those that are closely related (e.g., WebDAV [15], DASL [9], and DELTAV [35]), those that are less closely related (e.g., IPP [17], SWAP [30]), those that are based on partial clones of HTTP (e.g., SIP [16]), and those that are completely unrelated and based on the layering over HTTP of middleware systems of independent origin (e.g., COM, Java RMI, and some CORBA implementations) and of Web-conscious origin (e.g., XML-RPC [37], SOAP [4]). These other applications do not benefit from the parts of HTTP specific to TCWA, and because those parts are not well separated there are resulting inefficiencies and confusions. The parameter passing technique in HTTP is based on mail 'headers' [8] (excepting the one distinguished, optional parameter that is the MIME-typed 'body'). This parameter passing technique does not address structuring of recursive data, and requires a level of quoting/encoding to pass arbitrary application data. The use of HTTP for other applications invites confusions [29] between the other application and HTTP's document application. The following questions, which must be answered in the course of developing applications layered on top of HTTP, are symptoms of this confusion.

- Should the application use a different port than the HTTP default of 80?
- Should the application use traditional HTTP methods (GET, POST, etc.) or should it define new methods?
- Should the application use `http:` URLs or define its own?
- Should the application define its own MIME-types, or use something that already exists?

Answering questions like this has been a real problem. For example, this was a contentious issue in the development of the Internet Printing Protocol. The 1.0 version was taken off the Standards Track at the last minute by the Internet Engineering Steering Group, due partly to their disagreeing with the Working Group on choice of URI scheme ([17]: IESG Note, [20]).

The well known paradigm of explicit interfaces, as used in modern programming languages and RPC systems, would help manage the co-existence and evolution of the multiplicity of applications of HTTP, but HTTP does not support that paradigm. The closest it comes is the OPTIONS method, which only reveals 'communication options' that manifest themselves through response headers.

HTTP offers limited support for decentralized evolution. Decentralized evolution is what happens when no one organization is in engineering control of a widely deployed distributed system (such as the Web). Evolutionary changes are independently developed by multiple independent organizations. At any given point in time, multiple such changes are in the process of being incrementally rolled out into the deployed system. In general, any given client and server have some extensions in common, and each also has extensions not supported by the other. When such a client and server interact, it is desirable for them to automatically employ the extensions they both understand, without a lot of latency or code complexity due to negotiation. HTTP supports this, with its rule that extension headers are optional and ignorable. However, it is also desirable for 'mandatory' extensions to be possible. When one peer employs a mandatory extension, the other must either support that extension or signal an error. Again, it should be possible to employ multiple mandatory extensions without a lot of latency or code complexity due to negotiation. Mandatory extensions are always easy to support on the receiving side (it can raise an error on its own whenever desired). HTTP does not give senders much support for mandatory extensions. The only available technique is to use an entirely new method, which loses all the benefits of formally being an incremental change, notably including the automatic combination of multiple extensions.

1.2. Networking performance and fairness

HTTP has networking performance and fairness problems. These include inefficient use of the network, poor latency delivered to the users, and a tendency to abuse the network with multiple parallel TCP streams.

The use of verbose text-based representations for 'headers' and other protocol-level data, and the confusion between that layer and human-readable documents and mail messages, leads to unnecessarily high numbers of bytes used for protocol overheads and method parameters.

HTTP's use of TCP suffers from high latencies for three reasons. One is simply that it takes time to transmit the unnecessarily large number of bytes. The next reason follows from the use of multiple parallel TCP streams. Commonly deployed TCP implementations do not share congestion-avoidance state between parallel streams, leading to less efficient reactions to network conditions. In particular, the streams may ramp up to full speed more slowly than possible, and may provoke more congestion and consequent back-off than necessary; both increase the latency suffered by users. Finally, opening a TCP connection involves three messages over one and a half round trips; there have been proposals [5] for how to reduce this to just one message prepended to the data stream.

There is a tendency for browsers to open multiple parallel HTTP/TCP streams, for two reasons. One is that with the currently deployed router policies, this tends to deliver an unfairly large share of the available network bandwidth. No changes in HTTP can fix this; the needed fix is to router policies. But even if and when the unfairness is fixed, there is another reason for browsers to use parallel streams (with the undesirable consequences mentioned above as well as the current unfairness). When first fetching a new Web page with inlined images, it is advantageous to be able to quickly fetch the first few bytes of each inlined image because those bytes tend to contain metadata critical to computing the page's overall layout. Some browser vendors (e.g., Netscape) have chosen to do this by invoking GETs in multiple parallel connections. While it might appear that there is a viable alternative in using HTTP/1.1's `Range` header, there are some problems with that approach: (1) it is relatively recently standardized, so uniform server support cannot be assumed; and (2) the Range header's interactions with other features of HTTP are unclear or bad (e.g., HTTP/1.1 offers integrity checking on messages, not documents [28]).

1.3. URIs bound to protocol stacks

HTTP can, in principle, be used over a great variety of 'transport' substacks, but the 'http' URI scheme is bound specifically to TCP. There is another scheme ('https') bound to TLS/SSL over TCP. One could imagine other transport substacks (e.g., a wireless version of TCP). In the current architecture, each particular choice of transport substack requires a new URI scheme. New URI schemes are painful to deploy, because, among other things, each one forms its own name space. Further, it is inconceivable for a URI to have multiple schemes (e.g., to offer multiple alternative transport substacks). Without the possibility of multiple stacks, it is not possible to incrementally move the current Web onto a new transport substack — nor offer multiple alternatives for any other reason — except by using mechanisms (such as HTTP redirections or UPGRADE) that cost additional round trips.

1.4. Tunnelled traffic vs. firewalls

The practice of tunnelling general applications through HTTP makes the job of a firewall harder. We must be clear on the job of a firewall. A firewall, if it passes any traffic between them at all, cannot prevent collusion between an attacker inside the firewall and an attacker outside the firewall. Nor does a firewall benefit a trusted and trustworthy insider who fully secures his machines (this involves high administrative and operational burdens, and the use of security-bug-free software). A firewall's job is to make it easier for a trusted insider to be trustworthy, by enforcing certain limits on traffic between the inside and outside. The great variety and obscurity of ways of tunnelling general applications through HTTP makes it hard for a firewall to do anything with HTTP traffic.

1.5. Unifying the Web with COM, CORBA, and Java RMI

The prototype solution to the above problem areas is based on factoring HTTP into three layers: (1) transport of opaque byte or message streams; (2) application-independent remote method invocation; and (3) the document fetching/storing application. The lower two layers suffice to serve the needs of the other applications currently being layered over all of HTTP, and provide a more robust platform on which to deploy and evolve a large collection of applications. There is a significant overlap among the problems addressed by this platform and the problems addressed by COM, CORBA, and Java RMI. This suggests an intriguing possibility. It starts with making a single wire protocol able to carry COM, CORBA, and Java RMI as well as Web traffic. This provides interoperability, at least in the areas where the features of those systems overlap. Additionally, this could spur further convergence between those systems.

In the next section we present an overview of the prototype design, focussing on the lessons learned in solving the above problems. In Section 3 we present the experimental results, which show that it is indeed possible to improve performance even while using a design and implementation that are more modular. In Section 4 we briefly consider future and related work.

2. The prototype design

The prototype design shows a feasible way to make simultaneous improvements in all the problem areas above. This is largely done by straightforward application of well-known engineering principles. The first principle applied is divide-and-conquer. The major application of this principle is the division of HTTP's functionality into three conventional layers; this yields a significant dose of simplicity (i.e., modularity), and is key to realizing a deep unification of the Web with related middleware systems. The lowest layer addresses transport of opaque messages or streams, in a way that allows composition of 'transport filters'; included is a design of a particular multiplexing filter that addresses some shortcomings of current TCP and provides a service abstraction that can insulate higher layers from certain desirable and expected changes in the lower levels. The middle layer addresses application-independent RPC, including typed messages as a degenerate case. The highest layer expresses the Web as an application of the lower two layers.

We consider these layers in turn.

2.1. The transport layer

The transport layer addresses problems with modularity and extensibility, networking performance and fairness, transport flexibility, and even makes a contribution to unifying middleware systems. All this is easily done using familiar ideas, mainly: (1) a system of filters (as, e.g., in UNIX shell commands); and (2) multiplexing.

The transport layer, which is inspired by and very similar to the corresponding layer in ILU [21], addresses reliable ordered bidirectional transport of opaque byte or message streams. An HTTP-NG connection can employ a stack of *transport filters*. A transport filter implements reliable ordered bidirectional transport of opaque byte streams or of opaque messages. The filter may do this either by directly using the services of protocols outside the scope of this design (e.g., TCP) or indirectly by using the services of the next lower filter in the stack. A filter can have explicit parameters, such as the TCP port number to use.

This transport layer is modular and offers controlled evolution; its flexibility is part of the solution to the problem of the strong linkage between URIs and protocol stacks. The remainder of the solution appears in the middle layer, where the choice of stack is communicated in a way that is independent of object identifiers.

The prototype design details two particular transport filters. One implements byte streams by directly using TCP. This filter has two parameters, a host name or address and a port number. The other filter is a multiplexer, described in the next section.

2.2. The MUX filter

The MUX filter addresses network performance and fairness problems, and contributes to middleware system unification. It does these by adding to the functionality delivered by its underlying stack in three ways. The underlying stack delivers reliable ordered bidirectional transport of opaque byte streams (e.g., by TCP). The MUX filter adds: (1) the delimiting of messages; (2) the multiplexing of parallel message streams over a single underlying byte stream; (3) the ability of the accepting (server) side of the byte stream connection to initiate message stream connections in the reverse direction.

The multiplexing of parallel message streams into a single byte stream addresses some of the network performance problems of HTTP. By moving the multiplexing up a level, the problems associated with lack of sharing of congestion-avoidance state between parallel TCP streams are avoided. The MUX filter can open a new message stream over an existing byte stream with the sending of only one message, at the start of the message stream; this saves a round trip compared to the cost of opening a new parallel TCP stream. The higher layers can open parallel message streams without paying the penalties of parallel TCP streams.

The ability of a byte stream connection receiver to initiate message stream connections in the reverse direction may be useful both (1) to solve the same performance problems mentioned above and (2) to enable callbacks from servers to clients behind firewalls. This contributes to unifying COM with other middleware systems. COM is unique in that a method parameter may be a callback function. Of course, a callback function can be considered just a special case of an object, except for the interaction with firewalls. Calling an object normally requires the caller to open a connection to the object's server. For an object modelling a callback function, this server is the client of the outer call, and may well be behind a firewall. Firewalls typically do not pass TCP connections initiated externally. Carving out this exception is reasonable, because it only allows traffic that the protected party has specifically requested and will interpret. Enabling message streams to be initiated in the reverse direction thus eliminates a problem with using objects to deliver the functionality of COM's callback functions.

Introducing this new layer of multiplexing introduces new possibilities of interference between independent connections. This can be partly solved by adopting TCP's flow control design, but that does not eliminate all the possible bad interactions.

The MUX protocol applies flow control independently to each message stream. Thus, a stall in one message stream does not block other message streams multiplexed with it. Flow is controlled by limiting the sender to a window, in terms of the total number of message payload bytes sent, given by the receiver. This is essentially the same as TCP's flow control. TCP's congestion avoidance ('slow start') does not need to be repeated at the MUX layer, as its presence in the underlying stack (e.g., in TCP) is sufficient.

There remains one potentially significant bad interaction between parallel message streams. If the underlying byte stream (e.g., TCP) encounters a delay due to an internal re-transmission (e.g., due to a lost IP packet), then all of the message streams multiplexed over it suffer that delay, even if the lost packet contained only information relevant to one message stream.

The IETF has chartered a Working Group on 'Endpoint Congestion Management' [10], which is intended to develop a way for parallel connections (both TCP and other kinds) to share congestion-avoidance state. By solving the state-sharing problem where it arises, this would eliminate the need for another layer of multiplexing above TCP. It would not eliminate the need for the other two things the MUX filter does. The flexibility of HTTP-NG's transport layer would allow a switch from MUX over TCP to a MUX−− over TCP++ without significant disruption of the other layers.

Introducing a new layer of multiplexing requires a solution to the problems of identifying the streams multiplexed together, and of identifying which of potentially several targets a stream is connected to. The obvious and simple technique of using numeric IDs suffices. The HTTP-NG prototype design goes a bit further, exploring opportunities that come with associating further semantics with those numbers.

Among those multiplexed together, a message stream connection is identified by a number called a 'session ID'. The space of session IDs is divided in two: one half to be allocated by the byte stream initiator, the other by the byte stream acceptor.

The MUX filter supports the possibility of multiple message stream acceptors on each side of the byte stream, through a technique that is inspired by and extends TCP's notion of port numbers for passive sockets. Each message stream acceptor is identified by a number; the initiator sends this number as part of opening a new message stream connection. The extension is that these numbers are known as 'Protocol IDs', and may be used to support a simple form of negotiation for the protocol stack above the message stream. The space of Protocol IDs is divided into four parts: (1) one with an ID for each possible TCP port number; (2) one with an ID for each possible UDP port number; (3) one where the IDs are allocated by the server at its discretion; and (4) one where the IDs are associated by the initiator with a URI that identifies the protocol stack above. The value of the first two parts is that they provide a standard way to use the MUX protocol to tunnel TCP and UDP over TCP, fixing the performance problems above in a way that is transparent to applications. The third part of the Protocol ID space functions analogously to the accepting side's port number in TCP: the acceptor uses one that either is allocated by an external (to the MUX protocol) process or is purely ephemeral, and the way that the initiator learns of that number is outside the scope of the MUX protocol. The fourth part of the Protocol ID space is intended to enable a message stream acceptor to have dynamic flexibility in protocol stacks. The idea is that rather than allocate a number for every supported combination and parameterization of transport filters and higher protocols (with the ability to combine and parameterize filters, the number of supported superstacks could get quite high), the client simply states the desired superior stack at the start of a message stream. We have not yet explored this much further, but it costs little to carve out this piece of Protocol ID space.

An issue not fully explored is how to identify 'endpoints'. For the ability to initiate message stream connections in the reverse direction to be useful, it is helpful to allow the byte stream initiator to give the acceptor some identification of what services can be reached at the initiator side. To this end, the MUX protocol allows one peer to send the other a message listing *endpoints* that are available. The MUX protocol says about endpoints only that they are URIs, with hierarchy — if any is defined by the URI's scheme — respected. That is, if one side wishes to open a message stream connection to endpoint 'sch:X/Y' and has in hand a byte stream connection initiated by a peer that advertises endpoint 'sch:X/', that byte stream connection may be used for the new message stream connection. Plausible things that an endpoint might actually identify include: (1) a particular host; (2) a particular process (address space); and (3) a particular software module instance in a particular process.

2.3. The remote invocation layer

The middle layer of the prototype HTTP-NG design is an application-independent remote method invocation layer. It provides object-oriented method calls, similarly to COM, CORBA, and Java RMI; HTTP's document fetching/storing application becomes a definition of a particular network interface for that application (the third layer, discussed later). The middle layer addresses problems of modularity and extensibility, network performance, the binding of object identifiers to protocol stacks, the opacity of tunnelled traffic to firewalls, and the unification of the Web with related middleware systems.

One lesson to draw from this exercise is that familiar ideas about how to design RPC systems can easily be applied to the Web, and that doing so yields the benefits we describe. The very idea of RPC — particularly when done with explicit interfaces — makes a major improvement in the modularity and extensibility of the Web. The interfaces are explicitly identified on the wire, and this makes it easier for firewalls to do more discriminating filtering. Further details on this first lesson appear in the sections below.

Another lesson to draw is that it is not difficult to take great strides toward a deep unification of the Web with COM, CORBA, and Java RMI. The unification of which we speak is not at the level of wire protocols — where all three systems are hopelessly far apart now but their owners have shown considerable flexibility for the future — but rather the abstractions with which application developers work. By a 'deep' unification we mean the deployment of a system whose semantics essentially encompass those of the all unified systems; this may be contrasted to the more shallow unification achieved, for example, by having all those systems exchange their data encoded in XML over HTTP but without agreeing on common kinds of data or common encodings. Unification is discussed further in the section on the type system, where this issue chiefly appears.

The middle layer's design may be organized into three parts: (1) a type system for the data (including object values and references) passed in the calls; (2) a way of encoding those data in serial bytes; and (3) the call framing and other conventions needed to implement remote invocations in terms of opaque messages. We consider each of those parts in turn.

2.3.1. The data type system

The problems for the data type system to solve are: (1) be sufficient for good expression of TCWA as well as other applications being layered on HTTP; and (2) unify the type systems of COM, CORBA, and Java RMI. As this was only a feasibility study, the PDG was willing to overlook relatively obscure features of related middleware systems, and to explore advanced concepts that seemed to be on the upswing, on the grounds that the other systems might make such changes in the future. The HTTP-NG prototype's type system is described in [13] (see also [23]).

One lesson we drew from this design exercise is that a fairly conventional type system would indeed support the Web application and other applications being layered on HTTP, with one important caveat. This conclusion is based on exploratory work on expressing the Web application using the type system described here; this exploration is discussed more in Section 2.4. The important caveat concerns support for decentralized evolution, which is important for Internet-scale applications like the Web's. Supporting decentralized evolution requires considerable flexibility in the types used to characterize applications' expectations of data, because decentralized evolution introduces relatively complex patterns of changes to the data being exchanged. The best way to get such flexibility in a network interface expressed in a conventional type system is to use some form of property list as the type for a datum that may evolve in a decentralized way. Although this leaves the type system saying relatively little about the data in the property lists, it *is* a viable approach. For example, you see it in the application-level view of IPP. For another example, consider the popularity of dealing with XML through the DOM or SAX interfaces, both of which present (all at once or serially, respectively) the XML document as essentially a fancy tree-structured property list. However, it is possible for a type system to be more involved in managing decentralized evolution. The work on this was pursued somewhat independently and later, because it was not on the critical path to producing and measuring a prototype that captured the essence of the Web application as it existed at one point in time. See [31] for one example of how a type system might better support decentralized evolution, using a particular combination of ideas that are each familiar and in the spirit of strong object-oriented typing; that paper also briefly reviews what goes wrong when you try to use object subtyping to support decentralized evolution.

As mentioned earlier, another lesson we drew is that it is not difficult to make great strides toward unifying the type systems of COM, CORBA, and Java RMI. These type systems have significant overlap, and if you look carefully you can view their differences as mainly a matter of features being present in some of those systems but not others. Thus it is straightforward to unify them: offer a type system that includes every feature found in any of the systems to be unified. Because those systems were similar to begin with, this need not produce a terribly bloated result. However, it is important to avoid duplicating functionality that is packaged in different ways in those systems. This was done by unbundling features, taking a relatively orthogonalized view of those type systems and producing a relatively orthogonalized result. This is just another application of the principle of modularity. The PDG also ignored relatively obscure features that could conceivably be dropped in future revisions of the systems to be unified, as well as some that were simply not important to the application being prototyped. The experience reported suggests that taking an orthogonalized view could make it relatively easy to add any of these other features that are also desired. Following are some details of how the unification was achieved.

The biggest area in which the type systems to be unified contain differing packages of features is in types for 'objects'. Indeed, to proceed fruitfully we must even be careful about terminology. In CORBA, an object reference type is commonly called an 'interface', and a 'value type' describes objects passed by value. COM also has a concept of an 'interface', and it is semantically close to a CORBA 'interface'. In COM there is also recognition of a larger unit of software organization, one of which generally has multiple 'interfaces'. Both the terms 'object' and 'component' are variously used for these larger units; a type for these units is known as a 'coclass'. In the Java programming language there are two kinds of types for objects: 'interfaces' and 'classes'. In Java RMI, every type for objects passed by reference is an 'interface'; both 'interfaces' and 'classes' may be used as types for objects to be passed by value. In this report, the term 'object' is used consistently for the level of software organization known as an 'object' in CORBA and Java RMI, and the term 'object type' for a type for objects (both when typing objects passed by reference and objects passed by value).

One of the biggest areas of difference among the type systems to be unified is in the question of multiple inheritance for object reference types. In CORBA and Java RMI, object reference types can directly inherit from multiple supertypes. In COM, an 'interface' can inherit directly from at most one other, and user-defined ones tend to inherit from exactly one base, `IUnknown`. COM's `IUnknown` 'interface' addresses two areas of functionality: (1) reference counting of objects (COM's technique for memory management); and (2) navigation — via the `QueryInterface` method — among the 'interfaces' of a COM 'component'. Memory management is implicitly present for all object reference types in CORBA and Java RMI, and it is handled in a similar way (reference counting) for the programming language mappings in common with COM, so there is no real difference there. The HTTP-NG prototype allows multiple inheritance among object reference types, viewing COM's 'interfaces' and 'coclasses' as a limited usage pattern. The idea is that a COM 'component' is taken to be an object passed by reference, and both COM 'interfaces' and 'coclasses' are types for such references, where multiple inheritance is used in just one way (to construct a 'coclass' from multiple 'interfaces').

Another area of difference is the support for passing objects by value instead of by reference. Java RMI supports this, and CORBA does too, with an added feature, the ability to declare that a passed object may be truncated to certain of its supertypes (which might happen when the receiver has access to the code for only some of the object's supertypes). COM does not directly support passing objects by value, although an application can use COM's custom marshalling feature to get that effect. The solution taken is to allow objects passed by value. For the sake of simplicity, the prototype design makes objects passed by value truncatable at every inheritance link. The prototype design does not address custom marshalling, as it was not needed for the prototyped application.

A further area of difference concerns whether pointer equality is preserved. Java RMI preserves equality of all pointers within a 'serialization context', which for RPCs amounts to a call or reply message. CORBA preserves pointer equality among objects passed by value within a message, and nowhere else. In COM, preservation of pointer equality applies to some kinds of pointer types ('full' ones) and not others ('unique' and 'ref' pointers). As the preservation of pointer equality is linked to the type of the data, these systems are easily unified by allowing explicit declaration of whether pointer equality is preserved for a given type of data. For the sake of type system modularity, this is broken out as part of a separate 'reference' constructor: a pointer-equality-preserving type can be constructed from any 'base' type; non-reference types do not promise any pointer equality preservation. In COM the scope over which equality of full pointers is preserved is larger: i.e., an entire call. This is reported to be problematic enough that usage of full pointers is avoided. The prototype solution is to scope pointer equality as in CORBA and Java RMI, in hopes that COM may later adopt this preferred semantic.

A similar pattern of difference and solution occurs with regard to the issue of 'optional' data. In CORBA and Java RMI, every object type is implicitly 'optional', meaning that the `null` value is included in the type. However, in Java RMI arrays and strings are also implicitly optional, while in CORBA they are implicitly non-optional. In COM, some pointer types ('unique' and 'full' ones) include `null` and others ('ref' pointers) do not. The solution is to make every type implicitly non-optional, except that the reference constructor can make optional types.

There is a similar, but different, story for network garbage collection. In COM and Java RMI, objects are implicitly subject to network-wide garbage collection; in CORBA, no network garbage collection is available. Again the solution is based on explicit declaration, but it is directly attached to the object types. Any object type that inherits from a certain designated type (`HTTP-ng.GCCollectibleObject-Base`) is subject to network garbage collection; others are not.

In addition to differing over the preservation of pointer equality, the type systems to be unified differ on the question of whether objects passed by reference have meaningful identities. In Java RMI and in the Web, there is a strong notion of object identity. In COM and CORBA this is not emphasized, but identities *do* appear in the implementations. While some workers have argued that there is no useful generic definition of object identity for distributed systems [34], the problems raised in that argument can be viewed as saying only that a generic definition of object identity has limited — but non-zero — utility. For this reason, objects passed by reference have identities in the prototype design.

Another area of difference is in the handling of 'charsets' [1] for strings. In COM and CORBA, the charset of a string type is unspecified, and the charset of a string value is determined at runtime by 'locale' and negotiated and possibly converted in the course of remote messaging. In Java, the 'charset' of string types and values is fixed as the UTF-32 encoding of Unicode. The solution taken is to let the charset be unspecified in HTTP-NG string types and negotiated and possibly converted in HTTP-NG messages, letting Java peers be particularly hard-nosed negotiators.

One more area of difference concerns degenerate methods. COM offers 'message' methods; these have no results, they raise no exceptions, and the caller does not normally wait for completion but proceeds immediately after issuing the call. Message methods are tied into Microsoft Message Queuing, and several controls over the message queuing are available. CORBA offers returnless exceptionless 'ONEWAY' methods, whose distinction is that the call might not be reliably delivered; the issue of whether the caller may proceed immediately is not explicitly addressed in the specification, but private conversations with CORBA developers reveal an appreciation for this concept. Java RMI offers neither. The HTTP-NG prototype allows returnless exceptionless methods to be 'asynchronous', meaning only that the caller does not wait for a return.

A minor difference easily removed is the fact that only COM offers 'callback' function parameters. These were simply omitted in the HTTP-NG prototype, on the grounds that callback functions can be treated as a special case of object references.

We now turn our attention to the problem of encoding data for network transmission.

2.3.2. The data encoding

The data encoding defines how data of types described above are encoded into bytes for transport, and does so in a way that addresses network performance problems and the rigid binding between object identities and transport stacks. Familiar techniques are entirely adequate to achieve these objectives. A binary data encoding was chosen, for the sake of efficiency in bytes on the wire and in processing time. The encoding is described in [22], and can be considered an extension of XDR [32]. The encoding of an object reference has a structure similar to that in CORBA; this structure includes separate places for the object's (1) identity, (2) type information, and (3) contact information. Also like CORBA, the contact information is structured as a set of alternatives.

2.3.3. The RPC protocol

The RPC protocol defines the formats of the messages exchanged to effect RPCs, and does so in a way that addresses modularity/extensibility and network performance. Again, only familiar techniques are needed to improve on HTTP and help unify the Web with related middleware systems. The RPC protocol is also described in [22] (see also [23]).

The message formats facilitate modularity/extensibility by having an application-independent section of protocol extensions, analogous to 'service contexts' in CORBA's GIOP.

The RPC headers in a request message improve network performance by using sender-managed tables to reduce the bytes needed to transmit common values. These apply both to the operation identifier and to the identifier of the object whose operation is being invoked. The sender may associate an identifier with a table index, and then use that table index in place of the identifier in multiple messages.

2.4. The Web application layer

The highest layer of the prototype design expresses TCWA as an application of the lower two layers. The group did not produce a full design here, but did prototype an indicative subset of HTTP's functionality [26]. The purpose of that prototype was twofold: (1) test the lower two layers against the needs of TCWA; and (2) enable measurement of an actual prototype. The lower two layers did indeed prove adequate, with the proviso noted earlier about the quality of the support for decentralized evolution. The prototype interfaces attempt to use subtyping to organize some of HTTP's extensions beyond its basic functionality; for this reason there are a number of interfaces of increasing sophistication. At the base we can start with a very simple version of the application, which could be rendered in OMG IDL as follows:

```
module TCWA {
 interface Resource {
  status_code GET
      (out Entity resp_ent);
  status_code PUT
      (in Entity req_ent);
  status_code POST
      (in Entity req_ent,
       out Entity resp_ent);
 };
};
```

More sophisticated versions are rendered as subtypes with cloned operations with added parameters relevant to the various advanced features of HTTP, such as caching, content negotiation, and so on.

One particular development explored in the prototype interfaces shows that although one might not expect this from the RPC paradigm, it is possible to write interfaces that pass documents by streaming rather than all at once. When a document is to be returned by streaming, the client passes a callback object that is the consumer of the stream. The server repeatedly calls an asynchronous method of the callback, passing chunk after chunk of the document body. The use of asynchronous methods means each call simply amounts to a message passed from server to client. That message stream differs from a direct byte stream of document content mainly in the addition of message framing and a little other per-chunk overhead, all of which is small. The first call back passes a control object reference to the client, who can call on it to make the server pause or abort the message stream — without having to close any connections — or back up for error recovery.

3. Experimental results

Although modularity and flexibility can have a negative impact on performance, the PDG produced and measured a prototype that shows it is possible to simultaneously improve performance *and* make the other reported improvements in HTTP. The comparison was between the prototype HTTP-NG protocols and both HTTP/1.0 and HTTP/1.1.

The main prototypes were built using a distributed object toolkit called ILU [21]. This toolkit is implemented in ANSI C, and runs on top of either a POSIX UNIX API or a Win32/WinSock API, and supports the system of transport stacks present in the lowest layer of the HTTP-NG design. ILU also supports alternatives at the RPC layer, and the main comparisons were done using ILU implementations of the middle layer of HTTP-NG as well as the corresponding parts of HTTP/1.0 and HTTP/1.1. For the tests reported here, a network interface (`NgRendering.NgRenderable` [26]) that supports the caching and content negotiation features of HTTP was used, although those features were not specifically measured. The operation (`GetRendering`) that returns the result all at once was used.

To exercise these interfaces on the most basic use of the Web, fetching a document, the PDG created two ANSI C programs, 'nggetbot' and 'ngwebserver'. 'ngwebserver' acts as a very simple Web server, managing a file base. It exports the TCWA interface via a number of different wire protocols, including HTTP 1.0, HTTP 1.1, HTTP-NG, CORBA's IIOP 1.0, and Sun RPC. The program 'nggetbot' acts as a testing client. It reads lists of URLs, and fetches them. An optional delay can be specified for each URL, which specifies how long the client will wait before it fetches the next URL. The client can be

Table 1
Comparing the HTTP/1.1 and HTTP-NG protocols

Test	Notes	Time, seconds (std. dev.)	Overhead bytes	TCP connections used
HTTP 1.1 (ILU)	+B, +P, −M	0.408 (0.012)	14,817	1
HTTP NG (ILU)	+B, −P, +M	0.306 (0.026)	7,935	1

directed to spread its fetches across multiple concurrent threads; ten threads were used in the ILU-based tests reported here.

The tests were run on a small network consisting of (1) two Sun Ultra-30 Model 250 computers, each having a 248 MHz UltraSPARC-II processor, 128 megabytes of memory, and running Solaris 2.6, (2) two Compaq Deskpro 6000 computers, each having a 300 MHz Pentium II processor, 64 MB of memory, and running Windows NT (Service Pack 3), and (3) a Xylan OmniSwitch switched-packet Ethernet router, using the ESM-100C-12W-2C fast Ethernet module. This network was connected to the regular PARC network, but the Xylan switch removed traffic not directed to the machines on the test network. The tests were mainly run on the two Sun machines, using one as a server and the other for the client programs. Some of the tests were also duplicated using the Compaq machines, to check for problems having to do with endian-ness, and between the Sun and Compaq machines. The results reported here were measured on the Sun machines using the 100 Mbit switched Ethernet.

This network is unflattering for the HTTP-NG protocols, which address concerns that are non-issues on this network. Because the network amounts to a direct connection between the client and server, there is no congestion to avoid, so it does not matter that the MUX filter improves the handling of congestion information. The network is very fast, so the number of bytes on the wire is not much of an issue, and round trips take very little time; thus HTTP-NG's conservation of these things matters very little.

The primary test was the fetch of a single Web page. This page had been developed as part of earlier performance testing work with HTTP 1.1 [12]. Called the *'Microscape site'*, it is a combination of the home pages of the Microsoft and Netscape Web sites. It consists of a 43 KB HTML file, which references 41 embedded GIF images (actually 42 embedded GIF images, but in our tests the image 'enter.gif' was not included, as libwww's webbot did not fetch it as a result of fetching the main page). Thus a complete fetch of the site consists of 42 HTTP GET requests. Our base performance measures were the time it took to fetch this page, and the number of bytes actually transferred. We repeated this test with HTTP 1.0, HTTP 1.1, and HTTP-NG.

There are inherent differences in the protocol stacks tested. Some of particular note are in the use or non-use of batching, pipelining, and the MUX filter. Pipelining is the practice of sending a series of requests without waiting for intervening replies. HTTP/1.0 lacks this feature, but it was added in 1.1. It allows a single TCP connection to serve some of the needs that prompt use of multiple parallel connections in HTTP/1.0. With batching, transport buffers are not flushed until an overflow, timeout, or specific prompt forces them out, which means that several pipelined or multiplexed call or reply messages can go in one network packet.

Table 1 compares the HTTP/1.1 and HTTP-NG protocols in the ILU-based test harness. The 'Notes' column indicates whether batching, pipelining, and/or the MUX filter were used. The 'time' column gives elapsed time. It is the average of 10 runs done in rapid succession. The bytes transferred and the number of connections used remained constant from run to run. The 'overhead bytes' gives the result of subtracting from the total number of bytes transferred, in both the request and the reply, the constant size in bytes of the HTML document and the associated GIF images (a total of 171,049 bytes); the remaining bytes consist of the data headers transferred with the requests and responses. The HTTP-NG protocols make a considerable improvement in both elapsed time and in overhead bytes.

Table 2 shows better results for both HTTP/1 and for HTTP-NG. At least two effects probably contribute to the speed improvements. One is that ILU's batching functionality lacks a critical piece: there is no way for the server side to indicate it is

Table 2
Better results for both HTTP/1 and for HTTP-NG

Test	Notes	Time, seconds (std. dev.)	Overhead bytes	TCP connections used
HTTP 1.0 (ILU)	−B, −P, −M	0.181 (0.003)	14,817	42
HTTP NG (ILU)	−B, −P, +M	0.194 (0.011)	7,935	1

done producing replies, and thus buffers occasionally languish until a timeout (the timeout used was 0.05 seconds). Another is that pipelining involves exclusive access to the connection on the client side at a higher level in the software than does multiplexing in the MUX filter or in the kernel's IP implementation, and we can expect less concurrency the higher the level at which access is exclusive. Discarding the problems associated with ILU's batching speeds up both HTTP/1 and HTTP-NG. The times for the two protocol approaches end up in the same ballpark; it is not yet known whether the small advantage of HTTP/1.0 is due to the use of many parallel connections and/or other factors. HTTP-NG could be run over parallel connections if desired. Recall that the network environment of these tests does not exercise some of the strengths of the HTTP-NG protocols. What Table 2 shows is that even in this unflattering network environment, HTTP-NG improves significantly on bytes on the wire and does not have a significant speed disadvantage.

To check that nothing was grossly wrong in the ILU-based test programs, the PDG also tested the 'webbot' program from the libwww-5.1m release, together with the 1.2 release of the Apache Web server. This gave comparison figures, reported in Table 3, for reasonably good HTTP 1.1 client and server implementations. Compared to the best result for HTTP-NG, this HTTP/1.1 result shows a larger elapsed time and larger overhead in bytes. However, there are some important differences between the two code bases, so the comparison is very rough. The webbot parses the fetched HTML and this in turn causes it to fetch the inline GIFs; the nggetbot is instead driven immediately from a list of URIs, and so has fewer delays built in. The webbot also produces more diagnostic output, which naturally costs elapsed time (even though it was directed to a file instead of a terminal). In the other direction, the ILU-based code is not particularly tuned for performance; this can be seen from the significant difference between the ILU-based 1.1 performance and the webbot/Apache 1.1 performance. While these factors affect the comparison of elapsed time, they do not affect the overhead bytes, for which the HTTP-NG protocols show a clear improvement.

A more complete description of the tests, along with the data collected for the results, is available [27]. In this file, the HTTP 1.1 (ILU) test case is 'Pipelined-HTTP', the HTTP-NG + B test case is 'Base-NG', the HTTP 1.0 test case is referred to as 'Multi-connection-HTTP', the HTTP-NG − B test case is 'Batchless-NG', and the HTTP 1.1 (libwww/Apache) test case is 'libwww-webbot'. The code used for the tests is available as part of the ILU distribution [21], in the directory ILUSRC/examples/ngtest/.

Finally, we have also talked about HTTP becoming a substrate for the carriage of popular distributed-object systems such as CORBA, DCOM, and Java RMI. To get an idea of how well that would work, we took the 'test1' test case from the ILU system, and ran the ANSI C client from that test against the ANSI C server from that test, using both the CORBA IIOP 1.0 protocol and the HTTP-NG protocol. Again, the application code and application interface used in that test were identical; only the wire protocol and transport stacks were changed. This test is an artificial application designed mainly to utilize a number of features such as distributed garbage collection,

Table 3
Testing libwww-5.1m and the 1.2 release of Apache

Test	Notes	Time, seconds (std. dev.)	Overhead bytes	TCP connections used
HTTP 1.1 (libwww/Apache)	+B, +P, −M	0.231 (0.003)	17,918	1

Table 4
The 'test1' test

Test	msec/call (std. dev.)	Total bytes transmitted	TCP connections used
test1-IIOP 1.0	1.718 (0.598)	566,876	3
test1-HTTP-NG	1.631 (0.405)	170,040	2

floating point numbers, strings, object references, union types, arrays, and asynchronous method calls. Note that HTTP-NG supports all of those concepts directly, without any need for the 'tunnelling' used, for example, in RMI over HTTP. We ran the 'test1' test 100 times in sequence, for each protocol stack, running the server on one of our Sun machines and the client on the other. This is a total of 1500 synchronous requests, with replies, and 100 asynchronous requests, without replies. Table 4 shows the results.

The timings were roughly the same, and with a fairly high variance, but IIOP used significantly more bytes than HTTP-NG to make the same calls. These bytes in this case include both the data payloads of the calls and the request and reply header 'overhead bytes'. Again, this should be regarded as indicative rather than definitive, but it is worth noting that the HTTP-NG protocol was carrying the same information as the IIOP protocol while using less than one-third the bandwidth. Much of this reduction is due to HTTP-NG's more efficient marshalling of object references. The reduction in TCP connections used is due to the ability in HTTP-NG of a server to 'call back' to a client through the same TCP connection that the client used to talk to the server.

4. Future and related work

Further work can, and is, being done both on solving HTTP problems and on unifying the Web with other middleware systems.

The Protocol Design Group attempted only to produce a prototype for use in studying feasibility. There are several areas in which the prototype design is only a preliminary guesstimate and could use improvements. This includes further work on simplifying and modularizing the middle layer (the designs for strings and exceptions are particularly preliminary). This also includes further work on making type systems better support decentralized evolution, and on integrating that work with the rest of the middle layer design. The unification of the Web with other middleware systems would profit from further work on the middle layer of HTTP-NG as well as on the other systems, to help them all converge. A complete proposal for network interfaces for TCWA is also needed, as is the formulation of WebDAV as an HTTP-NG application.

Further testing to more fully explore the performance relations is warranted.

Other workers have taken on parts of the problem space addressed by the HTTP-NG PDG. The IETF's 'Endpoint Congestion Management' Working Group [10] has already been noted. Others have undertaken to address part of the transport flexibility problem by adding a facility, known as 'TCP Filters' [3,2], for dynamically negotiating transport stacks. This is limited to transport stacks built on TCP, and does not address the issue of decoupling stacks from resource identifiers. There has been a long history of trying to establish a standard for mandatory extensions to HTTP; the latest is known as the 'HTTP Extension Framework' [14].

The idea of unifying the Web with other middleware systems has captured a lot of attention. For example, there is a series of related designs — each more elaborate and specific than the preceding — for doing RPC via XML over HTTP: XML-RPC, SOAP, and Windows DNA 2000 [36]. However, these fail to address the underlying problems with HTTP, and make only a limited contribution to unifying COM with the other popular middleware systems (the biggest limit is that no attention is paid to object types from the other systems).

5. Conclusion

The Protocol Design Group produced a prototype that showed that it is not difficult to make progress in all the addressed problem areas simultaneously, and that suggests that unification of the Web with COM, CORBA, and Java RMI is possible. Further work can, and is, being done on both solving HTTP problems and on unifying the Web with other middleware systems.

Acknowledgements

The work reported above was a collaboration of many people. The other major contributors were Jim Gettys, Dan Larner, and Henrik Frystyk Nielsen. Daniel Veillard did the integration of the HTTP-NG prototype with Apache. Andy Begel worked on flexible typing issues. Paul Bennett, Larry Masinter, and Paula Newman were also valuable collaborators. Thanks are also due to Doug Terry for reviewing drafts of this paper.

References

[1] H. Alvestrand, IETF policy on character sets and languages, Internet Society, RFC 2277, January 1998.

[2] G. Belingueres et al., Internet-Draft draft-belingueres-tcpsec-00.txt, TCP Security Filter (work in progress), Internet Society, November 1999.

[3] S. Bellovin et al., Internet-Draft draft-bellovin-tcpfilt-00.txt, TCP Filters (work in progress), Internet Society, October 1999.

[4] D. Box et al., Internet-Draft draft-box-http-soap-00.txt (work in progress), Internet Society, September 1999.

[5] R. Braden, T/TCP–TCP extensions for transactions, functional specification, Internet Society, RFC 1644, July 1994.

[6] K. Brockschmidt, Inside OLE, second edition, Microsoft Press, Redmond, WA, 1995.

[7] COM, in: Microsoft Developer Network Online Library (http://msdn.microsoft.com/library/default.htm), Platform SDK, Component Services, Microsoft, 1999.

[8] D. Crocker, Standard for the format of ARPA Internet text messages, Internet Society, RFC 822, August 1982.

[9] DAV searching and locating (dasl) charter (http://www.ietf.org/html.charters/dasl-charter.html), IETF Secretariat, 1999.

[10] Endpoint congestion management (ecm) charter (http://www.ietf.org/html.charters/ecm-charter.html), IETF Secretariat, 1999.

[11] R. Fielding et al., Hypertext transfer protocol – HTTP/1.1, Internet Society, RFC 2616, June 1999.

[12] H. Frystyk Nielsen et al., Network performance effects of HTTP/1.1, CSS1, and PNG, http://www.w3.org/Protocols/HTTP/Performance/Pipeline.html, W3C, June 1997.

[13] H. Frystyk Nielsen et al., Internet-Draft draft-frystyk-httpng-arch-00.txt, HTTP-NG Architectural Model (work in progress), available on ref. 23, Internet Society, August 1998.

[14] H. Frystyk Nielsen et al., Internet-Draft draft-frystyk-http-extensions-03.txt, HTTP Extension Framework (work in progress), Internet Society, March 1999.

[15] Y. Goland et al., HTTP extensions for distributed authoring – WEBDAV, Internet Society, RFC 2518, February 1999.

[16] M. Handley et al., SIP: session initiation protocol, Internet Society, RFC 2543, March 1999.

[17] R. Herriot et al., Internet printing protocol/1.0: encoding and transport, Internet Society, RFC 2565, April 1999.

[18] http://www.w3.org/Protocols/HTTP-NG/Activity-199905.html, W3C, October 20, 1999.

[19] http://www.w3.org/Protocols/HTTP-NG/Activity.html, W3C, October 24, 1999.

[20] Internet printing protocol working group charter, http://www.ietf.org/html.charters/ipp-charter.html, IETF Secretariat, 1999.

[21] B. Janssen et al., Inter-Language Unification home page, ftp://ftp.parc.xerox.com/pub/ilu/ilu.html. Xerox, 1999.

[22] B. Janssen et al., Internet-Draft draft-janssen-httpng-wire-00.txt, w3ng: Binary Wire Protocol for HTTP-NG (work in progress), available on ref. 23, Internet Society, August 1998.

[23] B. Janssen et al., Current HTTP-NG Resources, http://www.parc.xerox.com/istl/projects/http-ng/current-httpng-resources.html, Xerox, 1999.

[24] Java remote method invocation, http://java.sun.com/products/jdk/rmi/, Sun Microsystems, 1999.

[25] C. Kindel, Distributed component object model protocol – DCOM/1.0, in: Microsoft Developer Network Online Library (http://msdn.microsoft.com/library/default.htm), Specifications, Technologies and Languages, Microsoft, 1997.

[26] D. Larner, Internet-Draft draft-larner-nginterfaces-00.txt, HTTP-NG Web Interfaces (work in progress), available on ref. 23, Internet Society, August 1998.

[27] D. Larner, http-ng-test-results-round2.tar.gz, available on ref. 23, Xerox, 1999.

[28] J. Mogul, What's wrong with HTTP and why it doesn't matter, at 1999 USENIX Annual Technical Conference, http://www.usenix.org/events/usenix99/invitedtalks.html.

[29] K. Moore et al., Internet-Draft draft-iesg-using-http-00.txt, On the use of HTP as a substrate for other protocols (work in progress), available on ref. 23, Internet Society, August 5, 1998.

[30] S. Reddy, SWAP Working Group (proposed) home page, http://www.ics.uci.edu/ ietfswap/, October, 1999.

[31] M. Spreitzer et al., More flexible data types, in: Proc. 8th IEEE Int. Workshop on Enabling Technologies: Infrastructure for Collaborative Enterprises, IEEE Computer Society, Los Alamitos, CA, June 1999.

[32] R. Srinivasan, XDR: external data representation standard, Internet Society, RFC 1832, August 1995.

[33] The common object request broker: architecture and specification; revision 2.3, The Object Management Group (OMG), Framingham, MA, June 1999.

[34] A. Watson, Green paper on object identity ftp://ftp.omg.org/pub/docs/om/97-04-01.pdf, OMG, April 1997.
[35] Web versioning and configuration management (deltav) charter (http://www.ietf.org/html.charters/deltav-charter.html), IETF Secretariat, 1999.
[36] Windows DNA home page, http://www.microsoft.com/dna/, Microsoft, 1999.
[37] XML-RPC home page, http://www.xmlrpc.com/, UserLand Software, 1999.

Mike Spreitzer works at the Xerox Palo Alto Research Center, in the areas of distributed systems, security, and programming languages.

William C. Janssen Jr., is a member of the research staff of the Information Systems and Technologies Laboratory at Xerox's Palo Alto Research Center. He is a principal of the PARC Inter-Language Unification project, which investigates different approaches to language-independent object-oriented program component systems, and leads the PARC HTTP-NG project. His research interests include object interface systems, distributed object systems, programming language design, and group coordination systems.

Customized Internet radio

Venky Krishnan *, S. Grace Chang

Hewlett-Packard Laboratories, 1501 Page Mill Road, Palo Alto, CA 94304, USA

Abstract

Today's Internet radio breaks down geographic boundaries and lowers the barrier for audio broadcasting. The listener now has access to a huge growing number of radio stations. However, there are very few mechanisms in place that aid the listener in identifying audio broadcasts of his choice. Furthermore, unlike the traditional FM radio, radios on the network should exploit the Internet and provide features based on information about the content, the content providers and the listener. The Customized Internet Radio (CIR) proposes a framework for managing and customizing audio broadcast content on the Internet. The CIR, by managing the metadata of the broadcast content, provides the listener a dynamically selected and personalized radio program. This paper introduces the notion of a CIR Station, an Internet radio station with tools to create and manage program schedules for Internet audio broadcasts. The framework manages broadcast content originating from both local and remote sources. It allows specific radio stations or genre to be scheduled in time-slots, and provides alerts and dynamic changes based on the availability of a specified content. CIR, by caching live content, also enables program time-shifting. The CIR uses the Session Announcement Protocol (SAP) to advertise the station information. These announcements contain information used by the client to receive the dynamically changing content. An implementation example of CIR illustrates the enhanced listener and content manager experience.

Keywords: Internet radio; SAP; SDP; Media delivery; Media management; Customization; Dynamic content

1. Introduction

With the advent of the explosive growth of the Internet, we see a plethora of media delivery platforms such as the Internet radio. Broadcasting audio over the Internet is extremely popular. Today, there are approximately 2300 radio stations worldwide broadcasting live content and about 1500 stations broadcasting pre-recorded music. These numbers are growing at a rapid pace. There are several factors that contribute to this growth of Internet-based radio stations.

(1) Internet radio eliminates the coverage restriction found with FM radio stations. A radio station on the network can be accessed from any computer with Internet access. This wide coverage capability of Internet radio broadcast is very appealing to broadcasters. This has resulted in many FM radio broadcasters setting up a parallel Internet radio presence.

(2) It has become increasingly easy to set up a radio station server. Cheap hardware (networked PC and CD-ROM) and Internet access along with free/low-cost high-quality audio streaming software tools enable even a naive user to create an audio broadcast presence on the network.

Internet radio stations broadcast their content either using unicast or multicast. A station typically

* Corresponding author. E-mail: venky@hpl.hp.com

gives information describing the attributes (metadata) of (1) the station (e.g. genre, description), (2) the audio content (e.g. the program name and airtime, song and artist name), and (3) the data (e.g. the bandwidth, the data encoding format). Client software (such as WinAmp, RealPlayer, and MediaPlayer) use this information to (a) select the appropriate audio decoder and (b) to provide the listener with information on the content such as the station name and current playlist. There are several mechanisms by which a station advertises its metadata.

(1) Listeners select well-known IP addresses or Web sites to access the radio station. Typically, this information is obtained by advertisement, word of mouth, or from portal sites, search engines, and content provider sites (e.g. broadcast.com [2]).
(2) A radio station can register itself with a well-known Directory Server. Examples of this model include Nullsoft's Shoutcast system [13] (the server complement of the Nullsoft's Winamp MP3 player), and its open source replica called Icecast [8]. These systems provide a Directory Server that maintains a database keeping track of radio stations and their attributes, as well as a mechanism for a radio station to register itself.
(3) The radio station is hosted on a well-known address. Companies like live365.com [9] host radio stations on their site. They provide benefits such as reliability, high availability, robust servers, and fast connection.
(4) The station can announce its attributes using the Session Announcement Protocol (SAP) [7] on a well-known multicast address. The attributes include information on the broadcast such as the IP address of the data channel, the start and end time, the data encoding format, and the source of the broadcast.

The Internet radio listeners, while benefiting from the abundance of audio content, now have to sieve through many stations to find one that suit their preferences. Traditional AM/FM radio listeners rely on radio personalities like Disc Jockeys to filter the broadcast content for them. Traditional radio also has some powerful features like re-broadcasting content from a central content provider. For example, KQED, a local SF radio station, re-broadcasts the evening news from NPR in Washington. These are features of traditional radio that are lacking in today's Internet radio.

Moreover, a network-based audio broadcast should exploit the features of the Internet. Some of the key features that will enhance the listeners' experience are the following.

(1) *Event-based content switching*. Today, Internet radio provides static listening. Once tuned to a station, the listener needs to actively change stations. There is no mechanism of changing stations automatically based on attributes such as the time, listener location, alert messages (e.g. for weather and traffic reports), genre, content provider, etc.
(2) *Ease in accessing and reusing available content*. There is plenty of content on the network. Tools to assist in accessing the content would provide immense added-value. For example, the HP Labs Media Communications Department should be able to create an HP Labs Radio Station easily. The DJ of this station should be able to create the station's broadcast program based on content available on the network. The station itself does not need to create its own content. A listener of the HP Labs Radio Station thus will access content from different sources.
(3) *Content-caching for playback*. A radio station on the Internet should be able to cache content and playback this time-shifted content based on the listeners' needs.
(4) *Content/Station/Listener awareness*. Unlike a traditional radio, Internet radio should exploit information about the content, the station, and the listener's preferences to provide customized content to the listener.

The Customized Internet Radio (CIR) attempts to address the above-mentioned shortcomings of today's Internet radio. CIR is a framework for customizing and creating a 'radio station' with event-based dynamic content access. It allows the station creator to manage the content based on the specified preferences (like genre, time of day, priority), and leverage the content available on the Internet from other providers as well as locally generated content. Once created, this radio station announces its presence and schedule so that its subscribers receive dynamic content as well. The various events that trigger a change in radio stations are (1) the expiration of a scheduled time-slot for a program, (2) an alert for the availability of a radio station or a Webcast event, or (3) a location-specific event.

2. Basic framework

In the Customized Internet Radio framework, there are three entities: the radio station servers (CIRServer), the radio client (CIRClient), and the 'virtual' radio station (CIRVirtualStation), which is at the heart of the CIR framework. The CIRServer and the CIRClient are rather like the traditional server and client, with one serving the content and the other receiving the content. The CIRVirtualStation entity can be thought of as an intermediary Radio Station Program Manager, which gathers information (metadata) about the available radio stations and their content. It then compiles a schedule with programs from different sources and advertises this schedule to listening CIRClients or other CIRVirtualStations. Fig. 1 shows the relation between these three entities. In the following, we describe the functions of each entity, and their relations with each other. More details about the architecture will be presented later in Section 3.

2.1. CIRServer

A CIRServer is the radio station server from which the audio content originates. In the CIR framework, it represents the audio content provider. In today's Internet radio, the content providers stream out data using, for example, Real Network's RealServer [12], NullSoft's Shoutcast server [13], multicast conferencing tools (e.g. sdr [5]), or any other streaming audio servers. A server announces its presence typically in two mechanisms. It can register itself with a directory service such as yp.shoutcast.com or yp.icecast.org. It can also announce its attributes via multicast announcement protocols such as using SAP [7] and SDP [6], a mechanism provided by the tool sdr.

The CIRServer comes in two flavors: (1) a radio server that sends metadata information about its broadcast, and (2) a wrapper for existing servers. In both cases, the metadata sent include time of radio broadcast, URL, genre, priority, etc. The wrapper for an existing server gathers information about the server and its content, and transforms it to the CIR compatible format. For example, the Wrapper for the Shoutcast Server parses the list of radio stations on the Web page, http://yp.shoutcast.com, and creates announcements for each of the listed stations. The current incarnation of CIRServer does not announce fine grain metadata like details of songs (writer, singer, name, etc.) for a music radio station but these enhancements can be easily added.

2.2. CIRClient

A CIRClient is the audio player. The listener interacts with the CIRClient to select his choice of radio station (server). This can either be a CIRServer or CIRVirtualStation. Based on the metadata broadcasted by the selected server, the CIRClient tunes to the appropriate audio content stream from the content provider. The CIRClient has two parts: (1) a wrapper that interfaces with the CIR server components, and (2) off-the-shelf audio players (e.g. RealNetwork's RealPlayer, NullSoft's Winamp MP3 player, FreeAmp [4]). In order to be a CIRClient in the Customized Internet Radio framework, there needs to be a wrapper which understands directives from the CIRServer and CIRVirtualStation. A CIRClient also contains several audio players for encoding different audio data formats, so that it can be format-independent.

2.3. CIRVirtualStation

A CIRVirtualStation is an intermediary entity that acts as a Radio Station Program Manager, scheduling programs from different sources based on the preferences of the Disc Jockey (DJ). The DJ uses a user interface to set his preferences of the CIRVirtualStation. For example, the HP Labs DJ can specify that he wants to 'broadcast' BBC from 9 AM to 5 PM, and classical music from 5 PM to 9 PM. He can also specify that if there are traffic or weather report channels available relevant to the listener's current location, he wants the listener to be notified of these alerts. The CIRVirtualStation interacts with CIRServers to get their program schedules and sends out its own program announcements (metadata) based on the DJ's settings. A CIRVirtualStation can also receive an-

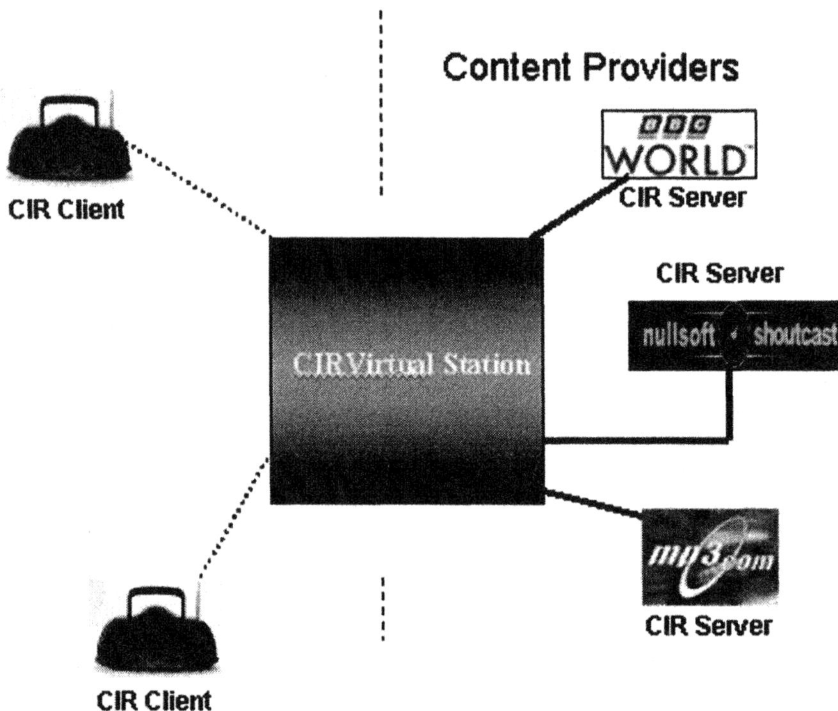

Fig. 1. Relations between CIRServers, CIRClients, and CIRVirtualStations.

nouncements from other CIRVirtualStations and can advertise its own local audio content.

A CIRClient listening to a CIRVirtualStation will get automatically tuned to the content provider identified by the metadata sent by the CIRVirtualStation. In the example above, if the listener 'tunes' his CIRClient to the HP Labs CIRVirtualStation, then between 9 AM and 5 PM, his Internet radio will be tuned to the BBC radio station. At 5 PM, the CIRClient will switch to the classical station chosen by the HP Labs CIRVirtualStation. Throughout the day, he will receive alert broadcasts of the traffic and weather updates for his location.

In the descriptions thus far, the DJ and the listener are two distinct persons. Our model also supports the notion of the listener being his own DJ. In such a scenario, the CIRClient and the CIRVirtualStation components run on the same system. The listener can personalize his radio station to suit his needs. For example, Venky (an HP Labs employee) can configure his Personal Station (CIRVirtualStation) to tune to the audio broadcast as selected by the HP Labs radio station when he is in his office and switch to the top rock station listed on the Shoutcast directory when he is at home. Venky's current location can be gotten either by manually indicating to the CIRClient or by integrating with a location-aware device like GPS.

To summarize, the CIRVirtualStation is at the core of the Customized Internet Radio framework. It enables a flexible and customized programming of the radio stations. To achieve this, the CIRVirtualStation needs to have mechanisms for the discovery of radio stations and their attributes (address, genre, bit rate, location, data format, etc.), and information about their content (descriptions of the songs and programs). It also has mechanisms for a DJ to create a radio station program schedule based on time, genre, location, and alerts. Lastly, it needs to communicate its schedule, or playlist, to listening CIRClients, so that the listener gets dynamically selected radio stations. The audio content can come from either the original CIRServers or it can be collected by the CIRVirtualStation and then re-transmitted to the CIRClients. In the latter case, the CIRVirtualStation provides the additional functionality of content caching, to allow time-shifting of radio programs. For example, Venky wants to listen to the NPR 6 o'clock news at 9 PM when he is at home. In this case, Venky's personal radio (CIRVirtualStation) will cache the 6 PM content and re-broadcast the news at 9 PM.

The fundamental idea behind the CIR is the notion of a passive broadcast. The metadata describing a radio station are broadcasted to whoever is interested. The client programs (listeners or other stations) that access this information can utilize these data as best as they see fit. The notion of a Radio Station Program Manager (CIRVirtualStation) facilitates an environment that enhances listener experience and content management.

3. Architecture

3.1. CIRVirtualStation

The architecture of the CIRVirtualStation is illustrated in Fig. 2. It consists of four parts: a DJ Profiler module, a Discovery module, a Scheduler module, and an Announcement module. The DJ Profiler module provides the DJ a graphical user interface to enter his preferences. The DJ can select a radio station, program the preferred time-slot for it, and set its priority. If a station is set with a high priority, its broadcast becomes an alert that overrides other stations of normal priority. The DJ can set a default genre which will cause a station of that genre to be randomly selected. A station can also be set to default, and will be played when no other stations have been selected for that given time. The DJ Profiler module saves this profile upon exiting and loads it upon start up.

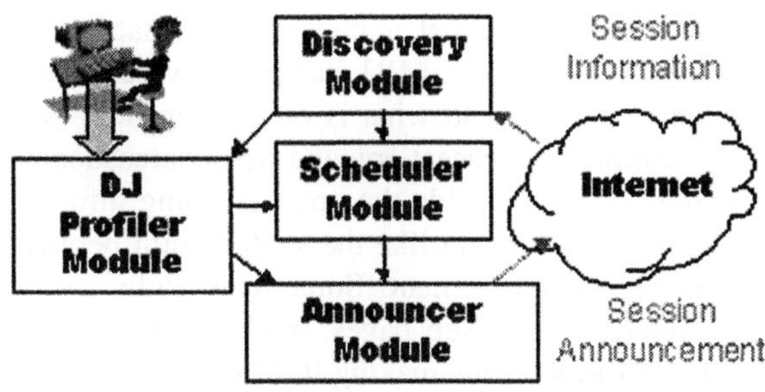

Fig. 2. Architecture of a CIRVirtualStation.

The Discovery module is responsible for discovering what radio stations are available. There are several mechanisms for discovery. One way is to fetch the lists of radio stations from directory servers such as yp.shoutcast.com [13] and yp.icecast.org [8], content hosts such as broadcast.com, or radio station search engines. These listings are often in the form of HTML pages, and can be parsed for the station's content URL, name, genre, description, data format, bit-rate, and other attributes. Another way of discovery is to listen to well-known multicast addresses used for announcing multicast sessions. For example, the popular multicast conferencing tool, sdr, announces and listens to the address 224.2.127.254 and port 9875 for SAP session announcements. Each SAP packet contains an SDP payload that describes session attributes such as the session originator, the data channel and format, the session name and description, the contact information of the session creator, and the time duration of the session. Lastly, the user can add a new station to the Discovery module by providing the necessary information (the name and the data channel, at least). This module also contains some pre-specified well-known channels such as the BBC (http://www.broadcast.com/bbc) news channel, and the weather channels. The Discovery module presents to the DJ Profiler module the discovered list, and lets the DJ select from the list in a convenient manner. The DJ can also specify different views based on genre, time, alphabetical, etc.

After the profile has been specified, the Scheduler parses this profile and decides what station should be played at what time, then generates a TV-guide-like playlist for the given profile. When the profile contains alerts (i.e. high-priority items), the Scheduler module queries the Discovery module to see whether these stations have become available. If so, and the alert conditions have been satisfied, then the Scheduler selects the alert station and interrupts the normal programming. When there are no alerts, then the scheduling is straightforward, as it only needs be concerned with the selected program times and the default genre and station.

A CIRVirtualStation needs to communicate its playlist to a CIRClient in order for the latter to receive the dynamic content. It achieves this by sending out its playlist via multicast announcements using SAP, with the payload being the playlist. This choice of playlist announcement has the advantage in that it provides scalability over the traditional client–server negotiation. A design issue is to decide how much information to announce and how often, in order to provide the CIRClients with a timely view of the schedule for the near future, without flooding the network with the playlist metadata. Currently we are investigating into using three types of announcements: long-term, medium-term and short-term. Medium-term announcements are on the order of minutes and convey programs in the proximity of several hours. Long-term announcements can contain, say, the schedule of the day, and it can be an HTML page at an announced URL or can be an infrequent multicast announcement. Short-term announcements are for alert messages that notify listener of an event that has just occurred or will occur in a matter of seconds (such as the availability of a traffic report that has just come on-line).

Once the CIRClient receives the playlist, it needs to parse and understand this playlist. The actual audio content can reach the client in two mechanisms. First, it can come from the CIRServer that serves out the original content, thus the CIRClient understands from the playlist when and where to receive a particular station, and tunes to it. In this model, the audio content does not go through the CIRVirtualStation, and the CIRVirtualStation manages the *metadata* about the audio content rather than the content itself. The CIRClient instructs its player to tune in to the current station, knows when to switch to the next scheduled program, and provides buffering in between for an uninterrupted transition. In the second case, the audio content from a CIRServer is cached in the CIRVirtualStation, who then re-transmits the audio content either immediately or at a later time. This mechanism is akin to the VCR recording, and allows the content to be broadcasted at a later time. It also allows transformation of the content at the CIRVirtualStation, such as re-coding the content to a lower bit-rate for low-bandwidth clients, or transcoding it to a different audio format for which the client has a player.

3.2. *CIRClient*

The architecture for a CIRClient is shown in Fig. 3, and it consists of two parts: a player and a wrapper. The player part includes many audio decoding tools (including those that can decode MP3, Real Audio format, and RTP), so that it can be as format-independent as possible. The wrapper includes a user interface that lets the listener set the radio station and other settings. This radio station can be a CIRServer or it can be a CIRVirtualStation. The wrapper also includes a parser that parses the playlist announcement from the CIRVirtualStation it subscribes to. Based on the announcement, it invokes the appropriate audio decoder and instructs it to tune to the selected station. Because it has the knowledge of the next program from the playlist, it can prepare for the next program by (possibly) invoking a different player, and buffer the content for a smooth transition.

As discussed earlier, our architecture allows a straightforward integration of the CIRVirtualStation and the CIRClient. This integration results in a customized radio client that achieves all the functions of the CIRVirtualStation personalized to the listener.

3.3. *CIRServer*

A CIRServer can be any currently available radio station (content provider) on the Internet without any modification. In our framework, we only need to be able to discover this station, and know its data channel. The CIRServer then creates an announcement for this content provider. Thus, any currently available server using, say, NullSoft's Shoutcast server, the multicast conferencing tool sdr, or the RealServer, can become CIRServers with a simple front–end wrapper that parses their listings and SAP announcements and changes to the CIR-compatible format.

In the current state of Internet radio, the server simply transmits the audio content, without sending information about what is playing and what will be played. At best, some MP3 stations provide what is currently playing and what is coming up next (see, for example, yp.icecast.org and yp.shoutcast.com), but they do not provide the precise timing information about the content like the switch point between songs and advertisement. Sometimes audio events are advertised on Web pages, but they are not in a standard format, thus making it difficult to automatically parse this information. If the next generation

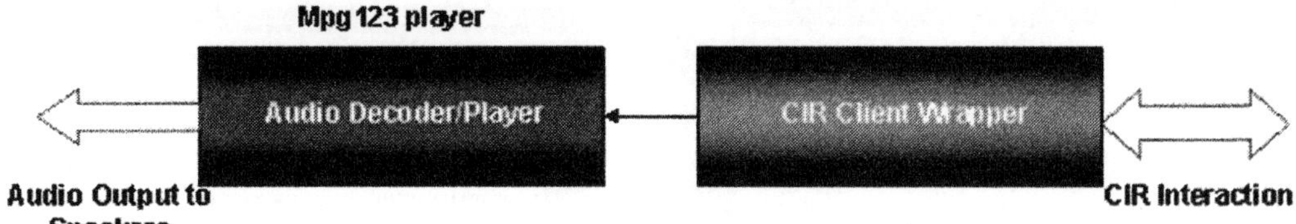

Fig. 3. Architecture of a CIRClient.

audio servers transmit in-band information on the data being currently broadcast, the CIRVirtualStation can exploit this fine granularity to do a more precise scheduling and enable features like advertisement insertion.

4. Implementation

4.1. CIRVirtualStation

The components in CIR have been implemented in Java to achieve platform independence. Fig. 4 shows a screen dump of the various pieces of the CIRVirtualStation that the DJ interacts with to manage the radio station's program schedule. The main window shows the current radio station playing, along with detailed information on the station when the 'Properties' button is pressed. From this window, one can also edit the profile by activating the 'Edit Profile' button. In the Profiler, the DJ enters the name of this CIRVirtualStation and the DJ's name. A new program can be added by selecting a station, specifying its start and end time and its priority. A high-priority entry means that if it is available, it will interrupt the normal programming. The DJ can set a default genre and a default station. When no station has been programmed for a time-slot, the Scheduler selects a radio station of the default genre if this property has been set. Otherwise, it plays the default station. The Profiler allows the DJ to browse a list of stations provided by the Discovery module or manually add a new one. After the profile has been edited, one can view a TV-guide-like schedule of today, tomorrow, or another specified date.

Recall that the CIRVirtualStation consists of a Discovery module, a Profiler module, a Scheduler module, and an Announcer module. The Profiler is the part most visible to a user. The other modules are background daemons. The Discovery module (DM) discovers radio stations on the network and passes the radio listings to the other modules in the CIRVirtualStations. The DM currently has three mechanisms to discover a radio stations.

(1) *SAP Announcement Listings*. Conferencing tools like sdr send SAP packets with an SDP payload on well-known multicast addresses. An SDP description of a session is a string of key–value pair attributes. The attributes include the scheduled air-time, content source, media type (audio vs. video), data encoding, additional information Web site location, etc. CIRVirtualStations use a description similar to SDP in their announcements, but include additional information like the genre and priority, and allow the concatenation of descriptions of several radio stations (see more details later in this section). These announcements are from varied types of content providers — live interactive classes and seminars, audio news, music radio stations, video clips, CIRVirtualStations, etc. The DM parses only the audio broadcast announcements — this includes the CIRVirtualStation announcements. Other announcements are ignored. The filtered announcements are sent to the other modules of the CIRVirtualStation.

(2) *Web-based Directory Listings*. An alternate model used in advertising a radio station is by registering it with a well-known directory server. yp.icecast.org and yp.shoutcast.com are examples of such directory servers that list registered radio stations on a Web site. These sites typically contain a list of radio stations, each entry including the name of the radio station, a short description, the genre, the URL of the data channel, the URL of the radio station, and perhaps the bit-rate, the uptime, and the number of listeners. The DM parses these Web sites and sends the

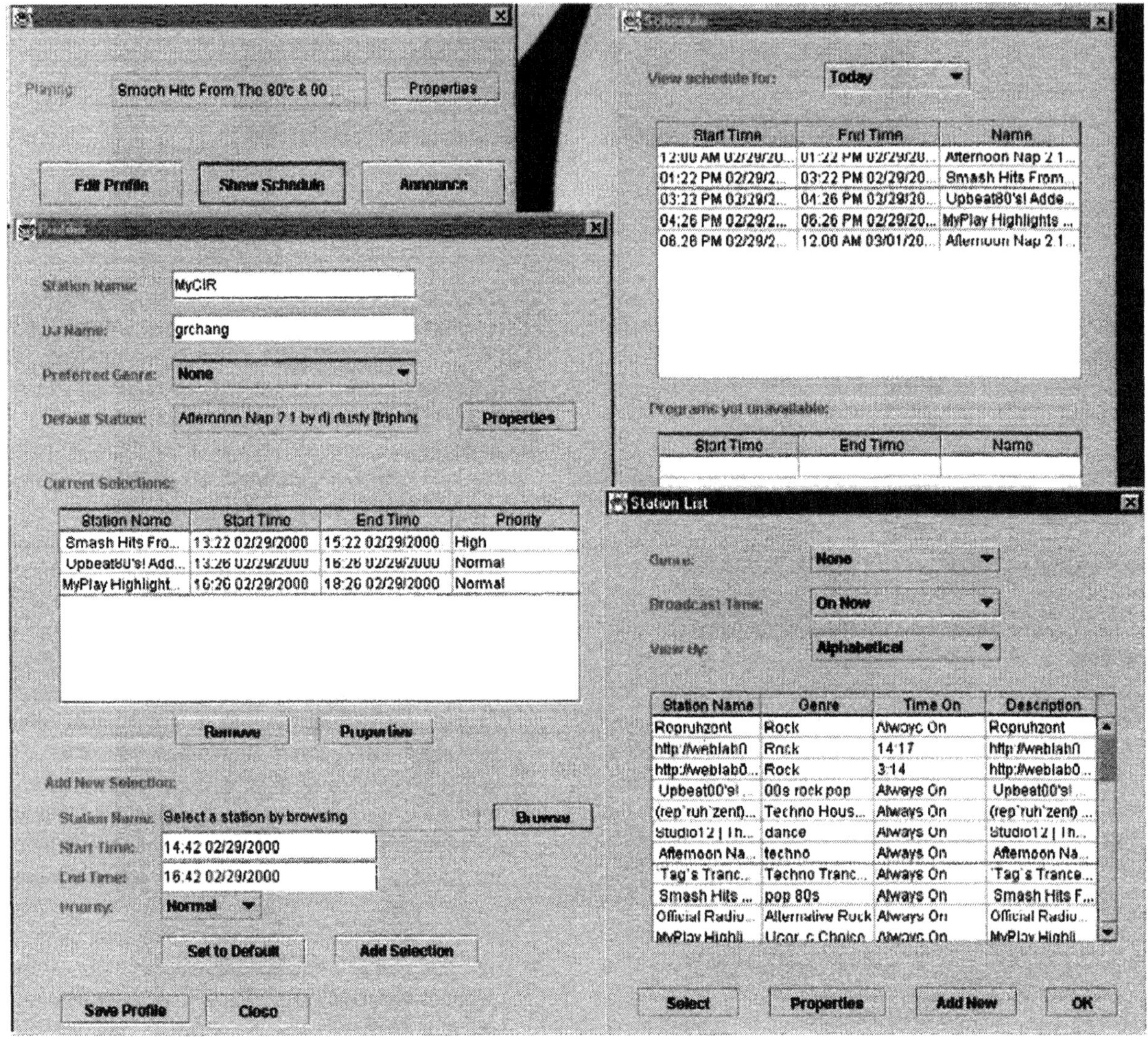

Fig. 4. The GUI of the CIRVirtualStation.

radio lists to the rest of the CIRVirtualStation. There are several other directory list servers on the Web but due to lack of any format standardization, the listing content is ad hoc. This necessitates writing a separate parser specific to each list server. Our current implementation handles only the two aforementioned directory servers.

(3) *Hard-coded Radio Station Listing*. The DM also provides the ability to add audio broadcasts from hard-coded sources. This is especially useful for adding audio broadcast locally: live feed from the CIRVirtualStation, playback of cached content, etc. The DM, based on input from either the user interface or configuration information creates listings for the broadcasts and passes them to the rest of the CIRVirtualStation.

The Scheduler module parses the profile and decides when and what gets played at a given time. It also gets notified by the Discovery module when the discovered list of stations has changed. The order of precedence for a station to be chosen at a given time is as follows: (1) a station of high priority, (2) a station of normal priority, (3) a station of genre equal to the default genre, and (4) the default station. If a station is not available, then the Scheduler goes to the next highest precedence to find an available station.

Once a schedule (or playlist) is formed, the CIRVirtualStation needs to announce it via its Announcer module. The announcements are sent out as multicast SAP packets, at the CIR-specified multicast address and port number. The payload is a modified form of SDP, which is an ASCII string of attributes each described in the `<key>=<value>` format. The CIR announcement contains a header describing the origin CIRVirtualStation. This header includes the station name, DJ username, message id, description, announcement session name, informational URL, etc. This header is followed by the program listing scheduled for this hour and the following four hours. The program listing is a concatenation of radio station descriptions, each including information such as the program name, program description, data address, start and end time, genre, informational URL, data format, bandwidth, referrer, and other extensible attributes. As mentioned earlier, the announcements from a CIRVirtualStation are not only received by CIRClients, but can also be parsed by other CIRVirtualStations.

4.2. CIRClient

The CIRClient is the CIR component that the listener uses to access the audio broadcasts. Our implementation of the CIRClient consists of an audio player (including the FreeAmp MP3 player and the GUI-less version of RealPlayer), a wrapper that listens to CIRVirtualStation announcements and controls the audio player, and a User Interface to control the CIRClient.

The wrapper listens to the multicasted CIR announcements, and extracts from the announcement the data format, the address of the data channel, and the start and end time of the current session. It then instructs the audio player to play.

The User Interface includes a Web interface for user control. This control is used to (1) set the CIRClient to the desired CIRVirtualStation or CIRServer, (2) configure the personal information (in the personalized radio case), and (3) configure the audio controls of the radio (like volume, balance, etc.).

As one of the sub-goals of the CIR, we built a Radio Appliance. The Radio Appliance is a Linux-based single board computer with wireless connectivity (using either a modem or Wireless LAN like WaveLAN) and audio interface (speakers and microphone). This appliance runs the CIRClient part of the CIR framework. The CIRClient code is implemented on top of Hewlett-Packard's ChaiServer [3], a Web-based software infrastructure for controlling and managing appliances. The ChaiServer library includes access to the infrared port, thus we have also implemented a user interface via IrDA, where the user can 'e-squirt' the stations and the volume control to the appliance. The appliance also has a 'beacon' that emits its current status via IrDA. Note that the CIRClient software component can be installed on any computer as well, not just on our customized Radio Appliance.

4.3. CIRServer

Currently, the CIRServers are the existing radio servers on the Web. We have also created a few radio stations in our network using the Shoutcast server and the sdr multicast conferencing tool. In our next generation implementation, the CIRServer will provide fine grain audio broadcast information, giving details like the start and stop time of songs, and details of the song name and singer, etc. An instance of this has been implemented by [1], which inserts the start and stop signals of a song in the RTP packet level. This allows the precise detection of a song or program, and facilitates a more precise scheduling of songs or programs, as well as enabling advertisement insertion.

5. Related work

There are wide and varied projects on different aspects of the Internet radio. The SDP-related projects [5–7] form the basic building blocks for the CIR architecture. The CIR framework uses SAP and descriptions similar to SDP to build program announcements. The MarconiNet project [10] deals with Internet-based audio broadcast but with a focus on creating ad-based channel broadcast where the content is always re-directed through the channel servers. The Information Discovery Graph [14] work discusses a scalable hierarchical resource directory through announcement and query. For example, the top level directory contains information of categories like sports, news and music. Then one queries the music directory to find more specific classes like classical music, rock, jazz, and so on. The CIR framework currently uses a simplistic single-address multicasting scheme. Future work will research the scalability issues regarding program announcements and description. [4,8,11–13], provide information on MP3 and RealAudio media formats and players.

6. Conclusion and future work

The CIR framework is a scalable Internet audio broadcast environment for managing, customizing, and communicating audio content. It enables features like dynamic content access, ease in creation and management of audio content, and program time-shifting. This research provides valuable insight into various aspects of audio broadcast on the network: exploiting the Web for multimedia information access, building of Web-based appliances and providing a consumer-centric view of the network. Some of our next steps include the following points.

- Extension of the CIR to accommodate other media (like video). This should be reasonably straightforward as our framework is out-of-band metadata management.
- Facilitate advertisement insertion. This would involve using RTP in-band information needed for dynamic ad insertion.
- Integrate RTP and other data format for audio streaming.
- Fine-tune the SAP messages in terms of frequency of broadcast and efficiency.
- Improve the switch-over from one audio stream to another. Currently, this switch-over is abrupt: we stop one stream and start another. By buffering the next stream and merging it with the previous one, we can make the transition smoother. This requires changes to the audio streaming software.
- Handle issues of scalability, security and authorization. Content ownership has currently been overlooked. However, as business models for Internet audio broadcast are developed, content distribution rights is a major issue. To facilitate this, both the content and the metadata management have to be done in a secure environment with a payment model as an integral part of this infrastructure. The different models for this domain will be researched.
- Enable location-aware services for the listener. This entails installing a device such as GPS on the client and integrating the location information with the CIRClient. There needs to be a register mechanism for the CIRVirtualStation to become aware of a CIRClient and provide appropriate services.

Acknowledgements

The authors would like to thank Scott Yam, who helped us develop a prototype during the summer of 1999.

References

[1] J. Brassil, The Media Siphon Project, Hewlett-Packard Laboratories, Palo Alto, CA.
[2] Broadcast.com, http://www.broadcast.com.
[3] Chai: a Web-based software infrastructure, http://www.chai.hp.com.
[4] FreeAmp Audio Player, http://www.freeamp.org.
[5] M. Handley, The sdr Session Directory: an Mbone conferencing scheduling and booking system, http://mice.ed.ac.uk/mice/archive/sdr.html.
[6] M. Handley and V. Jacobson, SDP: Session Description Protocol, IETF RFC 2327, Apr. 1998.
[7] M. Handley, C. Perkins and E. Whelan, SAP: Session Announcement Protocol, IETF draft, draft-ietf-mmusic-sap-v2-05.txt, Feb. 2000.
[8] Icecast, http://www.icecast.org.
[9] live365, http://www.live365.com.
[10] MarconiNet: Next-Generation Internet Radio Network, http://www.cs.columbia.edu/dcc/marconinet.
[11] mp3.com, http://www.mp3.com.
[12] Real Networks, http://www.real.com.
[13] Shoutcast, http://www.shoutcast.com.
[14] N.R. Sturtevant, N. Tang, L. Zhang, The Information Discovery Graph: towards a scalable multimedia resource directory, in: Proc. WIA'99 IEEE Workshop on Internet Applications, July 1999, pp. 72–79.

Running the Web backwards: appliance data services

Andrew C. Huang [a,1], Benjamin C. Ling [a,*,1], John J. Barton [b,2], Armando Fox [a,1]

[a] *Stanford University, Gates 252, Computer Science Department, Stanford, CA 94305, USA*
[b] *Hewlett-Packard Laboratories, 1501 Page Mill Road, Palo Alto, CA 94304-1126, USA*

Abstract

'Appliance' digital devices such as handheld cameras, scanners, and microphones generate data that people want to put on Web pages. Unfortunately, numerous complex steps are required. Contrast this with Web output: handheld Web browsers enjoy increasing infrastructural support such as user-transparent transformation proxies, allowing unmodified Web pages to be conveniently viewed on devices not originally designed for the task. We hypothesize that the utility of input appliances will be greatly increased if they too were 'infrastructure enabled'. Appliance Data Services attempts to systematically describe the task domain of providing seamless and graceful interoperability between input appliances and the Web. We offer an application architecture and a validating prototype that we hope will 'open up the playing field' and motivate further work. Our initial efforts have identified two main design challenges: dealing with device heterogeneity, and providing a 'no-futz' out-of-the-box user experience for novices without sacrificing expressive power for advanced users. We address heterogeneity by isolating device and protocol heterogeneity considerations into a single extensible architectural component, allowing most of the application logic to deal exclusively with Web-friendly protocols and formats. We address the user interface issue in two ways: first, by specifying how to tag input with commands that specify how data are to be manipulated once injected into the infrastructure; second, by describing a late-binding mechanism for these command-tags, which allows 'natural' extensions of the device's UI for application selection and minimizes the amount of configuration required before end-users benefit from Appliance Data Services. Finally, we describe how to leverage existing services in the infrastructure; our prototype is based on HTTP and Java but our architecture could also leverage services connected via Jini or CORBA. We also describe an implemented prototype of parts of the architecture and a specific application.

Keywords: Information appliances; Infrastructure enablement; Ubiquitous computing; Internet services

1. Background, motivation, and challenges

Much recent work has focused on accessing the Internet from 'post-PC' devices, especially 'information appliances' such as PDAs, cell phones, and palmtop computers [3]. Surveying that work, we see that these devices, despite their inherent hardware, software, and network limitations, can interoperate with the rest of the Internet through infrastructure support. In particular, software such as transformation proxies [4,5,9] and wireless protocol gateways [8,11] enable these devices to leverage the enormous installed infrastructure of servers, content, and interactive services. In the words of one mobile computing project [7], '*Access* is the killer app' for such devices. We capture this effect by saying that the post-PC devices have become more useful because they are now *infrastructure enabled.* Conversely, and

* Corresponding author.
[1] E-mail: {ach, bling, fox}@cs.stanford.edu
[2] E-mail: John_Barton@hpl.hp.com

partially as a result of infrastructure enablement, the Internet has begun to adapt to these devices and we are now seeing services tailored for their use, such as **Yahoo Mobile**[3] and a variety of sites that feature 'Palm-friendly' pages in addition to their desktop content. These new mobile computing devices are no longer isolated 'islands' of computation; they are participants in an Internet system.

1.1. Infrastructure enablement for input-centric devices

Almost all of the work on device access to the Internet has been focused on devices as Web browsers. We can say that it is focused on output from the Web. Our goal is to achieve infrastructure enablement for digital input-centric consumer appliances; we believe that Web-like infrastructure provides a good model for this enablement. Thus we aim to 'run the Web backwards', adding infrastructure to support input from portable input-centric digital devices.

By input-centric we refer to devices whose primary function is not to extract and browse digital information, but to create it. Examples include digital still cameras and video cameras, handheld scanners, and portable audio recorders. In part because of the pervasiveness and success of the established Internet infrastructure, much of the data created by these devices ends up in the Internet infrastructure, e.g. posted on Web sites. However, although much has been done to simplify the process of *extracting* information from the Internet to a variety of devices, the process for injecting data *from* devices into the infrastructure is extremely painful. We propose a framework and software components for facilitating this process, to stimulate further work that will allow input-centric devices to enjoy the same success as information browsing appliances enjoyed by becoming infrastructure-enabled. We call the resulting system 'Appliance Data Services'.

1.2. Contributions

The three main contributions of this paper are a systematic identification of the problem space, an architecture for the infrastructure-enablement of input appliances, and an implemented prototype of parts of the architecture. Our discussion of the problem space was informed by experiences with existing Web-input approaches and the process of formulating the architecture and prototype described here. The architecture attempts to reconcile the diversity of devices and protocols to be supported, the desired flexibility in selecting from a wide range of available Web applications, and the requirement of an unobtrusive 'no-futz' user experience in operating the device and connecting it to the Web. In particular we identify *command tagging* as a fundamental requirement for Appliance Data Services (ADS), describe an implemented approach to tagging that is extensible to a range of devices and communication protocols, and propose *command canonicalization* and *late binding* as specific architectural mechanisms to address the user experience concerns. We describe our proposed framework in light of the technical and usability challenges it addresses, describe our experience with a working prototype, and use it to motivate further research.

Our prototype implementation sketches all the elements of ADS so that we can experiment with an end-to-end prototype. We tried to avoid dependency on a particular software framework for the application logic; as we describe, a number of such frameworks are either commercially available or under development as research projects, and we wish to enable interoperation with as many of these as possible. The architectural mechanisms we describe can be implemented in the context of any of these frameworks.

The remainder of this section motivates the problem and identifies design challenges through a simple scenario, and introduces command tagging as a fundamental requirement for ADS. The second section describes the architecture and our implemented prototype, identifying ADS as a particular application domain for *infrastructure software frameworks* such as Jini [1] and Ninja [6], which we describe briefly. We conclude by describing our proposed extensions, lessons learned from the initial prototype, and discussion of work in progress.

1.3. Running the Web backwards

Imagine that we have taken a photo with a digital still camera and that we would like to publish the photo on the Web. Many current digital cam-

[3] mobile.yahoo.com

eras are equipped with infrared transceivers, which can be used to communicate photo data to another IR-equipped device such as a laptop or desktop PC. In an ideal world, we would point the camera's IR at the Internet-connected laptop or desktop, press a button to 'squirt' the photo data out of the camera, and sit back while infrastructure-deployed software reads the image, converts it to a Web-compatible encoding, authenticates itself to a remote server using your credentials, posts the image file there, and arranges for an HTML link on a designated 'photo album' page to point to it.

The reality is considerably uglier, as we found when we helped a California elementary school publish their 'Science Fair' results on the Web. We photographed each of 156 student posters with a digital camera and scanned one key item from each poster using a handheld scanner. To upload the data to the Web, we pointed the IR transceivers on the camera and scanner to an IR-equipped laptop connected to the wired Internet. Unfortunately, we had to install and learn to use different IR receiving software for each device. Furthermore, the uploaded images were only identifiable through serial numbers embedded in their file names on the laptop, leading to manual file copying and filename manipulation to coordinate the two data streams. The scanner's TIFF files had to be manually converted to JPEG for Web publishing. Finally, the school's Web server allowed only FTP write-once access, so that changes after uploading required manual intervention by a site administrator.

Taking these obstacles together, it is not surprising that the Web has so far failed to magnify the impact and usefulness of these input devices as it has for (e.g.) PDAs and cell phones. Small-scale attempts such as the **PhotoNet** [4] and **Cartogra** [5] Web sites are attempting to simplify this problem, but they provide only a solution for a very specific application, namely the publishing of photos to a site-maintained album in one of a limited set of presentation formats. We would like a more general solution that

(1) handles devices other than cameras such as hand-held scanners and digital audio recorders,
(2) allows the user to specify what happens to the data (how it is manipulated) once it enters the infrastructure, providing an easy-to-use interface for the novice user without sacrificing expressive power for the advanced user, and
(3) is able to coordinate the input from multiple devices.

Such an infrastructure would make it possible to have photos automatically routed to 'the science fair application', which would combine them with scanner images from the project's conclusion and add them in a predefined format to the Science Fair Web site. Selected photos might also be routed to the user's personal photo album, perhaps maintained on a site such as PhotoNet or Cartogra.

1.4. Design challenges

Recording the science fair was painful for two reasons. First, at a low level, appliances do not understand Internet standards such as HTTP and HTML, although this is slowly changing. Second and more importantly, at a higher level, there is no deployed application infrastructure that automatically performs the data transformations, protocol conversion, and data routing in a way that is largely transparent from the end-user's point of view.

This observation leads us to identify two specific design challenges for deploying software infrastructure to address this problem.

(1) *Dealing with device heterogeneity.* This challenge involves being able to handle the various data formats and protocols chosen by device vendors (e.g. JetSend [12], IRDA [13], and cradle synchronization [14]). This aspect is further complicated when we want to be able to merge multiple data streams from different devices, as in the 'Science Fair' scenario. In addressing this challenge, we leverage significant prior work on dealing with heterogeneity in the context of information delivery to post-PC devices [3]. As in the prior work, it is important that we provide an extensible solution that will generalize to other devices and protocols.
(2) *Providing 'no-futz', out-of-the-box operation.* Task-specific devices such as digital cameras have quite limited user interfaces by design: unobtrusive and familiar interface metaphors, such as the 'point and shoot' metaphor for a camera, make the devices easy to use. However, it

[4] www.photonet.com
[5] www.cartogra.com

seems intrinsic to this task domain that users need to be able to specify what should happen to the data they are 'injecting' into the infrastructure. The challenge is how to provide a flexible mechanism for specifying this without adding obtrusive features to the device UI, or while accommodating devices like digital microphones whose UI's may be essentially non-extensible. As a corollary, we want to enable devices to exhibit some reasonable 'out-of-the-box' behavior with zero user configuration, to allow new users to immediately begin experiencing the value of combining the device with Internet services.

Our answer to these challenges is an Appliance Data Service application architecture.

2. Architecture

Before describing the architecture in detail, we clarify our use of two specific terms: 'infrastructure' and 'service framework'.

By 'infrastructure' we refer to the deployed collection of hardware and software accessible directly or indirectly via an Internet (usually Web) programmatic interface. In addition to supporting 'destination applications' such as Web content, Web-accessible services (banking, etc.) and Web-accessible databases, the infrastructure includes 'faceless' application components. For example, most Web users never interact directly with Web-content caches or accelerators, but they are deployed throughout the infrastructure and programmatically accessed by destination sites. As another example, many portal sites that provide a search or query feature implement the feature by performing the search on a remote machine operated by a different vendor, and reformat the results in HTML for presentation to the user. In other words, the Internet infrastructure is, roughly speaking, the collection of all codes that implements or supports Internet sites, and the software and hardware mechanisms by which they communicate.

By 'service framework' we refer to any programmatic framework for deploying new services in the infrastructure. An example of a somewhat ad-hoc framework that emerged early in the Web's development is the collection of mechanisms used for Web-site intercommunication and code execution: HTTP, CGI-bin, SSL handshaking, etc. In this framework, each HTTP-accessible Web service can be considered a 'service module', and the modules communicate via HTTP and SSL. Various frameworks under development in academic research and industry, including Jini [1], Ninja [6], ChaiServer [2] and **HP e-speak** [6], feature a richer set of programmatic abstractions. Typically, a service framework provides three sets of mechanisms.

(1) The ability to compose services, either by writing a metaservice that calls each subservice, or by providing a way to name and execute a pipeline-like composition of services.
(2) An inter-service communication mechanism (HTTP, Java Remote Method Invocation, etc.) that may provide specific features such as authentication, security, etc.
(3) A registration/discovery service that tracks which services are available and allows services to be looked up by attribute value.

The ADS architecture, shown in Fig. 1, was developed to address the challenges outlined in the previous section. The envisioned use of such a framework begins with a user transferring data into the system via an *Access Point*, a network-connected hardware/software gateway that receives data from the user's appliance. The Access Point passes the data, user identifier and command-tag associated with the data to an *Application Controller*, which determines how the data is to be handled. The Application Controller activates the necessary infrastructure-resident *Modular Composable Services* that process and store the data. Each of these components mentioned in this usage model is justified and described in detail in the following sections.

2.1. Access point

The Access Point is the point of entry for data that is to be pushed into the system. It consists of necessary hardware and software to receive data from appliances. Hardware might include an IR transceiver, RF basestation hardware, or a cradle or cable for 'docking' an appliance. Software includes both hardware-specific drivers and the Access Point functionality described below. The Access Point could be

[6] www.e-speak.hp.com

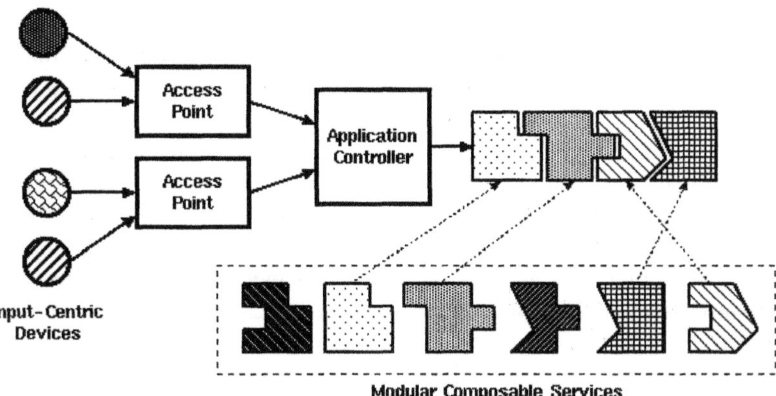

Fig. 1. Conceptual diagram of the ADS architecture. Devices and services are joined through Access Points and the Application Controller.

implemented as a commodity PC outfitted with the appropriate hardware interfaces, or it could be designed as a special-purpose 'network appliance'.

The main architectural role of the Access Point is to isolate device heterogeneity considerations in a single architectural component. By presenting a device-independent interface to the user and to the rest of the system, the Access Point converts a potentially large configuration space of handheld digital input devices into a small number of server-digestible data types. To allow *every* wireless device to send data without manually loading device-specific software on the receiver or receiver-specific software on the device, the Access Point must be extensible. Although we have deliberately avoided a design that assumes that appliances can run Java (to avoid an artificial dependence on a not-yet-deployed technology), a mechanism such as Jini that supports downloading of communication protocol code into the Access Point could be explored to provide such extensibility.

Along with the actual data, the Access Point must obtain a *user identifier* and *command-tag* from the device and attach these to incoming data in a client-protocol-specific manner. These metadata are necessary for a number of reasons.

(1) Application selection. The command-tag names the high-level application that the user wants to perform on the data (e.g. 'Send picture to my public_html directory'), using a binding mechanism described later. However, the command-tag alone is not sufficient to define the application since different users may have different meanings for the same tag, or result in different semantics in the interpretation of the tag (e.g. 'My Web site' maps to different URLs for different users). Thus, a user identifier is required to fully specify the desired application.
(2) Access control. The user identifier is also required to determine what credentials are to be attached to the application request. For example, a user should be allowed to push data into her own public_html directory, but not necessarily those of other users. Furthermore, some services may be accessible only to authorized users. Thus, the system needs some identifier to attach credentials to the request.
(3) Other service features requiring a command-tag and user identifier include billing, security, and personalization. Although we have not investigated the implementation of such features, we have left the user identifier as a necessary 'hook' for adding these capabilities later.

A simple example of a command-tag is text metadata that results from the user choosing a particular menu item on the device. A more sophisticated tag is possible with recent models of digital cameras that allow the embedding of audio-coded metadata in each image. In the latter example, the Access Point receives images from the camera and extracts the audio metadata for use as the command-tag. We also hope to explore merging of command-tag inputs from one device with data from another device.

Some devices have such limited user interfaces that there is no graceful way to specify a different command-tag with each device input. In this case, the Access Point attaches the special command-tag 'default' to the incoming data. We describe later why this is important architecturally.

2.2. *Service modules and application controller*

Once the typed data, command, and user identifier are available from the Access Point, they are handed off to the application infrastructure for application execution. In our system the 'application' relies on standalone or composable Internet service modules; for example, an image format translation service might take an image and some parameters as input, and deliver the image in a different encoding. Since ADS is an application architecture and not a service framework *per se*, our architecture *does not define* which service framework should be used to construct and execute the application. We believe that there are good engineering reasons to construct the application out of composable building blocks, but nothing in our architecture requires this. Architecturally, it suffices to distinguish one service module that acts as an ADS Application Controller, which must have the following functionality.

- Command-tag canonicalization. Since the command-tag can be one of several MIME-types, format conversion may be required to convert it into a simple string. For example, an audio file may be sent through an audio-to-text conversion service to produce a tag the Controller can use. Note that a composable-modules infrastructure that transforms data can be used to transform command-tags as well, without any modifications to the architecture. This concept is discussed in further detail in the following subsection.
- Command-tag resolution. The canonicalized command-tag is used to select a high-level application, by lookup in a *command database*. The representation of the application to be selected (URL naming a server, list of service modules to compose, etc.) is necessarily framework-specific. We describe later the XML-based 'work order' representation used in our prototype.
- Application execution. Instantiating the application is, again, framework-specific. For example, in a composable modular framework, execution involves matching the data input types to the needs of the application, finding a composition of available services such as format conversion and data storage that satisfies the data type constraints, and invoking the service modules.

We re-emphasize that there are many possibilities for executing code in the infrastructure, and we do not prescribe any particular method. Depending on the mechanisms used, the Application Controller may be a separate service module, or it may simply be a designated entry point into a piece of monolithic code in a larger service module, perhaps executed directly by an HTTP server as a CGI-bin script. However, the two Application Controller tasks of command canonicalization and command resolution are fundamental to our architecture, so we describe these in more detail before moving on to the description of specific mechanisms used in our implemented prototype.

2.3. *Command canonicalization*

The reason that command canonicalization and late binding are fundamental concepts in the architecture, although the implementation media may vary, is that together they effectively address the problem of command tagging without complicating the user experience. We first describe how each of the two architectural mechanisms works as shown in Fig. 2, and then give examples illustrating how they support an unobtrusive user experience.

Much recent work on information delivery (Web output) has focused on sophisticated data transformation services in the infrastructure. We have already described some ADS applications that make use of data transformation. Less obviously, but advantageously from the point of view of providing natural extensions to device UIs, we can also leverage the transformation infrastructure to transform command-tags into a canonical form. For example, recent digital camera models such as the Kodak DC265 [10] allow the embedding of audio-coded metadata in each image, in the form of a short audio clip. We can use an infrastructure speech-to-text service (operating against a fixed and very limited size vocabulary) to transform a spoken command word or phrase into a string, which is then looked up in the template database.

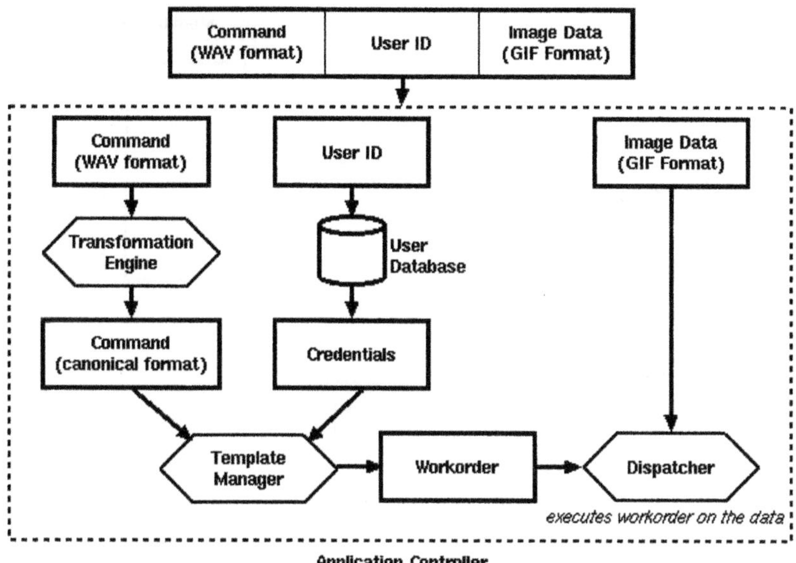

Fig. 2. A diagram of command transformation using late binding.

Command transformation is appealing because it decouples the method used to specify commands from the resolution of commands for application selection. Command transformation potentially allows each device's UI to be extended for command tagging in the way that is most natural for that device.

2.4. Command resolution using late binding

Commands are 'bound' to application descriptions in a separate template database, itself accessible via an infrastructural (e.g. Web) interface. This Web-accessible database is used to resolve a command into a script template ('work order' in our prototype, but machinery may vary according to the infrastructure framework used). Late binding of commands in a separate database contributes to a 'no-futz' user experience in at least two ways.

First, users can change or add command behaviors by modifying the database directly through a familiar Web interface. Even if an appliance is Web-configurable (e.g. using vendor-supplied software), centralized configuration frees users from having to configure each device independently. In fact, we envision third-party template databases that free the average user from worrying about how to construct new behaviors. Late binding therefore expands the repertoire of potential behaviors available to services, without burdening each device with the obligation of supporting a UI flexible enough to distinguish among all available commands, perhaps presenting only a subset at any given time.

Second, by modifying the binding of the special command-tag 'default', a user can modify the behavior of data coming from devices with non-extensible UIs. Thus, for digital cameras that provide no convenient metadata mechanism in which a command can be embedded to accompany a photo, the user can simply re-bind the default behavior to a new application in the command database, which has the same result as redefining the camera's (non-configurable) behavior.

3. Prototype implementation

This section describes the prototype implementation of the components shown in Fig. 3: Access Point, Application Controller, and Modular Services.

To make the description more concrete, the components are described in the context of the implemented application, a Web site displaying attendees of a conference. This application involves taking pictures and scanning business cards of conference attendees to be published on the conference Web site.

Using the ADS system, the user takes a picture of

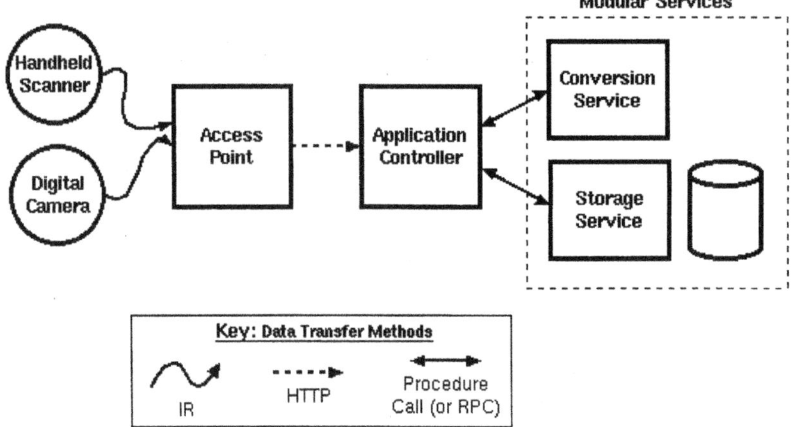

Fig. 3. ADS prototype implementation.

each person attending the conference and scans the attendees' business cards. The user then goes to an ADS Access Point, points the camera to the IR port, pushes a button on the camera to transfer the picture, and does the same with the handheld scanner. After repeating this process for each attendee, the appropriate data has been injected into the system. Within ADS, the appropriate transformations are applied and the resulting files are stored on the conference Web site. The end result is a page containing all the attendees' pictures and business cards.

3.1. *Implementation of the Access Point*

This section describes the implementation of the Access Point and the role it plays in the ADS system. The Access Point is separated into two modules, in order to decouple its two main concerns: device heterogeneity and management of hard state. These two modules, shown in Fig. 4, are:

- Information Daemon (InfoD) — interacts directly with devices using device-specific adaptors;
- Aggregator — receives data and command-tags from the InfoD, stores a user's pending data, and dispatches service requests upon receipt of a user's command-tag.

How these components — devices, InfoD, and Aggregator — interact is better understood in the context of a sample application such as the conference attendee list.

After the user has taken a picture of an attendee, the user points the camera's IR port at the InfoD. In the prototype, the InfoD is implemented on an IR-equipped laptop running Windows 98. The user then pushes a button on the camera to transfer the data into the system. The InfoD and camera do the necessary handshaking to begin transmission, and the data is passed from the camera to the InfoD. To accomplish this, the InfoD has various device adaptors that handle communication with the appropriate devices. Currently, the InfoD supports digital cameras, handheld scanners, PalmOS, and WinCE devices that use Hewlett-Packard's JetSend IR data transfer protocol.

The InfoD as we have described it is stateless and configurationless, which makes it appealing to deploy as (e.g.) a publicly available kiosk or Web-centric service. In fact, the InfoD looks very much like a reverse Web browser, its role being to read device-

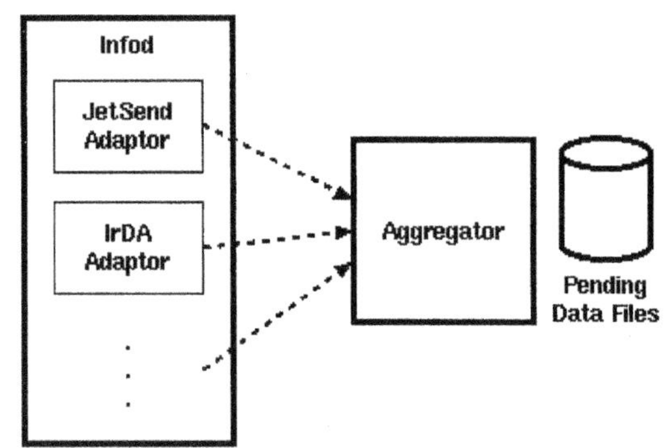

Fig. 4. Two components of the Access Point: Information Daemon and Aggregator.

specific data and write MIME-typed data streams to the rest of the system.

When the InfoD receives the data and extracts the relevant metadata, it uses HTTP POST to send the information to the Aggregator. The Aggregator is implemented as a Ninja service running on a Linux workstation. Using HTTP allows the InfoD to include whatever meta-information is available. However, the Aggregator does require the following headers:

- Content-Type
- Content-Length
- X-User-Id
- X-Data-Class

Using HTTP POST as the API between Device Adaptors and the Aggregator provides more flexibility than a strongly typed API. First of all, the HTTP POST API allows the InfoD to send any metadata it receives from the device without knowing what information the Aggregator can handle. Secondly, this API facilitates backwards compatibility. New adaptors can send newly defined parameters in headers or multipart MIME, while old adaptors continue sending the same information as before. Thus, only the Aggregator, rather than all adaptors, needs to be changed to handle both the new and old API.

The Content-Type and Content-Length headers are standard HTTP headers that are used to describe the data. The X-User-Id field is used by the Aggregator to associate the incoming data with the correct user; furthermore, as mentioned earlier, this field is required by other system components to fully define the command-tag received. Finally, the X-Data-Class field is used to differentiate actual data (e.g. jpeg image, text file) from command-tag data.

For each piece of data received (e.g. Data-Class = 'data'), the Aggregator archives the entire POST request. When a command-tag arrives, denoted by 'X-Data-Class: cmd-tag', the Aggregator attaches the command-tag to each piece of data pending for the current user. Each triple is then sent in an HTTP POST request to the Application Controller.

3.2. Application Controller

The Application Controller receives data from the Access Point Aggregator and executes the requested service command on the data. This component, shown in Fig. 5, contains the following three modules:

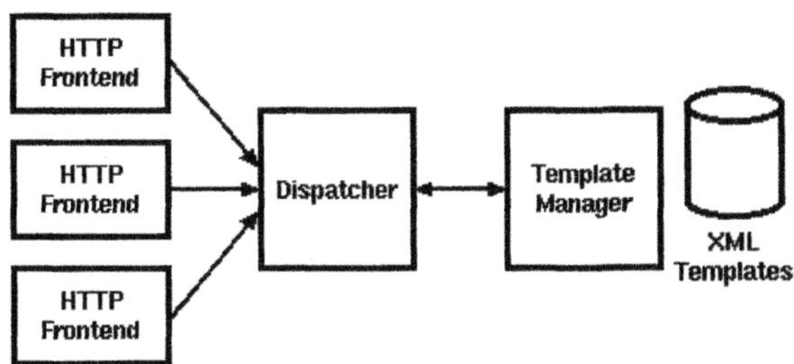

Fig. 5. The three components of the Application Controller: HTTP Frontend, Dispatcher, and Template Manager.

- HTTP Frontend — receives data posted from the Access Point;
- Dispatcher — invokes services on the data;
- Template Manager — manages the template database.

Again, we return to the attendee list application to describe how these three components interact with one another and how the Application Controller interacts with other components in the ADS system. When the Application Controller receives data from the Access Point it performs the following steps.

(1) The HTTP Frontend parses the HTTP POST request to extract the data, user-id, and command-tag. The Frontend then passes this data to the Dispatcher.
(2) Upon receipt of this information, the Dispatcher passes the user-id and command-tag to the Template Manager.
(3) The Template Manager finds the XML work order, whose format is described below, that corresponds to the user-id and command-tag given.
(4) The Dispatcher parses the work order using IBM's XML4J package. It extracts the relevant information such as service name, arguments, return type, etc.
(5) For each service listed in the work order, the Dispatcher does the following:
    - obtains a handle to the remote service using the Ninja service loader;
    - uses the Java Reflection API to obtain a handle to the service's main method;
    - calls the main method via Java RMI;
    - labels the corresponding entry in the work order as 'finished'; the labelled work order can be used for such things as intermediate

Workorder Format:

```
<template>

  <command>
    <service>[service name]</service>
    <method>[method name]</method>
    <arglist num="[number of arguments]">
      <arg type="[arg1 type]">[arg1]</arg>
      <arg type="[arg2 type]">[arg2]</arg>
      ...
    </arglist>
    <return>[return mimetype]</return>
  </command>

  <command>
    ...
  </command>

</template>
```

Sample Workorder:

```
<template>

  <command>
    <service>ads.services.Convert</service>
    <method>convert</method>
    <arglist num="3">
      <arg type="byte[]">$1</arg>
      <arg type="java.lang.String">$2</arg>
      <arg type="java.lang.String">gif</arg>
    </arglist>
    <return>image/gif</return>
  </command>

  <command>
    <service>ads.services.Store</service>
    <method>store</method>
    <arglist num="2">
      <arg type="byte[]">$1</arg>
      <arg type="java.lang.String">img.gif</arg>
    </arglist>
  </command>

</template>
```

Fig. 6. The work order format and a sample work order that converts images from jpg to gif and stores the resulting image.

status information, bookkeeping, billing, and possibly, error detection.

The XML work order returned by the Template Manager and used by the Dispatcher to execute the correct services on the data is shown in Fig. 6.

Note that the only difference between a template and a work order is that in a work order, service descriptions are bound to service handles. The reason that the current Template Manager returns work orders is that service discovery and lookup mechanisms have not yet been integrated into the ADS system. For this, we intend to explore the possibility of using Ninja's Service Discover Service (SDS) and/or Ninja's automatic path creation mechanisms.

3.3. Composable services

Our services are simple Ninja services that are invoked using Java RMI. Invoking services via procedure calls makes it easy for service writers to implement new services quickly. Furthermore, Ninja places minimal constraints on the service implementations; all that is required are `init()` and `destroy()` methods. The following services have been implemented for use in the attendee list application:

- ConvertService — uses the UNIX command 'convert' to convert between arbitrary image formats;
- ScalingService — scales images by a user-specified amount;
- ThumbnailService — re-sizes images to thumbnail size;
- StoringService — stores files on the local drive.

For each attendee's picture or business card, the Application Controller invokes the appropriate data-formatting services on the data. The Application Controller then uses the StoringService to store the file at the conference Web site.

4. Discussion

We set out to explore the potential for combining the new generation of digital input devices with emerging Internet services but using Web infrastructure for input rather than output. Our experience in constructing the Science Fair Web site without infrastructure support convinced us that such support would be essential for successful integration. This section presents some observations in trying to build such infrastructure.

The main objective in designing the Access Point was extensibility. Since there are many widely deployed protocols, it must be relatively simple to write Device Adaptors for the Access Point. We believe that using HTTP POST for the API between device adaptors and the Aggregator provides a good balance of simplicity and flexibility. However, more experience in writing device adaptors is required to test this hypothesis.

The Application Controller is still in an early stage; the balance between end-user ease-of-use and application generality will be a great challenge. Our attendee list application revealed many issues in robustness and usability that remain to be tackled, some of which we describe in Section 5.

There is also a larger issue to consider. This Web-input experience might be considered inappropriate for setting the requirements for Appliance Data Services. Arguably, a school science fair or conference attendee list is not a typical 'killer app', and the constraints imposed by the experience might not represent the bulk of applications of a Web-based data-input services systems in the future. However, we argue that this is instead a glimpse at the future on two grounds.

- Science fairs and attendee lists may not have great economic value, but the simplicity and ubiquity of the Web is what motivated the effort to record these events there in the first place. If we design a data-input system sufficiently simple and useful, then many marginally economic data-input activities suddenly become valuable. For example, consider the construction of auction house catalogs, recording inventory, insurance claim recording, and collaborative content authoring.
- The constraints of these applications, rather than being odd, may reflect constraints imposed on such systems in the future. We choose to tackle a system with heterogenous devices, multiple inputs to coordinate, and 'open' services as the application components. A single device with a single communications protocol and a closed application would not explore the potential challenges of deploying and operating real systems.

The Web's simplicity allowed it to quickly evolve from a simple way for researchers to publish static content to a universal interface for sophisticated services such as banking, shopping, and mapping. By analogy, we hope that ADS — which 'runs the Web backwards' — will make the 'trivial' task of data-input simple enough that applications that leverage it become more widespread and compelling.

5. Open issues

ADS is an early-prototype first step toward infrastructure support for appliance data services. Although we believe that we have identified some fundamental architectural mechanisms for such applications, we have barely begun to explore the issues involved in making ADS 'real'.

Failure semantics. An issue we have yet to tackle is how to report success or failure of the application to the user. This is a problem of semantics, not just implementation: only an end-to-end indicator of application success or failure is likely to be useful ('The photo got posted' or 'it did not'), but in some cases the application may be sufficiently long-running that it is unreasonable to expect the user to wait for an end-to-end check. A real concern is making sure the user's expectations are set correctly: in the digital-camera scenario, if the user successfully injects camera data into the infrastructure, the user may feel it is then safe to erase the camera's memory. In fact this is only safe if the application can make *some* guarantee about the persistence of the injected data, if not the success of complete application execution, so that recovery can be attempted later. We speculate that the application logic could include a separate end-to-end acknowledgment delivered to the user 'out of band' with respect to ADS; perhaps the user can be sent e-mail upon successful completion of the application.

Security and privacy. Although we envision the Access Point as a public shared resource, the user identifier accompanying the data entering the Access Point is sufficient to bootstrap a secure connection to the rest of the infrastructure. Because we have not yet investigated how best to provide secure and private service, we have deliberately avoided specifying the format of the user identifier. It might, for example, consist of an identification token accompanied by a challenge/response pair that the AP can use to authenticate itself to the Application Controller. This mechanism, which does not require a user's secret key to be revealed to the AP, is analogous to the mechanism used for roaming in the GSM cellular telephone system. In any case, the user has to trust the Access Point not to maliciously eavesdrop or tamper with the data coming from the device. Since users currently appear to be willing to read their e-mail on shared kiosks in airports and hotels, we do not expect trusting the Access Point to be a major obstacle to deployment.

6. Conclusion

Our overarching goal has been to enable the same level of innovation in connecting input-centric appliances to the Web as has been achieved in the last few years for Web information delivery appliances. To this end, we identified specific design challenges and proposed solutions to them in the context of an enabling architecture.

- Device and protocol heterogeneity. By handling the heterogeneity in the Access Point and producing a uniform representation (typed data, typed command-tag, user ID) of device input in a Web-digestible protocol, we isolate heterogeneity concerns in a single architectural component. The rest of the software infrastructure can deal exclusively with Web-friendly standard protocols and formats.
- Unobtrusive user experience. We have described how command canonicalization via transformation can be used to gracefully extend the functionality of a device's existing UI, and how late binding of commands in a database can be used to separate device configuration from the specification of new application behaviors.
- Leveraging Web services. By building an open system for data-input support we hope to allow for and thus encourage an economy of service providers to support data input, leading to a spiral of better devices and services to support them.

We hope and anticipate that our initial work on ADS will encourage others to leverage the Web to magnify the usefulness of input-centric appliances.

Acknowledgements

We thank Patrick Arnold of Hewlett Packard and the rest of the HP JetSend team for early access to JetSend protocol code for our Access Point implementations.

References

[1] K. Arnold, B. O'Sullivan, R.W. Scheifler, J. Waldo and A. Wollrath, The Jini Specification, Addison-Wesley, Reading, MA, 1999.

[2] ChaiServer system described on http://www.chai.hp.com

[3] A. Fox, S.D. Gribble, Y. Chawathe and E.A. Brewer, Adapting to network and client variation using active proxies: lessons and perspectives, IEEE Personal Communications (invited submission), Aug. 1998, Special Issue on Adapting to Network and Client Variability.

[4] A. Fox, S.D. Gribble, Y. Chawathe, E.A. Brewer and P. Gauthier, Cluster-based scalable network services, in: Proc. of the 16th ACM Symposium on Operating Systems Principles (SOSP-16), St. Malo, October 1997.

[5] A. Fox, I. Goldberg, S.D. Gribble, A. Polito and D.C. Lee, Experience with Top Gun Wingman: a proxy-based graphical web browser for the Palm Pilot PDA, in: IFIP International Conference on Distributed Systems Platforms and Open Distributed Processing (Middleware '98), Lake District, UK, September 15–18, 1998.

[6] S.D. Gribble, M. Welsh, E.A. Brewer and D.E. Culler, The NINJA project pages, January 1999, http://ninja.cs.berkeley .edu

[7] R.H. Katz and E.A. Brewer et al., The bay area research wireless access network (barwan), in: Proc. Spring COMPCON Conf. 1996.

[8] Metricom Corp., Ricochet Wireless Modem, 1995, http://w ww.ricochet.net

[9] ProxiNet, Inc., ProxiWeb Thin Client Web Browser, 1997, http://www.proxinet.com

[10] See product information for the Kodak DC265 camera on http://www.kodak.com

[11] WAP Forum, Wireless application protocol (WAP) forum, http://www.wapforum.org

[12] The JetSend communication protocol is described on http://www.jetsend.hp.com

[13] http://www.irda.org/

[14] For example, see the Intellisync software at http://www.pu matech.com/intellisync.html

Andrew C. Huang received his B.S. degree in Electrical Engineering and Computer Sciences from UC Berkeley in 1998. He is currently a second-year Ph.D. student in the Stanford University Computer Science Department and is a member of the Software Infrastructures Group headed by Professor Armando Fox. His current research involves enabling ubiquitous computing devices (such as PDAs, digital cameras, etc.) to access Internet services using software infrastructure support.

Benjamin C. Ling holds a B.S. in Electrical Engineering and Computer Sciences from UC Berkeley. He received the Bechtel Achievement Award at UC Berkeley, and is currently an Department of Defense Fellow. He is a second-year Computer Science Ph.D. student at Stanford University, and is also a member of the Software Infrastructures Group. His current research involves enabling ubiquitous computing devices to access Internet Services using software infrastructure support.

John J. Barton works on software infrastructure to support coordinated data input from digital appliances like cameras and PDAs. This work is part of the HP Labs Cooltown (www.hp.cooltown.com) project. Before joining HP in 1998, he worked at IBM's T.J. Watson Research Center. There he wrote the Jalapeno Java Virtual Machine boot image writer and managed the Java Technology group. Before that he worked on the 'Montana' research project that led to IBM's VisualAge C++ v 4.0 product and co-authored 'Scientific and Engineering C++' with Lee R. Nackman. He has a Ph.D. degree in Chemistry from the University of California at Berkeley and a Master's degree in Applied Physics from the California Institute of Technology.

Armando Fox joined the Stanford faculty as an Assistant Professor in January 1999, after getting his Ph.D. from UC Berkeley as a researcher in the Daedalus wireless and mobile computing project. His research interests include the design of robust Internet-scale software infrastructure, particularly as it relates to the support of mobile and ubiquitous computing, and user interface issues related to mobile and ubiquitous computing. In previous lives, Armando received a BSEE from M.I.T. and an MSEE from the University of Illinois, and worked as a CPU architect at Intel Corp. He is also an ACM member and a founder of ProxiNet, Inc. (now a division of Puma Technology), which is commercializing thin client mobile computing technology developed at UC Berkeley.

Latency-sensitive hashing for collaborative Web caching

Kun-Lung Wu [*,1], Philip S. Yu [1]

IBM T.J. Watson Research Center, 30 Saw Mill River Road, Hawthorne, NY 10532, USA

Abstract

Many geographically distributed proxies are increasingly used for collaborative Web caching to improve performance. In hashing-based collaborative Web caching, the response times can be negatively impacted for those URL requests hashed into geographically distant or overloaded proxies. In this paper, we present and evaluate a latency-sensitive hashing scheme for collaborative Web caching. It takes into account latency delays due to both geographical distances and dynamic load conditions. Each URL request is first hashed into an anchor hash bucket, with each bucket mapping to one of the proxies. Secondly, a number of nearby hash buckets are examined to select the proxy with the smallest latency delay to the browser. Trace-driven simulations are conducted to evaluate the performance of this new latency-sensitive hashing. The results show that (1) with the presence of load imbalance due to skew in request origination or hot-spot references, latency-sensitive hashing effectively balances the load by hashing into geographically distributed proxies for collaborative Web caching, and (2) when the overall system is lightly loaded, latency-sensitive hashing effectively reduces latency delays by directing requests to geographically closer proxies.

Keywords: Latency-sensitive hashing; Proxy caching; Collaborative Web caching; Performance; Load balancing

1. Introduction

The growth of the Internet has really been exploding. As a consequence, user response times for accessing the Web have become increasingly unsatisfactory. One popular approach to improving the Web performance is to deploy proxy cache servers between clients and content servers. With proxy caching, most of the client requests can be serviced by the proxy caches, reducing latency delays. Network traffic on the Internet can also be significantly reduced, eliminating network congestion. In fact, many commercial companies are providing hardware and software products and solutions for Web caching, such as Inktomi, Network Appliance and Akamai Technologies. Some of them are using geographically distributed data centers for collaborative Web caching. Namely, many geographically distributed proxies are increasingly used to cooperate in Web caching.

To cooperate in Web caching, a coordinating protocol is generally required. Hash routing, such as the cache array routing protocol (CARP) [12,13] and consistent hashing [10], is an emerging approach to coordinating a collection of cooperating proxy caches. Hashing partitions the entire URL space among the caches, creating a single logical cache. Each cache is responsible for requests belonging to the assigned partition. Requests are sent to the proper proxy caches based on the hash values of the corresponding URLs. Hashing can be computed ei-

* Corresponding author.
[1] E-mail: {klwu,psyu}@us.ibm.com

ther by the browsers or by the domain name servers (DNS).

As more and more geographically distributed proxies are used in collaborative Web caching, however, response times tend to be negatively impacted for those requests hashed into geographically distant proxies or overloaded proxies. Distant proxies tend to incur longer network latency delays. Overloaded proxies can cause significant delays as well, no matter how close they are to the browsers. As a result, the overall system response times can be significantly degraded. Therefore, there is a strong need to consider the latency issue in hashing-based Web caching among geographically distributed proxies.

One obvious solution to this latency problem is to avoid hashing requests into geographically distant proxies. In [10], a user's geographical region is encoded into the hash value and sent by the browser to a DNS in its geographical region. The DNS then maps the encoded hash value to a proxy cache within the same region. Thus, requests are served only by proxies in a geographically close region. In this paper, we refer to this approach as the *geographically clustered hashing*, or GCH. It works well if the proxies within a region can adequately service all the requests originated within the same region. However, if workloads are skewed among regions, proxies in one region may be overloaded while those in another region are under-loaded. As a result, the degree of collaboration among proxies is limited by geographical locations.

In contrast, one can simply hash requests into all cooperating proxy caches regardless of geographical locations. This approach is referred to, in this paper, as the *geographically distributed hashing*, or GDH. Compared with GCH, load tends to be more balanced among all the geographically distributed cooperating caches. However, GDH does not take into account network latency delays due to geographical distances. It does not deal with hot spots, either. In the presence of hot spots, all the references to the hot spots are hashed into the same proxies. As a result, the proxies that handle the hot spots can easily become overloaded.

In this paper, we propose a new *latency-sensitive hashing*, or LSH, for collaborative Web caching. Similar to GDH, it hashes requests into all proxies. But, it takes into account latency delays and potential overloaded proxies. In latency-sensitive hashing, a request is first hashed into an anchor hash bucket. Each hash bucket is mapped to one of the geographically distributed proxies. Secondly, a selection algorithm is used to pick a proxy among a small number of hash buckets adjacent to the anchor hash bucket. The selection is based on an objective to reduce network latency and to avoid creating overloaded proxies.

Trace-driven simulations were conducted to evaluate latency-sensitive hashing. We compared the average response times of client requests using the three hashing schemes. Specifically, we examined the impacts of skew in request origination (more browsers are active in one geographical region than in other regions) and hot-spot references (a particular URL is accessed by many browsers). The results show that (1) in the presence of high skew in request origination, the geographically clustered hashing scheme suffers the most because of limited collaboration, (2) in the presence of hot-spot references, both geographically clustered hashing and geographically distributed hashing degrade in performance because they cannot effectively balance the load, and (3) latency-sensitive hashing is very effective in dealing with skew in request origination and hot-spot references because it takes into account not only network latency but also potential load imbalance.

As an alternative to hashing, a class of query-based approaches can also be used to coordinate a collection of geographically distributed proxies [1,5,8,14]. Such query-based approaches use the *Internet Cache Protocol* (ICP) to ask its neighboring proxies for a missed object. A client browser sends its request to a configured proxy cache. If found locally, the requested object is returned. Otherwise, the configured proxy asks, on the browser's behalf, its neighboring proxies for a copy of the missed object using multi-casting. As more geographically distributed proxies are used for collaborative Web caching, the overhead of locating an object from neighboring proxies increases. For more detailed comparisons of query-based and hashing-based approaches to collaborative Web caching, readers are referred to [12].

There are many other papers on various issues of collaborative Web caching, such as [8,11,12,15,17].

However, none has dealt specifically with the network latency issues. Various load-balancing techniques have also been proposed for the Web, such as [2–4,6,9,16]. Most of them try to distribute requests evenly among a local cluster of servers. None has considered the latency issue of geographically distributed proxies.

The paper is organized as follows. Section 2 describes the details of the new latency-sensitive hashing scheme. Section 3 then presents our approach to evaluating the latency-sensitive hashing, including the simulation model, system parameters and workload characteristics. Section 4 shows the results from trace-driven simulations. Finally, Section 5 summarizes the paper.

2. Latency-sensitive hashing

To understand the basic idea of the new latency-sensitive hashing, let us first look at the geographically distributed hashing, GDH, through an example. Fig. 1 shows three geographically distributed clusters of proxies. Each cluster contains three proxies. The proxies within the same cluster are geographically close to each other and to the browsers residing in the same geographical region. Fig. 2 shows an example of hashing two requests, $u1$ and $u2$, originated from the proximity of cluster 1. It includes the latency delays of requests to all the proxies due to network distance for requests originating from region 1. The latency delays are 0.2 s to proxies a, b and c, 1.0 s to proxies d, e and f and 1.0 s to proxies g, h and i.

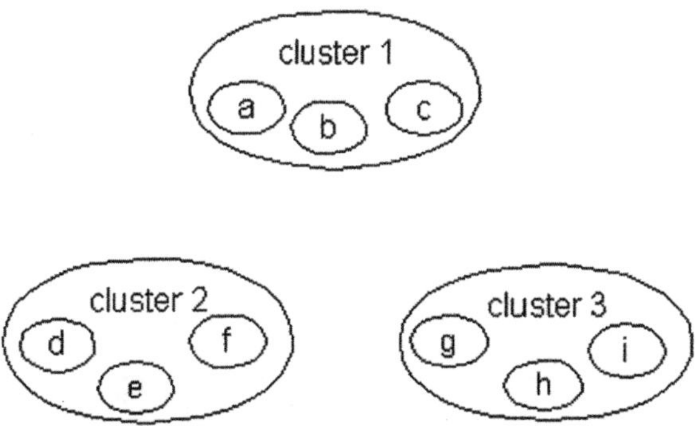

Fig. 1. Three geographically distributed clusters of proxies.

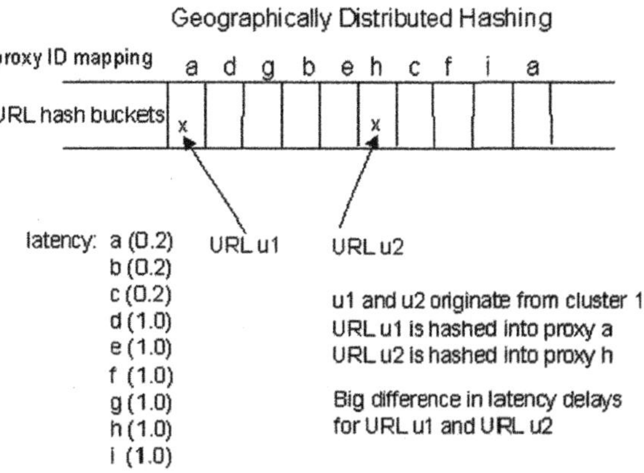

Fig. 2. An example of a geographically distributed hashing.

Assume that the hash values are partitioned into a sufficiently large number of hash buckets and each hash bucket is mapped to a proxy. Fig. 2 shows that $u1$ is hashed into proxy a and $u2$ is hashed into proxy h. Assuming both requests can be found locally in their respective proxy caches, the response times can still differ quite substantially. For request $u2$, the network latency of 1.0 s is substantially larger than 0.2 s for request $u1$. This example illustrates the potential problem of hashing requests into more and more geographically distributed proxies. For those that are hashed into geographically distant proxies, the network latency can be a problem.

Such network latency issue can be solved if it is taken into account during hashing. Fig. 3 shows an example of applying latency-sensitive hashing to the same requests in Fig. 2. In Fig. 3, requests

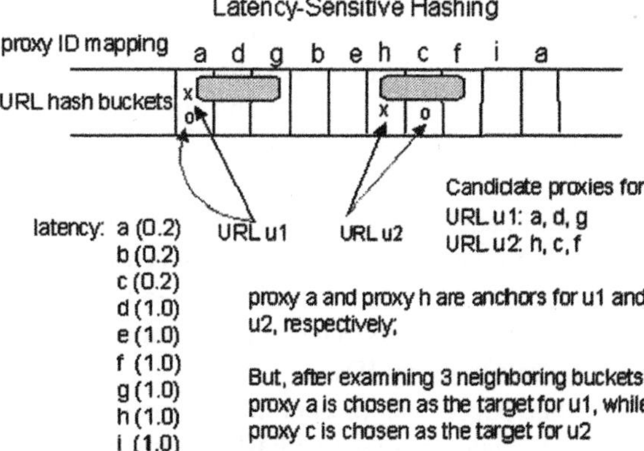

Fig. 3. An example of a latency-sensitive hashing.

are first hashed into anchor hash buckets, similar to Fig. 2. For example, request $u1$ is hashed into the hash bucket mapped to proxy a and $u2$ is first hashed into the one mapped to proxy h. However, a selection algorithm is then applied to a small number of hash buckets that are close to the anchor hash bucket to pick a proxy that can lower the latency delay. For example, in Fig. 3, after examining three hash buckets that are mapped to proxies h, c and f, proxy c is chosen to serve request $u2$ because proxy c can lower the latency. For request $u1$, however, the same proxy a will be chosen since it provides the smallest latency delay. Note that we are examining neighboring hash buckets of the anchor bucket in the hash value space. We are not examining the geographically neighboring proxies of the one mapped to the anchor hash bucket.

Obviously, in latency-sensitive hashing, both the mapping of hash buckets to proxies and the selection window size are important to its performance. These two issues are interdependent. With proper assignment, the window size need not be large. The objective is to have, for every request, a high probability of finding within the selection window size a proxy that is geographically close to the browser. If we model the geographical distribution of cooperative proxies as distributed clusters, similar to Fig. 1, then each hash bucket can be mapped to one proxy from each cluster in a round-robin fashion. And the selection window size can simply be the number of clusters. For instance, in Figs. 1 and 2, we assign one proxy from each cluster to every consecutive hash bucket in a round-robin fashion. As a result, any selection window of size 3 will have a proxy from each one of the three clusters.

If each cluster contains the same number of proxies, the mapping of hash buckets to proxy IDs is relatively simple. The proxy IDs can be directly assigned to the hash buckets in a straightforward manner. However, the number of proxies within a cluster can be different. In such cases, the mapping of hash buckets to proxies for latency-sensitive hashing is not obvious if the requests are to be evenly distributed to all proxies. As a result, we need a general mechanism to map hash buckets to proxy IDs.

In this paper, we present an indirect mapping scheme for latency-sensitive hashing. Instead of directly mapping each hash bucket into a proxy ID, we map each hash bucket to an index of a proxy ID array. From this proxy ID array, we then obtain the proxy ID for the hash bucket. Once we hash an URL to a proxy ID through this indirect mapping, we can select a proxy within the proxy ID array to lower the latency delay as well as balance the load. The indirect mapping scheme consists of two parts. The first part is the construction of the proxy ID array, PA. The second part is the assignment of the indices of the proxy ID array to hash buckets. Let us assume that there are N total clusters and the number of proxies in each cluster is denoted as C_i, $i = 0, 1, \ldots, N-1$.

The proxy ID array is constructed as follows. Proxy IDs are selected in a two-level round-robin fashion. Namely, first we select a cluster and then within each cluster we select a proxy ID, all in a round-robin manner. The size of PA is computed as $N \cdot \mathrm{LCM}_c$, where LCM_c is the l.c.m. of C_i, $i = 0, 1, \ldots, N-1$. As an example, assume we have two clusters, with one cluster containing two proxies a, b, and the other cluster containing three proxies, c, d, e. Fig. 4 shows the assignment of proxy IDs to the proxy ID array. There are a total of 12 elements in the proxy ID array since the l.c.m. of 2 and 3 is 6. For the proxy ID array, we also show the indices to the array elements. If we treat the proxy ID array as a circular array, then any window size of N in the proxy ID array will have at least one proxy from each cluster.

After the proxy ID array is constructed, we can then create the mapping of hash buckets to the in-

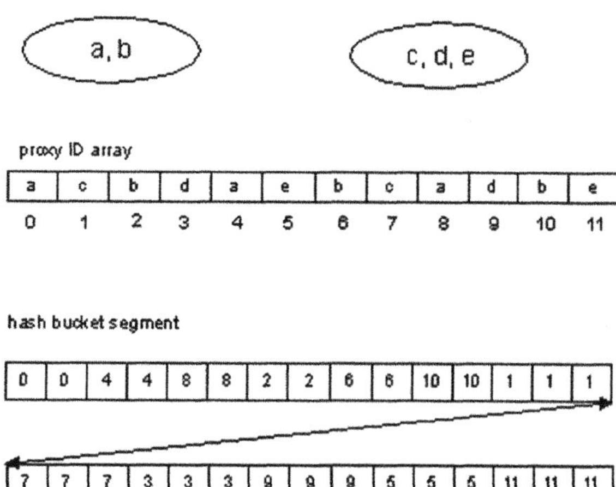

Fig. 4. An example of an indirect mapping scheme for LSH.

dices of the proxy ID array. We first construct a segment of hash buckets. Each hash bucket is assigned with an index of the proxy ID array. This segment is then repeated for a large enough number of times, say a few hundreds, to achieve good hashing results. Let us denote that the number of times a proxy ID from cluster j appears in the proxy ID array is n_j. The construction of the hash bucket segment is to create the indirect mapping such that each proxy ID is mapped to LCM_p hash buckets, where LCM_p is the l.c.m. of n_j, $j = 0, 1, \ldots, N-1$. Therefore, the total size of the hash bucket segment is $\mathrm{LCM}_p \cdot \sum C_i$.

As an example, Fig. 4 also shows the assignment of the indices of a proxy ID array to a hash bucket segment. Note that a proxy from the first cluster appears three times and a proxy from the second cluster appears two times in the proxy ID array. Each proxy ID will be assigned to six hash buckets in the segment. Therefore, the size of the hash bucket segment is $5 \times 6 = 30$. Since proxy a appears three times in the proxy ID array and the indices to them are 0, 4 and 8, we simply assign the first two hash buckets with 0, the second two hash buckets with 4 and the next two hash buckets with 8. Similarly, proxy c appears two times in the proxy ID array and the indices to these are 1 and 7. So, we assign 1 to three hash buckets and 7 to another three hash buckets.

This indirect mapping scheme can be easily generalized to the case where each cluster has proxies with unequal processing powers. Let R_i be the relative processing power of proxies in cluster i. The total size of the hash bucket segment becomes $\mathrm{LCM}_p \cdot \sum C_i R_i$. In the above example in Fig. 4, if proxies in the first cluster are twice as powerful as those in the second cluster, the size of the hash bucket segment is $6(2 \times 2 + 3) = 42$. And we will assign four hash buckets with 0, four hash buckets with 4 and another four hash buckets with 8.

Note that the example shown in Fig. 2 represents a special case of the indirect mapping. For example, the size of the proxy ID array for the case of Fig. 1 would have been $3 \times 3 = 9$. Since each proxy ID would appear in this proxy ID array only once, the size of the hash bucket segment would be $1 \times 9 = 9$. As a result, there is a one-to-one correspondence between the hash bucket segment and the proxy ID array. Therefore, we can directly map the proxy IDs to the hash buckets as indicated in Fig. 2. For the rest of this paper, we assumed that each cluster contains the same number of proxies.

Finally, besides network latency delays, load balancing is also important in the latency-sensitive hashing. If load balancing is not considered, all the requests from the proximity of a cluster might be hashed into the proxies in the same cluster. And it degenerates into the geographically clustered hashing, GCH. So, in latency-sensitive hashing, the load conditions of the proxies being examined need to be considered. If the load of a proxy is too high, then it should not be selected. Generally, it is easier for the DNS to obtain the load conditions of all the proxies. Thus, the DNS should be a better place to implement the latency-sensitive hashing, especially during the selection step.

3. Performance evaluation

We implemented a trace-driven simulator that models the three hashing schemes, GCH, GDH and LSH. There were a total of nine proxies, organized into three geographical clusters (see Fig. 1). Each cluster has three proxies. Each proxy has the same amount of computing resources.

A request originates from the proximity of one of the proxies, say proxy $p1$. Then it is hashed into one of the proxies, say $p2$, incurring a latency delay, L. If the requested object can be found locally, then the request is returned to the browser, incurring another latency delay. If not found locally, then a cache miss delay, C_{miss}, is added for the proxy to obtain the object from the content server. Both L and C_{miss} were assumed to be uniformly distributed. The mean latency delay is determined by a latency matrix that models the network latency delays among the proxies. A request from the proximity of proxy $p1$ hashed into proxy $p2$ incurs a network latency delay which is uniformly distributed with the mean specified in the matrix between $p1$ and $p2$. Note that the latency matrix can be dynamically updated by the DNS to reflect the changing network and load conditions.

For each proxy, we implemented a CPU server and a cache manager. For the cache manager, we implemented an LRU stack. For the CPU server, there is an FIFO service queue. The service time for processing an HTTP request or reply is defined as T_{http}; the service time for looking up an object from its cache or storing an object into its cache is defined as T_{cache}. As a result, the response time for a request whose object can be found locally is $(L + T_{\text{http}} + T_{\text{cache}} + T_{\text{http}} + L + Q)$. Here, Q represents the queue delay the request incurs waiting for the CPU. On the other hand, the response time is $(L+T_{\text{http}}+T_{\text{cache}}+C_{\text{miss}}+T_{\text{cache}}+T_{\text{http}}+L+Q)$, if the requested object is a cache miss. In the simulations, we assumed that T_{cache} is $\frac{1}{2} \cdot T_{\text{http}}$.

In our simulations, we conducted experiments to see the impacts of skew in request origination and hot-spot reference. For request origination skew, we assumed that the distribution of client IDs around the proximity of proxies follows a Zipf-like distribution [16,18]. Zipf(x, M) is a parametric distribution where the probability of selecting the ith item is proportional to $1/i^{(1-x)}$, where x is a parameter and i belongs to $\{1, \ldots, M\}$. Fig. 5 shows three distributions of clients around the proximity of the nine proxies, including Zipf(1.0, 9), Zipf(0.5, 9) and Zipf(0.25, 9). Zipf(1.0, 9) represents no skew and corresponds to a uniform distribution. Namely, client IDs are uniformly distributed around all proxies. Zipf(0.25, 9) represents the high skew case. In other words, a great majority of clients are in the proximity of proxies a, b and c.

To model references to a hot spot, we injected additional requests to a specific page from different

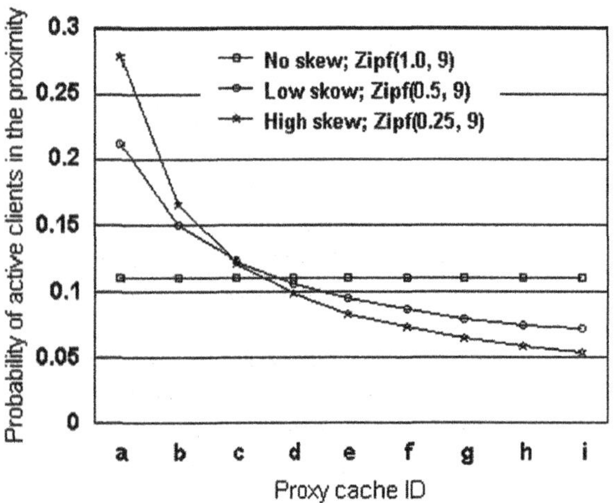

Fig. 5. Distributions of clients around the proximity of each proxy cache.

clients during the simulations. Each client is equally likely to generate such requests to the hot-spot object. We varied the percentage of total references to this hot page in the simulations. For example, a 5% hot-spot reference means that for each request from the trace, there is 95% chance that the next request for the simulation will be also from the trace, while a 5% chance it will be a request for the hot spot. The arrival time of a hot-spot reference was determined as follows. For each trace entry, a probability function was used to determine if a hot-spot reference should be issued at the moment. The client ID for such a hot-spot reference was chosen randomly from all clients, indicating that every client is equally likely to issue requests for the hot spot.

The proxy traces collected between 08/29/1996 and 09/09/1996 from Digital [7] were used to drive our simulations. The sizes of these 12 days' traces vary from about 300 K to over 1.3 M entries per day. The results are similar for each trace. For this paper, we concentrated our reports on two of the largest traces with over 1.3 M entries, 09-04 and 09-06 traces. These traces were used to represent requests made to the nine proxies traces.

To determine the proper cache sizes for our simulations, we computed through simulation the maximal buffer size needed for each proxy cache if no replacement were to be required. For large traces, the size is about 620 M bytes per cache. As a result, we used 310 M bytes as the default cache size for most of our simulations.

The mean latency delays between any pair of proxies were defined in a latency matrix. The matrix element (a, a) represents the mean latency delay for a request originated in the proximity of proxy a and hashed also into proxy a. In the simulations, we assumed that mean intra-cluster latencies are all the same. Namely, any request originated in the proximity of a cluster will have the same mean latency delay to all the proxies in the same geographical cluster. Moreover, the mean inter-cluster latency is 1.0 s, compared with the mean intra-cluster latency of 0.2 s. In order to illustrate the issue of latency, we also assumed that the mean cache miss delay is 1.0 s, same as the mean inter-cluster latency delay.

In the simulations, we first assigned each client to the proximity of a proxy so that we can compute the latency delay from the latency matrix. The default

CPU service time for processing an HTTP request, T_{http}, was set to be 0.045 s. This was chosen so that the average CPU utilization during the peak hours (between 5:00 am and 12:00 noon PDT) is around 65–70%, representing a moderately loaded system. But, we also used 0.030 s to examine the performance of a more lightly loaded system.

For the latency-sensitive hashing, the default selection window size was 3. The selection algorithm was very simple. If a proxy within the selection window improves latency and it is not currently overloaded, then it is chosen. Note that the mean intra-cluster latency delay of 0.2 s is much smaller than the mean inter-cluster latency delay of 1.0 s. Thus, so long as a proxy within the selection window is not overloaded and is in the same cluster as the browser originating the request, it will be chosen. In our simulations, the DNS collects the CPU load conditions of all proxies every 5 s.

We considered a proxy as being overloaded if (1) the maximum utilization of all proxies, i.e., the utilization of the most heavily utilized proxy at the moment, exceeds 80% and the utilization of the proxy exceeds the mean utilization of all proxies, or (2) the maximum utilization of all proxies is smaller than 80% and the utilization of the proxy is 20% greater than the mean utilization of all proxies. Note that the utilization of the most heavily utilized proxy indicates the level of load imbalance over the system. The idea was to be more conservative in selecting a geographically closer proxy if the overall system is highly skewed. On the other hand, if the overall system is less skewed, then we want to be more aggressive in hashing requests into geographically closer proxies. We did vary the parameters for the overload conditions and found that the results were not very sensitive to them. However, the performance of the latency-sensitive hashing is sensitive to the time interval between collecting the CPU load conditions.

4. Simulation results

4.1. Impact of request origination skew

Fig. 6 shows the average response times of the three hashing schemes under different degrees of skew using the 09-04 trace. The skew was generated following the Zipf-like distributions described in Fig. 5. As the degree of skew in request origination increases, the average response time of the geographically clustered hashing increases significantly. In GCH, requests originated in one cluster are serviced only by the proxies in the same cluster. As a result, the proxies in cluster 1 become overloaded while those in cluster 3 are under-loaded. Therefore the average response time over all requests for the GCH scheme is much worse than the other two schemes under high skew condition. This problem can also be seen in Fig. 7 in the coefficient of variation of response time. The coefficient of variation is defined as the ratio of the standard deviation of the

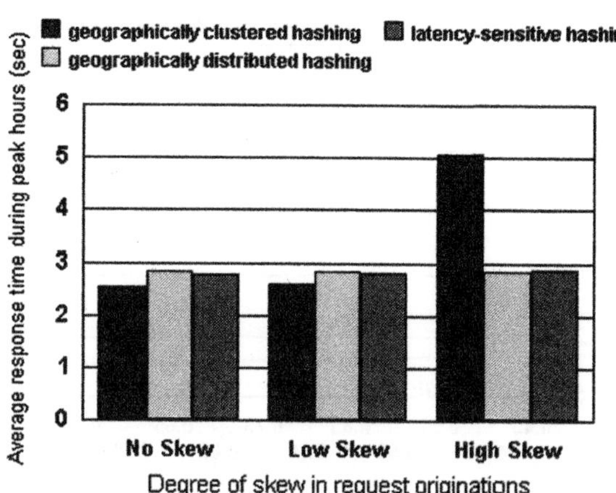

Fig. 6. The impact of request origination skew on average response time.

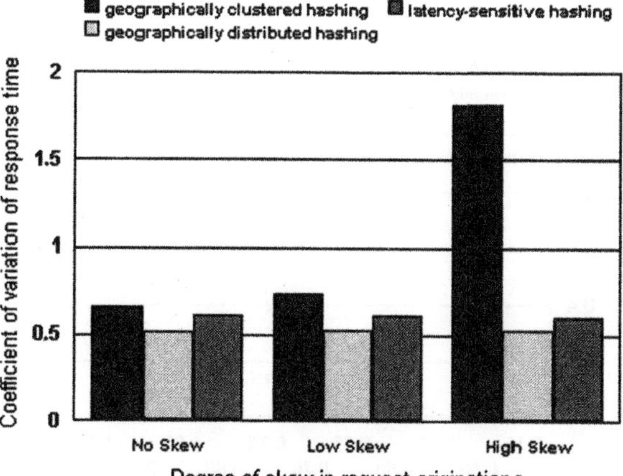

Fig. 7. The impact of request origination skew on coefficient of variation.

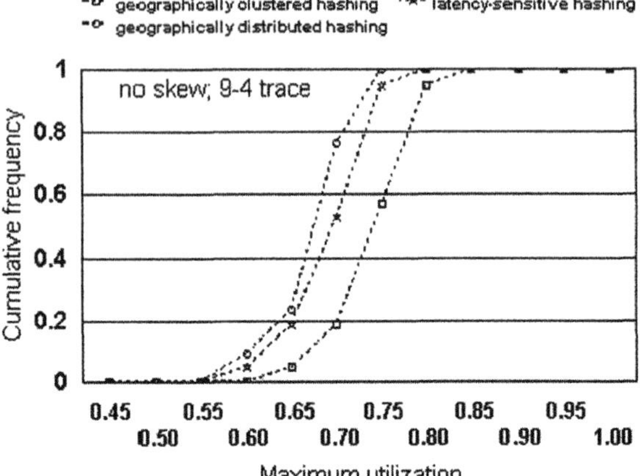

Fig. 8. The level of load imbalance with no skew.

response time over the mean response time. It measures the variation of a response time about the mean response time. In the case of GCH under the high skew condition, the coefficient of variation is substantially larger than those of the other two schemes. Even in the case of no skew in request origination, the coefficient of variation of response time is still higher for GCH. This suggests that load tends to be more unbalanced for GCH, even in the case of no skew in request origination.

Figs. 8 and 9 show the level of load imbalances of the three hashing schemes under no skew in request origination and high skew in request origination, respectively. In these two figures, we show the cumulative frequency of the maximal utilization among the proxies during the peak hours. The idea is that, by looking at the most utilized proxy, one can deduce if the load level of a collection of proxies is balanced or not [4]. The server with the maximum utilization changes over time. However, if the maximum utilization is low, it means that no proxy is overloaded during that time period. In general, the load level of the system is more balanced if the cumulative frequency chart moves towards the upper-left corner and less balanced if it moves towards the lower-right corner. For example, in Fig. 8, the probability of the maximum utilization being less than or equal to 70% is only 0.2 for GCH. This indicates that there is an 80% chance that the maximum utilization is greater than 70% for GCH. In contrast, there is only about 22% chance that the maximum utilization exceeds 70% during the observation period for GDH. Thus, the geographically clustered hashing GCH is less balanced while the geographically distributed hashing GDH is more balanced. The dramatic degradation of GCH in the average response time and the coefficient of variation due to request origination skew can be clearly explained by the dramatic level of load imbalance shown in Fig. 9.

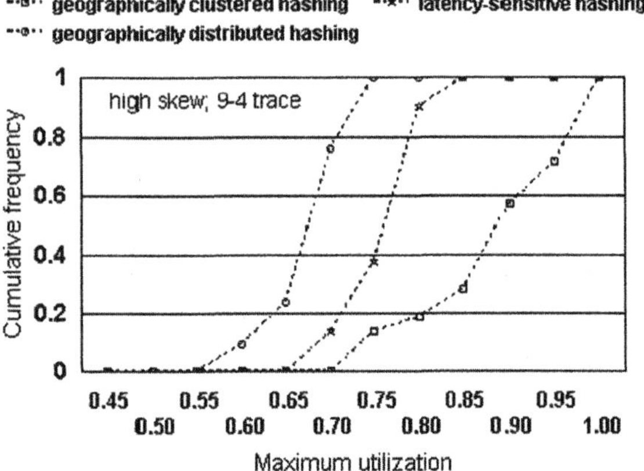

Fig. 9. The level of load imbalance with high skew.

From Figs. 6–9, it clearly shows that GCH is very sensitive to skew in request origination. Because requests originating from one cluster are only serviced by the proxies within the same geographical cluster, GCH cannot effectively utilize proxies in other clusters to help balance the load. One the other hand, GDH is immune to the skew in request origination. This is because hashing is based on URL and thus the load distribution among the proxies remains the same regardless of skew in request origination.

Similar to GDH, the latency-sensitive hashing LSH can distribute requests among all the proxies. As a result, LSH handles skew in request origination much better than GCH. However, compared with GDH, LSH is slightly less balanced (see Figs. 6–9). This is because, in order to lower latency delays, LSH tends to choose a proxy within the same cluster as the browser originating the request. Nevertheless, LSH performs almost as good as GDH even in the presence of high skew in request origination.

4.2. *Impact of hot-spot references*

Even though GDH is not susceptible to skew in request origination, it can be very sensitive to refer-

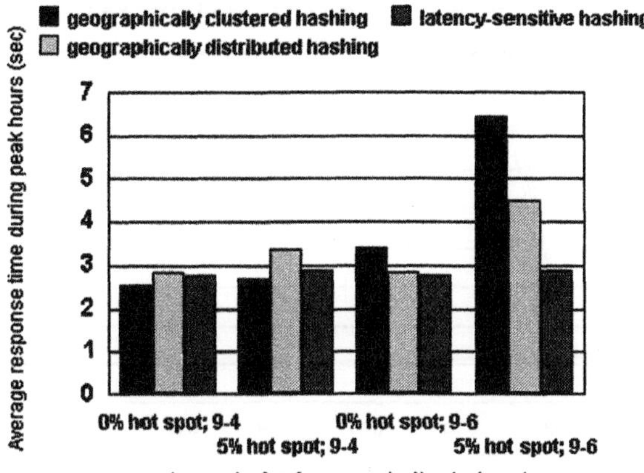

Fig. 10. The impact of hot-spot references on average response time.

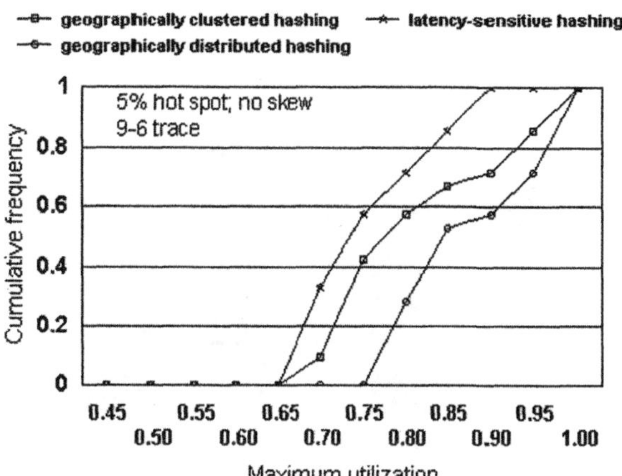

Fig. 11. The level of load imbalance with hot-spot references.

ences to hot spots. Because each URL is hashed into the same proxy cache no matter which browser issues the request, GDH can become quite unbalanced in the presence of hot-spot references.

Fig. 10 shows the average response times of the three hashing schemes in the presence of hot-spot references for both the 9-4 and 9-6 traces. For these experiments, there was no skew in request origination. For both traces, with 5% hot-spot references, the performance of GDH degrades significantly. On the other hand, GCH is less susceptible to hot-spot references for the 9-4 trace while highly sensitive for the 9-6 trace. For both traces, the latency-sensitive hashing handles hot-spot references rather effectively and is almost insensitive to them. This is due to the fact that LSH can select different proxies to offload the hot-spot references originating from different browsers.

Fig. 11 shows the impact of hot-spot references on the level of load imbalance for the 9-6 trace. For these experiments, 5% references to the hot-spot were introduced. But, there was no skew in request origination. As indicated in Fig. 11, GDH becomes extremely unbalanced in the presence of 5% hot-spot references. In contrast, the latency-sensitive hashing is the most balanced among the three.

4.3. *Impact of selection window size*

Now that we have demonstrated that the latency-sensitive hashing effectively handles skew in request origination as well as hot-spot references, we want to show the impact of some system design parameters specific to LSH. Here, we examined the selection window size, w. We define w to be the number of hash buckets that LSH examines, including the anchor bucket. Thus, LSH with $w = 1$ is equivalent to geographically distributed hashing, GDH. Namely, requests are hashed into the proxies mapped to the anchor hash buckets. In his section, we examined cases of $w = 1$, $w = 2$, $w = 3$ and $w = 4$.

Fig. 12 shows the average response times for both the 9-4 and 9-6 traces under different values of w. For these experiments, there was no skew in request origination and no hot-spot references. Furthermore,

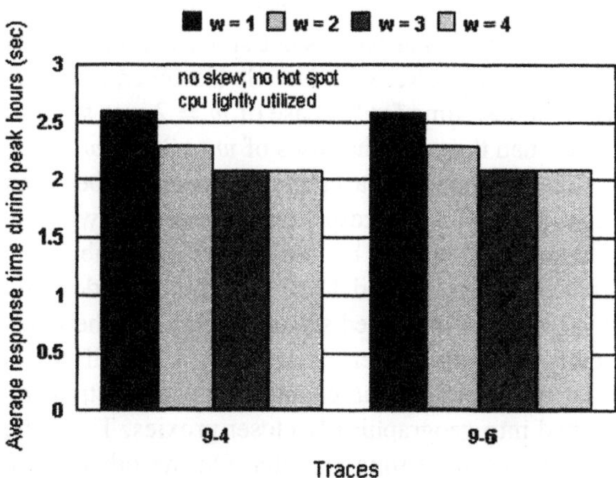

Fig. 12. The impact of selection window size when the system is lightly loaded and balanced.

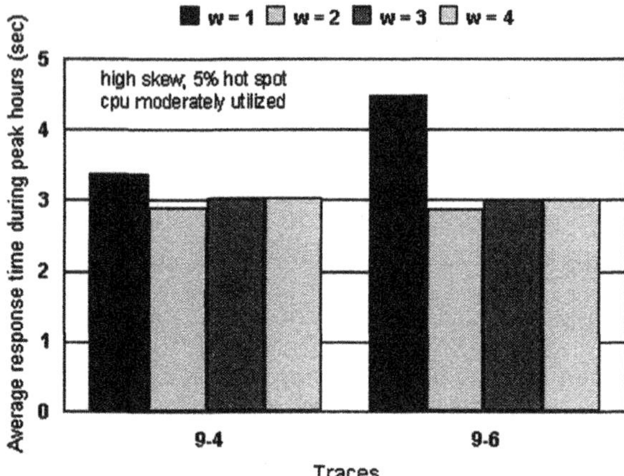

Fig. 13. The impact of selection window size when the system is moderately loaded and unbalanced.

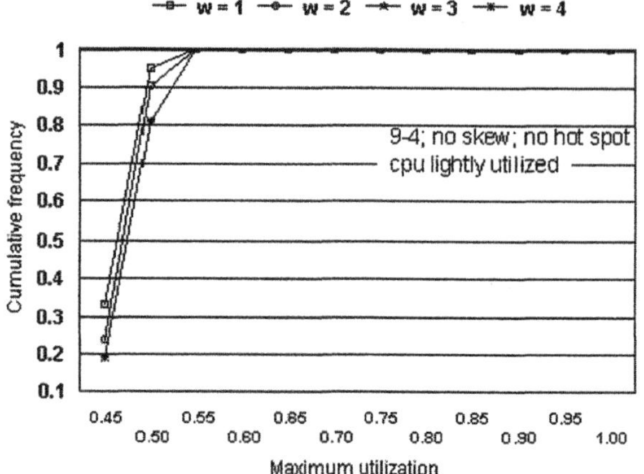

Fig. 14. The level of load imbalance when the system is lightly loaded and well balanced.

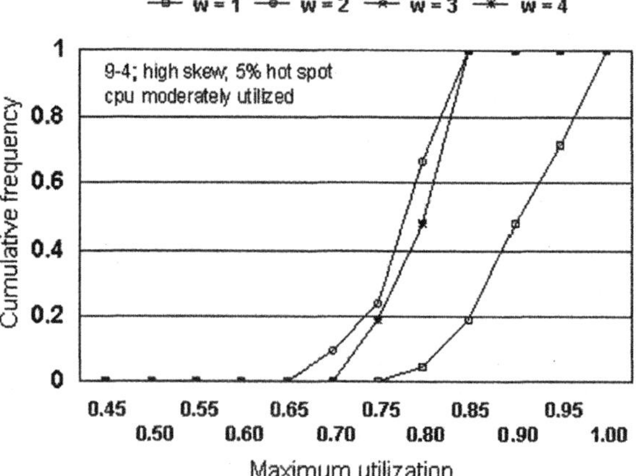

Fig. 15. The level of load imbalance when the system is moderately loaded and unbalanced.

T_{http} was set to be 0.03 s so that the overall system is lightly loaded. The overall CPU utilization during the peak hours was about 45%. Under such lightly loaded and well-balanced conditions, LSH performs better when the selection window size increases from 1 to 3. Since we only use three clusters in our experiments, LSH performs the same for $w = 3$ and $w = 4$.

Fig. 13 also shows the average response times of latency-sensitive hashing with various values of w, but when the overall system is relatively unbalanced. In contrast to Fig. 12, for the experiments in Fig. 13, there were 5% hot-spot references and high skew in request origination. Moreover, the system was moderately loaded with T_{http} set to be 0.045 s. The average CPU utilization among the proxies were about 65–70%. In the presence of high skew in request origination as well as hot-spot references, LSH also performs better with $w = 1$. However, the average response time for the case of $w = 2$ was slightly better than those for the cases of $w = 3$ and $w = 4$.

The differences in average response time between Figs. 12 and 13 with respect to the selection window size can be explained by the level of load imbalance shown in Figs. 14 and 15. For a lightly loaded and relatively well balanced system in Fig. 14, the maximum utilization never exceeded 55% for all cases. As a result, a larger w enables more requests to be hashed into geographically closer proxies. Thus, the average response time is better. On the other hand, for a moderately loaded and unbalanced system in Fig. 15, the chance that the maximum utilization exceeds 80% is very high for all cases. Therefore, compared with $w = 2$, the selection window size of 3 may cause too many requests to be hashed into geographically closer proxies, resulting in slightly less balanced system. However, it is still beneficial to have the selection choice with $w = 1$, because the system is highly unbalanced without choice for the case of $w = 1$.

5. Summary

In this paper, we have presented a new latency-sensitive hashing scheme for collaborative Web caching. Latency-sensitive hashing is very important as more and more geographically distributed proxy caches are being used for collaborative Web caching. It takes into account latency delays due to network distances as well as skew in workload. It first hashes a request into an anchor hash bucket. Then, it selects a proxy from a small number of hash buckets with the goal to reduce the latency delay and improve load balance.

Trace-driven simulations were used to evaluate latency-sensitive hashing (LSH). We compared latency-sensitive hashing with geographically clustered hashing (GCH) and geographically distributed hashing (GDH). GCH hashes requests originated from one region into proxies within the same region. GDH hashes requests to all proxies regardless of geographical locations. The results show that (1) in the presence of skew in request origination among geographical regions, GCH performs poorly because collaboration is limited within the same region, (2) in the presence of hot-spot references, GDH fails because hot-spots are hashed into the same proxies, (3) LSH effectively handles both skew in request origination and hot-spot references by hashing requests among geographically distributed proxies, and (4) when the overall system is lightly loaded, LSH effectively reduces latency delays by hashing requests into geographically closer proxies.

References

[1] C.M. Bowman et al., The Harvest information discovery and access system, in: Proc. of 2nd Int. World Wide Web Conference, 1994, pp. 763–771.

[2] P. Cao and S. Irani, Cost-aware WWW proxy caching algorithm, in: Proc. of USENIX Symp. on Internet Technologies and Systems, 1997, pp. 193–206.

[3] Cisco Systems, Scaling the Internet Web servers, Nov. 1997, white paper, http://www.cisco.com/.

[4] M. Colajanni, P.S. Yu and D. Dias, Analysis of task assignment policies in scalable distributed Web-server system, IEEE Trans. Parallel Distrib. Syst. 9 (6) (1998) 585–600.

[5] P. Danzig, NetCache architecture and deployment, http://www.netapp.com/technology/level3/3029.html.

[6] D.M. Dias et al., A scalable and highly available Web server, in: Proc. of IEEE COMPCON Conf. on Technologies for the Information Superhighway, 1996, pp. 85–92.

[7] Digital Equipment Corporation, Digital's Web proxy traces, 1996, http://ftp.digital.com/pub/DEC/traces/proxy/webtrace s.html.

[8] L. Fan et al., Summary cache: a scalable wide-area Web cache sharing protocol, in: Proc. of ACM SIGCOMM 98, 1998, pp. 254–165.

[9] G. Goldszmidt and G. Hunt, NetDispatcher: A TCP Connection Router, Technical Report, RC 20853, IBM T.J. Watson Research Center, May 1997.

[10] D. Karger et al., Web caching with consistent hashing, in: Proc. of 8th Int. World Wide Web Conference, 1999, pp. 125–135.

[11] R. Malpani, J. Lorch and D. Berger, Making World Wide Web caching servers cooperate, in: Proc. of 4th World Wide Web Conference, 1995.

[12] K.W. Ross, Hash-routing for collections of shared Web caches, IEEE Network Mag (Nov.–Dec. 1997) 37–44.

[13] V. Valloppillil and K.W. Ross, Cache array routing protocol v1.0, Internet draft, Feb. 1998, http://ircache.nlanr.net/Cac he/ICP/draft-vinod-carp-v1-03.txt.

[14] D. Wessels, Squid Internet object cache, 1998, http://squid.nlanr.net/Squid/.

[15] K.-L. Wu and P.S. Yu, Load balancing and hot spot relief for hash routing among a collection of proxy caches, in: Proc. of IEEE Int. Conf. on Distributed Computing Systems, 1999, pp. 536–543.

[16] K.-L. Wu and P.S. Yu, Local replication for proxy Web caches with hash routing, in: Proc. of ACM Int. Conf. on Information and Knowledge Management, 1999, pp. 69–76.

[17] P.S. Yu and E.A. MacNair, Performance study of a collaborative method for hierarchical caching in proxy servers, Comp. Networks ISDN Syst. 30 (1998) 215–224.

[18] G.K. Zipf, Human Behaviour and the Principles of Least Effort, Addison-Wesley, Cambridge, MA, 1949.

Kun-Lung Wu received his B.S. degree in Electrical Engineering from the National Taiwan University, Taipei, Taiwan, in 1982, and his M.S. and Ph.D. degrees in Computer Science from the University of Illinois at Urbana-Champaign, in 1986 and 1990, respectively. Since 1990, he has been with the IBM Thomas J. Watson Research Center, Yorktown Heights, NY, where he is a member of the Software Tools and Techniques Group. His current research interests include infrastructure design issues of the World Wide Web, personalization and data mining tools for the World Wide Web, Internet applications and pervasive computing. He has published extensively in the areas of Web caching, database performance, disk subsystems, transaction and query processing, multimedia systems, mobile computing and reliable computing. Dr. Wu has published more than 50 papers in refereed journals and conferences and over 30 research reports. He holds or has applied for 15 US patents. Dr. Wu is a member of the ACM and the IEEE Computer Society. He has served as an organizing and program committee member on various conferences. He has received various IBM awards, including Research Division Award and Invention Achievement Awards.

Philip S. Yu received his B.S. Degree in E.E. from the National Taiwan University, Taipei, Taiwan, his M.S. and Ph.D. degrees in E.E. from Stanford University, and his M.B.A. degree from

New York University. He is with the IBM Thomas J. Watson Research Center and currently manager of the Software Tools and Techniques group. His current research interests include data mining, Internet applications and technologies, database systems, multimedia systems, parallel and distributed processing, disk arrays, computer architecture, performance modeling and workload analysis. Dr. Yu has published more than 270 papers in refereed journals and conferences. He holds or has applied for 92 US patents. Dr. Yu is a Fellow of the ACM and a Fellow of the IEEE. He is a member of the IEEE Data Engineering steering committee. He is on the advisory board of IEEE Transactions on Knowledge and Data Engineering. He was an editor of IEEE Transactions on Knowledge and Data Engineering and also a guest co-editor of the special issue on mining of databases. In addition to serving as program committee member on various conferences, he was the program co-chair of the 11th Int. Conference on Data Engineering and the program chair of the 2nd Int. Workshop on Research Issues on Data Engineering: Transaction and Query Processing. He served as the general chair of the 14th Int. Conference on Data Engineering. He has received several IBM and external honors including Best Paper Award, two IBM Outstanding Innovation Awards, an Outstanding Technical Achievement Award, two Research Division Awards and 30th plateau of Invention Achievement Awards. He also received an IEEE Region 1 Award for contributions of 'New Concepts in Electrical Engineering'. Dr. Yu is an IBM Master Inventor and was recognized as one of the IBM's ten top leading inventors in 1999.

Proactive Web caching with cumulative prefetching for large multimedia data

Jaeyeon Jung [a,*,1], Dongman Lee [b,2], Kilnam Chon [a,1]

[a] Korea Advanced Institute of Science and Technology, Department of Computer Science, Taejon 305-701, South Korea
[b] Information and Communication University, Computer and Information Systems Group, Taejon, South Korea

Abstract

Web proxy caching provides an effective way to reduce access latency and bandwidth consumption, and thus improve performance of the World Wide Web. Due to the simplicity of incorporating various types of data into the Web, non-negligible access for large multimedia data is observed. Large multimedia data transfer, requiring a long-lived connection with consecutive data transmissions, often fails over wide area networks. Repetitive attempts to fetch large objects through proxy caches would waste network resources with no success guaranteed. In this paper, we propose on-demand cumulative prefetching to enhance proxy caches for better data availability of large multimedia files. Our analysis shows that on-demand cumulative prefetching can be performed within a few trials with minimal additional bandwidth requirement. The experimental results demonstrate that the proposed scheme substantially reduces error rate and increases byte hit rate for large multimedia data.

Keywords: Web proxy caching; Prefetching; Data availability; Cumulative

1. Introduction

As incorporation of multimedia data prevalent, the Web exhibits variability in workload characteristics [1,2,13]. In particular, the Web object sizes extremely vary in the range of 10^2 to 10^8 bytes according to media types. HTML documents and embedded images are in the range of 1 Kbyte to 10 Kbyte but executable binary and multimedia data such as mp3 audio and mpeg video files easily exceed 1 Mbyte [9]. Analyses done previously [1,2,11,13] show that non-negligible access is made for large multimedia data though the majority of Web data access is for small text and image data objects.

Often fails large multimedia data transfer via a wide area network like the Internet where it is hard to support a long-lived connection with consecutive data transmissions. As shown in Fig. 1, transfer error rate increases exponentially as the object size becomes larger than 100 Kbyte and the error rate of objects larger than 10 Mbyte is over 80%.

Proxy caching provides an effective way to reduce access latency and bandwidth requirements for Web content transfer. It copies the recently accessed data to a location closer to clients and improves data availability. However, conventional proxy caches stop fetching and send an error message to a client immediately when an error occurs. The partially fetched objects up to that point are discarded from the cache. We analyzed traces taken from real world proxies and observed that independent of object sizes, users are highly likely to access again the data

* Corresponding author
[1] {jyjung,chon}@cosmos.kaist.ac.kr
[2] dlee@icu.ac.kr

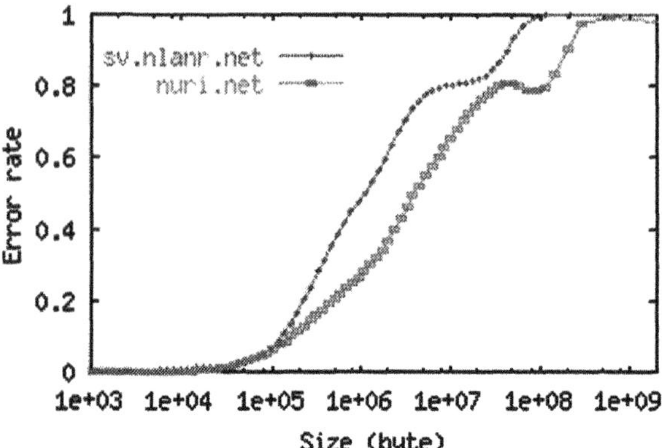

Fig. 1. Error rate by object size, both for sv.nlanr.net and nuri.net traces. The plots are smoothed to eliminate small spikes. Size is shown on a log scale.

that they have accessed more than once (see more detail, in Section 3). Subsequent requests for the same objects would follow the same fate unless the network condition gets improved much since then. Consequently, repetitive attempts to fetch these large objects through proxy caches would waste network resources with no success guaranteed.

In this paper, we propose an enhanced proxy cache that improves data availability of large multimedia, leveraging the observed user access pattern — as soon as a request fails twice, the proposed scheme starts prefetching the failed data and makes the subsequent requests successful data. In addition, to reduce abusive use of network bandwidth due to high transfer failure rate when transferring large data, we take advantage of cumulative fetching which augments data in successive retrievals. Since a proxy cache is located at an aggregate point of the Web traffic from a large network user community, the cache that employs some mechanism to prefetch data is naturally able to adapt user access patterns. While we consider conventional caching passive, we consider the proposed scheme proactive. The proactive caching with on-demand prefetching can improve the performance of a proxy cache as well as the data readiness of large multimedia data.

We have developed an on-demand cumulative prefetching mechanism within a popular proxy cache, Squid [15], and evaluated its performance using various methods. The analysis shows that the proposed scheme makes the requested data available within a few trials and requires much less additional bandwidth than the conventional scheme. The experimental results exhibit that the proposed scheme substantially reduces error rates by 40%, saves network bandwidth by 13.18% and enhances byte hit rates by 8.1% for large multimedia data.

The rest of this paper is organized as follows. Section 2 discusses related work. Section 3 describes workload characteristics to motivate the use of on-demand prefetching and cumulative fetching within a proxy cache. Section 4 presents the numerical analysis over the static network, where the probability of an error in a unit-transmission does not change over time. The model is applied for estimating bandwidth cost and any improvements in byte hit rate of the proposed scheme. Then, we outline the design and implementation of the on-demand prefetching mechanism and demonstrate its performance benefits using both experiments and trace-driven simulations in Section 5. Conclusion and future directions follow in Section 6.

2. Related work

There have been many proposals on using prefetching and caching for latency reduction [8,10,17]. By prefetching objects into proxy caches, the references to the prefetched objects can be satisfied without further communication to the server, thus reducing network latency. Kroeger et al. analyzed the efficiency of an approach combining caching and prefetching based on proxy logs [10]. They found that the combined approach reduces latency by up to 60% when the entire reference is known at the beginning. In fact, prediction does not encompass all of future reference and there is a finite chance of false prediction. Wang and Crowcroft examined that relationship between bandwidth consumption and the probability of correct prediction [17]. Using a queuing model, their analysis shows that bandwidth utilization rapidly increases for ensuring network latency reduction.

Mirroring is a common way to avoid abusive bandwidth consumption due to repetitive failures in caching large multimedia data. It predicts error-prone data and copies them before an actual request is made. Mirroring operations are usually scheduled when large bandwidth is available (e.g. in the middle of the night), so users can get fast responses from the mirrored copies during daytime. We call it *off-line* prefetching. Mirrored copies would avoid most failures caused by network congestion as mirror servers are located before bottleneck points. However, the effectiveness of the mirroring is limited on the accuracy in predictability because of the dynamics and high rate of change in traffic patterns of the World Wide Web [5]. Responding to changing traffic patterns is extremely costly, if not impossible [3].

Feldmann et al. analyzed the amount of wasted bandwidth by aborted connection using simulations [6]. They focused on bandwidth saving rather than improving data availability by a proxy cache. We present further analysis on the effects of resuming broken download in accordance with user access characteristics in the following sections.

3. On-demand prefetching

In this section, we present the analysis results of real-world proxy behavior and explore these results for the on-demand prefetching mechanism. We obtained log files from 18 nuri.net caches, a set of caches on one of the major backbone networks in Korea, and sv.nlanr.net cache [12], a root cache at vBNS [16]. Fig. 2 shows the cumulative distribution of the number of accesses and the amount of traffic volume by object size. The traffic volume of the objects larger than 1 Mbyte represents more than 40% of the total traffic, which is a significant amount considering less than 1% access counts. Combining this with Fig. 1, we can expect that large amounts of traffic would be wasted due to errors. Table 1 lists a summary of analysis results.

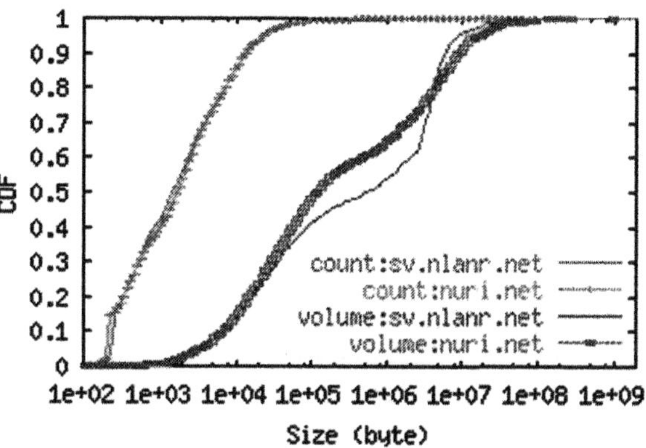

Fig. 2. Number of accesses vs. amount of traffic volume.

First, about 50% of the failed data objects are re-accessed within a day. Table 1 shows the percentage of re-access for each data set. Highly repeated attempts make the on-demand prefetching comparable to the off-line one. In other words, we do not have to delay prefetching until nighttime to determine prefetchable objects from the analysis of log files. Instead, the on-demand mechanism initiates prefetching at any time, thus improving the performance by prompt reaction to user demands. Second, most failures are temporal. In the analysis, we classify failures either as a connection error or as a transmission error based on the length of a fetched object. Objects with a zero length count up the number of connection errors. Table 1 indicates that only less than 4% are caused by connection errors. Connection errors include server failures and network partitioning, which involves special efforts. On the other hand, transmission errors are mainly caused by network congestion, which is automatically resolved by TCP mechanisms. Thus, we define

Table 1
Summary of analysis results (percentages in parentheses are relative to the category above it)

Total statistics	Value	Value
Data set	nuri.net	sv.nlanr.net
Date	1999/5/20	1999/9/30–1999/10/6
Objects fetched	4,022,575 (100%)	4,010,773 (100%)
Objects fetched with errors	49,445 (1.22%)	35,334 (0.88%)
Objects fetched with zero object length	466 (0.94%)	1,162 (3.28%)
Bytes fetched (Kbyte)	61,836,404 (100%)	66,903,016 (100%)
Bytes fetched with errors (Kbyte)	8,652,600 (13%)	14,654,932 (21%)
Percentage of objects re-accessed	49%	44%

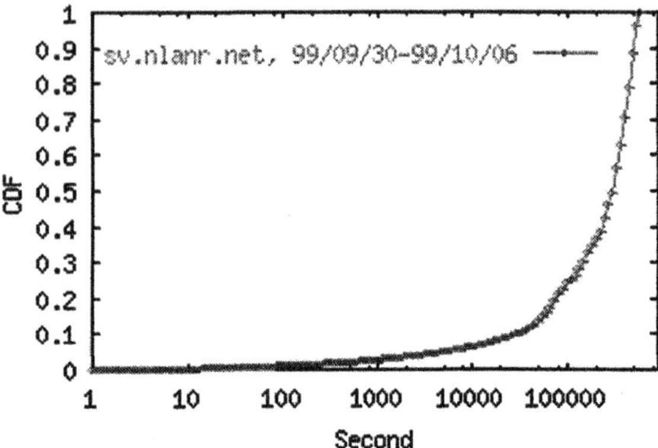

Fig. 3. Cumulative distribution of inter-access time.

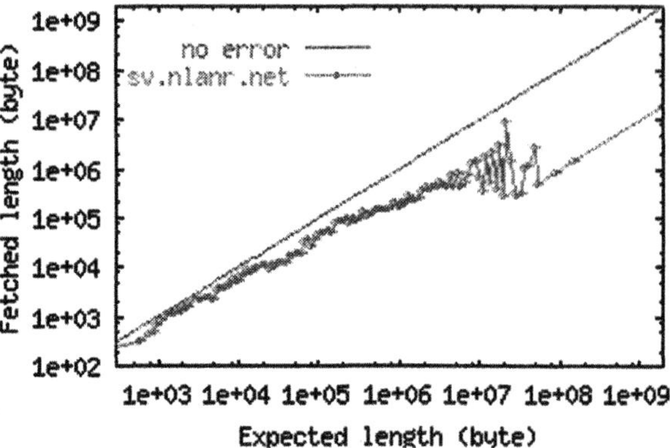

Fig. 4. Fetched length vs. expected length.

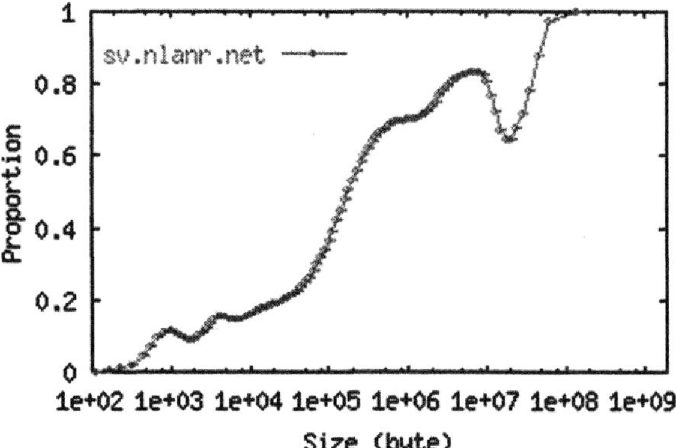

Fig. 5. The average proportion of data requests having errors more than twice.

prefetchable objects as failed objects with a non-zero length.

The performance of the proposed method depends on how fast it can accomplish prefetching, while the performance of off-line prefetching depends on the prediction accuracy. Fig. 3 shows the distribution of inter-access time for the broken data objects. If prefetching is done in 1000 s after the first error occurs, we can ensure 97% of following requests against subsequent errors. Unlike off-line prefetching, where prefetching is usually done when relatively large bandwidth is available, on-demand prefetching competes for bandwidth against user transactions. It is important to minimize network resource consumption.

For a cost-effective and higher performance prefetching a cumulative fetching strategy is introduced. When an error occurs, existing techniques stop transmitting and send an error message to a client. A portion of files fetched up to that point is discarded from a cache. Instead, cumulative fetching invokes the *range request* specified in HTTP/1.1 [7] to fetch the rest of the data and make them up into a complete one.

We expect two significant benefits from the cumulative fetching. First, it is possible to reduce bandwidth demands because of retrieving only necessary data with an offset from the beginning of the data. Fig. 4 shows the average amount of data fetched before errors over data size spectrum. The straight line represents the expected length referred from the *content-length* field in an HTTP reply header. On average, 38% of the fetched data fails after more than 50% of the expected amount is retrieved. This implies that a considerable amount of data is trashed which otherwise would be saved if cumulative fetching was used.

Second, a smaller number of trials are required for prefetching entire data. Since the error rate increases in proportion to the object size at the given network conditions, repeated attempts are also more likely to fail. Fig. 5 shows the average proportion of data requests which failed more than twice. It clearly illustrates that chances for the same requests to fail increase as data objects get bigger. On the other hand, cumulative fetching reduces failures since the amount to fetch gets smaller in the subsequent fetches. Thus data can be retrieved with fewer trials and bandwidth consumption can be minimized. The following section describes numerical analysis of data fetching over error-resilience network links and compares cumulative fetching with the conventional approach to bandwidth consumption and number of trials.

4. Analysis of bandwidth requirement and byte hit rate of on-demand prefetching

4.1. Model

To understand the correlation between an error rate and an object size, we develop a numerical model for the bandwidth requirement and the number of trials required to fetch data completely. We assume that data are composed of n units and that each unit has the same failure probability during transmission. To simplify the model, we consider a static network, i.e. the network condition does not change over time. Transmission of the entire data is considered successful if all of consecutive n transmissions are performed without errors. Let p be an error probability of each unit and P_n an error probability of data with n units, then:

$$P_n = \sum_{i=1}^{n} p(1-p)^{i-1} = \sum_{i=1}^{n} P_i^e,$$

$$P_n = 1-(1-p)^n, \quad 0 < p < 1.$$

Therefore, the average number of units that are successfully delivered during the transmission is:

$$N_n = N_{n|\text{error}} P_n + N_{n|\text{success}}(1-P_n),$$

$$N_{n|\text{error}} = \sum_{i=1}^{n} (i-1)\frac{P_i^e}{P_n} = \frac{p}{1-(1-p)^n} \sum_{i-1}^{n} (i-1)(1-p)^{i-1},$$

$$N_{n|\text{error}} = \frac{(1-p)-[1-p+(n-1)p](1-p)^{n-1}}{p[1-(1-p)^n]}, \quad 0 < p < 1,$$

$$N_{n|\text{success}} = n.$$

Fig. 6 compares P_n from the error model with real data. In this figure, we assumed that n linearly increases with the object size. Although the error rate increases more sharply with object size, the numerical model well explains the correlation between error rate and object size.

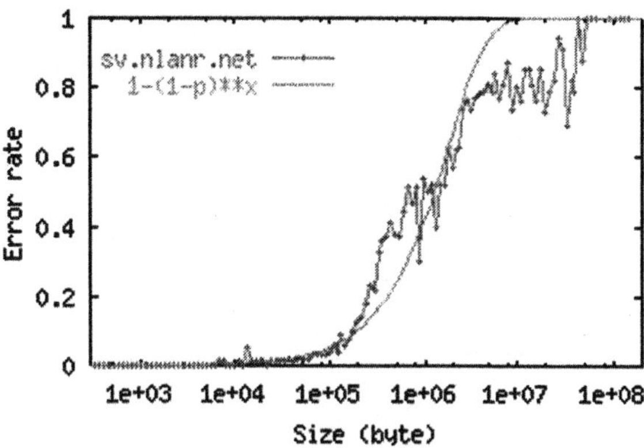

Fig. 6. Error rate vs. object size. The solid line represents the error rate calculated.

4.2. Cumulative fetching vs. repetitive fetching

In order to compare the bandwidth consumption of different strategies, we define bandwidth cost for a given value of P_n. Bandwidth cost is considered the number of units that are being transmitted on links. We assume that transmission is repeated until the entire data set is fetched. Then, the total bandwidth cost of the repetitive fetching is the sum of bandwidth costs of all trials. That is:

$$E_n^{(\text{RF})} = \sum_{i=1}^{\infty} [N_{n|\text{error}}(i-1) + N_{n|\text{success}}] P_n^{i-1}(1-P_n)$$

where $N_{n|\text{error}}(i-1) + N_{n|\text{success}}$ is the average bandwidth cost when the fetching is accomplished in the ith trial with a probability $P_n^{i-1}(1-P_n)$.

Similarly, the average number of trials is given by:

$$T_n^{(\text{RF})} = \sum_{i=1}^{\infty} i P_n^{i-1}(1-P_n).$$

As the cumulative fetching resumes data fetching at a point where an error occurs, the total bandwidth cost is simply n:

$$E_n^{(\text{CF})} = n$$

and the average number of trials can be described as:

$$T_n^{(\text{CF})} = \sum_{i=1}^{\infty} i\left(1 - P_{n-\sum_{i=1}^{j-1} F_i}\right) \prod_{j=1}^{i-1} P_{n-\sum_{i=1}^{j-1} F_i},$$

$$F_j = \left\lfloor N_{(n-\sum_{i=1}^{j-1} F_i)|\text{error}} \right\rfloor \quad (j = 1, 2, \ldots), \quad F_0 = 0$$

where F_j represents the number of units fetched at the jth trial when the transmission ends up with an error. In this case, the number of units to be transmitted at the ith trial is decreased by the amount

$$n - \sum_{j=1}^{i-1} F_j$$

so the probability that transmission is successful in ith trial becomes:

$$\left(1 - P_{n-\sum_{i=1}^{j-1} F_i}\right) \prod_{j=1}^{i-1} P_{n-\sum_{i=1}^{j-1} F_i}.$$

Figs. 7 and 8 depict bandwidth consumption and the number of trials in each strategy. The results show that repetitive fetching of error-prone data significantly consumes bandwidth and the number of trials increases as the error rate goes higher. The cumulative fetching requires constant bandwidth cost

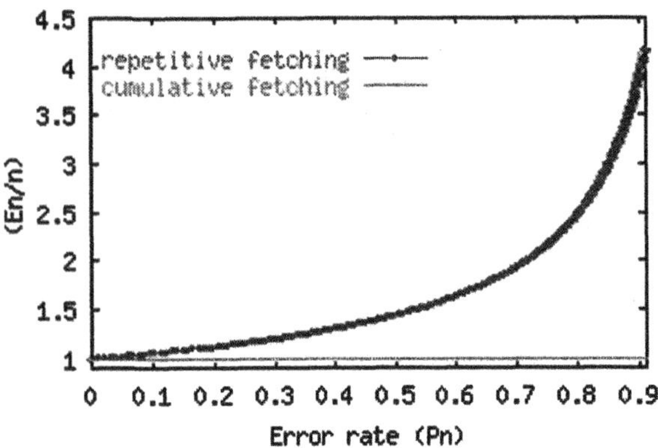

Fig. 7. Bandwidth requirement vs. error rate.

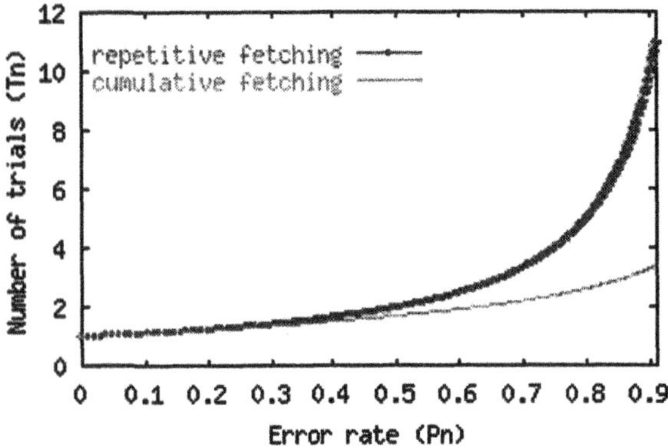

Fig. 8. Number of trials vs. error rate.

independent of error rate and allows prefetching to be done within a couple of trials even when the error rate is 80%.

4.3. Prefetching vs. non-prefetching

For the assessment of user access characteristics on the effect of cumulative prefetching, we take the probability of future references into consideration. We assume that prefetching is done before the next request arrives. Let M be an access frequency, then byte hit rate by the cumulative prefetching is simply:

$$\mathrm{BHR}^{(\mathrm{PF})} = \frac{M-1}{M}.$$

And the bandwidth cost is constant, n:

$$\mathrm{BC}^{(\mathrm{PF})} = N_{n|\mathrm{success}} = n.$$

The byte hit rate without cumulative prefetching depends on the number of trials to fetch complete data. If the number of accesses to the objects is smaller than the number of trials, then the byte hit rate becomes zero and the average bandwidth cost is

$$\mathrm{BHR}^{(\mathrm{NP})} = 0 \quad (M < T_n),$$

$$\mathrm{BC}^{(\mathrm{NP})} = N_{n|\mathrm{error}} \times M \quad (M < T_n).$$

When the number of accesses exceeds the number of trials, a proxy cache can successfully serve subsequent accesses after the transfer is done (T_n). Thus, no additional traffic is required from servers and bandwidth cost does not increase over M and the cost is:

$$\mathrm{BC}^{(\mathrm{NP})} = N_{n|\mathrm{error}} \times (T_n - 1) + N_{n|\mathrm{success}} \quad (M \geq T_n).$$

The byte hit rate can be written as:

$$\mathrm{BHR}^{(\mathrm{NP})} = \frac{N_{n|\mathrm{success}} \times (M - T_n)}{[N_{n|\mathrm{error}}(T_n - 1) + N_{n|\mathrm{success}}] + N_{n|\mathrm{success}}(M - T_n)} \quad (M \geq T_n)$$

where $N_{n|\mathrm{success}}(M - T_n)$ is the amount of traffic satisfied from a proxy cache.

Fig. 9 depicts the additional bandwidth cost of cumulative prefetching compared with non-prefetching according to $M = 1, 2, 5, 10$ and 20. The additional bandwidth cost increases as does an error rate when $M = 1$. This is because that the fraction of file to be prefetched is large for a high error rate and this

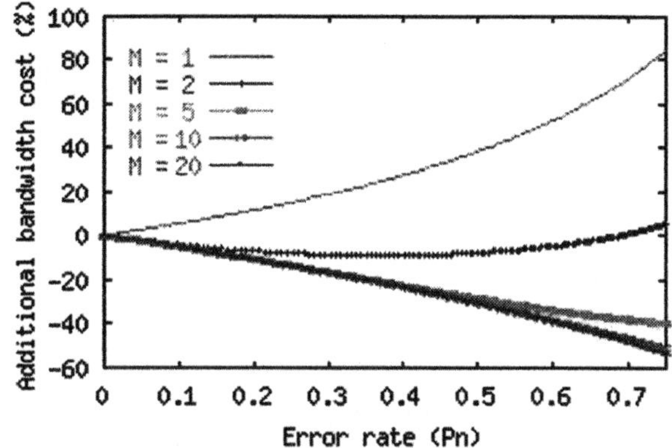

Fig. 9. Bandwidth cost vs. access frequency.

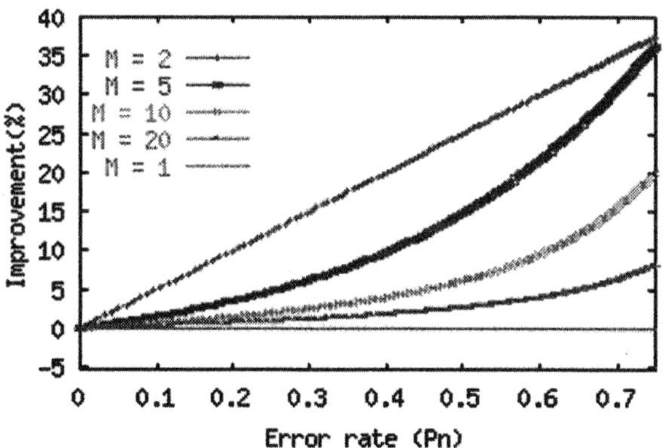

Fig. 10. Byte hit rate vs. access frequency.

amount of traffic is wasted for the wrong prediction. However, the additional cost can be compensated for by bandwidth saving when M is greater than or equal to 2. For example, when M is 2 and P_n is 0.69, traffic amounts to 0.2% of the total number of bytes in the file is wasted due to prefetching, but the byte hit rate is increased from 16% to 50%. The improvement in byte hit rate is shown in Fig. 10. The improvement is always positive except when M is 1.

5. Experimental results

We implemented the on-demand cumulative prefetching scheme in Squid [15], a public proxy cache software. A proxy cache accepts user requests, determines the location of a target object and delivers it through the Internet. The prefetching module monitors every transaction and attaches a prefetch-flag to the object entity that is broken during transmission. The *range request* in HTTP/1.1 is used for cumulative prefetching. A server with HTTP/1.1 parses range headers and transmits requested data bytes from the offset. Then, fractions of the object entity are summed up at the proxy and the complete object is swapped out to the local storage.

Fig. 11 shows a state transition diagram for the prefetching module. There are four states: prefetch-none, prefetch-needed, prefetch-pending and pre-

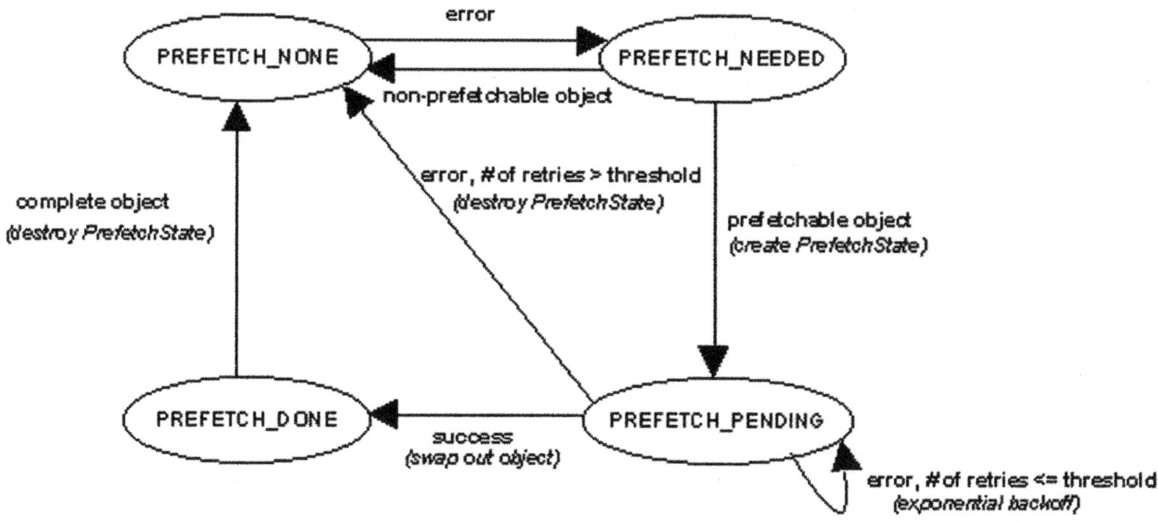

Fig. 11. State transition diagram for prefetching.

Fig. 12. Experimental environment.

fetch-done. Each state transition is initiated by events which may have actions associated with them. Prefetching is triggered when the fetched object length is less than the content length at the end of the transmission. The object is *prefetchable* if it is cacheable and has a non-zero positive fetched length. With the creation of *PrefetchState*, the prefetch timer is set to an initial value. To avoid frequent data fetching over congested links, we apply exponential back-off to prefetch-pending data objects. When the timer expires, we connect to the server and request the remaining bytes of the objects. If retrieving data is done successfully then the complete object is swapped out for future references. Otherwise, we repeat fetching until the number of trials reaches a threshold. Finally, *PrefetchState* is destroyed.

To evaluate the performance of the on-demand prefetching mechanism, we tested our implementation over an emulated network environment. Fig. 12 illustrates an experimental environment. We used Dummynet [14] on a FreeBSD operating system for emulating packet losses, communication delay and bandwidth limitation. In Dummynet, most features of the emulated network are simply controlled and configured via a command line interface. We conducted various experiments on a Pentium 300 MHz PC with 128 MB physical memory.

In each experiment, packet loss rate is controlled to get a different error rate. Wget [18] is customized to retrieve the same data repeatedly through a proxy cache with some time intervals. Fig. 13 shows the error rate observed using different packet loss rates. The error rate changes sensitively to a small range of the packet loss rate. In the first set of experiments, we disabled the on-demand prefetching module in Squid and measured the number of trials varying the packet loss rate. Then, the second set of experiments was done enabling the on-demand prefetching module. Fig. 14 shows the result. The number of trials is significantly reduced with the prefetching especially with high error rates, which is expected in the numerical analysis. On average 3.2 attempts were required to transmit the entire data by cumulative prefetching, compared with 9.5 attempts using the non-prefetching method when the error rate is 0.8.

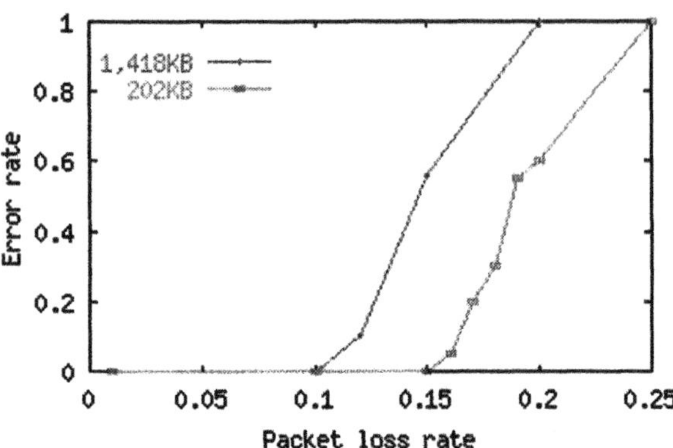

Fig. 13. Error rate vs. packet loss rate.

5.1. Trace-driven simulation

We demonstrated the performance benefits of the on-demand cumulative prefetching through trace-driven simulations. We computed data availability, the amount of traffic saved and the byte hit rate over six different fetching strategies.

The simulations draw on log files [12] of sv.nlanr.net caches for seven days. There are two types of log files. The access log contains request time, URL, and the number of bytes transmitted to clients. The store log records the expected length and the fetched length for each file when an object

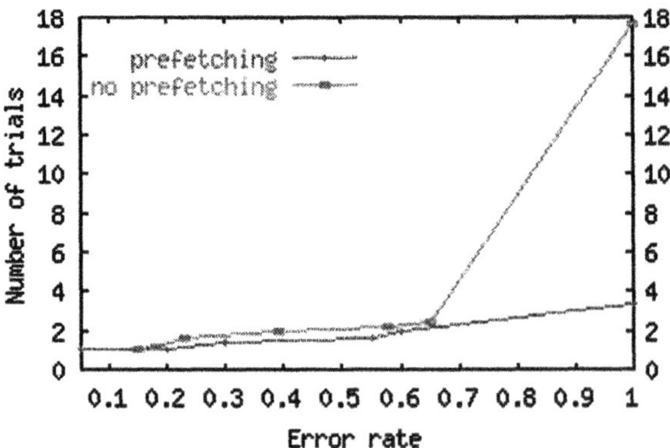

Fig. 14. Number of trials vs. error rate.

Table 2
Fetching strategies

Name	Description
RF	Repetitive fetching
CF	Cumulative fetching
OFCP	Off-line cumulative prefetching. Prefetchable objects are limited to the objects that are to be requested at least once during their lifetime (entire access sequence is known at the beginning)
ONCP	On-demand cumulative prefetching. Prefetching is initiated immediately for the failed object transmission
2ONCP	On-demand cumulative prefetching with 2 lookaheads. Prefetching is initiated for the objects having two consecutive failed transmissions.
3ONCP	On-demand cumulative prefetching with 3 lookaheads. Prefetching is initiated for the objects having three consecutive failed transmissions.

is transferred from a server into a local storage. By combining these two sets of files, we can figure out data objects that failed to be fetched, and the expected length and the number of requests followed to those objects. Table 2 lists six fetching strategies and each description used in the simulation. Fig. 15 illustrates the error rates according to fetching strategies. Compared with the existing repetitive fetching method (RF), the other five methods have improved data availability from 21% to 60%. On-demand cumulative prefetching (ONCP) and the off-line cumulative prefetching method (OFCP) provide the maximal improvement since a hit is guaranteed from the second time access of the broken objects in those two cases. For example, the reduction in error rate for 10 Mbyte data is 50%.

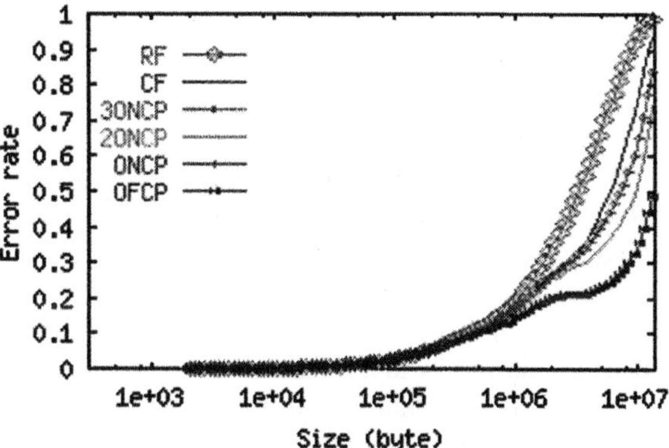

Fig. 15. Data availability. Error rates are plotted for each fetching strategy.

Table 3 lists the amount of traffic saved and the improvement of byte hit rates by each strategy. 'Traffic saved' represents how much network traffic is saved between a proxy cache and servers compared with the repetitive fetching method (RF). 'Improvement' represents the difference between byte hit rate obtained by repetitive fetching (RF) and that obtained by each method. The cumulative fetching method (CF) provides the most effective way to save network bandwidth from a proxy cache to servers because it resumes fetching at the point of break-off of the last attempt. However, it does not give us much benefit in terms of data availability. On-demand cumulative prefetching (ONCP) is a straightforward method to ensure high data availability. This method performs equivalently to the off-line cumulative prefetching method (OFCP) which pro-

Table 3
Simulation results

Name	Byte prefetched (Kbyte)	Traffic saved (%)	Byte hit (Kbyte)	Byte hit rate (%)	Improvement (%)
RF	8,925,617	–	18,996,144	68.03	–
CF	7,358,957	17	22,439,856	75.30	7.27
OFCP	7,771,162	12	27,061,904	77.69	9.66
ONCP	9,005,303	−0.8	27,061,904	75.03	7.00
2ONCP	7,748,413	13.18	24,717,797	76.13	8.10
3ONCP	7,747,897	13.19	23,528,840	75.23	7.20

vides the maximal availability for the given access characteristics. But it can be achieved at the cost of extra bandwidth consumption between a proxy cache and servers. In this simulation, it is shown that 0.8% extra traffic is taking place because of false prediction. Therefore, we leverage the user access pattern to reduce the false prediction. The 2ONCP method looks ahead past two records including the current one before initiating prefetching for the broken objects. Table 3 and Fig. 15 show that the 2ONCP method saves a data traffic amount to 13.18% and improves the byte hit rate by 8.10%, while reducing the error rate to 42% in the best case.

6. Conclusion

To avoid abusive bandwidth demands by repetitive failures of large multimedia data, we have proposed the on-demand prefetching for a proxy cache. We have analyzed bandwidth consumption of different strategies over error-resilience network links. The analysis shows that bandwidth consumption by repetitive trials of data fetching with non-zero error probability increases rapidly as the error probability goes higher. On the other hand, on-demand cumulative prefetching can be performed within a few trials with no additional bandwidth requirement. To assess user access patterns on the effects of prefetching, we compute byte hit rate and bandwidth cost varying access frequency. The results indicate that improvement in byte hit rate increases in any case while the additional bandwidth cost depends on the access pattern.

We have measured the performance of the proposed scheme over the network emulating a wide area network environment like the Internet. The experiments show that on-demand prefetching can be effectively achieved by cumulative fetching. Finally, trace-driven simulations explore traffic saved, improvement in the byte hit rate and data availability. The results show substantial reductions in error rates for large multimedia data. Error rates are reduced by 60% to 21% depending on fetching strategies. The network traffic between a proxy and servers is saved by 17% to −0.8%. Byte hit rate is also increased by 9.66% to 7.00%.

We plan to extend the presented model in terms of user-perceived latency that is one of ultimate evaluation metrics for the performance of Web proxy caches. This will allow us to elaborate our prefetching strategy to increase performance as well as to reduce client latency.

The cumulative prefetching could be combined with the rate controlled prefetching [4] to minimize the queuing delay in networks due to prefetching. We plan to monitor network conditions at a proxy cache to tailor the rate allocation to traffic for each request.

Acknowledgements

We would like to thank the anonymous referees for valuable comments. This work would not be possible but for the logs provided by Jaeho Yang at the Inet and the National Laboratory for Applied Network Research supported by National Science Foundation grants NCR-9616602 and NCR-9521745.

References

[1] M. Arlitt and C. Williamson, Web server workload characterization, in: Proc. ACM SIGMETRICS 96, San Francisco, CA, November 1996.

[2] P. Barford and M. Crovella, Generating representative Web workloads for network and server performance evaluation, in: Proc. SIGMETRICS 98, Wisconsin, June 1998.

[3] J. Chung and M. Sirbu, Distributed network storage with quality of service guarantees, in: Proc. INET99, San Jose, CA, 1999.

[4] M. Crovella and P. Barford, The network effects of prefetching, in: Proc. IEEE Infocom 98, San Francisco, CA, 1998.

[5] F. Douglis, A. Feldmann, B. Krishnamurthy and J. Mogul, Rate of change and other metrics: a live study of the World-Wide Web, in: Usenix Symp. on Internet Technologies and Systems, Monterey, December 1997.

[6] A. Feldmann, R. Caceres, F. Douglis, G. Glass and M. Rabinovich, Performance of Web proxy caching in heterogeneous bandwidth environments, in: Proc. INFOCOM 99, 1999.

[7] R. Fielding, J. Gettys, J. Mogul, H. Frystyk and T. Berners-Lee, Hypertext Transfer Protocol HTTP/1.1, RFC2068, January 1997.

[8] J. Gwertzman and M. Selter, The case for geographical push caching, Paper presented at the 5th Annual Workshop on Hot Operating Systems, 1995.

[9] J. Jung, Enhancing Web Caching Architecture with the Replication of Large Objects, Masters thesis, Korea Advanced Institute of Science and Technology, Korea, February 1998.

[10] T.M. Kroeger, D.D.E. Long and J.C. Mogul, Exploring the bounds of Web latency from caching and prefetching, in: Usenix Symp. on Internet Technologies and Systems, Monterey, December 1997.

[11] D. Menasce and V. Almeida, Web and intranet performance: a quantitative analysis, tutorials in: Usenix Technical Conf., New Orleans, June 1998.

[12] NLANR, Proxy cache log traces, October 1999, ftp://ircache.nlanr.net/Traces/

[13] J. Pitkow, Summary of WWW characterizations, in: Proc. WWW8, April 1998.

[14] L. Rizzo, Dummynet: a simple approach to the evaluation of network protocols, ACM Computer Communications Review 27 (1) (1997).

[15] Squid Web Proxy Cache, http://www.squid-cache.org, 1999.

[16] vBNS, very High Speed Backbone Network Service, http://www.vbns.net

[17] Z. Wang and J. Crowcroft, Prefetching in the World Wide Web, in: Proc. IEEE Global Internet, London, 1996.

[18] GNU Wget, http://sunsite.auc.dk/wget/

Jaeyeon Jung is a PhD student in computer science at the Korea Advanced Institute of Science and Technology (KAIST). Her research interests include Web workload analysis and characterization, caching visualization and scalable information dissemination architecture.

Dongman Lee received a BS in computer engineering from Seoul National University in 1982, and a MS and PhD in computer science from KAIST in 1984 and 1987, respectively. He worked at HP as a technical contributor from 1988 to 1997. He is associate professor at the Information and Communications University (ICU) since 1998. His research interests include distributed object computing, distributed collaborative environments, multimedia multicast protocols, fault-tolerance, group communications, and mobile computing.

Kilman Chon received a PhD in computer science from UCLA in 1974, in addition to a BS in engineering science from Osaka University. He worked at Rockwell International as distributed computer system designer in the late 60s, and at the Jet Propulsion Laboratory as member of the technical staff in the area of advanced mission control in the late 70s. He is a professor at the Computer Science Department at KAIST since 1982. He worked on network systems including the Internet since the early 80s, and contributed to form various regional organizations in the Internet such as APAN and APTLD, of which he is the founding chair. He is also co-chairing the Coordination Committee of Intercontinental Research Networking (CCIRN).

ELSEVIER

Protocol considerations for a prefix-caching proxy for multimedia streams

Stephane Gruber [a], Jennifer Rexford [*,b], Andrea Basso [c]

[a] *Lysis, 8, Cotes de Montbenon, 1003 Lausanne, Switzerland*
[b] *AT&T Labs — Research, 180 Park Avenue, Room A169, Florham Park, NJ 07931, USA*
[c] *AT&T Labs — Research, 100 Schulz Drive, Room 3-203, Red Bank, NJ 07701, USA*

Abstract

The increasing popularity of multimedia streaming applications introduces new challenges in content distribution. Web-initiated multimedia streams typically experience high start-up delay, due to large protocol overheads and the poor delay, throughput, and loss properties of the Internet. Internet service providers can improve performance by caching the initial segment (the prefix) of popular streams at proxies near the requesting clients. The proxy can initiate transmission to the client while simultaneously requesting the remainder of the stream from the server. This paper analyzes the challenges of realizing a prefix-caching service in the context of the IETF's Real-Time Streaming Protocol (RTSP), a multimedia streaming protocol that derives from HTTP. We describe how to exploit existing RTSP features, such as the Range header, and how to avoid several round-trip delays by caching protocol information at the proxy. Based on our experiences, we propose extensions to RTSP that would ease the development of new multimedia proxy services. In addition, we discuss how caching the partial contents of multimedia streams introduces new challenges in cache coherency and feedback control. Then, we briefly present our preliminary implementation of prefix caching on a Linux-based PC, and describe how the proxy interoperates with the RealNetworks server and client.

Keywords: Caching; Multimedia streaming; Proxy; RTSP; RTP; RTCP

1. Introduction

The popularity of Internet multimedia applications has grown dramatically in the past several years, spurred by the penetration of the Web and the increasing capacity of backbone and local-access networks. Although HTTP can be used to transfer audio and video content, most multimedia transmissions are simply initiated on the Web. Then, the client's player contacts the multimedia server using a different set of protocols that are better suited to streaming applications. For example, the RealNetworks client and server communicate using the Real-Time Streaming Protocol (RTSP) [17], an IETF draft standard that derives from HTTP. RTSP is used in a number of commercial streaming media applications, including the RealNetworks client and server.

Despite the advent of new multimedia protocols, today's audio and video applications typically experience high start-up delay, due to protocol overheads and the poor delay, throughput, and loss properties of the Internet. The route from the server to the client often traverses multiple ISP domains, giving the client's service provider little control over the

* Corresponding author. E-mail: jrex@research.att.com

end-to-end performance. Instead, response time can be reduced by caching popular streams at proxies near the requesting clients (e.g., at the head-end of the access network). The ISP can carefully provision the proxy–client path for good quality of service, and protect the client from the vagaries of the server–proxy path. Although proxy caching of text and image data has been widely explored in the past several years, proxy services for multimedia streams introduce new challenges — very large objects, strict timing requirements, and new protocols.

The large size of most multimedia streams makes conventional Web caching techniques inappropriate. Rather than storing the entire contents of a large audio or video clip, the proxy could cache a set of frames from the beginning of the stream (i.e., the prefix of the clip) [18]. This allows the proxy to initiate transmission to the client while simultaneously requesting the remainder of the stream (the suffix) from the server. The prefix could be cached while satisfying a client request, prefetched from the server upon access to the enclosing Web page, or pushed explicitly by the server. The prefix should be large enough to hide the round-trip delays, jitter, and small time-scale fluctuations in server–proxy throughput (e.g., 5-second prefix). Caching a larger prefix reduces the amount of traffic between the server and the proxy on subsequent client requests, and allows the proxy to support additional functions, such as transcoding or workahead transmission, without introducing client delay.

For ease of deployment, multimedia proxy services, such as prefix caching, should not require changes to existing client/server software or network mechanisms and should operate in the context of standard protocols. This paper investigates the challenges of realizing the prefix-caching service in the context of the RTP, RTSP, and RTCP family of IETF protocols. Section 2 briefly reviews the RTP, RTCP, and RTSP protocols. In Section 3 we describe how to exploit existing RTSP features, such as the Range header, and how to avoid several round-trip delays by caching protocol information at the proxy. Then, in Section 4 we discuss how caching partial contents at the proxy introduces new challenges in cache coherency and feedback control. Drawing on the protocol analysis, Section 5 briefly describes the architecture and preliminary implementation of our prefix-caching proxy on a Linux-based PC. We used the RealNetworks G2 server and player as a source and sink for testing the proxy. To aid other researchers in experimenting with multimedia proxy services, we describe how to coax the RealNetworks implementation of RTSP, including how to coax the RealServer to stream with RTP and RTCP, rather than the proprietary RDT protocol. Section 6 concludes the paper with a discussion of future research directions.

The paper complements recent work on multimedia caching and proxy services. Earlier research on multimedia caching proposed storing a sliding interval of successive frames to satisfy client requests that arrive close together in time [3,9,19]. Other recent work proposed having the proxy cache a fixed subset of frames, such as the prefix of the stream or a subset of frames in high-bandwidth regions of the stream, to reduce the overhead of transmitting to the client [4,12,13,18,20]. Our paper complements these studies by focusing on the protocol issues that arise in caching partial contents. Other recent work has introduced multimedia proxy services that operate within existing streaming protocols, including systems that perform transcoding, retransmission, workahead smoothing, and insertion [1,2,11,14]. We complement this work by focusing on the unique challenges of performing prefix caching at a proxy.

2. Multimedia streaming protocols

The RTP, RTCP, and RTSP suite of protocols supports multimedia streaming in the Internet, and serves as the starting point for our work on prefix caching.

2.1. Real-Time Transport Protocol (RTP)

RTP [16] provides the basic functionality for transferring real-time data over packet networks. Since RTP does not include mechanisms for reliable delivery or flow control, transport of RTP packets must rely on underlying protocols such as UDP and TCP. RTP typically runs over UDP, though TCP is sometimes used for reliable transport or to stream across firewalls that discard UDP packets. RTP provides source identification (randomly chosen SSRC identifier), payload type identification (to signal the appropriate decoding and playback information to the client), sequence numbering (for ordering packets and detecting losses), and timestamping (to control the playback time and measure jitter). Data packets contain a generic RTP header with these fields, as well as payload-specific information to improve the quality of delivery for specific media (e.g., MPEG). Interpretation of some header fields, such as the timestamp, is payload dependent. The RTP header may also identify contributing sources (CSRCs) for the payload carried in the packet; such a list is typically inserted by mixers or translators.

2.2. Real-Time Control Protocol (RTCP)

RTCP [16] monitors the delivery of RTP packets. The protocol provides feedback on the quality of data distribution, establishes an identification (CNAME) for each participant, scales the control packet transmission with the number of participants (to avoid generating excessive feedback traffic in large multicast groups), and provides minimal session control information. RTCP packets consist of source descriptors, sender reports, receiver reports, BYE packets (signifying the end of participation in a session), and APP packets (for application-specific functions). Receiver reports include the stream's SSRC, the fraction of RTP packets lost, the sequence number of the last RTP packet received, and the packet interarrival jitter. Senders can use this information to modify their transmission rates or to switch to a different encoder. The sender reports include the stream's SSRC, the sequence number of the last RTP packet sent, the wallclock time of the last transmission, and the number of RTP packets and bytes sent. The client can use the RTP timestamp and wallclock time information for media synchronization.

2.3. Real-Time Streaming Protocol (RTSP)

RTSP [17] coordinates the delivery of multimedia files, acting as a 'VCR remote control'. RTSP typically runs over TCP, though UDP can also be used. Though conceptually similar to HTTP/1.1 [5], RTSP is stateful and has several different methods. The OPTIONS method inquires about server capabilities (e.g., RTSP version number, supported methods, etc.), and the DESCRIBE method inquires about the properties of a particular file (e.g., Last-Modified time and session description information, typically using SDP [7]). Client and server state machines are created with the SETUP method, which also negotiates transport parameters (e.g., RTP over unicast UDP on a particular port). The client sends a SETUP message for each stream (e.g., audio and video) in the file. Streaming of the file is initiated with the PLAY method, which can include a Range header to control the playback point. The TEARDOWN method terminates the session, releasing the resources at the server and client sites. The protocol also includes a number of recommended or optional methods.

3. Prefix caching in RTSP

In this section, we describe how to reduce client delay by caching protocol information at the proxy, and how to use the RTSP Range header to fetch the suffix of the stream. The discussion draws on Fig. 1, which illustrates the handling of RTSP messages when the proxy has cached the prefix of each stream (e.g., audio and video), the description of the presentation, and the options supported by the server.

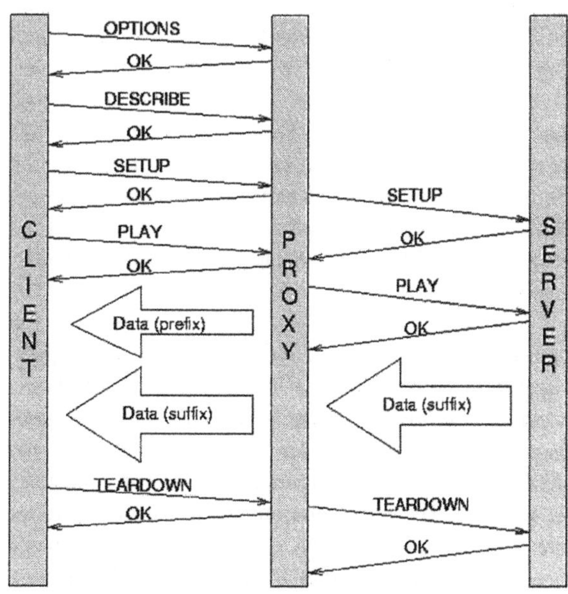

Fig. 1. Protocol exchange under proxy prefix caching.

3.1. Basic RTSP operation

The handling of client requests depends on whether or not the proxy has cached the prefix and the related RTSP information. The client uses the OPTIONS message to learn which methods are supported by the server. The server (and therefore the proxy) should support the basic methods such as OPTIONS, DESCRIBE, SETUP, PLAY, and TEARDOWN. The proxy can respond directly to the client's OPTIONS request, avoiding the delay in contacting the server, as shown in Fig. 1. In particular, the proxy could respond with a list of methods that were cached during a previous interaction with the server. Alternatively, the proxy could respond with a default list of basic methods. In either case, the proxy may occasionally send an incorrect list of methods (e.g., if the server ceases to support some method). If the client later attempts to invoke the unsupported method, the server would simply respond with an error message (response code 405 'Method not allowed') that includes the current list of methods, which the proxy can cache and forward to the client. Note that this error would not cause streaming to fail.

The DESCRIBE message is used to retrieve information about the particular presentation, which consists of one or more underlying streams (e.g., audio, video). Like the OPTIONS message, the DESCRIBE message is optional and does not affect the RTSP state machine at the client or the server. If the description resides in the cache, the proxy can respond directly to the client; otherwise, the proxy must contact the server. However, note that the cached DESCRIBE information may not be up-to-date. The proxy can employ a variety of techniques to reduce the likelihood of stale information, as discussed in Section 4.1.

The SETUP request is used to negotiate the transport parameters, including the transport protocol (e.g., RTP) and the TCP/UDP port numbers. Upon receiving the client's SETUP message, port numbers are generated for the proxy's end of the RTP and RTCP connections, and a session identifier is selected. The port numbers and session identifier are sent to the client. In the meantime, the proxy generates a separate SETUP message to the server. Each stream in the multimedia presentation results in separate connections on both the proxy–client and server–proxy paths, and consists of TCP or UDP connections for RTP and RTCP. The proxy could request that the server stream the RTP packets over TCP (or a related semi-reliable transport protocol), since the cached prefix could hide transient periods of TCP congestion where the server does not send packets fast enough for continuous playback. To coordinate the transfer of RTP and RTCP messages, the proxy must maintain a mapping table to direct messages to the appropriate outgoing connection (and with the appropriate session identifier), as discussed in Section 5.1.

The client can send the PLAY message after receiving the proxy response to the SETUP request. If the prefix is cached, the proxy can respond immediately to the PLAY request and initiate the streaming of RTP and RTCP messages to the client. The client can begin playback, without waiting for the proxy to communicate with the server. Note that the proxy may or may not have received the SETUP response from the server, depending on the delay on the server–proxy path. Once the proxy has received a SETUP response from the server, indicating the server's session identifier, the proxy can send the PLAY request to the server, with the appropriate Range header, as discussed in more detail in Section 3.2. After transmitting the prefix of the stream to the client, the proxy can start sending the RTP packets in the suffix retrieved from the server.

Depending on the size of the prefix, the proxy may decide to wait longer before asking the server to transmit the suffix. Fetching the suffix too early would require extra storage resources at the proxy, and may result in extra server load and network traffic if the client eventually pauses or stops the transfer of the presentation. Yet, the suffix should be requested sufficiently ahead of when the proxy would need to start transmitting this data to the client. Requesting the suffix a bit early allows the proxy to hide the server–proxy round-trip delay (which can be estimated from RTCP reports), or additional delays for other functions such as smoothing or transcoding.

3.2. Linking the prefix and suffix

When the entire stream resides in the cache, the proxy acts as a server in responding to the client

PLAY request. When the cache does not contain any portion of the requested resource, the proxy forwards the PLAY request to the server and simply shuttles messages back and forth between the server and the client, acting as an application-level router. The operation of the proxy becomes more interesting when the cache stores only the prefix of the stream. In this case, the proxy can reply to the client PLAY request and initiate transmission of RTP and RTCP messages to the client, while requesting the suffix from the server. Fetching the suffix requires the proxy to initiate a Range request for the appropriate portion of the stream. As part of linking the prefix and suffix, the proxy must specify the appropriate Range and handle inaccuracies in the server response.

As part of caching multimedia content, the proxy keeps track of the size of the prefix in terms of the timestamps in the RTP packets. The RTSP Range request is defined for both SMPTE relative timestamps and NPT (Normal Play Time). SMPTE has the format hours:minutes:seconds:frames.subframes with the origin at the beginning of the clip. In contrast, NPT time consists of a decimal fraction, where the left part of the decimal may be expressed in either hours, minutes or seconds, and the right part of the decimal point measures fractions of a second. These formats require the proxy to convert the RTP timestamps into time, by applying the payload-specific clock rate [15]. According to the protocol specification, servers supporting the Range header must understand the NPT range format and should understand the SMPTE range format. In most cases, the SMPTE format is preferable, since it supports more indexing into individual packets within a frame. But, the proxy could easily avoid the need for such fine-grain indexing by ending the prefix at frame boundaries.

The proxy does not know in advance whether or not the server supports Range requests for a particular presentation (some streams do not allow seek operations), and whether or not the SMPTE format is supported. The proxy can learn, and cache, this information for each presentation by sending Range requests to the server and noting the response (e.g., the server sends a 426 'Header Field Not Valid For Resource' response when Range is not supported). The proxy could avoid polling the server for this information if the RTSP SETUP or PLAY response included information about support for Range requests. To avoid changing existing RTSP implementations, providing the information about Range support could be optional, since the proxy could always infer the information and/or decline to cache partial contents when the information is not provided.

In addition, RTSP does not require the server to handle the Range request precisely. For example, the request may identify a starting time that does not correspond to any particular frame, forcing the server to initiate transmission from the previous or subsequent frame. In addition, the server may not support arbitrary indexing to individual frames. (For example, an MPEG stream typically consists of I, P, and B frames within a group of pictures (GOP). The server may not precisely satisfy a Range request that starts in the middle of a GOP. In fact, allowing clients to index to any arbitrary frame could introduce substantial overhead at the server (to maintain fine-grain indices, or to parse the content to sequence to the appropriate frame), particularly for variable-bit-rate streams, or streams without a fixed GOP structure.) The RTSP protocol does not dictate how accurately the server must handle the Range header, and does not provide a way for the server to indicate in advance how much inaccuracy could be introduced. As such, the proxy should be conservative, and ensure that the transmission to the client does not have duplicate or missing packets. Fortunately, the server reply includes a Range response header that indicates what range of time is currently being played. If the beginning of the suffix contains frames that are already at the end of the prefix, the proxy discards the overlapping packets. To avoid a gap between the prefix and the suffix, the proxy could initiate a conservative Range request, or issue a second request if a gap arises.

3.3. Seamless transmission of RTP packets

In order to link the prefix and the suffix, all RTP headers must be consistent, otherwise the client will not associate the two parts to the same stream. The sensitive fields are sequence numbers, timestamps, and source identifier (SSRC), which have been selected separately by the proxy (for the prefix) and the server (for the suffix). Therefore, the proxy will have to change the RTP header fields of the suffix to match the SSRC it chose for the prefix, and the timestamps and sequence numbers to indicate that the suffix must be played after the prefix. In streaming the suffix, the proxy overwrites the SSRC field in each RTP packet with the value it selected as part of initiating transmission of the prefix. The proxy knows the timestamp and sequence number used in transmitting the last RTP packet of the prefix. The base timestamp and sequence number for the server's transmission of the suffix are provided in the RTP-Info header in the PLAY response. The proxy can then add/subtract the appropriate constant for the timestamp and sequence number fields of each packet in the suffix.

4. Decoupling of client and server

Prefix caching decouples the server transmission from client reception. Caching partial contents of the stream, and overlapping the prefix transmission on the proxy–client path with the suffix on the server–proxy path, introduces new challenges in cache coherency and feedback control. This section identifies the key issues and presents several possible solutions.

4.1. Cache coherency

Caching RTSP messages and multimedia content at a proxy introduces potential coherency problems when the server changes this information. Cache coherency is a critical issue in the Web, where many resources change very frequently. The problem is arguably less important for multimedia presentations, which may change less frequently — the server could simply assign a new URL when new content is created. Still, the paradigms for authoring and updating multimedia content are not well understood, and the use of proxies should not place additional restrictions on how servers are managed. As such, the proxy should incorporate mechanisms to prevent the transmission of a suffix that does not come from the same version of the presentation as the cached prefix.

The proxy could reduce the likelihood of introducing an inconsistent stream by sending a DESCRIBE message to the server for every client request, and checking that the Last-Modified time matches the cached prefix. However, the additional exchange with the server would increase client start-up latency, which would partially defeat the purpose of prefix caching. Instead, the proxy could apply a timeout (time-to-live) to the cached information, revalidating (with an 'If-Modified-Since' request) only if the timeout has expired. To avoid forcing the client to wait for the proxy to check with the server, the proxy could periodically validate the cached information, even if no client has requested the stream. To reduce the overhead of creating a TCP connection to the server, the proxy could freshen the DESCRIBE information during other communication with this server (e.g., while coordinating the transmission of another stream from the same server). Such piggyback cache validation has proved to be a very effective technique for controlling the consistency of Web resources [10].

To ensure that a client never receives a suffix that does not match with the prefix, the proxy could send a DESCRIBE request to the server just after requesting the suffix. This would allow the proxy to verify that the suffix comes from the same presentation as the cached prefix. In the rare event that the suffix comes from a more recent version of the presentation, the proxy could terminate the transmission to the client rather than send inconsistent information. Note that this approach does not delay transmission to the client in the common case when the presentation has not changed. From the client's point of view, the disruption of the transmission would appear as a transient server error. For example, the proxy could send a '500 Internal Server Error', '502 Bad Gateway', or '503 Service Unavailable' message. Note that the proxy could also send such an error message if the server does not respond to the proxy's request for the suffix, or is unable to devote resources to satisfying the proxy's request. After receiving the error message from the proxy, the client could optionally initiate the request a second time, and receive a fresh copy of the presentation from the server.

Finally, cache inconsistency can be avoided with additional support from the server. The simplest approach would be to have the server indicate an expiration time for the presentation, and ensure that the contents will not change in the meantime. An alternative solution would be to allow additional communication between the server and the proxy. For example, the server could push the prefix of each popular multimedia presentation to interested proxies, perhaps using multicast to distribute the content. In this case, the proxy acts as a (partial) replica of the server content, rather than as a conventional cache. The server could indicate the expiration time for the presentation, or promise to send updates as part of changing the presentation. The proxies could subscribe to receive updates for a particular content of interest.

4.2. Relaying RTCP sender/receiver reports

Prefix caching introduces additional challenges in generating accurate and timely reports of server and client performance. If the entire stream resides in the cache, the proxy acts as a server in generating sender RTCP reports and responding to the client's receiver reports. On a cache miss, the proxy acts as an application-level router and simply forwards the reports generated by the server and the client. Yet, the appropriate behavior is less clear when the proxy sends the prefix of the stream and fetches the suffix from the server. On the one hand, the proxy could view the server–proxy and proxy–client paths as distinct, and have two unrelated RTCP sessions with the server and the client, respectively. Despite the conceptual appeal of this approach, the proxy runs the risk of hiding important information about performance problems on the server–proxy or proxy–client paths. Instead, the proxy could generate and receive reports while transmitting the prefix, and switch to forwarding reports while transmitting the suffix. In forwarding the server-generated reports, the proxy would need to map the key fields, such as the SSRC, timestamp, and sequence number, that have a different base in the suffix than in the prefix.

Forwarding server and client RTCP reports during transmission of the suffix has the advantage of informing the server about the performance experienced by the client. However, the information could be rather out of date, since the suffix is not sent to the client until transmission of the prefix is complete. The proxy has a number of possible options to control the RTCP reports sent to the server. Reporting transient performance problems (e.g., burst of loss) on the proxy–client path may not be particularly relevant, especially if this information is out-of-date. Instead, the proxy could choose to report only persistent problems that require a response by the server (e.g., to switch to a lower bandwidth version of the stream). In generating these reports, the proxy must be careful to reflect the delay that has been introduced in sending the RTP packets in the suffix to the client. Otherwise, the server may think that a large number of packets have not been received. The proxy could achieve these goals by basing the receiver reports on the packets that have been received by the proxy (even if they have not all been sent to the client), while using the loss rate experienced by the client to compute the number of lost packets to report to the server.

4.3. Proxy adaptation

Correctly modifying the RTCP receiver reports is a delicate process. Instead, the proxy could take advantage of the cached prefix to change the properties of the server–proxy and proxy–client paths. The proxy could take advantage of the prefix cache to hide the delay for explicit retransmission of lost packets on the server–proxy path. For example, the proxy could issue a Range request (perhaps on a separate connection) to retrieve a previously requested interval of frames from the server. This would isolate the client from the loss on the server–proxy path. Rather than issuing RTSP Range requests (which is arguably a rather coarse-grain way to effect packet retransmissions), the proxy could have the server transmit RTP packets over a TCP connection (by requesting TCP in the initial SETUP message). The TCP connection would ensure a reliable transmission of the RTP packets, and would obviate the need for an RTCP session between the server and the proxy. The proxy could still use UDP for transferring RTP packets to the client.

To address potential performance problems on the proxy–client path, the proxy could perform additional functions, such as transcoding and workahead smoothing. Transcoding [1] would reduce the bandwidth requirements of the stream by lowering the quality. The proxy could perform transcoding either by discarding a subset of the incoming packets, or by reencoding the stream (e.g., by discarding high-frequency components in each MPEG slice). In contrast, workahead smoothing would involve transmitting frames into the client playback buffer ahead of the playout time [14]. The cached prefix allows the proxy to transmit frames ahead of time without incurring additional client playback latency. The transmission of additional frames would allow time for slower transmission of large frames (smoothing out a burst) or retransmission of lost packets (based on the receiver reports). The proxy could perform these functions on the proxy–client path without involving the server. If the proxy sends RTCP receiver reports to the server, these messages should reflect the improvements made in the proxy–client path, to avoid triggering conflicting recovery operations at the server.

5. Prefix caching implementation

This section describes the architecture of the proxy and identifies the key implementation issues. We describe the session data structure, the operation of the cache, and the scheduling of processor and link resources. A preliminary implementation of the prefix-caching proxy has been implemented in C on a Linux-based PC, and successfully tested using the RealServer and RealPlayer (from www.real.com) as a source and sink.

5.1. Per-session state

The client sends RTSP messages directly to the proxy by configuring the player with the proxy's IP address. The client has a TCP connection to/from the proxy for RTSP operations, a UDP connection from the proxy to receive RTP packets, and a UDP connection to/from the proxy for RTCP. Having the client contact the proxy explicitly has advantages over transparent caching, where the proxy must lie in the path of client messages that are directed to the server. In addition, transparent caching would also introduce extra complexity and overhead for the proxy to intercept and modify all of the client and server packets, including reconstruction of the TCP stream for the RTSP messages. These challenges, while important, are beyond the scope of our initial implementation effort.

The proxy coordinates communication with the client and the server using a data structure that stores key information about the ongoing session. The fields in this data structure are populated as the session progresses. A session can include multiple streams, simultaneously or back-to-back; for example, a presentation often includes both an audio and a video stream, and perhaps a third stream for subtitles. The reply to the OPTIONS message contains cacheable information about the server, but does not include any session-level information. The reply to the DESCRIBE message includes cacheable information about a resource, such as its URI and Last-Modified Time. For illustration, we describe how the session data structure is populated on a cache miss:

- Client RTSP connection: upon establishing a TCP connection with the client, the proxy records the client IP address and the identifier for the TCP socket.
- First client RTSP request: the first RTSP message could be an optional OPTIONS or DESCRIBE message, or a SETUP message. The proxy extracts the server name and performs a gethostbyname() to learn the server IP address. The proxy establishes a TCP connection to the server and stores the identifier for the TCP socket.
- Client SETUP request: the client SETUP message(s) includes information about the transport protocol and port numbers that the client wishes to use (e.g., for RTP and RTCP). After binding the two UDP sockets, the proxy records the two sets of client and proxy port numbers, and replies to the client. In the meantime, the proxy generates and records the port numbers for its UDP connections with the server, and sends a SETUP message to the server.
- Server SETUP response: after receiving the server reply, the proxy records the server port numbers for the UDP connections and binds the UDP sockets. The proxy also stores the session identifier, generated by the server.
- Client TEARDOWN request: the proxy closes the sockets to the client, forwards the TEARDOWN to the server, and deletes the session data structure.

The session structure also includes a number of flags that indicate whether or not the requested streams are in the cache, and which packet should be sent next. The session data structure is populated in a similar manner when the proxy cache contains the prefix, except that the session identifier, base timestamp, and base sequence number are chosen by the proxy.

5.2. Caching architecture

The desire to efficiently transmit cached multimedia content to a large collection of clients drives most of the design decisions for the caching architecture. For example, the proxy caches RTP packets, rather than raw multimedia content. This obviates the need to parse the body of the RTP packets and repacketize the content, at the expense of additional storage overhead for RTP headers. Each item in the cache represents a particular multimedia resource, including the DESCRIBE information and a linked list of RTP packets, ordered by sequence number. In the simplest case, the incoming RTP packets are appended to the linked list as they arrive. Since packets sometimes arrive out of order, the proxy could insert each packet in the appropriate place in the list based on the sequence number field in the RTP packet header.

Each time a stream is transmitted from the cache, the proxy must select an SSRC and a base timestamp and sequence number (at random). As such, the proxy must alter these header fields in the cached RTP packets before transmitting to the client. To avoid extra data copying, the proxy can send the packet using a gather function (e.g., writev()) that can combine buffers from multiple locations. However, not all systems have efficient support for the gathering function. In this case, the proxy can overwrite the RTP header fields directly in the cache, and initiate a regular socket send operation for the entire packet. To avoid alteration or deletion of the packet during the copy into the socket buffer, each packet includes a lock bit to indicate that a (non-blocking) transmission is in progress; the lock bit is cleared after completion of the socket call. Also, since the proxy overwrites certain RTP header fields, the cache stores additional information to allow computation of the sequence number and timestamp fields for subsequent transmissions of the packet.

5.3. Processor and link scheduling

To handle requests from multiple clients, the proxy must have an effective way to allocate memory, processing, and I/O resources between different sessions. Our prototype implementation has an event-driven architecture, where the proxy coordinates all activity between client–server pairs in a single process. This avoids the overheads (and jitter) introduced by context switching between the processes, and simplifies the sharing of the cache amongst all of the sessions. In addition, the event-driven architecture enables the proxy to have greater control over resource allocation, by sending and receiving RTP data for each session in proportion to the bit-rate requirements. Instead of having a process scheduler implicitly allocate resources to each session, the event-driven approach shares resources by scheduling socket operations. The proxy can time-share the system by performing accounting of the number of bytes handled for each stream.

The proxy, like a server, must carefully schedule transmission of RTP packets to avoid underflow and overflow at the client site. If the proxy sends packets to the client over a TCP connection, the TCP flow control could implicitly pace the transmission. However, sending UDP packets requires greater care. The proxy schedules packets based on the RTP timestamps and packet sizes. The timestamp clock rate is payload dependent [15], requiring the proxy to maintain a mapping between payload types and clock rates to determine how many packets to transmit during a given time interval.

Ideally, the proxy could schedule the transmission of each packet at the appropriate departure time. However, such fine-grain scheduling is typically not possible, and is arguably not necessary. Instead, the proxy should pick an appropriate time interval (say, one second) for coordinating packet transmissions for each session. When streaming multimedia content to multiple clients, the proxy can sequence through the set of sessions, transmitting the appropriate number of packets for each active session. A system with kernel support for multimedia streaming could explicitly support packet scheduling [8]. Ideally, in addition to allowing per-session scheduling and variable transmission rates, the kernel could conceivably compute the appropriate rate directly from the RTP timestamps, payload-specific clock rate, and packet sizes. Such system support would aid in scaling the proxy to support a larger number of sessions.

5.4. Testbed and implementation status

Testing the prototype proxy requires multimedia clients and servers that implement RTP, RTCP, and RTSP. Currently, reference RTSP software is available for a source and a sink. However, the reference source cannot support multiple simultaneous clients, and the reference client does not display the multimedia stream; in addition, the reference code implements an earlier version of RTSP. Rather than extending the reference code, we decided to experiment with the RealNetworks server and player, which both support RTSP/1.0. This provided an opportunity to test the interoperability of our proxy with the dominant Internet multimedia components, and to study the RealNetworks RTSP implementation. Our testbed consists of a Windows NT 4.0 PC running a trial version of RealServer G2 (version 6.0.3.353), and a Windows 95 PC running RealPlayer G2 (version 6.0.3.143).

The RealPlayer is configured with the IP address and port number of the proxy. The decision to experiment with a local copy of the G2 server, rather than with existing multimedia servers in the Internet, was motivated by several issues. First, during the development and testing of our proxy software, we did not want to risk generating incorrect RTSP messages that might crash an operational G2 server. The G2 server in our testbed did crash a few times during our initial development of the proxy. Second, AT&T Research has a firewall that filters UDP packets. This would force RTP and RTCP transfers to use TCP, whereas we wish to experiment with UDP; later, we could conceivably put the proxy outside of the firewall, or experiment with RTP and RTCP transfers over TCP. Third, our initial implementation operates on a private Ethernet, to prevent accidental generation of excess traffic on the local area network; as such, the proxy does not have direct access to the larger Internet.

Although the RealServer can generate RTP and RTCP packets, the server typically employs a proprietary transport protocol called RDT. The selection of the transport protocol is initiated by the client SETUP message. For example, the SETUP message in Fig. 2 shows three candidate transport protocols, starting with RDT. Upon receiving this message, the server selects RDT as the transport protocol. To convince the server to send RTP and RTCP packets, the proxy modifies the Transport header to include only the RTP protocol. Then, the server selects RTP as the transport protocol, and transmits RTP and RTCP messages after receiving the PLAY request. Modifying the SETUP message is sufficient to convince the server to use RTP for most encoding formats (e.g., .wav, .au, and .avi files). However, the RealServer will not send RealNetworks files (e.g., .ra or .rm) using RTP. We discuss our experiences with the RealNetworks components and present a complete trace of the RTSP messages between the client and server in [6].

The initial prototype of proxy prefix caching implements a subset of the architecture, along with the modifications necessary for interacting with the RealNetworks server and player. Using the basic implementation, we can successfully process client RTSP messages, requesting the full contents from

```
SETUP rtsp://135.207.15.90:554/g2video.rm/streamid=0 RTSP/1.0
CSeq: 3
RealChallenge2: 7c7687849ca62b5a063fd037f9d13d7a01d0a8e3,
sd=78920df3
Transport: x-real-rdt/udp;client_port=6970;mode=play,
           x-pn-tng/udp;client_port=6970;mode=play,
           rtp/avp;unicast;client_port=6970-6971;mode=play
If-Match: 31278-2
```

Fig. 2. SETUP message

the server on a cache miss, or partial contents when a portion of the stream resides in the cache. The playback at the client is seamless in both cases. The proxy can sustain continuous transmission to multiple clients. In addition to viewing the stream at the client, we also verified the continuity of the RTP stream by packet inspection. The prototype is sufficient to test our uses of the RTP and RTSP protocols. However, supporting the full use of the protocols and scaling to a large number of simultaneous sessions would require enhancements to our implementation. The current prototype transfers RTSP messages over TCP, and RTP and RTCP messages over UDP, and assumes that a session has at most two simultaneous streams. The proxy forwards RTCP messages between the client and server, but does not generate reports itself. For simplicity, transfers of RTP packets to the client use a blocking send call. Future work can focus on extending the implementation and evaluating the performance.

6. Conclusions

Prefix caching offers an effective way for Internet service providers to improve user performance and network efficiency, without requiring additional support from the client, the server, or the network. The service can operate within existing standard protocols. Still, the service would benefit from improvements in the capabilities exchange in RTSP to provide more up-front information about the supported submethods, such as the Range header and acceptable time representations. In addition, prior knowledge of a bound on the server's inaccuracy in satisfying Range requests would be useful. These features could be added to RTSP, or supported in an alternate protocol with similar functionality.

As part of our ongoing work, we are pursuing these possible extensions to the RTSP standard, and are studying the cache coherency and RTCP feedback issues in greater detail. These issues become more complicated when the server can dynamically adjust the quality of the media stream in response to network congestion or server load. In addition, we are investigating how to combine prefix caching with other multimedia proxy services, such as workahead smoothing, retransmission, and transcoding.

Acknowledgements

We would like to thank Ethendranath Bommaiah and Kobus Van Der Merwe for their help in working with the RealNetworks RTSP messages, and Henning Schulzerinne for discussions about the current version of RTSP and possible extensions. Thanks also to Shubho Sen for his comments on an earlier version of the paper.

References

[1] E. Amir, S. McCanne and H. Zhang, An application level video gateway, in: Proc. ACM Multimedia, November 1995.

[2] J. Brassil, S. Garg and H. Schulzrinne, Program insertion in real-time IP multicasts, ACM Computer Communication Review 29 (1999) 49–68.

[3] A. Dan and D. Sitaram, Multimedia caching strategies for heterogeneous application and server environments, Multimedia Tools and Applications 4 (1997) 279–312.

[4] D. Eager, M. Ferris and M. Vernon, Optimized regional caching for on-demand data delivery, in: Proc. Multimedia Computing and Networking, January 1999.

[5] R. Fielding, J. Gettys, J.C. Mogul, H. Frystyk, L. Masinter, P. Leach and T. Berners-Lee, Hypertext transfer protocol — HTTP/1.1, Request for Comments 2616, June 1999.

[6] S. Gruber, J. Rexford and A. Basso, Design considerations for an RTSP-based prefix caching proxy service for multimedia streams, Tech. Rep. 990907-01, AT&T Labs — Research, September 1999.

[7] M. Handley and V. Jacobson, SDP: Session description protocol, Request for Comments 2327, April 1998.

[8] G. Hjalmtysson and S. Bhattacharjee, Control on demand: an efficient approach to router programmability, IEEE Journal Selected Areas in Communications, September 1999.

[9] M. Kamath, K. Ramamritham and D. Towsley, Continuous media sharing in multimedia database systems, in: Proc. International Conference on Database Systems for Advanced Applications, April 1995.

[10] B. Krishnamurthy and C.E. Wills, Study of piggyback cache validation for proxy caches in the World Wide Web, in: Proc. USENIX Symposium on Internet Technologies and Systems, December 1997, pp. 1–12.

[11] N.F. Maxemchuk, K. Padmanabhan and S. Lo, A cooperative packet recovery protocol for multicast video, in: Proc. International Conference on Network Protocols, October 1997.

[12] Z. Miao and A. Ortega, Proxy caching for efficient video services over the Internet, in: Proc. Packet Video Workshop, April 1999.

[13] R. Rejaie, M. Handley, H. Yu and D. Estrin, Proxy caching mechanism for multimedia playback streams in the Internet, in: Proc. International Web Caching Workshop, March 1999.

[14] J. Rexford, S. Sen and A. Basso, A smoothing proxy service for variable-bit-rate streaming video, in: Proc. Global Internet Symposium, December 1999.

[15] H. Schulzrinne, RTP profile for audio and video conferences with minimal control, February 1999, Internet Draft ietf-avt-profile-new-05.txt (work in progress).

[16] H. Schulzrinne, S. Casner, R. Frederick and V. Jacobson, RTP: a transport protocol for real-time applications, Request for Comments 1889, January 1996.

[17] H. Schulzrinne, A. Rao and R. Lanphier, Real time streaming protocol (RTSP), Request for Comments 2326, April 1998.

[18] S. Sen, J. Rexford and D. Towsley, Proxy prefix caching for multimedia streams, in: Proc. IEEE INFOCOM, April 1999.

[19] R. Tewari, H.M. Vin, A. Dan and D. Sitaram, Resource-based caching for Web servers, in: Proc. SPIE/ACM Conference on Multimedia Computing and Networking, January 1998.

[20] Y. Wang, Z.-L. Zhang, D. Du and D. Su, A network conscious approach to end-to-end video delivery over wide area networks using proxy servers, in: Proc. IEEE INFOCOM, April 1998.

Using Memex to archive and mine community Web browsing experience

Soumen Chakrabarti [*,1], Sandeep Srivastava [1], Mallela Subramanyam [1], Mitul Tiwari [1]

Department of Computer Science and Engineering, Indian Institute of Technology Bombay, Powai, Mumbai 400076, India

Abstract

Keyword indices, topic directories, and link-based rankings are used to search and structure the rapidly growing Web today. Surprisingly little use is made of years of browsing experience of millions of people. Indeed, this information is routinely discarded by browsers. Even deliberate bookmarks are stored passively, in browser-dependent formats; this separates them from the dominant world of HTML hypermedia, even if their owners were willing to share them. All this goes against Vannevar Bush's dream of the *Memex*: an enhanced supplement to personal and community memory. We present the beginnings of a Memex for the Web. Memex blurs the artificial distinction between browsing history and deliberate bookmarks. The resulting glut of data is analyzed in a number of ways. It is indexed not only by keywords but also according to the user's view of *topics*; this lets the user recall topic-based browsing contexts by asking questions like 'What trails was I following when I was last surfing about *classical music*?' and 'What are some popular pages related to my recent trail regarding *cycling*?' Memex is a browser assistant that performs these functions. We envisage that Memex will be shared by a community of surfers with overlapping interests; in that context, the meaning and ramifications of topical trails may be decided by not one but many surfers. We present a novel formulation of the *community taxonomy synthesis problem*, algorithms, and experimental results. We also recommend uniform APIs which will help managing advanced interactions with the browser.

Keywords: Community memory; Collaborative taxonomy synthesis; Browsing assistant

1. Introduction

What are the basic sources of information available from the Web? First-generation search engines (**Alta Vista** [2]) initially exploited the tokens on each page as the sole source of information. Second-generation search engines (**Google** [3], **Clever** [4]) use hyperlink structure as well.

Popular search sites answer tens of millions of queries per day. We speculate that the total number of browser clicks per day is at least three orders of magnitude larger. This third source of information has a scale that dwarfs the Web itself, and yet is perhaps as rich and valuable as text and links. Some centralized services (**Alexa** [5], **Third Voice** [6]) distribute a browser plug-in to monitor clicks and add page reviews. Others (**Hotbot** [7], **WiseWire** [8])

* Corresponding author.
[1] E-mail: {soumen, sandy, manyam, mits}@cse.iitb.ernet.in
[2] http://www.altavista.com
[3] http://google.com
[4] http://www.almaden.ibm.com/cs/k53/clever.html

[5] http://www.alexa.com
[6] http://www.thirdvoice.com
[7] http://www.hotbot.com
[8] http://www.wisewire.com

monitor clicks limited within their site to improve relevance ranking or dynamically reorganize content.

Nevertheless, most of the information latent in years of clicking by millions of surfers is carelessly discarded by browsers, unless they are deliberately bookmarked. Even bookmarks are stored passively, in browser-dependent formats; this separates them from the dominant world of HTML hypermedia, even if their owners were willing to share them.

In 1945, Vannevar Bush dreamt of *Memex*: an enhanced, intimate supplement to personal and community memory [5]. Memex would unobtrusively archive, analyze, and index our complete experience, covering books, movies, music, conversation, etc. Since then this theme of a 'living' hypermedium into which we 'weave ourselves' has been emphasized often, e.g., by **Douglas Engelbart**[9] and **Ted Nelson**[10], and of late by **Tim Berners-Lee**[11].

Assisted by a Memex for the Web, a surfer can ask the following questions:

- What was the URL I visited six months back regarding compiler optimization at Rice University?
- What was the Web neighborhood I was surfing the last time I was looking for resources on classical music?
- Are their any popular sites, related to my (Web) experience on classical music, that have appeared in the last six months?
- How is my ISP bill divided into access for work, travel, news, hobby and entertainment?
- What are the major topics relevant to my workplace? Where and how do I fit into that map? How does my bookmark folder structure that map on to my organization?
- In a hierarchy of organizations (by region, say), who are the people who share my interest in recreational cycling most closely and are not likely to be computer professionals?

We propose an architecture of a Memex for the Web which can answer the above questions. Memex is a large project involving hypertext data mining, browser plug-in and applet design, servlets and associated distributed database architecture, and user interfaces. In this paper we will give an overview of the major features of Memex, together with the architecture and design decisions.

We have validated the design using a prototype implementation. We will give examples of some of the features using screen shots and measurements on our prototype. The **Memex**[12] service will be made publicly accessible.

1.1. Architecture overview

The main function of Memex are personalization and community formation. Personalization in our context is different from the myriad *MyXYZ* portal sites, which involve manual selection of topic directories from a catalog. In our case, personalization is for both individuals and groups, and is done automatically by mining archives of community browsing experience, thus nurturing communities with clustered topical interest.

A major issue is the level at which communities are defined and analyzed. On one extreme, a central service may be provided. This would be a poor solution, not only owing to the formidable scale of operation, but also the diversity of the population and their interests. At the other extreme, individual browser-level plug-ins have limited access to behavior of anyone other than the user.

We therefore believe that the most successful community formation and personalization tool is at an intermediate level, such as an organization or geographical divisions of an ISP. Trust is not as major an issue at this level as on the Web at large; after all, most of us (have to) trust the administrator of our proxy cache and/or firewall machine. At the same time, the problems of sparse, noisy data from just one user is ameliorated somewhat by a larger user population.

The present release of Memex consists of client and server-side code, communicating via the applet–servlet protocol. The server-side code needs Apache with servlet support and a relational database, such as Oracle or IBM Universal Database installed. We avoid CGI-style solutions because the state exchanged between client and server is rather complex compared to HTML form data, and extended sessions with state are often useful. We anticipate that

[9] http://jefferson.village.virginia.edu/elab/hfl0035.html

[10] http://www.sfc.keio.ac.jp/ ted/

[11] http://www.w3.org/1999/04/13-tbl.html

[12] http://www.cs.berkeley.edu/~soumen

each logical organization or group will install a server.

We prefer not to assign the role of the Memex server to the proxy or firewall computer. The latter are already heavily loaded with their primary tasks. In the database world, software is separately architected for day-to-day transaction processing (OLTP) as against data analysis tools (warehousing, OLAP and mining). We believe a similar division of labor will be successful for Memex as well.

Unlike earlier browser plug-ins, for maximum portability, the client-side code is a JDK1.2-compliant applet. The applet polls the browser's location and sends the URL and other processed data through an encrypted connection to the server, where more analysis takes place. Java cannot steer us away from platform-dependent code, especially owing to the diverse browser security APIs. The applet runs on Netscape Communicator 4.5+ and Internet Explorer 4+. (A HotJava port is being planned.)

We use Javascript on UNIX and Dynamic Data Exchange (DDE) on Windows to interact with the browser, unlike some other systems like Web Browser Intelligence (WBI) [3] or Third Voice which install a client-side proxy. Unlike PowerBookmarks, we do not use a server-side proxy for monitoring clicks. Memex monitors the network performance and reassigns page fetching and analysis jobs dynamically between client and server. We believe this is an essential feature because a client may wish to connect to a geographically remote server which has a poorer Internet connection, or vice versa.

1.2. Features for archiving and analysis

Memex provides a platform for capturing hypertext and meta-data based on content as well as surfing events, in a structured manner. This lets us build a collection of interrelated and cooperative programs that mine the Memex traces. We discuss the major functions below.

*Bookmarks **are** history.* Browsers make an unnecessary distinction between *history* and *bookmarks.* The prevalent view is that bookmarks are valuable links deliberately archived by the user, whereas history is the list of all visited pages, long and mostly useless, therefore suitable for purging now and then. However, the rapidly increasing volume-to-cost ratio of disks makes it unnecessary to discard *anything* from our personal browsing trails, if only the resulting mass of data can be organized and analyzed usefully and effectively (features browsers do not provide).

Note that Memex does not directly undertake to archive the actual contents of the surfed pages. Our design should make it quite simple to interface Memex to other content and usage archives such as **Alexa Internet**[13] or the **Internet Archive**[14]. This will give additional benefits like never losing an obsolete page.

Learning folder structure. We claim that users create bookmarks sparingly only because of the complexity of creating and maintaining structure in their bookmark collection. If the user has a collection of topically coherent *folders*, Memex will learn to guess, using a hypertext topic learning algorithm, the best placement of new history entries. Thus the entire browsing experience of the user will be structured into topics[15].

Proposing folder structure. Interests and topics evolve with time. A narrow topic may grow until it becomes diffused, warranting a finer subdivision. Memex can propose, based on document similarity, a subdivision of pages belonging to a folder, which can lead to a better (re-)organization of the subtopics associated with that folder.

Trails and topical contexts. An extremely common question, unanswered by current browsers, is of the form: 'Where was I when I was last browsing about classical music?' Studies have shown that visiting Web pages is most strongly visualized using spatial metaphors: your context is 'where you are' and where you are able to go next [22].

Once Memex analyzes history as described above, it becomes possible to reconstruct the recent behavior of the user w.r.t. any topic. This is a valuable feature to return to a goal-directed browsing session and resume with context.

Synthesizing a taxonomy for the community.

[13] http://www.alexa.com

[14] http://www.archive.org/

[15] It has been pointed out that users may create folders which are not dependent on the contents of pages, but other features. If these features cannot be exposed to our learning programs, there is little hope for the learners. But content-based classification is by far the most common case we have seen.

Memex is best distinguished from bookmark archival services by its ability to synthesize a topic taxonomy from the browsing and bookmarking habits of a user community. This can be used in turn for better folder management and additional discovery of relevant resources from the Web.

1.3. Related work

1.3.1. Bookmark storage services

Internet start-ups have been quick to discover the annoyance of surfers maintaining multiple bookmark files and the opportunity of a central, networked bookmark server. We can list several sites which, using Javascript or a plug-in, import existing Netscape or Explorer bookmarks and thereafter let the surfer visit their Website and maintain it using CGI and Javascript: **Yahoo Companion** [16], **YaBoo** [17], **Baboo** [18], **Bookmark Tracker** [19] and **Backflip** [20] are some examples. Some services like Third Voice enable surfers to attach public or private annotations to any page they visit.

Netscape [21] itself has a 'roaming access' feature which is a convenient utility that can 'FTP' (actually LDAP and HTTP are used) the user's configuration, history and bookmarks to the client at the beginning of a session and 'FTP' them back to the server at the end of the session. No content-based analysis is involved.

Purple Yogi [22] will provide a private client-side browser assistant which will monitor browsing and searching actions and use this data to refine future search results. The technology is not published and the system is not available at the time of writing. No community-level mining seems involved.

Our work is closest in spirit to three well-known and similar systems, VistaBar, PowerBookmarks and the Bookmark Organizer.

VistaBar [23] is a browsing assistant application (later integrated into **Alta Vista Discovery** [23]) that lives on the Microsoft Windows desktop and attaches to the active browser using the DDE (Dynamic Data Exchange) interface. It provides bookmarking, annotation, indexing, find-similar, find-referrer, and classification into a shared Yahoo topic taxonomy. We have been greatly influenced by VistaBar's technique of interaction with the browser.

PowerBookmarks [24] [20] is a semi-structured database application for archiving and searching bookmark files. By visiting the PowerBookmarks site, the user gets 'a browser within the browser' which has controls for navigation and bookmarking that are provided as CGI forms by the PowerBookmarks site. PowerBookmarks uses Yahoo! for classifying the bookmarks of all users. In contrast, Memex preserves each user's view of their topic space, and reconciles these diverse views at the community level. Furthermore, PowerBookmarks does not use hyperlink information for classification or for synthesizing communities.

The Bookmark Organizer [21] is a useful client-side solution for personal organization via clustering and classification, but does not provide community-level themes or topical surfing contexts.

1.3.2. Mapping tools

Several visualization tools have been designed recently that explore a limited radius neighborhood and draw clickable graphs. These are often used for site maintenance and elimination of dead links. Mapuccino and Fetuccino from IBM Haifa are well known examples [4,15]. There is also a mature research literature on *graph drawing*: embedding graphs in the plane or in 3-D space so as to enhance some desirable properties such as reduced edge crossing, hierarchy separation, etc. Spring and Clan Graph Decomposition are some of the well-known techniques [17,27]. Our context viewer could benefit from better drawing techniques.

1.3.3. Supervised and semi-supervised learning

Supervised learning of document topics has been researched extensively in recent years [1,2,6,10,14, 19]. However, less is known about how to best integrate hypertextual features, and specifically how to exploit diverse patterns of individual bookmarking as

[16] http://www.yahoo.com/r/cm
[17] http://www.yaboo.dk
[18] http://www.baboo.com
[19] http://www.bookmarktracker.com
[20] http://www.backflip.com
[21] http://www.netscape.com
[22] http://purpleyogi.com
[23] http://discovery.altavista.com/
[24] http://www.ccrl.neclab.com/webdb/

new features. Unsupervised clustering is a classical field for structured data sources [16]. The clustering problem becomes harder in high-dimensional spaces such as text. Some well-known systems for clustering text are HyPursuit [28], Grouper [29] and Scatter-Gather [11]. Clustering is also related to structure discovery [25].

1.3.4. Resource discovery

Content- and hyperlink-based Web resource discovery has been extensively researched since 1996 [7,9,18]. In most such systems, discovery is deliberate: either a keyword-based query has to be entered (as in the HITS and Clever topic distillation systems) or topic nodes in a taxonomy have to be explicitly populated with examples and marked for exploration (as in the **Focused Crawler** [25]). For ad-hoc similarity search, Netscape's browser provides a 'find similar' button. However, a single page may not provide sufficient context information to discover important, related resources. Dean and Henzinger have provided an enhanced 'find-similar' algorithm [12].

Memex is well-suited to drive the resource discovery process. By synthesizing a topic taxonomy specific to the interest of a user community, Memex provides input for topic-based resource discovery algorithms [9].

[25] http://www.cs.berkeley.edu/~soumen/focus

1.4. Organization of this paper

The paper is organized as follows. Section 2 discusses the architecture and implementation details, design decisions, etc. It also introduces the look-and-feel of the Memex client to the end-user. Section 3 elaborates on the back-end mining techniques used to provide the client features. These involve understanding statistical relations between terms, documents and folders. Section 4 concludes the paper, with a wish-list for uniform and robust APIs for applets to interact with browsers, and a summary of ongoing and future work.

2. System architecture

Using the Memex client (Fig. 1) should not need any software installs or browser updates. In view of secure firewalls, proxies, and ISPs' restrictions on browser setups, the client should communicate with the server over HTTP. The data transferred should be encrypted if desired to preserve privacy.

On the server side (Fig. 1), the system should be robust and scalable. It is important that the server recovers from network and programming errors quickly, even if it has to discard one or two client events. For both client and server we also want a rapid prototyping environment. It should be possi-

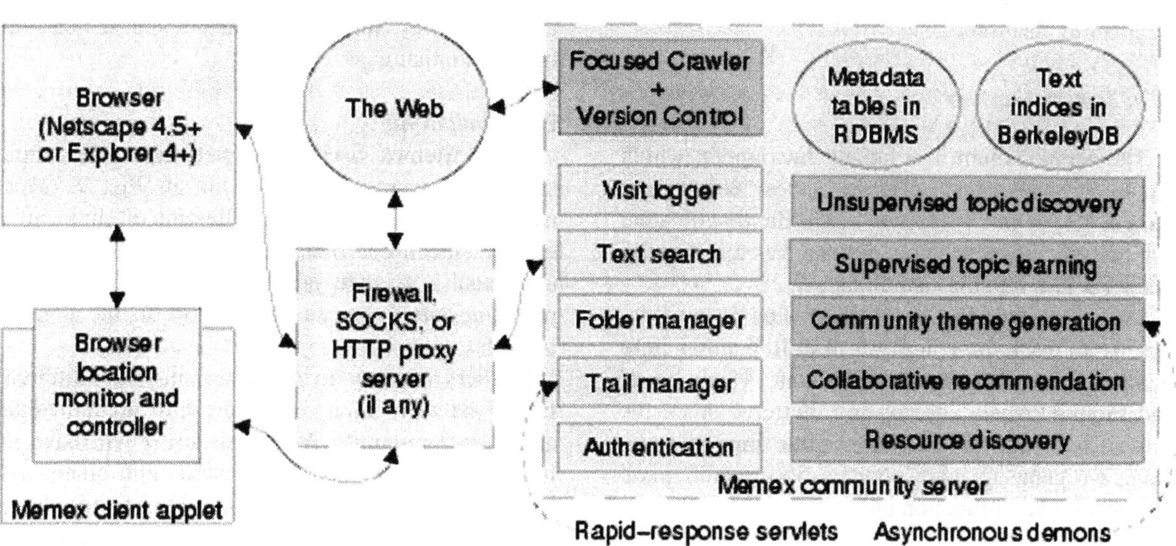

Fig. 1. Block diagram of the Memex system.

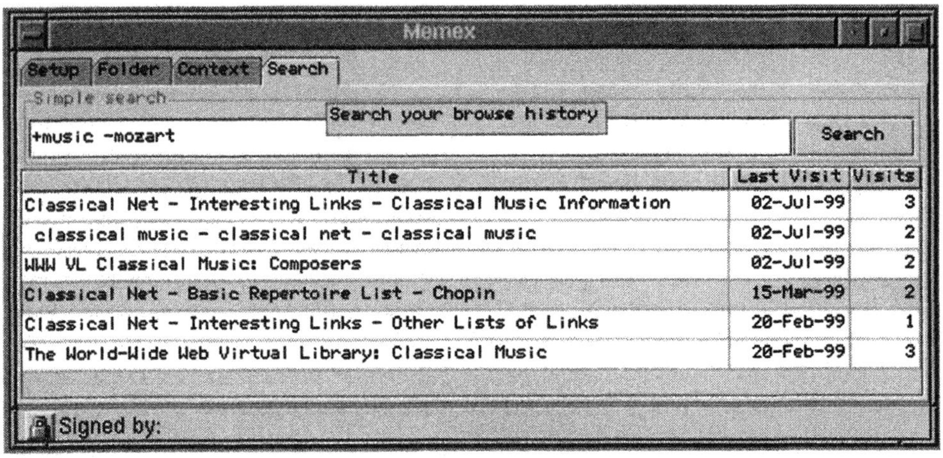

Memex

Setup | Folder | Context | Search

Simple search

+music -mozart

Search your browse history

Search

Title	Last Visit	Visits
Classical Net - Interesting Links - Classical Music Information	02-Jul-99	3
classical music - classical net - classical music	02-Jul-99	2
WWW VL Classical Music: Composers	02-Jul-99	2
Classical Net - Basic Repertoire List - Chopin	15-Mar-99	2
Classical Net - Interesting Links - Other Lists of Links	20-Feb-99	1
The World-Wide Web Virtual Library: Classical Music	20-Feb-99	3

Signed by:

Fig. 2. The Search tab enables boolean and free text search over all archived surfing history. Results can be sorted by various columns.

ble to distribute updates and new features effortlessly to users.

The Memex client is an applet that interacts with the browser and connects to the Memex server over HTTP. The server consists of servlets that perform various archiving and mining functions autonomously or triggered by client action. An important aspect of the engineering is the division of labor between the client and the server. Another interesting aspect of the server architecture is the loose data consistency model supported across text and user metadata in a relational database and text indices stored in lightweight storage managers. More details are given in Section 2.2.

2.1. Client-side design

The Memex client is a signed Java applet which can be invoked from a Memex server Website, or using a `.html` and a `.jar` or `.cab` file downloaded to local disk (a faster option, but one has to manually check for new versions and updates).

The main challenge with client-side system design is to pack in a host of useful features into small and precious screen real estate. Many users find browser panels already too cluttered since the days of Lynx and Mosaic. After quite some dummy trials, we came up with about a 500-by-400 pixel panel with several function tabs.

2.1.1. Search tab

Memex shows a three-way privacy choice: the user can choose not to archive clicks, to archive them as his/her private data, or share it with others. If and when the user so permits, page visits are reported to the server. The client and server cooperate to populate server-side tables with node, link, and visit meta-data, as well as a full-text index. Currently we handle only HTML, but we plan to add PS and PDF, which will be very useful for users in the academic community. The Search tab, shown in Fig. 2, enables boolean and free text search over the full text of surfing history. The responses can be sorted in a number of ways and clicking on a response takes the browser to that page.

2.1.2. Folder tab

Each Memex user has a personal folder/topic space shown in the Folder tab in Fig. 3. Most users will already have a collection of links in a browser-specific format. Memex can import these and attach it to their personal space as shown (Import-*timestamp*), it can also export to the popular formats.

Folders are key to characterizing and differentiating between topics of interest to an individual and to a community. Yet, some users will have no folder structure in their bookmarks, and others will keep accumulating bookmarks which are not placed in any folder (by default, in the root folder which characterizes 'any topic').

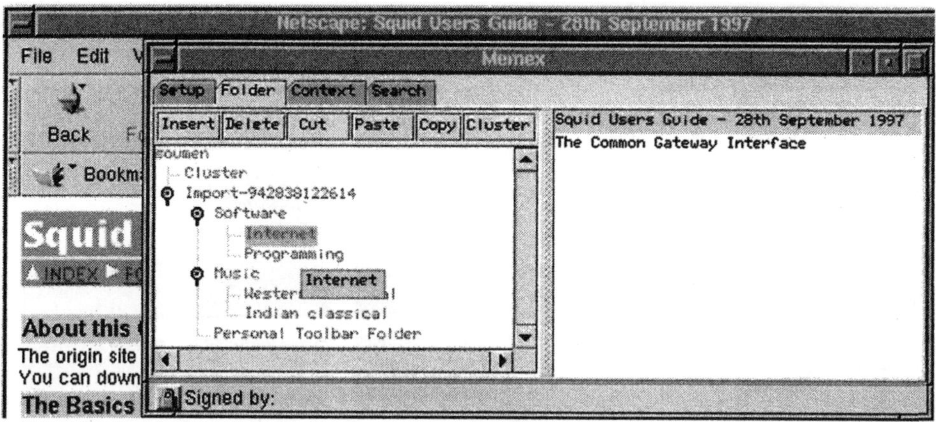

Fig. 3. Each user has a personal folder/topic space. The user can import existing browser-specific bookmark folders into Memex, which by default go into the '*log-in*/Import-*timestamp*' directory. Folders and their contents can be edited freely. The special 'Cluster' folder is explained later in Section 3.3.2.

Thus for both initial and continual use, surfers need two functions: *discovering* a topic taxonomy and *maintaining* it. If the user needs suggestions for (re-)organizing a set of URLs, s/he copies them into the special folder marked 'Cluster' in Fig. 3 and clicks the Cluster button. The user can then evaluate the result and cut and paste acceptable folders into the regular space.

Users will not manually classify most of their history. Memex will do this lazily in the background, populating the right panel with URLs whose folder membership has been 'guessed,' visually flagged. The user can then correct mistakes in folder assignment by cutting and pasting [26]. This constitutes valuable training by the user, and helps Memex more accurately reflect the user's notion of topics.

2.1.3. Context tab

Studies have shown that visiting Web pages is best expressed using spatial metaphors: your context is 'where you are' and 'where you are able to go' next [22]. Users surf on many topics with diverse priorities. Because browsers have only a transient context (one-dimensional history list), surfers frequently lose context when browsing about a topic after a time lapse.

[26] We cannot use drag-and-drop in many places because the full set of Java Foundation Classes functionality is not available from most browsers' JVM.

Once Memex has guessed the folders for unclassified history pages, providing a topical context becomes possible. Figs. 4 and 5 show how selecting a folder lets the user resume their browsing on a topic 'from where they left off'. A user-configurable parameter determines how many of the most recent nodes are shown.

As the user continues on the trail, new nodes get added to the graph. It may not be possible to classify these in real time. New nodes will be added to the display, and if/when the server responds with a folder assignment, nodes that do not belong to the currently selected folder may be dropped from the display.

Apart from restriction by topic, it is also possible to restrict context by site. Web surfing often involves fanning out and backing up. Mapping a small neighborhood of the current page being viewed lets the user perform these maneuvers with less effort. We also plan to integrate backlinks into the Context tab [8].

2.2. Server-side design

System design on the server side is guided by the concerns of robustness and scalability. We used a 3-tier approach (applet communicates with servlets which use JDBC to connect to relational databases) for two main reasons.

HTTP tunneling. Firewalls and proxies will often forbid non-HTTP traffic. Although several data-

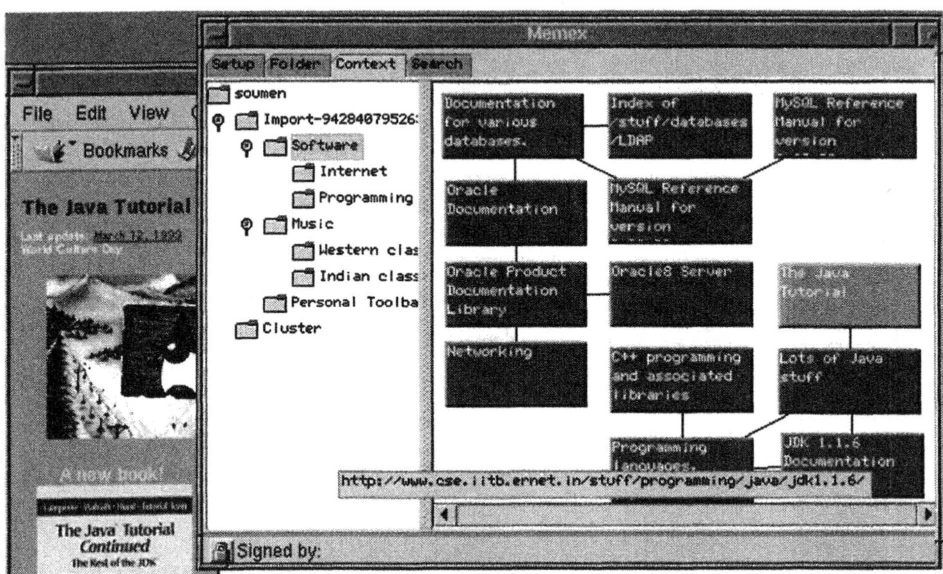

Fig. 4. The Trail tab shows a read-only view of the user's current folder structure. All pages visited by the user are (lazily) classified by Memex into the folders. When the user selects a folder, Memex shows (a configurable number of the) most recently browsed pages which belong to the selected topic, reminding the user of the latest topical context. In the screen-shot above, the chosen folder is */Software.*

base and middleware vendors are starting to provide HTTP tunneling support with JDBC, we wanted a lightweight solution for simplicity and efficiency.

Authentication and access control. Relational databases provide table- and view-level access control to users having log-in IDs on the host machine. In our case, access control information is itself in the tables.

Fig. 6 shows the basic entities represented in the Memex server: users, Web pages, visits, links, and folders. The database design needs to address the issues of efficient history archival taking care of user preferences, authentication, and storage of semi-structured HTML documents.

Server state is managed by two storage mechanisms: a relational database (RDBMS) such as Oracle or DB2 for managing meta-data about pages, links, users, and topics, and a lightweight Berkeley DB storage manager to support fine-grained term-level data analysis for clustering, classification, and text search. Storing term-level statistics in an RDBMS would have overwhelming space and time overheads.

An interesting aspect of the Memex architecture is the division of labor between the RDBMS and Berkeley DB. Planning the architecture was made non-trivial by the need for asynchronous action from diverse modules. There are some servlet events that must be guaranteed immediate processing. Typically, these are generated by a user visiting a page, or deliberately updating the folder structure. With many users concurrently using Memex, the server cannot analyze all visited pages, or update mined results, in real time. Background demons continually fetch pages, index them, and analyze them w.r.t. topics and folders. The data accesses made by these demons have to be carefully coordinated. This would not be a problem with the RDBMS alone, but maintaining some form of coherence between the meta-data in the RDBMS and several text-related indices in Berkeley DB required us to implement a loosely consistent versioning system on top of the RDBMS, with a single producer (crawler) and several consumers (indexer and statistical analyzers). Fig. 1 shows a block diagram of the system.

3. Mining the Memex archive

In this section we describe the core algorithms that run on the databases maintained by the Memex front-end. We also report on our experiences with

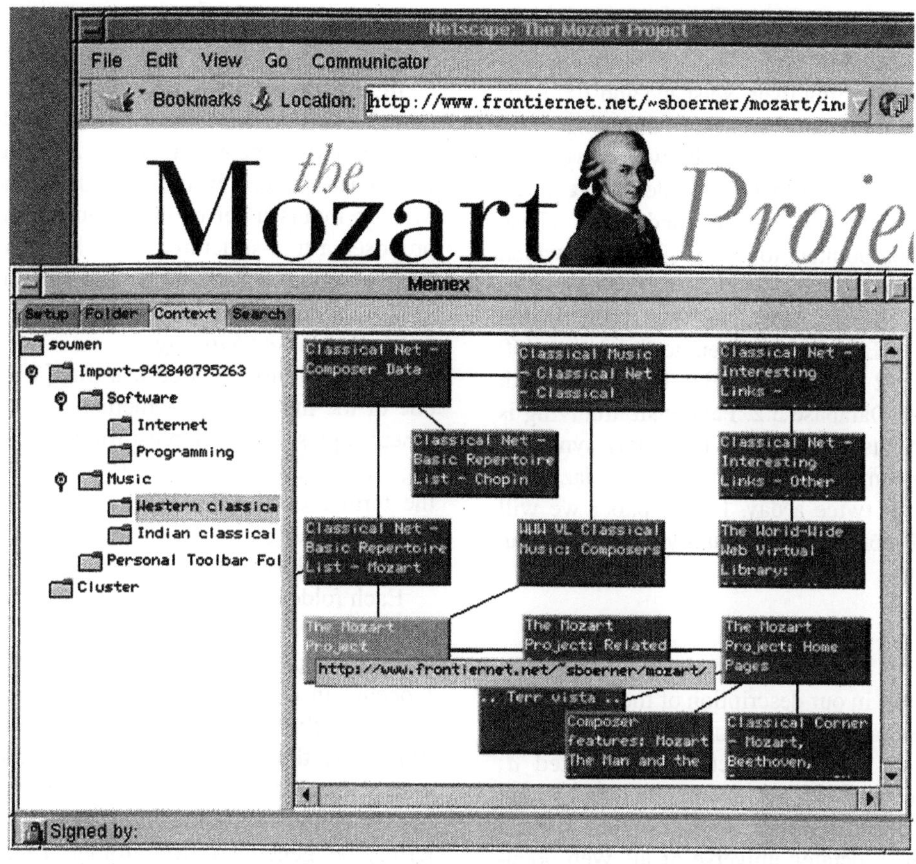

Fig. 5. Changing the selection to */Music/Western Classical* instantly gives the user a new topical context. The current/latest page is highlighted.

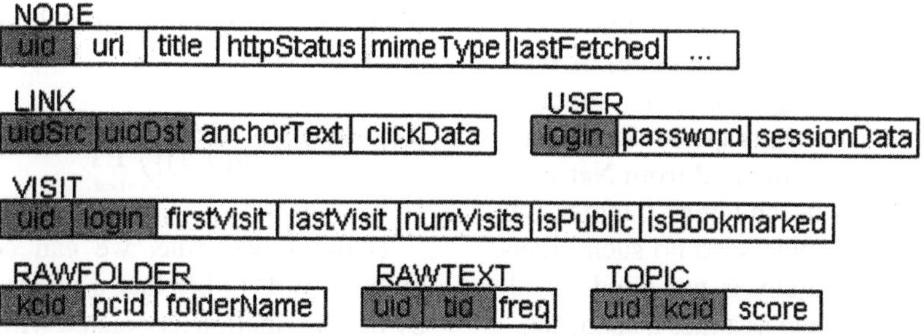

Fig. 6. The schema for server-side data. RAWFOLDER, TOPIC and RAWTEXT are processed into text indices for search, clustering and classification. Primary keys are dark. RAWTEXT is stored as a gzipped binary object for space efficiency. Inverted indices and folder are stored in Berkeley DB.

some of these algorithms. Most of our client features concern the analysis of relations between people, pages and folders (topics). (Although we provide a text-search capability over the history, we regard this as a standard feature.)

3.1. Experimental test-bed

For continuity, we shall inline our experimental results into the following subsections as we formulate problems and design solutions. For our experiments we obtained bookmark files from 23 Web surfers. They are Web-savvy but not computer scientists. After converting their Netscape and Explorer bookmark to a common format and throwing away default folders inserted by those browsers, we were left with 223 folders. All but two folders were at the first level; for simplicity we flattened those. These folders together pointed to 1693 URLs, of which 1424 were distinct.

Memex server-side code has been implemented in Java and JDBC. It has been tested on a 450 MHz Pentium 2 running RedHat Linux 5.2 with IBM Universal Database 5.2. Page visit archiving is real-time, but classification and taxonomy synthesis take several minutes. These are performed lazily by demons once or twice a day. In this paper we will be concerned more with the quality of results than running times.

3.2. Data models

As mentioned in our description of the Memex architecture (Section 2), the main entities represented in our analyses are Web documents, denoted d; hyperlinks, denoted (d_1, d_2); people, denoted p; and folders, also called topics or classes, denoted f. Each person has an associated universe of all Web documents s/he has ever seen, called the history $H(p)$. These documents are connected by hyperlinks, some of which have been traversed by the user.

Each person also owns a tree-structured hierarchy of folders (which may be just the root node). A typical user will start by importing their folder structure from their browser. Because Netscape bookmarks are stored in a flat file, a folder imported from Netscape will have an ordering on its children. Internet Explorer uses directories for folders, so no such ordering exists. The folder hierarchy is not fixed for all time, but our discussion below assumes a snapshot.

Folders reflect the owner's notion of topics and their refinement. Some of the documents in the history are 'bookmarked'; these are denoted $B(p)$. Bookmarks belonging to a particular folder are called $B(p, f)$. This means that a hyperlink to such a document is placed in some folder by a person. A document can be bookmarked by many people, but a person can only place a document in one folder. (In ongoing work we are relaxing this restriction.)

3.3. Learning and discovering topics

In supervised learning, the goal is to use the association between $B(p)$ and the folders to learn to assign documents in $H(p)\backslash B(p)$ to the user's predefined folders. In unsupervised topic discovery, Memex inputs a set of documents from $H(p)$ and proposes a tree-structured topic hierarchy that clusters the documents based on their contents.

3.3.1. Supervised learning

Statistical model-based learning [13,24] has been one of the most effective methods for learning document topics. In its simplest form, our text classifier regards a document d as a bag or multi-set of terms: the term t occurs $n(d, t)$ times and the document has a total length of $n(d) = \sum_t n(d, t)$. We do not consider multi-term phrases as features (yet).

Each folder f has an associated parameter $\theta(f, t)$ for each term t over a suitably large universe T of terms. Roughly, $\theta(f, t)$ is the rate at which term t occurs in documents belonging to folder f, and can be estimated from $B(p, f)$. One can regard $\theta(f, t)$ as the probabilities on the face of a die with T-faces, where $\sum_t \theta(f, t) = 1$. A document d that is known to belong to folder f (in statistical terms, be generated from folder f) is written as follows: first an arbitrary length $n(d)$ is decided, then the above die is tossed so many times, and the terms corresponding to the faces that come up written down. Thus the probability of generation of the document is:

$$\Pr(d|f) = \binom{n(d)}{\{n(d,t)\}} \prod_{t \in d} \theta(f, t)^{n(d,t)}. \tag{1}$$

Using Bayes rule, we can conversely find the probability $\Pr(f|d)$ that a document was generated by the distribution associated with a given folder.

It turns out that modeling the text alone does not give sufficient classification accuracy, because people tend to bookmark pages with little textual and much graphical content, as well as many links. In Section 3.3.3 we will discuss how to improve the accuracy of folder assignment using co-placement of URLs in folders. The Memex engine continually scans the `NODE` table in search of new classifications to do, and updates the `TOPIC` table.

3.3.2. Unsupervised learning

Topics will change with time, and users will reorganize their folder structure. The most common requirement for reorganization is refinement of a topic: the user's initial notion of a topic may be broad and shallow, but with time, the user collects a large number of links under that topic, which now needs to be refined into subtopics. This is a classic case of unsupervised learning or clustering [16].

An extension of the vector space model [26], similar to the bag-of-words model is used for clustering documents. In the basic vector space model, each document d is represented as a point in multi-dimensional Euclidean space; each dimension is a term t, and the coordinate in that dimension is $n(d, t)$[27]. Documents are normalized to have L_2 norm equal to one.

The similarity $s(d_1, d_2)$ between unit-length documents d_1 and d_2 is the cosine of the angle between their vectors, i.e., the inner product $\langle d_1, d_2 \rangle$. Since the role of clustering is to find large similar sets of documents, we use the definition of self-similarity of a set Γ from the Scatter-Gather system [11]:

$$s(\Gamma) = \frac{1}{|\Gamma|(|\Gamma| - 1)} \sum_{d_1, d_2 \in \Gamma, d_1 \neq d_2} s(d_1, d_2). \qquad (2)$$

[27] Various scale factors such as term frequency times inverse document frequency (TFIDF) are often used, but we omit these details for clarity.

We use a hierarchical agglomerative approach [11,16,21], in which we initially have each document to be clustered in its own group Γ, and at each step, that pair (Γ, Δ) is merged which leads to the maximum $s(\Gamma \cup \Delta)$. This step is repeated until only one group is left with all documents in it.

3.3.3. Exploiting hints from folder membership

Suppose a page d has to be classified for a person p_1, where d has already been bookmarked in some folder c_2 by another user p_2. Suppose many other members of c_2 have been bookmarked by p_1 as being in folder c_1; then there is reason to guess that d may belong to c_1 too. More generally, regarding p_2's folders as a *reference* taxonomy (such as Yahoo!), we can take all of p_1's bookmarked pages, and run them through p_2's classifier. We also run d through p_2's classifier, obtaining its class $c_{p_2}(d)$. We consider all documents D from p_1 which are in this same class, and guess the most frequently occurring class label (from p_1's folder system) as the class for d.

This experiment was performed with the first level of Yahoo!. The results shown in Fig. 7, while intuitive, are quite instructive: almost half the time, user folders are pairwise consistent at the first level of Yahoo! There is also a mild locality effect: if the folder is represented in HTML (as in Netscape) and two URLs are a short distance apart, this makes it more likely that their Yahoo-topics are the same.

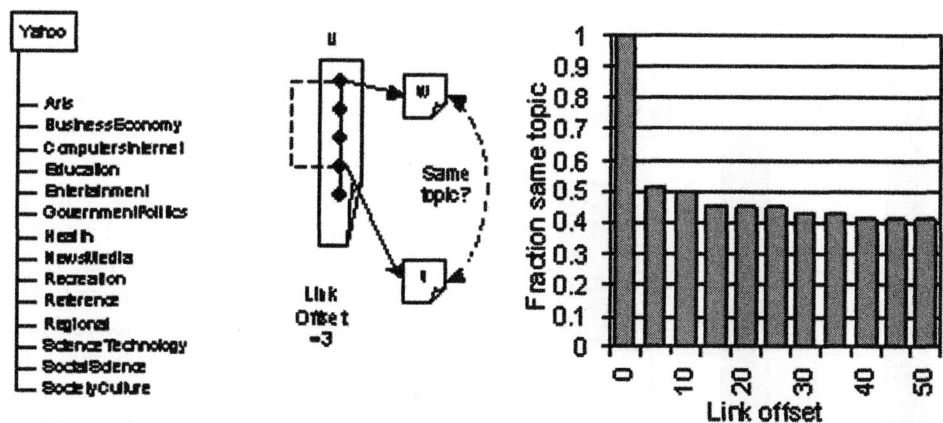

Fig. 7. Verification that folders tend to be reasonably coherent as judged by a reference taxonomy. Pairs of URLs were selected from our Netscape bookmark collection, the page fetched, its frequent terms formed into a query, and this query classified using Yahoo, to see if both belong to the same Yahoo class. The fraction of times this happens is plotted against the distance (in number of intervening out-links) between the two URLs.

This suggests the following algorithms:

(1) Build text-based classifiers for all users p.

(2) We are given a document d to classify under p_1. Find d in other users' folders to find a set of folders C_2. (If d is not found in anyone else's folders then fail.) Next we have two variants, *folder* and *locality*.

(3) (Folder) Classify all documents under each folder in C_2 as per p_1's folder system. Consider the majority class as the class for d.

(4) (Locality) Suppose d is found in a folder c_2. Call this offset zero. Scan left and right until d_{-i} and d_{+j} are found in c_2, such that d_{-i} and d_{+j} are classified under p_1. If these classes are the same, output this class, otherwise, fail.

We measured recall (coverage) and precision (for what fraction of documents was the proposed class approved by the user). The results are shown in Fig. 8. Because the algorithm might flag a failure, recall is not perfect, but, in the cases where it can generate a folder assignment, the answer is significantly more accurate than using the text accumulated by user p_1 alone. Basically, an extended vocabulary contributed by the whole community makes far more accurate classification. We also verified that our collection of bookmarks were reasonably spread out across Yahoo's taxonomy, hitting eight of the fourteen classes of Yahoo shown in Fig. 7.

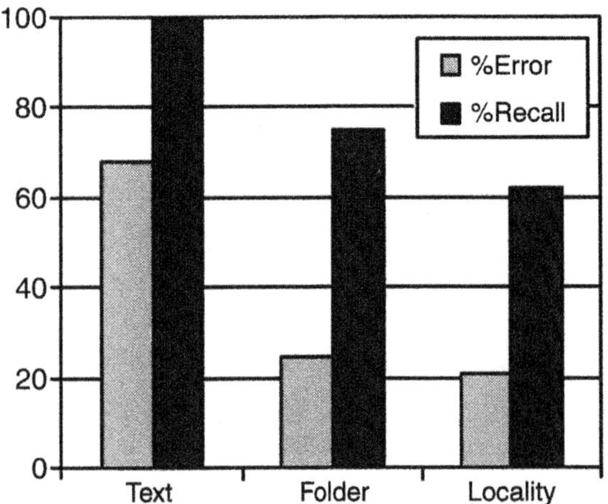

Fig. 8. Results of exploiting folder co-location and link locality for classifying history.

3.4. The community taxonomy synthesis problem

The results above clearly show that *relations* between pages (such as being placed in same or different folders) are quite important as features for learning. HyPursuit [28] recognized this, but only offered hand-tuned weights for different feature types. Similar issues also arise in combining text, HTML tags, and hyperlinks into one model. Basically, we want to exploit the fact that co-location of documents in a folder hint at a semantic similarity which should be factored in together with our text-based similarity in Eq. 2).

3.4.1. Problem formulation

The input to the problem is the following initial graph N with three layers of nodes, D for documents, G for groups, and F for folders. Initially, there are as many groups as documents, and each document is in its own group. We convert the original bipartite relation between folders and documents into a tripartite representation to help standardize the graph cost models in our algorithms (in Section 3.4.2). There is a many-to-many mapping between folders and groups. A folder maps to at least one group and vice versa. The F-to-G and G-to-D mappings induce each folder f to include a set of documents D_f; these sets can be overlapping. D_f induces a term distribution T_f for folder f. We have various choices for characterizing T_f, some will be discussed later.

The goal of taxonomy synthesis is to derive a new three-layer graph N'. In N', $D' = D$ and $F' = F$, but G' and the connecting edges have been modified. Groups no longer contain a single document in general. The F-to-G' mapping is many-to-many as before. Associated with such three-layer graphs is a cost model. N has some initial cost. N' has some (hopefully) lower cost. Our goal is to derive N' with as small a cost as possible (see Fig. 9).

Now we design the cost model. The cost of a graph is the sum of the *distortion* and *mapping* costs. Distortion is a measure of how much the new term distribution T'_f of a folder differs from the 'true' distribution T_f (i.e., what is the penalty for changing the red subgraph). Distortion is denoted $D(T'_f \| T_f)$, also called the Kullback–Leibler distance. For the initial graph, distortion is zero by definition. The

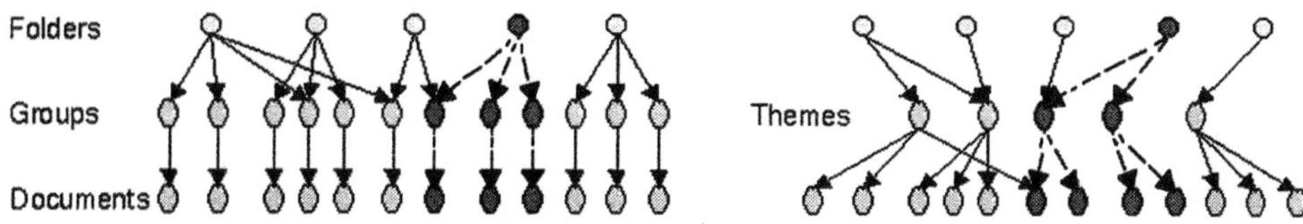

Fig. 9. A formulation for the community taxonomy synthesis problem. Initially, each document is a group or theme by itself. Finally, we want a highly compressed representation of the tripartite mappings while distorting the term distributions for original folders (induced by the dark subgraphs with dotted edges) as little as possible.

mapping cost is a measure of the complexity of specifying G or G' and the edges in the graph.

Why do we seek to minimize the total cost? This leads to the 'simplest' description of the data, which is the best model, according to the Minimum Description Length principle. For many formulations of the distance measure, the problem is at least as hard as set-cover. Hence we resort to fast heuristics.

3.4.2. Heuristics and experience

The first problem is with the KL-distance. Over the set of terms T, let I_{T} range through the set of all possible *document events*; i.e., all possible vectors of term counts. The KL distance of a distribution T' with reference to another distribution T is:

$$D(T' \| T) = \sum_{I_{\mathsf{T}}} \Pr_T(I_{\mathsf{T}}) \log \frac{\Pr_T(I_{\mathsf{T}})}{\Pr_{T'}(I_{\mathsf{T}})}. \qquad (3)$$

The KL distance is not symmetric; however, it is non-negative and zero only for $T = T'$. The sum over all I_{T} is impractical to compute; even with the binary model, there will be $2^{|\mathsf{T}|}$ terms in the sum. Therefore, we take recourse to inter-term independence as in the bag-of-words model, except we use a *binary* document model, where word counts are ignored for simplicity.

$$D(T' \| T) = \sum_t \phi_t(\log \phi_t - \log \phi'_t) + (1-\phi_t)(\log(1-\phi_t) - \log(1-\phi'_t)) \qquad (4)$$

where $\phi_t = \Pr_T(t)$ and $\phi'_t = \Pr_{T'}(t)$.

Mapping costs for the edges can be approximately estimated by encoding the vertex IDs using a Shannon-optimal code. Details are omitted for lack of space.

With this two-part cost model in mind, we will compare three heuristics: *LeafUnion*, *SingleBest* and *Bicriteria*, as specified next.

LeafUnion. This is the trivial mapping corresponding to each folder simply maintaining a 'link' to the original documents. The distortion cost is zero by definition, but the mapping cost is large. The mapping is not exploiting document similarities at all.

SingleBest. Once the hierarchical agglomerative cluster tree (dendogram) is built, each folder is assigned to exactly one node in the dendogram. Here we are trying to cut down on mapping cost, hoping that the clustering step will bring related documents under the same subtree so that few links will suffice. This may entail significant distortion.

Bicriteria. This heuristic recognizes the tension between mapping and distortion cost. It starts similar to hierarchical agglomerative clustering (HAC) with a frontier of groups, each with one document. In the end, it has a smaller frontier, with the original folders mapping to the surviving groups. Unlike in *SingleBest*, a folder can map to many groups.

The algorithm is a greedy cost-based sequence of merges. When two groups Γ and Δ on the frontier are evaluated for merging, we do not use $s(\Gamma \cup \Delta)$ as the goodness measure. Assuming all folder pointing to either Γ or Δ will point to their union, we estimate

- the decrease in mapping cost because of edges saved by the merger,
- the increase in distortion because of extraneous documents in Γ and Δ, and
- perform that merge with minimum increase in overall cost.

Sample results are shown in Fig. 10. As expected, *LeafUnion* pays too much in mapping cost and *SingleBest* pays too much in distortion cost. Although evaluation of discovered themes is necessarily subjective at this point, inspection of *Bicriteria* results showed that themes *were* being factored out of partially overlapping topics corresponding to folders of different users.

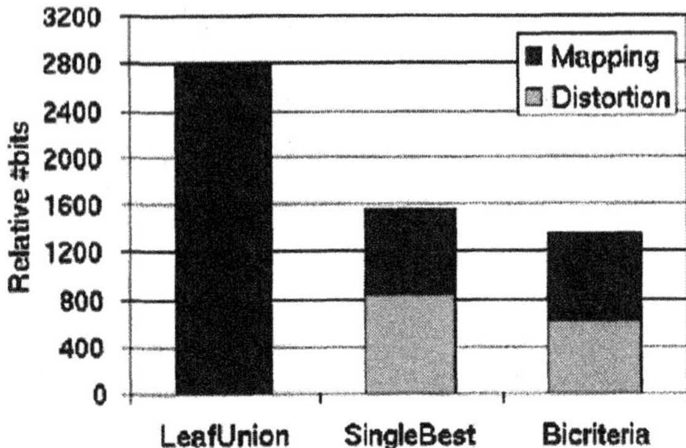

Fig. 10. Results for taxonomy synthesis, showing that both collocation in folders and term distribution are important features.

4. Conclusion

We have reported on the design and implementation of Memex, a companion on the Web for individuals and communities. We have demonstrated that Memex is effective in archiving and analyzing surfing patterns to bring out useful organization of surfing history. Specifically, Memex helps organize history into coherent topics, and relate topics between different users. It also enables search over the entire surfing history.

4.1. Status report

Memex is currently being tested by local volunteers after which we will make the service available for beta-testing. The client-side code runs on Netscape and Internet Explorer. A port is planned for HotJava and the JDK1.2 plug-in. Initial user feedback is that the client is intuitive and easy to use. However, the server is non-trivial to set up; knowledge of Apache, JServ, and some relational database like Oracle is needed. We wish to make server installation much simpler using scripts.

4.2. Recommendations for browser vendors

Anyone who develops serious Java code for browsers knows that Java's promise is sadly distant. The leading browsers differ significantly in their security API, as well as the API through which applets can get access to browser information. Dealing with this lack of standardization was quite difficult. Even Javascript differs across browsers; on Explorer there is a dialect called JScript.

The Memex client monitor module communicates with the browser using DDE on Windows and LiveWire (Java-to-Javascript communication tool) on UNIX, to read browser state variables.

We hope that our experiences with grafting Memex into the two most popular browsers will encourage the vendors of these browsers to evolve a more friendly and uniform browser interaction API which they or we can use for more advanced browser assistants. Specifically, we recommend that trusted applets get a handle to a `Browser` object which can then be used to interact closely with the browser:

```
import com.netscape.browser.*;
// or import com.ms.browser.*;
Browser b = Browser.getBrowser();
Vector wl = b.getBrowserWindows();
BrowserWindow bw = (BrowserWindow) wl.elementAt(0);
bw.addPageLoadListener(new PageLoadListener() {
    public void actionPerformed(LoadEvent le) {
        URL location = le.getURL(), referrer = le.getReferrer();
        String title = le.getTitle();
        Vector outLinkList = le.getOutlinks();
        // use these ...
    }
};
```

It goes without saying that the non-standard security and browser interaction interfaces cause much grief and prevent any serious browser-based Java developer from writing simple, clean code. The Java

2 plug-in will remove the security-related problems, but not the browser interaction issues.

4.3. Interaction with other systems and meta-data

Planned extensions to Memex involve integration with a caching proxy using ICP (Internet Caching Protocol). Currently, proxies associate URLs with content, and run variants of weighted LRU strategies. We believe that Memex, by analyzing content, can more intelligently advice the proxy about prefetching and eviction policies, thus tuning to the community that it serves. Memex can also help proxy servers detect mirror sites, reducing pressure on the cache. This will in turn help Memex to get its bulk of document fetches from the proxy.

The **Resource Description Framework** [28] (RDF), based on XML, provides a uniform syntax for defining and exchanging meta-data about Web pages in a format that can be manipulated by programs. Various communities are defining and agreeing on resource descriptions suited to their applications. In the context of Memex, a description language for topic taxonomies and associated resources, such as developed by the *Open Directory*, would be very useful. We intend to adapt that format to the description of individual and community interest profiles as well, through designing suitable description formats for folders and synthesized taxonomies.

Our premise is that Memex servers will find utility at the workgroup or organization level. In the next phase, we plan to develop and design protocols for interaction between distributed Memex servers for consolidating documents, topics, and communities across diverse geographical regions. Such cooperative analysis will help generate strategies for bandwidth and cache management for long-haul ISPs as well.

Acknowledgements

Thanks to S. Sudarshan for helpful discussions, to Hannes Marais for tips on using DDE, and to the reviewers for helping improve the presentation of the paper. Thanks to the School of Information Technology, IIT Bombay, for providing supplementary network resources during the work. Memex builds upon many pieces of public domain software: HTTPClient, Cryptix, JFlex, and Berkeley DB.

[28] http://www.w3.org/RDF/

References

[1] C. Apte, F. Damerau and S.M. Weiss, Automated learning of decision rules for text categorization, ACM Transactions on Information Systems, 1994, IBM Research Report RC18879.

[2] C. Apte, F. Damerau and S.M. Weiss, Towards language independent automated learning of text categorization models, in: SIGIR, 1994, IBM Research Report RC19481.

[3] R. Barrett and P.P. Maglio, Intermediaries: new places for producing and manipulating web content, in: 7th International World Wide Web Conference, Brisbane, 1998, Online versions: HTML, PDF.

[4] I. Ben-Shaul, M. Herscovici, M. Jacovi, Y.S. Maarek, D. Pelleg, M. Shtalheim, V. Soroka and S. Ur, Adding support for dynamic and focused search with Fetuccino, in: 8th World Wide Web Conference, Toronto, May 1999.

[5] V. Bush, As we may think, The Atlantic Monthly, July 1945, Online at http://www.theatlantic.com/unbound/flashbks/computer/bushf.htm.

[6] S. Chakrabarti, B. Dom, R. Agrawal and P. Raghavan, Scalable feature selection, classification and signature generation for organizing large text databases into hierarchical topic taxonomies, VLDB Journal, Aug. 1998, Invited paper, online at http://www.cs.berkeley.edu/~soumen/VLDB54_3.PDF.

[7] S. Chakrabarti, B. Dom, D. Gibson, J. Kleinberg, P. Raghavan and S. Rajagopalan, Automatic resource compilation by analyzing hyperlink structure and associated text, in: 7th World Wide Web Conference (WWW7), 1998, Online at http://www7.scu.edu.au/programme/fullpapers/1898/com1898.html.

[8] S. Chakrabarti, D.A. Gibson and K.S. McCurley, Surfing the Web backwards, in: WWW, Vol. 8, Toronto, May 1999, Online at http://www8.org.

[9] S. Chakrabarti, M. van den Berg and B. Dom, Focused crawling: a new approach to topic-specific web resource discovery, Computer Networks 31 (1999) 1623–1640 (first appeared in the 8th International World Wide Web Conference, Toronto, May 1999), Available online at http://www8.org/w8-papers/5a-search-query/crawling/index.html.

[10] W.W. Cohen, Integration of heterogeneous databases without common domains using queries based on textual similarity, in: SIGMOD, Seattle, WA, 1998, ACM.

[11] D.R. Cutting, D.R. Karger and J.O. Pedersen, Constant interaction-time scatter/gather browsing of very large document collections, in: Annual International Conference on Research and Development in Information Retrieval, 1993.

[12] J. Dean and M.R. Henzinger, Finding related pages in the

world wide web, in: 8th World Wide Web Conference, Toronto, May 1999.

[13] R. Duda and P. Hart, Pattern Classification and Scene Analysis, Wiley, New York, 1973.

[14] S. Dumais, J. Platt, D. Heckerman and M. Sahami, Inductive learning algorithms and representations for text categorization, in: 7th Conference on Information and Knowledge Management, 1998, Online at http://www.research.microsoft.com/~jplatt/cikm98.pdf.

[15] M. Hersovici, M. Jacovi, Y.S. Maarek, D. Pelleg, M. Shtalheim and S. Ur, The Shark-Search algorithm — an application: tailored web site mapping, in: 7th World Wide Web Conference, Brisbane, Apr. 1998, Online at http://www7.scu.edu.au/programme/fullpapers/1849/com1849.htm.

[16] A.K. Jain and R.C. Dubes, Algorithms for Clustering Data, Prentice-Hall, Englewood Cliffs, NJ, 1988.

[17] T. Kamada and S. Kawai, An algorithm for drawing general undirected graphs, Information Processing Letters 31 (1989) 7–15.

[18] J. Kleinberg, Authoritative sources in a hyperlinked environment, in: ACM–SIAM Symposium on Discrete Algorithms, 1998, Online at http://www.cs.cornell.edu/home/kleinber/auth.ps.

[19] D. Koller and M. Sahami, Hierarchically classifying documents using very few words, in: International Conference on Machine Learning, Vol. 14, Morgan-Kaufmann, Los Altos, CA, July 1997, Online at http://robotics.stanford.edu/users/sahami/papers-dir/ml97-hier.ps.

[20] W.-S. Li, Q. Vu, D. Agrawal, Y. Hara and H. Takano, PowerBookmarks: a system for personalizable Web information organization, sharing and management, Computer Networks 31, May 1999 (first appeared in the 8th International World Wide Web Conference, Toronto, May 1999), Available online at http://www8.org/w8-papers/3b-web-doc/power/power.pdf.

[21] Y.S. Maarek and I.Z. Ben Shaul, Automatically organizing bookmarks per content, in: Fifth International World Wide Web Conference, Paris, May 1996.

[22] P.P. Maglio and T. Matlock, Metaphors we surf the Web by, in: Workshop on Personalized and Social Navigation in Information Space, Stockholm, 1998.

[23] H. Marais and K. Bharat, Supporting cooperative and personal surfing with a desktop assistant, in: Proc. of UIST'97, ACM, Oct. 1997, pp. 129–138, Online at http://www.research.digital.com/SRC/personal/Johannes_Marais/pub/uist97/uist97paper.pdf.

[24] T. Mitchell, Machine Learning, McGraw-Hill, New York, 1997.

[25] R.R.P. Pirolli and J. Pitkow, Silk from a sow's ear: extracting usable structures from the web, in: ACM CHI, 1996.

[26] G. Salton and M.J. McGill, Introduction to Modern Information Retrieval, McGraw-Hill, New York, 1983.

[27] F.-S. Shieh and C. McCreary, Directed graphs by clan-based decomposition, in: Graph Drawing, 1995, pp. 472–482.

[28] R. Weiss, B. Velez, M.A. Sheldon, C. Nemprempre, P. Szilagyi, A. Duda and D.K. Gifford, HyPursuit: a hierarchical network search engine that exploits content-link hypertext clustering, in: Proc. of the Seventh ACM Conference on Hypertext, Washington, DC, Mar. 1996.

[29] O. Zamir and O. Etzioni, Grouper: a dynamic clustering interface to Web search results, in: 8th International World Wide Web Conference, Toronto, May 1999, pp. 283–296, Elsevier, Amsterdam.

Soumen Chakrabarti received his B.Tech in Computer Science from the Indian Institute of Technology, Kharagpur, in 1991 and his M.S. and Ph.D. in Computer Science from the University of California, Berkeley in 1992 and 1996. At Berkeley he worked on compilers and runtime systems for running scalable parallel scientific software on message passing multiprocessors. He was a Research Staff Member at IBM Almaden Research Center between 1996 and 1999. At IBM he worked on hypertext analysis and information retrieval. He designed the *Focused Crawler* and part of the *Clever* search engine. He is currently an Assistant Professor in the Department of Computer Science and Engineering at the Indian Institute of Technology, Bombay. His research interests include hypertext information retrieval, Web analysis and data mining.

Sandeep Srivastava, **Mallela Subramanyam**, and **Mitul Tiwari** are junior-year students in the Computer Science and Engineering Department at IIT Bombay. Their research interests include hypertext databases and data mining.

Web-collaborative filtering: recommending music by crawling the Web

William W. Cohen [a,*], Wei Fan [b,1]

[a] AT&T Shannon Laboratories, 180 Park Avenue, Florham Park, NJ 07974, USA
[b] Department of Computer Science, Columbia University, New York, NY 10027, USA

Abstract

We show that it is possible to collect data that are useful for collaborative filtering (CF) using an autonomous Web spider. In CF, entities are recommended to a new user based on the stated preferences of other, similar users. We describe a CF spider that collects from the Web lists of semantically related entities. These lists can then be used by existing CF algorithms by encoding them as 'pseudo-users'. Importantly, the spider can collect useful data without pre-programmed knowledge about the format of particular pages or particular sites. Instead, the CF spider uses commercial Web-search engines to find pages likely to contain lists in the domain of interest, and then applies previously proposed heuristics to extract lists from these pages. We show that data collected by this spider are nearly as effective for CF as data collected from real users, and more effective than data collected by two plausible hand-programmed spiders. In some cases, autonomously spidered data can also be combined with actual user data to improve performance.

1. Introduction

One key issue facing the field of computer science is how to exploit the vast amount of knowledge available on the Web. The main problem, of course, is that the bulk of information on the Web is designed to be read by humans, not by machines.

To date, most programs that collect knowledge from the Web fall into two classes. The first class of knowledge-collection programs are the spiders employed by search engines (like AltaVista) to index the Web. These spiders have limited understanding of the pages they collect, and hence only limited use (for instance, keyword search) can be made of the collected data. However, because the spiders are simple, and because they can access all sites equally well, large amounts of data can be easily collected. Below, we will call this the 'oblivious spider' approach to data collection.

The second class of knowledge-collection programs are those employed by Web-based 'information integration systems' (e.g., Whirl [2], Ariadne [8], and others). These systems extract information from selected Web pages, and then store the information in an internal database. This approach allows more complex queries to be answered; however, to extract database-like information from a Web page requires either learning (e.g., [9,12]) or programming (e.g., [6]) a special 'wrapper' for that page. Because constructing wrappers is time-consuming, Web-based information integration systems tend to operate in limited domains.

Below we will call this data collection strategy the 'programmed spider approach'. We use this term to emphasize the difference between this approach

* Corresponding author. E-mail: wcohen@research.att.com
[1] E-mail: wfan@cs.columbia.edu

to data collection and the use of oblivious, search-engine-like spiders, which do not need to be modified in any way to work on a new domain.

In this paper, we show that oblivious spiders can collect data that are useful for the task of 'collaborative filtering' (CF) [7,15–17]. In collaborative filtering, entities are recommended to a new user based on the stated preferences of other, similar users. (For example, a CF system might suggest the band 'The Beatles' to the user 'Fred' after noticing that Fred's tastes are similar to Kumar's tastes, and that Kumar likes the Beatles.) More specifically, we will describe an oblivious spider that uses heuristics to collect lists of musical artists from the Web. These lists can be used to supplement or replace user ratings in a collaborative filtering system. Using actual user-log data, we measure the performance of several CF algorithms. We show that running a CF algorithm using data collected from an oblivious spider is nearly as effective as using data collected from real users, and better than using data collected by two plausible programmed spiders. In some situations, the oblivious-spider data can also be combined with user-log data to improve CF performance.

The work reported here complements previous research demonstrating that CF can be improved by using 'content' features obtained from the Web by programmed spiders (e.g., [1,5]). The main novel contribution of this paper is to show that CF can also be performed using data collected by oblivious spiders. The main technical innovations exploited in this paper are new, robust methods for extracting lists of entities from HTML pages [3]. The list-extraction methods we use here were originally developed to facilitate building 'wrappers' (that is, programmed spiders) for information integration systems.

2. A collaborative filtering problem

2.1. The dataset

We elected to explore the issues discussed above for a specific CF problem — the problem of recommending music. The primary dataset we used was drawn from user logs associated with a large (2800 album) repository of digital music, which has been made available for limited use within the AT&T intra-net for experimental purposes. A server log records which files were downloaded by which IP addresses. Files on the repository obey certain naming conventions, which can (usually) be used to determine which musical artist — i.e., performer or composer — is associated with a downloaded file. (Some files are not associated with any single artist, but rather with some group or collection of artists. In the experiments reported below, downloads of these files were simply discarded.) Thus, by analyzing the log, it is easy to build up a record of which musical artists each client IP address likes to download.

We took 3 months worth of log data (June–August 1999), and split it into a baseline 'training set' and a 'test set' as follows. The test set consists of all downloads over the 3-month period associated with IP addresses that connected for the first time in August. The training set consists of all remaining downloads, i.e., downloads associated with IPs connecting in June or July; hence, the IP addresses in the training and test sets are disjoint. Recall that CF involves recommending 'entities' (e.g., movies, books, etc.) to 'users'. In our experiments, we take musical artists to be entities, and assume that each client IP address corresponds to a different user. We constructed binary preference ratings by further assuming that a user `U` 'likes' an artist `A` if and only if `U` has downloaded at least one file associated with `A`. We will denote the 'rating' for artist `A` by user `U` as `rating(U,A)`: hence `rating(U,A)=1` if IP address `U` has downloaded some file associated with `A` and `rating(U,A)=0` otherwise. If `rating(U,A)=1` then we say `U` has given `A` a 'positive' rating; otherwise, we say `U` has given `A` a 'negative' rating.

The baseline datasets are fairly large: there are 5095 downloads from 353 IP addresses in the test set, 23,438 downloads from 1028 IP addresses in the training set, and a total of 981 different artists associated with these downloads. It should be noted that in this dataset, almost all ratings (nearly 98%) are negative; thus, one would expect that more information about a user's preferences would be conveyed by a positive rating than by a negative rating.

It should also be noted that the baseline training and test datasets are only an approximate reflection of real user preferences. One problem is the assumption that each IP address corresponds to a distinct user. In fact, while many IP addresses are static and correspond to a single-user workstation, some of the IP addresses are dynamic, and hence correspond to a session by some user, or worse, to a set of distinct sessions by different, unrelated users. Further, some users also access music from several fixed IP addresses (e.g., a home PC and a work PC), and conversely some fixed IP addresses might be used by several distinct users (e.g., a home PC that is used by several family members). Another issue is that many users only download a handful of files; in this case, it is certainly wrong to assume that all artists *not* downloaded are disliked.

However, although the data are noisy, it seems reasonable to believe that metrics based on it can be used for comparative purposes. We note also that CF systems which can learn from this sort of noisy 'observational' data (e.g., [10,14]) are potentially far more valuable than CF systems that require explicit noise-free ratings.

2.2. Evaluation method

Many different evaluation metrics have been proposed for CF [5]. In choosing an evaluation metric we found it helpful to assume a specific interface for the recommender. Currently, music files are typically downloaded from this server by a browser, and then played by a certain 'helper' application. By default, the most popularly used helper-application 'player' will play a file over and over, until the user downloads a new file. We propose to extend the player so that after it finishes playing a downloaded file, it calls a CF algorithm to obtain a new recommended artist `A`, and then plays some song associated with artist `A`. If the user allows this song to play to the end, then this will be interpreted as a positive rating for artist `A`. Alternatively, the user could download some new file by an artist `A'`, overriding the recommendation. This will be interpreted as a negative rating for artist `A`, and a positive rating for `A'`.

For the sake of completeness, we will assume that the player can also be invoked without specifying the first song to be downloaded, leading to the following user interaction with the proposed 'smart player':

For `t=1,...,T`:

(1) PLAYER: call the CF algorithm to get a recommended artist, `A[t]`. Play some song by `A[t]`.

(2) USER: either
- reject the song, by explicitly requesting another music file, or
- accept the song (implicitly), by allowing it to play to completion.

This interaction can be simulated using the test user-log data. To simulate a user's actions, we accept a recommendation for `A` if `A` is rated positively by the test user, and reject it otherwise. When a recommendation is rejected, we simulate the user's choice of a new file by picking an arbitrary positively rated artist. We continue the interaction until every artist rated positively by the test user has been recommended (or else has been explicitly requested by the test user). We denote the total number of trials `T` associated with the simulated interaction as `LEN(U)`.

Note that `LEN(U)` is bounded by the number of artists rated positively by `U`. (We assume that the CF algorithm will recommend each artist at most once.) For most of the users, `LEN(U)` is relatively small: the median value of `LEN(U)` is only 10. This is shown in Fig. 1, which plots `T` against the total number of users `U` in the test set such that `LEN(U)>=T`. We will typically truncate all of our result graphs at `T=50`, as beyond this point there are only a handful of distinct users.

We define the 'accuracy' of a simulated interaction between a CF method `M` and a test user `U`, denoted `ACC(M,U)`, to be the number of times the user accepts a recommendation, divided by `LEN(U)`. For instance, if ten recommendations were made, and three were accepted, then accuracy would be 30%. We define `ACC(M,U,t)` to be the accuracy over the first `t` trials. To simplify notation, we will drop the first argument and write `ACC(U)` or `ACC(U,t)` when `M` is clear from context.

3. Baseline experimental results

3.1. Algorithms used

The CF algorithms we used all have the following behavior. For each trial `t`, the algorithm is called with two inputs:

(1) a list of artists `A[1],...,A[t-1]` that have been explicitly rated by some user `U`; and

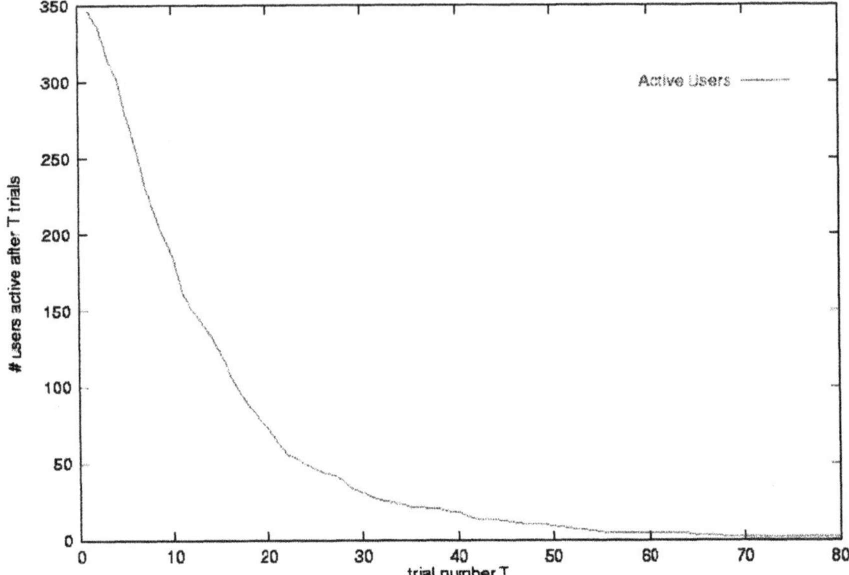

Fig. 1. The number of test-set users active at trial t.

(2) the ratings for these artists: rating(U,A[1]), ...,rating(U,A[t-1]).

The algorithm then associates a numeric 'score' with each artist A. A higher score is interpreted as stronger recommendation for A. Finally, a specific artist A[t] is recommended by picking the highest-scoring A that does not appear in the list of previously rated artists, A[1],...,A[t-1]. Below we will denote the score of A by SCORE(A).

The algorithms used were the following.

• *Popularity* (POP). This algorithm simply scores each artist according to the total number of users in the training set that rate the artist favorably. That is, if U[1],...,U[n] are all the users in the training set, then:

SCORE(A) = rating(U[1]) + ··· + rating(U[n])

This algorithm is perhaps the simplest plausible recommendation scheme that depends on the training set; it is analogous to using the 'Billboard Top-40' to pick music or the New York Times' best-seller list to pick books. Although it pre-dates any academic research on CF, it is often hard to beat according to objective standards of performance.

• *K-nearest neighbor* (K-NN). This algorithm first finds the k users U[1],...,U[k] whose preferences are most similar to U. Specifically, we define the 'distance' between U and U′ relative to the set of artists A[1],...,A[t-1] to be:

DIST(U,U′) =

|rating(U,A[1])-rating(U′,A[1])| + ···

+ |rating(U,A[t-1])-rating(U′,A[t-1])|

The K-NN algorithm first finds the k users U[1], ...,U[k] in the training set that are closest to U according to this metric. Ties are broken by preferring neighbors U[i] with fewer positive ratings. (Recall that most ratings are negative; hence agreement on positive ratings is less likely a priori than agreement on negative ratings.) Artists are then scored according to their popularity in this set of neighboring users:

SCORE(A) = rating(U[1],A)+ ···

+ rating(U[k],A)

The K-NN method is one of the most widely used CF algorithms (e.g., [7,16]). In our experiments we used k=10.

• *Weighted majority* (WM). This is a slight modification of a recommendation algorithm suggested by Nakamura and Abe [13]. This algorithm has strong formal foundations [4], and can be implemented quite efficiently (at least in principle). It is based on computing 'weights' for a large number of very simple recommendation strategies called 'experts', each of which predicts ratings for some subset of artists and users. Let `r` be a learning rate, where `0<r<1`. If an expert `E` has made `p` correct predictions and `n` incorrect predictions in the past, then the 'weight' of `E`, denoted `WT(E)`, is defined as

```
WT(E) = (2-r)^p * r^n
```

Now fix an artist `A` and a test user `U`, and let `E[1],...,E[m]` be all the experts that predict `rating(U,A)=1`, and let `F[1],...,F[n]` be all the experts that predict `rating(U,A)=0`. Then the score of `A` is defined to be the difference of the total weight on the 'positive' (`E`) experts and the total weight on the 'negative' (`F`) experts:

```
SCORE(A) = WT(E[1]) + ··· + WT(E[n])
         - WT(F[1]) - ··· - WT(F[n])
```

In our implementation we used `r=0.5`, and these experts:

(1) For each pair of artists `A[i]` and `A[i′]`, we define an 'expert' `E[i,i′]` which predicts that all users will rate `A[i]` and `A[i′]` identically.

(2) For each pair of users `U[j]` and `U[j′]`, we define an 'expert' `E[j,j′]` which predicts that `U[j]` and `U[j′]` will rate all artists identically.

(3) For each artist `A[i]`, we define an expert `E[i]` which predicts that all users will rate `A[i]` positively.

The first two sets of experts follow Nakamura and Abe [13], and the final set of experts was added to improve performance on the first few trials for a user. (Without these experts, performance is no better than random guessing when `t=1`.) We also found that performance was somewhat better when the number of correct predictions `p` assigned to an expert did not include cases in which a negative training-set rating was correctly predicted on the basis of another negative training-set rating. (Again, since most ratings are negative, this sort of agreement is quite likely to happen by random chance.) In recommendation, experts are trained on all ratings from the training set, as well as the known preferences from the test user `U`.

• *Extended direct Bayesian prediction* (XDB). This algorithm was motivated by the observation that, under relatively weak statistical assumptions, it is possible to recommend optimally (or nearly so) in the first two trials of each interaction. For instance, on trial `t=1`, the optimal prediction is clearly the one made by POP, if one assumes that users are i.i.d. For trial `t=2`, the situation is only slightly more complicated. Here we have one positive rating by the test user. Depending on the outcome of the first trial, we may or may not have one negative rating; however, since negative ratings carry little information, in either case we will ignore this. Now consider what the optimal behavior is given a single positive rating, i.e., a single artist `A[i]` that user `U` is known to like. Again assuming that users are i.i.d., the probability that `U` will like artist `A[j]` is simply:

```
Prob(rating(U′,A[j])=1 |
  rating(U′,A[i])=1)
```

where the probability is taken over all possible users `U′`. This probability can be easily estimated from the training data. In the experiments, we use an 'm-estimate' [11] for this probability, where `m=1` and the prior is simply the prior probability of a positive rating. Let `R(A[j],A[i])` denote this estimate. (Informally, `R(*,*)` measures the 'relatedness' of two artists.) For trial `t=2`, it is natural to use the scoring function `SCORE(A[j])=R(A[j],A[i])` in making a recommendation.

Unfortunately, this approach is hard use on later trials; after many artists have been rated, it is unlikely that there will be any previous users that exactly match all of a user's ratings, and so it becomes difficult to estimate the necessary statistics. Thus, we experimented with a simple ad hoc extension and approximation of this 'direct Bayesian' recommendation scheme. Consider an arbitrary trial `t`, and let `L[1], ... L[t-1]` be the artists that have been positively rated by `U`. The scoring system used by XDB for `t=1` is the same as that used by POP, and for `t>1` the scoring function is

```
SCORE(A) = 1-(1-R(A,L[1])) * ···
             * (1-R(A,L[t-1]))
```

Informally, `SCORE(A)` can be understood as `1-PENALTY(A)`, where `PENALTY(A)` is the probability that `A` is *not* 'related' to any `L[i]`, assuming independence of the `L[i]`'s. Notice that `SCORE(A)` equals `R(A,L[1])` when `n=1`. Empirically, XDB works quite well, particularly when `t` is small.

3.2. Collaborative filtering with user data

Before describing how oblivious spidering can be used to collect training data for CF algorithms, we will first evaluate these algorithms by training them on the baseline training data derived from the server logs, and then testing them on the baseline test data. Fig. 2 plots a trial number `t` on the x axis, and records on the y axis the average value of `ACC(U,t)` over all `U` such that `LEN(U)>=t`.

To summarize, all of the methods far outperform random guessing (which has an accuracy of about 0.02 on these data) and appear to give usefully accurate recommendations. XDB and K-NN perform best, while WM's performance is generally at best comparable to POP.

In order to determine if the difference between two CF methods `M1` and `M2` is statistically significant, we used a paired `t`-test to test the null hypothesis that the expected values of `ACC(M1,U)` and `ACC(M2,U)` are the same. According to this test, XDB and K-NN are both statistically significantly better than POP. However, XDB is not statistically significantly better than K-NN. Further experiments will focus on the behavior of XDB and K-NN.

In passing, we note that these curves are *not* conventional learning curves, in which prediction performance on a single problem is measured as a function of the amount of training data; in these curves, performance is averaged over a *different* set of users at each point `t`. This effect explains, for example, the upward-sloping shape of the results for POP, a non-adaptive recommendation strategy; clearly, it is easier to correctly guess preferred musical artists for users with many positive ratings than for users with few positive ratings.

3.3. Collaborative filtering with programmed spiders

As an additional baseline, we also implemented two recommendation systems based on data collected from programmed spiders. We wrote spiders that traversed a large on-line music database (Allmusic.com) and extracted information about the 'genre' and 'musical style' of each artist. Genres are broad categories of music, like 'jazz' or 'country', and

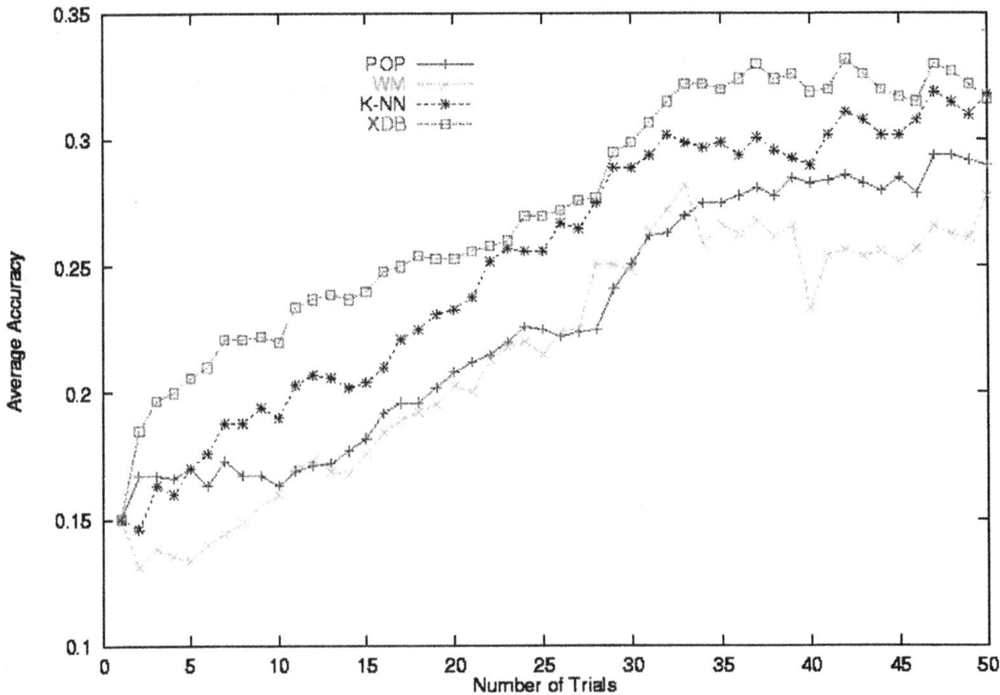

Fig. 2. Baseline results for four CF methods using server-log data.

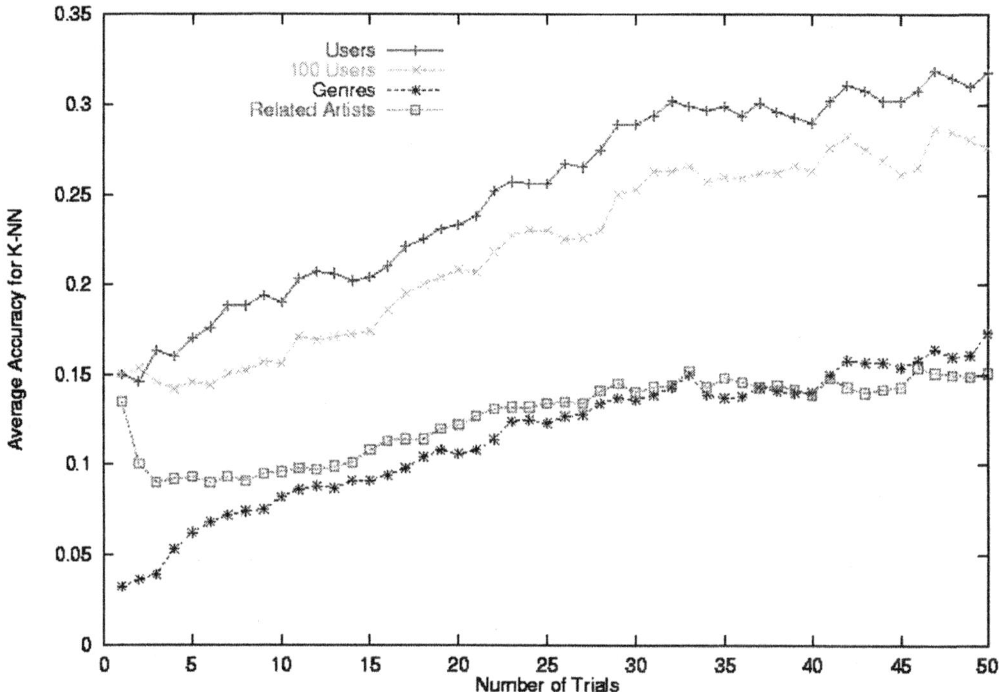

Fig. 3. Results for the K-NN algorithm using data collected by a programmed spider.

styles are narrow groupings of artists, like 'country boogie'. For each artist A, a list of 'related artists' was also extracted. Our spider used a relatively broad definition of 'related'; every artist that is mentioned in the on-line description of A is considered to be 'related to' A.

One plausible way to use genre or style information is to find genres that correlate with the user's preferences, and then recommend artists in these genres. We implemented a genre-based recommendation system using the K-NN algorithm described above. For each genre, we constructed a 'pseudo-user' that rates everything in the genre positively, and everything not in the genre negatively. We then used the standard K-NN algorithm described above, trained on these pseudo-users rather than the baseline training set, to make recommendations.

Used in this way, K-NN first finds genres (pseudo-users) that are correlated with the test user's positive ratings, and then recommends artists that play in these genres. The heuristics described above lead to a preference for relying on narrower groupings of artists, rather than broader categories (i.e., a preference for styles to genres), and for recommending artists that play in more than one correlated genre.

A similar approach was used to build a recommender that uses the related-artist information. In this case, each pseudo-user gives a positive rating to some artist A plus all artists 'related to' A. The K-NN algorithm was again used for recommendation. Thus our related-artist recommendation system is much like the genre-based recommendation system, where each set of related artists acts like a (very narrow) genre.

The results for these systems are shown in Fig. 3, which compares the genre-based recommender, the related-artist recommender, and the baseline K-NN recommender (trained on the user data). We also show results for K-NN trained on a subset of the baseline User dataset including only 100 distinct users. The 100-User subset is approximately equal in size to the related-artist and genre datasets (see Table 1). To summarize, the two programmed-spider recommendation systems are comparable in performance, with the related-artist system perhaps making slightly better recommendations when t is small.

Table 1
Sizes of the various datasets

Dataset	Nr. of users	Nr. of pos. ratings
User (baseline)	1,028	21,977
100 User	100	4,315
SPIDER/Log	1,539	26,917
SPIDER	1,894	48,878
SPIDER/Large	2,333	63,815
SPIDER/Phase 1	2,519	13,527
Related artist	639	5,104
Genre	613	4,623

However, performance with the programmed-spider datasets is statistically significantly worse than with either the User or 100-User datasets.

Similar results (not shown) are obtained if K-NN is replaced with the XDB or WM algorithm. We also note that there is relatively little difference between the baseline training set, with 1000-odd users, and the 100-user training set. This shows that the learning curve for CF in this domain is relatively flat; i.e., that little is gained by simply increasing the size of the training set.

4. An oblivious spider that collects CF data

In the experiments above, each training set could be represented as a set of users (or pseudo-users), together with a list, for each user, of the set of artists rated positively by that user. In the baseline experiments, these artist-lists were obtained by analyzing log data. Collecting this data requires the substantial effort of serving a large user community for a long period of time. It is natural to ask if there are any other ways in which sets of 'favorite artists' might be obtained, other than by examining user logs.

One possibility would be to conduct a series of Web searches with the goal of finding Web pages entitled something like 'My favorite musical artists', and then extracting the list of artists in that page by some automated means. Further reflection suggests that other pages which contain lists of musical artists could at least plausibly be used to train a CF algorithm like K-NN. As examples, a user interested in country blues might find her preferences are well correlated with a page titled 'Musical Influences of Robert Johnson'; a user interested in 'new age' music might find that her preferences are correlated with a page titled 'Top-selling New-Age Albums for the Week of September 13'.

We thus elected to build an oblivious spider that simply looks for lists of musical artists, or more generally, lists of items of some known type. The list-extraction part of our spider is based on heuristics for list-extraction introduced by Cohen [3]. The remaining portions rely on exploiting commercial Web-search engines to find pages likely to contain lists.

4.1. Extracting lists from a set of Web pages

We will first describe the heuristics for extracting lists from a set of Web pages. The page in Fig. 4 will be used as a running example.

Our routine for list extraction, henceforth `Find-Lists`, takes as input a set `N` of entity names and a set `URL[1],...,URL[n]` of URLs, and operates as follows.

```
<head>...</head>
<body>
<h1>Biff's Favorite Bands</h1>
<ul>
<li><b>Alice in Chains</b> - completely awesome!
<li><b>Smashing Pumpkins</b> - these d00des rock!!!
<li><b>Barry Manilow (NEW)</b> - check out all these
             great <a href="biffmp3.htm">MP3's</a>!!!
...
</ul>
</body>
```

Fig. 4. Part of an HTML page containing a list of musical artists.

Program `FindLists(N,URL[1],...,URL[n])`:

(1) Download each `URL[i]`, and parse the HTML markup of the downloaded Web page. (Web pages are parsed using the HTML parser included in Perl's `libwww` module.)

(2) For each HTML-tree node `n` that contains no more than 250 characters of non-markup text below it, construct a pair of the form `(Pos(n),Text(n))`, where `Text(n)` is all non-markup text that appears below node `n`, and `Pos(n)` is the concatenation of the URL for the page and the sequence of HTML tags that appear on the path from the root of the HTML-tree to `n`. The intuition here is that `Text(n)` is a candidate entity name (e.g., the name of some musical artist), and `Pos(n)` identifies a list of objects.

For instance, consider the sample HTML page above. The pairs extracted in this stage might include those in Table 2.

(3) From the set `S` of `(Pos,Text)` pairs computed above, and the set `N` of entity names, construct all tuples of the form `(Pos,Text,A)` such that `(Pos,Text)` is a tuple in `S`, `A` is an entity name in `N`, and the 'cosine similarity' between `Text` and `A` is at least 0.8.

'Cosine distance' is a measure of textual similarity that is widely used in information retrieval. We use the variant of cosine distance implemented in the WHIRL system [2], which can be conveniently used to perform the tuple-construction operation defined above.

For the sample HTML page above, the output of this stage would include the triples in Table 3.

Table 4
Final output

(http://lusers.com/~biff+body.ul.li.b,	'Alice in Chains')
(http://lusers.com/~biff+body.ul.li.b,	'The Smashing Pumpkins')
(http://lusers.com/~biff+body.ul.li.b,	'Barry Manilow')
...	

(4) Note that the tuples are now very close to being in the desired format, namely, entity names paired with lists to which they belong. The final step of `FindLists` is to filter the list of triples constructed above by removing all triples associated with positions that appear less than 4 times, and discarding the second component of each triple. The resulting set of position–entity pairs is the output of `FindLists`.

For the sample HTML page above, the final output of this stage would be the pairs in Table 4.

This output can be used as the input of a CF algorithm. Specifically, each position `P` represents a list of entities, and hence can be represented as a pseudo-user, where the pseudo-user for `P` rates positively exactly those entities that appear on the list `P` (that is, the set of entities `A` that appear in a pair with the position `P`).

While our example for `FindLists` is a single page, the implementation operates on a set of URLs, as some operations can be performed more efficiently if a large number of pages are processed in parallel. Experiments in a somewhat different context suggest that this sort of list extraction (based on

Table 2
Pairs extracted

(http://lusers.com/~biff+body.h1,	'Biff's Favorite Bands')
(http://lusers.com/~biff+body.ul.li,	'Alice in Chains - completely awesome!')
(http://lusers.com/~biff+body.ul.li.b,	'Alice in Chains')
(http://lusers.com/~biff+body.ul.li,	'Smashing Pumpkins - these (d00des rock!!!')
(http://lusers.com/~biff+body.ul.li.b,	'Smashing Pumpkins')
...	

Table 3
Output triples

(http://lusers.com/~biff+body.ul.li.b,	'Alice in Chains',	'Alice in Chains')
(http://lusers.com/~biff+body.ul.li.b,	'Smashing Pumpkins',	'The Smashing Pumpkins')
(http://lusers.com/~biff+body.ul.li.b,	'Barry Manilow (NEW)',	'Barry Manilow')
...		

HTML parse-tree positions and similarity to known entity names) is reasonably accurate [3]. For the purpose of CF, however, it is probably the case that a good deal of inaccuracy in the extraction step can be tolerated, simply because CF algorithms are tolerant of noise.

4.2. Design of the spider

The CF spider uses the FindLists routine to extract lists from Web pages identified using certain simple heuristics. The spider has two phases. Phase 1 constructs an initial set of entity-lists. This set of lists can be used in CF, but tends to have statistics very different from the user data described above, which limits its utility in CF. Phase 2 uses the Phase-1 entity-lists to build a second group of entity-lists with more representative statistics.

In Phase 1, the CF spider performs these actions.

(1) For each artist `A`, a Web search engine is invoked with the artist's name, and the top 100 URLs returns are recorded. In the music domain, this resulted in a list of 85,362 candidate URLs (using AltaVista as the search engine).

(2) The candidate URLs are filtered to find URLs that appear at least twice. (The assumption here is that these URLs are more likely to be lists.) In the music domain, there were 5268 duplicated URLs.

(3) The duplicate URLs are then passed to `FindLists`. In the music domain, this produced 2519 pseudo-users with a total of 13,527 positive ratings (i.e., position–entity pairs).

The entity-lists constructed by `FindLists` could be used directly in CF. Unfortunately, these lists tend to have somewhat unnatural statistics; in particular, due to the systematic nature of the search on artist names, obscure artists tend to be over-represented, and popular artists are under-represented, relative to the user data on which we intend to test the system. Phase 2 is intended to construct a more representative set of pseudo-users.

In Phase 2, the CF spider performs these actions.

(1) The CF spider finds the 1000 pairs of entity names that co-occur most frequently in the entity-lists constructed in Phase 1. This step was suggested by the observation that searching for a pair of artist names is likely to produce Web pages that are lists; furthermore, the co-occurrence statistics for the Phase-1 entity-lists are not too different from the co-occurrence statistics for the user data.

(2) The first few entries from this list of pairs are manually inspected, and pairs consisting of different artists with highly similar names (according to cosine distance) were removed. (Such pairs are an unfortunate by-product of the `FindLists` method.) In the music domain, four pairs were removed. We conjecture that results would be similar if this step were not performed.

(3) For each such pair `A[i],A[j]`, another Web-search was performed on this *pair* of names, in this case retrieving the top 10 URLs. We used Northern Lights as the search engine here, resulting 4326 unique downloadable URLs in the music domain.

(4) Finally, these URLs were processed with `FindLists`. This produced 1894 pseudo-users, with 48,878 positive ratings.

5. Results using obliviously collected Web data

Fig. 5 plots the performance of the K-NN algorithm using obliviously collected datasets. For comparison, we also plot the performance of K-NN on the baseline User training set, the 100-User subset of the baseline training set, and the related-artist dataset. The results for K-NN and the output of the oblivious CF spider are shown on the line labeled SPIDER. To summarize, SPIDER performs statistically significantly better than the related-artist dataset, but significantly worse than the User dataset. SPIDER is statistically indistinguishable from to the 100-User dataset.

We also evaluated two other obliviously collected datasets. SPIDER/Phase 1 is the output of Phase 1 of the spider. Results on this dataset are significantly worse than with SPIDER, demonstrating that Phase 2 is useful. SPIDER/Logs is the output of running Phase 2, starting with the baseline User training set instead of the output of Phase 1. Unlike the SPIDER dataset, the SPIDER/Log dataset cannot actually be constructed without having access to user logs, so it is not a viable replacement for this log data; however, it is nonetheless informative to consider

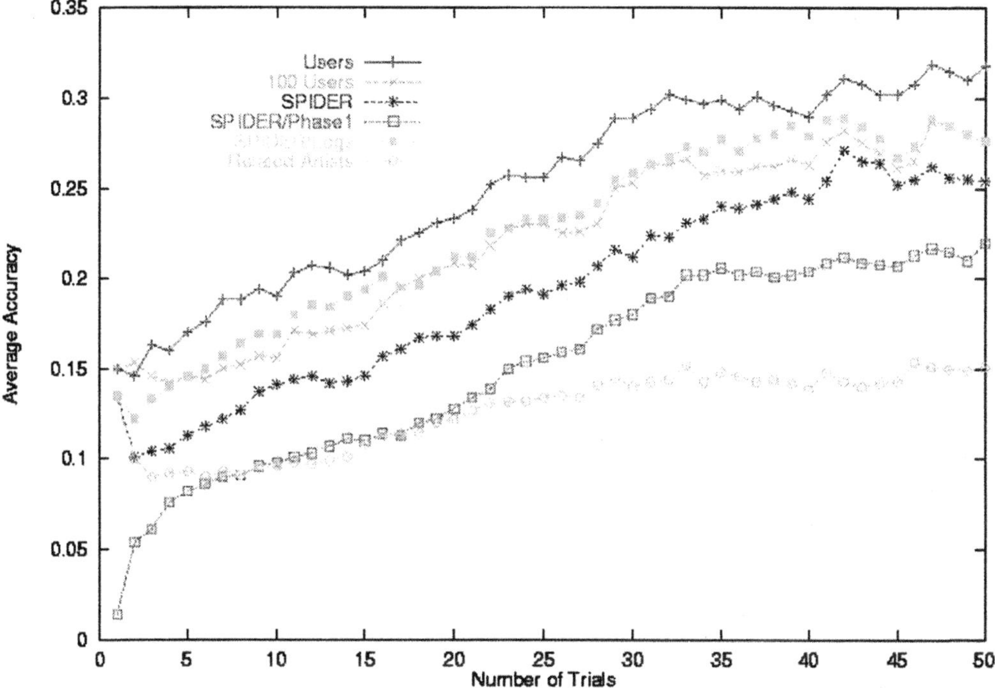

Fig. 5. Performance of the K-NN algorithm with User data, compared to data collected by an oblivious spider.

its performance. Performance with SPIDER/Logs is significantly better than with the SPIDER dataset, even though it is smaller (26,917 pairs with 1539 pseudo-users). This may indicate that even after Phase 2, the statistics of the data are still somewhat skewed relative to the user data. (We note that users of the music server are primarily employees of AT&T Research, a rather atypical population.)

Qualitatively similar results were obtained with the XDB, WM and POP algorithms. The results for XDB are shown in Fig. 6. In this case the SPIDER dataset is significantly better than the genre and related-artist datasets, but significantly worse than both the User and 100-User datasets.

XDB with the SPIDER/Logs dataset also performs quite well — in this case, significantly better than with the 100-User dataset. XDB with the SPIDER dataset is again somewhat better than K-NN with the SPIDER dataset; however, the difference is not significant.

Table 1 summarizes the size of the datasets explored thus far. Here the datasets are sorted by performance. We note that it is hard to construct a natural dataset of predetermined size, due to the wide variability in the size and quality of web pages unearthed by the SPIDER, and also the wide variability in `LEN(U)`. However, as previously noted, the learning curve appears to be fairly flat for this problem; e.g., the average difference in `ACC(u)` between the User and 100-User datasets is only about 2.5%. We thus conjecture that the primary differences between datasets is based on the nature of the information they contain, not their sizes. Note that the best-performing SPIDER datasets are comparable in size to the User dataset.

As an additional test of this conjecture, we built a larger SPIDER dataset (SPIDER/Large in the table) by repeating Phase 2 of the CF spider, using Google as the search engine, and collecting the top 30 URLs for each artist pair. (In building SPIDER, we collected the top 10 URLs.) Performance with SPIDER/Large is not significantly better than with SPIDER for any of the K-NN, XDB, or POP algorithms (in fact performance is slightly worse for two of the three algorithms) confirming the flatness of the learning curve.

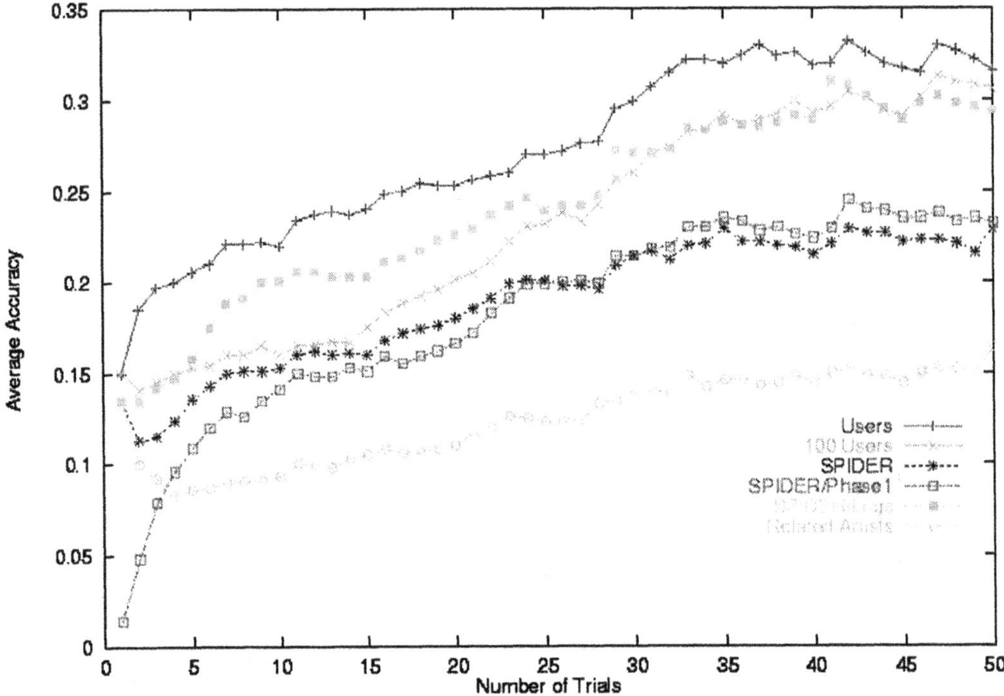

Fig. 6. Performance of the XDB algorithm with User data, compared to data collected by an oblivious spider.

6. Combining user data and obliviously collected data

We have thus far considered *replacing* user data for a CF algorithm with data collected by spiders. We will now consider *augmenting* user data with data collected by spiders, where 'augmenting' simply means adding to the first dataset all the pseudo-users from the second dataset. In augmenting user data with obliviously collected data, we primarily used the Spider/Log dataset, which was constructed by running Phase 2 of the CF spider with the user-log data as input.

Our results thus far are preliminary, but intriguing. Fig. 7 shows the result of combining the smaller 100-User training set with the Spider/Log dataset, and then using the K-NN algorithm. The augmented dataset shows a statistically significant improvement over the 100-User baseline.

Another statistically significant improvement (not shown) was gained by repeating this experiment with the XDB algorithm. Performance of the XDB algorithm was also significantly improved by augmenting the 100-User dataset with the related-artist dataset, or by the genre dataset. Interestingly, however, K-NN's performance did *not* improve by combining the 100-User dataset with either the related-artist dataset or the genre dataset. This suggests that obliviously collected data is in some settings more valuable than 'content' features.

Unfortunately, augmenting the complete User dataset with the SPIDER/Log data did not improve performance for either K-NN or XDB: in both cases, performance on the combined dataset is statistically indistinguishable from performance on the User dataset alone. However, the WM algorithm *is* statistically significantly improved by augmenting the User baseline training set with the Spider/Log dataset, as can be seen in Fig. 8.

7. Conclusions

We have considered replacing or augmenting user data for a collaborative filtering (CF) algorithm with data collected by spiders from the Web. This is a spe-

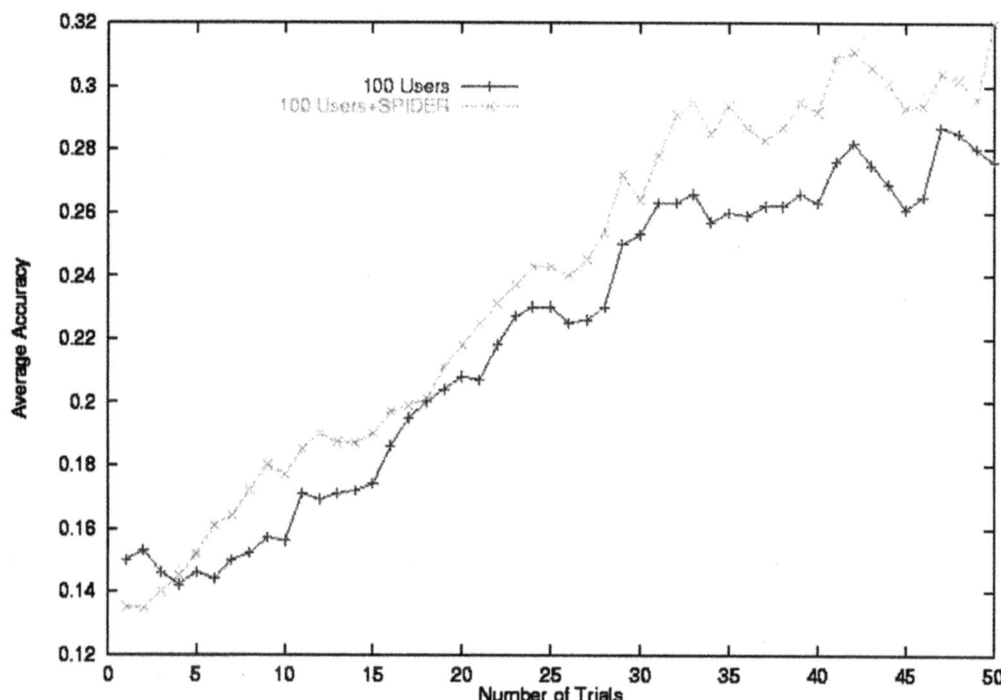

Fig. 7. Performance of the K-NN algorithm using the 100-User dataset augmented with obliviously collected Web data.

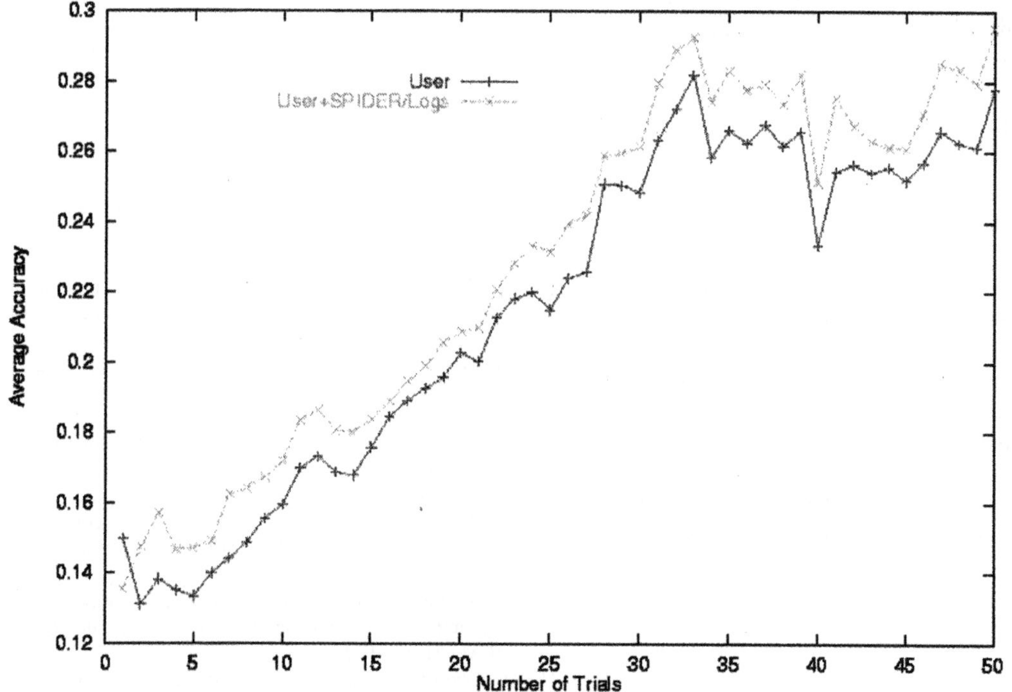

Fig. 8. Performance of the WM algorithm using User data augmented with obliviously collected Web data.

cial case of what we believe to be an extremely important research problem: namely, using automated methods to effectively exploit the vast amounts of information available on the Web.

Previous work has shown that CF can be improved by combining user data with 'content' features obtained from the Web by special-purpose 'programmed' spiders (e.g., [1,5]). In our experiments we have shown that CF algorithms can also exploit data collected by an 'oblivious' spider. In fact, in our experiments, the obliviously collected data leads to substantially better recommendation performance than the programmatically collected data. This result holds (1) even though the 'programmed' spider uses extensive knowledge to extract data from a high-quality site filled with expert recommendations, (2) even though the oblivious spider relies on very simple heuristics to extract information from Web pages, and (3) even though the number of pages from which information was actually extracted by the oblivious spider is rather small. (In the experiments, data from less than three thousand Web pages was actually used by the CF algorithms.) The result holds for several different widely used CF algorithms, including K-NN, an implementation of the weighted majority algorithm, and a simple popularity-based recommender.

Further experiments show that recommendation performance can sometimes be improved by augmenting user data with obliviously collected Web data. This seems to hold in several interesting situations (although not when the best-performing CF algorithm is trained on all available user data).

The results of this paper suggest that collaborative filtering methods may be useful even in cases in which there is no explicit community of users, and in fact, no user data at all. Instead, it may be possible to build useful recommendation systems that rely solely on information spidered from the Web by simple 'oblivious' spiders, much like the spiders employed by search engines to index the Web. This would greatly extend the range of problems to which collaborative filtering methods could be applied.

References

[1] C. Basu, H. Hirsh and W. Cohen, Recommendation as classification: combining social and content-based information in recommendation, in: Proc. of the 15th National Conference on Artificial Intelligence (AAAI-98).

[2] W.W. Cohen, Integration of heterogeneous databases without common domains using queries based on textual similarity, in: Proc. of ACM SIGMOD-98.

[3] W.W. Cohen, Recognizing structure in Web pages using similarity queries, in: Proc. of the 16th National Conference on Artificial Intelligence (AAAI-99).

[4] S. Goldman and M. Warmuth, Learning binary relations using weighted majority voting, Machine Learning 20 (1995) 245–271.

[5] N. Good, J.B. Shafer, J.A. Konstan, A. Borchers, B. Sarwar, J. Herlocker and J. Riedl, Combining collaborative filtering with personal agents for better recommendations, in: Proc. of the 16th National Conference on Artificial Intelligence (AAAI-99).

[6] J. Hammer, H. Garcia-Molina, J. Cho and A. Crespo, Extracting semistructured information from the Web, in: D. Suciu (Ed.), Proc. of the Workshop on Management of Semistructured Data, Tucson, AZ, 1997.

[7] W. Hill, L. Stead, M. Rosenstein and G. Furnas, Recommending and evaluating choices in a virtual community of use, in: Proc. of ACM CHI'95, 1995, pp. 194–201.

[8] C.A. Knoblock, S. Minton, J.L. Ambite, N. Ashish, P.J. Modi, I. Muslea, A.G. Philpot and S. Tejada, Modeling web sources for information integration, in: Proc. of the 15th National Conference on Artificial Intelligence (AAAI-98).

[9] N. Kushmerick, D. Weld and R. Doorenbos, Wrapper induction for information extraction, in: Proc. of the 15th International Joint Conference on Artificial Intelligence (AAAI-98).

[10] H. Liebermann, Letizia: An agent that assists Web browsing, in: Proc. of the 14th International Joint Conference on Artificial International (IJCAI-95), Montreal.

[11] T. Mitchell, Machine Learning, McGraw-Hill, New York, 1997.

[12] I. Muslea, S. Minton and C. Knoblock, Wrapper induction for semistructured, web-based information sources, in: Proc. of the Conference on Automated Learning and Discovery (CONALD).

[13] A. Nakamura and N. Abe, Collaborative filtering using weighted majority prediction algorithms, in: Machine Learning: Proc. of the 15th International Conference (ICML'98), Madison, WI, 1998, Morgan Kaufmann, Los Altos, CA.

[14] M. Perkowitz and O. Etzioni, Adaptive Web sites: an AI challenge, in: Proc. of the 15th International Joint Conference on Artificial International (IJCAI-97).

[15] P. Resnick, N. Iacovou, M. Sushak, P. Bergstrom and J. Riedl, GroupLens: an open architecture for collaborative filtering of Netnews, in: Proc. of Computer Supported Cooperative Work Conference (CSCW), 1994, pp. 175–186.

[16] U. Shardanand and P. Maes, Social information filtering: algorithms for automating 'word of mouth', in: Proc. of ACM CHI'95, 1995.

[17] I. Soboroff, C. Nicholas and M. Pazzani, eds., Proc. of the SIGIR-99 Workshop on Recommender Systems, Berkeley, CA, 1999.

Mining the Web for relations

Neel Sundaresan [a,*], Jeonghee Yi [b,1]

[a] *IBM Almaden Research Center, San Jose, CA, USA*
[b] *University of California, Los Angeles, CA, USA*

Abstract

The Web is a vast source of information. However, due to the disparate authorship of Web pages, this information is buried in its amorphous and chaotic structure. At the same time, with the pervasiveness of Web access, an increasing number of users is relying on Web search engines for interesting information. We are interested in identifying how pieces of information are related as they are presented on the Web. One such problem is studying patterns of occurrences of related phrases in Web documents and in identifying relationships between these phrases. We call these the duality problems of the Web. Duality problems are materialized in trying to define and identify two sets of inter-related concepts, and are solved by iteratively refining mutually dependent coarse definitions of these concepts. In this paper we define and formalize the general duality problem of relations on the Web. Duality of patterns and relationships are of importance because they allow us to define the rules of patterns and relationships iteratively through the multitude of their occurrences. Our solution includes Web crawling to iteratively refine the definition of patterns and relations. As an example we solve the problem of identifying acronyms and their expansions through patterns of occurrences of (acronym, expansion) pairs as they occur in Web pages.

Keywords: Mining; Crawling; XML; Relation; Duality

1. Introduction

The World Wide Web is a vast source of information. However, the Web consists of an ever-growing set of pages authored by people with vastly differing cultures, interests, and educational levels, while the goal of the individual Web page author is to furnish information. Web crawlers visit these Web pages and index the crawled pages to serve search engines. As these crawlers analyze these Web pages they could look for and learn interesting pieces of information which remain buried in these pages. For instance, a crawler could analyze link information in Web pages to identify how many pages point to a Web page, and how many pages a Web page points to. Based upon this information, the crawler can identify pages that are authorities on certain topics and pages that are starting points (hubs) for such authorities [3,6]. This technique can be extended to identify communities on the Web which consist of pages that point to each other in particular ways [9].

Links are only one type of relations that link entities (Web pages in this case) of the Web. There could be other kinds of relationships of a semantic nature between entities. Identifying these relationships and the patterns of occurrences of these relationships can help provide valuable information buried in the Web.

* Corresponding author. E-mail: nsundare@hotmail.com
[1] E-mail: jeonghee@cs.ucla.edu

This will be increasingly the case as access to the Web becomes pervasive and as end users rely on the Web to look for information with expectation of reliability. For instance, one may be interested in searching the Web to find out the author of a particular book, or to find all books written by a particular author [2]. Such information is typically not easily served by search engines of today.

The vision of a semantic Web [1] includes collaborations that extend to machines that are capable of analyzing all the data on the Web for content, links, and transactions. We are not anywhere near realizing this vision yet, but we do have some loose structure in the form of text, structure, and links in HTML. We would like to exploit what is available to find interesting information.

The rest of this paper is organized as follows. Section 2 discusses duality problems in the World Wide Web. Section 3 formalizes the duality problem of patterns and relations. Section 4 extends this to higher-level duality problems. In Section 5 we solve a *2-level* duality problem of finding acronyms and their expansions in detail. Section 6 discusses the issues in mining over structures and links. Section 7 further generalizes the duality problem and formulates how to discover new relationships. In Section 8 we discuss related research work and in Section 9 we draw conclusions and discuss work in progress and future work.

2. Duality problems in the World Wide Web

Duality problems are materialized in trying to identify two sets of inter-related concepts. Consider the problem of extracting a relation of books — (author, title) pairs from the Web [2]. Intuitively, the problem can be solved as follows.

(1) Begin with a small seed set of (author, title) pairs.
(2) Find all occurrences of those pairs on the Web.
(3) Identify patterns for the citations of the books from these occurrences.
(4) Then, search the Web for these patterns to recognize more new (author, title) pairs.
(5) Repeat the steps with the new (author, title) pairs.

Here, we try to solve the problem of extracting (author, title) relations for books, by iteratively refining mutually dependent coarse definitions of these concepts.

Note that, on the Web, the duality exists in two forms: (1) one induced by static link topology, and (2) the other occurring, in the text of Web documents, in the form of *relations* and *patterns*.

The first form of duality was identified as the notion of hubs and authorities [6,8]. The second form of duality is induced by a specific type of relation of information, such as (book, author) relation or (acronym, expansion) relation, and the patterns that signify the relations. Identifying these relations and patterns can help uncover valuable information in the Web. This will be increasingly more valuable as access to the Web becomes more common and as end users rely on the Web to look for more sophisticated information. For instance, one may be interested in studying business practices of companies as they do commerce on the Web or study hobbies of people and their geographic location through their Web pages for purposes of targeted marketing.

2.1. Some duality already explored

HITS (Hyperlink-Induced Topic Search) identifies authoritative Web pages by iteratively identifying *hub* pages and *authority* pages [6,8]. A *hub* page is a Web page that points to many authority pages. An *authority* page is one that is pointed to by many hub pages. In the world of research literature hubs can be identified with survey papers, and authorities with seminal papers. HITS starts with a small set of Web pages with their hub and authority scores set equal. At each iteration, it computes a list of hub pages by updating the hub score of each page on the basis of authority scores of its immediate neighbors. Likewise, it computes a list of authority pages on the basis of hub scores of its neighbors. The iteration continues until it converges.

DIPRE (Dual Iterative Pattern Relation Expansion) is applied to extract relations of (author, title) pairs for books from the Web, as described earlier [2]. The same framework can be applied to build a directory of people, a database of products, a bibliography of academic works, and many other useful resources.

3. Duality of relations and patterns on the Web

Let $\boldsymbol{W}$ be a large database of documents such as the Web. Let $R = \{r_i \mid i = 1, \ldots, n\}$ and $P = \{p_j \mid j = 1, \ldots, m\}$ be sets of relations and patterns, respectively. A relation is a pair of interrelated concepts, such as (acronym, expansion) pairs. A pattern is the way in which relations are marked up in Web pages. r_i occurs in $\boldsymbol{W}$ at least one time with one (or possibly more) pattern(s) p_j. A pattern p_j signifies at least one (or more) relation(s) r_i.

We iteratively identify two sets R and P, starting with R_0 and P_0 the initial definitions of R and P. R_i and P_i $(i > 0)$ are computed as follows:

$$R_i = R_{i-1} \cup f(P_{i-1}, \boldsymbol{W}_i),$$

$$P_i = P_{i-1} \cup g(R_{i-1}, \boldsymbol{W}_i)$$

where $\boldsymbol{W}_i$ is a subset of $\boldsymbol{W}$ that was not seen until the current iteration i. f and g are functions extracting new relations and patterns, respectively. Patterns are applied to $\boldsymbol{W}_i$ in order to find relations, and so are relations to find patterns. The computation of R_i's and P_i's is repeated until they converge towards R and P. The ultimate convergence is achieved if the following conditions are satisfied:

$$R_{i+1} = R_i \text{ and } P_{i+1} = P_i$$

after iterating the process on the domain of Web pages. The iterations themselves may be defined by full or partial steps in a Web crawling exercise.

We can think of several examples of R and P. R can be the set of (author, book) pairs and P can be the set of patterns using which pairs in R are defined [2]. Or R can stand for a set of community pages (high quality Web pages that talk about a particular topic like 'tennis' or 'fishing') and P is a set of ways they can point to each other. In the HTML world, P is a simple set of 'anchor tag' relationships using which Web page may point to another Web page.

4. Higher level duality problems

It is possible to define higher-level dualities when the mutually recursive relation between R and P is through another set, say S. Here an approximation to R in a particular iteration may depend on an approximation to P in a previous iteration, which in turn may depend on an approximation to S in a previous iteration. The approximation of S itself may come from R. Thus we can define a *2-level* duality as:

$$R_i = R_{i-1} \cup f(P_{i-1}, \boldsymbol{W}_i)$$

$$P_i = P_{i-1} \cup g(S_{i-1}, \boldsymbol{W}_i)$$

$$S_i = S_{i-1} \cup h(R_{i-1}, \boldsymbol{W}_i)$$

P R S

The figure on the right side depicts the dependencies between entities.

This can be further generalized to an *n-level* duality problem. An example of a *2-level* duality problem can be found in discovering pairs of acronyms and their expansions.

5. Solving a 2-level duality problem: mining the Web for acronyms

Here we give an experiment we ran with solving the *2-level* duality problem. We apply the duality to identify acronyms and their expansions. We call the occurrences of (acronym, expansion) relations *AE-pairs*. An acronym comes from the space of words defined by the regular expression [A–Za–z0–9][A–Za–z0–9]*. An expansion is a string of words that stands for an acronym. Acronym *formation rule* is a rule which specifies how an acronym is formed from its expansion. The acronym identification problem involves two kinds of duality:

(1) one between *AE-pairs* and their patterns (1-level duality), and

(2) another between *AE-pairs*, acronym *formation rules*, and patterns (2-level duality).

The dualities are depicted in Fig. 1.

We start off with base sets of *AE-pairs*, patterns, and acronym formation rules. Using the base set of patterns, we crawl the Web to look for new *AE-pairs* that conform the patterns in the base set. From the set of *AE-pairs*, new formation rules are extracted. Moreover, we identify new patterns that associate the acronyms, in the *AE-pairs* set, with their expansions. With the extended sets of *AE-pairs*, patterns, and the rules, we continue crawling the Web in order to discover more of them.

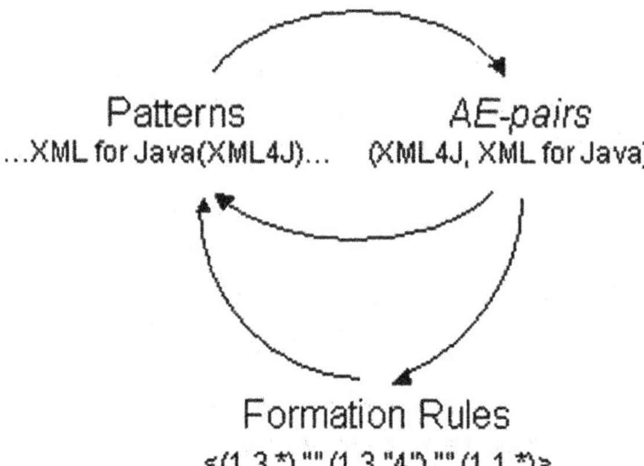

Fig. 1. Dualities for acronym mining: one between *AE-pairs* and their patterns, and another between *AE-pairs*, formation rules, and patterns.

5.1. Why acronyms?

Our work was motivated by the task of engineering a search engine targeted for XML (eXtensible Markup Language)-related information [5,14]. The search engine is available from http://www.ibm.com/xml. The **search engine** [1] is for developers and users of XML and its related technologies. It responds to queries for XML-related pages, documents, DTDs (Document Type Definition), and the like. XML is a meta-markup language and allows several domain-specific definitions of the language with their own definitions of element names and nesting structures. As a result, the crawler for the topic-specific search engine must include all Web pages that pertain to domain specific languages built on XML (e.g., MathML (Mathematical Markup Language) or CML (Chemistry Markup Language)) or XML instances. The automated and dynamic discovery of such language names and their relevant systems is a challenging problem. We notice that the domain of XML is acronym-driven. Thus automatic discovery of acronyms is a basis for discovering relevant concepts defined by the terms of acronyms. The discovered acronyms provide the domain (or scope) of mining the concepts relevant to the target topic.

[1] www.ibm.com/developer/xml

5.2. Problem definition

The acronym identification problem can be solved as a dual iterative problem where we start with a base set of *AE-pairs*, patterns, and the *formation rules* of the *AE-pairs*, in which the expansions occur in relation to the acronyms in Web pages.

We crawl the Web to look for new *AE-pairs* in the Web pages based upon the patterns described in the base set. We learn new *formation rules* from the new set of *AE-pairs*. In addition, we also identify additional patterns which associate the acronyms with their expansions in the base set of *AE-pairs*. Thus, after the first iteration, we would have identified new sets of *AE-pairs*, *formation rules*, and new sets of patterns in which the *AE-pairs* occur. Using the results in the first iteration, we continue crawling the Web to identify more *AE-pairs*, more *formation rules*, and more patterns. The goal is to identify as many *AE-pairs* and patterns of their occurrences while minimizing false identifications of acronyms, their expansions, *formation rules*, or patterns of their occurrences. We would also like to identify *good patterns* (patterns that identify the most *AE-pairs* with least false identifications) and identify *good relationships* (relationships that are identified by good patterns).

In this duality problem of identifying *AE-pairs*, it is possible to determine whether an expansion is a good expansion for an acronym. This can be automatically done through looking at the acronyms and their expansions. Since there is a reasonably well-known way how typical acronyms are built, this can be automatically done in our software system. In addition, since ours is a learning system, we define another duality problem, where we start with a base set of rules for how expansions for acronyms are provided. As we mine more acronyms and their expansions, we can also automatically refine the set of formation rules in our system.

5.3. The mining algorithm

Let W be a database of unstructured, or semi-structured documents such as the Web. Let R, P, and S be sets of target relations, patterns, and formation rules. Each relation, r (r in R), defines an *AE-pair*. An r can occur in one or more patterns. Each s in

1. initial set of *AE-pairs*: $R_0 = \{r_i \mid r_i \text{ is an } AE\text{-}pair,\ i = 1, \ldots, n_0\}$
   initial set of *patterns*: $P_0 = \{p_j \mid p_j \text{ signifies at least one tuple in } R_0,\ j = 1, \ldots m_0, m_0 \leq n_0\}$
   initial set of *formation rules*: $S_0 = \{s_k \mid k = 1, \ldots, l_0, l_0 \leq n_0\}$
2. Set $i = 1$
3. Let W_i be a new Web page (or a set of new Web pages) crawled.

   $R_i = R_{i-1} \cup f(P_{i-1}, W_i)$
   $S_i = S_{i-1} \cup h(R_{i-1})$
   $P_i = P_{i-1} \cup g(R_{i-1}, S_{i-1}, W_i)$

   where f, g, and h are relation, pattern, and formation rule extraction functions, respectively.
4. Set $i = i + 1$
5. If (steady state) stop, otherwise go to step 3.

Fig. 2. Acronym mining algorithm.

S specifies how an acronym of an expansion is determined. The acronym mining algorithm is given in Fig. 2. This is a specialized algorithm from the general duality algorithms discussed in Sections 3 and 4. The algorithm incorporates the double dualities, i.e., the 1-level duality between *AE-pairs* and their patterns, and the 2-level between *AE-pairs*, acronym *formation rules*, and patterns, into the mining.

New patterns have two ways of being identified: by either the *1-level* duality or by the *2-level* duality we identified at the beginning of this section. We combined the two cases into one-step as shown in step 3 of Fig. 2. For the mining of *formation rules*, a set of *AE-pairs* is sufficient without the lookup of Web pages.

The steady state is reached when *W* is repeatedly crawled and no new acronyms, patterns, or formation rules are discovered. In practice, we might not look for ultimate convergence. Alternatively, we may set a threshold on the rate of new knowledge discovered, on time, or on other resources, to determine the steady state. Since the set of Web pages is ever increasing, and typical crawlers do not terminate, this algorithm may be a constantly running process.

5.4. Acronym formation rules

An *acronym formation rule*, or, simply *formation rule*, is a rule by which an acronym is formed from its expansion. It consists of a list of *replacement rules*.

A *replacement rule* specifies how one or more characters in the acronym comes from a word in its expansion and can be encoded by a three-tuple

(*substr_bPos*, *substr_ePos*, *replacer*)

where *substr_bPos* (or *substr_ePos*) is the position of the leading (or ending) character of the substring of expansion word to be replaced. *Replacer* replaces the substring of the expansion word from *substr_bPos* to *substr_ePos* to form the acronym. If no replacement takes place, *replacer* is represented by '*'. For (*XML*, *eX*tensible *M*arkup *L*anguage) pair, for example, the replacement rule from '*Extensible*' to '*X*' is (1, 2, *X*), which indicates that the substring 'Ex' is retained in the acronym after being replaced with '*X*'.

A *formation rule* consists of a sequence of replacement rules interspersed with *intermediates*. An *intermediate* is a substring of an expansion that is ignored in making its acronym. For the (*PICS*, Platform for Internet Content Selection) pair, for example, '*for*' is an intermediate. The formation rule of the pair is <(1,1,*), 'for', (1,1,*), "", (1,1,*), "", (1,1,*)>.

5.5. Patterns

A *pattern* is a three-tuple

(*a_pattern*, *e_pattern*, *formation_rule*)

where *a_pattern* and *e_pattern* are acronym and expansion patterns, respectively, and are composed of two types; *text patterns* and *structure patterns*. *Formation_rule* is the formation rule of its acronym.

Patterns in Web document appear in text, or are embedded in structure tags. Patterns with HTML tags require more information than those with plain text only.

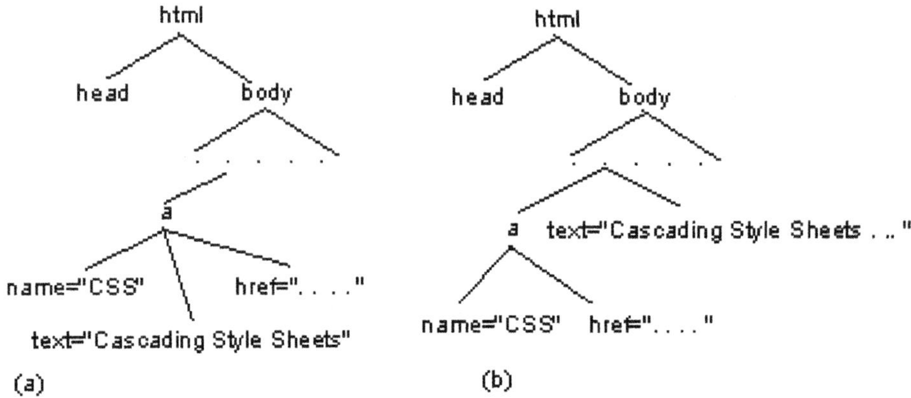

Fig. 3. HTML document hierarchies containing *AE-pair* definitions. In (a), expansion is defined at the *same* level as the acronym, such as '... <a name="CSS" href="...">Cascading Style Sheet</a>...'; in (b), expansion is defined in the *parent* level of the acronym, such as '... <a name="CSS" href="..."</a> Cascading Style Sheet...'.

5.5.1. Text patterns

a_pattern and *e_pattern* for flat text are defined as follows:

(1) *a_pattern* is a pair *(a_prefix, a_suffix)*, where *a_prefix* and *a_suffix* are characters surrounding an acronym;

(2) *e_pattern* is a pair *(e_prefix, e_suffix)*, where *e_prefix* and *e_suffix* are characters surrounding the expansion.

5.5.2. Structure patterns

In Web documents many *AE-pairs* are embedded in the structure of HTML, as in:

<a name="CSS" href="...">Cascading Style Sheet
</a>

This pattern is a sub-hierarchy of the entire document hierarchy. In this case only the sub-hierarchy, not the full hierarchy, needs to be stored as the pattern.

- *a_pattern* is a four-tuple: (*a_tag*, *a_attr*, *a_prefix*, *a_suffix*), where *a_tag* and *a_attr* are an HTML tag and its attribute, respectively, in which the acronym occurred. *a_prefix* and *a_suffix* are the surrounding characters of the acronym.
- *e_pattern* is a five-tuple: (*e_hier*, *e_tag*, *e_attr*, *e_prefix*, *e_suffix*), where *e_tag* and *e_attr* correspond to an HTML tag and its attribute in which the expansion occurred. *e_hier* is the relative position of the occurrence of the expansion, in the document hierarchy, in comparison to that of the acronym. *e_hier* has one of the four values [same | sibling | parent | child].

Fig. 3 shows patterns where *e_tag* is *same* and *parent*, respectively.

Note that the text pattern is the special case of the structure pattern where the values of *a_tag, a_attr, e_hier, e_tag*, and *e_attr* are all null.

5.6. Experiments on pattern learning

We conducted experiments on acronym learning in the context of a topic-specific search engine for XML-related information. (The search engine is available from http://www.ibm.com/xml.) The Web pages used for acronym mining were gathered by a targeted crawler [20] that crawls the Web for information related to XML. The crawler is started off with the *AE-pairs* given as seeds in Table 1.

Table 1
Initial set of *AE-pairs* and patterns provided for duality mining

(DCD, Document Content Description)	'Document Content Description (DCD)'
(CSS, Cascading Style Sheets)	'Cascading Style Sheets (CSS)'
(XML, eXtensible Markup Language)	'eXtensible Markup Language (XML)'

Unlike the conventional Web crawlers that visit all hyperlinks contained in the previously downloaded Web pages, the goal of a targeted crawler is to crawl ideally only and all the Web pages that are relevant to the given topic. In order to achieve the goal, our crawler system (1) incrementally defines the target topic, and (2) identifies and crawls the Web pages that qualify under each level of this topic definition. Typically a target topic consists of many sub-topics. In addition, it includes many other topics that are relevant because they share some property with the target topic. The system discovers the sub-topics and relevant topics using data mining techniques. It applies association mining on hyperlink metadata of the Web pages and various filtering techniques on the mined data. The system starts off with initial definition of target topic and a small set of seed pages. With the mining, the system enhances the definition incrementally by adding newly discovered topic terms, such as sub-topics and relevant topics. For example, the system is initially provided with a coarse definition of topic with a few basic terms, such as {XML, DTD}. As the crawling proceeds, the system discovers and adds new relevant topic terms to the topic definition like XSL (XML Speech Language) or JSML (Java Speech Markup Language).

The targeted crawler needs to be directed in order to avoid drifting away from the target topic. The crawler is guided on the basis of hyperlink metadata of the URLs. The system utilizes various prediction algorithms that compute the likelihood of the relevance of a Web page to the topic, without actually visiting the page, on the basis of its hyperlink metadata. That enables the system to prioritize the visiting order of URLs and thus prune irrelevant links without page lookup.

Table 2 demonstrates the progressive learning of *AE-pairs* and patterns, iteration-by-iteration, for the first five iterations. The new *AE-pairs* and patterns are listed for each iteration (columns 4 and 5). Due to space limitation, we omit listing of formation rules identified. For readability, the patterns are given as they appear in documents, rather than as in their formal definition. In our experiments we saw that learning through duality has far outperformed our initial expectation with respect to both quantity and quality of the discovery.

5.7. Good patterns and noise patterns

In Section 5.2 we defined *good patterns* as those that identify the most (acronym, expansion) pairs with least false identification, and *good relations* as the relations identified by good patterns. In our experiments, we hardly found any false identification of (acronym, expansion) relationships by any given pattern, mainly because our patterns require strict formation rules as well as well-defined prefixes and suffixes. Almost all acronyms conforming to any pattern indeed turned out to be acronyms. Therefore, we measure only the number of (acronym, expansion) relations to measure the goodness of patterns and relations.

5.7.1. Effectiveness of the acronym mining by duality

Table 3 summarizes the mining results in a nutshell. A single-threaded crawler implemented in JAVA ran on a PC with a 399 MHz Pentium II processor and 128 M RAM. The crawler downloaded and analyzed 13,628 Web pages, from which 2694 unique *AE-pairs* and 948 unique patterns were identified. A new *AE-pair* was discovered for every 5 pages, and a new pattern was discovered for every 14.5 Web pages.

In the experiment, no false identification of *AE-pairs* has occurred, except one case, achieving virtually zero error-rate, thanks to the strict pattern specification that requires strict formation rules, structure pattern, as well as well-defined prefixes and suffixes. The incorporation of formation rules specific to acronym and expansion into the general framework of patterns lifted the accuracy of the learning significantly. In general, in order to achieve high-quality learning, it is important to refine the definition of patterns specific to the target of the learning.

However, the system does discover some patterns that are not so useful to discover new relations. One reason is that our pattern is too strict, a trade-off for low error-rate of relation discovery. It is also due to the ambiguity in Web documents. For instance, from the text <a href = ".../*xml*.html">*XML: Extensible Markup Language*</a>, the system extracts two patterns: one from only the anchor text, and another from the entire anchor tag. The latter is an unnecessary duplicate. Though the unnecessary patterns may increase computational complexity, this is not a

Table 2
New *AE-pairs* and new patterns identified by first five iterative mining process [a]

Iteration	Number of AE-Pairs used	Number of Patterns Used	New Acronyms	New patterns discovered
seeds			DCD CSS	XML Document Content Description (DCD) Cascading Style Sheets (CSS) Extensible Markup Language (XML)
1	3	1	ACSS	Cascading Style Sheets, CSS, XML: Extensible Markup Language <a name="CSS">Cascading Style Sheets</a> <a href=".../CSS/">W3C:Cascading Style Sheets</a>
2	4	5	DOM, DTE, RDF, SAX, SDML, SMIL, VML, XSL	The Cascading Style Sheets (CSS) XSL - the eXtensible Stylesheet Language <cite>Document Content Description for XML</cite> <a name="DCD"></a>Document Content Description <a href="...dcd"><cite>Document Content Description</cite></a>
3	12	10	ANSI, ATM, BAWG, BRAN, CTM, DECT, DVB, ECBS, ECMA, EWG, FPLMTS, HLSQ, ICC, IEC, IEV, ISSS, ITPWG, PICS, PTS, TIPHON, TMWG	
4	33	10	DDML, ICE, ATHML, WIDL	<area ... href="...dcd" alt="Document Content Description...>
5	38	11	AIML, AML, CBL, CML, ICE, JSML, RDF, OMG, TML, XBEL, XLF, XLL	Document Content Description for XML (DCD) Extensible Markup Language [XML] DOM, Document Object Model CGM (Computer Graphics Metafile) "XML" The Extensible Markup Language <a ...>DOM</a>Document Object Model

[a] The 2nd and 3rd columns list the number of *AE-pairs* and patterns, respectively, known a-priori. The 4th column lists the new acronyms discovered in the iteration. The 5th column lists the occurrences of new patterns discovered. Starting off with 2 *AE-pairs* and 3 patterns, the duality mining discovered 1, 8, 21, 4, and 12 new *AE-pairs*, and 4, 5, 0, 1, and 6 new patterns from iteration 1 to 5, respectively.

major concern as the process is mostly communication-bound rather than computation-bound.

The next experiment compares the result sets of *AE-pairs* discovered with and without duality-based mining. For the comparison, we recrawled the same set of URLs by applying 10 a-priori acronym patterns and some variations of the conventions without duality-based mining process. Table 4 lists the result. Note that the a-priori patterns in the table are more general than our earlier definition of *pattern* in the sense that one pattern in the table may correspond to many patterns discovered by the system. Note that the sum of all *AE-pairs* discovered individually by the patterns is more than the entire *AE-pairs* discovered because of duplicates.

Table 3
AE-pairs and patterns extracted from Web documents

Number of URL downloaded	13628
Number of unique AE-pairs	2694
Number of unique patterns	948

AE-pairs are discovered at the rate of one every 5 pages, and new patterns are discovered at the rate of one every 14.5 pages.

The result shows that the mining by duality extracts twice as many *AE-pairs* as the extraction

Table 4
The coverage of a-priori patterns for AE-pairs

Pattern	Number of AE-pairs extracted by each pattern
expansion (acronym)	896
acronym (expansion)	332
acronym-expansion	98
acronym: expansion	31
expansion [acronym]	9
(acronym) expansion	6
acronym [expansion]	5
acronym, expansion,	5
(expansion) acronym	2
[acronym] expansion	1
	1385*

	Number of new AE-pairs
without duality-based mining	1033**
with duality-based mining (from Table 3)	2694***

The sum of all AE-pairs discovered (*) is greater than the entire AE-pairs discovered (**) because the same AE-pair is discovered by multiple patterns. The number of AE-pairs identified with duality-based mining (***) is more than 2.5 times of that without the mining (**).

without the mining. Moreover, we found that many acronyms are defined in unusual ways. Sometimes, they are used without explicit intention of defining it. For example,

```
<CENTER>
    <H1><font size=16>Center for Image
        Processing Research</font></H1>
    <IMG ALIGN=CENTER
        SRC="images/cipr_logo_200t.gif">
</CENTER>
```

Our system would mine the pair (CIPR, Center for Image Processing Research) from these data. This would not easily be recognizable without our mining technique.

6. Mining over structures, duality-links, and metadata

In the acronym-expansion formation we saw two kinds of patterns: text patterns and HTML structure patterns. In the text patterns we described the occurrence of acronyms and their expansions in terms of tuples of regular expressions representing character strings. In HTML structure patterns, we described patterns using element/attribute names and values and parent/child/sibling relationships. For generalized relationships between two entities we need a description language that describes how two entities are related over arbitrary tree or graph structures. The simplest way to describe such a pattern is through a pair of path expressions starting at the root or at a key node in the tree. A syntax as seen in WebL [7], XPath [17,19] or a proposed XML Query language [13] may be used for this purpose.

Other relationships could occur over link structures. These relationships may be defined by the annotations around the anchor tags in HTML. The anchor tag has attributes like ALT, HREF, NAME, ONMOUSEOVER, and TITLE. In addition there are annotations like the anchor text and the surrounding text. One can define a pattern language for describing how two entities are related over an anchor link.

Finally, text patterns, structure patterns, and link patterns have to be combined to be able to describe the relationship between two entities that are in two document fragments and, within their individual fragments, are embedded in some structure and, within that structure there is a text pattern that is required to define the relationship.

As the Web becomes increasingly XML-enabled these relationships would be over XLinks [16] and XPointers [18]. As we realize the vision of the semantic Web, metadata graphs would be used for mining.

7. Proposal for discovering new relations

So far in our discussion we have kept the notion of relation fixed in any instance of mining. For example, the relationship between acronyms and their expansions or between acronyms and theirs formation rules is fixed. These two relationships together define the overall relationship of the acronym problem that we are solving. We mine Web pages iteratively to find entities that substantiate that relationship. However, if we were to treat relations themselves as variables that can be mined and defined iteratively, we can come up with new relations.

Here we formalize this as follows. Let D be the

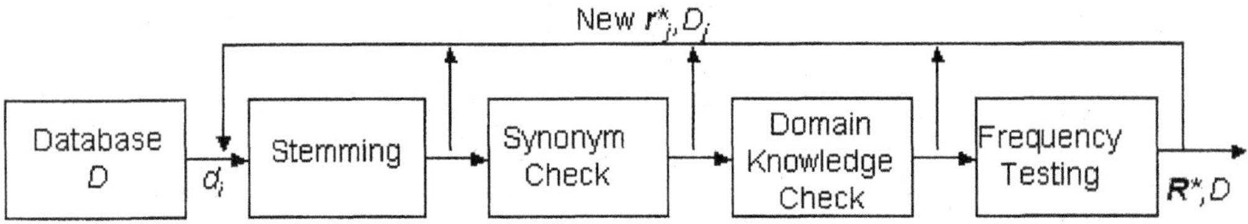

Fig. 4. Block diagram of the relationship identification process.

set of the pairs, (r, p), where relation r is a pair of entities, such as (person, company) or (book, author), and p is a phrase in which the relation is defined, such as 'John is an employee of IBM'. Let R be the set of relations and P be the set of phrases. Let $\boldsymbol{R}^*$ denote the set of relationships, r, in D. Formally, the terms are defined as follows:

(1) Database of Relations: $R = \{r \mid r = (e_1, e_2)$, where e_1 and e_2 are entities$\}$,
(2) Database of Phrases: $P = \{p\}$,
(3) Database of Relationships: $\boldsymbol{R}^* = \{\boldsymbol{r}^*\}$,
(4) Database of (relation, phrases): $D = \{d \mid d = (r, p), r \text{ in } R, p \text{ in } P\}$

The problem is

(1) to identify $\boldsymbol{R}^* = \{\boldsymbol{r}_1^*, \boldsymbol{r}_2^*, \ldots, \boldsymbol{r}_n^*\}$, from D, and
(2) to partition D into classes $D_1, D_2, \ldots, D_n$, such that all pairs in D_i pertain to the same relationship and D is the union of all D_is.

Informally, the problem can be solved as follows. We start with D and an empty set R. For the first pair of D, d_1, we

(1) create a new relationship of d_1, and
(2) create D_1 and add d_1 to D_1. Suppose d_1 = ((John, IBM), 'is employed by').

We create a new relationship, $\boldsymbol{r}_1^*$ = 'employment', and $D_1 = \{d_1\}$.

For a new d_i,

(1) if its relationship is already identified as $\boldsymbol{r}_j^*$, add it to the corresponding class D_j, or
(2) if it does not belong to any known relationship, create a new relationship, $\boldsymbol{r}_k^*$, and a new class D_k, and add d_i to D_k.

For example, suppose d_i = ((Mary, IBM), 'works for'). Since 'works for' represents employment relationship, d_i is added to D_1. If d_i = ((Smith, Smith Software), 'owns') and suppose an ownership relationship has not been identified, we create $\boldsymbol{r}_j^*$ = 'ownership', and place d_i into D_j.

The following paragraphs describe the techniques for identifying the relationship of d. The techniques are applied to each d_i. Fig. 4 illustrates the block diagram of the relationship identification process.

Stemming. This process strips content terms of common suffixes (such as -s or -ing or -ed) that indicate plurality, verb tense, conjugation, and so on, and leaves only the root of the term. The content terms after stemming is used to determine the relationship. For example, 'employee', 'employer', and 'employed' all become 'employ' after stemming and belong to 'employment' relationship.

Synonym check. This process identifies synonyms of a relationship word on the basis of the definition in a thesaurus, such as [12] and [15]. Phrases with synonyms are classified into the same relationship. For example, 'works for' is a synonym of 'employed by'. Both are classified in 'employment' relationship.

Domain knowledge checking. Some phrases convey multiple relationships. For example, a phrase 'by' can convey many relationships, such as '(a book) by (author)' for authorship, '(a house) by (the lake)' for locational proximity. For those phrases, we can apply available domain knowledge that specifies the qualification of entities. For example, the author entity in the authorship relationship has to be a person. Therefore, the (A,B) relation in the 'A by B' phrase cannot be an authorship relationship, unless B is a person.

Frequency testing. When a phrase implies multiple relationships, and is not resolved by the domain knowledge checking, we make a statistical judgment of the relationship on the basis of the frequency. That is, for a new instance of (relation, phrases) with the phrase with multiple relationships, such as 'by', with no other domain knowledge, we classify it as the most frequent relationship among those signified by the phrase. For example, suppose we have an (A,B) relation in an 'A by B' phrase, i.e., d_i = ((A,B), 'by'), and we have no knowledge about A or B. Further we assume that there are two relationships identified by the phrase 'by', r_j^* and r_k^* (such as *authorship* and *locational proximity*) where the number of relations of the form 'X by Y' that belongs to r_j^* is greater than that of r_k^*. Then, d_i is classified as relationship r_j^*.

7.1. The relationship mining algorithm

(1) Let R be a database of Relations, $R = \{r \mid r = (e_1, e_2)$, where e_1 and e_2 are entities$\}$.
Let R^* be a database of Relationships. Set R^* to empty set.
Let P be a database of Phrases, $P = \{p\}$.
Let D be a given database of (relation, phrases), $D = \{d \mid d = (r, p), r \in R, p \in P\}$
(2) Set $i = 1$.
(3) Stem the content word of phrase (p_i) of d_i, and determine the relationship of the stemmed term. If the relationship, r_j^* ($j \leq i$), is already identified, add d_i to D_j and go to step (8).
(4) Look up the synonyms of terms in p_i, and determine the relationship, r_j^* ($j \leq i$), of the synonyms. If the relationship is already identified, add d_i to D_j, and go to step (8).
(5) Look up domain knowledge of d_i, if available. If the domain knowledge uniquely determines the relationship, and the relationship, r_j^* ($j \leq i$), is already identified, add d_i to D_j, and go to step (8).
(6) If the relationship of d_i is ambiguous, but identified by other pairs, choose a relationship r_j^* ($j \leq i$) with highest frequency, and add d_i to D_j,
(7) Create a new relationship for d_i, called r_j^* ($j \leq i$), and a new class D_j, and add d_i to D_j.
(8) $i = i + 1$.
(9) If ($i \leq |D|$) go to (3); otherwise exit.

8. Related work

Bibliometrics [10] studies the world of authorships and citations through measurement. Bibliometric coupling measures similarity of two technical papers based upon their common citations. Co-citation strength is a measure of the number of times two papers are cited together. Statistical techniques are used to compute these and other related measures [11]. In typical bibliometric situations the citations and authorships are explicit and do not have to be learned or derived as in our system.

HITS (Hyperlink-Induced Topic Search) [6,8] is a system that identifies authoritative Web pages based upon the link structure of Web pages. It iteratively identifies hub pages (pages which point to authorities) and authority pages (pages which are pointed to by hub pages). The difference between HITS and our system is that in HITS the 'pattern' space is the links (anchor tags) in a Web page. Also, the 'hub' pages and the 'authority' pages are of the same kind — they are all Web pages. In our formulation of a general duality problem the related entities are not restricted to Web pages. For instance, neither acronyms nor their expansions stand for Web pages. They just occur close to each other in Web pages and form a tuple for our measure. In an interesting extension of our problem we could define the notion of 'goodness' as defined in HITS. For instance, we can formulate good acronyms and their expansions, good patterns of their occurrences, and good rules of acronym formation as follows.

Good (acronym, expansion) pairs are those that are identified by a large number of good patterns. Good patterns are those that identify large number of good (acronym, expansion) pairs. Similarly, good acronym formation rules are those that identify a large number of good (acronym, expansion) pairs; and good (acronym, expansion) pairs are those that are identified by a large number of good formations.

DIPRE (Dual Iterative Pattern Relation Expansion) [2] addresses the problem of extracting (author, book) relations. Brin [2] observed that given a set of pattern P with high coverage and low error rate, a very good approximation to R can be constructed simply by finding all matches to all the patterns. This system mines just the text in the pages to identify the relations. Unlike our system, this system does not involve strict formation rules and double duality which enhances the quality of our results.

Collins and Singer [4] use unlabeled examples on inducing lexicons or other knowledge sources from large corpora. The task is to learn a function which classifies an input string to one of the following categories: *Person, Organization*, or *Location,* with only small seed rules. They leverage natural redundancy in the unlabeled data either in *spelling* or *contextual* rules. For example, in

..., says **Mr. Cooper**, a vice president of ...

both a spelling feature (that the string contains *Mr.*) and a contextual feature (that *president* modifies the string) are strong indications that **Mr. Cooper** is of the type *Person.*

9. Conclusions and future work

In this paper we studied the duality problem of how entities are related on the Web. Given that the Web is a great source of information where the information itself is buried under the visual markups, texts, and links of the Web pages, discovering relationships between entities is an interesting problem. The repeated occurrences of loosely defined structures and relationships help us define these entities with increased confidence. In this paper we formalized the iterative process of mining for patterns and relations over text, structures, and links. We defined and solved the (acronym, expansion) two-level duality problem. We also proposed ideas on mining for new relations. Currently we are working on generalizing our implementation to work for arbitrary user-defined relations and on improving our pattern language over structures and links. We anticipate the seamless adoption of XML in the future and are working on support for XML-style well-formed structures and links [16,18]. In the future, as the Web evolves from a structural Web to a semantic Web, we envision such duality mining over data and metadata to identify higher-level metadata as a key area of research.

References

[1] T. Berners-Lee, Weaving the Web, Harpers, San Francisco, CA, 1999.

[2] S. Brin, Extracting patterns and relations from the World Wide Web, in: Proc. WebDB '98, Valencia, 1998.

[3] S. Chakrabarti, M. van de Berg and B. Dom, Focused crawling: a new approach to topic-specific Web resource discovery, in: Proc. 8th World Wide Web Conference '99 (WWW8), Toronto, 1999.

[4] M. Collins and Y. Singer, Unsupervised models for named entity classification, in: EMNLP 99, 1999.

[5] Extensible Markup Language (XML) 1.0, W3C Recommendation, T. Bray, J. Paoli and C.M. Sperberg-McQueen (Eds.), Feb. 1998, available from http://www.w3.org/TR/1998/REC-xml-19980210.

[6] D. Gibson, J. Kleinberg and P. Raghavan, Inferring Web communities from link topology, in: HyperText '98, Pittsburgh, PA, 1998, pp. 225–234.

[7] T. Kistler and H. Marais, WebL: a programming language for the Web, in: Proc 7th World Wide Web Conference '98 (WWW7), Brisbane, 1998.

[8] J. Kleinberg, Authoritative sources in a hyperlinked environment, in: Proc. 9th ACM–SIAM Symposium on Discrete Algorithms, May 1997.

[9] R. Kumar, P. Raghavan, S. Rajagopalan and A. Tomkins, Trawling the Web for emerging cyber-communities, in: Proc. 8th World Wide Web Conference '99 (WWW8), Toronto, 1999.

[10] R. Larson, Bibliometrics of the World Wide Web: an exploratory analysis of the intellectual structure of cyberspace, Technical Report, School of Information Management and Systems, University of California, Berkeley, 1996, http://sherlock.sims.berkeley.edu/docs/asis96/asis96.html.

[11] K. McCain, Mapping authors in intellectual space: a technical overview. Journal of the American Society for Information Science 41 (1990) 433–443.

[12] Miller, Introduction to WordNet: an on-line lexical database, ftp://ftp.cogsci.princeton.edu/pub/wordnet/5papers.ps.

[13] QL'98 — The Query Languages Workshop, available from http://www.w3.org/TandS/QL/QL99.

[14] W3C Technical Reports and Publications, available from http://www.w3.org/TR/.

[15] Webster Online, available from http://work.ucsd.edu:5141/cgi-bin/http_webster.

[16] XML Link Requirements 1.0, W3C Working Draft, S. De Rose (Ed.), Feb. 1999, available from http://www.w3.org/TR/NOTE-xlink-req/.

[17] XML Path Language Version 1.0, W3C Recommendation, Nov. 1999, available from http://www.w3.org/TR/xpath.

[18] XML XPointer Requirements 1.0, W3C Working Draft, S. De Rose (Ed.), Dec. 1999, available from http://www.w3.org/TR/xptr.

[19] XSL Transformations Version 1.0., W3C Recommendation, Nov. 1999, available from http://www.w3.org/TR/xslt.

[20] J. Yi, N. Sundaresan and A. Huang, Using data mining techniques for building a topic-specific web search engine (submitted for publication).

Neel Sundaresan is a research manager of the eMerging Internet Technologies Department at the IBM Almaden Research Center. He has been with IBM since December 1995 and has pioneered several XML and internet related research projects. He was one of the chief architects of the Grand Central Station project at IBM Research for building XML-based search engines. He received his Ph.D. in computer science in 1995. He has done research and advanced technology work in the area of compilers and programming languages, parallel and distributed systems and algorithms, information theory, data mining and semi-structured data, speech synthesis, agent systems, and internet tools and technologies. He has over 30 research publications and has given several invited and refereed talks and tutorials at national and international conferences. He has been a member of the W3C standards effort.

Jeonghee Yi is a Ph.D. candidate in computer science at the University of California, Los Angeles. She is a researcher at IBM Almaden Research Center, San Jose, California since July 1998. Her current research interests include data mining, Web mining, internet technologies, semi-structured data, and database systems. She received a BS and a MS degrees in Computer Science from Ewha Woman's University, Korea, in 1986 and 1988, respectively, and a MS degree in computer science from the University of California, Los Angeles in 1994. The work described here was partially supported through an IBM Graduate Fellowship.

Presenting tailored resource descriptions: will XSLT do the job?

Alison Cawsey [1]

Department of Computing and Electrical Engineering, Heriot-Watt University, Edinburgh EH14 7AS, UK

Abstract

The problem of finding *relevant* resources from those available across the World Wide Web is well recognised. Improved search engines provide part of the answer, but we also need to support the user in assessing for themselves the relevance of documents suggested by a search engine, prior to download. One way to do this is to provide them with descriptions tailored to their profile and query. This paper presents examples of how XSLT may be used to create tailored descriptions from RDF metadata, and explores whether XSLT is an adequate tool for this task.

Keywords: Metadata; RDF; XSL; Information retrieval; Personalisation

1. Introduction

The problem of finding *relevant* resources from those available across the World Wide Web is well recognised. A search engine may be able to suggest a set of potentially relevant resources given a query, but the user is left with the job of trawling through this set to find those that meet his/her need. Often the information provided by the search engine about each resource is not sufficient to allow the user to assess its possible relevance prior to download. We are interested in how more informative, but concise, resource descriptions may be provided to the users to aid them in assessing resource relevance.

There is already some work addressing this problem. Within the information retrieval community there is work on producing *query-directed summaries* that summarise document content in a way that depends on the user's query (perhaps highlighting information of likely interest). In this work, summaries are extracted from the text of the document (e.g., [8]). However, the summaries produced are limited to what can be extracted from the text, and thus ignore information *about* the resource which may be external to it. Also, as the summarisation methods work by extracting text fragments, they are not useful for multimedia resources where the text represents but a small part of the information content of the resource.

Another approach that is currently being pursued to support better search and retrieval is the use of rich *metadata* — data *about* the resource, such as the title, topic, author, and date of last modification. While some of this information may be repeated within the resource itself, it is useful to have it represented in a structured, explicit form, allowing very focused queries to be made (e.g., find resources where topic = T, author = A and where title contains W). Standards both for the vocabulary to be used in metadata (e.g., Dublin Core [5], and IMS [7]), and languages for the representation of metadata (RDF [11]) are now in place. We expect increased use

[1] E-mail: alison@cee.hw.ac.uk; http://www.cee.hw.ac.uk/~alison

of metadata as tools are developed based on these standards.

Metadata are normally embedded in a document, not visible to the user. Yet some holders of resource collections recognise the utility of metadata to the user, to help them assess relevance, and make those metadata accessible (see, for example, *The Gateway to Educational Materials* [6]). We believe that these metadata presentations may be more effective in allowing users to assess relevance if they are tailored to the user and query, so the user can influence which elements are presented. This is particularly important where the metadata available are complex, and could not all be concisely displayed; the IMS/IEEE metadata specification [7], for example, includes over 50 elements/subelements that may be included in a formal description of an educational resource. While not all would be used for a particular resource instance, it illustrates the complexity of the information that may be available.

The simplest way to present metadata is as a table (see Fig. 1 for a simple presentation of some Dublin Core metadata). Yet the same information may often be presented more concisely as a text description. We have explored how personalised resource descriptions may be produced, both in table and text form.

Description of: http://www.dlib.org	
Title	D-Lib Program — Research in Digital Libraries
Description	The D-Lib program supports the community of people with research interests in digital libraries and electronic publishing.
Publisher	Corporation For National Research Initiatives
Date	1995-01-07
Subject	Research; statistical methods
	Education, research, related topics
	Library use Studies
Type	World Wide Web Home Page
Format	text/html
Language	en

Fig. 1. Example metadata table.

We assume that the metadata will be represented using the Resource Description Framework (RDF) XML serialisation. RDF is a W3C standard for representing metadata [14], allowing clear specification of metadata vocabularies, and rich structure within the formal description. We focus on rich metadata describing individual resources, and in particular those describing educational resources, such as IMS and GEM [6,7]. Although there are currently very scarce rich metadata in RDF format, it is a standard which is likely to be quickly adopted, as the problems with existing methods (e.g., use of HTML meta tag) become apparent.

The paper explores how far we can get using XSLT to present RDF metadata in a personalised and concise fashion, suggesting some current limitations with how stylesheets are associated with documents. XSLT is the transformation part of a general stylesheet language for XML [12]; it allows quite complex tree transformations by matching on an input tree and creating an output tree, through the application of templates. It is currently used primarily to transform XML to HTML, allowing presentation via current browsers.

2. Presenting RDF to the user — simple tables

Our first investigation focused on how XSLT could be used to present RDF metadata to the user. We used the examples from the RDF specification document as input. Fig. 2 illustrates a typical example. It is very straightforward to develop XSLT stylesheets to present these data as a nested table. Templates are written to deal with each element from the RDF namespace (e.g., Description, Bag, Resource), and for each metadata property element (e.g., Author) that we wish to be displayed to the user. A simplified fragment is given in Fig. 3, with output illustrated in Fig. 1. This example also serves to illustrate XSLT for those not familiar with it. Each template matches on some elements of the input tree (e.g., RDF:Description elements). The body of the template mixes elements to be inserted in the output tree (e.g., Table) with XSLT processing instructions (e.g., xsl:apply-templates, which results in templates being applied to child nodes in the input tree). Further demonstration output is available on http://www.cee.hw.ac.uk/~alison/

```
<rdf:RDF
  xmlns:rdf="http://www.w3.org/1999/02/22-rdf-syntax-ns#"
  xmlns:dc="http://purl.org/metadata/dublin_core#">
  <rdf:Description about="http://www.dlib.org">
    <dc:Title>D-Lib Program - Research in Digital Libraries</dc:Title>
    <dc:Description>The D-Lib program supports the community of people
    with research interests in digital libraries and electronic
    publishing.
    </dc:Description>
    <dc:Publisher>Corporation For National Research Initiatives</dc:Publisher>
    <dc:Date>1995-01-07</dc:Date>
    <dc:Subject>
      <rdf:Bag>
        <rdf:li>Research; statistical methods</rdf:li>
        <rdf:li>Education, research, related topics</rdf:li>
        <rdf:li>Library use Studies</rdf:li>
      </rdf:Bag>
    </dc:Subject>
    <dc:Type>World Wide Web Home Page</dc:Type>
    <dc:Format>text/html</dc:Format>
    <dc:Language>en</dc:Language>
  </rdf:Description>
</rdf:RDF>
```

Fig. 2. Simple RDF example.

```
<?xml version='1.0'?>
<xsl:stylesheet
  xmlns:xsl="http://www.w3.org/XSL/Transform/1.0"
  xmlns:RDF="http://www.w3.org/1999/02/22-rdf-syntax-ns#"
  xmlns:DC="http://purl.org/metadata/dublin_core#">
...
<xsl:template match="RDF:Description">
  <TABLE border="2">
    <xsl:apply-templates />
  </TABLE>
</xsl:template>

<xsl:template match="DC:subject">
  <tr>
    <th> Subject </th>
    <td> <xsl:apply-templates /> </td>
  </tr>
</xsl:template>
</xsl:stylesheet>
```

Fig. 3. Partial style sheet for displaying RDF.

mirador/xml/demo.html (note: these examples were tested with version 19990721 of XT, an implementation of XSLT).

The fragment in Fig. 3 can be improved and developed in many ways. We can reasonably assume in RDF that property element names (including the namespace) will be URIs pointing to a definition of that element (either an RDF schema, or an English definition). Links to these definitions can be easily added, as can links to the resource being de-

```
<rdf:Description ID="Title">
   <rdf:type rdf:resource="http://www.w3.org/1999/02/22-rdf-syntax-ns#Property"/>
     <rdfs:label>Title</rdfs:label>
     <rdfs:comment>The name given to the resource, usually by the Creator
          or Publisher.
     </rdfs:comment>
</rdf:Description>
```

Fig. 4. Fragment of RDF schema for Dublin Core.

scribed, and also any property values specified using rdf:resource. As an example, given a property element DC:subject, the following XPath functions [13] (used by XSLT) inserts a suitable link to the definition of the Dublin Core subject element:

```
<A HREF= "{namespace-uri()}
     {local-name()}">
   <xsl:value-of select="local-name()"/>
</A>
```

If we want the stylesheet to handle all of RDF, it should be able to handle all the abbreviated syntaxes. This makes RDF somewhat awkward to handle; the abbreviated syntax for typed nodes, for example, introduces difficulties. It seems to make sense, therefore, to 'normalise' RDF (eliminating abbreviated syntax) prior to application of the stylesheets. This can be done using XSLT again, and separates out one subproblem, making all stylesheets easier to construct. Handling abbreviated typed nodes in XSLT is possible, just difficult; prior to applying XSLT to present the data we should use XSLT to transform it into the syntax simplest to handle.

The stylesheet illustrated in Fig. 3 requires that templates are defined for each property element that we want displayed. There are two ways this can be managed, without requiring the stylesheet author to create all such templates 'by hand'. The first way is to use the RDF *schema* [14]. An RDF schema will define all the property elements associated with a particular metadata element set. An example fragment of a schema for Dublin Core is given in Fig. 4. We can use an XSLT stylesheet (applied to the schema) to *generate* another XSLT stylesheet suitable for the presentation of RDF instances based on that schema. Fig. 5 illustrates a fragment of such a stylesheet generating stylesheet. The example relies on XSLT namespace aliases being used for the XSLT namespace itself (so we can distinguish XSLT instructions and parts of the result tree), and the namespace of the target element set.

So far we have only explored generating stylesheets that cover one RDF schema. Yet a particular metadata record may be based on several schemas. In general we would want to access all these schemas (via the namespace URL) and create a merged stylesheet that covers all the element types that might occur in the record. This should be reasonably straightforward, exploiting the possibility in XSLT of having multiple input documents. The second way we have attempted dealing with arbitrary property elements is to create a general stylesheet which is based on the assumption that any non-RDF/XML namespace refers to property ele-

```
<xsl:template match="Description[RDF:type/@RDF:resource =
        'http://www.w3.org/1999/02/22-rdf-syntax-ns#Property']">
   <litxsl:template match="ElNameSpace:{@ID}">
      <tr>
         <th> <xsl:value-of select="RDFS:label"/> </th>
         <td> <litxsl:apply-templates /> </td>
      </tr>
   </litxsl:template>
</xsl:template>
```

Fig. 5. XSLT fragment to create stylesheet for RDF instance from RDF schema.

ments. We therefore have a single general template for property elements. However, this approach will not be able to use information from the schemas (e.g., the *label* of property elements). Also this (and the previous approach) results in all metadata being displayed; yet much of an RDF record may refer to cataloguing and indexing information of little interest to the user. We need methods of easily defining which elements are of interest.

3. Simple tailored descriptions

We can easily 'hardwire' our stylesheets so, for example, they only present a subset of a particular metadata element set (perhaps missing out Language and Format). Yet different users (making different types of information search) are likely to be interested in different subsets. One way to support this is to allow users to set up their own stylesheet. In a preliminary study (18 subjects) users appeared to value the facility of specifying which resource metadata elements to present following a search.

It is straightforward to create a form interface allowing metadata elements to be selected (e.g., author, title), and a cgi-program to create a personalised XSLT file. However, it is more interesting, and more easily adapted to other metadata element sets, if the form is generated automatically. We can do this using XSLT to present the contents of an RDF schema (defining a metadata element set) as an HTML form (for element selection). All RDF property elements in the schema are translated into appropriate checkboxes (see Fig. 6). A general cgi-program can then be used to create the personalised XSLT for display of metadata.

This allows personal stylesheets to be created given an RDF schema, which should be accessible via the property element names in a particular RDF document. It would be a useful facility for users interested primarily in a particular type of document (e.g., educational), with a specified metadata element set defined in an RDF schema. However, we are left with the question of how to associate that personalised schema with an RDF document. This is straightforward when using XSLT on the server side (using XT); we can easily specify which XSLT file to apply to the RDF, and return the resulting HTML. However, it is less straightforward when using XSLT on the client side, using Internet Explorer. The existing methods and standards for associating a stylesheet with a document [15] do not make it easy to flexibly select which stylesheet to use. One answer is to use cookies, with the stylesheet instruction in the RDF referring to a CGI program which will look up the name of the users own personalised stylesheet, via their cookie.

```
<?xml-stylesheet type="text/xsl"
  href="findmystylesheet.cgi">
<RDF... >
```

However, this is of limited flexibility; unless the user can specify a stylesheet independently of the source XML document, much of the power of XML

```
<xsl:template match="Description[RDF:type/@RDF:resource =
        'http://www.w3.org/1999/02/22-rdf-syntax-ns#Property']">
   <tr>
      <th align="left">
         <xsl:value-of select="RDFS:label"/>
      </th>
      <td>
         <input type="checkbox">
            <xsl:attribute name="name">
               <xsl:value-of select="@ID"/>
            </xsl:attribute>
         </input>
      </td>
   </tr>
</xsl:template>
```

Fig. 6. XSLT fragment to create property element selection form from RDF schema.

is lost. (As a very different example of this, we might want to have a stylesheet which can create output particularly suitable for screen readers/speech synthesiser, with the appropriate markup for intonation and voice. We want the (possibly visually impaired) user reading the document to be able to specify that this speech-enhanced stylesheet should be used, without relying on the XML author to provide an alternative version of the document with that stylesheet specified.)

4. Tailored textual resource descriptions

Producing tables to present metadata is in fact a rather verbose and inflexible approach. Consider the following metadata:

Title	The Moon and Stars
Author	Jane Smith
Subject	Astronomy
Type	Lesson Plan
Grade	5, 6, 7

This can be presented much more concisely as a single sentence:

> "The Moon and Stars, by Jane Smith, is an astronomy lesson plan for grades 5 to 7."

Text-based output also opens up possibilities to go beyond the literal facts when presenting the data, commenting on, comparing and adding to the raw facts (e.g., "Unlike 'Stars today' it is . . . ").

However, generating coherent text from raw facts is a complex problem, addressed in the natural language processing community (see [4]). If the input data are very consistent (i.e., every set of input facts contains the same sort of data) it is possible to create a fill-in-the-blanks template to slot data in (illustrated in XSLT in Fig. 7).

However, typically different authors will use a different subset of the available metadata elements when describing their resources. Where the metadata property values are arbitrary strings (rather than from a controlled vocabulary) this introduces further uncertainty, as the length, and even syntactic constructions used by different authors for the same type of element may vary. If we add to that the desire to allow personalised output, containing just those facts of interest to the particular user, we find that simple template-based methods are pushed to their limits. We can easily create grammatically correct text by expressing each fact as a single sentence, or substituting contentless expressions when facts are omitted. But our initial studies with users suggest that poor-quality text provides no value over tabular output [1].

The problem is then, given an arbitrary subset of facts (from a reasonably well defined set), how to combine them coherently into a small number of concise sentences. This is a classic natural language generation problem — that of aggregation. While some good work has been done on algorithms for aggregation (e.g., [9]), we are interested in whether we can exploit some of the basic ideas of natural language generation, using XSLT, to at least improve on the simple template-based approach, allowing reasonably coherent text from varying input data. Does XSLT provide sufficient power to make headway?

A standard approach to use in natural language generation is to separate out the problems of content selection and 'realisation' (as English sentences). Two, or often three, stages may be used [2], each creating intermediate representations which will be input to the next. This seems to make equally good sense when presenting information using XSLT (whether that output is in table, or other format). Typically stylesheets merge the two functions of

```
<xsl:template match="RDF:Description">
  <xsl:value-of select="DC:Title"/>
  by <xsl:value-of select="DC:Author"/>,
  is a <xsl:value-of select="GEM:Subject"/>
  <xsl:value-of select="GEM:Type"/>
  for grades <xsl:value-of select="GEM:grades"/>
</xsl:template>
```

Fig. 7. XSLT template for text output.

Astronomy is a Science Lesson Plan for grades 5, 6. It is published by AskERIC, an OnlineProvider (Email: askeric@askeric.org). The following resources will be needed: Meter sticks, Styrofoam pellets, Cotton balls, Black poster board, Black umbrella, Star chart, Dictionary.

Constellations is another Science Lesson Plan but for grades 3, 4, 5, 6. It is also published by AskERIC.

Fig. 8. Example natural language output.

content selection and presentation. If we can have two separate stylesheets, one concerned with picking out the sections of an XML document that are to be presented, and one with transforming those data into a suitable realisable surface form, then we have a much improved modular structure allowing presentation and content selection to be revised independently of one another, and combined in more flexible ways. This is (like many things) straightforward using XSLT on the server side; the stylesheets may be simply piped together. Yet this rather obvious procedure is currently difficult on the client side (though can be managed within Javascript for example). This again points to limitations in the way stylesheets are currently associated with documents. As more and more applications require multiple transformations there will be pressure for better support for this.

Separating out these two processes, we have one (simple) stylesheet for selecting content, and one more complex one for composing sentences from that content. The latter can assume that *all* the data in the input tree are to be expressed. We can also require that the first (content selection) stylesheet, while not imposing a rigid final order on the information, does order and group information. This simplifies certain things, so that the second stylesheet can check whether facts have already been expressed, simply by examining the input tree. (XSLT does not allow access, in its decisions, to the tree being constructed.) The templates required are a little inelegant, but do allow simple decisions to be made to enhance the coherence and conciseness of the next (e.g., using 'also' for repeated values; omitting information already expressed). Fig. 8 illustrates example (simplified) output, showing how previous resources are referred to, and publisher details can be omitted in the second description using this approach.

Separating out content selection from realisation certainly clears some ground. But there are many more issues to be addressed when creating quality text. For example, since an easily readable and concise paragraph should contain little redundancy, we want to be able to choose from the several ways in which an object may be referred to. Some of these choices will be informed by whether (and how) it has been mentioned before. The simplest case of this concerns the use of pronouns (e.g., "*It* is published ..."). The second sentence above would not make sense if the first sentence was omitted (perhaps due to the non-availability of data on subject, type and grades in the input tree). We really need to determine when to use pronouns dynamically, based on what has already been expressed.

The simplest algorithm for pronoun selection just looks to see if a particular entity (e.g., 'Astronomy') has been mentioned in the previous sentence; if so a pronoun is used. However, even this apparently simple task proves quite difficult in XSL, due to the unavailability of the output tree, and limited variable mechanisms. One approach is to push more of the problem into the content selection stylesheet, so the output from that contains information on objects (to be) mentioned — we add 'focus' elements to the tree, containing a specification of the expected main subject of a description (e.g., 'Astronomy' or 'AskERIC'). But this approach will only work if the order of information in the content tree is strictly maintained in the output.

Taking this approach to its rational conclusion would result in numerous stylesheets being used, each making some progress on transforming the input tree, adding more contextual information to the tree as required. This fits reasonably with current proposals for architectures for natural language generation [2], but is hardly an expected way of using XSL.

While certain problems appear difficult to handle, others have a more natural solution. One issue in language generation is how to handle the fact that a particular fact may be expressed in many different ways, and the way to express it should depend on how it is being combined with other facts. XSLT conveniently provides a 'mode' mechanism that at least allows one to separate cleanly different ways

```
<xsl:template match="dc:Subject" mode="pp">
  on the subject of
  <xsl:value-of select="."/>
</xsl:template>

<xsl:template match="dc:Subject" mode="adjective">
  <xsl:value-of select="."/>
</xsl:template>

<xsl:template match="dc:Subject" mode="sentence">
  The subject category is:
  <xsl:value-of select="."/>.
</xsl:template>
```

Fig. 9. Using modes to define different syntactic constructions for same input.

of expressing the same content. Fig. 9 illustrates how this may be used when defining a template for realising Dublin Core subject information.

While these 'tricks' and others may provide some mileage in creating reasonable output text given varied input, allowing stylesheets to be written that work fairly well for a particular element set, ultimately natural language generation is a problem that requires complex algorithmic solutions; it involves optimisation — choosing the best output given varied quality criteria. XSLT does not allow this type of processing. One approach, used in related work on generating multilingual text from a common input representation, is to make use of Java/Javascript functions, which may be called from XSL. However, making extensive use of this facility results in code that might just have well been written without the XSLT layer. Where quality texts are required we need to turn to other methods, using a general purpose programming language (or specific natural language generation toolkit (e.g., [10]) that can take parsed XML or RDF and determine how it can be coherently expressed.

5. Looking beneath the surface: should we use the RDF data model?

In the discussion so far we have considered how to give a fairly direct presentation of a selected subset of RDF metadata using XSLT. We work with the surface (XML) syntax of RDF (acknowledging the utility of first converting this to a non-abbreviated normal form), and have only considered fairly simple uses of RDF for representing tables of attributes and values. Yet RDF allows richer underlying structures to be represented, and allows inferencing on the knowledge encoded. RDF has a well specified data model, and parsing RDF will result in a set of triples which provide a canonical representation that allows further inference. An example of triples based on the RDF in Fig. 1 is given in Fig. 10. This is generated using the standard RDF parser, SiRPAC [16].

There have been various attempts to present useful visualisations of the information from this data model [16]. Furthermore, as mentioned, working with a canonical representation with defined semantics would allow inference to be done which relates the metadata to the user or query in more sophisticated ways.

Although working with RDF triples does provide more power, it also involves some loss of information (e.g., order of element attributes). We are interested in how to present the information back to the user. But the surface RDF syntax may be closer to a 'human-readable' form, making hierarchical structure and decomposition explicit; and RDF authors (or authoring tools) may be influenced by readability issues when structuring their metadata (e.g., defining 'important' property elements first). One of the first things that would have to be done when working with the triples of the data model would be to reconstruct (normalised) trees.

We believe that for our purposes there is currently much to be gained from doing fairly simple personalisation, and ensuring that the descriptions output

```
triple('http://purl.org/metadata/dublin_core#Title',
       'http://www.dlib.org/',
       'D-Lib Program - Research in Digital Libraries').
triple('http://purl.org/metadata/dublin_core#Description',
       'http://www.dlib.org/',
       'The D-Lib program supports the community of people
        with research interests in digital libraries and electronic
        publishing.').
triple('http://purl.org/metadata/dublin_core#Publisher',
       'http://www.dlib.org/',
       'Corporation For National Research Initiatives').
triple('http://purl.org/metadata/dublin_core#Date',
       'http://www.dlib.org/',
       '1995-01-07').
...
```

Fig. 10. Triples of the RDF data model.

are concise and coherent. In our initial work we have therefore worked entirely with the surface (XML) syntax, and leave to further work the possibility of reasoning more deeply with the parsed representation (as for example in the SiLRI project [3] for querying RDF data).

Whether or not we work with the RDF data model, there may be significant gains in making more use of the RDF schema for a given metadata element set — currently we just insert HTML links in our descriptions to the appropriate sections of the schema. In principle an RDF schema allows definition of a simple ontology, and property values may refer to concepts in this ontology rather than being literal strings. If this facility is widely used, then it will be important in presenting RDF to, at the least, look up the appropriate label of schema-defined concepts and use that in the description, and possibly do further reasoning using the ontology to decide just how best to refer to a concept within a given context.

6. Conclusions

XSLT, despite its complexity and power, has limitations as a tool for creating tailored resource descriptions from metadata. For tabular descriptions, the limitations seem to lie partly in current standards for associating stylesheets with documents; these make it awkward to 'mix-and-match' stylesheets and documents, to allow personalised output, and also make it difficult to specify that a sequence of stylesheets should be piped together (which seems rational modular development, allowing separation of content selection and presentation).

When creating coherent textual output, the limitations become more apparent. To produce quality text from varying input data is a complex problem, and though we can come up with various useful tricks to make this tractable when the input is fairly constrained (e.g., using modes; creating intermediate tree structures), XSLT is not suitable for less constrained input, when we need to turn to general purpose programming languages or natural language generation tools.

Generating descriptions from RDF metadata is complicated somewhat by the range of alternative abbreviated syntaxes allowed in the current RDF recommendation. These can be 'normalised' out, but their existence appears to do no one any favours, making both machine processing and human interpretation more difficult.

Many of the methods described in this paper, while developed for presenting resource descriptions from metadata, should apply to many related applications where structured data in XML syntax are to be presented flexibly to the user. For example, e-commerce applications may want tailored product descriptions from product data represented in XML. We would expect that XML schemas [17] would provide information on structures that could be used in setting up stylesheets and presenting the data.

Acknowledgements

This work was partially funded by EPSRC grant GR/M23106. Richard Tobin provided advice on XML and XSLT (and much more).

References

[1] D. Bental, A. Cawsey, S. Rock and P. McAndrew, The need for natural language generation techniques to produce resource descriptions in MIRADOR, IEE Colloquium on Searching for Information: Artificial Intelligence and Information Retrieval Approaches, November 1999, Glasgow.

[2] L. Cahill et al., In search of a reference architecture for NLG systems, in: Proc. European Workshop on Natural Language Generation, Toulouse, May 13–14, 1999.

[3] S. Decker, D. Brickley, J. Saarela and J. Angele, A query and inference service for RDF, in: QL'98 — The Query Languages Workshop, 1998.

[4] The Dublin Core Metadata Initiative, http://www.purl.org/DC.

[5] The Gateway to Educational Materials, http://www.geminfo.org/.

[6] IMS Metadata Specification, http://www.imsproject.org/.

[7] E. Reiter and R. Dale, Building applied natural-language generation systems, Journal of Natural-Language Engineering 3 (1997) 57–87.

[8] M. Sanderson, Accurate user directed summarization from existing tools, in: Proc. 7th Int. Conf. on Information and Knowledge Management (CIKM 98), 1998, pp. 45–51.

[9] J. Shaw and K. McKeown, An architecture for aggregation in text generation, in: Proc. 15th Int. Joint Conf. on Artificial Intelligence, Poster Session, 1997.

[10] M. White and T. Caldwell, EXEMPLARS: a practical, extensible framework for dynamic text generation, in: Proc. 9th Int. Workshop on Natural Language Generation, Niagara-on-the-Lake, 1998, pp. 266–275.

[11] World Wide Web Consortium, Resource description framework (RDF) model and syntax, http://www.w3.org/TR/REC-rdf-syntax/, 1999.

[12] World Wide Web Consortium, XSL transformations (XSLT) W3C recommendation, http://www.w3.org/TR/xslt, 1999.

[13] World Wide Web Consortium, XML path language (XPath), http://www.w3.org/TR/xpath, 1999.

[14] World Wide Web Consortium, Resource description framework (RDF) schema specification (W3C proposed recommendation), http://www.w3.org/TR/PR-rdf-schema/, 1999.

[15] World Wide Web Consortium, Associating stylesheets with XML documents, W3C recommendation, http://www.w3.org/TR/xml-stylesheet/, 1999.

[16] World Wide Web Consortium, SiRPAC — simple RDF parser and compiler, http://www.w3.org/RDF/Implementations/SiRPAC/, 1999.

[17] World Wide Web Consortium, XML schema, Part 1: Structures, W3C working draft, http://www.w3.org/TR/xmlschema-1/.

Alison Cawsey was awarded a Ph.D. in artificial intelligence in 1989, from the University of Edinburgh. Since then she has worked at Cambridge and Glasgow Universities, and is currently a lecturer in computer science at Heriot-Watt University. Her research has mainly focused on techniques to generate tailored descriptions and explanations, for education and medical applications.

SilkRoute: trading between relations and XML

Mary Fernández [a,*,1], Wang-Chiew Tan [b,2], Dan Suciu [a,1]

[a] *AT&T Labs – Research, 180 Park Avenue, Florham Park, NY 07932, USA*
[b] *University of Pennsylvania, Philadelphia, PA, USA*

Abstract

XML is the standard format for data exchange between inter-enterprise applications on the Internet. To facilitate data exchange, industry groups define public document type definitions (DTDs) that specify the format of the XML data to be exchanged between their applications. In this paper, we address the problem of automating the conversion of relational data into XML. We describe SilkRoute, a *general*, *dynamic*, and *efficient* tool for viewing and querying relational data in XML. SilkRoute is general, because it can express mappings of relational data into XML that conforms to arbitrary DTDs. We call these mappings *views*. Applications express the data they need as an XML-QL query over the view. SilkRoute is dynamic, because it only materializes the fragment of an XML view needed by an application, and it is efficient, because it fully exploits the underlying RDBMs query engine whenever data items in an XML view need to be materialized.

Keywords: Data exchange; XML; Relational databases; XML queries

1. Introduction

XML can serve many purposes: as a more expressive mark-up language than HTML; as an object-serialization format for distributed object applications; or as a data exchange format. In this work, we focus on the role of XML in data exchange, in which XML documents are generated from persistent data then sent over a network to an application. Numerous industry groups, including health care and telecommunications, are working on document type definitions (DTDs) that specify the format of the XML data to be exchanged between their applications[3]. The aim is to use XML as a 'lingua franca' for data exchange between inter-enterprise applications, making it possible for data to be exchanged regardless of the platform on which it is stored or the data model in which it is represented.

In this paper, we address the problem of exporting existing data into XML. Most data is stored in relational or object-relational database management systems (RDBMs) or in legacy formats. To realize the full potential of XML, we need tools that can automatically convert the vast stores of relational data into XML: we call the resulting XML document a *view*. We believe that such tools must be *general*, *dynamic*, and *efficient*. Relational data is tabular, flat, normalized, and its schema is proprietary, which

* Corresponding author.
[1] E-mail: {mff,suciu}@research.att.com
[2] E-mail: wctan@saul.cis.upenn.edu

[3] Dozens of such applications can be found at http://www.oasis-open.org/cover/

makes it unsuitable for direct exchange. In contrast, XML data is nested and unnormalized, and its DTD is public. Thus, the mapping from relational data to an XML view is often complex, and a conversion tool must be *general* enough to express complex mappings. Some commercial systems fail to be general, because they map each relational database schema into a fixed, canonical DTD. This approach is limited, because no public DTD will match exactly a proprietary relational schema. In addition, one may want to map one relational source into multiple XML documents, each of which conforms to a different DTD. Hence a second step is required to transform the data from its canonical XML form into its final XML form, e.g., using XSLT.

Our second requirement is that tools must be dynamic, i.e., only the fragment of the XML document needed by the application should be materialized. In database terminology, the XML view must be *virtual*. The application typically specifies in a query what data item(s) it needs from the XML document, and these items are typically a small fraction of the entire data. Some commercial products allow users to export relational data into XML by writing scripts. According to our definition, these tools are general but not dynamic, because the entire document is generated all at once.

Finally, to be efficient, such tools must exploit fully the underlying RDBMs query engine whenever data items in the XML view need to be materialized. Query processors for native XML data are still immature and do not have the performance of highly optimized RDBMs engines.

In this paper, we describe SilkRoute, a general, dynamic, and efficient tool for viewing and querying relational data in XML. SilkRoute is a particular instance of a mediator system, as defined by Wiederhold [21]. In SilkRoute, data is exported into XML in two steps. First, an XML view of the relational database is defined using a declarative query language, called RXL (Relational to XML Transformation Language). The resulting XML view is virtual. Second, some other application formulates a query over the virtual view, extracting some piece of XML data. For this purpose, we use an existing XML query language, XML-QL. Only the result of that XML-QL query is materialized.

The core of SilkRoute is RXL, a powerful, declarative data-transformation language from flat relations to XML data. On the relational side, RXL has the full power of SQL queries and can express joins, selection conditions, aggregates, and nested queries. On the XML side, RXL has the full power of XML-QL, and can generate XML data with complex structure and with arbitrary levels of nesting. It can also specify arbitrary grouping criteria, using nested queries and Skolem functions. Typical RXL queries are long and complex, because they express general transformations from the relational store to the XML view. RXL has a block structure to help users organize, structure, and maintain large queries.

Once the virtual XML view is defined, SilkRoute accepts XML-QL user queries and *composes* them automatically with the RXL query. The result of the composition is another RXL query, which extracts only that fragment of the relational data that the user requested. Query composition is the most important technical contribution of this work, and our solution to this problem is general enough to be used in other systems requiring virtual XML views. In relational databases, composition is straightforward and not considered a problem; for example, Ramakrishnan [19] describes how to reformulate SQL queries over SQL virtual views as SQL queries over base relations. For XML, however, this problem is more complex, and, to the best of our knowledge, no solution has been published. We present a sound, complete, and conceptually simple algorithm that when given an RXL query and an XML-QL query, produces a new RXL query equivalent to their composition. We place some restrictions on aggregate functions in RXL queries, but they can be used freely in XML-QL queries.

Finally, when an RXL query is evaluated, most of the processing is done by the underlying relational engine. To do this, the RXL query is split into a collection of SQL queries, each of which produces a set of tuples. The SQL queries are sent to the RDBMS, and their flat, sorted results are merged in a single pass to construct the nested XML output. In summary, this paper makes the following contributions:

- it describes a general framework for mapping relational databases to XML views to be used in data exchange;
- it describes a new query language, RXL, for mapping relational sources to XML views;

```
<?xml encoding="US-ASCII"?>
<!ELEMENT supplier (company, product*)>
<!ELEMENT product (name, category, description, retail, sale?, report*)>
<!ATTLIST product ID ID>
<!ELEMENT company (#PCDATA)>
<!ELEMENT name    (#PCDATA)>
<!ELEMENT retail  (#PCDATA)>
<!ELEMENT sale    (#PCDATA)>
<!ELEMENT report  (#PCDATA)>
<!ATTLIST report code (size|defective|style) #REQUIRED>
```

Fig. 1. `supplier.dtd`: DTD of XML data exported by suppliers to resellers.

- it describes a sound and complete query composition algorithm that, when given an RXL query and an XML-QL query, generates a new RXL query equivalent to their composition;
- it describes a technique in which most of the work of an RXL query can be shipped to the underlying database engine.

To motivate this work, we present in the next section an example scenario from electronic commerce. In Section 2, we describe SilkRoute's architecture, its various components and the view-definition language, RXL. In Section 3, we give an informal discussion of our query composition algorithm by describing the pattern matching and query rewriting steps of the algorithm in detail. A brief discussion of aggregates appears in Section 3.4. Section 4 includes descriptions of related systems. A pseudo-code description of query composition can be found in Appendix A.

1.1. Motivating example

We motivate SilkRoute with a simple example from electronic commerce, in which *suppliers* provide product information to *resellers*. For their mutual benefit, suppliers and resellers have agreed to exchange data in a format that conforms to a particular DTD, depicted in Fig. 1. It includes the supplier's name and a list of available products. Each product element includes an item name, a category name, a brief description, a retail price, an optional sale price, and zero or more trouble reports. The contents of a `retail` or `sale` element is a currency value. A trouble report includes a code attribute, indicating the class of problem; the report's content is the customer's comments. Most importantly, this DTD is used by suppliers and resellers, and it is a public document.

Consider now a particular supplier whose business data is organized according to the relational schema depicted in Fig. 2. The `Clothing` table contains tuples with a product id (the table's key), an item name, category name, item description, price, and cost. The `SalePrice` table contains sale prices and has key field `pid`; the `Problem` table contains trouble codes of products and their reports. This is a third-normal form relational schema, designed for the supplier's particular business needs. The schema is proprietary: for example, the supplier may not want to reveal the attribute `cost` in `Clothing`. The supplier's task is to convert its relational data into a valid XML view conforming to the DTD in Fig. 1 and make the XML view available to resellers. In this example, we assume that the supplier exports a subset of its inventory, in particular, its stock of winter outer-wear that it wants to sell at a reduced price at the end of the winter season.

Once the XML views of suppliers' data are available, the reseller can access that data by formulating

```
Clothing(*pid, item, category, description, price, cost)
SalePrice(*pid, price)
Problems(pid, code, comments)
```

Fig. 2. Schema of supplier's relational database (* denotes key).

queries over the XML view. Some examples of such queries are:

- retrieve products whose sale price is less than 50% of retail price;
- count the number of 'defective' reports for a product;
- compute minimum and maximum cost of outerwear stock.

As these queries suggest, the reseller is typically interested only in a small subset of the information provided by the suppliers. Readers familiar with SQL will recognize that these queries could be formulated as SQL queries over the supplier's relational database, but relational schemas differ from supplier to supplier and are not accessible by the reseller.

2. Silkroute's architecture

SilkRoute's architecture is depicted in Fig. 3. It serves as middleware between a relational database (RDBMS) and an application accessing that data over the Web. The database administrator starts by writing an RXL query that defines the XML virtual view of the database. This is called the *view query* and it is typically complex, because it transforms the relational data into a deeply nested XML view. The resulting view query is virtual, meaning that it is not evaluated, but kept in source code.

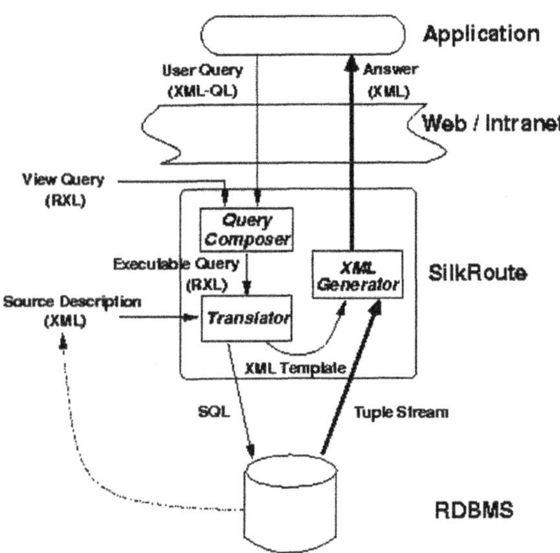

Fig. 3. SilkRoute's architecture.

Typically, applications contact SilkRoute to request data. An application only 'sees' the virtual XML view, not the underlying relational database. To access the data, it formulates a *user query* in XML-QL over the virtual view and sends it to SilkRoute. Together, the RXL view query and the XML-QL user query are passed to the *query composer*, the most complex module in SilkRoute. The composer computes the composition and produces a new RXL query, called the *executable query*. The answer to the executable query typically includes only a small fragment of the database, e.g., one data item, a small set of data items, or an aggregate value. Its result is an XML document, as specified by the user XML-QL query.

Once computed, the executable query is passed to the *translator*, which partitions it into a data-extraction part, i.e., one or more SQL queries, and an XML-construction part, i.e., an XML template. The translator also takes as input a description of the relational schema.

Until now, SilkRoute has manipulated only query source code, but no data. At this point, the SQL queries are sent to the RDBMS server, which returns one tuple stream per SQL query. The *XML generator* module merges these tuple streams and produces the XML document, which is then returned to the application.

This scenario is probably the most common use of SilkRoute, but minor changes to the information flow in Fig. 3 permit other scenarios. For example, the data administrator may export the entire database as one, large XML document by materializing the view query. This can be done by passing the view query directly to the translator. In another scenario, the result of query composition could be kept virtual for later composition with other user queries. This is useful, for example, when one wants to define a new XML view from an existing composed view. In the rest of this section, we describe the system's components in more detail.

2.1. The view query: RXL

In this section, we describe RXL (Relational to XML transformation Language). RXL essentially combines the extraction part of SQL, i.e., a `from` and a `where` clause (possibly followed by `sort by` and/or `group by` clauses) with the construction part of XML-QL [9], i.e., the `construct` clause.

As a first example, consider this RXL query, which defines a fragment of an XML view:

```
from Clothing $c
where $c.category = "outerwear"
construct  <product>
              <name>$c.item</name>
              <category>$c.category
                           </category>
              <retail>$c.price</retail>
           </product>
```

Given a database like that in Fig. 2, the query will produce an XML fragment like the following:

```
<product> <name>...</name>
   <category>...</category>
   <retail>...</retail>
</product>
<product> <name>...</name>
   <category>...</category>
   <retail>...</retail>
</product>
...
```

A root element is missing; we will explain later how to add one.

As in SQL, the `from` clause declares *variables* that iterate over tables. Variable names start with a `$`. In this example, `$c` is a tuple variable that iterates over the `Clothing` table. The `where` clause contains zero or more *filters* (Boolean predicates) over *column expressions*. The column expression `$c.item` refers to the `item` attribute value of `$c` and in this case, requires that it equals the string `"outerwear"`. The `construct` clause specifies the XML value, called an *XML template*, in terms of the bound column expressions.

RXL has three powerful features that make it possible to create arbitrarily complex XML structures: nested queries, Skolem functions, and block structure. An example of a *nested query* is:

```
construct <view> {
  from Clothing $c
  construct
    <product>
      <name>$c.item</name>
      { from Problems $p
        where $p.pid = $c.cid
        construct
          <report>$p.comments</report>
      }
    </product>
} </view>
```

The outer query has no `from` or `where` clauses, only a `<construct>` clause for the root element `<view>`. The first sub-query builds one `<product>` element for each row in `Clothing`. Its inner sub-query creates zero or more `<report>` sub-elements, one for each report associated with that product. Readers familiar with SQL may recognize this as a left-outer join of `Clothing` with `Problems` followed by a `group by` on `Clothing`.

Skolem functions [14] allow us to control the way elements are grouped. Recall that in XML an attribute with type `ID` contains a value that uniquely identifies the element in the document, i.e., a *key*. In RXL, the distinguished attribute `ID` always has type `ID`, and its value is a Skolem term, which is used to control grouping and element creation. For example, in the following:

```
from Clothing $c
construct
     <category
          ID=Cat($c.category)
          name=$c.category>
        <product>$c.item</product>
     </category>
```

`Cat` is a Skolem function and `Cat($c.category)` is a Skolem term whose meaning is that only one `<category>` element exists for every value of `$c.category`, and it includes all products in that category:

```
<category><product>p1</product>
          <product>p2</product>
</category>
<category><product>p3</product>
          <product>p4</product>
</category>
...
```

Without the `ID` attribute and its Skolem term, the query would create one `<category>` element for each row in `Clothing`:

```
construct
  <view ID=View()>
    { from Clothing $c
      construct <product ID=Prod($c.item)>
                  <name ID=Name($c.item)>$c.item</name>
                  <price ID=Price($c.item, $c.price)>$c.price</price>
                </product> }
    { from Clearance $d
      where $d.disc > 50
      construct <product ID=Prod($d.prodname)>
                  <name ID=Name($d.prodname)>$d.prodname</name>
                  <discount ID=Discount($d.prodname,$d.disc)>$d.disc</discount>
                </product> }
  </view>
```

Fig. 4. Multi-block RXL view query.

```
<category><product>p1</product>
</category>
<category><product>p2</product>
</category> ...
```

When Skolem terms are missing, RXL introduces them automatically. Since Skolem terms could be used to define arbitrary graphs, RXL enforces semantic constraints that guarantee that a view always defines a tree, and therefore, a well-formed XML document. For example, the Skolem term of a sub-element must include all the variables of its parent element.

Finally, the *block structure* allows RXL to construct parts of complex elements independently. The query in Fig. 4 contains two blocks. The first block creates elements of the form:

```
<product><name>n</name>
         <price>p</price>
</product>
```

for each product name in Clothing. The second block creates elements of the form:

```
<product><name>n</name>
         <discount>d</discount>
</product>
```

for each product name in Clearance. (Here, we assume Clearance(*prodname, disc) is part of the supplier's schema.) When the same product name occurs both in Clothing and Clearance, then the two elements will have the same ID key and are merged into:

```
<product><name>n</name>
         <price>p</price>
         <discount>d</discount>
</product>
```

Readers familiar with SQL will recognize this as an outer join.

Fig. 5 contains the complete view query for our supplier example in Section 1.1. Lines 1, 2, and 27 create the root <supplier> element: notice that the Skolem term Supp() has no variables, meaning that one <supplier> element is created. The outer-most clause constructs the top-level element supplier and its company child element. The first nested clause (lines 4–26) contains the query fragment described above, which constructs one product element for each 'outerwear' item. Within this clause, the nested clause (lines 13–17) expresses a join between the Clothing and SalePrice tables and constructs a sale element with the product's sale price nested within the outer product element. The last nested clause (lines 18–24) expresses a join between the Clothing and Problem tables and constructs one report element containing the problem code and customer's comments; the report elements are also nested within the outer product element. Notice that the Skolem term of product guarantees that all product elements with the same identifier are grouped together. Usually, Skolem terms are inferred automatically, but we include them explicitly, because they are relevant to query composition described in Section 3.

```
construct
<supplier ID=Supp()>
  <company ID=Comp()>"Acme Clothing"</company>
  {
    from Clothing $c
    where $c.category = "outerwear"
    construct
      <product ID=Prod($c.pid)>
        <name ID=Name($c.pid,$c.item)>$c.item</name>
       <category ID=Cat($c.pid,$c.category)>$c.category</category>
       <description ID=Desc($c.pid,$c.description)>$c.description</description>
       <retail ID=Retail($c.pid,$c.price)>$c.price</retail>
      { from SalePrice $s
        where $s.pid = $c.pid
        construct
        <sale ID=Sale($c.pid,$s.pid,$s.price)>$s.price</retail>
      }
      { from Problems $p
        where $p.pid = $c.pid
        construct
        <report code=$p.code ID=Prob($c.pid,$p.pid,$p.code,$p.comments)>
        $p.comments
        </report>
      }
    </product>
  }
</supplier>
```

Fig. 5. RXL view query (V).

2.2. *The user query: XML-QL*

Applications do not access the relational data directly, but through the XML view. To do this, they write *user queries* in XML-QL, a query language for XML [9]. XML-QL queries contain a `where` clause followed by a `construct` clause. The `where` clause contains an arbitrary number of XML *patterns* and filters. The `construct` clause is identical to that in RXL.

In our example, the reseller can retrieve all products with a sale price less than half of the retail price using the XML-QL query in Fig. 6. The `where` clause consists of a pattern (lines 3–10) and a filter (line 11). A pattern's syntax is similar to that of XML data, but also may contain variables, whose names start with `$`. Filters are similar to RXL (and SQL). The meaning of a query is as follows. First, all variables in the `where` clause are bound in all possible ways to the contents of elements in the XML document. For each such binding, the `construct` clause constructs an XML value. Grouping is expressed by Skolem terms in the `construct` clause. In this example, the `construct` clause produces one `result` element for each value of `$company;` each `result` element contains the supplier's name and a list of `name` elements containing the product names.

It is important to notice that answer to the user query includes a small fraction of the relational database, i.e., only those products that are heavily discounted.

2.3. *The query composer*

SilkRoute's query composer takes a user query and the RXL view query and generates a new RXL query, which is equivalent to the user query evaluated on the materialized view. In our example, the view query is in Fig. 5, the user query in Fig. 6, and the composed query is in Fig. 7. The composed query combines fragments of the view query and user query. Those fragments from the user query are highlighted. The composed query extracts data from the relational database in the same way as the view

```
construct
 <results> {
   where <supplier>
           <company>$company</company>
            <product>
             <name>$name</name>
             <retail>$retail</retail>
             <sale>$sale</sale>
            </product>
           </supplier> in "http://acme.com/products.xml",
           $sale < 0.5 * $retail
    construct
           <result ID=Result($company)>
             <supplier>$company</supplier>
             <name>$name</name>
           </result>
  } </results>
```

Fig. 6. XML-QL user query (U).

```
construct
  <results>
  { from Clothing $c, SalePrice $s
    where $c.category = "outerwear",
          $c.pid = $s.pid,
          $s.price < 0.5 * $c.retail
    construct
      <result ID=Result("Acme Clothing")>
        <supplier>"Acme Clothing"</supplier>
        <name ID=Name($c.pid, $c.item)>$c.item</name>
      </result>
  }
  </results>
```

Fig. 7. Composed RXL query (C).

query. It also includes the user filter `$s.price < 0.5 $c.retail` and structures the result as in the user query. The details of composition are subtle, and a complete description of the composition algorithm is given in Section 3.

We call the composed query *executable*, because it is typically translated into SQL queries and sent to the relational database engine. Notice that the answer of the executable query is quite small — the same as that of the user query. In general, it is more efficient to execute the composed query, instead of materializing the view query, because composed queries often contain constraints on scalar values that can be evaluated using indexes in the relational database. Such indices are of little or no use when evaluating a view query. For example, consider a user query that specifies the condition: `$s.price between 80 and 100`. This condition is propagated into the executable query, and then into the SQL query, and can be evaluated efficiently if an index exists on `price`. In contrast, an index on `price` is useless when materializing the view query directly.

2.4. Translator and XML generator

The *translator* takes an RXL query and decomposes it into one or more SQL queries and an XML template. The SQL queries are executed by the relational engine, and their flat results (streams of tuples) are converted into XML by the *XML generator*.

The translator also takes a source description, which is an XML document specifying systems information needed to contact the source: the protocol (e.g., JDBC), the connection string, and a source-specific query driver. The driver translates RXL expressions into the source's query language, which is typically a dialect of SQL, but other query languages can be supported. For example, the executable RXL query in Fig. 7 is translated into the SQL query:

```
select   c.pid as pid,
         c.item as item
from     Clothing c, SalePrice s
where    c.category = "outerwear",
         c.pid = s.pid,
         s.price < 0.5 * c.retail
sort by  c.pid
```

and into the XML template:

```
<results>
 <result ID=Result("Acme Clothing")>
    <supplier>"Acme Clothing"
    </supplier>
    <name ID=Name($pid, $item)>$item
    </name>
  </result>
</results>
```

where the variables `$pid` and `$item` refer to the attributes `pid` and `item` in the SQL query's `select` clause; we describe the template generation in more detail in Section 3.1. After translation, the SQL query is sent to the relational engine, and the resulting tuple stream is fed into the XML generator, which produces the XML output.

In this example, the translation requires only one SQL query. In general, there may be several ways to translate a complex RXL query into one or more SQL queries and to merge tuple streams into the XML result. Choosing an efficient evaluation strategy may be important when the RXL query returns a large result, e.g., if the entire XML view if materialized. Currently, SilkRoute has one evaluation strategy, which generates one SQL query for each disjunct of an RXL sub-query, which must be in disjunctive-normal form (DNF). Each SQL query has a `sort by` clause, making it possible for the XML generator to merge them into an XML document in a single pass.

2.5. Alternative approaches

We have described what we believe to be the most general approach for exporting relational data into XML. Other approaches are possible, and in some cases, may be more desirable.

Currently, the most widely used Web interfaces to relational databases are HTML forms with CGI scripts. User inputs are translated by a script into SQL queries, and their answers are rendered in HTML. The answers could be generated just as easily in XML. Forms interfaces are appropriate for casual users, but inappropriate for data exchange between applications, because they limit the application to only those queries that are predetermined by the form interface. Aggregate queries, for example, are rarely offered by form interfaces.

In another alternative, the data provider can either precompute the materialized view or compute it on demand whenever an application requests it. This is feasible when the XML view is small and the application needs to load the entire XML view in memory, e.g., using the DOM interface. However, precomputed views are not dynamic, i.e., their data can become stale, and are not acceptable when data freshness is critical.

A third alternative is to use a native XML database engine, which can store XML data and process queries in some XML query language. XML engines will not replace relational databases, but a high-performance XML engine might be appropriate to use in data exchange. For example, one could materialize an XML view using SilkRoute and store the result in an XML engine that supports XML-QL, thus avoiding the query composition cost done in SilkRoute. We do not expect, however, XML engines to match in performance commercial SQL engines anytime soon. In addition, this approach suffers from data staleness, and incurs a high space because it duplicate the entire data in XML.

3. Query composition

In this section, we describe the query composition algorithm. Recall that an RXL query, V, takes as input a relational database and returns as output an XML document. The XML-QL user query, U,

```
construct
  <supplier ID=Supp()>
    <company ID=Comp()>"Acme Clothing"</company>
    {
      from Clothing $c
      where $c.category = "outerwear"
      construct
        <product ID=Prod($c.pid)>
        <name ID=Name($c.pid,$c.item)>$c.item</name>
        <category ID=Cat($c.pid,$c.category)$c.category</category
        <retail ID=Retail($c.pid,$c.price)>$c.price</retail>
          { from SalePrice $s
             where $s.pid = $c.pid
             construct
               <sale ID=Sale($c.pid,$s.pid,$s.price)>$s.price</sale>
          }
          { from Problems $p
             where $p.pid = $c.pid
             construct
             <report code=$p.code ID=Prob($c.pid,$p.pid,$p.code,$p.comments)>
               $p.comments
             </report>
          }
        </product>
    }
  </supplier>
```

Fig. 8. RXL view query (V) with patterns from XML-QL query (U) highlighted.

is written against V; it takes as input an XML document and returns an XML document. For any database D, we can compute the result of U by first materializing $V(D)$, denoted as *XMLD*, and then computing U(*XMLD*). The query composition problem is to construct an equivalent RXL query C, where $C = U \circ V$. In other words, we would like to construct an RXL query C that is guaranteed to yield the same result as U and V for any database D, that is, $C(D) = U(V(D))$. Notice that C takes as input a relational database and returns an XML document. With C, we skip the construction of the intermediate result *XMLD*. As a running example, we use V from Fig. 5, and U from Fig. 6; the result of the composition, C, is shown in Fig. 7.

Before describing the details, we give a brief intuitive description. An important observation is that all XML components (tags, attributes, `#PCDATA`) present in *XMLD* are explicitly mentioned in the `construct` clause(s) of V. When U is evaluated on *XMLD* its patterns are matched with these components. The key idea is then to evaluate U on V's templates directly, without constructing *XMLD*. During this evaluation we only consider the patterns, not the filters occurring in U. In our example, U has a unique pattern that mentions `<supplier>`, `<company>`, `<product>`, `<name>`, `<retail>`, and `<sale>` with a particular nesting, and all these tags indeed occur in V's templates under the same nesting. We show V again in Fig. 8, after the matching, with the matched tags highlighted in bold. Once the matching is done, we `construct` the composed query C in a second step, as follows. C's `construct` clause is the same as U's `construct` clause, modulo variable renaming. Its `from` and `where` clauses consist both of the 'relevant' `from` and `where` clauses in V and of all the `where` filter conditions in U, modulo variable renaming. This completes the construction of C. In our example, the 'relevant' `from` and `where` clauses are (see Fig. 8):

```
from Clothing $c, SalePrice $s
where $c.category = "outerwear",
      $s.pid = $c.pid
```

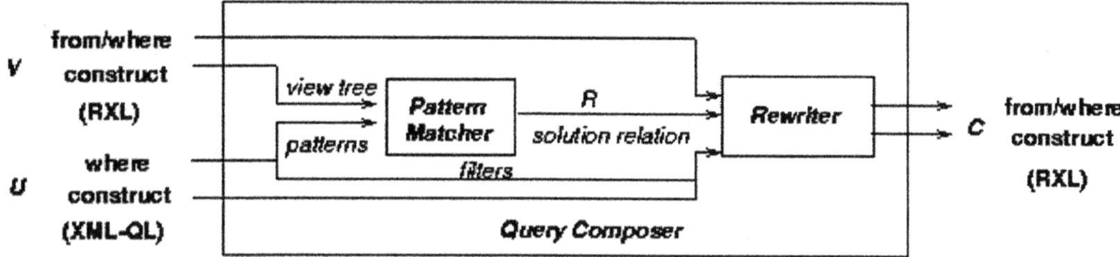

Fig. 9. Diagram of query composition.

and the `where` filter condition from U is `$sale < 0.5 * $retail` becomes the following after variable renaming:

```
where $s.price < 0.5 * $c.retail
```

The reader may check that, together, they form the `from` and `where` clauses in Fig. 7.

Fig. 9 depicts the architecture of query composition. The *pattern matcher* implements the first step; it evaluates U on V by matching U's patterns with V's templates. The result is a *solutions relation*, R, in which each tuple represents one match. Multiple matches may occur if the patterns contain alternation, e.g., `<company|organization>`, or Kleene-star operators, e.g., `<*.supplier>`, or tag variables `<$elm>`. The second step is implemented by the *rewriter*. It takes the remaining clauses (V's `from` and `where` and U's `construct`) and the relation R, and rewrites each solution tuple into one RXL block. The result is the composed query C.

We notice that our query composition technique can be viewed as an example of *partial evaluation*: the patterns are evaluated at *composition time* (a.k.a. compile time) on V's templates, and the filters and constructors are evaluated *at run time* when the new RXL view is evaluated. The remainder of this section describes the internal representation of view and user queries and gives a detailed description of the composition algorithm. A pseudo-code version of the algorithm appears in Appendix A.

3.1. Step 1: pattern matching

In Step 1, we construct the solutions relation R that contains all matchings of U's patterns with V's templates.

3.1.1. Construct the view tree

For the composition algorithm, we represent V by a data structure called a *view tree*, which consists of a global template and a set of datalog rules. The global template is obtained by merging all V's templates from all its `construct` clauses: nodes from two different templates are merged if and only if they have the same Skolem function, hence each Skolem function occurs exactly once in the view tree. The datalog rules are non-recursive. Their heads are the Skolem functions names, and their bodies consist of relation names and filters. The datalog rules are constructed as follows. For each occurrence of a Skolem function F in V, we construct one rule of the form $F(x, y, \ldots)$ `:-` *body*, where *body* is the conjunction of all `from` and `where` clauses in the scope where F occurs. When a rule is associated with a Skolem function, we say that the rule *guards* that function and its corresponding XML element. In both the template and datalog rules, we replace the tuple variables used in RXL by column variables.

Fig. 10 contains the view tree for our example. The unique `supplier` element is guarded by the rule `Supp():- true`, which is always `true`, because no predicate expression guards the element's creation. The `retail` elements are guarded by the rule:

```
Retail($cpid, $cprice):-
  Clothing($cpid, _, $category, _,
           $cprice),
  $category = "outerwear"
```

which means that one `retail` element is created for each value of `cpid` and `cprice` that satisfies the table expression on the right-hand side. There is only one datalog rule for each Skolem function, because each function occurs once in V (Fig. 5).

```
<supplier ID=Supp()>                                Supp() :- true
  <company ID=Comp()>Acme Clothing</company>        Comp() :- true
  <product ID=Prod($cpid)>                          Prod($cpid) :- Clothing($cpid, _, $category, _, _),
                                                                   $category = "outerwear"
    <name ID=Name($cpid,$citem)>                    Name($cpid, $citem) :- Clothing($cpid, $citem, c$ategory, _, _),
      $citem                                                                $category = "outerwear"
    </name>
    <category ID=Cat($cpid,$ccategory)>             Cat($cpid, $ccategory) :- Clothing($cpid, _, $category, _, _),
      $ccategory                                                               $category = "outerwear"
    </category>
    <retail ID=Retail($cpid,$cprice)>               Retail($cpid, $cprice) :- Clothing($cpid, _, $category, _, $cprice),
      $cprice                                                                  $category = "outerwear"
    </retail>
    <sale ID=Sale($cpid,$spid,$sprice)>             Sale($cpid, $spid, $sprice):-
      $sprice                                             Clothing($cpid, _, $category, _, _), $category = "outerwear",
    </sale>                                               SalePrice($spid, $sprice), $cpid = $spid
    <report ID=Prob($cpid,$ppid,$pcode,$pcmnts) Rep($cpid, $ppid, $pcode, $pcmnts):-
            code=$pcode>                                  Clothing($cpid, _, $category, _, _), $category = "outerwear",
      $pcmnts                                             Problems($ppid, $pcode, $pcmnts), $cpid = $ppid
    </report>
  </product>
</supplier>
```

Fig. 10. View tree for the RXL query in Fig. 5: template (left) and datalog rules (right).

```
<supplier ID=$t1>
  <company ID=$t2>$company</company>
    <product ID=$t3>
      <name ID=$t4>$name</name>
      <retail ID=$t5>$retail</retail>
      <sale ID=$t6>$sale</sale>
    </product>
</supplier>
```

Fig. 11. Adding one temporary variable for each element in the pattern.

3.1.2. Evaluate U on the view tree

Next, we match U's patterns with V's template. To simplify presentation, we assume that U consists of a single block:

$U =$ construct <elm>
where { P, W construct T } </elm> (1)

where T denotes the template, P denotes all patterns, and W denotes all filters. For each element in U's patterns, we introduce one new, temporary variable for the element's ID attribute. In our example, U has a single pattern and we add six new variables shown in Fig. 11. We discuss the necessity of these variables and how to handle multi-block user queries in Section 3.3.

Next, we evaluate U's patterns on V's template in the standard way of evaluating patterns on a tree [9]. In general, there may be zero, one, or more results, and we represent them as a table R, with one column for each variable in U, and one row for each result. The values in the table are #PCDATA, Skolem terms, variables, tag names, attribute values, and attribute names, which occur in V's template. In our example, this step results in the following table R:

\$t1	\$t2	\$company	\$t3
Supp()	Comp()	"Acme Clothing"	Prod (\$cpid)

\$t4	\$name	\$t5
Name(\$cpid, \$cprice)	\$citem	Retail(\$cpid, \$cprice)

\$retail	\$t6	\$sale
\$cprice	Sale(\$cpid, \$spid, \$sprice)	\$sprice

The column names correspond to the variables in U's pattern in Fig. 11. The single row in R means that there exist only one matching of U's pattern with V's template. The row specifies that U's variable $name is bound to $citem in V, the variable $t3 is bound to the Skolem term Prod($cpid), and the variable $company is bound to the text data Acme Clothing.

3.2. Step 2: query rewriting

In Step 2, we use the table R to construct the composed query C. Each row in R represents one match, and C is the union of all possible matches. In particular, C consists of several parallel blocks, which denote union in RXL. In each block, the from and where clauses contain the 'relevant' datalog rules, which are the rules for the Skolem functions in the corresponding row. The block's construct clause contains U's template. Recall that U consists of a single block, Eq. 1, and that T denotes its template, P its patterns, and W its filters. Let the rows in R be $r_1 \ldots r_k$. Then C consists of several parallel blocks:

$C =$ construct {<elm>{B_1}...{B_k} </elm>}

with one or more blocks corresponding to each row r_i. Next, we show how to construct the blocks corresponding to one row, r_i, in R.

3.2.1. Construct one block

We first represent one block's from and where clauses as one datalog rule. Let $F_1 \ldots F_n$ be the Skolem functions that occur in the row r_i. Recall that the view tree associates one or more datalog rules to each Skolem function. Assume that there is a unique datalog rule for each Skolem function:

$F_1 :\text{-}\ body_1\ \ldots\ F_n :\text{-}\ body_n$

The block's construct clause is $S_0(T)$ where S_0 is a variable substitution defined below. For each datalog rule F_i, we apply one variable substitution S_i. The body of the new datalog rule is the union of all bodies after variable substitution, plus $S_0(W)$. Thus, the new rule has the form:

$Q(S_0(x), S_0(y), \ldots) :\text{-}$
$S_0(W), S_1(body_1), \ldots, S_n(body_n)$

where $x, y, \ldots$ are the variables in U's template T. Next, we minimize Q, and rewrite it as a from–

`where` clause: all relation names appear in the `from` clause, and all filters in the `where` clause. This completes the construction of one block.

3.2.2. Variable substitutions

Next, we define the substitutions S_0 and $S_1 \ldots S_n$. For all the datalog rules $F_1 \ldots F_n$, we construct the substitutions $S_1 \ldots S_n$ so that the expressions $S_1(body_1) \ldots S_n(body_n)$ all have distinct variables, with one exception. For every two columns t_j, t_k in R, where the variable t_j corresponds to an element that is the parent of t_k's element, all variables in $S_j(F_j(\ldots))$ must be shared with $S_k(F_k(\ldots))$. To compute S_0, we apply the substitutions $S_1 \ldots S_n$ to the entire row r_i and drop all columns in r_i that correspond to the temporary variables `$t1 ... $t2`. The new row is S_0, which maps U's variables to column variables, constants, and Skolem terms.

When there is more than one datalog rule per Skolem function, we must convert the resulting datalog program into disjunctive normal form, i.e., a disjunction of multiple conjunctive datalog rules, before generating the RXL blocks. For each conjunctive rule, we apply the construction above to obtain one block and take the union of all such blocks. In this case, we obtain more than one block for one row r_i.

In our example, table R has one row that contains the Skolem terms `Supp()`, `Comp()`, `Prod($cpid)`, `Name($cpid, $citem)`, `Retail($cpid, $cprice)`, and `Sale($cpid, $spid, $sprice)`. Their corresponding datalog rules are in Fig. 10. Now we compute the substitutions $S_1, \ldots, S_6$ such that the rules have disjoint variables with the exception of variables that have parent/child relationships. In our example, the variable `$t3` is the parent of variables `$t4, $t5, $t6` (Fig. 11). Therefore, the Skolem term `Prod($cpid)` must share the variable `$cpid` with that in `Name($cpid, $citem)`, `Retail($cpid,$cprice)`, and `Sale($cpid, $spid, $sprice)`. Otherwise, all variables must be distinct. The modified rules are:

```
Supp()                         :- true
Comp()                         :- true
Prod($cpid)                    :- Clothing($cpid, _, $category1, _, _),
                                  $category1= "outerwear"
Name($cpid, $citem)            :- Clothing($cpid, $citem, $category2, _, _),
                                  $category2= "outerwear"
Retail($cpid, $cprice)         :- Clothing($cpid, _, $category3, _, $cprice),
                                  $category3= "outerwear"
Sale($cpid, $spid, $sprice) :- Clothing($cpid, _, $category4, _, _),
                                  $category4= "outerwear",
                                  SalePrice($spid, $sprice), $cpid = $spid
```

The substitution S_0 is obtained directly from the table R, by dropping all columns corresponding to the new variables `$t1,...,$t6`: $S_0 =$

`$company`	`$name`	`$retail`	`$sale`
`"Acme Clothing"`	`$citem`	`$cprice`	`$sprice`

U's template T is in Fig. 6 and its filter W is `$sale < 0.5 * $retail`. Only the variables `$company` and `$name` occur in T, so we have to include S_0`($company)` and S_0`($name)` in the rule's head; *company*, however, is a constant, therefore the rule becomes:

```
Q($citem):-    Clothing($cpid, _, $category1, _, _), $category1= "outerwear",
               Clothing($cpid, $citem, $category2, _, _), $category2= "outerwear",
               Clothing($cpid, _, $category3, _, $cprice), $category3= "outerwear",
               Clothing($cpid, _, $category4, _, _),
               $category4= "outerwear", SalePrice($spid, $sprice), $cpid = $spid,
               $sprice < 0.5 * cprice
```

The last line is $S_0(W)$. We minimize Q (see e.g., [1]) and obtain the equivalent query:

```
Q($citem):- Clothing($cpid, _, $category3, _, $cprice),
   $category3= "outerwear",
   SalePrice($spid, $sprice),
   $cpid = $spid,
   $sprice < 0.5 * cprice
```

Finally, we convert it into from and where clauses, and add a construct clause whose template is $S_0(T)$:

```
from     Clothing($cpid, _, $category3, _, $cprice),
         SalePrice($spid, $sprice)
where    $category3 = "outerwear",
         $cpid = $spid,
         $sprice < 0.5 * cprice
construct
     <result ID= Result("Acme Clothing")>
        <supplier>Acme Clothing</supplier>
        <name>$citem</name>
     </result>
```

Lastly, we replace column variables by tuple variables, and we obtain the single-block query C in Fig. 7.

3.3. Details

Our example illustrates the simplest cases of query composition. Here, we give several other examples, which illustrate more complex cases.

3.3.1. View tree for multi-block query

Consider the two-block RXL query in Fig. 4.

```
<view ID=View()>                                 View():- true
 <product ID=Prod($name)>                        Prod($name):- Clothing($name, _)
                                                 Prod($name):- Clearance($name, $ddisc),
                                                     $ddisc > 50
  <name ID=Name($name)>                          Name($name):- Clothing($name, _)
   $name                                         Name($name):- Clearance($name, $ddisc),
  </name>                                            $ddisc > 50
  <price ID=Price($name, $cprice)>               Price($name,$cprice):-
   $cprice                                           Clothing($name, $cprice)
  </price>
  <discount ID=Discount($name, $ddisc)>          Discount($name, $ddisc):-
   $ddisc                                            Clearance($name, $ddisc),
  </discount>                                        $ddisc > 50
 </product>
</view>
```

Its view-tree template is on the left and its datalog rules on the right. In the RXL query, the Skolem functions Prod and Name occur twice. In the view tree, each function has two corresponding datalog rules, but in the template, they occur once.

3.3.2. Multiple rows

In general, R may contain multiple rows. To illustrate, we use the query V (in Fig. 10) and compose it with the following XML-QL user query U':

```
construct <results> {
  where <supplier.product.(retail|sale)>$val</> in "http://acme.com/products.xml"
  construct <price>$val</price>
} </results>
```

The regular expression `supplier.product.(retail|sale)` matches a `retail` or a `sale` element nested in a `product` element, which is nested in a `supplier` element. It is analogous to the XPath expression `/supplier/product/retail|sale`. There are two matches of U with V, which produce two rows in R:

$t1	$t2	$t3	$val
Supp()	Prod($cpid)	Retail($cpid,$cprice)	$cprice
Supp()	Prod($cpid)	Sale($cpid,$spid,$sprice)	$sprice

The temporary variables `$t1`, `$t2`, `$t3` are for `supplier`, `product`, and `retail|price`, respectively. The composed query C has two blocks:

```
C = construct <results> { B1 } { B2 } </results>
```

The relevant datalog rules for the first row are those for `Supp`, `Prod` and `Retail` (Fig. 10). No variables are renamed, because `$t2` is the parent of `$t3`. The generated datalog rule after minimization is:

```
Q($cprice):- Clothing($cpid, _, $category, _, $cprice), $category = "outerwear"
```

and it produces C's first block $B1$:

```
B1 = from Clothing $c
     where $c.category="outerwear"
     construct <price>$c.price</price>
```

The relevant datalog rules for the second row are those for `Supp`, `Prod`, and `Sale`. As before, no variables are renamed, and the datalog rule is:

```
Q($sprice):- Clothing($cpid, _, $category, _, _), $category="outerwear",
             SalePrice($spid, $sprice), $cpid = $spid
```

which produces C's second block $B2$:

```
B2 = from Clothing $c, SalePrice $s
     where $c.category="outerwear", $c.pid = $s.pid
     construct <price>$s.price</price>
```

3.3.3. Adding template variables

The temporary variables added to U's patterns play an important role, as revealed by the next example. The query V, written directly with column variables, is:

```
V = construct <v ID=H()> { from T($x,$y)
                           construct <a ID=F($x)>
                                       <b ID=($x,$y)>$y</b>
                                     </a>
                         } </v>
```

and we consider two XML-QL queries U, U':

```
U = construct <results> { where <v><a><b>$z1</b> <b>$z2</b></a></v>
                          construct <result><z1>$z1</z1> <z2>$z2</z2></result>
          } </results>

U'= construct <results> { where <v> <a><b>$z1</b></a> <a><b>$z2</b></a> </v>
                          construct <result><z1>$z1</z1> <z2>$z2</z2></result>
          } </results>
```

Both return pairs of <b> values, but the first query returns pairs where both <b>'s are nested in the same <a> element. Without temporary variables in U's patterns, the relation R would be the same for U and U'. After introducing the new variables, the two relations R have different column names, and as expected, they produce two distinct composed queries.

3.3.4. Renaming variables in datalog rules

Continuing the previous example, we illustrate the need for the substitutions $S_1, S_2, \ldots$. First, we build V's view tree:

```
<v ID=H()>              H()      :- true
 <a ID=F($x)>           F($x)    :- T($x, _)
  <b ID=G($x,$y)>       G($x,$y):- T($x, $y)
   $y
  </b>
 </a>
</v>
```

We illustrate the composition with U'. We add five temporary variables and its pattern becomes:

```
<v ID=$t1>
    <a ID=$t2><b ID=$t3>$z1</b></a>
    <a ID=$t4><b ID=$t5>$z2</b></a>
</v>
```

Matching the pattern with the template produces one row in R:

\$t1	\$t2	\$t3	\$z1	\$t4	\$t5	\$z2
H()	F(\$x)	G(\$x,\$y)	\$y	F(\$x)	G(\$x,\$y)	\$y

Intuitively the variable `$y` in the `$z1` column is different from `$y` in the `$z2` column, because they match different <b> elements, possibly in different <a> elements. This distinction is made precise by the renaming step. Thus, after variable substitution, the five relevant datalog rules become:

```
H()           :- true
F($x1)        :- T($x1, _)
G($x1, $y1):- T($x1, $y1)
F($x2)        :- T($x2, _)
G($x2, $y2):- T($x2, $y2)
```

and the composed query C, after query minimization, is:

```
construct
  <results> from T($x1, $y1),
                 T($x2, $y2)
   construct
     <result><z1>$y1</z1>
             <z2>$y2</z2>
     </result>
  </results>
```

3.3.5. XML-QL queries with block structure

In general, U may have several blocks, both nested and parallel. For multi-block user queries, we construct a different table R for each block in U, in the same way in which the XML-QL query processor handles multiple blocks. Tables corresponding to parallel blocks are independent; for nested blocks, there is a distinct inner table that corresponds to each row in the outer table. The composed query C follows the same block structure, except that one block in U may generate multiple parallel blocks in C, as described earlier in this section.

3.3.6. Query minimization

Query minimization eliminates redundancies in queries, such as duplicate conditions. Query minimization can be expensive, because it is NP-complete. Commercial database systems often do not perform minimization, because users typically do not write redundant queries. In SilkRoute, the composed query C is generated automatically. One condition in a view query V may appear in multiple datalog rules, and, hence be propagated as multiple copies in the generated query C. To avoid query minimization, one could trace these repetitions to the original RXL query, but care is needed to deal with variable renaming. For RXL queries with large parallel blocks, however, query minimization may be unavoidable.

3.4. Aggregation queries

We briefly describe how aggregations in XML-QL queries can be 'pushed' into composed RXL views and evaluated by the target RDBMs. In both XML-QL and RXL, we use Skolem terms to specify the values by which aggregate expressions are grouped.

Suppose a reseller wants to count the total number of reports for each defective product. This can be expressed in XML-QL as follows:

```
where <supplier.product ID=$pid>
        <name>$n</>
        <report>$r</>
      </> in "http://acme.com/
                              products.xml"
construct <product ID=F($pid)>
            <name ID=G($pid,$n)>$n</>
            <totaldefects ID=
                      H($pid)>count(*)</>
          </>
```

The Skolem term `F($pid)` in `<product ID=F($pid)>` asserts that all bindings for the variables `$pid`, `$n` and `$r` are grouped by `$pid`'s value. Similarly, the Skolem term `H($pid)` specifies the grouping attributes for the aggregate function `count(*)`, which counts the total number of bindings. This idea is similar to the group-by construct in SQL. XML-QL and RXL's semantics guarantee that only one element is produced for each value of a Skolem term, e.g., one `name` element is emitted for each value of `$n`.

We use a simple extension to datalog that accommodates aggregate functions [1]. An example of a datalog rule that uses a 'generator' to count values is:

```
C(p,q,COUNT(*)):- R(p,q)
```

Only the last argument in the head can be an aggregate function; the other arguments specify the grouping attributes. The meaning is that C contains the set of triples (p, q, r) where r is the number of tuples in the group corresponding to values (p, q) in the relation R.

Using our composition algorithm, the XML-QL query above can be rewritten as:

```
from Clothing $c, Problems $p
where $c.pid = $p.pid
construct
    <product ID=F($c.pid)>
      <name ID=G($c.pid, $c.item)>
        $c.item</>
      <totaldefects ID=H($c.pid)>
        count(*)</>
    </product>
```

Note that the aggregate function is 'pushed' into the RXL view. When this view is materialized, the aggregation will be evaluated by the relational engine. Most importantly, this query can be evaluated efficiently, because commercial database systems are often highly optimized for aggregation queries.

4. Related research and systems

Bosworth [3] discusses the need for tools that export relational data into XML views. Several commercial tools already exist. The ODBC2XML tool allows users to define XML documents with embedded SQL statements, which allows them to construct an XML view of the relational data. Such views are materialized, however, and cannot be further queried with an XML query language like XML-QL. Alternatively, Oracle's XSQL tool defines a fixed, canonical mapping of the relational data into an XML document, by mapping each relation and attribute name to an XML tag and tuples as nested elements. Such a view could be kept virtual, but the approach is not general enough to support mappings into arbitrary XML. IBM's DB2 XML Extender provides a Data Access Definition (DAD) language that supports both composition of relational data in XML and decomposition of XML data into relational tables. DAD's composition feature, like RXL, supports generation of arbitrary XML from relational data. Unlike RXL, the criterion for grouping elements is implicit in the DAD and DAD specifications cannot be nested arbitrarily. More significantly, XML Extender does not support query composition; however,

```
// Top-level invocation of compose function
X_env = new [("$viewtree", Root())]
S = new []
R_block_list = compose(X_env, S, X_block)

fun compose(Env X_env, VarMap S, XMLQL X_block): [ RXL ] {
  (X_patterns, X_filters, X_template) = decompose(X_block);

  // Get pairs of (parent, child) variables from XML-QL patterns
  X_parent_child_vars = getHeadTargetMap(X_patterns);

  // Evaluate pattern on view tree
  R = evalPattern(X_patterns, X_env);

  // Consider each potential solution
  R_blocks = new []
  for each r_i in R {
    // Extend current environment with new variable bindings
    X_env' = appendList(X_env, r_i);

    // Compute new S variable substitution from X_nodemap
    S' = newVariables(X_env', X_parent_child_vars, S);

    // Compute RXL block for potential solution
    R_blocks = listAppend(oneSolution(X_env', S', X_block, r_i), R_blocks)
  }
  return R_blocks
}
```

Fig. 12. Composition algorithm: top-level `compose` function.

DAD could be used as a view-definition language in a SilkRoute architecture.

XML-QL was first proposed as a W3C technical note [8], then published in [9]. It is the first complete query language specifically designed for XML, borrowing ideas from the research area on semistructured data [2,4,11]. Other query languages for XML include XSL [5,6], XQL [20], Lorel [15], XMAS [13], and YaTL [7].

Query composition is simple for select-project-join queries [1,19], and for the relational calculus [1], in general. In the context of semistructured data, Papakonstantinou et al. first address the problem in the framework of MSL [16], a datalog-like language. Their composition algorithm, called *query decomposition and algebraic optimization*, uses a unification algorithm on the view's head and the query's body. Deutsch et al. [10] and Papakonstantinou and Vassalos [18] address query composition in the more complex setting of query rewriting for semistructured data. Our solution borrows ideas from [10].

5. Discussion

SilkRoute is a general, dynamic, and efficient framework for viewing and querying relational data in XML. We believe it is the first XML-export tool to support arbitrarily complex, virtual views of relational data and to support XML user queries over virtual views. The ability to support arbitrary views is critical in data exchange between inter-enterprise applications, which must abide by public DTDs and cannot reveal the underlying schemas of their proprietary data. The main contribution of this work is a sound and complete algorithm for composing virtual views and user queries. SilkRoute has many benefits: (1) only the relational data requested by a user query is ever materialized; (2) that data is always produced on demand; and (3) the relational engine performs most of the computation efficiently.

We have not addressed two important open problems: general techniques for translating of RXL into efficient SQL and minimization of composed RXL

```
// Return new RXL block for potential solution in r_i
fun oneSolution(Env X_env, VarMap S, XMLQL X_block, Env r_i): [ RXL ] {
  R_conditions = new []
  // For each XML-QL variable X_v in X_block
  foreach X_v in getVariables(X_block) {
    // Get view-tree node bound to X_v
    R_node = project(r_i, X_v);
    // Get rule associated with view-tree node
    (R_tag, R_rule, R_children) = R_node
    // Get body of rule
    (R_head, R_body) = R_node;
    foreach R_condition in R_body {
      R_condition' = makeCopy(R_condition)
      // Rename head variables in R_condition' and add to R_conditions
      R_conditions = cons(rewriteR(S, R_condition'), R_conditions)
    }
  }
  // Rename variables in X_filters and add to R_conditions
  foreach X_filter in X_filters
    R_conditions = cons(rewriteX(X_env, S, X_filter), R_conditions)

  // Put conditions in disjunctive normal form, i.e., [[ Condition ]]
  R_disjuncts = to_DNF(R_conditions)

  // Rename variables in X_template
  R_template = rewriteX(X_env, S, X_template)

  R_blocks = []
  // Construct new RXL block: solution conditions + RXL template
  foreach R_conjunct in R_disjuncts
    R_blocks = cons(new RXL(R_conjunct, R_template), R_blocks)

  return RXL_blocks
}
```

Fig. 13. Composition algorithm: `oneSolution` function.

views. As discussed in Section 2.4, SilkRoute has one translation strategy, which generates one SQL query for each RXL sub-query, which must be in disjunctive-normal form (DNF). In practice, RXL view queries can be arbitrary Boolean combinations of table and filter expressions; for example, parallel RXL blocks often construct parts of complex elements independently, i.e., they express unions. User queries over such views often produce composed queries with many unions. Currently, we normalize any RXL sub-query into multiple sub-queries in DNF, which is a quadratic increase in the number of sub-queries to evaluate. In practice, we may be able to translate multiple queries in DNF directly into SQL, for example, by using SQL's union-join constructs. Similarly, nested RXL queries often express left-outer joins, e.g., the parent sub-query is the left relation and the child sub-query is the right relation. Currently, we generate two SQL queries, one for parent and child, but clearly one SQL query suffices. In addition to reducing the number of SQL queries, we want to minimize each individual RXL sub-query, i.e., eliminate all redundant expressions, so that the resulting SQL query is also minimal. Techniques exist for query minimization [1], but general algorithms are NP-complete. We expect heuristic algorithms to be effective for RXL queries, because RXL's nested block structure can help identify those expressions that most likely are redundant. Our future research will focus on these problems and on applying SilkRoute to large-scale applications.

```
// rewriteX rewrites XML-QL expression as RXL expression
fun rewriteX(Env X_env, VarMap S, X_Expr E) {
  fun substX(E) {
    case E of
      Var(v)              = lookupMap(S, v)
      Const(c)            = new Const(c)
      Element(T, X)       = new Element(T, mapList(substX, X))
      Relop(op,E1,E2)     = new Relop(op, substX(E1), substX(E2))
      // Cases for all types of BoolExprs ...
      // Recursively compose and rewrite nested XML-QL query
      NestedQuery(X_block) = new NestedQuery(compose(X_env, S, X_block))
  }
  return substX(E)
}
// rewriteR renames RXL variables.
fun rewriteR(S varmap, R_Expr E) {
  fun substR(E) {
    case E of
      Var(v)                = lookupMap(S, v)
      TableExpr(name, vars) = new TableExpr(name, mapList(substR, vars))
      Filter(b)             = new Filter(substR(b))
      Or(l1, l2)            = new Or(mapList(subst, l1), mapList(substR, l2))
      // Cases for all types of BoolExprs...
      NestedQuery(RXL(conditions, template)) =
        new NestedQuery(new RXL(mapList(substR, conditions), substR template))
  }
  return substR(E)
}
```

Fig. 14. Composition algorithm: `rewrite` function.

5.1. Availability

XML-QL and SilkRoute are implemented in Java. SilkRoute has drivers for Oracle and MySQL database servers. XML-QL can be downloaded from http://www.research.att.com/sw/tools/xmlql. SilkRoute should be available publicly in 2000.

Appendix A. Composition algorithm — pseudo-code

In the formal description of the algorithm, we need a notation for describing the types of values that are manipulated, e.g., view trees, XML-QL blocks. We denote types by grammar rules, like the following:

```
Node      :- Tag, Rule, [ Node ]
Rule      :- SkolemTerm, [ Condition ]
Condition:- TableExpr(String, [ Var ])
        | Filter
        | Or([ Condition ],[ Condition ])
Filter    :- And(Filter, Filter) |
             Or(Filter, Filter) | Not(Filter) | Term
             RelOp Term
```

These rules specify that a view tree `Node` is composed of a tag, a rule, and a list of children nodes; a `Rule` is composed of a Skolem term (its head) and a conjunctive list of conditions (its body); and a `Condition` is either a table expression, a filter expression, or the disjunction of two lists of conjuncts.

An XML-QL block is represented by a list of patterns, a list of filters, and a template, and an RXL block by a list of conditions and a template:

```
XMLQL:- [ Pattern ], [ BoolExpr ],
        Template
RXL   :- [ Condition ], Template
```

A template is either a constant string, a variable, an element which includes a tag and list of nested templates, or a nested query. To simplify presentation, templates are polymorphic, i.e., an XML-QL template contains only a nested XML-QL block and similarly so for an RXL template.

```
Template:- Const(String)
         | Var(String)
         | Element(Tag, [ Template ])
         | NestedQuery(XMLQL)
         | NestedQuery(RXL)
```

Finally, a canonical pattern is represented by the head variable (that occurs on the right-hand side of `in`), a regular-path expression over strings, and the target variable (that occurs in the body of an element):

```
Pattern:- Var, RegPE, Var
RegPE   :- String | Concat(RegPE, RegPE) |
           Alt(RegPE, RegPE) | Star(RegPE)
```

Regular-path expressions can be combined with the concatenation (`.`), alternation (`|`), and Kleene-star (`*`) operators, similar to those used in regular expressions.

The composition function `compose` in Fig. 12 takes two *environments*, which are lists of (XML-QL variable, value) pairs. The initial environment (`X_env`) maps the distinguished variable `$viewtree` to the root of the view tree referenced by the user query U. The initial variable-substitution `S` that maps XML-QL variables to RXL expressions is empty, and `X_block` is the top-level XML-QL block (lines 1–3). In our example, `$viewtree` is bound to the root of the tree in Fig. 10. The result of `compose` is a list of RXL blocks. In the pseudo-code, XML-QL expressions are prefixed by `X_` and RXL expressions by `R_`.

Function `compose` (line 7) decomposes `X_block` into its patterns, filters, and template. New temporary variables are introduced to represent the intermediate nodes in the nested pattern.

On line 13, the patterns are evaluated in the current environment, producing `R`, which maps U's variables to nodes and constants in V. Each tuple in `R` represents one possible rewriting of U over the view. For each tuple `r_i`, the current environment is extended with the new variable bindings (line 19).

Function `newVariables` (line 22) computes the new mappings of XML-QL and RXL variables to common RXL variables. In summary, `newVariables` recovers the correspondence between Skolem terms that share a common ancestor in the XML-QL pattern; this correspondences determines the mappings for RXL variables. For XML-QL variables, the mapping is simple: if the corresponding value is a leaf node or constant value, the variable is replaced by its value in the substitution mapping S, as described in Section 3.2. If the corresponding value is an internal node, the variable is replaced by the complete RXL expression that computes that element under the substitution S. Lastly, function `oneSolution` (line 25) takes the new environment and computes the new RXL blocks, which are appended to the list of other potential solutions.

Function `oneSolution` in Fig. 13 constructs the RXL block(s) in four steps. First, for each XML-QL variable `X_v` in `X_block`, it projects `X_v`'s value from the solution tuple `r_i`; its value is a view-tree element and an associated rule, whose head and body are projected in `R_head` and `R_body` (a list of conditions). Function `makeCopy` (line 13) assigns fresh variable names to all free variables in `R_condition`, i.e., those that do not occur in the rule's head. Function `rewriteR` (line 15) rewrites the new rule, using the variable mapping `S`. The new condition is added to the conjunctive conditions in `R_conditions`. Second, the function `rewriteX` (line 20) rewrites the XML-QL filters in `X_filters` and adds those to `R_conditions`. Third, the function `to_DNF` (line 22) puts the new conditions in disjunctive normal form. On line 26, `rewriteX` rewrites the XML-QL template to produce the new RXL template. Finally, one new RXL block is created for each list of conjuncts in `R_disjuncts`, and the union of all these blocks is returned.

The `rewriteX` and `rewriteR` functions in Fig. 14 replace XML-QL and RXL variables by their new names in `S`. The 'helper' functions `substX` and `substR` perform the variable substitutions. Note that `rewriteX` calls `compose` recursively to rewrite a nested XML-QL block into an equivalent nested RXL block.

References

[1] S. Abiteboul, R. Hull and V. Vianu, Foundations of Databases, Addison-Wesley, Reading, MA, 1995.

[2] S. Abiteboul, D. Quass, J. McHugh, J. Widom and J. Wiener, The Lorel query language for semistructured data, International Journal on Digital Libraries 1 (1) (1997) 68–88.

[3] A. Bosworth and A. L. Brown, Microsoft's vision for XML, IEEE Data Engineering Bulletin (Sept., 1999) 37–45.

[4] P. Buneman, S. Davidson, G. Hillebrand and D. Suciu, A query language and optimization techniques for unstructured data, in: Proc. of ACM-SIGMOD International Conference on Management of Data, 1996, pp. 505–516.

[5] J. Clark, XML path language (XPath), 1999, http://www.w3.org/TR/xpath.

[6] J. Clark, XSL transformations (XSLT) specification, 1999, http://www.w3.org/TR/WD-xslt.

[7] S. Cluet, C. Delobel, J. Simeon and K. Smaga, Your mediators need data conversion! in: Proc. ACM-SIGMOD International Conference on Management of Data, 1998, pp. 177–188.

[8] A. Deutsch, M. Fernández, D. Florescu, A. Levy and D. Suciu, Xml-ql: a query language for XML, 1998, http://www.w3.org/TR/NOTE-xml-ql/.

[9] A. Deutsch, M. Fernández, D. Florescu, A. Levy and D. Suciu, A query language for XML, in: Proc. of the 8th International World Wide Web Conference (WWW8), Toronto, 1999.

[10] A. Deutsch, M. Fernández and D. Suciu, Storing semistructured data with STORED, in: Proc. of the ACM SIGMOD International Conference on Management of Data, 1999.

[11] M. Fernández, D. Florescu, J. Kang, A. Levy and D. Suciu, Catching the boat with Strudel: experience with a web-site management system, in: Proc. of ACM-SIGMOD International Conference on Management of Data, 1998.

[12] L. Haas, D. Kossmann, E. Wimmers and J. Yang, Optimizing queries across diverse data sources, in: Proc. of VLDB, Athens, 1997.

[13] B. Ludaescher, Y. Papakonstantinou, P. Velikhov and V. Vianu, View definition and DTD inference for xml, in: Workshop on Semistructured Data and Nonstandard Data Formats, January 1999.

[14] D. Maier, A logic for objects, in: Proc. of Workshop on Deductive Database and Logic Programming, Washington, DC, August 1986.

[15] J. McHugh and J. Widom, Query optimization for XML, in: Proc. of VLDB, Edinburgh, September 1999.

[16] Y. Papakonstantinou, S. Abiteboul and H. Garcia-Molina, Object fusion in mediator systems, in: Proc. of Very Large Data Bases, September 1996, pp. 413–424.

[17] Y. Papakonstantinou, H. Garcia-Molina and J. Widom, Object exchange across heterogeneous information sources, in: IEEE International Conference on Data Engineering, March 1995, pp. 251–260.

[18] Y. Papakonstantinou and V. Vassalos, Query rewriting for semistructured data, in: SIGMOD 1999, Proc. ACM SIGMOD International Conference on Management of Data, Philadelphia, PA, June 1999, ACM Press, pp. 455–466.

[19] R. Ramakrishnan and J. Gehrke, Database Management Systems, McGraw-Hill, New York, 1999, 2nd ed.

[20] J. Robie, The design of XQL, 1999, http://www.texcel.no/whitepapers/xql-design.html.

[21] G. Wiederhold, Mediators in the architecture of future information systems, IEEE Computer (March, 1992) 38–49.

Mary Fernández is Senior Technical Staff Member in Large-Scale Programming Research at AT&T Labs.

Dan Suciu is Principal Technical Staff Member in Information Systems and Analysis Research at AT&T Labs.

Wang-Chiew Tan is a Ph.D. candidate in Computer Science at University of Pennsylvania.

Millau: an encoding format for efficient representation and exchange of XML over the Web

Marc Girardot [a,*,1], Neel Sundaresan [b,2]

[a] *Institut Eurécom, Sophia Antipolis, France*
[b] *IBM Almaden Research Center, San Jose, CA, USA*

Abstract

XML is poised to take the World Wide Web to the next level of innovation. XML data, large or small, with or without associated schema, will be exchanged between increasing number of applications running on diverse devices. Efficient storage and transportation of such data is an important issue. We have designed a system called *Millau* for efficient encoding and streaming of XML structures. In this paper we describe the *Millau* algorithms for compression of XML structures and data. *Millau* compression algorithms, in addition to separating structure and text for compression, take advantage of the associated schema (if available) in compressing the structure. *Millau* also defines a programming model corresponding to XML DOM and SAX for XML APIs for *Millau* streams of XML documents. Our experiments have shown significant performance gains of our algorithms and APIs. We describe some of these results in this paper. We also describe some applications of XML-based remote procedure calls and client-server applications based on *Millau* that take advantage of the compression and streaming technology defined by the system.

Keywords: Binary XML; Compression; Tokenization; Streaming; Proxy server; RPC

1. Introduction

As the World Wide Web transitions from just being a medium for browsing to a medium for commerce, XML (eXtensible Markup Language) [7] has emerged as the standard language for markup. Business to business applications over the Internet are increasingly adopting XML as the de facto standard for expressing messages, schema, and data. Consequently, XML is being increasingly used for Web based applications as an exchange wire format. On the other hand, with the popularity of the World Wide Web and increasing dependency on it to find information and to conduct business, the network bandwidth is being tested to its limit. One approach to address this bandwidth problem is to compress data on the network. Traditional data compression algorithms (e.g. Huffman coding [11] or LZ77 [25]) can achieve good compression rates on large text files but are less effective towards small sized files like the ones that may be typical in many *eBusiness* applications. Moreover, they cannot always treat data as a continuous stream. To be really efficient, they need to work on the entire file of a Web object. This is incompatible with the real time constraints of the Web. Finally, these compression systems do

* Corresponding author.
[1] girardot@eurecom.fr
[2] neel@almaden.ibm.com

not retain this structural information in the data they exchange. Thus there is a need for compression and streaming system that works in the Internet context with structured data. These requirements motivate our design for *Millau.*

The Wireless Application Protocol (WAP) [19] defines a format to reduce the transmission size of XML documents with no loss of functionality or semantic information. For example, it preserves the element structure of XML, allowing a browser to skip unknown elements or attributes. *Millau* extends this format to adapt it to business to business applications while improving on the compression algorithm itself. It separates structure compression from text compression. Further, it takes advantage of the schema and data types to enable better compression. To be compliant with the XML standards, it defines a parsing model based on both DOM and SAX at the same time taking advantage of the compression of the document.

This paper is organized as follows. In Section 2, we present the work related to compression and more precisely to XML compression. In Section 3 we describe the *Millau* compression algorithm. We discuss the DOM and SAX support in *Millau* in Section 4. In Section 5 we study performance of the *Millau* system and discuss experimental results. In Section 6 we briefly discuss some applications of our system. We describe a compression/decompression proxy server system for efficient data exchange and an XML remote procuedure call (RPC) engine which takes advantage of the *Millau* compression model. In Section 7 we draw conclusions on our work so far and describe work in progress and future research.

2. Related work

A lot of work has already been done on lossless data compression [15]. Researchers have developed fast and powerful algorithms for data compression. Their principles are mostly based on Claude Shannon's Information Theory. A consequence of this theory is that a symbol that has a high probability has a low information content and will need fewer bits to encode. In order to compress data well, you need to select models that predict symbols with high probabilities. Huffman coding [11] achieves the minimum amount of redundancy possible in a fixed set of variable-length codes. It provides the best approximation for coding symbols when using fixed-width codes. Huffman coding uses a statistical modeling because it reads and encodes a single symbol at a time using the probability of that character's appearance. A dictionary-based compression scheme uses a different concept. It reads in input data and looks for groups of symbols that appear in a dictionary. If a string match is found, a pointer or index into the dictionary can be output instead of the code for the symbol. The longer the match, the better the compression ratio. In LZ77 compression [25], for example, the dictionary consists of all the strings in a window into the previously read input stream. The deflate algorithm [4] uses a combination of the LZ77 compression and the Huffman coding. It is used in popular compression programs like GZIP [5] or ZLIB [3].

One drawback of these text compression algorithms is that they perform compression at the character level. If the algorithm is adaptive (as, for example, with LZ77), the algorithm slowly learns correlations between adjacent pairs of characters, then triples, quadruples and so on. The algorithm rarely has a chance to take advantage of longer range correlations before either the end of input is reached or the tables maintained by the algorithms are filled to capacity, specially with small files. To address this problem, Horspool and Cormack explore the use of words as basic units of the algorithm [10]. In most implementations of dictionary-based compression, the encoder operates on-line, incrementally inferring its dictionary of available phrases from previous parts of the message. An alternative approach proposed by Larsson and Moffat [13] is to infer a complete dictionary off-line to optimize the choice of phrases so as to maximize compression performance.

The Wireless Application Protocol Forum [19] has proposed an encoding format for XML based on a table (the *code space*) that matches tokens to XML tags and attribute names [22]. It takes advantage both of the off-line approach (the *code space* can be built off-line) and of the word-based compression (tags and attribute names are usually the most frequent words in an XML document). Moreover, unlike the previous compression algorithms, it retains the structure of XML documents. But it does not compress at all the character data content nor the attribute values which are not defined in the DTD. Moreover, it does not suggest any strategy to build the code space in an efficient way. The *Millau* encoding format addresses both of these drawbacks: it is designed to compress character data and defines a strategy to build code space.

3. The *Millau* compression model

The *Millau* encoding format is an extension of the WAP binary XML format. The WBXML (Wireless Application Protocol Binary XML) content format specification [22] defines a compact binary representation of XML. This format is designed to reduce the transmission size of XML documents with no loss of functionality or semantic information. For example, WBXML preserves the element structure of XML, allowing a browser to skip unknown elements or attributes. More specifically, the WBXML content encodes the tag names and the attributes names and values with tokens (a token is a single byte).

In WBXML format, tokens are split into a set of overlapping 'code spaces'. The meaning of a particular token is dependent on the context in which it is used. There are two classifications of tokens: global tokens and application tokens. Global tokens are assigned a fixed set of codes in all contexts and are unambiguous in all situations. Global codes are used to encode inline data (e.g., strings, entities, opaque data, etc.) and to encode a variety of miscellaneous control functions. Application tokens have a context-dependent meaning and are split into two overlapping 'code spaces', the 'tag code space' and the 'attribute code space':

- The tag code space represents specific tag names. Each tag token is a single-byte code and represents a specific tag name. Each code space is further split into a series of 256 code spaces. Code pages allow for future expansion of the well-known codes. A single token (SWITCH_PAGE) switches between the code pages.
- The attribute code space is split into two numeric ranges representing attribute prefixes and attribute values respectively. The *Attribute Start* token (with a value less than 128) indicates the start of an attribute and may optionally specify the beginning of the attribute value. The *Attribute Value* token (with a value of 128 or greater) represents a well-known string present in an attribute value. Unknown attribute values are encoded with string, entity or extension codes. All tokenized attributes must begin with a single attribute start token and may be followed by zero or more attribute value, string, entity or extension tokens. An attribute start token, a LITERAL token or the END token indicates the end of an attribute value.

In *Millau* format, an *Attribute Start* token is followed by a single *Attribute Value* token, string, entity or extension token. So there is no need to split the attribute token numeric range into two ranges (less than 128 and 128 or greater) because each time the parser encounters and *Attribute Start* token followed by a non-reserved token, it knows that this non-reserved token is an *Attribute Value* token and that it can be followed only by an END token or another *Attribute Start* token. Thus instead two overlapping code spaces, we have three overlapping code spaces:

- the tag code space as defined in the WAP specification,
- the attribute start code space where each page contains 256 tokens,
- the attribute value code space where each page contains 256 tokens.

Notice that, in WBXML format, character data is not compressed. It is transmitted as strings inline, or as a reference in a string table which is transmitted at the beginning of the document. In *Millau* encoding format, character data can be transmitted on a separate stream. This allows to separate the content from the structure so that a browser can separately download the structure and the content or just a part of each. This further allows to compress the character data using traditional compression algorithms like deflate [4]. In the structure stream, character data is indicated by a special global token (STR or STR_ZIP) which indicates to the *Millau* parser (see Section 4) that it must switch from the structure stream to the content stream if the user is interested in content and whether the content is compressed (STR) or uncompressed (STR_ZIP). Optionally, the length of the content is encoded as an integer in the structure stream right after the global token (STR_L or STR_ZIP_L). If the length is not indicated, the strings contained in the structure must terminate with a End Of String character or a null character.

We described how *Millau* encoding format efficiently represent character data but we must also take in consideration the fact that, in typical business to business communications, most of the attribute values are of primitive type like Boolean, byte, integer or float. For example, in a set of typical business to business XML messages provided by the Open Application Group [16], 70% of the attribute values are of primitive type. These attribute values should not be transcoded in strings in a binary representation of an XML document. So in *Millau*, we use the extension codes to prefix primitives types like bytes, integers or floats. The following table reminds the meanings given to the global tokens by the WBXML encoding specification and also precises the meanings of the extension tokens which have been redefined for the needs of *Millau* (these tokens appear in bold in Table 1).

The following is an example of a simple tokenized XML document. Here is the source document:

```
<?xml version="1.0" encoding="UTF-8"?>
<!DOCTYPE Book [
 <!ELEMENT Book (Title, Chapter+,
   Picture+)>
 <!ATTLIST Book
  Author CDATA #REQUIRED
  Genre (literature|science|history|
    cartoons) #REQUIRED >
 <!ELEMENT Title (#PCDATA)>
 <!ELEMENT Chapter (#PCDATA)>
 <!ATTLIST Chapter
  id ID #REQUIRED>
 <!ELEMENT Picture (#PCDATA)>
 <!ATTLIST Picture
  Caption CDATA #REQUIRED>
]>

<Book Author="Anonymous"
   Genre="literature">
 <Title>Sample Book</Title>
```

Table 1
Global WBXML and *Millau* tokens

Token name	Token	Description
SWITCH_PAGE	0	Change the code page for the current token state. Followed by a single u_int8 indicating the new code page number.
END	1	Indicates the end of an attribute list or the end of an element.
ENTITY	2	A character entity. Followed by an integer encoding the character entity number.
STR_I	3	Inline string. Followed by a string.
LITERAL	4	An unknown tag or attribute name. Followed by an integer that encodes an offset into the string table.
FALSE	**40**	Encodes the Boolean value false.
TRUE	**41**	Encodes the Boolean value true.
FLOAT	**42**	Inline float. Token is followed by an integer representing the floating-point argument according to the IEEE 754 floating-point 'single precision' bit layout.
PI	43	Processing instruction.
LITERAL_C	44	Unknown tag, with content.
STR_L	**80**	Indicates that uncompressed character data has been written to the content stream. Followed by an integer indicating the number of characters.
STR_ZIP_L	**81**	Indicates that compressed character data has been written to the content stream. Followed by an integer indicating the number of characters.
EXT_T_2	**82**	Inline integer. Token is followed by an integer.
STR_T	83	String table reference. Followed by an integer encoding a byte offset from the beginning of the string table.
LITERAL_A	84	Unknown tag, with attributes.
STR	**C0**	Indicates that uncompressed character data has been written to the content stream.
STR_ZIP	**C1**	Indicates that compressed character data has been written to the content stream.
BYTE	**C2**	Inline byte. Followed by a single byte.
BINARY	**C3**	Binary data. Followed by an integer indicating the number of bytes of binary data.
LITERAL_AC	C4	Unknown tag, with content and attributes.

Table 2
Code space example

Tag code space		Attribute name code space		Attribute value code space	
Tag name	Token	Attribute name	Token	Attribute value	Token
Book	5	Author	5	Literature	5
Title	6	Genre	6	Science	6
Chapter	7	Number	7	History	7
Picture	8	Caption	8	Cartoons	8

```
 <Chapter Number="1">
  This is chapter 1. It is not very
    long or interesting.
 </Chapter>
 <Chapter Number="2">
  This is chapter 2. Although it is
    longer than chapter 1, it is not
    any more interesting.
 </Chapter>
 <Picture Caption="Nice picture">
  [base 64 encoded binary data]
 </Picture>
</Book>
```

Tokens for the tag code space, the attribute names code space, and the attribute value code space are defined in Table 2.

Tokenized form (numbers in hexadecimal) follows:

```
01 01 6A 00 C5 05 03 "Anonymous" 06 05
   01 46 C1 C7 07 C2 01 01 C1 01 C7 07
   C2 02 01
C1 01 C8 08 03 "Nice picture" 01 C3 ...
   01 01
```

4. *Millau* API: specification and implementation

The *Millau* format is designed to represent XML documents in a compact way using tokens to represent tags and attributes instead of strings. We built parsers for documents encoded using this format implementing the two standard APIs DOM [6] and SAX [17]. DOM is the tree model API used to represent and process parsed XML document trees. The SAX API has an event-based streaming model typically used to process large XML documents without actually building a parse tree.

We provide two variants of SAX parsers. The first one produces traditional SAX events, as defined by the SAX API. This means that each time it encounters a tag token, it generates a *startElement* event passing the name of the tag. The name matching the tag token is found in the code spaces. We will describe later how the code spaces are built in our implementation. The second SAX parser, which we call the *Millau* BSAX (Binary SAX) parser, extends the SAX API by providing events which pass tokens instead of strings. This parser has been designed for applications that are able to handle tokens instead of strings. We show later how applications using tokens perform better than those using strings only.

We also provide two DOM-based parsers. The first one creates a conventional DOM tree from a *Millau* stream. The second one creates what we call a BDOM tree (Binary DOM tree). A BDOM tree is like a DOM tree but instead of storing node names it stores, for each node, a pair (*page number*, *token*) which uniquely identifies the node. Here follows a description of how each parser works.

4.1. The Millau SAX parser

A conventional SAX parser parses an XML stream and throws SAX events (e.g. *characters*, *startElement*, *endElement*) that can be handled by a specific handler. Parameters can be passed through these events (e.g. the element name is passed through the startElement and endElement events). These events and their associated parameters are defined by the SAX API [17]. The *Millau* SAX parser has been designed to parse a *Millau* stream. It implements the SAX API. In the following paragraphs, we describe how it works.

Before reading tokens from the binary input stream, the *Millau* SAX parser creates a LIFO (last in, first out) stack in which it puts the names of the

Table 3
Millau element tokens decision table

Token	Action taken
Switch page	Read the next token which gives the current code page.
String inline	Read the inline string that follows and throw a character event.
Extension	Read the following content according to its type, translates it into a string and throw a character event.
End token	Remove the last element of the tag names stack and throw an *endElement* event with the tag name which has been removed from the stack.
Not a reserved token	If the token is not a reserved token, then it is a tag token, so the parser looks for the corresponding tag name in the element code space (if not found, an exception is raised). It then calls a method which returns an attributes list. Eventually, it throws a *startElement* event with the tag name and its corresponding attribute list (if the element has attributes).

element that are opened and not yet closed. This is so that it can get the name of an element when it ends and send it to the handler. Then it reads tokens from the input stream until the stack is empty. When the stack is empty, it means that the root element has been closed. Table 3 specifies the action taken for each token type.

The *getAttribute* method tests the most significant bit of the tag token to know if this element has attribute. If the bit is 0, the element has no attribute and the method returns an empty list. If the bit is 1, the element has attributes and the method reads the attribute tokens from the input stream.

While the most significant bit of the next read tokens is 0, the parser knows that these tokens are not attribute value token. The tokens are processed, based upon their types, as described in Table 4.

The attribute value can be encoded as a token value, as an inline string (compressed or not) or as a primitive type like byte, integer, float, or Boolean.

4.2. The Millau binary SAX parser

It is expected that parsing a compressed *Millau* stream using our SAX parser is faster than decompressing a compressed XML stream and then parsing it with a conventional SAX parser. But it could take more time than parsing a non compressed XML stream with a conventional SAX parser. We observed that the part of the processing which takes the most time with *Millau* SAX parser is the translation of the tokens in elements and attributes names. The reason for this it that, for each received token, the parser must search the code spaces for the corresponding strings. For example, if it receives an element token, it must search the corresponding element name in the element code space and this can take a lot of time, especially if there are many elements in the element code space. Skipping this translation step could make the encoded XML parsing faster. These tokens do not really need to be translated into strings at all. In fact, they can be directly processed by appropriate handlers which recognize the tokens. The design of such handlers and the efficiency aspects will be discussed later.

A *Millau* binary SAX parser is like a SAX parser but instead of studying character based XML streams it operates on the binary encoded XML. Instead of passing tag names and attribute names and values to the handler, it passes encoding tokens without translating them into strings. More precisely, each time it throws a *startElement* event or an *endElement* event, it passes a pair (*code page*, *element token*) which uniquely identifies the element (see WBXML encod-

Table 4
Millau attribute tokens decision table

Token	Action taken
Switch page	Read the next token which gives the current code page.
Not a reserved token	If it is not a reserved token, then it is an attribute name token. So the parser looks for the corresponding name in the attribute name code space (if not found, an exception is raised). It then reads the attribute value.
End token	End of the attribute list identified; return the attributes list.

Table 5
Comparison between *Millau* conventional and binary SAX parsers

Interface	*Millau* conventional SAX parser	*Millau* binary SAX parser
Handler	startElement(String name, AttributeList)	startElement(int token, BAttributeList)
AttributeList	getName(int i) returns the name	getNameToken(int i) returns a token
AttributeList	getValue(int i) returns the value	getValueToken(int i) returns a token getValue(int i) returns an Object

ing specification [22] or Section 2). For a *startElement* event, it also passes a *Millau* binary attribute list which is a variant of the XML SAX attribute list implementation. A *Millau* attribute list, instead of containing triples (*attribute name*, *attribute type*, *attribute value*) contains triples (*attribute name uid*, *attribute type*, *attribute value uid*) if the type of the attribute is 'enumerated' or triples (*attribute name uid*, *attribute type*, *attribute value*) if the type of the attribute is 'CDATA'. A 'uid' (unique identifier) is a pair (*code page*, *token*). It can uniquely identify an attribute name or an attribute value. Table 5 illustrates the differences between the two parsers.

A *Millau* SAX handler must be able to recognize (*code page*, *token*) to trigger special processing adapted to the element or the attribute. It is faster than a conventional handler because, instead of comparing two strings (a time consuming operation), it just has to compare two pairs of bytes.

4.3. The Millau DOM parser

The DOM parser is able to build a DOM tree dynamically from a binary XML stream. The top-level architecture of the DOM parser is almost the same as the architecture of the SAX parser. Like the SAX parser, the DOM parser creates a LIFO stack to store the names of the opened elements. Then it reads tokens from the input stream until the stack is empty. It differs from the SAX parser in the processing which is done for each type of token. Table 6 gives the details.

The *getAttributes* method reads the attribute tokens from the binary XML stream. While the most significant bit of the next read tokens is 0, the parser knows that these tokens are not attribute value tokens. Table 7 describes the action taken on different kinds of tokens.

The attribute value can be encoded as a token value or as an inline string (compressed or not).

4.4. The Millau binary DOM parser

The *Millau* binary DOM parser uses the binary DOM (BDOM) API. Table 8 describes the action taken by the parser on different types of tokens.

4.5. The Millau binary DOM API

The binary DOM API implements all the interfaces of the DOM API as defined by the World Wide

Table 6
Millau DOM parser decision table for element tokens

Token	Action taken
Switch page	Read the next token which gives the current code page.
String inline	Reads the inline string that follows and creates a text node and appends this text node to the last opened element (the first element of the LIFO stack).
Extension	Read the content following the content according to its type, translates it into a string, creates a text node and appends it to the last opened element.
End token	Just remove the last element of the tag names stack.
Not a reserved token	If this is not a reserved token, then it is a tag token, so looks for the corresponding tag name in the element code space (if not found, an exception is raised). It then creates an element node. If the stack is empty, it means that this element is the root of the document, so it is appended to the document node. If the stack is not empty, the element is appended to the last opened element (the first in the LIFO stack). Eventually, the parser tests the last bit of the token, if it is 1, it invokes a method which gets the attributes for this element.

Table 7
Millau DOM parser decision table for attribute tokens

Token	Action taken
Switch page	It reads the next token which gives the current code page.
End token	This is the end of the attribute list. The method exits.
Not a reserved token	If it is not a reserved token, then it is an attribute name token. So the parser looks for the corresponding name in the attribute name code space (if not found, an exception is raised). It then reads the attribute value. Eventually, it adds this attribute to the current element.

Web Consortium [6]. The main advantage of a binary DOM tree is that the tag and attribute names are stored not as strings but as tokens and is space-efficient. The correspondence between names and pairs (*code page*, *token*) is stored in the code spaces so that names can be normally retrieved for every element or attribute nodes. Attribute values can be stored as tokens, if available, as strings, or as primitive types. The primitive types currently supported by the BDOM API are Boolean, byte, integer (4 bytes), and float. Element contents can also be stored as primitive types. For element contents, we have defined one more binary node, the binary data node, which stores binary data without base 64 encoding, thus avoiding the 33% overload of the base 64 encoding. This is useful for binary files like images embedded in an XML document.

In addition to the methods of the DOM API, the BDOM API also provides methods for creating or retrieving elements or attributes by tokens instead of strings. This is useful for applications which have been designed to work with *Millau* format (see Section 6). For example the class *BElement* (for Binary Element) which implements the DOM interface *Element* has also a method *getTagToken()* which returns a short where the first byte is the code page and the second page is the tag token. For convenience, the class *BDocument* which implements the DOM interface *Document* provides a method *writeBinaryXML(OutputStream)* which write the BDOM tree in *Millau* format to the *OutputStream*.

4.6. The Millau code spaces

The choice of the data structure to represent the code spaces is also important for good performance of the system. The translation time is mostly influenced by the time it takes to look up in the code spaces for a token or for its corresponding string. Depending of what the program needs to do, translating strings into tokens or tokens into strings, different data structure may be used. For example, to convert strings into tokens quickly, strings must be found quickly in a table. For this, it is better to use a hash table where the keys are the strings and the values are the corresponding tokens. But, if given a page number and an index in a code page the corresponding string must be found quickly, the best data

Table 8
Millau binary DOM parser decision table

Token	Action taken
Switch page	No change
String inline	No change
Extension	The BDOM parser can create a primitive type node (Boolean, byte, integer, float, binary data) defined by the BDOM API by invoking the methods *createBooleanNode*, *createByteNode*, *createIntegerNode*, *createFloatNode* or *createBinaryData* of the class *BDocument*. This node is then appended to the last opened element by invocation of the method appendChild.
End token	No change
Tag token	The BDOM parser creates a *BElement* node by invoking the method *createElement* of the class *BDocument* with a short as parameter. The first byte (most significant) of this short is the code page of the tag and the second byte is the tag token.

structure is a two dimensional array indexed by page numbers and indexes in pages. If we need to be able to find a string from a token quickly or a token from a string, then we need to sort the table and then do a binary search to find a string corresponding to a token.

Next we describe the method to fill in the hash table for element code space. First, the page number variable is set to 0 and the index variable to 5 (the first four indexes are reserved for global tokens). For each element declaration, the system gets the element name, adds it in the hash table with the element name as the key and (56 $\times$ pageNumber + index) as the value. The system increments the index by 1. The size of a page for elements is 64 because the last two bits of the index are reserved so when the index reaches the value 64, the system increments the page number by 1 and resets the index to 5. When the page number reaches its maximum value 255, an exception is raised.

For each element declared, the system gets the corresponding attribute declaration from the previously built DOM tree. It adds the attribute name in the hash table with the attribute name as the key and (256 $\times$ pageNumber + index) as the value. If the attribute type is enumerated (enumerated attribute types are NOTATION or NAME_TOKEN_GROUP), then the system looks for the values of this enumerated attribute. For each value, it adds the attribute value in the hash table with the attribute value as the key and (256 $\times$ pageNumber + index) as the value. The system increments the index for the value by 1. The size of a page for attribute value is 128 so when the index reaches the value 128, the system increments the page number by 1 and resets the index to 5. When the page number reaches its maximum value 255, an exception is raised. If there are no values or when the values have been successfully added to the attribute value code space, the system increments the index for the name by 1. The size of a page for attribute name is 128 so when the index reaches the value 128, the system increments the page number by 1 and resets the index to 5. When the page number reaches its maximum value 255, an exception is raised.

Next, the method to fill in the 2-dimensional array for element code space is described. First, we set the page number variable to 0 and the index variable to 5 (the first four indexes are reserved for global tokens). For each element declaration, the system gets the element name, adds it in the elements array at position (page number, index). The system increments the index by 1. The size of a page for elements is 64 because the last two bits of the index are reserved so when the index reaches the value 64, the system increments the page number by 1 and resets the index to 5. When the page number reaches its maximum value 255, an exception is raised.

The attribute names code space and the attribute values code space can be merged into one so that each pair (*attribute name*, *attribute value*) is a single token instead of two tokens (name and value). The code space is filled as follows. For each element declared, the system gets the corresponding attribute declaration from the previously built DOM structure. If the attribute type is not enumerated (no specific value is declared for this attribute), then the system adds the attribute name in the attribute code space (hash table for the server, array for the client). If the attribute type is enumerated, then the system looks for the values of this enumerated attribute. For each value, it adds the pair (*attribute name*, *attribute value*) with a specific token in the attribute code space. When the server comes across an attribute with a value, it looks in the attribute code space for the couple (*attribute name*, *attribute value*). If it can find it, it sends this token. If it cannot find it, it looks for the attribute name in the attribute code space. If the name is found, the server sends the corresponding token for this name followed by a string inline token followed by the attribute value encoded in the charset specified at the beginning of the binary XML stream. If the name is not found, an exception is raised.

Attributes may be mandatory (*#REQUIRED*), optional (*#IMPLIED*), or can have fixed values (*#FIXED*). For mandatory or fixed attributes, it is not necessary to transmit tokens. To achieve this optimization the system can store in the element code space the names of the required or fixed attributes with the element name. For example, if attributes *Author* and *Genre* are required for element *Book*, the element code space stores the triplet (*Book*, *Author*, *Genre*) at the entry *Book*. This element code space is filled as follows. For each element declaration, the system gets the element name and the required and fixed attributes. It adds the element names and the required and fixed attribute names to the element code space. For the fixed attributes, it also adds their value. In the attribute code space, only the implied attributes will be stored with their corresponding values (if defined).

Notice that for applications which can work with tokens without translating them into strings, there is no need for code spaces. This saves memory and CPU. However, to facilitate the task of the developer of the application, the tokens can be stored as static variables with explicit names.

5. Experimental results

In this section we study the performance of the *Millau* system.

5.1. Theoretical compression rate

First we compute the theoretical size of *Millau* streams. Suppose:

- there is a total of N occurrences of elements of which M have empty contents and K are elements with attributes,
- there are a total of T text elements,
- there are a total of A attribute occurrences,
- S is the total size of the text elements in bytes,
- H is the size of the header and,
- P is the number of page switches.

The size W of the token encoded document can be computed as:

$$W = 2N - M + 2A + K + T + S + 2P + H.$$

The following explains the origin of each term in the above formula:

- $2N$: each element is represented by an element token plus and end token (2 bytes);
- M: empty elements do not need an end token;
- $2A$: each attribute is represented by a name token and either an attribute token, a string inline token plus a string or an extension token plus a primitive type (at least 2 bytes per attribute);
- K: every attribute list ends with an end token;
- T: each text element is introduced by a string inline token;
- S: size of all the text which has no corresponding token (it can be text elements or unknown attribute values);
- $2P$: each page switch means one switch token plus one byte for the new page number;
- H: the header is composed of a version number (one byte), a document public identifier (1 to 4 bytes or one byte plus a string), a character set (1 to 4 bytes), a string table (1 to 4 bytes plus possibly the strings).

The first five parameters N, M, A, K, and T depend only on the document so we cannot change these parameters for a given document. The size of the text can be a large parameter. First of all, the number of unknown attribute values must be minimized. This can be done by encoding the attribute values given by the DTD for the attribute of the type enumerated. Another improvement is to pre-parse the document and look for the attribute values which are not in the DTD and appear more than once in the document. These attribute values can be put in the string table so that they will appear only one time in the binary XML stream.

The best solution to text compression is to separate the text from the document structure and compress it with an algorithm like GZIP [5]. The same can also be done for the unknown attribute values but it can cost in terms of processing time to have to switch to another stream for each attribute value. The size of the header depends mainly of the use of a string table: a string table contains the most frequently used strings in the document. They are then referenced in the document by an offset in the string table. The experiments show that the number of page switches can constitute a large overhead (a page switch is two bytes). This number can be further reduced by putting sibling elements on the same page. The DTD can be used to perform this optimization. (The number of page switches cannot be larger than $2(N + 2A)$ because there cannot be more page switches than the number of elements and attributes names and values.)

The following formula now gives a good estimate of the size X of the XML stream:

$$X = (2N - M)n + A(a + v) + S$$

where n is the mean length of an element name, a is the mean length of an attribute name, and v is the mean length of an attribute value.

The theoretical estimated compression rate is thus given by this formula:

$$C = \frac{W}{X} = \frac{2N - M + 2A + K + T + S + 2P + H}{(2N - M)n + A(a + v) + S}$$

We can compute a better estimate by using the exact size X of the XML stream if it is known. Usually, it is not an unknown parameter. We will use this value in the experimental computations. We observe that C is a function of the size of the markup. If elements and attributes are given long and explicit names in the original XML document, the compression rate can be very good.

5.2. *Experimental compression rate*

To measure the performance of our compression system, we have built a test package which considers the following parameters:

- number of elements;
- number of empty elements;
- number of attributes;
- number of elements with attributes;
- number of text elements (also termed PCDATA elements);
- number of page switches;
- compression rate for the structure stream encoded in *Millau* format;
- compression rate for the data stream compressed with GZIP algorithm;
- compression rate for the whole document processed by our compression system;
- compression rate for the whole document compressed with GZIP;
- compression rate for the structure stream compressed with GZIP;
- time to parse an uncompressed XML stream;
- time to parse an XML streamed compressed with GZIP;
- time to parse a *Millau* stream;
- time to parse a *Millau* stream without decoding the name and value tokens.

We ran our experiments with XML documents of varying sizes. We first discuss a typical set of results obtained with a 3 MB technical manual marked up in XML. This document is a valid XML document which means that it comes with a DTD which can be used to efficiently build the code spaces. Table 9 presents the results.

Table 9
Size of the markup for a technical documentation

Size of the document (in bytes)	3 093 194
Size of the markup (in bytes)	2 038 952
Size of the character data (in bytes)	1 052 242
Number of elements	73 591
Number of empty elements	9 485
Number of attributes	25 611
Number of elements with attributes	22 529
Number of PCDATA elements	64 588

From the above table, we can compute a lower bound for the theoretical compression rate for the markup (PCDATA excluded) as defined previously. This is a lower bound and not an exact value because the number of page switches is not known a priori. Moreover, we assume that there are no attribute values encoded as strings (which is usually not true). In other words, we assume that every attribute value has a corresponding token. The lower bound of the size of the markup encoded in *Millau* format is thus given by: $2 \times 73\,591 - 9485 + 2 \times 25\,611 + 22\,529 + 64\,588 = 276\,036$ bytes. Subsequently, the lower bound of the theoretical compression rate for the markup is given by: $276\,036/2\,038\,952 = \mathbf{13.5\%}$.

Notice that the number of page switches cannot be larger than: $2 * (73\,591 + 2 * 25\,611) = 249\,626$ bytes. So the upper bound for the *Millau* size is (if there are no attribute values encoded as strings): $276\,036 + 249\,626 = 525\,662$ bytes. Subsequently, the higher bound of the theoretical compression rate for the markup is: $525\,662/2\,038\,952 = \mathbf{25.7\%}$. This seems reasonably good for a worst case measure.

Table 10 shows the experimental compression rate achieved by *Millau* algorithm and GZIP algorithm (sizes are given in bytes).

The figures compared are the compression rate of the markup using *Millau* encoding and using GZIP encoding (figures in bold in the chart). It can be seen that the compression rate achieved by *Millau* encoding is reasonable (18.0% is usually considered as a good compression rate for text). But we can also notice that the compression rate achieved by the GZIP algorithm for the same markup is very good (8.6%). Actually, this is not very surprising because the GZIP algorithm takes advantage of the

Table 10
Comparison of the compression rates achieved by *Millau* and GZIP algorithms

	Initial document size	*Millau* document size	*Millau* compression (%)	GZIP document size	GZIP compression (%)
Whole document	3 093 194	593 795	19.2	401 518	13.0
Markup only	2 038 952	367 321	**18.0**	175 044	**8.6**
Data only	1 052 242	226 474	21.5	226 474	21.5

redundancy of a document to compress it and the XML markup is highly redundant. There are a few tags which are repeated a large number of times in this large document. This is why the compression rate for GZIP outperforms the compression rate for *Millau*. But at the same time, GZIP does not retain structure of the document which is a disadvantage for fast documents processing.

To improve the compression rate of *Millau*, we can limit this number of page switches (about 30 000) by reordering the code spaces so that opening tags which are close to each other in the document appear on the same code space page. We do not care about the closing tags because there are encoded with the reserved token END in *Millau* format. The code space optimization can be done from the DTD or from the XML document itself. To formalize the problem of optimizing from the XML document itself, we consider an ordered set T of n possible tags where n is bigger than the size p of a code space page. The document can be represented as a series of tags (ti) where each ti is element of T. We want to find a permutation of T that minimizes the number of page switches inside of this document. The first approach is to find the most frequent pair (ti, tj) (a pair is two different tags that appear next to each other in the XML document) and put them in the same page. A better approach consists in computing the mean distance between two tags for each pair (ti, tj) and then grouping tags in fixed-size clusters using a clustering algorithm. Each cluster here represents a code space page.

We are currently working on optimizing the code spaces from the DTD. From the DTD, we can estimate the probability that a tag follows another tag. The next step is to compute the probability that two tags will follow each other in less than p hops (where p is a page size). From these probabilities, we can compute mean distances between tags in order to apply a clustering algorithm as we do with the XML document itself.

An alternative to the code spaces approach is to encode the tags with variable length tokens. One or several bytes encode a tag according to its occurrence frequency. The 128 most frequent tags will be encoded with a single byte. The formats of these bytes is similar to the byte format of UTF-8 [24]. Table 11 shows the byte sequences:

5.3. *Influence of the document size*

In the previous section we computed the compression rate for a big XML document. This experiment has shown that, for this big document, GZIP was more efficient than *Millau* as regards the compression rate because GZIP takes advantage of the

Table 11
UTF-8 byte sequences

Token length	Byte sequence
1 byte	`0xxxxxxx`
2 bytes	`110xxxxx 10xxxxxx`
3 bytes	`1110xxxx 10xxxxxx 10xxxxxx`
4 bytes	`11110xxx 10xxxxxx 10xxxxxx 10xxxxxx`
5 bytes	`111110xx 10xxxxxx 10xxxxxx 10xxxxxx 10xxxxxx`
6 bytes	`1111110x 10xxxxxx 10xxxxxx 10xxxxxx 10xxxxxx 10xxxxxx`

redundancy induced by the XML markup. It has also highlighted some theoretical problems that will need to be solved in further investigation. In this section we run experiments on a set of small XML files like the ones exchanged in business transactions and see if *Millau* can be more efficient with this kind of files than traditional compression algorithms like GZIP.

We have tested *Millau* compression algorithm on a set of 118 XML reference files from the Open Applications Group [16]. These sample files represent the typical files which are used in business transactions (e.g. sales orders, bills, payments). There sizes range from 1 KB to 14 KB. They all come with a specific DTD. We compressed them, first using GZIP algorithm [5] with a buffer size of 512 bytes, then using *Millau* on the XML stream. The *Millau* code spaces have been built from the DTDs provided with the XML sample files. On the diagram of Fig. 1, we represented the size of the compressed files with respect to the initial size. The red points are for GZIP while the blue ones are for *Millau*.

First, we observe that the size of the *Millau* compressed file grows linearly with the file of the uncompressed file (the correlation coefficient between the *Millau* compressed size and the initial size is 0.9918 which is very close to 1). This means that the compression ratio is roughly constant (~20%) with respect to the document size. On the other hand, the compression rate of GZIP grows with the size of the initial document. This is because GZIP (like other lossless traditional compression algorithms) is designed to take advantage of the redundancy of character strings inside of a document. That is also why the compression of GZIP does not grow linearly (the còrrelation coefficient between the GZIP compressed size and the initial size is only 0.8995 to compare to 0.9918). Although it is true that the redundancy is high on large XML documents because of the limited number of allowed tags, it is also found that the occurrence frequency of repeated characters in a small XML document (like a sales order) might not be very high (because of the limited size of the document). So one can think that it is beneficial to map XML tags to tokens and that this mapping must be done off-line from the DTD. The experience proves that this is beneficial for small documents (typically documents which size ranges from 0 to 5 KB — according to the crossing point between the two regressions lines — this is the case of most of the documents exchanged in business transactions — here, only 20 of the 118 documents of our eBusiness test set are bigger than 5 KB).

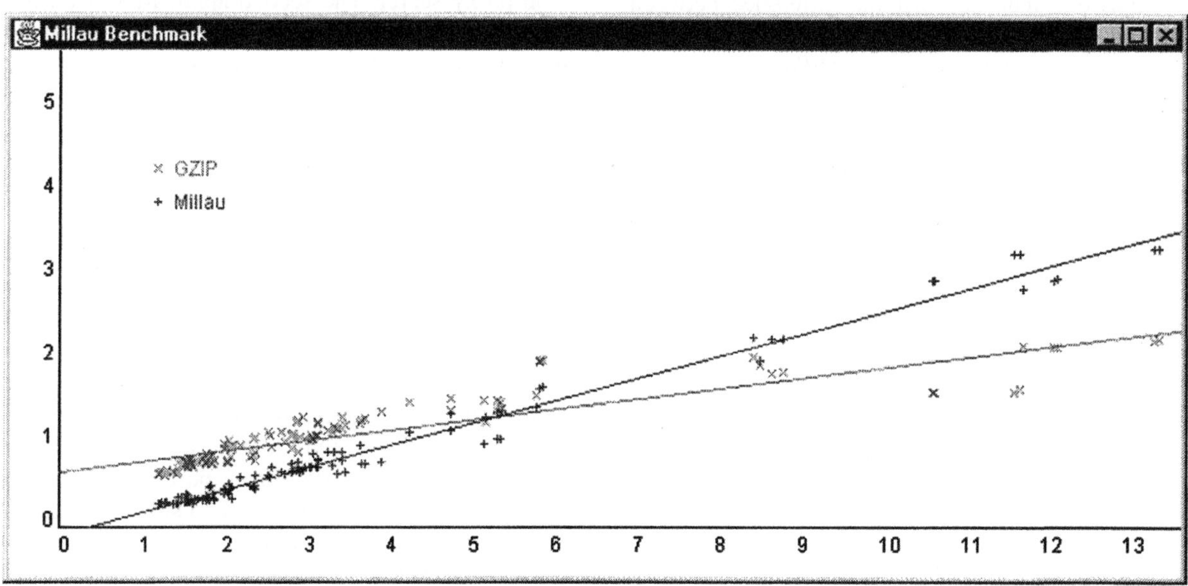

Fig. 1. Size in KB of the compressed file (× = GZIP, + = *Millau*) versus the initial size.

5.4. Processing times

The third experiment measures the time to parse an XML stream (with and without compression) and compares that time to the time needed to parse a *Millau* stream. For the XML stream, we have used the SAX driver of the IBM XML parser [12]. For the *Millau* stream, we have obtained measurements with two kinds of parsers:

- a *Millau* SAX parser,
- a *Millau* BSAX parser.

As a reminder, the *Millau* SAX parser implements the Parser interface defined by SAX so it must translate every token to its corresponding string. On the other hand, the *Millau* BSAX parser generates events with tokens instead of strings so it does not make any translation (see Section 4).

For the measurements, the XML stream is created from a 3 MB technical manual marked up in XML and served of a local disk. It is better to use a large file for timing experiments because the experiments have shown that the method *currentTimeMillis* of the Java class *System* was not able to measure time differences smaller than 10 ms. SAX events are handled by basic handlers which do no processing at all. We measured the time to parse the stream from the creation of the stream to the endDocument event. Table 12 summarizes the results.

First, this indicates that the difference between parsing a compressed or uncompressed stream is negligible. Secondly, parsing a *Millau* stream is at least five times faster than parsing an ASCII XML stream. This result was initially somewhat surprising. However, this result can be explained by the fact that the operations performed during the parsing of a token stream are easier and less time consuming than the operations needed to parse a text XML stream: the parsing of a text stream involves string comparisons, a time consuming operations while the parsing of binary stream involves bytes comparison. Moreover, the fact that the content stream (which does not need any parsing) is separated from the structure stream makes the parsing more efficient. The processing speed is one of the greatest strengths of *Millau* and is the main reason why this model is particularly well adapted for business applications as well as streaming applications.

We can also observe that the time needed to translate tokens into strings by performing a look-up in the code space (3 s to compare with 5 s to parse the stream) is not a large overhead. This can be done if the application has not been designed to work with tokens. But for efficiency purposes it is preferable to work with tokens instead of strings as the time needed by the handler to compare two strings can be much larger than the time needed to compare two tokens.

Table 12
Parsing time comparison using IBM SAX parser and *Millau* SAX parser

Time to parse the uncompressed XML stream	40 seconds
Time to parse the XML stream compressed with GZIP	40 seconds
Time to parse the *Millau* stream using a *Millau* SAX parser	8 seconds
Time to parse the *Millau* stream using a *Millau* BSAX parser	5 seconds

6. Applications using *Millau* streams

We have built two applications using the *Millau* APIs. The first application is a *Millau* compression proxy server and its companion *Millau* decompression proxy server. The second application is an implementation of the XML-RPC using *Millau* as an exchange data format. For these two applications, we discuss the implementation design and why these are good applications of *Millau* encoding format.

6.1. Millau compression proxy server

Studies have been made in prior research work in using HTTP proxy servers to compress data on the network [2,14,20]. These demonstrate that about 33% of the bandwidth can be saved easily by compressing the data exchanged on the network. In these studies, they have used conventional compression algorithms like ZLIB and GZIP to compress the text data. The fact that a significant portion of the Web objects electronic commerce have a small size makes these compression algorithms not efficient for this purpose. So it has been suggested that compression proxy server uses a static table that maps the frequently used HTML strings into tokens. However, they do not have a systematic scheme like ours to compress any XML document. Here, we investigate the architecture and the performances of an HTTP proxy server based on *Millau* binary XML.

The system is composed of two proxy servers: a *client proxy server* and a *server proxy server*. The client proxy server is located 'close' to the client, and the server proxy server is located 'close' to the server. In an extreme situation the client proxy server may be merged with the client, and the server proxy server with the server. Also if there is seamless XML data flow between two locations in both directions there may be possibly more than one compression proxy server and decompression proxy server. We built our proxy servers using the WBI (Web Intelligence) proxy architecture system [1].

Before describing the architecture with more details, we introduce the architecture of WBI. WBI is a programmable HTTP request and HTTP response processor. WBI's data model is based on the request/response structure of HTTP version 1.0. Each request and each response consist of a *structured* part and a *stream* part. The structured part corresponds to the header and the stream part corresponds to the body. *Millau* mainly works on the stream part which is here supposed to be XML content. Notice that HTML content can be converted to XML thanks to an already existing WBI plug-in so that *Millau* can then process this stream. WBI receives an HTTP request from a client, such as a Web browser, and produces an HTTP response that is returned to the client. The processing that happens in between is controlled by the modules programmed into WBI. A typical WBI transaction flow goes through three basic stages: request editors (RE), generators (G), and editors (E). A request editor receives a request and has the freedom to modify the request before passing it along. A generator receives a request and produces a corresponding response (i.e. a document). An editor receives a response and has the freedom to modify the response before passing it along. When all the steps are completed, the response is sent to the originating client.

The diagram of Fig. 2 shows the architecture of the *Millau* compression–decompression client proxy server and its associated compression–decompression server proxy server.

Here, we describe the flow for a request–response transaction between a client and a server. The client

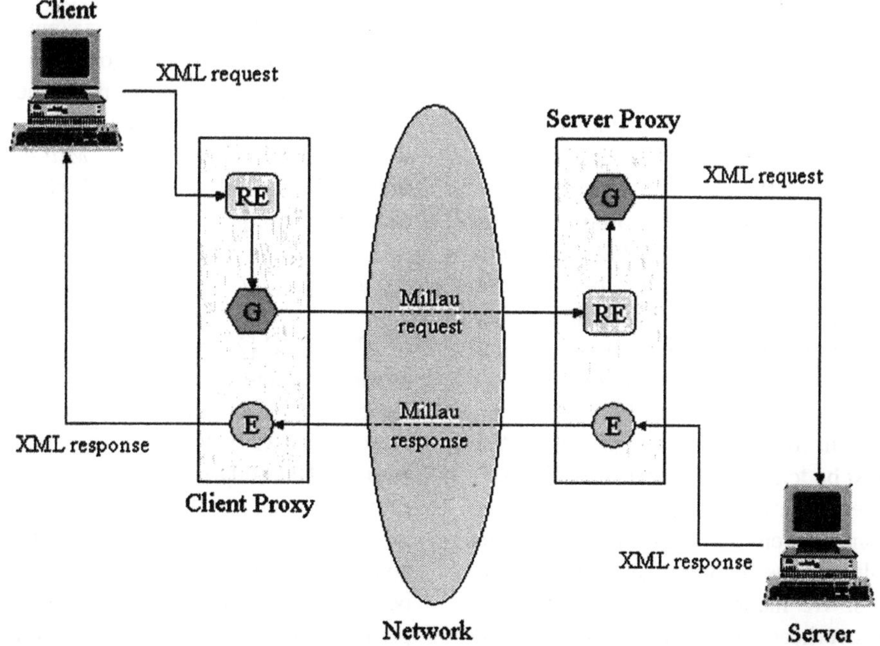

Fig. 2. Workflow path of a Web request and its response in the *Millau* compression–decompression WBI proxy environment.

Table 13
Millau compression–decompression time compared to transmission time on a 56 Kbits/s modem line

Document type	Mean size (bytes)	Transmission time (ms)	Compression–decompression (ms)
Uncompressed small document	3 647	521	N/A
Compressed small document	886	126	98
Uncompressed large document	213 160	30 451	N/A
Compressed large document	148 269	21 181	1554

The compression–decompression and transmission of a *Millau* stream is faster than the transmission of an uncompressed stream.

generates an XML request and expect an XML response from the server. In the client proxy, the Request Editor (RE) compress the XML body of the HTTP request into a *Millau* stream using a *Millau* XML Tokenizer. The request is then handled by the Generator (G) which forward the request, now in *Millau* format, to the server proxy. In the server proxy, the *Millau* request is received by the request editor which decompresses the *Millau* stream using a *Millau* SAX parser. The request, now in XML format, is handled by the generator which forwards the request to the server. The server produces a response which is received by the Editor (E) of the server proxy. The editor compresses the response in *Millau* format using an XML tokenizer and send this encoded response to the originated client (the client proxy). The editor of the client proxy decodes the response using a *Millau* SAX parser and send it to the client.

Notice that the client proxy is actually a simple WBI plug-in that can be embedded in a LAN proxy cache machine or that can also be running directly on the client machine. An important issue is that the client proxy is 'close' to the client machine. By 'close' we mean that the connection between the client machine and the client proxy machine is fast compared to the connection between the client and the server (typically an Internet connection). For example, the client proxy machine must be on the same LAN than the client machine. In the same way, the server proxy must be 'close' to the server machine.

To test the efficiency of this architecture, we compare the compression–decompression overhead with the download time saving that *Millau* compression realizes. We measured this compression–decompression overhead on a large set of small and big XML documents. The results show that the compression–decompression overhead is small compared to the download time that can be saved, specially on a low bandwidth connection like a modem connection. In the following table, we present mean results for small eBusiness documents and for large text documents (Shakespeare's plays encoded in XML by John Bosak [18]). The transmission time was computed for a 56 Kbits/s modem line. Table 13 shows the results.

A typical eBusiness transaction is composed of a short request followed by a short answer. Without *Millau*, the transmission takes 1042 ms. With *Millau*, it takes 368 ms including the compression–decompression overhead giving a saving of 65% of the time. This can account for a significant portion on a large number of transactions. Note that the compression–decompression system has been implemented in Java. With an algorithm like GZIP which current implementation is in C, the compression–decompression time is smaller. We are working on a C implementation of the *Millau* compression–decompression algorithms which would allow a faster processing.

6.2. *Millau XML remote procedure call*

XML-RPC [23] is a very simple protocol for performing remote procedure calls over HTTP. It was designed by Userland Software, working with Microsoft. An XML-RPC message is an HTTP-POST request. The body of the request is in XML. A procedure executes on the server and the value it returns is also formatted in XML. Procedure parameters can be scalars, numbers, strings, dates, etc., and can also be complex record and list structures. In our implementation, the body of the request is in *Millau* binary XML.

The *Millau* encoding format appears to be particularly well adapted to the XML-RPC because the exchanged messages are usually very short and may not contain redundant tags. So, as demonstrated in the previous section, the traditional compression algorithms have usually poor performances in term of compression rate with these kind of messages. On the other hand, XML-RPC uses a limited set of tags (20 different tags) and no attributes. All the tags can hold on one code page so there is no switch page. Actually, because *Millau* RPC has been designed to work with tokens, it is not necessary to store the code page in memory. Moreover, most of the content is of primitive type and *Millau* RPC can thus take advantage of the possibility of transmitting primitive types without text encoding. All these features make that the processing of XML-RPC requests and answers is efficient.

The *Millau* XML-RPC system is composed of a client which generates *Millau* requests and gets the answers in *Millau* format from the XML-RPC server and of a server which gets the requests for the clients, invokes the corresponding method (if found) and sends the response in *Millau* format or an error message (for example if the method is not found). The HTTP requests are first handled by a Java Servlet which passes the *Millau* body to the server.

The *init* method of the servlet creates the server which does all the work. It also registers the handler object which methods can be called from the client side. The server provides a *register* method to register handler object with a specific name and a *remove* method to remove a specific handler object from its name. References to the handlers are stored in a hash table on the server side. Each time the servlet receives a request, it passes the input stream to the server. The server parses the request encoded in *Millau* binary XML-RPC format using a *Millau* BDOM parser. We are currently working on a version using a *Millau* BSAX parser instead of BDOM for improved efficiency. The server tries to find the handler object and the method corresponding to the method name of the request. If it finds it, it calls this method and encodes the response in *Millau* binary XML-RPC format using the previously described *Millau* BDOM API. It then calls the method *writeBinaryXML* of this API which generates a *Millau* stream that can be sent as the body of the response.

To create a *Millau* XML-RPC client, the user passes the URL of a valid *Millau* XML-RPC server. Then the client can open a persistent connection with the server. The user can then call the *invoke* method of the client, passing the name of the method as 'handler.method' and a vector of the parameters. Details on the type mapping between XML-RPC and Java can be found in [21]. From the method name and the parameters, the client will generate a *Millau* XML-RPC request using the *Millau* BDOM API. Then, it invokes the *writeBinaryXML* method on the BDOM tree to generate a *Millau* stream that can be sent to the *Millau* XML-RPC server through the previously opened socket. The client listens on the socket port to receive the response from the server. If it is a valid *Millau* XML-RPC response message, it is parsed and the result sent to the user; if it is an error message, the error is reported to the user. Notice that the error messages are also encoded in *Millau* XML-RPC format.

Table 14
Performance comparison between *Millau* XML-RPC and Helma XML-RPC

XML-RPC platform	Mean number of calls per second
Millau binary XML-RPC	27
Helma XML-RPC	12

To evaluate the performance of this implementation, we made a benchmark which sends an array of 100 integers as a parameter and receives the same array as a return value. We compared the performances of our implementation with the Helma XML-RPC system [21]. The performance measure is given in Table 14.

Notice that HTTP may not be the best protocol to implement RPC because of the HTTP header which can be big compared to the binary XML payload, specially if there are few parameters in the request. In case of very small requests, the performance improvement will not be significant because of the HTTP header overhead. A solution is to use persistent HTTP connections.

7. Conclusion

As large number of XML documents are exchanged and streamed over the Internet medium, techniques for compact and efficient representation and exchange for this data become essential. In this paper, we describe a system called *Millau* for efficient encoding and streaming of XML structures. While traditional data compression algorithms lose the structure of the documents, *Millau* keeps the XML hierarchical structure. Moreover, *Millau* enables the separation of the content from the structure in order to be able to compress the text or multimedia data separately from the XML structure. This allows achieving better compression rates. This further allows an application to do some processing on the structure without having to download large volume of data. Moreover, our experiments show that, though traditional data compression algorithms are able to perform high compression rate on large XML files, they are much less effective towards small sized XML documents like the ones exchanged in eCommerce transactions. *Millau* achieves better compression rates for such documents.

To allow manipulation of *Millau* encoded XML documents at a layer transparent from the application, we provide both a SAX API and a DOM API conform to the standards of the Web. Additionally, we provide for both APIs methods for allowing applications to work directly with tokens instead of processing strings. Our experiments have shown that the processing of *Millau* tokens where up to five times faster than the processing of XML tags. We also developed data structures to efficiently map tags to tokens and to store the tokens. We provide algorithms to build the code spaces from the associated XML DTDs in an efficient way. We are currently working on taking better advantage of the document structure to limit the number of page switches inside of a document and so to improve the compression rate.

To demonstrate the advantages of *Millau* encoding format, we built two applications on top of the previously mentioned APIs. The first one is a compression-decompression proxy server which takes advantage of the compact representation of XML that *Millau* provides to save Internet network bandwidth and also of the ease of processing. The second one, the *Millau* XML-RPC uses the methods which return token instead of strings for faster processing of parameters marshaled in XML. Moreover, it allows saving network bandwidth because of the compact format. These applications must be seen as a first step toward eBusiness transaction on the Internet.

Because it retains the structure of XML documents and because it is designed to be processed as a continuous stream, *Millau* encoding format can also be used for efficiently streaming structured multimedia content. For example, we built a solution for fragmenting a *Millau* document, associating a priority to each fragment, streaming each fragment independently, and rebuilding the whole document or parts of the document according to the user's preferences or the browser capabilities. We applied this solution to the streaming of structured multimedia documents. We also designed a simple tool for the browsing and searching of XML structure and retrieval of multimedia content. This subject has been discussed in [8,9].

Acknowledgements

The authors would like to express their gratitude to Prof. Bernard Mérialdo for his help during the prior work done in [8]. We would also like to thank Anita Huang and Sami Rollins who reviewed this paper and helped improve the final version.

References

[1] R. Barrett, P. Maglio, J. Meyer, S. Ihde and S. Farrell, WBI development kit, http://www.alphaworks.ibm.com/tech/wbidk

[2] C.-H. Chi, J. Deng and Y.-H. Lim, Compression proxy server: design and implementation, in: 2nd USENIX Symp. on Internet Technologies and Systems.

[3] P. Deutsch and J. Gailly, ZLIB Compressed Data Format Specification Version 3.3, RFC 1950, May 1996, http://www.ietf.org/rfc/rfc1950.txt

[4] P. Deutsch, DEFLATE Compressed Data Format Specification version 1.3, RFC 1951, Aladdin Enterprises, May 1996, http://www.ietf.org/rfc/rfc1951.txt

[5] P. Deutsch, GZIP file format specification version 4.3, RFC 1952, Aladdin Enterprises, May 1996, http://www.ietf.org/rfc/rfc1952.txt

[6] Document Object Model (DOM) Level 1 Specification Version 1.0, W3C Recommendation 1 October, 1998, http://www.w3.org/TR/REC-DOM-Level-1/

[7] Extensible Markup Language (XML) 1.0, W3C Recommendation 10 February 1998, http://www.w3.org/TR/REC-xml

[8] M. Girardot, Efficient representation, streaming and exchange of XML content over the Internet medium, Master Thesis, Eurecom Institute, September 1999.
[9] M. Girardot and N. Sundaresan, Efficient representation and streaming of XML content over the Internet medium, in: IEEE Int. Conf. on Multimedia and Expo 2000, December 1999.
[10] R.N. Horspool and G.V. Cormack, Constructing word-based text compression algorithms, IEEE Trans. Inf. Theory (1992).
[11] D.A. Huffman, A method for the construction of minimum-redundancy codes, Proc. IRE 40 (9) (1952) 1098–1101.
[12] IBM XML Parser for Java, http://www.alphaworks.ibm.com/tech/xml4j
[13] N.J. Larsson and A. Moffat, Offline dictionary-based compression, IEEE Trans. Inf. Theory (1999).
[14] J.C. Mogul, F. Douglis, A. Feldmann and B. Krishnamurthy, Potential benefits of delta-encoding and data compression for HTTP, in: Proc. ACM SIGCOMM '97 Conf., September 1997.
[15] M. Nelson, The Data Compression Book, M and T Books, 1992.
[16] Open Applications Group, http://www.openapplications.org/
[17] SAX 1.0: The Simple API for XML, http://www.megginson.com/SAX/
[18] Shakespeare's plays encoded in XML by J. Bosak from Sun Microsystems, http://metalab.unc.edu/bosak/xml/eg/shaks200.zip
[19] The Wireless Application Protocol (WAP) Forum, http://www.wapforum.org/
[20] J.R. Velasco, L.A. Velasco Luciañez, Benefits of compression in HTTP applied to caching architectures, in: Proc. 3rd Int. WWW Caching Workshop, 1998, http://wwwcache.ja.net/events/workshop/32/manchester.html
[21] H. Wallnöfer, XML-RPC Library for Java, http://helma.at/hannes/xmlrpc/
[22] WAP Binary XML Content Format, W3C NOTE 24 June 1999, http://www.w3.org/TR/wbxml/
[23] XML-RPC Home Page: http://www.xml-rpc.com/
[24] F. Yergeau, UTF-8, a transformation format of ISO 10646, RFC 2279, Alis Technologies, January 1998, http://www.ietf.org/rfc/rfc2279.txt
[25] J. Ziv and A. Lempel, A universal algorithm for sequential data compression, IEEE Trans. Inf. Theory 23 (3) (1997) 337–343.

Marc Girardot is a research intern at the IBM Almaden Research Center, California, USA. He holds a D.E.A. honors degree in Networking and Distributed Applications from the University of Nice, France and a telecommunications engineering degree (major: Multimedia Communications) from the Ecole Nationale Supérieure des Télécommunications, Paris, France. His areas of research interests and expertise include multimedia, virtual reality, information theory, and Internet technologies with focus on XML.

Neel Sundaresan is a research manager of the eMerging Internet Technologies department at the IBM Almaden Research Center. He has been with IBM since December 1995 and has pioneered several XML and Internet related research projects. He was one of the chief architects of the Grand Central Station project at IBM Research for building XML-based search engines. He received his Ph.D. in CS in 1995. He has done research and advanced technology work in the area of compilers and programming languages, parallel and distributed systems and algorithms, information theory, data mining and semi-structured data, speech synthesis, agent systems, and internet tools and technologies. He has over 30 research publications and has given several invited and refereed talks and tutorials at national and international conferences. He has been a member of the W3C standards effort.

An entropy approach to unintrusive targeted advertising on the Web

John A. Tomlin [1]

IBM Research Division, Almaden Research Center, K53/802, 650 Harry Road, San Jose, CA 95120-6099, USA

Abstract

This paper describes the formulation of a new model for unintrusive targeted advertising on the web, extending the linear programming approach taken by Langheinrich et al. [M. Langheinrich, A. Nakamura, N. Abe, T. Kamba and Y. Koseki, Unintrusive customization techniques for Web advertising, in: Proc. of World Wide Web 8, 1999]. A feature of our model is that it avoids unrealistic solutions of the type which may show ads to only a too-narrow group of users. This is accomplished by using a statistically derived entropy maximization model, which incorporates a form of randomization in associating advertisements with targetable groups of users, as well as considering click-through probability. It is then shown that this nonlinear entropy model can be embedded in larger models for the purpose of optimal management of web advertisement portfolios by agencies or brokerages.

Keywords: World Wide Web; Electronic commerce; On-line advertising; Optimization; Statistics; Entropy; Equilibrium

1. Introduction

This paper outlines the formulation of some entropy models for directed advertising on the Web [9], and in particular for unintrusive targeted advertising. The initial aim is to build an optimization model which can be used to compute frequencies for showing advertisements to groups of users to *stably* optimize click-throughs or revenue. A feature of the model is that it is formulated to avoid unrealistic, 'over-targeted' solutions. To illustrate what this means, and to motivate the rest of this paper, let us consider a very simple example.

Suppose we have 100 identical banner ads to be presented to two distinguishable types, or groups, of users, who view the page on which the ad may be displayed in equal numbers, and who have estimated click-through probabilities of 51% and 49%. How many of the ads should we show to each type of user to maximize the expected number of click-throughs?

If we let x_1, x_2 be the number of ads shown to users of type 1 and 2, this problem can be expressed as a tiny *linear program* (LP):

$$\begin{aligned} \text{Maximize} \quad & 0.51x_1 + 0.49x_2 \\ \text{subject to} \quad & x_1 + x_2 = 100 \\ & x_i \geq 0 \end{aligned}$$

The obvious 'optimal' solution is $x_1 = 100$, $x_2 = 0$, in other words to show all the ads to the first group of users, to achieve an expected 51 click-throughs. The second group are shown no ads at all.

Is this solution realistic or desirable? If the click-through probabilities and ratio of users were known with perfect accuracy, perhaps. But in the real world such data are uncertain. Suppose the uncertainty in the click-through probabilities is a modest 5%. Then in the worst case, the actual probabilities might be 46% and 54%, the coefficients in the function to be

[1] E-mail: tomlin@almaden.ibm.com

maximized would be 0.46 and the 0.54, rather than 0.51 and 0.49, and the 'optimal' solution would be *completely different* — to show all of the ads to the second group of users ($x_1 = 0$, $x_2 = 100$). This would result in 54 expected click-throughs, whereas our previous solution with $x_1 = 100$ would result in only 46. These drastic differences in solution are clearly unsatisfactory, and we shall refer to 'all-or-nothing' solutions of this type as 'over-targeted'.

It might be thought that one way out of this dilemma is to specify a minimum allocation of ads to each group — to demand that (say) each group is shown at least 10 ads (i.e. $x_i \geq 10$). However, the effect of this is that once each group has been assigned its minimum 10 ads, the remaining 80 will again be assigned on an all-or-nothing basis as before, and our solution will be ($x_1 = 90$, $x_2 = 10$) — only slightly more stable under changes in the probabilities than before. We might improve the situation by increasing the lower bound further, but we have no guidance on how much.

Faced with the above situation, the commonsense approach is to "more or less evenly distribute the ads between the groups of users, but with a bias toward the group(s) with the higher click-through probability". We must then ask how this is to be expressed mathematically. The results of Section 3 of this paper suggest that instead of solving the tiny linear program (LP)above, we should solve the following tiny *non-linear program* (NLP):

$$\begin{aligned} \text{Maximize } & 0.51x_1 + 0.49x_2 \\ & - 0.5x_1 \ln(x_1) - 0.5x_2 \ln(x_2) \\ \text{subject to } & x_1 + x_2 = 100 \\ & x_i \geq 0 \end{aligned}$$

The solution (to 4 figures) to this NLP is $x_1 = 51.00$, $x_2 = 49.00$, yielding an expected number of 50.00 click-throughs — one less than in the LP optimum, but much more robust under changes in the data. Under the worst case 5% variation in probabilities considered above, the extreme cases — when the probabilities are (0.56, 0.44) and (0.46, 0.54) — yield solutions of (55.97, 44.03) and (46.01, 53.99) with expected click-throughs of 50.72 and 50.32 — a far more stable outcome. The nonlinear terms in the NLP objective have accomplished the goal of "more or less evenly distributing the ads between the groups of users", which we might more formally describe as *randomization*, but the linear terms still give us a "bias toward the group(s) with the higher click-through probability". While the concept of randomizing may at first appear odd in the advertising context, any Web surfer will have observed that portals do in fact serve up mixtures of ads.

The first priority of this paper is then to formulate optimization models which avoid 'over-targeted' solutions by a technique which allows for randomization, as well as considering click-through probability, and which is suitable for much larger (and less contrived) problems than our example, involving many types of users and ads. We use a statistical argument in deriving this model, following the lead given in other modeling areas — notably transportation planning. These models also have the advantage that efficient algorithms are available for their solution, making them attractive in practice.

A further advantage of this formulation is that it provides a fundamental building block for more far-reaching objectives in Web-based advertising. In particular we will describe how this linear-logarithmic model can be embedded in a larger model for the purpose of optimal management of Web advertisement portfolios by agencies or brokerages.

In the next section we move beyond the highly simplified LP model described above, and outline the quite general linear programming model formulated by Langheinrich et al. [10] for their ADWIZ system. This is followed by a derivation of the entropy approach and a description of the form of the solutions. We then describe how this model may be embedded in a prototype multi-time-period planning model for an advertising campaign. Finally we summarize some of the many interesting areas of further exploration associated with the entropy modeling approach.

2. The ADWIZ LP model

Langheinrich et al. [10] have described a system for 'unintrusive customization' of Web advertising — unintrusive in the sense that only impersonal information, such as use of a search keyword, or accessing of a page, is required. This system consists of a number of elements. Those of most interest to us here are a *Selection Engine* and a *Learning System*.

The first of these components uses a set of weights in a *Relevancy Computation* to compute the probability of displaying a particular ad to a user, the user being associated with certain keywords or pages.

The component of principle interest here is a 'learning' system, which computes display weights based on current estimates of click-through probabilities, the keyword list and the ad inventory. The components and formulation of the model (but with the indices reversed here) are as follows:

Indices
$i = 1, \ldots, m$ The keywords;
$j = 1, \ldots, n$ The ads available.

Data
h_j The desired display rate for ad j (normalized over all ads);
k_i The keyword input probabilities (normalized over all keywords);
c_{ij} Click-through probability for ad j and keyword i.

Variables
d_{ij} The display probability of ad j for keyword i.

Constraints

$$\begin{aligned} &\sum_{j=1}^{n} d_{ij} = 1 && (i = 1, \ldots, m); \\ &\sum_{i=1}^{m} k_i d_{ij} = h_j && (j = 1, \ldots, n); \\ &d_{ij} \geq 0 && (i = 1, \ldots, m;\ j = 1, \ldots, n). \end{aligned} \tag{1}$$

Maximize

$$\sum_{i=1}^{m} \sum_{j=1}^{n} c_{ij} k_i d_{ij}.$$

Note that the first equation in (1) above can be multiplied through by k_i, followed by a change of variable:

$$\rho_{ij} = k_i d_{ij}$$

to produce the equivalent constraints:

$$\begin{aligned} &\sum_{j=1}^{n} \rho_{ij} = k_i && (i = 1, \ldots, m); \\ &\sum_{i=1}^{m} \rho_{ij} = h_j && (j = 1, \ldots, n); \\ &\rho_{ij} \geq 0 && (i = 1, \ldots, m;\ j = 1, \ldots, n). \end{aligned} \tag{2}$$

and objective:

$$\text{Maximize} \sum_{i=1}^{m} \sum_{j=1}^{n} c_{ij} \rho_{ij}. \tag{3}$$

This is a classic 'transportation problem' (see e.g. [3]), and we shall work with this and subsequent models in this form. The model may be complicated in practice by contractual requirements setting a minimum on certain ad display rates. Such constraints, of the form

$$\rho_{ij} \geq L_{ij}$$

where L_{ij} is a constant, do not significantly complicate the model. This is fortunate, because although efficient algorithms exist for general linear programs, there exist algorithms which are orders of magnitude faster for the transportation problem (see [8]). Since these models may become quite large, or need to be solved frequently, this is an important practical consideration.

Despite the virtues of this model — simplicity and fast solution time — it suffers from much the same weakness as the LP model in the introduction. Linear programming theory (see [3]) tells us that a model like this, with $(m + n)$ linear constraints on mn variables, has optimal solutions in which at most $(m + n)$ of the variables are away from their lower bound (usually zero). Thus for realistically large values of m and n we expect only a small fraction of the variables to be nonzero. In other words we expect the same phenomenon of over-targeting; on an even larger (if less extreme) scale. Once again we must regard such solutions as unrealistic and unsatisfactory, with many of the ads not being shown at all for most keywords. Langheinrich et al. [10] recognized this, and resorted to the technique of applying rather arbitrary lower bounds on all the variables. As we saw in the small example, this can remove the immediate symptom — where many or most ad/keyword combinations never appear — but it is far from clear in what sense such solutions can be described as 'optimal'.

3. A statistical theory

In this section we shall employ a methodology used in Traffic Theory for the distribution of vehicles from origins (sources) to destinations (sinks). Following the description (but not the notation) of Wilson [13] in the traffic context, let us define a total number of trips A_i originating at origin node i, and require B_j trips to end at destination j. Let x_{ij} be the number of trips for the origin-destination pair (i, j), further let c_{ij} be some generalized cost or impedance of travelling from i to j. Then clearly we require:

$$\begin{aligned} &\sum_{j=1}^{n} x_{ij} = A_i \quad (i = 1, \ldots, m); \\ &\sum_{i=1}^{m} x_{ij} = B_j \quad (j = 1, \ldots, n); \\ &x_{ij} \geq 0 \quad (i = 1, \ldots, m;\ j = 1, \ldots, n) \end{aligned} \tag{4}$$

and for feasibility we must have:

$$X = \sum_{i=1}^{m} A_i = \sum_{j=1}^{n} B_j \tag{5}$$

where X is the total number of trips.

We shall also assume for the time being that another constraint is satisfied:

$$\sum_{i=1}^{m} \sum_{j=1}^{n} c_{ij} x_{ij} = C. \tag{6}$$

The basic assumption is that the probability of the distribution $\{x_{ij}\}$ occurring is proportional to the number of states $w(x_{ij})$ of the system which give rise to this distribution. The number of distinct arrangements of individuals which give rise to a distribution $\{x_{ij}\}$ is:

$$w(x_{ij}) = (X!) \Big/ \Big(\prod_{ij} x_{ij}! \Big). \tag{7}$$

Now finding the maximum of this function is equivalent to finding the maximum of the log of w, which after applying Stirling's formula, and neglecting constant terms, requires us to:

$$\text{Maximize } -\sum_{i=1}^{m} \sum_{j=1}^{n} x_{ij} \ln(x_{ij}) \tag{8}$$

subject to (4) and (6). The function appearing in (8) is an *entropy function*.

Without going into detail, the solutions of this entropy maximization problem can be shown to be of the form:

$$x_{ij} = a_i A_i b_j B_j \exp(-\beta c_{ij}) \tag{9}$$

where β is the Lagrange multiplier for equation (6). In practice it is not necessary to know the value of β. An efficient iterative (scaling) procedure is available (see [11,5]) which enables us to solve the problem without having to resort to more expensive general nonlinear programming methods. It can also be shown that for practical values of the A_i, B_j that this maximum is sharp [13].

The maximum entropy solution discussed above is one form of *equilibrium solution*.

The applicability of this model to the targeted advertising problem should now be clear. If we take trips originating at origins as analogous to 'buckets' of users, with A_i users in each bucket, and the destinations as groups of ads to be shown, with B_j ads of each type, and consider the c_{ij} as click-through probabilities with C as the total number of clicks required, we obtain an unnormalized extension of the model discussed in Section 2. Once again, contractual lower bounds may be imposed on particular ad/user pairings (as long as feasibility is not lost). However, there is no 'all-or-nothing' nature to the solution, and over-targeting may be avoided without any requirement for arbitrary lower bounds. Indeed, since the model involves the logarithm of the x_{ij}'s, they must necessarily be positive.

Another statistical model of interest here has also arisen in traffic theory, and is perhaps even more appropriate (see [12]). We proceed by analogy with the Helmholtz free-energy function, which is at a minimum for a system in equilibrium in conditions of constant volume and temperature. This function is of the form:

$$F = E - K \ln w \tag{10}$$

where K is a constant, E is the internal energy, and w is the number of states as defined in (7). We are interested in maximizing click-through, or equivalently, minimizing non-click-through probability. Again using Stirling's formula, and defining

$$\bar{c}_{ij} = \left[\max_{pq} c_{pq}\right] - c_{ij} \tag{11}$$

if we identify these 'cost' values as the analogue of energy we obtain:

$$F = \text{constant} + \sum_{i=1}^{m} \sum_{j=1}^{n} x_{ij} \left(\bar{c}_{ij} + \gamma \ln(x_{ij}) \right). \tag{12}$$

Here γ is a constant, replacing K, whose value is yet to be determined. We now assert that the equilibrium distribution is that which minimizes F subject to (4). The constraint (6) is no longer needed, and the parameter γ accommodates a range of cases, from the extreme of $\gamma = 0$, which gives us the unnormalized version of the LP model in Section 2, to a completely proportional model, giving the solution

$$x_{ij} = A_i B_j / X \tag{13}$$

when γ is taken to be arbitrarily large. The general form of the solution to this model can be shown to be of form

$$x_{ij} = \hat{a}_i \hat{b}_j \exp(-\bar{c}_{ij}/\gamma) \tag{14}$$

which is of the same form as (9). We must then choose a value for γ. It is shown in [12] that under certain assumptions the *weighted mean* of the cost values (as defined in (11)) provides a good fit for the analogous traffic problem, and we shall initially assume so here. This allows us to use an iterative procedure (in γ) to solve the problem. A good initial value for γ has proved to be simply the mean of these cost values for some models, and sometimes this is even a good enough estimate to obtain good agreement between the model and real data. (We used this value in the tiny NLP example in the introduction). Once again the solution to (14) for any γ can be obtained by an efficient iterative (scaling) procedure.

Thus far we have stated this form of the statistical model as a minimization problem. Once γ has been chosen this is of course equivalent to the maximization problem:

$$\text{Maximize} \quad \sum_{i=1}^{m} \sum_{j=1}^{n} x_{ij} \left(c_{ij} - \gamma \ln(x_{ij}) \right) \tag{15}$$

subject to (4), and we shall also use the model in this form.

This form of the statistical model offers significant advantages over that stated in (4)–(8). The constraints are those of the classical transportation problem, and the rather arbitrary constraint (6) has been replaced by a parameter in the linear–logarithmic objective function for which we have some rationale for assigning a value. For either case, we have a self-contained, easily solvable, constrained optimization model which can be embedded in more complex models which we may now consider building for the management of Web advertising campaigns.

Note that we have made no assumptions on how the 'buckets' of users are defined. They may correspond to search keywords, states or histories. Similarly, the assigning of the ads to groups may be by individual or classes of ad. The key pieces of data are the number of users or ads in each bucket or group and the click-through probabilities. The question of maximizing revenue then naturally arises, and can be answered by applying revenue weights to the c_{ij} term in the objective. This will be seen in the more general model of the next section.

4. An embedded model

We will consider the environment in which our models are to be used — the ad supply chain — to be made up of three segments:

Advertisers
: who hire the agencies to display their ads as effectively as possible to users at the various properties.

Agencies/Brokerages
: who choose and display ads at a property, using what information there is available on the users (if any).

Properties
: The particular pages, typically at a portal, where banner ads are displayed by the agency/broker(s).

For concreteness, let us formulate a model which considers only the first two of these specifically — an agency and a number of advertisers who wish to present ads to users in (at least some of) the same buckets. We also broaden the model to multiple time periods. The aim of the agency is to obtain ads from the advertisers which will maximize their net revenue, given the expected number of users in each bucket per time period, and the click-through probabilities for ads in each time period. The components of this model are:

Indices

$i = 1, \ldots, m$ The buckets of users;
$j = 1, \ldots, n$ The ad types available;
$k = 1, \ldots, K$ The advertisers;

$t = 1, \ldots, T$ Time periods.

Data

A_{it} The number of expected users in bucket i in period t;
c_{ij} Click-through probability for ad j by user i in period t;
R_{ijt} Revenue from click-through for ad j by user i in period t;
D_{ijt} Revenue (or Cost) for displaying ad j by user i in period t;
P^+_{jt} Penalty for shortfall of shown ads type j at end of period t;
P^-_{jt} Penalty for excess of shown ads type j at end of period t;
M_{jkt} Agency's cost of obtaining ads of type j from advertiser k to be shown in period t;
U_{jkt} Upper limit on ads of type j from advertiser k in period t;
L_{jkt} Lower limit on ads of type j from advertiser k in period t;
γ_t Entropy weight for period t.

Variables

x_{ijt} The displays of ad j for user type i in period t;
y_{jkt} The number of ads j bought by advertiser k for display in period t;
z_{jt} The number of ads j shown to all users in period t;
s^+_{jt} Inventory of unshown ads of type j at end of period t;
s^-_{jt} Excess of shown ads of type j at end of period t.

Constraints

Material balance:

$$s^+_{jt} - s^-_{jt} = s^+_{j,t-1} - s^-_{j,t-1} + \sum_{k=1}^{K} y_{jkt} - z_{jt} \quad \text{for all } j, t;$$
$$\sum_{j=1}^{n} z_{jt} = \sum_{i=1}^{m} A_{it} \quad \text{for all } t. \tag{16}$$

Supply and demand:

$$\sum_{j=1}^{n} x_{ijt} = A_{it} \quad \text{for all } i, t;$$
$$\sum_{i=1}^{m} x_{ijt} = z_{jt} \quad \text{for all } j, t. \tag{17}$$

Bounds:

$$s^+_{jt}, s^-_{jt}, x_{ijt}, z_{jt} \geq 0 \quad \text{for all } i, j, t,$$
$$L_{ijt} \leq y_{ijt} \leq U_{ijt} \quad \text{for all } i, j, t. \tag{18}$$

Maximize

$$\sum_{i,j,t} x_{ijt}(D_{ijt} + R_{ijt}c_{ijt} - \gamma_t \ln(x_{ijt})) - \sum_{jt}(P^+_{jt}s^+_{jt} + P^-_{jt}s^-_{jt}) - \sum_{jkt} M_{jkt}y_{jkt}. \tag{19}$$

Although the broader questions of costing of Web advertising (see [1,7]) are beyond the scope of this paper, note that by allowing revenues (or costs) to be associated with ads that are clicked on or otherwise (via the D_{ijt} and R_{ijt} coefficients), as well as marketing costs M_{jkt}, considerable flexibility is provided.

This prototype model needs some further specifications to complete it. For example dummy ads may need to be added to make sure that the second material balance constraint can be satisfied, but the above description gives us a sufficiently detailed model to examine its structure. Clearly it can grow quite large quite quickly if T becomes large, or if m or n are taken to be large. However the model has a definite structure. If we let H represent an m by n transportation problem coefficient matrix, the structure of the entire problem coefficient matrix is of the form:

$$\begin{pmatrix} A^{(0)} & & & & \\ A^{(1)} & H & & & \\ A^{(2)} & & H & & \\ \vdots & & & \ddots & \\ A^{(T)} & & & & H \end{pmatrix}$$

where the $A^{(k)}$ are coefficients corresponding to the y_{jkt}, z_{jt}, s^+_{jt} and s^-_{jt} variables only. This structure is well known in the optimization community to be amenable to a technique known as *Generalized Benders Decomposition* (see [6]). Without going into too much technical detail, for this model the decomposition leads to solving multiple subproblems of the form (4), (15) in only the x_{ijt} variables, with the right hand sides B_{jt} now determined by the 'master' z_{jt} values, and a 'master' problem in the y, z, s^+, s^- variables, with constraints derived from the $A^{(k)}$ matrices and the 'cuts' generated by the subproblems. We expect the overall solution procedure to very efficient, even for large problems.

It is important to note that the Generalized Benders approach can be applied in a wider context. It is not limited in applicability to the maximum entropy submodels we have considered. Any procedure for displaying groups of ads to buckets of users which can notionally be expressed as an optimization problem in our x_{ijt} variables, subject to constraints only on those variables, is a candidate for this treatment. Thus some form of Markovian model (see [2]) may be just as amenable as the entropy model(s) we have discussed.

5. Refinements and extensions

There are many possible extensions to the embedded targeting model described above, to encompass more of the ad supply chain. It is relatively straightforward to extend it to consider properties on multiple portals by stratifying the buckets of users (say by adding an index p) and considering not only variables x_{pijt}, etc., but stratified revenues R_{pijk}, etc. Such a model, incorporating agencies, advertisers and properties/portals will still have the basic matrix structure shown above, and be amenable to treatment by decomposition.

There are other statistical techniques, again grounded in transportation studies, which might well be considered for application in targeted advertising applications. One of these is the 'intervening opportunities' model (see [13]) which ranks, in this context, groups of ads in decreasing attractiveness for each bucket of users, and using a probability that opportunities of a certain rank will be passed up, constructs an exponential decay model for associating users with groups of ads.

It should be considered that the model(s) formulated here deliberately assume (since they are 'unintrusive') that very little is known about individual users — only the bucket to which they belong and the click-through probabilities for that bucket of users. If we relax the unintrusivity requirement it may well be that we can *stratify* users by information level — some with the information level we have used above, some with limited information available through cookies, and others for which a detailed click-trail is available. Once again, it is possible to extend the model to accommodate this stratification, modifying it to vary the weight on the entropy terms for the different strata, without losing the matrix structure which promises efficient solution.

Other extensions of this model involve examining the structure of the costs which we have so far considered constant. Especially when multiple advertisers and multiple portals are considered, there is an opportunity to use the model to evaluate some forms of nonlinear pricing for yield management (see [4,14]).

6. Conclusion

We have shown that entropy models, and potentially other modeling techniques from other areas of Operations Research, can provide useful tools in the context of Web advertising campaigns, either in a single time-slice application, or more generally, at a strategic level in the management over time of entire campaigns and portfolios.

As in any large scale optimization application, data availability is critical. This work is at an early stage. The next step is the acquisition of suitable data to test and calibrate the models we have described.

The author is indebted to Prabhakar Raghavan and Sridhar Rajagopalan for valuable discussions in the course of this work.

References

[1] R. Briggs and N. Hollis, Advertising on the Web: is there response before click-through? J. Advert. Res. 37 (2) (1997) 33–45.

[2] M. Charikar, R. Kumar, P. Raghavan, S. Rajagopalan and A. Tomkins, On targeting Markov segments, in: Proc. of the ACM Symposium on Theory of Computing, ACM Press, 1999.

[3] G.B. Dantzig, Linear Programming and Extensions, Princeton University Press, Princeton, NJ, 1963.

[4] S. Daudel and G. Vialle, Yield Management: Applications to Air Transport, Institut du Transport Aerien, Paris, 1994.

[5] S. Erlander, Optimal spatial interaction and the gravity model, Lecture Notes in Economics and Mathematical Systems 173, Springer, Berlin, 1980.

[6] A.M. Geoffrion, Generalized benders decomposition, J. Optimization Theory Appl. 10 (1972) 237–260.

[7] B. Harvey, The expanded ARF model: bridge to the accountable advertising future, J. Advert. Res. 37 (2) (1997) 11–20.

[8] J.L. Kennington and R.V. Helgason, Algorithms for Network Programming, Wiley, New York, 1980.
[9] Y. Kodha and S. Endo, Ubiquitous advertising on the WWW: merging advertisement on the browser, in: Fifth International World Wide Web Conference, Paris, France, May 1996, see also: http://www5conf.inria.fr/fich_html/papers/P52/Overview.html.
[10] M. Langheinrich, A. Nakamura, N. Abe, T. Kamba and Y. Koseki, Unintrusive customization techniques for Web advertising, in: Proc. of World Wide Web 8, 1999, available at: http://www8.org/w8-papers/2b-customizing/unintrusive/unintrusive.html.
[11] R.B. Potts and R.M. Oliver, Flows in Transportation Networks, Academic Press, New York, 1972.
[12] J.A. Tomlin and S.G. Tomlin, Traffic distribution and entropy, Nature 220 (1968) 974–976.
[13] A.G. Wilson, A statistical theory of spatial distribution models, Transport. Res. 1 (1967) 253–269.
[14] R.B. Wilson, Nonlinear Pricing, Oxford University Press, Oxford and New York, 1993.

John Tomlin gained his B.Sc. (Hons) and Ph.D. in Mathematics at the University of Adelaide, South Australia. Since then he has worked continuously in the areas of operations research, applied optimization and optimization software. He joined the IBM Research Division in 1987. He is a member of ACM, INFORMS and the Mathematical Programming Society.

A Web marketing system with automatic pricing

Naoki Abe *, Tomonari Kamba [1]

NEC C&C Media Research Laboratories and Human Media Research Laboratories, 4-1-1 Miyazaki, Miyamae-ku, Kawasaki 216-8555, Japan

Abstract

We propose a new scheme of 'automatic pricing' for digital contents, and describe an implemented system as well as concrete pricing algorithms for it. Automatic pricing refers to a methodology of automatically setting sales prices to optimal prices, based on past prices and sales. In particular, we consider the case in which automatic pricing is done in order to maximize the profit of an on-line marketing site. We describe a demo site for on-line marketing with automatic pricing, which we call 'digiprice'. We will also describe the concrete pricing algorithms we employ in digiprice, and report on preliminary performance evaluation experiments we conducted using simulated data. The results of experimentation verify that our methods are practical in terms of both the speed of convergence to the optimal price and computational efficiency.

Keywords: Electronic commerce; On-line marketing; Automatic pricing; Machine; Learning; On-line learning

1. Introduction

With the recent technological and social developments surrounding the World Wide Web, it is fast developing as a medium for commerce as well as a medium for information exchange. Electronic commerce not only helps lubricate economical activities, but is bringing about a fundamental change to the practice of commerce that we have been familiar with over many centuries. Shopping sites on the Internet began at first as a mere copy of the off-line shops that make sales with fixed prices, but soon auction sites such as ebay and priceline [5,10] became well-accepted, and now 'reverse auction' sites are gaining popularity. Such forms of commerce did exist before the emergence of the World Wide Web, but these on-line marketing sites are qualitatively different from their off-line counterparts, due to the substantially greater reach they enjoy. These on-line sites are also attracting attention as a medium for community formation.

Electronic commerce is affecting what is being sold in addition to the way it is sold. Consumers can now purchase pictures, music and software as digital contents by downloading them from on-line sites. For manufacturers, digital contents allow mass-production with virtually no additional cost. Furthermore, electronic commerce is affecting the mechanism of pricing, one of the fundamental elements of commerce. On-line auction and reverse auction sites, by their large audience size, are affecting the existing practices of pricing. The prices are more and more determined by the consumers, rather than the manufacturers. Conceptually, this property is shared by any capitalist economy, but the speed and the

* Corresponding author. E-mail: abe@ccm.cl.nec.co.jp

[1] kamba@hml.cl.nec.co.jp

manner by which the consumers can affect pricing in electronic commerce make it qualitatively different.

In this paper, we propose a new scheme of 'automatic pricing' for digital contents, and describe an implemented system as well as concrete pricing algorithms. Automatic pricing refers to a methodology of automatically setting sales prices to optimal prices, based on past prices and sales. In particular, we consider the case in which automatic pricing is done in order to maximize the profit of an on-line marketing site. In what follows, we begin by giving an outline of a demo site for on-line marketing with automatic pricing, which we call 'digiprice'. We will then describe the concrete pricing algorithms we employ in digiprice, and report on performance evaluation experiments we conducted using simulated data.

2. Digiprice: a Web-marketing system with automatic pricing

Digiprice is an on-line shopping server equipped with an automatic pricing function. The electronic payment function has not yet been implemented in the system and the site is operating internally on an intranet. It is therefore not freely available on the Internet. Fig. 1 shows the overall system architecture. As shown in this figure, a seller is expected to specify conditions of sales for each item, such as the initial price and the minimum possible price, and the system automatically adjusts the sales price so as to maximize the sales revenue within those conditions. For this purpose, the system keeps the time of sales in addition to the quantity of sales in its database. This is because how the amount of sales per unit time changes as the price is adjusted plays a key role in automatic pricing. The system constantly calculates the current sales price for each item, based on the past records of prices and sales and the conditions specified by the seller.

Fig. 2 shows the top page of digiprice. Fig. 3 gives a page for a seller to register an item for on-line sales, and Fig. 4 shows an example page for a consumer to select an item, to purchase or to examine. As shown in Fig. 4, a consumer can check to see how the prices of a given content have changed in the past, and refer to comments made by other users. In particular, Fig. 5 depicts what can happen, when the user clicks on the 'check market' button on the page shown in Fig. 4. The past prices of the specified item are plotted over time in the graph. The users can, for example, view this graph, try and predict what will happen to the price in the near future, and make their decision on whether and when to buy a given item. Fig. 6 shows an example of a page that appears when a user has requested to purchase a certain item. Purchase of an item can mean different things depending on what is being bought. For example, if it is a digital picture that is being purchased, then it may mean downloading of a high-quality digital picture file. If it is music, then it may mean downloading music data, which can then be enjoyed on a publicly available software.

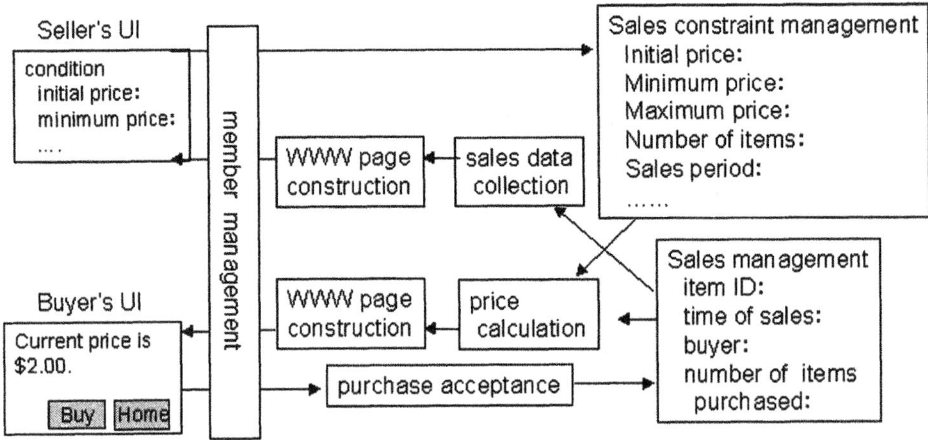

Fig. 1. System architecture of digiprice.

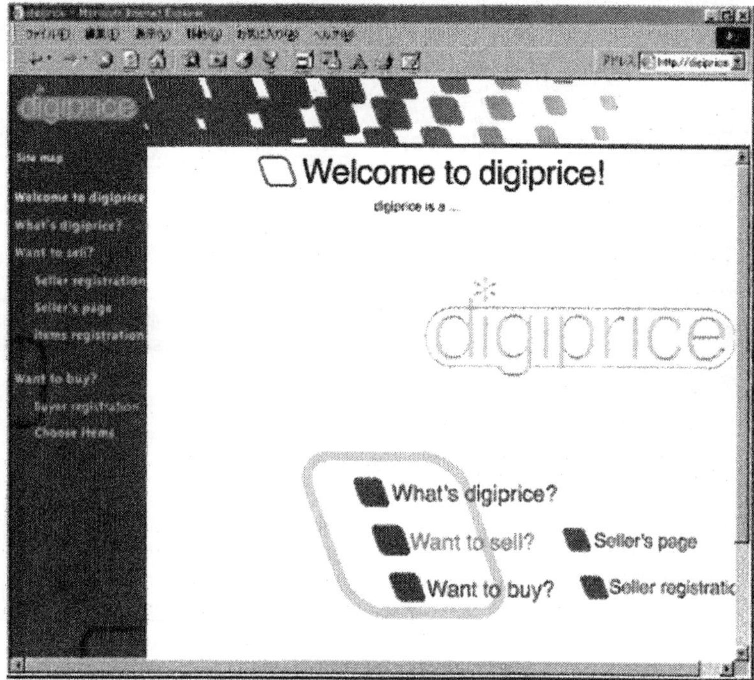

Fig. 2. Top page of digiprice.

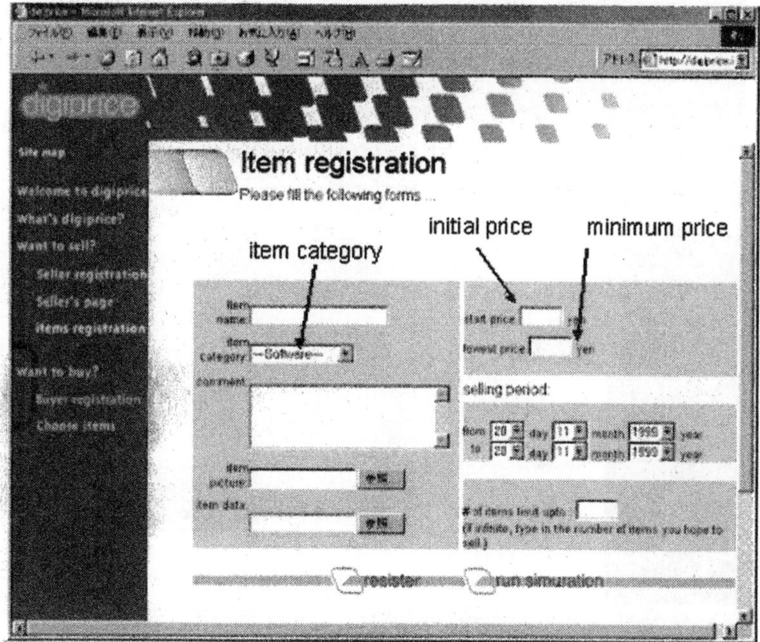

Fig. 3. Seller's page of digiprice.

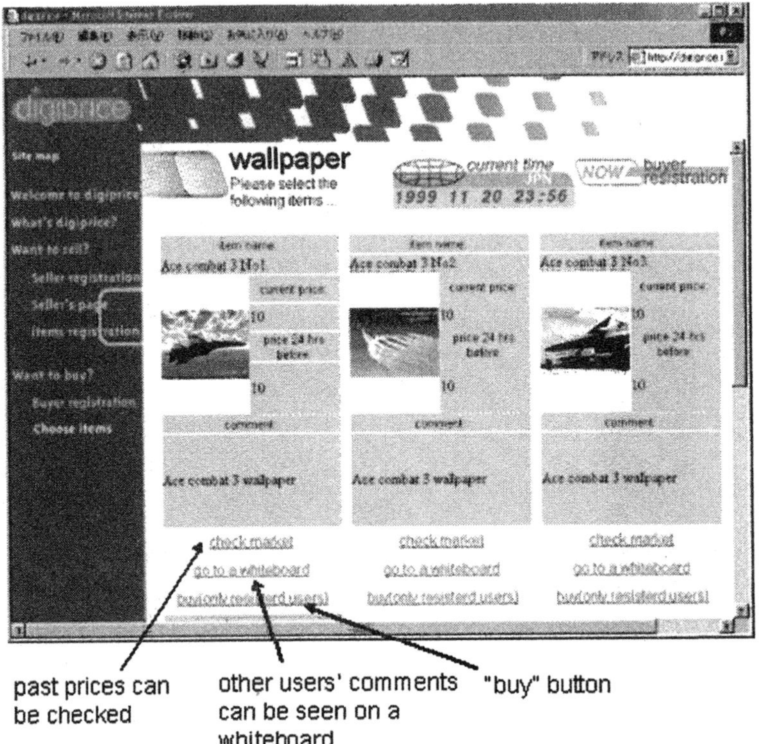

Fig. 4. User's page of digiprice.

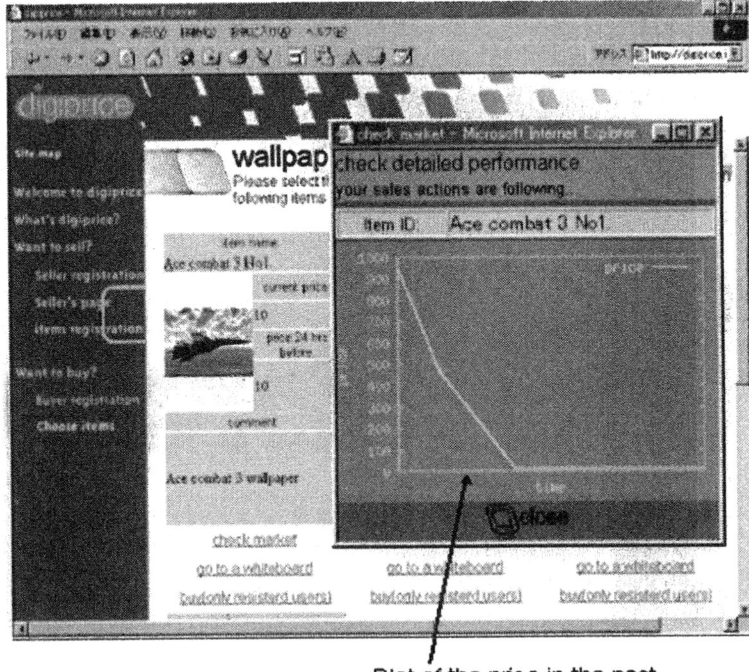

Fig. 5. 'Check market' page of digiprice.

Fig. 6. Purchase page of digiprice.

3. Automatic pricing methods employed by digiprice

The automatic pricing methods that we propose and that are implemented as part of 'digiprice' are the following three.

(1) A pricing method that determines the price of each item independently, without using any attributes associated with them.
(2) A pricing method that determines the prices of all items at once, as a function of their attributes.
(3) A couple of selection methods that determine which items to display in order to optimize the trade-off between selling more immediately and estimating better the pricing function. This is to be used in combination with the above attribute-based method as the pricing method.

3.1. A pricing method for individual goods

With some exceptions, it is generally believed that the amount of commercial goods sold is a decreasing function of their prices. Let us denote the amount of sales per unit time of (a fixed item) by $S(p)$, at price p. Some goods are more sensitive to the price than others, and thus $S(p)$ is unknown a priori to an on-line Web marketing system. An especially desirable feature of on-line marketing is that it allows us to observe the amount of sales as a function of the price and optimize the price in an on-line fashion.

In general, profit per sales depends on the price as well as the amount of sales. In reality, this dependence is complicated due to factors such as economy to scale. Here, for simplicity, we suppose that the total profit can be approximated by the following function of price p and amount of sales $S(p)$, where we use $C(p, N)$ to denote the production cost (per item) at price p and amount of sales N.

$$P(p) = S(p) \cdot \big(p - C(p, S(p))\big).$$

We further assume that the total cost does not depend on the amount of sales, allowing us to simplify the above to:

$$P(p) = S(p) \cdot p - C.$$

This assumption is reasonable for digital contents.

Now the goal of an automatic pricing method is to find a price p that maximizes $P(p)$ quickly, and set the price accordingly. That is, it wishes to find p^* such that

$$p^* = \arg\max_p P(p).$$

We emphasize here that the goal is to quickly find p^*, and not necessarily to estimate the entire function $P(p)$.

Below, we will describe a pricing method that estimates p^* for each item independently, and sets the price automatically.

3.1.1. A pricing method based on stochastic approximation

Stochastic approximation is a general methodology for on-line function optimization, which estimates the maximum of a regression function by testing and obtaining the (estimate of) function values at points of its choice, and gradually converge to the optimum point (cf. [12]). In this section, we propose an automatic pricing method based on this general technique.

The basic idea of stochastic approximation is as follows. In trying to maximize $f(x)$, which dictates the expected reward at point x, it estimates the value of the derivative $f'(x)$ at its current point x, and determines the next point by updating the current position as $x + af'(x)$. Since we cannot observe the values of $f(x)$ directly, one need take care to ensure that the estimation of the derivative is credible. We basically follow the idea of the Kiefer–Wolfowitz method. Having set the initial point x to be some arbitrarily chosen point, this method repeats the following process.

(1) For step size Δ, appropriately determined as a decreasing function of the number of trials (up to that point), test at two points $x+\Delta$ and $x-\Delta$, and obtain rewards $\hat{f}(x-\Delta)$ and $\hat{f}(x+\Delta)$, whose expectations are dictated by the function f.

(2) Update x as follows:

$$x := x + a\frac{\hat{f}(x+\Delta) - \hat{f}(x-\Delta)}{\Delta}.$$

Here, in order to ensure that the x's so obtained converge to the (local) maximum point of f, certain constraints must be satisfied by the values of a and Δ, as will be specified later.

Based on this general idea, we propose a pricing method for a single good. As indicated above, we assume that the profit function can be approximated as

$$P(p) = S(p) \cdot p - C.$$

For maximization of $P(p)$, C can be ignored, so we further simplify the above to obtain

$$P(p) = S(p) \cdot p.$$

In other words, we are simply to maximize the total revenue.

There can be legal constraints on pricing (against dumping, for example), so we assume that there are maximum and minimum possible prices, $p_{\max}$ and $p_{\min}$, given a priori to the system. We assume also that the system is given a reasonable price p_{init} as the initial price. Based on these minimal pieces of information, our first pricing method (StochPrice: Stochastic Pricing) repeats the following process.

(1) Using step size Δ, determined as a decreasing function of the number of trials so far (for example, $\Delta = I^{-1/3}$, where I is the current trial number), conduct on-line sales at both prices $p+\Delta$ and $p-\Delta$ for a certain fixed period of time, and based on the amount of sales obtained during these periods, $S(p+\Delta)$ and $S(p-\Delta)$, calculate the profits (revenues) obtained for the respective prices:

$$P(p+\Delta) = S(p+\Delta) \cdot (p+\Delta),$$

$$P(p-\Delta) = S(p-\Delta) \cdot (p-\Delta).$$

(2) Update the current price p as follows:

$$p := p + \frac{A}{\Delta}\frac{P(p+\Delta) - P(p-\Delta)}{2T}.$$

Here, A is an update interval, set as a decreasing function of the trial number (for example $A = c \cdot I^{-1}$), and T is a measure of the duration of each trial. (To be precise, the size of T depends strongly on what time unit is used. In our experiments, we actually used the average number of visits to the site in a unit period as the value of T.)

(3) If p is either above $p_{\max}$ or below $p_{\min}$, then clamp its value so that it falls within these bounds.

In order to ensure convergence of the obtained prices to the (local) optimum, it suffices to see that the following conditions hold on A and Δ described above [12]:

$$\sum_{I=1}^{\infty} A(I) = \infty,$$

$$\sum_{I=1}^{\infty} \frac{A(I)^2}{\Delta(I)^2} < \infty.$$

Note that both of these conditions are met by the examples we gave earlier of $A = c \cdot I^{-1}$ and $\Delta = c \cdot I^{-1/3}$.

We give the details of this method as a pseudocode below.

Algorithm: StochPrice

(p_{init}, $p_{\min}$, $p_{\max}$, T: Unit sales period)

1. Initialization
   1.1. Initial price $p := p_{\text{init}}$
   1.2. Trial number $I := 1$
2. **Repeat for** $I = 1$ until forever
   2.1. Set Δ as follows: $\Delta := I^{-1/3}$
   2.2. For a period of T, set the price to $p + \Delta$.
   2.3. Let $S(p+\Delta)$ be the amount of sales during this time.
   2.4. For a period of T, set the price to $p - \Delta$.
   2.5. Let $S(p-\Delta)$ be the amount of sales during this time.

2.6. Calculate the obtained profit as follows:

$$P(p+\Delta) = S(p+\Delta)\cdot(p+\Delta)$$

$$P(p-\Delta) = S(p-\Delta)\cdot(p-\Delta)$$

2.7. Set the update interval A as follows:

$$A := \frac{1}{I}$$

2.8. Update the current price as follows:

$$p := p + \frac{AP(p+\Delta) - P(p-\Delta)}{2T\Delta}$$

2.9. If necessary, clamp the value of p between the maximum and minimum possible prices.

$$p := \min\{p_{\max} - \Delta, \max\{p_{\min} + \Delta, p\}\}$$

3.2. *Attribute-based automatic pricing method*

The pricing method proposed in the previous section suffers from the shortcoming that each new product will basically have to be priced from scratch. Using attributes associated with goods and users, it is supposed that earlier experiences can be used to price new items more intelligently. In this section, we propose such a method.

Let us write X for a (binary) attribute vector associated with a fixed item, and write x_i for its ith component. These attributes can be attributes of the good, such as its category, those of a user, such as their demographic attributes, and their combinations. For example, based on attributes like $y_1 = 1$ iff cosmetics, $y_2 = 1$ iff woman, combined attributes like $x_1 = y_1 \cdot y_2$ can be obtained. Strictly speaking, therefore, these attributes are not attributes of the goods alone, but are attributes of potential 'sales,' consisting of a user, a good and possibly the environment. In digiprice, we use binary attributes of the contents, those of the users, and their logical combinations (conjunctions).

The basic idea behind the pricing method we propose here is that the optimal price of a good can be approximated by a linear function of its attributes. That is, there is a weight vector W having the same dimensionality as their associated attribute vectors, such that for an arbitrary item, its profit function $P_X(p)$ approximately attains a maximum at $W \cdot X$, where X is its associated attribute vector, i.e.

$$p_X^* = \arg\max_p P(p) = W \cdot X.$$

Here, we emphasize that this assumption is much weaker than an assumption that $P_X(p)$ itself can be approximated by a simple function. In general, it is supposed that $P_X(p)$ will take a complicated form, but it is reasonable to suppose that its optimal price can be linearly approximated. Since the goal of an automatic pricing method is not necessarily to estimate $P_X(p)$ but that of p_X^*, this assumption helps us design a simple method for it.

3.2.1. *Automatic pricing method based on linear approximation of optimal price*

The pricing method we propose here is based on the Kiefer–Wolfowitz method as before, but here the search for optimality is done in a higher dimensional attribute space.

(1) For each item, calculate its associated vector based on its attributes and those of the current user.
(2) For each item i, set the initial price $p(i)$ to $W \cdot X(i)$, using the weight vector W.
(3) For each item i, generate a random vector $\vec{\Delta}(i)$ of length Δ. Here, Δ is a step size, determined as a decreasing function of the trial number I (for example, $\Delta = c \cdot I^{-1/3}$).
(4) Using the vector $\vec{\Delta}(i)$ thus obtained, set the current price for each item i as follows:

$$p(i) := (W + \vec{\Delta}(i)) \cdot X.$$

Here, for each item, if $p(i)$ goes above the maximum price or below the minimum price, then clamp the vector $\vec{\Delta}(i)$ so that this is not so.
(5) Conduct on-line sales at the above price for a certain period.
(6) Next, conduct on-line sales for the same period, with the price set as follows:

$$p(i) := (W - \vec{\Delta}(i)) \cdot X(i).$$

Here, too, $\vec{\Delta}(i)$ should be clamped if necessary.
(7) For each item, for the respective prices, calculate the total profits, based on the amount of sales obtained for each of the above periods, $S(W + \vec{\Delta}(i))$ and $S(W - \vec{\Delta}(i))$:

$$P(W+\vec{\Delta}(i)) = S(W+\vec{\Delta}(i)) \cdot X(i)(W+\vec{\Delta}(i))$$

$$P(W-\vec{\Delta}(i)) = S(W-\vec{\Delta}(i)) \cdot X(i)(W-\vec{\Delta}(i))$$

(8) Once for each i, update the weight W using the value of $\vec{\Delta}(i)$, as follows:

$$W := W + \frac{A\vec{\Delta}(i)}{|\vec{\Delta}(i)|}\frac{P(W + \vec{\Delta}(i)) - P(W - \vec{\Delta})(i)}{2T}$$

Again, A is an update interval set as a decreasing function of I (for example, $A = c \cdot I^{-1}$).

The details of this method, FeaturePrice(Feature-based Pricing) are shown as a pseudo-code below.

Algorithm: FeaturePrice

(W_{init}: initial weight vector; T: unit sales period)

1. Initialization
   1.1. Set weight vector $W := W_{\text{init}}$
2. **Repeat for** $I = 1$ until forever
   2.1. **For** item $i = 1$ until N (number of items)
      2.1.1. $X(i) :=$ attribute vector for item i
      2.1.2. $p(i) := W \cdot X(i)$
      2.1.3. $\Delta := I^{-1/3}$
      2.1.4. $\vec{V}(i) =$ Random-Vector()
      2.1.5. $\vec{\Delta}(i) = \Delta \cdot (\vec{V}(i))/(|\vec{V}(i)|)$
   2.2. For a time period of T, set the price of each item (i) to $p(i) := (W + \vec{\Delta}(i)) \cdot X(i)$ and conduct sales.
   2.3. Let $S(W + \vec{\Delta}(i))$ be the amount of sales thus obtained for each item (i).
   2.4. For a time period of T, set the price of each item (i) to $p(i) := (W + \vec{\Delta}(i)) \cdot X(i)$ and conduct sales.
   2.5. Let $S(W - \vec{\Delta}(i))$ be the amount of sales thus obtained for each item (i).
   2.6. For each item i, calculate the revenue raised during this time.

$$P(W + \vec{\Delta}(i)) = S(W + \vec{\Delta}(i)) \cdot X(i)(W + \vec{\Delta}(i))$$

$$P(W - \vec{\Delta}(i)) = S(W - \vec{\Delta}(i)) \cdot X(i)(W - \vec{\Delta}(i))$$

   2.7. **For** $i = 1$ until number of items
      Update the weight vector W as follows:

$$W := W + \frac{A}{\Delta}\frac{P(W + \vec{\Delta}(i)) - P(W - \vec{\Delta})(i)}{2T}$$

3.3. Methods for selecting goods to display

We have so far discussed how to automatically set the prices of goods for on-line marketing, in order to maximize the resulting revenue. When the number of items to be sold at a particular site is large enough, however, there is the additional issue of which items to 'display on the show window'. Even if, in principle, the number of items that can be displayed on an on-line marketing site is unlimited, the degree of exposure to the user is heavily influenced by whether they are displayed on the top page, etc. In this section, we consider how to optimize both the prices and the selection of items to display, in order to maximize the total revenue obtained at an on-line marketing site.

At the heart of the issue raised here, is the trade-off known as the 'Exploration–Exploitation trade-off' in the literature on on-line learning (reinforcement learning in particular [7]), formulated below for the current problem of our concern.

(1) If one wishes to maximize the immediate revenue, one should select those items estimated to have the maximum expected revenue.
(2) If one wishes to maximize the total revenue obtained in the long run, one should also take care to display a variety of items, so that their optimal prices, and hence their expected maximum revenues, can be reliably estimated.

The issue of the Exploration–Exploitation trade-off has been addressed by a number of authors in the literature [1–3,6,8], but the work in [1,8], in particular, does so in the context of on-line learning of (probabilistic) linear functions, and is closely related to the problem studied here.

In trying to resolve this trade-off, we consider the following three measures.

(1) *The immediate pay-off of each item.* In particular, we use the profit obtained during the last sales period ($2T$) for each item, i.e.:

$$\text{PTotal}(i, W) = (P(W + \vec{\Delta}(i)) + P(W - \vec{\Delta}(i)).$$

(2) *Variety of attribute vectors.* We use the sum of Hamming distances among the vectors in the set of items selected to be displayed, i.e.:

$$H(S) = \sum_{u,v \in S} \sum_{i} |X(u)_i - X(v)_i|.$$

(3) *Uncertainty of estimating the optimal price function.* We use the difference between the revenues obtained in the first half and the second half of the last sales period:

$$\mathrm{PDiff}(i, W) = |P(W + \vec{\Delta}(i)) - P(W - \vec{\Delta}(i))|.$$

By combining (1) and (2), and (1) and (3) of these three measures, we propose two methods for selecting the items to display.

(1) *Variety Selection.* From among the set of candidate items, select a set of items such that the weighted sum of the variety measure and the immediate pay-off measure is maximized, that is, select S such that

$$\sum_{i \in S} \lambda_1 \mathrm{PTotal}(i, W) + \lambda_2 H(S).$$

Here, λ_1 and λ_2 are parameters controlling the relative contributions of the two measures.

(2) *Uncertainty Selection.* From among the set of candidate items, select the top N items, maximizing the sum of the immediate pay-off and the uncertainty measure:

$$\begin{aligned} &\mathrm{PTotal}(i, W) + \mathrm{PDiff}(i, W) \\ &\quad = P(W + \vec{\Delta}(i)) + P(W - \vec{\Delta}(i)) \\ &\qquad + |P(W + \vec{\Delta}(i)) - P(W - \vec{\Delta}(i))| \\ &\quad = 2 \cdot \max\{P(W + \vec{\Delta}(i)), P(W - \vec{\Delta}(i))\}. \end{aligned}$$

Thus, this method coincides with that of maximizing the larger of the revenues raised for the two different prices.

Since Variety Selection is a strategy that is more oriented towards exploration, we generally switch from Variety Selection to the method of selecting those expected to bring most immediate revenues, after an initial 'exploration' phase. For Variety Selection, strict maximization of $\sum_{i \in S} \lambda_1 \mathrm{PTotal}(i, W) + \lambda_2 H(S)$ would be computationally infeasible. Thus, we settle with the following heuristic. We start with the set consisting with the top N items in terms of the immediate pay-off, and then repeatedly perform random swaps, if such a swap results in increasing the value of the above objective function.

Algorithm: Variety Selection

(W: current weight vector; G: set of items; n: number of items to be displayed; N: number of iterations)

1. Initialization
   1.1. Sort G in increasing order of $\mathrm{PTotal}(i, W)$.
   1.2. $S := \mathrm{First} - n(G, n)$
   1.3. $\overline{S} := \backslash S$
2. **Repeat for** $i = 1$ until N
   2.1. Randomly select item $j \in \overline{S}$.
   2.2. If there exists item k such that exchanging j, k would result in increasing the value of

   $$\sum_{i \in S} \lambda_1 \mathrm{PTotal}(i, W) + \lambda_2 H(S)$$

   then make that exchange and update S and $\overline{S}$.
3. Output S.

We refer to the resulting on-line marketing strategy, consisting of good pricing and selection, by such names as StochPrice (Uncertainty) and FeaturePrice (Variety).

4. Performance evaluation

4.1. Experimental procedure

4.1.1. Consumption model

We model the consumption behavior of users by the following stochastic process.

At each time t and price p, do the following:

(1) Determine the number of visits $V(t)$ in a unit time interval to the marketing site in question, according to a normal distribution with a fixed average and variance.

(2) Determine the probability of purchase by the following function of time t since the beginning of sales and price p:

$$p(t, p) := F(t) \cdot G(p)$$

where the exact forms of $F(t)$ and $G(p)$ will each take one of three possible forms (to be described shortly). The idea is that the purchase probability is governed by a time-dependent factor and a price-dependent factor, which are relatively independent of one another.

(3) Determine the number of sales $S(t, p)$ in a given time period T by:

$$S(t, p) := V(t) \cdot p(t, p).$$

We considered the following three forms for $F(t)$.

(1) $F(t)$ is constant.

$$F(t) = C$$

(2) $F(t)$ decreases exponentially in time.

$$F(t) = C\ \exp\{-Kt\}$$

(3) $F(t)$ is normally distributed.

$$F(t) = C\ \exp\{-K(t-c)^2\}$$

For $G(p)$, we assume one of the following three forms.

(1) $G(p)$ is constant.

$$G(p) = C$$

(2) $G(p)$ decreases exponentially in price.

$$G(p) = C\ \exp\{-Kp\}$$

(3) $G(p)$ is a logistic function (smooth step function).

$$G(p) = C\frac{1}{1+\exp\{K(p-c)\}}$$

For most of the experimental results we reported on, we used the first choice for $F(t)$ and the last choice for $G(p)$.

4.1.2. Generation of attributes

The attributes associated with goods are generated by either of the following two methods: the independent method, and the random walk method. In the independent method, we generate each attribute vector by randomly generating a bit (0 or 1) by a fair coin. In the random walk method, we first generate a random attribute vector as above. We then generate the next vector by probabilistically flipping each bit independently, with a small fixed probability. This process is repeated until the desired number of vectors are obtained.

We then use these attributes to determine the consumption model for each item, so that items having similar attribute vectors tend to have similar consumption patterns. More concretely, we determine each of the constants (such as C, K, c) determining $F(t)$ and $G(p)$ as the product of the attribute vector and a real valued vector, which is randomly generated for each run.

4.1.3. Site visits

The number of site visits $V(t)$ is determined independently for each item (by a normal distribution), when there is no issue of selecting items to display. When a subset of items is to be selected for display, the number of site visits for the selected items, and those for the items not selected, are determined by two different normal distributions. We ensure that the distribution of $V(t)$ for the selected items has a much higher mean than for the non-selected ones.

4.2. Experimental results

For all cases we consider, we basically used the total (cumulative) revenues obtained, for a fixed item or an ensemble of items, as the performance measure for our pricing methods. In most cases. we compared the performance of the proposed pricing methods against that of the method of just keeping the initial price, and the ideal method of using a near optimal price from the beginning. Since the 'optimal price' was not available in closed form for most of our experiments, in our plots, we substituted the optimal price by the estimated optimal price, as obtained by our pricing methods. The performance plots are averaged over five randomized runs, unless otherwise noted.

4.2.1. Results on StochPrice

Fig. 7 plot the cumulative and instantaneous (per unit sales period) revenues obtained by the following three methods as a function of the number of trials: (1) keeping the initial price; (2) using StochPrice; and (3) using a near-optimal price from the beginning. In this experiment, various parameters of StochPrice were set as follows. The constants within F and G, which determine the purchase probability, were set as $C = 1.0$, $K = 0.5$, and $c = 20$. This means that the purchase probability is at most 0.5 and is around 0.1 for prices that are two units higher than the optimal price (which is around 16). The number of site visits per unit time, $V(t)$, was set to be distributed around 300 visits. Thus, at each unit sales period, a typical number of sales is in the tens.

Note that the third method is an ideal and impractical method, since the near optimal price is not available a priori. It is clearly seen in these graphs that after suffering a small initial loss due to the ne-

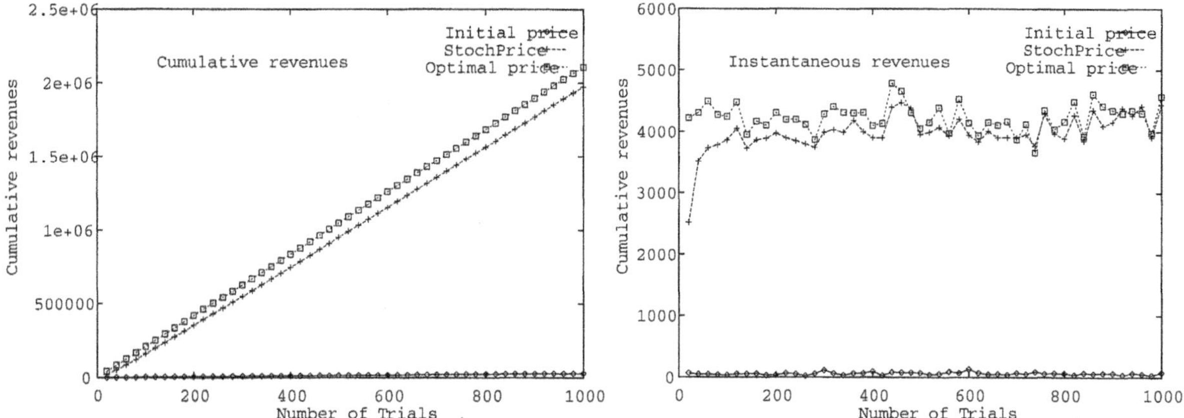

Fig. 7. Cumulative revenues (left) and instantaneous revenues (right) obtained by (1) keeping the initial price, (2) using StochPrice, and (3) using a near-optimal price from the beginning.

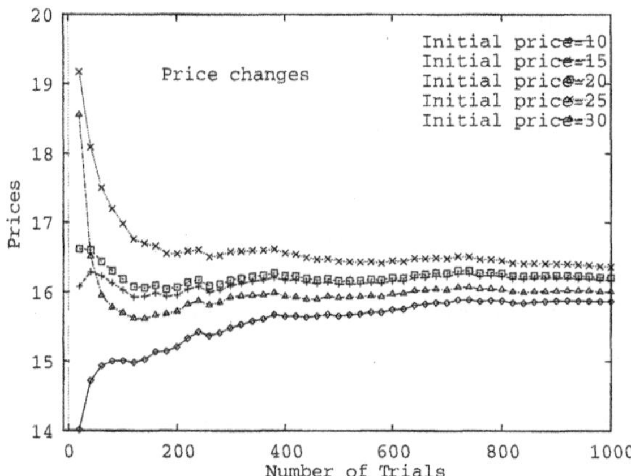

Fig. 8. Price changes made by StochPrice over 1000 trials as a function of the initial price.

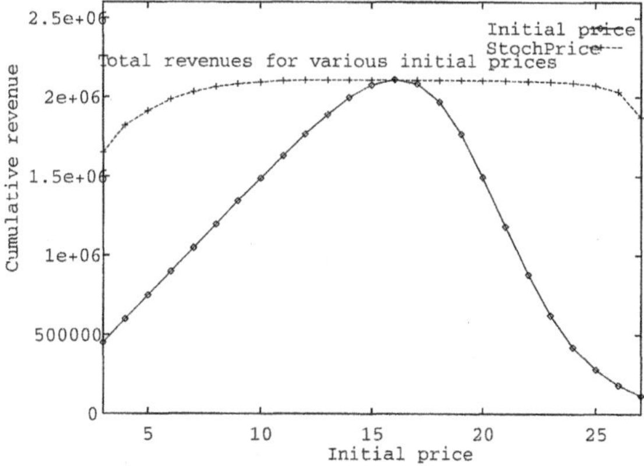

Fig. 9. Cumulative revenues obtained by StochPrice and by keeping the initial price, as a function of the initial price.

cessity to learn the optimal price, StochPrice quickly catches up with the ideal method in its performance.

Fig. 8 shows how the price of a particular item changes over time (on a particular run) using StochPrice, for a variety of choices of the initial price. It is seen that the optimal price is approximately 16 dollars, and whatever the initial price is (within the range shown here), they converge to the optimal price. Fig. 9 plots how the cumulative revenue obtained by StochPrice over 1000 trials changes as a function of the initial price. In the graph, this is compared with how the revenue changes if one kept the initial price, also as a function of the initial price. A rather dramatic difference is observed: when the initial price is kept, the total revenue quickly falls off when the initial price is wrongly set, but using StochPrice, one can see that the total revenue is insensitive to the choice of the initial price for a good range of initial prices.

4.2.2. *Results on FeaturePrice*

As before, we plot the cumulative and instantaneous (per unit sales period) revenues obtained by the following methods: (1) keeping the initial price, (2) using FeaturePrice, and (3) using a near optimal price from the beginning (see Fig. 10). In this experiment, the number of items was set to be 30, and the number of attributes was 10. Other parameters

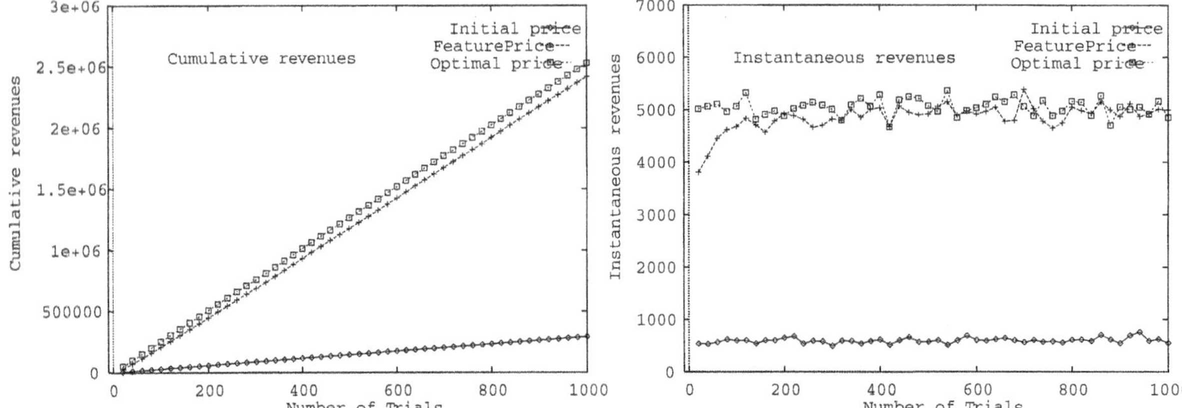

Fig. 10. Cumulative revenues (left) and instantaneous revenues (right) obtained by (1) keeping the initial price, (2) using FeaturePrice, and (3) using a near-optimal price from the beginning.

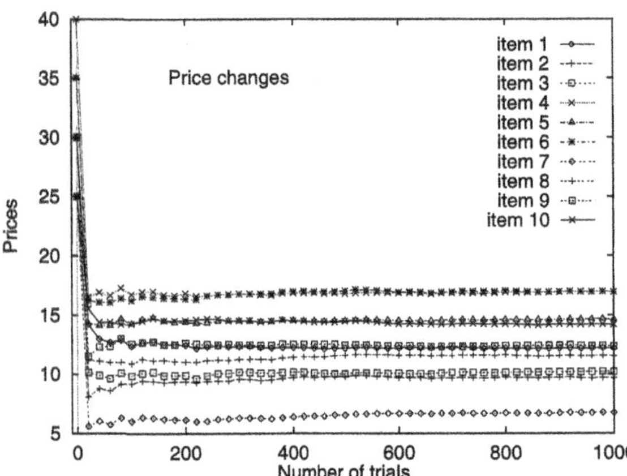

Fig. 11. Price changes made by FeaturePrice for 10 out of the 30 items, over 1000 trials.

controlling F and G were set as follows: $C = 1.0$, $K = 0.9$, and $c = 0.37$. $V(t)$ was set to be averaged at 300 as before.

It is clearly seen that FeaturePrice also improves the revenue of a marketing site significantly. Whether the prices computed by FeaturePrice converge to the respective optimal price is harder to see, but we plotted how the prices are changed by FeaturePrice: Fig. 11 exhibits how the prices are changed by FeaturePrice for 10 (chosen unintentionally) out of the 30 items used in the above experiment. One can see here that although the pricing is done via learning of a single target vector, a great variety of pricing is realized by utilizing the attributes attached to the items being sold. We plan in the near future to compare the performance of FeaturePrice with that of StochPrice in realistic settings, which we will report on in a full paper.

4.2.3. *Results on Good Selection methods*

We compared the revenues obtained by the two methods we propose to address the Exploration–Exploitation trade-off, namely Uncertainty Selection and Variety Selection, with the method of always selecting those items that are estimated to bring about the maximum revenue (MaxProfitSelection). Here, the exploration period for Variety Selection was set at 200 out of the 1000 trials in total. The parameters controlling F and G and $V(t)$ were set identically to the experiment for FeaturePrice.

Fig. 12 shows the cumulative and instantaneous revenues obtained by each of the three methods. It is seen that the revenues obtained by both Uncertainty Selection and Variety Selection significantly out-perform that of MaxProfit, with Uncertainty Selection being the favored one for the experimental conditions we tried. Since Uncertainty Selection is computationally cheaper than Variety Selection, it appears to be the method of choice.

5. Concluding remarks

We have proposed a new concept of on-line marketing with automatic pricing. In particular, we ex-

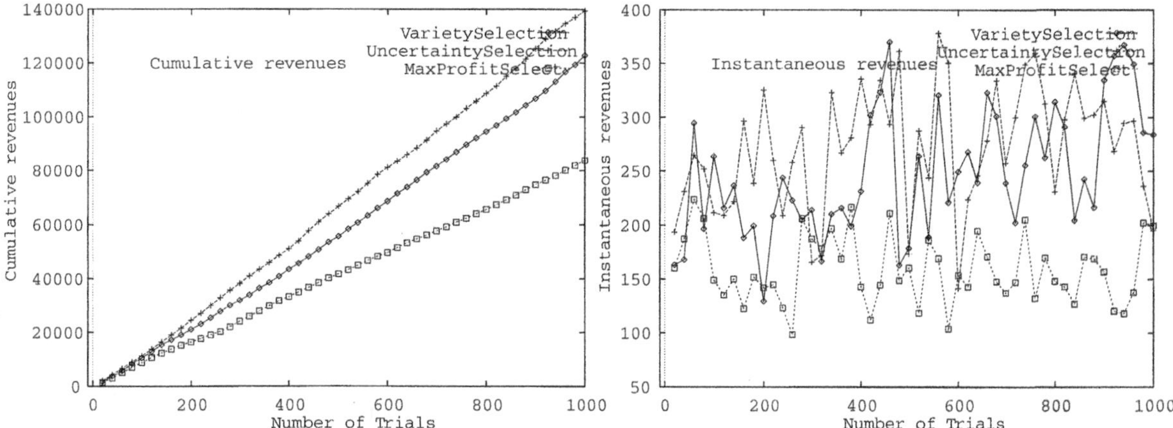

Fig. 12. Cumulative revenues (left) and instantaneous revenues (right) obtained by VarietySelection, UncertaintySelection and MaxProfit-Selection.

hibited an implemented system and concrete pricing algorithms designed to maximize the profit of the sellers. The proposed scheme of automatic pricing is distinguished from other forms of dynamic pricing that are currently employed by on-line marketing sites on the Internet. Most Web-marketing sites with dynamic pricing schemes base their pricing on the demand–supply information that is available via the Internet. Auction [5,10] and reverse auction sites [9], as well as other pricing information services [4] share the property that the pricing is determined as a result of competition between buyers and sellers. Among those Web-marketing sites that are currently operating on the Internet, perhaps 'OutletZoo' [11] employs a pricing scheme that is most closely related to ours. In particular, OutletZoo offers a dynamic pricing scheme they call 'Automatic Drop'. It is a means to ensure that excess merchandises that manufacturers wish to sell are eventually all sold, and it works by simply making "prices fall at a seller determined percentage at regular intervals until everything is sold". A variation of our automatic pricing scheme which is sensitive to constraints posed by the amount of goods in stock may prove to be a viable alternative. In the future, we wish to investigate extensions of the proposed pricing scheme to other scenarios and purposes, such as in a two-way interactive marketing environment like auction or in the presence of physical stock constraints. We believe that, through such extensions and variations, the concept of automatic pricing we propose in this paper can be developed into a model of on-line marketing that can truly benefit the buyers as well as the sellers.

Acknowledgements

We would like to thank Phil Long of National University of Singapore for valuable discussions on topics related to this paper. We also thank the anonymous referees for providing invaluable information. We wish to thank Dr. Doi, Dr. Koseki, Dr. Koike, Dr. Sakata, and Dr. Goto of NEC for their encouragement for this research. Finally, we thank Mr. Omoto and Dr. Takada of NIS for their programming efforts.

References

[1] N. Abe and P. Long, Associative reinforcement learning using linear probabilistic concepts, in: Proc. 16th International Conference on Machine Learning, 1999, pp. 3–11.

[2] N. Abe and J. Takeuchi, The 'lob-pass' problem and an on-line learning model of rational choice, in: Proc. 6th Annual ACM Conference on Computational Learning Theory, 1993, pp. 422–428, 1994, pp. 1198–1204.

[3] D.A. Berry and B. Fristedt, Bandit Problems, Chapman and Hall, New York, 1985.

[4] Dealtime, An Internet marketing service site, http://dealtime.com/.

[5] Ebay, An Internet auction site, http://www.ebay.com/.

[6] D.P. Helmbold, N. Littlestone and P.M. Long, Apple tasting and nearly one-sided learning, in: Proc. 33rd Annual Symposium on the Foundations of Computer Science, 1992.

[7] L. Kaelbling, Associative reinforcement learning: functions in k-DNF, Machine Learning 15 (3) (1994) 279–298.
[8] P.M. Long, On-line evaluation and prediction using linear functions, in: Proc. 10th Annual Conference on Computational Learning Theory, 1997, pp. 21–31.
[9] Nextag, An Internet reverse auction site, http://nextag.com/.
[10] Priceline, An Internet auction site, http://www.priceline.com/.
[11] OutletZoo, An Internet marketing site, http://outletzoo.com/.
[12] M.T. Wasan, Stochastic Approximation, Cambridge University Press, Cambridge, 1969.

Naoki Abe received his B.S. and M.S. degrees from Massachusetts Institute of Technology in 1984, and his Ph.D. degree from the University of Pennsylvania in 1989, all in computer science. After holding a postdoctoral researcher position at the University of California, Santa Cruz, he joined the NEC Corporation in 1990, where he is currently principal researcher in the C&C Media Research Laboratories. He is also a visiting associate professor in the department of computational intelligence and systems science of Tokyo Institute of Technology. His research interests include theories and applications of machine learning to various domains, including Internet information mining and navigation.

Tomonari Kamba received his B.E., M.E. and Ph.D. in electronics from the University of Tokyo in 1984, 1986 and 1997, respectively. He joined the NEC Corporation in 1986, and he has been engaged in user interface design methodology, multimedia user interface, software agent, and Internet information service technology. He was a visiting scientist at the Graphics, Visualization and Usability Center at the College of Computing, Georgia Institute of Technology, from 1994 to 1995. He is now research manager in the Human Media Research Laboratories. Dr. Kamba is a member of ACM SIGCHI and the Information Processing Society of Japan.

MicroISPs: providing convenient and low-cost high-bandwidth Internet access

José Brustoloni [*,1], Juan Garay [1]

Information Sciences Research Center, Bell Laboratories, Lucent Technologies, 600 Mountain Avenue, Murray Hill, NJ 07974, USA

Abstract

We present MicroISP, a novel architecture for Internet Service Providers suitable for installation in airports, hotels, conference centers, cafés, and office or apartment buildings. Users access a MicroISP via a low-cost, high-bandwidth LAN, e.g. Ethernet or WaveLAN. A router connects the MicroISP's LAN to a shared high-bandwidth access link (e.g., DSL or cable) to a conventional ISP. For this service, a MicroISP charges its clients. The architecture supports a variety of payment methods, both offline (e.g., cash, credit card, or billing to a hotel room account) and online (e.g., *e*Cash, SET, IBM Micro Payments, or Millicent). MicroISPs use IPSec's IKE protocol for securely exchanging authentication keys with paying users. Paying users use IPSec's AH protocol in tunnel mode to authenticate each packet they send. Therefore, MicroISPs can easily detect and drop packets of nonpaying users. A MicroISP must present to users a certificate signed by a recognized authority, but a user may simply present a self-signed certificate, as long as the user pays for service. Regardless of how online payment is implemented, it runs on the user's authenticated tunnel, and therefore can be securely bound to it. The MicroISP protocol allows users to monitor and control usage and supports recovery in case of a MicroISP or user computer crash.

Keywords: Internet Service Provider; Mobile access; Electronic commerce; Security and privacy

1. Introduction

Users typically connect to the Internet via Internet Service Providers (ISPs). In the conventional ISP architecture, illustrated in Fig. 1, each user pays for the installation and maintenance of an access link connecting the user's computer(s) to an ISP's POP (Point of Presence). Alternatives for access links include dial-up PSTN (Public Switched Telephone Network) or ISDN (Integrated Services Digital Network) telephone lines, dedicated telephone lines (e.g., T1), DSL (Digital Subscriber Line), and cable. A contract between user and ISP lasts typically at least a month and often much longer than that.

The conventional ISP architecture has two shortcomings. First, access link costs are significant, i.e., correspond to a considerable fraction of the user's total Internet connection cost. Second, mobility support is poor, especially for higher access bandwidths. On the one hand, dedicated telephone lines, DSL, and cable can provide high bandwidths, but are available only where the user installs them (e.g, office or home). On the other hand, dial-up lines allow access wherever there is a phone, but phones may be unavailable, inconvenient, or expensive to use and, in any case, provide low bandwidth. For example, the number and location of pay-phones in airports, con-

* Corresponding author.

[1] E-mail: {jcb,garay}@research.bell-labs.com

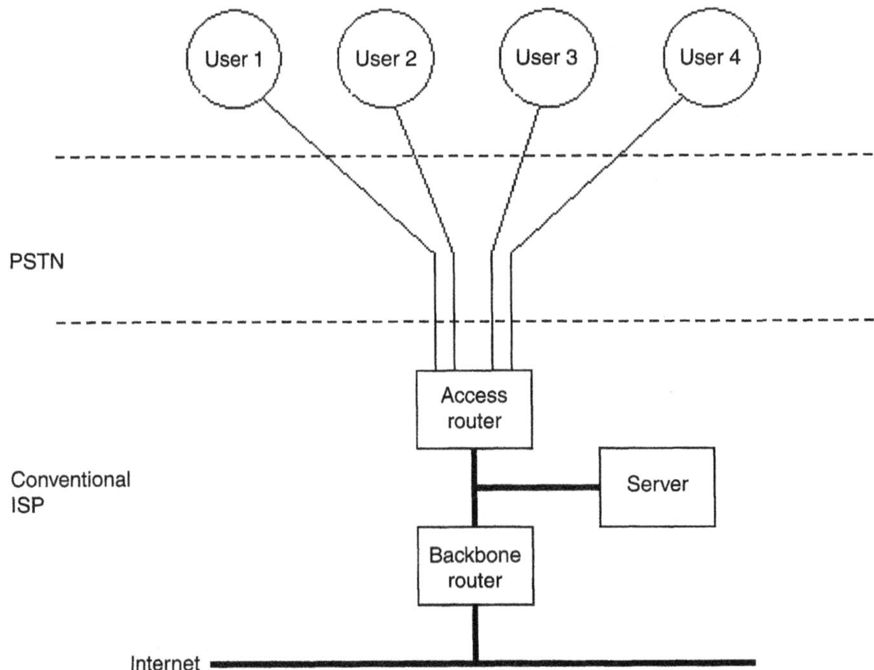

Fig. 1. Dial-up PSTN lines are still the most common ISP access links. They provide low bandwidth and usually require one access link and ISP account per computer. When the user is mobile, dial-up PSTN lines may be unavailable, inconvenient, or expensive to use.

ference centers, and cafés is often adequate for short conversations but inappropriate for laptop hookups and Web browsing. Wireless phones are convenient in such situations, but are expensive to use for more than a few minutes. Additionally, long-distance calls may be necessary to dial-up the nearest POP of the user's ISP.

This paper introduces a novel architecture, MicroISP, that overcomes the above-mentioned shortcomings of conventional ISPs. A MicroISP reduces access costs by amortizing among many users the cost of a high-bandwidth access link to a conventional ISP. Users access a MicroISP via a low-cost, high-bandwidth Local Area Network (LAN), e.g., Ethernet or WaveLAN, as shown in Fig. 2. The bandwidth dynamically allocated to each user is likely to be similar to that which many users enjoy at work, and much better than that afforded at home by a dial-up PSTN line. A router connects the MicroISP's LAN to the shared high-bandwidth access link, which may be, e.g., DSL or cable. For this service, the MicroISP charges its clients. The architecture supports a variety of offline and online payment methods. MicroISPs support the needs of transient (mobile) users because, unlike conventional ISP contracts, MicroISP contracts can be short-term (e.g., may last only 15 min). The low investment necessary to set up a MicroISP and the potential profitability encourage widespread deployment.

A challenge in this type of architecture is how to prevent a nonpaying user from gaining free service or charging his or her Internet usage to a paying user. For example, if the MicroISP's LAN uses a shared medium, e.g. Ethernet or WaveLAN, a nonpaying user n might be able to communicate with another host h by (1) snooping in the LAN to find the IP address of an active (paying) user p, (2) sending packets to h by spoofing them, i.e., making the source address equal to p, and (3) receiving packets from h by snooping in the LAN to find packets with source equal to h and destination equal to p. The MicroISP architecture uses IPSec's standard Authentication Header protocol (AH) in tunnel mode [18] to solve this problem. MicroISPs and paying users securely exchange authentication keys using IPSec's IKE (Internet Key Exchange) protocol [15,

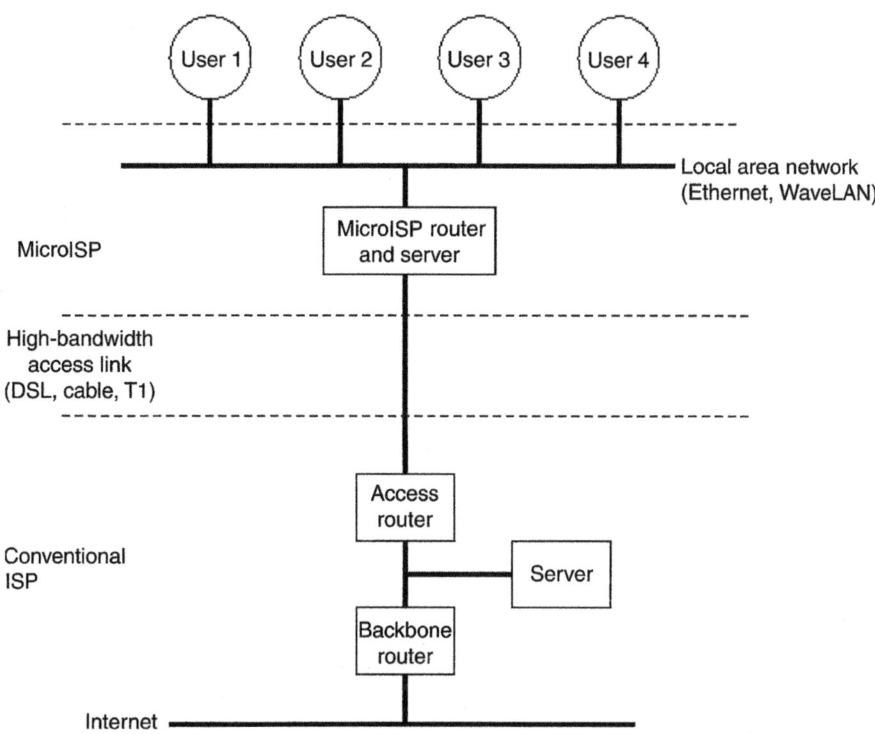

Fig. 2. A MicroISP amortizes among many users the cost of a high-bandwidth access link (e.g., DSL). MicroISPs require little investment and space and therefore may be deployed widely and in convenient locations. MicroISPs support mobile users by allowing short-term contracts.

23]. Paying users then use AH with such keys to authenticate each packet they send. No application (e.g., browser) modifications are necessary because IPSec is configured and operates at the network layer [7,19]. Because AH authentication includes the packet's source address, and nonpaying users do not have authentication keys, the MicroISP can easily detect and drop spoofed packets, shutting off nonpaying users.

The MicroISP architecture uses IKE with certificate-based authentication. A MicroISP must present to users a certificate signed by a recognized MicroISP Certifying Authority (CA). Users, on the other hand, need not incur the cost or trouble of obtaining certificates from a recognized CA. A user may present to MicroISPs a self-signed certificate and may thus remain anonymous if the payment method also preserves anonymity (e.g., cash or *e*Cash [9]).

A potential source of complexity and implementation difficulty is the need to accommodate within the architecture the many different usage metrics and payment methods that may be desirable in a given MicroISP. Usage metrics may be, e.g., elapsed or usage time, or number of bytes or packets transmitted. Payment methods may be offline (e.g., cash or credit card) or online (e.g., *e*Cash [9], SET [28], IBM Micro Payments [16], or Millicent [12]). The MicroISP architecture defines a carefully designed protocol that supports these and other options. In particular, the MicroISP protocol does not require modifications in online payment method implementations, because the protocol automatically and securely binds online payment (however implemented) with the above-mentioned AH tunnel.

Another potential pitfall is how to recover from computer crashes. In many scenarios, crashes are actually expected. For example, a guest at a hotel or conference center may turn her laptop on and off several times until her contract with the local MicroISP expires. The MicroISP protocol allows graceful recovery by issuing the user a *receipt* after the user pays. The MicroISP authenticates the receipt using a secret key. If the usage metric is simply elapsed time (flat fee until an expiration time), the receipt contains all the information necessary for recovery and, except for online payments, the MicroISP need not commit user state to stable storage. Recovery of crashes between the time the user sends online payment to the MicroISP and the time the user commits the respective receipt to stable storage is handled according to the respective payment method.

As mentioned above, MicroISPs use the services of conventional ISPs. MicroISPs may be able to reduce substantially the cost of such services by implementing NAPT (Network Address Port Translation) [29] in the router between the MicroISP LAN and the shared high-bandwidth access link. In this case, all MicroISP users use the same global IP address and appear to the conventional ISP as a single host.

1.1. Related work

Cybercafés are a competing alternative to ISPs. Typically, cybercafés lease to users desktop computers connected to the Internet. Like MicroISPs, cybercafés allow short-term service contracts. Cybercafés require much greater investment than do MicroISPs because cybercafés own the computers used and need space for them, whereas MicroISPs simply provide Internet access to user-owned laptop or desktop computers and therefore need negligible space. Consequently, MicroISPs may be deployed more widely and in more convenient locations. An additional advantage of MicroISPs is that users may find their own computers more familiar and secure to use than are those provided by a cybercafé. A hybrid service model, MicroISP café, is also possible, and would accommodate the latter users as well as users who do not have their computers with them.

Unlike conventional ISPs, cybercafés and MicroISPs do not themselves provide to users local content and e-mail or Web page hosting services. However, this is becoming hardly a disadvantage, because users can easily find on the Web portals or servers that provide such services for free (e.g., www.yahoo.com, hotmail.com, and www.geocities.com). Web-based services have the advantage of being accessible wherever the user may be.

1.2. Organization of the paper

The rest of this paper is organized as follows. Section 2 gives an overview of the MicroISP protocol and its phases. Sections 3–8 describe each of the phases in greater detail: networking configuration, secure tunnel establishment, control channel establishment, contract establishment and binding, usage metering, and settlement. Section 9 discusses implications of using NAPT, and Section 10 discusses some other variations in the MicroISP design. Finally, Section 11 reports the performance of a prototype implementation, and Section 12 concludes.

2. MicroISP protocol overview

As shown in Fig. 2, the main components of the MicroISP architecture are a high-bandwidth LAN, a router, a server, a shared high-bandwidth access link, and a protocol for communication between user computers and the MicroISP server and router. Although server and router can in general be implemented separately, in this paper we assume that the server is implemented within or as an adjunct to the router, and the term ‘MicroISP’ is used to refer to that combination when communicating with users.

This section gives an overview of the MicroISP protocol. Its design was influenced by the following constraints.

- *Use of standard hardware and protocols.* MicroISP access will typically be based on a shared medium, and it is tempting to design special network cards, protocols, tokens, or smartcards to guarantee secure access and payment in such networks. For example, cable access networks are also based on a shared medium and use special, certified cable modems and a special protocol (BPI+ [4]) to secure communications between cable modems and cable head-ends. (An offline process binds a certified cable modem with a user account, to which Internet usage is billed.) However, special hardware makes installation costly, and special protocols may not be as well scrutinized and secure as standard ones. For example, the protocol initially used in cable systems did not authenticate the cable head-end, leaving an important security hole. In contrast, MicroISPs interoperate with standard LAN cards that many users already own (e.g., Ethernet or WaveLAN), and use IETF's standard IPSec protocols [19]. IPSec is supported by most current operating systems, including Windows 2000, NT 5, and Linux.

- *Use of existing online payment method implementations.* There are many proposals for online payment methods (e.g., *e*Cash [9], SET [28], CyberCash [3], IBM Micro Payments [16], or Millicent [12]). Some proposals are proprietary and no proposal has achieved wide use. Embedding specific online payment methods into MicroISP implementations would therefore involve considerable licensing and maintenance difficulties. These difficulties are avoided by MicroISP's secure binding of payments received by independently designed and implemented processes.
- *Support for offline payment.* Depending solely on online payment could adversely delay MicroISP deployment, given that adoption of online payment methods has been slow. Additionally, offline payment would be quite natural in many scenarios, e.g. when a user checks in at an airport, hotel, or conference, or comes into a lounge or café.

Consequently, the MicroISP protocol actually combines several underlying protocols and processes, some of which may be offline.

The MicroISP protocol defines the following phases.

(1) *Networking configuration.* Before a user's computer can communicate with the MicroISP, some of its networking parameters need to be configured, e.g. the IP addresses of the user's computer and of the default router. MicroISP uses the standard Dynamic Host Configuration Protocol (DHCP) [8] to achieve this configuration.

(2) *Secure tunnel establishment.* MicroISP uses IPSec's AH protocol in tunnel mode to authenticate user packets. The tunnel guarantees that all packets received by the MicroISP from a certain IP address correspond to the same user. The identity of that user is immaterial to the MicroISP, provided that the user pays for the MicroISP services. Therefore, the user may present a self-signed certificate. On the other hand, before paying, users may want to verify that they are communicating with a bona fide MicroISP. Therefore, MicroISPs must present a certificate signed by a recognized MicroISP certifying authority. Users are also given the option of privacy on the MicroISP's LAN. When this option is selected, the tunnel encrypts packets between the user's computer and the MicroISP's router, using IPSec's Encapsulating Security Payload (ESP) protocol [20].

(3) *Control channel establishment.* The MicroISP needs a secure control channel to send to the user the MicroISP's price list before payment and a receipt after payment. The user also uses this channel to control his or her Internet usage. If the tunnel established in the previous phase uses ESP, the control channel is simply a TCP connection; otherwise, the control channel uses the TLS protocol [5].

(4) *Contract establishment and binding.* In this phase, (1) the MicroISP presents to the user a list of options for service (e.g., usage metrics: elapsed or usage time, or number of bytes or packets transmitted) and payment (e.g., *e*Cash, SET, IBM Micro Payments, or Millicent) and the respective prices, (2) the user selects the desired options, (3) the user makes a deposit payment, and (4) the MicroISP gives a receipt to the user. This phase is skipped entirely if the user's computer already has the receipt of an outstanding contract and the user, e.g., is reconnecting to the MicroISP again after turning his or her computer off. Steps 1 to 3 are skipped if the user presents a valid password, received from the MicroISP in offline processing of those steps (e.g., payment by cash, credit card, or billing to a hotel room account). Step 3 may be performed over channels other than the one established in the previous phase (e.g., in the case of independent online payment method implementation). However, any online payment will necessarily use the tunnel established in phase 2, and therefore can be securely bound to it.

(5) *Usage metering.* Until a user's Internet usage reaches the amount selected in the previous phase, the user can send or receive packets to the Internet using the MicroISP's facilities. To monitor and control his or her usage, the user may exchange messages with the MicroISP, using the control channel established in phase 3.

These messages may, for example, suspend, resume, or terminate service.

(6) *Settlement*. When service to a user terminates, the net amount paid by the user should be equal to his or her actual usage. If the deposit of phase 4 is greater than the net amount, the user may be due a refund. This settlement is performed in this final phase.

The following sections describe each phase in greater detail.

3. Networking configuration

This section describes in greater detail phase 1 of the MicroISP protocol.

In this phase, MicroISPs use DHCP for configuring the networking parameters of dynamically connected user computers. When user computers boot or restart, they broadcast in the LAN DHCP packets requesting configuration. A MicroISP server replies with the necessary parameters, including network mask and broadcast address, IP addresses of the user's computer and of the default router, and possibly the IP addresses of a DNS (Domain Name System) server, NTP (Network Time Protocol) server, and line printer server. MicroISPs use DHCP's dynamic IP address allocation, so that IP addresses assigned to a user's computer remain valid only during a specified lease time. User computers must periodically renew their leases to preserve their IP addresses. Expired IP addresses may be reused. In MicroISPs, the list of unallocated addresses is maintained in FIFO order.

DHCP makes MicroISPs easy to use. A user may, for example, link her laptop to the Ethernet or WaveLAN in an airport lounge or conference room, reboot the computer, and automatically be configured to access the Internet. DHCP is supported by most current operating systems, including Windows 2000, NT, and Linux.

4. Secure tunnel establishment

This section describes phase 2 of the MicroISP protocol and the use of IPSec [19] in MicroISPs.

IPSec defines two protocols for secure data communication: AH [18] and ESP [20]. These protocols are implemented at the network layer and therefore do not require modifications in user applications. AH can provide authentication of packet origin, proof of integrity of packet data, and protection against packet replay. ESP can provide, in addition to AH's services, encryption of packet data and limited traffic flow confidentiality. However, unlike AH's authentication, ESP's does not include the packet's source and destination IP addresses. Therefore, to guarantee that an IP address is always used by the same user while the address is allocated or bound to a contract, MicroISPs use the AH protocol to authenticate all packets sent from that address. If the user so selects, MicroISPs also use ESP encryption for all packets sent to or received from the user's address. This option preserves privacy on the MicroISP's LAN.

AH and ESP can be used in either transport or tunnel mode, as illustrated in Fig. 3. Transport mode provides end-to-end security between the packet's source and destination. In contrast, tunnel mode encapsulates packets and thus provides security between the nodes where the packet is encapsulated and decapsulated. MicroISPs use tunnel mode between user computers and MicroISP routers. A user may establish other IPSec tunnels *within* the user's MicroISP tunnel. A user may do this, e.g., when using the MicroISP and Internet to communicate securely with an IPSec gateway into the Intranet of the user's employer.

Another IPSec protocol, IKE [15], establishes security associations that define the algorithms and cryptographic keys used by AH and ESP. Security associations have a specified lifetime, after which they are terminated and need to be replaced [19]. The MicroISP protocol uses IKE authenticated with signatures. The initiator is always the user. Using this method, MicroISP and user perform a Diffie–Hellman [6] key exchange for securely establishing a shared secret, from which AH and ESP keys are derived. Each party then authenticates the other by verifying the other's signature [25] on a message containing the other's certificate. A party's certificate contains that party's public key, which is necessary for verifying that party's signatures. A party's certificate also contains that party's identity and is itself usually signed by a certifying authority (CA) whose public key is widely known, so that any party can

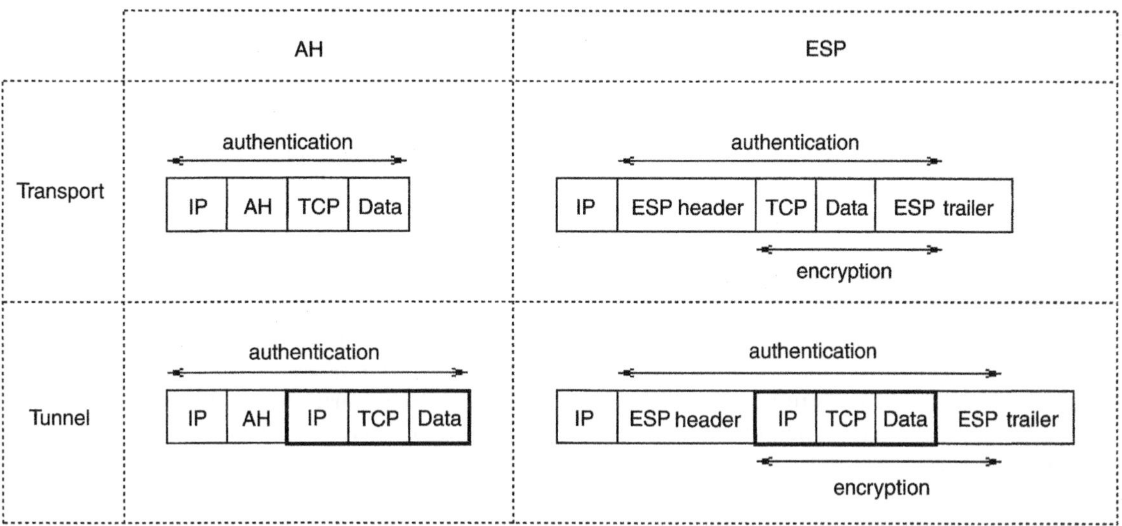

Fig. 3. IPSec packet format depends on protocol (AH or ESP) and mode (transport or tunnel). The portion of the packet that is authenticated or encrypted is different for AH or ESP. The encapsulated packet is shown in bold.

verify the certificate. Certificate formats are defined, e.g., in the X.509 standard [32]. Authentication is necessary to prevent 'person-in-the-middle' attacks, where an intruder would pretend to be the user when communicating with the MicroISP and to be the MicroISP when communicating with the user. Therefore, MicroISPs must present certificates signed by a recognized MicroISP CA, which maintains registration procedures appropriate for such certification. In a PKIX-based implementation [17], these certificates would contain a policies extension with explicit-text user notice. This notice should be displayed to the user [17] and informs about the location and type of LANs supported by the MicroISP. On the other hand, the MicroISP does not really need to authenticate the user's identity in this phase; the MicroISP's only requirement is that the user pay in phase 4 of the protocol, and that no other user be able to use that payment to gain service. Therefore, the MicroISP can be configured to accept self-signed user certificates in IKE exchanges. Using such certificates, users can remain anonymous.

IPSec security policies are defined in a Security Policy Database (SPD) per network interface [19]. Each SPD entry specifies a selector and a rule. Selectors may match, e.g., packets that have a certain protocol and source and destination IP addresses and port numbers (ranges and wild cards are allowed for these values). Actions may be to drop the packet, bypass IPSec, or apply specified IPSec protocols to the packet. The SPD of the LAN interface of MicroISP routers is configured, in the incoming case, to bypass IPSec in the cases of DHCP and IKE packets destined to the MicroISP, to perform AH and optionally ESP processing to packets whose source address is bound (phase 4) to an active contract or whose destination is the MicroISP, and to drop remaining packets. In the outgoing case, the SPD is configured to bypass IPSec in the cases of DHCP and IKE packets whose source is the MicroISP, to either bypass IPSec or apply ESP processing to packets whose source is the MicroISP or whose destination address is bound to an active contract, and to drop remaining packets. While a user's computer is accessing a MicroISP, the SPD of the computer's LAN interface is similarly configured, with the incoming and outgoing cases reversed.

5. Control channel establishment

This section briefly covers phase 3 of the MicroISP protocol.

Because of its uses in the MicroISP protocol, the control channel should guarantee message authenticity and privacy in both directions. Privacy is needed, e.g., to prevent the eavesdropping of receipts and their later use by nonpaying users. If the user selected the privacy option in phase 2, all communication over the user's tunnel is already secured in both directions by ESP. Therefore, the user establishes the control channel by simply opening a TCP connection to a well-known port in the MicroISP. Otherwise, the tunnel established in phase 2 does not provide all the required security (i.e., only authenticates user packets to the MicroISP). Therefore, the user employs the TLS [5] protocol for establishing a secure control channel over the user's tunnel. The principals of the TLS channel are guaranteed to be the same as those of the AH tunnel: the MicroISP is authenticated using its certificate, while the user is authenticated by AH.

6. Contract establishment and binding

This section describes how a contract between MicroISP and user is established in offline and online cases and how the IP address assigned to the user in phase 1 and secured in phase 2 is bound to the user's contract in phase 4 of the MicroISP protocol. (Note: frameworks for online price negotiation and payment selection have been discussed in the e-commerce literature and there are proposals for their standardization, e.g. JEPI [31] and SEMPER [27].)

The contract is established in the following four steps.

(1) *MicroISP offer.* The MicroISP presents to the user a contract form containing a serial number, the current date and time, available service options, including acceptable usage metrics (e.g., elapsed or usage time, or number of bytes or packets transmitted) and the respective prices, and acceptable payment methods (e.g., in offline cases: cash, credit card, or billing to an account, such as a hotel room account; or in online cases: *e*Cash [9], SET [28], IBM Micro Payments [16], or Millicent [12]). A contract is always subject to an expiration time. Prices may depend, e.g., on whether the user has selected phase 2's privacy option, on the amount of usage, on the payment method selected, and on the current or anticipated MicroISP load.

(2) *User request.* The user completes the form indicating the desired usage metrics, soft and hard usage limits, and payment method. In offline cases, if the payment method is not cash, the user physically signs the form.

(3) *User deposit.* The user employs the selected payment method to deposit with the MicroISP an amount equal to the selected hard usage limit. If the payment method is credit card or SET, this deposit is implemented by an authorization transaction. In certain online cases (which do not include SET or *e*Cash), the MicroISP may need to allow the user to communicate directly with external servers before paying. In IBM Micro Payments [16], for example, the user may need to contact his or her issuer to obtain the user's daily certificate, which is necessary for making payments. As another example, in Millicent [12], the user may need to contact his or her broker to convert broker scrips into MicroISP scrips (scrips are Millicent's merchant-issued payment instruments). To enable the latter payment methods, modifications in IPSec's SPDs may be necessary (e.g., permitting user communication with certain supported issuers or brokers for a limited time).

(4) *MicroISP receipt.* The MicroISP gives to the user a copy of the contract and password (offline cases) or a receipt (online cases). The user commits the receipt to stable storage. The receipt is a data structure that includes the contract's serial number, date and time, expiration, selected usage metrics and limits, and payment parameters. The MicroISP authenticates the receipt with a Message Authentication Code (MAC). MAC computation uses a secret key with, e.g., the DES-MAC [26], keyed-MD5 [30], or HMAC [1] algorithms.

Phase 4 of the MicroISP protocol is executed as follows. If the user's stable storage contains the receipt of an outstanding contract, the user sends the receipt over the control channel to the MicroISP, which verifies that the contract is still outstanding, is not bound to an IP address, and is not being settled. The MicroISP then binds the contract with the user's IP address, concluding this phase. Otherwise, if the user sends over the control channel the password of an unbound outstanding offline contract, the MicroISP binds the contract with the user's IP address and returns the corresponding receipt. The user then commits the receipt to stable storage, concluding this phase. Otherwise, the user sends over the control channel a request for online contract establishment, triggering the four steps described above. The contract is bound to the user's IP address in step 4.

7. Usage metering

This section describes phase 5 of the MicroISP protocol, usage metering. Metering depends on contract and IP address states. Therefore, this section discusses the possible states and the events that trigger state transitions (e.g., user commands).

Metering is greatly simplified when the usage metric is elapsed time. In such cases, the MicroISP does not need to commit contract state and usage to stable storage in order to be able to recover from MicroISP crashes: the receipts themselves contain all the necessary information. If the MicroISP's shared link to a conventional ISP is charged on a similar basis, this is probably the best alternative. However, if the MicroISP is charged according to number of bytes or packets transmitted, it may need to do the same with respect to its clients.

In general, users monitor and control contract state by sending commands to the MicroISP. Available commands include report usage, start/resume, suspend, or terminate a contract, and extend a contract's soft limit up to its hard limit. The MicroISP replies to these commands include the accumulated usage and the soft and hard limits. The MicroISP may also send asynchronous warning messages when a contract's accumulated usage reaches its soft or hard limit or expires, or when a user on a different IP address presents the contract's receipt on phase 4 of the MicroISP protocol. All these messages contain the contract's serial number and are sent over the control channel.

A contract is *outstanding* between its establishment and settlement, and becomes *extinguished* when it expires, has accumulated usage that reaches its hard limit, or after settlement, as shown in Fig. 4. An outstanding contract can be *unbound*, *bound*, or *in settlement*. An outstanding contract is initially unbound. An unbound contract becomes bound to an IP address when a receipt for that contract is sent to or from that IP address in phase 4 of the MicroISP protocol. A bound contract becomes unbound when the user's computer lets the respective DHCP lease or IPSec security association expire (e.g., because of a crash). An unbound or bound contract becomes in settlement when the user issues a terminate command.

A bound contract can be *suspended*, *active*, or *delinquent*. A bound contract is initially suspended. A suspended contract becomes active when the user issues a start/resume command. An active contract becomes suspended when the user issues a suspend command, and becomes delinquent when the usage reaches the soft limit. A delinquent contract becomes active when the user issues a valid extend command.

An IP address can be *unallocated*, *allocated*, or *bound* to a contract, as shown in Fig. 5. IP addresses are initially unallocated. An unallocated IP address becomes allocated when DHCP allocates it to a user's computer. An allocated IP address becomes unallocated again if the user's computer allows the respective DHCP lease or IPSec security association to expire. An allocated IP address becomes bound to a contract when the converse is true. A bound IP address b becomes unallocated when the respective contract becomes unbound or extinguished or: (1) a user on a different IP address d presents the contract's receipt on phase 4 of the MicroISP protocol; and (2) the MicroISP repeatedly warns b but b does not respond, which suggests that the user's computer crashed and is now recovering on a different address.

The MicroISP meters a contract's usage time only while the contract is active. The MicroISP router forwards to or from the Internet and meters the number of bytes or packets only of packets that use an IP address bound to an active contract. The MicroISP also allows packets whose source or destination is the MicroISP.

8. Settlement

This section describes phase 6 of the MicroISP protocol. This is the final phase.

If the user lets the contract expire or uses the contract fully to its hard limit, the MicroISP retains the whole deposit. If the payment method is credit card

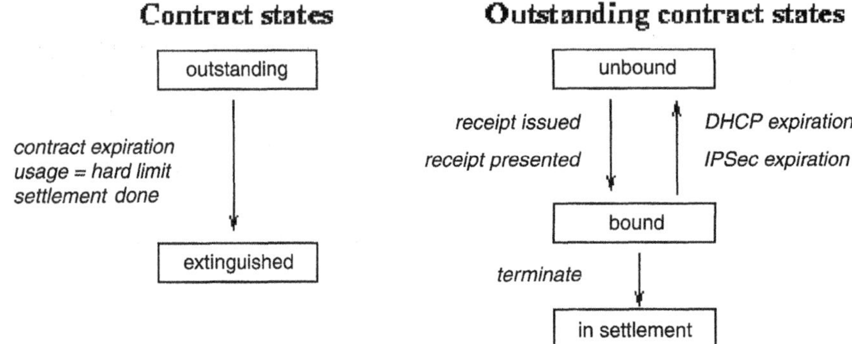

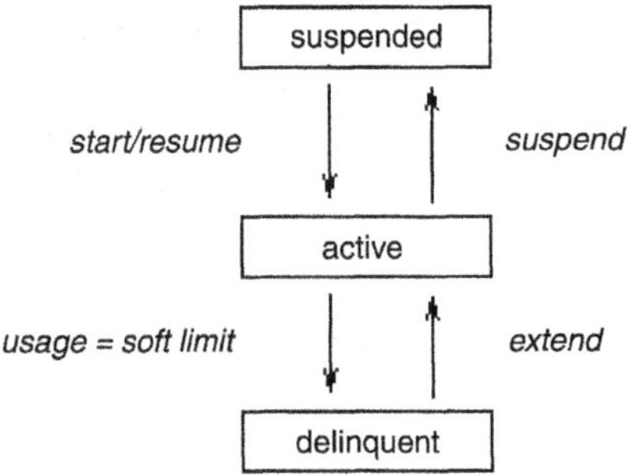

Fig. 4. Contract states and transitions. The initial states are the top ones.

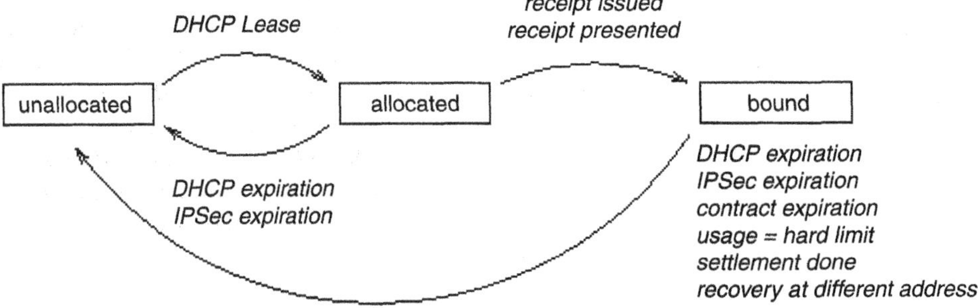

Fig. 5. IP address states and transitions. The initial state is unallocated.

or SET, the MicroISP automatically performs a settlement transaction for that value. On the other hand, if the usage is below the hard limit, an adjustment or refund is necessary, and will be processed according to the payment method. In offline cases other than cash, the user physically signs a new form. In the credit card and SET cases, a settlement transaction for the value of the actual usage is performed. In the cash, *e*Cash [9] and Millicent [12] cases a refund is returned to the user. In the cases of offline billing to an account and of IBM Micro Payments [16], the MicroISP simply adjusts its billing records.

9. NAPT (Network Address Port Translation)

MicroISPs have to allocate one IP address per contract that is bound or in settlement. In order to get more than one IP address from a conventional ISP, the MicroISP will typically need to pay extra. A cost-saving alternative is to have the MicroISP router implement NAPT (Network Address Port Translation) [29] so that all MicroISP users share a single global IP address. However, NAPT may not support certain protocols, as discussed in this section.

If a MicroISP implements NAPT, the IP addresses that it allocates to user computers are private (unregistered and possibly not globally unique) [24]. NAPT translates respectively the source or destination IP addresses and port numbers (between private and global) in packets sent to or received from the Internet. NAPT builds a translation table such that all local hosts share the same global IP address, and destinations of packets received from the Internet can be determined by the global port numbers.

NAPT is not transparent to application-layer protocols that include host addresses or port numbers within their payloads (e.g., FTP). For each such protocol, NAPT requires a corresponding Application Level Gateway (ALG) that knows how to modify the application-level payloads. ALG support has been increasing, but NAPT may still not interoperate with certain protocols [29].

NAPT is also not transparent with respect to most of IPSec's protocols and modes. (However, note that NAPT does not affect the AH tunnel used in the MicroISP protocol, which terminates at the router.) NAPT address translations invalidate AH's authentication, whose scope includes the source and destination addresses. NAPT address translations can also invalidate TCP or UDP checksums of ESP packets in transport mode, which are calculated including the packet's source and destination addresses. An ALG for these cases is not possible because it would need to know the cryptographic keys used, which would violate end-to-end security. NAPT can, however, interoperate with ESP in tunnel mode, where the entire packet is encapsulated and NAPT's translations do not affect the encapsulated checksum. VPN Masquerade [14] is a NAPT implementation that provides such support. VPN Masquerade uses a number of heuristics for demultiplexing incoming traffic. These heuristics are subject to race conditions and may, in some cases, fail, causing packet misdelivery. However, packet misdelivery does not break security any more than eavesdropping in the LAN would.

We recently proposed [2] a DHCP extension that allows hosts to lease from NAPT, e.g., global IP addresses and port numbers. Using that extension, IPSec implementations can always interoperate correctly with NAPT. Another alternative currently being considered is to replace NAPT by RSIP (Realm-Specific IP) [29]. We believe that either solution will go a long way toward eliminating NAPT's current interoperation difficulties. Therefore, the cost-reducing option of using a single global IP address in MicroISPs may soon become even more attractive.

10. Other design variations

Many details in the MicroISP design can be altered without essentially impacting in the overall functionality. This section discusses some of the possible modifications.

An obvious variation is to use another protocol for authentication and/or encryption in the secure tunnel. The new protocol must be able to encapsulate and decapsulate packets. For example, instead of AH, a MicroISP might employ ESP's authentication option to authenticate packets sent by paying users. In either case, ESP's encryption is optional, and tunnel mode is used. Unlike AH, ESP's authentication does not cover the packet's source and destination IP addresses. However, ESP's authentication does cover the entire encapsulated packet. Therefore, ESP's authentication is sufficient for spoofing prevention [13].

Another variation would be to set up the control channel *before* the secure tunnel. The control channel might allow, for example, the transmission of cryptographic keys to be used in the tunnel. In this case, IKE authentication could, e.g., use a pre-shared key, instead of digital signatures.

Other variations include using a solution other than the DHCP protocol for configuring networking parameters of user computers, using a solution other than the IKE protocol for establishing the secure tunnel's cryptographic algorithms and keys, using a firewall, instead of IPSec's SPDs, for dropping packets of nonpaying users, or using a protocol other than TLS (e.g., TLS's predecessor, SSL [11]) for the secure control channel.

11. Performance

An important practical question is how powerful a computer would be necessary for implementing a MicroISP router/server. To answer this question, we built a PC-based MicroISP router/server prototype and report its performance in this section.

Our prototype is based on a low-cost PC with a 400 MHz Pentium II CPU and 64 MB of main memory. The prototype uses the freely available Linux 2.2.12 operating system and the FreeS/WAN 1.1 IPSec implementation [10].

To circumvent limitations of our prototype environment, we used several of the design alternatives discussed in the previous section. First, we used SSL instead of TLS because we had an SSL implementation easily available. Second, the prototype uses SSL to establish the control channel *before* the secure tunnel, because FreeS/WAN 1.1 does not fully implement IKE. The control channel securely transmits randomly generated keys for FreeS/WAN authentication using pre-shared keys.

We connected a client and a server Linux PC to the MicroISP prototype using separate 10 Mbps Ethernets, and measured the TCP throughput between the client and server. For control, we also measured the TCP throughput between client and server when connected on the same 10 Mbps Ethernet (without the MicroISP): 6.4 Mbps. When client and server were connected through the prototype implementing only routing and NAPT (no MicroISP functionality), the TCP throughput dropped slightly to 6.2 Mbps, and the CPU utilization on the prototype was 4%. With MicroISP functionality and packet authentication between client and MicroISP (using AH with MD5 [22]), the TCP throughput between client and server was 5.8 Mbps and the CPU utilization on the prototype was 26%. (Note: for ease of implementation, in the latter experiment AH was used in both directions; results would probably improve significantly if AH were used only from client to MicroISP, as described in Section 4.) Finally, with MicroISP functionality and both authentication and encryption between client and MicroISP (using ESP with MD5 and triple DES [21]), the TCP throughput between client and server was 5.3 Mbps, and the CPU utilization on the prototype was 70%.

We also measured the time necessary for a client to connect to the MicroISP prototype (steps 1 to 4 of the MicroISP protocol), as well as the load imposed on the prototype's CPU by such connections (with no other network or CPU activity). We simultaneously started connections from two 100 MHz Pentium clients and one 700 MHz dual-processor Pentium III client. Connection took 0.5 s for the fast client and 1.9 and 2.1 s for the slow clients. The prototype CPU was 31% utilized during these connections.

These measurements suggest that even a modest PC can handle the loads that may be expected on a MicroISP router/server. Access links such as T1, DSL and cable provide bandwidths from 0.6 to 7 Mbps downstream and from 0.6 to 1.5 Mbps upstream (cable can theoretically support up to 27 Mbps downstream, but cable modems usually limit a client's bandwidth to 1 Mbps). Such bandwidths are one to two orders of magnitude greater than those enabled by PSTN (57 Kbps downstream and 33 Kbps upstream), but still represent only a moderate load for today's processors.

The measurements also justify charging a premium price for privacy on the MicroISP's LAN: ESP's authentication (MD5) and encryption (triple DES) imposed a much higher load on the MicroISP prototype than did AH's authentication (MD5) alone.

12. Summary

We described MicroISP, a novel architecture that allows Internet access services to be securely provided and charged for over standard shared-medium LANs, e.g. Ethernet or WaveLAN. Such LANs can be easily installed in convenient locations, e.g. airports, hotels, conference centers, lounges, and cafés. Standard protocols automatically configure user computers so that they can access the Internet. A router connects the MicroISP LAN to a shared high-bandwidth access link (e.g., DSL or cable) to a conventional ISP. Because a MicroISP amortizes the cost of the access link among many users, it can also reduce the cost of Internet access in offices and apartment buildings. The bandwidth dynamically allocated to each user is likely to be similar to that enjoyed by many users at work, and much better than that provided by a dial-up PSTN line. The architecture supports a variety of payment methods, both offline (e.g., cash, credit card, or billing to a hotel room account) and online (e.g., *e*Cash, SET, IBM Micro Payments, or Millicent). MicroISPs use IPSec's IKE protocol for securely exchanging authentication keys with paying users. Paying users use IPSec's AH protocol in tunnel mode to authenticate each packet they send. Therefore, MicroISPs can easily detect and drop packets of nonpaying users. A MicroISP must present to users a certificate signed by a recognized MicroISP certifying authority. However, MicroISPs can accept users who do not have a certificate by a recognized authority or who choose to remain anonymous, as long as those users provide valid payment. The MicroISP protocol can use independent online payment method implementations because, regardless of how online payment is implemented, it runs on the user's authenticated tunnel, and therefore can be securely bound to it. The MicroISP protocol allows users to monitor and control usage and supports recovery in case of a MicroISP or user computer crash.

Acknowledgements

We thank Sumit Garg for his help in the prototype implementation.

References

[1] M. Bellare, R. Canetti and H. Krawczyk, Keyed hash functions and message authentication, in: N. Koblitz (Ed.), Advances in Cryptology — Crypto '96, Lecture Notes in Computer Science 1109, Springer-Verlag, Berlin, 1996, pp. 1–15.

[2] J. Brustoloni and J. Garay, Application-independent end-to-end security in shared-link access networks, in: Proc. IFIP Networking'2000, Lecture Notes in Computer Science, Springer-Verlag, Berlin, 2000.

[3] CyberCash, Home page at http://www.CyberCash.com/.

[4] Data-Over-Cable Service Interface Specifications, Baseline Privacy Plus Interface Specification, SP-BPI+-101-990316, CableLabs, 1999, available at http://www.cablemodem.com.

[5] T. Dierks and C. Allen, The TLS Protocol Version 1.0, IETF, RFC 2246, Jan. 1999.

[6] W. Diffie and M.E. Hellman, New directions in cryptography, IEEE Transactions on Information Theory IT-22 (1976) 644–654.

[7] N. Doraswamy and D. Harkins, IPSec: The New Security Standard for the Internet, Intranets and Virtual Private Networks, Prentice-Hall, Englewood Cliffs, NJ, 1st ed., 1999.

[8] R. Droms, Dynamic Host Configuration Protocol, IETF, RFC 2131, Mar. 1997.

[9] *e*Cash Technologies, Inc., Home page at http://www.ecashtechnologies.com/.

[10] FreeS/WAN, Homepage at http://www.xs4all.nl/~freeswan/.

[11] A. Freier, P. Karlton and P. Kocher, The SSL Protocol Version 3.0, Netscape, Mar. 1996, available at http://home.netscape.com/eng/ssl3/ssl-toc.html.

[12] S. Glassman, M. Manasse, M. Abadi, P. Gauthier and P. Sobalvarro, The Millicent protocol for inexpensive electronic commerce, in: Proc. 4th International World Wide Web Conference, W3C, Boston, MA, Dec. 1995, available at http://www.w3.org/conferences/WWW4/.

[13] R. Glenn and S. Kent, The NULL Encryption Algorithm and its Use with IPsec, IETF, RFC 2410, Nov. 1998.

[14] J. Hardin, Linux VPN Masquerade, Homepage at http://www.wolfenet.com/~jhardin/ip_masq_vpn.html.

[15] D. Harkins and D. Carrel, The Internet Key Exchange (IKE), IETF, RFC 2409, Nov. 1998.

[16] A. Herzberg and H. Yochai, MiniPay: charging per click on the Web, in: Proc. 6th International World Wide Web Conference, W3C, Santa Clara, CA, 1997, available at http://www.scope.gmd.de/info/www6/, Now called IBM Micro Payments, Home page at http://www.hrl.il.ibm.com/mpay/.

[17] R. Housley, W. Ford, W. Polk and D. Solo, Internet X.509 Public Key Infrastructure Certificate and CRL Profile, IETF, RFC 2459, Jan. 1999.

[18] S. Kent and R. Atkinson, IP Authentication Header, IETF, RFC 2402, Nov. 1998.

[19] S. Kent and R. Atkinson, Security Architecture for the Internet Protocol, IETF, RFC 2401, Nov. 1998.

[20] S. Kent and R. Atkinson, IP Encapsulating Security Payload (ESP), IETF, RFC 2406, Nov. 1998.

[21] C. Madson and N. Doraswamy, The ESP DES-CBC Cipher Algorithm with Explicit IV, IETF, RFC 2405, Nov. 1998.

[22] C. Madson and R. Glenn, The Use of HMAC-MD5-96 within ESP and AH, IETF, RFC 2403, Nov. 1998.

[23] D. Maughan, M. Schertler, M. Schneider and J. Turner, Internet Security Association and Key Management Protocol (ISAKMP), IETF, RFC 2408, Nov. 1998.

[24] Y. Rekhter, B. Moskowitz, D. Karrenberg, G.J. de Groot and E. Lear, Address Allocation for Private Internets, IETF, RFC 1918, Feb. 1996.

[25] R. Rivest, A. Shamir and L. Adleman, A method for obtaining digital signatures and public-key cryptosystems, Communications of the ACM 21 (2) (1978).

[26] B. Schneier, Applied Cryptography, Wiley, New York, 1996, 2nd. ed.

[27] Secure Electronic Marketplace for Europe (SEMPER), Homepage at http://www.semper.org/.

[28] SET, Homepage at http://www.setco.org/.

[29] P. Srisuresh and M. Holdrege, IP Network Address Translator (NAT) Technology and Considerations, IETF, RFC 2663, Aug. 1999.

[30] G. Tsudik, Message authentication with one-way hash func-

tions, in: Proc. INFOCOM '92, IEEE, 1992, pp. 2055–2059.
[31] W3C Joint Electronic Payments Initiative (JEPI), Homepage at http://www13.w3.org/ECommerce/Overview-JEPI.html.
[32] Recommendation X.509 (1197 E), Information Technology — Open Systems Interconnection — The Directory: Authentication Framework, ITU-T.

José C. Brustoloni received his Ph.D. in computer science from Carnegie Mellon University in 1997 and has been with Bell Labs since then, where he works in the Network Systems Research Department. His main research interests are in access networks, quality of service and billing, programmable networks, protocol performance, and embedded systems.

Juan A. Garay received his Ph.D. in computer science from Penn State University in 1989. Before joining the Secure Systems Research Department at Bell Labs, he was with IBM's T.J. Watson Research Center in Yorktown Heights, NY. His areas of interest include the design and analysis of cryptographic protocols, distributed computing, and fault tolerance.

Object browsing using the Internet Imaging Protocol

Kirk Martinez [a,*], Steve Perry [b,1], John Cupitt [c,2]

[a] Electronics and Computer Science Department, University of Southampton, Southampton, UK
[b] ANT Ltd., Cambridge, UK
[c] Scientific Department, The National Gallery, London, UK

Abstract

This paper builds on the results from the Viseum project where we built an image server/client system to allow browsing of very large images. In the follow-on European ACOHIR project we built systems capable of acquiring colour-calibrated high-resolution views of objects from many positions. A Java viewer allows the user to closely examine objects in a similar way to Quicktime VR but with much higher resolution. The Internet Imaging Protocol is used to allow the viewer to request 64×64 pel tiles on demand to allow fast browsing of the objects in a Web browser. The original image data occupy typically around 200 MBytes yet we can provide almost instantaneous views with zooming and acceptable performance across the Internet or a modem. The approach taken in the Java viewer is modular and easily customised using JavaScript. Caching at both the server and client provide improved performance. This paper shows how the techniques developed for large images have been applied and modified to handle high-resolution object views.

Keywords: Object movies; Java; JavaScript; Internet Imaging Protocol

1. Introduction

Previous research into high-resolution imaging [1,6] has produced systems capable of creating very large colorimetric images of works of art. These could be as large as 1.6 GBytes each and were colour calibrated. This means that the images can be reproduced accurately and show fine detail. The problem of how to browse these large 2D images over the Web was tackled in the Euro–Canadian project Viseum [7,11]. This designed a client–server system for displaying the images and investigated the effects of long distance ATM networking. Since then the European project ACOHIR has worked on imaging 3D objects and placing high-quality views on the Web. This included making systems with high-quality digital cameras and controllable turntables to capture the object views. These are colour calibrated to CIE Lab but stored compressed as sRGB values. The multiresolution tiled JPEG in TIFF format from Viseum is still used and the client–server system has been enhanced to cope with the object data.

The aim of the ACOHIR project was to provide high-quality images of 3D objects, in particular sculptures from the Louvre and Greek museums, furniture and porcelain in Spain and archaeological finds used in teaching. These often have fine details such as scratch marks or engravings. To capture a

* Corresponding author. E-mail: km@ecs.soton.ac.uk
[1] stephen@ant.co.uk
[2] john.cupitt@ng-london.org.uk

texture mapped 3D graphics model of an object with a sufficiently high level of detail would require expensive hardware. It also requires a 3D processor at the client in order to display the data. The approach used in Apple's Quicktime VR [8] is to capture images of objects from many views and store them as a movie. For this reason they are often known as object movies. This is played in a special way so that a sequence of 30 frames for example is seen as rotating an object and moving it in the up/down axis is handled by jumping to different 30 frame segments. This approach provides a very fast interface and the images can be quite detailed for each view compared to a rough 3D object. High-quality images give a much better idea of surface texture which is very difficult to do with 3D graphics. Companies such as Kadian [4] also produce a wide range of hardware to help capture objects including turntables with controllable camera arms to automate the whole process. Companies such as Live Picture [5] make software to produce and browse object movies and panoramas.

In ACOHIR we wanted to be able to use images of around 3k $\times$ 2k resolution for each view so that 'zooming' into details was possible. This makes sending a full set of images to the client impractical: 36 views of 3k $\times$ 2k three times would make 216 MBytes of raw data which could be compressed to around 20 MBytes. Transmitting this is impractical on the Internet compared to our solution which initially only transmits around 25 kBytes and only ever send the areas the user requires. We decided to adapt the technique used before for high resolution images: to supply images on demand.

2. Capturing object views

In ACOHIR new turntables were designed by AIDIMA in Spain, the Louvre used a heavy turntable capable of handling very large sculptures, while Southampton made a low-cost turntable shown in Fig. 1 below. Existing hardware can also be used to capture images which can then be colour calibrated using our software and a MacBeth Colorchecker chart [2].

We decided to standardise on Kodak professional digital cameras in order to provide an integrated cap-

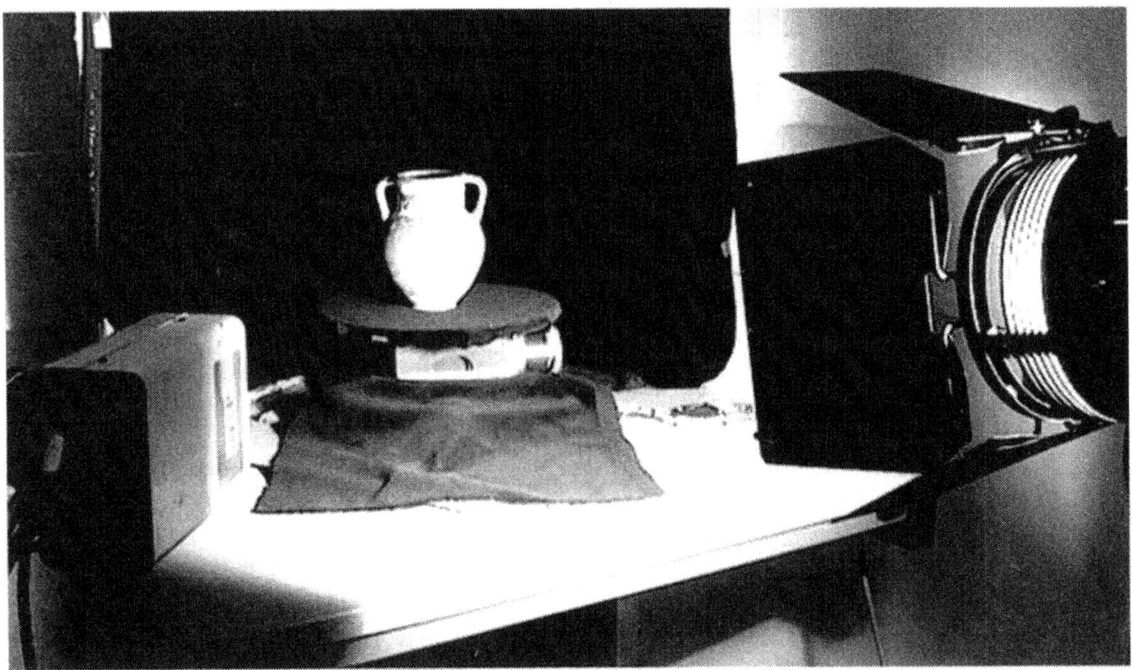

Fig. 1. The imaging system in Southampton.

ture package which worked with a range of their cameras. These range from the DCS410 to the DC-S560, although the camera shown above is a Kontron camera from the Vasari project. A 'consumer' Kodak DC265 has also been tested for a low-cost solution. The colour calibration is described elsewhere [3,9]. The colour calibration and compression of 10k $\times$ 10k paintings (approx. 300 MBytes) was always time-consuming and in this project it is still the case: the 216 MByte example cited above is comparable in size.

3. The use of sRGB

The use of device-independent colour has increased considerably, with the general aim of more consistent colour reproduction across devices. sRGB is a fairly new colour space which is used in printers and some cameras as it provides a standard RGB. Unlike CIE colour spaces which we commonly use, sRGB can be displayed well without any computation, which is a great benefit when unknown systems are used.

In the Viseum project we allowed the client to register a colour profile (ICC) with the server so that it could transform CIE colour spaces specifically for the client's display. This allowed the images to be kept in a wider colour space such as CIE Lab but placed a small extra load on the server, as well as adding complexity. This functionality has been kept but now we also allow sRGB images to be stored at the server. This relies on the user making their display conform to sRGB which includes an ambient luminance level of around 64 lux and a display gamma of 2.2. The server does not need to carry out any computation in this case.

4. Storage format

For compressed files we generally use a TIFF format file with multiple images for each resolution, each tiled to 64 $\times$ 64 and each tile JPEG compressed. This provides quick access to 64 $\times$ 64 pel tiles at full, half, quarter etc. resolutions, and the JPEG compression is particularly useful for sending images to the Java viewer. Fig. 2 illustrates the format with multiple images within the file. Most commercial packages only load the first image and few support JPEG in TIFF although it is supported by the TIFF standard and common libraries. The compression can also be LZW or ZIP as the tiles can be recompressed at the server before transmission to the viewer. Although we sometimes refer to these images as a pyramid there is no inter-resolution com-

Fig. 2. Representation of multiresolution tiled JPEG TIFF file.

pression as used in PhotoCD for example, which is a true pyramidal coding scheme. The major advantage of using TIFF is that it is an open standard.

5. The Java viewer

The viewer has been written in Java, as it runs on a number of different platforms, and can be embedded in Web pages to provide an easy way to present the acquired objects to the largest possible audience. The applet is highly configurable, and the user interface can be created either as components of the applet itself, or using HTML on the page in which the applet is embedded which communicates with the applet using JavaScript. The viewer reads image tiles from the server and displays them in a window. As the window is typically considerably smaller than the actual size of the image, the viewer facilitates navigation around the image, to different resolutions and to different frames in the image sequence. A cache of tiles is kept at the client to prevent unnecessary requests to the server and to increase performance. When dealing with a multiframed image, this cache may optionally be preloaded with low-resolution tiles. Thus, when the user changes the current frame being displayed in that resolution the tile will quickly be retrieved from the cache rather than the server, and so a smooth turning effect can be achieved.

Fig. 3 shows the viewer in use for a typical archaeological object with descriptive text. The page consists of two Java applets rather than a new applet containing two image areas with a fixed layout and controls. The small top view has hidden controls and is for turning the object around. The applets search for all compatible applets and communicate with each other to update views. When it is released it sends a position update message to the lower applet which shows the appropriate view. The user controls the viewer in one of four ways — either by clicking in the viewing window, using keyboard shortcuts, activating the controls seen at the bottom of the screen, or by activating JavaScript code which communicates with the viewer. The lower viewer also has its internal controls hidden and JavaScript is used in text links instead. Clicking and dragging with the left mouse button in the viewing window allows the user scroll the viewport around the image, and clicking and dragging with the middle button changes the current frame (Alt is used with single button mice). For a zoomed-out view with the tiles for each frame in the cache, dragging the middle button results in a smooth rotation of the object. The frame containing the image views is generated dynamically in the browser using JavaScript, by passing the object name and other details as parameters to the page. This make it possible to easily generate a Web page for viewing any object from a database for example, without having to manually write it. This combination of JavaScript controlling modular applets means the user interface can easily be tailored for different applications or image types without modifying any Java code.

In the text frame on the right of the image, hyperlinks in the text may be used to update the current view. When the link is activated a piece of JavaScript code instructs the viewing applets to change to the appropriate location and frame. This enables the person viewing the document to easily refer to the correct part of the object to which the author is referring. In the example shown, four of the links may be used to zoom in and show details of the surface of the pot.

Pages containing applets are typically partially created using JavaScript to enable a number of integration facilities such as personal linking. In this situation the Web page may contain a link or button which invokes JavaScript to query the applet for its current location. It can then add this to a list on the page created using HTML forms, entries in which when clicked will update the viewer to the stored location. This can be useful for temporarily 'bookmarking' interesting locations within an object which may be returned to later.These bookmarks are stored using cookies, and when the user returns to a page which has been visited previously the bookmarks are reloaded and are again available for selection. In addition to placing links on the page, the author of the document can also define a set of initial bookmarks to be present in the list. This is achieved by creating a special links file for the page which the server is aware of. Whenever a page is requested, the server checks for the existence of a links file, and if present encodes the information within into a cookie which is then sent to the browser

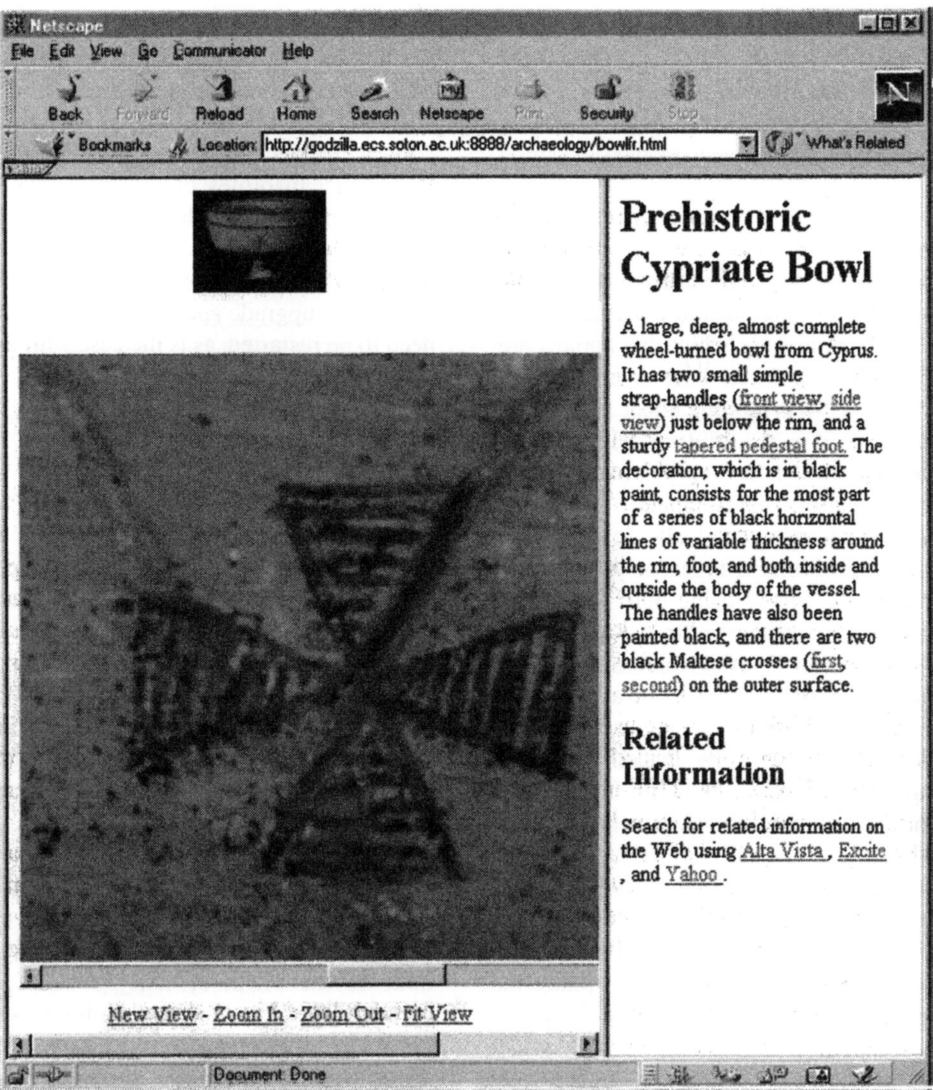

Fig. 3. Screendump of viewer.

and presented in the bookmarks list by the JavaScript that is used when creating the page.

6. IIP server

Our image server uses the Internet Imaging Protocol (IIP) [10] which provides a framework for CGI calls to request parts of images and details about the image such as its resolution. We added extensions to handle directories with object images. Each view of the object is usually stored as a multiresolution JPEG tiled TIFF image, although other or no compression can be used. The client requests `get_image_resolutions` and then `get_num_images` to initialise. It can then request JFIF tiles, using JTL requests from the appropriate TIFF file. The server is capable of handling other formats but the efficiency will be very low if it is not tiled or multiresolution. It can decompress tiles from the source file and recompress them to JFIF, which means the user could request a higher compression or other processing. The server is written in C and runs as a permanently resident fastCGI process. It has been tested under Solaris, Linux and Irix. On a SUN e450 the server load is usually under 1% per user. The load on the client always seems higher, with a 450 MHz Pentium II, running NT, being loaded to around 80% decompressing and displaying images.

The other more advanced server is written in Java. It is completely self contained, and acts as a combined Web and IIP server, and is therefore capable of serving not only the high-resolution images, but also the HTML documents in which the applets are embedded. Alternatively, the Java server may simply be used as a set of servlets running under any servlet capable Web server. This flexibility provides a convenient single step solution to the problem of serving images in a cross-platform environment.

The Java server uses dynamically loaded code to enable a variety of image types to be handled. JPEG images may be served using pure Java code, although this is rather slow due to the lack of tiling in the images, and the fact that decompression, tiling, and recompression must be done in Java. For optimal performance tiled TIFF images are usually used, and the server uses dynamically loaded native libraries for handling the JPEG and TIFF image files. These libraries are themselves extremely portable and run under a number of platforms, including Linux, Solaris, Irix, and Windows 95/98/NT. Although marginally slower than the native C server, in practice the Java server is more advanced for a number of reasons. It is highly cross-platform, and will run on any system possessing a Java virtual machine. Additionally, the only native code that needs to be ported are the image handling libraries rather than the whole server itself, as is the case with the C server. The use of Java also provides a convenient mechanism for accessing the underlying threading capabilites of the host platform, thereby giving considerably enhanced multiuser performance when running on a multiprocessor system. One side benefit of the standalone Java server has been that it is easier to upgrade and maintain as Apache does not need to be restarted, as is the case with the C version.

7. Caching strategies

The effective use of caching has a significant effect on the system's performance. Each image tile is flagged as not cacheable to prevent them flooding the browser's cache, so a separate cache in the Java client maintains recently used tiles using a simple scoring algorithm. This also reduces the possibility of a potentially slow disc access. The scoring prevents images from the top levels of the pyramid which may also be used for the object overview being discarded at the expense of a tile further down the pyramid.

Prefetching commonly visited areas while the viewer is quiet can improve performance at the cost of higher network use. The server can maintain statistics of tile usage in each image and provide hints to the client at start-up which are used to prefetch later. Fig. 4 shows an image with the most

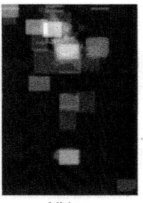

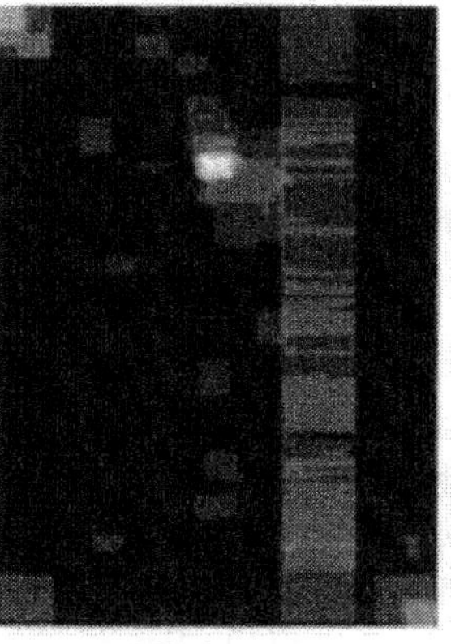

Fig. 4. Showing statistics of image use.

visited areas marked to illustrate this idea, for example in this case most people visit the mirror in the background at high resolution.

An IIP extension allows the viewer to get a list of tiles to preload during quiet periods. This is made easier by the threaded nature of the cache filling code, which can be interrupted to provide better response. The server stores tile usage statistics to generate the cache hints. If the user looks at the low-resolution image and the controls for a while before doing anything then most of the popular tiles for an image such as the one in Fig. 4 can be preloaded. This has the effect of an instant response if the user follows a typical browsing pattern but places a heavier load on the viewer's caching system and network if they do not. This is more complex for objects due to the large number of images involved but the principle is the same. However, the heavy preloading of the small images for the icon applet places a heavy load on the client already, so any further prefetching will have to take place in other quiet periods.

8. Conclusions and future work

A new way of serving and browsing images of 3D objects has been successfully produced. This is a logical high-quality step up from object movies as used in Quicktime-VR. Any number of views can be taken at any resolution to provide higher detail views of objects than has been available so far on the Web. In practice the system is usable over modems and long distances on the Internet. The initial load of the image area only involves around 25 kBytes and on a 56 kbaud modem the first screen fills in around 6 s. The Java code load of 50 kBytes is actually more time-consuming but only happens once. On our Lan the pot image shown above is loaded with its Java in 10 s with the small view completing in a further 7 s. The low load on the server is significant as it means that the system could cope with many users, which is an important consideration with new types of service such as this. A demonstration server runs at http://ernie.ecs.soton.ac.uk/~km/iipdemos/

A small tool will eventually be included in the viewer to shift the user's display gamma to closer to 2.2. At the moment we rely on external third party programs. The viewer will continually gain small improvements such as more controls, hyperlinks and painting unavailable tiles with expanded old lower-resolution ones. The caching should be user-configurable, as not everyone would want his network loaded by prefetches. It will also become more sophisticated, for example prioritising cached tiles from lower resolutions rather than a simple least recently used algorithm. The release of JPEG2000 will provide interesting improvements due to its inherently multiresolution nature (it uses wavelet compression) but probably issues of support in Java once again. When hyperlink areas are included on the images these will optionally come from a linkbase rather than simply coded in the applet's parameters at startup.

Acknowledgements

Thanks to Nick Lamb for his work on the prefetching. The partners of ACOHIR: ATC, Cobax, AIDIMA, Barco, ENST, Lladro, LRMF, Vasari Ltd., The National Gallery, Aristotle University of Thessaloniki, The Christian and Byzantine Museum in Athens, Museum of Cycladic Art. ACOHIR was funded by the European Commission's ESPRIT programme. Thanks also to the IIP community for many helpful discussions.

References

[1] J. Cupitt, K. Martinez and D. Saunders, A methodology for art reproduction in colour: the MARC project, Computers and the History of Art Journal 6 (2) (1996) 1–20.

[2] Gretag: www.gretagmacbeth.org.

[3] Internet Imaging Protocol, Hewlett Packard, Live Picture and Eastman Kodak, 1997 — available from www.digital imaging.org.

[4] Kadian: www.kadian.com.

[5] Live Picture: www.livepicture.com/.

[6] K. Martinez, J. Cupitt and D. Saunders, High resolution colorimetric imaging of paintings, Proc. SPIE, 1901, Jan. 1993, pp. 25–36.

[7] K. Martinez, J, Cupitt and S. Perry, High resolution colorimetric image browsing on the Web, Computer Networks and ISDN Systems 30 (1998) 399–405, online.

[8] Quicktime VR: www.apple.com/quicktime/.

[9] D. Saunders, J. Cupitt, R. Pillay and K. Martinez, Maintaining colour accuracy in images transferred across the

Internet, in: L.W. MacDonald and M.R. Luo (Eds.), Colour Imaging: Vision and Technology, Wiley, New York, 1999, pp. 215–231.

[10] M. Stokes, M. Anderson, S. Chandrasekar and R. Motta, A Standard Default Color Space for the Internet, 1996 — www.color.org/sRGB.html.

[11] Viseum project, www.InfoWin.org/ACTS/RUS/PROJECTS/ac238.htm and www.ecs.soton.ac.uk/~km/projs/viseum.

Kirk Martinez gained a B.Sc. in physics from the University of Reading and a Ph.D. in image processing at the University of Essex. He has worked on several European projects such as VASARI, MARC and Viseum. His research interests include high-resolution colorimetric imaging, parallel image processing, Web multimedia. He is director of the Centre for Digital Libraries Research at the University of Southampton.

Stephen Perry obtained a B.Sc. in computer science and a Ph.D. in image and multimedia from the University of Southampton, and subsequently worked on a number of European projects including VISEUM and ACOHIR. He is currently working for ANT Ltd. on their embedded Web browser, Fresco.

John Cupitt, since completing his Ph.D. in theoretical computer science at the University of Kent, has worked in the Scientific Department of the National Gallery London on the European Community-funded VASARI, MARC and VISEUM projects. He has published papers on camera calibration, image processing I/O systems, user-interface design, the measurement of colour change in paintings and infrared imaging of paintings.

ELSEVIER

Discovering the gap between Web site designers' expectations and users' behavior

Takehiro Nakayama *,[1], Hiroki Kato [1], Yohei Yamane [1]

Fuji Xerox Corporate Research Laboratories, 430 Sakai, Nakai-machi, Ashigarakami-gun, Kanagawa 259-0157, Japan

Abstract

This paper proposes a technique that discovers the gap between Web site designers' expectations and users' behavior. The former are assessed by measuring the inter-page conceptual relevance and the latter by measuring the inter-page access co-occurrence. The discovery of pages that are conceptually related but rarely co-occur in visits suggests areas where Web site design improvement would be appropriate. Further, the technique suggests how to apply quantitative data obtained through a multiple regression analysis that predicts hyperlink traversal frequency from page layout features. The effectiveness of the technique is validated by case studies.

Keywords: Web site design; Conceptual relevance; Access co-occurrence; Regression analysis

1. Introduction

The World Wide Web has grown explosively since its creation. Having gained the attention of millions of people across social and geographical boundaries, the Web is now frequently used by companies attempting to succeed in the global market. Many companies maintain their own Web site, and emphasize its importance for their business.

Business Web sites generally contain a wide range of topics to provide information for users who have different interests and goals. Hypertext on the Web is a convenient means of integrating multiple topics because it allows users to navigate through multiple paths according to their own preferences. Web site designers carefully construct a site structure with the aim of facilitating effective user navigation. However, designing a good Web site is not a simple task because hypertext structures can easily expand in a chaotic manner as the number of pages increases. Thus, many techniques to improve the effectiveness of user navigation have been proposed. They can be broadly classified into two types. One type is described as client-side assistance, and the other as server-side assistance. The former helps users to browse the hypertext structure effectively. For example, Botafogo [3] reconstructs the hypertext structure by employing clustering algorithms based on a graph theory, Lieberman [8] tracks users' browsing behavior to anticipate items of interest by exploring hyperlinks from a user's current position, and Li et al. [7] parse metadata from bookmarked pages for personalized indexing and classification. On the other hand, the latter type helps Web site designers to construct an effective site structure. In this paper, techniques of this type are studied. Before describing our approach, we first review related work.

* Corresponding author.

[1] {takehiro.nakayama,hiroki.kato,yohei.yamane}@fujixerox.co.jp

1.1. Related work

Extracting user navigation patterns is an essential task to assist Web site designers in understanding the preferences of users for further redesign activities. When users interact with a Web site, data recording their accesses are stored in Web server logs. The access log data include the client's IP address, the URL of the page requested, and the time the request is received. By identifying individual users' sessions from access log data, it is possible to infer user navigation patterns. For example, Chen et al. [5] convert access log data into a set of consecutive references to find frequent navigation patterns. Borges and Levene [2] model access log data as a directed graph where nodes correspond to pages and arcs to hyperlinks. This graph is weighted and the weight of an arc represents the probabilities that reflect user interaction with the Web site. Further, association rules developed in the data mining field [1] are modified to extract navigation patterns from the graph.

These techniques basically attempt to find access paths that a number of users have followed. However, user session identification from access log data is not always accurate because accesses from search engine robots and proxy servers are also recorded in the log data. The former exhaustively traverse hyperlinks regardless of page contents to collect as many pages as possible, and the latter represent activities of multiple users. Even if accesses from a real user are distinguished by using heuristics, user session identification is still inaccurate because of the caching functionality at the client side, i.e., backward references are not recorded in the access log data. Moreover, frequent navigation patterns only indicate how a Web site of current design is being used. Thus, Web site designers still need to interpret these patterns to improve the site quality.

To assist the interpretation of frequent navigation patterns, some features that can characterize these patterns must be employed. The use of user classification is one approach, where frequent navigation patterns are interpreted differently based on the importance of users. For example, Spiliopoulou et al. [12] compare navigation patterns of customers (Web site users who have purchased something) with those of non-customers. This comparison leads to rules on how the site's topology should be improved to turn non-customers into customers. Another approach uses hyperlink connectivity. For example, Perkowitz and Etzioni [10] find clusters of pages that tend to co-occur in visits but are not connected. For each cluster, an index page consisting of hyperlinks to the pages in the cluster is generated. In this way, more effective traversal between these pages will be achieved.

One drawback of these approaches is that they lack techniques to evaluate infrequent navigation patterns. In other words, they extract no navigation patterns that should be frequent (in the ideal Web site) but are actually infrequent because of poor site design. To find navigation patterns that should be frequent, we presume that page content analysis, as well as access log analysis, will be important.

Another drawback is that these approaches mostly concentrate on the hypertext topology and suggest no clues to improving the site design at the page layout level. In other words, if pages suggested for further improvement are already connected, Web site designers have to work on them without any help. Because the quality of page layout is dependent on many factors (e.g., topics, objectives, users, size, languages, the use of multimedia techniques, visual/logical consistency with other pages, and so forth), analysis of site-specific page layout features will be necessary.

1.2. Our approach

Under our assumption, Web site designers expect that conceptually related pages should co-occur in visits if their site is well designed. Thus, the finding that some conceptually related pages rarely co-occur would suggest a set of pages that should be improved in terms of Web site design. By employing the vector space model [11] which translates conceptual relevance into a numerical value based on word frequency, we first measure inter-page conceptual relevance for each pair of pages in the Web site. Second, by modifying the vector space model, we measure inter-page access co-occurrence. Third, we compare conceptual relevance with access co-occurrence for each pair. This process can be viewed as discovering the gap between Web site designers' expectations and users' behavior.

Given page pairs with a significant gap, Web site

designers can focus their redesign activities effectively. However, they still need to know how they can improve the site design because the cause of the gap is not known. If page pairs are not connected by a hyperlink, making a connection or generating an index page that references them as proposed by Perkowitz and Etzioni [10] is an intuitive solution. However, if page pairs are already connected, Web site designers probably do not know how they should work on each page. Therefore, we analyze the correlation between hyperlink traversal frequency and page layout features to give quantitative suggestions on redesigning the page layout. Further, by using the statistical data obtained above, Web site designers can simulate the effect of redesigning without involving users.

The rest of the paper is organized as follows. Section 2 describes the technique that discovers the gap between Web site designers' expectations and users' behavior. Section 3 studies how the site should be improved, and describes a system that gives quantitative suggestions about page layout design for better user navigation. Section 4 discusses the validation of our approach by means of case studies. Section 5 concludes the paper and gives suggestions for future work.

In this paper, we use **Fuji Xerox's** [2] public Web site as a source of experimental data. It consists of 2825 textual pages most of which are written in Japanese. The topics include corporate philosophy, recruiting, products, research activities, office location, and so forth. We use access log data that consist of 235,413 accesses after excluding accesses from robots or proxies. We also use JMP (SAS Institute Inc.) for statistical computation.

2. Discovering the gap between Web site designers' expectations and users' behavior

In this section, we introduce a technique that discovers the gap between Web site designers' expectations and users' behavior. In our approach, the former is assessed by measuring the inter-page conceptual relevance whereas the latter by measuring the inter-page access co-occurrence as described above.

[2] http://www.fujixerox.co.jp

2.1. Measurement of conceptual relevance

We employ the vector space model to measure the inter-page conceptual relevance. Given a Web site, we first remove HTML tags from each page. Second, we obtain content words (nouns, verbs, and adjectives) by performing morphological analysis and stop-word removal. Third, we compute the frequency of content words for each page. Fourth, we generate a list of content words weighted with their frequency. This list is viewed as a vector that represents page contents,

$$p_i = (\omega_{i,1}, \omega_{i,2}, \ldots, \omega_{i,k}, \ldots, \omega_{i,n})$$

where $\omega_{i,k}$ is the weight of the kth content word, and n is the number of distinct content words found in the Web site.

We finally measure the inter-page conceptual relevance (Sim$C$) for each page pair p_i and p_j using the cosine similarity formula as follows:

$$\mathrm{Sim}C(p_i, p_j) = \frac{\sum_{k=1}^{n} (\omega_{i,k} \cdot \omega_{j,k})}{\sqrt{\sum_{k=1}^{n} (\omega_{i,k})^2 \cdot \sum_{k=1}^{n} (\omega_{j,k})^2}}$$

where Sim$C$ is 0 if one of the pages contains no content words.

If the number of content words that appear in both pages is 0, the value of Sim$C$ is also 0. If two pages contain identical content words with the same frequency (i.e., vectors of two pages are identical), the value of Sim$C$ is 1. Note that all pages are equally informative in the vector space model because of the page length normalization.

2.2. Measurement of access co-occurrence

We modify the vector space model to measure the inter-page access co-occurrence. Given access log data, we first remove accesses from search engine robots and proxy servers using heuristics (e.g., access to /robots.txt; exhaustive access in a short period). Second, we count IP addresses for each page. Third, we generate a list of IP addresses weighted with their frequency. This list is viewed as a vector that represents page users. We finally measure the inter-page access co-occurrence (Sim$A$) for each page pair using the aforementioned cosine similarity formula,

$$\mathrm{Sim}A(p_i, p_j) = \frac{\sum_{k=1}^{t} (\lambda_{i,k} \cdot \lambda_{j,k})}{\sqrt{\sum_{k=1}^{t} (\lambda_{i,k})^2 \cdot \sum_{k=1}^{t} (\lambda_{j,k})^2}}$$

where $\lambda_{i,k}$ is the weight of the kth IP address that visited p_i, and t is the number of distinct IP addresses found in the access log data. Sim$A$ is 0 if one of the pages has never been visited by anyone.

If the number of users who visit both pages is 0, the value of Sim$A$ is also 0. If two pages are visited by identical users with the same frequency, the value of Sim$A$ is 1. Note that the inter-page access co-occurrence in this model is independent of the page popularity because the number of visits is normalized. It is also independent of hyperlink connectivity.

2.3. *Gap discovery*

Before comparing the inter-page conceptual relevance with the access co-occurrence for each pair of pages, we introduce the notions of *content page* and *index page*. While the former is an ordinary page that conveys conceptual contents to users, the latter is a functional page for navigational help. In general, the index page has multiple references to content pages of various topics, and tends to include content words of various topics without conceptual consistency. Consequently, measuring the conceptual relevance between the content page and the index page (or between two index pages) generates noisy data with a meaningless value. We therefore discard index pages in advance. The question here is how we should distinguish index pages. Because many pages actually have characteristics of both a content page and an index page, the boundary between them can be subjective. In this paper, we use the number of references in a page as a guide, based on the intuitive idea that an index page should have more references than a content page. We consider a page with more than N references as an index page. To determine the optimal value of N, we compute the correlation coefficient (R_{CA}) between the inter-page conceptual relevance (Sim$C$) and the access co-occurrence (Sim$A$) using the following formula:

$$R_{CA} = \frac{s_{CA}^2}{\sqrt{s_C^2 \cdot s_A^2}} \qquad (-1 \le R_{CA} \le 1)$$

where

$$s_{CA}^2 = \sum_{i=1}^{m} \left(\mathrm{Sim}C_i - \overline{\mathrm{Sim}C}\right)\left(\mathrm{Sim}A_i - \overline{\mathrm{Sim}A}\right),$$

$$s_C^2 = \sum_{i=1}^{m} \left(\mathrm{Sim}C_i - \overline{\mathrm{Sim}C}\right)^2,$$

$$s_A^2 = \sum_{i=1}^{m} \left(\mathrm{Sim}A_i - \overline{\mathrm{Sim}A}\right)^2$$

where SimC_i is the value of conceptual relevance for the ith pair of pages, SimA_i is the value of access co-occurrence for the ith pair of pages, and m is the number of page pairs.

The correlation coefficient (R_{CA}) measures the degree of linear relationship between two variables (Sim$C$ and Sim$A$). If there is an exact linear relationship, it is 1 or -1 depending on whether the variables are positively or negatively related. If there is no relationship, it is 0 (see [6] for more detail). Thus, if index pages (which generate noisy data) are properly discarded, the correlation coefficient will tend toward 1. Fig. 1 shows the result of this computation, where we used the Fuji Xerox Web site. The peak is observed at $N = 8$, i.e., pages with more than eight references can be considered as index pages in this Web site.

The correlation coefficient above can also be used as a criterion to indicate the overall design quality of

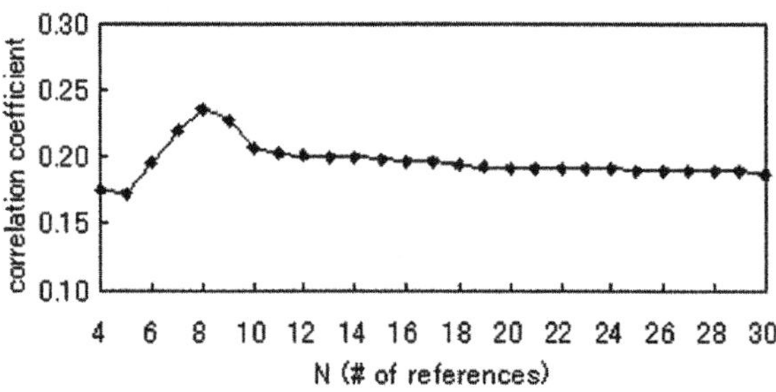

Fig. 1. Index page determination.

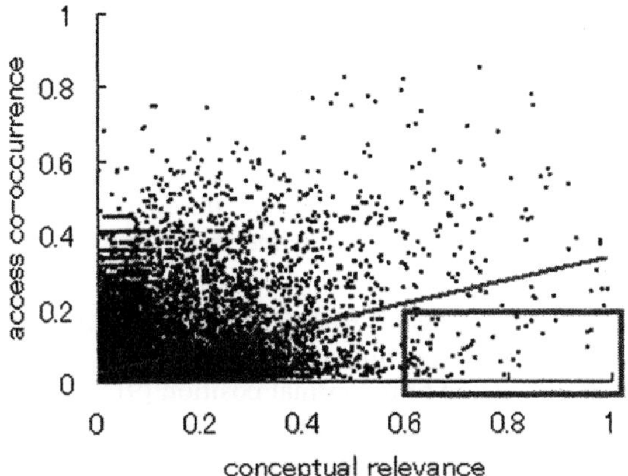

Fig. 2. Conceptual relevance versus access co-occurrence.

the Web site. It would tend toward 1 if the overall site design were ideal. However, it does not indicate where the Web site requires improvement. For this purpose, we plot the inter-page conceptual relevance versus the access co-occurrence for each page pair as shown in Fig. 2. The straight line in the figure is a fit to the plot using least square regression. The markers on the lower right show the page pairs that rarely co-occur in visits even though they are conceptually related. Web site designers can locate the URLs of these pages by pointing at the markers.

Our technique, depending on the size and quality of the Web site, may find many page pairs that should be improved, but it can also give a structural view for browsing assistance. The technique first transforms the set of page pairs into a set of distinct pages, then applies a content-based agglomerative hierarchical clustering algorithm [13] to the new set. It finally shows page clusters, which can help Web site designers to understand the design problem at a more abstract level. For example, we found that many pages in the lower right area in Fig. 2 were about products of the company.

3. Web site design improvement

There are two levels of assistance for Web site design improvement. One is hyperlink topological improvement, and the other is page layout improvement. For example, 67 page pairs of 74 in the lower right rectangle region (conceptual relevance > 0.6; access co-occurrence < 0.2) in Fig. 2 are not connected, and they will require hyperlink topological improvement. On the other hand, the rest are connected, and they will require page layout improvement for effective user navigation.

3.1. Hyperlink topological improvement

If page pairs are not connected, creating a new hyperlink between them or making the path length shorter is an intuitive solution. To provide empirical validation for this solution, we investigate the Web site mentioned above. For each pair of pages, we compute the path length (the number of hyperlinks required to reach from one page to the other). Obviously, there can be multiple paths between any two pages in the hypertext system. However, since considering all paths would be computationally expensive, we compute only the shortest path, taking account of the hyperlink direction. Fig. 3 plots the path length versus the access co-occurrence for each page pair. The straight line is a fit to the plot us-

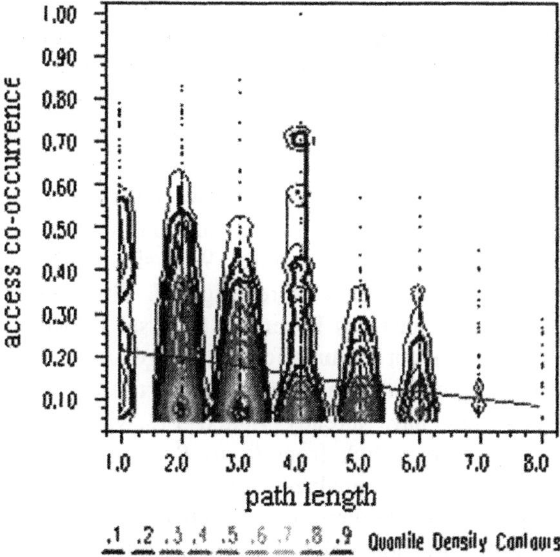

Fig. 3. Path length versus access co-occurrence. Since it was hard to see patterns in the original plot because of the marker density, we used the quantile density contours in 5% intervals. This means that 5% of the markers are below the lowest contour, 10% are below the next contour, and so forth. The highest contour has 95% of the markers below it.

ing least square regression, where we can observe a negative correlation as expected.

3.2. Page layout improvement

When page pairs are already connected, Web site designers have to consider the improvement of page layout design. This is a hard task since there are two basic problems as follows:

- *No standards regarding good page design.* The quality of page layout is dependent on many factors (e.g., topics, objectives, users, size, languages, the use of multimedia techniques, visual/logical consistency with other pages, and so forth). Therefore, Web site designers probably do not know how to improve it most effectively.
- *User involvement in evaluation.* Even if Web site designers redesign the page layout based on experience (or by trial and error), they still need to evaluate whether or not it is improved in terms of effective user navigation. Designers typically upload redesigned pages to the site, then wait for several days to collect a sufficient amount of access log data for evaluation. If the result of evaluation is not satisfactory, they will repeat the process above. This may damage the reputation of the site if the redesigned pages are of worse quality than the original ones. Further, frequent changes in design may confuse users who often visit the site.

To mitigate these problems, we built a system that gives quantitative suggestions on redesigning the page layout, and enables Web site designers to simulate the effect of redesigning. The system, in advance, analyzes hyperlink traversal frequency and page layout features for each page in the Web site. The former is the probability of users visiting P_2 if they have already visited P_1, where there must be a hyperlink from P_1 to P_2. Given a page pair, the system analyzes the hyperlink traversal frequency in both directions if there exist hyperlinks for both directions. Note that this is different from the inter-page access co-occurrence that can be used for page pairs regardless of hyperlink connection.

As regards the page layout features, we have selected the following five features. They are all computable, i.e., the system can automatically extract these features.

- *The number of distinct hyperlinks.* When many hyperlinks are embedded in a page, the probability of individual hyperlink selection will decrease. Note that because we discard index pages that contain more than N hyperlinks in the gap discovery process as described in Section 2, the maximum number of distinct hyperlinks here is N.
- *The position of a hyperlink.* It is empirically proven that the importance of a sentence in a text is related to its ordinal position [9]. By analogy, the selection probability of a hyperlink may be related to its ordinal position. We presume that a hyperlink in an earlier position will have a higher probability of selection.
- *The size of a hyperlink.* We consider the hyperlink size, which is measured by the number of characters between the anchor tags, as a feature. If the anchor text contains many characters, the region it occupies in the Web browser will increase. Consequently, we expect that it has a higher probability of selection.
- *Conceptual relevance between anchor text and the referred page.* If hyperlink anchor text appropriately describes the content of the referred page, user navigation will be more successful. We measure the relevance between anchor text and the referred page using the vector space model mentioned in Section 2.
- *Conceptual relevance between text preceding a hyperlink and the referred page.* If sentences preceding a hyperlink appropriately describe the content of the referred page, user navigation will be more successful. The region of the text is delimited by an HTML tag.

Our system employs multiple regression analysis to predict the hyperlink traversal frequency from a linear combination of these page layout features. Since no features are infallibly informative for this purpose, the system uses the *stepwise forward selection procedure* (see [6]) to remove uninformative ones. This procedure adds the page layout features one at a time, until no more features explain significant variation. By applying the procedure to the Fuji Xerox Web site, the system added all the features except hyperlink size which was not significant at the *probability to enter* value of 0.25. This means that hyperlink size is not an informative feature, at least in this Web site. In the remainder of this paper, we use the other features for experiments.

Next, the system obtains the following regression equation:

$$Y = b_0 + \sum_{i=1}^{p} b_i X_i$$

where Y is hyperlink traversal frequency, X_i is the score on the ith page layout feature, b_0 is the regression constant, b_i is the weight corresponding to the ith page layout feature, and p is the number of remaining page layout features after the stepwise procedure.

This equation reflects the site-specific characteristics of page layout design in terms of user navigation. In other words, hyperlink traversal frequency can be predicted when these page layout features are known.

Given a pair of pages (from the lower right area in Fig. 2), the system analyzes the page layout features, and substitutes them for the corresponding X_i in the regression equation. If one feature (kth feature) is not substituted at this step, the regression equation will be a linear equation of a single variable as follows:

$$Y = b_0' + b_k X_k$$

where

$$b_0' = b_0 + \sum_{i=1}^{k-1} b_i X_i + \sum_{i=k+1}^{p} b_i X_i.$$

For each page layout feature, the system obtains the equation above, and displays each graph as shown in Fig. 4. When x_1 is the current value of X_k,

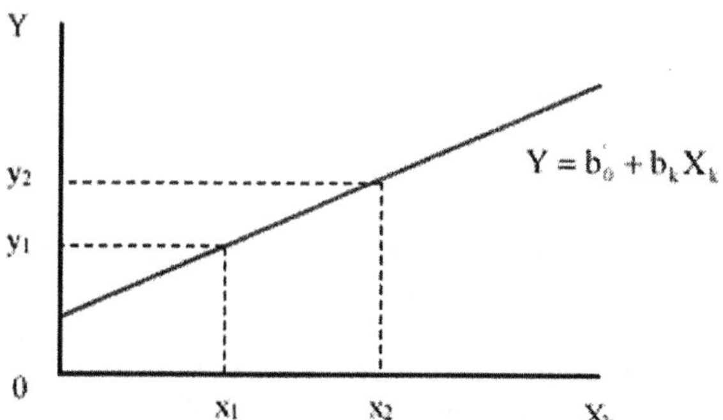

Fig. 4. Hyperlink traversal frequency (Y) as a function of page layout feature (X_k).

y_1 is the predicted value of Y. To increase y_1 to y_2, this graph suggests that the value of X_k should be x_2 as long as other features never change.

When multiple features are simultaneously redesigned, the system reanalyzes the page layout features, and repeats the procedure above. If the effect of redesigning activities is simulated in this manner, Web site designers need not upload redesigned pages to the real Web site for evaluation. Consequently, they can avoid possible damage to the reputation of the Web site.

4. Case study

In this section, we describe and discuss some cases that indicate the advantages (and disadvantages) of our approach.

4.1. Case 1: hyperlink topological improvement

We examined page pairs in the lower right area in Fig. 2. As described above, they are conceptually relevant but rarely co-occur in visits. Fig. 5 shows one of these page pairs that are not connected to each other. Each page explains the technical features of a different product (multiple function copier/fax/printer), respectively. Since these two products are very similar to each other except for the printing speed, the contents of both pages are also similar. In fact, the value of their conceptual relevance was 0.95 (very high). Probably, users who are interested in purchasing one of the products are also interested in the other. However, the value of access co-occurrence between the pages was only 0.13. This can be explained by their hyperlink connectivity. The hyperlink distance was eight for their shortest path, i.e., at least eight clicks were needed to visit both pages. By understanding this situation, Web site designers can create a shortcut between the pages for better user navigation.

This case study shows the advantages of our gap discovery technique described in Section 2. Since the cause of the situation is clear, Web site designers can easily understand what they should do in this case.

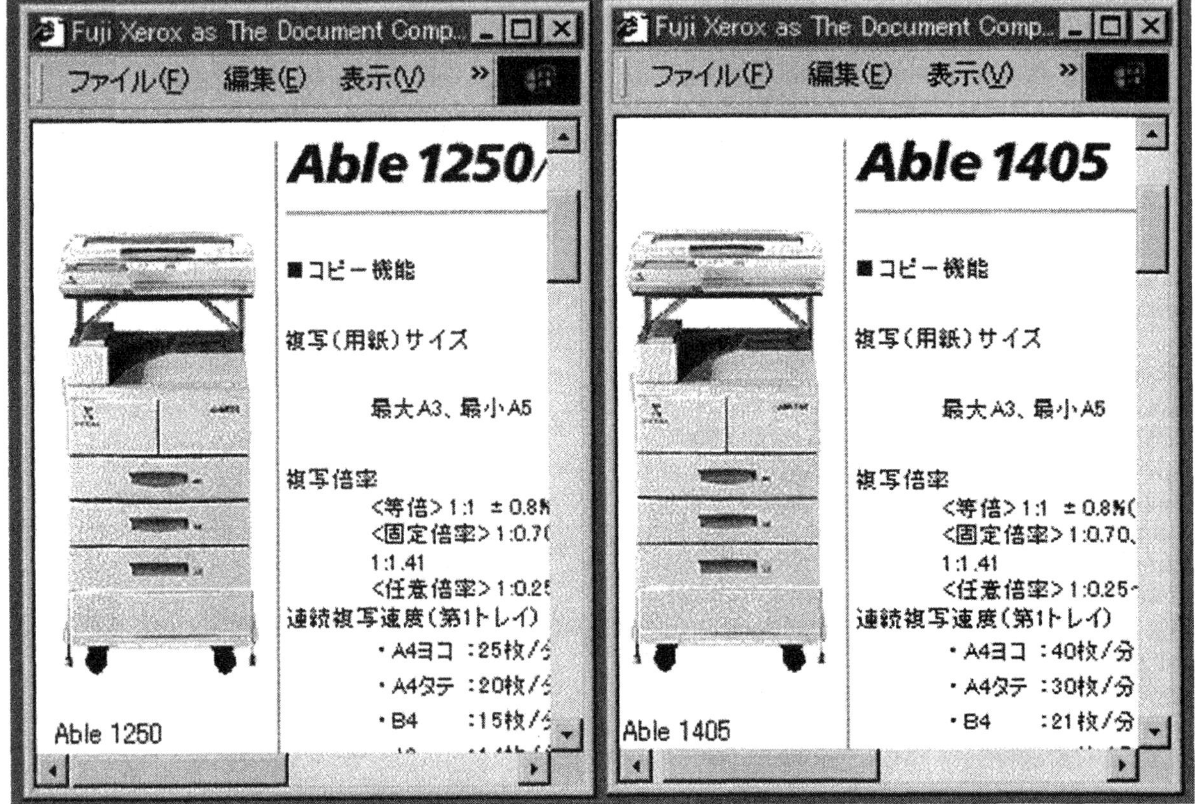

Fig. 5. Case study 1: pair of pages that are not connected.

4.2. Case 2: page layout improvement

Fig. 6 shows one of the page pairs in the lower right area in Fig. 2. The left page is a general introduction to engineering printing systems, whereas the right is a concrete explanation of one system. They are conceptually related, and the value of their conceptual relevance was as high as 0.65. On the other hand, the value of access co-occurrence was 0.17. Unlike in the previous case, there is a hyperlink connection from left to right. We therefore presume that few users who visited the left page followed the hyperlink (labeled *BrainTech8180a*).

To investigate this situation, our system uses the multiple regression equation to predict the hyperlink traversal frequency as described in Section 3. The equation obtained for this Web site was as follows:

$$Y = 0.1004 - 0.0025X_1 + 0.0011X_2 + 0.1196X_3 + 0.0841X_4$$

where Y = hyperlink traversal frequency, X_1 = the number of distinct hyperlinks, X_2 = the position of a hyperlink, X_3 = conceptual relevance between anchor text and the referred page, X_4 = conceptual relevance between text preceding a hyperlink and the referred page.

Note that X_2 has a positive coefficient, which is contrary to our aforementioned anticipation that a hyperlink in an earlier position will have a higher probability of selection. This can be interpreted to mean that users of this Web site tend to scroll (to read the whole page), then decide which hyperlink to follow. This interpretation is also supported by a recent research study that indicates that users spend a great deal of time scrolling [4].

Given the pair of pages in Fig. 6, the system extracted the value of each feature as follows.

$X_1 = 8$ (the number of hyperlinks in the left page); $X_2 = 6$ (the ordinal position of the hyperlink labeled *BrainTech 8180a*); $X_3 = 0.56$ (the concep-

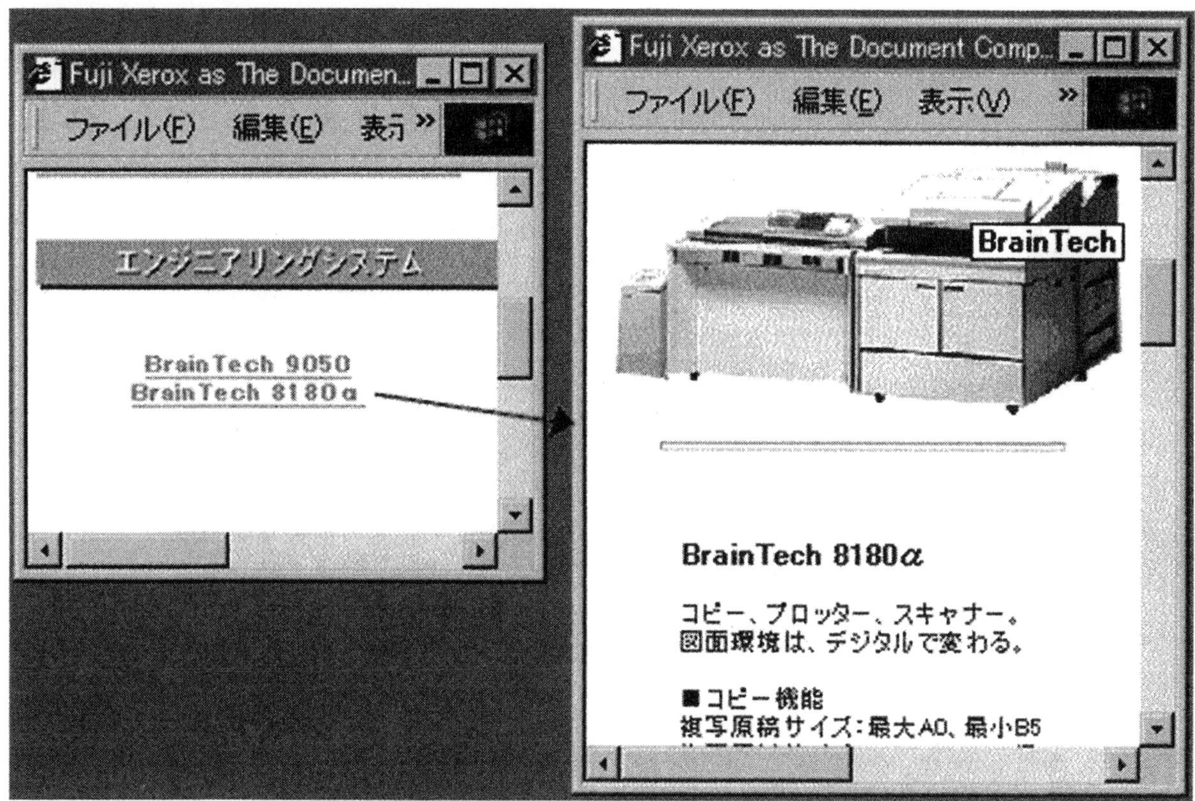

Fig. 6. Case study 2: pair of pages that are connected.

tual relevance between the anchor text (i.e., *BrainTech 8180a*) and the right page); $X_4 = 0$ (the value is 0 because there is no text preceding the hyperlink).

By substituting these values for the variables in the equation above, the system obtained $Y = 0.154$ (the predicted value of hyperlink traversal frequency). This value means that 15.4% of users who visit the left page are predicted to follow the hyperlink.

Further, the system gives the regression equation between Y and X_k ($k = 1, 2, 3, 4$) as described in Section 3. Fig. 7 shows the equation for each feature as a quantitative suggestion. Web site designers can now understand what they should do to increase the value of Y. If they remove several hyperlinks from the page (reduce the value of X_1), Y will increase. However, if $Y = 0.2$ is required, this redesign is still insufficient. Designers need to consider another feature (or multiple features) for that purpose. If, for example, the value of X_4 is increased from 0 to 0.55 by adding a paragraph that describes the system (*BrainTech 8180a*), the purpose will be achieved. When we tried copying the first paragraph in the right page (in Fig. 6) to the space before the hyperlink in the left page, the system reanalyzed the value of X_4 to return $X_4 = 0.48$ and $Y = 0.194$. If Web site designers are still not satisfied with this value of Y, they can consider further redesign with a new quantitative suggestion based on reanalysis.

This case study shows the advantages of our system for page layout improvement as well as gap discovery. By using our system, Web site designers can understand what they should do based on quantitative suggestions. Moreover, they can simulate their redesign activities without involving real users, i.e., they need not collect access log data for each redesign step for the purpose of evaluation.

4.3. Case 3: higher access co-occurrence despite less conceptual relevance

In this section, we investigate page pairs in the upper left area in Fig. 2. Unlike those in the lower

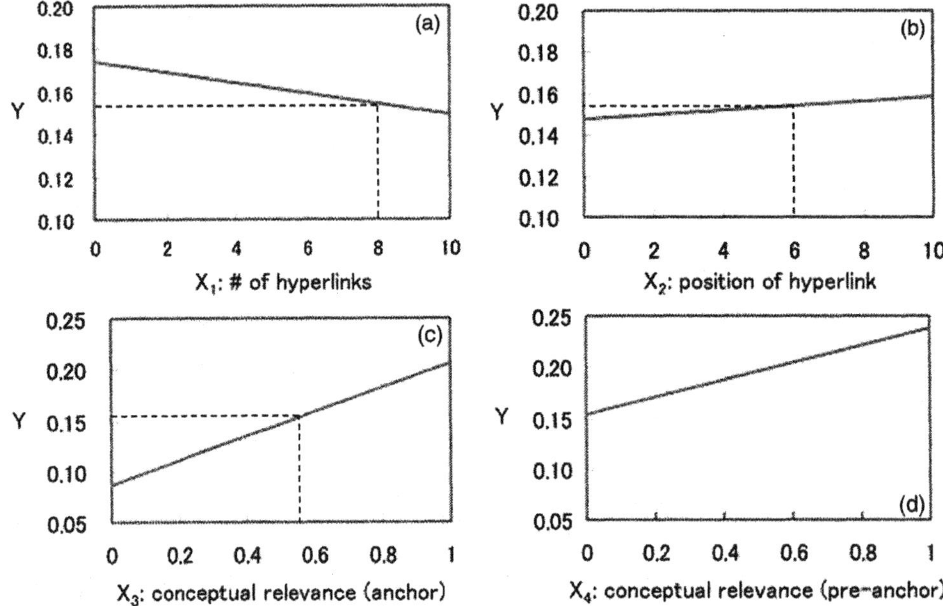

Fig. 7. Quantitative suggestion for each feature. The dotted line indicates the value of each feature (X_k) and the predicted value of hyperlink traversal frequency (Y: 0.154).

right area, these pairs are conceptually less related but frequently co-occur in visits. In these cases, we assume that some users are navigating through the Web site with a goal that cannot be characterized by the page content analysis based on the vector space model.

Fig. 8 shows one of the page pairs in the upper left area in Fig. 2. Each page shows the location of a different office. Perhaps some users were interested in the offices of Fuji Xerox, and visited both these pages. However, the value of their conceptual relevance was only 0.16. This is because the vector space model depends only on the frequency of surface words. These pages contain the office address, but contain no words that explicitly express the meaning of location. Thus, the value did not reflect the abstract notion of location.

This case study shows the disadvantage of our system that employs the vector space model for the measurement of inter-page conceptual relevance. To solve this problem, semantic analysis for exploring contents at a deeper level is needed. However, this approach is unrealistic given the current natural language understanding technology.

For a realistic solution, the use of metadata that describes page contents would be a good approach. If Web site designers embed machine-readable metadata in each page, we can use these data to measure conceptual relevance. Because the W3C has introduced the **Resource Description Framework**[3] as a world-wide standard, the use of metadata is being encouraged.

5. Conclusions and future work

We have presented a technique that discovers the gap between Web site designers' expectations and users' behavior. The former are assessed by measuring the inter-page conceptual relevance and the latter by measuring the inter-page access co-occurrence. Further, plotting both on the same graph reveals the gap, and we have shown that removing index pages, which can be identified by the number of outgoing hyperlinks, prevents the generation of noisy data.

We have also presented a system that gives quantitative suggestions for page layout improvement. The system uses multiple regression analysis to pre-

[3] see http://www.w3.org/RDF/

Fig. 8. Case study 3: pair of pages that are considered conceptually less relevant.

dict hyperlink traversal frequency from selected page layout features. Web site designers can simulate the redesigning process using the system without involving real users. We have validated the effectiveness of our approach using case studies.

As a future work, we suggest the examination of the use of metadata for measuring inter-page conceptual relevance. If Web site designers utilize metadata by which they explicitly describe page contents, the measurement of inter-page conceptual relevance will accurately reflect their expectations.

We also suggest investigation of other page layout features to predict hyperlink traversal frequency. For example, color and multimedia usage are possible features. However, because these features cannot be represented in a continuous/ordinal scale but in a nominal scale, multiple regression analysis is not directly applicable. Thus, a technique that transforms the data so that the transformed variables have good distributional properties is necessary.

Acknowledgements

This study was conducted as part of the Fuji Xerox Document Mining research project led by Yoshihiro Ueda, who provided us with essential support.

References

[1] R. Agrawal, T. Imielinski and A. Swami, Mining associations between sets of items in massive databases, in: Proc. ACM SIGMOD International Conference on Management of Data, 1993.

[2] J. Borges and M. Levene, Mining association rules in hypertext databases, in: Proc. 4th International Conference on Knowledge Discovery and Data Mining, 1998.

[3] R.A. Botafogo, Cluster analysis for hypertext systems, in: Proc. 16th Annual International ACM SIGIR Conference on Research and Development in Information Retrieval, 1993.

[4] M.D. Byrne, B.E. John, N.S. Wehrle and D.C. Crow, The

tangled web we wove: a taskonomy of WWW use, in: Proc. ACM CHI Conference: Human Factors in Computing Systems, 1999.
[5] M.S. Chen, J.S. Park and P.S. Yu, Data mining for path traversal patterns in a Web environment, in: Proc. 16th IEEE International Conference on Distributed Computing Systems, 1996.
[6] C.J. Huberty, Applied Discriminant Analysis, Wiley, New York, 1994.
[7] W.S. Li, Q. Vu, D. Agrawal, Y. Hara and H. Takano, PowerBookmarks: a system for personalizable Web information organization, sharing, and management, in: Proc. 8th International World Wide Web Conference, 1999.
[8] H. Lieberman, Letizia: an agent that assists Web browsing, in: Proc. International Joint Conference on Artificial Intelligence, 1995.
[9] C.Y. Lin and E. Hovy, Identifying topics by position, in: Proc. 5th ACL Conference on Applied Natural Language Processing, 1997.
[10] M. Perkowitz and O. Etzioni, Adaptive Web sites: automatically synthesizing Web pages, in: Proc. 15th National Conference on Artificial Intelligence, 1998.
[11] G. Salton, Developments in automatic text retrieval, Science 253 (1991).
[12] M. Spiliopoulou, C. Pohle and L.C. Faulstich, Improving the effectiveness of a Web site with Web usage mining, in: Proc. Workshop on Web Usage Analysis and User Profiling, 1999.
[13] E.M. Voorhees, Implementing agglomerative hierarchical clustering algorithms for use in document retrieval, Information Processing and Management 22 (1986).

Takehiro Nakayama is a member of the research staff at Fuji Xerox Corporate Research Laboratories. Prior to that, from 1992 to 1996, he was a member of the research staff at FX Palo Alto Laboratory. He received his M.S. in Information Science from Kyushu University in 1989. His interests include Web site analysis, information retrieval, natural language processing, and document image understanding.

Hiroki Kato is a member of the research staff at Fuji Xerox Corporate Research Laboratories. He received his M.S. from Tokyo Institute of Technology in 1997. His research interests lie in Artificial Intelligence, especially in Machine Learning. His current research includes Web mining and personal assistant agent for the Web.

Yohei Yamane is a member of the research staff at Fuji Xerox Corporate Research Laboratories. He received his M.S. from Nara Institute of Science and Technology (NAIST), where he studied natural language processing, in particular anaphora resolution and centering theory. Presently, he works on Web site analysis.

What is this page known for? Computing Web page reputations

Davood Rafiei [1], Alberto O. Mendelzon [*,1]

Department of Computer Science, University of Toronto, Toronto, ON M5S 3H5, Canada

Abstract

The textual content of the Web enriched with the hyperlink structure surrounding it can be a useful source of information for querying and searching. This paper presents a search process where the input is the URL of a page, and the output is a ranked set of topics on which the page has a reputation. For example, if the input is www.gamelan.com, then a possible output is 'Java'. We propose several algorithmic formulations of the notion of reputation using simple random walk models of Web-browsing behavior. We give preliminary test results on the effectiveness of these algorithms.

Keywords: Reputation ranking; Searching; Random walks; PageRank; Hubs and authorities

1. Introduction

The idea of exploiting the 'reputation' of a Web page when searching has recently attracted research attention and has even been incorporated into some search engines [2,3,5,11,15]. The idea is (1) that pages with good reputations should be given preferential treatment when reporting the results of a search, and (2) that link structure can be mined to extract such reputation measures, on the assumption that a link from page a to page b is, to some degree, an endorsement of the contents of b by the creator of a.

We consider a different question in this paper: given a page (or a Web site), on what topics is this page considered an authority by the Web community? There are many potential applications for such computations. For example, organizations routinely expend a great deal of effort and money in determining how they are perceived by the public; evaluating the reputation of their Web site on specific topics, or determining those topics on which its reputation is highest (or abnormally low) could be a valuable part of this self-evaluation. A second application is page classification: determining that a page has high reputation on a certain topic is evidence that the page is, first of all, *about* that topic, and also a good candidate to be included in a directory of resources on the topic. Yet another application is the analysis of the reputation of personal home pages to determine what topics a person is known for, say for tenure hearings or recruiting.

However, there are some difficulties in formalizing the concept of 'reputation' effectively. The assumption that links are endorsements suggests that the number of incoming links of a page indicates its reputation. But in practice, links represent a wide variety of relationships such as navigation, subsumption, relatedness, refutation, justification, etc. In addition, we are interested not just in the overall reputation of a page, but in its reputation on certain topics. In the next subsection we give an overview of our approach to dealing with these difficulties.

* Corresponding author.

[1] E-mail: {drafiei, mendel}@cs.toronto.edu

1.1. Overview

We focus on two problems: (1) computing the reputation rank of a page, whether overall or for specific topics; (2) identifying those topics for which a page has a good reputation. We address these problems in the framework of simple probabilistic models of user behavior that simulate the way pages are created or searched.

We propose two methods for computing the reputations of a page. Our first method is based on one-level weight propagation, generalizing the PageRank model [3]. The reputation of a page on a topic is proportional to the sum of the reputation weights of pages pointing to it on the same topic. In other words, links emanating from pages with high reputations are weighted more. For example, a page can acquire a high reputation on a topic because the page is pointed to by many pages on that topic, or because the page is pointed to by some high-reputation pages on that topic.

Our second method is based on two-level weight propagation, generalizing the Hubs and Authorities model [11]. In this model, a page is deemed an *authority* on a topic if it is pointed to by good *hubs* on the topic, and a good hub is one that points to good authorities.

We formulate both these methods in terms of random walks on the Web graph. Our random walk formulation of the first method is an extension of the one used to define PageRank [3]; unlike PageRank our formulation allows computing the reputation rank of a page on a specific topic. Our random walk formulation of the second method is novel; to the best of our knowledge, there is no random walk formulation of a hubs-and-authorities model in the literature. We present algorithms for computing page reputations both in the case where a large crawl of the Web is available and when it is not. We also provide preliminary experimental results on the effectiveness of our formulations.

1.2. Related work

Recent work on analyzing the link structure of the Web suggests that hyperlinks between pages often represent relevance [5,15] or endorse some authority [2,3,11].

Brin and Page [3] suggest a recursive method for ranking the importance of a Web page based on the importance of its incoming links. The ranking is based on simulating the behavior of a 'random surfer' who either selects an outgoing link uniformly at random, or jumps to a new page chosen uniformly at random from the entire collection of pages. The PageRank of a page corresponds to the number of visits the 'random surfer' makes to the page. The Google search engine [9] adopts PageRank as part of its ranking system. Our first model of ranking is an extension of PageRank; the main difference is that we do ranking with respect to a topic instead of computing a universal rank for each page.

Kleinberg [11] proposes an algorithm that, given a topic, finds pages that are considered strong authorities on that topic. For example, given the term 'Java', the system built around this algorithm, known as HITS, finds *www.gamelan.com* among other pages. The algorithm is based on the intuition that for broad topics, authority is conferred by a set of *hub pages*, which are recursively defined as a set of pages with a large number of links to many relevant authorities. The basic idea is to compile a root set of pages that contain the query terms, extend this set by adding pages linked to/from these pages, build the adjacency matrix A of the link graph, and compute the eigenvectors of $A^{T}A$ and AA^{T}. These vectors, respectively, correspond to the weights of authorities and hubs. We provide a probabilistic formulation of this search mechanism which also allows us to go in the opposite direction, i.e. given the URL of a page, we can find the topics the page is an authority on.

The literature reports analyses and improvements over Kleinberg's original algorithm. Gibson et al. [8] investigate the dependence between top authorities and hubs identified by HITS and the choice of the root set. Bharat and Henzinger [2] suggest the use of link weights to adjust the influence of pages based on their relevance to the query. To measure the relevance of a page to a query, they use the normalized *cosine* measure of similarity between the page and an estimated query page, computed by concatenating the first 1000 words of pages retrieved in the root set.

Based on the hub-and-authority structure of a community, Kumar et al. [13] show that a large number of such communities can be identified from their signatures in the form of complete bipartite subgraphs of the Web. Chakrabarti et al. [4] show the benefit of using linkage information within a small neighborhood of documents to improve the accuracy of a text-based statistical classifier. Dean and Henzinger [5] suggest algorithms to find related pages of a given page solely based on the linkage structure around the page. Finally, Henzinger et al. [10] use random walks on the Web to measure the quality of pages stored in an index.

The view of the Web as a directed-graph database allows a large number of database techniques to be applied to the Web. Several query languages have been proposed for both querying and restructuring Web documents. A recent survey by Florescu et al. [7] gives an overview of this area.

2. Random walks on the Web

Given a set $S = \{s_1, s_2, \ldots, s_n\}$ of states, a *random walk* on S corresponds to a sequence of states, one for each step of the walk. At each step, the walk either switches to a new state or remains in the current state. A random walk is *Markovian* if the transition at each step is independent of the previous steps and it only depends on the current state. A random walk on the Web is in the form of navigation between pages, where each page represents a possible state, and each link represents a possible transition.

2.1. One-level influence propagation

Consider a 'random surfer' who wanders the Web, searching for pages on topic t. At each step, the surfer either jumps into a page uniformly chosen at random from the set of pages that contain the term t, or follows a link uniformly chosen at random from the set of outgoing links of the current page. If the random surfer continues this walk forever, then the number of visits he or she makes to a page is its reputation on t.

Intuitively, pages with relatively high reputations on a topic are more likely to be visited by the random surfer searching for that topic. A justification for this is that the reputation of a page on a topic naturally depends both on the number of pages on the same topic that point to it, and on the reputations of these pages on the same topic as well. The number of visits the surfer makes to a page depends on the same two factors.

2.1.1. Formal model

We want to *define* the reputation of a page p on topic t as the probability that the random surfer looking for topic t will visit page p. For this we formulate the following random walk model.

Suppose at each step, with probability d the random surfer jumps into a page uniformly chosen at random from the set of pages that contain the term t, and with probability $(1-d)$ he or she follows an outgoing link from the current page. Let N_t denote the total number of pages on the Web that contain the term t. Intuitively, the probability that the surfer at each step visits page p in a random jump is d/N_t if page p contains term t and it is zero otherwise. Let $q \to p$ denote a link from page q to page p, and $O(q)$ denote the number of outgoing links of page q. Intuitively, the probability that the surfer visits page p at step n after visiting page q and through the link $q \to p$ is $((1-d)/O(q))\, R^{n-1}(q,t)$ where $R^{n-1}(q,t)$ denotes the probability that the surfer visits its page q for topic t at step $n-1$. We can write the probability of visiting page p for topic t at step n of the walk as follows:

$$R^n(p,t) = \begin{cases} \dfrac{d}{N_t} + (1-d) \displaystyle\sum_{q \to p} \frac{R^{n-1}(q,t)}{O(q)} & \text{if term } t \text{ appears in page } p, \\ (1-d) \displaystyle\sum_{q \to p} \frac{R^{n-1}(q,t)}{O(q)} & \text{otherwise.} \end{cases} \tag{1}$$

Definition 1. The one-level reputation rank of page p on topic t is the equilibrium probability $\pi_{p,t}$ of visiting page p for topic t, i.e.

$$\pi_{p,t} = \lim_{n \to \infty} R^n(p,t) \tag{2}$$

Theorem 1. *The notion of one-level reputation rank is well-defined, i.e. for every term t with $N_t > 0$ and every parameter $d > 0$, there is a unique probability distribution $\pi_{p,t}$ satisfying Eq. (2), provided that every page has at least one outgoing link.*

Proof. Given a term t and a parameter $d > 0$, consider the base set of pages that contain the term t, and add to this set every page which can be reached from a page in the base set. Construct the matrix U of transition probabilities for the random walk process with each entry u_{ij} representing the probability of directly going from page i to page j as follows: first, if there is no link from p_i to p_j, then set entry u_{ij} of the matrix to 0, otherwise set it to $(1-d)/O(j)$; second, add d/N_t to every entry u_{ij} where p_j contains the term t. Clearly U is a square stochastic matrix with non-negative elements and unit row sums due to the assumption that every page has at least one outgoing link. Thus, both U and U^{T} have eigenvectors with eigenvalue 1. If we denote the weights of pages in the current step of the walk with vector x, then the weights in the next step of the walk will be $x = U^{\mathrm{T}}x$. Therefore, we are seeking an eigenvector of U associated with the eigenvalue 1.

Furthermore, because of the parameter $d > 0$, the transition matrix is both irreducible (i.e. every page is reachable from every other page) and aperiodic (see, for example [16], for details). Therefore, according to the convergence theorem ([16], theorem 1.8.3), starting from any distribution x, $(U^{\mathrm{T}})^{(n)}x$ will converge to the stationary probability $\pi_{p,t}$ of pages induced by the random walk process when $n \to \infty$. □

In the setting of the Web, our assumption that every page has at least one outgoing link may not be true; there are often pages that have no outgoing link, or the outgoing links may not be valid. A solution to accommodate these pages is to implicitly add links from every such page to all pages in the base set, i.e. the set of pages that contain the term. The interpretation here is that when the surfer reaches a dead end, he or she jumps to a page in the base set chosen uniformly at random.

2.2. Two-level influence propagation

We return to the 'random surfer' who wanders the Web, searching for pages on topic t. The surfer's behavior is a bit more involved now. Define a *transition* as one of (a) jump to a page on topic t chosen uniformly at random from the whole collection, or (b) follow an outgoing link of the current page chosen uniformly at random. When the current page is p, the surfer has two choices: either make a transition out of page p, or randomly pick any page q that has a link into page p and make a transition out of page q. The intuitive justification is this: when the surfer reaches a page p that seems useful for topic t, this does not mean that p is a good source of further links; but it does mean that pages q that point to p may be good sources of links, since they already led to page p.

To make our presentation slightly more formal, we say the surfer follows links both *forward* (out of page p) and *backward* (into page q). The walk alternates strictly between forward and backward steps, except that after option (a) is chosen, the direction of the next step is picked at random.

If the random surfer continues the walk forever, then the number of forward visits he or she makes to a page is its *authority* reputation and the number of backward visits he or she makes to a page is its *hub* reputation. Clearly pages with relatively high authority reputations on a topic are more likely to be visited through their incoming links, and pages with relatively high hub reputations on a topic are more likely to be visited through their outgoing links. Intuitively the authority reputation of a page p on topic t depends not only on the number of pages on topic t that point to p, but on the hub reputations of these pages on topic t as well.

2.2.1. Formal model

We want to define the authority reputation of a page p on a topic t as the probability that the random surfer looking for topic t makes a forward visit to page p and the hub reputation of a page p on topic t as the probability that the random surfer looking for topic t makes a backward visit to page p. For this we formulate the following random walk model.

Suppose at each step, with probability d the random surfer picks a direction and jumps into a page uniformly chosen at random from the set of pages on topic t, and with probability $(1-d)$ the surfer follows a link. Intuitively, the probability that at each step the surfer makes a forward visit (and similarly a backward visit) to page p in a random jump is $d/2N_t$ if page p contains term t and it is zero otherwise. Let $p \to q$ denote a link from page p to page q, $O(p)$ denote the number of outgoing links of page p, and $I(p)$ denote the number of incoming links of page p. Let us denote with $A^{n-1}(p,t)$ the probability of a forward visit into page p at step $n-1$ and with $H^{n-1}(p,t)$ the probability of a backward visit into page p at step $n-1$. Intuitively, the probability that the surfer makes a forward visit to page p at step n after visiting page q and through a link $q \to p$ is $((1-d)/O(q))\, H^{n-1}(q,t)$. Similarly, the probability that the surfer makes a backward visit to page q at step n after visiting page p and through a link $q \to p$ is $((1-d)/I(p))\, A^{n-1}\,(p,t)$. We can write the probabilities, $A^n(p,t)$ and $H^n(p,t)$, of visiting page p for topic t at step n as follows:

$$A^n(p,t) = \begin{cases} \dfrac{d}{2N_t} + (1-d)\displaystyle\sum_{q\to p} \dfrac{H^{n-1}(q,t)}{O(q)} & \text{if term } t \text{ appears in page } p, \\ (1-d)\displaystyle\sum_{q\to p} \dfrac{H^{n-1}(q,t)}{O(q)} & \text{otherwise,} \end{cases} \tag{3}$$

$$H^n(p,t) = \begin{cases} \dfrac{d}{2N_t} + (1-d)\displaystyle\sum_{p\to q} \dfrac{A^{n-1}(q,t)}{I(q)} & \text{if term } t \text{ appears in page } p, \\ (1-d)\displaystyle\sum_{p\to q} \dfrac{A^{n-1}(q,t)}{I(q)} & \text{otherwise.} \end{cases} \tag{4}$$

Definition 2. The two-level reputation rank $r \in \{$*authority, hub*$\}$ of page p on topic t is the equilibrium probability $\pi^r_{p,t}$ of visiting page p for topic t in the direction associated to r (forward for authority and backward for hub), i.e.

$$\pi^{\text{authority}}_{p,t} = \lim_{n\to\infty} A^n(p,t), \tag{5}$$

$$\pi^{\text{hub}}_{p,t} = \lim_{n\to\infty} H^n(p,t). \tag{6}$$

Theorem 2. *The notion of two-level reputation rank is well-defined, i.e. for every term t with $N_t > 0$ and every parameter $d > 0$, there is a unique probability distribution $\pi^r_{p,t}$ satisfying Eqs. (5) and (6), if every page has at least an incoming or an outgoing link.*

Proof. Given a term t and a parameter $d > 0$, consider the base set of pages that contain the term t, and add to this set every page which is reachable from a page in the base set by repeatedly following links in one of the *back–forth* or the *forth–back* order. To construct the matrix U of transition probabilities for the random walk process, we allocate two states for each page p_i, say i^{f} to denote the state of the page when it is visited in the forward direction and i^{b} to denote the state of the page when it is visited in the backward direction. Entries of matrix U are set as follows: (1) $u_{i^{\text{f}}j^{\text{f}}} = u_{i^{\text{b}}j^{\text{b}}} = 0$; (2) if there is a link from page p_i to page p_j, then $u_{i^{\text{b}}j^{\text{f}}} = (1-d)/O(p_i)$ and $u_{j^{\text{f}}i^{\text{b}}} = (1-d)/I(p_j)$; otherwise $u_{i^{\text{b}}j^{\text{f}}} = u_{j^{\text{f}}i^{\text{b}}} = 0$; (3) add $d/2N_t$ to every entry in column j if p_j is on topic t.

Clearly U is a square stochastic matrix with non-negative elements and unit row sums due to the assumption that every page has at least an incoming or an outgoing link. Thus, both U and U^{T} have eigenvectors with eigenvalue 1. Therefore, we are seeking an eigenvector of U associated with the eigenvalue 1.

The transition matrix U is both irreducible and aperiodic; therefore, according to the convergence theorem ([16], theorem 1.8.3), starting from any distribution x, $(U^{\text{T}})^{(n)}x$ will converge to the stationary probability $\pi^r_{p,t}$ of pages induced by the random walk process when $n \to \infty$. □

In the setting of the Web, our assumption that a page has at least either one incoming link or one outgoing link may not hold. However, since we are dealing with collections of pages collected by crawling, we feel justified in assuming that they all have at least one incoming link.

3. Computing reputations of pages

The probabilistic models presented in the previous section provide a natural way of measuring the reputations of a page, but there are computational issues which need to be addressed. The first issue is within which set of pages should the ranks be computed. The second issue is what is the set of topics on which to compute reputations. It is not enough to look for terms or phrases that appear in a page, as a page might have a high reputation on a topic, but the term denoting that topic may not be explicitly mentioned anywhere in the page. For example, Sun Microsystems has a high reputation on 'Java', but the term does not appear in *www.sun.com*. In this section, we address both problems. Section 3.1 deals with the situation where we have access to a large crawl of the Web, as is the case, for example, when the computation is performed by a search engine. Section 3.2 deals with the situation where we do not have access to such a crawl or cannot afford the time to do the full computation of Section 3.1.

3.1. Computing reputation ranks

Given a collection of pages, for example the result of a relatively large crawl of the Web, and a parameter d, we can compute the reputation ranks using one of the two influence propagation models. The ranks in the one-level influence propagation model are in the form of a sparse matrix, say R, with rows representing Web pages and columns denoting each term or phrase that appears in some document (after removing stop words, etc.) The computation involves initializing R and repeatedly updating it until convergence.

Algorithm 1. (computing one-level reputation ranks)

For every page p and term t,
Initialize $R(p,t) = 1/N_t$ if t appears in page p; otherwise $R(p,t) = 0$.
While R has not converged,
Set $R'(p,t) = 0$ for every page p and term t,
For every link $q \to p$,
$R'(p,t) = R'(p,t) + R(q,t)/O(q)$
$R(p,t) = (1-d)R'(p,t)$
for every page p and term t,
$R(p,t) = R(p,t) + d/N_t$
if term t appears in page p.

Since each column of R converges to the principal eigenvector of the matrix of transition probabilities for a term t, the algorithm is guaranteed to converge. The principal eigenvector associated to each term is the stationary distribution of pages in the random walk process, provided every page has at least one outgoing link and $d > 0$.

The ranks in the two-level influence propagation model can be represented in the form of two sparse matrixes, say H and A, respectively denoting the hub and the authority reputations of pages. The computation can be arranged as follows:

Algorithm 2. (computing two-level reputation ranks)

For every page p and term t,
Initialize $H(p,t) = A(p,t) = 1/2N_t$ if t appears in page p; otherwise $H(p,t) = A(p,t) = 0$.
While both H and A have not converged,
Set $H'(p,t) = A'(p,t) = 0$
for every page p and term t,
For every link $q \to p$,
$H'(q,t) = H'(q,t) + A(p,t)/I(p)$
$A'(p,t) = A'(p,t) + H(q,t)/O(q)$
$H(p,t) = (1-d)H'(p,t)$ *and*
$A(p,t) = (1-d)A'(p,t)$
for every page p and term t,
$H(p,t) = H(p,t) + d/2N_t$ *and*
$A(p,t) = A(p,t) + d/2N_t$
if term t appears in page p.

Again, the computation for each term is guaranteed to converge to the principal eigenvector of the matrix of transition probabilities for that term. The principal eigenvector is the stationary distribution provided every page has at least one incoming or outgoing link and $d > 0$. Next we discuss how to obtain an approximate estimation of reputation when we do not have access to a large crawl of the Web.

3.2. Identifying topics

The two algorithms presented in the previous section not only compute the reputation ranks but also identify topics of reputations. However, in practice we may not have access to a large crawl of the Web, or we may not be able to afford the full computation. In this section, we show that it is still possible to approximately find the topics a page has a high reputation on, although the ranks will not reflect the real probability distributions.

Given a page p and a parameter $d > 0$, suppose we want to find the reputations of the page within the one-level influence propagation model. If the page acquires a high rank on an arbitrarily chosen term t within the full computation of Algorithm 1, then at least one of the following must hold: (1) term t appears in page p; (2) many pages on topic t point to p; or (3) there are pages with high reputations on t that point to p. This observation provides us with a practical way of identifying the candidate terms. We simply start from page p and collect all terms that appear in it. We then look at the incoming links of the page and collect all possible terms from those pages. We continue this process until we get to a point where either there is no incoming link or the incoming links have very small effects on the reputations of page p. Let us denote the maximum number of iterations by k. The algorithm can be expressed as follows.

Algorithm 3. (approximating one-level reputation)

$R(p, t) = d/N_t$ for every term t that appears in p
For $l = 1, 2, \ldots, k$
  $d' = d$ if $l < k$, 1 otherwise
  For every path $q_l \to \ldots \to q_1 \to p$ of length l and every term t in page q_l,
  $R(p, t) = 0$ if term t has not been seen before
  $R(p, t) = R(p, t) + \left((1-d)^l / \prod_{i=1}^{l} O(q_i)\right)(d'/N_t)$
Report every term t with $R(p, t) > 1/N_t$.

The parameter k can be chosen such that $(1-d)^k$ becomes very close to zero; i.e. there is no need to look at a page if the terms that appear in the page have little or no effect on the reputations of page p. Similarly, the hub and the authority reputations of a page can be approximated within the two-level influence propagation model as follows.

Algorithm 4. (approximating two-level reputation)

$H(p, t) = A(p, t) = d/(2N_t)$ for every term t that appears in p
For $l = 1, 2, \ldots, k$
  $d' = d$ if $l < k$, 1 otherwise
  If l is odd
    For every path $q_l \to q_{l-1} \leftarrow q_{l-2} \ldots \to p$ of length l and every term t in page q_l,
      $A(p, t) = 0$ if term t has not been seen before
      $A(p, t) = A(p, t) + \left((1-d)^l/(O(q_l)I(q_{l-1})\ldots O(q_1))\right) d'/(2N_t)$
    For every path $p \to \ldots q_{l-2} \leftarrow q_{l-1} \to q_l$ of length l and every term t in page q_l,
      $H(p, t) = 0$ if term t has not been seen before
      $H(p, t) = H(p, t) + \left((1-d)^l/(I(q_l)O(q_{l-1})\ldots I(q_1))\right) d'/(2N_t)$
  else
    For every path $q_l \leftarrow q_{l-1} \to \ldots \to p$ of length l and every term t in page q_l,
      $A(p, t) = 0$ if term t has not been seen before
      $A(p, t) = A(p, t) + \left((1-d)^l/(I(q_l)O(q_{l-1})\ldots)\right) d'/(2N_t)$
    For every path $p \to \ldots \to q_{l-1} \leftarrow q_l$ of length l and every term t in page q_l,
      $H(p, t) = 0$ if term t has not been seen before
      $H(p, t) = H(p, t) + \left((1-d)^l/(O(q_l)I(q_{l-1})\ldots)\right) d'/(2N_t)$
Report every term t with $A(p, t) > 1/N_t$ or $H(p, t) > 1/N_t$.

In both algorithms 3 and 4, we have adopted a breadth-first search of the pages that can affect the reputations of a page p, i.e. all pages within depth l are visited before any page in depth $l+1$. A benefit of this ordering is that the user can stop the search at any point and be sure that pages that are expected to have a high influence on p are visited. This may happen, for example, if the search takes longer than expected. However, it should be noted that the algorithm needs to remember the number of outgoing or incoming links for each page being visited, if this information is not already stored. An alternative to a breadth-first search is to conduct a depth-first search, if we can assume that, for example, the search engine always gives us the same set of pages with the same ordering. The only benefit of such a search is that the algorithm only needs to remember the current path. However, this assumption usually does not hold for real search engines. In addition, there is the danger of spending most of the time on pages that have a very small effect on the reputations of page p before visiting more important pages.

4. Duality of terms and pages

Our main objective so far has been to find the topics on which a page has a strong reputation, but our random walk models also allow us to compute the pages that have high reputation on a given topic, as proposed by Kleinberg and others for enhancing search engine performance.

Indeed, if we fix p in Eqs. 1, 3 and 4 to a specific page, we will find the reputation ranks of the page for every possible topic t. We may then report the topics with the highest reputation ranks. If we fix instead t in the same equations to be a specific topic, we will find the reputation ranks of every page on topic t. Again, we may report those pages with high reputation ranks first in the answer to a query.

In terms of rank computations, our algorithms presented in Section 3.1 already compute the reputations of every page p on every topic t. Therefore, the highly weighted pages for a given topic can be easily identified. In practice, however, we may not be able to afford the full computation for every possible term; or an approximate solution might be as good as an exact solution. In Section 3.2 we presented algorithms to approximately find the topics on which a page has a high reputation. In the rest of this section, we show how we can approximately find pages with relatively high reputations on a given topic.

Given a topic t, an arbitrarily chosen page p can potentially acquire a relatively high rank, within the one-level influence propagation model, on topic t if at least one of the following holds: (1) term t appears in page p; (2) many pages on topic t point to p; (3) there are pages with relatively high reputations on t that point to p. Thus, a page with high reputation on topic t must either contain term t or be reachable within a few steps from a large set of pages on topic t. An approximate way of computing the one-level reputation ranks of pages on topic t is as follows: (1) identify pages that are either on topic t or reachable within a short distance from a page on topic t; (2) construct the matrix U of transition probabilities for the resulting set of pages, as described in Section 2.1; (3) compute the principal eigenvector of U^{T}. The principal eigenvector will give the approximate ranks of pages that are expected to have high reputations; i.e. every page which is not identified in Step 1 is assumed to have a rank of zero. This is more general than the PageRank computation, which determines the overall reputation of a page, but not its reputation on specific topics.

For the two-level influence propagation model, given a topic t, an arbitrarily chosen page p can acquire a relatively high rank on topic t if either term t appears in page p or it is reachable within a short path of alternating forward and backward links (or vice versa) from a large set of pages on topic t. An approximate way of computing the two-level reputation ranks of pages on topic t is as follows: (1) identify pages that are either on topic t or reachable within a few steps from a page on topic t, alternately following links forward and backward or vice versa; (2) construct the matrix U of transition probabilities for the resulting set of pages, as described in Section 2.2; (3) compute the principal eigenvector of U^{T}. The principal eigenvector will give the approximate ranks of pages that are expected to have high reputations. Again, every page which is not identified in Step 1 is assumed to have a rank of zero. Note that the hubs-and-authorities computation of Kleinberg is a special case of this method; it is based on only identifying pages that either contain term t or are reachable within one link from one such page.

5. Experimental evaluation

In this section, we describe a preliminary evaluation of our approach. Since we did not have access to a large crawl of the Web, it was not feasible to do the full rank computations of Section 3.1. We also did not fully implement the approximate algorithms suggested in Section 3.2 due to the limitations imposed by the search engines we used, either on the maximum number of entries returned for a query or on the response time.

Instead, we implemented a simplified version of Algorithm 3 (and also part of Algorithm 4 that computes the authority reputation of a page) where we set k to 1, d to 0.10 and $O(q_i)$ for every page q_i to 7.2, the estimated average number of outgoing links of a page [12]. The best value for parameter d needs to be determined empirically. Further details of the implementation are as follows.

(1) Only a limited number of incoming links are

URL : java.sun.com — 500 links examined (out of 128653 available)
Highly weighted terms: Developers, JavaSoft, Applets, JDK, Java applets, Sun Microsystems, API, Programming, Solaris, tutorial
Frequent terms: Java, Software, Computer, Programming, Sun, Development, Microsoft, Search
URL : sunsite.unc.edu/javafaq/javafaq.html — 500 links examined (out of 1541 available)
Highly weighted terms: Java FAQ Java, comp.lang.java FAQ, Java Tutorials, Java Stuff, Applets, IBM Java, Javasoft, Java Resources, API Java, Learning Java
Frequent terms: Java, Programming, FAQ, Sun, Computer, Language, Tutorial, Java FAQ, Software

Fig. 1. Authorities on (java).

examined; we obtain at most 500 incoming links of a page, but the number of links returned by the search engine, currently Alta Vista [1], can be less than that.

(2) For each incoming link, terms are extracted from the 'snippet' returned by the search engine, rather than the page itself. A justification for this is that the snippet of a page, to some degree, represents the topic of the page. In addition, the number of distinct terms and as a result the number of count queries needed to be sent to the search engine are dramatically reduced.
(3) Internal links and duplicate snippets are removed.
(4) Stop words and every term t with $N_t < (1 + r \times L)$ are removed, where L is the number of incoming links collected and r is the near-duplicate ratio of the search engine, currently set to 0.01. This reduces the number of count queries and also removes unusual terms such as 'AAATT' that rarely appear in any page but might acquire high weights.

Despite all the simplifications, the experience with our prototype has been quite encouraging in terms of approximating both the one-level reputation and the two-level authority reputation of a page. Next we report our experiments with the prototype, called **TOPIC** [2].

5.1. Known authoritative pages

In our first experiment, we picked a set of known authoritative pages on queries (*java*) and (*+censorship +net*), as reported by Kleinberg's HITS algorithm [11], and computed the topics that each page was an authority on. As shown in Fig. 1, the term 'java' is the most frequent term among pages that point to an authority on Java. There are other frequent terms such as 'search' or 'Microsoft' which have nothing to do with the topic; their high frequency represents the fact that authorities on Java are frequently cocited with search engines or Microsoft. This usually happens in cases where the number of links examined is much less than the number of links available. However, the highly weighted terms for each page in both Figs. 1 and 2 largely describe the topics that the page is an authority on, consistently with the results of HITS.

In another experiment, we used Inquirus [14], the NECI meta-search engine, which computes authorities using an unspecified algorithm. We provided Inquirus with the query ('*data warehousing*') and set the number of hits to its maximum, which was 1000, to get the best authorities, as suggested by the system. We picked the top-four authorities returned by Inquirus and used our system to compute the topics those pages have high reputations on. The result, as shown in Fig. 3, is again consistent with the judgments of Inquirus.

5.2. Personal home pages

In another experiment, we selected a set of personal home pages and used our system to find the high reputation topics for each page. We expected this to describe in some way the reputation of the owner of the page. The results, as shown in Fig. 4, can be revealing, but need to be interpreted with

[2] This can be tried online at http://www.cs.toronto.edu/db/topic

URL : www.eff.org — 500 links examined (out of 181899 available) **Highly weighted terms**: Anti-Censorship, Join the Blue Ribbon, Blue Ribbon Campaign, Electronic Frontier Foundation, Free Speech
URL : www.cdt.org — 500 links examined (out of 12922 available) **Highly weighted terms**: Center for Democracy and Technology, Communications Decency Act, Censorship, Free Speech, Blue Ribbon, Syllabus, encryption
URL : www.vtw.org — 500 links examined (out of 7948 available) **Highly weighted terms**: decision is near in the fight to overturn the Communications Decency Act, Blue Ribbon Campaign, Censorship, American Civil Liberties Union, free speech
URL : www.aclu.org — 500 links examined (out of 22087 available) **Highly weighted terms**: ACLU, American Civil Liberties Union, Communications Decency Act, Amendment, CDA, Criminal Law, Censorship

Fig. 2. Authorities on (+censorship +net).

some care. Tim Berners-Lee's reputation on the 'History of the Internet', Don Knuth's fame on 'TeX' and 'Latex' and Jeff Ullman's reputation on 'database systems' and 'programming languages' are to be expected. The humor site *Dilbert Zone* [6] seems to be frequently cited by Don Knuth's fans. Alberto Mendelzon's high reputation on 'data warehousing', on the other hand, is mainly due to an online research bibliography he maintains on data warehousing and OLAP in his home page, and not to any merits of his own.

5.3. Unregulated Web sites

In our last experiment, we selected the home pages of a number of computer science departments on the Web. The main characteristic of these pages is that the sites are unregulated, in the sense that users store any documents they desire in their own pages. The results, as shown in Fig. 5, can be surprising. The Computer Science Department at the **University of Toronto** [3] has a high reputation on 'Russia' and 'Images', mainly because a Russian graduate student of the department has put online a large collection of images of Russia, and many pages on Russia link to it. The high reputation on 'hockey' is due to a former student who used to play on the Canadian national women's hockey team. The Faculty of Mathematics, Computer Science, Physics and Astronomy at the **University of Amsterdam** [4] has a high reputation on 'Solaris 2 FAQ' because the site maintains a FAQ on the Solaris operating system. It also has a high reputation on the musician Frank Zappa because it has a set of pages dedicated to him and the FAQ of the alt.fan.frank-zappa newsgroup. The Computer Science Department of the **University of Helsinki** [5] has a high reputation on Linux because of the many pages on Linux that point to Linus Torvalds's page.

5.4. Limitations

There are a number of factors that affect our page reputation computations. The first factor is how well a topic is represented on the Web. A company, for instance, may have a high reputation on a specific topic, or a person may be well known for his or her contribution in a specific field, but their home pages may not receive the same recognition mainly because the topic or the field is not well represented on the Web; or even if it is, it may not be visible among other dominant topics. This can be easily seen in some of our experiments.

The second factor is how well pages on a topic are connected to each other. There are two extreme cases that can affect the convergence of a topic in our com-

[3] www.cs.toronto.edu

[4] www.wins.uva.nl

[5] www.cs.helsinki.fi

URL : www.dw-institute.com — 390 links examined (out of 785 available) **Highly weighted terms**: TDWI, Data Warehousing Information Center, www.dw-institute.com, Data Warehousing Institute, data warehouse
URL : pwp.starnetinc.com/larryg — 500 links examined (out of 1017 available) **Highly weighted terms**: Data Warehousing Information Center, OLAP and Data, Analytical Processing, Data Mining, data warehouse, Decision Support Systems
URL : www.datawarehousing.com — 188 links examined (out of 229 available) **Highly weighted terms**: Data Warehousing Information, OLAP, Data Mining
URL : www.dmreview.com — 270 links examined (out of 1258 available) **Highly weighted terms**: Data Warehouse 100, Powell Publishing, Review Magazine, Data Warehousing, Business Intelligence, Cognos, Data Mining, Product Review

Fig. 3. Authorities on ('data warehousing').

URL : www.w3.org/People/Berners-Lee — 500 links examined (out of 933 available) **Highly weighted terms**: History Of The Internet, Tim Berners-Lee, Internet History, W3C
URL : www-cs-faculty.stanford.edu/~knuth — 500 links examined (out of 1733 available) **Highly weighted terms**: Don Knuth, Donald E Knuth, TeX, Dilbert Zone, Latex, ACM
URL : www-db.stanford.edu/~ullman — 238 links examined (out of 466 available) **Highly weighted terms**: Jeffrey D Ullman, Database Systems, Database Management, Data Mining, Programming Languages, Computer Science, Stanford University
URL : www.cs.toronto.edu/~mendel — 139 links examined (out of 259 available) **Highly weighted terms**: Alberto Mendelzon, Data Warehousing and OLAP, SIGMOD, DBMS

Fig. 4. Personal home pages.

URL : www.cs.toronto.edu — 500 links examined (out of 7814 available) **Highly weighted terms**: Russia, Computer Vision, Linux, Images, Orthodox, Hockey
URL : www.wins.uva.nl — 500 links examined (out of 6174 available) **Highly weighted terms**: Solaris 2 FAQ, Wiskunde, Frank Zappa, FreeBSD, Recipes
URL : www.cs.helsinki.fi — 500 links examined (out of 9664 available) **Highly weighted terms**: Linux Applications, Linux Gazette, Linux Software, Knowledge Discovery, Linus Torvalds, Data Mining

Fig. 5. Computer science departments.

putations. At one extreme, there are a few pages such as the Microsoft home page (www.microsoft.com) with incoming links from a large fraction of all pages on the Web. These pages end up having high reputation on almost every topic represented in the Web; it is not reasonable to identify a small set of highly weighted topics for them.

At the other extreme, there are pages with no

more than a few incoming links; according to some estimates (e.g. [13]), a large number of pages fall in this category. Depending on where the incoming links of a page are coming from and the reputations of those links, they can have various effects on the reputation of a page according to our models. Our current implementation, however, may not report any strong reputations on any topic for these pages because all incoming links are simply weighted equally.

6. Conclusions

We have introduced general notions of page reputation on a topic, combining the textual content and the link structure of the Web. Our notions of reputation are based on random walk models that generalize the pure link-based ranking methods developed earlier. For instance, our ranking based on the one-level weight propagation model becomes PageRank if the rank is computed with respect to all possible topics. We have presented algorithms for identifying the topics that a page has highest reputation on and for computing the reputation rank of a page on a topic. Our current work concentrates on refining the implementation of TOPIC to achieve more accurate rankings and better performance.

Acknowledgements

This research was supported by the Communications and Information Technology of Ontario and the Natural Sciences and Engineering Research Council of Canada.

References

[1] Alta Vista, http://www.altavista.com

[2] K. Bharat and M.R. Henzinger, Improved algorithms for topic distillation in hyperlinked environments, in: Proc. 21st Int. ACM SIGIR Conf. on Research and Development in Information Retrieval, 1998, pp. 104–111.

[3] S. Brin and L. Page, The anatomy of a large-scale hypertextual web search engine, in: Proc. 7th Int. World Wide Web Conf., Brisbane, April 1998, Elsevier, Amsterdam, pp. 107–117.

[4] S. Chakrabarti, B. Dom and P. Indyk, Enhanced hypertext categorization using hyperlinks, in: Proc. ACM SIGMOD Int. Conf. on Management of Data, Seattle, WA, 1998, pp. 307–318.

[5] J. Dean and M.R. Henzinger, Finding related pages on the Web, in: Proc. 8th Int. World Wide Web Conf., Toronto, May 1999, Elsevier, Amsterdam, pp. 389–401.

[6] Dilbert Zone, http://www.unitedmedia.com/comics/dilbert

[7] D. Florescu, A. Levy and A. Mendelzon, Database techniques for the World Wide Web: a survey, ACM SIGMOD Record 27 (3) (September 1998) 59–74.

[8] D. Gibson, J.M. Kleinberg and P. Raghavan, Inferring Web communities from link topology, in: Hypertext, Pittsburgh, PA, June 1998, pp. 225–234.

[9] Google, http://www.google.com

[10] M.R. Henzinger, A. Heydon, M. Mitzenmacher and M. Najork, Measuring index quality using random walks on the Web, in: Proc. 8th Int. World Wide Web Conf., Toronto, May 1999, Elsevier, Amsterdam, pp. 213–225.

[11] J.M. Kleinberg, Authoritative sources in a hyperlinked environment, in: Proc. ACM–SIAM Symp. on Discrete Algorithms, January 1998, pp. 668–677.

[12] R. Kumar, P. Raghavan, S. Rajagopalan and A. Tomkins, Extracting large-scale knowledge bases from the Web, in: Proc. 25th Int. Conf. on Very Large Databases, September 1999, pp. 639–650.

[13] R. Kumar, P. Raghavan, S. Rajagopalan and A. Tomkins, Trawling the Web for emerging cyber-communities, in: Proc. 8th Int. World Wide Web Conf., rence, Toronto, May 1999, Elsevier, Amsterdam, pp. 403–415.

[14] S. Lawrence and C.L. Giles, Context and page analysis for improved Web search, IEEE Internet Computing 2 (4) (1998) 38–46.

[15] Netscape Communications Corporation, What's related, Web page, http://www.netscape.com/escapes/related/faq.html

[16] J.R. Norris, Markov Chains, Cambridge University Press, 1997.

Davood Rafiei completed his undergrad in Computer Engineering at Sharif University of Technology, Tehran, in 1990, received his master in Computer Science from the University of Waterloo in 1995 and his Ph.D. in Computer Science from the University of Toronto in 1999. He is currently a post-doctoral fellow at the University of Toronto. His research interests include information retrieval on the Web and non-traditional data management.

Alberto Mendelzon did his undergraduate work at the University of Buenos Aires and obtained his Master's and Ph.D. degrees from Princeton University. He was a post-doctoral fellow at the IBM T.J. Watson Research Center and since 1980 has been at the University of Toronto, where he is now Professor of Computer Science and member of the Computer Systems Research Group. He has spent time as a visiting scientist at the NTT Basic Research Laboratories in Japan, the IASI in Rome, the IBM Toronto Lab, and AT&T Bell Labs Research in New Jersey. Alberto's research interests are in database systems, database query languages, Web-based information systems, and information integration.

Author Index

Subject Index

Printed and bound by CPI Group (UK) Ltd, Croydon, CR0 4YY
03/10/2024
01040327-0020